Medieval Damascus

Plurality and Diversity in an Arabic Library

Edinburgh Studies in Classical Islamic History and Culture
Series Editor: Carole Hillenbrand

A particular feature of medieval Islamic civilisation was its wide horizons. In this respect it differed profoundly from medieval Europe, which from the point of view of geography, ethnicity and population was much smaller and narrower in its scope and in its mindset. The Muslims fell heir not only to the Graeco-Roman world of the Mediterranean, but also to that of the ancient Near East, to the empires of Assyria, Babylon and the Persians – and beyond that, they were in frequent contact with India and China to the east and with black Africa to the south. This intellectual openness can be sensed in many interrelated fields of Muslim thought: philosophy and theology, medicine and pharmacology, algebra and geometry, astronomy and astrology, geography and the literature of marvels, ethnology and sociology. It also impacted powerfully on trade and on the networks that made it possible. Books in this series reflect this openness and cover a wide range of topics, periods and geographical areas.

Titles in the series include:

Arabic Materia Medica*: Arabian Drugs in Medieval Mediterranean Medicine*
Zohar Amar and Efraim Lev

Keeping the Peace in Premodern Islam: Diplomacy under the Mamluk Sultanate, 1250–1517
Malika Dekkiche

Medieval Damascus – Plurality and Diversity in an Arabic Library: The Ashrafiya Library Catalogue
Konrad Hirschler

The Popularisation of Sufism in Ayyubid and Mamluk Egypt, 1173–1325
Nathan Hofer

Defining Anthropomorphism: The Challenge of Islamic Traditionalism
Livnat Holtzman

Lyrics of Life: Sa'di on Love, Cosmopolitanism and Care of the Self
Fatemeh Keshavarz

A History of the True Balsam of Matarea
Marcus Milwright

Ruling from a Red Canopy: Political Authority in the Medieval Islamic World, from Anatolia to South Asia
Colin P. Mitchell

www.edinburghuniversitypress.com

Medieval Damascus

Plurality and Diversity in an Arabic Library

The Ashrafīya Library Catalogue

Konrad Hirschler

EDINBURGH
University Press

Hevin'e ve Hüseyin'e

Edinburgh University Press is one of the leading university presses in the UK. We publish academic books and journals in our selected subject areas across the humanities and social sciences, combining cutting-edge scholarship with high editorial and production values to produce academic works of lasting importance. For more information visit our website: www.edinburghuniversitypress.com

Edinburgh University Press Ltd
The Tun – Holyrood Road
12 (2f) Jackson's Entry
Edinburgh EH8 8PJ

First published in hardback by Edinburgh University Press 2016

Typeset in 11/15 Adobe Garamond by
Servis Filmsetting Ltd, Stockport, Cheshire,
and printed and bound in Great Britain by
CPI Group (UK) Ltd, Croydon CR0 4YY

A CIP record for this book is available from the British Library

ISBN 978 1 4744 0877 6 (hardback)
ISBN 978 1 4744 2639 8 (paperback)
ISBN 978 1 4744 0878 3 (webready PDF)
ISBN 978 1 4744 0879 0 (epub)

Published with the support of the Edinburgh University Scholarly Publishing Initiatives Fund.

Contents

Illustrations

Tables

Maps

Figures

Plates

Situated between pages 142 and 143

Acknowledgements

Researching and writing this book relied on so many informal academic exchanges that it did indeed take a village to complete it. Editing a medieval manuscript catalogue with titles across the full range of human knowledge inevitably becomes a series of short-term collaborations as its author tiptoes cautiously through unfamiliar landscapes of numerous disciplines and fields. I can only express my heartfelt gratitude to all those colleagues who have responded to my obscure queries linked to an even more obscure project. In the course of Chapter 4 I have acknowledged the help of individuals in identifying specific titles, but it is not unfair to single out one colleague who shared his time and expertise with a generosity that went well beyond what one could reasonably expect: Geert Jan van Gelder (the University of Oxford). From when I presented the first tentative ideas on this project he stayed closely involved and not only advised on anything to do with poetry, but also read drafts of this lengthy chapter. At SOAS Doris Behrens-Abouseif has always kept a close interest in the project and helped me in a variety of ways.

Writing a book requires extended periods of research leave and I have to thank three institutions that enabled this: My home institution, SOAS, granted me research leave in 2010/11 when I started the project. A three-month stay as fellow at the Annemarie-Schimmel-Kolleg in Bonn in 2013 provided me with the tranquil environment to push the project ahead when it was about to stall. Finally, the British Academy granted a mid-career fellowship for 2014/15, which allowed me to bring the book to conclusion. My thanks to these institutions is particularly sincere as they were willing to support a stand-alone project at a time when funding is increasingly focused on large-scale research groups and networks – a funding approach that does not always sit easily with the research culture in the Humanities.

The audiences' questions and comments at conferences and workshops where I presented parts of this book, especially in Ghent (Colloquium on the History of Egypt and Syria in the Fatimid, Ayyubid and Mamluk Eras (CHESFAME) 2011), Denver (Middle East Studies Association (MESA) 2012), Bonn (Annemarie-Schimmel-Kolleg 2012), Oxford (Islamic World Subject Group 2013), Cambridge, UK (Islamic Manuscript Conference 2013) and Madrid (Histories of Books Conference 2015) have helped me rethink its main arguments. Here I would like to underline that the time spent at the Annemarie-Schimmel-Kolleg with a group of colleagues specialising in medieval Middle Eastern history was especially helpful. In particular I have to thank Mohammad Gharaibeh, Élise Franssen and Tarek Sabra. It goes without saying that any remaining mistake in this book is my sole responsibility.

Crucial for this project was the support I received from librarians and it is particularly appropriate to highlight this in a book on a medieval library. At SOAS, Dominique Akhoun-Schwarb made sure that even rather dated titles and those published in uncommon places found their way to our bookshelves. In Bonn, Sarah Spiegel kept track of all those interlibrary loans, which – contrary to my optimistic predictions – only increased in number. The catalogue around which this book is written is held in Istanbul in the Süleymaniye library, which made the catalogue available to me without hesitation. During my research stay its staff provided crucial support and a word of praise is in order for what is a splendid library for research on medieval Arabic manuscripts. The project received further support from Eyad Hamid in Istanbul who helped in tracking Ashrafiya manuscripts, from Paula Manstetten and Christopher Bahl in London who built most of the Ashrafiya database and from Suzanne Ruggi who copy-edited the book manuscript.

I would also like to thank the two anonymous reviewers at Edinburgh University Press for their constructive comments, especially on how to present the material. The different members of staff at Edinburgh University Press who were involved in this project greatly contributed to bringing this work to publication. Finally, I am very grateful to family and friends for their patience and support throughout the years of my work on this project.

Introduction

This is the story of a medieval Arabic library. Positioned in the centre of seventh-/thirteenth-century Damascus, part of an educational institution and endowed by members of the political and social elite there is nothing too unusual about the Ashrafiya library. In many ways it is a run-of-the-mill library of which dozens probably existed in Damascus and hundreds more in the various Syrian and Egyptian cities. Yet this library differs in one significant way from all of its counterparts: its catalogue has come down to us. Library catalogues do not sound like the most exciting documents we can lay our hands on and this book is certainly not the Middle Eastern equivalent to Umberto Eco's *Name of the Rose* (although the first *shaykh* to preside over the library's mother institution did fall victim to a highly suspicious and unsolved murder). Rather this library catalogue is so valuable because it opens a door into a pre-print world of books and shelves, which was at the very heart of society but was hitherto largely inaccessible.

For the first time we are able to gain a detailed insight into what books were held in such a medieval Arabic library and thus its intellectual profile. William of Baskerville would not have found Aristotle's *Book on Comedy* on the library's shelves, but at least eighteen other titles ascribed to Aristotle, Plato, Galen and Socrates would have been available to him among the 2,000 books in its stock. The catalogue also allows us to understand for the first time how the books were actually organised on the shelves (How do we make the books retrievable?) and it allows us to grasp the spatial dimensions of a medieval library (How do we cram all of these books into such small places?). Finally, for the first time one can follow the nuts and bolts of founding a medieval library in the Arabic Middle East (From where do we get the books?) and of running it in the subsequent decades and centuries (How do we prevent those folks from running off with the books?). The catalogue was known to the great scholar of manuscripts Ramazan Şeşen, who briefly cited it in some of his publications from the 1970s onwards. On the basis of his work the catalogue was referred to in subsequent publications by other scholars such as Ṣalāḥ al-Dīn al-Munajjid, who mentioned it in a Syrian training manual for librarians published in the 1970s.[1] This early work laid the basis for some of the misunderstandings that have circulated in scholarship on this library and its catalogue.[2] In the late 2000s the catalogue was studied more intensively in the framework of an Egyptian PhD thesis on pre-modern Arabic library catalogues.[3] However, as it has neither been edited nor been the subject of an in-depth study, this catalogue is still awaiting its appropriate place in scholarship as a unique insight into medieval Arabic cultural life.

Research Context and Approach

Arabic societies, at least those in Syria and Egypt, arguably belonged to the most literate and bookish societies worldwide when the Ashrafiya library was founded in the seventh/thirteenth century.[4] In the third/ninth and fourth/tenth centuries Middle Eastern societies had experienced a book revolution, partly driven by a significant fall in paper prices and accompanied by the spread of new cultural practices.[5] This in turn led to a 'reading revolution', where the written word became increasingly central and spread to wider sections of society. Although literacy rates are virtually impossible to determine with the source material currently at hand, the ubiquity of reading suggests that it became a two-digit number in the cities of Egypt and Syria.[6] One of the salient features of the intertwined processes of textualisation and popularisation was the rise of a new type of library in the Middle Period, the local endowed library. In contrast to the previously dominant royal libraries, these local endowed libraries offered a large number of venues spread across the region's cities where broader reading audiences could access books. As this development gained pace in the seventh/thirteenth century, the Ashrafiya library sat at the very heart of the increasing availability and circulation of the written word and it itself was in no way an outstanding book collection. As we will see in the course of Chapter 1, it was rather a minor library set in a mausoleum and contemporaries did not consider it to be very remarkable. This very averageness (or perhaps even below-averageness) is what makes the Ashrafiya so interesting: we are not necessarily dealing with an outlier or with an exceptional institution, but with a library that can typologically stand for hundreds of counterparts in Syria and Egypt.

The number of books held in the Ashrafiya is a good example of why this library's averageness matters. The Ashrafiya held a remarkably large collection of more than 2,000 'books', many of them multi-volume works (more on this number in Chapter 2). To put this number into perspective, on the British Isles the number of books in medieval monastic libraries typically did not exceed the low to mid-hundreds. In the late fourteenth century the largest Friars' library, the Austin library of York, held 646 volumes; the catalogue of the Cistercian library of Meaux listed 363 volumes; the Benedictine Dover Priory's library stocked 450 volumes; and the Augustinian library of Lanthony had 508 volumes.[7] In this period, more than a century after the Ashrafiya was founded, only the most remarkable libraries had a collection that came close to 2,000 volumes: Norwich cathedral's priory arguably held more than 1,600 volumes; Christ Church cathedral in Canterbury and St Augustine's abbey both boasted some 1,800 volumes; and Bury St Edmunds more than 2,000.[8] As late as the fifteenth century, all of the libraries of Cambridge University taken together possessed no more than 2,000 volumes.[9] Although we do not have numbers for other Arabic libraries, the fact that the library of this rather unremarkable institution in Damascus was of a magnitude only matched a century later by the most prestigious institutions in medieval Britain gives a taste of how bookish life in Syria was.

The Ashrafiya catalogue is of outstanding importance for another very simple reason, namely that it has survived. Although libraries in Britain were clearly of a comparatively modest size, a large number of medieval library catalogues and inventories have come down. Certainly a large number of catalogues have been lost: of the 130 Cistercian abbeys and priories a mere three catalogues have survived; the same number has been preserved for the 50 Premonstratensian houses; and there is not a single catalogue for the 25 Gilbertine institutions.[10] Nonetheless, the surviving material is so large that the wide-ranging edition project of the *Corpus of British Medieval Library Catalogues* could be undertaken. For the pre-1500 Arabic Middle East, by contrast, the number of known surviving catalogues in a strict sense is easy to enumerate: two. In consequence, we face the absurd situation that our ability to write the history of the much larger and much more numerous book collections in the Middle East is severely curtailed compared with what we know about those in the relatively book-poor British lands.

The question why these catalogues have had a low survival rate is part of the much wider debate on document survival and archival practices in Middle Eastern societies and is beyond the scope of the present discussion.[11] However, with regard to the field of book studies two points need to be made that are to some degree also relevant for other fields of historical enquiry. First, although numbers are relatively low this cannot be a reason for sidelining documentary evidence and falling back on the more easily available narrative sources. The fact that the Ashrafiya catalogue has not been edited yet is a typical example of how crucial documents remain on the margins of scholarship while numerous research articles and monographs on Middle Eastern libraries continue to plough the depleted soil of a narrow band of narrative sources.[12] To give but one example of problems associated with narrative sources we only need to return to the issue of the actual size of medieval Arabic libraries. Narrative sources repeatedly gave outlandish numbers going into several hundred thousand volumes or even more than a million for one specific library. For instance, when the founder of the Ayyubid dynasty, Saladin, conquered the northern Mesopotamian town of Amad (Diyarbakir) in 579/1183 he supposedly found the rather unlikely number of 1,040,000 books in the library.[13] While the topos-like quality of these numbers is a fascinating topic in itself, to rely on them for writing the history of libraries in the Middle Period will contribute little to furthering our knowledge of the past. The reliance on narrative sources has also led to highly questionable statements on the Ashrafiya library itself. For instance, in his seminal work on Damascus, Louis Pouzet briefly remarks that 'we know of several madrasas in Damascus [including the Ashrafiya] to which books were endowed even though these institutions did not have a real library in the sense as it is generally understood today'.[14] On the contrary, as the following will show, there is no doubt that even according to the narrowest of definitions the Ashrafiya was very much a 'real library'.

The second point to be made on the use of documents in book studies is that there is a danger – as much as in other fields – of reproducing Eurocentric research paradigms by looking for pendants with source genres in Latin European societies. The relative absence of library catalogues clearly does not indicate a poor literary life and rather than lamenting the absence of what is presumably not there scholarship should instead mobilise the source genres that we do have for Middle Eastern societies. In the field of book and library studies these are, in particular, the rich marginal notes on the numerous medieval manuscripts, which give insight into their production, circulation and use.[15] It is this source genre that will drive most progress in research on medieval Arabic literary culture in the foreseeable future. In the field of medieval library studies Youssef Eche first pursued this approach in what is still a towering achievement: his *Les bibliothèques arabes publiques et semipubliques en Mésopotamie, en Syrie et en Égypte au Moyen Âge* from 1967. Although heavily reliant on narrative sources he put his knowledge of manuscripts as former director of the Syrian national collection (currently al-Assad National Library) to very good use. With this he offered the first diachronic account of the development of medieval Arabic libraries even though the earliest catalogue Eche was aware of was a late eighteenth-century catalogue from Aleppo.

Against this background there is little need to underline the importance of the Ashrafiya catalogue: written in the 670s/1270s it is not only the earliest-known Arabic medieval library catalogue, but it is – in a much wider perspective – one of very few pre-Ottoman book-related documents that are available at all. The only other known medieval Arabic catalogue is the inventory of the mosque library in the North African city of Kairouan from 693/1293–4, which only had 125 titles. If we broaden the search and include book-related documents other than catalogues there is more material: the largest such document is a list of more than 900 titles selected from Aleppo's libraries written in 694/1294, although its authenticity is in my view doubtful. In addition we have book lists of scholars' private collections, which range from brief informal notes with a few entries, via estate inventories to endowment lists with several hundred entries.[16] The largest number of medieval Middle Eastern book lists known so far comes from the Cairo Genizah, the depository for disused writings in the Ben Ezra synagogue, and the authoritative monograph on this material lists more than one hundred of them. These documents are mostly from the period from the eleventh century to the thirteenth century and most likely come from the usual Genizah territories of Egypt and southern Syria. Yet among these lists there are only four that refer to book holdings of institutions – works held in synagogues – in contrast to inventories of private collections, lists of categories of books, price-lists, legacies, and registers of loans. Furthermore, these four documents are difficult to use for comparative purposes in the framework of the present study as they are not catalogues, but rather inventory lists of all the property, including books, in a given synagogue. Compared with the Ashrafīya catalogue they are not only distinctively shorter, but they are much more concerned with the physical aspects of the books (size and format of paper, bound or unbound, number of volumes and pages). Concomitantly, they are also less concerned with developing a system of ordering the books according to criteria such as alphabet or theme – quite similar to the brief Kairouan catalogue-cum-inventory.[17]

The most recent survey of Arabic library 'catalogues' by Saᶜīd al-Jūmānī is only able to identify the frustratingly small number of twenty-five documents for the entire period up to the nineteenth century and only five of them, including the Ashrafīya and the Kairouan catalogues, belong to the pre-Ottoman period.[18] In addition it is problematic to apply the phrase 'library catalogue' to all of them as some refer to private collections and others are endowment lists, rather than library catalogues. For instance, one of the largest pre-Ottoman documents refers to the endowment of the Damascene scholar Ibn ᶜAbd al-Hādī (d. 909/1503). This endowment was made for the benefit of a madrasa library, but the document itself is not a catalogue composed for the use of a librarian and readers. It is first and foremost a legal document.[19] While it is thus highly problematic to compare the Ashrafīya catalogue with such chronologically and functionally diverse material, the following pages will occasionally refer to this 'Jūmānī-corpus'.

In addition to book-related documents, bibliographical book lists were composed by individuals during the medieval period, most famously the *Fihrist* of the fourth-/tenth-century Baghdadi bookseller Ibn al-Nadīm. It is likely that these lists expressed the accumulated knowledge of books gained by an individual over the course of many years in various cities and numerous collections. Confusingly, scholars have suggested that such book lists can provide insight into a specific 'library'.[20] Obviously this is highly misleading, as we have no indication whatsoever that the books known to the author of any such list were held in one single collection. In this sense Ibn al-Nadīm's work is comparable with the fourteenth-century *Catalogus* of Henry of Kirkstede, the prior of Bury St Edmunds. In this work Henry listed hundreds of authors and thousands of works leaving a fascinating bibliography, but certainly not a library catalogue. In the same vein it is debatable to what extent the seventeen Genizah book lists written by Joseph Rosh ha-Seder in about the late sixth/twelfth and early seventh/thirteenth century can be considered 'catalogues'.[21]

Middle Eastern library catalogues only survive in large numbers – or rather many more are known – from the Ottoman period onwards. The work of Ismail Erünsal has greatly contributed to our knowledge of libraries and their catalogues from the late ninth/fifteenth century onwards.[22] However, the Ottoman catalogues generally refer to collections in the non-Arabic provinces – as is also evident from the small size of Arabic catalogues in the Jūmānī-corpus. Istanbul collections appear over and over, but also those in other cities such as Bursa, Skopje, Konya and Edirne.[23] One of the most fascinating early Ottoman catalogues is the palace library inventory of 1502/3, which is the subject of a forthcoming publication edited by Gülru Necipoğlu, Cemal Kafadar and Cornell Fleischer. As there is no indication of a steep cultural decline in the Arabic provinces, the relative paucity of catalogues from these areas is most likely a result of academic preferences, with the Ottoman period in the Arabic lands still a relatively under-researched field.

Although we have Ottoman catalogues they are of limited relevance for this study, which will avoid drawing together material from a wide variety of regions and periods to develop the idea of a 'Muslim' library. Rather, it is an explicit aim of this book not to label the Ashrafiya as a 'Muslim' library that is supposedly representative of book collections in the vast geographical area influenced by Islam. To eschew such essentialist categories is no longer noteworthy in most fields of Middle Eastern history, but they are surprisingly durable in small sub-fields such as book studies and library studies. Work based on narrative sources is still very prone to adopt this label – largely because the net needs to be cast wide enough to reach a critical mass of source material.[24] However, the Ashrafiya was set up and run in a specific local context that is fundamental to any satisfying analysis: its setting in the urban topography of Damascus and its arrangement by an outstanding librarian played just as crucial a role as the background of the two endowers. The present study is in this sense very much meant to show that the Ashrafiya is best understood with a micro-historical approach.

To write a book on the basis of a unique document poses considerable challenges as there are hardly any points of comparison. While I will make occasional references on the basis of narrative sources to other libraries, mostly in Syria and Egypt, the different nature of the information available makes a far-reaching contextualisation simply impossible. The more promising strategy has thus been to compare the findings on the Ashrafiya with a case where similar source material has survived and has been made accessible. Here contemporaneous Latin European history offers ample material, but rather than using 'Latin Europe', an essentialist category that has gained significant traction in recent work on Middle Eastern history, this study draws comparisons with one specific region. The *Corpus of British Medieval Library Catalogues* offers a series of editions and studies on catalogues that are very similar to the Ashrafiya catalogue. Now standing at fifteen titles with hundreds of medieval catalogues they give a unique insight into the history of medieval libraries in one specific region. These documents are not only contemporaneous with the Ashrafiya catalogue, but they are – in contrast to many of the Arabic documents in the Jūmānī-corpus – in function and intent identical with it.

Keeping these introductory remarks in mind, the present study has three main aims: to provide the historical context for the Ashrafiya library, to make the catalogue available for future research and to propose how the catalogue may be fruitfully employed in such research. Chapter 1 discusses the library's foundation in the Ayyubid period with particular emphasis on the possible origins of its book stock. It further follows the library's history in the following centuries until it gradually disappears from the educational landscape of Mamluk Damascus in the middle of the ninth/fifteenth century. Surviving manuscripts and the notes on them are then used to examine the collection's fate in the Ottoman period. In Chapter 2 the catalogue is analysed in order to understand the organisation of this medieval library, in particular how the books were arranged on the shelves. This close reading of the catalogue makes it possible to reconstruct the library's spatiality and thus offers the first insights into questions such as where books were kept in educational institutions and how shelves were arranged. The building that once housed the Ashrafiya was torn down in the early twentieth century. However, combining the catalogue with surviving survey data, contemporaneous illustrations and reports in narrative sources gives us a unique understanding of what a medieval Damascene library looked like. Chapter 3 turns to the holdings of this library and seeks to ascertain the intellectual profile of its books. The catalogue is used here to offer an insight into the holdings of an educational library – a discussion that has hitherto been impossible simply because of the lack of adequate sources. Most intriguingly it shows that this library held a diversity and plurality of titles, which go well beyond the subjects typically associated with madrasa teaching.

The catalogue itself is at the heart of Chapter 4 and here the individual entries are identified. In many cases a title's identification is unproblematic and straightforward. Yet in numerous cases the identification is debatable and what Richard Sharpe stated with reference to medieval British catalogues and book lists is easily applicable to the Middle Eastern context: 'Entries in medieval booklists can sometimes seem like a fiendish species of crossword, demanding to be solved but providing incomplete or otherwise inadequate clues.'[25] This is especially true because the number of Arabic works in circulation during the period when the Ashrafiya catalogue was prepared was considerably larger and more multifaceted than the titles that circulated on the British Isles in this period. The Ashrafiya cataloguer repeatedly used short titles to refer to books, which leaves considerable room for interpretation. Ascribing an entry to a known title is thus to situate it on a spectrum with reasoned argument at one end, conjecture in the middle and informed guess at the other end. The rationale for identifying the specific titles is provided in Chapter 4 and the reader can thus see my line of argument. By contrast, Chapters 1 to 3 do not indicate in each case how secure a given book's identification is. In some cases I may be wrong – and it would rather be surprising if this was not the case – but I am confident that systematic thematic, regional or chronological bias does not underlie any such mistakes. Individual erroneous identifications should therefore not undermine the broader arguments made in these chapters.

Finally, Chapter 5 provides a diplomatic edition of the catalogue, which should be read in conjunction with the catalogue's facsimile-reproduction (Plates 6–54). The reproductions allow readers to follow my arguments on title identification and, more importantly, they show the catalogue's organisation, which cannot be adequately reflected in an edition. The indexing of such a large document is inevitably unsatisfying and cannot possibly cater for the various ways researchers may want to use it. In consequence, the data contained in Chapter 4 is available as an open-resource database, which allows users to manipulate the information commensurate with their research questions. As there is nothing as unreliable and unstable as references to internet links in printed works, the interested reader is invited to locate it with the search terms 'The Ashrafiya Library Database'.

Historical Context

At the point when the Ashrafiya library was founded, that is, the seventh/thirteenth century, Damascus was arguably the hub of cultural activities in the Arabic Middle East. Syria and its cities had emerged in the course of the sixth/twelfth century as one of the main centres of Arabic literary life, scholarship and manuscript production. This was in some sense an atypical position for Damascus and other Syrian cities, as they had been traditionally overshadowed by regional heavyweights Baghdad and Cairo. It was in these two cities that political control was traditionally located – best exemplified by the Fatimid and 'Abbasid Caliphates who took full advantage of the rich economic resources provided by the irrigated lands in their vicinity. However, the regionalisation of political control in the wider Middle East had opened up new windows of opportunity for hitherto marginalised regions such as Syria. From the fourth/tenth century onwards Baghdad was suffering from lower agricultural returns in Mesopotamia due to overexploitation of the lands.[26] While this process did not necessarily entail an overall economic decline – the rich cultural activities under the Saljuq rulers in the fifth/eleventh and sixth/twelfth centuries would have hardly been feasible within such a decline context – it clearly reduced the relative prominence of Baghdad in the wider region. In the same vein Egypt was embroiled for most of the sixth/twelfth century in intricate infighting, which substantially reduced its trans-regional political and also its cultural role.

In this period from the mid-sixth/twelfth to the mid-seventh/thirteenth century, what may be called the 'Syrian Century', the Syrian lands achieved first under the Zangid and subsequently under the Ayyubid dynasties a large degree of autonomy from the dominance of neighbouring regions, especially Egypt. This unusual degree of autonomy and the prominence of the region, and in particular Damascus, was to gradually disappear with the foundation of the Mamluk Empire, when Syrian cities became increasingly subordinate to the political centre in Egypt. Egypt emerged at this point in the seventh/thirteenth century not only as the leading political but also the main cultural region in the Arabic-speaking Middle East and was to remain in this position for the following centuries. At the same time the Mongol Ilkhanid rulers in Iraq and further to the east inaugurated a new epoch where Persian increasingly became the main written language and where cities such as Tabriz emerged as cultural hubs.[27]

The Syrian Century was not characterised by a highly centralised political structure. On the contrary, the pattern of political organisation can best be understood in terms of a 'post-Saljuq' political culture where sovereignty was seen to rest within the ruling family at large. In consequence, there was little tendency towards centralisation and sovereignty was generally parcelled out to the various households that clustered around the family's powerful men (and sometimes women).[28] The Ayyubid family confederation is a clear example of this political structure where a shared dynastic identity only became effective in times of external threats. On account of the high number of small lordships, the political map of Syria during the Ayyubid period was, to say the least, colourful. After the heavyweights of Damascus, Aleppo and northern Mesopotamia around Mayyāfāriqīn (northeast of Diyarbakir), came two second-rank lordships, Hama and Homs, and finally a third layer of more or less ephemeral lordships with little land such as al-Karak/Crac (Transjordan), Boṣrā (southeast of Damascus), Bāniyās (southwest of Damascus), Baʿlbakk (north of Damascus), Manbij (northeast of Aleppo), al-Ruhā/Edessa (modern-day Urfa) and Sarūj/Sorogia (southwest of al-Ruhā/Edessa). Added to this was a fourth level of mostly non-Ayyubid lords of castles who, time and time again, succeeded in carving out semi-independent minuscule lordships.

This multitude of autonomous lordships in Syria had a strong impact on scholarly and artistic activities, as the various lords were in fierce competition to furnish their often quite extravagant claims to political hegemony with artistic patronage. This led also to intensive building activities across the various Ayyubid cities and towns. For instance, a total of 74 mausolea and 76 teaching institutions alone were founded in the eighty-five years that Damascus was under Ayyubid control.[29] The intensity of these building activities, as much as scholarly and artistic activities, are testament to the economic upsurge in the region that began in the sixth/twelfth century and reached its peak in the first half of the seventh/thirteenth century. The economic blossoming of the period was accompanied by far-reaching monetary reforms that ensured stable currencies in the region, including the introduction of the region's first weight-controlled silver dirham for three centuries.[30] The Syrian Century was thus more than just a period of political autonomy; it was underlain by sustained economic growth and an outstandingly rich cultural life.

It was in this world that the eponym of the Ashrafiya library, al-Malik al-Ashraf, forged his career. As a son of al-Malik al-ᶜĀdil, Saladin's brother who had successfully monopolised political control of most of the Ayyubid lands for himself and his offspring, he clearly belonged to the winning branch of the family.[31] It was in Diyār Muḍār, the northern Mesopotamian region bordering Syria, that al-Malik al-Ashraf entered political life in 597/1200 when he was around twenty years of age. With the towns of Ḥarrān and Ruhāᵓ/Edessa as his power base, he gradually expanded his territories to build up an impressive principality that was to dominate all of northern Mesopotamia. He first acted as his father's deputy, then gradually came to rule in his own name and finally became one of the main players in the Ayyubid family confederation. Marriage alliances within the intricate northern Mesopotamian political landscape buttressed his strong position: His first wife, who he married in 600/1203–4, was the sister of the Zangid ruler in Mosul, Arslanshāh; and his second wife was the daughter of the Kurdish, turned Armenian, turned Georgian commander Ivane.[32] In light of his formidable position it is therefore slightly surprising that he relinquished half of these lands in exchange for Damascus in 626/1229. In so doing, he neutralised his role as the main rival to his brother, al-Kāmil, who already ruled Egypt and could now embark on extending informal influence in Syria. Al-Malik al-Ashraf, by contrast, now had geographically separated realms around Damascus and in northern Mesopotamia, which significantly reduced his military capacities. Even though he retained several castles in northern Mesopotamia and continued to participate in every major campaign in the area, he had effectively relinquished his political home turf.[33]

When al-Malik al-Ashraf arrived in Damascus he did so with a slightly tainted reputation. Together with al-Kāmil he had ruthlessly ousted his predecessor and nephew al-Malik al-Nāṣir Dāwūd, certainly one of the most tragic figures of the Ayyubid period, who so often found himself to be a member of the losing political coalition. As al-Nāṣir came under increasing pressure he not only drew on his late father's popularity in the city, but successfully exploited the fact that al-Malik al-Ashraf had been promised Damascus in the framework of broader political dealings that involved Frederick II. It did not require too much effort from al-Nāṣir to have al-Ashraf and al-Kāmil condemned in large preaching assemblies for allying with a Christian ruler who came under the banner of a Crusade. Although al-Ashraf's reputation was thus initially blemished he proved to be an effective ruler who secured years of stability for the city and kept it out of military conflicts until he died heirless in 635/1237.

With the inauguration of his mausoleum, al-Malik al-Ashraf's posthumous career became intertwined with that of another al-Ashraf, namely al-Ashraf Aḥmad whose book collection also became part of the Ashrafīya library. The relevant point here is that al-Ashraf Aḥmad is representative of the civilian elite that did very well during the Syrian Century. Local political autonomy combined with an expanding economy allowed members of the urban civilian elites, among others, to play a crucial role as patrons of the arts and scholarship in general and as founders of local endowed libraries in particular.[34] Al-Ashraf Aḥmad was the son of one of the most famous administrators in the early Ayyubid period, al-Qāḍī al-Fāḍil. In his early life he worked in administrative roles continuing the family tradition and became vizier to al-Malik al-ᶜĀdil, but after the ruler's death he devoted most of the rest of his life to scholarly activities. The enormous wealth that he had inherited from his father also allowed him to act as patron of established scholars and students.[35]

The establishment of the Ashrafīya library was thus inscribed in the confluence of the period's main trends with respect to supporting cultural activities, namely the active patronage of local rulers and of members of the civilian elites. It is far from clear whether the more than one hundred teaching institutions and mausolea that were founded in Damascus during the Ayyubid period had libraries that were as large as that of the Ashrafīya and, in some cases, whether they even had libraries at all. However, it is likely that the size of the Ashrafīya's collection is exemplary of broader trends as we only know of it because of the survival of its catalogue. The narrative sources alone do not give any indication as to this library's size, but since they are also silent on other institutions' libraries this cannot be taken to indicate a small size. The overall number of mausolea and teaching institutions founded in Egypt and Syria during the Ayyubid period alone is close to 300,[36] to which we have to add book collections in mosques and palaces as well as private collections. By the late Ayyubid period the number of books in circulation in these lands could thus have easily been in the high hundreds of thousands; the Ashrafīya catalogue, at least, leaves little doubt that a reader in Damascus would have had access to tens of thousands of books in libraries alone.

Notes

1. Şeşen, 'Cāḥīz'in Eserleri' and Şeşen, *Salahaddin'den*, 336; al-Munajjid, *Qawāʿid*, 20–1. Other references include Sayyid, *al-Kitāb al-ʿarabī al-makhṭūṭ*, II, 526–7 and Gacek, 'Cataloguing', 173.
2. For instance, Touati, *L'armoire à sagesse*, 302–3, who states that the catalogue supposedly ends with the letter *mīm* and that it gives the full name of the author and codicological information for each entry.
3. Al-Jūmānī, 'al-Fahāris al-makhṭūṭa' and al-Jūmānī, 'Fihrist'.
4. The term 'Syria' as used in this book does not refer to the modern nation-state of Syria, but to historical Bilād al-Shām, which includes the modern nation-states of Lebanon, Palestine, Israel, Jordan, Syria (except for northern Mesopotamia) and parts of southern Turkey.
5. On these developments see, in particular, Gründler, *Book Revolution*; Shatzmiller, *Early Knowledge Economy*; Ali, *Arabic Literary Salons*.
6. Hirschler, *Written Word*, 29.
7. York: Humphreys, *Friars' Libraries*, 11–154; Meaux: Bell, *Cistercians, Gilbertines and Premonstratensians*, 34–82; Dover: Stoneman, *Dover Priory*; Lanthony: Webber and Watson, *Augustinian Canons*, 34–94.
8. Sharpe et al., *Benedictine Libraries*, XXV and Sharpe, 'Medieval Librarian', 228.

9. Lovatt, 'Introduction', XXX.
10. Bell, *Cistercians, Gilbertines and Premonstratensians*, XXIII.
11. For the relevant literature see Hirschler, 'Archival Practices'.
12. For instance, Ghanem, *Bibliotheksgeschichte*; ᶜAbd al-Mahdī, *al-Ḥaraka al-fikrīya*; Sibai, *Mosque Libraries*; Ibn Dohaish, 'Islamic Libraries'; Elayyan, 'Arabic-Islamic Libraries'; Pourhadi, 'Muslim Libraries'; Kügelgen, 'Bücher und Bibliotheken'; Green, 'History of Libraries'.
13. Abū Shāma, *al-Rawḍatayn*, III, 146.
14. Pouzet, *Damas*, 170.
15. This area of research has been in particular pursued by Boris Liebrenz for the Ottoman period, e.g. 'Die Rifāʿīya'. See also Görke and Hirschler, *Manuscript Notes*. Earlier examples of using notes from library history are patchy and include, for instance, Vajda, 'Trois manuscrits'.
16. Kairouan: Kairouan catalogue-cum-inventory, MS Raqqāda, Centre d'Études de la Civilisation et des Arts Islamiques, 289 discussed by Shabbūḥ, 'Sijill qadīm' and Voguet, 'L'inventaire'. (I thank Élise Voguet for having granted me access to the document's copy.) On the Aleppo list, *al-Muntakhab*, ed. Sbath, see Chapter 4. For an excellent example of the use of a private 'catalogue', albeit very small, see D'Ottone, 'La bibliothèque d'un savant Yéménite'. Another example of a library catalogue fragment is discussed in Nef, 'L'histoire des "mozarabes"'. Estate inventory: Haarmann, 'Library' and MS Jerusalem, al-Ḥaram al-sharīf 61, 180 and 532. Endowment list: Ibn ᶜAbd al-Hādī (d. 909/1503), *Fihrist al-kutub*, MS Damascus, al-Assad National Library, 3190 (written before 896/1491).
17. Allony, *Jewish Library*. I thank Miriam Frenkel for giving further background on these catalogues.
18. Al-Jūmānī, 'al-Fahāris al-makhṭūṭa'.
19. Ibn ᶜAbd al-Hādī, *Fihrist al-kutub*, MS Damascus, al-Assad National Library, 3190 (written before 896/1491).
20. Kohlberg, *Ibn Ṭāwūs*.
21. Rouse and Rouse, *Henry of Kirkestede*; Joseph Rosh ha-Seder: Allony, *Jewish Library*, nos. 97–114.
22. Erünsal, 'Catalogues and Cataloguing'; Erünsal, 'The Establishment and Maintenance of Collections'; Erünsal, 'History and Organization'.
23. Erünsal, *Ottoman Libraries: A Survey of the History*, 143–62; Stanley, 'Books of Umur Bey'.
24. See, for instance, the studies by Ibn Dohaish, 'Islamic Libraries'; Elayyan,

'Arabic-Islamic Libraries'; Pourhadi, 'Muslim Libraries'; Kügelgen, 'Bücher und Bibliotheken'.

25. Sharpe, *Titulus*, 83.
26. For a good overview of the relevant literature see Wing, 'Rich in Goods', 301–20.
27. Pfeiffer, *Tabriz*.
28. Chamberlain, 'Military Patronage States', 135–53.
29. Korn, *Ayyubidische Architektur*, I, 115.
30. Heidemann, 'Economic Growth'.
31. The best overview of Ayyubid politics, including the career of al-Ashraf, remains Humphreys, *From Saladin to the Mongols*, on which this summary is mostly based. To this add Kaya, 'Artuklu Melikleri ile Ilişkileri'.
32. First wife: Al-Nuᶜaymī, *al-Dāris*, I, 129; second wife: Eastmond, *Tamta's World*.
33. Humphreys, *From Saladin to the Mongols* and Kaya, *Anadolu'da Eyyûbiler*.
34. Hirschler, *Written Word*, 139–40.
35. For al-Ashraf Aḥmad see TI, 641–50, pp. 149–51 and the sources given there.
36. Korn, *Ayyubidische Architektur*, I, 48.

1

The Making and Unmaking of a Medieval Library

The Ayyubid period was one of extensive building activity during which many cities of Syria and Egypt were substantially redeveloped. Damascus was at the very centre of these activities and the city continually witnessed the erection of new edifices, especially educational institutions. The patrons of these 'constructions of power and piety' belonged mostly to the military and political elites.[1] Al-Malik al-Ashraf was no exception and when he passed away in 635/1237 he had prominently inscribed himself into the urban texture of Damascus. His most visible legacy was two Dār al-ḥadīths, institutions dedicated to the study of the Prophetic tradition, which al-Malik al-Ashraf had built in the decade that he ruled the city. The inaugurations of the two institutions were important moments in the city's life and the buildings were to remain focal points of scholarly and devotional activities in the decades and centuries to come.

Their position within the urban landscape of Damascus was carefully chosen: Al-Ashraf built his first Dār al-ḥadīth intra muros and close to the citadel, the seat of military and political might in Damascus (number 164 in Map 1.1). Its significance went well beyond the scholarly and social elite as it housed a relic that al-Malik al-Ashraf had brought to Damascus, the Prophet's sandal. This sandal was a central element of the increasing Muḥammad veneration that characterised the religious life of Damascus and Syria during this period. It remained for almost two centuries, until it was carried off by Tamerlane (Tīmūr (d. 807/1405)), one of the city's major attractions.[2] Al-Malik al-Ashraf's second Dār al-ḥadīth was placed outside the city walls on the slope of Qāsyūn Mountain to the northwest of the city.

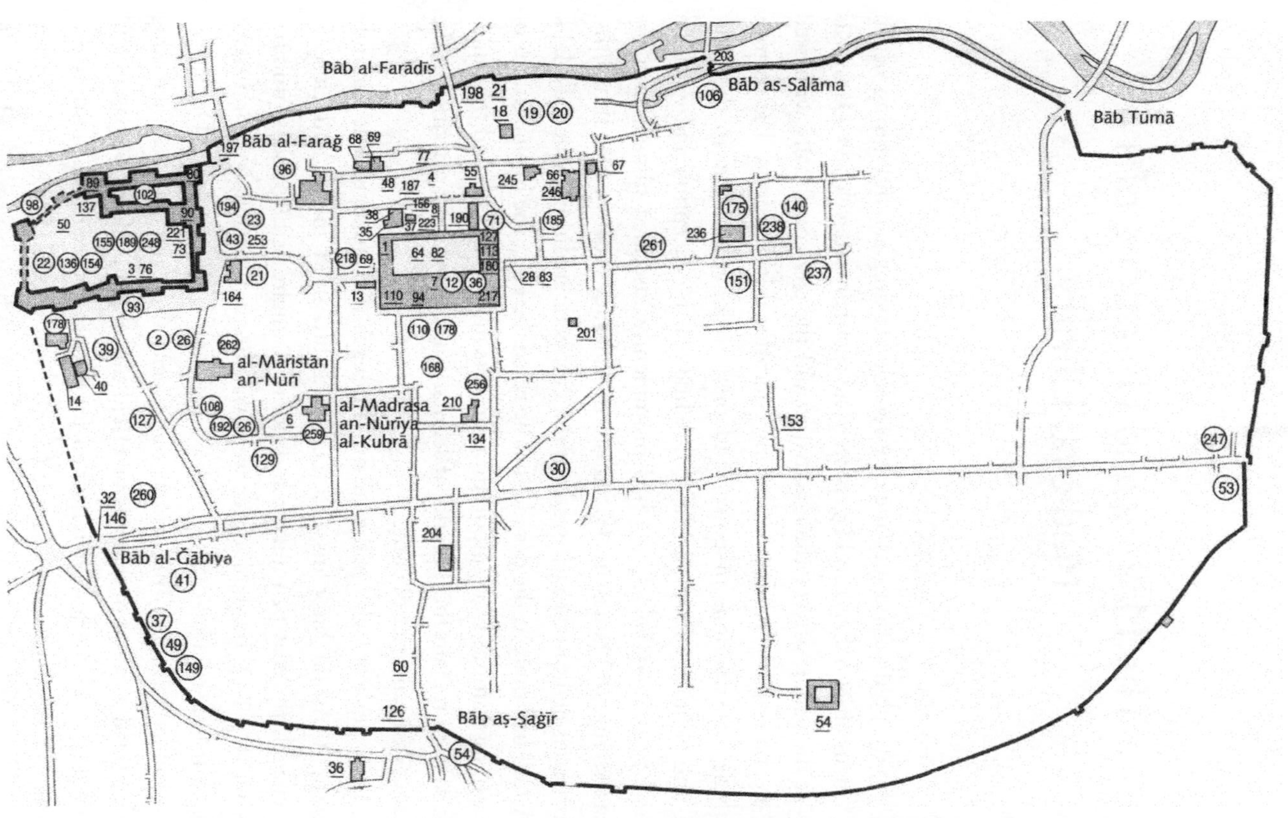

Map 1.1 Ayyubid buildings in Damascus (Ashrafiya mausoleum = no. 187). © Korn, *Ayyubidische Architektur*, I, 110

In the previous decades the Ṣāliḥīya suburb on Qāsyūn had witnessed rapid development and was a flourishing part of Damascus when he was ruling the city. Al-Malik al-Ashraf further deepened his devotional footprint by building or rebuilding several mosques across the city.

To set up an endowment such as a Dār al-ḥadīth not only inserted the founder into the urban topography, but also positioned him or her as a – or preferably *the* – patron of the city's civilian elites. Positions in the larger endowments were so prestigious and lucrative that the great scholarly families – or rather dynasties – of Damascus competed fiercely for positions within these institutions.[3] The significance of founding the Qāsyūn Dār al-ḥadīth thus went well beyond inserting a building into one of the most rapidly developing areas of Damascus. It enabled al-Malik al-Ashraf to act as patron of the city's second *madhhab*, the Hanbalites, which had started to monopolise the area. His endowment for the Qāsyūn Dār al-ḥadīth was so large that the most important of all Hanbalite families, the Maqdisīs, ensured their control of its *mashyakha* (professorship). The citadel Dār al-ḥadīth, in turn, was controlled by the Shafiᶜites, the city's premier *madhhab*, but here no single family was ever able to dominate and the city's great Shafiᶜi families competed for its professorship.[4]

Al-Malik al-Ashraf had thus secured himself a long-lasting and multifaceted legacy at two crucial sites in the city. Yet it was the provisions for his third monument, his own mausoleum, that brought him closer to what was the undisputed centre of religious life in Damascus, the Umayyad Mosque. On account of the mosque's prestige the area around it was crammed with endowments of madrasas, mausolea, Dār al-ḥadīths and oratories. Rulers and other members of the political elite tended to leave their legacy close to the mosque's northern wall, the Kallāsa quarter, in a sense the 'Mausoleum Lane' of Ayyubid Damascus: the Zangid Sultan Nūr al-Dīn endowed the Kallāsa madrasa (B on Map 1.2); Saladin's mausoleum was at this site; his son al-Malik al-ᶜAzīz founded a madrasa (both D); Saladin's secretary and confidant al-Qāḍī al-Fāḍil erected a Dār al-ḥadīth (C); and al-Fāḍil's son al-Ashraf Aḥmad endowed an 'oratory' (labelled in contemporaneous texts with the nondescript term '*makān*').[5]

Al-Malik al-Ashraf was adamant that his mausoleum would lie at the very heart of this nexus of religious, political and cultural prestige. This was

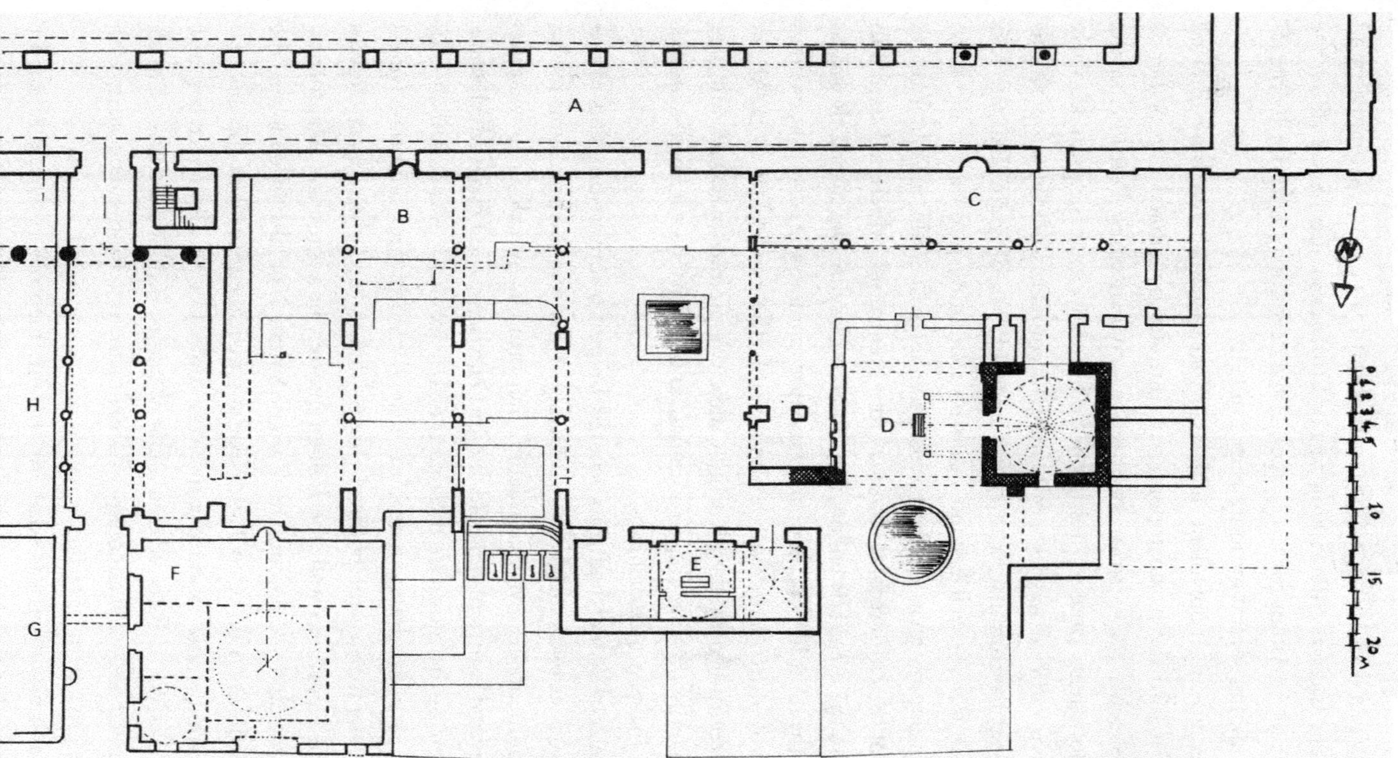

Map 1.2 Kallāsa quarter north of Umayyad Mosque with Ashrafiya mausoleum (E). © Moaz, 'Mausolée de Saladin', planche 1, with the permission of the French Institute for the Near East (Ifpo)

difficult as there was little space left in the Kallāsa quarter. The builders thus had to incorporate al-Ashraf Aḥmad's oratory into the design of al-Malik al-Ashraf's mausoleum to put it in close proximity to Saladin's mausoleum.[6] In this way the Ashrafiya mausoleum (E) was prominently positioned at the northern end of the courtyard formed by the aforementioned educational and funerary institutions. The mausoleum consisted of a central domed hall with a room on each side. The different sizes of the rooms, which made the building asymmetric, were probably the outcome of the difficulties the builders faced when squeezing the mausoleum into the Kallāsa quarter. Most of the building must have been destroyed at some point between 1917 (when Karl Wulzinger and Carl Watzinger surveyed it) and the death of ᶜAbd al-Qādir Ibn Badrān, who stated that only the dome survived, in 1927.[7] In the following decades this dome disappeared as well and today only the bare grave (*qabar*) remains (Plate 1). From the plan made by Wulzinger/Watzinger (that is the basis for Map 1.2) it is clear that the Ashrafiya mausoleum had retained the original orientation towards the courtyard mentioned by contemporaneous authors. The door for both rooms as well as the large window (*c.*2.5m by 3m) of the domed hall containing al-Malik al-Ashraf's tomb opened on to this court.[8]

The Ashrafiya mausoleum had two main purposes: to commemorate the deceased ruler and to support scholarship. Although its endowment deed has not come down to us and it is not quoted in the period's texts, the rich biographical tradition clearly shows this dual purpose. To commemorate was to recite the Koran at the tomb day and night, and we have the name of several individuals who were charged with this remunerated task.[9] With the large window facing the Umayyad Mosque and thus the Kallāsa quarter's central court, this was a very public commemoration contributing to the area's aural soundscape. In addition to these reciters the presence of the library most likely intensified commemorative recitation: the endowment notes on manuscripts of a Damascene mausoleum set up in the late seventh/thirteenth century stipulated that users were to recite the opening sura of the Koran and thrice the *ikhlāṣ* sura before reading the book.[10]

The second purpose, much more important within the scholarly hierarchy of the city, inserted the mausoleum into the Damascene landscape of teaching as provisions were made for a professorship. The scholarly field that the postholder was to teach refers back to the first purpose, as the post was dedicated to teaching Koran recitation. As seen above, the professorship in an endowment could carry considerable prestige and members of the grand scholarly families competed for them. The Maqdisīs monopolised the positions in al-Malik al-Ashraf's Qāsyūn Dār al-ḥadīth and, in the same vein, the first Dār al-ḥadīth that had been founded in Damascus by Nūr al-Dīn in the previous century, the Dār al-hadīth al-Nūrīya, remained in the hands of the ᶜAsākir family. The list of office-holders in al-Malik al-Ashraf's citadel Dār al-ḥadīth also reads like a Who's Who of the city's very best (Shafiᶜi) scholars: the first professor was Ibn al-Ṣalāḥ, author of the most important manual for *ḥadīth* study of his period; in the following decades we find al-Nawawī, one of the greatest *ḥadīth* scholars of the Mamluk period; ᶜAbd al-Karīm Ibn al-Ḥarastānī, scion of one of the prominent scholarly families of Damascus; and Taqī al-Dīn al-Subkī, member of one of the trans-regional scholarly families so typical of the Mamluk period.[11]

The post in the Ashrafīya mausoleum, by contrast, never attracted prominent scholars and the great families of Damascus did not compete for the one modest teaching position it offered. The first office-holder, Abū Shāma, was at least a local scholar of some repute and the second, al-Sulamī, belonged to one of the great families, although he himself died too young to gain any standing. But their successors are without exception minor scholars. Repeatedly they are newcomers to the city, from North Africa (number six in *Table 1.1*), northern Mesopotamia (number eight) and Iraq (number nine), but sometimes they are so obscure that we are lacking even the most basic biographical data, for instance in the cases of number seven and number eleven. The scholarly reputation of some postholders was quite dubious, such as number twelve who 'was not distinguished in this field [Koran recitation] . . . and nobody learned anything from him'.[12]

The Ashrafīya mausoleum clearly was a scholarly institution and contemporaneous texts interchangeably designated it as 'mausoleum' or 'madrasa'. However, in contrast to Nūr al-Dīn's mausoleum further to the south, which is clearly a 'funerary madrasa', the Ashrafīya was first and foremost a commemorative mausoleum, with some additional educational activities. It was thus a rather marginal run-of-the-mill endowment with a single professorship for teaching Koran recitation. The additional positions for reciting the Koran were low-level positions held by unimportant scholars who mostly remain

Table 1.1 Ashrafiya mausoleum, shaykhs of Koran recitation

1	ᶜAbd al-Raḥmān b. Ismāᶜīl Abū Shāma	(d. 665/1268)
2	Muḥammad b. Isrāʾīl al-Sulamī	(d. 671/1272–3)
3	ᶜAlī b. Muḥammad Kamāl al-Dīn	(d. 692/1292)
4	Ibrāhīm b. Falāḥ al-Iskandarānī	(d. 702/1303)
5	Ibrāhim b. Ghālī Jamāl al-Dīn	(d. 708/1308)
6	Abū Bakr b. Muḥammad al-Tūnisī	(d. 718/1318–19)
7	Muḥammad b. Baḍḥān Badr al-Dīn	(d. ?)
8	Muḥammad b. ᶜAlī al-Mawṣilī	(d. 727/1327)
9	Muḥammad b. Aḥmad al-Raqqī	(d. 742/1341)
10	Aḥmad Shihāb al-Dīn Ibn al-Naqīb	(d. 764/1363)
11	ᶜAbd al-Wahhāb b. al-Salār Amīn al-Dīn	(d. ?)
12	Shaᶜbān b. ᶜAlī al-Ḥanafī	(d. 803/1400–1)
13	Aḥmad b. Aḥmad al-Ramlī[a]	(d. 923/1517)

a 1: Al-Nuᶜaymī, *al-Dāris*, II, 291–8. 2: Ibn al-Jazarī, *Ghāyat al-nihāya*, II, 100. 3: TI, 691–700, pp. 163–4. 4: al-Dhahabī, *Maᶜrifat al-qurrā*ʾ, I, 381. 5: Ibn Ḥajar, *al-Durar*, I, 54. 6: TI, 701–46, pp. 165–6. 7: Ibn Kathīr, *al-Bidāya*, XIV, 101. 8: al-Dhahabī, *Muᶜjam*, II, 255 who left the position to return to his hometown. 9: al-Dhahabī, *al-ᶜIbar*, IV, 126. 10: Ibn Kathīr, *Bidāya*, XIV, 345. 11: Ibn Kathīr, *al-Bidāya*, XIV, 345. 12: Ibn al-Jazarī, *Ghāyat al-nihāya*, I, 325. 13: Ibn al-ᶜImād, *Shadharāt*, X, 168.

anonymous. The other employees were an administrator (*nāẓir*), who managed the endowment's finances, and those who did the menial housekeeping tasks.[13] However, it seems that there were no provisions for students, which would have been obligatory had the endowment played a more salient role in the city's intellectual life. The Ashrafiya mausoleum thus clearly ranked towards the bottom end of the educational institutions in the city. That only one paid teaching position existed and that no provisions were made for students is also relevant for developing an understanding of the library's role. This library clearly did not primarily serve a small group of scholars and students resident in the building or closely attached to this institution. Rather, users coming from the outside were meant to read its considerable holdings – a feature to which we will repeatedly return in this and the following chapters.

Stocking the Ashrafiya I: The Royal Library of al-Malik al-Ashraf

While it is relatively easy to trace an endowment's development and position within the urban topography (including the city's soundscape) and the scholarly landscape, the case is very different for libraries for several reasons.

Narrative sources are not terribly interested in the details of how a library was set up or, most importantly for our purposes here, from where its books were sourced. In the same vein, even if the mausoleum's endowment deed had come down to us it would have been in all likelihood of no significance for this question; surviving deeds from the subsequent Mamluk period only contain very limited information on books in an institution's library.[14] Furthermore, understanding the process of how a library stock was built up is complicated by the fact that books were not produced 'in-house' in scriptorium-like practices: neither the narrative sources nor the identifiable Ashrafiya manuscripts give any evidence in this regard.

The foundation of medieval libraries has thus been a closed book and in the absence of positive evidence, secondary literature has repeatedly assumed that a library's stock was provided by the endowment's founder. While this assumption seems commonsensical, the analysis of the Ashrafiya catalogue shows a more complex picture, namely that its books were sourced from two very different collections: al-Malik al-Ashraf's royal, or Sultanic, library, as may be expected, and the book collection of al-Ashraf Aḥmad. It has to be underlined that in general there was no scarcity of books with which to stock a medieval Arabic library. Even though many books were endowed and thus, to take the literal Arabic translation of *mawqūf* theoretically 'immobilised', books did remain highly mobile and could easily move between various collections. One may describe this in terms such as theft, fraud and misappropriation, but it is more useful to think of this process in terms of 'reconstitution'. Many endowed books that were 'mobilised' in breach of the endowment's stipulations ultimately made their way back to the shelves of another endowment library.[15]

Royal libraries have not yet been studied and even Youssef Eche remains conspicuously silent on this issue in his seminal study of everything library-related in medieval Damascus.[16] The narrative sources provide no clues where al-Malik al-Ashraf (or other Ayyubid rulers) may have held his books while he resided in Damascus (or in northern Mesopotamia in the earlier stages of his career) and at what point they were moved to the mausoleum. That Ayyubid Sultans had their own libraries is evident from notes on manuscripts, which refer, for instance, to 'the library of the victorious ruler . . . Saladin' or 'the noble, Sultanic and royal library of al-Afḍal'.[17] The narrative sources also repeatedly mention such libraries, for instance the library of al-Malik al-Ashraf's brother and predecessor in Damascus, al-Malik al-Muᶜaẓẓam.[18] The statement that the scribe Ḥasan al-Qaylawī was in the service of al-Malik al-Ashraf in Ḥarrān and Damascus and 'was charged with the libraries in them', refers to running the ruler's royal library at the court in northern Mesopotamia and subsequently Damascus.[19] Consequently, we find on one of the manuscripts, which al-Qaylawī copied and that ultimately found its way into the Ashrafiya library, the dedication to 'the Sultanic and royal library of al-Ashraf'.[20] Other dedication notes on manuscripts, usually superbly executed and written in gold, refer to this royal library as 'the library of our lord the Sultan al-Malik al-Ashraf'.[21] In Damascus this royal library was certainly housed in the citadel and this is probably also true for the other principalities.[22] However, it is only with the Ottoman conquest of the Mamluk lands some three centuries after al-Malik al-Ashraf's rule that we find the first documentary evidence for such a citadel library. This is a protocol from 923/1517 listing the books held in the formerly Mamluk 'library in the citadel' of Aleppo, which were to be taken to Istanbul or disposed of.[23]

The main point concerning al-Malik al-Ashraf's royal library is that analysis of the Ashrafiya catalogue shows that substantial parts of this collection made its way into the mausoleum. As may be expected, the period's chronicles and biographical dictionaries do not mention the collection's role in building up the library at all. Yet its role is evident in three characteristic features of the Ashrafiya mausoleum's collection: namely, the prominence of authors from the ruler's entourage, reflected also in panegyrics; the relative prominence of authors linked to northern Mesopotamia, where al-Malik al-Ashraf had ruled previously and where he continued to hold lands while ruling Damascus; and finally the presence of particularly expensive manuscripts. The library has more than a dozen works of panegyric verse and prose that were most likely dedicated to al-Malik al-Ashraf, among them several by his panegyric and secretary Ibn al-Nabīh, but also by other poets of the period (see Chapter 4).[24] The importance of al-Malik al-Ashraf's collection is also reflected in the panegyric poetry for other rulers on the shelves of the Ashrafiya library. This poetry is first and foremost dedicated to Ayyubid rulers while individual rulers of earlier dynasties make only occasional appearances, such as the Zangids, the Saljuqs and possibly the Fatimids.[25]

Among the works dedicated to Ayyubid rulers the most prominent are those addressed to the Ayyubid dynasty's founder, Saladin, and to his successor and al-Malik al-Ashraf's father, al-Malik al-ᶜĀdil.[26] Their inclusion in the library's holdings is linked to the crucial role that these two figures played in al-Malik al-Ashraf's strategies of legitimisation. Presenting oneself as the heir to Saladin was central to warding off claims by non-Ayyubid contenders and al-Malik al-Ashraf had to deal with many of those in northern Mesopotamia. Before he came to Damascus in 626/1229 he had spent the better part of three decades dealing with local rivals, especially Artuqids, Zangids and Georgians. The claim to Saladin's legacy was visually and aurally expressed in al-Malik al-Ashraf's final resting place itself as he positioned his mausoleum right next to that of his uncle. Celebrating his father al-ᶜĀdil, in turn, was indispensable for inner-dynastic competition as it justified the exclusion of Saladin's offspring from playing a prominent role in the Ayyubid family confederation. The other main Ayyubid ruler represented in a panegyric work in this library is al-Kāmil, al-Malik al-Ashraf's brother and close ally, who had been instrumental in securing al-Malik al-Ashraf's rule of the city.[27] It is thus not surprising that this Damascene library did not hold a single panegyric for al-Malik al-Ashraf's nephew and predecessor in the city, the before-mentioned tragic al-Nāṣir Dāwūd, who had been ousted by the alliance between al-Kāmil and al-Malik al-Ashraf. The same applies to al-Malik al-Muᶜaẓẓam, al-Nāṣir's father. Although al-Muᶜaẓẓam and al-Nāṣir were both lavishly praised by poets in Damascus, the inclusion of poetry celebrating the most prominent targets of al-Malik al-Ashraf's close alliance with al-Kāmil would clearly have been inopportune.

The role of al-Ashraf's royal library is not only evident in panegyrics, but also in the issue of patronage. This is writ large right at the beginning of the catalogue: its very first title is the summary of Muslim's *ḥadīth* collection that his ally al-Kāmil had authored. Held in Damascus during al-Malik al-Ashraf's reign this collection played a vital role in establishing the political elite's credentials to act as scholarly patrons. More pertinent for the present discussion are those titles that were written by the entourage of al-Malik al-Ashraf or directly dedicated to him. Panegyric poetry has been discussed above, but this is not the only way that the ruler's patronage was reflected in the Ashrafiya library. We thus find literature typical of court culture, such as a book of falconry most likely dedicated to al-Malik al-Ashraf, a mirror for princes definitely dedicated to him, a medical work composed by a Damascene physician who served at the city's Ayyubid court and a historical work on al-Ashraf's reign.[28] A second set of works dedicated to him deals with religious topics in a narrow sense, such as edifying writings, religious poetry, sermons and invocations for the ruler during Friday sermons.[29] Finally, we have literary works in the widest sense of the term composed for al-Malik al-Ashraf including titles dealing with love and with Arabic–Persian word puzzles.[30] Prose panegyric literature may also be included in this group, such as a treatise on the ruler's victory over the Khwarazmshah Jalāl al-Dīn Mingburnu in Anatolia in 627/1230 and two further unknown works with a title indicating (probably prose) panegyric content.[31]

That al-Malik al-Ashraf had built up such a royal library is never explicitly mentioned in the narrative sources, but they do mention his role as active patron of scholarly activities at his court. Although his reputation in modern scholarship has been rather as a narrow-minded and 'orthodox' ruler, as we will see in Chapter 3, he clearly enjoyed a courtly life of entertainment and songs. In addition to his constructions of power and piety, he also built several pleasure palaces in the surroundings of Damascus, which 'captivate and amaze the beholder'.[32] More importantly, he had a broad interest in different fields of knowledge, including mathematics.[33] This is expressed in anecdotes involving the ruler. In one such anecdote a scholar proudly reported that he had washed off all manuscripts of Ibn Sīnā's encyclopaedia of natural history, mathematics and philosophy, *The Book of Healing* (*al-Shifāʾ*), in Baghdad's libraries. When the conversation later turned to the high number of deaths on account of diseases in Baghdad, the ruler dryly commented: 'How could it be otherwise as you destroyed the *Shifāʾ*?'[34] It does not come as a surprise that this work sat on the shelves of the Ashrafiya library.[35]

The importance of al-Malik al-Ashraf's royal collection in setting up the Ashrafiya library is also evident in a second characteristic feature, namely the distinct role of works from northern Mesopotamia. As seen in the Introduction, al-Malik al-Ashraf's career started in this region and he remained deeply involved in its local politics throughout his career. Except for Mosul, which al-Malik al-Ashraf never controlled, northern Mesopotamia was by no means a centre of scholarship. The minor towns of the region could not compete at all with the trans-regional heavyweights of Damascus, Aleppo and Baghdad, and they were also easily overshadowed by regional second-rate towns such as Homs and Hama, which were better able to provide the posts and stipends in educational endowments that fostered local scholarship. However, cultural life in northern Mesopotamia did experience a relative blossoming for the same reason that we have seen before in the Syrian context, namely a highly regionalised political landscape with numerous local courts in fierce competition to attract poets, musicians and scholars.[36] As the dominant political player in the region's colourful political landscape, al-Malik al-Ashraf eagerly participated in this race for prestige among local rulers. This was expressed in the panegyric poetry discussed above, in particular the work of Ibn al-Nabīh, who died before al-Malik al-Ashraf moved to Damascus. Narrative sources mention other scholars, especially physicians, who dedicated works to al-Ashraf at his northern Mesopotamian court. A rather obscure member of the northern Mesopotamian scholarly al-Athīr dynasty, Sharaf al-Dīn Ibn al-Athīr authored an anthology of prose and poetry for al-Ashraf. His patronage during these years in the north also stretched beyond his realms to Aleppo from where he had books sent to him and where book traders offered books to him.[37]

In the Ashrafiya library itself the northern Mesopotamian connection is especially evident in those works that have a very clear local character, such as an epistle referring to one of al-Malik al-Ashraf's castles in the region and poems sent to al-Malik al-Ashraf while he was busy expanding his influence in northern Syria.[38] At least two works in the Ashrafiya library, with poetry and on medicine, addressed al-Malik al-Ashraf as 'King of the Armenians' (Shāh Arman) in their titles, a title he specifically used during the northern Mesopotamian period of his career. Similarly northern Mesopotamian are those texts that show patronage by local rulers other than al-Ashraf, but would not have made it to Damascus without his involvement. Panegyrics for the Zangid ruler of the principality of Sinjār, al-Malik al-Manṣūr, arguably found their way into the library because al-Malik al-Ashraf took over this principality – and its local literary tradition – in 617/1220.[39] Other texts in the library may also have been authored in the region, including panegyrics for the Rum Saljuq Sultan ᶜAlāᵓ al-Dīn, poetry composed under the patronage of a local Kurdish lord and an autobiographical account written under the patronage of the Ayyubid ruler of Mayyāfāriqīn, al-Malik al-Muẓaffar Ghāzī.[40]

This northern Mesopotamian profile of the Ashrafiya is also evident when we consider not only the content of the texts, but also information on their production. For instance, the Ashrafiya manuscript of a prose and verse anthology was written in the year 628/1231 in the northern Mesopotamian town of Dunaysir.[41] Dunaysir is a typical example of a rather unremarkable provincial market town that gained prominence under its local (Artuqid) rulers and their attempts to gain cultural prestige. By the early seventh/thirteenth century it was prospering and had become a modest intellectual centre with a madrasa. Even more importantly it boasted the quintessential expression of claims to partake in trans-regional scholarly prestige – a biographical dictionary of the scholars and literati associated with the town.[42] That the manuscript's scribe explicitly underlined that he had copied it in Dunaysir shows some provincial pride and that it made its way into al-Ashraf's royal library (and ultimately into the Ashrafiya) underlines al-Ashraf's close involvement in the regional race for cultural prestige.

The legacy of al-Malik al-Ashraf's royal collection is finally evident in a third characteristic feature, namely the presence of particularly valuable manuscripts. Although not all such manuscripts were necessarily linked to the royal library – al-Qāḍī al-Fāḍil was certainly also a connoisseur of splendid books – it is at least likely that some of this material goes back to the ruler's library. The first examples are the valuable books ascribed to grand calligraphers, in particular Ibn Muqla, Ibn al-Bawwāb and al-Juwaynī. Books in their hand traded for extraordinarily high prices and were thus also subject to fraud.[43] It is certainly for this reason that the cataloguer added comments in entries (supposedly) written by the grand calligraphers, which we do not find anywhere else in the catalogue: For instance, he reassuringly stated that a given manuscript was 'without doubt' by Ibn al-Bawwāb and he expressed elsewhere some doubt by adding that 'it is written [on the manuscript] that it is in the hand of Ibn al-Bawwāb'.[44]

A second group of particularly valuable manuscripts are those that were illustrated and of these we have eleven specimens, all of which the cataloguer explicitly describes as illustrated. There certainly were more illustrated manuscripts that the cataloguer did not flag up, such as a copy of the geographical

The Climes' Illustrations.[45] Further valuable manuscripts included those with gilded folia. The cataloguer mentions some of these, but again the library held certainly more. In general, they are only explicitly indicated as such if the cataloguer deals with generic titles such as 'prayer book' and here he refers to the entry's materiality to differentiate it from those with similar titles.[46]

To find a considerable number of illustrated manuscripts in this library is not too surprising as illustrated Arabic books appear in larger number from the end of the sixth/twelfth century, in particular in Iraq, Syria and Egypt.[47] Among those in the Ashrafīya library were some typical for courtly culture, namely on falconry (*bayzara*) and equitation (*furūsīya*). Other illustrated books are closely linked with the *Kalīla wa-dimna* collection of fables, the most commonly illustrated medieval text: *The Singer and the Wailer* by Ibn al-Habbārīya, which was inspired by *Kalīla wa-dimna*, in two copies, and *The Emulation of Kalīla and Dimna* by al-Yamanī in one copy.[48] A (probably pharmacological) treatise in the collection is also quite common among illustrated manuscripts, but a book of illustrated reports of the Buyid poet Ibn al-Ḥajjāj is a highly uncommon piece.[49] The work on *Pilgrimage Rituals* most likely contained illustrations similar to those found on contemporaneous pilgrimage certificates, first and foremost depictions of the sacred landscape of Mecca.[50] Finally, we have *The Prophet's Genealogy*, which probably included genealogical trees and would thus make the Ashrafīya manuscripts one of the earliest known examples to use this visual device.[51] These illustrated manuscripts possibly have a northern Mesopotamian connection, as competition there for artistic patronage would have led to increased production of such works. The most famous examples of such (most likely) northern Mesopotamian illustrated manuscripts are the splendid copies of the *Book of Antidotes* (595/1190) and the *Book of Songs* (early seventh/thirteenth century).[52]

Al-Malik al-Ashraf thus built up, as is evident from the three characteristic features, a very clearly profiled royal library in the course of his career, part of which made its way into his mausoleum. The case of this royal library in particular allows us to make two general comments on rulers' book collections in the period. First, it seems that royal libraries were not bound to a specific place, but rather moved with the ruler. The northern Mesopotamian profile of the Ashrafīya collection shows that al-Malik al-Ashraf had transferred all or at least parts of the book collection that he had built up while ruling the northern lands. With the shift to Damascus as his seat of rule his book collection must have been transported to the city. Second, the status of a royal library at the ruler's death was highly volatile, as the successor was entirely free to dispose of it at his will. Royal books were clearly the ruler's personal property and, in contrast to books in libraries of educational institutions, not endowed. It is not even clear what the legal status of al-Ashraf's royal collection was once it reached his mausoleum. Significantly, the Ashrafiya catalogue and surviving Ashrafiya manuscripts do not state anywhere that the books in the mausoleum were endowed. The rather vague terms employed in the catalogue – this is the 'catalogue of the Ashrafiya library that is in the mausoleum of al-Malik al-Ashraf' – recalls the terminology employed in the above-cited Ottoman protocol from Aleppo, which listed the books held in the 'library in the citadel'.

As a royal library was privately owned there were no legal restrictions concerning its use. The considerable number of works in the Ashrafiya dedicated to other Ayyubid rulers of Damascus indicates that al-Malik al-Ashraf took over their royal libraries (or rather *the* royal library that his predecessors had built up in the citadel). Chief among these was the library of his brother al-Malik al-Muᶜaẓẓam, probably the most learned of all Ayyubid rulers of Damascus. Such a line of continuity is indicated in the Ashrafiya collection by a historical work on him held in two copies, as well as poetry composed by him and a prayer book written by the head of his chancery. There are also works dedicated to him such as, arguably, three different copies of a pharmacological manual.[53] That al-Ashraf inherited al-Muᶜaẓẓam's collection also explains the relative prominence of Hanafi works among the legal books in the library as al-Muᶜaẓẓam, in contrast to al-Malik al-Ashraf, strongly supported this *madhhab*.[54]

However, al-Malik al-Ashraf did not hand over the royal library to his successor, his brother al-Ṣāliḥ Ismāᶜīl, and thus ended what must have been a decade-long process of building up this book collection. Rather, he decided to change its status from private ownership to (possibly) endowment and, more importantly, to move it out of the citadel to new locations. As these new locations were his educational endowments the books came to emphasise the prominent role that he had given himself in the urban topography of Damascus. Some of the books made it to his citadel Dār al-ḥadīth and a second set of books was set up in the Ashrafiya.[55] That al-Malik al-Ashraf broke up the royal library was certainly linked to the fact that he left no male heir. As dynastic succession was thus impossible, and as he was rather suspicious of al-Ṣāliḥ Ismāᶜīl's loyalty, the ruler may have preferred for his books to be integrated into the buildings that were part of his legacy. That the books did indeed leave the citadel after al-Ashraf's death and that none of his successors subsequently 'de-endowed' (or 'mobilised') the books to bring them back is perhaps even more remarkable. The main reason for this was arguably that the Ayyubid family confederation descended into a prolonged period of infighting after al-Malik al-Ashraf's death, Stephen Humphrey's 'Third Civil War'.[56] This conflict was very much centred on the control of Damascus and the city's ruler changed no less than seven times within a decade; for instance, al-Ṣāliḥ Ismāᶜīl ruled for just over four months. It is likely that none of these short-term rulers had the time to focus on matters such as appropriating the royal library while they were engaged in complex diplomatic and military manoeuvres to ensure their very political survival.

Stocking the Ashrafiya II: The Personal Library of al-Ashraf Aḥmad

The second of the library's sources is al-Ashraf Aḥmad's personal library, which he endowed in his father's sanctuary but was subsequently merged with the Ashrafiya library. Al-Ashraf Aḥmad was a student of *ḥadīth* who combined his scholarly interests with extended bouts of serving as Ayyubid administrator. He was, for example, vizier to al-Malik al-ᶜĀdil, and al-Kāmil employed him as envoy to Baghdad. As the son of the arguably most influential early Ayyubid administrator, al-Qāḍī al-Fāḍil, he was certainly wealthy, as is also clear from his considerable number of servants.[57] Despite his wealth and position he was never prominent enough to act as patron of scholars who would have dedicated works specifically to him. At first glance the role of his private collection within the Ashrafiya library thus seems more difficult to trace than that of al-Malik al-Ashraf with its explicit dedications. However, this absence of dedicated works is easily compensated by evidence from narrative sources, exactly the kind of evidence that is missing for al-Malik al-Ashraf. If there is one family in Ayyubid Damascus whose history of book collecting is documented in chronicles and biographical dictionaries it is that of al-Qāḍī al-Fāḍil. In al-Ashraf Aḥmad's case it is thus possible to match the evidence of the catalogue with these narrative sources.

The story of al-Ashraf Aḥmad's books has a surprising start for a collection that was to become part of a Damascene library placed in the mausoleum of an Ayyubid and Sunni ruler: it goes right back to Fatimid Cairo. While Saladin put a gradual end to the Isma^cili (or Sevener Shi^cite) Fatimid dynasty from 1169 to 1171, the royal family's properties, including the palace library, were undergoing large-scale removal and sale. The crucial figure in disposing of the Fatimid books was Saladin's secretary al-Qāḍī al-Fāḍil, who helped himself during the library's dissolution.[58] While the outlandish numbers of books ascribed to his collection in the sources are symbolic and of no factual value, there is little doubt that al-Qāḍī al-Fāḍil and his family were in possession of considerable private libraries in the next decades that originated, at least in part, in Fatimid Cairo. Al-Qāḍī al-Fāḍil himself endowed the Fāḍilīya madrasa in Cairo with a large library in 580/1184, some ten years after the end of Fatimid rule. His brother ᶜAbd al-Karīm, al-Ashraf Aḥmad's uncle, had another massive book collection, which was only equalled by that of al-Qāḍī al-Fāḍil himself.[59]

More pertinent for us is that al-Qāḍī al-Fāḍil bequeathed a significant part of his (non-endowed) collection to his son al-Ashraf Aḥmad. The latter's book collection again met a turbulent fate: the Ayyubid ruler of Cairo confiscated part of it in 626/1229 to build up his own royal library in the citadel. Another chunk was also confiscated, but subsequently returned to al-Ashraf Aḥmad who, in turn, endowed some of these books in his father's sanctuary (*maqṣūra*) in the Kallāsa quarter from where they made their way into the Ashrafiya library. More precisely, when al-Ashraf Aḥmad built his 'oratory' (*makān*) for the recitation of Koran and *ḥadīth* in 628/1231 at the northern end of the Kallāsa quarter courtyard, he positioned it right next to his father's sanctuary. In order to build al-Malik al-Ashraf's mausoleum seven years later this sanctuary was torn down and the oratory was incorporated into the mausoleum's mosque (*masjid*) together with 'bookcases', presumably al-Ashraf Aḥmad's endowment in the sanctuary.[60] And thus his collection became, in combination with the books from al-Malik al-Ashraf's collection, the foundation stock of the library. As al-Ashraf Aḥmad was still alive when his oratory became part of the mausoleum and when his books were transferred he must have – voluntarily or involuntarily – consented.

The connection between the Isma^cili Fatimid palace library in Cairo and the Sunni Ashrafīya library in Damascus, via al-Qāḍī al-Fāḍil and al-Ashraf Aḥmad, is not only evident from the narrative sources. We find in the Ashrafīya a number of works that clearly reflect intellectual life at the Fatimid court. In medicine, the works by two Fatimid court physicians were held, one on pulse and urine, while the other is an otherwise unknown medical treatise. Books by Ibn al-Zubayr, a Fatimid administrator, are repeatedly represented, as are those by a head of the Fatimid chancery.[61] In the same vein, poets who composed in close proximity to the Fatimid court feature prominently: including again Ibn al-Zubayr; the Fatimid vizier Ṭalā^ᵓi^c b. Ruzzīk al-Malik al-Ṣāliḥ; poetry by the Fatimid panegyric al-Ballanūbī; and the diwan by the court poet Abū al-Qāsim Muḥammad Ibn Hāni^ᵓ. Individuals attached to the Fatimid court do not only appear as authors, but also as scribes of specific manuscripts mentioned in the catalogue, such as another head of the Fatimid chancery. Finally, we find works by Fatimid Caliphs, for example the letter by the Caliph al-Mu^cizz to his general Jawhar al-Ṣiqillī and prayers of invocation arguably ascribed to the Caliph.[62] There are no distinctively theological Isma^cili texts in the Ashrafīya, which would establish a further link. However, it is by now apparent that such texts circulated in the Egyptian and Syrian lands and Yahya Michot has first drawn attention to Ibn Taymīya quoting the Isma^cili *Keys of Sovereignty* (*al-Aqālīd al-malakūtīya* or *Kitāb al-maqālīd*) by al-Sijistānī about one generation after the Ashrafīya catalogue was written.[63] In the meantime, further evidence of Ibn Taymīya having access to Isma^cili book has emerged.[64] We do not know where such Isma^cili texts were held in Damascus and they were certainly not in the Ashrafīya library. However, the Ashrafīya shows at least that Fatimid texts made their way into such institutions of learning and it was certainly not unique in having received books from the former Fatimid library (or rather libraries).

Apart from the salient Fatimid profile of this library, al-Ashraf Aḥmad's role in stocking the library is also reflected in other less prominent features. For instance, the catalogue repeatedly mentions that Mawhūb b. Aḥmad Ibn al-Jawālīqī, a scholar from Baghdad, is the scribe of specific manuscripts. This is noteworthy because the cataloguer only provides the name of the scribes in seventy-three cases (some 3.5 per cent of the entries) and with nine entries Ibn al-Jawālīqī is the most prominent among them.[65] Ibn al-Jawālīqī certainly was a sought-after scribe in Damascus during this period. For instance, the contemporaneous Damascene scholar Ibn Khallikān held in his personal library ten works in Ibn al-Jawālīqī's hand.[66] However, the high number of works in the Ashrafiya library can be more specifically linked to al-Ashraf Aḥmad who studied with Ibn al-Jawālīqī in Baghdad.[67] Arguably, the cataloguer emphasised the manuscripts copied by Ibn al-Jawālīqī not only because they were highly priced in Damascus at this point, but also because they were an outstanding feature of the collection. Finally, the role of al-Ashraf Aḥmad is also evident from autographs. We have at least one preserved Ashrafiya manuscript, the adab anthology *Treasures of Insightful Perception* by al-Tawḥīdī, which was written in his own hand.[68]

Stocking the Ashrafiya III: The Damascene Profile

In analysing the Ashrafiya collection the emphasis has so far been on the characteristics that facilitated the detection of its two principal sources, the libraries of al-Malik al-Ashraf and al-Ashraf Aḥmad. This has emphasised trans-regional aspects, be they links to northern Mesopotamia or Egypt, at the expense of the library's local profile. However, the Ashrafiya is very much part of the local book market and intellectual scene in Damascus and there is a very strong Damascene flavour to its collection.

If we consider the library's seventh-/thirteenth-century books, for instance, Damascene authors play a very prominent role. The Maqdisī family, encountered earlier as the office-holders in al-Malik al-Ashraf's Qāsyūn Dār al-ḥadīth, is well represented among the recent books with at least five titles ranging from a biography of the Prophet Muḥammad to *ḥadīth* collections and prayer books.[69] The same Damascene focus appears when considering specific thematic clusters. The Ashrafiya had twelve *jihād*-related titles of which eight have identifiable authors. Three of these titles were authored by ᶜAlī Ibn ᶜAsākir, the founding father of the Damascene ᶜAsākir family that came to dominate the Dār al-ḥadīth of Nūr al-Dīn, and a fourth title was authored by a close colleague of his, ᶜAlī b. Sulaymān al-Murādī. Two further works were composed by 'trans-regional' Egyptian-Syrian authors who cannot be described as belonging to any specific city in the area. Finally, the only two works with a clearly non-Damascene profile were written two to four centuries before the establishment of the Ashrafiya library.[70]

That the only two clearly non-Damascene *jihād* works date to the third/ninth and fifth/eleventh centuries highlights an important chronological caveat to the argument that the Ashrafiya has a parochial nature. The parochial character of the collection is restricted to books composed some two centuries before the writing of the catalogue, that is, by those authors who roughly died after 500/1106. By contrast, works authored prior to this period have no distinct regional profile and there is little that is specifically Damascene about them. These works were mostly the 'classics' of Arabic–Islamic culture from the perspective of the seventh/thirteenth century. However, few works from the more immediate past had already entered the literary canon. This solidly Damascene character of the recent works in the Ashrafiya collection helps us understand the intellectual life of the central Arabic lands during this period in general, especially for questions of trans-regional knowledge exchange. The parochial character of the Ashrafiya – heavily focused on Damascus, including Syria, and on account of its specific background also having a fair representation of Egypt and northern Mesopotamia – contradicts the hackneyed image of innumerable Muslim scholars constantly on the move seeking knowledge and thus creating tightly-knit long-distance networks of knowledge exchange.

As will be seen in Chapter 4, the parochial character of the Ashrafiya's more recent titles also appeared in the bio-bibliographical texts used to identify its books. The Damascene or Syrian works of the period by Ibn Khallikān, Yāqūt al-Ḥamawī, Ibn al-Qifṭī and Ibn Abī Uṣaybiʿa were indispensable for understanding the Ashrafiya catalogue and identifying its texts and authors. Again and again they listed the exact books held in this library. Another very promising text was *The Precious Pearls* (*al-Durr al-thamīn*) by the librarian Ibn al-Sāʿī, an author contemporaneous with the foundation of the Ashrafiya. His work is basically an extended list of books and is thus exactly what is needed for working through a library catalogue. However, hardly any recent titles from the Ashrafiya catalogue could be identified via this work of an author who lived and worked in Baghdad. Just as the Ashrafiya library gives a rather local impression of knowledge production the recent intellectual world of Baghdad as seen by Ibn al-Sāʿī was also very restricted in regional terms.

The Ashrafiya catalogue is only an example of one library, but it is noteworthy that the first documented library does show such a regional profile. Furthermore, this regional profile goes hand in hand with other research that is based on specific case studies. In his analysis of the bibliography of a work written in sixth-/twelfth-century Bukhara Shahab Ahmed showed the heavily regionalised profile of the recent works. Virtually all of the books cited in the bibliography that were written in the previous 200 years came from the surrounding area. Even neighbouring Iran was barely represented and Iraq, Syria, Egypt and al-Andalus further to the west were virtually absent from the author's intellectual map.[71]

The Ashrafiya's Damascene character appears not only in the profile of its recent authors, but also in the regional background of the scribes named in the catalogue. Of a total of seventy-three manuscripts carrying such information, ten pertaining to the seventh-century *hijrī* have scribes with an identifiable regional background. Two of these were copied by Ibn Rīsh, a minor Damascene *ḥadīth* scholar, one by Ibn Shīth, al-Malik al-Muᶜaẓẓam's head of chancery, and four more were produced by renowned Damascene calligraphers, the above-mentioned Ḥasan al-Qaylawī and Muḥammad b. Khazraj al-Dimashqī.[72] The remaining three manuscripts bring us away from Damascus, but, for two of them, no further than Aleppo. Only a single manuscript was copied by a clearly non-Syrian individual who spent his life in Baghdad.[73] Just as it took time for an author's work to enter the literary canon, it also took time for a scribe to emerge with a trans-regional reputation – and the small number of Ashrafiya entries with named scribes shows that one needed quite a reputation before the cataloguer was willing to give their name.

Beyond doubt, we do see some examples of the transfer of recent trans-regional knowledge, yet this is very much limited to the absolute bestsellers of the period. A typical example of this is al-Ghazālī (d. 505/1111), who spent most of his career in Baghdad and further to the east. Although he is a relatively recent author his thirty entries easily bring him into the top 20 of the most popular authors in the Ashrafiya library (see *Table 3.4*). Yet by this period al-Ghazālī had already become a 'classical' author with a trans-regional profile similar to the top two authors in the library: al-Thaᶜālibī (d. 429/1038) with forty-six entries and al-Jāḥiẓ (d. 255/868–9) with thirty-one entries.

This was especially true in the case of Damascus, which experienced in the seventh/thirteenth century 'a productive period of Ghazālī reception'.[74] A similar case is that of the Baghdadi scholar Ibn al-Jawzī (d. 597/1200): with his twenty-three titles, putting him in fifth place, he is the only sixth-/twelfth-century author to make the top 20. However, this must again be seen within the regional context of Damascus, as his grandson, Sibṭ Ibn al-Jawzī, became one of the most influential Damascene scholars, was closely linked to the city's Ayyubid rulers and artfully promoted his grandfather's legacy when the Ashrafiya library was founded. A specific Damascene background is evident in another group of books, which at first glance seems to indicate trans-regional processes of knowledge transmission. Books from the western Islamic world, al-Andalus and the Maghreb, constitute a noteworthy group in the Ashrafiya, although no author from this region even came close to the most popular authors in terms of entries. This has to be seen in the framework of the strong Maghrebian migration to Damascus and the salient role that this group played in the city's scholarly life of the seventh/thirteenth century.[75]

A final indicator for the very Damascene background of parts of the Ashrafiya collection is the importance of specific fields of knowledge. For instance, works linked to political thought are well represented on this library's shelves. More than seventy entries in this field cover a wide spectrum: including works ascribed to the classical authors, Aristotle, Plato and Socrates; the big names from the Umayyad and ᶜAbbasid periods, Ibn al-Muqaffaᶜ, al-Sarakhsī, al-Thaᶜlabī and al-Māwardī; as well as more contemporaneous authors such as al-Ghazālī, al-Ṭurṭūshī, Ibn Ẓafar and Sibṭ Ibn al-Jawzī. This very strong field of works is arguably linked to the intensive interest in questions of just and legitimate rule in Damascus during the late Ayyubid and early Mamluk periods. Ibn Jamāᶜa (d. 733/1333) authored his *Summary of the Rules to Govern the People of Islam* in the course of his trans-regional career spanning Egypt and Syria. Better known are the Hanbali groups of authors in Damascus clustered around Ibn Taymīya (d. 728/1328) and Ibn Qayyim al-Jawzīya (d. 751/1350). The large cluster of works in the Ashrafiya thus underlines the role of Damascus in late Ayyubid and early Mamluk political thought.

The Damascene character of the Ashrafiya as evident from authors, scribes and its intellectual profile is an outcome of the fact that its two main sources had been built up to some extent in Damascus. Al-Ashraf Aḥmad had certainly complemented his inherited Fatimid collection while living in Damascus and the same is true for al-Malik al-Ashraf, who played an active role in the city's intellectual life acting as patron for scholars and purchasing books. As in northern Mesopotamia he again found himself in Syria within a very colourful landscape of principalities where local courts strongly competed for artists and scholars. With Damascus he held without doubt the main principality of Syria, but Aleppo was not far behind in terms of intellectual life; Hama and Homs were serious players and even third-ranking principalities such as Karak could attract scholars of considerable standing. Karak certainly could not compete with the regional heavyweights; the renowned jurisprudent Ibn ᶜAbd al-Salām poignantly refused an invitation to join its court with the words, 'Your lands are too small for my knowledge,' before moving on to Egypt. However, such small courts were able to carve out niches in specific disciplines and in the case of Karak in the late 620s to early 630s/first half of 1230s, for instance, this was astronomy. Another poignant example of the vivid patronage at the various Ayyubid courts is evident when considering the careers of physicians who could easily move between numerous patrons.[76]

How the Ashrafiya was stocked thus goes back to two main processes that are typical of the development of local endowed libraries in this period: On the one hand, patronage within the framework of a highly regionalised political landscape played a crucial role. This is evident in the development of al-Malik al-Ashraf's royal library and the inclusion of previous royal libraries. On the other hand, the constant transfer of books between different ownership statuses greatly contributed to building up what ultimately became the Ashrafiya book collection. Many of the books that al-Ashraf Aḥmad 'contributed' to the Ashrafiya collection had had a rather eventful journey in the preceding sixty years. They were originally housed in the Fatimid royal library in Cairo, went into the ownership of his father al-Qāḍī al-Fāḍil, were bequeathed to al-Ashraf Aḥmad, confiscated by the Ayyubid ruler of Egypt al-Malik al-Kāmil, subsequently returned, endowed by al-Ashraf Aḥmad in his father's sanctuary in Damascus and integrated – whatever form this 'integration' took – into the Ashrafiya collection. As argued above, such a process where books repeatedly changed their legal status, several times back and forth between endowed and private, was a regular phenomenon for medieval book collections. As is evident from the books going into the Ashrafīya, and as we will see further down with regard to the destination of the Ashrafīya collection, there is little point in framing this in terms of 'plunder' or 'theft'. Rather, the changing status often ensured that books survived over longer periods as the new political and social elites included them into better-kept collections.

Sustaining the Library: The Mamluk Period

The Ashrafīya mausoleum was officially 'opened' some five months after the ruler's death when his corpse was transferred from its temporary burial site in the citadel in 635/1238.[77] The mausoleum must have had a library from the very moment of its inauguration as al-Qāḍī al-Fāḍil's sanctuary with al-Ashraf Aḥmad's book endowment was incorporated into the building and as al-Malik al-Ashraf's royal library in the citadel had lost its patron. Despite the mausoleum's minor status within the scholarly landscape of Damascus it is now evident that the Ashrafīya library housed a substantial and splendid library. What appears at first glance to be a paradox, a minor institution equipped with a major book collection, seems to have been quite ordinary in this period: Contemporaneous texts and those of the following centuries did not single out the library in their few references to the Ashrafīya mausoleum. We have some isolated comments by bibliophilic scholars on specific titles that they only found in this collection,[78] but compared with the libraries of the period's major institutions such comments are few.

More importantly, we do not have a single documented case of a 'supplementary endowment' indicating that further books were bequeathed to the Ashrafīya mausoleum.[79] Although this was common practice for the city's prominent institutions, such as al-Malik al-Ashraf's citadel Dār al-ḥadīth, individuals clearly did not consider the Ashrafīya library to be of sufficient prestige to place them there. Even the mausoleum's own professor, Abū Shāma, preferred to endow his books in the more prestigious ᶜĀdilīya madrasa.[80] That the Ashrafīya would not be a target for supplementary endowments is arguably also reflected in the catalogue itself: it made no attempt to provide space for future additions, but it very confidently stated that this was the catalogue of *the* library in the Ashrafīya and not just of the al-Malik al-Ashraf/al-Ashraf Aḥmad endowment. Either the cataloguer assumed that a new catalogue would be prepared after a few years or he correctly assumed that any future additions to the mausoleum's stock would be rather unlikely.

Yet the initial library of the Ashrafīya was so substantial that its endowment must have provided for a librarian and its terms in this regard were probably similar to those that the endowment deed set out for al-Malik al-Ashraf's citadel Dār al-ḥadīth. We do not have the original deed for this Dār al-ḥadīth either, but its provisions are at least quoted in a later text. According to these provisions, the librarian was not very well paid compared with other positions. He was entitled to eighteen dirhams per month and was thus on a comparable level with the doorkeeper (*bawwāb*) at fifteen dirhams. Yet he was some way off the earnings of the professor, who received ninety dirhams, and the servant of the Prophet's sandal, who was entitled to forty dirhams.[81] This low income is very much in line with the information that we have on librarians in other endowments in Syria and Egypt during the Ayyubid and Mamluk periods. A librarian was a low-ranking position, comparable to a teacher in a children's school.[82] The tasks of the librarian as set out in the deed of al-Malik al-Ashraf's Dār al-ḥadīth were to keep the books in good repair, to discuss the required expenditure with the administrator and to appoint scribes as necessary to correct and collate manuscripts.[83] While the Ashrafīya librarian certainly had to fulfil the same tasks, we can expect his salary to have been even more modest, as the mausoleum's overall endowment must have been significantly smaller than that of the Dār al-ḥadīth.

As in medieval Europe we only know of very few librarians from medieval Arabic libraries by name, as they were generally not prominent enough to make their way into the narrative sources. Those librarians who are known by name were either employed in the large libraries, became prominent later in their career or belonged to prominent families.[84] The Ashrafīya library conforms to this pattern and only two of its librarians are known to us. One of them is Ṣadr al-Dīn al-Āmadī who taught at various madrasas and was also administrator in several endowments. Of more interest at this point is Abū al-ʿAbbās Aḥmad al-Anṣārī (d. 683/1284). He was the son of the city's chief judge Muḥammad Ibn al-Ṣāʾigh and certainly destined for a more prominent role in the city than a low-ranking librarian in a low-ranking institution. However, some ominous 'well-known affairs' prevented him from becoming his father's deputy judge and he died at a relatively young age. Arguably, al-Anṣārī held the Ashrafīya librarianship as a convenient low-profile position while waiting for the 'affairs' – whatever they may have been – to pass. Yet even if this position was a mere stop-gap it did not prevent him from becoming an outstandingly assiduous and diligent caretaker of the library's book collection, according to the generous praise of his obituaries. For instance, when one reader lost a copy of *The Singer and the Wailer* by Ibn al-Habbārīya, which he had borrowed from the Ashrafīya, al-Anṣārī forced him to produce another copy although the library held almost ten copies of this work.[85]

Al-Anṣārī was also the most likely author of the Ashrafīya catalogue, as sources refer to the fact that 'owing to his approach the library became very well ordered'.[86] It is also noteworthy that the Ashrafīya catalogue exactly matches information given in al-Anṣārī's biography on the almost ten copies of *The Singer and the Wailer*, as the catalogue notes two illustrated copies and seven non-illustrated copies.[87] Unless his successors in the post were as diligent as al-Anṣārī, which is possible but not very likely, this library would not have continued to hold on to the same number of manuscripts of this work in the following centuries. Further evidence of his authorship comes from the catalogue itself: it is highly likely that its writer had a background in the judiciary, as he remarked at one point that the organisation of a specific work resembles that found in a *sijill* (court register).[88] This again matches the profile of al-Anṣārī, who had acted for a while as his father's deputy judge. A final indicator of the catalogue's early Mamluk origin is the fact that it is bound in a multiple-text manuscript, which contains other texts from this period (see Chapter 5). The dating of the catalogue is obviously crucial for the argument built up in these chapters. Previous remarks in scholarship have suggested a later date for its composition and Ramazan Şeşen placed it, without arguing his case, in the eighth/fourteenth century. Saᶜīd al-Jūmānī, by contrast, thought it to have been written in the ninth/fifteenth century and seemingly relies on one single entry for this argument.[89]

However, these later dates do not match the internal evidence from the catalogue, which strongly indicates a date of composition in the second half of the seventh/thirteenth century. There are no entries from the eighth/fourteenth century or later, but eighty-five entries dating to the seventh/thirteenth century (see *Figure 3.1*). Dividing the seventh *hijrī* century into three brackets of thirty-three years each it is evident that the majority of the works pertain to the first bracket 600–33, some thirty-four to the second bracket 634–66 and only nine to the final 667–99 bracket.[90] It is also remarkable that the catalogue has only two dated entries, which both refer to the early seventh/thirteenth century.[91] Finally, there is indirect evidence for the origin of the catalogue in this century from Ashrafiya books, which circulated in the seventh/thirteenth century but have subsequently been lost. For instance, the chronicle *Governors of Khurasan* was last used by Ibn al-Athīr in the early seventh/thirteenth century (incidentally in northern Mesopotamia), but then lost soon after the Mongol invasions in the later seventh/thirteenth century. Unless we deal with an unknown later copy of the work, its presence in the Ashrafiya thus very well fits the dating of the catalogue to this century.[92]

We do not know when al-Anṣārī took over the librarianship, but taking into account that he died at a young age in the early 680s/1280s it could not have been before the 670s/1270s. It is thus most likely that the catalogue was written some three to four decades after the mausoleum's (and thus the library's) opening and that the catalogue still reflected the initial book holdings to a large extent, although not exactly. The similarity between the library's initial stock and the stock as documented in the catalogue is especially likely because of the low number of books from the third bracket and the absence of any reports on supplementary endowments.

The Ashrafiya library thus had an auspicious start: its position in a ruler's mausoleum provided some protection from the books being swiftly 'mobilised' towards a new collection and its outstandingly diligent librarian helped to provide some stability. However, our knowledge of the Ashrafiya library is very patchy for the following decades and centuries. Obviously no other library catalogue exists for the Ashrafiya and nor does the catalogue by al-Anṣārī demonstrate any dateable signs of later revisions. The narrative sources also show little awareness of the library after the foundation period in the seventh/thirteenth century. Even their references to specific rare and/or valuable manuscripts housed in the Ashrafiya dwindle away. While the contemporaneous Ibn Khallikān mentions the library three times, in the following century al-Ṣafadī (d. 764/1362) and Ibn Kathīr (d. 774/1373) make only one reference each.[93] No later author mentions the Ashrafiya library or its manuscripts again, except for the second known librarian of the Ashrafiya in the early ninth/fifteen century.[94] The silence of the sources must always be treated with caution and this is especially true for the case of narrative Damascene texts in the Mamluk period. On account of the gradual centralisation of political control in Cairo and the subsequent rise of this city's scholarly life, chronicles and biographical dictionaries become increasingly Cairo-focused. In such texts local libraries beyond Cairo were to a large extent below the authors' radar. It is thus highly pertinent that al-Ṣafadī and Ibn Kathīr were not only the last authors to mention manuscripts from the Ashrafīya library, but also the last two grand historians of the Damascene line of historiography that reaches back to the sixth/twelfth century uninterrupted. While we know little about the Ashrafīya's fate in the later eighth/fourteenth and ninth/fifteenth centuries there is no reason to take this as evidence that the library was dissolved at some point. We are at least able to trace a more or less continuous succession of those holding the professorship in Koran recitation in the institution for some 150 years (*Table 1.1*) and the library most likely existed in parallel with these teaching activities.

There is, however, little doubt that teaching activities in the Ashrafīya mausoleum largely stopped in the early ninth/fifteenth century. A certain Aḥmad al-Ramlī al-Shāfiʿī is named a century later, but he is isolated; there is a century with no names available before him and complete silence after him. In consequence it is fair to assume that teaching mostly stopped with the continuous succession of traceable postholders. This does not necessarily mean that the entire endowment was dissolved, but rather that the endowment income was not seen to be sufficient to keep up the professorship in Koran recitation. The priority would have been to sustain the principal purpose of the mausoleum, to commemorate its founder. Indeed we still have information on individuals attached in some way to the mausoleum for the next century. Tellingly, the information on these individuals cannot be taken as evidence that the mausoleum was still functioning as a scholarly institution. One al-Sayyid al-Ḥāḍirī al-Maghribī al-Mālikī, a migrant to Damascus, was merely said to have 'resided' in it. Ḥasan b. Yūnis al-Ghazzī became its administrator in 938/1531, so the endowment itself was clearly still working at this point.[95]

The impression of the Ashrafīya turning into a non-teaching endowment is reinforced by the best late Mamluk/early Ottoman source on Damascene educational endowments, *al-Dāris fī ta'rīkh al-madāris* by al-Nuᶜaymī. al-Nuᶜaymī does not name any *shaykhs* at the Ashrafiya beyond the early ninth/fifteenth century, but he discusses the mausoleum at considerable length and clearly refers to it as an existent institution.[96] However, in the other Damascene late Mamluk/early Ottoman texts the al-Ashraf mausoleum is conspicuously absent.[97] Aḥmad al-Ramlī al-Shāfiᶜī was probably able to take on the professorship in the early tenth/sixteenth century either because the endowment income had briefly gone up or because he profited from a short-lived shift in how the endowment income was spent. From the second half of the tenth/sixteenth century, however, there is complete silence on the Ashrafiya mausoleum either as a teaching institution, a non-teaching institution or a library. This cannot be explained by an absence of Damascene sources during the Ottoman period. Works by authors such as Ibn Ṭūlūn, (d. 953/1546), al-Ghazzī (d. 1061/1650–1), Ibn al-ᶜImād (d. 1089/1679) and al-Muḥibbī (d. 1111/1699) have a lot to say on local affairs yet they never mention the Ashrafiya.[98] However, the Ashrafiya mausoleum remained known under this name up to the early twentieth century, and up to the present day the last vestige of this site, al-Malik al-Ashraf's tomb itself, is still standing (Plate 1). The Ashrafiya mausoleum thus petered out as an educational institution without a decisive moment of dissolution.

Off to New Shores: Ashrafiya Manuscripts and the Library's Dissolution

The most pressing question for the present book is what happened to the Ashrafiya library when the mausoleum's educational function was coming to a slow end? When and in what ways were its manuscript holdings 'mobilised' to facilitate their move to new book collections? To answer this question we can obviously not turn to the narrative sources, which are frustratingly silent on any library-related matters in the Ashrafiya from the early ninth/fifteenth century onwards. The only evidence for the collection's fate is the movement of the manuscripts themselves through the identification of where Ashrafiya manuscripts have been housed in recent centuries. Answering this question comprehensively is not feasible for a medieval library such as the Ashrafiya with more than 2,000 books simply because of the lack of adequate resources. Ashrafiya manuscripts, as much as those of any other medieval Arabic library, could today be housed in Damascus, Aleppo, Cairo or Istanbul, Paris or

Princeton, and, more recently, on the Arabian Peninsula, to name but a few possibilities. A full understanding of the manuscripts' trajectories would only be possible if these collections were comprehensively catalogued (that is often not the case), if these catalogues were accessible in digital format (that is a process in its early stages) and most crucially if these catalogues included information on manuscript notes, particularly those on endowments and purchases (that they do occasionally).

However, for the Ashrafiya collection we have one crucial indicator as to where its manuscripts may have moved, namely the present-day location of its catalogue in Istanbul in the Süleymaniye library. As will become evident in the following the catalogue did not make its way to Istanbul (or rather Constantinople at this point) by chance, but was taken there with a substantial number of Ashrafiya manuscripts. Most likely this transfer took place after the Ottoman conquest of Syria in 922/1516 and the catalogue was used to facilitate the inclusion of Ashrafiya manuscripts into the Topkapı palace library. To make this argument on the move of Ashrafiya manuscripts to Istanbul requires some explanation of the methodology involved because most medieval Arabic manuscripts do not carry what would have been the most helpful indicator – a note explicitly linking a manuscript to a specific library. We do not systematically find pre-Ottoman stamps or notes that would establish such a link, nor endowment notes by individuals, which would allow a manuscript to be linked to a library they had set up. There are certainly examples where we do find such indicators, mostly in the form of splendid frontispieces with dedication notes. The patrons of these works are generally rulers, officers and viziers, that is, members of the military and political elite.[99] However, there are few occurrences of such frontispieces from the Ayyubid and earlier periods, perhaps because later owners of the manuscripts removed them. At any rate, some later owners had no quibbles about adding their own frontispieces, implying patronage even though it is evident that the manuscript was written earlier.[100]

In the absence of such explicit notes, or 'smoking guns', linking a manuscript presently held in the Süleymaniye collection with the same manuscript mentioned in the Ashrafiya catalogue requires a more nuanced approach. In consequence the manuscripts were divided into three categories, each of which indicates the degree of certainty of the link according to the contextual information found on the manuscript: 1) Possible: The manuscript was copied before the year 680 and no place is mentioned or it was written/circulating in Damascus[101] and no date is mentioned. This category is indicated in Chapter 4 with * [single asterisk]. 2) Likely: The manuscript was written before the year 680 and was written/circulating in Damascus. This category is indicated in Chapter 4 with ** [two asterisks]. 3) Secure: The manuscript explicitly mentions the Ashrafīya mausoleum, al-Malik al-Ashraf or al-Ashraf Aḥmad. This category is indicated in Chapter 4 with *** [three asterisks]. These criteria can obviously not be employed across the board for all manuscripts that are both mentioned in the catalogue and also appear in the Süleymaniye as there is a very high chance that medieval 'bestsellers', such as al-Ghazālī's *Revival of the Religious Sciences*, would fall in category 1 or 2 without ever having had a link with the Ashrafīya library.[102]

After seeing the initial results it became apparent that the manuscripts are not randomly distributed across the historical collections that are today in the Süleymaniye library. Rather there were two very distinct clusters of Ashrafīya manuscripts in the Fatih and the Ayasofya collections. As it is evident that a substantial number of Ashrafīya manuscripts made their way into these 'host' collections the classification system was amended for manuscripts in these two collections as follows: 1) codicological features make a seventh-/thirteenth-century origin certain; 2) the manuscript was written before the year 680 or it was written/circulating in Damascus and no date is mentioned; or 3) the manuscript was written before the year 680 and was written/circulating in Damascus.

To illustrate how this search for smouldering guns was applied in practice, let us consider some examples. An exceptionally clear case is al-Jawharī's *Sound* [Dictionary]. On a Süleymaniye manuscript of this work the above-mentioned al-Ḥasan al-Qaylawī states that he produced it in the year 609/1212 for al-Malik al-Ashraf's royal library.[103] Al-Qaylawī admittedly does not state that he produced this manuscript for the Ashrafīya mausoleum library, but it is reasonable to assume that it was part of the royal collection transferred to the mausoleum. Even though the manuscript today is in neither of the two host collections the link between this Ashrafīya catalogue entry and this manuscript can be classified as 'secure'. A slightly more complex case is [The Book] *Composed for al-Malik Ashraf Concerning Translated*

Word Puzzles. This link is classified as 'secure' too, even though the manuscript is undated and no manuscript notes geographically locate it or make a direct link to al-Ashraf. The reason for this classification is that this is a very rare work specifically written for al-Malik al-Ashraf and that it is held in one of the host collections, the Fatih collection. In addition it is now part of a multiple-text manuscript, which includes several titles that exactly match at least five entries in the Ashrafiya catalogue. It is thus very likely that what were initially individual texts subsequently came to be bound into one single volume either while they were still in Damascus or after they had moved to Istanbul.[104]

To move to another set of examples, among the many manuscripts in the Süleymaniye that were classified as not having belonged to the Ashrafiya is the only copy of *The Repentants*. This manuscript was copied in the year 652/1254 and would thus potentially fit. However, it was produced in Aleppo and is not held in either of the two host collections, so it seemed prudent to discard it.[105] A typical example of the discarded bestsellers is the *Signposts of Revelation*. The Süleymaniye collection holds one copy produced in the year 572/1176 in Aleppo and a note shows that this manuscript was in Damascus in the year 650/1252 – so again a potentially very good fit.[106] However, in light of the many copies that were produced of this work this is not sufficient proof to consider it an Ashrafiya manuscript.

On the basis of these criteria, 143 Ashrafiya manuscripts were identified in the Süleymaniye library. This considerable number is particularly noteworthy because the Ashrafiya library did not have the benefit of institutional continuity until the present or at least the recent past, but was most likely dissolved in the tenth/sixteenth century. How disastrous such an absence of institutional continuity can be for the survival rate of manuscripts is evident from the case of British medieval libraries. With the dissolution of monasteries in the sixteenth century their libraries were dispersed and for one of the most important monastic libraries, the Austin library of York, only nine manuscripts are traceable. The state of affairs is similar for the roughly 550 books known to have been held in other Friars' libraries, of which only twelve are traceable. The number of 360 surviving manuscripts, which have been ascribed to one of the 130 Cistercian houses, seems at first glance considerable. Yet this is less than the number of books held in the Meaux library alone. This enumeration continues with twenty surviving manuscripts out of the 450 held in the late fourteenth century in the Dover Priory or the less than twenty manuscripts known to have survived of more than 1,000 held in Leicester library in the late fifteenth century.[107]

Furthermore, it must be added that the number of 143 identified Ashrafiya manuscripts is really the minimum and additional manuscripts will certainly come to light. The Süleymaniye library is among the best libraries with Arabic manuscripts in terms of making its holdings available. However, the researcher has to rely on the computer catalogue, which has a highly inconsistent transliteration system and where entries are repeatedly incomplete and occasionally simply wrong. For instance, the Ashrafiya manuscript of *Astute Men* by Ibn al-Jawzī is entered under the generic title 'Kitāb al-Jawzī' and only by looking at the manuscript itself – a clearly impossible task to carry out systematically for all the tens of thousands of Süleymaniye manuscripts – can one find its correct title.[108] In addition, the Ashrafiya catalogue was written in the late seventh/thirteenth century, that is, more than two centuries before the transfer from Damascus to Istanbul took place. During this long period some manuscripts were undoubtedly discarded or moved to new locations, so they were not part of the early Ottoman Ashrafiya. More importantly, other manuscripts were without doubt added to the Ashrafiya collection after the catalogue was drafted in the late seventh/thirteenth century and are thus not identifiable as Ashrafiya manuscripts. Therefore, it is very likely that the true number of Ashrafiya manuscripts held today in the Süleymaniye is higher. Finally, this research has focused on manuscripts held in the Süleymaniye and the presence of the catalogue in this library provided a strong rationale to do so. Nevertheless, more manuscripts will appear when considering other collections in Istanbul, especially those in the Topkapı palace, as well as in Damascus and Cairo.

The 143 Ashrafiya manuscripts are not randomly distributed across the various collections that are today held in the Süleymaniye. As stated above, we have rather two host collections where Ashrafiya manuscripts cluster with the Fatih collection holding forty-seven of them and the Ayasofya collection forty-three. This is not the place to discuss in detail the trajectory of the Ashrafiya manuscripts from their transfer to Istanbul to their becoming part of the Süleymaniye library. However, it is possible to argue that the Ashrafiya manuscripts came to Istanbul as imperial booty and were initially deposited in the Topkapı palace library. Consequently, the manuscripts were closely linked with the imperial court and it is this link that explains the clusters of Ashrafiya manuscripts in the Fatih and Ayasofya libraries: both were imperial foundations set up during the reign of Sultan Mahmud I (r. 1730–54), who endowed a large number of books to them. In addition, the Galata Palace College library, itself another imperial foundation set up by Mahmud I, was split between the Fatih and the Ayasofya libraries in 1837.[109] The Galata library, in turn, had been established specifically for the education of the empire's administrative personnel so that it had particular strengths in subject areas such as grammar, poetry and history – a profile that fits well the Ashrafiya's library's profile, as we will see in Chapter 3.[110] The connection between Ashrafiya manuscripts and the imperial court is corroborated by other imperial foundations, which also contain a noticeable number of such manuscripts. For instance, the Laleli library, founded by Sultan Mustafa III (r. 1757–74), has eight Ashrafiya manuscripts and the Reisülküttab library, founded during the reign of Mahmud I by one of his main administrators, contains four.

The Ashrafiya manuscripts thus retained some degree of historical identity as a unit after their transfer to Istanbul and while moving through various Ottoman libraries until they reached their current location in the Süleymaniye. This historical identity was not just retained in the sense that they moved between a few collections, but even within the new collections the manuscripts retained some bonds. This is evident from the class marks that were assigned when catalogues were published during the reign of Abdülhamid II (r. 1876–1908) for most Istanbul libraries. For instance, in the Fatih collection only nine Ashrafiya manuscripts fall between the class marks 1 to 3,500, but twenty-six Ashrafiya manuscripts cluster between the class marks 3,501 and 4,500. Despite an eventful trajectory of almost 800 years and in the absence of institutional continuity at least parts of the collection thus retained a remarkable degree of shared history. This shared history within the Ottoman collections of Istanbul cannot be discussed in detail here, but to give just one further example: the Fatih manuscript, which included the Ashrafiya catalogue itself, carries an endowment note by 'merhum Celebizade Mevlana Derviş Mehmed', who is arguably the Ottoman Turkish official and Grand Vizier who spent most of his career under Mahmud I and died in 1761. Identical endowment notes appear on fourteen other Ashrafiya manuscripts, all of them in the Fatih collection, so this official must have had a sizeable number of Ashrafiya manuscripts in his possession before they made their way into the Fatih collection.[111]

There is one final point to be made on the Ottoman chapter in the history of the Ashrafiya manuscripts, which brings us back to the Ashrafiya catalogue. If we map those entries that are identifiable in the Süleymaniye it is evident that they are not evenly distributed across the catalogue. Most strikingly, there are three types of work that feature in the catalogue but are rarely identifiable in Istanbul, either because they did not appeal to the Ottomans who transferred the manuscripts or as a result of cataloguing methods: first, very few incomplete manuscripts made their way to Istanbul; this is not too surprising as they were neither prestigious enough nor valuable enough to be transferred there. They must have remained in Syria for transfer to other libraries or have been sold off on the scrap paper market or been deposited in Genizah-style depositories such as the Qubbat al-khazna in the Umayyad Mosque. Second, relatively few collections of poetry are traceable in Istanbul even though – as will become apparent in the following chapters – the Ashrafiya library was stuffed with such collections. Seemingly in the new Ottoman context Arabic pre-Islamic and 'tribal' poetry commanded much less of a standing than in seventh-/thirteenth-century Damascus. As they did not hold the same prestige and value in the new political and cultural context into which the Ashrafiya collection was taken, they too stayed in Damascus. Finally, there are works that are non-identifiable, not so much because the historical context changed, but on account of medieval and modern bibliographical practices. This is the case for prayer books, which al-Anṣārī mostly entered with a simple generic title in the Ashrafiya catalogue. When the Istanbul collections were catalogued in the late nineteenth century – and the modern Süleymaniye catalogue partly relies on these catalogues – the works were entered with similar generic titles. Among the thousands of prayer books it is thus virtually impossible to match an Ashrafiya entry with a modern Istanbul entry with any degree of confidence.

The Ashrafiya library as it existed in the early tenth/sixteenth century was thus clearly moved from Damascus to Istanbul, most likely in the aftermath of the Ottoman conquest. This is the first documented proof of the early modern movement of manuscripts to Istanbul, apart from the above-cited protocol from 923/1517 listing the books of the Aleppo citadel library. In the case of this protocol it is evident that no inventory existed and that one had to be drawn up to accompany the transfer. In the case of the Ashrafīya, however, the task proved to be significantly easier. The existing catalogue, although dated, could be taken to identify titles and was sent with the books to Istanbul. Rather than going through a large collection, which was probably still in the thousands, it seemed significantly easier to ship off the most interesting pieces and to have it sorted out in Istanbul.

The question of book transfers (or 'plundering') from Syria and Egypt after the Ottoman conquest is a highly contentious issue that has been poorly researched. Like the Ottoman conquest in general, the transfer of books has been set into a narrative of decline and intellectual stagnation and has become embroiled in national discourses. However, there is just too little systematic research to make a convincing case for even a rough estimate of the amount of manuscripts that were transferred or to make a statement on specific libraries – apart from the Ashrafīya that is. Even those modern authors who claim that a massive transfer took place are only able to refer to a few concrete examples.[112] In addition, a short passage from the chronicle by Ibn Iyās on plundering from Cairene libraries is repeatedly cited. However, plundering libraries and book collections is a recurring topos of conquest narratives and an isolated passage from one chronicle does not inspire much confidence on such a general point.[113] Those vehemently refuting the claims of Ottoman 'plundering' again do not refer to actual manuscripts but make rather broad assumptions that local book traders were willing to sell individuals manuscripts taken from libraries to whoever offered the best price.[114]

With the above study of the Ashrafīya manuscripts' trajectory there is now one case study that can be considered in relation to the question of Ottoman 'plunder'. What happened in Damascus and who decided which manuscripts should be shipped to Istanbul is impossible to reconstruct. However, it is striking that the Ottoman conquerors turned to what was clearly a minor library, rather than targeting one of the more prestigious ones. Although substantial holdings of the Ashrafīya library were transferred to Istanbul after the Ottoman conquest the story of its unmaking does not fit into narratives of plunder and decline. Some 200 years after its foundation the Ashrafiya had increasingly become a non-teaching institution owing to diminishing income from the endowment. When the books were transferred to Istanbul in the early tenth/sixteenth century the Ashrafiya had not been an educational institution for about a century. The Ottoman elite in search of books turned to a library that had lost its educational function. Rather than taking books from the educational heavyweights of the scholarly landscape, a decision that would have been decisively more controversial, the new elites transferred books from what had anyway been a minor scholarly institution and become dysfunctional by the early tenth/sixteenth century. And in this way the Ashrafiya manuscripts continued a journey that had started in numerous libraries in late sixth-/twelfth-century Artuqid northern Mesopotamia, Fatimid Cairo and seventh-/thirteenth-century Ayyubid Syria.

Notes

1. Tabbaa, *Constructions of Power and Piety.*
2. Dickinson, 'Ibn al-Ṣalāḥ al-Shahrazūrī'.
3. Chamberlain, *Knowledge and Social Practice.*
4. On these two Dār al-ḥadīths and the relevant primary sources see Pouzet, *Damas.*
5. Korn, *Ayyubidische Architektur*, nos. 8, 34, 38; Moaz, 'Mausolée de Saladin'.
6. Abū Shāma, *al-Mudhayyal*, II, 20.
7. Different sizes: The western room measured 4.5m x 7.5m, i.e. *c.*33.75m^2 and the eastern room 7m x 7.5m, i.e. *c.*52.5m^2. Wulzinger and Watzinger, *Damaskus*, 64 (Abb. 7) (Sack, *Damaskus*, 97 (2.23) merely quotes Wulzinger and Watzinger). Ibn Badrān (d. 1346/1927), *Munādamat al-aṭlāl*, 353.
8. Ibn Wāṣil, *Mufarrij*, V, 145.
9. For instance, Yūsuf al-Wāsiṭī al-Aᶜraj al-Muqriᵓ (d. 656/1258); Abū Shāma, *al-Mudhayyal*, II, 124 and al-Kamāl al-Qazwīnī (d. 659/1261); Abū Shāma, *al-Mudhayyal*, II, 160. 'Day and Night': Ibn Wāṣil, *Mufarrij*, V, 145.
10. MS Istanbul, Süleymaniye Library, Fatih 4097/1 (fols. 1a–39a): *al-Maqāmāt al-arbaᶜūn* by al-Hamadhānī endowed to mausoleum library of Maḥfūẓ b. Maᶜtūq Ibn al-Buzūrī (d. 694/1294; TI, 691–700, pp. 231–2). The same notes from this endowment are on manuscripts in al-Assad National Library (Damascus), cf. Eche, *Bibliothèques arabes*, 239–40.

11. Ibn al-Ṣalāḥ (d. 643/1245); al-Nawawī (d. 676/1277); Ibn al-Ḥarastānī (d. 669/1264); al-Subkī (d. 756/1355).
12. Ibn al-Jazarī, *Ghāyat al-nihāya*, I, 325: '*wa-lam yataqaddam fī hādhā al-ᶜilm . . . wa-lā intafaᶜa aḥadun bihi*'.
13. We only know two *nāẓirs* by name: the officer Sharaf al-Dīn Qayrān (d. 709/1309) who got the position after having been demoted (al-Yūnīnī, *Dhayl*, II, 843) and Ḥasan b. Yūnis al-Ghazzī al-Shāfiᶜī who became *nāẓir* in 938/1531 (al-Ghazzī, *al-Kawākib*, II, 137). The only known menial post-holder was the doorkeeper Muḥammad b. Yūsuf al-Ḥawrānī (d. 738/1338) (al-Dhahabī, *Muᶜjam*, II, 306), who was also the mausoleum's muezzin.
14. Hirschler, *Written Word*.
15. Hirschler, *Written Word*, 131–4.
16. Eche, *Bibliothèques arabes*.
17. '*Bi-rasm khizānat al-Malik al-Nāṣir . . . Ṣalāḥ al-Dīn*', al-Ṭarsūsī, *al-Tabṣira fī al-ḥurūb*, MS Oxford, Bodleian Library, Huntington 264, fol. 208v–209r. '*Al-khizāna al-sharīfa al-sulṭānīya al-malikīya al-Afḍalīya*.' Dedication by Ibn Nubāta (d. 768/1366) to al-Malik Afḍal in Hama in 732/1331 in his *Sulūk duwal al-mulūk* (Bauer, 'Means of Communication', 27–8).
18. MU, V, 2349: '*khizānat al-Malik al-Muᶜaẓẓam*', which the author visited in person (see also MU, II, 659).
19. Ḥasan al-Qaylawī (d. 633/1236): *al-Wāfī*, XII, 219; see Fihrist al-Ashrafiya, Engl. tr. no. 257, 533, 698, 1253 for copies in his hand.
20. '*Al-khizāna al-sulṭānīya al-malakīya al-Ashrafīya*': MS Istanbul, Süleymaniye Library, Süleymaniye 1008, fol. 1a (=Fihrist al-Ashrafiya, Engl. tr. no. 698).
21. '*Khizānat mawlānā al-Sulṭān al-Malik al-Ashraf*': MS Istanbul, Süleymaniye Library, Rağıp Paşa 1180, fol. 1a (*Kitāb al-shiᶜr wa-al-shuᶜarāᵓ* by ᶜAbd Allāh b. Muslim al-Dīnawarī Ibn Qutayba, d. 276/889).
22. In Mamluk Cairo the Sultan al-Malik al-Muᵓayyad Shaykh set up his madrasa/mausoleum in 823/1420 (ᶜAbd al-Ḥalīm, *al-ᶜImāra al-islāmīya*) and built up its library by transferring books from the citadel.
23. MS Istanbul, Topkapı Palace Museum Archives, D.9101, no. 1. Cf. Erünsal, *Ottoman Libraries: A Survey of the History*, 30.
24. Ibn al-Nabīh (d. 619/1222): Fihrist al-Ashrafiya, Engl. tr. nos 190, 288, 315, 863, 868, 1049; Ibn (al-)Amsīnā?: nos 484, 875; Ibn Māḍī?: no. 1130; al-Yārūqī: no. 1147; anonymous: nos 977, 1122, 1369.
25. Zangids: Fihrist al-Ashrafiya, Engl. tr. nos 1151 and 1294b; Saljuqs: no. 1609; Fatimids: no. 648 (panegyric?).

26. Saladin: Fihrist al-Ashrafiya, Engl. tr. nos 873, 1094, 1224a, 1226d; al-Malik al-ᶜĀdil: nos 874, 1054, 1055.
27. Fihrist al-Ashrafiya, Engl. tr. no. 376.
28. Fihrist al-Ashrafiya, Engl. tr. nos 215, 301, 1325c, 319.
29. Fihrist al-Ashrafiya, Engl. tr. nos. 458, 864, 381, 375.
30. Fihrist al-Ashrafiya, Engl. tr. nos. 474 and 1115.
31. Fihrist al-Ashrafiya, Engl. tr. nos. 516, 977, 1369.
32. Ibn Wāṣil, *Mufarrij*, V, 143–4.
33. Ibn Wāṣil, *Mufarrij*, V, 138–49.
34. Al-Dhahabī, *Siyar*, XXII, 376–7.
35. Fihrist al-Ashrafiya, Engl. tr. no. 1471.
36. For a case study see Korn, 'Artuqid Courts'.
37. The physician Sadīd al-Dīn Maḥmūd (d. 635/1237–8) served al-Malik al-Ashraf for many years in Mayyāfāriqīn and Damascus. He composed *al-Qaṣīda al-bāhīya* for al-Ashraf, including a commentary, in Mayyāfāriqīn in 615/1218–9 (IAU, IV, 271–95). The ophthalmologist Ḥakim al-zamān ᶜAbd al-Munᶜim b. ᶜUmar (d. 620/1223–4 in al-Ruhā) composed panegyrics for al-Ashraf (IAU, IV, 77). Ibn al-Athīr (d. 622/1225): IKH, V, 397. Book sent: *Ḍawʾ al-ṣabāḥ fī al-ḥathth ᶜalā al-samāḥ* by Ibn al-ᶜAdīm (d. 660/1262; Ibn Shākir, *Fawāt*, III, 127 and MU, V, 2086); books offered: 12-volume administrative Fatimid manual (MU, V, 2035).
38. Fihrist al-Ashrafiya, Engl. tr. nos. 1240a and 868.
39. Shāh Arman: Fihrist al-Ashrafiya, Engl. tr. nos. 315, 1354; al-Malik al-Manṣūr: Fihrist al-Ashrafiya, Engl. tr. no. 1151.
40. Fihrist al-Ashrafiya, Engl. tr. nos. 1585, 776, 778.
41. Fihrist al-Ashrafiya, Engl. tr. no. 855: MS Istanbul, Süleymaniye Library, Ayasofya 3359, fol. 190b.
42. EI², D. Sourdel, 'Dunaysir' and EI², A.H. de Groot, 'Ḳoč Ḥiṣār'; biographical dictionary: ᶜUmar b. al-Khiḍr, *K. Ḥilyat al-sarīyīn min khawāṣṣ al-Dunaysarīyīn*, MS Berlin, Staatsbibliothek, We. 1099 (Ahlwardt 9851).
43. Ibn Muqla (d. 328/940); Ibn al-Bawwāb (d. 413/1022); al-Juwaynī (d. 586/1190?); fraud: Touati, *L'armoire à sagesse*, 100–13.
44. Fihrist al-Ashrafiya, Engl. tr. nos. 1662, 454.
45. Fihrist al-Ashrafiya, Engl. tr. no. 1467.
46. Fihrist al-Ashrafiya, Engl. tr. no. 365 (Koran: 'lavishly gilded'), no. 450 (prayer book: 'gilded in the beginning and the end') and no. 1066 (al-Muntakhal: 'gilded').

47. Gacek, *Vademecum*, 183; Contadini, 'Ayyubid Illustrated Manuscripts'.
48. Falconry and equitation: Fihrist al-Ashrafīya, Engl. tr. nos 214 and 833; Ibn al-Habbārīya and al-Yamanī: nos 701 and 1021. On *Kalīla wa-dimna* illustrations see O'Kane, *Early Persian Painting*.
49. Fihrist al-Ashrafīya, Engl. tr. nos. 858 and 62.
50. Fihrist al-Ashrafīya, Engl. tr. no. 1470. On pilgrimage certificates see Sourdel and Sourdel-Thomine, *Certificats de pèlerinage*.
51. Fihrist al-Ashrafīya, Engl. tr. no. 1367. On genealogical trees see Binbaş, 'Structure and Function'.
52. Book of Antidotes: *Kitāb al-diryāq*, MS Paris, Bibliothèque Nationale, arabe 2964; Book of Songs: Touati, *L'armoire à sagesse*, 67.
53. On al-Muᶜaẓẓam and learning see Humphreys, *From Saladin to the Mongols*, 189–92; Pouzet, *Damas*, 67–70; Yılmaz, 'Dımaşk Eyyubi', 329–47; historical work: Fihrist al-Ashrafīya, Engl. tr. no. 47; poetry: no. 664; prayer book: no. 425; pharmacological manual: nos. 105, 193, 1479.
54. Fihrist al-Ashrafīya, Engl. tr. nos. 358, 944, 946, 1160a, 201.
55. For the citadel Dār al-ḥadīth's library see Eche, *Bibliothèques arabes*, 214–17.
56. Humphreys, *From Saladin to the Mongols*, 239–81.
57. The most complete biographies of al-Ashraf Aḥmad are in: TI, 641–50, pp. 149–51; IKH, III, 163; *Wāfī*, VII, 57–8. The names of his servants are registered in reading certificates such as in Ibn ᶜAsākir, *Taʾrīkh madīnat Dimashq*, LIV, 183 (samāᶜ no. 6).
58. Bora, 'Fatimids' Books' and Hirschler, *Written Word*, 124–63.
59. ᶜAbd al-Karīm (d. 621/1224–5): *Wāfī*, XIX, 82.
60. The details are given by the contemporaneous scholar and first *shaykh* of recitation in the mausoleum, Abū Shāma, *Mudhayyal*, II, 20.
61. Medicine: Fihrist al-Ashrafīya, Engl. tr. nos. 264 and 1032; Ibn al-Zubayr: nos. 462, 502, 744; head of chancery (Ibn Khayrān): no. 497.
62. Ibn al-Zubayr: Fihrist al-Ashrafīya, Engl. tr. no. 1615; Ṭalāʾiᶜ: no. 1611; al-Ballanūbī: no. 648; Ibn Hāniʾ: no. 398; scribes: Fihrist al-Ashrafīya, Engl. tr. no. 1607 (Ibn al-Khallāl, cf. IKH, VII, 219–25); al-Muᶜizz (r. 341–65/953–75)/al-Ṣiqillī (d. 381/992): no. 893; al-Muᶜizz/prayers: nos. 151, 1170c, 1198b, 1661.
63. Michot, 'Mamlūk Theologian's Commentary' referring to Ibn Taymīya's commentary on Avicenna's *Aḍḥawīya*.
64. Ibn Taymīya, *Sharḥ al-Iṣfahānīya* where he quotes as well al-Sijistānī's *al-Maqālīd* (Walker, 'An Ismāᶜili Answer', 198). Ibn Taymīya, *al-Risāla*

al-ṣafadīya, I, 276, 301 and II, 3, quoting al-Sijistānī's *K. al-ifitkhār* and again his *Maqālīd.* Ibn Taymīya, *Minhāj*, VIII, 27 quoting the *Maqālid.* I thank Paul Walker (Chicago) and Rodrigo Adem (Chicago) for directing me to these references.

65. Fihrist al-Ashrafīya, Engl. tr. nos. 296, 297, 459, 498, 557b, 853, 900, 953a, 978.
66. IKH, V, 342.
67. TI, 541–50, p. 150.
68. Fihrist al-Ashrafīya, Engl. tr. no. 204; MS Istanbul, Süleymaniye Library, Fatih 3695–7 (628/1231).
69. Fihrist al-Ashrafīya, Engl. tr. nos. 574, 918, 1335, 805, 1241f.
70. Ibn ᶜAsākir (d. 571/1176): Fihrist al-Ashrafīya, Engl. tr. nos. 229, 840, 842; al-Murādī (d. 544/1150): no. 2; Egyptian-Syrian authors: nos. 353 and 841; non-Damascene profile: no. 6 and 8.
71. Ahmed, 'Mapping the World', 24–43.
72. Ibn Rīsh: Fihrist al-Ashrafīya, Engl. tr. nos. 153, 168; Ibn Shīth: no. 425; al-Qaylawī: nos. 533, 698; al-Dimashqī (d. 654/1256): nos. 715, 1392.
73. Aleppo: Fihrist al-Ashrafīya, Engl. tr. nos. 198, 1653; Baghdad: no. 821.
74. Griffel, *Philosophical Theology*, 76.
75. Pouzet, 'Maghrébiens à Damas'.
76. Ibn ᶜAbd al-Salām (d. 660/1262): al-Subkī, *Ṭabaqāt*, VIII, 210; Karak: Hirschler, *Medieval Arabic Historiography*, 59; physicians: Brentjes, 'Ayyubid Princes'.
77. Al-Nuᶜaymī, *al-Dāris*, II, 292.
78. IKH, I, 214 (Dīwān Abū Saᶜādāt Asᶜad b. Yaḥyā al-Sinjārī, Fihrist al-Ashrafīya, Engl. tr. no. 800); IKH, IV, 450 (Dīwān Muḥammad b. ᶜAlī b. al-Ḥasan Ibn Abī al-Ṣaqr al-Wāsiṭī, no. 1062); *Wāfī*, III, 37 (referring to a work copied by the Syrian calligrapher Muḥammad b. Khazraj al-Anṣārī, no. 1392); Ibn Kathīr, *al-Bidāya*, XIII, 129 (Dīwān Ibrāhīm b. al-Muẓaffar al-Baznī (d. 622/1225, also TI, 621–30, pp. 99–100): Iraqi scholar, student of Ibn al-Jawzī, author of ascetic poetry; possibly IKH, IV, 24–6 (Shiᶜr al-Shihāb Fityān, no. 1070).
79. Al-Nuᶜaymī, *al-Dāris*, II, 291–8 makes a mistake recurrent in medieval texts, namely to confuse the 'Ashrafīya' mausoleum with one of the 'Ashrafīya' Dār al-ḥadīths. He mentions a scholar who endowed books to the 'Ashrafīya' in his entry on the mausoleum, yet as TI, 681–90, pp. 435–6 clarifies this is the Dār al-ḥadīth. This mistake is often uncritically reproduced in modern secondary literature, e.g. al-Jūmānī, 'Fihris', 72.

80. Al-Yūnīnī, *Dhayl*, XVIII, 10.
81. Al-Subkī, *Fatāwā*, II, 109.
82. Hirschler, *Written Word*, 137–8.
83. Al-Subkī, *Fatāwā*, II, 109.
84. Hirschler, *Written Word*, 137.
85. Al-Āmadī (d. 816/1413): al-Nuᶜaymī, *al-Dāris*, I, 506; al-Anṣārī: TI, 681–90, p. 136; al-Yūnīnī, *Dhayl*, XIX, 248–9; lost copy: al-Yūnīnī, *Dhayl*, XIX, 248.
86. '*Wa-ḥaṣala bi-ṭarīqīhi lahā ḍabṭ ᶜaẓīm*' (al-Yūnīnī, *Dhayl*, XIX, 248).
87. Illustrated copies: Fihrist al-Ashrafīya, Engl. tr. no. 701; non-illustrated copies: no. 705.
88. Fihrist al-Ashrafīya, Engl. tr. no. 1694.
89. Şeşen, *al-Makhṭūṭāt al-ᶜarabīya al-nādira*, 893. Al-Jūmānī, 'Fihris', 73. Regrettably, he does not provide details on where his main proof, 'a book by al-Bāᶜūnī (d. 871)', would be in the catalogue. See also my comments in Chapter 4 on the issue of identifying book titles in medieval library catalogues.
90. 667–99 bracket: Fihrist al-Ashrafīya, Engl. tr. nos. 466, 534, 813, 1115, 1171b, 1230f, 1238d, 1328c, 1549.
91. Fihrist al-Ashrafīya, Engl. tr. nos. 258 ('*year 625/1227–8*') and 1694 ('*after the year 620[/1223–4]*').
92. Fihrist al-Ashrafīya, Engl. tr. no. 1378. Bosworth, 'Arabic, Persian and Turkish Historiography', 143.
93. IKH, I, 214 (Fihrist al-Ashrafīya, Engl. tr. no. 800); IKH, IV, 450 (no. 1062); and possibly IKH, IV, 24–6 (no. 1070); *Wāfī*, III, 37 (Fihrist al-Ashrafīya, Engl. tr. no. 1392); Ibn Kathīr, *al-Bidāya*, XIII, 129 (Dīwān Ibrāhīm b. al-Muẓaffar al-Baznī).
94. Ṣadr al-Dīn al-Āmadī (d. 816/1413); al-Nuᶜaymī, *al-Dāris*, I, 506.
95. Al-Mālikī (d. 943/1536–7): Ibn al-ᶜImād, *Shadharāt*, X, 357; al-Ghazzī, *al-Kawākib*, II, 137.
96. Al-Nuᶜaymī, *al-Dāris*, II, 291–8.
97. For instance, al-Buṣrawī (d. 905/1500), *Taʾrīkh* and al-Badrī (d. 909/1503?), *Nuzhat*.
98. On this period's historiography, cf. Winter, 'Historiography in Arabic'.
99. For example, rulers: MS Istanbul, Süleymaniye Library, Rağıp Paşa 1180 (620/1223); officers: Fatih 3646 (510/1116–17), Ayasofya 1686 (559/1164), Fatih 5297 (624/1227), Ayasofya 4824/3 (649/1251); vizier: Fazıl Ahmed Paşa 215 (6th/12th century).
100. For example, MS Istanbul, Süleymaniye Library, Fazıl Ahmed Paşa 663 and

Fatih 691. For a fascinating case directly relevant to the Ashrafiya library, see Fihrist al-Ashrafiya, Engl. tr. no. 204.

101. On account of al-Malik al-Ashraf's career, a north Syrian (especially Aleppo) and northern Mesopotamian place of production/circulation was also taken to be an indicator in the case of manuscripts written in the early 7th/13th century.
102. The criteria for assigning a given manuscript one of the three categories are partly given in Chapter 4 and are listed in the *The Ashrafiya Library Database.*
103. Fihrist al-Ashrafiya, Engl. tr. no. 698; MS Istanbul, Süleymaniye Library, Süleymaniye 1008, fol. 1a.
104. Fihrist al-Ashrafiya, Engl. tr. no. 1115; MS Istanbul, Süleymaniye Library, Fatih 5300/4 (fols. 89a–118b).
105. Fihrist al-Ashrafiya, Engl. tr. no. 232; MS Istanbul, Süleymaniye Library, Murad Buhari 332/3 (fols. 147b–198b).
106. Fihrist al-Ashrafiya, Engl. tr. no. 916; MS Istanbul, Süleymaniye Library, Süleymaniye 139.
107. Humphreys, *Friars' Libraries*; Bell, *Cistercians, Gilbertines and Premonstratensians*, XXXIII; Stoneman, *Dover Priory*; Leicester: Webber and Watson, *Augustinian Canons*, 104–399.
108. Fihrist al-Ashrafiya, Engl. tr. no. 59; MS Istanbul, Süleymaniye Library, Fatih 4024.
109. For Ottoman libraries, see the numerous publications by Erünsal, specifically *Ottoman Libraries: A Survey of the History*, 53–8, 77.
110. Erünsal, *Ottoman Libraries: A Survey of the History*, 155–6.
111. MS Istanbul, Süleymaniye Library, Fatih 2214 (ex libiris), 3439, 3695–3699, 3724, 3738, 3900, 3942 & 3943, 3946, 3959, 4022, 4024, 4090, 4828/2, 5303 (=Fihrist al-Ashrafiya, Engl. tr. nos. 1376, 862, 204, 253, 335, 83, 669, 670, 675, 888, 59, 1110, 1646, 257). It goes without saying that his endowment note also occurs on Fatih manuscripts, which have no link with the Ashrafiya, such as Fatih 1456, 4079, 4097, 5194, 5306.
112. Sayyid, *Dār al-kutub al-miṣrīya*, 16–17 (referring only to four examples of transfers).
113. Ibn Iyās (d. c.930/1524), *Badāʾiʿ*, V, 176.
114. Erünsal, 'Vakıf Kütüphaneleri'.

2

Organising the Library: The Books on the Shelves

With its large library collection the Ashrafiya had to have some system of how to arrange and organise its books. This was paramount for two reasons: first, space was – as we will see below – a scarce resource in such an endowment and the books had to be stocked in an efficient way to avoid unnecessarily wasting it. Perhaps even more importantly a collection holding more than 2,000 books had to provide some reliable system to retrieve specific titles in order to be of any use to its librarian and readers. Smaller collections could afford the luxury of organising their books into rough categories and could also, arguably, afford to use comparatively inefficient library furnishings such as book chests. The only other surviving catalogue from this period pertaining to the mosque library in the North African city of Kairouan only listed 125 books. On account of its small size, there is no real organisation to speak of apart from grouping the copies of the Koran.[1] However, a library such as the Ashrafiya required a sophisticated and highly developed system for storing and retrieving its books. Its catalogue of forty-eight pages was a crucial tool in achieving these goals and the present chapter will analyse its structure to present the organisation of this library and its spatial arrangement. As the catalogue was most likely written by the librarian al-Anṣārī in the 670s/1270s, I will in the following repeatedly talk of al-Anṣārī's role in organising the library. This is not meant to imply that he completely reorganised the library on his own, but rather to put a name to a process, which certainly began with the foundation of the library some four decades earlier and involved more than one individual in subsequent years.

So far the document at the heart of this book, the *fihrist*, has been consistently called a 'catalogue'. This conscious choice was made in order to argue against the assumption that a medieval library's '*fihrist* is a legal register' in the first place[2] and functions as a catalogue as a by-product, if at all. In this vein the Ashrafiya catalogue has been described as a 'failure in being a veritable tool for retrieving books, but it rather leans towards being a mere tool for listing them'.[3] For Ottoman library catalogues the judgements are strikingly similar, as they 'were made not to facilitate the work of the librarian or to help the reader to locate a book, but rather because the legal status of foundation libraries required that inventories of endowed books were drawn up at various stages as a means of exercising control over the collection'.[4] The main argument presented in the following is that the Ashrafiya catalogue, on the contrary, was first and foremost a practical tool – composed by a librarian with the intention of facilitating the use of the library. Al-Anṣārī was extremely brief in his 'introduction' to the Ashrafiya *fihrist* and he did not indicate in any way why he chose to prepare it. However, it is evident that it was clearly not a legal document for the purpose of registering the books endowed in the mausoleum. The absence of the term 'endowment' anywhere in the Ashrafiya catalogue as well as the absence of any other feature of legal documents (attestation by the judge or signatures of witnesses) leaves little doubt that it has no legal dimension.

Furthermore, the Ashrafiya catalogue is not a celebration of 'our city's learnedness', which seems very much the driving force behind the composition of the seventh-/thirteenth-century inventory of libraries in Aleppo. This text listed a selection of titles in the city's libraries, but its author did not specify in which of the city's many libraries a given title could be found. In contrast to the almost contemporaneous *Registrum Anglie*, the 'union catalogue' of books in English, Scottish and Welsh libraries, the Aleppo inventory thus lacked any practical dimension for its readers as an aid for retrieval.[5] Finally, the Ashrafiya catalogue is also not a panegyric or commemorative text celebrating its endowers, which would have circulated within the social and political elite of the city. This is not only evident from its format, but al-Anṣārī also dispensed with any panegyrics for the endowers in the catalogue's two-line 'introduction' and even the ritual formulae were kept to an absolute minimum. After the *basmallāh* he went straight on to state what this is all about, namely to provide the 'catalogue of the Ashrafiya library'.[6]

The practical character of the catalogue is very much inscribed in its format. Rather unusually for Arabic-language manuscripts of this period it is *safina*-shaped, that is, an oblong format bound at the top or bottom of the folia with the lines running horizontal to the spine. *Safina*-shaped manuscripts were typically used for 'notebook' purposes when a scholar collected material and first ideas in preparation for drafting the finished work. Examples of such *safina*-shaped notebooks include the well-known eighth-/fourteenth-century *Tadhkira* by al-Ṣafadī.[7] In the Ashrafiya catalogue, to cite a second 'notebook-example', one entry is described as being '*safina-shaped*' and very fittingly so it is an entry without a title, which appears to be a notebook drawing together various material on the recitation of the Koran.[8] As for the Ashrafiya catalogue itself, choosing the unusual *safina* format reinforces the argument that the cataloguer intended it to be a functional text for himself and the library users. A *safina* format would have been very unusual, and arguably inappropriate, for a panegyric text.

That this is not a panegyric text or a text to celebrate the learnedness of Damascus is also evident from the document's mise-en-page. There is not the slightest attempt to have a standard number of lines per page and they vary from fifteen to twenty-one (*Figure 2.1*). The Aleppo-inventory, by contrast, always has twenty lines on each of its sixty-three pages.[9] Consequently, the Ashrafiya catalogue has no sign of a more or less regular and straight rectangular block for the body text. The space between the top and the bottom lines varies from *c.*161mm to *c.*178mm (see Chapter 5). In addition, the

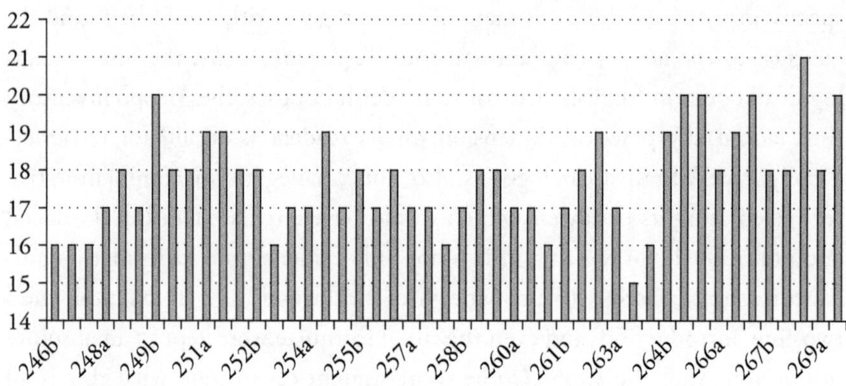

Figure 2.1 Ashrafiya catalogue, lines per page

left margin is jagged throughout the catalogue and even the right margin barely resembles a straight line (for example, folio 264b; Plate 43). The use of catchwords, repeating the last word of a folio at the beginning of the next folio to ensure the correct order of the folia, is also rather haphazard. Such catchwords are used for the first three folia, ignored on the next thirteen folia with two exceptions in between (folia 255b/256a, 256b/257a; Plates 25/6, 27/8), reappear on four folia (folia 262b/263a, 263b/264a, 264b/265a, 266b/267a; Plates 39/40, 41/2, 43/4, 47/8) and are then forgotten for good.

In contrast to the rich tradition of splendid book-making in this period, the catalogue was clearly a very modestly produced text. The absence of an aesthetic programme in writing the catalogue is also apparent in the one case where we have two near-identical pages. Al-Anṣārī started his catalogue on the folio's verso probably to leave space on the recto for a title page. However, after completing seven folia he must have mixed up the order and mistakenly continued on the page he had reserved for the title. Only when he turned the folio over did he realise his mistake, cross out the page (folio 246a; Plate 6) and start a new folio (folio 253a; Plate 20). Luckily, he was not willing to rewrite the entire catalogue, giving us the two near-identical pages. Although al-Anṣārī dealt with exactly the same material on these two pages the line-break already starts to differ from the very first line. In the same vein the use of margins is different and the same goes for the number of lines on each page with seventeen lines on the erroneous folio 246a and sixteen lines on folio 253a. The Ashrafiya catalogue was thus a functional and practical text and we will see in the following how it reflected the library's organisation and thus helped the library users to navigate its shelves. Although al-Anṣārī hardly introduced the catalogue it is not difficult to see his task in the same vein as an early Ottoman catalogue where the librarian stated, 'I was, for my part, now ordered to prepare a new catalogue which would represent the books as they are to be found in the library, that it too may be placed in this library.'[10] To what extent the practical nature of the Ashrafiya catalogue was a more widespread phenomenon in the medieval Arabic lands can only be answered once more catalogues are discovered.

Although the Ashrafiya catalogue had a practical purpose, the surviving version was clearly not used in the library's daily workings. This version is in such pristine condition that it cannot have served as a working tool for either librarian or library users for an extended period. It was definitely never used as a lending register, nor could it have been intended as one with the little space it provided for any further notes. More remarkably, it has no later additions or changes, which would have reflected the library's changing holdings on account of loss and theft as well as new acquisitions and replacement copies. How to integrate such additions into a medieval catalogue is demonstrated well in the late twelfth-century example of the Benedictine library of Bury St Edmunds.[11] It is evident that al-Anṣārī never intended the Ashrafīya catalogue to be a similar document representing work-in-progress. As he left no space for further additions within the course of the catalogue or in the margins, it would have been simply impossible to keep the document up to date.[12] It is thus most likely that a separate document was kept for lending purposes and that a new catalogue was drawn up when the holdings had changed to such an extent that the old catalogue had become obsolete. Considering the amount of work that must have gone into preparing the catalogue and that it was not used for an extended period, the most likely scenario is that a new catalogue was drawn up shortly after al-Anṣārī finished his work on the version that has come down to us.

The Order of Books

Aiming to prepare a practical tool, al-Anṣārī (or his predecessors) faced the question of how to organise the catalogue (and library) to make it useable. We know from narrative sources that catalogues had been prepared for centuries in Arabic libraries[13] and even book collections held by individuals, such as those in the family of al-Qāḍī al-Fāḍil, were recorded in a systematic fashion.[14] However, authors of narrative sources are not terribly interested in giving too many details on the organisation of these catalogues. When a librarian prepared a catalogue (*fihrist*) for his madrasa in Basra some four decades after al-Anṣārī he was said to have 'followed a good method', but there is no indication what this method may have been.[15] Nevertheless, from these descriptions it is at least evident that there was no single system of how to structure catalogues. Many earlier catalogues had been organised thematically, such as the library of the Buyid Sultan ᶜAḍud al-Dawla, the Fatimid library in Cairo, a contemporaneous madrasa-library in Baghdad and also the book endowment by a seventh-/thirteenth-century scholar in

Damascus.[16] Yet at the same time we have examples of book lists, which like the above-mentioned seventh-/thirteenth-century inventory of libraries in Aleppo were organised alphabetically.[17] Some libraries had specific catalogues for sub-collections attached to the original endower; others had independent catalogues for specific thematic fields.

When al-Anṣārī prepared the Ashrafīya catalogue in the late seventh/thirteenth century ample examples of library catalogues were thus available and al-Anṣārī would certainly have at least been aware of those in Damascus. However, although he did not have to invent the wheel, no paradigmatic system existed for him to copy. The freedom to develop one's own system is also evident from the Jūmānī-corpus: about half of these lists had an explicit thematic organisation, while the other half did not use subject matter as a principal criterion for organising the collection.[18] Among those lists that did use a thematic organisation there is again no uniform approach as to what categories were used. The plurality of how book lists and catalogues were organised also emerges from descriptions in narrative sources. In the late Mamluk period, for instance, the librarian of a madrasa found a pragmatic solution to the various possibilities of how to organise the stock and composed both a thematic and an alphabetic catalogue.[19] That Arabic medieval library catalogues were organised in many ways is not surprising. Different catalogue structures were favoured depending on the collection's size, historical development, thematic homogeneity or heterogeneity, situation in one room or several locations, endowment by one or several benefactors and a range of other factors. This is also true for the well-documented case of medieval British catalogues. Even among monastic libraries from the same orders, for instance the Friars' libraries, there was no unified approach towards cataloguing and the same is true for the various medieval libraries of the University of Cambridge.[20]

The Ashrafīya catalogue allows us for the first time to see how a large-scale medieval Arabic library was organised and what we see is a remarkably sophisticated three-tier system organising the books by alphabet, theme and size. No description of another medieval Arabic library catalogue mentions such a three-tier system and it is certainly one of the fascinating aspects of this document. The absence of similar descriptions should not be taken as evidence that it was necessarily a unique system. As seen above, narrative sources were not terribly interested in how pre-seventh/thirteenth-century library catalogues were organised and this changed little in the following centuries. We would know nothing of the Ashrafiya's catalogue structure – or even be aware of its existence – were it not for the chance survival of its catalogue. The fact that none of the book lists and catalogues in the Jūmānī-corpus had a system similar to the Ashrafiya's three-tier system should also not be given too much weight. The vast majority do not refer to large-scale institutional libraries such as the Ashrafiya, but rather to book collections by specific individuals. It may well be that other institutional libraries in the vast number of teaching institutions in medieval Syria and Egypt adopted a similar system.

However, as will become repeatedly evident in the course of the following discussion, this three-tier organisation was certainly not a well-established or widespread system copied by al-Anṣārī for his purposes. The drafting of the catalogue was in many ways rather an experiment for him: He repeatedly aborted attempts to include specific bits of information and the whole sophisticated system very much crashed towards the end. Even in a rather minor library such as the Ashrafiya, librarians were thus clearly playing around with various possibilities to introduce some order to the books. The role of individual librarians in developing new systems is also evident if we look at the development of British medieval catalogues. Only from 1100 onwards did they slowly grow in sophistication to become more than simple book lists. It is as late as the fourteenth century that catalogues started to display a clearer interest in the arrangement of the books and provided data concerning their location in the library.[21] The Dover Priory catalogue from 1389 was outstanding in its sophistication, offering press-marks for each volume, but also providing the library user with a thematic and alphabetical list of the works held. It is a marked departure from the pedestrian approaches of its predecessors and contemporaries, yet it is unclear where the library's precentor John Whytefelde got the idea to develop this structure. Some decades earlier another outstanding librarian, Henry of Kirkstede, prepared a similarly sophisticated classification system for the Bury St Edmunds library.[22] However, there is no sense of interdependence among these systems and they did not serve as a paradigmatic example in the subsequent decades. With al-Anṣārī's Ashrafiya catalogue the main difference is that he prepared it a century earlier than the Dover and the Bury St Edmunds systems. The sophistication of the Ashrafiya catalogue is yet another expression of the more bookish character of Syrian and Egyptian urban society where even second-rate libraries routinely had to deal with large numbers of books.

The Ashrafiya catalogue's first and main level of organisation was the alphabetical order of titles running through all letters from *alif* to *yāʾ*. Under each of the letters a second level of organisation subdivided the entries by size into either normal format (the default category) or small format (occasionally explicitly highlighted as '*ṣighār*'). Each of the resulting fifty-six categories (twenty-eight letters with two sections for size) was further subdivided by a third organisational level of subject-matter. For this third level the writer of the catalogue introduced fifteen thematic categories for the normal-sized books and eight for the small-sized books. For instance, normal books in category 5 were mainly concerned with history. This combination of twenty-eight letters, two sizes and fifteen or eight thematic categories gave a potential 644 'class-marks', albeit a term that was neither used in the catalogue nor in the period's literature at large.[23] A book that was found under the letter *alif*, normal size, category 5 was most likely a historical work that could be labelled with the class-mark A/n/5. The actual number of class-marks in the Ashrafiya catalogue was significantly lower than the potential number. For instance, the letter *ḍād* was entirely missing, the letter *thāʾ* only had one entry and other letters had so few entries that the librarian dispensed with the second and third organisational level. The letter *ẓāʾ* with its three entries had no further subdivisions according to size or subject.[24] Despite these missing categories the catalogue used a total of 276 class-marks, about 40 per cent of those potentially available, and thus offered its users a highly specific system.

The alphabetical order of the titles was relatively straightforward to record, especially as there is no secondary alphabetical order within each letter, which would have significantly complicated things. Al-Anṣārī was willing to bend the system when expedient. This appears in one of the most intriguing 'cross-references' in the catalogue (although the term is being stretched here). In the letter *alif*, al-Anṣārī places the title *Qiṣṣat Dalla al-Muḥtāla* (*The Story of Dalla the Crafty*), which clearly did not belong there, but rather to the *qāf* section.[25] However, this was not an alphabetical mix-up: as this story was already seen to be part of the *Alf layla wa-layla, 1001 Nights*, the cataloguer thought the entry would be most appropriately placed in the *alif* section.

Readers looking for a copy of the *1001 Nights* would go to this letter and thus come across the Dalla story. Another example of creatively adapting the system occurs under the letter *ᶜayn*, where a number of entries starting with other letters suddenly occur.[26] What seems at first glance to be another mistake[27] is in fact a grouping of Persian language (*ᶜajamīya*) works under the appropriate letter – as deemed appropriate by al-Anṣārī and arguably the library users. A final and third example is an obscure commentary on the poetry of the *ghazal* poet Ibn Hāniᵓ. As al-Anṣārī had little hope that readers would look for it under its title *Durr al-maᶜānī* (*Pearl of Meanings*) he rather put it under the letter *ghayn* and gave it the generic title *Ghazal Ibn Hāniᵓ*.[28]

Although alphabetical order proved to be initially unproblematic and gave the cataloguer sufficient flexibility, it started to pose considerable challenges for al-Anṣārī once he arrived at the letter *mīm*. After having successfully completed more than two-thirds of the complete books his system hit the wall when dealing with multiple-text manuscripts (*majāmīᶜ*), which he encountered in large numbers at this point.[29] He had already previously dealt with the occasional multiple-text manuscript. Here he had found ways of working around the problem of having to catalogue two (or more) texts, which were of the same size (as they were bound together), but did not match alphabetically in most cases and in some cases did not match thematically. In these cases al-Anṣārī tried to maintain the alphabetical order by using cross-references. For instance, when he catalogued a historical work bound together with early Islamic poetry under the letter *tāᵓ* he stated that 'we will mention it [as well] in [the section on the letter] *qāf*'. This entry under the letter *qāf* simply reversed the order of this multiple-text manuscript's two texts, which ensured that both texts had their correct alphabetical and thematic place.[30]

However, when al-Anṣārī came to the considerable section of multiple-text manuscripts under the letter *mīm*, he did not even try to implement this system, which would obviously have demanded a considerable degree of planning prior to preparing the catalogue. This was especially the case because the multiple-text manuscripts in this section contained considerably more texts and the largest has sixteen of them.[31] He thus abandoned the alphabetical order according to titles and prioritised these books' textual format instead, placing them all under *mīm* for *majāmīᶜ*. For the library's readers this differentiation between single-text and multiple-text manuscripts would not have come as a surprise as narrative texts drew a similarly sharp distinction. When describing the book endowment of a scholar in Damascus some years before al-Anṣārī prepared the Ashrafīya catalogue, a chronicler clearly differentiates between the '*kutub*' and the '*majāmīʿ*'.[32] Al-Anṣārī not only abandoned the alphabetical system at this point, but also dropped the third, the thematic, level of organisation. As he was not able to find a workable solution for manuscripts containing texts from very different fields of knowledge, he just randomly assigned the multiple-text manuscripts to one of the three 'thematic' categories 7, 8 and 9. These categories were thus of no real thematic significance in this section, but functioned rather as residual categories.[33]

That al-Anṣārī did not find a neater solution for dealing with multiple-text manuscripts is not too surprising as it was also a problem encountered by cataloguers of British medieval catalogues. Even though multiple-text manuscripts were much more frequent in British catalogues (in the Ashrafīya they constituted just 8 per cent of the entries), cataloguers generally failed to come up with no more a sophisticated solution than only taking into consideration a volume's first text and ignoring the rest. We have only few examples where cataloguers successfully engaged with the problems raised by these manuscripts. John Whytefelde's catalogue, for instance, had a section with an alphabetically organised location list for all texts including those in multiple-text manuscripts, considerably improving the library's usability.[34] The Peterborough *Matricularium* from the late 1390s, to cite another example, routinely omits the first text and was thus a dedicated list of secondary items and shorter texts. It was most likely a complement to another – lost – catalogue listing these first texts, which in combination with the former gave a complete overview of the texts held in the library.[35] However, most medieval British catalogues were just organised according to the first text and to a large extent disregarded the challenges posed by the other texts in the same volume. Al-Anṣārī was thus not alone in facing or failing to resolve the integration of multiple-text manuscripts in medieval library catalogues.

The second tier of organisation, normal or small size, was the most unproblematic level to implement. It was common to differentiate between the two basic formats in contemporaneous literature. We find, for instance, the same underlying concept in an advice book for students on right manners (adab), which differentiates between large (*al-qaṭ*ᶜ *al-kabīr*) and small (*al-qaṭ*ᶜ *al-ṣaghīr*) formats.[36] In the illustrations from al-Ḥarīrī's *Maqāmāt* we can see how this differentiation played out in a library setting in this period. Plate 2 clearly shows how the works on a library's shelves could be organised by size. If we take this bookcase's lowest row of shelves starting from the right, the first two bookcases contain small-sized books, each with two piles of books, followed by the third bookcase with one pile of normal-sized books, followed by three bookcases for small-sized books and so on. That the book piles on the shelves were reasonably neat very much depended on the books' binding: in contrast to loose piles of quires and sheets the books in the illustration are almost all bound and thus gave sufficient stability. On the Ashrafiya library's shelves most books were bound as well and the cataloguer only mentions in some cases that specific books were without binding ('*bi-ghayr jild*').[37] Tellingly, these are only three cases and they all occur in the section on incomplete manuscripts so that bound volumes must have been the norm in this library.

It is worth mentioning here that the bookcases were organised horizontally and not vertically, that is, the catalogue recorded the books in all bookcases on one shelf from right to left before moving (up or down) to the next shelf. Below we will see that the catalogue itself referred to a 'second shelf' (*ṣaff*) and, as importantly, Plates 4 and 5 have horizontally staggered bookcases, which would make any vertical organisation in these libraries impossible. When taking a closer look at Plates 4 and 5 another striking feature emerges, namely that in these bookcases there is no differentiation according to size. At first glance this contradicts the argument on the importance of space as an element in organising a medieval Arabic library. However, it is evident that the book piles are highly simplified in this illustration for aesthetic reasons. The identical and impeccable shape of almost all book piles is highly unlikely in a library that was actually in use. Especially the wasted space on the shelf in Plate 4, where there is just a single pile of small books, suggests that this can hardly reflect actual storage practices.

Differentiation by size was for practical reasons and was of particular importance in a book culture where horizontal stacking of books was the preferred – and almost exclusive – option. There is no indication that books were ever organised vertically in the medieval period and this is also reflected in Plates 2 to 5. This absence of vertically placed books is noteworthy, especially in Plate 2, which presents the books in a messier but more realistic arrangement on the shelves than the other illustrations. The dominance of horizontal book storage is also evident from the advice book for students mentioned above, which gave considerable detail on the most appropriate way to stack books on different subjects.[38] The differentiation according to size allowed piles to be built up of books with a similar format, which was important for two main reasons. The first of these was the need to have stable piles relatively unlikely to collapse. Stacking normal format books on top of those of a small format was certainly a risky affair and could result in all sorts of damage if the piles tipped over. The mixed-size pile in Plate 2, top shelf, second case from left certainly looks like an accident waiting to happen. The advice book for students explicitly warned against putting large-sized volumes on those of a small format to prevent such accidents.[39]

More importantly, piles of homogeneously sized books significantly increased the storage capacity of the shelves. As the Ashrafiya library was a very crowded place, storage was a major issue, as it probably was in most libraries of similar size. If Plate 4 does indeed reflect actual storage practices this library must have been, by contrast, in blessed possession of virtually unlimited availability of space. For reasons of efficiency the Ashrafiya – and arguably most Middle Eastern libraries of a similar size – thus organised their shelves by size so that books could be tightly packed in a single pile of normal-sized books or two piles of small-sized books. In the Kairouan catalogue-cum-inventory there is no indication of any such differentiation, but its books were most likely also stored in size-appropriate piles. However, as this library was of a very modest size, and as the document thus did not primarily have to serve as a catalogue, the librarian seemingly saw no need to reflect this in the document.[40]

The Ashrafiya catalogue dispenses with the differentiation between the two book sizes under the letters with few entries. For instance, the letter *hāʾ* has only three entries, which are all entered as 'small', while the letter *yāʾ* lists all of its five entries as normal size.[41] This could either indicate chance and all the books under letters with few entries were of the same size, or more likely that these few books were all in one single bookcase irrespective of their size. Consequently, librarians and users would have piled the different

Table 2.1 Ashrafiya library, thematic categories, normal-sized books (This table does not include those entries mentioned in the sections of multiple-text manuscripts and incomplete manuscripts, 'makh')

No.	Subject matter	Number of entries
1	transmitted sciences, esp. Koran, *ḥadīth*	115 (11.5%)
2	transmitted sciences, esp. *ḥadīth*, sermons	78 (7.5%)
3	transmitted sciences, esp. *fiqh*	39 (4%)
4	philological sciences, esp. grammar, lexicography	67 (6.5%)
5	philological sciences, esp. history	37 (3.5%)
6	poetry, esp. pre-Islamic and early Islamic	112 (11%)
7	adab	46 (4.5%)
8	adab	97 (9.5%)
9	rational sciences, esp. astronomy, oneiromancy	47 (4.5%)
10	rational sciences, esp. medicine, pharmacology	78 (7.5%)
11	poetry, esp. late ᶜAbbasid and following periods	18 (2%)
12	poetry (esp. late ᶜAbbasid and following periods) and prayers	83 (8%)
13	poetry, esp. anthologies	87 (8.5%)
14	adab (cat. mostly used in annex of incompl. MS)	3 (0.3%)
15	adab, poetry, commentary on poetry	112 (11%)

formats in one single alphabetical stack; a differentiation according to size in the catalogue would not have made retrieving the books any easier. The pragmatic handling of the catalogue's organisation with regard to size is a good example that the Ashrafiya catalogue is very much a functional tool. It was not meant to impose a strict system on the book collection, but to assist users of the library.

The third tier of organisation, subject matter, profiled the book collection in a thematic way and is a fascinating attempt by a librarian to impose order on his collection. Al-Anṣārī used fifteen categories to subdivide the entries under each letter according to broad thematic areas, as shown in *Table 2.1*. In his work on the Ashrafiya, al-Jūmānī explains the fifteen categories in a very different manner. Nowhere does he touch upon the thematic clustering within each group; rather he sees the categories as fifteen bookcases, so that the numbering system represents a location system. Theoretically, the two explanations are reconcilable in the sense that thematic bookcases may have existed in the Ashrafiya library. However, the uneven distribution of the library's books in the various categories makes a bookcase system rather unlikely. With numbers of entries varying between eighteen (category 11) and more than one hundred (category 1) a bookcase system would be very awkward to organise on account of its inflexibility. More importantly, if the Ashrafīya library really did have a fixed location system one would expect it to be referred to on a regular basis in the catalogue. However, there are only four unambiguous spatial references, which refer to the 'second shelf' as discussed below and there is not a single explicit reference to a bookcase.

The categories were thus attempts to classify the numerous fields of knowledge into workable units, but as with any classification of knowledge the system that we encounter in the Ashrafīya was far from an exact science. Categories 1, 2 and 3 were clearly concerned with the transmitted sciences and specific foci are evident. For instance, category 1 was particularly concerned with the fields of knowledge linked to the Koran so the vast majority of the works in fields such as Koran recitation and Koran commentary can be found here. Yet such works also occasionally appear in category 2. In the same vein, works on *ḥadīth* appear in both category 1 and category 2. Al-Anṣārī was well aware of how tenuous his classification system was; he classified the first copy of a book on stories of the Prophets (*qiṣaṣ al-anbiyāʾ*) under category 1 and the second copy under category 2.[42]

The most important point of the Ashrafīya's thematic classification system is again that this system was developed with an eye on the practical use of a library. In contrast to the abstract and theoretical classification systems of scholars such as al-Fārābī, al-Ghazālī and Ibn Khaldūn, the Ashrafīya system aimed first and foremost at providing easy and uncomplicated access to its books. Al-Ghazālī's differentiations between theoretical (*naẓarī*) and practical sciences (*ᶜamalī*) or those obligatory for every individual (*farḍ ᶜayn*) and those obligatory only for individuals able to master them (*farḍ kifāya*) could not have been of relevance for the organisation of the Ashrafīya collection.[43]

However, the Ashrafīya system was evidently influenced by these schemes and most of its fifteen categories can be linked to them in one way or the other. Three of the categories directly belong to the transmitted sciences (*al-ᶜulūm al-naqlīya*). Categories 1 to 3 were directly concerned with the understanding of divine revelation (Koran and *ḥadīth* categories 1 and 2) or its translation into legal norms (legal category 3). The following two categories dealt with philological concerns (*ᶜilm al-lisān*/*al-ᶜulūm al-ᶜarabīya*). Category 4 provided the ancillary lexicographical and grammatical knowledge necessary to master the language and category 5 offered the ancillary historical knowledge.

In the same vein, categories 9 and 10 appear familiar from the theoretical schemes. These categories grouped works belonging to the sciences variously labelled as ancient, foreign or rational (*ᶜulūm al-awāʾil/al-ᶜajam, al-ᶜulūm al-qadīma/al-ᶜaqlīya*). In category 10, library users could find medical works on human medicine, including pharmacology, toxicology and dietetics, or veterinary medicine, including falconry and equitation. Category 9 was a much more colourful mix with astronomy, oneiromancy, geomancy, mathematics, chess, mechanics, warfare, agriculture, geography and also some medicine and pharmacology. In addition, this category was also the main deposit for the above-discussed illustrated manuscripts in the library as diverse as a work on poetry, *The Singer and the Wailer*, a pharmacological title, a work on the *Rituals of the Pilgrimage* and *The Emulation of Kalīla and Dimna*.[44] The two illustrated veterinary titles are in category 10 and the illustrated small-sized work on *The Prophet's Genealogy*, finally, is in category 5, but – as discussed below – the small-sized thematic categories differed anyway to some extent from those in the normal-sized section.

The practical character of the Ashrafiya classification system really emerges from the remaining categories 6 to 8 and 11 to 15. These categories housed works showing the mastery of language in the fields of adab and poetry. That adab and poetry received the majority of the categories in the catalogue reflects the fact that they represented the largest number of works in the library. Yet if we consider the theoretical classification systems adab and poetry are either marginal or entirely absent. In al-Fārābī's system, for example, poetry is merely one sub-category within the philological sciences (*ᶜilm al-lisān*), which itself is only one of five main categories.[45] The Ashrafiya system thus allows us to look beyond the well-trodden paths of the theoretical thinkers in order to understand how relatively low-level scholars tried to come to terms with the mass of knowledge available in their age – a mass of knowledge that clearly did not sit very well with the abstract classifications. However, even if we move beyond such abstract attempts to classify the different fields of knowledge there are no obvious precedents. For instance, the ten books (*maqāla*) in Ibn al-Nadīm's *Fihrist*, arguably a practical attempt to order books in fourth-/tenth-century Baghdad, does not easily map on to the Ashrafīya catalogue. Book I (language, Jewish and Christian scriptures, the Koran) is much broader than the Ashrafīya's category 1. Ibn al-Nadīm's books V (theology), IX (other religions) and X (alchemy) simply do not have an equivalent in the Ashrafīya and, by contrast, Ibn al-Nadīm's *Fihrist* lacks the highly differentiated poetry and adab categories.[46]

One may expect to find a system more similar to that of the Ashrafīya in the period closer to its foundation. Although we do not have other catalogues, we do have at least the profile of a contemporaneous Damascene scholar's personal library, which – even more interestingly – is given in the chronicle of the Ashrafīya's first *shaykh*, Abū Shāma. In his description of this personal library, Abū Shāma classifies the works into seven groups: Koranic sciences (*ᶜulūm al-qurʾān*), *ḥadīth*, *fiqh*, lexicography (*lugha*), poetry, grammar and morphology (*taṣrīf*) and finally sciences of the ancients (*ᶜulūm al-awāʾil*).[47] The first four categories are roughly identical with those given in the Ashrafīya with the only exception that the Ashrafīya's fourth category also includes grammar and morphology. In addition, the Ashrafīya has two categories for the sciences of the Ancients and rational sciences (instead of one). However, the most striking difference is again that the Ashrafīya has four categories for poetry (instead of one) and four adab categories (instead of none). While this scholar's library has a similar profile to the Ashrafīya it seems that the Ashrafīya system was an innovative and pragmatic response to the library's specific stock. That the catalogue was a pragmatic answer to a specific collection is very much evident in the relatively even distribution of books throughout its categories. If the system had been taken over from a generic model one would have expected more categories to be virtually empty. The catalogue is thus one of a few examples that show how the abstract classifications of sciences were translated into practical systems on the ground.

However, this system was certainly part of a wider culture of sophisticated library organisation in the Middle East. Arguably, this is also evident from the library illustrations, which all show rather small bookcases with narrowly spaced vertical supports. These numerous vertical supports certainly served a practical function, preventing the bookshelves from sagging under the weight of too many books on relatively thin shelf boards. However, the small bookcases were also well adapted to spatially reflect a highly differentiated organisation such as the Ashrafīya's three-tier system. The breakdown of the collection according to alphabet, size and subject meant the resulting 'class-marks' often had very few books. Using broader bookcases would have meant that each bookcase would have had more class-marks, which in turn would have reduced the library's usability. Small bookcases, by contrast, allowed the user to go through the shelves without spending too much time trying to identify which categories a bookcase contained. Although we will never know what systems were in place in the libraries the artists had in mind when preparing the illustrations (if there was indeed any specific example), the small bookcases indicate that highly differentiated class-mark systems must have been a common feature.

Although part of a wider library culture, the organisation of the Ashrafiya was to some extent experimental in combining the two main systems of organising libraries, alphabetical and thematic, and also in coming up with a set of fifteen thematic categories. This was an experiment not without risks: we saw above that the librarian hit the wall when he came to multiple-text manuscripts, which could not be fitted into the alphabetical and thematic systems. The catalogue furthermore indicates that al-Anṣārī felt some need to explicate at least part of the library's thematic system to the users – or at the very least felt the need to make notes in it to reassure himself. When he first introduces thematic category 6 he adds 'sixth [thematic category], which is the beginning of [the books concerned with] genealogy'.[48] Indeed the following entries are tribal diwans and thematic category 6 is where such material is generally found. Al-Anṣārī's note suggests that he was not entirely confident that the library users were familiar with the system laid out in the catalogue.

The Ashrafiya system was an experiment that clearly presented al-Anṣārī with challenges: this is evident from minor changes he made to the cataloguing system as he progressed. For instance, in the beginning the cataloguer has a rather cumbersome system to enumerate several copies of manuscripts; according to this system, four copies of a manuscript would be indicated 'second copy, third copy, fourth copy', for example. Not too far into the catalogue, after seven pages, he changed to a more efficient system just stating 'six copies'.[49] As the *fihrist* was new territory for al-Anṣārī he clearly had to find his way. Right in the beginning he forgot to insert the very first category heading (A/1), which he then had to add in the margins. On the second folio he again forgot a category heading, which he had to squeeze between the lines.[50] In the same vein we see that he was changing the headings for thematic categories in the course of the catalogue. When first using the headings for the small-sized manuscripts he flagged them up with 'the first [thematic category] of the small[-sized manuscripts]', 'the fourth [thematic category] of the small[-sized manuscripts]' and 'the fifth [thematic category] of the small[-sized manuscripts]'.[51] He quickly decided that this was too cumbersome and henceforth only stated 'the first', 'the fourth', 'the fifth' and so on.

More relevant, at least from the point of view of potential users, were two ways in which the three-tier system was abandoned or at least substantially modified. The first of these applies to all of the entries for small books in the catalogue. While these are in the correct alphabetical place, and obviously the right place for their size, al-Anṣārī here adapted his use of thematic categories (see *Table 2.2*). He got rid of seven categories (2, 10, 11, 12, 13, 14 and 15) entirely and removed the thematic function of three further categories, instead using them to group books according to external criteria (primarily multiple-text manuscripts, but also incomplete and Persian-language manuscripts) irrespective of their content (7, 8 and 9). The five remaining categories do not directly overlap with those for normal-sized books. Category 1s is clearly geared towards poetry, with some emphasis on pre-Islamic and early Islamic poetry. Category 3s by contrast is quite mixed, with an emphasis on poetry and adab, but also history. Prayer books feature very prominently in category 4s.

Table 2.2 Ashrafiya library, catalogue's thematic categories, small-sized books (The numbers in brackets include those entries mentioned in the sections of multiple-text manuscripts and incomplete manuscripts, 'makh')

No.	Subject matter	Number of entries
1	poetry, esp. pre-Islamic and early Islamic	11 (29)
2	category does not exist	0
3	poetry, adab	36 (27)
4	prayer books	56 (0)
5	adab, poetry (esp. panegyric)	68 (29)
6	adab, esp. epistles	31 (10)
7	multiple-text and incomplete manuscripts	6 (69)
8	multiple-text manuscripts	2 (54)
9	multiple-text and Persian manuscripts	27 (72)
10–15	categories do not exist	0

Category 5s is again very much an adab and poetry category with a preference for panegyric works. Category 6s brings together epistolary literature.

To apply two different thematic systems within one and the same library seems rather awkward and exceedingly complicated. However, there was good reason to do so because book size and theme were to some extent linked. For instance, the majority of prayer books came in small format (roughly two-thirds of all prayer books), while the proportion of small-sized books in the overall Ashrafiya collection is only about a quarter. It thus made sense to introduce a category specific to these books in the small-sized section. By contrast, it seems that books on the transmitted sciences linked to the Koran, *ḥadīth* and *fiqh* (categories 1, 2 and 3 for normal-sized books) rarely came in small format. For instance, there were only five small-sized titles on Koranic fields of knowledge and since they were all bound in multiple-text manuscripts they could not be thematically classified anyway.[52] Likewise there were only eight small-sized *ḥadīth*-related titles of which four were bound in multiple-text manuscripts.[53] Here again it made perfect sense to abandon categories 1, 2 and 3 as they were used in the normal size section. Overall, the two different thematic systems for normal and small-sized books underlines again the very pragmatic character of the Ashrafiya catalogue.

The second point where al-Anṣārī substantially modified his system was in the section on incomplete manuscripts. This section constitutes an appendix to the main catalogue (folia 266b–270a; Plates 47–54) and shows significant differences to the main catalogue. In this section there is no attempt to impose an alphabetical order and the manuscripts are only organised according to size and thematic category. There is one isolated case where the cataloguer tried to find a solution for this awkward organisation, which made it considerably more difficult for readers to identify a specific work's location. This is found in the catalogue's main section where the reader is referred to the annex section in order to find the work: '*incomplete* [manuscript], *mentioned in the* [catalogue's section on] *incomplete manuscripts*'.[54] However, like cross-referencing for the multiple-text manuscripts this would have required substantial planning prior to preparing the catalogue and al-Anṣārī clearly was not willing or not in a position to spend so much time on drafting the catalogue.

Similar to the approach with multiple-text manuscripts he prioritised the books' textual format, their incomplete nature, by placing them all in one section. Yet al-Anṣārī could have provided references for duplicate copies the other way round, from the incomplete section to the complete section. This would have been quite easy to implement and there were numerous titles, which featured in both the complete and incomplete sections. When he started the incomplete section he indeed added after the third entry '*mentioned under the letter ᶜayn*'[55], but this comment remained isolated and is another example of the cataloguer experimenting with different ways to organise the catalogue. The absence of further cross-references can certainly not be blamed on a sloppy librarian, who would be in insufficient control of his collection. On the contrary, al-Anṣārī knew his books very well and this is evident throughout the catalogue. To give just one minor example from the section on incomplete manuscripts: when he registered the *Prayers of Invocation for the Seven Days* he assiduously added that this was the '*fourth copy, incomplete in the end*', as he had already previously registered three other copies of the work in various sections of the catalogue.[56]

However, in contrast to the section with multiple-text manuscripts he did not entirely give up the thematic level of organisation for the incomplete manuscripts. Most categories are identical with those in the catalogue's main section, such as category 2 (*ḥadīth*), 3 (*fiqh*), 4 (philology) and 5 (history). Yet the annex section did entail some modification of the classification system. While many books are exactly where one would expect them to be, categories 6 and 14 are now used as residual categories into which nearly anything could be entered – quite similar to the categories 7, 8 and 9 in the *majāmīᶜ* section. In category 6, for instance, we find works related to Koran and *ḥadīth*, but also pre-Islamic and Umayyad poetry. The residual character of category 14 is made clear when the cataloguer initially listed fragments of two historical works where one would expect them to be, in category 5. However, he was clearly not satisfied with this and decided to move them to one of his residual categories, which he made explicit with the words '*moved to category 14*'.[57] Similarly, the *Path of Eloquence* (*Nahj al-balāgha*) with sayings attributed to the fourth Caliph and imam ᶜAlī b. Abī Ṭālib in its complete form was put into thematic category 2 and al-Anṣārī duly had it in the same category in the section of incomplete manuscripts. Yet he again stated that he moved it to the residual category 14.[58]

While the modification of the classification system for the small-sized books had some scholarly rationale, the case is different for these incomplete books. We can only speculate as to why al-Anṣārī took this approach: did his term as a librarian come to an end? Did he succumb to the illness that led to his early death? Did he simply lose interest in his cataloguing project and try to finish off this annex as quickly as possible by opting for the easiest solution? Whatever the exact reason may have been, there are similar changes such as the deteriorating quality of his writing throughout the catalogue. In the beginning the hand is very clear and the mise-en-page shows some care, for example, a justified right margin. However, as the catalogue progressed this changed and the writing shows clear signs of haste. In the same vein he wrote with an increasingly worn pen in the later part of the manuscript. Rather than sharpening the nib he just continued for two pages in a larger script, so this section has the lowest number of lines.[59] Most tellingly, the catalogue just stops with the last entry. While the introduction to the catalogue is brief there is at least some attempt to set the scene. There is nothing comparable at the end of the catalogue and not even a brief conclusion is offered.

The reasonably consistent cataloguing system in the Ashrafīya catalogue went hand in hand with the practical role that it played for library users. With its combined alphabetical and thematic ordering system the reader could identify with relative ease the place of a given work on the shelves. For instance, if a reader was to look for the *Manṣūrī Book of Medicine* (*Kitāb al-ṭibb al-Manṣūrī*) by al-Rāzī (Rhazes) it would not take too long to identify it in thematic category 10 under the letter *mīm*. The reader would have to check both the normal and small formats to be on the safe side. However, arguably even this step was often unnecessary as some distinct relations between topics and formats existed, as seen above with regard to prayer books. Compared with the overall ratio of 25 per cent small-sized books in the Ashrafīya collection, only 10 per cent of the works of medical literature were small-sized books, so an experienced reader would first check the section for normal-sized books.

The Ashrafīya catalogue offered first and foremost the relative location of a specific book so that the user roughly knew where to start the search. Yet in a few scattered places the catalogue even provides information on fixed locations. Before starting category 6 of the normal-sized books under the letter *khāʾ* the cataloguer states, for instance, 'sixth [thematic category], which is the beginning of the second shelf'.[60] In three other instances he has a slightly briefer version: 'sixth [thematic category], which is the beginning of the second [shelf]'.[61] It is remarkable that the comments on fixed locations always refer to the same category, 6, and always start on the second row of shelves. It thus seems that a few absolute markers referring to specific shelves supplemented the catalogue's information on relative locations and helped the library user to navigate the library's room. An experienced library user would thus know that certain categories are broadly linked to specific rows, although it is unlikely that the library was organised so schematically that category 1 always started on the first shelf, category 6 always on the second shelf and category 11 always on the third shelf. The different number of works within each category would simply preclude such a clear system as it would have entailed wasting a lot of shelf space. However, a user looking for category 6 would at least know that the second shelf would be a good place to start.

Not all readers would necessarily look for a specific title and the beauty of the Ashrafiya catalogue is that it also allowed thematic browsing even though its first level of organisation was the alphabet. A reader looking for medical literature would still need to check category 10 under each letter and category 9 in the annex with the incomplete manuscripts. But al-Anṣārī's use of abbreviated titles in the catalogue points to another device in the library that would enable users to quickly find works.[62] Contemporaneous scholarly advice literature encouraged the practice of labelling books' edges with abbreviated titles, and illustrations (Plate 3) show that this was indeed done.[63] This system facilitated the identification of the titles on the shelves as it enabled users to scan them at some speed. Although this labelling cannot be directly gleaned from the Ashrafiya catalogue, short titles are used throughout the catalogue that may very well reflect the titles used on the edges. Apart from labelling books, another device to facilitate browsing and identifying specific books in the Ashrafiya were possibly book lists for each shelf as is reported on other large libraries.[64]

The Ashrafiya catalogue itself was visually presented in a way that made searching and browsing the collection less cumbersome, with al-Anṣārī putting discernible effort into making it easily searchable. The main tool to facilitate navigation of the catalogue was his use of display script. The letters signalling the start of a new alphabetical section as well as the thematic sections were clearly signposted, generally with an elongated final letter. For this purpose al-Anṣārī always spelt out the numbers for thematic organisation, even though he used numerals elsewhere in the catalogue for other purposes. In addition, he generously spaced these section markers, which thus became clear navigating points. The markers for thematic sections were always written as ordinal numbers, for instance 'the fifth [category of the letter] *alif*', and they were always in the feminine, giving them a regular appearance throughout the catalogue. Furthermore, the spelt-out numbers for thematic categories helped the user to quickly understand whether s/he was in the section on normal-sized or small-sized manuscripts. The ordinal numbers generally carry the article in the former case, while they are without article in the sections on the small manuscripts. Grammatically, this works well as the writer assumed that the ordinal numbers are here a genitive construction's first noun and hence in the status constructus ('[the] fifth [category of the letter] *alif* of the small [manuscripts]'). With this simple but very effective tool the catalogue itself could be navigated at considerable speed.[65]

The use of display script is another example of why the catalogue was a rather experimental undertaking, as discussed above. The display system just described worked very well in most sections of the catalogue. However, when al-Anṣārī came to the *majāmī*ᶜ section within the letter *mīm* this usage of display script became obsolete with the breakdown of his three-tier organisation. In a de facto abandonment of the thematic numbering system the catalogue here became nothing but a very long series of titles with hardly any visual aids for the user. Al-Anṣārī made sure that he left a space between two multiple-text manuscripts to offer some visual markers, but this was clearly only minimal compensation for dropping the much clearer mise-en-page of previous sections. After proceeding with this minimal system for some five and a half folia of *majāmī*ᶜ (folio 260b, line 9 to folio 263b, line 4; Plates 35 to 41) he started to put the term *majmū*ᶜ itself into display script so that it took over the visual function that the now defunct letter and thematic categories had played in earlier sections. As a result, the remaining multiple-text section allows the user a distinctively faster navigation (up to folio 265b, line 17; Plate 45).

Overall, al-Anṣārī displayed great care when preparing the catalogue. There is only one passage where he got things quite substantially wrong without correcting them. Under the letter *rāʾ* he started running through the normal-sized categories as usual, but then considerably jumps to record entries for the small-sized category 6. He then realised that he had overlooked some books and had to make second headings for normal-sized categories 7, 8, 9 and 15 to fit in the books he had missed.[66] As this mistake occurred on a verso page, he clearly had no appetite for binning the folio, which would have meant rewriting a substantial section. However, this turned out to be one of those days: it was exactly at this point, when he had finished this verso page (successfully avoiding rewriting it) and moved to the next folio, that he mistakingly took the empty verso of the first folio where he had left space for the title page – and, as seen above, he had to rewrite that page. In other cases he strove to rectify minor mistakes, such as under the letter *ḥāʾ* where he missed the entries for thematic category 14. He thus had to put category 14 after 15, but at least added '*al-adab* in [category] 14' to highlight the error to the user.[67]

In addition to the three-tier system, the Ashrafiya catalogue has another intriguing system for providing data on the book collection. It provided information on the physical space taken up by the individual books and for this end employed a dual-numbering system. While the numbers for the thematic categories are always spelt out in the catalogue, al-Anṣārī worked here with numerals in order to clearly differentiate between the two systems. These numerals are placed directly after the respective title so that in contrast to the thematic categories, which create larger groups of several entries, the numerals are always entry-specific. The two sets of numerals used in this system fall into two groups: those in the first group range from one to eight while those in the second are typically in the high thirties/low forties. The most probable reading of these numerals is that the first group – placed directly after the title – indicated the number of volumes/*mujallad* constituting an individual work (some 90 per cent of the numerals given in the first group are 1)[68] whereas the second numeral indicated the number of quires/ *juzʾ* (about three-quarters of the numerals given in the second group range from 35 to 45).[69] The few instances where the preposition '*fī*' connects the first and second numerals support the argument that we are dealing with a volume-quire system. Here al-Anṣārī states, for instance, '1 [volume] in 12 [quires]'.[70] This reading of the numerals is also supported by the only instance where the cataloguer indicates the number of volumes for a work's two copies first by spelling out the term and subsequently by simply giving a numeral: 'The Life of the Prophet (May Peace be upon him) [in] two volumes, a second copy [of the same work in], 6 [volumes].'[71]

The alternative would be to read these numerals as a location system, as suggested by al-Jūmānī, who argues that they refer to shelves. In his explanation he does not refer to the numerals of the first group, but only to the larger numbers of the second group.[72] However, a system to indicate fixed locations is very unlikely, as the Ashrafiya catalogue was organised in a way that reflected the relative locations of books. In consequence, such a system for providing information on fixed locations would have been quite superfluous and potentially cumbersome. More importantly, the numbers provided are so repetitive that they cannot possibly refer to locations – unless there were very large piles of books on shelves 35 to 45 and empty shelves in other places.

As we do not have a comparable library catalogue it is difficult to assess to what extent al-Anṣārī was again experimenting with a new – or at least reworked – system when using the volume-quire numerals. These numerals are very irregularly used, become less and less frequent as the catalogue progresses and they entirely disappear halfway through from folio 257a (Plate 28) onwards. These numbers are thus another indicator that the Ashrafiya catalogue was quite experimental and that al-Anṣārī developed and refined some aspects of the catalogue's structure as he went along. Yet he most likely grew weary of the volume-quire system and dispensed of it as he advanced his project. The point of this system was to provide the librarian with data in order to ascertain that books were still complete. Loss of individual volumes or quires could happen between two inventories in the library, especially whenever a book was lent out. As the Ashrafiya was – similar to most libraries in the medieval Middle East – a lending library its librarian spent a lot of his time preventing books from disappearing or from being returned with parts missing. And as seen in Chapter 1, al-Anṣārī was so renowned for his great care in looking after the collection that he forced a lender to replace a book he had lost.[73]

The most likely scenario for the Ashrafiya's volume-quire system is, however, not linked to lending but rather with an eye on a revision, which took place shortly after the catalogue had been prepared. This is evident from the small 'ṣ'-sign for *ṣaḥḥa* or *ṣaḥīḥ* (correct) on top of many of the first numerals. This sign indicates that the librarian earmarked some of the books to be checked at a later point. He must have done so while he was drawing up the catalogue, as the two-digit system required substantial space behind the title. Yet the numerals have ample space and hardly ever seem to be squeezed in, which they would have been had they been added during a later revision. The reasons as to why al-Anṣārī earmarked some entries for later revision is unclear, but these were perhaps slightly damaged volumes that needed some care.

All in all, what emerges from the Ashrafiya catalogue is thus a highly sophisticated document written by a very able librarian. Although it was a catalogue it also served as an inventory for the librarian who could revise the library's stock on its basis. Yet the most remarkable feature is how it facilitated the retrieval of its titles. The three-tier system allowed readers to identify specific titles via the first alphabetical level, but also to browse for books on specific subjects via the third thematic level. Although the catalogue did not have press-marks, it reflected the relative locations of books so that library users would have had few problems in identifying a given book's location. This clear and systematic organisation of a considerable part of its holdings indicates that the Ashrafiya library was not envisioned as a severely restricted space in terms of its users. It was clearly not meant to be used by a small circle of initiated readers whose access depended on the librarian's willingness to share his insider knowledge of where books were located. Rather the Ashrafiya strove to offer an arrangement of its books that would allow reasonably easy access to those titles held in complete single-text manuscripts even to a reader visiting for the first time. The Ashrafiya mausoleum only provided for a single teaching position and it had no resident students. Its library was thus in all likelihood meant to cater for outside users and it was with an eye on these users that the library not only developed such sophisticated organisation, but also laid it open through its catalogue.

The practical function of the Ashrafiya catalogue can be more clearly highlighted by contrasting it with the other large-scale documentary book list from pre-Ottoman Syria, the Ibn ᶜAbd al-Hādī endowment from the late ninth/fifteenth century. On its fifty-nine folia Ibn ᶜAbd al-Hādī, who himself drafted this document, enumerates thousands of titles, most of them in multiple-text manuscripts (*majāmīᶜ*). In contrast to the Ashrafiya catalogue there is no alphabetical order, there is no thematic system and there is no differentiation according to size. There were single-text manuscripts, but again there is not even an attempt to separate them from the multiple-text manuscripts, being interspersed without an evident system. As a legal document this list was never intended as a finding tool for books and I doubt that anybody except Ibn ᶜAbd al-Hādī himself would have ever been able to navigate it to retrieve a title. Providing access to outside users was clearly no concern when this document was written.[74]

The Space of Libraries

The present section is primarily concerned with the wider spatial setting of a medieval Arabic library. This is of relevance for one very simple reason: we do not have a surviving library in situ that would afford us – even taking into account all the possible changes over the centuries – a rough idea of what such a library may have looked like. In addition, research has not yet systematically established in the surviving Ayyubid and Mamluk-period buildings with rooms that might have been used for library purposes. The most detailed survey of building activities in Syria and Egypt in the seventh/thirteenth century, for instance, has nothing to say on this issue.[75] The best-documented library spaces so far are from late-Mamluk Cairo. For instance, the endowment complex of Mamluk Sultan Faraj b. Barqūq, dating to the early ninth/fifteenth century, provided library space in the form of two small rooms 3m high and with a base of about $3.2m^2$.[76] In the following century the madrasa in the endowment complex by Mamluk Sultan al-Ghūrī had a library room of some $9.4m^2$.[77] However, these are rather small spaces and it is unlikely that they were the only spaces where books were stored within such massive complexes. Their book collections were most likely dispersed across various buildings similar to many medieval British libraries. The most important point for us is that libraries did not have a dedicated architecture that would have clearly set them apart for this function. As we will see in the following, the Ashrafiya is a clear example of this, even though all of its books were in a single space. Books were stored in wooden bookcases, which could easily be moved about within the library, so few lasting architectural features remain – libraries were a fleeting affair.[78]

By the seventh/thirteenth century book collections had become so large that books were generally stored in dedicated spaces. There is little doubt that such library rooms existed earlier in the grand royal libraries of ᶜAbbasid Baghdad, Fatimid Cairo and Umayyad Cordoba. In a similar vein, when a seventh-/thirteenth-century Damascene author referred to an individual who 'sat down in the mosque's library (*khizānat kutubihā*)' to choose books he was clearly referring to a dedicated room, not a bookcase[79] – a differentiation in vocabulary that will be explained below. Designated library spaces only come into existence when book collections start to outgrow more ad hoc arrangements of storing books in chests or small bookcases. In medieval Britain such designated library spaces are only traceable from the fifteenth century onwards and previously books were stored in a variety of locations. For instance, at Durham cathedral priory books could be found throughout the building, including the cloister, near the refectory, the lodgings, the infirmary and at various altars in the cathedral church. However, with the growth of book collections designated library spaces came into being and among the forty surviving catalogues of Friars' libraries only that of the Franciscans in London from 1421 undoubtedly refers to a dedicated library space. In a similar vein, it was only in the late fifteenth century that the libraries of the University of Cambridge started to be housed in separate rooms.[80]

As Arabic medieval libraries tended to have dedicated rooms, although not a dedicated architecture, books were generally stored in bookcases (generally described as *khazāʾin*). Storing books in chests (generally described as *ṣanādīq*, but sometimes also as *khazāʾin*) was rather rare – in contrast to earlier medieval British libraries where chests and wall recesses played an important role owing to smaller collections and the concomitant absence of dedicated rooms.[81] Although we have references to chests in earlier Arabic libraries, by the seventh/thirteenth century they had come to be used primarily in small collections of individual scholars or small sub-collections within a larger institution.[82] To give two examples, when a scholar in Aleppo left one '*khizāna*' of books to each of his two sons and when only four books were found in another scholar's '*khizāna*' it can be assumed that the author is referring to chests. Contemporaries also explicitly speak of a 'chest' (*ṣundūq*) when describing endowments of specific collections, which were to retain their own identity, in mosques.[83] However, the term *khizāna* (pl. *khazāʾin*) referred much more frequently either to the library room or bookcases. Of relevance here are those cases where documentary and narrative sources employ the term for individual bookcases. For instance, a reference as early as the fourth/tenth century clearly refers to shelves in a library when employing the term '*khizāna*' and another in a seventh-/thirteenth-century endowment note on a Damascene manuscript clearly refers to a specific bookcase in a madrasa.[84]

A crucial indicator that bookcases had become the standard furniture for book storage is the contemporaneous illustrations of libraries. These leave little doubt that during this period books were stored on shelves (Plates 2–5) and chests never appear as library furniture. This is also reinforced by the few explicit comments in the Ashrafiya catalogue on spatial arrangements quoted above where al-Anṣārī refers to the 'second shelf'. More importantly, the sheer number of books in the Ashrafiya would have made it simply impossible to store books in chests. While chest storage may work for smaller collections, for a collection with well over 2,000 books it would be a nightmare for both librarian and readers. Heavy chests could not have been stacked on top of one another as many book searches would have required moving them to access a lower chest. In consequence, storage space would be very restricted and the Ashrafiya building's size, discussed below, would not have allowed for all of the library's books to be stored in a single row of chests along its walls. Annoyingly for the librarian and reader, considerable time would have been spent rummaging through a chest to access the books stored at the bottom. In a collection as massive as the Ashrafiya there would have been few convincing alternatives to the method of storage depicted in the illustrations: stacked on open shelves and clearly labelled in order to prevent librarian and reader from spending the best part of their day looking for books.

These bookcases must have taken up considerable space within the mausoleum as the Ashrafiya held so many books. While it is possible to say that it held *many* books the exact number of books and the space they took up is obviously more complicated to determine. The Ashrafiya has in total 2,096 clearly identifiable entries in the catalogue. This number is informative as to the titles held in the library, but it is not very helpful when it comes to the number of volumes actually on the shelves. Many of these entries were bound within multiple-text manuscripts and if we discount the secondary, tertiary, and so forth texts within multiple-text manuscripts, a total of 389, this brings down the total number to 1,707 books. However, many of the single-text books in the Ashrafiya, 163 in total, were held in multiple copies and there could be up to fifteen copies of a single title in the library. Taking these – 431 – multiple copies into account brings the total number of books in the Ashrafiya up to 2,138.[85]

Yet this number still provides a far from clear idea of the space needed to store the library's holdings because each book could require a very different space on the shelf. They were not only of different sizes but, more importantly, consisted of one or several volumes. Regrettably, the catalogue gives only incomplete data on the number of volumes per title. Most importantly, the volume-quire system was not systematically employed throughout the catalogue. Additional explicit comments on the numbers of volumes are mostly made in the section on incomplete manuscripts (fourteen out of twenty-one comments), which was so chaotic that al-Anṣārī used physical features to make clear which book he was referring to. For instance, in order to unequivocally identify a manuscript of Ibn Sīnā's *Canon* he stated that it consists of 'sixteen bound volumes, overlapping, in different hands and different formats'.[86] Comments on physical features in the 'complete section' of the catalogue are generally only provided to differentiate between multiple copies of the same work. One case aims to indicate that one copy of a specific title – seemingly in contrast to the other copy – consisted of two volumes and in another case to identify an entry for which the author could not come up with a title.[87] These explicit comments are again so rare that they do not allow for even a rough estimate of volume numbers and the space required. However, as argued elsewhere, documentary evidence suggests that the number of actual physical volumes in a library is some 25 per cent higher than the number of books.[88] In the case of the Ashrafiya this would mean that some 2,700 volumes were on its shelves. For spatial purposes the final step is to convert the number of volumes into a normal-size equivalent value. As seen above, bookcases containing small-sized volumes could hold two piles so that for spatial purposes the number of small-sized volumes has to be halved in order to arrive at a standardised value. Taking also into account multiple-text manuscripts and multiple copies of the same title, this gives a figure of 1,868 normal-size equivalent books.[89] Adding the 25 per cent to the relevant sections of the catalogue, this gives a number of 2,269 volumes.[90]

Although al-Anṣārī did not provide systematic data on the space taken up by the library or by parts of the collection, he – inadvertently – provided another indicator that is far more helpful for these purposes. While working on the first letter of the alphabet, *alif*, he committed a glaring mistake when he suddenly started to record manuscripts starting with the letter *dāl*, the eighth letter of the alphabet. After five rows he realised the slip, crossed out this section and returned to the titles starting with the letter *alif*.[91] To make such a mistake is by itself not that surprising and almost inevitable in a document as long, as complex and as repetitive as this library catalogue. What is surprising is that it took al-Anṣārī so long to realise that he was entering the wrong titles. It is very unlikely that he just jumped seven letters when going through the shelves to take down his catalogue. Most likely, al-Anṣārī finished with one bookcase and intended to move on (after a break?) to the next. At this point he must have accidentally skipped one bookcase (or several), mechanically writing down the wrong titles and only later realising his mistake.

With this glitch al-Anṣārī inadvertently marked the transition from one bookcase to another in the Ashrafiya library and allows us to get some sense of its spatiality. Before he made the mistake at the end of the bookcase, al-Anṣārī had registered 129 normal-sized books.[92] After he corrected his mistake, he registered another 275 normal-size equivalent books before he came to the letter *dāl*, returning to the bookcase to which he had mistakenly jumped.[93] Looking at the two numbers it may be hypothesised that the writer had finished the 129 books of the first bookcase in the Ashrafiya before he made his mistake and went for whatever reason to the fourth bookcase. After he had realised his mistake he returned to the second bookcase and subsequently registered the second and third bookcases' titles, which seem to have each held some 137 normal-size equivalent books. That a number of about 135 normal-sized books is not an entirely arbitrary number for the books contained in one bookcase is also evident from contemporaneous Plate 2. Here we find the equivalent of 133 normal-sized books on the shelves.[94] In the same vein, a late Mamluk endowment of books in Cairo provided two book chests for a total of 263 titles.[95]

If the 2,269 volumes were to be distributed in bookcases holding an average of 135 normal-size equivalent books this would give slightly less than seventeen bookcases for the Ashrafiya. It is very unlikely that all of the bookcases in a library were as ornate and sophisticated as the one in Plate 2, but it gives a rough idea of what contemporaries considered to be a reasonable size of such a bookcase. Taken together with reports in narrative sources on library furnishing, a length of about 1.5m per bookcase is a realistic estimate, so the bookcases in the Ashrafiya would have required a total wall space of just over 25m.[96] Most likely these bookcases would have been quite tall: contemporaneous illustrations uniformly depict even the lowest shelf of bookcases a metre from the ground. Consequently, these bookcases often reached the ceiling and Plate 3 shows a ladder as part of the library's furnishings.

How can we visualise the arrangement of these bookcases in the Ashrafiya mausoleum? A library can either have its bookcases arranged in a wall system parallel to the outside walls and/or in a stall system perpendicular to the outside walls.[97] A combination of the wall and stall systems provides maximum storage space, but it depends on a crucial feature in a library's set-up: light. Natural light was a prime factor in making any library workable as artificial light posed a significant danger. Accidental fires in libraries were a recurrent danger and certainly well known to those managing libraries. For instance, the books in the most famous early madrasa-library, the Niẓāmīya in Baghdad, were only just saved from a fire in 510/1116–17 by the scholars who carried them outside.[98] Closer to home, many of those manuscripts that were confiscated from al-Ashraf Aḥmad in 626/1229 to build up the royal library in the citadel in Cairo perished in a fire in 691/1292.[99] The reluctance to use candles and lanterns explains in part why madrasa-teaching normally took place during the day-time while devotional practices, which did not necessarily require the written word, took place later in the day.[100]

Looking at the mausoleum's layout (Map 1.2) it is evident that the library could only have fitted in either the western or the eastern room. The central domed hall with al-Malik al-Ashraf's tomb would not have been considered appropriate for library purposes and its (later?) separation into two rooms made it unsuitable for practical reasons anyway. A further argument for the placement of the library in one of the rooms comes from one of the rare contemporaneous descriptions, which indicates the position of a library within a Damascene madrasa. In the Rawāḥīya madrasa the eastern room was reserved for the founder's lodging and the western room for the library.[101] In the case of the Ashrafīya, the eastern room, due to its larger size, would have been the natural home for the library, as it would have allowed for more teaching and reading space. Assuming that the plans as we have them reflect the original architecture of windows and doors, natural light could only come into this room – and the other rooms in the mausoleum – via the large window in the doomed hall and through the rooms' external doors. Facing southwards these openings provided ample light during day-time, but they clearly excluded a stall system of bookcases. With the light coming from only one side, any bookcases projecting into the room would have put a significant proportion of the collection into shade.

The books in the Ashrafīya were thus similar to the description of a late-Mamluk madrasa, in a large room 'for the storage of books, with shelves on the right, left, and at the back'.[102] It was in the eastern room that the walls offered just sufficient space with about twenty-five metres of shelves (if we leave some space adjacent to the door). However, the eastern room was certainly full to the brim with the books listed in the Ashrafīya catalogue and, as seen above, it was assumed when the library was founded that it would not grow considerably. The shelf space in the eastern room was limited to perpendicular shelves not only because of the limited light, but also because the library room functioned at the same time as a mosque. When the mausoleum's first *shaykh*, Abū Shāma, described that the builders incorporated al-Ashraf Aḥmad's oratory into the mausoleum, he said that this oratory was added to the mausoleum's mosque (*masjid*). This oratory, he continued 'remained and *ḥadīth* is recited in it and in it are the bookcases (*khazāʾin kutub*)'.[103] The library room thus co-functioned as the mausoleum's prayer room and without doubt also as the mausoleum's teaching room. Despite having a massive library the Ashrafīya thus conformed to the overall picture that libraries were generally not housed in dedicated spaces. No architectural feature in the two rooms or the hall clearly indicated either of them as a space for storing books.

That library spaces were somewhat unmarked may also be linked to a further feature peculiar to the Middle Eastern library, namely the absence of any furnishings specifically for the library user. Although contemporaneous illustrations and narrative sources do mention bookcases or chests for storing books, reader-specific furnishings are missing. Readers are always depicted as sitting on the ground floor while lecterns, so consistently found in libraries in Latin Europe, are absent. Of the four contemporaneous library illustrations only Plate 3 shows a reader not sitting on the floor, but this is only because he is handing down a book from one of the top shelves. Contemporaneous advice literature also consistently assumes that the reader is sitting on the ground.[104] The absence of furnishing for readers meant that there were few architectural requirements to house a library. A room equipped with lecterns and desks obviously has to ensure that reading places have sufficient light and would thus require windows where necessary. However, ensuring access to light in the various parts of the building had clearly not been a major concern when constructing the Ashrafiya. Apart from the south-facing openings (and most likely openings in the dome for the central room) there is no indication in any narrative source or in the building's description by Wulzinger/Watzinger that additional windows had existed.

This absence of windows is linked to the fact that the library was used in two ways. On the one hand the library was certainly a teaching and reading space where books were read in situ. The illustrations mostly depict teaching scenes centred on one single book, but Plate 4 (and arguably also Plate 3) is of interest here as it shows individual readers immersed in their books. The absence of bulky desks, lecterns and other furnishings opened up a wide space framed by the bookcases so that the Ashrafiya could accommodate a considerable number of readers who could take advantage of the light provided by the door. Yet the Ashrafiya was also a lending library and users could take books out to read them elsewhere. Borrowing books was a common feature of Middle Eastern libraries and the idea of restricting the use of books within the institution housing the library or even to chain reference books to reading desks, as seen in Latin European libraries, never gained currency. We see instead an altogether different atmosphere: books could be taken out for several weeks, normative treatises discussed the etiquette of book lending, scholars revoked provisions of those endowments trying to restrict use of the books to their institution, and endowment notes laid out specific conditions for borrowing for individual books.[105] Even if book lending was prohibited by an endowment deed, narrative sources show that the actual practice could be very different. When one of the mausoleum's *shaykhs* endowed his books in another Damascene institution, for instance, he stipulated such restrictive conditions that they were simply disregarded.[106]

Although we do not have the Ashrafiya's endowment deed, the report on its librarian requesting that a user replace a lost copy clearly shows that the Ashrafiya was a typical lending library. The anecdote in no way implies that the act of lending itself breached the deed or was inappropriate. On the contrary, in libraries attached to mausolea lending books could be spiritually beneficent for the deceased. As we have seen above, endowment notes on books belonging to another late seventh/thirteenth mausoleum in Damascus stipulated that those taking them out had to recite parts of the Koran for the benefit of the endower and his parents' souls. The same notes stipulate that the lender had to leave a deposit twice the value of the book, which explains how the Ashrafiya's librarian was able to force the reader to replace the lost copy.[107]

That endowment libraries were often lending libraries is linked to the increasing use of the written word during this period. With regard to the library's three-tier organisation we have seen that the systematic arrangement of its stock has to be seen as an attempt to cater for a larger group of readers, not all of whom were intimately linked with the library. This larger group, not affiliated with the institution, could only systematically take advantage of the library because books could be taken out. This is also of relevance when it comes to the Ashrafiya's spatiality: as books could be taken out, reading spaces were not restricted to the mausoleum itself, but on a much larger scale. Readers took the library's books not only to their homes and other learned institutions, but reading could take place in mosques, markets, gardens and other open spaces.[108]

Looking at the sheer number of educational institutions and private collections life in medieval Damascus, and other Middle Eastern cities, could anyway be a quite bookish affair. Yet the Kallāsa quarter as part of the Umayyad Mosque area was probably as bookish as a place could get in the Middle East, offering ample opportunities to read. The proximity of the city's book market to the Umayyad Mosque[109] guaranteed a steady supply of new and second-hand copies. It is thus not by chance that a rare purchase note on a manuscript produced in the year 619/1223 states that the manuscript was bought in the Kallāsa quarter.[110] In the same vein, a deceased scholar's descendants, who had fallen into poverty during the Ilkhanid occupation of Damascus in 699/1299–1300, decided to auction off his books right in front of the Ashrafiya mausoleum.[111] The Umayyad mosque just opposite the Ashrafiya held so many individual book endowments that the rulers of Damascus repeatedly – and rather unsuccessfully – tried to merge them into a single large book collection.[112] The educational institutions in the Kallāsa quarter offered further books in their libraries. And the written word was so deeply embedded in the quarter's topography that we find here a Genizah-style book cemetery: the Qubbat al-khazna in the Umayyad Mosque's courtyard held thousands of texts that their owners had disposed of in numerous languages, including Arabic, Hebrew, Armenian, Coptic, Syriac, Aramaic, Greek, Latin and Old French.[113]

Users taking books out from the Ashrafiya thus immediately passed through numerous spaces where reading or copying books was central, be it the Umayyad Mosque, other institutions or the market – and this is evident from Ashrafiya manuscripts themselves: for instance, the copy of Ibn Abī al-Dunyā's *Mudārāt al-nās* was, as transmission notes testify, read in the Umayyad Mosque while it was part of the Ashrafiya library.[114] The limited provision of natural light in the Ashrafiya mausoleum was closely linked to the fact that its reading space went well beyond its walls. A local endowment library such as the Ashrafiya was not an enclosed and restricted space. Rather its reading space expanded beyond the topography of its immediate neighbourhood and into the wider topography of Damascus where its books circulated.

Notes

1. Kairouan catalogue-cum-inventory, MS Raqqāda, Centre d'Études de la Civilisation et des Arts Islamiques, 289.
2. Eche, *Bibliothèques arabes*, 321.
3. Al-Jūmānī, 'Fihris', 87.
4. Erünsal, *Ottoman Libraries: A Survey of the History*, 143.

5. *Al-Muntakhab*, ed. Sbath (see ch. 4 for comments on its authenticity). For the Registrum Anglie, see Rouse and Rouse, *Registrum Anglie*.
6. Fihrist al-Ashrafīya, fol. 246b, l. 2.
7. This notebook has been worked on by F. Bauden and also É. Franssen, who presented her paper 'Aṣ-Ṣafadī: His Personality, Methodology and Literary Tastes, Approached through the 49th Volume of his Taḏkirah' at the 9th Islamic Manuscript Conference in Cambridge, September 2013.
8. Fihrist al-Ashrafīya, Engl. tr. no. 1282.
9. *Al-Muntakhab*, ed. Sbath, XI.
10. Erünsal, *Ottoman Libraries: A Survey of the History*, 151.
11. Sharpe *et al.*, *Benedictine Libraries*, 50–87.
12. The only space intentionally left in the catalogue is on fol. 253a, l. 2 within the letter 'r' (Plate 20). Here we have a heading, 'third [thematic category] of the small [books]', but there is no entry. This is the previously discussed section, which the writer initially put on to the first folio's recto (fol. 246a; Plate 6) and then rewrote on fol. 253a after he had realised his mistake. On fol. 246a the same space occurs in exactly the same position. Arguably, the cataloguer assumed that a corresponding title existed, which he intended to add at a later stage. One possible explanation why this never happened is that the title had been lent out at the point of the catalogue's composition, but was never returned.
13. The best overview of this topic is al-Jūmānī, 'al-Fahāris al-makhṭūṭa'. Examples of earlier catalogues include the seven-volume *fihrist* in the library of the Buyid vizier and scholarly patron Abū al-Qāsim Ismāʿīl Ibn ʿAbbād (d. 385/995; MU, II, 662) and the catalogue for the Andalusian library of al-Ḥakam II (d. 366/976) containing 44 quires with 20 folio each (Kügelgen, 'Bücher und Bibliotheken', 158).
14. Library of ʿAbd al-Karīm (d. 621/1224–5), al-Ashraf Aḥmad's uncle, seen by Yāqūt (MU, II, 810).
15. Fakhr al-Dīn Ibrāhīm b. Ḥasan b. al-Bawwāb, 714/1314, catalogue for Bashīrīya madrasa (Ibn al-Fuwaṭī, *Talkhīṣ*, IV/3, 57).
16. ʿAḍud al-Dawla (d. 372/982): al-Muqaddasī, *Aḥsan al-taqāsīm*, 449; Fatimid library: Abū Shāma, *al-Rawḍatayn*, II, 444–5; Baghdad: Ibn al-Fuwaṭī (pseudo), *al-Ḥawādith*, 53–7 refering to the Mustanṣirīya madrasa in 631/1237 (*ithbāt al-kutub*); Damascus: Abū Shāma, *al-Rawḍatayn*, I, 275.
17. *Al-Muntakhab*, ed. Sbath.
18. Al-Jūmānī, 'al-Fahāris al-makhṭūṭa'.

19. Ibn Ḥajar al-ᶜAsqalānī (d. 852/1449); al-Sakhāwī, *Jawāhir*, 283–4.
20. Humphreys, *Friars' Libraries*; Cambridge: Lovatt, 'Introduction', XLIX.
21. Sharpe, 'Library Catalogues and Indexes', 197–218.
22. Whytefelde: Stoneman, *Dover Priory*; Kirkstede: Sharpe, *Library Catalogues and Indexes*, 204–18.
23. The first catalogue to use class-marks in the Jūmānī-corpus is the 19th-century catalogue of Ibrāhīm Ḥalīm Pāshā's library in Cairo (al-Jūmānī, 'al-Fahāris al-makhṭūṭa', 58).
24. Letter *thāʾ*: Fihrist al-Ashrafiya, Engl. tr. no. 288; letter *ẓāʾ*: nos. 717–19.
25. Fihrist al-Ashrafiya, Engl. tr. no. 188.
26. Fihrist al-Ashrafiya, Engl. tr. no. 757–83.
27. Al-Jūmānī, 'Fihris', 74 considers this to be the case.
28. Fihrist al-Ashrafiya, Engl. tr. no. 795.
29. Fihrist al-Ashrafiya, fols. 260a–265b; Engl. tr. no. 1142–1332. To integrate multiple-text manuscripts was a recurrent headache for cataloguers as evident from the manifold examples in the Jūmānī-corpus (al-Jūmānī, 'al-Fahāris al-makhṭūṭa', 60–1).
30. Fihrist al-Ashrafiya, Engl. tr. nos. 280 and 869.
31. Fihrist al-Ashrafiya, Engl. tr. no. 1230.
32. Ibn Kathīr, *al-Bidāya*, XIII, 230 when describing the endowment by the scholar al-Yaldānī (d. 665/1257).
33. For more detail cf. Hirschler, 'Concepts of the Arabic Book'.
34. Stoneman, *Dover Priory*.
35. Friis-Jensen and Willoughby, *Peterborough Abbey*.
36. Ibn Jamāᶜa, *Tadhkirat*, 172.
37. Fihrist al-Ashrafiya, Engl. tr. nos. 1509, 1527, 1688.
38. Ibn Jamāᶜa, *Tadhkirat*, 170–1.
39. Ibn Jamāᶜa, *Tadhkirat*, 170–1.
40. Kairouan catalogue-cum-inventory, MS Raqqāda, Centre d'Études de la Civilisation et des Arts Islamiques, 289.
41. Letter *hāʾ*: Fihrist al-Ashrafiya, Engl. tr. nos. 1369–1371; letter *yāʾ*: 1387–1391. The same phenomenon can be observed under the letter *ẓāʾ* with all three entries in normal format (Fihrist al-Ashrafiya, Engl. tr. nos. 717–19), letter *ṭāʾ* with all eight entries in normal format (nos. 709–16) and letter *zāʾ* with all eleven entries in normal format (no. 536–46).
42. Koran in category 2: Fihrist al-Ashrafiya, Engl. tr. nos. 290, 466, 1339; *Qiṣaṣ al-anbiyāʾ*: Fihrist al-Ashrafiya, Engl. tr. no. 720.

43. For systems of classification, see Bakar, *Classification of Knowledge*.
44. *The Emulation of Kalīla and Dimna* in a non-illustrated version was to be found in the thematic category 8 (Fihrist al-Ashrafīya, Engl. tr. no. 1009). On the role of the category 9 for illustrated manuscripts see also no. 62 (*Akhbār Ibn Ḥajjāj – Reports on Ibn Ḥajjāj*). The main (non-illustrated) entry of this work is in category 7, but the cataloguer explicitly mentions that '*a second copy of it* [is] *illustrated* [and] *in* [thematic category] *9*'.
45. Al-Farābī, *Iḥṣā*.
46. Stewart, 'Structure of the *Fihrist*'.
47. Abū Shāma, *al-Mudhayyal*, I, 275.
48. Fihrist al-Ashrafīya, fol. 247a, l. 5 (=Fihrist al-Ashrafīya, Engl. tr. no. 48).
49. Fihrist al-Ashrafīya, Engl. tr. no. 251.
50. Fihrist al-Ashrafīya, fol. 247a, l. 10–11 (see Fihrist al-Ashrafīya, Engl. tr. no. 56). The last forgotten heading is on fol. 251a, l. 10 (see no. 359).
51. Fihrist al-Ashrafīya, fol. 248a, l. 3 and 8; fol. 249a, l. 6.
52. Fihrist al-Ashrafīya, Engl. tr. nos. 1163a, 1171a, 1172a, 1236, 1282.
53. Fihrist al-Ashrafīya, Engl. tr. nos. 1170a, 1189a, 1191a, 1274a.
54. For the reference, see Fihrist al-Ashrafīya, Engl. tr. no. 339 (*al-Ḥayawān* by al-Jāḥiẓ) and for the actual manuscript see nos. 1535, 1604.
55. Fihrist al-Ashrafīya, Engl. tr. no. 1394.
56. Fihrist al-Ashrafīya, Engl. tr. nos. 151, 1170c, 1198b, 1661.
57. Fihrist al-Ashrafīya, Engl. tr. nos. 1428 and 1429 (fol. 267a, l. 8–9).
58. Category 2: Fihrist al-Ashrafīya, Engl. tr. no. 1336; category 14: no. 1393.
59. Fihrist al-Ashrafīya, fol. 263b–264a.
60. Fihrist al-Ashrafīya, fol. 251a, l. 11–12: Before this entry the cataloguer inserts '*al-sādisa wa-hiya al-ūlā min al-ṣaff al-thānī*' (see Fihrist al-Ashrafīya, Engl. tr. no. 364). The same comment is on fol. 267a, l. 9–10 in the section on incomplete manuscripts, but here it is crossed out (see no. 1430).
61. Fihrist al-Ashrafīya, fol. 249a, l. 14; fol. 251b, l. 2–3; fol. 252b, l. 1: '*al-sādisa wa-hiya ūlā al-thānīya*'. The feminine '*al-thānīya*' does not fit '*ṣaff*', yet no other reading is convincing (esp. reading '*al-thānīya*' as referring to the thematic category).
62. For these short titles, see Serikoff, 'Marginal- und Schnitttitel'.
63. Ibn Jamāᶜa, *Tadhkirat*, 171.
64. Fatimid library in Cairo: Ibn al-Ṭuwayr, *Nuzhat*, 126–8.
65. A rare case where the cataloguer does not follow this system is Fihrist al-Ashrafīya, fol. 251b, l. 12.

66. Fihrist al-Ashrafīya, fol. 252b, l. 4-fol. 253a, l. 2. For instance, the first heading for thematic category 7 is Fihrist al-Ashrafīya, Engl. tr. no. 473 and the second heading is no. 501a; the first heading for category 8 is nos. 474–6 and the second is nos. 502–4.
67. Fihrist al-Ashrafīya, fol. 251a, l. 1–3. For the comment see Fihrist al-Ashrafīya, Engl. tr. no. 341a.
68. This is clearly not the letter *alif* as numbers can appear in this place.
69. A number about 40 matches well the number of quires given by contemporaneous authors. Yāqūt al-Ḥamawī, for instance, repeatedly described volumes with quires in the 40s: MU, I, 330; MU, I, 332; MU, I, 333; MU, V, 2270.
70. For instance, Fihrist al-Ashrafīya, fol. 248a, l. 11 (=Fihrist al-Ashrafīya, Engl. tr. no. 118).
71. Fihrist al-Ashrafīya, fol. 253b, l. 9 (=Fihrist al-Ashrafīya, Engl. tr. no. 547).
72. Al-Jūmānī, 'Fihris', 86. In addition, he misreads the number 5 as an inverted 'B' arguing without further explanation that it also indicated a book's location. For the Hindu-Arabic numerals used in the catalogue see Gacek, *Vademecum*, 125.
73. Al-Yūnīnī, *Dhayl*, XIX, 248.
74. Ibn ᶜAbd al-Hādī, *Fihrist al-kutub*, MS Damascus, al-Assad National Library, 3190 (written before 896/1491).
75. Korn, *Ayyubidische Architektur*.
76. Mostafa, *Kloster und Mausoleum*, 21–2 and 110.
77. Alhamzah, *Late Mamluk Patronage*, 66.
78. In Mamluk libraries in Cairo these bookcases were often recessed in walls or books were stored in chests (*karāsī al-kutub*) (Al-Nashshār, *Taʾrīkh al-maktabāt*, 119–26). However, neither possibility is relevant for a collection as large as the Ashrafīya.
79. IKH, IV, 390.
80. Durham: Lovatt, 'Introduction', XLIII; Humphreys, *Friars' Libraries*; Cambridge: Lovatt, 'Introduction', L.
81. Gameson, 'Medieval Library'.
82. Earlier examples of chests in the Middle East include the royal libraries of the ᶜAbbasid Caliph al-Muᶜtaḍid (d. 289/902), where a sub-collection was held in chests (Ibn al-ᶜAdīm, *Bughyat*, I, 41–2) and the Samanid library in Bukhara on which Ibn Sīnā reported in the early 5th/11th century: 'I entered a house (*dār*) with numerous rooms (*buyūt*). In every room were bookcases (*ṣanādīq*) positioned on top of each other' (IAU, III, 74/5).

83. Aleppo: MU, V, 2071 and IV, 1781; chest: Al-Rāfiʿī (d. 623/1226), *Tadwīn*, I, 52–3. However, authors could also employ the term *khizāna* in such instances; see, for instance: MU, IV, 1775 (Umayyad Mosque in Damascus).
84. Fourth/Tenth century: al-Muqaddasī, *Aḥsan al-taqāsīm*, 449; seventh-/thirteenth-century: Eche, *Bibliothèques arabes*, 227 (endowment by Muḥammad b. al-Ḥasan b. Sallām (d. 630/1232) for the benefit of the Ḍiyāʾīya madrasa).
85. Al-Jūmānī, 'Fihris', 73 calculates the total number of books to be 2127.
86. Fihrist al-Ashrafīya, Engl. tr. no. 1477.
87. Two volumes: Fihrist al-Ashrafīya, Engl. tr. no 547; identifying: no. 1144. The same link between multiple copies and detailed description is evident in the contemporaneous catalogue from the Kairouan library, where the more than 50 copies of the Koran are described in much detail, but the titles held in single copies get a very brief entry (Kairouan catalogue-cum-inventory, MS Raqqāda, Centre d'Études de la Civilisation et des Arts Islamiques, 289).
88. Hirschler, *Written Word*, 128.
89. 1,200 normal-sized entries minus 24 in multiple-text manuscripts plus 422 multiple copies: 1,598. In addition, there were 896 small-sized entries minus 365 in multiple-text manuscripts plus 9 multiple copies: 540, halved for spatial purposes: 270 normal-size equivalent books, which give a total of 1,868.
90. The 25% factor can be applied to the catalogue's main section. In the case of the multiple-text manuscripts the factor cannot be applied, as they are generally single volume manuscripts. However, the catalogue has almost all multiple-text manuscripts in small categories and, as seen before, the categories had lost their function in this section of the catalogue. The 25% factor is thus retained here to compensate for the undervalued number of normal-size multiple-text manuscripts. The 25% factor cannot be applied to the section of incomplete manuscripts (265 normal-size equivalent books).
91. Fihrist al-Ashrafīya, fol. 248a, l. 5–10.
92. 114 entries plus 15 multiple copies.
93. 190 normal-sized entries minus 3 in multiple-text manuscripts plus 49 multiple copies: 236. In addition, there were 82 small-sized entries minus 4 in multiple-text manuscripts: 78, halved for spatial purposes: 39 normal-size equivalent books, which give a total of 275.
94. 79 normal-sized books, plus 108 small-sized books equal to another 54 normal-sized books.
95. ʿAlī al-Abshādī al-Azharī, 919/1513: Ibrāhīm, 'Maktaba fī wathīqa'.
96. Al-Muqaddasī, *Aḥsan al-taqāsīm*, 449 describes the wooden bookcases in the

library of the Buyid Sultan ᶜAḍud al-Dawla (d. 372/982) to be of 3 cubits (between 50 and 60 cm) length.

97. On these and numerous other issues discussed in this section see Petroski, *Book on the Bookshelf.*
98. Ibn al-Athīr, *al-Kāmil*, X, 523.
99. Al-Maqrīzī, *al-Khiṭaṭ*, III, 683.
100. Examples cited in Berkey, *Transmission of Knowledge*, 81.
101. Abū Shāma, *al-Mudhayyal*, I, 391.
102. Alhamzah, *Late Mamluk Patronage*, 66.
103. Abū Shāma, *al-Mudhayyal*, II, 20. There are several examples of Ayyubid mausolea with *masjids* in Ayyubid Damascus (see Korn, *Ayyubidische Architektur*, 66).
104. Ibn Jamāᶜa, *Tadhkirat*, 172.
105. Hirschler, *Written Word*, 141–3.
106. Al-Yūnīnī, *Dhayl*, XVIII, 10.
107. MS Istanbul, Süleymaniye Library, Fatih 4097/1 (fols. 1a–39a): *al-Maqāmāt al-arbaᶜūn* by al-Hamadhānī endowed to mausoleum library of Maḥfūẓ b. Maᶜtūq Ibn al-Buzūrī (d. 694/1294; TI, 691–700, pp. 231–2). The same notes from this endowment are on manuscripts in al-Assad National Library (Damascus); cf. Eche, *Bibliothèques arabes*, 239–40.
108. See Hirschler, *Written Word*, 69 for different reading spaces.
109. Touati, *L'armoire à sagesse*, 208.
110. MS Istanbul, Süleymaniye Library, Beşir Ağa (Eyüp) 194/1 (fols. 1a–28b). The untrained script clearly indicates that the buyer was only an occasional writer.
111. Al-Yūnīnī, *Dhayl*, XIX, 225.
112. See Eche, *Bibliothèques arabes*, 202–8 for the various book collections. For an attempt to centralise the endowments in the mosque see Abū Shāma, *al-Mudhayyal*, I, 359.
113. D'Ottone, 'Manuscripts as Mirrors'; Soden, 'Bericht'; Mayer, 'Abū ᶜAlīs Spuren'; Bandt and Rattmann, 'Damaskusreise'.
114. MS Istanbul, Süleymaniye Library, Laleli 3664 (fols. 110a–121b): *samāᶜ*, fol. 121a (year 634/1236) and *samāᶜ*, fol. 120b (year 667/1269).

3

Plurality and Diversity: The Profile of a Medieval Library

We have seen who put the books on the Ashrafiya's shelves and how these books were organised; the present chapter will now turn to the books themselves. The Ashrafiya catalogue provides the first opportunity for scholarship to access and gain an insight into the thematic profile of a large-scale medieval Arabic educational library and this discussion centres on just that: what kind of texts were available and what the library's thematic profile tells us about its function within the literary topography of a medieval Middle Eastern city. Until now scholarship has not recognised the originality and breadth of the collection and its potential contribution to understanding medieval libraries and this is for two main reasons: the Ashrafiya's eponym has had a rather 'anti-intellectual' reputation in modern scholarship, so without this catalogue the library's diet of books would have been assumed to be rather meagre. Yet, as will be seen in the following, a rather colourful mixture of books surrounded al-Malik al-Ashraf in his final resting place. More important for Middle Eastern history beyond the case of this one specific ruler and his intellectual outlook is that the library was part of a run-of-the-mill mausoleum-cum-madrasa, which scholarship has not considered to have had particularly interesting book collections.

Al-Malik al-Ashraf's reputation in modern scholarship – not that there is much of a reputation – has been dented by his dismissal of the leading theologian and theoretical jurisprudent Sayf al-Dīn al-Āmidī. Louis Pouzet considered this as a pivotal moment of 'the "traditionalist" and anti-intellectual reaction, which accompanied the accession [of al-Malik al-Ashraf]' in Damascus. In a similar vein, Stephen Humphreys argued that al-Malik al-Ashraf did not share the 'tolerance' of his brother and predecessor al-Muᶜaẓẓam, but that he rather pursued a 'constant policy to rid his capital of rationalist philosophizing in its madrasas and of "extremist" Sufis in its popular life'. In consequence, 'his patronage extended only to the narrowest form of scholarship, the study of *hadith*' in line with 'the strict and puritanical tone of his public administration'. This line of argument was subsequently taken up by Yasser Tabbaa who described al-Malik al-Ashraf succinctly as 'the most orthodox of the Ayyubids of Damascus'. And I myself adopted a similar line of argument in one of my previous publications.[1]

Such descriptions obviously do not inspire confidence in the thematic breadth of a library housed in this ruler's mausoleum – even if one disagrees with the notion that the study of *ḥadīth* is necessarily the narrowest form of scholarship. However, Sonja Brentjes recently showed that the demise of al-Āmidī was much more complex than previously thought and was basically centred on questions of patronage rather than part of an orthodox strategy.[2] The origin of al-Ashraf's image as an 'orthodox' ruler goes back not only to his dismissal of al-Āmidī, but also to how some intensively used narrative sources portrayed this ruler. Here his edict that in the madrasas 'none of the jurisprudents should study anything except Koranic interpretation, tradition and jurisprudence' and his threat to exile anyone who 'studies logic or the sciences of the Ancients' played a crucial role.[3] However, as seen in Chapter 1 with regard to al-Malik al-Ashraf's role as scholarly patron, if one starts to take into consideration more varied narrative texts and the manuscript evidence, a more nuanced portrayal emerges. In addition, the rather colourful mixture of books he chose for his own mausoleum would have been peculiar if al-Malik al-Ashraf had indeed exclusively adopted the narrow intellectual outlook some contemporaneous sources and modern scholarship have ascribed to him.

The second reason why this library's thematic profile would not have sounded too colourful takes us beyond the immediate case of the Ashrafiya and brings up how scholarship has studied libraries in educational institutions in general. Middle Eastern history has certainly moved away from the idea that the madrasa necessarily had a narrow and restricted curriculum, as was expressed in the words of George Makdisi that 'neither the madrasa nor its cognate institutions harboured any but the religious sciences and their ancillary subjects' and in those of Heinz Halm that 'teaching at the madrasa was always limited to religious knowledge. The instruction and study of medicine or astronomy, algebra or geometry, took place elsewhere.' The now classic study of Jonathan Berkey and a set of other contributions have convincingly laid this idea to rest.[4] This scholarship has also both liberated the madrasa from sweeping associations with the Saljuq-period Sunni Revival and being seen primarily as a tool in the hands of the political and military elites. However, in the absence of catalogues, this rethinking of educational institutions has not yet satisfyingly tackled the question of their libraries. Some scholarship has thus continued with an outdated framework that sees library collections in madrasas as having a narrow canon of disciplines, especially law, so that books on ancient fields of knowledge, for example, would have played only a marginal role.[5] From this perspective, the Ashrafiya library would have seemed even less promising, as it was housed in an institution that was first and foremost a commemorative endowment rather than a teaching endowment. Youssef Eche, for instance, assumed that on account of the close link between an institution and its library's profile, libraries in such mausolea basically 'received endowments of prayer books and pious works'.[6]

The Ashrafiya's Overall Thematic Profile

With the Ashrafiya catalogue we are now able to test these assumptions on mausolea and madrasa libraries with reference to a specific book collection. This section will do so by comparing qualitative and quantitative data obtained from several approaches used to categorise and profile the collection. Some approaches developed in the course of writing this book complement others adopted by the cataloguer himself. In order to thematically profile this library we can start by considering al-Anṣārī's thematic categories, which we saw in Chapter 2. The 'pious' works Eche mentioned would most likely fall into the Ashrafiya catalogue's thematic categories 1–3 where especially titles on Koran, *ḥadīth* and law were held. If we turn to *Table 2.2* it is evident that these three categories, which are largely synonymous with the transmitted sciences, do contain a significant number of books, namely 232. However, in contrast to what one may expect of a madrasa library, books from these thematic fields are far from constituting the majority and represent only 23 per cent of the Ashrafiya's total collection. Even if we add the ancillary subjects of the philological categories 4 and 5, the share does not increase to more than 33 per cent. By contrast, there are more than twice as many books in the remaining categories 6–15 (683), which encompass medicine, pharmacology, falconry, mathematics, agriculture, geography and, most importantly, adab and poetry. The very fact that the catalogue only apportioned three thematic categories to the transmitted sciences is by itself testament to the quantitative (un)importance of these fields on the library's shelves. It would be entirely ahistorical and a misrepresentation of the contemporaneous intellectual world to impose a schematic 'pious'/religious vs. 'secular' divide on this collection. For instance, to some extent the adab works contained material that would fit perfectly well into categories 1–3. To divide poetry along such lines would more often than not be equally impossible. However, it is striking that the first documented library of an educational institution has its emphasis in fields of knowledge that have traditionally not been associated with the intellectual activities of madrasas.

The multifariousness of the Ashrafiya collection becomes even clearer if we move beyond these thematic categories, which only catch half of the library's books as they are exclusively concerned with normal-sized, complete and stand-alone works. As shown in Chapter 2, the catalogue's system of thematic categories broke down when it came to many other entries, in particular the incomplete works and those in multiple-text manuscripts. In consequence, Chapter 4 assigns what will hereafter be called an 'external thematic category' to each entry so that the collection can be considered as a whole. In methodological terms these external categories have two main caveats: as the identification of titles is in many cases tentative the content of these works can also be only tentatively classified, and as numerous works are encyclopaedic in nature it is often impossible to pin them down with one single term. On account of these problems, the numbers in *Table 3.1* are only indicative, but they do at least give an impression of the overall thematic distribution in the Ashrafiya. The broad validity of these external thematic categories is indicated by the fact that their numbers are strikingly similar to those in the catalogue's own thematic categories. For instance, the 23 per cent of books in the transmitted sciences according to al-Anṣārī's own classification system is very similar to the 20 per cent of books found in these same fields of knowledge according to the external thematic categories.

Table 3.1 Ashrafiya library, external thematic categories (percentages rounded to .5)

Thematic category	No. of entries	Percentage
poetry[a]	674	32%
transmitted sciences[b]	421	20%
adab	341	16.5%
philological sciences[c]	194	9.5%
medicine[d]	106	5%
history[e]	88	4%
political thought	72	3.5%
philosophy/theology[f]	50	2.5%
Astronomy	24	1%
miscellany[g]	72	3.5%
unknown	54	2.5%

a Including commentary on poetry, but excluding explicitly devotional poetry.
b Including prayer book (99 entries), *ḥadīth* (65), *fiqh* (52), Koran (51), Ṣufism (27), sermons (24), biography (21), history (19), poetry (9), oneiromancy (10), rituals (8), ᶜAlī – sayings attributed to (8), ethics – Islamic (8), eschatology/afterlife (5), *qiṣaṣ al-anbiyāʾ* (4), Prophet Muḥammad – devotional (3), biographical dictionaries of scholars (3), *uṣūl al-dīn* (2), *jihād* (2), pre-Islamic revelation (1).
c Including lexicography (84), grammar (78), rhetoric (19), morphology (6), philology (6), phonetics (1).
d Including human medicine (69), veterinary medicine (13), pharmacology (24).
e Including history (72), biography (9), biographical dictionaries of poets (6), biographies (2), autobiography (2), onomastics (2).
f Including philosophy (29), theology (10), mathematics (8), logic (2), natural philosophy (1).
g Including ethics (14), administrative handbook (12), falconry (8), music (7), (prose) panegyric (6), mineralogy (4), warfare (4), equitation (4), geography (3), agriculture (2), calligraphy (3), trade handbook (1), geomancy (1), chess (1), dates (1), chemistry (1).

The 20 per cent of entries that clearly fit into the fields of transmitted sciences (most importantly, law, *ḥadīth*, Koran, biography of the Prophet, early Islamic history, Islamic ethics, eschatology, rituals, sermons, Sufism, prayer books, devotional poetry, *uṣūl al-dīn*) constitute some 420 entries in the library. This is again a significant number and prayer books (ninety-nine entries) as well as works on *ḥadīth* (sixty-four), *fiqh* (fifty-two) and the Koran (fifty-one) clearly reflect devotional and scholarly concerns that have been traditionally associated with madrasas. Yet when considering all the entries according to the external thematic categories the number of books in the transmitted sciences remains strikingly low as they do not constitute more than a fifth of the library's total stock. Adding the books in the philological fields brings the share close to 30 per cent, but again does not significantly alter the overall picture. By contrast, poetry represents some 32 per cent, adab is not far behind the transmitted sciences with 16 per cent and even medicine is relatively well represented at 5 per cent.

The relatively low representation of the transmitted sciences is even more accentuated if we take a different approach, namely considering whether multiple copies were held of the same work, and, if so, how many. If more than one copy of a work is held it indicates a work's relative popularity in the library's cultural setting – although it is difficult to differentiate whether the reading interests of those who set up a library and provided the books matched the reading interests of those who used the library. It is no surprise that multiple copies were held in medieval libraries, but the information we have, based on narrative sources, can be quite fanciful. For instance, more than 1,220 copies of al-Ṭabarī's universal chronicle were supposedly held in the Fatimid library of Cairo.[7] Numbers in the Ashrafīya library were significantly lower, but they have the advantage that they are not only more realistic, but more importantly allow more detailed insights into the wider collection.

The Ashrafīya held 163 works in multiple copies in total and these were not evenly distributed across the external thematic categories (*Table 3.2*). While the transmitted sciences comprise 20 per cent of the total entries, this share drops by almost a half to one-eighth of the total of multiple copies. By contrast, three fields increase their share when looking at multiple copies: poetry moves further up and represents half of all works in multiple copies, adab slightly increases its share to move to second rank and medicine has the strongest increase in relative terms moving to fourth rank, a particularly striking shift in the relative weighting of the two fields. While the total number of entries for the transmitted sciences was four times that of the field of medicine, in terms of multiple-copy works it is less than double.[8]

The relative weighting changes again when the number of copies held of a specific work is taken into account, a range of two to fifteen copies. If we consider those works with six or more copies (*Table 3.3*) we see that now the transmitted sciences and medicine are on an equal footing, both represented by two entries. Yet there are slightly more copies of the most

Table 3.2 Ashrafiya library, works in multiple copies according to thematic categories (percentages rounded to .5)

Thematic category	No. of entries	Percentage
poetry	77	47%
adab	29	18%
transmitted sciences	21	13%
medicine	12	7.5%
philological sciences	10	6%
history	5	3%
political thought	3	2%
philosophy/theology	0	0%
astronomy	0	0%
miscellany	6	3.5%

popular medical titles than of those in the transmitted sciences: Ibn Buṭlān's *Almanac of Health* ranks sixth in the library with eleven copies and Ibn Jazla's pharmacological *Method of Demonstrating* has eight copies. From the fields of transmitted sciences the highest placed is Muslim's *Sound Collection* in eight copies followed by al-Sharīf al-Raḍī's *Path of Eloquence* in six copies. Multiple copies in the fields of transmitted sciences tend to be *ḥadīth* collections, such as the other highly placed works al-Quḍāʿī's *The Flame* and al-Bukhārī's *Sound Collection* with five copies each. However, not a single work on Koran recitation – the scholarly raison d'être of the Ashrafiya – is held in multiple copies. The only works associated with the Koran held in at least two copies were the fifth-/eleventh-century Koran commentaries by al-Wāḥidī and al-Sharīf al-Murtaḍā.[9]

The Ashrafiya library raises a rather surprising side question, namely how many copies of the Koran were held in such a madrasa-cum-mausoleum and where they were held. The catalogue only mentions two complete copies (one copied by the famous calligrapher Ibn al-Bawwāb and the other said to be a lavishly gilded scroll) and one incomplete copy.[10] One could argue that copies of the Koran in the library were not mentioned unless they had a specific value, but why then is the incomplete copy mentioned? The low number of copies of the Koran is particularly vexing in an endowment where the Koranic text features so prominently. The likelihood is that either there was an independent collection of Koran copies elsewhere in the building,

Table 3.3 Ashrafiya library, most popular titles by multiple copies[b]

	Title	Author	Thematic category	D. date	No. copies
1	Shiʿr	Salāma b. Jandal	poetry – pre-Islamic		15
1	Maqāmāt	al-Ḥarīrī	adab	516/1122	15
3	Dīwān (al-Ṣūlī)	Abū Nuwās	poetry	*c.*200/815	12[a]
3	Shiʿr	al-Mawj b. al-Zimmān	poetry – early Islamic		12
3	Fiqh al-lugha	al-Thaʿālibī	lexicography	429/1038	12
6	Taqwīm al-ṣiḥḥa	Ibn Buṭlān	medicine	458/1066	11
7	Dīwān	Ibn Ḥayyūs	poetry	473/1081	10
7	Ḥamāsa	Abū Tammām	poetry	c.231/845	10
7	Dīwān	Ibn Hāniʾ	poetry	362/973	10
10	Dīwān	Mihyār	poetry	428/1037	9
10	Dīwān	al-Buḥturī	poetry	284/897	9
12	Siqṭ al-zand	al-Maʿarrī	poetry	449/1058	8
12	Ṣaḥīḥ	Muslim	ḥadīth	261/875	8
12	Minhāj al-bayān	Ibn Jazla	pharmacology	493/1100	8
12	Dīwān	al-Mutanabbī	poetry	354/955	8
16	Mujmal	Ibn Fāris	lexicography	395/1004	7
16	Shiʿr	al-Mutalammis	poetry – pre-Islamic		7
18	Tatimmat al-Yatīma	al-Thaʿālibī	poetry/adab	429/1038	6
18	Nahj al-balāgha	al-Sharīf al-Raḍī	ʿAlī – sayings	406/1016	6
18	Ghazal	al-Sharīf al-Raḍī	poetry	406/1016	6
18	Dīwān	Kushājim	poetry	*c.*350/961	6
18	al-Ṣādiḥ wa-al-bāghim	Ibn al-Habbārīya	poetry/adab	*c.*509/1115	6
18	Dīwān	Ṣurradurr	poetry	465/1074	6

a In addition to the 12 copies in the transmission of al-Ṣūlī, 4 copies were held in the transmission of Ḥamza and 1 copy in the transmission of Tūzūn.

b Only multiple copies of exactly the same format are counted, as they are highlighted by the cataloguer. The numbers would be slightly different if additional copies in multiple-text manuscripts and incomplete manuscripts were taken into account we well. For instance, al-Thaʿālibī's *Yatīmat al-dahr* has eight (mostly incomplete) copies at different points in the catalogue.

which was not part of the library, or, more likely, the teaching and practice of recitation relied to such a large extent on oral forms of transmission and performance that the written text played a very marginal role. Whatever the reason, the almost complete absence of the Koran from the library is another intriguing aspect of its book holdings.

Returning now to the library's collection as a whole, the most striking feature of the Ashrafiya is the salience of works of poetry and adab, with some 680 and 340 entries thus constituting 32 per cent and 16 per cent of the collection, respectively. And works from these fields were more frequently held in more than one copy; poetry represents 47 per cent of the 163 works held in multiple copies and adab 18 per cent (*Table 3.2*). Furthermore, poetry dominates the list of the most popular works in terms of multiple copies (*Table 3.3*): among the twenty-three works of which there were six or more copies in the library fourteen are poetry and two more are anthologies of poetry and prose texts. If the Ashrafiya had a key feature in its thematic profile it was thus to offer its users poetry that did not directly fall within the fields of the transmitted sciences.

As stated previously it would be impossible to clinically separate poetry and adab works from the transmitted sciences, but taking a closer look at specific sub-categories helps to clarify the point made here. For instance, more than eighty entries within the field of poetry refer to pre-Islamic poetry, which is more than the numbers for any specific field of the transmitted sciences except prayer books: Just over sixty entries were on the shelves for all aspects of *ḥadīth* study and respectively just over fifty for the fields associated with the Koran and for those on law. This salience of pre-Islamic poetry is particularly evident when looking at the most popular works in terms of multiple copies. Salām b. Jandal, the celebrated warrior poet, is joint first with fifteen copies and al-Mutalammis is sixteenth with seven copies. The frequency of pre-Islamic poetry held in multiple copies continues with five copies of Zuhayr b. Abī Sulmā's poetry, four copies of that of the brigand-poet al-Shanfarā and Ḥātim al-Ṭāʾī, three copies of Imruʾ al-Qays b. Ḥujr al-Kindī and so on.

The presence of pre-Islamic poetry on the Ashrafiya's shelves can be explained by a variety of factors, chief among them a philological interest in mastering the linguistic context in which the Koran emerged. In addition, the meaning of pre-Islamic poetry evidently changed over time and by the third/ninth century it served as a positive marker of Arabness and Arab authenticity.[11] Nevertheless, as recent scholarship has argued, by the sixth/twelfth century the pre-Islamic period became increasingly associated with the pejorative idea of *jāhilīya*, or age of ignorance.[12] It is thus quite remarkable that a library placed in this mausoleum-cum-madrasa held the works of so many pre-Islamic poets. The multiple copies indicate furthermore that they must have been among the period's most popular

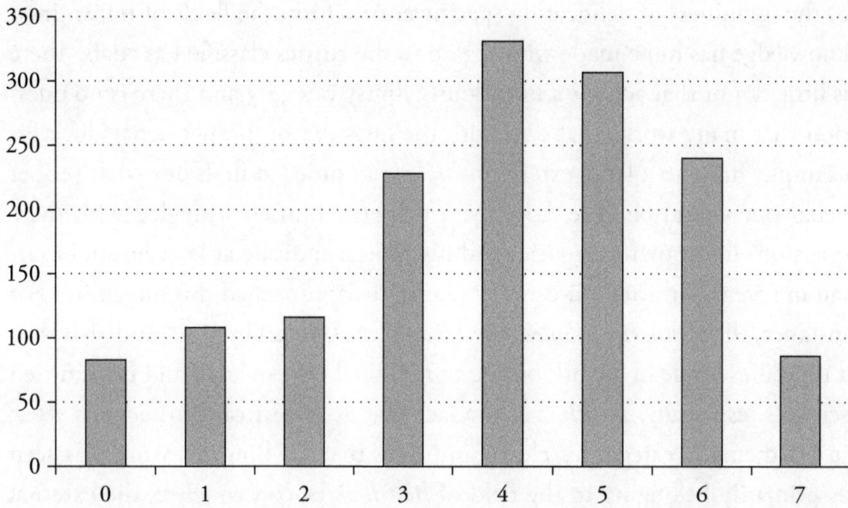

Note: As it is impossible to ascertain the exact date of composition for these works they are assigned to *hijrī* centuries. For this end the author's death date is taken. As not all authors died upon finishing their work, twenty years are deducted from the death date to have a more realistic average value. Titles ascribed to early Islamic individuals are registered as belonging to the first *hijrī* century. All pre-Islamic works are bundled under '0'

Figure 3.1 Ashrafiya library, chronological distribution of dateable works (1,498 entries out of 2,096) by *hijrī* century

books – or at least among the most frequently lent out works in this library. The main point here is not that the Ashrafiya library held poetry deemed to be problematic in its collection – certainly more research would be needed on contemporaneous attitudes towards this material to make such a point. The main point is rather one of relative distribution among the various fields, namely that with more than eighty titles, pre-Islamic poetry is better represented in the collection than virtually any field within the transmitted sciences. The salience of pre-Islamic literature in general is also underlined by taking a slightly different approach, namely looking at the chronological distribution of works in the Ashrafiya library (*Figure 3.1*). Here we see that the numbers of entries ascribed to pre-Islamic authors (83) is not far from those ascribed to the formative first century of Islam (108).

Whatever the reason behind this solid appearance of pre-Islamic poetry in the catalogue, it is at least obvious that these entries can be separated with some justification from the fields of the transmitted sciences. The same point of the usefulness of delineating specific entries from the fields of transmitted knowledge has to be made with regard to the entries classified as adab. The is little doubt that adab is a notoriously flimsy category and there is no question that many works that deal with the question of 'proper behaviour', for example, draw to a large extent on *ḥadīths* in order to flesh out what proper behaviour would be. The Ashrafīya cataloguer himself struggled with these questions in his own categories and his choices indicate at least how a librarian in seventh-/thirteenth-century Damascus approached this quagmire. For instance, the *Gatherings' Splendour* (*Bahjat al-Majālis*) by Ibn ᶜAbd al-Barr is a typical example of a work on the borderline between adab and transmitted sciences, especially *ḥadīth*. Yet the fact that al-Anṣārī categorised this work in his thematic category 2 clearly indicates that for him this work was seen as primarily belonging to the field of *ḥadīth*.[13] In consequence, the external thematic category chosen for such a borderline work was also in the first instance *ḥadīth*. In general, the choice of external thematic categories for such borderline cases took al-Anṣārī's category as an important indicator.

There are well over 300 entries classified in the external thematic category for adab and again we find numerous multiple copies, although to a lesser extent than among the poetic works. However, compared with the works from the field of the transmitted sciences it is again striking how often the library offered its readers several copies of the same adab work. Tellingly, in joint first place in terms of multiple copies together with Salām b. Jandal's poems is the widely popular adab work *The Sessions* (*Maqāmāt*) by al-Ḥarīrī (d. 516/1122). And among the library's 163 works in multiple copies twenty-nine were adab works, compared to twenty-one from all the fields of transmitted sciences. Yet the importance of adab is not primarily apparent from multiple copies, but rather from looking at the library's most popular authors by entries (*Table 3.4*): Here we find two classical adab scholars right at the top of the list: al-Thaᶜālibī as the number one by a wide margin and al-Jāḥiẓ in second place.

This discussion has so far looked at the representation of works in the transmitted sciences, poetry and adab in the collection. The fourth most important category in the Ashrafīya by external thematic categories is works belonging to the philological sciences with 9 per cent. Here we find the standard works of grammar and lexicography for anybody dealing with the

Table 3.4 Ashrafiya library, most popular authors by entries

	Author	D. date	No. entries
1	al-Thaᶜālibī	429/1038	46
2	al-Jāḥiẓ	255/868-9	31
3	al-Ghazālī	505/1111	30
4	Ibn Durayd	321/933	24
5	Ibn al-Jawzī	597/1200	23
6	Abū al-ᶜAlāᵓ al-Maᶜarrī	449/1058	20
7	al-Rāzī (Rhazes)	*c.*313/925	18
8	al-Sharīf al-Raḍī	406/1016	13
9	Abū al-Fatḥ Ibn Jinnī	392/1002	13
10	al-Aṣmaᶜī	213/828	12
11	Ibn Sīnā	428/1037	11
11	Abū Tammām	*c.*231/845	11
11	Abū Ḥayyān al-Tawḥīdī	414/1023	11
14	al-Khaṭīb al-Tibrīzī	502/1109	10
14	al-Ḥātimī	388/998	10
14	al-Mutanabbī	354/955	10
17	Abū al-Faraj al-Iṣfahānī	356/967	9
17	ᶜAbd Allāh Ibn al-Muᶜtazz	296/908	9
17	Ibrāhīm b. Hilāl al-Ṣābiᵓ	384/994	9
17	Ibn Qutayba	321/933	9

Arabic language. The relative importance of works from these fields is also reflected in the list of the most popular works in terms of multiple copies, where we find al-Thaᶜālibī's *Understanding of Lexicography* highly ranked with twelve copies as well as Ibn Fāris' *Summary on Lexicography* with seven copies. In the same vein, authors who were particularly active in these fields feature in the list of the most popular authors by entries (*Table 3.4*), such as Ibn Durayd in fourth place and Ibn Jinnī in fifth. If there is an outstanding feature in this category it is the bilingual Persian–Arabic works. The Ashrafiya held an otherwise unknown lexicographical work for Persian speakers entitled *Chosen Arabic Terms that Enter Phrases and Books* to which al-Anṣārī added 'and these are difficult expressions explained in Persian'. Another work in this group is one that catered for Arabic-speakers and had, in three copies, a lexicographical work on Arabised words from Persian.[14]

These lexicographical works were well placed in a library that had a noteworthy number of Persian-language entries. The forty-four entries, representing 2 per cent of the overall collection, are distributed across the various fields of knowledge, including poetry (first and foremost), adab, medicine, theology, *fiqh*, sermons and Koranic exegesis. Among them featured a Persian version of *Kalīla wa-Dimna*, the famous collection of animal fables. As seen in Chapter 2, these Persian-language works were important enough for the author to make the only explicit break in his system of organising the library as he introduces a special category for them: 'Books in Persian in [thematic category] nine'.[15] The presence of these Persian works in a Damascene library is the outcome of a boom in Persian literature, which goes back to the fifth/eleventh century and witnessed a high degree of Persian–Arabic intertextuality.[16] This movement was increasingly felt in Syria from the late decades of this century when it became part of the Saljuq sphere of influence. The Ayyubid rulers, coming from a Kurdish-/Persian-speaking background, reinforced this tendency: just looking at the Damascene case, it is evident that the Ayyubid elite acted as patrons of Persian–Arabic translations. Al-Muᶜaẓẓam encouraged the translations of at least two Persian works into Arabic, the great *Shāh-nāma* and the abridgment of ᶜImād al-Dīn al-Iṣfahānī's history of the Saljuqs.[17]

The relative salience of these Persian works can be more specifically ascribed to the immediate context of the library and its patron al-Malik al-Ashraf. For instance, one bilingual work on Arabic–Persian word puzzles was specifically dedicated to him.[18] Especially in the northern Mesopotamian environment, of the first decades of his political career al-Ashraf found himself in a strongly bi- or rather multilingual context. Damascus was also certainly far from monolingual in this period. The manuscripts in a myriad of languages originally housed close to the Ashrafiya in the Qubbat al-khazna in the Umayyad Mosque's courtyard are 'mirrors of a multilingual and multicultural society' in the city.[19] However, not everybody mastered Persian and the library's cataloguer al-Anṣārī most likely did not: one of the few instances where he got a word completely wrong and had to cross it out is in the entry for the Persian anthology of pre-Islamic gnomes *Jāwīdhān Khirad*. It is also noteworthy that Persian entries tend to be very generic and al-Anṣārī often provided conspicuously less detail for them than he did for the neighbouring Arabic titles. Finally, al-Anṣārī repeatedly records the Persian entries not in Persian but with an Arabised title. This certainly reflects the bi-lingual environment of his day, as the Persian mirror for princes *Baḥr al-Fawāʾid*, probably written in Aleppo in the mid-sixth/twelfth century, also has an Arabic title and Arabic chapter headings. Other contemporaneous Arabic authors tended to quote Persian books with Arabic titles as well, such as Ibn al-Sāᶜī from Baghdad and the Syrian Yāqūt al-Ḥamawī.[20]

The main point emerging from the discussion so far is not so much that the Ashrafiya held particularly odd titles. The salience of poetry, including pre-Islamic poetry, and adab as well as the presence of medical works is by itself not necessarily surprising in a madrasa context. The striking feature is rather the relative distribution of the Ashrafiya's books across the various thematic categories. The low proportion of works directly addressing the transmitted sciences stands in clear contrast to the purported main focus of such a teaching institution. Especially in a library attached to an institution dedicated to the devotional commemoration of a ruler and the teaching of Koran recitation one would expect works on the Koran and possibly also *ḥadīth* and *fiqh* to take the bulk of the shelf space. Rather, what we encounter is a very broad range of titles where works from the transmitted sciences take a backseat, whether we look at the overall distribution of entries, the number of multiple copies or the most popular authors.

The distinctiveness of this thematic profile of a teaching institution's library such as the Ashrafiya can be further underlined by comparing it with other medieval book collections. The first comparative angle to be taken looks to entirely different shores. If there is a Latin European equivalent to the important role that libraries in medieval Middle Eastern educational institutions played in making books available it is ecclesiastical libraries, especially those attached to monasteries and cathedrals. Focusing on the comparative case chosen for this study the question of the thematic profile of British medieval libraries arises. Here we can consider the monastery libraries from the late twelfth century to the fourteenth century analysed by David Bell (*Table 3.5*). These libraries show a wide variation in the numbers of books they held in the different fields of knowledge, so they cannot just be treated as one coherent unit. Furthermore, any direct comparison is rendered difficult by the different concepts of classifying works. However, there is one continuous line relevant for the present discussion emerging out of these British catalogues, namely that in these institutions works on theology, which roughly maps on to the fields of transmitted sciences, were by far the largest

Table 3.5 Thematic categories in selected medieval British libraries (Bell, Cistercians, Gilbertines and Premonstratensians, *XXV)*

	Meaux	Rievaulx	Lanthony	Peterborough	Bradsole	Welbeck
Theology	81.3	85.3	61.0	73.0	58.6	77.0
Grammar and Logic	5.3	3.3	7.3	4.3	2.1	5.0
Philosophy	2.6	1.05	4.1	2.6	0.7	1.6
Law (Civil and Ecclesiastical)	2.7	2.3	9.5	4.5	11.7	3.3
Classics	1.8	1.05	5.8	5.5	6.9	0
Science and Medicine	2.9	3.0	9.0	6.8	19.3	11.5
History	3.4	4.0	3.3	3.3	0.7	1.6

category. Starting with almost 60 per cent at the Premonstratensian house of Bradsole in the late thirteenth century they rise to well over 80 per cent in the Cistercian house of Rievaulx in the late twelfth century. That it was that high and late medieval British monastery libraries held mostly theological works and that philosophy, classics and medicine played a substantial but subordinate role is not a particularly groundbreaking discovery. However, it helps to highlight that the library profile of the Ashrafiya as a mausoleum with teaching activities geared towards Koran recitation is indeed remarkable if seen in a wider perspective, as in its titles it embraced far more intellectual breadth.

A second comparative angle that can be taken in order to highlight the distinctiveness of the Ashrafiya library brings us back to the Middle East and looks at the profiles of private book collections. As argued elsewhere, these collections have a distinctively different profile: in private collections owned by scholars, the transmitted sciences dominate in a way that is reminiscent of the weight of theological works in the medieval British monastery libraries.[21] The low ratio of the transmitted sciences in the Ashrafiya is by no means an expression that these fields were of low importance to the scholarly elite. They clearly held these works in their private libraries and these fields took centre stage in many of their scholarly endeavours. However, a library such as the Ashrafiya simply did not reflect these interests – in the same way as it did not simply reflect the stated central devotional and scholarly aims set out in its endowment.

This point is crucial, as the Ashrafiya was arguably not the odd one out among the libraries of educational institutions, although one could certainly argue that the special circumstances of its foundation as shown in this book make it a unique case. Especially its close links with the royal library of al-Malik al-Ashraf on the one hand and with the Fatimid library of Cairo on the other, could be taken as an argument that this library cannot be compared with other libraries of the period. However, the case of the Ashrafīya is the first example where the history of a medieval Arabic library is traced in such detail and we simply do not know enough about other libraries to put its thematic profile down to idiosyncrasy. There is, for instance, little doubt that books from the Fatimid library made their way to other madrasa libraries, such as that of the Fāḍilīya madrasa in Cairo, one of the best provisioned libraries of the city.[22] There is also little doubt that royal collections of other rulers made their ways into madrasa libraries. Even al-Ashraf himself divided his collection between his mausoleum and his citadel Dār al-ḥadīth so that the latter's library is at least as 'royal' as that of the mausoleum. If we thus consider the Ashrafīya mausoleum's profile we cannot a priori assume that it is unique among educational institutions of the period. Rather its library's profile does match the limited information that we do have on other Arabic libraries in educational institutions of the period. Although it would be premature to take this profile as an established overall trend of the period, until further catalogues have come to light, it is at least possible to say that no contrary evidence has come up so far.[23]

To conclude this discussion of the Ashrafīya's overall thematic profile two points have to be made: first, the Ashrafīya's distinct library profile (and arguably that of educational institutions in general) brings up the question of the function of these libraries. In contrast to private libraries, which were obviously primarily restricted to the owner's use, and monastery libraries, which also granted only restricted access, the Ashrafīya can justifiably be called a public library. As argued in Chapter 2, this library was embedded within the literary topography of the Kallāsa quarter with its book market, open reading spaces, libraries and depositories for worn-out books. Most importantly, it was embedded in the wider reading culture of Damascus as it was a lending library. The Ashrafīya's profile has thus not to be seen exclusively as part of the intellectual interests of the religious scholars, the *ᶜulamāᵓ*, but rather as reflecting the wider literary interests as they existed in a city such as Damascus. Its users certainly came from among the *ᶜulamāᵓ*, but crucially this was a period when the written word was experiencing rapid expansion with more and more groups starting to gain access to it so the library's users also came from the wider population. The Ashrafiya profile thus only looks odd if one assumes that the library of an educational institution necessarily reflected this institution's teaching profile and if one sidelines the relatively high degree of literacy in a medieval Middle Eastern city such as Damascus.

The second issue brought up by the Ashrafiya's profile is the intellectual horizons of the *ʿulamāʾ* themselves. This takes us back to the issue raised at the beginning of this chapter, namely the changed view of the scholarly activities in madrasas, which are now seen to be much wider than was traditionally assumed. The plurality of the Ashrafiya's library sits comfortably with this revised vision of scholarly activities and the substantial presence of medical works with its numerous multiple copies, for instance, goes well with the argument that medicine could very well be part of madrasa-teaching.[24] In the same vein, it explains the noteworthy presence of 'ancient' authors, of which we have thirty-four entries in the library: including works on astronomy by Euclid; on philosophy by Plato; on medicine by Galen, Hippocrates and Rufus of Ephesus; on political thought by Socrates and Aristotle; on oneiromancy by Artemidorus of Ephesus; and on warfare by Aelianus Tacticus.[25]

While the general diversity of scholars' interests allows us to account for the library's plurality, it does not satisfyingly explain the exact profile of the library, especially the salience of poetry and adab. In order to explain the specific salience of poetry and adab the dual process recently described as the 'adabisation' of religious scholars and the 'ulamisation' of adab is most relevant. This process started in the fifth/eleventh century when functions in the administration that had hitherto been dominated by a distinct group of secretaries were increasingly taken over by religious scholars. At the same time, scholars also appropriated the cultural heritage of what had previously been the main field of activity of secretaries. In consequence, adab became unequivocally part of the literary corpus that 'religious' scholars – an increasingly awkward translation for many '*ʿulamāʾ*' the further we move into the Middle Period – were interested in. In the same vein, these scholars started composing the type of poetry that had previously rather been associated with courtly life and the secretarial milieu.[26] This process was well established by the Mamluk period and the Ashrafīya arguably provides strong documentary evidence for the impact that the adabisation of *ᶜulamāᵓ* had on libraries.

The Obscene and the Ambiguous

So far the discussion of the Ashrafīya has focused on its broad thematic profile and the relative importance of the various fields of scholarly activity. This approach has allowed the library's characteristic features to be highlighted, but has the inherent danger of obfuscating the remarkable diversity in this collection's content in terms of smaller thematic units and individual works. The best place to start this more detailed enquiry is the library's most popular field, poetry. This poetry must very much be seen as part of the adabisation of the *ᶜulamāᵓ* and the prominence of pre-Islamic poetry discussed above is certainly part of the reconfigured profile of what knowledge an average religious scholar should master and what was seen to be appropriate. The nature of poetry held in the Ashrafīya is also strikingly diverse if we move to poets in the Islamic period. For instance, the library contained poetry by Kaᶜb b. al-Ashraf, an opponent of the Prophet Muḥammad who was killed for his satirical verses. Again from the early Islamic period the love poems by Suḥaym ᶜAbd Banī al-Ḥasḥās are on the shelves, which a modern critic described as 'obscene'. From the ᶜAbbasid period there is no lack of wine poetry, such as the *Khamrīyāt* of Abū Nuwās or verses by Ibn al-Muᶜadhdhal, who was also renowned for his satirical and invective poems. Closer to the period of the Ashrafīya library itself are the poems of Ibn Quzmān, which were held in one complete and three incomplete copies. This Andalusian poet established a highly ironic counter-genre with a strong interest in the lower strata of society and popular events such as carnivals. For his celebration of wine drinking, satirising of scholars and clashing with members of the political elite he spent time in prison and was condemned – although not put – to death.[27]

To hone in on the issue of poetry, the oeuvre by the Buyid poet and student of Abū Nuwās, Ibn al-Ḥajjāj can be considered in more detail. The Ashrafīya held five incomplete manuscripts of his poetry and two (complete) books of narrations concerned with his poems. He was again famous for his sexually explicit poetry and was 'perhaps the most notoriously obscene poet in Arabic', which is quite a reputation to achieve. One of the Ashrafīya books of narrations came with illustrations; one can only speculate as to what these may have depicted. On account of the nature of Ibn al-Ḥajjāj's poetry, a sixth-/twelfth-century author of a *ḥisba* treatise on the right and the wrong enjoined teachers to keep children from this poetry and a scribe later regretted that he had produced copies of Ibn al-Ḥajjāj's poems. This attitude may seem understandable in light of verses such as 'My cock calls for the forenoon prayer inside her ass and prays at noon'.[28]

However, despite occasional quibbles, the poetry held in the Ashrafīya had circulated for centuries in Arabic–Muslim societies and it would be entirely misguided to present this library as holding extraordinary texts. Kaᶜb b. al-Ashraf had been highly valued for his eloquence and Abū al-Faraj al-Iṣfahānī praised him in his monumental *Book of Songs*.[29] In the same vein, Ibn Quzmān was a hugely successful and esteemed poet of his time. Ibn al-Ḥajjāj was for a time the *muḥtasib*, market-inspector, of Baghdad – an ironic position in light of the later censure of his poetry in a *ḥisba* treatise – and apart from isolated criticism his verses were, as Sinan Antoon has shown in detail, highly valued in the following centuries.[30] The main point here is not that such poetry, which may contravene modern notions of how to talk about sexuality and religion, were in circulation and passed down. The main point is rather that they were held in this mausoleum-cum-madrasa library. The presence of these works on the library's shelves again links to the public character of the library, but also to the widening interest of *ᶜulamāᵓ* in all forms of literature. While poetry such as that by Ibn al-Ḥajjāj had been produced very much in a courtly and an elite literary culture, the adabisation of the 'religious' scholars brought his verses into wider circulation and even on to the shelves of a library such as the Ashrafīya.

In addition to explicit poetry, a second field to be considered in more detail is verse that challenged prevailing dogma. Abū al-ᶜAlāᵓ al-Maᶜarrī provides a case in point for the wide variety of such poetry on the Ashrafīya's shelves. Certainly a maverick he also had a dubious reputation as to his faith, as he expressed doubts about tenets such as bodily resurrection and the value of prophethood.[31] There is no doubt that he was greatly esteemed for his mastery of Arabic and the Ashrafīya's contemporaneous Ibn Khallikān almost unequivocally praises him in his biographical dictionary. But another author who wrote only a few decades earlier is much more restrained about al-Maᶜarrī and underlines that 'he did not believe in prophethood and resurrection'.[32]

The most controversial of his works was his second poetic diwan, *Self-Imposed Constraints* (*Luzūm mā lā yalzam*), which aroused such criticism that he felt the need to refute allegations of unbelief with a follow-up work *Chiding the Barking Dog* (*Zajr al-nābiḥ*).[33] The Ashrafiya had a remarkably high number of works from al-Maᶜarrī's oeuvre – twenty – among them four copies of *Self-Imposed Constraints*, two complete and two incomplete.[34]

Further examples of poets accused of deviant beliefs and whose poetry was on the Ashrafiya's shelves include the 'freethinker' Ibn al-Rīwandī (Rāwandī/Rawandī). Most famous for his book against prophecy, *Book of the Emerald* (*al-Zumurrud*), some scholars contemporaneous with the Ashrafiya had no quibbles about describing him as a 'heretic' (*zindīq*). Also, the Ashrafiya held no less than nine copies of the diwan of the Buyid-period poet Mihyār b. Marzawayh al-Daylamī, in addition to further collections of his oeuvre. Again a remarkable presence for an author about whom it was said that his conversion to Islam merely meant that, on account of his poetry, he 'passed from one corner of hell to another'. Finally, the poetry of Ṣāliḥ b. ᶜAbd al-Quddūs al-Baṣrī and of Bashshār b. Burd, both executed by the ᶜAbbasid Caliph al-Mahdī for unbelief, was kept in the library.[35]

Dogmatically, diverse texts did not only come in verse, but also in prose. For instance, we see a number of authors with a Muᶜtazilite background represented on the Ashrafiya's shelves. The Muᶜtazila as a school of rationalist Islamic theology was central to the development of theology from the second/eighth century onwards, but scholarship traditionally argued that it vanished from the fifth/eleventh century onwards. With the rise of the Saljuqs the Muᶜtazila did indeed lose official support and its rationalism was increasingly seen to be contrary to more scriptural approaches. However, it is by now evident that Muᶜtazilite ideas survived – although on a much lesser scale – in Baghdad itself, but also more importantly in other regions in the eastern Islamic world and also Yemen.[36] The survival of Muᶜtazilite ideas and texts was in part due to the impact they had had on different groups within Islam, especially Twelver and Zaydi Shiᶜism, and without Islam, especially Judaism.[37]

It is thus of crucial importance to see Muᶜtazilite works represented in this Damascene library in chronological (seventh/thirteenth century), regional (Syria) and religious (Sunni madrasa) contexts, where this theological school is said to have vanished entirely. Among these works was, most surprisingly, what seems to be the lost exposition of Muᶜtazilite doctrine by the fourth-/tenth-century Muᶜtazilite theologian Ibn Khallād, his *Book of Principles* (*Kitāb al-uṣūl*). We also find the polemical defence of Muᶜtazilism by al-Jāḥiẓ, although not under its original title, *Kitāb al-tarbīᶜ wa-al-tadwīr*, but rather described as a 'treatise'. Particularly noteworthy are Muᶜtazilite doxographical texts from the third/ninth century, including a short version of the lost *Tracts* by the Baghdadi Muᶜtazilite theologian al-Nāshiᵓ al-Akbar. The Ashrafiya also held another lost doxographical work, *The Difference in the Teachings*, by the marginal author al-Mismaᶜī Zurqān. A final work of early Muᶜtazilite doxography, again lost, is *The Principles* by Jaᶜfar b. Ḥarb, which was most likely held in a Persian version. Yet the Ashrafiya did not only hold early Muᶜtazilite texts, which one may see as mere vestiges of times gone by. Rather its shelves also contained the exegetical *Revealer* by al-Zamakhsharī, one of the last great representatives of the Muᶜtazila in its classical period. Finally, the Muᶜtazilite works were not just isolated texts, but the library also contained anti-Muᶜtazilite polemical works, including an unknown treatise.[38]

The circulation of such texts in Damascus should not come as a major surprise in light of the recent rediscovery of Muᶜtazilite ideas beyond this school's 'classical' period. What is surprising is that these texts were held in this library. In contrast to the adabisation trend outlined above what we find here goes to the very core of religious scholarship and religious knowledge. In contrast to both the traditional view of the madrasa as part of a Sunni 'orthodox' revival and the traditional view of this madrasa's patron as 'anti-intellectual', its shelves were equipped with material that discussed a distinctively rationalist way of approaching theological questions. The importance of this material should not be overstated, as we do not have hundreds of such titles, but it is crucial to underline that they were not isolated phenomena. The Ashrafiya also contained works influenced by other theological schools such as the Karāmīya, of which hardly any texts have survived and that is seen to be extinct by the seventh/thirteenth century. Perhaps equally important when talking about Muᶜtazilite rationalist theology are those texts that draw on classical Greek philosophy, such as, for instance, *The Philosophers' Manual* by Ḥunayn b. Isḥāq, a collection of letters, anecdotes and sayings ascribed to Greek philosophers or the anonymous *Aristotle's Letter to Alexander the*

Great, which according to Miklós Maróth has, in contrast to other such texts ascribed to Aristotle, little Muslim flavour, but is entirely framed within a Greek world with pagan Gods.[39]

The diversity and plurality of the material held in the Ashrafiya is more remarkable still for the absence of any indication of a distinction between 'right' and 'wrong' texts. One could easily imagine a library where such works would be clearly marked as problematic, for instance by moving them into one category and perhaps even physically separating them from the main collection. Moving the works into a distinct category would have been no problem, as al-Anṣārī shows for the example of Persian-language titles, for which he just created a new section. However, the catalogue and its system of organising the books do not give the slightest indication that such an approach was taken. Rather all these works were slotted into their appropriate places according to alphabetical order, size and thematic category. In consequence, all of the works listed in the catalogue were equally accessible to library users and were possibly all available for loan – at least there is no sign in the catalogue or in the narrative sources that this was not the case.

In addition to the question of rationalist theology, a further striking thematic characteristic of the Ashrafiya, which brings up the issue of religious diversity, is the presence of – what seems to be – Shiᶜite works. These works are more specifically linked to Twelver Shiᶜism, whereas Ismaᶜili or Sevener Shiᶜite works are rarely on the shelves. There are two main thematic clusters in the Ashrafiya where the presence of such works is particularly salient. The first one is a considerable number of works linked to ᶜAlī b. Abī Ṭālib, especially sayings and poetry attributed to him. These works have a wide variety of titles: some are simply called *Sayings* (*Amthāl* and *Kalām*), some are more poetically entitled *Gems of Sayings* (*Jawāhir al-kalām*) and *Signs of Wisdom* (*Dustūr maᶜālim al-ḥikam*), but most importantly the library includes the well-known *Path of Eloquence* (*Nahj al-balāgha*).[40] It is debatable to what extent all of these titles are necessarily associated with Twelver Shiᶜism, but it is at least clear that passages in the *Nahj al-Balāgha* laying out ᶜAlī's claim to the caliphate and his superiority over the three other early Caliphs Abū Bakr, ᶜUmar and ᶜUthmān, for instance, may cause some concern in traditionalist circles. This is especially so as ᶜAlī's sayings and poetry came in companion of works that have a very distinct Shiᶜite profile, such as those proving his imamate, extolling his virtues, legal decisions by him and the Prophet appointing him as trustee. Further works refer to his sons and successors, Ḥasan and Ḥusayn, and ᶜAlī's final advice to them is held in multiple copies. Ḥasan and Ḥusayn appear also as poets, and a martyrological treatise deals with *The Killing of al-Ḥusayn.*[41]

The second salient Shiᶜite thematic cluster in the Ashrafiya consists of works referring to imams other than ᶜAlī. The imams' popularity is particularly evident when turning to books with prayers of invocation (*duᶜāʾ*), of which the library held nearly one hundred. Most of these books are not ascribed to a specific figure and carry generic titles such as *Prayers of Invocation*, *Noble Prayers of Invocation* and *Prayers of Invocation for the Seven Days* and those that are ascribed to a specific person generally refer to Muḥammad. Only eighteen of these prayer books are ascribed to somebody other than Muḥammad and these are of interest here as ten of them refer to one of the imams succeeding ᶜAlī. Chief among them is the fourth imam Zayn al-ᶜĀbidīn with five entries, particularly with his famous *Whispered Prayers* (*munājāt*). He is followed by the sixth imam Jaᶜfar al-Ṣādiq with four entries and finally the fifth imam Muḥammad b. Zayn al-ᶜĀbidīn with one entry.[42] One of the few prayer books with an identifiable author is, furthermore, *Conduct during the Month of Rajab* by the Shiᶜite author Ibn ᶜAyyāsh al-Jawharī, which contains prayers ascribed to Twelver Shiᶜite imams. However, the imams do not only appear in devotional texts, but cover a much wider range of topics. Jaᶜfar al-Ṣādiq appears, for instance, as the author of *Gnomic and Paraenetic Sayings*, of a work for drawing prognostications from verses of the Koran, *Benefits of the Koran*, and of a polemical work of theology.[43] Poetry by one of his sons, who was unable to establish himself as a successful claimant to the imamate, is as present on the shelves as *The Golden Treatise*, a work of Shiᶜite medicine ascribed to ᶜAlī b. Mūsā al-Riḍā, the eighth imam.[44]

Furthermore, a large corpus of works in the Ashrafiya is by Twelver Shiᶜite scholars and the most prominent among them is al-Sharīf al-Raḍī, who authored the above-mentioned *Path of Eloquence*. In addition to this work the Ashrafiya held his *Commentary* on jurisprudence and, in line with the overall thematic profile of the library, his poetry appears again and again on its shelves.[45] In consequence, his works are among the library's most popular works: his *Path of Eloquence* and his *ghazal*-poetry are both held in six copies and his diwan in three. His brother and theologian al-Sharīf al-Murtaḍā is also represented with his commentary on poetry and, more interestingly, his work on the Koran and *ḥadīth* in two copies – as mentioned above, one of only two works on the Koran held in multiple copies in the Ashrafiya library.[46]

The presence of these Twelver Shiᶜite works in the Ashrafiya obviously raises questions as to why they were included. There are several possible lines of argument, one of them being that they are simply remnants from the Fatimid library that came to Damascus via al-Qāḍī al-Fāḍil and his son al-Ashraf Aḥmad. The presence of devotional prayers ascribed to a Fatimid Caliph makes this explanation tantalising. However, in the majority they are clearly Twelver Shiᶜite works and as very few distinctively Ismaᶜili Shiᶜite works made their way into the Ashrafiya this explanation is unconvincing. A second line of argument would be that Shiᶜite works were included in order to 'know the enemy' for polemical purposes. While this cannot be entirely excluded for any single work, there are two points that make this argument rather unlikely: first, as we have seen in the context of the Muᶜtazilite works, there is no indication whatsoever that 'problematic' works were perceived as such and pigeonholed in separate categories. More importantly, in the present context a very substantial body of these Shiᶜite works were devotional texts and not scholarly treatises on points of ritual or dogma. Texts such as prayer books would certainly not have been the first choice if one were to engage polemically with a religious opponent.

A more fruitful way to understand the inclusion of such texts in a madrasa library is to question to what extent they were actually perceived to be 'Shiᶜite' texts. For this purpose, it is useful to look farther to the east where the lines between Sunnism and Shiᶜism became increasingly blurred in the late medieval Persianate world. Scholarship has termed this de-confessionalisation of religious identities variously as confessional ambiguity, Twelver Sunnism, Shiᶜi-Sunnism or imamophilism.[47] This development was to some extent driven by the interpenetration of Sufism and Shiᶜism, where the Sufi *shaykh* increasingly resembled the Shiᶜite imam with a shared concept of *wilāya* or sanctity. Matthew Melvin-Koushki has highlighted the occult sciences as an area where confessional boundaries became more and more meaningless.[48] For the present discussion, it is particularly relevant that this trend towards confessional ambiguity was specifically characterised by ᶜAlid loyalism and a trans-confessional veneration of the twelve imams.[49]

For the Arabic lands, scholarship has only started to tentatively consider comparable developments. The traditional viewpoint is very much embodied in Louis Pouzet's study, where religious life in Damascus is basically seen to be synonymous with Sunnism. Anything else is clearly cordoned off in a very brief separate chapter dealing with the rest, whether they are *sharīfs*, Twelver Shiᶜites, Ismaᶜilis or 'heretics' (*zanādiqa*). However, Daniella Talmon-Heller has drawn together evidence that complicates this rather straightforward approach and has suggested that more research is needed on this topic. In his sixth-/twelfth-century pilgrimage guide to Syria, for instance, a Sunni author includes the shrines of the Shiᶜite imams.[50] In the same vein, her work on the interpenetration of Sufism and Sunnism, especially with regard to *wilāya*, could be taken further to look at how Shiᶜite elements appeared in Sunni practice and thought.[51] From the scholarship emerging on this issue it is evident that devotional practices, such as the example of the veneration of the Prophet's relics in Damascus, are key to confessional ambiguity in a Syrian context. And here the twelve imams, including ᶜAlī, are again of particular importance: Kazuo Morimoto has highlighted in this regard a Damascene work contemporaneous with the Ashrafiya library, namely Sibṭ Ibn al-Jawzī's *Tadhkirat al-khawāṣṣ*, a book on the merits of ᶜAlī and the ᶜAlids, which devotes many pages to Ḥusayn and also discusses all the other imams. This trend may have been reflected in the remarkable spread of ᶜAlid shrines in Syria from the fifth/eleventh to seventh/thirteenth centuries, many of them under Sunni patronage. Stephennie Mulder has argued that these shrines had a 'supra-sectarian' appeal across various sections of the population beyond Sunni-Shiᶜite distinctions.[52] Although she does not link this process with a possible trend towards confessional ambiguity, it is noteworthy that it did not only appear in the more Shiᶜite-influenced north of Syria, but was also prominent in Damascus itself.

When combining these Syrian trends with the profile of the 'Shiᶜite' books in the Ashrafiya library, they indicate a development towards confessional ambiguity or imamophilism, which may be comparable with that established for the eastern Islamic world. The context of the Ashrafiya library was as Sunni as could be: There is not the slightest doubt as to al-Malik al-

Ashraf's allegiance and the same goes for al-Ashraf Aḥmad. The scholars who taught in this mausoleum and who were associated with it, such as al-Anṣārī, were all Sunnis. Yet the numerous texts ascribed to ᶜAlī and the following imams, or venerating them, depict a devotional landscape where a term such as Twelver Sunnism does seem appropriate. This is further reinforced by the fact that these texts were to some extent domesticated for Sunni consumption. Whenever one of the imams is mentioned, the catalogue adds '*raḍiya Allāh ᶜanhu*' (may God be pleased with him), an invocation clearly distinct from the '*ᶜalayhi al-salām*' (may peace be upon him) one would expect in a clearly Shiᶜite context. It may be that al-Anṣārī changed the invocations from what was on the manuscripts in line with his own preferences and those of the catalogue's future users. Yet there is also a very strong possibility that the cataloguer copied the invocations as they were on the manuscripts, which may indicate a genre of Sunni–imami texts circulating in Damascus. At least to al-Anṣārī, arguably to library users and most certainly to al-Malik al-Ashraf, whose final resting place was among these books, there was seemingly nothing 'non-Sunni', 'un-Sunni' or even 'anti-Sunni' about them.

Scholarship on confessional ambiguity in the eastern Islamic world has set about determining the extent to which this process can indeed be generalised over the entire late medieval period and whether it was interrupted by moments of confessional polarisation.[53] It would be misguided to argue for a corresponding, ill-defined and poorly delimitated equivalent farther to the west. Yet the evidence specifically emerging for Syria during the sixth/twelfth and seventh/thirteenth century does at least indicate that the mellowing of confessional borders was a discernible phenomenon. This is not the place to consider the trend's origin in more detail, but it seems at least likely that it was in part linked to Fatimid influence. As has recently been suggested, the legacy of Fatimid rule was not so much that Shiᶜism in a narrow sense was spread in the lands under the dynasty's control, but rather that devotional practices were influenced and reconfigured.[54] In addition to a possible Fatimid influence, Twelver Shiᶜite learning itself flourished during the sixth/twelfth century in Syria, especially in Tripoli and Aleppo, and the region emerged as one of its intellectual centres alongside those in Persia.[55] The wider influence of Twelver Shiᶜism is evident in the Jewish–Karaite reception of theological works such as those by al-Sharīf al-Murtaḍā in both Egypt and

Syria.[56] The subsequent rise of the post-Saljuq Zangid and Ayyubid dynasties in the region only put a gradual end to this prominence of Shiᶜite life.[57] A madrasa library such as the Ashrafiya may thus have been one of those places where 'Shiᶜite' devotional practices and learning became very much intermingled with those of their 'Sunni' counterparts.

Conclusion

A library's collection is never entirely haphazard; it has to respond to the social world to which it belongs. It is underlain by a 'grammar', to borrow a term from Houari Touati, which structures the individual titles into a coherent whole.[58] The social world of the Ashrafiya is clearly seventh-/thirteenth-century Damascus and the insights we gain from this library can certainly not be transferred to other 'Islamic' libraries in Egypt, Anatolia, Iraq, Persia or Khurasan. It is also debatable whether the Ashrafiya was typical of wider trends in Syria or even Damascus during this century, as we do not have comparable catalogues for contemporaneous libraries. Neither do we have scholarship that traces the making of a specific library in comparable detail. In consequence, it would be premature to argue that the specific set of circumstances, most importantly the transfer of the royal library and the Fatimid library connection, make the Ashrafiya an atypical library. However, a ruler such as al-Malik al-Ashraf, who clearly played on his credentials as a Sunni ruler, certainly saw his mausoleum and its library as a crucial representation of his rule. The library shelves were in the immediate vicinity of his final resting place, which was carefully chosen to embed him into a topographical narrative of piety and power.[59] There is little doubt that he had an opinion on what parts of his royal library should go into his mausoleum and what parts should go to into his citadel Dār al-ḥadīth.

Even though we cannot determine the Ashrafiya's typicality or atypicality, this chapter has shown that the Ashrafiya's highly diverse and plural holdings can be connected to broader literary, cultural and intellectual trends detected in recent scholarship, including the adabisation of *ᶜulamāʾ*, the acceptance of 'obscene' poetry and the question of confessional ambiguity. Drawing together the various elements of the Ashrafiya library's remarkable diversity and plurality invites us to take a broader look at what this may signify. Thomas Bauer recently suggested that 'tolerance of ambiguity' was one of the most characteristic features of intellectual life in Middle Eastern societies of the Middle Period.[60] This tolerance made it possible to accept opposing systems of values and norms without necessarily insisting on the exclusive truth of one's own system. Intellectual life in these societies was thus less characterised by the quest for the one and only truth, but rather by searching for probable and likely answers. In consequence, actors could ascribe different meanings to a term, an action or an object, and it was not in principle seen as a problem; most importantly, a significant number of actors in these societies were willing to accept two or more such meanings at the same time.

The thematic profile of the Ashrafiya should thus not be seen to vary from or be in opposition with what one would have expected such a Sunni madrasa-cum-mausoleum to contain. Rather, it expresses the very wide variety of texts that circulated and were read in the city's literary, scholarly and cultural worlds. The intellectual world one can envisage from this medieval Arabic library is vivid, it is varied and, most importantly, it is an invitation to rethink assumptions about the wider scholarly and cultural life in a medieval Middle Eastern city.

Notes

1. Al-Āmidī (d. 631/1233). Pouzet, *Damas*, 36; Humphreys, *From Saladin to the Mongols*, 208, 210–11, 214; Tabbaa, *Constructions of Power and Piety*, 100, note 4; Hirschler, *Medieval Arabic Historiography*, 44.
2. Brentjes, 'Ayyubid Princes', 347–51. A similar line of argument is suggested by EI[3], Bernard G. Weiss, 'Sayf al-Dīn al-Āmidī'.
3. Ibn Kathīr, *al-Bidāya*, XIII, 164.
4. Makdisi, *Rise of Colleges*, 77; Halm, *Traditions of Learning*, 71; Berkey, *Transmission of Knowledge*. Among the most relevant recent work is that of Brentjes, 'Ayyubid Princes' and Brentjes, 'Prison of Categories'.
5. Kügelgen, 'Bücher und Bibliotheken', esp. 164–5 and 170.
6. Eche, *Bibliothèques arabes*, 294.
7. Abū Shāma, *al-Rawḍatayn*, II, 210.
8. This shift is even more distinct when taking into account the catalogue's own thematic categories: here categories 1–3 represent 23% of all entries compared with 7.5% in category 10 (the main medical category), but in terms of multiple copies the margin decreases to 11.5% and 8%.
9. Ibn Buṭlān: Fihrist al-Ashrafiya, Engl. tr. no. 267; Ibn Jazla, *Method*: no. 1030;

Muslim: no. 695; al-Sharīf al-Raḍī: no. 802; al-Quḍāʿī: no. 576; al-Bukhārī: no. 696; al-Wāḥidī: no. 1373; al-Sharīf al-Murtaḍā: no. 790.

10. Fihrist al-Ashrafiya, Engl. tr. nos. 364, 365, 1454.
11. Drory, 'Abbasid Construction'.
12. Webb, 'Uncertain Times' and Ron-Gilboa, *Ǧāhilī Brigands*.
13. Ibn ʿAbd al-Barr (d. 463/1070); Fihrist al-Ashrafiya, Engl. tr. nos. 196 and 1527.
14. *Chosen Arabic Terms*: Fihrist al-Ashrafiya, Engl. tr. no. 754; arabised words: no. 953a.
15. Fihrist al-Ashrafiya, fol. 256a, l. 3 (Fihrist al-Ashrafiya, Engl. tr. nos. 757–83).
16. Behmardi, 'Arabic and Persian Intertextuality'.
17. R. S. Humphreys, Ayyubids, in *Encyclopædia Iranica* (online version, accessed 27/2/2015).
18. Fihrist al-Ashrafiya, Engl. tr. no. 1115.
19. D'Ottone, 'Manuscripts as Mirrors'.
20. *Jāwīdhān Khirad*: Fihrist al-Ashrafiya, fol. 264a, l. 5–6 (=Fihrist al-Ashrafiya, Engl. tr. no. 1263a); examples of Persian 'super-generic' entries are Fihrist al-Ashrafiya, Engl. tr. no. 1254a 'most of it are Persian poems', 1273b 'Poems in Persian', 1284b 'Prose and Verse'; *Baḥr al-Fawāʾid*: Meisami, *Sea of Precious Virtues*, XVIII; Ibn al-Sāʿī, *al-Durr*, repeatedly states that a specific book is in Persian, but gives an Arabic title: p. 401, l. 8/9; p. 402, l. 1; p. 402, l. 2/3; p. 402, l. 18/9. See also p. 246 l. 4, 6, 7, 8, 9/10; p. 356, l. 6/7. MU, VI, 2632. However, the example of the MU shows that Syrian authors of this period could quote the Persian title – they probably did so if a book was (?better) known by this title (MU, I, 128).
21. Hirschler, *Written Word*, 145–56.
22. Bora, 'Fatimids' Books'.
23. Hirschler, *Written Word*, 145–56.
24. Brentjes, 'Prison of Categories'.
25. Euclid: Fihrist al-Ashrafiya, Engl. tr. no. 718; Plato: no. 1143; Galen: nos. 104, 272, 1211b, 1211e, 1476, 1481; Hippocrates: nos. 887, 1031b, 1211d; Rufus of Ephesus: no. 892; Socrates: no. 515; Aristotle: nos. 509, 554, 1237a; Artemidorus of Ephesus: no. 1475; Aelianus Tacticus: no. 1390.
26. EI^3, Thomas Bauer, 'Adab c) and Islamic scholarship after the "Sunnī revival"' and Bauer, 'Literarische Anthologien'.
27. Kaʿb b. al-Ashraf: Fihrist al-Ashrafiya, Engl. tr. no. 628; Suḥaym (d. 37/657–8): nos. 602, 972, 1332a; EI^2, A. Arazi, 'Suḥaym'; Abū Nuwās: nos. 1250c

and 1258b; Ibn al-Muᶜadhdhal (d. 240/854–5): no. 1251b; Ibn Quzmān (d. 555/1160): nos. 120, 1490, 1589, 1594; D.C. Young 'Ibn Quzman', in: Meri, *Medieval Islamic Civilization*, I, 364–5; EI², G.S. Colin, 'Ibn Ḳuzmān'.

28. Ibn al-Ḥajjāj (d. 391/1001); Fihrist al-Ashrafīya, Engl. tr. nos. 62, 1496, 1599, 1649, 1672, 1688; 'notoriously obscene': v. Gelder, *Bad and the Ugly*, 110; Ḥisba: al-Shayzarī, *Nihāyat*, 104; Scribe: TI, 501–20, pp. 160–1; Ibn al-Ḥajjāj quote: Antoon, *Poetics*, 35.
29. Kilpatrick, *Making*, 123.
30. Antoon, *Poetics*.
31. Abū al-ᶜAlāᵓ al-Maᶜarrī (d. 449/1058); Lindstedt, 'Anti-Religious Views'.
32. IKH, I, 113–16; MU, I, 303.
33. V. Gelder and G. Schoeler, 'Introduction', in Abū al-ᶜAlāᵓ al-Maᶜarrī, *Epistle*, XV–XXVIII.
34. Fihrist al-Ashrafīya, Engl. tr. nos. 899, 905, 1505, 1525.
35. Ibn al-Rīwandī: Fihrist al-Ashrafīya, Engl. tr. no. 1047. On this author see Stroumsa, *Freethinkers of Medieval Islam*; Heretic: MU, VI, 2684; Mihyār (d. 428/1037): Fihrist al-Ashrafīya, Engl. tr. nos. 396, 798, 1613; Hell: IKH, V, 359; Ṣāliḥ (d. 167/783)/Bashshār (d. 167/783): Fihrist al-Ashrafīya, Engl. tr. nos. 1494, 1495.
36. Schwarb, 'Age of Averroes'.
37. Adang et al., *Common Rationality*.
38. Ibn Khallād: Fihrist al-Ashrafīya, Engl. tr. no. 15 (see comments in Chapter 4 on this title's identification); al-Jāḥiẓ: no. 531b; al-Nāshiᵓ al-Akbar (d. 293/906): no. 943; Mismaᶜī Zurqān (d. 278/891): no. 1329b; Jaᶜfar b. Ḥarb (d. 236/850): no. 759; al-Zamakhsharī (d. 538/1144): no. 1434; anti-Muᶜtazilite: no. 1318d.
39. Karāmīya: Fihrist al-Ashrafīya, Engl. tr. no. 1165b; Ḥunayn (d. 260/873): no. 93; *Aristotle's Letter*: no. 509; Maróth, *Aristotle and Alexander the Great*.
40. Sayings: Fihrist al-Ashrafīya, Engl. tr. no. 14b; Gems: nos. 289, 312, 1134, 1658; Signs: no. 382; Path: no. 1336; poetry: nos. 282, 617.
41. Imamate: Fihrist al-Ashrafīya, Engl. tr. no. 19; virtues: no. 936; legal decisions: no. 851; trustee: no. 1218b; final advice: nos. 1161b, 1382, 1384, 1663; poets: no. 618; killing: no. 931.
42. Zayn al-ᶜĀbidīn (d. 94/712?): Fihrist al-Ashrafīya, Engl. tr. nos. 154, 424, 438, 1136, 1200c; Jaᶜfar al-Ṣādiq (d. 148/765): nos. 321, 430, 433, 1269c; Muḥammad b. Zayn al-ᶜĀbidīn (d. *c.*117/735): no. 431. The eight remaining entries are: Fihrist al-Ashrafīya, Engl. tr. nos. 151, 1170c, 1198b, 1661 (Fatimid Caliph and Ismaᶜili imam al-Muᶜizz (r. 341–65/953–75)?), no. 182

(al-Shāfi[c]ī, d. 204/820), 1441 (al-Ṭabarānī, d. 360/971), 1164b (Ibn al-Jawzī, d. 597/1200), 1335 (al-Maqdisī, d. 600/1203).

43. Al-Jawharī (d. 401/1010–11): Fihrist al-Ashrafīya, Engl. tr. no. 751; *Gnomic*: no. 346; *Benefits*: no. 930; theology: no. 1320a.
44. Poetry: Fihrist al-Ashrafīya, Engl. tr. no. 1669; medicine: no. 511.
45. Jurisprudence: Fihrist al-Ashrafīya, Engl. tr. no. 237; poetry: nos. 394, 799b, 802, 1086.
46. Commentary: Fihrist al-Ashrafīya, Engl. tr. no. 713; Koran/*ḥadīth*: no. 790.
47. For confessional ambiguity see Woods, *Aqquyunlu*. Melvin-Koushki, *Occult Philosophy*, 73.
48. Melvin-Koushki, *Occult Philosophy*, 69–77.
49. The term '[c]Alid loyalism' was first used by Hodgson, *The Venture of Islam*, 2–446.
50. Talmon-Heller, *Islamic Piety*, 197.
51. Morimoto, 'Prophet's Family'.
52. Relics: Mouton, *Damas et sa principauté*, 341–5; Mouton, 'Quelques reliques'; Morimoto, 'How to Behave'; Mulder, *Shrines of the [c]Alids*.
53. Pfeiffer, 'Confessional Ambiguity vs. Confessional Polarization'.
54. As suggested by D. Talmon-Heller in her paper at the Jerusalem and the Crusades Conference, Jerusalem, 6–11 December 2014.
55. Ansari and Schmidtke, 'Al-Shaykh al-Ṭūsī'.
56. Schmidtke, 'Jewish Reception'; Schwarb, 'al-Tustarī's Kitāb al-Īmā[ᵓ]'.
57. Hillenbrand, 'Shī[c]īs of Aleppo'.
58. Touati, *L'armoire à sagesse*, 62–100.
59. On royal libraries and symbolic value see Touati, *L'armoire à sagesse*, especially 193–5.
60. Bauer, *Kultur der Ambiguität*.

4

The Ashrafīya Catalogue: Translation and Title Identification

This chapter presents the data contained in the Ashrafīya catalogue in a standardised form. The central challenge in preparing this list, and in working with medieval book lists and catalogues in general, is the identification of titles. In many cases this is a straightforward endeavour, as titles are given with a reasonable degree of detail and are sufficiently well known: an entry such as *Adab al-dīn wa-al-dunyā* (*On Conduct in Religious and Worldly Matters*) by al-Māwardī is unequivocal and requires no further research.[1] Easily identifiable titles are especially found whenever al-Anṣārī provides the author's name, which is the case for almost half of the catalogue's entries (965). In these cases modern reference and overview works such as the *Encyclopaedia of Islam*, Baghdādī's *Īḍāḥ al-maknūn*, Sezgin's *Geschichte des arabischen Schrifttums*, al-Kaḥḥāla's *Mu*ʿ*jam al-Mu*ʾ*allifin*, Brockelmann's *Geschichte der arabischen Litteratur* and al-Ziriklī's *al-A*ʿ*lām* are generally sufficient if combined with early modern bio-bibliographical works such as Ḥājjī Khalīfa's *Kashf al-ẓunūn* as well as subject-specific and author-specific works such as Ullmann's *Die Medizin im Islam*, Gutas's *Avicenna and the Aristotelian Tradition*, Pellat's *Nouvel essai d'inventaire de l'oeuvre Ǧāḥiẓienne* and Alwajī's *Mu*ʾ*allafāt Ibn al-Jawzī*. However, in many other cases the identification is far from straightforward and rather resembles, as quoted in the Introduction, a fiendish species of crossword. In these cases the information on the author is generally absent and the title given poses particular problems. From my experience of working with the Ashrafīya catalogue and other medieval book lists, the titles of these problematic cases broadly fall into four main categories: the generic title, the popular title, the 'book-in-the-making' title and the key word title.

The first category of generic titles includes entries such as *Multiple-Text Manuscript with Poems and Reports* (*Majmūᶜ ashᶜār wa-akhbār*), *Stories, Poems and Anecdotes* (*Akhbār wa-ashᶜār wa-nawādir*) and *Persian Correspondence* (*Tarassul ᶜajamī*).[2] In these cases an author is not given and it is simply impossible to exactly reconstitute what texts these entries contained. Most prayer books also belong to this category; they are often simply entitled *Prayers of Invocation* (*Adᶜiya*) without any further clue as to whom they are ascribed.[3] The generic 'title' is thus often interchangeable with, or at least similar to, a description of the entry's content. With these entries one generally hits the wall and in most cases they have to remain unidentified. While it is frustrating to have a substantial number of unidentifiable titles on the shelves, it is important to underline that al-Anṣārī himself was not able to provide more specific data on author or text for them. The absence of such data indicates in my view that these entries had no fixed textual form when the catalogue was composed, as many of them were arguably 'ad-hoc' anthologies. Such ad-hoc anthologies were compiled for a specific occasion or for personal use and brought together a writer's preferred prayers, poems, reports, anecdotes and so on. In contrast to works with unproblematic titles, these entries were thus not aimed at 'publishing' a book with a reasonably stable text.

Al-Anṣārī himself found these entries somewhat unsatisfying and it is for this reason that he especially – although not exclusively – provided information on the materiality of the manuscripts. He did so arguably in order to compensate for the lack of data on author and text and he also did so out of a very practical concern, that is to match such a generic title at a later point with the actual manuscript, be it for the purpose of lending out or revising the stock. His comments on the manuscripts' materiality consequently includes information on number of volumes or folia,[4] writing material (paper or parchment),[5] age,[6] layout,[7] format,[8] script,[9] and condition.[10] A second strategy to allow later identification, which we again find in particular for generic titles, was that he described the manuscript's content in greater detail.[11] Generic titles appear throughout the catalogue, but there are significantly fewer in the last section on incomplete manuscripts. This noteworthy absence is for three main reasons: generic titles seem to refer to short one-volume texts, so there was no danger of a volume being lost; if they were incomplete they were certainly prone to being discarded rather than preserved; and finally these works often had an ad-hoc quality and did not claim a clearly defined textual format so that missing folia were seemingly not seen as a major issue.

Problematic entries in the second category have specific non-generic titles making them in some ways the exact opposite of the generic title. However, these titles, such as *Kernels of Kernels* (*Lubāb al-lubāb*) and the *Merits of Jerusalem* (*Faḍāʾil al-Quds*), were popular and used by many medieval authors.[12] If al-Anṣārī does not provide the author's name after such a title – and he often does not – one simply has to list the various possibilities. For the *Merits of Jerusalem* entry, for instance, there are so many possibilities that it is impossible to make an informed guess as to which text is among the catalogue's entries. Nevertheless, occasionally it is possible to make a contextual argument on the basis of clues offered by the catalogue and/or on the basis of our knowledge of the literary culture in seventh-/thirteenth-century Damascus. A title such as *The Sound/Correct* (*al-Ṣiḥāḥ*), for example, can theoretically refer to a large number of works. Yet the cataloguer clearly assumes that it is known to library users and does not name the author.[13] Contemporaneous narrative sources show that there were two well-known books with this title in seventh-/thirteenth-century Damascus and one of them was the *ḥadīth* compendium *al-Ṣiḥāḥ* by Razīn b. Muʿāwiya al-ʿAbdarī.[14] However, the entry is in the catalogue's thematic category 4, which focuses on the philological sciences, especially grammar and lexicography, so it most likely refers to the second work, the famous lexicographical *al-Ṣiḥāḥ* by al-Jawharī.

The third problematic category constitutes entries that also have non-generic titles, but ones that cannot be found in any of the period's sources or in modern scholarship. In a number of cases this is surely nothing but an oversight on my part and identification may very well be possible. However, in many other cases the impossibility of identifying such titles is informative of the period's literary culture as they are what can be called 'books-in-the-making'. These are relatively recent texts that were in the process of becoming well-established books with a clearly defined textual format. Yet this crystallisation process was unsuccessful; they never gained popularity and the titles were quickly forgotten. In the other cases where this process was successful, by contrast, the books became stable and their 'books-in-the-making' status was soon forgotten. A typical book-in-the-making is a collection entitled *Selection of Poems of the Eloquent among the Arabs* compiled and written by al-Ḥasan b. ᶜAlī al-Juwaynī who has several comparable entries in the catalogue.[15] No such title is identifiable for this calligrapher so seemingly this work never became a stable book. Without the name of the compiler/writer – and in many other cases this information is not given in the catalogue – the identification of such a title would have remained highly speculative. While books-in-the-making pose a challenge to presenting the catalogue in a neat and standardised form, they are fascinating evidence for marginal titles, which would otherwise have remained unknown.

The final broad category of difficult identifications comprises entries with a key word title.[16] These come in a variety of forms in the catalogue and, as mentioned in Chapter 2, they may occasionally reflect the titles used on the books' edges.[17] The clearest way of altering a title is that al-Anṣārī chooses a title's key word and follows it with *fī* (*on*) and the subject matter. For instance, the cataloguer notes Ibn al-Muqaffaᶜ's famous mirror for princes *The Unique Pearl* (*al-Durra al-yatīma*) at one point as *The Unique on the Conduct of Kingship* (*al-Yatīma fī siyāsat al-mulk*).[18] It is evident that deciding on the key word was often ad hoc so that the very same mirror for princes can be referred to elsewhere in the catalogue as *The Pearl* (*al-Durra*).[19] The identification of such key word titles often heavily depends on contextual arguments. For instance, the *Elucidation on the Pulse and Urine* (*al-Tabṣira fī al-nabḍ wa-al-tafsira*) is a typical 'key word + *fī* + subject matter' entry, which is not found as such in contemporaneous or modern literature. However, the subject matter is clearly medical and the book is indeed in the catalogue's thematic category 10. It is thus most likely the medical work *al-Tabṣira* by the Fatimid court physician Manṣūr b. Sahlān. The link between the Ashrafiya library and the Fatimid library makes this identification very probable, especially since the book was used in contemporaneous teaching sessions in Damascus by a scholar who became the court physician at the city's Ayyubid court.[20]

Apart from these four categories the main challenge in identifying book titles is obviously the instability or flexibility of premodern titles. One and the same book can be referred to in different ways in the various documentary and narrative sources – and as seen this occurs also within the Ashrafīya catalogue itself: another example is the compendium of a Fatimid court musician, which is given at one point as *Ḥāwī al-funūn* (*The Comprehensive* [Book] *on the Arts*) and elsewhere as *Dhāt al-funūn* ([The Book] *Containing the Arts*).[21]

When encountering problematic entries, and the above four categories are just the most common forms, there are sometimes a wide variety of possible ascriptions. Here the early modern and modern works are not only of limited help, but can be rather misleading.[22] As shown in the above examples, such titles can only be identified with a reasonable degree of certainty with reference to the specific context in which the Ashrafīya catalogue was prepared in Damascus during the late Ayyubid and early Mamluk period. This context is the period's literary world, which is accessible via manuscript catalogues and contemporaneous narrative sources, especially biographical dictionaries, written in chronological and spatial proximity to the catalogue. These biographical dictionaries include most importantly two Damascene works, the *Wafayāt al-aᶜyān* by Ibn Khallikān from Damascus (who was contemporaneous to the catalogue, had very broad thematic interests and frequented the Ashrafīya library[23]) and the *ᶜUyūn al-anbāᵓ* by Ibn Abī Uṣaybiᶜa (who was again contemporaneous to the catalogue and was particularly interested in medicine and the sciences). Two further works of crucial importance come from northern Syria, namely the *Muᶜjam al-udabbāᵓ* by Yāqūt al-Ḥamawī (who died a decade or so before the library was endowed and who had a particular penchant for long lists of book titles) and the *Taᵓrīkh al-ḥukamāᵓ* by the vizier Ibn al-Qifṭī (who died a decade after the library had been endowed and was a notorious bibliomaniac).[24] Finally, two eighth-/fourteenth-century dictionaries, again from Damascus, proved to be of prime importance even though they were compiled some time after the catalogue was written: the *Taᵓrīkh al-Islām* by al-Dhahabī (who tends to include fewer book titles but has the advantage of drilling so deep that he included the most insignificant scholars of seventh-/thirteenth-century Damascus) and *al-Wāfī bi-al-wafayāt* by al-Ṣafadī (who had a unique knowledge of texts circulating in Damascus, including poetry and adab, and who frequented the Ashrafīya library as well).[25]

The usefulness of concentrating on texts written in close proximity to the Ashrafīya's setting is apparent, as argued in Chapter 1, when considering

The Precious Pearls (*al-Durr al-thamīn*) by the Baghdad librarian Ibn al-Sāʿī (d. 674/1275). It is exactly the kind of book that should have enhanced the identification of titles, as it is a contemporaneous list of book titles. Yet it proved to be a very poor source indeed and the main reason is, in my view, that its author lived and worked in Baghdad. Beyond doubt, manuscripts were often on the move, especially westwards from Baghdad when the city was in the process of losing its predominant cultural position in the course of the fifth/eleventh century. Yet the case of Ibn al-Sāʿī shows how provincial intellectual life could be. Another great moment for manuscript movement was that from Damascus to Cairo, when Damascus lost its central position in the intellectual life of the Arabic-speaking Middle East from the second half of the seventh/thirteenth century onwards. However, the cases of al-Dhahabī's and al-Ṣafadī's texts wonderfully show that things were again not that well connected: while their texts are indispensable to make sense of the Ashrafiya catalogue, the numerous works of their Egypt-focused contemporaries were of little help.

One source rarely used in the following, although it could have played a much more prominent role, is the Aleppo list. This 'inventory' from 694/1294 lists a selection of more than 900 titles in Aleppo's libraries and was edited by Paul Sbath in 1946 under the title *al-Muntakhab mimmā fī khazāʾin al-kutub bi-Ḥalab/Choix de livres qui se trouvaient dans les bibliothèques d'Alep (au XIIIe siècle)*. I have worked with this source for more than ten years, but I am growing increasingly suspicious as to its authenticity. Sbath gives precious little detail about the manuscript in his edition, only that he acquired it in 1939 in Cairo as part of a collection of 200 other manuscripts from Muṣṭafā al-Ḥalabī. He states that he would describe this manuscript, together with the other 200 manuscripts, 'dans le second Supplement de mon catalogue *al-Fihris*, que j'ai l'intention de publier prochainment' ('in the second Supplement to my catalogue *al-Fihris*, which I intend to publish soon'),[26] but it has never been published. The manuscript is neither in the *Sbath Collection* of the Vatican library nor is it traceable in the Salem foundation in Aleppo.[27]

The manuscript could simply be lost or misplaced, but there are several internal features in the text that seem somewhat odd. First, the work would be a real outlier in the literary production of Syria in the seventh/thirteenth and eighth/fourteenth centuries. Other authors who have written bibliographical works did so, as the above-mentioned titles show, in the framework of the bio-bibliographical 'genre'. If the Aleppo list did indeed exist it would have been a very remarkable piece and it is thus all the more astonishing that no contemporaneous text mentions it. Al-Ṣafadī, with his unique knowledge of the literary world in Damascus and Syria, may have at least slipped in a word. Second, the list is in many ways too good to be true and too neat to be medieval: the compiler lists all titles in alphabetical order – he never gets it wrong and, if necessary, follows the alphabetical order to the second or the third letter of the word. Almost every single title has an author and virtually all authors are identifiable and known. Better still the authors' names are always given with the same onomastic elements following the same standardised pattern: *kunya* + *ism* + *nasab* (preferably two or three generations back) + *nisba* (+ *shuhra*). Most impressively, if a given author has more than one entry his name is invariably given in exactly the same form throughout the list, so that the thirty-one entries for al-Jāḥiẓ all refer to 'Abū ᶜUthmān ᶜAmr b. Baḥr b. Maḥbūb al-maᶜrūf bi-Ibn Jāḥiẓ' – an indexer's dream. To me this all looks like a medieval proto-Carl Brockelmann composing a volume for his *Geschichte der arabischen Litteratur*. However, as the reader of the catalogue below, or the Kairouan catalogue-cum-inventory, will appreciate this does not even remotely look like a seventh-/thirteenth-century book list. Sbath may have 'corrected' and 'tidied' a list that was far messier in the original, but as he does not discuss the extent of his editorial intervention nor include a facsimile of at least one page this is impossible to assess.

Admittedly, the discussion so far has been highly speculative and certainly not by itself sufficient to discredit this list or to cast doubt on Sbath's scholarship. However, it seems that Sbath invented manuscripts in the *Fihris*, his three-volume catalogue of manuscripts, which he claimed to have seen mostly in private collections in Aleppo.[28] While no study on this question has been published, scholars working with the *Fihris* have repeatedly expressed their unease with his text in discussion fora. For instance, John Lamoreaux, Dedman College, argues that 'many of the manuscripts that [Sbath] claimed to have seen did not exist. Rather, he took citations of these manuscripts from a number of medieval works and pretended that he had seen them.'[29] In the same vein, Emilio Platti, Leuven University, states, 'I never came across any of these "Fihrist MSS". So, my conclusion is quite the same: we should forget about these MSS and not mention them any more.'[30] Taken together, the internal evidence from the *Muntakhab* and the doubt cast on his *Fihris* should be sufficient reason to only use Sbath's *Muntakhab* for the time being with utmost caution. While it is unlikely that Sbath invented titles ex nihilo it is far from certain that the manuscripts did indeed exist in seventh-/thirteenth-century libraries in Aleppo.

Even disregarding the Aleppo list we luckily still have sufficiently dense and rich Syrian material to contextualise the catalogue's entries. The above four problematic title categories have shown how tentative identification is in many cases and the comments on numerous entries in the below list reflect this. In order to illustrate the contextual information needed to identify titles in more detail, it is useful to turn to one example of a larger corpus of works, the panegyric poetry for al-Ashraf, which may at first glance seem straightforward. The authors of panegyric works are not generally given in the catalogue, which is not too surprising as al-Anṣārī could assume that they were well known. Furthermore, the catalogue lists them with definite titles implying that they were well-established and stable books. However, these titles are in most cases impossible to trace in any contemporaneous text and they are typical 'books-in-the-making'. They are found in large numbers in this library because of their link to the mausoleum's founder, but their transmission as identifiable books arguably came to an end shortly afterwards. In contrast to these titles, the poems themselves were not necessarily forgotten as a number of panegyrics for al-Ashraf can be found in various texts.

As the panegyric booklets mentioned in the catalogue have not survived (or at least it has not been possible to track them down), it is only possible to make tentative statements on the authorship of these pieces by considering the known panegyric poets of al-Ashraf. The poet who was most closely attached to al-Malik al-Ashraf was Ibn al-Nabīh who served the ruler as secretary during his northern Mesopotamian phase most presumably from 600/1204 onwards. The poetry in his diwan is mostly dedicated to al-Ashraf and contemporaneous chroniclers systematically quoted his panegyrics for al-Ashraf. Considering clues in the titles it is possible to attribute several entries in the catalogue to him with a reasonable degree of confidence.[31]

A number of further entries do not give specific clues and they may have been authored by Ibn al-Nabīh or one of the other poets connected to al-Malik al-Ashraf. Besides Ibn al-Nabīh there are six other known authors of Ashrafian panegyrics who are possible candidates for these entries. Chief among them is Ibn ᶜUnayn, although he was not on unproblematic terms with al-Ashraf. The ruler took one of his satires rather badly and ordered that the poet's tongue be cut off. While the poet escaped this ordeal he had to retire from public life. Despite this unglamorous end to his career, chroniclers cited the many panegyrics he had composed for al-Ashraf. A second poet who ran into trouble with al-Ashraf was al-Tallaᶜfarī, whose compulsive drinking and gambling habits made his position at the court increasingly untenable. However, before his fall into disgrace he composed panegyrics for the ruler and they may very well have made their way into the library. For the four other possible authors of these panegyric entries we have to move to the rather obscure side of literary life in Ayyubid Damascus. Ibn al-Ardakhl and Asᶜad al-Sinjārī were two minor poets and panegyrists who are at least represented in the library with clearly identifiable non-panegyric texts. Even more obscure are Sharaf al-Dīn Rājiḥ b. Ismāᶜīl al-Ḥillī whose panegyric pieces were cited by contemporaneous chroniclers and biographers, and the physician and poet Sadīd al-Dīn Maḥmūd Ibn Raqīqa, who was closely attached to al-Ashraf.[32]

Looking at this list of probable authors for the anonymous pieces, the strongest candidates are the three well-known poets Ibn al-Nabīh, Ibn ᶜUnayn or al-Tallaᶜfarī. This line of argument is rendered likely when we look at those three cases of panegyric poetry for al-Malik al-Ashraf where the authors were indeed named. In all three cases the individuals were minor figures who are difficult to trace in the contemporaneous sources. First we have an entry for *Ashrafiyan qaṣīdas* (*Qaṣīd Ashrafiya*) that is ascribed to Ibn (al-)Amsīnā (fl. 606/1209). This Iraqi author was an outsider to the Syrian literary scene and nothing is known about his career in Syria, but his name also appears as the author of *Ashrafiyan Epistles Alphabetically Organised* (*Rasāʾil Ashrafiya ᶜalā ḥurūf al-muᶜjam*).[33] The second entry, *Panegyrics on al-Ashraf*, is ascribed to a certain 'Ibn al-Māḍī', and no poet under this name is known. Most likely this work was authored by the scholar and literatus (*muʾaddib*) ᶜAbd Allāh Ibn Māḍī (d. 655/1257), a member of the Banū Māḍī who played a considerable role in the city as Hanbalite scholars.[34] The rather unusual origin of this piece is arguably due to the fact that the city's

Hanbalite circles looked upon the rule of al-Ashraf more favourably than that of his predecessor al-Muᶜaẓẓam.[35]

The third entry is simply called *Panegyrics* and it is ascribed to ᶜAlī b. ᶜUmar al-Yārūqī, who was a well-known panegyric of Ayyubid rulers. However, al-Yārūqī's diwan has no poems for al-Malik al-Ashraf, in contrast to his later poems for other Ayyubid rulers.[36] It is thus likely that al-Anṣārī felt the need to underline that these poems came from this rather unlikely poet. From the above examples it is thus evident that the cataloguer took care to identify pieces when he felt that their origin was too obscure for the users of the library. As he did not do so in the other cases it appears he was certain that they were sufficiently known to the users and they were thus most likely authored by one of the three prominent panegyric poets. The panegyric poems for al-Ashraf are obviously only a very small part of the overall collection, but they offer a good illustration of how the identifications offered in this chapter repeatedly depend on contextual arguments. Readers should be aware of this and should not necessarily take the (relative) neatness of the list below as one of rock-solid identifications.

The breaking-up of multiple-text manuscripts into distinct entries (a, b, c, and so forth) in the list below is unproblematic as long as they consist of clearly identifiable titles. However, these manuscripts repeatedly contain diverse material and al-Anṣārī described the content in generic terms, such as 'poems' and 'wise sayings' (*fawāʾid*). Such generic descriptions have in general not received a separate entry with a letter on its own, but are rather grouped together with the preceding or following identifiable title. However, if such general terms are further specified (e.g. 'Persian poetry') or fit a specific thematic category (e.g. prayers) they have received an entry on their own.

Plate 1 Tomb of al-Malik al-Ashraf (Damascus 1995). © Shihābī, *Mushayyadāt Dimashq*, 284

Plate 2 Library from al-Ḥarīrī, *Maqāmāt*, 634/1237. © Paris, BnF, MS arabe 5847, fol. 5b

Plate 3 Library from al-Ḥarīrī, *Maqāmāt*, first half 7th/13th century. © St Petersburg, Academy of Sciences, C. 23, fol. 13a

Plate 4 Library from al-Ḥarīrī, *Maqāmāt*, 654/1256? © The British Library Board, or. 1200, fol. 6b

Plate 5 Library from al-Ḥarīrī, *Maqāmāt*, second half 7th/13th century, Damascus. © The British Library Board, or. 9718, fol. 9

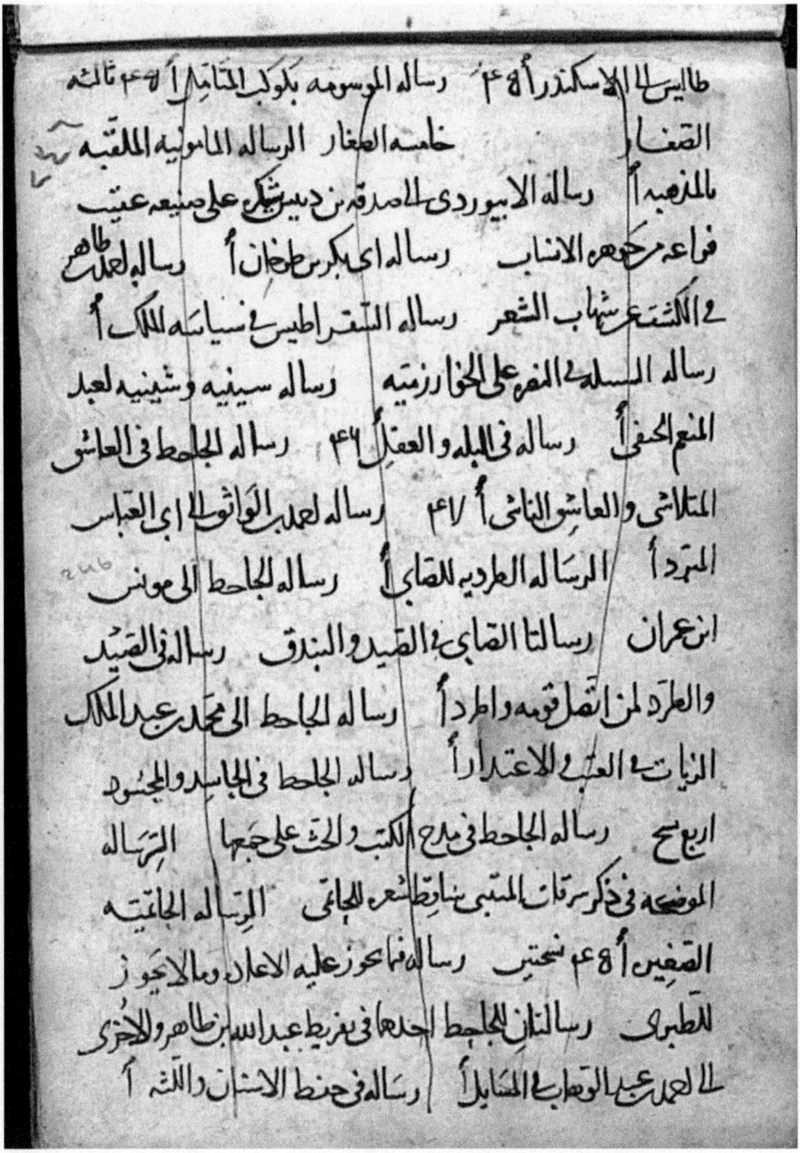

Plate 6 Ashrafiya catalogue (670s/1270s), fol. 246a. © Istanbul, Süleymaniye Yazma Eser Kütüphanesi, Fatih 5433

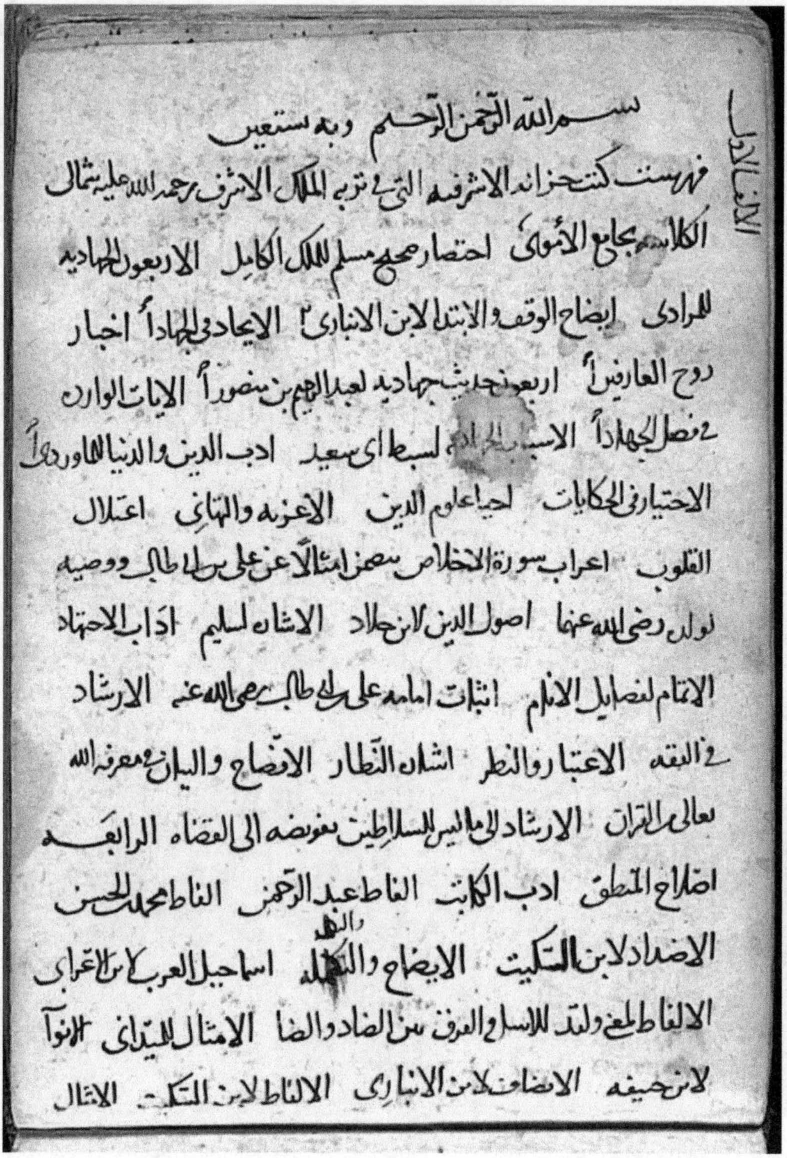

بسم الله الرحمن الرحيم وبه نستعين

فهرست كتب خزانة الاشرفية التي في تربة الملك الاشرف رحمه الله عليه بشمالي
الكلاسة بجامع الأموي اختصار صحيح مسلم للملك الكامل الاربعون الجهادية
للرادي ايضاح الوقف والابتدا لابن الانباري ٢ الايجاد في الجهاد ا اخبار
روح العارفين ا اربعون حديث جهادية لعبد الرحيم بن منصور ا الايات الواردة
في فضل الجهاد ا الاسباب [illegible] لسبط ابي سعيد ادب الدين والدنيا للماوردي ا
الاختيار في الحكايات احيا علوم الدين الاعزة والتهاني اعتلال
القلوب اعراب سورة الاخلاص [illegible] امثال الامام علي بن ابي طالب ووصية
لولده رضي الله عنهما اصول الدين لابن جلاد الاشارة لسليم اداب الاجتهاد
الاتمام لفضائل الانام اثبات امامة علي بن ابي طالب رضي الله عنه الارشاد
في الفقه الاعتبار والنظر اشارة النظار الايضاح والبيان في معرفة الله
تعالى من القران الارشاد الى ما ليس للسلاطين تفويضه الى القضاة الرابعة
اصلاح المنطق ادب الكاتب الفاظ عبد الرحمن الفاظ محمد بن الحسن
الاضداد لابن السكيت الايضاح والتكملة والذيل اساجيل العرب لابن الاعرابي
الالفاظ [illegible] للاسماع الفرق بين الضاد والظا الامثال للميداني الانواء
لابن حنيفة الانصاف لابن الانباري الالفاظ لابن السكيت الامثال

Plate 7 Ashrafīya catalogue (670s/1270s), fol. 246b. © Istanbul, Süleymaniye Yazma Eser Kütüphanesi, Fatih 5433

الامثال لحمزه   الامثال لابن عبيد   الامثال للمفضل   امثال الاصمعي

الانموذج في النحو   امثال حمزه الخامسه   الاوراق للصولي

الاستظهار امر القضاه وهو المستظهري   الاخبار الطوال لابي حنيفه

الملك

الدينوري   الاعمال لابن ماكولا   امثال امر المعظم ٤ ترجمه اخبار العجم ٥

نسخه ثانيه منه ٥ السادسه وهي الاولى من النسبه   اشعار فهم وعدوان ١

اشعار بني اسد بن خزيمه ١ نسخه ثانيه منه ١   الاعجاز ٣١ والايجاز ٣٩

نسخه ثانيه ٥٤ نسخه ثالثه نسخه رابعه ١٥   الاداب الذهبيه لابن للترا ١

اسم المفعول الثاني لابن جني ويعرف بالمعتصب ٩   اسما الاسل ورساله ابي العلا

وهي الاغريضيه ١   احال عوامل الاعراب لابن بري ١   الانوا لابن دريد ١

الابيات السائر مايه بخط ابن مقله ١   الاعيان والاماثل ١   ٤٣

السابع

الامتاع والمؤانسه ٣   ٤٣ الاذكيا لابن الجوزي ١   ٤٣ نسخه ثانيه

منه ١ ٤٤   الامثال والحكم للماوردي ١ ٣٨ نسخه ثانيه ١   ٤٤

نسخه ثالثه ١ ٤٤   اخبار وحكايات وامثال واشعار ١   اخبار

ابن حجاج ٩ نسخه ثانيه منه مصون في ٩   اجناس الاعداد والاخبار ١

ادبا الغربا ١٤٥   اختيارات ابن العميد من كتب الجاحظ ١٥ ٤ الثامن

اداب الملوك ١   ٤١ اخلاق الملوك ١   ٣٩   اختيار الوزرا ٤

Plate 8 Ashrafiya catalogue (670s/1270s), fol. 247a. © Istanbul, Süleymaniye Yazma Eser Kütüphanesi, Fatih 5433

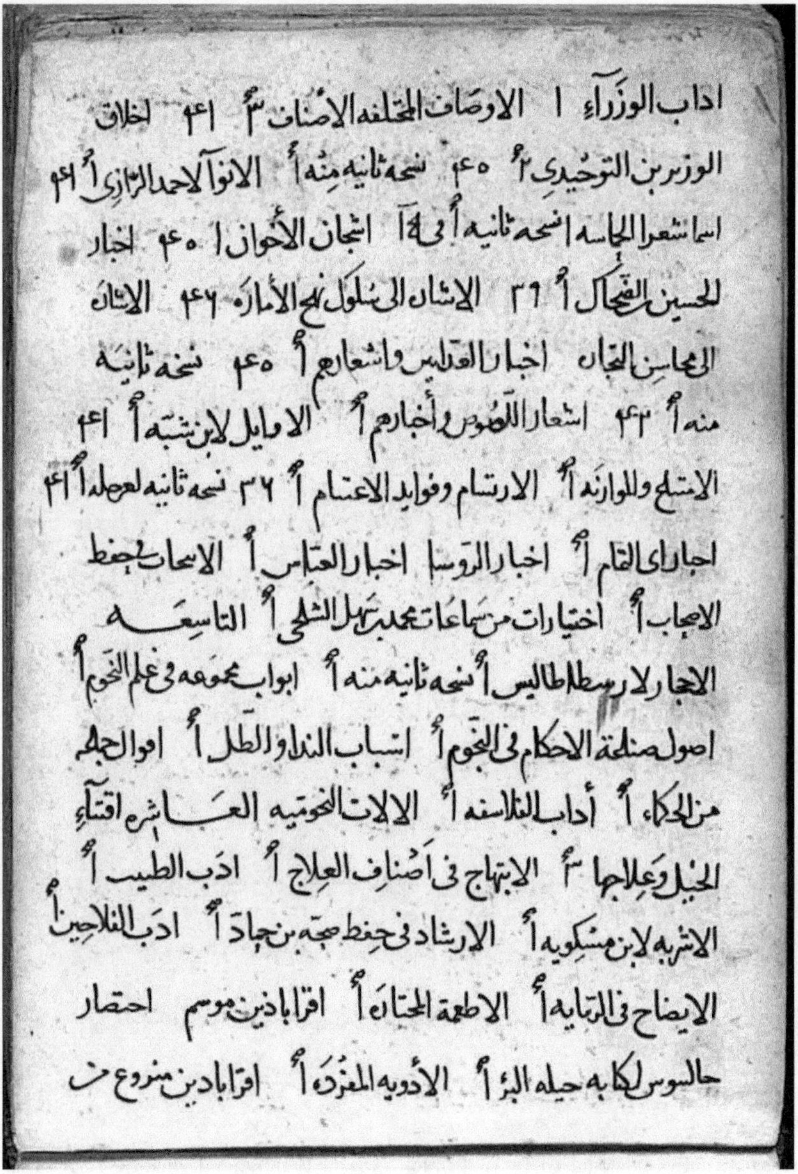

اداب الوزراء ١ الاوصاف المختلفه الاصناف ٣ ٤١ اخلاق

الوزير بن التوحيدي ٢ ٤٥ نسخه ثانيه منه ١ الانوا لاحمد الرازي ١ ٤١

اسما شعرا الحماسه ١ نسخه ثانيه ١ في ١ اشجان الاخوان ١ ٤٥ اخبار

الحسين الضحاك ١ ٣٦ الاشاره الى سلوك نهج الاماره ٤٦ الاشاره

الى محاسن الحجاب اخبار العدليس واشعارهم ١ ٤٥ نسخه ثانيه

منه ١ ٤٣ اشعار اللصوص واخبارهم ١ الاوايل لابن شبه ١ ٤١

الاسجاع والموازنه ١ الارتسام وفوايد الاغتنام ١ ٣٦ نسخه ثانيه لعرجله ١ ٤١

اخبار اهل القام ١ اخبار الروسا اخبار العباس ١ الاسعاف في حفظ

الاصحاب ١ اختيارات من ساعات محمد بن سهل الشلحي ١ التاسعه

الاحجار لارسطاطاليس ١ نسخه ثانيه منه ١ ابواب مجموعه في علم النجوم ١

اصول صناعة الاحكام في النجوم ١ اسباب الندا والطل ١ احوال الجم

من الحكماء ١ اداب الفلاسفه ١ الالات النجوميه العاشر اقتناء

الخيل وعلاجها ٣ الابتهاج في اصناف العلاج ١ ادب الطبيب ١

الاشربه لابن مسكويه ١ الارشاد في حفظ صحه بن جاد ١ ادب الفلاحين ١

الايضاح في الرمايه ١ الاطعمة الخيانه ١ اقراباذين موسى اختصار

جالينوس لكتابه حيله البر ١ الادويه المفرده ١ اقراباذين منروع

Plate 9 Ashrafiya catalogue (670s/1270s), fol. 247b.

من علق اقراباذينات ١ اقراباذين سابور ١ الاغذية لابن زهر ١
اظهار حكمة الرحمن في خلق الانسان وغيره ١ ابدال الادويه المفرده
والمركبه ١ الاكليل للرازي ١ اقراباذين يوحنا ١ الثانية عشره
اشعار الهذليين ٥ نسخه ثانيه منه ١١ الاغاني لابن الغنسيري ١
الثانيه دستور معالم الحكم ١ الدعا الحاملي ١ درر
السادسة وهي اول الثانيه الدريديه منكبة ١ نسخه اخرى وعالبق وفوايد
بخط ابن العصار ١ الثامنه دميه القصر ١ ٣٩ نسخه اخرى
الديارات للاصفهاني ١ التحبس ٣٨ نسخه ثانيه منه ١ ٥٠ التاسعه
الدلايل لابن البهلول ١ الحاديه عشره ٤٣ ديوان البحتري ١ نسخه
ثانيه ٢ الرجال المدعليس ١ موجز الازجال ١٢٤ الثالثة عشر مقلم
اشعار دوبيتي ١٢٤ اشعار دوبيتي ١٢٤ اشعار السته ١ الاعراض
في دار الاعراض ١ اشعار السته ١ اشعار واخبار جمع الثعالبي وبخطه
الخامسه عشر اخبار مجنون ليلى والشعراء ١ الاعجاز في الاحاجي
والالغاز ١ ازهار الانهار ٣ الآداب لابن شمس الخلافة ٣٨١ نسخه
ثانيه منه ١ اخبار الخاسه لابي رياش ١ ٤٦ آداب الملوك والعلما النجاح
اخبار ابي نواس ١ ٤٢ اخبار العذابين وسعاة العرب ١ اخبار
اللصوص احسن ما قيل في البلاغة ١ اجناس في التجنيس والمنهج للثعالبي ١

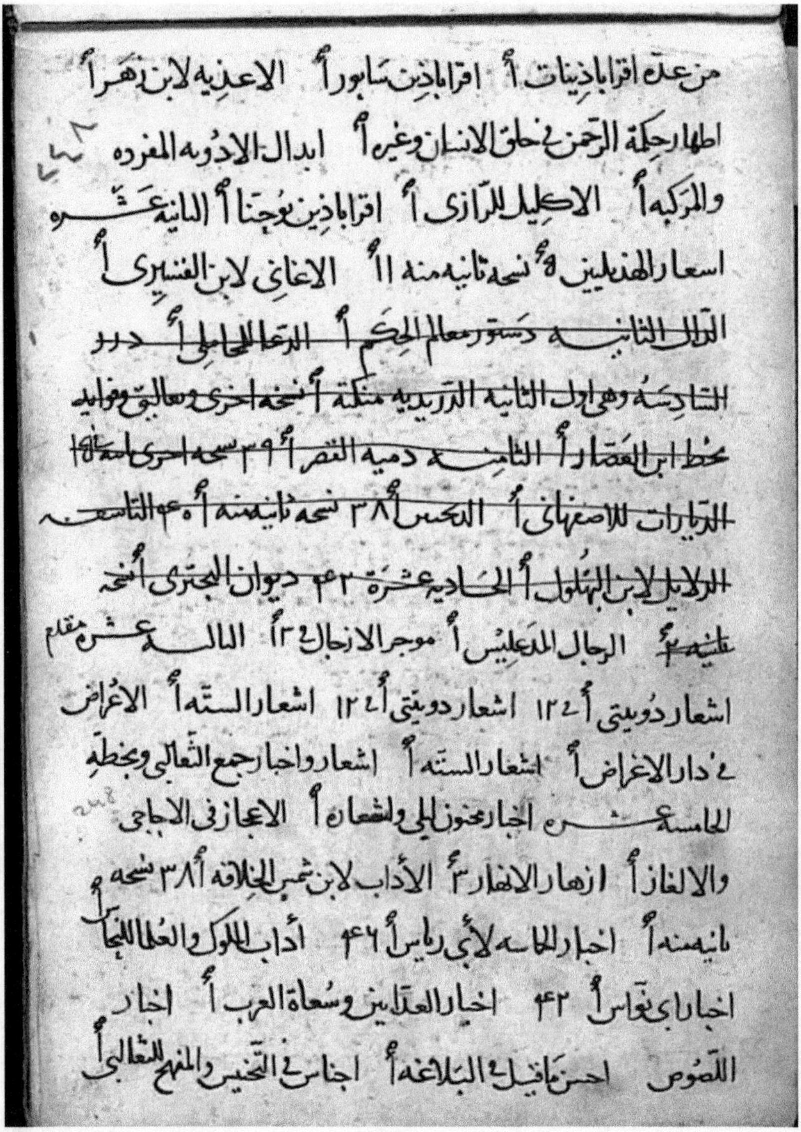

Plate 10 Ashrafiya catalogue (670s/1270s), fol. 248a. © Istanbul, Süleymaniye Yazma Eser Kütüphanesi, Fatih 5433

أدب للطالع ا ٤٥ افراد المعاني ا الات الرياسه ا أخبار
عبد الله بن جعفر ا اخبار واشعار ونوادر ا انيس الامير وجليس
الوزير ا ٤٢ أجزا حديث ا اول الصغار اشعار بني سعد بن
موعد ا ثالثه اشعار واخبار ونوادر بخط الجويني ا أختيارات
من كلام الحكماء بخط منوجهر ا اشعار في اهل البيت واخبار مستحسنه ا
اشعار وفقر منتخبه ا ٤٧ أخبار البحتري ا ٤٧ اسباب العز
الطاهر ا ٤٦ اشعار واخبار وفقر ا الالفاظ المقتضبات والكلمات
المهذبات ا رابعة الصغار اسما الله الحسنى ا أدعيه الايام
السبعه أدعيه شهيه ا ادعيه عن النبي صلى الله عليه وسلم خط ابن
ريش ا ادعيه ومناجاه علي بن الحسين ا ادعيه ماثوره ا ادعيه خط
ابن صدقه ا ادعيه النصر والاحتراس ا ادعيه شهيه مجربه لقضاء
الحوايج ا ادعيه شريفه مجربه عن السلف الصالح ا ادعيه بخط منسوب ا
ادعيه نثر ونظم ا ادعيه بخط كوفي ا ادعيه بخط كوفي ا ادعيه بخط
كوفي ا ادعيه مكتوبه باحمر واصفر واسود ردي ا ادعيه مباركه ا
ادعيه مباركه بخط منسوب ا ادعيه مباركه عن النبي صلى عليه وسلم بخط
ابن ريش ا ادعيه ماثوره كبيرة القطع ا الاصابه في الدعوات المستجابه ا
أدعيه مباركه ماثوره مرويه عن السلف ا أدعيه عن النبي عليه السلام
ادعيه منقوله من خط ابن البواب ا ادعيه بخط المراكشي أدعيه

Plate 11 Ashrafiya catalogue (670s/1270s), fol. 248b. © Istanbul, Süleymaniye Yazma Eser Kütüphanesi, Fatih 5433

ادعيه اوله ما جاء في فضل الدعوات ادعيه الوسايل الى المسايل أ

ادعيه هو دعاه يوم الاحزاب أ ادعيه مختار بخط سنجر أ ادعيه

شهيه ورش عن اهل البيت ادعيه عن السلف ٥ ادعيه مستجابه

عن النبي عليه السلام أ ادعيه عن الامام الشافعي رحمه الله أ اسما الناس

واسم أ ادعيه بخط المراكشي ادعيه مرويه عن النبي عليه السلم أ

خامسة الصغار اخبار وانشادات بخط عبد السلام البصري ٩١

اشعار في الجواد أ قصه دلة المحتاله أ اشعار وعظيه لابي العتاهيه أ

الالفاظ النحويه والمدايح الاشرفيه أ اغاني جر أ السادسه

الفاظ فائقه وكلمات رايقه في الرسايل أ السابعه الادويه

المفرده الباب الاول بستان المبتدي في القراات أ البعث لابن

الاشعث والمايه الشرحيه أ الثانيه بهجة المجالس لابن عبد البر ٢ بهجة

الاسرار مجهول المصنف أ بهجة الاسرار لابن جهضم خط ابن الشوا ٥ بدايه

الهدايه أ نسخه اخرى أ بستان العارفين أ الثالثه البحر الحاوي

لجوهر الفتاوي الخامسه البرق الشامي ٦ السادسه وهي اولي الثانيه

البساله اختيار ثعلب أ ٥ ٤ع الثامنه البصاير والذخاير التوحيدي

التاسعه البيان والتبيين ٤ع البشان والنداف أ البستان

وسع ١٧ ٣ بشورع دسا في الاثار العلويه أ العاشر

Plate 12 Ashrafiya catalogue (670s/1270s), fol. 249a. © Istanbul, Süleymaniye Yazma Eser Kütüphanesi, Fatih 5433

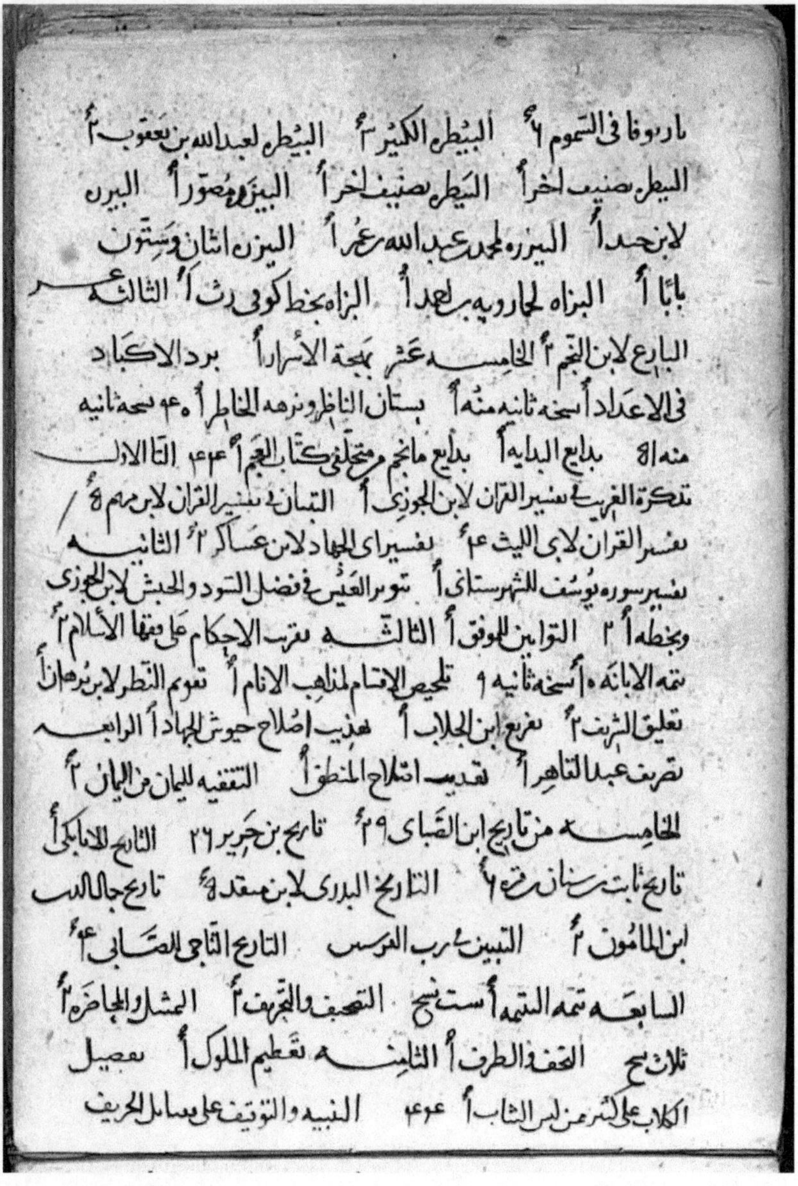

بادربوقا في السموم ٦ البيطرة الكبير ٣ البيطرة لعبد الله بن يعقوب ٢
البيطرة تصنيف اخر ١ البيطرة تصنيف اخر ١ البيزرة مصور ١ البيزرة
لابن حمدان ١ البيزرة لمحمد عبد الله بن عمر ١ البيزرة اثنان وستون
بابا ١ البزاة لجارويه بن عبد ١ البزاة بخط كوري رث ١ الثالث عشر
البارع لابن النجم ٢ الخامسة عشر بهجة الاسرار ١ برد الاكباد
في الاعداد ١ نسخة ثانية منه ١ بستان الناظر ونزهة الخاطر ١ ٥ ٤ نسخة ثانية
منه ١ بدايع البداية ١ بدايع ما نجم من تحلي كتاب العجم ١ ٤٣٤ التا الاول
تذكرة الغريب في تفسير القران لابن الجوزي ١ التبيان في تفسير القران لابن مهم ٤
تفسير القران لابي الليث ٤ تفسير اي الجهاد لابن عساكر ٢ الثانية
تفسير سورة يوسف للشهرستاني ١ تنوير الغبش في فضل السود والحبش لابن الجوزي
وبخطه ١ ٢ التوابين للموفق ١ الثالثة تقريب الاحكام على فقها الاسلام ٢
تتمة الابانة ٥ نسخة ثانية ٩ تلخيص الاقسام لمذاهب الانام ١ تقويم النظر لابن برهان ١
تعليق الشريف ٢ تفريع ابن الجلاب ١ تهذيب اصلاح جيوش الجهاد ١ الرابعة
تصريف عبد القاهر ١ تهذيب اصلاح المنطق ١ التقفية لليمان بن اليمان ٢
الخامسة من تاريخ ابن الصابي ٢٩ تاريخ ابن جرير ٢٦ التاريخ الاتابكي ١
تاريخ ثابت بن سنان ٦ التاريخ البلدي لابن مسعدة ٤ تاريخ جمال الدين
ابن المامون ٢ التبيين في رب العرش التاريخ التاجي للصابي ٤ ٤
السابعة تتمة التتمة ١ ست نسخ التصحيف والتحريف ٢ المثل والمحاضرة ٢
ثلاث نسخ التحف والطرف ١ الثامنة تعظيم الملوك ١ تفضيل
الكلاب على كثير ممن لبس الثياب ١ ٤ ٤ التنبيه والتوقيف على مسائل الحريف

Plate 13 Ashrafiya catalogue (670s/1270s), fol. 249b. © Istanbul, Süleymaniye Yazma Eser Kütüphanesi, Fatih 5433

التاسعه تقويم سنه خمس وعشرين وستمايه ا تحفه الملوك في التعبير ا تعبير
الرويا لعبد الواحد ا تعبير الرويا عن ابن سيرين ا تحويل المواليد وغيره ا
تركيب العود والعمل به ا العاشر التبصر في السحر والنشر ا التدارك لانواع
خطا التدبير ا التذكره الاشرفيه ا تقويم الصحه لاحد عشر نسخه تقويم الابدان
اربع نسخ التبصر في معرفه الجواهر ا الترياق الكبير خمس نسخ ترياق برشعثا ا
الثاني لشفا الامراض ا تدبير الصحه لحنين ا نسخه ثانيه ا تذكره الكحالين ا المختصر
لعلي بن عبد الله ا تقاسيم العلل وعلاجها ا تقاسيم مسايل حنين ا تفسير
اسنان الدواب ا الخامسه عشر توقيعات كسرى انوشروان ا ثالثه
الصفار تحفه الظرفا في تاريخ الخلفا ومعه تفضيل الاعشى وتذكره في القاف
رابعه تحفه العباد في بيان الاوراد ا ترجمه الناموس عن علي بن ابي طالب
رضي الله عنه ا تحفه الاديب وحليه الاريب ا ربع خامسه التوحيد
250 عن الايمه ا سادسه التسبات والطلب ا تنزيل الحصكفي ا سابعه
تدبير المسافرين وتنبيه المحلل لصحتي الابدان والاديان ا الثا الثالث عشر
الشا المشرقي بصفات الملك الاشرف ٢ الجيم الثانيه جواهر الكلام عن
علي بن ابي طالب كرم الله وجهه ا جواهر القران للغزالي ا الثالثه جامع شرايط
الاحكام ا الرابعه جمهره الامثال للعسكري ا جمل عبد القاهر ا
جمل الزجاجي ا الخامسه الجمع والبيان في اخبار القيروان ٢ السادسه
جزو حديث بخط ابن الجواليقي ا جزء اخر بخطه ايضا ا الجمان لابن فارس وبخطه ا

Plate 14 Ashrafiya catalogue (670s/1270s), fol. 250a. © Istanbul, Süleymaniye Yazma Eser Kütüphanesi, Fatih 5433

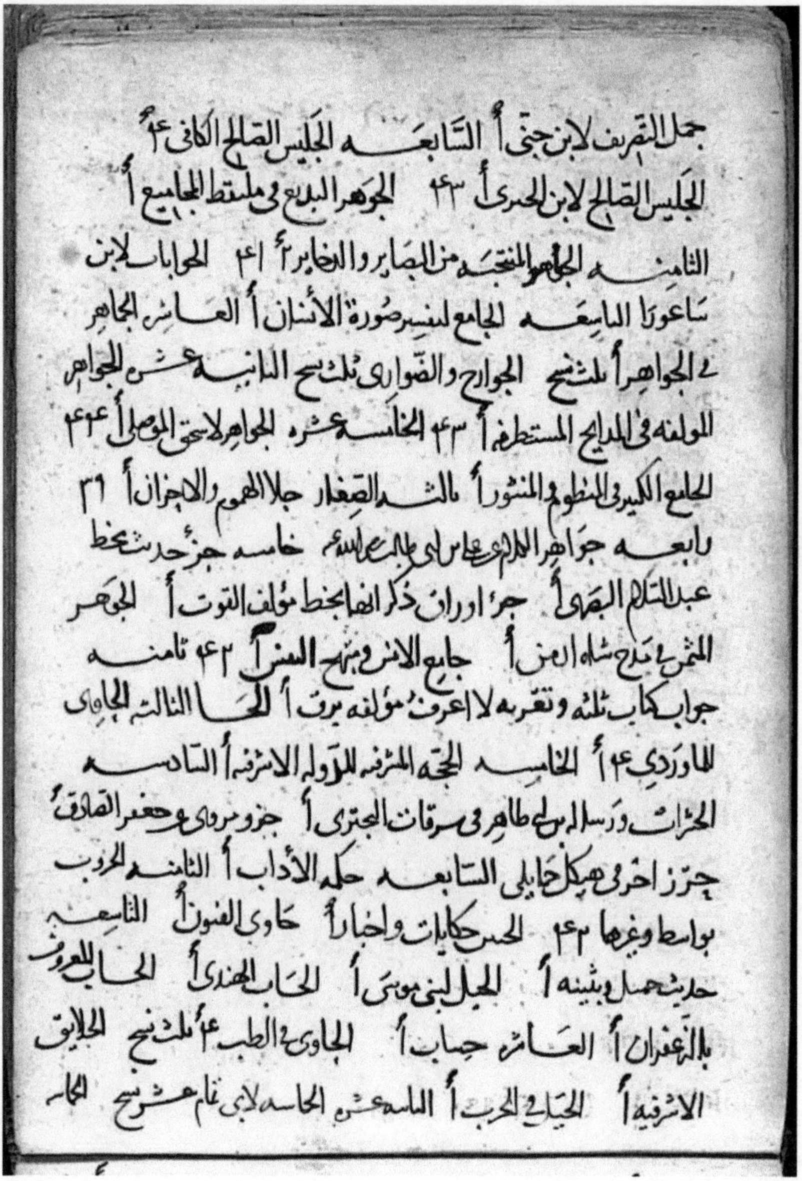

Plate 15 Ashrafiya catalogue (670s/1270s), fol. 250b. © Istanbul, Süleymaniye Yazma Eser Kütüphanesi, Fatih 5433

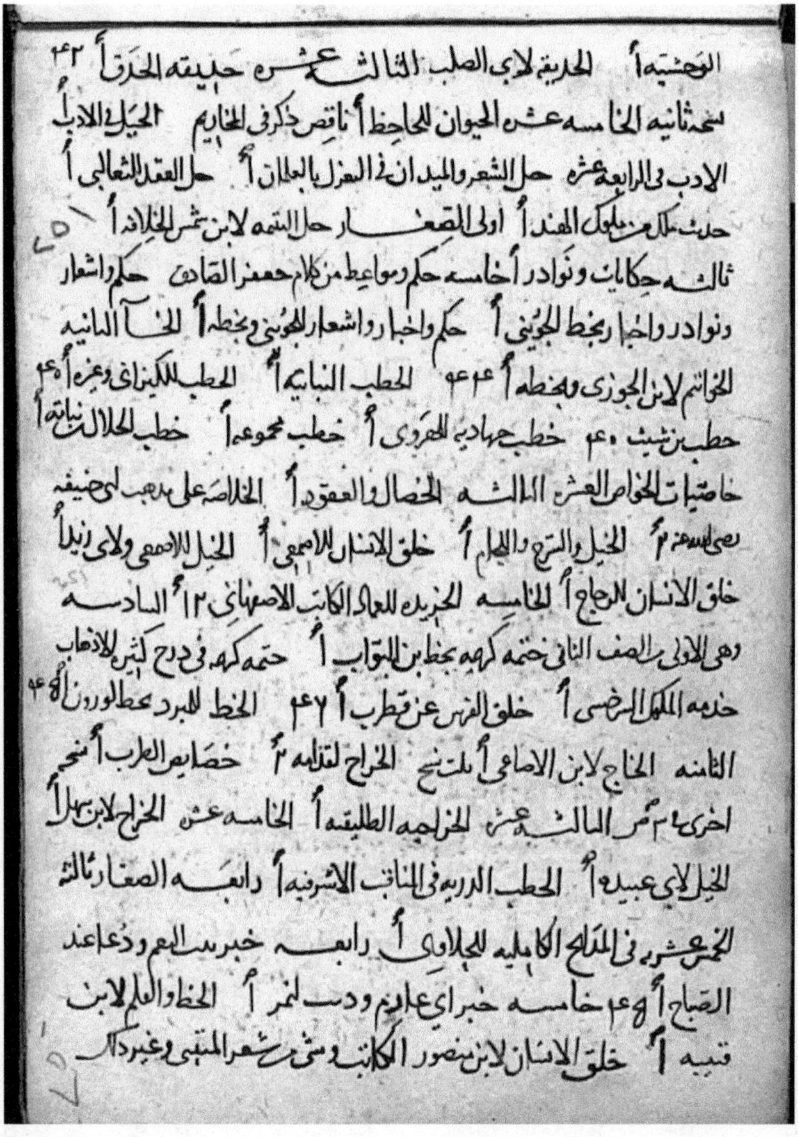

Plate 16 Ashrafiya catalogue (670s/1270s), fol. 251a. © Istanbul, Süleymaniye Yazma Eser Kütüphanesi, Fatih 5433

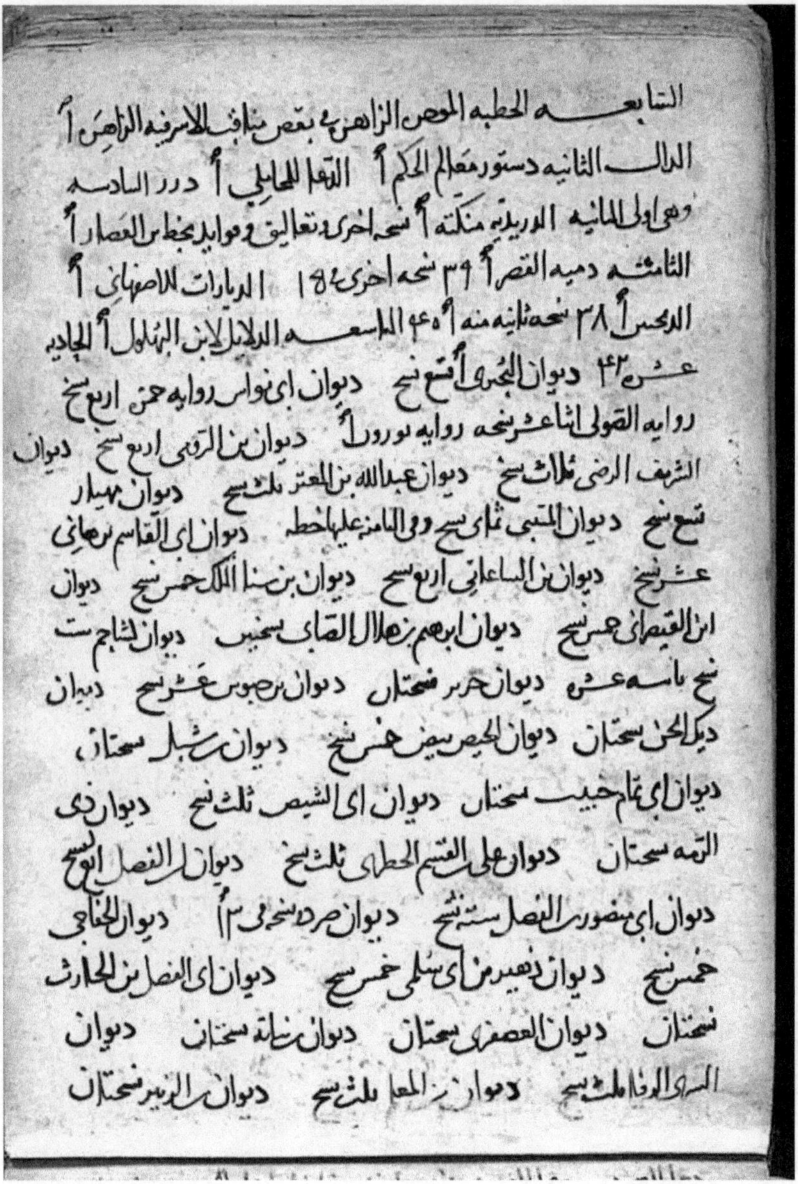

السابعه الخطبه الموصل الزاهر في بعض مناقب الاشرفيه الزاهره ا
الدالـــ الثانيه دستور معالم الحكم ا اللقعه الحائلي ا درر السادسه
وهي اولى الثانيه الوريديه منكته ا نسخه اخرى وتعاليق وفوايد بخط بن العصار ا
الثامنه دميه القصر ا ٣٩ نسخه اخرى ١٨٤ الزيارات للاصبهاني ا
الدبجس ا ٣٨ نسخه ثانيه منه ا ٤٠٥ التاسعه الدلايل لابن البهلول ا الحاديه
عشر ٤٢ ديوان البحتري اربع نسخ ديوان ابي نواس روايه حمزه اربع نسخ
روايه الصولي اثنا عشر نسخه روايه توزون ا ديوان بن الرومي اربع نسخ ديوان
الشريف الرضي ثلاث نسخ ديوان عبد الله بن المعتز ثلث نسخ ديوان مهيار
تسع نسخ ديوان المتنبي ثماني نسخ وفي الثامنه عليها خطه ديوان ابي القاسم بن هاني
عشر نسخ ديوان بن الساعاتي اربع نسخ ديوان بن سنا الملك خمس نسخ ديوان
ابن القيسراني خمس نسخ ديوان ابرهيم بن هلال الصابي نسختين ديوان كشاجم ست
نسخ باسه عشره ديوان جرير نسختان ديوان بن حيوس عشر نسخ ديوان
ديك الجن نسختان ديوان الحيص بيص خمس نسخ ديوان بن شبل نسختان
ديوان ابي تمام حبيب نسختان ديوان ابي الشيص ثلث نسخ ديوان ذي
الرمه نسختان ديوان علي بن العسم الخطاي ثلث نسخ ديوان ابن الفضل الوبج نسخ
ديوان ابي منصور بن الفضل سته نسخ ديوان صرده نسخ في ٣ ا ديوان الخفاجي
خمس نسخ ديوان زهير بن ابي سلمى خمس نسخ ديوان ابي الفضل بن الحارث
نسختان ديوان العصري نسختان ديوان بن نباتة نسختان ديوان
السري الرفا ثلث نسخ ديوان بن المعلم ثلث نسخ ديوان بن الزبير نسختان

Plate 17 Ashrafiya catalogue (670s/1270s), fol. 251b. © Istanbul, Süleymaniye Yazma Eser Kütüphanesi, Fatih 5433

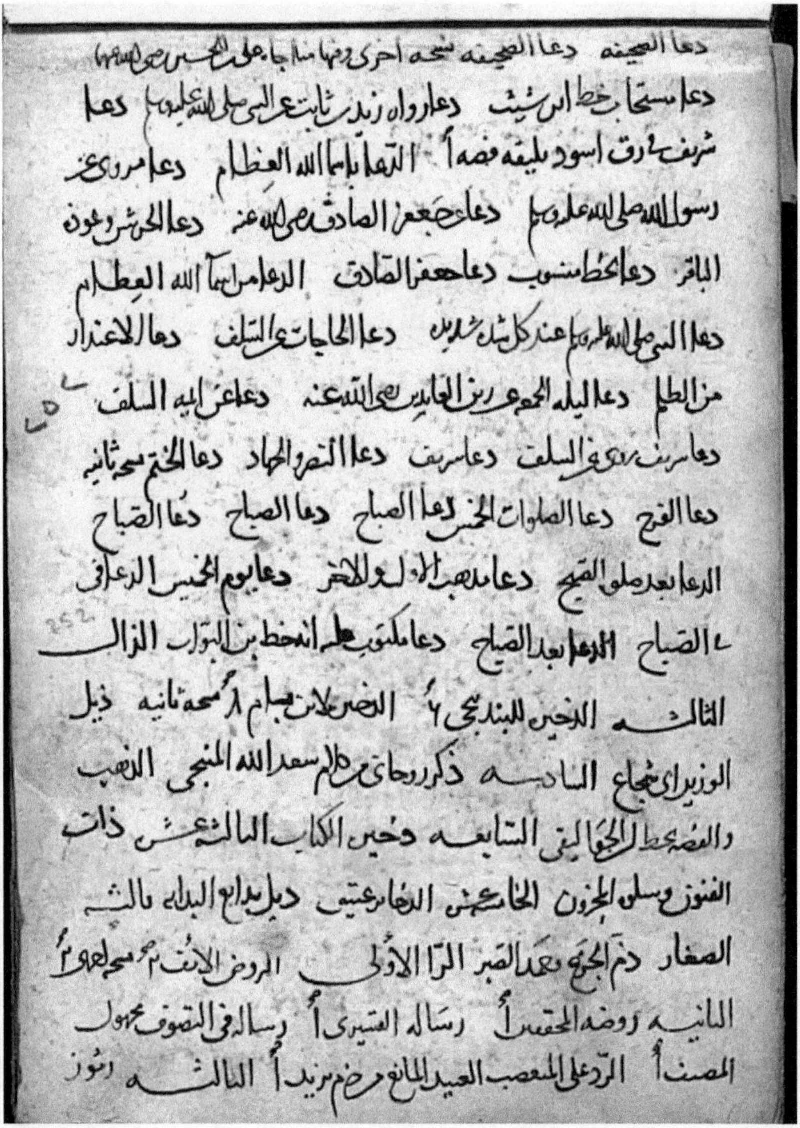

دعا الصحيفه دعا الصحيفه نسخه اخرى وفيها مناجاه على بن الحسين صلى الله عليه
دعا مستجاب خط ابن شيث دعا رواه زيد بن ثابت عن النبي صلى الله عليه وسلم دعا
شريف في رق اسود بليقه فضه أ اللهم انا باسما الله العظام دعا مروي عن
رسول الله صلى الله عليه وسلم دعا جعفر الصادق رضي الله عنه دعا الحرش وعوذ
الباقر دعا بخط منسوب دعا جعفر الصادق الدعا من اسما الله العظام
دعا النبي صلى الله عليه وسلم عند كل شدة شديدة دعا الحاجات عن السلف دعا الاعتذار
من الظلم دعا ليله الجمعه عن زين العابدين رضي الله عنه دعا عن ابيه السلف
دعا شريف روي عن السلف دعا شريف دعا النصر والجهاد دعا الختم نسخه ثانيه
دعا الفرج دعا الصلوات الخمس دعا الصباح دعا الصباح دعا الصباح
الدعا بعد صلوة الصبح دعا مذهب الاول والاخر دعا يوم الخميس الدعا في
الصباح الدعا بعد الصباح دعا مكتوب على انه خط ابن البواب الزال
252
الثالث الدخيره للبندنيجي ٦ الدخيره لابن بسام ٨ نسخه ثانيه ذيل
الوزير ابي شجاع السادس ذكر روحاني من كلام سعد الله المنجي الذهب
والفضه بخط الجواليقي السابعه دخيره الكتاب الثالث عشر ذات
الفنون وسلوه المحزون الخامس عشر الدخائر عتيقه ذيل بدايع البدايه الثالث
الصغار ذم الجزع وحمد الصبر الرا الاولى الروض الانق ٣ نسخه لعون ٢
الثانيه روضه المحتسب أ رساله القشيري أ رساله في التصوف مجهول
المصنف أ الرد على المتعصب العنيد المانع من ذم يزيد أ الثالثه رموز

Plate 18 Ashrafiya catalogue (670s/1270s), fol. 252a.

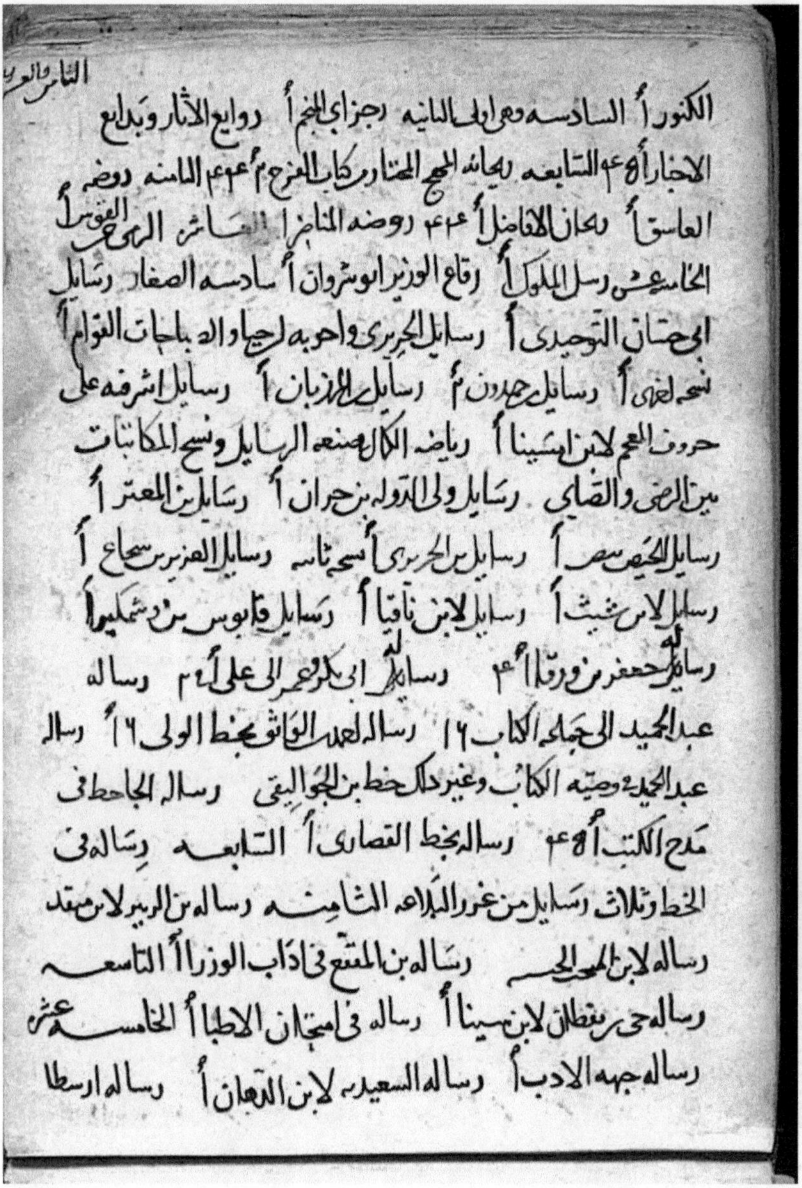

Plate 19 Ashrafiya catalogue (670s/1270s), fol. 252b. © Istanbul, Süleymaniye Yazma Eser Kütüphanesi, Fatih 5433

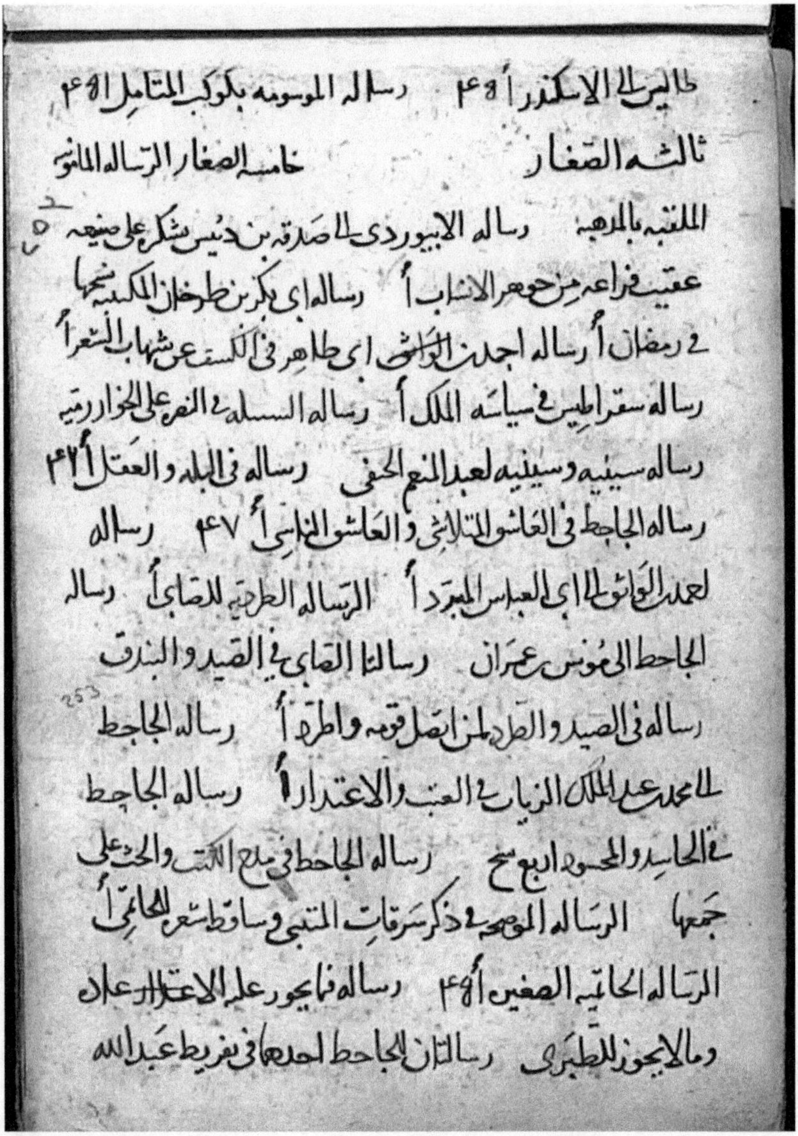

طالبين الى الاسكندر ١ ٤٨ رساله الموسومه بكوكب المتامل ١ ٤٨
ثالثه الصغار خامسه الصغار الرساله الملوسه
الملقبه بالمذهبه رساله الابيوردي الى صدقه بن دبيس شكر على صنيعه
عقيب قراءه من جوهر الانساب ١ رساله ابي بكر بن طرخان المكتبه شيخها
في رمضان ١ رساله احمد بن الواثق ابي طاهر في الكشف عن شهاب الشعرا ١
رساله سقراطيس في سياسه الملك ١ رساله السلسله في النفر على الخوارزميه
رساله سينيه وسينيه لعبد المنعم الحنفي رساله في البله والعقل ١ ٤٢
رساله الجاحظ في العاشق المتلاشي والعاشق الناسي ١ ٤٧ رساله
لاحمد بن الواثق الى ابي العباس المبرد ١ الرساله الطرديه للصابي ١ رساله
الجاحظ الى موسى بن عمران رساله الصابي في الصيد والبندق
رساله في الصيد والطرد لمن اتصل قومه واطرد ١ رساله الجاحظ
الى محمد بن عبد الملك الزيات في العتب والاعتذار ١ رساله الجاحظ
في الحاسد والمحسود اربع نسخ رساله الجاحظ في مدح الكتب والحث على
جمعها الرساله الموضحه في ذكر سرقات المتنبي وساقط شعره للحاتمي ١
الرساله الحاتميه الصغير ١ ٤٨ رساله فيما يجوز على الاعتلال ... وما لا يجوز للطبري رسالتان للجاحظ احدهما في تقريظ عبد الله

Plate 20 Ashrafiya catalogue (670s/1270s), fol. 253a. © Istanbul, Süleymaniye Yazma Eser Kütüphanesi, Fatih 5433

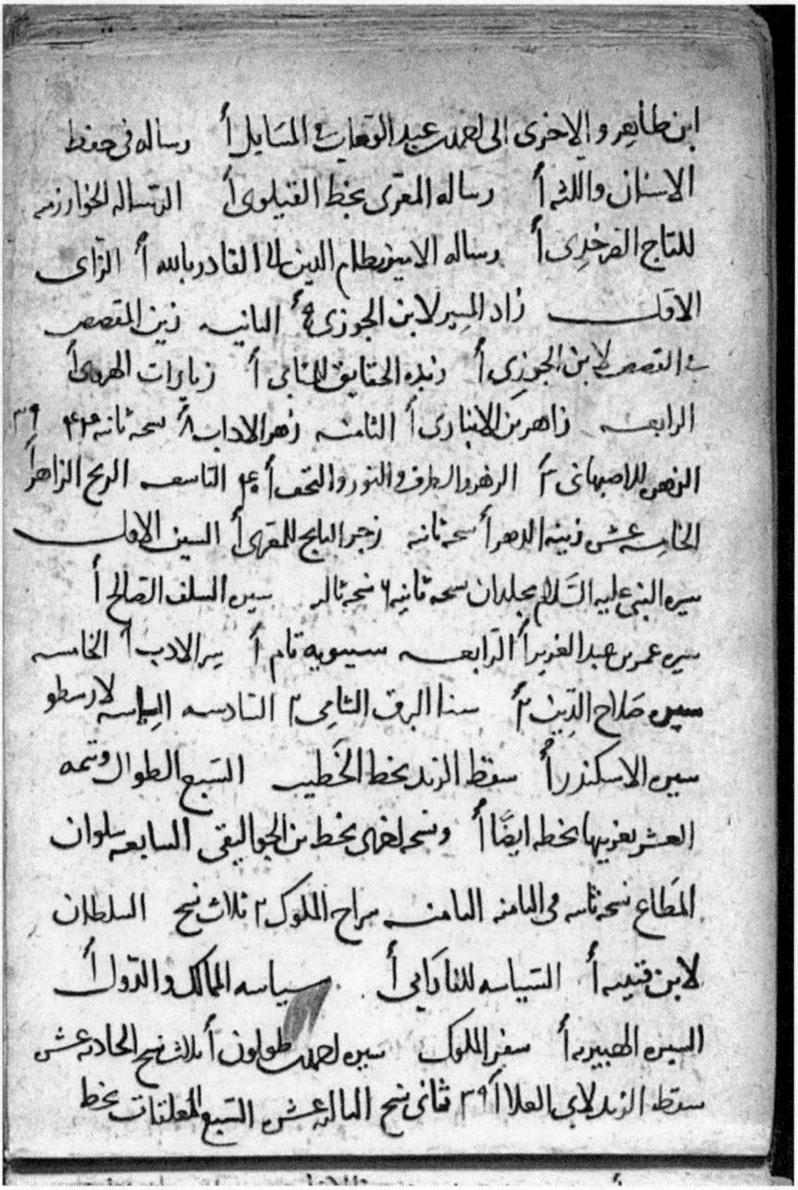

ابن طاهر والاخرى الى ابن عبد الوهاب في المسايل أ رساله في حفظ
اللسان واللثة أ رساله المعري بخط القيلوي أ الرساله الخوارزميه
للتاج الزمخشري أ رساله الامير بطلب الدين الى القادر بالله أ الزاي
الاول زاد المسير لابن الجوزي ٤ الثاني زين القصص
في القصص لابن الجوزي أ زبدة الحقايق للثاني أ زيارات الهروي
الرابع زاهر بن الانباري أ الثامن زهر الاداب ٨ نسخه ثانيه ٤٢ ٣٩ أ
الزهر للاصبهاني ٢ الزهر والطرف والنور والتحف أ التاسع الروح الزاهر أ
الحادي عشر زينة الدهر أ نسخه ثانيه زجر النابح للمعري أ السين الاول
سيره النبي عليه السلام لابن علان نسخه ثانيه نسخه ثالثه سير السلف الصالح أ
سيره عمر بن عبد العزيز أ الرابعة سيبويه تام أ سر الادب ٦ الخامس
سيره صلاح الدين ٢ سنا البرق الشامي ٢ السادس السياسه لارسطو
سيره الاسكندر أ سقط الزند بخط الخطيب السبع الطوال وتتمه
العشر بغريبها بخطه ايضا أ ونسخه اخرى بخط ابن الجواليقي السابع سلوان
المطاع نسخه ثانيه في المجلد الثامن سراج الملوك ٢ ثلاث نسخ السلطان
لابن قتيبه أ السياسه للثعالبي أ سياسه الممالك والدول أ
السيره الهبيريه أ سفر الملوك سيره احمد بن طولون أ ثلاث نسخ الحادي عشر
سقط الزند لابي العلا أ ٣٩ ثاني نسخه الثاني عشر السبع المعلقات بخط

Plate 21 Ashrafiya catalogue (670s/1270s), fol. 253b. © Istanbul, Süleymaniye Yazma Eser Kütüphanesi, Fatih 5433

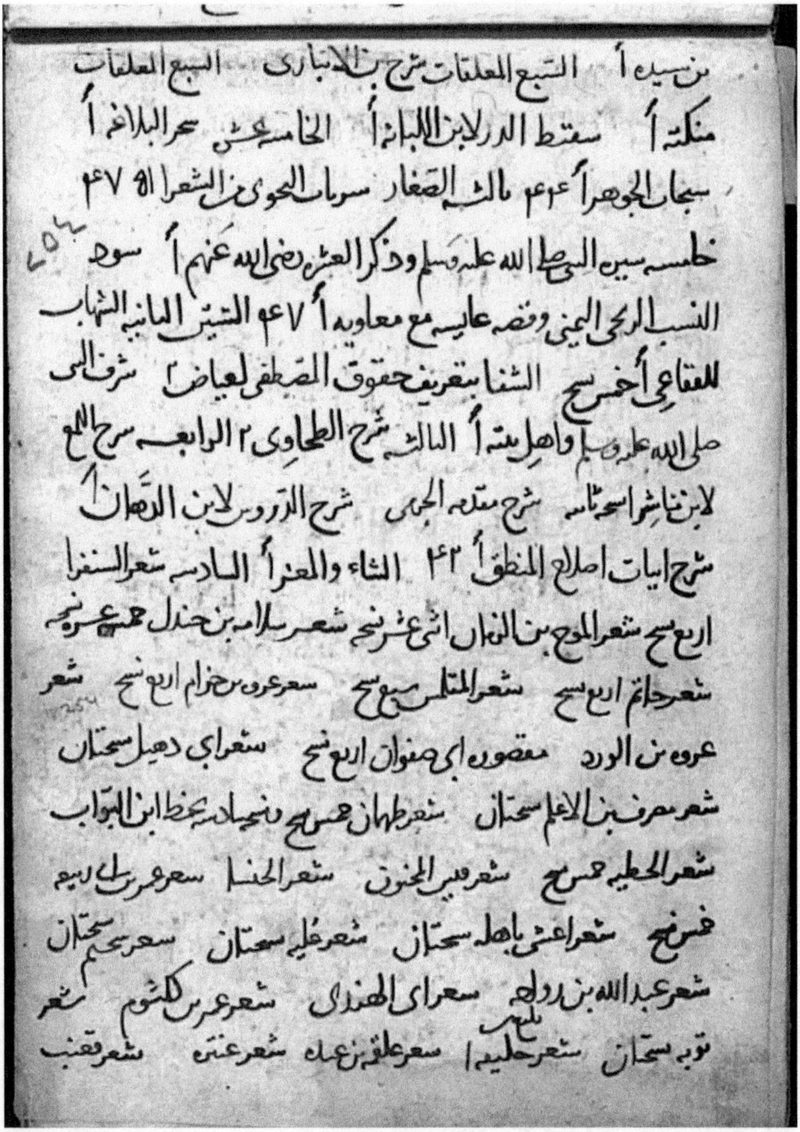

Plate 22 Ashrafiya catalogue (670s/1270s), fol. 254a. © Istanbul, Süleymaniye Yazma Eser Kütüphanesi, Fatih 5433

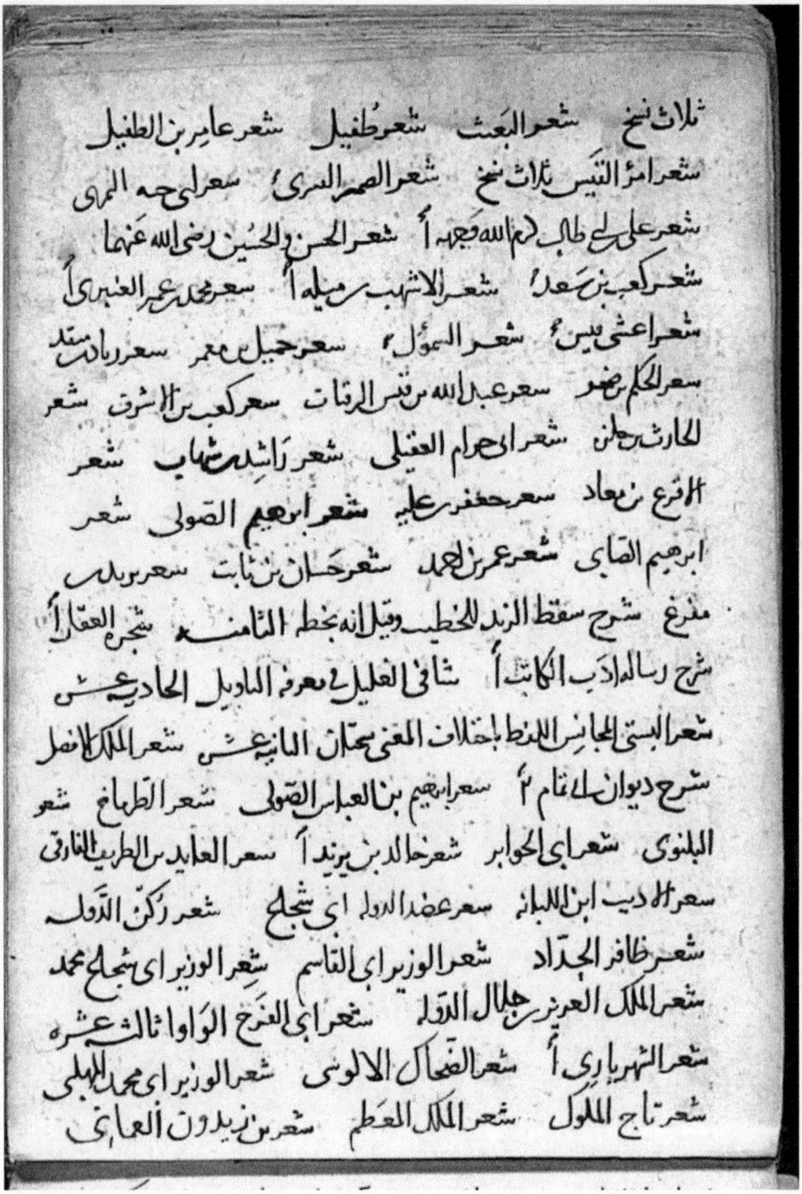

Plate 23 Ashrafiya catalogue (670s/1270s), fol. 254b. © Istanbul, Süleymaniye Yazma Eser Kütüphanesi, Fatih 5433

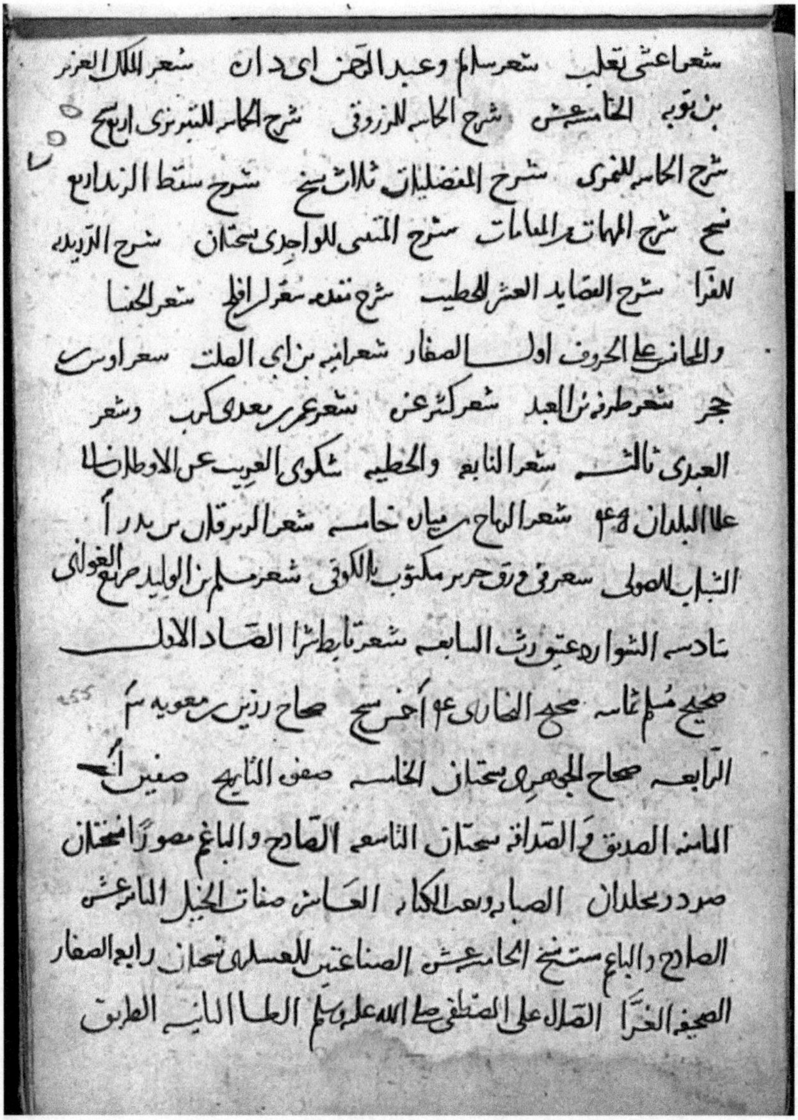

شعر اعشى تغلب شعر سالم وعبد الرحمن ابنى دارة شعر الملك العزيز
بن نوبة الخامس عشر شرح الحماسة للمرزوقي شرح الحماسة للتبريزي اربع
شرح الحماسة للنمري شرح المفضليات ثلاث نسخ شرح سقط الزند اربع
نسخ شرح المهمات ع المقامات شرح المتنبي للواحدي نسختان شرح الدريدية
للفرا شرح القصايد العشر للخطيب شرح نقدة شعر ابن افلح شعر الخنسا
والمجانس على الحروف اول الصفار شعر امية بن ابى الصلت شعر اوس
بن حجر شعر طرفة بن العبد شعر كثير عزة شعر عمرو بن معدي كرب وشعر
العبدي ثالث شعر النابغة والحطيئة شكوى الغريب عن الاوطان الى
علما البلدان عه شعر الرماح بن ميادة خامس شعر الزبرقان بن بدر ا
الشباب للصولي شعر في رق حرير مكتوب بالكوفي شعر مسلم بن الوليد صريع الغواني
سادس الشوارد عتيق رث السابع شعر تابط شرا الصاد الاول
صحيح مسلم ثامن صحيح البخاري عو اخر نسخ صحاح رزين بن معوية سم
الرابع صحاح الجوهري نسختان الخامس صفوة التاريخ صفين ا
الثامن الصديق والصداقة نسختان التاسع الصادح والباغم مصورا نسختان
صور دربخلدان الصبابة ونعت الكتاب العاشر صفات الخيل الحادي عشر
الصادح والباغم ست نسخ الخامس عشر الصناعتين للعسكري نسختان رابع الصفار
الصحيفة الغرا الصلاة على المصطفى صلى الله عليه وسلم العطا النابه الطريق

Plate 24 Ashrafiya catalogue (670s/1270s), fol. 255a. © Istanbul, Süleymaniye Yazma Eser Kütüphanesi, Fatih 5433

الثالث لابن الصبح ٤ الطريق المسلوك في وعظ الملوك الرابع الطيب

عن المفصل الخامس طريق الطليق ا الثامن طيف الخيال طرايف الاخبار

الحادي عشر طبقات الشعرا لعطا بن خزرج الطرايف واللطايف الظا

الطالات لعلي بن يوسف ا ع الطاهرات لاوقليدس الطرف والمتطرفين

للماوردي العين الاولى العرايس في المجالس للثعلبي الثاني العرايس نحو

ثالث علوم الحديث لابن الصلاح من عوالي الفراوي عوارف المعارف

للسهروردي الثالث العمل للنوراني العقيد الموسوم بالاحلية العقلية

للناشي الرابع عين العين للشيرازي السادس عرايس الادب لابن الهبارية

عروض بن عباد عنوان المآثر الجاهلية السابع العقد لابن عبد ربه

عجايب الاشعار وغرايب الاخبار ع٤٤٤ عقلا المجانين الثامن

عيون الاخبار لابن قتيبة ثمان العمدة لابن رشيق عبارات الاشارات

عهد اردشير لابن المقفع التاسع على تعبير الرويا بخط العتقي ا علم الرمل

لابن مدبلج العمل بالاصطرلاب الثاني عشر العراقيات لابي المظفر

الثالث عشر عيون الاشعار ا عيون الاشعار ط ا الخامس عشر عهد السلطان

العجايب والطرف والهدايا والتحف العروض لابن مرون العروض لعبد

الرحمن عهد اردبانوس الملك الى ابنه عهد الشاعر عرايس الادب

غطان الحاذق ما المرا الصغار عهد المامون رابعه العلاج رحب

عوذة النبي صلى الله عليه وسلم خامس عرايس الالباب وغرايس الاداب

العربيات

Plate 25 Ashrafiya catalogue (670s/1270s), fol. 255b. © Istanbul, Süleymaniye Yazma Eser Kütüphanesi, Fatih 5433

العربيات المنتخبات التي تدخل في العبارات والكتب وهي الفاظ غريبة مشروحة
بالعجمي أسادسه عدة الكتاب وفضل الاداب في الترسل سابعه عشرون مسئلة سيل
عنها الشافعي رضي الله عنه الكتب بالعجمي التاسعه دستور اللغة الكافي
في العروض اصول الحرب شعر الحكم الرومي وغيره ديوان الوشيد
وطواط الارشاد في الفقه مقامات سحبان وسيلة الطالب للمبادي
سحبان ديوان جمال الدين النتاس ديوان البيلقاني ديوان بندار
نزهة العشاق الديوان الاسدي الديوان العمري كليلة ودمنة ديوان
ابي المظفر قصص الانبيا دفع مضار الاغذية ترلع الافهام مجموع
شعر فرنه علوان مجموع شعر مجدول نفثة الصدور مجموع شعر مجموع
اخر ترسل عجمي مجموع شعر عتيق مجموع شعر عتيق الغين
الاولى غريب الحديث لابن الجوزي غريب الحديث لابن قتيبة
غريب الحديث لابن عبيد غريب القران لابن عزيز غريبا القران والحديث
للهروي اربع نسخ الثانيه غريب القران لابن عزيز ثلاث نسخ غرر الفوايد
للشريف المرتضى نسخة ثانية السابعه الغرة لعبدالله الثانية غرر
البراعات الثامنه الغارات مجلد التاسعه غزل ابن المعلم الثالثه
غزل بن هاني موارد المعاني في غزل بن هاني غزل بن قسيم الحموي غزل
ديوان النتاش غزل مهيار غزل البحتري والرضي غزل السنجاهي

Plate 26 Ashrafiya catalogue (670s/1270s), fol. 256a. © Istanbul, Süleymaniye Yazma Eser Kütüphanesi, Fatih 5433

غزل ابن الساعاتي غزل المرهف ست نسخ الخامس عشر العلان المغنين
سادس الصغار غرر البلاغة للصابي الثاني فضايل الاعمال للضيا
فضايل دمشق فضايل الصحابة واهل البيت فضايل القدس فضول
حيان في فضل شعبان لابن الحلبي الثالث غرايب المجالس المفرى الرابع
فقه اللغة للثعالبي اثنا عشر نسخة فرايد الخرايد الفروق بين الظا والضاد
لمحمد بن عبد الله الخامس فتوح ابن اعثم ٢ فتوح سيف بن عمر ٢ الفتح القسي ١
فتوح النواحي والبلدان للبلاذري فتوح الشام للازدي فضايل مصر وذكر
ما خصها الله تعالى به فهرست كتب الامام السادس فصل في فضل الفقر على الغنى
بخط شهاب الدين السهروردي الفتح على ابي الفتح السابع الفرج بعد الشدة
الفوايد وغرر الفرايد فنون الفوايد وهو مجموع اشعار وغيره الثامن فضل
زين الفتوة والمروة الفرايد والقلايد اربع نسخ العاشر القلايد ابن
حبيش الفروسية لمحمد بن يعقوب ٢ الفروسية في الطب فن في الفنون في معرفة
صفو العيون الفروسية مصور الفروسية لطر الفروسية لخبر الثالث عشر فرح
القلوب في مدايح بني ايوب الخامس عشر فلك المعاني لابن الهبارية فنون الفوايد
الفاضل في الادب الكامل للمبرد الصفار فضايل الجهاد وشهر رمضان لابن عساكر
فضايل الجهاد خامس فضايل الجهاد لابن عساكر فقر وحكم ونوادر السادس
فصوص الفصول وعقود العقول فصول البلغا فصول ستة في المكاتبات
فضل المجاهدين على القاعدين الثاني الاولى قراة يعقوب وع

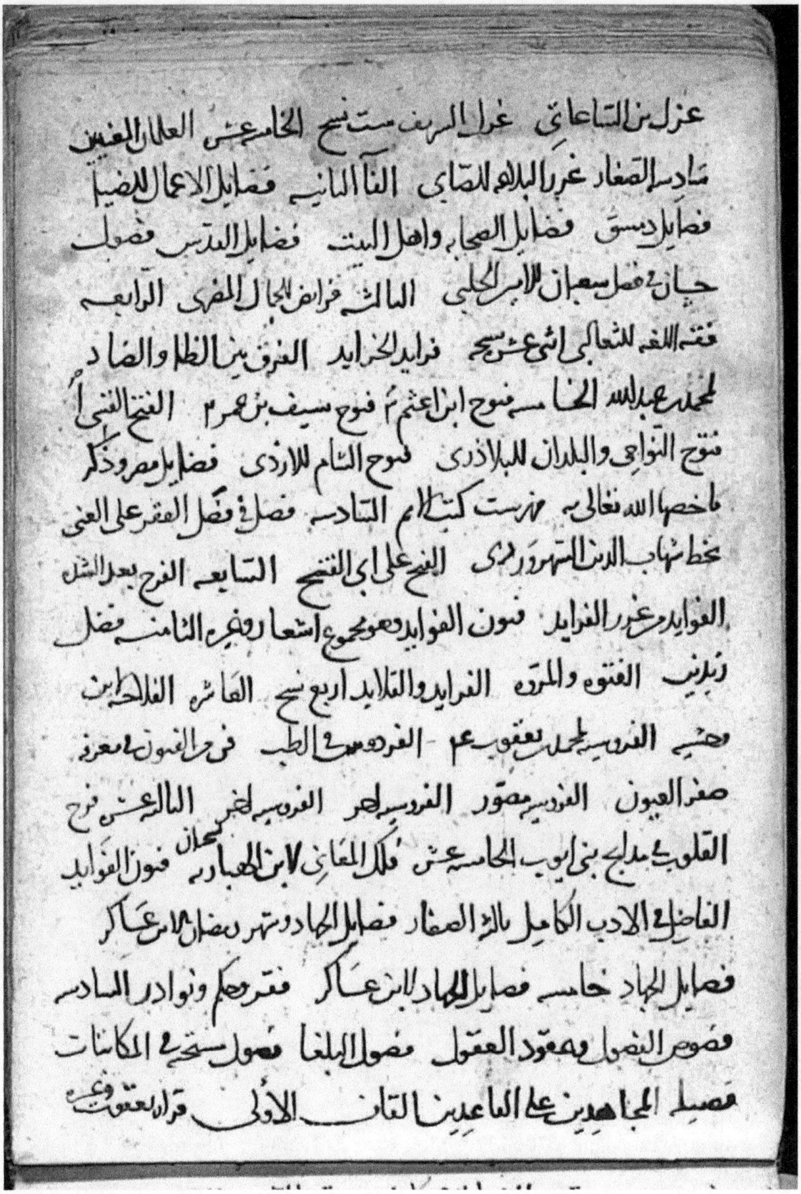

Plate 27 Ashrafiya catalogue (670s/1270s), fol. 256b. © Istanbul, Süleymaniye Yazma Eser Kütüphanesi, Fatih 5433

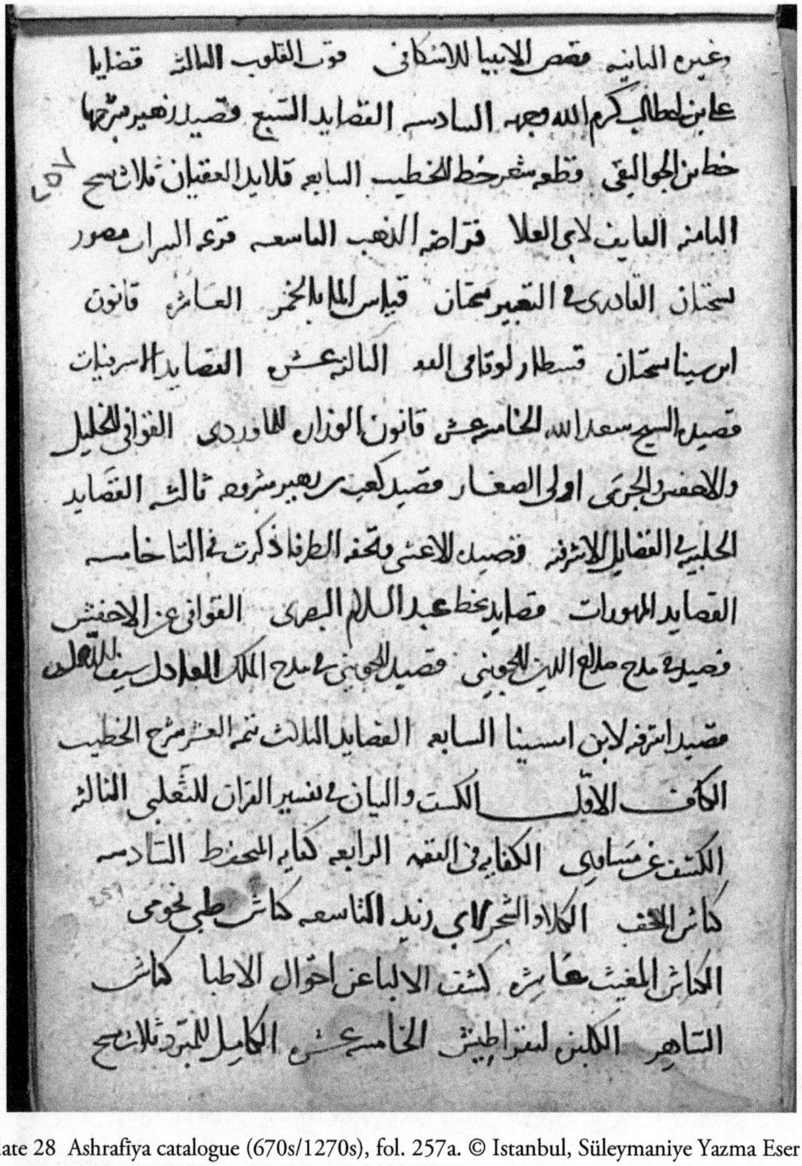

Plate 28 Ashrafiya catalogue (670s/1270s), fol. 257a. © Istanbul, Süleymaniye Yazma Eser Kütüphanesi, Fatih 5433

الكناء والتقريض الكافي في العروض بسحمان كنز الكتاب خامس الصغار
كتاب روض ... دلايل الصحة التي يحتاج اليها عند شرا المماليك كتاب
كسب المعز لدين الله تعالى لافتاه الكاتب جوهر كتاب عن المسترشد
اللام الحد الثانيه لوامع انوار القلوب لمع بن السراج في علوم الصوفيه
الرابعه لمع ابي الفتح بن جني الخامسه اللباب في تهذيب الانساب
السادسه لزوم ما لا يلزم اللبا واللبن خط ابن الجواليقي لمع بن جني
خط القاساني السابعه لب الاداب الثامنه اللالي المضيه في مناقب الحاكم
التاسعه لباب اللباب العاشره لزوم ما لا يلزم حاديه عشر لمح الملح للحظيري ثالثه عشر
لمح الملح لابن الصيرفي اللطايف للثعالبي لطايف المعارف مالي الصغار
لمع من اخبار البرامكه خامسه لمع من اخبار البرامكه اللطايف الحليه
المواقف العليه الجوي تاسعه لذ القلوب ونزهه لنشر المكروب لليم الاولى
مسند الدارمي مختصر زاد المسير في التفسير معالم التنزيل للبغوي الثانيه
مصابيح البغوي المتحابين في الله مسند الشافعي موطا رواية يحيى بن يحيى
موطا رواية معن موطا رواية ابي مصعب من عاش بعد الموت المستعذب في
القراات مشيخة ابن الجوزي الملخص لابن الجندي المبتدا للكسائي
مناقب الابرار لابن خميس مثير الغرام الساكن الى اشرف الاماكن منافع القراات
عن جعفر الصادق مقتل الحسين بن علي رضي الله عنهما الملاحم لابن المنادي

Plate 29 Ashrafiya catalogue (670s/1270s), fol. 257b. © Istanbul, Süleymaniye Yazma Eser Kütüphanesi, Fatih 5433

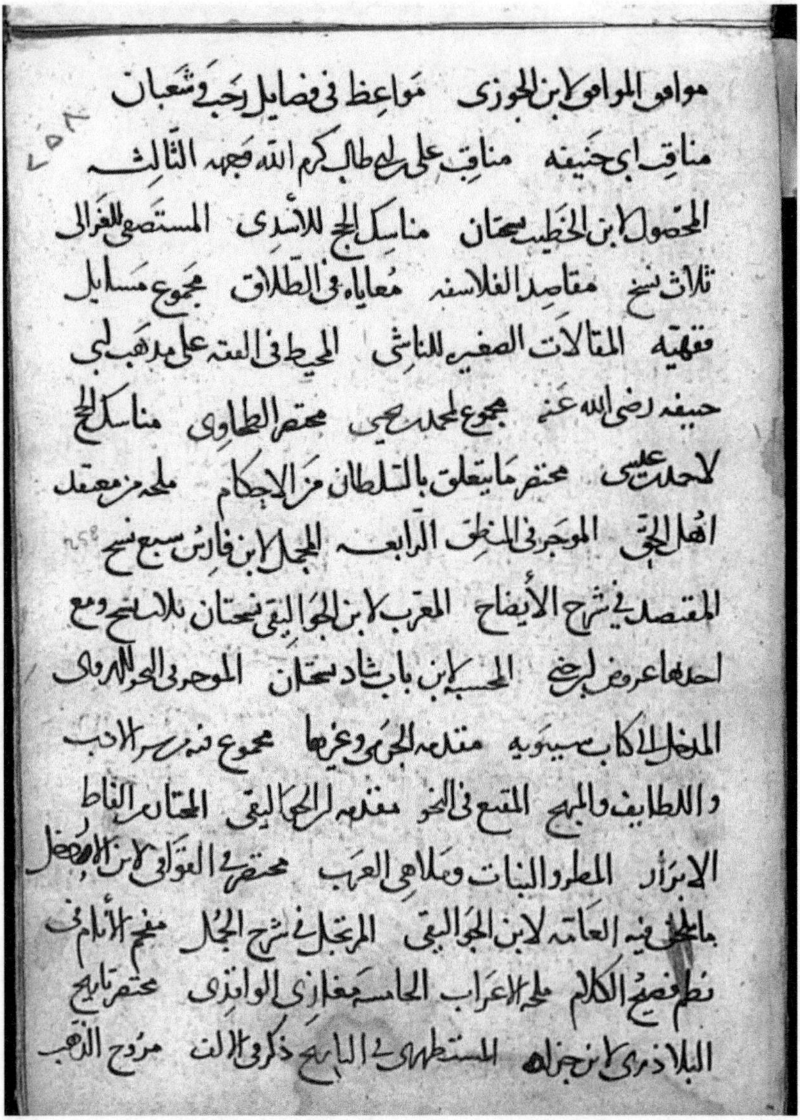

موافق المرافق لابن الجوزي   مواعظ في فضايل رجب وشعبان
مناقب ابي حنيفه   مناقب علي ابن ابي طالب كرم الله وجهه الثالث
المحصول لابن الخطيب نسختان   مناسك الحج للاسدي   المستصفى للغزالي
ثلاث نسخ   مقاصد الفلاسفه   معاياه في الطلاق   مجموع مسايل
فقهيه   المقالات الصغير للناشي   المحيط في اللغة على مذهب ابي
حنيفه رضي الله عنه   مجموع لمحمد بن يحيى   مختصر الطحاوي   مناسك الحج
لمحمد بن عيسى   مختصر ما يتعلق بالسلطان من الاحكام   ملحه من معتقد
اهل الحق   الموجز في المنطق   الرابعه   المجمل لابن فارس سبع نسخ
المقتصد في شرح الايضاح   المعرب لابن الجواليقي نسختان بلا شرح ومع
احدها عروض ابن جني   الحسبه لابن باب شاد نسختان   الموجز في النحو للهروي
المدخل الى كتاب سيبويه   مقدمه الجزولي وغيرها   مجموع فيه سر الادب
واللطايف والمبهج   المتسع في النحو   مقدمه ابن الجواليقي   المختار من الفاظ
الابرار   المطر والنبات وملاهي العرب   مختصر في القوافي لابن [illegible]
بما يلحن فيه العامه لابن الجواليقي   المرتجل في شرح الجمل   منهج الانام في
نظم فصيح الكلام   ملحه الاعراب   الحماسه   مغازي الواقدي   مختصر تاريخ
البلاذري لابن جزله   المستظهري في البايع   ذكرى الالف   مروج الذهب

Plate 30 Ashrafiya catalogue (670s/1270s), fol. 258a. © Istanbul, Süleymaniye Yazma Eser Kütüphanesi, Fatih 5433

ثلاث نسخ السادس مجموع بخط ابن المامون وشعر [illegible] والخالدي ومراثي

في النبي صلى الله عليه وسلم مقصورة ابي صفوان اربع نسخ مجموع بخطا في

اشعار جماعة من العرب اوله شعر عبد الله بن عتبة بن مسعود مجموع بخط ابن ابي [illegible]

ملح [illegible] في الفرق بين الظاء والضاد المعجز العربية في مناقب الدولة الاشرفية

مجموع بخط ابن الجواليقي فيه اخبار واسانيد وقصايد من [illegible] واستغفر

وغير ذلك مجموع فوايد تسع قوايم ذكر ان [illegible] بخط ابن [illegible] المطر

لابن دريد مجموع شعر فيه [illegible] بن [illegible] وغير ذلك المقصور والممدود

لابي علي الفارسي المسلة التي جرت بين سيبويه والكسائي السابعة

مجازات [illegible] ثلاث نسخ مجموع بخط [illegible] المعمرين لابي عبيد

ملح الممالح لابن [illegible] اربع نسخ ملح النوق مصارع العشاق [illegible]

المذهب [illegible] [illegible] الاجواد [illegible] الحديث

في الاغاني المدح للمرزباني المنتهى في الكمال المقتبس لابن دريد [illegible]

الثانية [illegible] جواهر السلوك معارف [illegible] المونس

اشعار المجموع [illegible] محاسن المحاضرات المكافاة على الحسن والقبيح

المحظوظ في الرزق والمحروس فيه المبهج للثعالبي مجموع اوله [illegible] رسول الله

صلى الله عليه وسلم [illegible] المادح والمذام [illegible] مضاهاه

كليلة ودمنة معالي [illegible] على الموازنة والترجيح في [illegible]

Plate 31 Ashrafīya catalogue (670s/1270s), fol. 258b. © Istanbul, Süleymaniye Yazma Eser Kütüphanesi, Fatih 5433

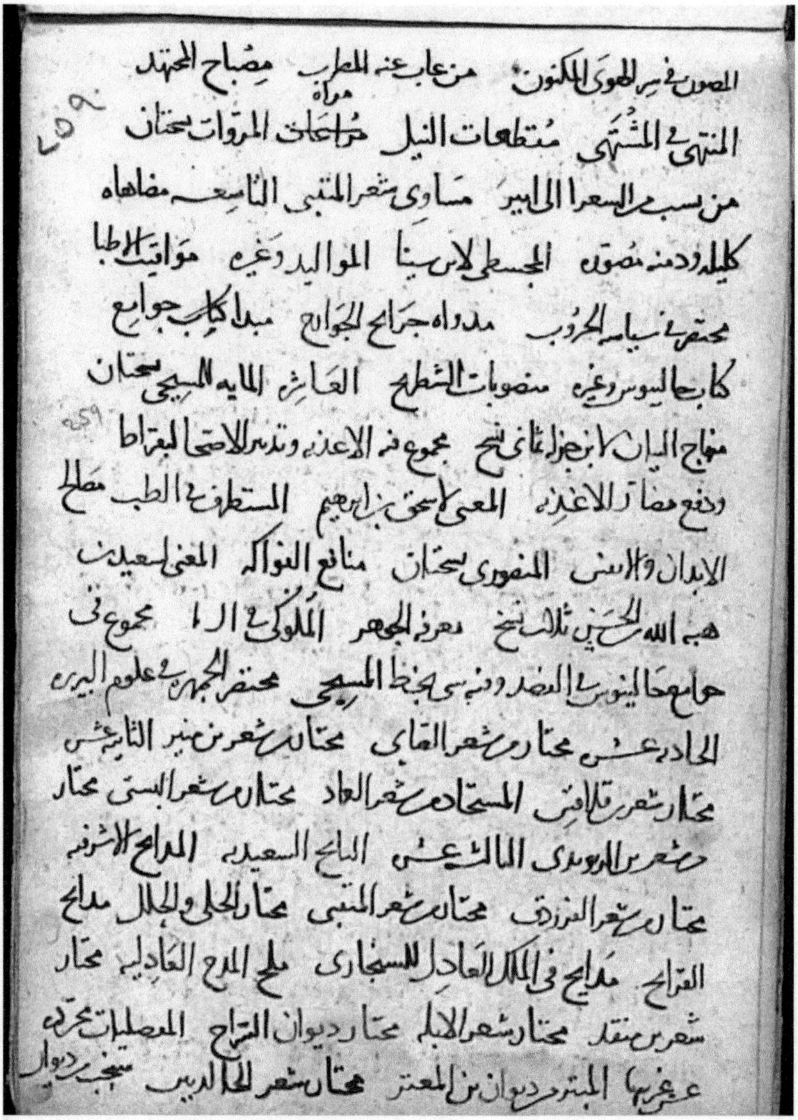

المصون في سر الهوى المكنون   من غاب عنه المطرب   مصباح المجتهد

مرآة

المنتهى في المشتهى   مقطعات النيل   مراعات المروات نسختان

من نسب من الشعرا الى امه   مساوي شعر المتنبي   التاسعة مضاهاه

كليلة ودمنة مصور   المجسطي لابن سينا   المواليد وغيره   مواقيت الاطبا

مختصر في سياسة الحروب   مداواة جراح الجوارح   مبدا كتاب جوامع

كتاب جالينوس وغيره   منصوبات الشطرنج   العاشر المائة للمسيحي نسختان

منهاج البيان لابن جزلة ثاني نسخ   مجموع في الاغذية وتدبير الاصحا لبقراط

ودفع مضار الاغذية   المغني لاسحق بن ابرهيم   المستطرف في الطب   مصلح

الابدان والانفس   المنصوري نسختان   منافع الفواكه   المغني لسعيد بن

هبة الله الحسين ثلاث نسخ   معرفة الجوهر   الملوكي في الرما   مجموع فيه

جامع جالينوس في الفصد وفيه شي بخط المسيحي   مختصر الجمهرة في علوم البديع

الحادي عشر   مختار من شعر العماني   مختار من شعر ابن منير   الثاني عشر

مختار شعر ابن قلاقس   المستجاد من شعر العماد   مختار من شعر البستي   مختار

من شعر ابن الرومي   الثالث عشر   المنايح السعيدية   المدائح الاشرفية

مختار من شعر الفرزدق   مختار من شعر المتنبي   مختار الحلي والحلل   مدائح

القراح   مدائح في الملك العادل للسنجاري   ملح المدح العادلية   مختار

شعر ابن منقذ   مختار شعر الابله   مختار ديوان التهامي   المفضليات مجردة

عن غريبها   البحتري   ديوان ابن المعتز   مختار شعر الخالديين   منتخب من ديوان

Plate 32 Ashrafiya catalogue (670s/1270s), fol. 259a. © Istanbul, Süleymaniye Yazma Eser Kütüphanesi, Fatih 5433

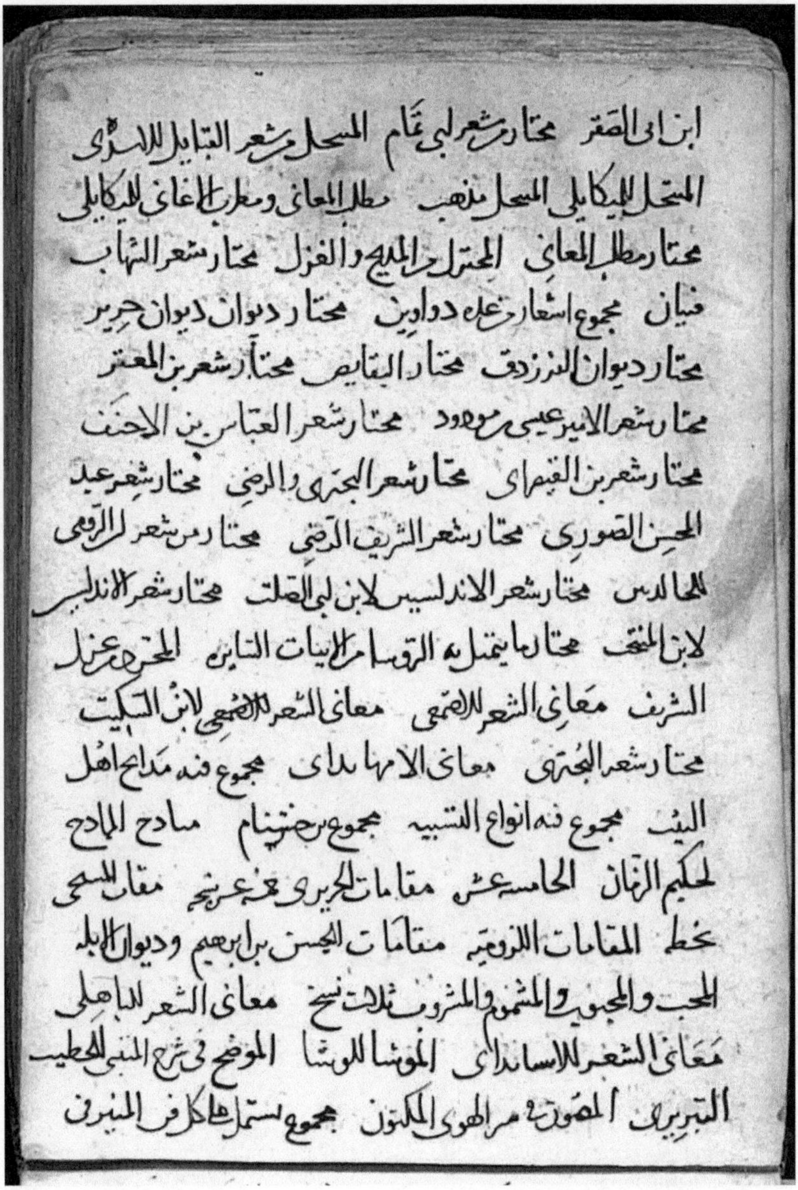

ابن ابى الصقر مختار من شعر ابى تمام المنتحل من شعر القبايل للاسرى
المنتحل للميكالى المنتحل مذهب مطلب المعانى ومطرب الاغانى للميكالى
مختار مطلب المعانى المختار المليح والغزل مختار شعر الشهاب
فتيان مجموع اشعار على دواوين مختار ديوان ديوان جرير
مختار ديوان الفرزدق مختار النقايض مختار شعر ابن المعتز
مختار شعر الامير عيسى بن مودود مختار شعر العباس بن الاحنف
مختار شعر ابن القيسرانى مختار شعر البحترى والرضى مختار شعر عبد
المحسن الصورى مختار شعر الشريف الرضى مختار من شعر الرقى
الجالدس مختار شعر الاندلسيين لابن ابى الصلت مختار شعر الاندلسى
لابن المنجف مختار ما يتمثل به الروساء من الابيات السايرة المحرر عند
الشريف معانى الشعر للاصمعى معانى الشعر للاصمعى لابن السكيت
مختار شعر البحترى معانى الاشناندانى مجموع فيه مدايح اهل
البيت مجموع فيه انواع التشبيه مجموع من حسن نظام مادح المادح
لحكيم الزمان الخامسة عشر مقامات الحريرى بخط غير منجم مقال السجى
بخط المقامات اللزومية مقامات الحسن بن ابرهيم وديوان الابله
المحب والمحبوب والمشموم والمشروب ثلاث نسخ معانى الشعر للباهلى
معانى الشعر للاشناندانى الموشا للوشا الموضح فى شرح المتنبى للخطيب
التبريزى المصون من الهوى المكنون مجموع يشتمل على كل فن المنثور

Plate 33 Ashrafiya catalogue (670s/1270s), fol. 259b. © Istanbul, Süleymaniye Yazma Eser Kütüphanesi, Fatih 5433

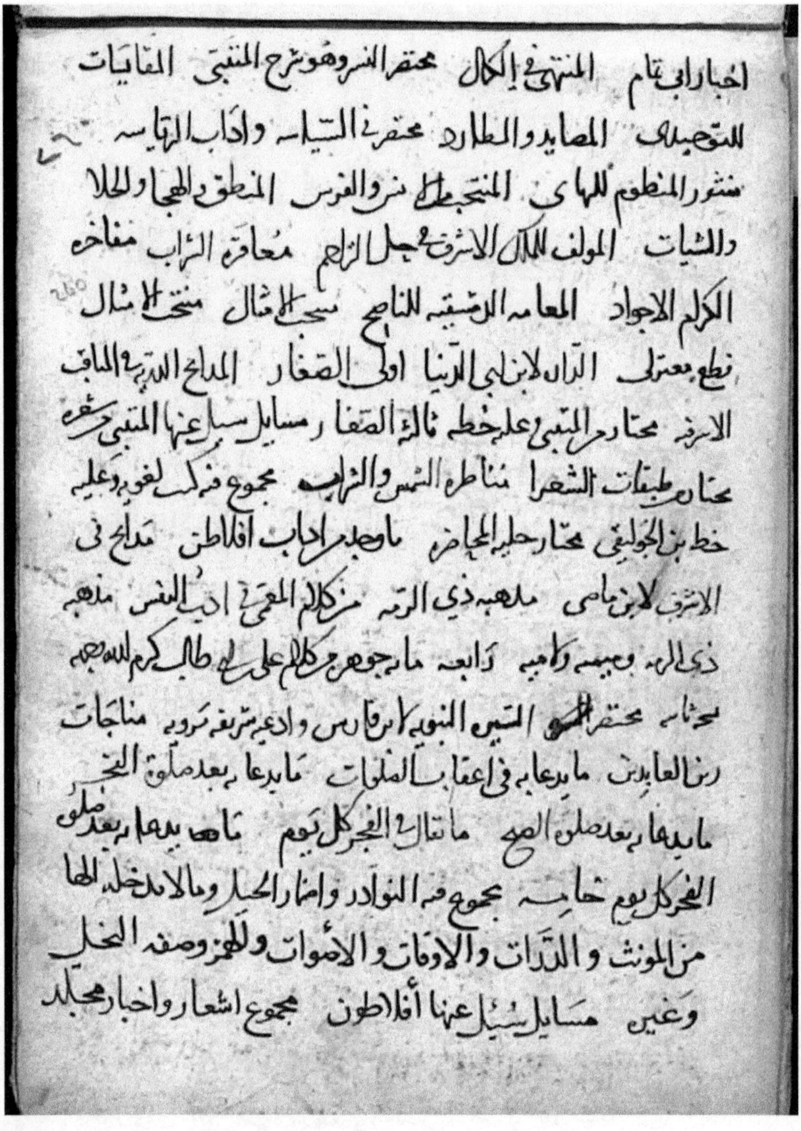

اخبار ابي تمام المنتهى في الكمال مختصر النثر وهو شرح المتنبي المقابسات
للتوحيدي المصايد والمطارد مختصر في السياسة واداب الرياسة
منثور المنظوم للبهائي المنتحل نثر والفرس المنطق والهجا والحلا
والشيات المولف للملك الاشرف في حل الزايج معاقرة الشراب مفاخرة
الكرام الاجواد المقامة الدمشقية للناصح سحب الامثال منتخب الامثال
نطع معتزلي الذال لابن ابي الدنيا اولي الصغار المدايح الدرية في المناقب
الاشرفية مختار من المتنبي على خط ثالثة الصفار مسايل سيل عنها المتنبي جز شعر
مختار من طبقات الشعرا مناظرة الشمس والتراب مجموع فيه كتب لغوية وعليه
خط ابن الجواليقي مختار حلية المحاضرة ما وجد من اداب افلاطن مدايح في
الاشرف لابن ماضي ملعبة ذي الرمة من كلام المعري في ادب النفس مذهبة
ذي الرمة بعينه ولامية رابعة ما جوهر من كلام علي بن ابي طالب كرم الله وجهه
ثانية مختصر المحو السيرة النبوية لابن فارس وادعية مروية مناجات
زين العابدين ما يدعا به في اعقاب الصلوات ما يدعا به بعد صلوة الفجر
ما يدعا به بعد صلوة الصبح ما يقال في الفجر كل يوم ما يدعا به بعد صلوة
الفجر كل يوم خامسة مجموع فيه النوادر واشعار الخيل وما لا يدخله الها
من المونث والذوات والاوقات والاصوات واللهو ووصف النخل
وغير مسايل سيل عنها افلاطون مجموع اشعار واخبار مجلد

Plate 34 Ashrafiya catalogue (670s/1270s), fol. 260a. © Istanbul, Süleymaniye Yazma Eser Kütüphanesi, Fatih 5433

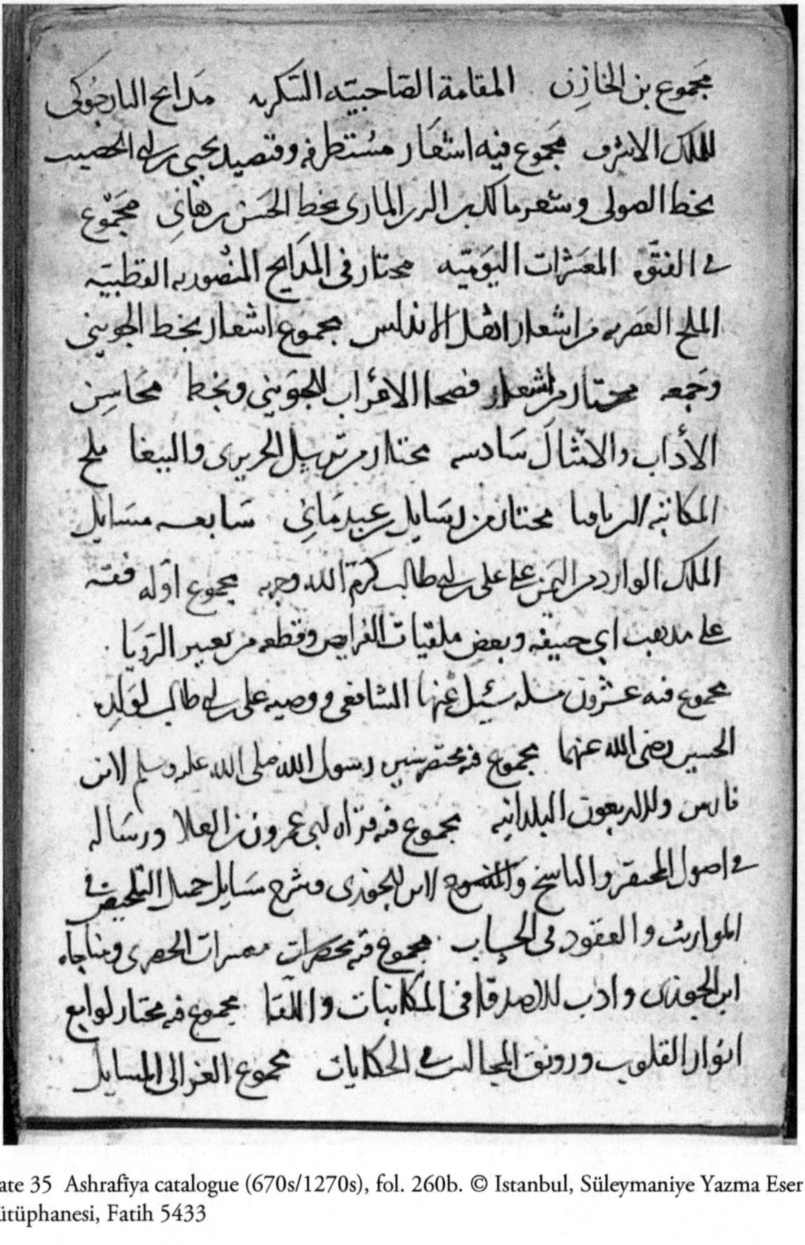
مجموع بن الخازن المقامة الصاحبية السكرية مدايح البارجوكي
للملك الاشرف مجموع فيه اشعار مستطرفة وقصيد يحيى بن ابي الحصيب
بخط الصولي وشعر ما كتبه الدر الماري بخط الحسن رهاني مجموع
في الفتوة المعشرات اليومية مختار في المدايح المنصورية القطبية
الملح العصرية من اشعار اهل الاندلس مجموع اشعار بخط الجويني
وجمعه مختار من اشعار فصحا الاعراب للجويني وبخطه محاسن
الاداب والامثال سادسه مختار من ترسيل الحريري والببغا ملح
المكاتبة الرياضية مختار من رسايل عبدمائي سابعه مسايل
الملك الوارد من اليمن على علي بن ابي طالب كرم الله وجهه مجموع اوله فقه
على مذهب ابي حنيفة وبعض ملغيات الفرايض وقطعة من تعبير الرويا .
مجموع فيه عشرون مسلة سيل عنها الشافعي ووصية علي بن ابي طالب لولده
الحسين رضي الله عنهما مجموع فيه مختصر سنن رسول الله صلى الله عليه وسلم الى
فارس والاربعون البلدانية مجموع فيه قراة ابي عمرو بن العلا ورسالة
في اصول الفقه والناسخ والمنسوخ ابن الجوزي وشرح مسايل جمل التلخيص في
المواريث والعقود في الحساب مجموع فيه مختصرات معمرات الحصري ومناجاة
ابن الجوزي وادب الاصدقا في المكاتبات واللقا مجموع فيه مختار لوامع
انوار القلوب ورونق المجالس في الحكايات مجموع الغزالي المسايل

Plate 35 Ashrafiya catalogue (670s/1270s), fol. 260b. © Istanbul, Süleymaniye Yazma Eser Kütüphanesi, Fatih 5433

البغداديه والمسايل الاخرويه والمسايل الاربعون والمصون والمصباح
وخواتيم الباطنه وابطال الدرر اللفظي مجموع للغزالي منهاج العابدين
ومعراج العارفين مجموع فيه تفضيل النسابين وتحصيل العارفين مجموع
مختصر اصول الفقه وجدل وتاسيس النظاير مجموع فيه الترغيب والترهيب
ومبادي الهدايه وادعية الايام السبعه مجموع فيه الناسخ والمنسوخ لهبة الله وقرات
مرموزه واراجيز في عدد اي القران مجموع فيه العنوان ومتشابه القران
مجموع فيه تلخيص الرضى ومفاتيح العلوم مذهب ذي الرمه وشرحها مجموع
فيه ديوان علي بن الجهم والمسومات والمتجاب والجمان والفرسان مجموع
فيه عهد اردشير وحديث خسروي ابرويز وابنه شيرويه وانتصاف دولة العجم
وابتدا امر جبير الانبيا العرالام مجموع شعر اشيا حسنه تعلق الحسن يوسف
الاماي مجموع فيه المخبر برجها وعلل الريح الحاموي عن تلم مجموع فيه فنا الغلا
ورحلة عبد القادر ولوعة المشتاق مجموع الفرايد والقلايد ورسالة في
العهود واليونانيه مجموع ديوان الرستمي وعدة شعر ابي فراس ومختار
شعر الرئيس والسماح والنجاح للواحدي مجموع فيه شعر ظافر ومن شعر
محيي محمد الصقلي ومن كلام الوهراني مجموع النجم العصري مجموع فيه ليل
الحقايق وفتح التقدير واعتراضات ابن سينا واجوبتها مجموع فيه شعر

Plate 36 Ashrafiya catalogue (670s/1270s), fol. 261a. © Istanbul, Süleymaniye Yazma Eser Kütüphanesi, Fatih 5433

طرفه ر ديوان لبيد وابن حلزه مجموع فيه اشعار مختلفه واسما العود
الذي يتخرب وغيره ذلك مجموع فيه برص القلوب وشرح حقايق التوبه
واللباب في شرح الشهاب مجموع ادبا الغربا والجارين والجارات
واخبار الطلسمات العشق والزيارات مجموع فضايل الاعمال للبكاري
ووعظ عجمي مجموع جدل الشريف مجموع درر السنيه ومنافع القران
والمنبهات مجموع المنثور البهاي والمبهج ووقعة الادهم مجموع فيه
نصر حميد الارقط وذكر النقعبي وسور الدب مجموع اخبار الخلفا
على خط حالي السنة تاريخ قديم مجموع الطيب والتطيب ومختصر الاستفاق
والرسالة المسجلة في تفسير لفظ الحماسة وايضاح مشكل شعر المتنبي وسر الصناعة
في الرمل مجموع جدل وقياس الخوارزمي مجموع الفرايد والقلايد ورسالة
في العهود وادعية الايام السبعة مناقب الشافعي وجزء عرود ومنامات ابن
ابي الدنيا مجموع عجمي ودقيقي وندبه زين العابدين ومقتل الحلاج مجموع شعر
مراثي مجموع مختار شعر البحتري وابي الشيص الخزاعي مجموع ملقى البيك
والمقصور لابن دريد وما لحن فيه العامة للكسايي وغير ذلك مختار من شعر ابي
منهف المعري المامنة مجموع رسالة وصف البيم والاخلاق ورسالة هفوات
الالبا وعثرات الاطبا مجموع اخبار وحكايات وطرف اشعار واول اخبار
المامون ورسالتان مجموع فيه رسايل الخوارزمي ورسالة ابن افلح في علم

Plate 37 Ashrafiya catalogue (670s/1270s), fol. 261b. © Istanbul, Süleymaniye Yazma Eser Kütüphanesi, Fatih 5433

الشعر وقطعة من شعره ومن شعر الارجاني وغير ذلك مجموع فيه نخل
الميكالي وخيل العرب ومحاسن نثر الدر والرائق والشائق ومنتخب
خاوندان وآداب ابن المعتز وغير ذلك مجموع منتخب من نزهة الفريد
فيه بيت المنسر ورقايق واخبار وحكايات وسمر نديم الفريد ووالى عهد
المامون وفوايد مجموع منتخب باخبار الخلفا اوله ذكر الصبوح والحزم من
النعوت مجموع طبي فيه الرهبان وجالينوس في علامات الطبايع والدلالات
على معرفة الاوجاع وعلامات الموت والادوية المسهلة مجموع فيه ما يجب برأي
الاذهر ومن محاسن الادوات مجموع فيه ديوان المتلمس وانشادات وغير
ذلك مجموع فيه فنون يشتمل على العقل والذات ونوادر الحكما وادعية واستغفار
مجموع فيه ديوان الافوه ومن شعر ابن ابي ربيعة وقصيد كعب ولامية الشنفرى
وشعر قيس الطفري مجموع فيه ميزان العروض للخطيب والجامع في النحو للخليل
ومختصر ما يجوز صرفه للشاعر مجموع يشتمل على مقالتي علام رجل في ماهية الشفاعات
وعللها وسبل التيسرات مجموع اوله من موالد النبي صلى الله عليه وسلم ووصيته
لعلي عليه السلام رضي الله عنه وبلاغات البحار وادعية وغيرها مجموع عوذ
وحروز وقلع الآثار من الخواص للتياني مجموع اشعار واخبار وحكم
ونوادر وحكايات وغير ذلك كما ذكر في ترجمة مجموع فيه الخيل ووصفها
والطير والخمار نخب المنوا الجاهر مجموع حد عروض الرهني وقوافي
ابن جني واللامات لابن فارس وفوايد وفحول العرب وآداب الوزرا والكتاب

Plate 38 Ashrafiya catalogue (670s/1270s), fol. 262a. © Istanbul, Süleymaniye Yazma Eser Kütüphanesi, Fatih 5433

المجاميع والجزاز

مجموع فيه الاعرابية وفوايد الوحوش للاصمعي وشعر ابن ابي سلمى

والمذهبة مجموع شعر لبعض شعرا اصلاح الدين اولى وشعر في عيوب الشعر والقوافي

وشرح المسايل الثلاث وشرح المسايل السبع ومخارج الحروف وغير ذلك مجموع

فيه الخط والقلم وتهاني وتعازي ووصايا مجموع اوله رسايل وعروض الخليل

والدروس فيها والقوافي وشعر الحادرة ومن شعر ابن ابي دسور وارجوزة

في صفات الخيل وادعية مجموع فيه مختار من اشعار الخازرة والازهار الذكية في

المباحث العباسية المصون للريحاني يشتمل على عدة كتب من تواليفه مجموع اخبار

واشعار ومن شعر الغزي وديوان امري القيس الكندي ومن شعر ابن الساعاتي

وابن النبيه وجرير مجموع فيه ملحمة ذي الرمة وقصيد دعبل والشنفرى

وكعب ونابغة ابن دريد وقصيدة في الطاءات وارجوزة في الفرق بين الضاد والظا

ومن شعر الحريري وقصيد دعبل امين وقصيد ابن السيد التي لا يعرف قايلها

ومقصورة ابن دريد وقصيد رثا ولم ينسخ ومذهبة والسبع وهل بالطلول

ويا دارمية وقصيد سويد مجموع شعر ابي الشاس واشعار واخبار

وغير ذلك مجموع اوزان الاشعار وقوافي المبرد وكنى الشعرا لثعلب

وطبقاتهم للجمحي ورسالة البيغا في الدواة مجموع الاخلاق لابن الهيثم

وزجر النفس لافلاطن وسياسة البدن وفضل الشراب مجموع اوزان

الافعال والاسما ورسالة ابن الحصارية الى الخطيب ناقصة ومقالة في النفس

وفوايد مجموع فيه الاقتباس من كلام رب الناس ومن امالي ابن دريد وغير

ذلك مجموع ذكر في ترجمته جزء فيه فضايل سور القران وفي الاصول

Plate 39 Ashrafiya catalogue (670s/1270s), fol. 262b.

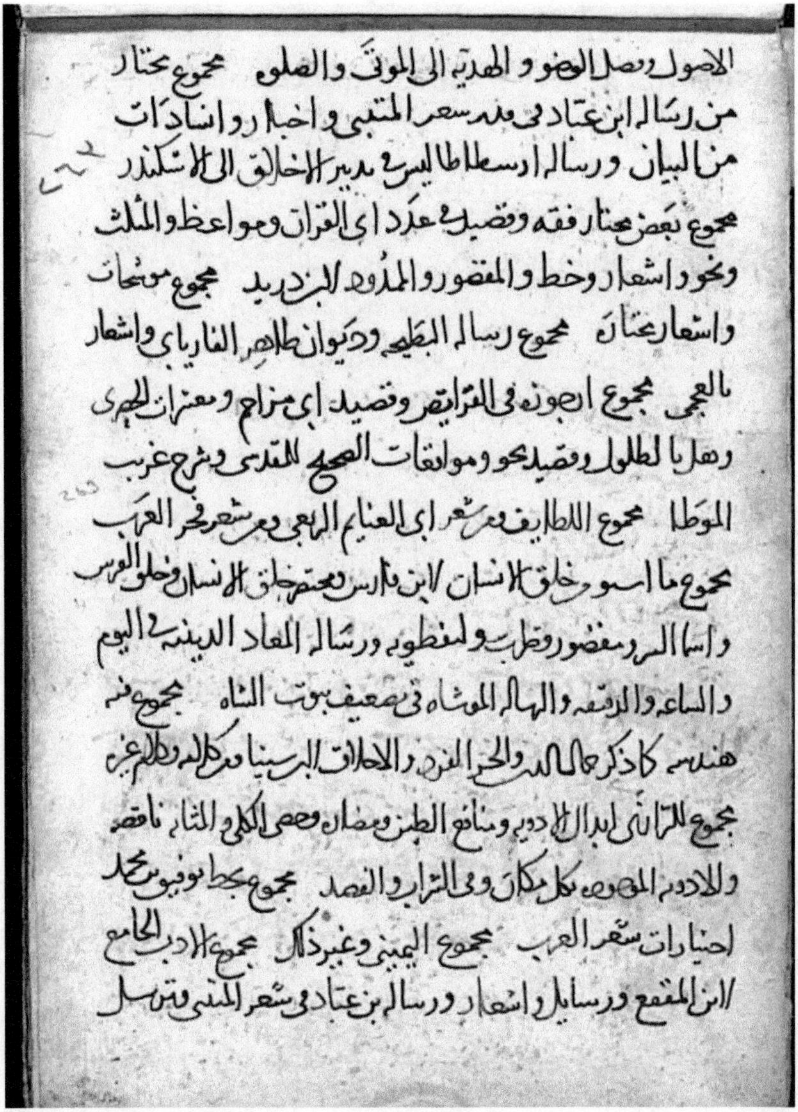

الاصول وفصل الوضوء والهدية الى الموثق والصلوة مجموع مختار
من رسائل ابن عباد في عدة شعر المتنبي واخبار وانشادات
من البيان ورسالة ارسطاطاليس في تدبير الاخلاق الى الاسكندر
مجموع بعض مختار فقه وقصيدة في عدد اي القران ومواعظ والمثلث
ونحو واشعار وخط والمقصور والممدود لابن دريد مجموع موشحات
واشعار مختارة مجموع رسائل البطليوسي وديوان طاهر الفاريابي واشعار
بالعجمي مجموع اجوبة في الفرائض وقصيدة ابي مزاحم ومعشرات الجبري
وهل بالطلول وقصيدة نحو وموافقات الصحيح للمقدسي وشرح غريب
الموطا مجموع اللطائف ومن شعر ابي الغنائم الرهمي ومن شعر فخر العرب
مجموع ما اسمه خلق الانسان لابن فارس وعنه خلق الانسان وخلق الفرس
واسماء البر ومقصور وقطرب والمقطوع ورسالة المعاد الدينية في اليوم
والساعة والدقيقة والهالة الموشاة في تضعيف بيوت الشاه مجموع فيه
هندسة كاذكر جمال الدين والجزء الفرد والاخلاق لابن سينا ومن كلامه وكلام غيره
مجموع للترياقي ابدال الادوية ومنافع الطين ومضار وخصي الكلى والمثانة ناقص
والادوية الموجودة بكل مكان وفي التراب والفصد مجموع بخط يونس بن محمد
اختيارات شعر العرب مجموع اليميني وغير ذلك مجموع الادب الجامع
لابن المقفع ورسائل واشعار ورسالة بن عباد في شعر المتنبي وترسل

Plate 40 Ashrafiya catalogue (670s/1270s), fol. 263a. © Istanbul, Süleymaniye Yazma Eser Kütüphanesi, Fatih 5433

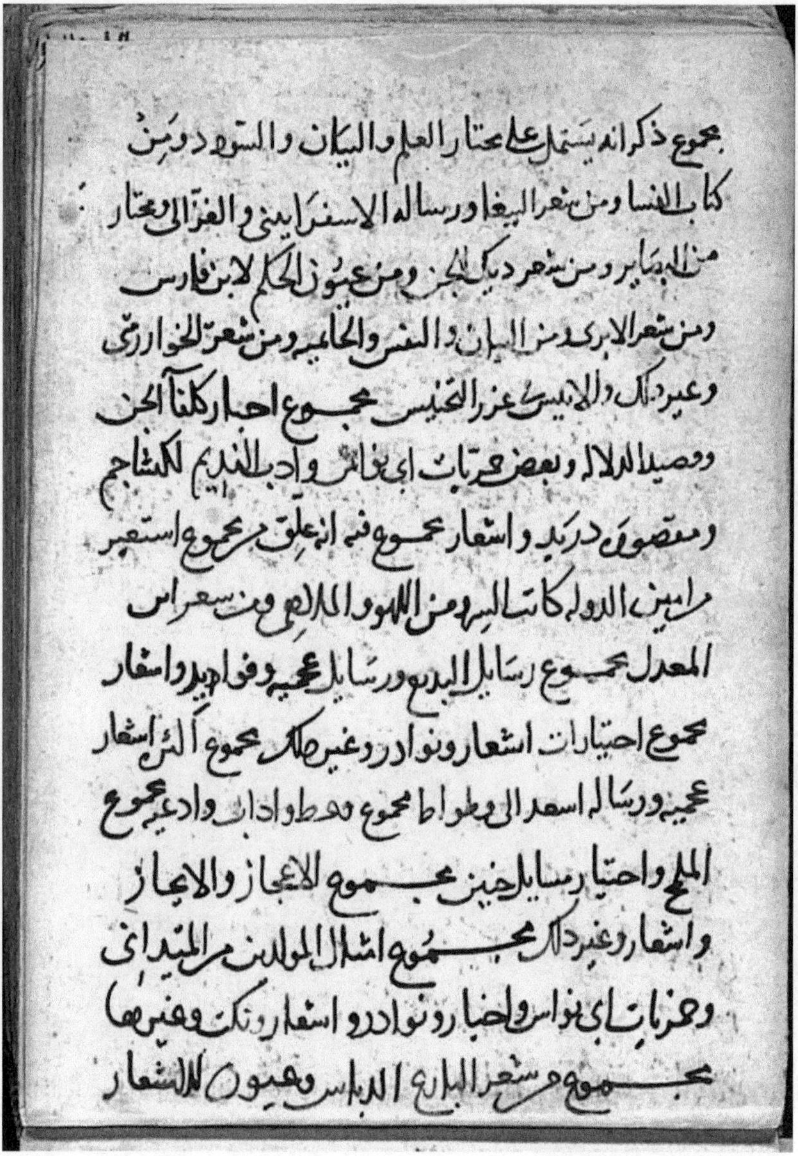

مجموع ذكر انه يشتمل على مختار العلم والبيان والشهود ومن
كتاب الفسا ومن شعر البيغا ورساله الاسفرايني والغزالي ومختار
من البصاير ومن شعر ديك الجن ومن عيون الحكم لابن فارس
ومن شعر الابيوردي من البيان والتبيين والحماسه ومن شعر الخوارزمي
وغير ذلك والانيس عن الجليس مجموع اخبار كلثم الجن
ووصيلا للالاه وبعض خمريات ابي نواس وادب النديم لكشاجم
ومقصوره دريد واشعار مجموع فيه انه علق من مجموع استعير
من امين الدوله كاتب السر من اللهو والملاهي ومن شعر ابن
المعدل مجموع رسايل البديع ورسايل عجميه وفوايد واشعار
مجموع اختيارات اشعار ونوادر وغير ذلك مجموع اكثر اشعار
عجميه ورساله اسعد الى وطواط مجموع وخط واداب وادعيه مجموع
الملح واخبار رسايل حنين مجموع للاعجاز والايجاز
واشعار وغير ذلك مجموع امثال المولدين من الميداني
وخمريات ابي نواس واخبار ونوادر واشعار ونكت وغيرها
مجموع من شعر البارع الدباس وعيون للاشعار

Plate 41 Ashrafiya catalogue (670s/1270s), fol. 263b. © Istanbul, Süleymaniye Yazma Eser Kütüphanesi, Fatih 5433

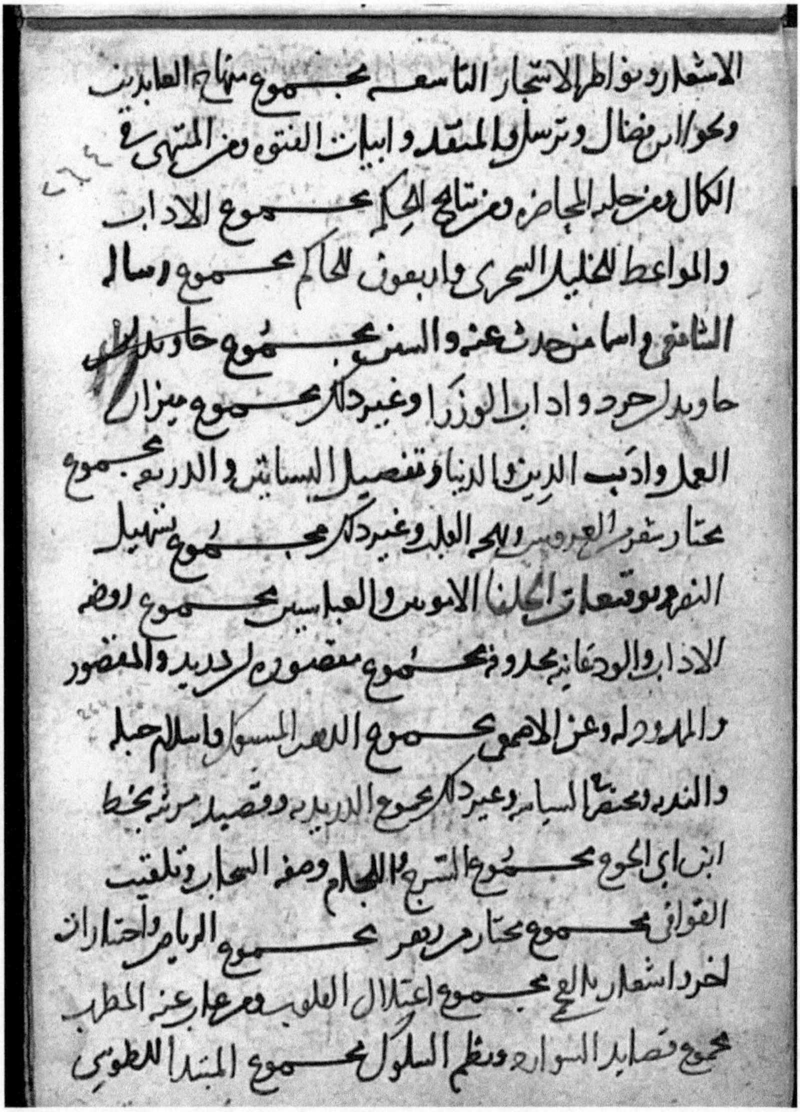

الاشعار ونوادر الاشجار التاسع مجموع منهاج العابدين
ونحو ابن فضال وترسل المستقد وابيات الفتوة ومن المنتهى في
الكمال ومن حلية المحاضرة ومن نتائج الحكم مجموع الاداب
والمواعظ للخليل السجزي والابعوث للحاكم مجموع رسالة
الشافعي واسما من حدث عنه والسنن مجموع جاويدان
جاويدان خرد واداب الوزرا وغير ذلك مجموع ميزان
العمل واداب الدين والدنيا وتفضيل البساتين والدروع مجموع
مختار شعر من العروس ولمح الملح وغير ذلك مجموع تسهيل
النظر وتوقيعات الخلفا الامويين والعباسيين مجموع روضة
الاداب والودعانية محذوف مجموع مقصورة ابن دريد والمقصور
والممدود له وعن الاصمعي مجموع اللعب المسلوك واسلاك حبل
والندب ومختصر السامر وغير ذلك مجموع الدريدية وقصيدة مرثية بخط
ابن ابي الجوع مجموع الشرح الكلام وصف السحاب وتلقيب
القوافي مجموع مختار من شعر مجموع الرياض واختيارات
لخرد اشعار بالفتح مجموع اعتلال القلوب ومن اخبار عزة المطلب
مجموع قصايد السوابح ونظم السلوك مجموع المبتدا للطوسي

Plate 42 Ashrafiya catalogue (670s/1270s), fol. 264a. © Istanbul, Süleymaniye Yazma Eser Kütüphanesi, Fatih 5433

ومن معاني الواقدي مجموع عصمة الانبيا عليهم السلام ومناقب
الشافعي مجموع الحاشية والخلاف بين صاحبي ابي عمر مجموع
حامل العروض للخطيب الاسا بداي مجموع مختار من ترسل [illegible]
ودوبيتي العماد ومن الحماسة مجموع من شعر ابن وكيع وغير ذلك
مجموع سفينة في القرانات مجموع فيه الادعية [illegible]
والحادي والمحاورات للاصبهاني مجموع درة ابن المقفع ونثر ونظم بالعجمي
مجموع من اشعار العرب ومختار من النقائض ومن المفضليات
مجموع اخلاق الملوك ومفاخرة الشتا والصيف مجموع
للجاحظ [illegible] والمضحك والملح وذم الهوى والحاسد والمحسود واستهدا
والحث على اتخاذ الكتب مجموع القادح والباغم ومن شعر الخالدي
مجموع شعر ابي الحكم وشعر الطريف الفارقي مجموع مختار
النقائض وشعر جرير والفرزدق مجموع فيه اشعار الانصار مجموع
التمسك والحاضر والاستمتاع للعجلي ورسالة في نوادر الحكما ومن كلامهم مجموع
اختيارات جماعة من شعرا العرب واشعارهم [illegible] مجموع مكاتبات ابن الشريف
والصابي وديوان ابن [illegible] مجموع ثمانية عشر قصيدة للعرب مجموع
مختار من شعر ثلثة عشر شاعرا من العرب اختيارهما بخط [illegible] مجموع خلق
الفرس للاصمعي والوحوش له والفاظ ابن الاعرابي بزيادات ابن خالويه وحديث [illegible]
مجموع مختار المتنبي والبحتري وابي تمام والملتقط من الامثال والملح
مجموع قصيدة ابن حلزة السبعة وقصيدة [illegible] وقصيدة عنترة مجموع رد

Plate 43 Ashrafiya catalogue (670s/1270s), fol. 264b.

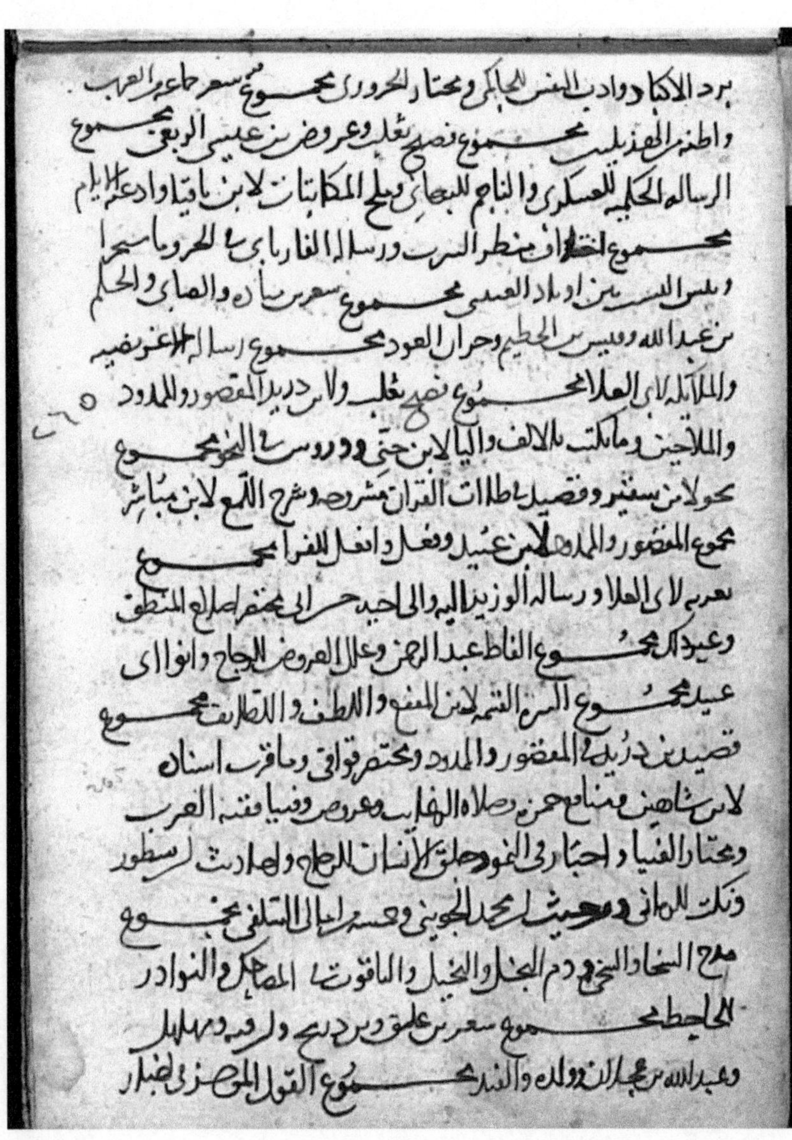

Plate 44 Ashrafiya catalogue (670s/1270s), fol. 265a. © Istanbul, Süleymaniye Yazma Eser Kütüphanesi, Fatih 5433

Plate 45 Ashrafiya catalogue (670s/1270s), fol. 265b. © Istanbul, Süleymaniye Yazma Eser Kütüphanesi, Fatih 5433

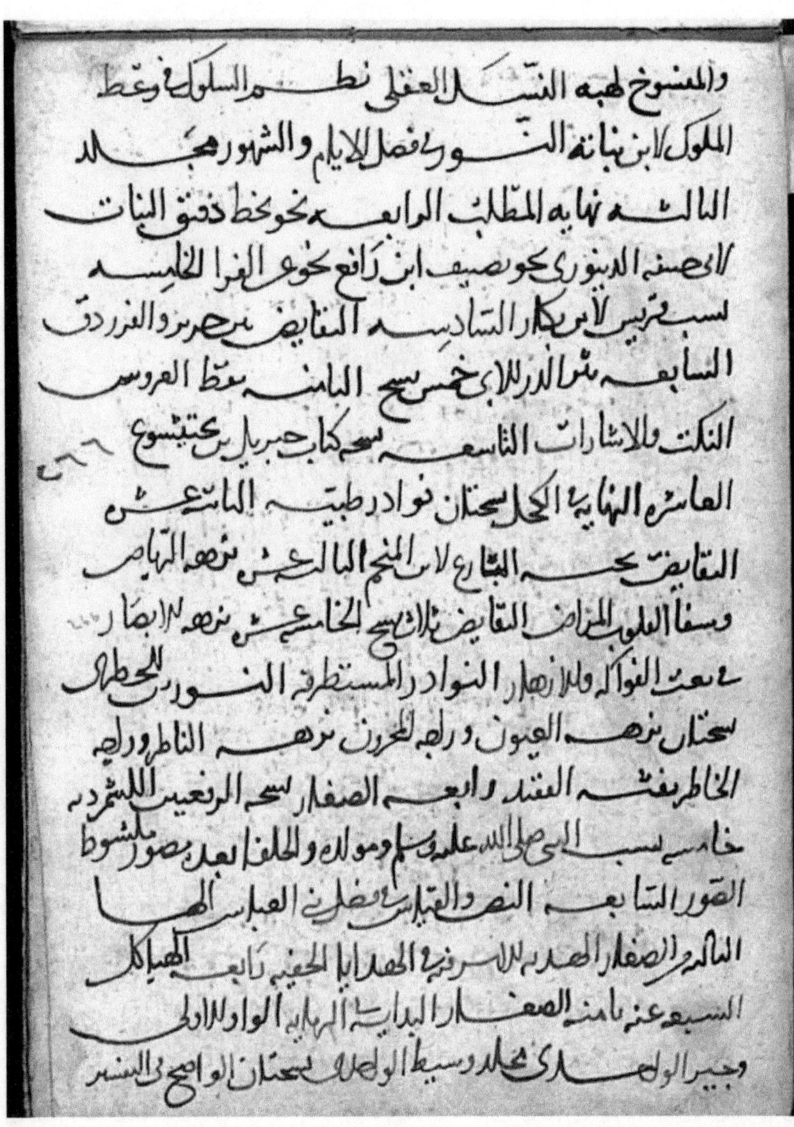

Plate 46 Ashrafiya catalogue (670s/1270s), fol. 266a. © Istanbul, Süleymaniye Yazma Eser Kütüphanesi, Fatih 5433

Plate 47 Ashrafiya catalogue (670s/1270s), fol. 266b. © Istanbul, Süleymaniye Yazma Eser Kütüphanesi, Fatih 5433

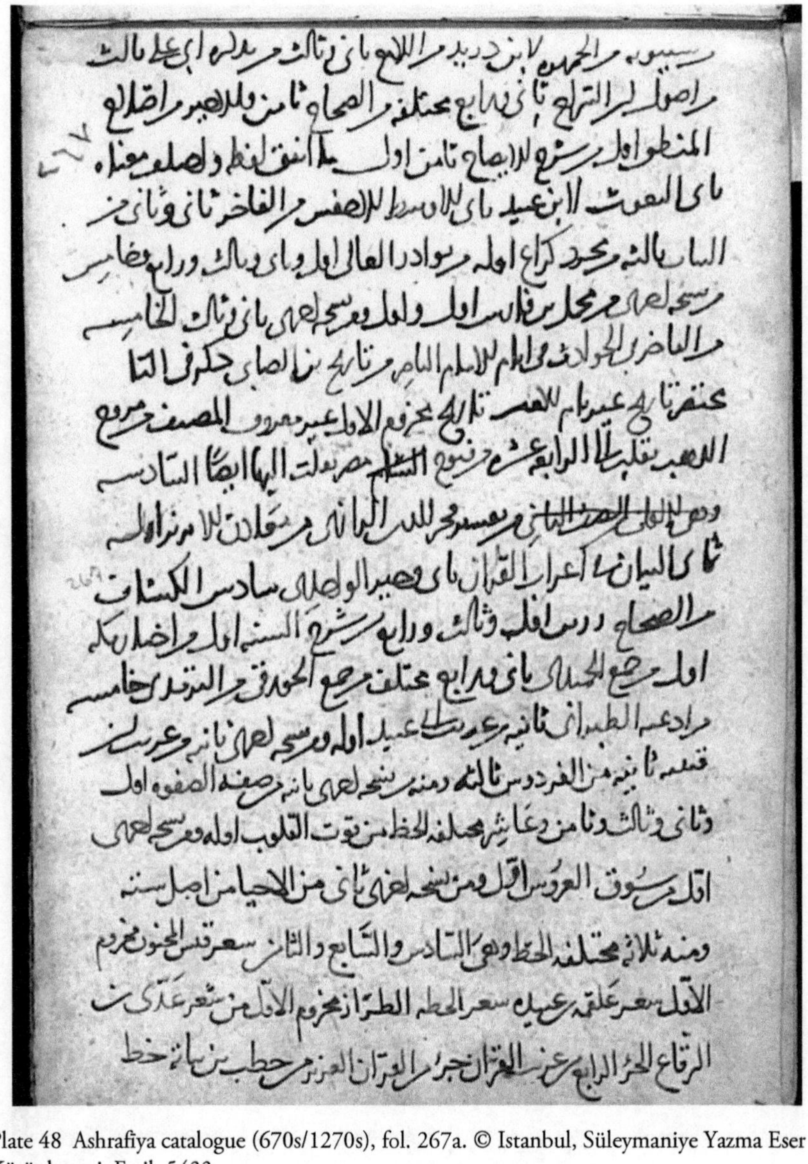

Plate 48 Ashrafiya catalogue (670s/1270s), fol. 267a. © Istanbul, Süleymaniye Yazma Eser Kütüphanesi, Fatih 5433

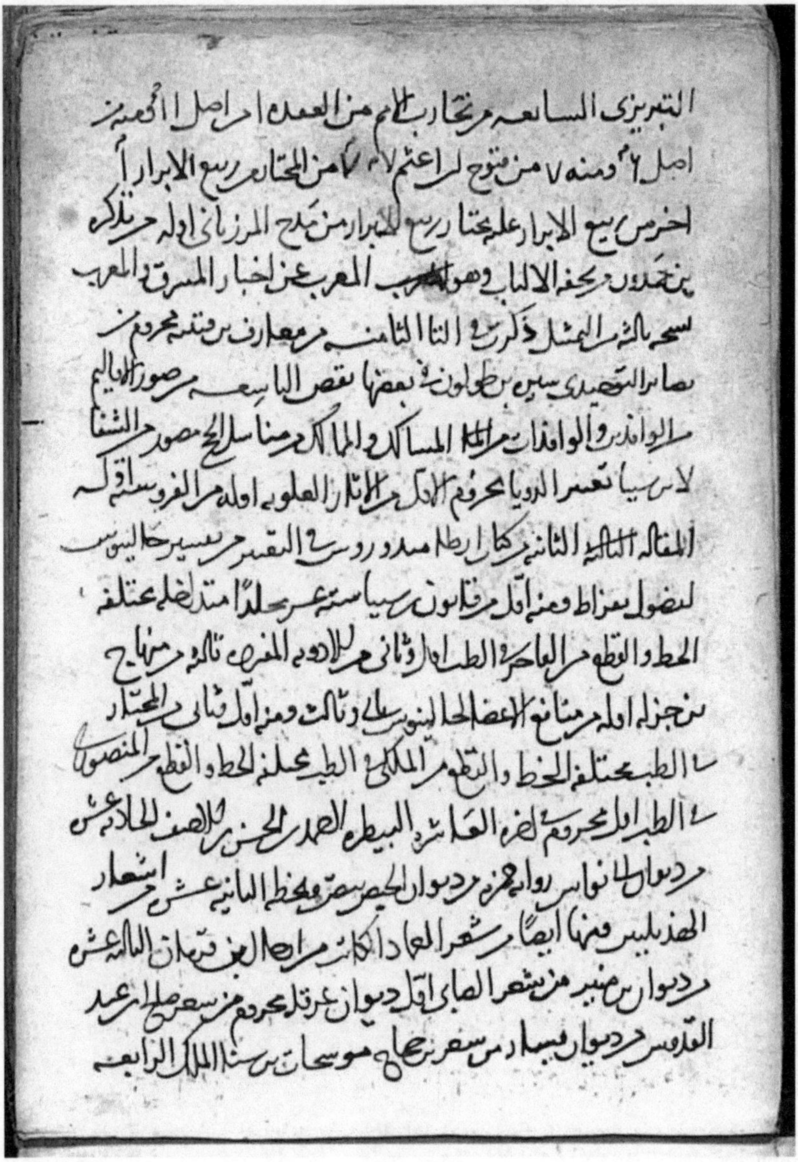

Plate 49 Ashrafiya catalogue (670s/1270s), fol. 267b. © Istanbul, Süleymaniye Yazma Eser Kütüphanesi, Fatih 5433

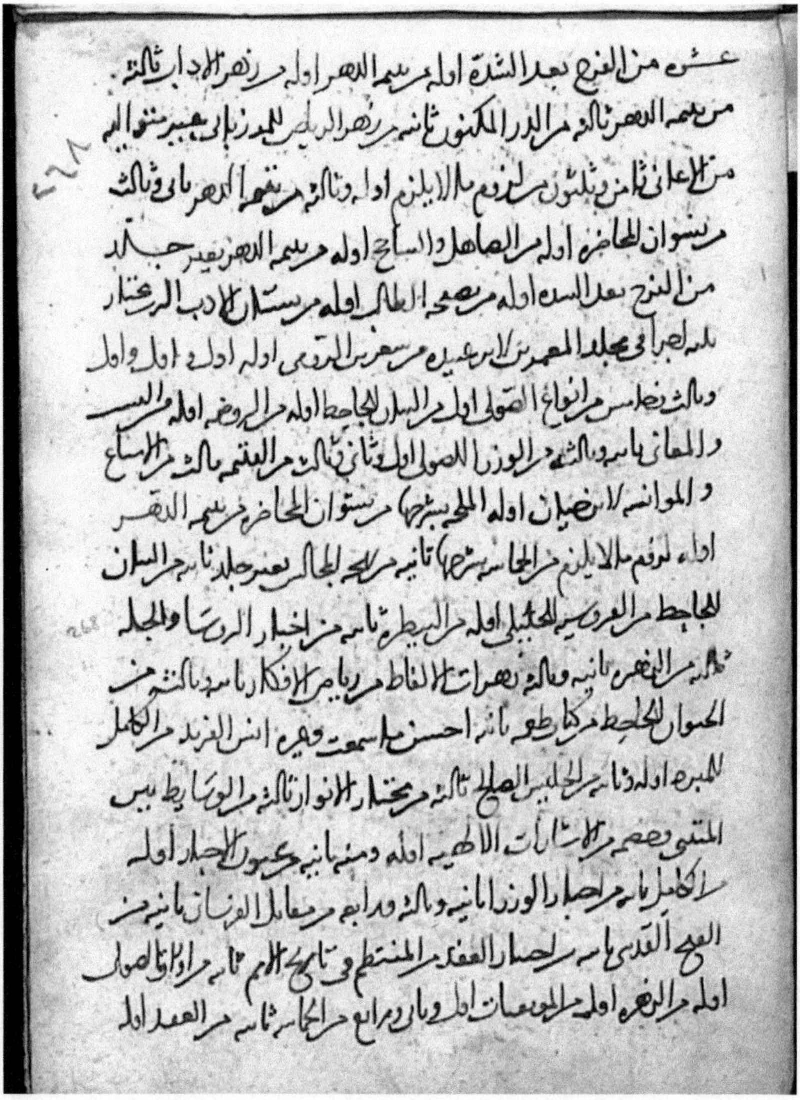
عشر من الفرج بعد الشدة اوله من يتيمة الدهر اوله من زهر الآداب ثالثة
من يتيمة الدهر ثالثه من الدر المكنون ثانيه من زهر الرياض للمرزباني بخبير مشتوا اليه
٢٦٨ من الاغاني ثامن وثلثون من لزوم ما لا يلزم اوله وثالثه من يتيمة الدهر ثاني وثالث
من ديوان الحاضر اوله من الصاهل والشاحج اوله من يتيمة الدهر بغير جلد
من الفرج بعد الشدة اوله من بهجة الطالب اوله من بستان الادب الى مختار
بلده مجلدا المعمرين لابي عبيدة من شعر ابن الرومي اوله اوله اول واول
وثالث وخامس من انواع الصلة اوله من البيان للجاحظ اوله من الروضة اوله من
والمعاني ثانيه وثالثه من الوزراء الصولي اول وثاني وثالث من العقيق ثالث من الاسجاع
والموازنه لابن ضيان اوله المحب من ديوان الحاضر من يتيمة الدهر
اوله لزوم ما لا يلزم من الحماسة ثانيه من الجالس بغير جلد ثانيه من البيان
للجاحظ من العروضية الحبلبلي اوله من البيطرة ثانيه من اخبار الرؤسا والجلة
ثالثه من البغرهم ثانيه وثالثه زهرات الالفاظ من رياض الافكار ثانيه ثالثة من
الحيوان للجاحظ من كتاب طبع ثانيه احسن ما سمعت انس العزيز من الكامل
للمبرد اوله وثانيه من الجليس الصالح ثالثه من مختار الانوار ثالثه من الوسايط بين
المتنبي وخصومه من الاشارات الالهيه اوله ومنه ثانيه من عيون الاخبار اوله
من الكامل ثانيه من اخبار الوزرا ثانيه وثالثه ورابعه من معالم الفرسان ثانيه من
الفتح القدسي ثانيه من اخبار العقد من المنتظم في تاريخ الامم ثانيه من اوائل الصواب
اوله من البغره اوله من الموضعات اول وثاني ورابع من الحماسه ثانيه من العقد اوله

Plate 50 Ashrafiya catalogue (670s/1270s), fol. 268a. © Istanbul, Süleymaniye Yazma Eser Kütüphanesi, Fatih 5433

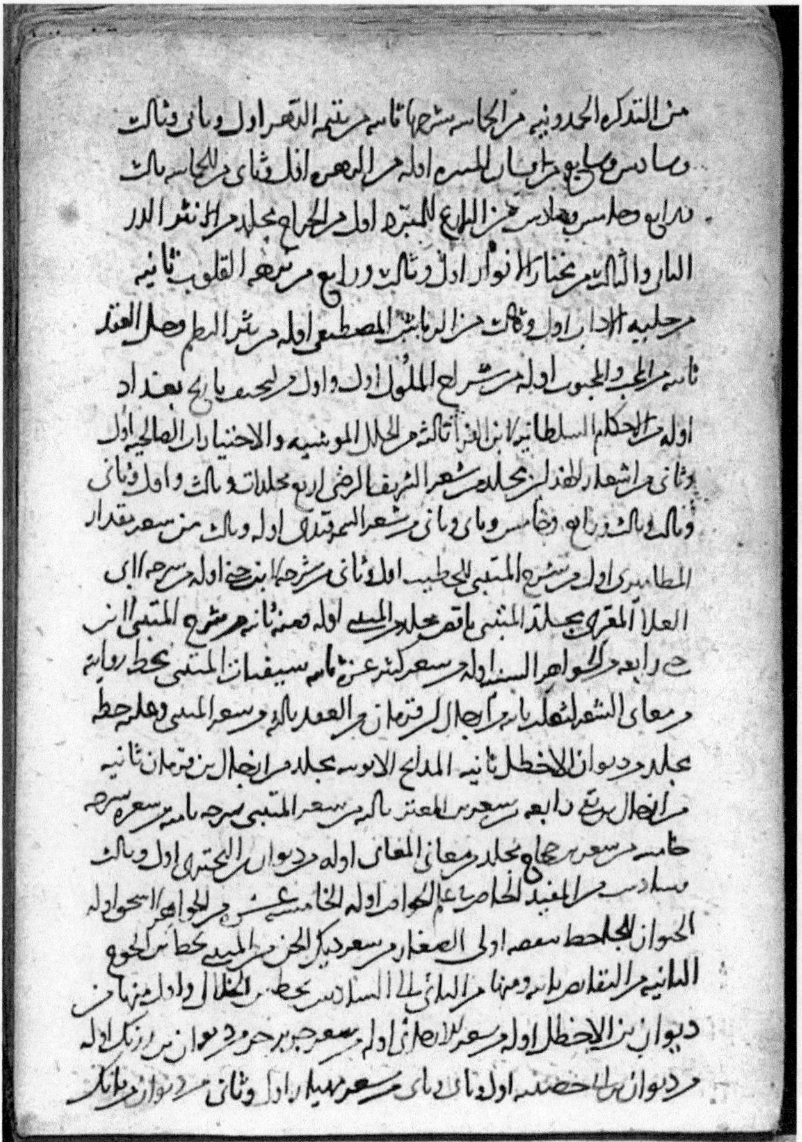

Plate 51 Ashrafiya catalogue (670s/1270s), fol. 268b. © Istanbul, Süleymaniye Yazma Eser Kütüphanesi, Fatih 5433

Plate 52 Ashrafiya catalogue (670s/1270s), fol. 269a. © Istanbul, Süleymaniye Yazma Eser Kütüphanesi, Fatih 5433

Plate 53 Ashrafiya catalogue (670s/1270s), fol. 269b. © Istanbul, Süleymaniye Yazma Eser Kütüphanesi, Fatih 5433

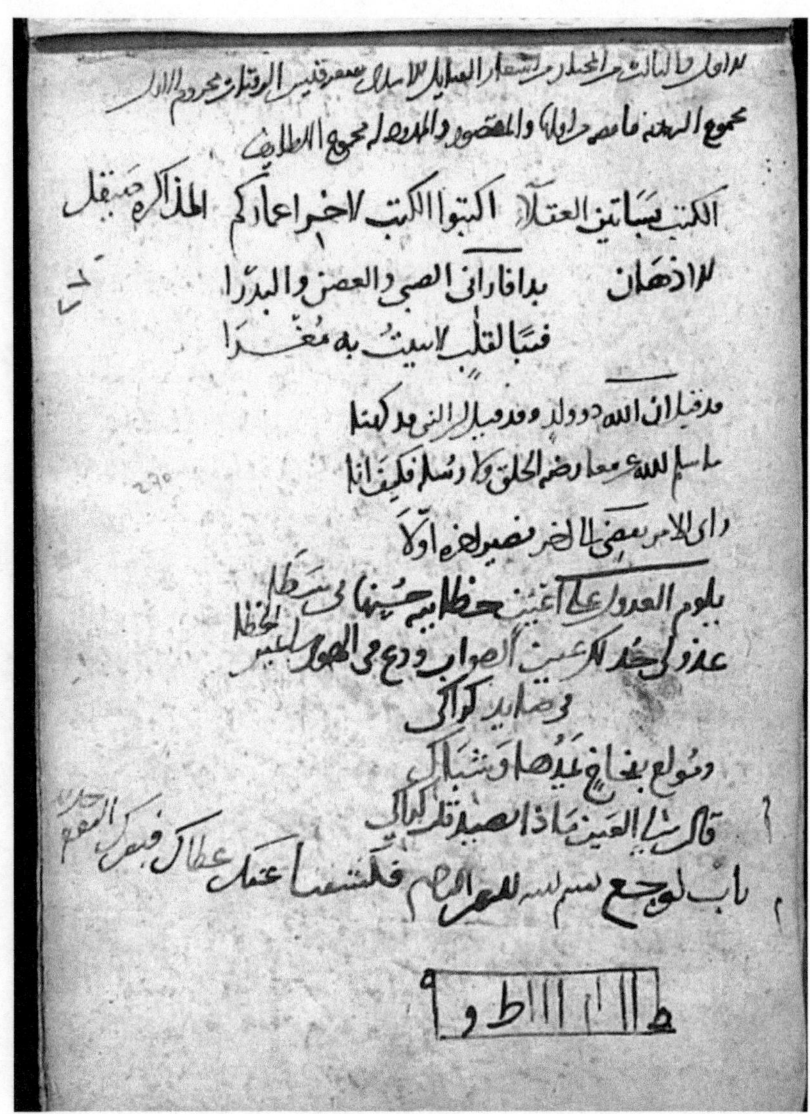

Plate 54 Ashrafiya catalogue (670s/1270s), fol. 270a. © Istanbul, Süleymaniye Yazma Eser Kütüphanesi, Fatih 5433

Abbreviations

Scr: scribe (if named, including terminology, for example '*bi-khaṭṭ*')
A: author (including collectors and creators of the work's content); the part of the name mentioned in the catalogue is underlined
S: source
MS: present-day manuscript location (asterisk classification explained in Chapter 1)
NC: number of copies (if more than one)
FI: further information on entry from the catalogue if provided, such as 'incomplete' and 'in different hands'
Q: number of quires (*juzʾ*, as given in the section on incomplete manuscripts)
L: language (if other than Arabic)
VQ: volume-quire numerals
Ṣ: *ṣaḥḥa*/*ṣaḥīḥ* sign given
C: external thematic category

K. = Kitāb
For abbreviations of authors, titles and publishing houses see bibliography.

Ashrafiya Catalogue

In the following list the standard structure of entries is as follows: consecutive entry number (assigned for the purpose of this book); 'class mark' with letter/thematic category/size; folio/line; Arabic transcription of title – English translation; comment on content; Scr; A; S; MS; NC; FI; Q; L; VQ; Ṣ; C. The reference(s) given under 'S' are in no way meant to be an exhaustive bibliography of what has been published on a specific title. Rather the aim is to provide the reader with a definitive reference for each individual title's identification. In many cases this reference is a modern edition (of which many are merely 'commercial' editions); in others this may be the most pertinent reference in a contemporaneous source or in modern scholarship.

In the name of God, the Beneficent, the Merciful, whom we ask for help. Catalogue of the books in the Ashrafiya library that is in the mausoleum of al-Malik al-Ashraf, may God's mercy be upon him, which is to the north of the Kallāsa in the [area of the] Umayyad Mosque.

(1) A/1 246b/3 *Ikhtiṣār ṣaḥīḥ Muslim – Abridgement of the Ṣaḥīḥ Muslim*; A: <u>al-Malik al-Kāmil</u> (d. 635/1238); S: Ibn Kathīr, *al-Bidāya*, XIII, 264 reports that al-Kāmil, al-Malik al-Ashraf's brother and ally, abridged the famous *ḥadīth* collection by Muslim (d. 261/875) in five volumes and that it was held in Damascus during al-Ashraf's reign. C: *ḥadīth* – collection.

(2) A/1 246b/3–4 *al-Arbaᶜūna al-jihādīya – Forty ḥadīth on jihād*; A: ᶜAlī b. Sulaymān <u>al-Murādī</u> (d. 544/1150; TI, 541–50, pp. 196–7), Damascene *ḥadīth* scholar and colleague of Ibn ᶜAsākir, the author of another *jihād* treatise (cf. no. 840); C: *ḥadīth* – collection (40, *jihād*).[37]

(3) A/1 246b/4 *Īḍāḥ al-waqf wa-al-ibtidāʾ* – *Elucidating Pauses and Beginnings*; A: Ibn al-Anbārī (d. 328/940); S: ed. M. ᶜA. Ramaḍān, Damascus: MLA, 1971; MS: Süleymaniye, Fazıl Ahmed Paşa 11***; VQ: 2; C: Koran – recitation. (cf. no. 1375)

(4) A/1 246b/4 *al-Injād*[38] *fī al-jihād* – *The Assistance in jihād*; A: ᶜAbd al-Raḥmān b. Najm Nāṣiḥ al-Dīn (d. 634/1236); S: MM, II, 125; another possibility would be Muḥammad b. ᶜĪsā al-Azdī al-Qurṭubī (d. 620/1223) who authored *K. al-injād fī abwāb al-jihād* (ed. Q.ᶜA. al-Wazzānī, Beirut: DGI, 2003), but the regional proximity and the fact that a second title by Nāṣiḥ al-Dīn was in the library (cf. no. 1118) makes him more likely. VQ: 1; Ṣ; C: sermons – jihād.

(5) A/1 246b/4-5 *Akhbār rūḥ al-ᶜārifīn* – *Reports on 'Rūḥ al-ᶜārifīn'*; probably A: Yūsuf Sibṭ Ibn al-Jawzī (d. 654/1256) who authored a commentary on the famous collection of seventy *ḥadīth*, *Rūḥ al-ᶜārifīn*, by the ᶜAbbasid Caliph al-Nāṣir li-Dīn Allāh (d. 622/1225) (ed. B.M. Fahd, Amman: DF, 2001) and who endowed another copy of this work in the mausoleum's sister institution in Damascus, the Dār al-ḥadīth al-Ashrafīya (Sibṭ Ibn al-Jawzī, *Mirʾāt*, XIV–XV, 541, 569). VQ: 1; Ṣ; C: *ḥadīth* – collection – commentary.

(6) A/1 246b/5 *Arbaᶜūna ḥadīth jihādīya* – *Forty ḥadīth on jihād*; A: the author is given as ᶜAbd al-Raḥīm b. Manṣūr and this could be a work by the *ḥadīth* scholar ᶜAbd al-Raḥmān b. Muḥammad b. Manṣūr (d. 271/884–5) (TI, 261–80, pp. 386–7) who transmitted *jihād*-relevant *ḥadīths* and is occasionally cited as ᶜAbd al-Raḥmān b. Manṣūr (see al-Ḥākim, *al-Mustadrak*, II, 104). However, this would be an unusually early work of this genre and it is more likely that this author belonged to the circle of Ibn ᶜAsākir like no. 2. That the cataloguer does not use the definite article for the title (in contrast to no. 2) indicates that this was a minor work. VQ: 1; Ṣ; C: *ḥadīth* – collection (40, *jihād*).[39]

(7) A/1 246b/5-6 *al-Āyāt al-wārida fī faḍl al-jihād* – *Koranic Verses on the Merits of jihād*; No such title is identifiable and this is probably a book-in-the-making. VQ: 1; Ṣ; C: Koran – collection of verses – jihād.

(8) A/1 246b/6 *al-Asbāb al-jihādīya* – *Occasions of jihād*; the author is arguably A: Muḥammad b. Hibat Allāh Ibn al-Warrāq al-Baghdādī Sibṭ Abū Saᶜīd

(d. 470/1078; TI, 461–70, pp. 338–9). While first and foremost a grammarian he had also some scholarly interest in *ḥadīth* (al-Suyūṭī, *Bughyat*, I, 255–6), the main source for such *jihād* works. C: *ḥadīth* – collection (*jihād*).[40]

(9) A/1 246b/6 *Adab al-dīn wa-al-dunyā – On Conduct in Religious and Worldly Matters*; A: al-Māwardī (d. 450/1058); S: ed. M. al-Saqqā, *Adab al-dunyā wa-al-dīn*, Beirut 1955; Germ. tr. by O. Rescher, Stuttgart 1932; VQ: 1; Ṣ; C: ethics. (cf. no. 1264b)

(10) A/1 246b/7 *al-Ikhtiyār fī al-ḥikāyāt – The Selection of Narrations*; no such title is identifiable and this is most likely either a generic or a key word title. '*Ḥikāyāt*' has a range of meanings (including narrations, stories, speeches and reports) and can refer to various fields of knowledge. On account of it being placed in category 1 and the preceding titles, this treatise is most likely a collection of edifying reports. C:?

(11) A/1 246b/7 *Iḥyāʾ ʿulūm al-dīn – The Revival of the Religious Sciences*; A: al-Ghazālī (d. 505/1111); S: ed. Cairo: Lajnat nashr al-thaqāfa al-islāmīya, 1937–9; C: sufism. (cf. no. 1448)

(12) A/1 246b/7 *al-Aʿziya wa-al-tahānī – Consolations and Congratulations*; possibly A: Muḥammad b. Sahl Ibn al-Marzubān al-Karkhī (d. c.345/956) whose *al-Muntahā fī al-kamāl* includes an *al-Tahānī wa-al-taʿāzī*; S: ed. I. al-Baṭshān, Burayda: Nādī al-qaṣīm al-adabī, 2003; C: adab – anthology. (cf. nos 995, 1107, 1260f)

(13) A/1 246b/7–8 *Iʿtilāl al-qulūb – Lovelornness [Concerning the Reports on Lovers]*; A: Muḥammad b. Jaʿfar al-Kharāʾiṭī (d. 327/939); S: *Iʿtilāl al-qulūb fī akhbār al-ʿushshāq*, ed. Gh. al-Shaykh, Beirut: DKI, 2001; C: ḥadīth – collection/love literature. (cf. no. 1274a)

(14a) A/1 246b/8 *Iʿrāb sūrat al-Ikhlāṣ – Inflexion of the sura 'al-Ikhlāṣ'*; probably an extract from one or several of the many *Iʿrāb al-Qurʾān* works (cf. IN, index); C: Koran – inflexion (*iʿrāb*).

(14b) 246b/8 *Amthāl ʿan ʿAlī b. Abī Ṭālib – Sayings of ʿAlī b. Abī Ṭālib*; such collections of moral maxims and proverbs attributed to ʿAlī (or other central religious figures) are generally anonymous. For one example see P. Heath, 'Aphorisms of ʿAli', in Renard (ed.): *House of Islam*, 149–55; FI: cataloguer, exceptionally so, remarks that the previous entry '*yataḍammana*'/'*contains*' these sayings, so that this is not a standard multiple-text entry; C: ᶜAlī – sayings attributed to.

(14c) 246b/8–9 *wa-Waṣīya li-waladihi raḍiya Allāh ᶜanhumā – Last Advice to His Son (may God be pleased with them)*; probably treatise on ᶜAlī's advice to his son Ḥasan, which was, for instance, included in the *Treasury of Virtues* (*Dustūr maᶜālim al-ḥikam*) by Muḥammad al-Quḍāᶜī (d. 454/1062) (Engl. tr. & ed. Qutbuddin, *Treasury of Virtues*, 89–93, 101); one example of this title is the undated manuscript Süleymaniye, Ayasofya 2790/6. C: political thought – *imāmate* theory. (cf. no. 1382)

(15) A/1 246b/9 *Uṣūl al-dīn – Principles of Religion*; A: Muḥammad al-Baṣrī Ibn Khallād (d. mid 4th/10th c.); S: IN, I/2, 627; the identification of this title is problematic for two reasons: Ibn Khallād's work is always cited as '*Kitāb al-uṣūl*', not as '*Uṣūl al-dīn*' and the work was lost much earlier (on this work see Ansari and Schmidtke, 'Zaydī Reception'). However, the reading of this entry is clear and there is no other possible author who authored such a work. C: uṣūl al-dīn.

(16) A/1 246b/9 *al-Ishāra – Guidance*; A: Salīm b. Ayyūb al-Rāzī (d. 447/1055); S: IKH, II, 397–9; C: fiqh – shāfiᶜī.

(17) A/1 246b/9 *Ādāb al-ijtihād – Rules of ijtihād*; no such title is identifiable and this book-in-the-making draws probably on the larger adab works for judges such as the 7th-/13th-c. work by Ibn Abī al-Dam, *Adab al-qaḍāʾ*. C: fiqh.

(18) A/1 246b/10 *al-Itmām li-faḍāʾil al-anām – Perfecting Man's Virtues*; A: Abū al-Ḥasan Muḥammad b. Yūsuf al-ᶜĀmirī (d. 381/992); S: Rowson, *Muslim Philosopher*, 10. This work is lost, but al-ᶜĀmirī refers to it in his own writings to refute the view (that he ascribes to unnamed philosophers and esotericists) that the sage can dispense with ritual obligations. C: theology?

(19) A/1 246b/10 *Ithbāt imāmat ᶜAlī b. Abī Ṭālib raḍiya Allāh ᶜanhu – Proof of ᶜAlī b. Abī Ṭālib's imamate (may God be pleased with him)*; arguably the *Ithbāt al-waṣīya li-l-Imām ᶜAlī b. Abī Ṭālib* that is also referred to as *Ithbāt al-imāma li-ᶜAlī b. Abī Ṭālib* (al-Ṭihrānī, *Dharīᶜa*, I, 85); attr. to A: ᶜAlī b. al-Ḥusayn al-Masᶜūdī (d. 345/956) (ed. Najaf, *c.*1955); C: political thought – imāmate theory. (cf. no. 1218b)

(20) A/1 246b/10-11 *al-Irshād fī al-fiqh – Guidance in Jurisprudence*; three main possibilities: 1) Muḥammad b. Aḥmad al-Hāshimī (d. 428/1037) (TI, 421–40, p. 240: '*Irshād*'); C: fiqh – ḥanbalī; 2) ᶜAlī b. ᶜUqayl al-Baghdādī (d. 513/1119) (Baghdādī, *Hadīyat*, I, 695); C: fiqh – ḥanbalī; 3) Muḥammad b. Muḥammad al-Shaykh al-Mufīd (d. 413/1032) (Engl. tr. Howard, *Book of Guidance*); C: fiqh – imāmī. (cf. no. 762)

(21) A/1 246b/11 *al-Iᶜtibār wa-al-naẓar – Consideration and Reflection*; no such title is identifiable. Placed in thematic category 1 it is most likely an extract from *fiqh* works dealing with legal reasoning, such as *Taʾsīs al-naẓar/ al-Mukhtalaf bayna aṣḥāb al-fiqh* by Abū al-Layth Naṣr b. Muḥammad al-Samarqandī (d. between 373/983–4 and 393/1002–3) (GAS, I, 450), *Taʾsīs al-naẓar* by ᶜAbd Allāh b. ᶜUmar al-Dabūsī (d. 430/1039) (GAS, I, 456) and *al-Iᶜtibār fī ibṭāl al-qiyās* by Ibrāhīm b. Aḥmad al-Ribāᶜī (d. 352/963) (IN, II/1, 66); C: fiqh.

(22) A/1 246b/11 *Ishārat al-nuẓẓār – Guidance for Theologians*; most likely *Irshād al-nuẓẓār ilā laṭāʾif al-asrār* by A: Muḥammad b. ᶜUmar Fakhr al-Dīn al-Rāzī Ibn al-Khaṭīb (d. 606/1210); S: al-Zarkān, *Fakhr al-Dīn al-Rāzī*, no. 9; C: theology.

(23) A/1 246b/11-12 *al-Ifṣāḥ wa-al-bayān fī maᶜrifat Allāh taᶜālā min al-Qurʾān – Elucidation and Clarification Concerning the Knowledge of God (may He be exalted) by the Koran*; no such title is identifiable and these are possibly two works bound together. If that is the case the first title would most likely refer to the *fiqh* compendium *al-Ifṣāḥ* by the Shafiᶜi jurisprudent al-Ḥasan/ al-Ḥusayn b. al-Qāsim al-Ṭabarī (d. 350/961) (IKH, II, 76) or the *ḥadīth* commentary by the ᶜAbbasid vizier Yaḥyā b. Muḥammad Ibn Hubayra (d. 560/1165) (IKH, VI, 233). The second title would be a title such as *al-Bayān fī ᶜilm al-Qurʾān* by al-Faḍl b. Ismāᶜīl al-Jurjānī (fl. 5th/11th c.) (MU, V, 2166) or *al-Bayān al-jāmiᶜ fī ᶜulūm al-Qurʾān* by Sulaymān b. Najāḥ (d. 496/1103) (MM, I, 798–9); C: fiqh – shāfiᶜī?/Koran – theology?

(24) A/1 246b/12 *al-Irshād ilā mā laysa li-l-salāṭīn tafwīḍuhu ilā al-quḍāt – Guidance on What Rulers Cannot Delegate to Judges*; no such title is identifiable. Most likely it is a treatise derived from advice for rulers literature on the question of delegating their prerogatives, for instance discussed in ᶜAbd Allāh Ibn al-Muqaffaᶜ's (d. 139/756?) *al-Ādāb al-kabīr* under the heading

al-Tafwīḍ ilā al-kufāh (see Tardy, 'd'al-Adab al-kabīr', §§ 23) and al-ᶜAskarī (d. *c.*400/1010) *K. mā iḥtakama bihi al-khulafāᵓ ilā al-quḍāh*, ed. & Fr. tr. Tillier, *Livre des Caliphes*. C: political thought – mirror for princes.

(25) A/4 246b/13 *Iṣlāḥ al-manṭiq – Correcting Speech*; A: Ibn al-Sikkīt (d. 244/858); S: ed. ᶜA.M. Hārūn, Cairo: DM, 1949; MS: Süleymaniye, Yeni Cami 933**; C: lexicography. (cf. no. 1414)

(26) A/4 246b/13 *Adab al-kātib – The Secretary's Manual*; several authors wrote works with this popular title. However, placed in category 4 with its heavy emphasis on philological fields of knowledge this is probably not one of those manuals focusing on administrative issues in a narrow sense, such as the one by Muḥammad b. Yaḥyā al-Ṣūlī (d. 335/947). Rather this is more likely a philologist's work focusing on correct grammatical and lexicographical usage, such as those by Ibn Qutayba (d. 276/889) (IN, I/1, 237) and Ibn Durayd (d. 321/933) (IN, I/1, 180). The outstanding popularity of the former's work, also evident from the number of surviving manuscripts, makes him by far the most likely author. A: ᶜAbd Allāh b. Muslim al-Dīnawarī Ibn Qutayba; S: ed. M. ᶜAbd al-Ḥamīd, Cairo: Dār al-Ṭalāᵓiᶜ, 2005; MS: Süleymaniye, Ayasofya 3770**; C: grammar/lexicography/manual for secretaries.

(27) A/4 246b/13 *Alfāẓ – Words*; A: ᶜAbd al-Raḥmān b. ᶜĪsā al-Hamadhānī (d. 320/932); S: IN, I/2, 425: '*al-Alfāẓ*'; ed. *K. al-Alfāẓ al-kitābīya*, Beirut: DKI, 1991; C: lexicography. (cf. no. 1311a)

(28) A/4 246b/13 *Alfāẓ – Words*; the author is given as Muḥammad b. al-Ḥasan but among the authors of *Alfāẓ* works (cf. e.g. indices in IN, IKH, MU) no scholar carries this name. As this is clearly a lexicographical work this may be A: Muḥammad b. al-Ḥasan al-Ḥātimī (d. 388/998) as MU, VI, 2507 refers to an unfinished '*kitāb fī al-lugha*' of his. C: lexicography.

(29) A/4 246b/14 *al-Aḍdād – Contranyms*; A: Ibn al-Sikkīt (d. 244/858); S: ed. A. Haffner, Beirut: MKa, 1913; IN, I/1, 220; C: philology.

(30a) A/4 246b/14 *al-Īḍāḥ – Elucidating [Grammar]*; A: Abū ᶜAlī al-Ḥasan al-Fārisī (d. 377/987); S: ed. K.B. al-Marjan, Beirut: AK, 1996; C: grammar.

(30b) 246b/14 *wa-al-Takmila – and The Completion*; A: Abū ᶜAlī al-Ḥasan al-Fārisī (d. 377/987); S: ed. K.B. al-Marjan, Mosul 1981; C: grammar.

(31) A/4 246b/14 *Asmāʾ khayl al-ᶜArab* – *Names of the Arabs' Horses*; A: Muḥammad b. Ziyād Ibn al-Aᶜrābī (d. c.231/846); S: ed. M.ᶜA. Sulṭānī, Beirut: MR, 1981; GAS, VIII, 127–8; C: lexicography. (cf. no. 1208b)

(32) A/4 246b/15 *al-Alfāẓ li-maghā wa-li-qadd al-asmāʾ fī al-farq bayna al- ḍād wa-al-ẓāʾ* – *Words for Pronouncing and Cutting Short Names: On the Difference between the Letters ḍād and ẓāʾ*; the reading of the title's first part is very tentative, but the second part clearly indicates the work's content. The most prominent work on this topic was authored by Ismāᶜīl Ibn ᶜAbbād (d. 385/995) (ed. M. Ḥ. Āl-Yāsīn, Baghdad 1958), which is held elsewhere in the library (cf. no. 976?). C: lexicography.

(33) A/4 246b/15 *al-Amthāl* – *Proverbs*; A: al-Maydānī (d. 518/1124); S: ed. M.M. ᶜAbd al-Ḥamīd, Beirut: DF, 1972; C: adab – proverbs.

(34) A/4 246b/15-16 *al-Anwāʾ* – *Setting and Rising of Asterisms*; A: Abū Ḥanīfa Aḥmad b. Dāwūd al-Dīnawarī (fl. 3rd/9th c.); S: IN, I/1, 238; GAS, VII, 349; C: lexicography/astronomy/meteorology.

(35) A/4 246b/16 *al-Inṣāf* – *[Book of] Equity [Concerning the Dispute between the Grammarians of Basra and those of Kufa]*; A: al-Anbārī (d. 577/1181); S: *al-Inṣāf fī masāʾil al-khilāf bayna al-naḥwīyīn al-Baṣrīyīn wa-al-Kūfiyīn*, ed. G. Weil, Leiden 1913; MS: Süleymaniye, Yeni Cami 1060*; C: grammar.

(36) A/4 246b/16 *al-Alfāẓ* – *Words*; A: Ibn al-Sikkīt (d. 244/858); S: IN, I/1, 220; C: lexicography. (cf. no. 1407)

(37) A/4 246b/16-247a/1 *al-Amthāl* – *Proverbs*; A: Ḥamza al-Iṣfahānī (d. after 350/961); S: *al-Durra al-fākhira fī al-amthāl al-sāʾira*, ed. ᶜA. Qaṭāmish, Cairo: DM, 1971–2; IN, I/2, 432; C: adab – proverbs. (cf. no. 42)

(38) A/4 247a/1 *al-Amthāl* – *Proverbs*; A: Abū[41] ᶜUbayd al-Qāsim b. Sallām al-Harawī (d. 224/838); S: ed. R. Sellheim, *Die klassisch-arabischen Sprichwörtersammlungen insbesondere die des Abū ᶜUbaid*, 's-Gravenhage 1954; C: adab – proverbs.

(39) A/4 247a/1 *al-Amthāl* – *Proverbs*; A: al-Mufaḍḍal al-Ḍabbī (d. 164/780 or 170/786); S: ed. I. ᶜAbbās, *Amthāl al-ᶜArab*, Beirut: DRA, 1981; C: adab – proverbs.

(40) A/4 247a/1 *[al-]Amthāl* – *Proverbs*; attr. to A: ᶜAbd al-Malik b. Qurayb al-Aṣmaᶜī (d. 213/828?); S: EI³, R. Weipert, 'al-Aṣmaᶜī'; C: adab – proverbs.

(41) A/4 247a/2 *al-Unmūdhaj fī al-naḥw* – *The Model on Grammar*; two main possibilities: 1) Maḥmūd b. ᶜUmar al-Zamakhsharī (d. 538/1144; ed. in al-Maydānī, *Nuzhat al-ṭarf fī ᶜilm al-ṣarf*, Beirut: DAJ, 1981) or 2) al-Maydānī (d. 518/1124; EI², R. Sellheim, 'al-Maydānī'); C: grammar.

(42) A/4 247a/2 *[al-]Amthāl* – *Proverbs*; A: Ḥamza al-Iṣfahānī (d. after 350/961); S: *al-Durra al-fākhira fī al-amthāl al-sāʾira*, ed. ᶜA. Qaṭāmish, Cairo: DM, 1971–2; IN, I/2, 432; C: adab – proverbs. (cf. no. 37)

(43) A/5 247a/2 *al-Awrāq* – *Book of Leaves*; A: Muḥammad b. Yaḥyā al-Ṣūlī (d. 335/947); S: part. ed. J. Heyworth-Dunne, London and Cairo 1934; IN, I/2, 464; MS: Süleymaniye, Şehid Ali Paşa 2141*; C: history/adab. (cf. no. 1551)

(44) A/5 247a/3 *al-Istiẓhār amr al-quḍāt* – *Assisting Judges' Decisions*; A: al-Ghazālī (d. 505/1111); S: ed. ᶜA. Badawī, Paris 2006; FI: '*wa-huwa al-Mustaẓhirī*' / '*and this is the Mustaẓhirī*'; C: political thought.[42] (cf. no. 970 for cross-reference to this work)

(45) A/5 247a/3-4 *al-Akhbār al-ṭiwāl* – *The Extended Reports*; A: Abū Ḥanīfa Aḥmad b. Dāwūd al-Dīnawarī (fl. 3rd/9th c.); S: ᶜA. ᶜĀmir, Cairo: DIKA, 1960; C: history – universal.

(46) A/5 247a/4 *al-Ikmāl* – *Completion*;[43] A: ᶜAlī b. Hibat Allāh Ibn Mākūlā (fl. 5th/11th c.); S: ed. ᶜA. al-Yamānī, Hyderabad: DMU, 1962–7; MS: Süleymaniye, Carullah 584*; C: onomastics.

(47) A/5 247a/4–5 *Amthāl amr al-Malik al-Muᶜaẓẓam fī tarjamat akhbār al-ᶜajam* – *Similitudes of al-Malik al-Muᶜaẓẓam's Affairs: The Translation of the Persians' History*; no such title is identifiable and this is clearly a local Ayyubid work dedicated to al-Malik al-Muᶜaẓẓam (r. 615/1218–624/1227), al-Malik al-Ashraf's predecessor in Damascus. The term *tarjama* could refer to either a biography or a translation. However, the latter is the obvious choice here partly because the term is used in this sense elsewhere in this catalogue (cf. no. 1115). The Persian-language works in this catalogue show that such texts circulated in Ayyubid Damascus to a considerable extent. NC: 2; VQ: 5; C: history.

(48) A/6 247a/5 *Ashᶜār Fahm wa-ᶜAdwān* – *Poems of the Fahm and ᶜAdwān Tribes*; A: al-Sukkarī (d. 275/888); S: IN, I/2, 498; GAS, II,

298; FI: '*al-sādisa wa-hiya al-ūlā min al-nisba*'/'*sixth [thematic category], which is the beginning of the [books concerned with] genealogy*';[44] VQ: 1; C: poetry – anthology – pre-Islamic.

(49) A/6 247a/6 *Ashᶜār Banī Badr b. Juwayya – Poems of the Badr b. [ᶜAmr b.] Juwayya Tribe*; the cataloguer was unsure about this entry as he refrained from using any diacritical marks, which is unusual for this section of the catalogue. No tribe called '*Banū ᵓ-b/t/th/n/y-d/dh-r/z*' is identifiable. For the tribal name suggested here see Kister, 'Tribes of Arabia', 39. NC: 2; VQ: 1; Ṣ; C: poetry – anthology – pre-Islamic.

(50) A/6 247a/6-7 *al-Iᶜjāz wa-al-ījāz – Inimitability and Conciseness*; A: al-Thaᶜālibī (d. 429/1038); S: ed. M.I. Salīm, Cairo: MQ, 1999; NC: 4; VQ: 39, 45, 15; C: adab – proverbs. (cf. no. 1257)

(51) A/6 247a/7 *al-Ādāb al-dhahabīya – Golden Book of Elegance*; no such title is identifiable, but this clearly refers to the *Ādāb* by A: ᶜAbd Allāh Ibn al-Muᶜtazz (d. 296/908); S: *al-Ādāb*, ed. S. Radīf, Baghdad: MḤ, 1972; VQ: 1; Ṣ; C: adab – proverbs. (cf. no. 1208f?)

(52) A/6 247a/8 *Ism al-mafᶜūl al-thulāthī – [The Book of] Hollow Roots*; FI: '*wa-yuᶜrafu bi-al-Muqtaḍab*'/'*known as al-Muqtaḍab*'; A: Abū al-Fatḥ Ibn Jinnī (d. 392/1002); S: *al-Muqtaḍab fī ism al-mafᶜūl min al-thulāthī al-muᶜtall al-ᶜayn*, ed. M. al-Mubārak, Damascus and Beirut: Dār Ibn Kathīr, 1988; VQ: 1; Ṣ; C: grammar.

(53a) A/6 247a/8 *Asmāᵓ al-asad – Names of the Lion*; A: two possibilities: 1) Ibn Khālawayh (d. 370/980–1; ed. M. J. al-Darwīsh, Beirut: MR, 1989) or 2) Muḥammad b. ᶜAlī al-Harawī (d. 433/1041; MU, VI, 2579); C: lexicography.

(53b) 247a/8–9 *wa-Risālat Abī al-ᶜAlāᵓ – Abū al-ᶜAlāᵓ's Epistle*; A: Abū al-ᶜAlāᵓ al-Maᶜarrī (d. 449/1058); S: al-Maᶜarrī, *Rasāᵓil*, I, 183–250; FI: '*wa-hiya al-Ighrīḍīya*'/'*and this is the Ighrīḍīya*'; VQ: 1; Ṣ; C: adab. (cf. nos 533, 1223a, 1306a)

(54) A/6 247a/9 *Ijmāl ᶜawāmil al-iᶜrāb – Summary of Words Affecting Desinential Syntax*; A: ᶜAbd Allāh Ibn Barrī (d. 582/1187) (IKH, III, 108); no such title is identifiable, but Ibn Barrī's teacher al-Shantarīnī (d. 550/1155–6) authored a *Talqīḥ al-albāb fī ᶜawāmil al-iᶜrāb* and this is arguably Ibn Barrī's summary of his teacher's work. VQ: 1; Ṣ; C: grammar.

(55) A/6 247a/9 *al-Anwāʾ – Setting and Rising of Asterisms*; A: Ibn Durayd (d. 321/933); S: IN, I/1, 180; VQ: 1; Ṣ; C: lexicography/astronomy/meteorology.

(56) A/7 247a/10 *al-Abyāt al-sāʾira [al-]miʾa – One Hundred Much-Quoted Verses*; this is a popular title and there are several possibilities for such an anthology of well-known and much-quoted verses that became proverbs (*amthāl*), such as Abū al-ᶜAmaythal (d. 240/854) (IN, I/1, 135) and al-Sukkarī (d. 275/888) (IN, I/1, 240); Scr('*bi-khaṭṭ*'): Muḥammad b. ᶜAlī Ibn Muqla (d. 328/940); VQ: 1; Ṣ; C: adab – proverbs.[45]

(57) A/7 247a/10 *al-Aᶜyān wa-al-amāthil – Prominent and Exemplary Persons*; A: Hilāl b. al-Muḥassin al-Ṣābiʾ (d. 448/1056); S: MU, VI, 2783: '*al-Amāthil wa-al-aᶜyān*'; VQ: 1–43; Ṣ; C: adab – collection of anecdotes.

(58) A/7 247a/11 *al-Imtāᶜ wa-al-muʾānasa – [The Book of] Delightful and Intimate Conversations*; A: Abū Ḥayyān al-Tawḥīdī (d. 414/1023); S: ed. A. Amīn/A. al-Zayn, Cairo: LTTN, 1953; VQ: 3–43; Ṣ; C: adab/philosophy. (cf. nos 81a, 1521)

(59) A/7 247a/11–12 *al-Adhkiyāʾ – Astute Men*; A: Ibn al-Jawzī (d. 597/1200); S: ed. M.A. Farshūkh, Beirut: DF, 1990; NC: 2; VQ: 1–43, 1–44; Ṣ; MS: Süleymaniye, Fatih 4024***; C: adab – anthology. (cf. no. 990)

(60) A/7 247a/12-13 *al-Amthāl wa-al-ḥikam – Proverbs and Pieces of Wisdom*; A: al-Māwardī (d. 450/1058); S: ed. F. ᶜA. Aḥmad, Doha: Dār al-amīn, 1983; NC: 3; VQ: 1–38, 1–44, 1–44; C: adab/proverbs.

(61) A/7 247a/13 *Akhbār wa-ḥikāyāt wa-amthāl wa-ashᶜār – Reports, Narrations, Proverbs and Poems*; anonymous work with generic title; VQ: 1; Ṣ; C: adab/proverbs/poetry.

(62) A/7 247a/13–14 *Akhbār Ibn Ḥajjāj – Reports on Ibn Ḥajjāj*; no such title is identifiable. It refers to the poet al-Ḥusayn Ibn al-Ḥajjāj (d. 391/1001) (IKH, II, 168–72), whom contemporary authors such as Ḥāzim al-Qarṭājannī (d. 684/1285) also cite as 'Ibn Ḥajjāj' without the article (cited in v. Gelder, *Bad and the Ugly*, 110). NC: 2; FI: '*nuskha thāniya minhu muṣawwara fī 9*'/'*a second copy of it [is] illustrated, in [thematic category] 9*'; VQ: 1; Ṣ; C: poetry – commentary.

(63) A/7 247a/14 *Ajnās al-aᶜdād wa-al-akhbār – Classes of Numbers and Reports*; no such title is identifiable and this is most likely a

book-in-the-making. Placed in category 7 this is probably an adab anthology. VQ: 1; Ṣ; C: adab?

(64) A/7 247a/15 *Adab*[46] *al-ghurabāʾ* – *Book of Strangers*; A: Abū al-Faraj al-Iṣfahānī (d. 356/967) (authorship disputed); S: ed. Ṣ. al-Munajjid, Beirut 1972; Engl. tr. by Moreh and Crone, *Medieval Arabic Graffiti*; VQ: 1–40[47]; C: adab – anthology. (cf. no. 1188a)

(65) A/7 247a/15 *Ikhtiyārāt Ibn al-ᶜAmīd min kutub al-Jāḥiẓ* – *Ibn al-ᶜAmīd's Selections from al-Jāḥiẓ's Books*; A: Abū al-Faḍl Ibn al-ᶜAmīd (d. 360/970); no such anthology of al-Jāḥiẓ's oeuvre is known. This may be a minor anthology authored in the circle of *adībs* gathered around this Buyid vizier and scholarly patron. VQ: 1–45; C: adab – anthology.

(66) A/8 247a/16 *Ādāb al-mulūk* – *Rules for Kings*; popular title with numerous possibilities – the most likely candidate, as he is one of the best-represented authors in this library, being: attr. to A: al-Thaᶜālibī (d. 429/1038); S: ed. J. al-ᶜAṭīya, Beirut 1990; VQ: 1–41; Ṣ; C: political thought – mirror for princes.

(67) A/8 247a/16 *Akhlāq al-mulūk* – *Morals of the Kings*; A: Muḥammad b. al-Ḥārith al-Thaᶜlabī (fl. 3rd/9th c.); S: Fr. tr. (attr. to al-Jāḥiẓ) Pellat, *Livre de la couronne*; VQ: 1–39; C: political thought – mirror for princes. (cf. no. 1286a)

(68) A/8 247a/16 *Ikhtiyār al-wuzarāʾ* – *The Choice of Viziers*; no such title is identifiable. This may be a chapter with this heading from a mirror for princes, such as, for instance, al-Qalᶜī, *Tahdhīb al-riʾāsa*, 134–43; VQ: 4; C: political thought – mirror for princes.

(69) A/8 247b/1 *Ādāb al-wuzarāʾ* – *Rules for Viziers*; possibly A: Aḥmad b. Jaᶜfar b. Shādhān (fl. 3rd/9th c.?); S: Kohlberg, *Ibn Ṭāwūs*, 99–100; VQ: 1; C: political thought – adab of vizier. (cf. no. 1263b for other *ādāb al-wuzarāʾ* entries)

(70) A/8 247b/1 *al-Awṣāf al-mukhtalifat al-aṣnāf* – *Descriptions of Different Kinds*; no such title is identifiable. Probably this is a key word title of a work entitled '*al-Awṣāf*' with the following two terms added by the cataloguer (or the scribe of the manuscript). The term *awṣāf* was repeatedly used in works on literature, but also on theological issues (see Zakeri, *Wisdom*, 204–12). As

this entry is placed in category 8 it is most likely that it belonged to the broad field of adab. VQ: 3–41; Ṣ; C: adab?

(71) A/8 247b/1–2 *Akhlāq al-wazīrayn* – *The Two Viziers' Morals*; A: Abū Ḥayyān al-Tawḥīdī (d. 414/1023); S: ed. M. al-Ṭanjī, Damascus: MIA, 1965; NC: 2; VQ: 2–40, 1; Ṣ; C: ethics.

(72) A/8 247b/2 *al-Anwāʾ* – *Setting and Rising of Asterisms*; A: Aḥmad b. Sulaym al-Rāzī; S: IN, I/1, 273; VQ: 1–41; Ṣ; C: astronomy/meteorology.

(73) A/8 247b/3 *Asmāʾ shuʿarāʾ al-Ḥamāsa* – *The Poets' Names in the Ḥamāsa [of Abū Tammām]*; probably A: Abū al-Fatḥ Ibn Jinnī (d. 392/1002) who authored *al-Manhaj fī ishtiqāq (or al-Mubhif fī sharḥ) asmāʾ shuʿarāʾ al-Ḥamāsa*; S: IKH, III, 247; MS: Süleymaniye, Fatih 5413/9 (fols. 168a–231a: *Tafsīr asmāʾ shuʿarāʾ al-Ḥamāsa*)**; NC: 2; FI: '*nuskha thāniya fī 15*'/'*a second copy is in 15 [quires?]*'; VQ: 1, 1; Ṣ; C: poetry – commentary – anthology. (cf. no. 1196b)

(74) A/8 247b/3 *Ashjān al-ikhwān* – *The Brothers' Anxieties*; no such title is identifiable and this is most likely a book-in-the-making. That it is in category 8 makes it likely that this is an adab anthology. VQ: 1–40; C: adab?

(75) A/8 247b/3–4 *Akhbār al-Ḥusayn b. al-Ḍaḥḥāk* – *Reports on al-Ḥusayn b. al-Ḍaḥḥāk*; no such title is identifiable. It refers to the poet al-Ḥusayn b. al-Ḍaḥḥāk (d. c.250/864) (IKH, II, 168–72); VQ: 1–39; Ṣ; C: poetry – commentary.

(76) A/8 247b/4 *al-Ishāra ilā sulūk nahj al-imāra* – *Guidance on How to Rule*; no such title is identifiable. Most likely this is A: Muḥammad b. al-Ḥasan al-Murādī (d. 489/1095–6); S: *al-Ishāra fī tadbīr al-imāra*, eds M.Ḥ. Ismāʿīl and A.F. al-Mazīdī, Beirut: DKI, 2003; VQ: 46; C: political thought – mirror for princes.

(77) A/8 247b/4-5 *al-Ishāra ilā maḥāsin al-tijāra* – *Merits of Trade*; A: Jaʿfar al-Dimashqī (fl. 5th/11th c.); S: ed. F. Saʿd, Beirut: Dār Alif Bā, 1983; C: trade handbook.

(78) A/8 247b/5-6 *Akhbār al-ʿAddāʾīn wa-ashʿāruhum* – *Reports on the Runners and Their Poems*; no such title is identifiable. The 'runners' were a group of pre-Islamic poets renowned for their proverbial speed, overlapping with the brigand-poets (see, for example, Khulayyif, *al-Shuʿarāʾ al-ṣaʿālīk*). Among the most famous representatives of this group were al-Shanfarā

(cf. no. 585 and elsewhere) and Taᵓabbaṭa Sharran (cf. no. 694). NC: 2; VQ: 1–40, 1–42; Ṣ; C: poetry – commentary – anthology. (cf. no. 130)

(79) A/8 247b/6 *Ashᶜār al-luṣūṣ wa-akhbāruhum* – *Poems and Reports of Thieves*; possibly A: al-Sukkarī (d. 275/888) (S: IN, I/1, 239: '*ashᶜār al-luṣūṣ*'); VQ: 1; Ṣ; C: poetry – commentary – anthology. (cf. nos 131, 1650b)

(80) A/8 247b/6 *al-Awāᵓil* – *Book of Firsts*; arguably the poet and historian A: ᶜUmar <u>b. Shabba</u> al-Baṣrī (d. 262/876). Although sources do not mention such a title for him (cf. IN, I/2, 344–6), the close connection between history and the *awāᵓil*-genre makes this identification likely. VQ: 1–41; Ṣ; C: history – *awāᵓil*.

(81) A/8 247b/7 *al-Imtāᶜ wa-al-muwāzana* – *[Book of] Delightful Conversations and [Book of] Weighing*; No such title is identifiable and this may be an erroneous rendering for *al-Imtāᶜ wa-al-muᵓānasa* by Abū Ḥayyān al-Tawḥīdī (d. 414/1023). However, as the cataloguer placed that work correctly under no. 58 it is more probable that this is a multiple-text manuscript of two works. In this case these would be most likely the following two works:

(81a) *al-Imtāᶜ [wa-al-muᵓānasa]* by A: Abū Ḥayyān al-Tawḥīdī (d. 414/1023); S: eds A. Amīn and A. al-Zayn, Cairo: LTTN, 1953; C: adab/philosophy. (cf. nos 58, 1521)

(81b) *al-Muwāzana [bayna Abī Tammām wa-al-Buḥturī]* by A: al-Ḥasan b. Bishr al-Āmidī (d. 370/980 or 371/981); S: ed. al-S.A. Ṣaqr, Cairo: DM, 1961–5 (vols 1 and 2), ed. ᶜA.Ḥ. Muḥārib, Cairo: MK, 1990 (vol. 3); VQ: 1; Ṣ; C: poetry – criticism.

(82) A/8 247b/7 *al-Irtisām wa-fawāᵓid al-ightinām* – *Obedience and the Benefits of Opportunism*; no such title is identifiable and this is most likely a book-in-the-making. NC: 2 ('*nuskha thāniya li-ᶜArqala*'). The reading of ᶜArqala is tentative and probably refers to the Damascene poet Ḥassān b. Numayr ᶜArqala al-Kalbī (d. *c.*567/1171–2; TI, 561–70, pp. 284–6; cf. no. 1493). This note does not indicate that ᶜArqala was the scribe of the second copy, as the cataloguer elsewhere explicitly refers to further copies in a different hand with '*bi-khaṭṭ*' (cf. nos 557b and 595b). This note thus most likely indicates an earlier ownership of the manuscript. Placed in category 8 this may be a minor adab anthology on this topic, although the two copies

indicate that it enjoyed some popularity in contemporaneous Damascus. VQ: 1–36, 1–41; Ṣ; C: adab?

(83) A/8 247b/8 *Akhbār Abī Tammām – Reports on Abū Tammām*; popular title with numerous possibilities (cf. GAS, II, 552–3) with a preference for A: Muḥammad b. Yaḥyā al-Ṣūlī (d. 335/947) on account of MS: Süleymaniye, Fatih 3900*, which was authored by him; VQ: 1; Ṣ; C: poetry – commentary.

(84) A/8 247b/8 *Akhbār al-ruʾasāʾ – Reports on Leading Men*; on account of the thematic category and the preceding titles this entry could be read as an anthology of poetry with explanatory anecdotal material. However, this is most likely *al-Anwār al-jalīya fī akhbār al-dawla al-murābiṭīya*, which later authors also referred to as *K. akhbār al-ruʾasāʾ bi-al-Andalus* (cf. no. 1531 for an explicit link between the two works). A: Yaḥyā b. Muḥammad Ibn al-Ṣayrafī (d. 570/1174); S: Ṭāhā, *al-Taʾrīkh al-andalusī*, 239; C: history – Andalusian. (cf. no. 1531)

(85) A/8 247b/8 *Akhbār al-ᶜAbbās [b. ᶜAbd al-Muṭallab] – Reports on al-ᶜAbbās [b. ᶜAbd al-Muṭallab]*; A: Hishām b. Muḥammad Ibn al-Kalbī (d. 204/819 or 206/821); S: *Wāfī*, XXVII, 363; VQ: 1; Ṣ; C: biography – ᶜAbbāsid.

(86) A/8 247b/8–9 *al-Intikhāb fī ḥifẓ al-aṣḥāb – The Choice on Preserving the Companions*; no such title is identifiable and it is most likely a title in the form of key word + *fī* + content description. In this case it refers arguably to a certain A: al-Ḥasan b. Muḥammad b. Faraj; S: al-Qāḍī ᶜIyāḍ b. Mūsā al-Yaḥṣubī, *Tartīb al-madārik*, VI, 98 '*K. al-intikhāb*', a work that contained biographical information on Andalusian scholars. Other possibilities are less likely on account of their thematic focus, such as 1) ᶜAlī b. ᶜAdlān al-Mawṣilī's (d. 666/1268) *al-Intikhāb li-kashf al-abyāt* (Arberry, *Second Supplementary Hand-List*, 1), which is on poetry and does thus not fit the content description. 2) Naṣr b. Ibrāhīm al-Maqdisī's (d. 490/1097) *al-Intikhāb al-Dimashqī fī al-madhhab* is on *fiqh* and is unlikely due to the thematic category 8 in which this book is placed. VQ: 1; Ṣ; C: biographical dictionary – scholars.

(87) A/8 247b/9 *Ikhtiyārāt min samāᶜāt Muḥammad b. Sahl al-Shilḥī – Selections from Muḥammad b. Sahl al-Shilḥī's Transmissions*; this compendium is not identifiable, but it is referring to the secretary and *adīb* Muḥammad b. Muḥammad b. Sahl al-Shilḥī (d. 423/1032) (TI, 421–30, pp. 116–17).

The term *samā*^c^*āt* seems to make reference to the field of *ḥadīth*, but the author's background and the thematic category 8 makes an adab work more likely. *Samā*^c^ is here probably used in a non-technical sense as in the poetry anthology no. 1537 and similar to the use of the term *ḥadīth* in several titles (cf. no. 140). VQ: 1; Ṣ; C: adab.

(88) A/9 247b/10 *al-Aḥjār – Stones*; A: Aristotle (attr.); S: ed. J. Ruska, *Das Steinbuch des Aristoteles*, Heidelberg 1912; NC: 2; VQ: 1, 1; Ṣ; C: mineralogy.

(89) A/9 247b/10 *Abwāb majmū*^c^*a fī* ^c^*ilm al-nujūm – Collected Chapters on Astronomy*; this is probably similar to the treatise Süleymaniye, Fatih 3439/20 (fols. 205a–217a) entitled *al-Madkhal ilā* ^c^*ilm al-nujūm* written in Mosul in 587/1191. The multiple-text manuscript Fatih 3439 contains other titles that are similar to or identical with Ashrafiya entries (cf. nos 94, 331, 862). VQ: 1; Ṣ; C: astronomy.

(90) A/9 247b/11 *Uṣūl ṣinā*^c^*āt al-aḥkām fī al-nujūm – Principles of the Art of Astrology*; possibly A: Kūshyār b. Lābbān al-Jīlī (fl. early 5th/11th c.; author of *Mujmal al-uṣūl fī aḥkām al-nujūm*); S: GAS, VI, 247; VQ: 1; Ṣ; C: astronomy.

(91) A/9 247b/11 *Asbāb al-nad*^ɔ^*a wa-al-ẓill – On the Formation of Halo and Shade*; no such title is identifiable. In line with category 9 this is probably a small treatise on astronomical/optical phenomena as discussed in Ibn al-Haytham's (d. 430/1039) treatises 'On the halo and the rainbow' and 'On the formation of shadows' (see al-Fārisī: *Tanqīḥ al-manāẓir*). VQ: 1; Ṣ; C: astronomy/optics.

(92) A/9 247b/11-12 *Aqwāl jamā*^c^*a min al-ḥukamā*^ɔ^ *– Sayings of Wise Teachers*; anonymous work with generic title; VQ: 1; Ṣ; owing to preceding works possibly C: astronomy?

(93) A/9 247b/12 *Ādāb al-falāsifa – Philosophers' Manual*; A: Ḥunayn b. Isḥāq (d. 260/873); S: ed. ^c^A. Badawī, Kuwait: MMA, 1985; VQ: 1; Ṣ; C: philosophy.

(94) A/9 247b/12 *al-Ālāt al-nujūmīya – Astronomical Instruments*; no such title is identifiable and this is most likely a treatise on the building/use of astronomical instruments similar to Süleymaniye, Fatih 3439/18 (fols. 190a–197a) entitled *Ālāt al-aṣṭurlāb* (late 6th/12th c.). The multiple-text

manuscript Fatih 3439 contains other titles that are similar to or identical with Ashrafiya entries (cf. nos 89, 331, 862). C: astronomy.

(95) A/10 247b/12-3 *Iqtināʾ al-khayl wa-ʿilājuhā – Purchasing Horses and Their Treatment*; no such title is identifiable. In contrast to the lexicographical works on horses (for example, nos 359, 361 and 374), this seems to be – in line with thematic category 10 – rather a practitioner's guide on the purchase and medical treatment of horses. VQ: 3; Ṣ; C: veterinary medicine.

(96) A/10 247b/13 *al-Ibtihāj fī aṣnāf al-ʿilāj – [Book of] Delight on the Different Kinds of Treatment*; no such title is identifiable. VQ: 1; Ṣ; C: medicine.

(97) A/10 247b/13 *Adab al-ṭabīb – Physician's Manual*; A: Isḥāq b. ʿAlī al-Ruhāwī (fl. 4th/10th c.?); S: ed. M. Saʿīd Murayzin ʿAsīrī, Riyad: MMF, 1992; VQ: 1; Ṣ; C: medicine.

(98) A/10 247b/14 *al-Ashriba – Book of Drinks*; A: Aḥmad b. Muḥammad Miskawayh (d. 421/1030?); S: TI, 551–60, p. 326, n. 7 referring to a summary of '*Kitāb al-ashriba li-Miskawayh*'; VQ: 1; Ṣ; C: pharmacology.

(99) A/10 247b/14 *al-Irshād fī ḥifẓ ṣiḥḥat Ibn Ḥammād – Guidance on Preserving Ibn Ḥammād's Health*; no such title is identifiable. Perhaps a treatise composed for a ruler of the Maghrebi dynasty of the Hammadids (405–547/1015–1152)? VQ: 1; Ṣ; C: medicine.

(100) A/10 247b/14 *Adab al-fallāḥīn – Peasants' Manual*; Arab authors quote the '*Adab al-fallāḥīn*' in their works and ascribe this to the Greek author A: Bolos Democritus of Mendes (fl. *c.*200 BCE); S: Ullmann, *Natur- und Geheimwissenschaften*, 428 who argues that this text was indeed translated into Arabic; VQ: 1; Ṣ; C: agriculture.

(101) A/10 247b/15 *al-Īḍāḥ fī al-rimāya – Elucidating the Accusation*; no such title is identifiable and it is most likely a title in the form of key word + *fī* + content description. As this is category 10 the most likely candidate is the *Īḍāḥ* by the Andalusian physician A: Zuhr b. ʿAbd al-Malik (d. 525/1131); S: Ullmann, *Medizin*, 162. This work is a refutation of Ibn Riḍwān's (d. *c.*453/1061) polemic against Ḥunayn b. Isḥāq (IAU, III, 284). VQ: 1; Ṣ; C: medicine.

(102) A/10 247b/15 *al-Aṭʿima al-mukhtāra – Selected Dishes*; no such title is identifiable and this is probably an anonymous summary of one of

the *aṭ*ᶜ*ima*-books by authors such as Galen (Ullmann, *Medizin*, 47) and al-Rāzī (Rhazes) (d. 313/925 or 323/935) (IN, II/1, 312); VQ: 1; Ṣ; C: medicine – dietetics.

(103) A/10 247b/15 *Aqrābādhīn marham – Antidotarium on Salves*; the reading of the second term is tentative. This seems to be an extract from one or several antidotaria on the making of salves (see Ullmann, *Medizin*, 297 on the use of the term). C: pharmacology.[48]

(104) A/10 247b/15-6 *Ikhtiṣār Jālīnūs li-kitābihi Ḥīlat al-bur*ᵓ *– Galen's Summary of His Book 'On the Therapeutic Method'*; A: Galen; S: IN, II/1, 278 (mentions *Ḥīlat al-bur*ᵓ); VQ: 1; Ṣ; C: pharmacology.

(105) A/10 247b/16 *al-Adwiya al-mufrada – Simple Drugs*; numerous authors have authored a book with this popular title. As the cataloguer does not provide any information on the author he was either at a loss or – more likely – this was a well-known work in his period. In this case it may be the medical work dedicated to al-Malik al-Muᶜaẓẓam, al-Malik al-Ashraf's predecessor in Damascus, by A: Rashīd al-Dīn Ibn al-Ṣūrī (d. 639/1242) who is mentioned elsewhere in this catalogue (cf. no. 1325c). S: *Wāfī*, XIV, 125; VQ: 1; Ṣ; C: pharmacology. (cf. no. 193, 1479)

(106) A/10 247b/16-248a/1 *Aqrābādhīn manzū*ᶜ *min* ᶜ*iddat aqrābādhīnāt – Antidotarium Derived from Several Antidotaria*; anonymous work with generic title; VQ: 1; Ṣ; C: pharmacology.

(107) A/10 248a/1 *Aqrābādhīn Sābūr – Sābūr's Dispensatory*; A: Sābūr b. Sahl (d. 255/869); S: ed. O. Kahl, *Sābūr ibn Sahl's Dispensatory in the Recension of the* ᶜ*Aḍudī Hospital*, Leiden 2009; VQ: 1; Ṣ; C: pharmacology.

(108) A/10 248a/1 *al-Aghdhiya – Book of Dietetics*; A: ᶜAbd al-Malik Ibn Zuhr (d. 557/1162); S: Azar, *Sage of Seville*, 33–6; VQ: 1; Ṣ; C: pharmacology.

(109) A/10 248a/2 *Iẓhār ḥikmat al-Raḥmān fī khalq al-insān wa-ghayruhu – The Benevolent's Wisdom in Creating Man and Other [Writings]*; physiology of human organs including their meaning and purpose as intended by God; A: ᶜĪsā b. Yaḥyā al-Masīḥī al-Jurjānī (d. 401/1010); S: IAU, III, 68; VQ: 1; Ṣ; C: medicine.

(110) A/10 248a/2–3 *Abdāl al-adwiya al-mufrada wa-al-murakkaba – Substitutes of Simple and Composite Drugs*; possibly A: al-Rāzī (Rhazes)

(d. 313/925 or 323/935); S: IN, II/1, 310; VQ: 1; Ṣ; C: pharmacology. (cf. no. 1245a)

(111) A/10 248a/3 *al-Iklīl – Melilot*; A: al-Rāzī (Rhazes) (d. 313/925 or 323/935); S: GAS, III, 292; VQ: 1; Ṣ; C: pharmacology.

(112) A/10 248a/3 *Aqrābādhīn Yūḥannā – Yūḥannā's Antidotarium*; A: Yūḥannā b. Sarābiyūn (fl. 3rd/9th c.); the treatise on compound drugs from the author's *Kunnāsh*, S: Ullmann, *Medizin*, 102–3; MS: Süleymaniye, Ayasofya 3716**; VQ: 1; Ṣ; C: pharmacology.

(113) A/12 248a/4 *Ashᶜār al-Hudhalīyīn*[49] *– Poems of Those Belonging to the Hudhalī Tribe*; S: *Dīwān al-Hudhalīyīn*, eds M. Abū al-Wafāᵓ and A. Zayn, Cairo: DKM, 1945–50; NC: 2; VQ: 5, 11; Ṣ; C: poetry – anthology – pre-Islamic/early Islamic. (cf. nos 1301, 1488, 1575)

(114) A/12 248a/4 *al-Aghānī – The [Book of] Songs*; an author 'Ibn al-Qushayrī' who would have authored such a title is not identifiable. These are most likely the pieces ascribed to the Umayyad poet A: al-Ṣimma b. ᶜAbd Allāh al-Qushayrī (d. *c.*90/708) (GAS, II, 342–3) and taken from Abū al-Faraj al-Iṣfahānī's (d. 356/967) *Book of Songs*. The cataloguer erroneously inserted an 'Ibn' and he probably did not know this poet as he had problems with this name in the catalogue's second entry on him as well (cf. no. 615). S: Kilpatrick, *Making*, 223–5; VQ: 1; Ṣ; C: poetry – Umayyad.

(115) A/12 248a/10 *Azjāl*[50] *Mudghalīs – Mudghalīs' Zajal Poems*; A: Mudghalīs (or Madghallīs, Madghalīs) (d. after 577/1181–2); S: W. Hoenerbach and H. Ritter, Neue Materialien zum Zacal. 2. Mudġalīs, *Oriens* 5 (1952), 269–301; VQ: 1; Ṣ; C: poetry – zajal.

(116) A/12 248a/10 *Mūjaz al-azjāl – Summary of Zajal Poems*; probably anonymous; VQ: *fī* 13; Ṣ; C: poetry – anthology – zajal.

(117) A/13 248a/11 *Ashᶜār dūbaytī*[51] *– Dūbaytī Poems*; anonymous work with generic title; VQ: 1 *fī* 12; Ṣ; C: poetry – anthology – dūbaytī.

(118) A/13 248a/11 *Ashᶜār dūbaytī – Dūbaytī Poems*; anonymous work with generic title; VQ: 1 *fī* 12; Ṣ; C: poetry – anthology – dūbaytī.

(119) A/13 248a/11 *Ashᶜār al-sitta – The Six Poems*; S: e.g. al-Baṭalyawsī, *Sharḥ al-ashᶜār al-sitta*; VQ: 1; Ṣ; C: poetry – anthology – pre-Islamic. (cf. no. 121)

(120) A/13 248a/11-12 *al-Aghrāḍ fī dhikr*[52] *al-aᶜrāḍ – Aims of Mentioning Good Reputations*; A: Muḥammad Ibn Quzmān (d. 555/1160); S: *Dīwān = El cancionero hispano-arabe de Aban Quzmán de Córdoba: Iṣābat al-aghrāḍ fī dhikr al-aᶜrāḍ*, ed. F. Corriente, Cairo: al-Majlis al-aᶜlā lil-thaqāfa, 1995; VQ: 1; Ṣ; C: poetry – zajal.

(121) A/13 248a/12 *Ashᶜār al-sitta – The Six Poems*; S: e.g. al-Baṭalyawsī, *Sharḥ al-ashᶜār al-sitta*; VQ: 1; Ṣ; C: poetry – anthology – pre-Islamic. (cf. no. 119)

(122) A/13 248a/12 *Ashᶜār wa-akhbār – Poems and Anecdotes*; Scr('*bi-khaṭṭ*') & A 'compiler' ('*bi-jamᶜihi*'): al-Thaᶜālibī (d. 429/1038); C: poetry – commentary – anthology.

(123) A/15 248a/13 *Akhbār Majnūn Laylā wa-ashᶜāruhu – The Reports on Majnūn Laylā and His Poems*; anonymous; S: *Dīwān Majnūn Laylā*, ed. A. Farrāj, Cairo: MMi, 1958; VQ: 1; Ṣ; C: poetry – commentary.

(124) A/15 248a/13–14 *al-Iᶜjāz fī al-aḥājī wa-al-alghāz – The Unique Book on Riddles and Word Puzzles*; A: Saᶜd b. ᶜAlī b. al-Qāsim al-Ḥaẓīrī Dallāl al-Kutub (d. 568/1172); S: MM, I, 757; VQ: 1; Ṣ; C: adab.

(125) A/15 248a/14 *Azhār al-anhār – Rivers' Blossoms*; A: Usāma b. Munqidh (d. 584/1188); S: cited in Ibn al-ᶜAdīm, *Bughyat*, III, 1361; VQ: 3; Ṣ; C: adab?

(126) A/15 248a/14–15 *al-Ādāb – Ādāb*; A: Jaᶜfar b. Shams al-Khilāfa al-Afḍalī (d. 622/1225); S: ed. M.A. al-Khānjī, Cairo: MK, 1930; NC: 2; VQ: 1–38, 1; Ṣ; C: adab – anthology.

(127) A/15 248a/15 *Akhbār al-Ḥamāsa – Reports on the Ḥamāsa [of Abū Tammām]*; A: Abū Riyāsh (d. 339/950–1); S: EI[3], G. J. van Gelder, 'Abū Riyāsh'; VQ: 1–46; Ṣ; C: poetry – commentary – anthology.

(128) A/15 248a/15 *Ādāb al-mulūk wa-al-ᶜulamāʾ – Rules for Kings and Scholars*; A: Aḥmad b. Muḥammad al-Naḥḥās (d. 338/950); S: MU, I, 469 '*adab al-mulūk*' (*Wāfī*, VII, 363 adds a *Adab al-kuttāb*); VQ: 1; Ṣ; C: political thought – mirror for princes/adab of scholars.

(129) A/15 248a/16 *Akhbār Abī Nuwās – Reports on Abū Nuwās*; popular title with numerous possibilities (cf. GAS, II, 544/5); VQ: 1–42; Ṣ; C: poetry – commentary.

(130) A/15 248a/16 *Akhbār al-ᶜAddāʾīn wa-Suᶜāt al-ᶜarab* – *Reports on the Runners*; no such title is identifiable. For the pre-Islamic poets known as 'runners' cf. no. 78. VQ: 1; Ṣ; C: poetry – commentary – anthology. (cf. no. 78)

(131) A/15 248a/16–17 *Akhbār al-luṣūṣ* – *Reports on the Thieves*; no such title is identifiable and this may be a collection of stories about thieves. Taking the previous entries into consideration it is, however, more likely that this is either (a) an extract from and commentary on *Ashᶜār al-luṣūṣ by* al-Sukkarī (d. 275/888) or (b) an extract from and commentary on *K. al-luṣūṣ* by al-Jāḥiẓ (d. 255/868–9). It is noteworthy that the above entry on *Reports on the Runners* was also followed by a work on *luṣūṣ* (cf. nos 78 and 79). C: poetry – commentary – anthology. (cf. nos 79, 1650b)

(132) A/15 248a/17 *Aḥsan mā qīla fī al-balāgha* – *The Best Said of Balāgha*; no such title is identifiable and it is either a collection of sayings from the field of *ᶜilm al-balāgha* (similar to the numerous *aḥsan mā qīla*-sections in works such as al-Thaᶜālibī's (d. 429/1038) *Yatīmat al-dahr*) or praise of a work entitled *al-Balāgha* (numerous possible authors, among them Muḥammad b. Yazīd al-Mubarrad, d. 286/900); VQ: 1; Ṣ; C: rhetoric.

(133) A/15 248a/17 *Ajnās fī al-tajnīs wa-al-minhaj* – *Classes of Paronomasia*; A: al-Thaᶜālibī (d. 429/1038); S: ed. ᶜA. al-Jādir, *Ajnās al-tajnīs*, Beirut: AK, 1997; VQ: 1; Ṣ; C: rhetoric. (cf. no. 1249l)

(134) A/15 248b/1 *Adab al-maẓālim* – *The Manual for Dispensing the Ruler's Justice*; no such title is identifiable and this is most likely an extract from/commentary on/elaboration of al-Māwardī's (d. 450/1058) section in his *al-Aḥkām al-sulṭānīya* on *maẓālim* jurisdiction (Engl. tr. Wahba, *Ordinances of Government*, 116–42). VQ: 1–45; Ṣ; C: political thought – mirror for princes.

(135) A/15 248b/1 *Afrād al-maᶜānī* – *Isolated Words from the Field of Rhetoric*; A: al-Thaᶜālibī (d. 429/1038); S: *Wāfī*, XIX, 196; VQ: 1; Ṣ; C: rhetoric.

(136) A/15 248b/1 *Ālāt al-riʾāsa* – *The Instruments of Leadership*; no such title is identifiable and this is most likely an anonymous treatise based on Muḥammad b. Idrīs al-Shāfiᶜī's (d. 204/820) saying that 'there are five instruments of leadership: truthfulness, secrecy, abiding agreements, heeding advice, providing protection'. This statement was quoted by broadly

contemporaneous Damascene sources such as *Siyar*, X, 42; VQ: 1; Ṣ; C: political thought – mirror for princes.

(137) A/15 248b/1-2 *Akhbār ᶜAbd Allāh b. Jaᶜfar – Reports on ᶜAbd Allāh b. Jaᶜfar*; referring to the nephew and son-in-law of ᶜAlī b. Abī Ṭālib; A: Abū Bakr Muḥammad b. Khalaf Ibn al-Marzubān (d. 309/921); S: IN, I/1, 267, I/2, 461; VQ: 1; Ṣ; C: biography – imāmate?

(138) A/15 248b/2 *Akhbār wa-ashᶜār wa-nawādir – Stories, Poems and Anecdotes*; anonymous work with generic title; VQ: 1; Ṣ; C: poetry/adab – anthology.

(139) A/15 248b/2–3 *Anīs al-amīr wa-jalīs al-wazīr – The Officer's Companion and the Vizier's Attendant*; no such title is identifiable. It may be an altered version of the work by al-Muᶜāfā b. Zakarīyāᵓ al-Jarīrī (d. 390/1000) that contemporaneous authors such as Ibn Khallikān (e.g. IKH, VI, 382) cite as *al-Jalīs wa-al-anīs* (*al-Jalīs al-ṣāliḥ al-kāfī wa-al-anīs al-nāṣiḥ al-shāfī*, ed. M. al-Khūlī/I. ᶜAbbās, Beirut: AK, 1981–7). However, the *Anīs al-jalīs fī al-tajnīs* by A: ᶜAlī b. al-Ḥasan Shumaym al-Ḥillī (d. 601/1204); S: MU, IV, 1691 is more likely, as this panegyric for Saladin would very well fit this library. An undated manuscript of this work is Süleymaniye, Nuruosmaniye 3682. VQ: 1–42; Ṣ; C: adab/poetry – panegyric – Ayyūbid – Ṣalāḥ al-Dīn?

(140) A/15 248b/3 *Ajzāᵓ ḥadīth – Quires with Narratives*; anonymous work with generic title; '*Ḥadīth*' could very well refer to Prophetic traditions, but the work is placed in thematic category 15. It thus most likely refers to either the field of adab or poetry. For using the term *ḥadīth* beyond Prophetic traditions in this catalogue cf. nos 296, 297, 313 and for a similar non-technical use of the term *samāᶜāt* cf. no. 87. VQ: 1; Ṣ; C: adab/poetry.

(141) A/1s 248b/3–4 *Ashᶜār banī Nahd b. Mawᶜid – Poetry of the Banū Nahd b. Mawᶜid*; GAS, II, 39 mentions a *K. Nahd* among tribal diwans listed by al-Ḥasan b. Bishr al-Āmidī (d. 370/980 or 371/981), but a 'Mawᶜid' (or other variant readings) is not identifiable. VQ: 1; Ṣ; C: poetry – anthology – pre-Islamic/early Islamic.

(142) A/3s 248b/4 *Ashᶜār wa-akhbār wa-nawādir – Poems, Reports and Anecdotes*; Scr('*bi-khaṭṭ*'): al-Ḥasan b. ᶜAlī al-Juwaynī (d. 586/1190?; MU,

II, 940–1; cf. nos 347, 348, 873, 874); anonymous work with generic title; VQ: 1; Ṣ; C: poetry/adab – anthology.

(143) A/3s 248b/4–5 *Ikhtiyārāt min kalām al-ḥukamāʾ* – *Selections from the Sayings of the Wise*; Scr(‘*bi-khaṭṭ*’): probably the *adīb* and secretary Abū al-Faḍl Manūjihr (d. 575/1179; MU, VI, 2731); anonymous work with generic title; VQ: 1; Ṣ; C: adab?

(144) A/3s 248b/5 *Ashʿār fī ahl al-bayt wa-akhbār mustaḥsana* – *Poems on the Prophet's Family and Reports Considered to Be Comely*; anonymous work with generic title; VQ: 1; Ṣ; C: poetry – anthology – praise of religious figures – ahl al-bayt.

(145) A/3s 248b/6 *Ashʿār wa-fiqar muntakhaba* – *Chosen Poetry and Prose*; anonymous work with generic title; VQ: 1-47; Ṣ; C: poetry/adab – anthology.

(146) A/3s 248b/6 *Akhbār al-Buḥturī* – *Reports on al-Buḥturī*; A: Muḥammad b. Yaḥyā al-Ṣūlī (d. 335/947); S: ed. Ṣ. al-Ashtar, Damascus: MIA, 1958; VQ: 1–47; Ṣ; C: poetry – commentary.

(147) A/3s 248b/6–7 *Asbāb al-ʿ. . . al-ṭ/ẓāhira*; unidentified; VQ: 1–46; Ṣ; C:?

(148) A/3s 248b/7 *Ashʿār wa-akhbār wa-fiqar* – *Poems, Reports and Prose*; anonymous work with generic title; VQ: 1; Ṣ; C: poetry/adab – anthology.

(149) A/3s 248b/7–8 *al-Alfāẓ al-muqtaḍabāt wa-al-kalimāt al-mahdīyāt* – *Sayings in the Muqtaḍabāt Metre and Rightly-Guided Words*; no such title is identifiable and this is most likely a book-in-the-making, most probably an anonymous collection of poetry and pious material. VQ: 1; Ṣ; C: poetry?

(150) A/4s 248b/8 *Asmāʾ Allāh al-ḥusnā* – *The Beautiful Names of God*; probably a work listing and explaining God's 99 or 100 ‘most beautiful names’. Owing to the following titles this is categorised as a prayer book. This entry may be identical with/similar to Süleymaniye, Ayasofya 1869 (dated 608/1211–12), *Sharḥ maʿānī asmāʾ Allāh al-ḥusnā* by Ibn Barrajān al-Andalusī (d. 536/1141). VQ: 1; Ṣ; C: prayer book.

(151) A/4s 248b/8–9 *Adʿiyat al-ayyām al-sabʿa* – *Prayers of Invocation for the Seven Days*; this looks like a generic title, but it is striking that exactly the same title appears in four different places in the catalogue. The cataloguer has one

of the four copies in the section on incomplete manuscripts (cf. no. 1661), which is remarkable as there are only three prayer books in total in that section. The two other titles are an authored prayer book (by al-Ṭabarānī, d. 360/971, cf. no. 1441) and a generic prayer book written by the grand calligrapher Ibn al-Bawwāb (cf. no. 1662). They were thus special works that were different from the mass of generic prayer books here in the catalogue's main section. In addition, the cataloguer states at that point that this is the 'fourth copy', i.e. he clearly sees the various copies with this title not as 'some' prayers for the seven days, but as all pertaining to one very specific work. In consequence, this is most likely the prayer book by A: Fatimid Caliph al-Muᶜizz (r. 341–65/953–75); S: ed. I.K. Poonawala, Beirut: DGI, 2006. The link between the Ashrafiya and the Fatimid library makes the presence of such a text on the former's shelves possible. In addition, another text in this library is explicitly ascribed to al-Muᶜizz (cf. no. 893). C: prayer book. (cf. nos 1170c, 1198b, 1661)

(152) A/4s 248b/9 *Adᶜiya sharīfa – Noble Prayers of Invocation*; generic title; VQ: 1; C: prayer book.

(153) A/4s 248b/9-10 *Adᶜiya ᶜan al-Nabī ṣallā Allāh ᶜalayhi wa-sallam – Prayers of Invocation from the Prophet* (*may God's blessing and peace be upon him*); generic title; Scr('*khaṭṭ*'): probably Aḥmad b. al-Ḥasan/al-Ḥusayn Ibn Rīsh, a minor Damascene *ḥadīth* scholar of the early 7th/13th c. (d. 646/1248) (TI, 641–50, p. 305; cf. no. 168); VQ: 1; Ṣ; C: prayer book.

(154) A/4s 248b/10 *Adᶜiya wa-munājāt – Prayers of Invocation and Whispered Prayers*; A: ᶜAlī b. al-Ḥusayn b. ᶜAlī b. Abī Ṭālib Zayn al-ᶜĀbidīn, the fourth Shiᶜite *imām* (d. 94/712?); S: Engl. tr. Chittick, *Psalms of Islam* (*munājāt*, pp. 232–59); VQ: 1; Ṣ; C: prayer book. (cf. nos 424, 1136)

(155) A/4s 248b/10 *Adᶜiya maʾthūra – Transmitted Prayers of Invocation*; generic title; VQ: 1; Ṣ; C: prayer book.

(156) A/4s 248b/10-11 *Adᶜiya – Prayers of Invocation*; generic title; probably Scr('*khaṭṭ*'): ᶜAlī b. al-Ḥasan b. Ṣadaqa (d. 554/1159) (praised, for instance, by MU, IV, 1689 for his calligraphy, cf. no. 1657); VQ: 1; Ṣ; C: prayer book.

(157) A/4s 248b/11 *Adᶜiyat al-naṣr wa-al-iḥtirās – Prayers of Invocation for Victory and Protection*; generic title; VQ: 1; Ṣ; C: prayer book.

(158) A/4s 248b/11-12 *Adᶜiya sharīfa mujarraba li-qaḍāʾ al-ḥawāʾij – Noble and Well-Tried Prayers of Invocation for Fulfilling Wishes*; generic title; VQ: 1; Ṣ; C: prayer book.

(159) A/4s 248b/12 *Adᶜiya sharīfa mujarraba ᶜan al-salaf al-ṣāliḥ – Noble and Well-Tried Prayers of Invocation on the Authority of the Pious Predecessors*; generic title; VQ: 1; Ṣ; C: prayer book.

(160) A/4s 248b/12 *Adᶜiya – Prayers of Invocation*; generic title; FI: '*bi-khaṭṭ mansūb*'/'*in proportioned script*'; VQ: 1; Ṣ; C: prayer book.

(161) A/4s 248b/13 *Adᶜiya nathr wa-naẓm – Prayers of Invocation in Prose and Verse*; generic title; VQ: 1; Ṣ; C: prayer book.

(162) A/4s 248b/13 *Adᶜiya – Prayers of Invocation*; generic title; FI: '*bi-khaṭṭ Kūfī*'/'*in Kufi Script*'; VQ: 1; Ṣ; C: prayer book.

(163) A/4s 248b/13 *Adᶜiya – Prayers of Invocation*; generic title; FI: '*bi-khaṭṭ Kūfī*'/'*in Kufi Script*'; VQ: 1; Ṣ; C: prayer book.

(164) A/4s 248b/13-14 *Adᶜiya – Prayers of Invocation*; generic title; FI: '*bi-khaṭṭ Kūfī*'/'*in Kufi Script*'; VQ: 1; Ṣ; C: prayer book.

(165) A/4s 248b/14 *Adᶜiya – Prayers of Invocation*; generic title; FI: '*maktūba bi-aḥmar wa-aṣfar wa-aswad*'/'*written in red, yellow and black*'; '*radīʾ*'/'*of inferior quality*'; VQ: 1; Ṣ; C: prayer book.

(166) A/4s 248b/14 *Adᶜiya mubāraka – Blessed Prayers of Invocation*; generic title; VQ: 1; Ṣ; C: prayer book.

(167) A/4s 248b/15 *Adᶜiya mubāraka – Blessed Prayers of Invocation*; generic title; FI: '*bi-khaṭṭ mansūb*'/'*in proportioned script*'; VQ: 1; Ṣ; C: prayer book.

(168) A/4s 248b/15–16 *Adᶜiya mubāraka ᶜan al-Nabī ṣallā Allāh ᶜalayhi wa-sallam – Blessed Prayers of Invocation from the Prophet (may God's blessing and peace be upon him)*; generic title; Scr('*bi-khaṭṭ*'): probably Aḥmad b. al-Ḥasan/al-Ḥusayn Ibn Rīsh (d. 646/1248) (TI, 641–50, p. 305; cf. no. 153); VQ: 1; Ṣ; C: prayer book.

(169) A/4s 248b/16 *Adᶜiya maʾthūra – Transmitted Prayers of Invocation*; generic title; FI: '*kabīrat al-qaṭᶜ*'/'*large format*'; VQ: 1; Ṣ; C: prayer book.

(170) A/4s 248b/16 *al-Iṣāba fī daᶜawāt al-mustajāba – The [Book of] Attainment Concerning Prayers of Invocation that Will Be Fulfilled*; such a

title is not identifiable. Al-Suyūṭī (d. 911/1505) has a strikingly similar title (*Sihām al-iṣāba fī al-da^{c}awāt al-mujāba*, ed. S. Ibn ^{c}Āyish, Beirut: DB, 2008) and maybe he appropriated/'plagiarised' a previously existing work and reissued it under his name? VQ: 1; Ṣ; C: prayer book.

(171) A/4s 248b/17 *Ad^{c}iya mubāraka maʾthūra marwīya ^{c}an al-salaf – Blessed Prayers of Invocation Transmitted from the [Pious] Predecessors*; generic title; VQ: 1; Ṣ; C: prayer book.

(172) A/4s 248b/17 *Ad^{c}iya ^{c}an al-Nabī ^{c}alayhi al-salām – Prayers of Invocation from the Prophet (may peace be upon him)*; generic title; C: prayer book.

(173) A/4s 248b/18 *Ad^{c}iya – Prayers of Invocation*; generic title; FI: '*manqūla min khaṭṭ Ibn al-Bawwāb*'/'*copied from Ibn al-Bawwāb's hand [d. 413/1022]*'; VQ: 1; Ṣ; C: prayer book.

(174) A/4s 248b/18 *Ad^{c}iya – Prayers of Invocation*; generic title; Scr('*bi- khaṭṭ*'): Muḥammad b. Maymūn al-Marrākushī al-Ḥimyarī (fl. 647/1249–50), on this otherwise unknown author of a manual for producing ink see al-Marrākushī, *K. al-azhār*, 45; C: prayer book. (cf. no. 184)

(175) A/4s 248b/18-249a/1 *Ad^{c}iya – Prayers of Invocation*; generic title; FI: '*awwaluhu mā jāʾa fī faḍl al-da^{c}awāt*'/'*in the beginning is a section on the virtues of prayers of invocations*'; C: prayer book.

(176) A/4s 249a/1 *Ad^{c}iyat al-wasāʾil ilā al-masāʾil – Prayers of Invocation for Attaining the Requests*; generic title; VQ: 1; Ṣ; C: prayer book.

(177) A/4s 249a/2 *Ad^{c}iya huwa da^{c}āhu yawm al-aḥzāb – Prayers of Invocation Said by Him [i.e. the Prophet] on Yawm al-Aḥzāb*; generic title referring to the battle of the confederates/trenches, year 5/627; VQ: 1; Ṣ; C: prayer book.

(178) A/4s 249a/2 *Ad^{c}iya mukhtāra – Selected Prayers of Invocation*; generic title; Scr('*bi-khaṭṭ*'): M-n-j-r? Maybe this is the misspelled name of the *adīb* and secretary Abū al-Faḍl Manūjihr (d. 575/1179; MU, VI, 2731) who was mentioned on the previous folio (cf. no. 143). VQ: 1; Ṣ; C: prayer book.

(179) A/4s 249a/2-3 *Ad^{c}iya sharīfa wurithat ^{c}an Ahl al-bayt – Noble Prayers of Invocation Inherited from the Prophet's Family*; generic title; C: prayer book.

(180) A/4s 249a/3 *Ad^{c}iya ^{c}an al-salaf – Prayers of Invocation from the [Pious] Predecessors*; generic title; VQ: 5; C: prayer book.

(181) A/4s 249a/3-4 *Adᶜiya mustajāba ᶜan al-Nabī ᶜalayhi al-salām – Prayers of Invocation from the Prophet (may peace be upon him) that are answered*; generic title; VQ: 1; Ṣ; C: prayer book.

(182) A/4s 249a/4 *Adᶜiya ᶜan al-imām al-Shāfiᶜī raḥimahu Allāh – Prayers of Invocation from al-Shāfiᶜī (may God have mercy upon him)*; A: Muḥammad b. Idrīs al-Shāfiᶜī (d. 204/820); VQ: 1; Ṣ; C: prayer book.

(183) A/4s 249a/4-5 *Asmāᵓ alf ism wa-ism – The Names of 1001 Names*; generic title referring to the Prophet's prayer of invocation known as *alf ism wa-ism*; VQ: 1; Ṣ; C: prayer book.

(184) A/4s 249a/5 *Adᶜiya – Prayers of Invocation*; generic title; Scr('*bi-khaṭṭ*'): Muḥammad b. Maymūn al-Marrākushī al-Ḥimyarī (fl. 647/1249–50; cf. no. 174); C: prayer book.

(185) A/4s 249a/5 *Adᶜiya marwīya ᶜan al-Nabī ᶜalayhi al-salām – Prayers of Invocation Transmitted from the Prophet (may peace be upon him)*; generic title; VQ: 1; Ṣ; C: prayer book.

(186) A/5s 249a/6 *Akhbār wa-inshādāt – Reports and Recitations*; anonymous work with generic title; Scr('*bi-khaṭṭ*'): probably ᶜAbd al-Salām al-Baṣrī (fl. 5th/11th c.; IKH, VII, 73); VQ: 1–5; C: adab – anthology. (cf. nos 313 and 871 on scribe)

(187) A/5s 249a/7 *Ashᶜār fī al-jawār – Poems on Female Slaves*; possibly A: Muḥammad b. Muḥammad al-Mufajjaᶜ (d. 327/939) who has an *Ashᶜār al-jawārī*; S: MU, V, 336–44; VQ: 1; Ṣ; C: poetry – anthology.

(188) A/5s 249a/7 *Qiṣṣat Dalla al-Muḥtāla – The Story of Dalla the Crafty*; anonymous work, subsequently absorbed into 1001 Nights, see Chapter 2; VQ: 1; Ṣ; C: adab – 1001 Nights.

(189) A/5s 249a/7 *Ashᶜār waᶜẓīya – Homiletic Poems*; A: Abū al-ᶜAtāhiya (d. 210/825 or 211/826); S: EI^{3}, R.S. Creswell, 'Abū l-ᶜAtāhiya'; VQ: 1; Ṣ; C: poetry – anthology – zuhdīya.

(190) A/5s 249a/8 *al-Alfāẓ al-taᶜzīya wa-al-madāᵓiḥ al-Ashrafīya – Words of Consolation and Praise of al-Ashraf*; placed in thematic category 5s this is most likely panegyric poetry for the mausoleum's patron al-Malik al-Ashraf. The most probable poet is al-Ashraf's secretary A: ᶜAlī b. Muḥammad Kamāl al-Dīn Ibn al-Nabīh (d. 619/1222) renowned for his *Ashrafīyāt* and the poet

with the largest corpus of panegyrics for al-Ashraf. S: al-Asᶜad, *Dīwān Ibn al-Nabīh*, 123–363; VQ: 1; Ṣ; C: poetry – panegyric – Ayyūbid – al-Malik al-Ashraf. (cf. nos 288, 315, 863, 868, 1049, 1055, 1229d)

(191) A/5s 249a/8 *Aghānī – Songs*; anonymous work with generic title; as the cataloguer recorded this 'title' without the definite article, he was clearly not sure about the entry (for another problematic *Aghānī*-entry cf. no. 114), giving a description of the work's content rather than a title. It does not refer to the famous *Book of Songs* by Abū al-Faraj al-Iṣfahānī (d. 356/967), which he gives the definite article elsewhere (cf. no. 1504). Q: '*juzʾ*'/'*one quire*'?; VQ: 1; Ṣ; C: adab – anthology.

(192) A/6s 249a/9 *Alfāẓ fāʾiqa wa-kalimāt rāʾiqa fī al-rasāʾil – Excellent Terms and Clear Words on Epistles*; anonymous work with generic title; VQ: 1; Ṣ; C: adab – epistle.

(193) A/7s 249a/9-10 *al-Adwiya al-mufrada – Simple Drugs*; see comments in no. 105; possibly A: Rashīd al-Dīn Ibn al-Ṣūrī (d. 639/1242); S: *Wāfī*, XIV, 125; C: pharmacology. (cf. nos 105, 1479)

(194) B/1 249a/10 *Bustān al-mubtadiʾ fī al-qirāʾāt – The Beginner's Garden on Koran Recitation*; A: Muḥammad b. Maḥmūd b. Abī Bakr al-Ṭūsī (fl. 620s/1220s); S: Ibn al-Jazarī, *Ghāyat al-nihāya*, II, 259; VQ: 1; Ṣ; C: Koran – recitation.

(195a) B/1 249a/10-11 *al-Baᶜth – Resurrection*; A: Sulaymān Ibn al-Ashᶜath al-Sijistānī (d. 275/889); S: al-Ziriklī, *al-Aᶜlām*, III, 182; C: eschatology/afterlife.

(195b) 249a/11 *al-Miʾa al-Shurayḥīya – Shurayḥ's Hundred [Ḥadīth]*; A: ᶜAbd al-Raḥmān b. Aḥmad Abī Shurayḥ (d. 392/1001–2); S: ed. Ay.ᶜA. al-Shurayda, MA thesis, Kuwait University/Kullīyat al-dirāsāt al-ᶜulyā, 2005; VQ: 1; Ṣ; C: ḥadīth – collection.

(196) B/2 249a/11 *Bahjat al-majālis – The Gatherings' Splendour*; A: Ibn ᶜAbd al-Barr (d. 463/1070); S: ed. M. al-Khūlī and ᶜA. al-Qiṭṭ, Cairo: al-Dār al-Miṣrīya, 1969–72; MS: Süleymaniye, Fatih 3708*; VQ: 2; Ṣ; C: ḥadīth/adab. (cf. no. 1527)

(197) B/2 249a/11-12 *Bahjat al-asrār – The Splendour of Secrets*; A: anonymous work ('*majhūl al-muṣannif*') with popular title; VQ: 1; Ṣ. (cf. nos 198, 221)

(198) B/2 249a/12 *Bahjat al-asrār* – *The Splendour of Secrets*; probably the Aleppian calligrapher Scr(‘*bi-khaṭṭ*’): ᶜAlī b. Abī Ṭālib Ibn al-Shawwāᵓ (d. 640/1242–3; TI, 631–40, p. 446); A: ᶜAlī Ibn Jahḍam (d. 414/1023); S: *Siyar*, XVII, 275–6; VQ: 5; C: sufism. (cf. nos 197, 221)

(199) B/2 249a/12-13 *Bidāyat al-hidāya* – *The Beginning of Guidance*; as this book is held in two copies and the author is not identified the cataloguer assumed that it was well known. This is thus most likely A: al-Ghazālī (d. 505/1111); S: ed. ᶜA. Darwīsh, Beirut: DṢ, 1998; NC: 2; VQ: 1, 1; Ṣ; C: ethics – Islamic. (cf. no. 1170b)

(200) B/2 249a/13 *Bustān al-ᶜārifīn* – *The Garden of the Knowledgeable*; A: Abū al-Layth Naṣr b. Muḥammad al-Samarqandī (d. between 373/983–4 and 393/1002–3); S: ed. ᶜA. Zayyāt, Cairo: Dār al-manār, 1995; VQ: 1; Ṣ; C: ethics – Islamic.

(201) B/3 249a/13–14 *al-Baḥr al-ḥāwī li-jawhar al-fatāwī* – *The Encompassing Ocean on the Essence of Fatwas*; this is most likely the *Jawāhir al-fatāwī* by A: Muḥammad b. ᶜAbd al-Rashīd al-Kirmānī (d. 565/1170); S: King Saud University, Riyad, MS 1437; C: fiqh – ḥanafī – fatwa collection.

(202) B/5 249a/14 *al-Barq al-Shāmī* – *The Syrian Bolt*; A: Muḥammad b. Muḥammad ᶜImād al-Dīn al-Kātib al-Iṣfahānī (d. 597/1201); S: eds M. al-Ḥayyārī and F. Ḥusayn, Amman 1987; VQ: 6; Ṣ; C: history – Ayyūbid.

(203) B/6 249a/15 *al-Basāla ikhtiyār Thaᶜlab* – *On Courage, Selected by Thaᶜlab*; no such title is identifiable, but Thaᶜlab refers to the theme of courage in his writings such as *Majālis Thaᶜlab*, ed. ᶜA.M. Hārūn, Cairo: DM; A: Aḥmad b. Yaḥyā Thaᶜlab (d. 291/904); VQ: 1–45; Ṣ; C: philology.[53]

(204) B/8 249a/15 *al-Baṣāᵓir wa-al-dhakhāᵓir* – *Treasures of Insightful Perception*; A: Abū Ḥayyān al-Tawḥīdī (d. 414/1023); S: ed. W. al-Qāḍī, Beirut: DṢ, 1984–8; MS: Süleymaniye, Fatih 3695–9***. (Each volume carries a splendid frontispiece claiming the manuscript was the possession of the private library of the Mamluk governor of Damascus Badr al-Dīn Baydarā (d. 693/1293). The volumes were copied in 628–9/1231, so Baydarā took possession of them several decades after they were written. There is no doubt that these manuscripts belonged to the Ashrafīya library: they are today in one of the host collections, carrying an endowment note by ‘merhum Celebizade

Mevlana Derviş Mehmed', and, most importantly, vol. 3 (Fatih 3697) carries the note that it was personally copied by one of the library's patrons, al-Ashraf Aḥmad (the same notes on 3695 and 3696 are hardly legible). The most likely scenario is that Baydarā took possession of this copy for his large private library and that it was returned to the Ashrafīya after his execution.); C: adab – anthology. (cf. nos 303, 1249e, 1465)

(205) B/9 249a/16 *al-Bayān wa-al-tabyīn – Book of Clarity and Clarification*; A: al-Jāḥiẓ (d. 255/868–9); S: ed. ᶜA.M. Hārūn, Cairo: MK, 1948–50; VQ: 1–4; Ṣ; C: adab – anthology. (cf. nos 1237b?, 1249i, 1516, 1528)

(206) B/9 249a/16 *al-Bishāra wa-al-nidhāra – Joyful Tidings and Warnings [Concerning Dream Interpretation]*; A: ᶜAbd al-Malik b. Muḥammad al-Khargūshī (d. 406/1015 or 407/1016); S: EI², A.J. Arberry, 'al-K͟hargūs͟hī': '*al-Bishāra wa-al-nidhāra fī taᶜbīr al-ruʾyā*'; MS: Süleymaniye, Ayasofya 1688*; VQ: 1; Ṣ; C: oneiromancy.

(207) B/9 249a/16–17 *al-Bustān wa-? al-A – The Garden and?*; the title's final two terms make no sense in Arabic. The following two entries in this catalogue refer to works originally in Syriac and they both pose considerable problems to the cataloguer. In consequence, this may be the case here as well and this is arguably a text in *garshūnī*, Arabic written in Syriac script. A strong candidate for this is *al-Bustān wa-shams al-adhhān* (Paris syr. 398; Briquel-Chatonnet, *Manuscrits syriaques*, 120), a collection of moralistic sayings attributed to various wise men. In this case the writer correctly deciphered '*al-Bustān wa-*', got the '*shams*' entirely wrong and gave up after deciphering the first three letters of '*al-a*'. VQ: 3; Ṣ; C: ethics.

(208) B/9 249a/17 *Yashūrᶜdnā fī al-āthār al-ᶜulwīya – Ishōᶜdnaḥ on Meteorological Phenomena*; an author or book title as given in the catalogue, B-sh-w-r-ᶜ, is not identifiable. This term is probably a corrupted version of Ishōᶜdnaḥ/Īshōᶜdĕnaḥ (fl. 3rd/9th c.), the Syriac Metropolitan of Basra. The cataloguer (or the scribe of this manuscript) must have got the Arabised (or *garshūnī*) version of the name wrong reading the initial 'b' for a 'y', adding a 'r' and dropping the final 'ḥ', thus writing بشورع دنا instead of يشوع دناح. Ishōᶜdnaḥ/Īshōᶜdĕnaḥ authored the *Book of Chastity* and also a lost book on logic (Fiey, 'Îchô'dnah'). It is thus feasible that he authored a book on meteorological phenomena or, more likely, that such a book was ascribed to him.

The text here may be the Syriac translation of Theophrastus's meteorological work (cf. Daiber, 'Meteorology of Theophrastus') that was subsequently translated into Arabic (GAS, VII, 223). VQ: 1; Ṣ; C: astronomy/meteorology (influence of the spheres).[54]

(209) B/10 249b/1 *Yārbūqā fī al-sumūm* – *Yārbūqā on Poisons*; the cataloguer was uncertain about this Syriac name, which has no diacritical marks, except for an erroneous '*fā*'' instead of the '*qāf*'. For the 'author' and his work translated by Ibn Waḥshīya see S: GAS, III, 179–81. VQ: 6; Ṣ; C: pharmacology – toxicology.[55]

(210) B/10 249b/1 *al-Bayṭara al-kabīr* – *The Large Book on Veterinary Medicine*; no 'large' *bayṭara* book is identifiable, although there are numerous possibilities for the title Bayṭara itself (cf. IN, index). VQ: 3; Ṣ; C: veterinary medicine.

(211) B/10 249b/1 *al-Bayṭara* – *[The Book on] Veterinary Medicine*; A: Abū ᶜAbd Allāh Muḥammad b. Yaᶜqūb Ibn Akhī Ḥizām al-Khuttalī (fl. late 3rd/9th c.); S: ed. & Germ. tr. Heide, *Hippiatrie*; MS: Süleymaniye, Ayasofya 2899*; VQ: 2; Ṣ; C: veterinary medicine.

(212) B/10 249b/2 *al-Bayṭara* – *[The Book on] Veterinary Medicine*; generic/popular title with numerous possibilities (cf. IN, index); FI: '*taṣnīf ākhar*'/'*a work by another [author]*; VQ: 1; Ṣ; C: veterinary medicine.

(213) B/10 249b/2 *al-Bayṭara* – *[The Book on] Veterinary Medicine*; generic/popular title with numerous possibilities (cf. IN, index); F: '*taṣnīf ākhar*'/'*a work by another [author]*'; VQ: 1; Ṣ; C: veterinary medicine.

(214) B/10 249b/2 *al-Bayzara* – *[The Book of] Falconry*; generic/popular title with numerous possibilities (cf. Möller, *Falknereiliteratur*); FI: '*muṣawwar*'/'*illustrated*'; VQ: 1; Ṣ; C: falconry.

(215) B/10 249b/2-3 *al-Bayzara* – *[The Book of] Falconry*; no author called Ibn J/Ḥ/Kh-b/t/th/n/y-d/dh is known in the field of falconry. However, the name must be familiar to the cataloguer and this may thus be a treatise written for al-Malik al-Ashraf, who had a strong interest in falconry, similar to the anonymous work (MS Istanbul, Süleymaniye, Ayasofya 3636) whose author was in Damascus during the reign of al-Ashraf (cf. Möller, *Falknereiliteratur*, 87–90). VQ: 1; Ṣ; C: falconry.

(216) B/10 249b/3 *al-Bayzara – [The Book of] Falconry*; A: Muḥammad b. ᶜAbd Allāh b. ᶜUmar Ibn al-Bāzyār (d. 245/859); S: eds A. Akasoy and S. Georges, *Das Falken- und Hundebuch des Kalifen al-Mutawakkil*, Berlin 2005; VQ: 1; Ṣ; C: falconry.

(217) B/10 249b/3-4 *al-Bayzara – [The Book of] Falconry*; generic/popular title with numerous possibilities (cf. Möller, *Falknereiliteratur*); FI: '*62 bāb*'/'*in 62 chapters*'; VQ: 1; Ṣ; C: falconry.

(218) B/10 249b/4 *al-Buzāt – [The Book of] Falcons*; A: Khumārawayh b. Aḥmad b. Ṭūlūn (d. 282/896); S: discussed in Möller, *Falknereiliteratur*, 93 and 120; VQ: 1; Ṣ; C: falconry.[56]

(219) B/10 249b/4 *al-Buzāt – [The Book of] Falcons*; popular title with numerous possibilities (cf. Möller, *Falknereiliteratur*); FI: '*bi-khaṭṭ Kūfī rathth*'/'*in Kufi script, worn-out [manuscript]*'; VQ: 1; Ṣ; C: falconry.

(220) B/13 249b/5 *al-Bāriᶜ – The Excellent Book*; A: Hārūn Ibn al-Munajjim (d. 288/901 or to 289/902); S: IN, I/2, 444; VQ: 2; Ṣ; C: poetry – anthology. (cf. no. 1357)

(221) B/15 249b/5 *Bahjat al-asrār – The Splendour of Secrets*; popular title with numerous possibilities; VQ: 1; Ṣ. (cf. no. 197)

(222) B/15 249b/5–6 *Bard al-akbād fī al-aᶜdād – Alleviating the Hearts Concerning Numbers*; A: al-Thaᶜālibī (d. 429/1038); S: ed. I. Thāmirī, Beirut: DIḤ, 2006; NC: 2; VQ: 1, 1; Ṣ; C: adab – anthology. (cf. no. 1300a)

(223) B/15 249b/6–7 *Bustān al-nāẓir wa-nuzhat al-khāṭir – The Beholder's Garden of Delight*; no such title is identifiable, but several titles include the same or similar combinations of terms, such as the chronicle *Nuzhat al-nāẓir wa-rawḍat al-khāṭir* by the north Syrian author ᶜAbd al-Qāhir b. ᶜAlawī (fl. 571/1176; Ibn al-ᶜAdīm, *Bughyat*, II, 741), the *fiqh* work *Rawḍat al-nāẓir* by ᶜAbd Allāh b. Aḥmad Ibn Qudāma al-Muwaffaq (d. 620/1223) and, in light of the category, the most likely adab/poetry/wisdom literature anthology *Rawḍat al-nāẓir wa-nuzhat al-khāṭir* by ᶜAbd al-ᶜAzīz al-Kāshī (fl. 7th/13th c.) (Marlow, *Hierarchy and Egalitarianism*, 141; cf. no. 476). NC: 2; VQ: 1–40, 1–5; Ṣ; C: adab/poetry – anthology?

(224) B/15 249b/7 *Badāʾiᶜ al-badāʾih – Marvels of the Beginning*; A: ᶜAlī Ibn Ẓāfir (d. 613/1216 or 623/1226); S: ed. M.A. Ibrāhīm, Cairo: Maktabat

al-Anjlū al-Miṣrīya, 1970; VQ: 1; Ṣ; C: adab – anthology of improvisations. (cf. no. 463 for continuation)

(225) B/15 249b/7 *Badāˀi^{c} mā najama min mutakhallifī kuttāb al-^{c}ajam – Marvels Originating from Later Persian Secretaries*; A: Muḥammad b. Muḥammad b. Sahl al-Shilḥī (d. 423/1032); S: MM, III, 645; VQ: 1–44; Ṣ; C: adab – anthology.

(226) T/1 249b/8 *Tadhkirat al-gharīb fī tafsīr al-Qurˀān – Uncommon Words: On Koran Exegesis*; A: Ibn al-Jawzī (d. 597/1200); S: ed. Ṭ. Sayyid, *Tadhkirat al-arīb fī tafsīr al-gharīb*, Beirut: DKI, 2004; VQ: 1; Ṣ; C: Koran – exegesis (*tafsīr*)/lexicography.

(227) T/1 249b/8 *al-Tibyān fī tafsīr al-Qurˀān – Exposition of Koran Exegesis*; A: Naṣr b. ^{c}Alī al-Shīrāzī Ibn Abī Maryam (fl. 565/1170). The authorship of Ibn Abī Maryam is debatable as he is not known to have authored an exegetical work with the keyword '*tibyān*'. The most famous exegetical work entitled *al-Tibyān* was rather authored by the Shi^{c}ite scholar Muḥammad b. al-Ḥasan al-Ṭūsī (d. 459 or 460/1066–7). However, as Ibn Abī Maryam is explicitly, although not correctly, mentioned and as he authored *al-Kashf wa-al-bayān fī tafsīr al-Qurˀan* his authorship is more likely. S: MM, IV, 23; VQ: 5; Ṣ; C: Koran – exegesis (*tafsīr*).

(228) T/1 249b/9 *Tafsīr al-Qurˀan – Koran Exegesis*; A: Abū al-Layth Naṣr b. Muḥammad al-Samarqandī (d. between 373/983–4 and 393/1002–3); S: eds ^{c}A. Mu^{c}awwaḍ and ^{c}Ā. ^{c}Abd al-Mawjūd/Z. al-Nūtī, *Tafsīr al-Samarqandī al-musammā Baḥr al-^{c}ulūm*, Beirut: DKI, 1993; VQ: 4; Ṣ; C: Koran – exegesis (*tafsīr*).

(229) T/1 249b/9 *Tafsīr āy al-jihād – Exegesis of the Jihad Verses*; A: ^{c}Alī Ibn ^{c}Asākir (d. 571/1176); this title is not mentioned in Ibn ^{c}Asākir's biographies or his own works. VQ: 2; Ṣ; C: Koran – exegesis (*tafsīr*).

(230) T/2 249b/10 *Tafsīr sūrat Yūsuf – Exegesis of the Joseph Verse*; A: Muḥammad b. ^{c}Abd al-Karīm al-Shahrastānī (d. 548/1143); S: Yāqūt, *Mu^{c}jam al-buldān*, III, 377 classifies this work as one of speculative theology (*kalām*) in which the author uses 'philosophical expressions'; VQ: 1; Ṣ; C: theology?

(231) T/2 249b/10-11 *Tanwīr al-ghabash fī faḍl al-sūd wa-al-ḥabash – Lightening Darkness Concerning the Merits of Blacks and Ethiopians*; Scr('*bi-*

khaṭṭihi') & A: Ibn al-Jawzī (d. 597/1200); S: ed. M. Ibrāhīm, Riyad: Dār al-sharīf, 1998; VQ: 1–2; Ṣ; C: ḥadīth – merits.

(232) T/2 249b/11 *al-Tawwābīn – The Repentants*; A: ʿAbd Allāh b. Aḥmad Ibn Qudāma al-Maqdisī al-Muwaffaq (d. 620/1223); S: ed. ʿA. al-Arnāʾūṭ, Damascus: Dār al-Bayān, 1969; VQ: 1; Ṣ; C: ḥadīth.

(233) T/3 249b/11 *Taqrīb al-aḥkām ʿalā fuqahāʾ al-islām – Presentation of Legal Decisions According to the Jurisprudents of Islam*; no such title is identifiable, but the two most famous legal works containing the term '*taqrīb*' were: 1) Aḥmad b. Ḥasan/Ḥusayn Abū Shujāʿ (fl. 5th/11th c.; ed. S. Keyser, *Précis de jurisprudence musulmane*, Leiden 1859) and 2) al-Qāsim b. Muḥammad al-Qaffāl al-Shāshī (d. 336/947) whose *taqrīb* is, for example, repeatedly cited by al-Subkī, *Ṭabaqāt*, III, 472–7; VQ: 2; Ṣ; C: fiqh – shāfiʿī.

(234) T/3 249b/12 *Tatimmat al-ibāna – Completion of the Explanation*; A: ʿAbd al-Raḥmān b. Maʾmūn al-Mutawallī (d. 478/1086); S: EI^{2}, D. Gimaret, 'al-Mutawallī'; NC: 2; VQ: 10, 9; Ṣ; C: fiqh – shāfiʿī.

(235) T/3 249b/12 *Talkhīṣ al-aqsām li-madhāhib al-anām – Summary of the Divisions Concerning the Schools of Law of the Creatures*; A: Muḥammad b. ʿAbd al-Karīm al-Shahrastānī (d. 548/1143); S: MM, III, 422; VQ: 1; Ṣ; C: fiqh – shāfiʿī.

(236) T/3 249b/12 *Taqwīm al-naẓar – Rectifying the View [Concerning Disputed Problems]*; A: Muḥammad b. ʿAlī Ibn al-Dahhān[57] (d. *c.*592/1196); S: *Taqwīm al-naẓar fī masāʾil khilāfiya*, ed. A. al-Azharī, Beirut: DKI, 2001; VQ: 1; Ṣ; C: fiqh – trans-madhhab.

(237) T/3 249b/13 *Taʿlīq al-Sharīf – Al-Sharīf's Commentary*; A: Muḥammad b. al-Ḥusayn al-Sharīf al-Raḍī (d. 406/1016); S: al-Najāshī, *K. al-rijāl*, II, 326: '*K. taʿlīq khilāf al-fuqahāʾ*'; VQ: 2; Ṣ; C: fiqh – imāmī.

(238) T/3 249b/13 *Tafrīʿ – Derivation of [Legal] Propositions*; A: ʿUbayd Allāh b. al-Ḥusayn Ibn al-Jallāb (d. 378/988); S: ed. *al-Tafrīʿ fī fiqh al-imām Mālik Ibn Anas*, Beirut: DKI, 2007; VQ: 1; Ṣ; C: fiqh – mālikī.

(239) T/3 249b/13 *Tahdhīb iṣlāḥ juyūsh al-jihād – Refinement of Reforming the Jihad Armies*; no such title is identifiable. Placed in category 3 this work most likely had a strong legal component. VQ: 1; Ṣ; C: jihād.

(240) T/4 249b/14 *Taṣrīf – Morphology*; A: ᶜAbd al-Qāhir b. ᶜAbd al-Raḥmān al-Jurjānī (d. 471/1078); S: ed. al-B. Zahrān, *al-ᶜUmud: K. fī al-taṣrīf*, Cairo: DM, 1988; VQ: 1; Ṣ; C: morphology.

(241) T/4 249b/14 *Tahdhīb iṣlāḥ al-manṭiq – Refinement of Correcting Speech*; A: Yaḥyā b. ᶜAlī al-Khaṭīb al-Tibrīzī (d. 502/1109); S: ed. F. Masᶜūd, Cairo: HMAK, 1986–7; VQ: 1; Ṣ; C: lexicography.

(242) T/4 249b/14 *al-Taqfiya – The Rhyme Book*; A: al-Yamān b. al-Yamān al-Bandanījī (d. 284/897); S: ed. Kh. al-ᶜAṭīya, *al-Taqfiya fī al-lugha*, Baghdad: MᶜA, 1976; MS: Süleymaniye, Ayasofya 4670**; VQ: 2; Ṣ; C: lexicography.

(243) T/5 249b/15 *Min Taʾrīkh Ibn al-Ṣābiʾ – [Parts] of Ibn al-Ṣābiʾ's Chronicle*; A: Hilāl b. al-Muḥassin al-Ṣābiʾ (d. 448/1056); S: IKH, V, 127; VQ: 29; Ṣ; C: history – Būyid. (cf. no. 1425)

(244) T/5 249b/15 *Taʾrīkh Ibn Jarīr – Ibn Jarīr's Chronicle*; A: Muḥammad b. Jarīr al-Ṭabarī (d. 310/923); S: Engl. tr. *The History of al-Ṭabarī*, Albany (NY) 1985–99; VQ: 26; C: history – universal.

(245) T/5 249b/15 *al-Taʾrīkh al-Atābakī – The Atabeg History*; A: ᶜAlī Ibn al-Athīr (d. 630/1233); S: *al-Taʾrīkh al-bāhir fī dawlat al-Atābakīya*, ed. ᶜA. Ṭulaymāt, Cairo: DKḤ, 1963; VQ: 1; Ṣ; C: history – Zangid.

(246) T/5 249b/16 *Taʾrīkh Thābit b. Sinān b. Qurra – Thābit b. Sinān b. Qurra's Chronicle*; A: Thābit b. Sinān b. Qurra al-Ṣābiʾ (d. *c.*363/974); S: MM, I, 466; VQ: 6; Ṣ; C: history – ᶜAbbāsid/Būyid.

(247) T/5 249b/16 *al-Taʾrīkh al-Badrī – History of the Battle of Badr*; A: Usāma b. Munqidh (d. 584/1188); S: TI, 581–90, p. 176; VQ: 5; Ṣ; C: history – early Islam.

(248) T/5 249b/16-17 *Taʾrīkh Jamāl al-Dīn b. al-Maʾmūn – Jamāl al-Dīn b. al-Maʾmūn's Chronicle*; A: Sharaf al-Khilāfa Jamāl al-Dīn Mūsā b. al-Maʾmūn al-Baṭāʾiḥī (d. 588/1192); S: ed. F. Sayyid, *Nuṣūṣ min akhbār Miṣr li-Ibn al-Maʾmūn*, Cairo: IFAO, 1983; VQ: 2; Ṣ; C: history – Fatimid. (cf. no. 1700b)

(249) T/5 249b/17 *al-Tabyīn fī nasab*[58] *al-Qurashīyīn – Clarification Concerning the Quraysh Tribe's Genealogy*; A: ᶜAbd Allāh b. Aḥmad Ibn Qudāma al-Maqdisī al-Muwaffaq (d. 620/1223); S: *Wāfī*, XVII, 38;

al-Tabyīn fī ansāb al-Qurashīyīn, ed. M.N. al-Dulaymī, Baghdad: MII, 1982; MS: Süleymaniye, Fatih 4239**; C: history – genealogy.

(250) T/5 249b/17 *al-Taʾrīkh al-Tājī – The Crown Chronicle*; A: Ibrāhīm b. Hilāl al-Ṣābiʾ (d. 384/994); S: EI^2, F.C. de Blois, 'Ṣābiʾ': '*al-Kitāb al-Tājī fī akhbār al-dawla al-daylamīya*'; VQ: 4; Ṣ; C: history – Būyid.

(251) T/7 249b/18 *Tatimmat al-Yatīma – Completion of the Yatīma*; A: al-Thaᶜālibī (d. 429/1038); S: ed. M. Qumayḥa, Beirut: DKI, 1983; NC: 6; VQ: 1; Ṣ; C: poetry/adab – anthology.

(252) T/7 249b/18 *al-Taṣḥīf wa-al-taḥrīf – Misspelling and Alteration*; arguably A: ᶜUthmān b. ᶜĪsā al-Balīṭī (d. 599/1202); S: TI, 591–600, pp. 396–8; alternative possibility is al-Ḥasan b. ᶜAbd Allāh b. Sahl al-ᶜAskarī (fl. 4th/10th c.), *Sharḥ mā yaqaᶜu fīhi al-taṣḥīf wa-al-taḥrīf*; placed in adab category 7 this work most probably referred to mistakes in literary prose texts and verse. VQ: 2; Ṣ; C: philology – orthography and spelling/adab.

(253) T/7 249b/18–19 *al-Tamthīl wa-al-muḥāḍara – The Book of Exemplification and Discussion*; A: al-Thaᶜālibī (d. 429/1038); S: ed. ᶜA. al-Ḥulw, Cairo: DᶜAK, 1983; MS: Süleymaniye, Fatih 3724*; NC: 3; VQ: 2; Ṣ; C: adab – anthology. (cf. nos 1292a, 1463)

(254) T/7 249b/19 *al-Tuḥaf wa-al-ṭuraf/ẓuraf – Rarities and Curiosities/ Gracious Objects*; 1) read as *ṭuraf* this is the work by Muḥammad b. Jaᶜfar Ibn al-Najjār (d. 402/1011?; MM, III, 196), 2) read as *ẓuraf* this is the work by Muḥammad b. Aḥmad al-Daylamī (d. 378/988; ed. ᶜI. al-Kubaysī, Baghdad: al-Jāmiᶜa al-Mustanṣirīya, 1991); VQ: 1; Ṣ; C: adab.

(255) T/8 249b/19 *Taᶜẓīm al-mulūk – Honoring Kings*; no such title is identifiable, but this may be an extract from an administrative handbook on how to address rulers in correspondence (cf. al-Qalqashandī, *Ṣubḥ al-aᶜshā*, V, 461 for such a passage) or a short treatise in this regard. VQ: 1; Ṣ; C: administrative handbook?

(256) T/8 249b/19-20 *Tafḍīl al-kilāb ᶜalā kathīr mimman labisa al-thiyāb – The [Book of] Preference for Dogs over Many Wearing Clothes*; A: Abū Bakr Muḥammad b. Khalaf Ibn al-Marzubān (d. 309/921); S: eds & Engl. trs G.R. Smith and M.A.S. Abdel Haleem, Warminster 1978; VQ: 1–44; Ṣ; C: adab.

(257) T/8 249b/20 *al-Tanbīh wa-al-tawqīf ᶜalā faḍāʾil al-kharīf – Alerting to and Insisting on Autumn's Virtues*; A: Aḥmad b. ᶜAlī al-Khaṭīb al-Baghdādī (d. 463/1071); S: MU, I, 387; MS: Süleymaniye, Fatih 5303/1 (fols. 1a–52b)***; the scribe of this manuscript is al-Ḥasan al-Qaylawī (d. 633/1236; TI, 631–40, p. 145), a renowned scribe of Damascus and librarian of al-Malik al-Ashraf who appears elsewhere as scribe in this library (cf. nos 533, 698, 1253) and who was also involved in the transmission of other copies (cf. no. 807). C: adab.

(258) T/9 250a/1 *Taqwīm sanat 625 – Ephemeris for the Year 625*; in contrast to calendarian sections in administrative and topographical works (see Pellat, *Calendriers égyptiens*) this *taqwīm* probably did not include information on fiscal issues and the liturgical year. It could be an agricultural almanac containing astronomical and astrological data for each day of the year 625/1227–8 in tabular form similar to the Yemenite almanac for the year 808/1405–6 (ed. Varisco, 'Rasulid Agricultural Almanac'). More likely, however, is that this is an ephemeris, displaying positions of the sun, moon and five planets for each day of the year similar to the Yemenite ephemeris for the year 727/1326/7 (King and Samsó, 'Astronomical Handbook'). VQ: 1; Ṣ; C: astronomy.[59]

(259) T/9 250a/1 *Tuḥfat al-mulūk fī al-taᶜbīr – The Kings' Precious Rarity on Interpreting Dreams*; A: Khalaf b. Aḥmad al-Sijistānī (d. 399/1008); S: MU, III, 1258; VQ: 1; Ṣ; C: oneiromancy.

(260) T/9 250a/1-2 *Taᶜbīr al-ruʾyā – Interpreting Dreams*; A: ᶜAbd al-Wāḥid b. Aḥmad (fl. 4th/10th c.). Most likely this is the dream manual by Ibn Qutayba (d. 276/889) (Lamoreaux, *Dream Interpretation*, 27–34), which was transmitted to his son Aḥmad and his grandson ᶜAbd al-Wāḥid (*Siyar*, XIV, 565–6) and that was here ascribed to the latter. VQ: 1; Ṣ; C: oneiromancy.

(261) T/9 250a/2 *Taᶜbīr al-ruʾyā – Interpreting Dreams*; A: Muḥammad Ibn Sīrīn (d. 110/728) (attrib.); S: Daïm, *L' oniromancie*; MS: Süleymaniye, Fatih 5300/1 (fols. 1a–47a)**; The multiple-text manuscript Fatih 5300 holds additional titles, which were identical with or similar to Ashrafiya titles (cf. nos 915, 1115, 1132, 1135a, 1256b). VQ: 1; Ṣ; C: oneiromancy.

(262) T/9 250a/2 *Taḥwīl al-mawālīd wa-ghayruhu – Preparing Horoscopes and Other [Writings]*; arguably referring to '*taḥwīl sinī al-mawālīd*', a popular

title with numerous possibilities (cf. IN, index); VQ: 1; Ṣ; C: astronomy/genethlialogy.

(263) T/9 250a/3 *Tarkīb al-ᶜūd wa-al-ᶜamal bihi – The Making of the ᶜŪd*; this may be an extract from a treatise on melodies ascribed to al-Kindī (d. *c.*252/866), which has a section entitled '*tarkīb al-ᶜūd*'. S: al-Kindī, *Risālat fī al-luḥūn wa-al-nigham*, ed. Z. Yūsuf, Baghdad: Maṭbaᶜat Shafīq, 1965; VQ: 1; Ṣ; C: music.

(264) T/10 250a/3 *al-Tabṣira fī al-nabḍ wa-al-tafsira – Elucidation on the Pulse and Urine*; A: Manṣūr b. Sahlān (fl. early 4th/10th c.); S: IAU, III, 368. Most likely this is a title in the form of key word + *fī* + description of content. Writings on the pulse and urine are well known, as is evident from IAU's title list (although the term for 'urine' in titles is generally *bawl*, except for *K. al-tafsira* by Ayyūb al-Ruhawī, fl. 216/832; Ullmann, *Medizin*, 102). There is only one identifiable medical work with the title *al-Tabṣira*. This work fits well into the history of this library for two reasons: Manṣūr b. Sahlān was the Fatimid court physician, the predecessor of Isḥāq b. Ibrāhīm (cf. no. 1032) and this book was used in the teaching sessions of the Damascene physician Shams al-Dīn Aḥmad b. al-Khalīl (d. 637/1240; IAU, IV, 115). Shams al-Dīn was not only near-contemporaneous to the library's foundation, but he became a court physician of al-Malik al-Muᶜaẓẓam (r. 615/1218–624/1227), al-Malik al-Ashraf's predecessor in Damascus. VQ: 1; Ṣ; C: medicine.

(265) T/10 250a/3–4 *al-Tadāruk li-anwāᶜ khaṭaʾ al-tadbīr – Preventing Various Mistakes in Treatment*; A: Ibn Sīnā (d. 428/1037); S: Gutas, *Avicenna and the Aristotelian Tradition*, 516; VQ: 1; Ṣ; C: medicine.

(266) T/10 250a/4 *al-Tadhkira al-Ashrafīya – The Ashrafian Treatise [on the Medical Profession]*; A: Ismāᶜīl b. al-Ḥasan al-Jurjānī (d. 531/1137); S: MM, I, 361: '*al-Tadhkira al-Ashrafīya fī ṣināᶜat al-ṭibbīya*'; VQ: 1; Ṣ; C: medicine.

(267) T/10 250a/4 *Taqwīm al-ṣiḥḥa – Almanac of Health*; A: al-Mukhtār b. al-Ḥasan Ibn Buṭlān (d. 458/1066); S: ed. & tr. H. Elkhadem, *Le Taqwīm al-ṣiḥḥa (Tacuini sanitatis)*, Leuven 1990; NC: 11; C: medicine.

(268) T/10 250a/4–5 *Taqwīm al-abdān – The Arrangement of Bodies [for Treatment]*; A: Yaḥyā b. ᶜĪsā Ibn Jazla (d. 493/1100); S: *Taqwīm al-abdān*

bi-tadbīr al-insān, ed. S. al-Shammāᶜ, Cairo: al-Dār al-thaqāfīya, 2007; NC: 4; C: medicine.

(269) T/10 250a/5 *al-Tabṣira fī maᶜrifat al-jawāhir* – *Elucidation on the Knowledge of Precious Stones*; no such title is identifiable. This is arguably a commentary on al-Bīrūnī's (d. after 442/1050) mineralogical treatise *al-Jamāhir fī maᶜrifat al-jawāhir*; VQ: 1; Ṣ; C: mineralogy. (cf. nos 306, 1038)

(270) T/10 250a/5 *al-Tiryāq al-kabīr* – *The Large Book on Antidotes*; A: Aḥmad b. Muḥammad Ibn al-Rūmīya; S: IAU, III, 339–40. Books with this popular title were also authored by other scholars such as Muḥammad b. Aḥmad b. Saᶜīd (fl. 370/980; *Wāfī*, II, 81). However, the five copies held in this library indicate a distinct regional popularity and it is thus more likely that Ibn al-Rūmīya, who composed *al-Tiryāq al-kabīr* for al-Malik al-ᶜĀdil in Egypt in 613/1216–17, is the author. NC: 5; C: pharmacology – toxicology.

(271) T/10 250a/5 *Tiryāq* – *Antidotes*; A: al-Muwaffaq Abū al-Barakāt Ibn Shaᶜthāᵓ (fl. early 7th/13th c.); S: IAU, III, 461 (شعيا/شعثا in manuscripts); VQ: 1; Ṣ; C: pharmacology – toxicology.

(272) T/10 250a/6 *al-Taᵓattī li-shifāᵓ al-amrāḍ* – *Healing Illnesses*; A: Galen/ Ḥunayn b. Isḥāq (d. 260/873); S: ed. M. Sālim, *K. Jālīnūs ilā Ghlūqun fī al-taᵓattī li-shifāᵓ al-amrāḍ: maqālatān*, Cairo: HMAK, 1982; VQ: 1; Ṣ; C: medicine.

(273) T/10 250a/6 *Tadbīr al-ṣiḥḥa* – *Guide to Good Health*; probably the author's *K. tadbīr al-aṣiḥḥāᵓ bi-al-maṭᶜam wa-al-mashrab*; A: Ḥunayn b. Isḥāq (d. 260/873); S: Ullmann, *Medizin*, 199; NC: 2; VQ: 1, 1; Ṣ; C: medicine – dietetics.

(274) T/10 250a/6 *Tadhkirat al-kaḥḥālīn* – *Treatise for Ophthalmologists*; A: ᶜAlī b. ᶜĪsā al-Kaḥḥāl (d. after 400/1010); S: ed. Gh. al-Qādarī al-Sharafī, Hyderabad: DMU, 1964. VQ: 1; Ṣ; C: medicine.

(275) T/10 250a/6-7 *al-Taḥbīr* – *The Embellishment*; no such title is identifiable with the author's name given here and it is clearly a key word title. As this is thematic category 10 this is most likely a minor medical work by the Syrian physician, secretary and *adīb* A: ᶜAlī b. Abī ᶜAbd Allāh ᶜĪsā (d. 574/1178); S: IAU, IV, 90–3 and TI, 571–80, pp. 151–2; VQ: 1; Ṣ; C: medicine.

(276) T/10 250a/7 *Taqāsīm al-ᶜilal wa-ᶜilājuhā – Categories of Illnesses and Their Treatment*; A: al-Rāzī (Rhazes) (d. 313/925 or 323/935); S: ed. Ṣ. Ḥammāmī, Aleppo: Jāmiᶜat Ḥalab, 1992; VQ: 1; Ṣ; C: medicine.

(277) T/10 250a/7 *Taqāsīm masāʾil Ḥunayn – Divisions Concerning the Questions of Ḥunayn*; possibly a commentary or summary of Ḥunayn's al-*Masāʾil fī al-ṭibb li-l-mutaᶜallimīn*; A: Ḥunayn b. Isḥāq (d. 260/873); S: eds M. Abū Rayyān, M. ᶜArab and J. Mūsā, Cairo: DJM, 1978; VQ: 1; Ṣ; C: pharmacology. (cf. no. 1256)

(278) T/10 250a/7-8 *Tafsīr asnān al-dawābb – Explaining the Life Stages of Animals*; no such title is identifiable, but being placed in category 10 this is most likely a minor treatise on veterinary medicine. VQ: 1; Ṣ; C: veterinary medicine.

(279) T/15 250a/8 *Tawqīᶜāt Kisrā Anūshirwān – The Decrees of the Sasanian King Anūshirwān*; answers questions on issues such as politics, social justice and administration (see Zakeri, 'Persian Apophthegma'); VQ: 1; Ṣ; C: ethics.

(280a) T/3s 250a/9 *Tuḥfat al-ẓurafāʾ fī taʾrīkh al-khulafāʾ – The Refined People's Precious Rarity on the History of the Caliphs*; arguably the *Bulghat al-ẓurafāʾ fī taʾrīkh al-khulafāʾ*; A: ᶜAlī b. Muḥammad b. Abī al-Surūr al-Rawḥī (d. after 648/1250); S: ed. ᶜI. Hilāl, Cairo: Wizārat al-awqāf, 2004; C: history – Islamic. (cf. no. 869b)

(280b) 250a/9 *Qaṣīdat al-Aᶜshā – Al-Aᶜshā's Qaṣīda*; most likely A: Maymūn b. Qays al-Aᶜshā (d. after 625); S: EI³, B. Jockers, 'al-Aᶜshā'; FI: '*wa- nadhkuruhu fī al-qāf*' / '*we will mention it [as well] in [the section on the letter] qāf [cf. no. 869]*'; C: poetry – early Islamic. (cf. no. 869a)

(281) T/4s 250a/10 *Tuḥfat al-ᶜibād fī bayān al-awrād – The Servants' Gift on Elucidating Litanies*; no such title is identifiable, but in line with thematic category 4s this seems to be a treatise on prayers, here supererogatory personal devotions (*wird*), possibly similar to the prayer book *al-Awrād* by ᶜUmar al-Suhrawardī (d. 632/1234) (GAL, I, 441) or to one of the commentaries on it, such as *Kanz al-ᶜibād fī sharḥ al-awrād* (GAL S, I, 790). VQ: 1; Ṣ; C: prayer book.

(282) T/4s 250a/10–11 *Tarjamat al-Nāqūs ᶜan ᶜAlī b. Abī Ṭālib raḍiya Allāh ᶜanhu – The Interpretation of the Sound of ᶜAlī b. Abī Ṭālib's Clapper (may God be pleased with him)*; on ᶜAlī interpreting the sound of a clapper in the form

of a short moralistic poem consisting only of long syllables. attr. to A: ᶜAlī b. Abī Ṭālib, the fourth Caliph and first Shiᶜite *imām* (d. 40/661); S: Gelder, *Sound and Sense*, 108–23; VQ: 1; Ṣ; C: poetry – early Islamic.

(283) T/4s 250a/11 *Tuḥfat al-adīb wa-ḥilyat al-arīb* – *The Man of Letter's Gift and the Proficient's Ornament*; no such title is identifiable. The entry may refer to two separate works. In this case the second may be the *Ḥilyat al-arīb fī mukhtaṣar al-gharīb* by the philologist ᶜAbd al-ᶜAzīz al-Lakhmī al-Andalusī (d. 616/1219) (Baghdādī, *Hadīyat*, II, 110), a summary of the lexicographical *ḥadīth* work *Gharīb al-ḥadīth* by Isḥāq b. Mirār al-Shaybānī (d. *c.*213/828). However, on account of the rhymed title this is more likely one single adab anthology. VQ: 1 *min* 4; Ṣ; C: adab.

(284) T/5s 250a/11–12 *al-Tawḥīd ᶜan al-aʾimma* – *The Book of Affirming God's Unity Transmitted from the Imams*; this is a key word title with numerous possibilities of books carrying the popular key word '*Tawḥīd*' (IN alone lists nineteen of them). The cataloguer seems unable to ascribe this entry to a specific author and thus merely states that it was transmitted from the *imāms*/grand scholars of the past. VQ: 1; Ṣ; C: theology?

(285) T/6s 250a/12 *al-Tashbībāt wa-al-ṭalab* – *Pleasing Openings and Elegant Requests*; possibly A: Muḥammad b. Sahl Ibn al-Marzubān al-Karkhī (d. *c.*345/956) whose *al-Muntahā fī al-kamāl* includes a section *al-Tashbībāt wa-al-ṭalab*; S: *al-Tashbībāt wa-al-ṭalab*, ed. ᶜU. Ṣiddīqī, Beirut: DB, 2013; VQ: 1; Ṣ; C: adab – anthology.

(286) T/6s 250a/12 *Tarassul al-Ḥaṣkafī* – *Al-Ḥaṣkafī's Letters*; no reading of the word *t-z/r/d/dh-b/t/th/n/y-l* makes sense. *Tarassul* is the only approximate reading that matches the author's literary output and also the 'epistle category' 6s. A: al-Khaṭīb Yaḥyā b. Salāma al-Ḥaṣkafī (d. *c.*551/1156); S: MU, VI, 2818; VQ: 1; Ṣ; C: adab – epistle?[60]

(287a) T/7s 250a/13 *Tadbīr al-musāfirīn* – *Regimen for Travellers*; A: Ibn Sīnā (d. 428/1037); S: Gutas, *Avicenna and the Aristotelian Tradition*, 518; MS: Süleymaniye, Ayasofya 4849/32 (fols. 153a-175b)*; C: medicine.

(287b) 250a/13 *wa-Tanbīh al-mukhtalisīn li-ṣiḥḥatay al-abdān wa-al-adyān* – *Warning the Pilferer for the Well-Being of Bodies and Faith*; No such title is identifiable. VQ: 1; Ṣ.

(288) Th/13 250a/14 *al-Thanāᵓ al-mushraf bi-ṣifāt al-Malik al-Ashraf – Exalted Praise of al-Malik al-Ashraf's Characteristics*; no such title is identifiable and this is most likely a book-in-the-making. Placed in thematic category 13 this is panegyric poetry for al-Malik al-Ashraf, the mausoleum's patron. In this case the most probable poet is al-Ashraf's secretary A: ᶜAlī b. Muḥammad Kamāl al-Dīn Ibn al-Nabīh (d. 619/1222) renowned for his *Ashrafiyāt* and the poet who has the largest corpus of panegyrics for al-Ashraf. S: al-Asᶜad, *Dīwān Ibn al-Nabīh*, 123–363; VQ: 3; Ṣ; C: poetry – panegyric – Ayyūbid – al-Malik al-Ashraf. (cf. nos 190, 315, 863, 868, 1049, 1055, 1229d)

(289) J/2 250a/14-15 *Jawāhir al-kalām ᶜan ᶜAlī b. Abī Ṭālib karrama Allāh wajhahu – Gems of ᶜAlī b. Abī Ṭālib's Sayings (may God honour his countenance)*; arguably the *One Hundred Proverbs* that also appear in the catalogue as *Miᵓat jawhara min kalām ᶜAlī b. Abī Ṭālib* (cf. no. 1134); attr. to A: al-Jāḥiẓ (d. 255/868–9); S: *One Hundred Proverbs* (*Miᵓat kalima min kalām amīr al-Muᵓminīn ᶜAlī b. Abī Ṭālib)*, in: Engl. tr. & ed. Qutbuddin, *Treasury of Virtues*, 220–33; VQ: 1; Ṣ; C: ᶜAlī – sayings attributed to. (cf. nos 312, 1134, 1658)

(290) J/2 250a/15 *Jawāhir al-Qurᵓān – Jewels of the Koran*; A: al-Ghazālī (d. 505/1111); S: ed. M. al-Qabbānī, Beirut: Dār iḥyāᵓ al-ᶜulūm, 1985; MS: Süleymaniye, Ayasofya 1816–19 (fols. 112a–130b)***; VQ: 1; Ṣ; C: Koran.

(291) J/3 250a/15–16 *Jāmiᶜ sharāᵓiṭ al-aḥkām – Collection of the Prerequisites of Rulings*; arguably the *Sharāᵓiṭ al-aḥkām* by A: ᶜAbd Allāh b. ᶜAbdān (d. 433/1041); S: al-Subkī, *Ṭabaqāt*, III, 234; VQ: 1; Ṣ; C: fiqh – shāfiᶜī.

(292) J/4 250a/16 *Jamharat al-amthāl – Compilation of Proverbs*; A: al-Ḥasan b. ᶜAbd Allāh b. Sahl al-ᶜAskarī (fl. 4th/10th c.); S: ed. A. Zaghlūl, Beirut: DKI, 1988; VQ: 1; Ṣ; C: adab – proverbs. (cf. no. 1404)

(293) J/4 250a/16 *Jumal – The Comprehensive [Grammar]*; A: ᶜAbd al-Qāhir b. ᶜAbd al-Raḥmān al-Jurjānī (d. 471/1078); S: *al-Jumal fī al-naḥw*, ed. Y. ᶜAbd Allāh, Beirut: DKI, 1990; VQ: 1; Ṣ; C: grammar.

(294) J/4 250a/17 *Jumal – The Comprehensive [Grammar]*; A: ᶜAbd al-Raḥmān b. Isḥāq al-Zajjājī (d. 337/948 or 339–40/949–50?); S: *al-Jumal fī al-naḥw*, ed. M. Ben Cheneb, Paris 1957; MS: Süleymaniye, Şehid Ali Paşa 2511/1 (fols. 1a–76b)*; VQ: 1; Ṣ; C: grammar.

(295) J/5 250a/17 *al-Jamʿ wa-al-bayān fī akhbār al-Qayrawān – Summarising and Elucidating the Reports on Kairouan*; A: ʿAbd al-ʿAzīz Ibn Shaddād (d. after 582/1186); S: IKH, VI, 211; this is probably the fuller edition of this author's chronicle that he composed (as argued by Brett, *Fitnat*, I, 387–425) after he had settled in Damascus. VQ: 2; Ṣ; C: history – Zīrid.

(296) J/6 250a/18 *Juzʾ ḥadīth – Volume with Narration*; '*ḥadīth*' could very well refer to Prophetic reports. However, placed in poetry category 6 and explicitly said to be copied by a litterateur who had no involvement in the study of *ḥadīth*, this is more likely an extract of (rhymed?) speech from a larger work. The term *ḥadīth* is used in a similar vein in the catalogue, e.g. *Ḥadīth malik min mulūk al-hind* (343), *Ḥadīth Khusraw Abarwīz wa-ibnuhu Shīrūya* (1176b) and *Ḥadīth Qays* (1297d). Scr('*bi-khaṭṭ*'): Mawhūb b. Aḥmad Ibn al-Jawālīqī (d. 539/1144; EI^2, H. Fleisch, 'al-Djawālīḳī'), who, similar to the scribe in no. 1153, may have also been the 'author'/'compiler' of this text; VQ: 1; Ṣ; C: adab. (cf. nos 140, 297, 313)

(297) J/6 250a/18 *Juzʾ [ḥadīth] ākhar – Another [Ḥadīth] Volume*; Scr('*bi-khaṭṭ*'): Mawhūb b. Aḥmad Ibn al-Jawālīqī (d. 539/1144; EI^2, H. Fleisch, 'al-Djawālīḳī'); VQ: 1; Ṣ; C: adab. (cf. nos 140, 296, 313)

(298) J/6 250a/18 *al-Jumān – The Pearls*; Scr('*khaṭṭ*') & A: Aḥmad Ibn Fāris (d. 395/1004); no such (key word) title by an Ibn Fāris is identifiable. However, the cataloguer repeatedly uses this name to refer to the famous philologist Ibn Fāris (cf. nos 951, 1135a, 1162a, 1222c, 1243a, 1423). This is thus most likely an anthology by Ibn Fāris himself, which, similar to no. 1249g, never acquired the status of an independent title (see the list of his works in Suʿūd, *Aḥmad ibn Fāris*, 99–126). As the cataloguer explicitly names Ibn Fāris as scribe and author it is rather unlikely that he confused this work with those bearing the same title such as *al-Jumān fī tashbīhāt al-Qurʾān* by ʿAbd Allāh b. Muḥammad Ibn Nāqiyā (d. 485/1092) (ed. A. Maṭlūb/ Kh. al-Ḥadīthī, Baghdad: Dār al-jumhūrīya, 1968) or *al-Jumān wa-al-ʿurf* by Ḥusayn b. Muḥammad al-Rāfiqī (d. 422/1031) (Ibn al-Sāʿī, *al-Durr*, 325–6). Placed in category 6, this is most likely a work of poetry. VQ: 1; Ṣ; C: poetry?

(299) J/6 250b/1 *Jumal al-taṣrīf – Sum of Morphology*; A: Abū al-Fatḥ Ibn Jinnī (d. 392/1002); S: ed. D. Saqqāl, *al-Taṣrīf al-mulūkī*, Beirut: DF, 1998; VQ: 1; Ṣ; C: morphology.

(300) J/7 250b/1 *al-Jalīs al-ṣāliḥ al-kāfi – The Good and Sufficient Companion [and the Intimate Adviser]*; A: Mu^cāfā b. Zakarīyā^ͻ al-Jarīrī (d. 390/1000); S: *al-Jalīs al-ṣāliḥ al-kāfi wa-al-anīs al-naṣīḥ al-shāfi*, ed. M. al-Khūlī/I. ͨAbbās, Beirut: AK, 1981–7; VQ: 4; Ṣ; C: adab/edifying.

(301) J/7 250b/2 *al-Jalīs al-ṣāliḥ – The Good Companion [and the Intimate Adviser]*; The MS has 'الحري' (or الجيزي\الجبري\الجنزي\الخبري etc.), but no author of a work with this title fits this *nisba*. It is most likely that the cataloguer rather meant A: Yūsuf Sibṭ Ibn al-Jawzī (d. 654/1256); S: *al-Jalīs al-ṣāliḥ wa-al-anīs al-nāṣiḥ*, ed. F. Fawwāz, London 1989. This reading is also likely because Sibṭ Ibn al-Jawzī dedicated this book, relying strongly on material from the early Islamic period, to al-Malik al-Ashraf in 613/1216 before al-Ashraf became ruler of Damascus. VQ: 1-43; Ṣ; C: political thought – mirror for princes. (cf. no. 1540)

(302) J/7 250b/2 *al-Jawhar al-badīͨ fi multaqaṭ al-majāmīͨ – The Novel Gem Concerning the Meeting Place for Assemblies*; No such title is identifiable and this is most likely a book-in-the-making. Judging from the thematic category and the title, this is most likely an adab anthology. VQ: 1; Ṣ; C: adab – anthology?

(303) J/8 250b/3 *al-Jawāhir al-muntakhaba min al-baṣāͻir wa-al-dhakhāͻir – Chosen Gems from the Treasures of Insightful Perception*; no such title is identifiable and this is most likely a summary of Abū Ḥayyān al-Tawḥīdī's (d. 414/1023) *al-Baṣāͻir wa-al-dhakhāͻir*; VQ: 2–41; Ṣ; C: adab – anthology. (cf. nos 204, 1249e)

(304) J/8 250b/3 *al-Jawābāt – Responsa*; A: Ibn Bāͨūrāͻ; no such title is identifiable and the reading of the author's name is tentative. Arguably the name refers to the legendary figure and sage of pre-Islamic Arabia Luqmān (EI^2, B. Heller and N.A. Stillmann, 'Luḳmān'). Luqmān became identified with Balͨam b. Bāͨūrāͻ, known from Koranic exegesis. The *Responsa* mentioned here most likely refers to the wisdom literature ascribed to him. C: adab – gnomic literature.

(305) J/9 250b/4 *al-Jāmiͨ li-tafsīr ṣūrat al-insān – The Compendium for Commenting on the Human Form*; no such (key word?) title is identifiable. The term *tafsīr* could refer to a wide vide variety of fields of knowledge ranging from exegesis to medicine. It is possible that the cataloguer substituted

here 'ṣ' for 's' (that would give *ṣūra* instead of *sūra*), a common phenomenon in Middle Arabic, which would make this an exegetical work. However, the cataloguer does not undertake similar substitutions elsewhere, and, more importantly, the work is classified in thematic category 9. This category includes a range of topics such as astronomy, medicine, oneiromancy and mathematics, but no exegetical works. A medical treatise is thus the most likely possibility. VQ: 1; Ṣ; C: medicine?

(306) J/10 250b/4–5 *al-Jamāhir fī al-jawāhir* – *The Essence of Knowledge Concerning Precious Stones*; A: al-Bīrūnī (d. after 442/1050); S: ed. H. Said, *K. al-Jamāhir fī ma*ᶜ*rifat al-jawāhir*, Karachi: Pakistan Historical Society, 2001; NC: 3; VQ: 1; Ṣ; C: mineralogy. (cf. no. 269, 1038)

(307) J/10 250b/5 *al-Jawāriḥ wa-al-ḍawārī* – *Birds of Prey and Hunting Dogs*; perhaps the anonymous *al-Zand al-wārī fī aḥwāl al-jawāriḥ wa-al-ḍawārī*; S: Baghdādī, *Īḍāḥ al-maknūn*, I, 614; NC: 3; C: falconry and hunting dogs.

(308) J/12 250b/5–6 *al-Jawāhir al-mu*ᵓ*allafa fī al-madā*ᵓ*iḥ al-mustaṭrafa* – *Gems Composed on Exquisite Eulogies*; no such title is identifiable. Placed in thematic category 12 this is probably an anonymous or little known collection of late ᶜAbbasid or later poetry, a book-in-the-making. The title clearly indicates that this is panegyric poetry, similar to the rarely mentioned and lost *al-Qalā*ᵓ*id al-durrīya fī madā*ᵓ*iḥ al-Musta*ᶜ*ṣimīya* by Ibn al-Sāᶜī (d. 674/1276) (Ibn al-Sāᶜī, *Durr*, 45); VQ: 1–43; Ṣ; C: poetry – panegyric.

(309) J/15 250b/6 *al-Jawāhir* – *Gems [of Speech]*; A: <u>Isḥāq</u> b. Ibrāhīm <u>al-Mawṣilī</u> (d. 235/849); S: IN, I/2, 437: '*Jawāhir al-kalām*'; Zakeri, *Wisdom*, 16; VQ: 1–44; Ṣ; C: adab – gnomic literature. (cf. no. 1603)

(310) J/15 250b/7 *al-Jāmi*ᶜ *al-kabīr fī al-manẓūm wa-al-manthūr* – *The Large Compendium on Poetry and Prose*; A: Ḍiyāᵓ al-Dīn Abū al-Fatḥ Naṣr Allāh Ibn al-Athīr (d. 637/1239); S: ed. ᶜA. Hindawī, *al-Jāmi*ᶜ *al-kabīr fī ṣinā*ᶜ*at al-manẓūm min al-kalām wa-al-manthūr*, Cairo: Dār al-āfāq al-ᶜarabīya, 2007; VQ: 1; Ṣ; C: rhetoric and stylistics.

(311) J/3s 250b/7 *Jalā*ᵓ *al-humūm wa-al-aḥzān* – *Dispersing Worries and Sorrows*; no such title is identifiable. The title recalls a book with prayer(s) of supplication, such as the one in Zayn al-ᶜĀbidīn's *Ṣaḥīfa* entitled '*idhā ḥazanahu amr wa-ahammatuhu al-khaṭāyā*' (Engl. tr. Chittick, *Psalms of Islam*, 76–9). However, the category 3s does not contain prayer books (these

are rather in 4s), but is rather reserved for works of adab and poetry. VQ: 1–39; Ṣ; C: adab/poetry – anthology?

(312) J/4s 250b/8 *Jawāhir al-kalām ᶜan ᶜAlī b. Abī Ṭālib raḍiya Allāh ᶜanhu – The Gems of ᶜAlī b. Abī Ṭālib's Sayings* (*may God be pleased with him*); arguably the *One Hundred Proverbs* that are also as *Miᵓat jawhara min kalām ᶜAlī b. Abī Ṭālib* in the catalogue (cf. no. 1134); attr. to A: al-Jāḥiẓ (d. 255/868–9); S: *One Hundred Proverbs* (*Miᵓat kalima min kalām amīr al-Muᵓminīn ᶜAlī b. Abī Ṭālib*), in: Engl. tr. & ed. Qutbuddin, *Treasury of Virtues*, 220–33; C: ᶜAlī – sayings attributed to. (cf. nos 289, 1134, 1658)

(313) J/5s 250b/8-9 *Juzᵓ ḥadīth – Ḥadīth Volume*; '*ḥadīth*' could very well refer to Prophetic reports. However, placed in poetry category 5s and said to be copied by a scholar who was not renowned for involvement in the study of *ḥadīth*, this is more likely a piece of poetry or adab (similar to nos 140, 296, 297). Scr('*bi-khaṭṭ*'): probably ᶜAbd al-Salām al-Baṣrī (fl. 5th/11th c.) (IKH, VII, 73); VQ: 1; Ṣ; C: poetry/adab? (cf. nos 186 and 871 on scribe)

(314) J/5s 250b/9 *Juzᵓ – Volume*; generic title; Scr('*dhukira annahā bi-khaṭṭ muᵓallif al-Qūt*'): probably Muḥammad b. ᶜAlī al-Makkī (386/998), author of *Qūt [al-qulūb fī muᶜāmalat al-maḥbūb wa-waṣf ṭarīq al-murīd ilā maqām al-tawḥīd]*, ed. ᶜA. Madkūr, Cairo: HMAK, 2007; FI: '*awrāq*'/'*loose folios*'; VQ: 1; Ṣ; C:?

(315) J/5s 250b/9–10 *al-Jawhar al-muthamman fī madḥ Shāh Arman – The Precious Gem Praising the Armenians' King*; the title 'Shāh Arman' was held by the members of the Turcoman dynasty in Akhlāṭ, eastern Anatolia, who ruled from 493/1100 to 604/1207 (EI², C. Hillenbrand, 'Shāh-i Arman'). This title was subsequently employed for the mausoleum's patron al-Malik al-Ashraf when he was ruling the lands in northern Mesopotamia and before he took Damascus (also cf. no. 1354 where a manuscript most likely employs this term for al-Ashraf). His main panegyrist in this period was his secretary Ibn al-Nabīh and the present title may refer to the panegyric where he uses the phrase *al-Jawhar al-muthamman* (al-Asᶜad, *Dīwān Ibn al-Nabīh*, 241–6, l. 6). A: ᶜAlī b. Muḥammad Kamāl al-Dīn Ibn al-Nabīh (d. 619/1222); VQ: 1; Ṣ; C: poetry – panegyric – Ayyūbid – al-Malik al-Ashraf. (cf. nos 190, 288, 863, 868, 1049, 1055, 1229d)

(316) J/5s 250b/10 *Jāmi^{c} al-uns wa-mubhij al-nafs – Compendium of Conviviality and What Delights the Soul*; no such title is identifiable, neither read as referring to one single work nor as referring to two separate works and it is most likely a book-in-the-making. The title and thematic category indicates an anthology of prose and verse. VQ: 1–42; Ṣ; C: poetry/adab?

(317) J/8s 250b/11 *Jawāb kitāb wa-ta^{c}ziya – Reply to a Letter/Treatise and an Elegy*; anonymous work (*'lā a^{c}rifu mu$^{\circ}$allifahu'/'I do not know its author'*) with generic title; FI: *'thuluthīya'/'in thuluth script'*, *'bi-raqq'/'parchment'*; the cataloguer was clearly unsure about this entry and thus adds additional information to identify this codex. The reading of *thuluthīya* is uncertain, but he may have been thinking of a term such as *qalam al-tawāqī^{c} al-thuluthīya* (Gacek, *Vademecum*, 264). VQ: 1; Ṣ; C:?

(318) Ḥ/3 250b/11-12 *al-Ḥāwī – The Comprehensive [Book]*; A: al-Māwardī (d. 450/1058); S: ed. M. Maṭrajī, Beirut: DF, 1994; MS: Süleymaniye, Ayasofya 1105 & 1106**; VQ: 4–1; Ṣ; C: fiqh – shāfi^{c}ī.

(319) Ḥ/5 250b/12 *al-Ḥujja al-mashrafīya li-l-dawla al-Ashrafīya – The Exalted Proof of al-Ashraf's Reign*; no such title is identifiable. This is probably a panegyric work for al-Malik al-Ashraf, the mausoleum's patron. Placed in category 5 it is unlikely that this would be poetry and the category rather indicates a historical prose text. VQ: 1; Ṣ; C: panegyric – Ayyūbid – al-Malik al-Ashraf?

(320a) Ḥ/6 250b/13 *al-Ḥasharāt – Insects*; popular title with numerous possibilities (cf. IN, index); C: lexicography.

(320b) 250b/13 *wa-Risālat Ibn Abī Ṭāhir fī sariqāt al-Buḥturī – Ibn Abī Ṭāhir's Treatise on al-Buḥturī's Plagiarisms*; A: Aḥmad Ibn Abī Ṭāhir Ṭayfūr (d. 280/893); S: IN, I/2, 452; VQ: 1; Ṣ; C: poetry – commentary.

(321) Ḥ/6 250b/13 *Ḥirz marwī ^{c}an Ja^{c}far al-Ṣādiq – Prayer Amulet Transmitted from Ja^{c}far al-Ṣādiq*; A: Ja^{c}far al-Ṣādiq, the sixth Shi^{c}ite *imām* (d. 148/765); A collection of such prayers for protection ascribed to the twelve imams can be found in the MS Süleymaniye, Ayasofya 3324. Ṣ; C: prayer book.

(322) Ḥ/6 250b/14 *Ḥirz ākhar – Another Prayer Amulet*; FI: *'fī haykal ḥamā$^{\circ}$ilī'/'to be worn as a necklace'*; C: prayer book.

(323) Ḥ/7 250b/14 *Ḥikmat al-ādāb – The Wisdom of Suitable Knowledge and Behaviour*; no such title is identifiable. VQ: 1; Ṣ; C:?

(324) Ḥ/8 250b/14–15 *al-Ḥurūb bi-Wāsiṭ wa-ghayruhā – The Battles at Wāsiṭ and Other [Writings]*; this is probably an anonymous work referring to the ᶜAbbasid siege of Wāsiṭ in the year 132/749–50 as mentioned by al-Ṭabarī (Williams (tr.): *The History of al-Ṭabarī*, XXVII, 185–94); VQ: 42; C: history – ᶜAbbāsid.

(325) Ḥ/8 250b/15 *al-Ḥanīn ḥikāyāt wa-akhbār – Home-sickness, Narrations and Reports*; probably anonymous compendium on the theme of *ḥanīn* (on this theme see Müller, 'al-Ḥanīn ilā l-awṭān'); VQ: 1; Ṣ; C: adab – anthology.

(326) Ḥ/8 250b/15 *Ḥāwī al-funūn – The Comprehensive [Book] on the Arts*; A: Muḥammad b. al-Ḥasan Ibn al-Ṭaḥḥān (d. after 449/1057); S: fac. ed. E. Neubauer, *Compendium of a Fatimid Court Musician*, Frankfurt (Main) 1990; VQ: 1; Ṣ; C: music. (cf. no. 461 where the same title appears as *Dhāt al-funūn*)

(327) Ḥ/9 250b/16 *Ḥadīth Jamīl wa-Buthayna – Jamīl and Buthayna*; S: Jagonak, *Bild der Liebe*; VQ: 1; Ṣ; C: poetry/love literature.

(328) Ḥ/9 250b/16 *al-Ḥiyal – Book of Ingenious Devices*; A: Banū Mūsā Ibn Shākir (3rd/9th c.); S: Engl. tr. D.R. Hill, Dordrecht 1979; VQ: 1; Ṣ; C: mechanics.

(329) Ḥ/9 250b/16 *al-Ḥisāb al-hindī – Indian Arithmetic*; popular title with numerous possibilities (cf. indices in IN and IAU); VQ: 1; Ṣ; C: mathematics.

(330) Ḥ/9 250b/16-17 *al-Ḥisāb al-maᶜrūf bi-al-Zaᶜfarān – [The Book on] Arithmetic Known as al-Zaᶜfarān*; 'Al-Zaᶜfarān' could either refer to a book title or a specific method of arithmetic, but neither of the two is identifiable. VQ: 1; Ṣ; C: mathematics.[61]

(331) Ḥ/10 250b/17 *Ḥisāb – Arithmetic*; popular title with numerous possibilities (cf. EI² 'ᶜIlm al-Ḥisāb'); the reading of the title is tentative as works on mathematics are generally in thematic category 9. The title clearly starts with the letter *ḥāᵓ* (alphabetical order) and ends with a *bāᵓ* (compare the previous entry for exactly the same final *bāᵓ*). The only two possibilities for this combination are *ḥabāb* and *ḥisāb*, but for the former term no book title is identifiable, whereas there is no lack of book titles with *ḥisāb* (cf. no. 329).

This entry is probably similar to the treatise Süleymaniye, Fatih 3439/21 (fols. 217b–234b) entitled *Risāla fī al-ḥisāb* written in Mosul in 587/1191. The multiple-text manuscript Fatih 3439 contains other titles that are similar to or identical with Ashrafīya entries (cf. nos 89, 94, 862). VQ: 1; Ṣ; C: mathematics.

(332) Ḥ/10 250b/17 *al-Ḥāwī fī al-ṭibb – The Comprehensive Book on Medicine*; A: al-Rāzī (Rhazes) (d. 313/925 or 323/935); S: ed. M. Dhākir, Tehran: Markaz-i taḥqīqāt-i ṭibb-i sunnatī, 2010; MS: Süleymaniye, Süleymaniye 850*; NC: 3; VQ: 4; Ṣ; C: medicine.

(333) Ḥ/10 250b/17–18 *al-Khalāʾiq*[62] *al-Ashrafīya – The Ashrafian Qualities*; no such title is identifiable. Placed in category 10 this is probably a medical work dedicated to the mausoleum's patron al-Malik al-Ashraf (similar to no. 1354). VQ: 1; Ṣ; C: medicine?

(334) Ḥ/10 250b/18 *al-Ḥiyal fī al-ḥarb – Ruses of War*; possibly A: ʿAlī b. Abī Bakr al-Harawī (d. 611/1215) who has another entry in this catalogue (cf. no. 353) and authored the *Tadhkira Harawīya fī al-ḥiyal al-ḥarbīya*; S: ed. Sourdel-Thomine, 'Conseils'; Süleymaniye, Âtıf Efendi 2018; VQ: 1; Ṣ; C: political thought – mirror for princes.

(335) Ḥ/12 250b/18 *al-Ḥamāsa – Bravery*; A: Ḥabīb b. Aws Abū Tammām (d. 231/845 or 232/846); S: ed. M. Khafājī, Cairo: ʿAlī Ṣabīḥ, 1955; MS: Süleymaniye, Fatih 3738***; NC: 10; C: poetry – anthology – ʿAbbāsid. (cf. nos 1280c, 1526, 1554, 1557, 1561)

(336) Ḥ/12 250b/18–251a/1 *al-Ḥamāsa al-waḥshīya – Bravery with Unfamiliar Poems*; A: Ḥabīb b. Aws Abū Tammām (d. 231/845 or 232/846); S: ed. ʿA. al- Rājkūtī, Cairo: DM, 1987; VQ: 1; Ṣ; C: poetry – anthology – ʿAbbāsid.

(337) Ḥ/12 251a/1 *al-Ḥadīqa – The Garden*; A: Abū al-Ṣalt Umayya b. ʿAbd al-ʿAzīz b. Abī al-Ṣalt al-Andalusī (d. 529/1134); S: IKH, I, 243: '*ʿalā uslūb Yatīmat al-dahr*'; C: poetry/adab – anthology.

(338) Ḥ/13 251a/1–2 *Ḥadīqat al-ḥadaq – The Irises' Garden*; arguably A: Hārūn al-Ṣamīrī who composed a lost poetry anthology quoted in S: al-Thaʿālibī (d. 429/1038), *Yatīmat al-dahr*, ed. M. ʿAbd al-Ḥamīd, Beirut: DKI, 1979, II, 218; NC: 2; VQ: 1–42; Ṣ; C: poetry – anthology.

(339) Ḥ/15 251a/2 *al-Ḥayawān – The Animals*; A: al-Jāḥiẓ (d. 255/868–9); S: ed. ᶜA. Hārūn, Cairo: MBḤ, 1938–45; FI: *'nāqiṣ dhukira fī al-makhārīm'/'incomplete [manuscript], mentioned in the [catalogue's section on] incomplete manuscripts'*; VQ: 1; Ṣ; C: adab. (cf. nos 1535, 1604)

(340) Ḥ/15 251a/2–3 *al-Ḥiyal fī al-adab – [The Book of] Stratagems Concerning Adab*; no such title is identifiable. This is most likely a title in the form of key word + *fī* + content description. The key word '*ḥiyal*' appears in several titles referring to *fiqh* in the sense of legal devices and in titles of mirror for princes (cf. no. 334), but this would not fit category 15, which has either adab or poetry. There is only one well-known adab work with this key word: A: ᶜAlī b. Muḥammad al-Madāᵓinī (d. 215/830?); S: IN, I/2, 322; VQ: 1; Ṣ; C: adab.

(341a) Ḥ/14 251a/3 *Ḥall al-shiᶜr – Prosifiying Poetry*; no such title is identifiable. This is arguably an extract from a larger work such as the first part of *al-Washī al-marqūm fī ḥall al-manẓūm* by Ḍiyāᵓ al-Dīn Abū al-Fatḥ Naṣr Allāh Ibn al-Athīr (d. 637/1239) (ed. J. Saᶜīd, Baghdad: MII, 1989) whose main oeuvre is represented in this library (for example, no. 310) and whose son Sharaf al-Dīn Muḥammad (585–622/1189–1225) authored a *majmūᶜ* for al-Malik al-Ashraf (IKH, V, 397). C: adab/poetry.[63]

(341b) 251a/3 *wa-al-Maydān fī al-ghazal bi-al-ghilmān – The Place Concerning Love Poetry on Boys*; no such title is identifiable and it is most likely a title in the form of key word + *fī* + content description. The key word '*maydān*' is reasonably frequent in book titles (see e.g. IN, index). However, none of the known titles matches the content description given here and this is thus probably a short-lived or anonymous anthology. VQ: 1; Ṣ; C: poetry – anthology – ghazal.

(342) Ḥ/14 251a/3 *Ḥall al-ᶜaqd – Prosifiying Poetry*; A: al-Thaᶜālibī (d. 429/1038); S: *Nathr al-naẓm wa-ḥall al-ᶜaqd*, ed. A. Tammām, Beirut: MKTh, 1990; VQ: 1; Ṣ; C: adab/poetry – Ghaznawid/Khwārazmshāh. (cf. no. 1569)

(343) Ḥ/14 251a/4 *Ḥadīth malik min mulūk al-hind – Words of an Indian King*; similar to the testament of the Persian monarch Ardashīr (*c.*226–40) and the treatise with a rebuttal and advice ascribed to the Persian monarch Khusraw II Parvīz/Abharvēz (r. 590–628) (cf. nos 1176a and 1176b), this is

most likely advice literature ascribed to a non-Islamic source. Such 'Indic' material was a prominent feature in Arabic mirror for princes (see Marlow, 'Greek and Indian Wisdom'). VQ: 1; Ṣ; C: political thought – non-Muslim.

(344) Ḥ/1s 251a/4 *Ḥall al-Tatimma – Prosifying the Tatimmat [al-Yatīma by al-Thaᶜālibī]*; A: Jaᶜfar b. Shams al-Khilāfa al-Afḍalī (d. 622/1225); S: TI, 621–30, pp. 103–4 (does not mention this work); VQ: 1; Ṣ; C: adab/poetry – anthology.

(345) Ḥ/3s 251a/5 *Ḥikāyāt wa-nawādir – Narrations and Anecdotes*; anonymous work with generic title; VQ: 1; Ṣ; C: adab – anthology.

(346) Ḥ/5s 251a/5 *Ḥikam wa-mawāᶜiẓ min kalām Jaᶜfar al-Ṣādiq – Gnomic and Paraenetic Sayings by Jaᶜfar al-Ṣādiq*; A: Jaᶜfar al-Ṣādiq, the sixth Shiᶜite *imām* (d. 148/765); VQ: 1; Ṣ; C: ethics – imāmate.

(347) Ḥ/5s 251a/5-6 *Ḥikam wa-ashᶜār wa-nawādir wa-akhbār – Pieces of Wisdom, Poetry, Anecdotes and Reports*; anonymous work with generic title; Scr('*bi-khaṭṭ*'): al-Ḥasan b. ᶜAlī al-Juwaynī (d. 586/1190?) (MU, II, 940–1); VQ: 1; Ṣ; C: adab/poetry – anthology. (cf. nos 142, 348, 873, 874)

(348) Ḥ/5s 251a/6 *Ḥikam wa-akhbār wa-ashᶜār – Pieces of Wisdom, Reports and Poetry*; Scr('*bi-khaṭṭ*') & A: al-Ḥasan b. ᶜAlī al-Juwaynī (d. 586/1190?) (MU, II, 940–1); VQ: 1; Ṣ; C: adab/poetry – anthology. (cf. nos 142, 347, 873, 874)

(349) Kh/2 251a/7 *al-Khawātim – Perorations [of Sermons]*; Scr('*bi-khaṭṭ*') & A: Ibn al-Jawzī (d. 597/1200); S: Hartmann, 'Sermonnaire ḥanbalite'; VQ: 1–44; Ṣ; C: sermons.

(350) Kh/2 251a/7 *al-Khuṭab al-Nubātīya – Ibn Nubāta's Sermons*; A: ᶜAbd al-Raḥīm b. Muḥammad Ibn Nubāta (fl. 4th/10th c.); S: ed. *Dīwān khuṭab*, Cairo: ᶜAbbās Shaqrūn, 1982; VQ: 1; Ṣ; C: sermons (*khuṭab*). (cf. nos 355, 1455)

(351) Kh/2 251a/7 *al-Khuṭab – Sermons*; A: Muḥammad b. Ibrāhīm al-Kīzānī (d. 562/1166) and others (*li-l-Kīzānī wa-ghayrihi*); S: TI, 561–70, pp. 134–5; VQ: 1–40; Ṣ; C: sermons (*khuṭab*).

(352) Kh/2 251a/8 *Khuṭab Ibn Shīth – Ibn Shīth's Sermons*; possibly the Ayyubid secretary and vizier A: ᶜAbd al-Raḥīm b. ᶜAlī Ibn Shīth (d. 625/1227) who appears elsewhere in this catalogue as author (cf. no. 491) and scribe

(cf. no. 425); His biographies (cf. TI, 621–30, pp. 231–2) do not mention any such work, but other *khuṭab*-works in this library were seemingly dedicated to al-Malik al-Ashraf (cf. nos 375, 381). VQ: 40; C: sermons (*khuṭab*).

(353) Kh/2 251a/8 *Khuṭab jihādīya – Sermons on Jihad*; possibly A: ᶜAlī b. Abī Bakr al-Harawī (d. 611/1215) who authored '*al-khuṭab al-harawīya*' and who authored another work in this library (cf. no. 334); S: IKH, III, 347; VQ: 1; Ṣ; C: sermons (*khuṭab*). (cf. no. 344)

(354) Kh/2 251a/8 *Khuṭab majmūᶜa – Collected Sermons*; anonymous work with generic title; VQ: 1; Ṣ; C: sermons (*khuṭab*).

(355) Kh/2 251a/8 *Khuṭab al-Jalāl Ibn Nubāta – Ibn Nubāta's Sermons*; A: ᶜAbd al-Raḥīm b. Muḥammad Ibn Nubāta (fl. 4th/10th c.); S: *Dīwān khuṭab*, Cairo: ᶜAbbās Shaqrūn, 1982; VQ: 1; Ṣ; C: sermons (*khuṭab*). (cf. nos 350, 1455)

(356) Kh/2 251a/9 *Khāṣṣīyāt al-khawāṣṣ al-ᶜashara – Characteristics of the Ten Selected [Companions Promised Paradise]*; this is arguably the *K. Khaṣāᵓiṣ al-ᶜashara al-kirām al-barara* by A: Maḥmūd b. ᶜUmar al-Zamakhsharī (d. 538/1144); S: ed. B.B. al-Ḥasanī, Baghdad: al-Muᵓassasa al-ᶜĀmma, 1968; C: ḥadīth – merits.

(357) Kh/3 251a/9 *al-Khiṣāl wa-al-ᶜuqūd – Virtues and Obligations*; A: al-Ḥasan b. Aḥmad Ibn al-Bannāᵓ (d. 471/1079); S: cited in al-Mardāwī, *Maᶜrifat al-rājiḥ*, III, 69: '*al-Khiṣāl wa-al-ᶜuqūd wa-al-aḥwāl wa-al-ḥudūd ᶜalā madhhab Abī ᶜAbd Allāh Aḥmad b. Ḥanbal*'; VQ: 1; Ṣ; C: fiqh – ḥanbalī.

(358) Kh/3 251a/9-10 *al-Khulāṣa ᶜalā madhhab Abī Ḥanīfa raḍiya Allāh ᶜanhu – The Finest Extracts According to the School of Abū Ḥanīfa (may God be pleased with him)*; probably summary of the *Mukhtaṣar* by the Hanafi scholar Aḥmad al-Qudūrī (d. 428/1037); A: ᶜAlī b. Aḥmad al-Rāzī al-Ḥanafī (d. 598/1201); S: ed. A. al-Dimyāṭī, *Khulāṣat al-dalāᵓil fī tanqīḥ al-masāᵓil*, Riyad 2007; VQ: 2; Ṣ; C: fiqh – ḥanafī.

(359) Kh/4[64] 251a/10 *al-Khayl wa-al-sarj wa-al-lijām – The Horse, Saddle and Reins*; numerous possibilities of authors who composed books with similar titles such as Ibn Durayd (d. 321/933), Ibn al-Sikkīt (d. 244/858) and ᶜAbd al-Malik b. Qurayb al-Aṣmaᶜī (d. 213/828?) as mentioned in IN; VQ: 1; Ṣ; C: lexicography.

(360) Kh/4 251a/10 *Khalq al-insān – Human Anatomy*; A: ʿAbd al-Malik b. Qurayb al-Aṣmaʿī (d. 213/828?); S: ed. A. Haffner, *Texte zur arabischen Lexikographie*, Leipzig 1905, 158–232; VQ: 1; Ṣ; C: lexicography.

(361) Kh/4 251a/10 *al-Khayl – The Horse*; A: ʿAbd al-Malik b. Qurayb al-Aṣmaʿī (d. 213/828?)/Abū Zayd Saʿīd b. Aws al-Anṣārī (d. 215/830) ('*li-l-Aṣmaʿī wa-Abī Zayd*'; are these two separate works bound together?); S: (al-Aṣmaʿī) ed. Hilāl Nājī, *al-Mawrid* 12/4 (1404/1983), 177–222; (al-Anṣārī) possible, although IN, I, 153–5, GAS, VIII, 76–80 and other sources do not mention such a work; VQ: 1; Ṣ; C: lexicography.

(362) Kh/4 251a/11 *Khalq al-insān – Human Anatomy*; A: Ibrāhīm b. al-Sarī al-Zajjāj (d. 311/923); S: ed. I. al-Sāmarrāʾī, Baghdad: MII, 1963; VQ: 1; Ṣ; C: lexicography. (cf. no. 1313j)

(363) Kh/5 251a/11 *al-Kharīda – The Pearl*; A: Muḥammad b. Muḥammad ʿImād al-Dīn al-Kātib al-Iṣfahānī (d. 597/1201); S: *Kharīdat al-qaṣr wa-jarīdat al-ʿaṣr*, ed. Sh. Fayṣal, Damascus: MLA, 1955 (al-Shām); ed. M.B. al-Atharī, Baghdad: MII, 1955 (al-ʿIrāq); ed. M. al-Marzūqī/M. al-Maṭwī/al-J. Yaḥyā, Tunis: DTu, 1966–72; VQ: 12; Ṣ; C: poetry – anthology.

(364) Kh/6 251a/12 *Khatma karīma – Koran*; Scr('*bi-khaṭṭ*'): Ibn al-Bawwāb (d. 413/1022); VQ: 1; Ṣ; C: Koran – text.[65]

(365) Kh/6 251a/12 *Khatma karīma – Koran*; FI: '*fī darj*'/'*scroll*',[66] '*kathīrat al-idhhāb*'/'*lavishly gilded*'; C: Koran – text.

(366) Kh/6 251a/13 *Khidmat al-mulūk – Serving Rulers*; A: Aḥmad b. al-Ṭayyib al-Sarakhsī (d. 286/899); S: IN, II/1, 197: '*Zād al-musāfir wa-khidmat al-mulūk*'; VQ: 1; Ṣ; C: political thought – mirror for princes?

(367) Kh/6 251a/13 *Khalq al-faras – Anatomy of the Horse*; A: Muḥammad b. al-Mustanīr Quṭrub (d. 206/821); S: IN, I/1, 148; VQ: 1–46; Ṣ; C: lexicography.

(368) Kh/6 251a/13 *al-Khaṭṭ – The Script*; Scr('*bi-khaṭṭ*'): Ibrāhīm b. Aḥmad Tūzūn (d. 355/966; MU, I, 39–40 who praises his hand); A: Muḥammad b. Yazīd al-Mubarrad (d. 286/900); S: IN, I/1, 171; VQ: 1–45; Ṣ; C: calligraphy.

(369) Kh/8 251a/14 *al-Kharāj*[67] – *Taxation*; arguably A: ʿUbayd Allāh b. Hibat Allāh Tāj al-Ruʾasāʾ Ibn al-Aṣbāghī (fl. 502/1108); S: *Wāfī*, XIX,

417; al-Iṣfahānī, *Kharīdat al-qaṣr* (al-ᶜIrāq), 135-9; NC: 3; the reading of *al-kharāj* is likely because of the following works with this title and because the author was employed in the ᶜAbbasid administration. Al-Iṣfahānī mentions that Ibn al-Aṣbāghī authored a book on penmanship ('*fī ᶜilm al-kitāba*') and that 'the secretaries of Iraq write the records according to his method' ('*kuttāb al-ᶜIrāq yaktubūna al-ḥisāb ᶜalā ṭarīqatihi*'). NC: 3; VQ: 1; Ṣ; C: administrative handbook.

(370) Kh/8 251a/14 *al-Kharāj – Taxation*; A: Qudāma b. Jaᶜfar (d. 328/939–40 or 337/948?); S: facs. ed. F. Sezgin, *Book on Taxation and Official Correspondence*, Frankfurt (Main) 1986; VQ: 2; Ṣ; C: administrative handbook.

(371) Kh/8 251a/14-15 *Khaṣāʾiṣ al-ṭarab – The Particularities of Music*; A: Maḥmūd Kushājim (d. c.350/961); S: MM, III, 803; NC: 2; FI: '*nuskha ukhrā fī 3 ṣ'l' another copy in 3 folia*';[68] VQ: 1; Ṣ; C: music.

(372) Kh/13 251a/15 *al-Kharājīya al-ṭalīqīya* (?); tentative reading; VQ: 1; Ṣ; C:?

(373) Kh/15 251a/15 *al-Kharāj – Taxation*; A: Aḥmad Ibn Sahl (d. 270/883); S: MM, I, 274; VQ: 1; Ṣ; C: administrative handbook.

(374) Kh/15 251a/16 *al-Khayl – The Horse*; A: Abū ᶜUbayda Maᶜmar b. al-Muthannā al-Taymī (d. between 207/822 and 213/828); S: ed. Hyderabad: DMU, 1939; VQ: 1; Ṣ; C: lexicography.

(375) Kh/15 251a/16 *al-Khuṭab al-durrīya fī al-manāqib al-Ashrafīya – Blazing Sermons on Ashrafian Virtues*; no such title is identifiable (including the variant reading *al-Khuṭab al-badrīya*), but it was most likely dedicated to the mausoleum's patron al-Malik al-Ashraf. Arguably, it was based on the invocations held during Friday sermons, one of which has survived from the Ayyubid period in the Damascus Papers (Sourdel and Sourdel-Thomine, 'Texte d'invocations'); VQ: 1; Ṣ; C: sermons (khuṭab) – panegyric – Ayyūbid – al-Malik al-Ashraf. (cf. no. 381)

(376) Kh/3s 251a/17 *al-Khams al-ᶜasharīya fī al-madāʾiḥ al-Kāmilīya – The Fifteen [Odes?] in Praise of al-Malik al-Kāmil*; probably for the Ayyubid ruler al-Malik al-Kāmil (d. 635/1238), the brother and ally of the mausoleum's patron al-Malik al-Ashraf; A: Aḥmad b. Muḥammad al-Ḥulāwī

(d. 656/1258); S: TI, 651–60, pp. 226–8 (title is not named, but poet was renowned for ‘praising the Caliphs and Kings’); VQ: 1; Ṣ; C: poetry – panegyric – Ayyūbid – al-Malik al-Kāmil.[69]

(377) Kh/4s 251a/17–18 *Khabar bayt al-ni^{c}am wa-du^{c}āʾ ^{c}inda al-ṣabāḥ – The Report on Paradise and The Morning Prayer of Invocation*; generic title; VQ: 1–45; Ṣ; C: prayer book.

(378a) Kh/5s 251a/18 *Khabar Abī ^{c}Ārim – The Report on Abū ^{c}Ārim*; referring to Abū ^{c}Ārim Ja^{c}far b. ^{c}Ulba al-Ḥārithī (fl. 2nd/8th c.) (Abū al-Faraj Iṣfahānī, *Mukhtār al-aghānī*, ed. I. Ibyārī, Cairo 1965, II, 311). Brief extracts from a ‘*khabar Abī ^{c}Ārim*’ are quoted by authors such as Ibn Sīda (d. 458/1066), *al-Muḥkam*, VI, 389 and VIII, 453. C: history?

(378b) 251a/18 *wa-Dhiʾb li-namir – [A Fable Called?] A Wolf [Said?] to a Leopard/Panther*; tentative reading and no such title is identifiable; this may be a fable drawing on material such as that found in *Kalīla wa-Dimna*. VQ: 1; Ṣ; C: adab?

(379) Kh/5s 251a/18–19 *al-Khaṭṭ wa-al-qalam – Script and Pen*; authorship disputed; A: ^{c}Abd Allāh b. Muslim al-Dīnawarī Ibn Qutayba (d. 276/889); S: *Risālat al-khaṭṭ wa-al-qalam*, ed. H.Ṣ al-Ḍāmin, Beirut: MR, 1989; VQ: 1; Ṣ; C: adab.

(380a) Kh/5s 251a/19 *Khalq al-insān – Human Anatomy*; A: ^{c}Abd Allāh b. Sa^{c}īd Abī[70] Manṣūr al-kātib al-Khawāfī (d. 480/1087); S: MM, II, 245; C: lexicography.

(380b) 251a/19 *wa-Shayʾ min shi^{c}r al-Mutanabbī wa-ghayr dhālika – Some of al-Mutanabbī's Poetry and Other [Texts]*; A: Aḥmad al-Mutanabbī (d. 354/955); S: *Dīwān al-Mutanabbī*, ed. ^{c}A. ^{c}Azzām, Cairo: LTTN, 1944; C: poetry – Ḥamdānid.

(381) Kh/7s 251b/1 *al-Khuṭba al-mūjaza al-zāhira fī ba^{c}ḍ manāqib al-Ashrafīya al-zāhira – The Bright and Concise Sermon on al-Malik al-Ashraf's Bright Virtues*; no such title is identifiable. Most likely it was similar to no. 375, dedicated to the mausoleum's patron al-Malik al-Ashraf. VQ: 1; Ṣ; C: sermons (khuṭab) – panegyric – Ayyūbid – al-Malik al-Ashraf.

(382) D/2 251b/2 *Dustūr ma^{c}ālim al-ḥikam – Signs of Wisdom*; referring to ^{c}Alī b. Abī Ṭālib, the fourth Caliph and first Shi^{c}ite *imām* (d. 40/661);

A: Muḥammad b. Salāma al-Quḍāʿī (d. 454/1062); S: *Dustūr maʿālim al-ḥikam wa-maʾthūr makārim al-shiyam min kalām Amīr al-Muʾminīn ʿAlī b. Abī Ṭālib*, ed. Cairo: Saʿāda, 1914; VQ: 1; Ṣ; C: ʿAlī – sayings attributed to.

(383) D/2 251b/2 *al-Duʿāʾ – Prayer of Invocation*; A: al-Ḥusayn b. Ismāʿīl al-Maḥāmilī (d. 330/941); S: ed. S. al-Qizqī, Beirut: DGI, 1992; VQ: 1; Ṣ; C: ḥadīth – collection.[71]

(384a) D/6 251b/3 *al-Duraydīya [fī al-maqṣūr wa-al-mamdūd] – Ibn Durayd's Qaṣīda [on the Short and Long Alif]*; A: Ibn Durayd (d. 321/933); S: *Dīwān*, ed. B. al-ʿAlawī, Cairo: LTTN, 1946, 29–37; MS: Süleymaniye, Laleli 1932/2 (fols. 135a–163b)*; NC: 2; FI: '*munakkata*' / '*with vowel marks*'; VQ: 1; Ṣ; C: grammar.[72] (cf. nos 384b, 676 *[sharḥ]*, 1203b, 1230j, 1238g, 1268b, 1307b, 1313a, 1326b)

(384b) 251b/3 *al-Duraydīya [fī al-maqṣūr wa-al-mamdūd] – Ibn Durayd's Qaṣīda [on the Short and Long Alif]*; Scr('*bi-khaṭṭ*'): arguably the calligrapher ʿAlī b. ʿAbd al-Raḥīm Ibn al-ʿAṣṣār (d. 576/1180) (IKH, III, 338); A: Ibn Durayd (d. 321/933); S: *Dīwān*, ed. B. al-ʿAlawī, Cairo: LTTN, 1946, 29–37; FI: '*wa-taʿālīq wa-fawāʾid*' / '*[with] notes and useful remarks*'; VQ: 1; Ṣ; C: grammar. (cf. nos 384a, 676 *[sharḥ]*, 1203b, 1230j, 1238g, 1268b, 1307b, 1313a, 1326b)

(385) D/8 251b/4 *Dumyat al-qaṣr – The Palace's Statue*; A: ʿAlī b. Ḥasan al-Bākharzī (d. 467/1075); S: *Dumyat al-qaṣr wa-ʿuṣrat ahl al-ʿaṣr*, ed. M. Altūnjī, Beirut: DJ, 1993; continuation of *al-Yatīma* by al-Thaʿālibī; MS: Süleymaniye, Ayasofya 3400**; NC: 2; FI: '*nuskha ukhrā fī 15*' / '*another [the second] copy is in 15 [volumes/quires]*'; VQ: 1–39; Ṣ; C: poetry/adab – anthology.

(386) D/8 251b/4 *al-Diyārāt – [The Book of] Monasteries*; ascribed to A: Abū al-Faraj al-Iṣfahānī (d. 356/967); S: ed. J. al-ʿAṭīya, London 1991; VQ: 1; Ṣ; C: adab – anthology. (cf. no. 1188e)

(387) D/8 251b/5 *al-Dulajīyīn* –?; no such title is identifiable and the reading is very tentative (see Ibn al-Athīr, *al-Lubāb*, I, 506 for the *nisba*). This is particularly unsatisfying because the cataloguer has the title in exactly the same form on folio 248a, l. 8 (where he erroneously inserted nine titles starting with the letter *dāl* in the *alif* section) and because the library held this work in two copies. As the term given here is in the genitive case, it is most likely the second term of a genitive construction with the first term (such as '*Akhbār*'

or 'Ashʿār') omitted. Placed in category 8 this is very probably a collection of prose and/or verse similar to the *Ashʿār al-Hudhalīyīn* (cf. nos 113, 1301, 1488, 1575) or the *Akhbār al-ʿAddāʾīn* (cf. nos 78, 130). However, no group of poems/authors with the *nisba* al-Dulajī is identifiable and other possible readings of the term (D-b/t/th/n/m/y-j/ḥ/kh) are not known as *nisba* forms. VQ: 1–38 1–40; Ṣ; NC: 2; C: poetry?

(388) D/9 251b/5 *al-Dalāʾil – The Signs*; A: al-Ḥasan b. (al-)Bahlūl (fl. 2nd half 4th/10th c.); S: GAS, VII, 332/2; VQ: 1; Ṣ; C: astronomy/meteorology.

(389) D/11[73] 251b/6 *Dīwān al-Buḥturī – Al-Buḥturī's Diwan*; A: al-Walīd al-Buḥturī (d. 284/897); S: ed. Ḥ. al-Ṣayrafī, Cairo: DM, 1963–5; NC: 9; VQ: 1; Ṣ; C: poetry – ʿAbbāsid. (cf. nos 1089, 1601)

(390) D/11 251b/6 *Dīwān Abī Nuwās riwāyat Ḥamza – Abū Nuwās' Diwan in the Transmission of Ḥamza [al-Iṣfahānī]*; A: al-Ḥasan b. Hāniʾ Abū Nuwās (d. between mid-198 and early 200/813–5); S: ed. E. Wagner and G. Schoeler, Wiesbaden and Beirut 1958–2006; MS: Süleymaniye, Hacı Ahmed Paşa 267*; NC: 4; C: poetry – ʿAbbāsid. (cf. no. 1486)

(391) D/11 251b/7 *[Dīwān Abī Nuwās] riwāyat al-Ṣūlī – [Abū Nuwās' Diwan] in the Transmission of al-Ṣūlī*; A: al-Ḥasan b. Hāniʾ Abū Nuwās (d. between mid-198 and early 200/813–5); S: ed. B. al-Ḥadīthī, Baghdad: Dār al-risāla, 1980; NC: 12; C: poetry – ʿAbbāsid.

(392) D/11 251b/7 *[Dīwān Abī Nuwās] riwāyat Tūzūn – [Abū Nuwās' Diwan] in the Transmission of [Ibrāhīm b. Aḥmad] Tūzūn [d. 355/966]*; A: al-Ḥasan b. Hāniʾ Abū Nuwās (d. between mid-198 and early 200/813–15); S: lithogr., Cairo 1277/1860; VQ: 1; Ṣ; C: poetry – ʿAbbāsid.

(393) D/11 251b/7 *Dīwān Ibn al-Rūmī – Ibn al-Rūmī's Diwan*; A: ʿAlī b. al-ʿAbbās Ibn al-Rūmī (d. 283/896?); S: ed. H. Naṣṣār, Cairo: HMAK, 1973–81; NC: 4; C: poetry – ʿAbbāsid. (cf. nos 1082, 1514)

(394) D/11 251b/7–8 *Dīwān al-Sharīf al-Raḍī – Al-Sharīf al-Raḍī's Diwan*; A: Muḥammad b. al-Ḥusayn al-Sharīf al-Raḍī (d. 406/1016); S: I. ʿAbbās, Beirut: DṢ, 1994; NC: 3; C: poetry – Būyid. (cf. nos 1079, 1081, 1181c, 1576, 1666)

(395) D/11 251b/8 *Dīwān ʿAbd Allāh Ibn al-Muʿtazz – ʿAbd Allāh Ibn al-Muʿtazz's Diwan*; A: ʿAbd Allāh Ibn al-Muʿtazz (d. 296/908); S:

ed. B. Lewin, Istanbul 1945–50; NC: 3; C: poetry – ᶜAbbāsid. (cf. nos 1060, 1075, 1596, 1617, 1638)

(396) D/11 251b/8-9 *Dīwān Mihyār – Mihyār's Diwan*; A: Mihyār b. Marzawayh al-Daylamī (d. 428/1037); S: ed. A. Nasīm, Beirut: MA, 1999; MS: Süleymaniye, Fazıl Ahmed Paşa 1243*; NC: 9; C: poetry – Būyid. (cf. nos 798, 1613)

(397) D/11 251b/9 *Dīwān al-Mutanabbī – Al-Mutanabbī's Diwan*; A: Aḥmad al-Mutanabbī (d. 354/955); S: ed. ᶜA. ᶜAzzām, Cairo: LTTN, 1944; NC: 8; FI: '*wa-fī al-thāmina ᶜalayhā khaṭṭuhu*'/'*the eighth [copy] has some writing in his [al-Mutanabbī's] hand*'; C: poetry – Ḥamdānid. (cf. nos 1582, 1583, 1591, 1606)

(398) D/11 251b/9–10 *Dīwān Abī al-Qāsim b. Hāniᵓ – Abū al-Qāsim b. Hāniᵓ's Diwan*; A: Abū al-Qāsim Muḥammad Ibn Hāniᵓ al-Andalusī (d. 362/973); S: ed. ᶜU.F. al-Ṭabbāᶜ, Beirut: DAr, 1998; NC: 10; C: poetry – Ḥamdūnid (Andalus)/Fatimid.

(399) D/11 251b/10 *Dīwān Ibn al-Sāᶜātī – Ibn al-Sāᶜātī's Diwan*; A: ᶜAlī b. Rustam Ibn al-Sāᶜātī (d. *c*.604/1207); S: ed. A. al-Maqdisī, Beirut: American Press, 1938–9; NC: 4; C: poetry – Zangid/Ayyūbid. (cf. nos 801, 1229c)

(400) D/11 251b/10 *Dīwān Ibn Sanāᵓ al-Mulk – Ibn Sanāᵓ al-Mulk's Diwan*; A: Hibat Allāh b. Jaᶜfar Ibn Sanāᵓ al-Mulk (d. 608/1211); S: ed. I. Naṣr, Cairo: DKA, 1967–9; NC: 5; C: poetry – Ayyūbid. (cf. no. 1628)

(401) D/11 251b/10–11 *Dīwān Ibn al-Qayṣarānī – Ibn al-Qayṣarānī's Diwan*; A: Muḥammad b. Naṣr Ibn al-Qayṣarānī (d. 548/1154); S: Muḥammad, *Shiᶜr Ibn al-Qayṣarānī*; NC: 5; C: poetry – Zangid.

(402) D/11 251b/11 *Dīwān Ibrāhīm b. Hilāl al-Ṣābiᵓ – Ibrāhīm b. Hilāl al-Ṣābiᵓ's Diwan*; A: Ibrāhīm b. Hilāl al-Ṣābiᵓ (d. 384/994); S: *Shiᶜr Abī Isḥāq al-Ṣābiᵓ*, ed. M. Gharīb, Alexandria: Markaz al-Babāṭīn, 2010; NC: 2; C: poetry – Būyid.

(403) D/11 251b/11–12 *Dīwān Kushājim – Kushājim's Diwan*; A: Maḥmūd Kushājim (d. *c*.350/961); S: ed. H. Maḥfūẓ, Baghdad: Wizārat al-iᶜlām, 1970; NC: 6; C: poetry – Ḥamdānid.

(404) D/12[74] 251b/12 *Dīwān Jarīr – Jarīr's Diwan*; A: Jarīr b. ᶜAṭīya (d. *c.*110/728–9); S: ed. N. Ṭaha, Cairo: DM, 1986; NC: 2; C: poetry – Umayyad. (cf. nos 1072, 1229e, 1290b, 1610, 1630, 1653)

(405) D/12 251b/12 *Dīwān Ibn Ḥayyūs – Ibn Ḥayyūs' Diwan*; A: Muḥammad b. Sulṭān Ibn Ḥayyūs (d. 473/1081); S: ed. Kh. Mardam, Damascus: MIA, 1951; NC: 10; C: poetry – Mirdāsid. (cf. no. 1629)

(406) D/12 251b/12-13 *Dīwān Dīk al-Jinn – Dīk al-Jinn's Diwan*; A: ᶜAbd al-Salām b. Raghbān Dīk al-Jinn (d. 235–6/849–51); S: ed. A. Qawwāl, Beirut: DKiA, 1992; NC: 2; C: poetry – ᶜAbbāsid. (cf. nos 1249f, 1605)

(407) D/12 251b/13 *Dīwān Ḥayṣa Bayṣa – Ḥayṣa Bayṣa's Diwan*; A: Saᶜd b. Muḥammad Ḥayṣa Bayṣa (d. 574/1179); S: ed. M. Jāsim/Sh. Shukr, Baghdad: Wizārat al-iᶜlām, 1974–5; NC: 5; C: poetry – Saljūq. (cf. nos 1487, 1618)

(408) D/12 251b/13 *Dīwān Ibn Shibl – Ibn Shibl's Diwan*; A: al-Ḥusayn b. ᶜAbd Allāh Ibn Shibl (d. 473/1080–1?); S: contemporaneous authors quote his poems at length (e.g. MU, III, 1078–86); NC: 2; C: poetry – Būyid.

(409) D/12 251b/14 *Dīwān Abī Tammām Ḥabīb – Abū Tammām Ḥabīb's Diwan*; A: Ḥabīb b. Aws Abū Tammām (d. 231/845 or 232/846); S: *Dīwān Abī Tammām bi-sharḥ al-Khaṭīb al-Tibrīzī*, ed. M. ᶜAzzām, Cairo: DM, 1957–65; MS: Süleymaniye, Ayasofya 3873**; NC: 2; C: poetry – ᶜAbbāsid. (cf. nos 1063, 1626)

(410) D/12 251b/14 *Dīwān Abī al-Shīṣ – Abū al-Shīṣ' Diwan*; A: Abū al-Shīṣ Muḥammad al-Khuzāᶜī (d. *c.*200/915); S: *Ashᶜār Abī al-Shīṣ al-Khuzāᶜī wa-akhbāruhu*, ed. ᶜA. al-Jubūrī, al-Najaf: Maṭbaᶜat al-Ādāb, 1386 *[1967]*; NC: 3; C: poetry – ᶜAbbāsid.

(411) D/12 251b/14–15 *Dīwān Dhī al-Rumma – Dhū al-Rumma's Diwan*; A: Ghaylān b. ᶜUqba Dhū al-Rumma (d. 117/735); S: *Dīwān*, ed. ᶜA. Abū Ṣāliḥ, Damascus: MLA, 1972–3; NC: 2; C: poetry – Umayyad – Bedouin. (cf. nos 1131, 1133, 1174, 1230, 1640)

(412) D/12 251b/15 *Dīwān ᶜAlī b. al-Qāsim al-Ḥaẓīrī – ᶜAlī b. al-Qāsim al-Ḥaẓīrī's Diwan*; A: Saᶜd b. ᶜAlī b. al-Qāsim al-Ḥaẓīrī Dallāl al-Kutub (d. 568/1172); S: MM, I, 757; NC: 3; C: poetry – Saljūq.

(413) D/12 251b/15 *Dīwān Abī al-Faḍl – Abū al-Faḍl's Diwan*; possibly A: Abū al-Faḍl ᶜUbayd Allāh b. Aḥmad al-Mīkālī (d. 436/1044); S: GAS, II, 643; NC: 4; C: poetry.

(414) D/12 251b/16 *Dīwān Abī Manṣūr b. al-Faḍl – Abū Manṣūr b. al-Faḍl's Diwan*; the cataloguer lists the same author in the following entry with his *shuhra*, the name by which a person is famous. Here he probably faithfully copied the different forms of the name as they appeared on the different manuscripts. A: Abū Manṣūr ᶜAlī b. al-Ḥasan Ibn al-Faḍl Ṣurradurr (d. 465/1074); S: facs. ed. Cairo: DKM, 1995; NC: 6; C: poetry. (cf. nos 415, 702)

(415) D/12 251b/16 *Dīwān Ṣurradurr – Ṣurradurr's Diwan*; A: Abū Manṣūr ᶜAlī b. al-Ḥasan Ibn al-Faḍl Ṣurradurr (d. 465/1074); S: facs. ed. Cairo: DKM, 1995; FI: '*nuskha fī 13*/'*a[nother] copy in 13 [folia/quires?]*'; the cataloguer specifies this copy's physicality in order to differentiate it from the previous six copies of the same work. C: poetry. (cf. nos 414, 702)

(416) D/12 251b/16-17 *Dīwān al-Khafājī – Al-Khafājī's Diwan*; A: ᶜAbd Allāh b. Saᶜīd al-Khafājī (d. 466/1074); S: ed. M. Nūwīwāt, Damascus: MLA, 2007; NC: 5; C: poetry.

(417) D/12 251b/17 *Dīwān Zuhayr b. Abī Sulmā – Zuhayr b. Abī Sulmā's Diwan*; A: Zuhayr b. Abī Sulmā Rabīᶜa al-Muzanī (d. 609 CE?); S: ed. K. al-Bustānī, Beirut: DṢ, 1960; NC: 5; C: poetry – pre-Islamic. (cf. no. 1223d)

(418) D/12 251b/17-18 *Dīwān Abī al-Faḍl b. al-Ḥārith – Abū al-Faḍl b. al-Ḥārith's Diwan*; possibly A: Abū al-Faḍl Yaḥyā b. Ziyād al-Ḥārithī (d. *c.*160/776); S: GAS, II, 467–8; NC: 2; C: poetry.

(419) D/12 251b/18 *Dīwān al-ᶜUṣfurī – Al-ᶜUṣfurī's Diwan*; no such diwan is identifiable, but this entry refers arguably to the poet A: ᶜAsal b. Dhakwān al-ᶜUṣfurī (fl. 3rd/9th c.); S: MU, II, 917 and IV, 1622; NC: 2; C: poetry – ᶜAbbāsid.

(420) D/12 251b/18 *Dīwān Ibn Nubāta – Ibn Nubāta's Diwan*; A: ᶜAbd al-ᶜAzīz b. ᶜUmar Ibn Nubāta (d. 405/1015); S: ed. ᶜA. al-Ṭāʾī, Baghdad: DḤ, 1977; The authorship of this poet is more likely than that of ᶜAbd al-Raḥīm b. Muḥammad Ibn Nubāta (fl. 4th/10th c.): ᶜAbd al-Raḥīm's diwan does not include poems, which all the other diwans in this section do, but rather sermons. NC: 2; C: poetry – Ḥamdānid. (cf. no. 1616)

(421) D/12 251b/18-19 *Dīwān al-Sarī al-Raffāʾ – Al-Sarī al-Raffāʾ's Diwan*; A: al-Sarī b. Aḥmad al-Raffāʾ (d. 362/972–3); S: ed. Ḥ. al-Ḥasanī, Baghdad: DR, 1981; NC: 3; C: poetry – Ḥamdānid/Būyid. (cf. no. 1625)

(422) D/12 251b/19 *Dīwān Ibn al-Muᶜallim – Ibn al-Muᶜallim's Diwan*; A: Muḥammad b. ᶜAlī Ibn al-Muᶜallim (d. 592/1196); S: IKH, V, 5–9; MS Bodleian Marsh. 516; NC: 3; C: poetry. (cf. nos 794, 1624)

(423) D/12 251b/19 *Dīwān Ibn al-Zabīr – Ibn al-Zabīr's Diwan*; A: ᶜAbd Allāh b. al-Zabīr b. al-Ashyam al-Asadī (d. 78/698?); S: *Shiᶜr ᶜAbd Allāh ibn al-Zabīr*, ed. Y. al-Jubūrī, Baghdad: DḤ, 1974; NC: 2; C: poetry – Umayyad.

(424) D/12 252a/1 *Duᶜāʾ al-ṣaḥīfa – The Ṣaḥīfa Prayer of Invocation*; A: ᶜAlī b. al-Ḥusayn b. ᶜAlī b. Abī Ṭālib Zayn al-ᶜĀbidīn, the fourth Shiᶜite *imām* (d. 94/712?); S: Engl. tr. Chittick, *Psalms of Islam*; NC: 2; FI: '*wa-fīhā munājāt ᶜAlī b. al-Ḥusayn raḍiya Allāh ᶜanhumā*' / '*in it [the second copy] are the Whispered Prayers by ᶜAlī b. al-Ḥusayn* (*may God be pleased with them*)'; C: prayer book. (cf. nos 154, 1136 for *munājāt*)

(425) D/12 252a/2 *Duᶜāʾ mustajāb – Prayer of Invocation That Is Answered*; generic title; Scr('*khaṭṭ*'): al-Malik al-Muᶜaẓẓam's head of chancery ᶜAbd al-Raḥīm b. ᶜAlī Ibn Shīth (d. 625/1227; TI, 621–30, pp. 231–2); C: prayer book.

(426) D/12 252a/2 *Duᶜāʾ rawāhu Zayd b. Thābit ᶜan al-Nabī ṣallā Allāh ᶜalayhi wa-sallam – Prayer of Invocation Transmitted by Zayd b. Thābit from the Prophet* (*may God's blessing and peace be upon him*); referring to Zayd b. Thābit (d. between 42/662–3 and 56/675–6); C: prayer book.

(427) D/12 252a/2–3 *Duᶜāʾ sharīf – Noble Prayer of Invocation*; generic title; FI: '*fī raqq aswad yalīquhu fiḍḍa*' / '*bound in black parchment with silver*'; VQ: 1; Ṣ; C: prayer book.

(428) D/12 252a/3 *al-Duᶜāʾ bi-asmāʾ Allāh al-ᶜiẓām – Prayer of Invocation with God's Magnificent Names*; generic title; C: prayer book.

(429) D/12 252a/3–4 *Duᶜāʾ marwī ᶜan Rasūl Allāh ṣallā Allāh ᶜalayhi wa-sallam – Prayer of Invocation Transmitted from the Prophet* (*may God's blessing and peace be upon him*); generic title; C: prayer book.

(430) D/12 252a/4 *Duᶜāʾ ᶜan Jaᶜfar al-Ṣādiq raḍiya Allāh ᶜanhu – Prayer of Invocation from Jaᶜfar al-Ṣādiq* (*may God be pleased with him*); A: Jaᶜfar al-Ṣādiq, the sixth Shiᶜite *imām* (d. 148/765); C: prayer book.

(431) D/12 252a/4–5 *Du*ᶜ*ā*ᵓ *al-jars wa-*ᶜ*ūdhat al-Bāqir – Whispered Prayer of Invocation and al-Bāqir's Protective Prayer*; referring to Muḥammad b. ᶜAlī Zayn al-ᶜĀbidīn (d. *c.*117/735) the fifth Shiᶜite *imām*; C: prayer book.

(432) D/12 252a/5 *Du*ᶜ*ā*ᵓ *– Prayer of Invocation*; generic title; FI: '*bi-khaṭṭ mansūb*'/'*in proportioned script*'; C: prayer book.

(433) D/12 252a/5 *Du*ᶜ*ā*ᵓ *Ja*ᶜ*far al-Ṣādiq – Ja*ᶜ*far al-Ṣādiq's Prayer of Invocation*; A: Jaᶜfar al-Ṣādiq, the sixth Shiᶜite *imām* (d. 148/765); C: prayer book.

(434) D/12 252a/5 *al-Du*ᶜ*ā*ᵓ *min asmā*ᵓ *Allāh al-*ᶜ*iẓām – Prayer of Invocation Using God's Magnificent Names*; C: prayer book.

(435) D/12 252a/6 *Du*ᶜ*ā*ᵓ *al-Nabī ṣallā Allāh* ᶜ*alayhi wa-sallam* ᶜ*inda kull shidda shadīda – The Prophet's Prayer of Invocation (may God's blessing and peace be upon him) for any Calamity*; generic title; C: prayer book.

(436) D/12 252a/6 *Du*ᶜ*ā*ᵓ *al-ḥājāt* ᶜ*an al-salaf – Prayer of Invocation for [Fulfilling] Needs from the [Pious] Predecessors*; generic title; C: prayer book.

(437) D/12 252a/6–7 *Du*ᶜ*ā*ᵓ *al-i*ᶜ*tidhār min al-ẓulm – Prayer of Invocation for Complaining about Injustice*; generic title; C: prayer book.

(438) D/12 252a/7 *Du*ᶜ*ā*ᵓ *laylat al-jum*ᶜ*a* ᶜ*an Zayn al-*ᶜ*Ābidīn raḍiya Allāh* ᶜ*anhu – Friday Night's Prayer of Invocation from Zayn al-*ᶜ*Ābidīn (may God be pleased with him)*; A: ᶜAlī b. al-Ḥusayn b. ᶜAlī b. Abī Ṭālib Zayn al-ᶜĀbidīn, the fourth Shiᶜite *imām* (d. 94/712?); S: Engl. tr. Chittick, *Psalms of Islam*; C: prayer book.

(439) D/12 252a/7 *Du*ᶜ*ā*ᵓ ᶜ*an a*ᵓ*immat al-salaf – Prayer of Invocation from the Foremost [Pious] Predecessors*; generic title; C: prayer book.

(440) D/12 252a/8 *Du*ᶜ*ā*ᵓ *sharīf marwī* ᶜ*an al-salaf – Noble Prayer of Invocation Transmitted from the [Pious] Predecessors*; generic title; C: prayer book.

(441) D/12 252a/8 *Du*ᶜ*ā*ᵓ *sharīf – Noble Prayer of Invocation*; generic title; C: prayer book.

(442) D/12 252a/8 *Du*ᶜ*ā*ᵓ *al-naṣr wa-al-jihād – Prayer of Invocation for Victory and Jihad*; generic title; C: prayer book.

(443) D/12 252a/8 *Du*ᶜ*ā*ᵓ *al-khatm – Prayer of Invocation on Occasion of Completing the Recitation of the Entire Koran*; NC: 2; C: prayer book.

(444) D/12 252a/9 *Duᶜāᵓ al-faraj – Prayer of Invocation When Sorrows Have Ceased*; generic title; C: prayer book.

(445) D/12 252a/9 *Duᶜāᵓ al-ṣalawāt al-khams – Prayer of Invocation of the Five Ritual Prayers*; generic title; C: prayer book.

(446) D/12 252a/9 *Duᶜāᵓ al-ṣabāḥ – Prayer of Invocation for the Morning*; generic title; C: prayer book.

(447) D/12 252a/9 *Duᶜāᵓ al-ṣabāḥ – Prayer of Invocation for the Morning*; generic title; C: prayer book.

(448) D/12 252a/9 *Duᶜāᵓ al-ṣabāḥ – Prayer of Invocation for the Morning*; generic title; C: prayer book.

(449) D/12 252a/10 *al-Duᶜāᵓ baᶜda ṣalāt al-ṣubḥ – The Prayer of Invocation after the Ritual Morning Prayer*; generic title; C: prayer book.

(450) D/12 252a/10 *Duᶜāᵓ – Prayer of Invocation*; generic title; FI: '*mudhahhab al-awwal wa-al-ākhir*'/'*gilded in the beginning and the end*'; C: prayer book.

(451) D/12 252a/10 *Duᶜāᵓ yawm al-khamīs – Thursday's Prayer of Invocation*; generic title; C: prayer book.

(452) D/12 252a/10-11 *al-Duᶜāᵓ fī al-ṣabāḥ – Prayer of Invocation in the Morning*; generic title; C: prayer book.

(453) D/12 252a/11 *al-Duᶜāᵓ baᶜda al-ṣabāḥ – Prayer of Invocation after the Morning*; generic title; C: prayer book.

(454) D/12 252a/11 *Duᶜāᵓ – Prayer of Invocation*; generic title; Scr('*maktūb ᶜalayhi annahu bi-khaṭṭ*'/'*on it is written that it is in the hand of*'): Ibn al-Bawwāb (d. 413/1022); C: prayer book.

(455) Dh/3 252a/12 *al-Dhakhīra – The Treasure*; A: al-Ḥasan b. ᶜAbd Allāh al-Bandanījī (d. 425/1034); S: MM, I, 559; Placed in category 3 this is most likely a legal work and al-Subkī's references to this work support this assumption (al-Subkī, *Ṭabaqāt*, III, 30; IV, 299; IV, 306). VQ: 6; Ṣ; C: fiqh – shāfiᶜī.

(456) Dh/3 252a/12 *al-Dhakhīra – Treasure [concerning the Andalusians' Virtues]*; A: ᶜAlī b. Bassām al-Shantarīnī (d. 543/1147); S: *al-Dhakhīra fī maḥāsin ahl al-Jazīra [Andalus]*, eds Ṭ. Ḥusayn and ᶜA. al-ᶜIbādī/ᶜA. ᶜIzām, Cairo 1939-42; NC: 2; This entry is rather surprising for category 3 and one

wonders whether the cataloguer confused this title and the Mālikī *fiqh* work *al-Dhakhīra* by Aḥmad b. Idrīs al-Qarāfī (d. 694/1285; ed. Beirut: DGI, 1994). VQ: 8; Ṣ; C: adab/poetry – anthology? (cf. no. 716?)

(457) Dh/3 252a/12-13 *Dhayl al-wazīr Abī Shujā^{c} – Vizier Abū Shujā^{c}'s Supplement*; continuation of Miskawayh's *Tajārib al-umam*; A: Abū Shujā^{c} Muḥammad b. al-Ḥusayn al-Rūdhrāwarī (d. 488/1095); S: eds & Engl. trs H.F. Amedroz and D.S. Margoliouth, *The Eclipse of the Abbasid Caliphate*, Oxford 1921. Category 3 is again rather surprising and the cataloguer may have forgotten to put in the heading for category 5, which usually holds historical works. C: history – Būyid.

(458) Dh/6 252a/13 *Dhikr rūḥānī min kalām Sa^{c}d Allāh al-Manbijī – Spiritual Recital from Sa^{c}d Allāh al-Manbijī's Words*; A: al-Shaykh Sa^{c}d Allāh b. Abī al-Fatḥ al-Manbijī (d. 651/1254), who composed a book for the mausoleum's patron al-Malik al-Ashraf, which 'included chapters from his words on *ḥaqīqa* and wisdom' and who later lived an ascetic's life in Damascus; S: Ibn al-^{c}Adīm, *Bughyat*, IX, 4239–40; C: sufism? (cf. no. 864)

(459) Dh/6 252a/13–14 *al-Dhahab wa-al-fiḍḍa – Gold and Silver*; no such title is identifiable. Placed in poetry category 6 and copied by a prominent litterateur who appears elsewhere in this catalogue as scribe of poetry manuscripts (cf. nos 557b, 853, 953b) this is most likely an anthology of poetry. Scr('*bi-khaṭṭ*'): Mawhūb b. Aḥmad Ibn al-Jawālīqī (d. 539/1144; cf. EI^{2}, H. Fleisch, 'al-Djawālīḳī', IKH, V, 342–4); C: poetry – anthology.

(460) Dh/7 252a/14 *Dhakhīrat al-kuttāb – The Secretaries' Treasure*; A: ^{c}Alī b. ^{c}Abd al-^{c}Azīz Ibn Ḥājib al-Nu^{c}mān (d. 423/1031); S: regularly cited in al-Qalqashandī, *Ṣubḥ al-a^{c}shā*; Al-Qalqashandī's citations show that this is primarily a pragmatic handbook for administrative matters, which also contains anecdotes and philological material. C: administrative handbook/adab. (cf. no. 755?)

(461) Dh/13 252a/14–15 *Dhāt al-funūn wa-salwat al-maḥzūn – [The Book] Containing the Arts*; probably A: Muḥammad b. al-Ḥasan Ibn al-Ṭaḥḥān (d. after 449/1057); S: fac. ed. E. Neubauer, *Compendium of a Fatimid Court Musician*, Frankfurt and Main 1990; MS: Süleymaniye, Ayasofya 3835/1 (fols. 1a–144b)*; C: music. (cf. no. 326 where the same title appears as *Ḥāwī al-funūn*)

(462) Dh/15 252a/15 *al-Dhakhā'ir – Treasures*; possibly A: Abū al-Ḥasan/Ḥusayn Aḥmad b. ᶜAlī b. Ibrāhīm Ibn al-Zubayr (d. 563/1167); S: ed. M. Ḥamīd Allāh, *K. al-Dhakhā'ir wa-al-tuḥaf*, Kuwait: MḤK, 1959; FI: '*ᶜatīq*'/'*old [manuscript?]*'. This comment may have been copied from the manuscript. For one such statement on a manuscript's age cf. MS Süleymaniye, Fatih 4189 (*Shiᶜr Tawba b. al-Ḥumayyir*, cf. no. 606), which has on folio 1a an ornamented octagon with the word '*ᶜatīq*' written in the centre and at each of its corners. Cf. nos 693, 782 and 783 for other manuscripts where the cataloguer uses this term. C: adab – Fatimid.

(463) Dh/15 252a/15 *Dhayl Badā'iᶜ al-badā'ih – Continuation of the Marvels of the Beginning*; this continuation of ᶜAlī Ibn Ẓāfir's (d. 613/1216 or 623/1226) anthology (cf. no. 224) is unidentifiable. C: adab – anthology of improvisations.

(464) Dh/3s 252a/16 *Dhamm al-jazaᶜ wa-ḥamd al-ṣabr – Censuring Impatience and Praising Endurance*; no such title is identifiable and it is probably a selection drawn from texts on Islamic ethics on laudable and blameworthy morals such as al-Jāḥiẓ's *Risāla fī al-akhlāq al-maḥmūda wa-al-madhmūma* (see Günther, 'Advice for Teachers', 111–12); C: ethics.

(465) R/1 252a/16 *al-Rawḍ al-unuf – Garden of Novelty*; A: ᶜAbd al-Raḥmān b. ᶜAbd Allāh al-Suhaylī (d. 581/1185); S: ed. ᶜA. al-Wakīl, *al-Rawḍ al-unuf fī sharḥ al-sīra al-nabawīya li-Ibn Hishām*, Cairo: DKḤ, 1967–70; MS: Süleymaniye, Carullah 1609–M*; NC: 2; VQ: 2, 2; Ṣ; C: biography of the Prophet (*sīra*). (cf. no. 1173a)

(466) R/2 252a/17 *Rawḍat al-muḥaqqiqīn – The Verifiers' Garden*; Placed in thematic category 2 this may be the exegetical *Rawḍat al-muḥaqqiqīn fī tafsīr al-kitāb al-mubīn*, although the author is rather late. A: Muḥammad b. ᶜAlī b. Muḥammad al-Jurjānī al-Astarābādhī (fl. 697/1298); S: MM, III, 536; VQ: 1; Ṣ; C: Koran – exegesis (tafsīr).

(467) R/2 252a/17 *Risālat al-Qushayrī – Al-Qushayrī's Epistle*; A: ᶜAbd al-Karīm al-Qushayrī (d. 465/1072); S: Germ. tr. R. Gramlich, *Das Sendschreiben al-Qušayrīs über das Sufitum*, Wiesbaden 1989; VQ: 1; Ṣ; C: sufism.

(468) R/2 252a/17–18 *Risāla fī al-taṣawwuf – Epistle of Sufism*; A: anonymous work ('*majhūl al-muṣannif*') with generic title; VQ: 1; Ṣ; C: sufism.

(469) R/2 252a/18 *al-Radd ᶜalā al-mutaᶜaṣṣib al-ᶜanīd al-mānīᶜ min dhamm Yazīd – Refuting the Obstinate Bigot Who Prohibited Cursing Yazīd*; refuting ᶜAbd al-Mughīth b. Zuhayr's (d. 583/1187) treatise forbidding the cursing of the Umayyad Caliph Yazīd (Ibn Rajab, *Dhayl*, II, 349–52); A: Ibn al-Jawzī (d. 597/1200); S: ed. H.ᶜA. Muḥammad, Beirut: DKI, 2005; VQ: 1; Ṣ; C: history – Umayyads.

(470) R/3 252a/18–252b/1 *Rumūz al-kunūz – The Treasures' Signs*; two main possibilities 1) ᶜAbd al-Razzāq b. Rizq Allāh al-Rasᶜanī al-Ḥanbalī (d. 661/1263) (ed. ᶜA. Ibn Duhaysh, Mecca 2008) on Koran Exegesis or 2) the lost summary that Sayf al-Dīn ᶜAlī al-Āmidī (d. 631/1234) (IKH, III, 294) made of his own *Abkār al-afkār*, which is on theology; VQ: 1; Ṣ; C:?

(471) R/6 252b/1 *Rajaz Abī al-Munajjim – Abū al-Munajjim's Verses in the Rajaz Metre*; A: Muḥammad b. Makkī al-Dārī Abū al-Munajjim (b. 417/1026); S: *Wāfī*, V, 57; VQ: 1; Ṣ; C: poetry – rajaz.[75]

(472) R/6 252b/1–2 *Rawāᵓiᶜ al-āthār wa-badāᵓiᶜ al-akhbār – Admirable Traditions and Marvellous Reports*; no such title is identifiable. Arguably this is the *Badāᵓiᶜ al-akhbār wa-rawāᵓiᶜ al-ashᶜār* by the man of letters A: Yaᶜqūb b. Sulaymān al-Khāzin (d. 488/1090); S: *Wāfī*, XXVIII, 497–8; VQ: 1–45; Ṣ; C: poetry/adab – anthology.

(473) R/7 252b/2 *Rayḥānat al-muhaj al-mukhtār min kitāb al-Faraj – The Souls' Fragrant Flowers Selected from the Book al-Faraj*; extract from al-Tanūkhī's (d. 384/994) *al-Faraj baᶜda al-shidda*; A: unknown; S: Arberry, *Handlist*, VII, 67 (no. 5211: *Rayḥānat al-muhaj min mukhtār kitāb al-Faraj*); VQ: 2–44; Ṣ; C: adab – anthology.

(474) R/8 252b/2-3 *Rawḍat al-ᶜāshiq – The Passionate Lover's Garden* [and the Tender Lover's Promenade]; composed for al-Malik al-Ashraf, the mausoleum's patron; A: Aḥmad b. Sulaymān b. Ḥumayd al-Kisāᵓī (fl. first half 7th/13th c.); S: GAS, II, 80: '*Rawḍat al-ᶜāshiq wa-nuzhat al-wāmiq*'; VQ: 1; Ṣ; C: adab/love literature.

(475) R/8 252b/3 *Rayḥān al-Afāḍil – al-Afāḍil's Fragrant Flower*; this is most likely the adab anthology *al-Rayāḥīn* by A: al-Qāsim b. al-Ḥusayn Ṣadr al-Afāḍil (d. 617/1220); S: MU, V, 2197; VQ: 1–44; Ṣ; C: adab.

(476) R/8 252b/3 *Rawḍat al-manāẓir – Garden of Observations*; the MS has *rawḍat al-manāḍir*, which is impossible. The reading *Rawḍat al-manāẓir* leads to a work with this title by Muḥammad b. Thābit al-Khujandī (d. 483/1090) (*Wāfī*, II, 281) or *Rawḍat [al-nāẓir wa-jannat] al-manāẓir [fī uṣūl al-fiqh ᶜalā madhhab al-imām Aḥmad Ibn Ḥanbal]* by ᶜAbd Allāh b. Aḥmad Ibn Qudāma al-Maqdisī al-Muwaffaq (d. 620/1223) (ed. ᶜA. al-Namla, Riyad 1993). However, a work on *fiqh* would be very unlikely for adab category 8. Thus this is more likely the adab/poetry/wisdom literature anthology *Rawḍat al-nāẓir wa-nuzhat al-khāṭir* by ᶜAbd al-ᶜAzīz al-Kāshī (fl. 7th/13th c.) (Marlow, *Hierarchy and Egalitarianism*, 141), which may appear elsewhere in this catalogue (cf. no. 223). VQ: 1; C: adab/poetry – anthology?

(477) R/10 252b/3 *al-Ramī ᶜan al-qaws – Archery*; no such title is identifiable. This is arguably an extract from a treatise on weapons such as *Tabṣirat arbāb al-albāb* by al-Ṭarsūsī (fl. 6th/12th c.), which contains a section on the bow (see Cahen, 'Traité d'armurerie'). VQ: 1; Ṣ; C: warfare.

(478) R/15 252b/4 *Rusul al-mulūk – The Kings' Envoys*; A: Muḥammad b. al-Ḥusayn Ibn al-Farrāᵓ (d. 458/1066); S: ed. Ṣ. al-Munajjid, *Rusul al-mulūk wa-man yaṣluḥu li-l-risāla wa-al-safāra*, Cairo: LTTN, 1947; VQ: 1; Ṣ; C: administrative handbook – etiquette of envoys.

(479) R/15 252b/4 *Riqāᶜ al-wazīr Anūshirwān – Vizier Anūshirwān's Decisions*; the Saljuq vizier A: Anūshirwān b. Khālid (d. 533/1138–9?) (EI³, C.L. Klausner, 'Anūshirwān b. Khālid'); no such title is identifiable. VQ: 1; Ṣ; C: administrative handbook?

(480) R/6s 252b/4–5 *Rasāᵓil Abī Ḥayyān al-Tawḥīdī – Al-Tawḥīdī's Epistles*; A: Abū Ḥayyān al-Tawḥīdī (d. 414/1023); S: ed. ᶜI. Aḥmad, *Min rasāᵓil Abī Ḥayyān al-Tawḥīdī*, Damascus: WTh, 2001; VQ: 1; Ṣ; C: adab – epistle.

(481) R/6s 252b/5–6 *Rasāᵓil al-Ḥarīrī wa-ajwibat Ibn Jiyā (wa-al-ṣabāḥāt al-qawām?) – The Epistles of al-Ḥarīrī and Ibn Jiyā's replies and?*; A: al-Qāsim b. ᶜAlī al-Ḥarīrī al-Baṣrī (d. 516/1122) and Muḥammad b. Aḥmad Ibn Jiyā (d. 579/1183); S: al-Ḥarīrī (contemporaneous authors mention a collection of his epistles: MU, V, 2207: '*Kitāb rasāᵓilihi al-mudawwana*', cf. nos 489, 1156, 1683); on Ibn Jiyā's replies: MU, VI, 2387–8; the second part of the title is not identifiable. NC: 2; VQ: 1, 1; Ṣ; C: adab – epistle.

(482) R/6s 252b/6 *Rasāʾil Ibn Ḥamdūn – Ibn Ḥamdūn's Epistles*; perhaps extract of this author's adab collection *al-Tadhkira* (cf. nos 1461, 1556)? A: Muḥammad b. al-Ḥasan Ibn Ḥamdūn (d. 562/1166–7); VQ: 2; Ṣ; C: adab – epistle.

(483) R/6s 252b/6 *Rasāʾil Ibn al-Marzubān – Ibn al-Marzubān's Epistles*; on account of no. 1684 arguably A: Abū ᶜAbd Allāh Aḥmad b. Khalaf Ibn al-Marzubān (d. 310/922); VQ: 1; Ṣ; C: adab – epistle. (cf. no. 1684)

(484) R/6s 252b/6-7 *Rasāʾil Ashrafiya ᶜalā ḥurūf al-muᶜjam – Ashrafiyan Epistles Alphabetically Organised*; the Ibn Amsīnā named here is probably A: Muḥammad b. Aḥmad b. ᶜAlī Ibn (al-)Amsīnā (fl. 606/1209). The fate of this secretary after he lost his position in the Caliphal administration in Baghdad in 606/1209 at the age of 57 (lunar) years (*Wāfī*, II, 109) is unknown. He may have moved to al-Malik al-Ashraf's court in northern Mesopotamia, where the latter had built up a major principality. The cataloguer clearly does not know these epistles, because he does not use – similar to the panegyrics by the same author in no. 875 – the definite article. VQ: 1; Ṣ; C: adab – epistle? (cf. no. 875)

(485a) R/6s 252b/7 *Riyāḍat al-kamāl fī ṣanᶜat al-rasāʾil – Accomplished Exercise on Composing Letters*; such a title is not identifiable, but this is most likely *al-Riyāḍa* by the secretary and author of administrative compendia on *kharāj* and *inshāʾ* A: Muḥammad b. Muḥammad b. Sahl al-Shilḥī (d. 423/1032); S: *Wāfī*, I, 116; C: adab – epistle.

(485b) 252b/7-8 *wa-Naskh al-mukātabāt bayna al-Raḍī wa-al-Ṣābiʾ – Copy of the Correspondence between al-Raḍī and al-Ṣābiʾ*; A: Muḥammad b. al-Ḥusayn al-Sharīf al-Raḍī (d. 406/1016) and Ibrāhīm b. Hilāl al-Ṣābiʾ (d. 384/994); S: *Rasāʾil al-Ṣābiʾ wa-al-Sharīf al-Raḍī*, ed. M. Najm, Kuwait: MḤK, 1961; C: adab – epistle. (cf. no. 1294a)

(486) R/6s 252b/8 *Rasāʾil Walī al-Dawla Ibn Khayrān – Walī al-Dawla Ibn Khayrān's Epistles*; A: Aḥmad b. ᶜAlī Walī al-Dawla Ibn Khayrān (d. 431/1039); S: MU, I, 380–4; VQ: 1; Ṣ; C: adab – epistle.

(487) R/6s 252b/8 *Rasāʾil Ibn al-Muᶜtazz – Ibn al-Muᶜtazz's Epistles*; A: ᶜAbd Allāh Ibn al-Muᶜtazz (d. 296/908); S: *Rasāʾil Ibn al-Muᶜtazz fī al-naqd wa-al-adab wa-al-ijtimāᶜ*, ed. M.ᶜA. Khafājī, Cairo: MBḤ, 1946; VQ: 1; Ṣ; C: adab – epistle.

(488) R/6s 252b/9 *Rasāʾil al-Ḥayṣa Bayṣa – Ḥayṣa Bayṣa's Epistles*; A: Saʿd b. Muḥammad Ḥayṣa Bayṣa (d. 574/1179); S: contemporaneous authors are aware of his *Dīwān al-rasāʾil* (MU, III, 1352–3) or at least his *Rasāʾil* (IKH, II, 363); VQ: 1; Ṣ; C: adab – epistle.

(489) R/6s 252b/9 *Rasāʾil Ibn al-Ḥarīrī – Ibn al-Ḥarīrī's Epistles*; A: al-Qāsim b. ʿAlī al-Ḥarīrī al-Baṣrī (d. 516/1122) who was also called 'Ibn' al-Ḥarīrī; S: contemporaneous authors mention a collection of his epistles: MU, V, 2207: '*Kitāb rasāʾilihi al-mudawwana*'; NC: 2; VQ: 1; Ṣ; C: adab – epistle. (cf. nos 481, 517, 1156, 1683)

(490) R/6s 252b/9 *Rasāʾil al-ʿAzīz b. Shujāʿ – Al-ʿAzīz b. Shujāʿ's Epistles*; A: Fātik b. ʿAbd Allāh al-Rūmī ʿAzīz al-Dawla (Abū) Shujāʿ (d. 413/1022); S: al-Ziriklī, *Aʿlām*, V, 322; VQ: 1; Ṣ; C: adab – epistle?

(491) R/6s 252b/10 *Rasāʾil li-Ibn Shīth – Ibn Shīth's Epistles*; A: ʿAbd al-Raḥīm b. ʿAlī Ibn Shīth (d. 625/1227); S: TI, 621–30, pp. 231–2; VQ: 1; Ṣ; C: adab – epistle.

(492) R/6s 252b/10 *Rasāʾil li-Ibn Nāqiyā – Ibn Nāqiyā's Epistles*; A: ʿAbd Allāh b. Muḥammad Ibn Nāqiyā (d. 485/1092); S: contemporaneous authors mention a *Dīwān rasāʾil* (IKH, III, 98); VQ: 1; Ṣ; C: adab – epistle.

(493) R/6s 252b/10 *Rasāʾil Qābūs b. Wushmagīr – Qābūs b. Wushmagīr's Epistles*; A: Qābūs b. Wushmagīr (d. 403/1012–13); S: *Kamāl al-balāgha: wa-huwa rasāʾil Shams al-Maʿālī Qābūs b. Wushmakīr*, ed. ʿA. al-Yazdādī, Baghdad/Cairo 1341 *[1922–3]*; VQ: 1; Ṣ; C: adab – epistle.

(494) R/6s 252b/11 *Risālat Jaʿfar b. Warqāʾ – Jaʿfar b. Warqāʾ's Epistle*; A: Jaʿfar b. Muḥammad Ibn Warqāʾ (d. 352/963); S: al-Ziriklī, *al-Aʿlām*, II, 123; VQ: 1–4; Ṣ; C: adab – epistle.

(495) R/6s 252b/11 *Risālat Abī Bakr wa-ʿUmar ilā ʿAlī – Abū Bakr and ʿUmar's Epistle to ʿAlī*; A: attr. Abū Bakr (d. 13/634); for one version see S: King Saud University Library MS 1620 '*hādhihī risālat Abī Bakr al-Ṣiddīq wa-atbāʿ ʿUmar b. al-Khaṭṭāb lahā ilā ʿAlī b. Abī Ṭālib*'; VQ: 1 *fī* 2; Ṣ; C: history – early Islamic.

(496) R/6s 252b/11–12 *Risālat ʿAbd al-Ḥamīd ilā jamāʿat al-kuttāb – ʿAbd al-Ḥamīd's Epistle to Secretaries*; A: ʿAbd al-Ḥamīd b. Yaḥyā (d. 132/750?);

S: ᶜAbbās, *ᶜAbd al-Ḥamīd*, 180–8 and 281–8 '*risālatuhu ilā al-kuttāb*'; VQ: 16; C: adab of secretary. (cf. no. 498)

(497) R/6s 252b/12 *Risālat Aḥmad b. al-Wāthiq – Aḥmad b. al-Wāthiq's Epistle*; Scr('*bi-khaṭṭ*'): arguably Aḥmad b. ᶜAlī Walī al-Dawla Ibn Khayrān (d. 431/1039) (MU, I, 380–4) who was head of the Fatimid chancery, kept close contact with the literati of Baghdad and whose epistles were also held in this library (cf. no. 486); A: ᶜAbbasid Caliph Abū ᶜAbd Allāh Aḥmad/ Muḥammad b. al-Wāthiq al-Muhtadī bi-Allāh (d. 256/870); S: contained in al-Mubarrad, *al-Balāgha*, ed. R. ᶜAbd al-Tawwāb, Cairo 1965; the reply by Muḥammad b. Yazīd al-Mubarrad (d. 286/900) is edited as *Risālat Abū al-ᶜAbbās Muḥammad Ibn Yazīd al-Mubarrad al-Shamāli al-Naḥwī ilā Aḥmad Ibn al-Wāthiq al-ᶜAbbāsī*, ed. M. Aḥmad, ᶜAlīgarh 1968. VQ: 16; Ṣ; C: rhetoric. (cf. no. 520)

(498) R/6s 252b/12–13 *Risālat ᶜAbd al-Ḥamīd fī waṣīyat al-kuttāb wa-ghayr dhālika – ᶜAbd al-Ḥamīd's Epistle with His Advice for Secretaries and Other [Writings]*; Scr('*khaṭṭ*'): Mawhūb b. Aḥmad Ibn al-Jawālīqī (d. 539/1144) (EI^2, H. Fleisch, 'al-Djawālīḳī'); A: ᶜAbd al-Ḥamīd b. Yaḥyā (d. 132/750?); S: ᶜAbbās, *ᶜAbd al-Ḥamīd*, 180–8 and 281–8 '*risālatuhu ilā al-kuttāb*'; C: adab of secretary. (cf. no. 496)

(499) R/6s 252b/13–14 *Risālat al-Jāḥiẓ fī madḥ al-kutub – Al-Jāḥiẓ's Epistle in Praise of Books*; A: al-Jāḥiẓ (d. 255/868–9); S: Pellat, 'D'inventaire', nos. 124–5; VQ: 1–45; Ṣ; C: adab. (cf. no. 527)

(500) R/6s 252b/14 *Risāla – An Epistle*; generic title; Scr('*bi-khaṭṭ*'): al-Qaṣṣārī (not identified); VQ: 1; Ṣ; C: adab – epistle.

(501a) R/7 252b/14–15 *Risāla fī al-khaṭṭ – An Epistle on Calligraphy*; anonymous work with generic title; C: calligraphy.[76]

(501b) 252b/15 *Thalāth rasāʾil min ghurar al-balāgha – Three Epistles from Ghurar al-balāgha*; A: Hilāl b. al-Muḥassin al-Ṣābiʾ (d. 448/1056); S: *K. ghurar al-balāgha*, ed. M. al-Dībājī, Beirut: DṢ, 2000; C: rhetoric. (cf. nos 804, 1323a)

(502) R/8 252b/15 *Risālat Ibn al-Zubayr – Ibn Zubayr's Epistle*; A: Usāma b. Munqidh (d. 584/1188), who corresponded with the Fatimid secretary and judge Aḥmad b. ᶜAlī al-Zubayr (d. 563/1167) after he had to leave Egypt

(Ibn Munqidh, *al-ᶜAṣā*, 420). This title is not mentioned in his *K. al-ᶜAṣā* or in Ibn Munqidh's biographies and it is probably a short piece originally deposited in the Fatimid library. C: adab – epistle.

(503) R/8 252b/16 *Risāla li-Ibn al-Munjib [illegible word] – An Epistle by Ibn al-Munjib*; as the entries in this section refer to epistles by secretaries this is most likely A: ᶜAlī b. (al-)Munjib Ibn al-Ṣayrafī (d. 542/1147). The illegible word probably identifies the content of this epistle, but none of his known titles (e.g. MU, V, 1971–2) matches this term. C: adab – epistle.

(504) R/8 252b/16 *Risālat Ibn al-Muqaffaᶜ fī ādāb al-wuzarā᾽ – Ibn al-Muqaffaᶜ's Treatise on the Rules for Viziers*; this is either a lost work or material drawn from the relevant parts of his *al-Ādāb al-kabīr*. A: ᶜAbd Allāh Ibn al-Muqaffaᶜ (d. 139/756?); S: Fr. tr. Tardy, 'd'al-Adab al-Kabīr', §§ 33–73; VQ: 1; Ṣ; C: political thought – adab of vizier.[77]

(505) R/9 252b/17 *Risālat Ḥayy b. Yaqẓān – The Tale of Ḥayy b. Yaqẓān*; A: Ibn Sīnā (d. 428/1037); S: ed. & Fr. tr. H. Corbin, *Avicienna et le récit visionnaire*, Tehran 1954; VQ: 1; Ṣ; C: philosophy/mysticism.

(506) R/9 252b/17 *Risāla fī imtiḥān al-aṭibbā᾽ – A Treatise on Examining Physicians*; possibly *Imtiḥān al-alibbā᾽ li-kāffat al-aṭibbā᾽* by A: ᶜAbd al-ᶜAzīz al-Sulamī Muwaffaq al-Dīn (d. 604/1208); S: eds & Engl. trs Leiser and Al-Khaledy, *Questions and Answers*; VQ: 1; Ṣ; C: medicine.

(507) R/15 252b/18 *Risālat jabhat al-adab – Epistle on Mistreating Adab*; A: Muḥammad b. al-Ḥasan al-Ḥātimī (d. 388/998). This is another title for al-Ḥātimī's epistle against al-Mutanabbī. S: *al-Risāla al-mūḍiḥa* (ed. M.Y. Najm, Beirut: DṢ, 1965). VQ: 1; Ṣ; C: poetry – commentary. (cf. nos 528, 1249j, 1278a)

(508) R/15 252b/18 *[al-]Risāla al-Saᶜīdīya – The Saᶜidian Treatise*; short title for *al-Risāla al-saᶜīdīya fī al-ma᾽ākhidh al-kindīya* on al-Mutanabbī's 'plagiarisms'; A: Saᶜīd b. al-Mubārak Ibn al-Dahhān (d. 569/1174); S: IKH, II, 382; VQ: 1; Ṣ; C: poetry – commentary.

(509) R/15 252b/18-253a/1 *Risālat Arisṭāṭālīs ilā al-Iskandar – Aristotle's Letter to Alexander the Great*; S: Maróth, *Aristotle and Alexander the Great*; VQ: 1–45; Ṣ; C: political thought – non-Muslim – mirror for princes/adab – epistle/history. (cf. no. 1237c)

(510) R/15 253a/1 *[al-]Risāla al-mawsūma bi-Kawkab al-Mutaʾammil – The Epistle Called the Star of He Who Contemplates*; on description of horses; A: Fakhr al-ʿArab Abū al-Muẓaffar Muḥammad b. Aḥmad al-Abīwardī (d. 507/1113); S: MU, V, 2365; VQ: 1–45; C: adab – epistle.

(511) R/5s 253a/2-3 *al-Risāla al-Maʾmūnīya al-mulaqqaba bi-al-dhahabīya – The Maʾmūnīya Treatise Called 'The Golden'*; A: ʿAlī b. Mūsā al-Riḍā, the eighth Shiʿite *imām* (d. 203/818); S: ed. Y.Ḥ. Zāmil al-Sāʿidī, *al-Risāla al-dhahabīya aw ṭibb al-imām al-Riḍā*, Baghdad: Muʾassasat al-Riḍā, 2004; Ullmann, *Medizin*, 190; C: medicine – imāmī.

(512) R/5s 253a/3-4 *Risālat al-Abīwardī ilā Ṣadaqa b. Dubays – Al-Abīwardī's Letter to Ṣadaqa b. Dubays*; A: Fakhr al-ʿArab Abū al-Muẓaffar Muḥammad b. Aḥmad al-Abīwardī (d. 507/1113) writing to Ṣadaqa b. Dubays (d. 501/1108), ruler of al-Ḥilla; FI: '*shakarahu ʿalā ṣanīʿihi ʿuqayba farāghihi min Jawhar al-ansāb*'/'*thanking him for his benefaction shortly after completing* Jawhar al-ansāb'; VQ: 1; Ṣ; C: adab – epistle.

(513) R/5s 253a/4–5 *Risālat Abī Bakr b. Ṭarkhān – Abū Bakr b. Ṭarkhān's Epistle*; A: Abū Bakr Muḥammad b. Ṭarkhān al-Turkī (d. 513/1119); S: *Siyar*, XIX, 423; *Wāfī*, III, 169; no specific epistle is known for this scholar, who wrote in the fields of *ḥadīth*, grammar, theology, jurisprudence and adab. However, placed in category 5s this is most likely a work of adab. FI: '*al-muktataba* (?) *naskhuhā fī Ramaḍān*'/'*written in Ramadan*'; VQ: 1; Ṣ; C: adab?

(514) R/5s 253a/5 *Risālat Aḥmad b. Abī Ṭāhir fī al-kashf ʿan shihāb al- shiʿr – Aḥmad b. Abī Ṭāhir's Epistle on Revealing the Brilliance of Poetry*; this title is not mentioned in the literature, but it is probably one of the epistles that Ibn Ṭayfūr wrote to the poets Ibrāhīm b. al-Mudabbir (d. 279/892–3, MU, I, 102–4) and ʿAlī b. Yaḥyā al-Munajjim (d. 275/888–9, MU, V, 2008–22); A: Aḥmad Ibn Abī Ṭāhir Ṭayfūr (d. 280/893); S: MU, I, 284: '*Risālatuhu ilā Ibrāhīm b. al-Mudabbir*', '*al-Risāla ilā ʿAlī b. Yaḥyā*'; VQ: 1; Ṣ; C: poetry – commentary.

(515) R/5s 253a/6 *Risālat Suqrāṭīs fī siyāsat al-malik – Socrates' Epistle on the Ruler's Governance*; A: Socrates; VQ: 1; Ṣ; C: political thought – non-Muslim.

(516) R/5s 253a/6 *Risālat al-sabīla* (?) *fī al-nuṣra ʿalā al-Khwārazmīya – The Treatise of the Path* (?) *Concerning the Victory over the Khwarazmshahs*; No

such title is identifiable and the reading of the term *al-sabīla* (even though we find it twice, on folia 246a, l. 6 and 253a, l. 6) is very tentative. It may be a work authored after the battle at Erzincan in 627/1230 when al-Malik al-Ashraf, in coalition with the Rum Saljuq Sultan ᶜAlāᵓ al-Dīn Kay Qubādh, defeated the Khwarazmshah Jalāl al-Dīn Mingburnu. Placed in this library it was most likely dedicated to al-Ashraf, but panegyric poetry for ᶜAlāᵓ al-Dīn was arguably held in this library as well (cf. no. 1585). This treatise may be similar to *al-Risāla al-Khwārazmīya* mentioned further down (cf. no. 534), which is also unknown. A possible ascription is given in the early modern bio-bibliographical *Kashf al-ẓunūn* where the author notes, just after mentioning a book translated into Arabic for al-Malik al-Ashraf's predecessor in Damascus al-Malik al-Muᶜaẓẓam and copied in 679/1280–1, that a certain Majd al-Dīn al-Bābārī al-Nasāᵓī authored an account of the battle with the Khwarazmshahs (Ḥājjī Khalīfa, *Kashf*, II, 1026).[78] C: history – Ayyūbid? – al-Malik al-Ashraf?

(517) R/5s 253a/7 *Risāla sīnīya wa-shīnīya – An Epistle Employing Only Words Containing the Letters sīn and shīn*; on the model of the famous *risāla sīnīya* by al-Qāsim b. ᶜAlī al-Ḥarīrī al-Baṣrī (d. 516/1122) (ed. in *al-Maqāmāt al-adabīya*, Cairo: MBḤ, 1950). There is no ᶜAbd al-Munᶜim al-Ḥanafī who is renowned as an author and the cataloguer did not determine the title so this was probably a book-in-the-making by a local author. It is thus feasible that the physician and *adīb* A: ᶜAbd al-Munᶜim b. ᶜUmar al-Jilyānī Ḥakīm al-Zamān (d. 602/1206), who has a title elsewhere in this catalogue (cf. no. 1094), is intended (TI, 601–10, pp. 120/1). C: adab – epistle.

(518) R/5s 253a/7 *Risāla fī al-balah wa-al-ᶜaql – An Epistle on Stupidity and Understanding*; no such title is identifiable. It is most likely an epistle on this issue drawing on material in adab works such as al-Jāḥiẓ's *al-Bayān wa-al-tabyīn* where he has a section on stupidity ('*min al-balah*', ed. ᶜA.M. Hārūn, Cairo: MK, 1948–50, II, 349–50); VQ: 1–42; Ṣ; C: adab – epistle.

(519) R/5s 253a/8 *Risālat al-Jāḥiẓ fī al-ᶜāshiq al-mutalāshī wa-al-ᶜāshiq al-nāshī – Al-Jāḥiẓ's Tale on the Inexperienced Lover and the Dwindling One*; A: al-Jāḥiẓ (d. 255/868–9); S: Pellat, 'D'inventaire', no. 44: '*K. al-ᶜĀshiq al-nāshī wa-al-mutalāshī*'; VQ: 1–47; Ṣ; C: adab – epistle.

(520) R/5s 253a/8-9 *Risālat Aḥmad b. al-Wāthiq ilā Abī al-ᶜAbbās al-Mubarrad – The Epistle of Aḥmad b. al-Wāthiq to Abū al-ᶜAbbās*

al- Mubarrad; A: ᶜAbbasid Caliph Abū ᶜAbd Allāh Aḥmad/Muḥammad b. al-Wāthiq al-Muhtadī bi-Allāh (d. 256/870); S: contained in al-Mubarrad (d. 286/900), *al-Balāgha*, ed. R. ᶜAbd al-Tawwāb, Cairo: Dār al-ᶜurūba, 1965; VQ: 1; Ṣ; C: rhetoric. (cf. no. 497)

(521) R/5s 253a/9 *al-Risāla al-ṭardīya – The Hunting Epistle*; A: Ibrāhīm b. Hilāl al-Ṣabiʾ (d. 384/994); S: Hachmeier, 'Letters', no. 423 describing a hunter; VQ: 1; Ṣ; C: adab – epistle/hunting.

(522) R/5s 253a/9-10 *Risālat al-Jāḥiẓ ilā Muways b. ᶜImrān – Al-Jāḥiẓ's Epistle to Muways b. ᶜImrān*; A: al-Jāḥiẓ (d. 255/868–9); S: Pellat, 'D'inventaire', no. 157 lists this work, but only with reference to this catalogue; C: adab – epistle.

(523) R/5s 253a/10 *Risālatā al-Ṣābiʾ fī al-ṣayd wa-al-bunduq – Al-Ṣābiʾ's Two Epistles on Hunting and the Crossbow*; A: Ibrāhīm b. Hilāl al-Ṣabiʾ (d. 384/994); S: Hachmeier, 'Letters', no. 424 on weapons used for hunting (see also Ibrāhīm b. ᶜAlī al-Ḥuṣrī al-Qayrawānī, *Nūr al-ṭarf wa-nūr al-ẓarf*, ed. L.ᶜA. Abū Ṣāliḥ, Beirut: MR, 1996 on a lengthy quote from the *risāla* on the crossbow) and no. 430 on *ṣayd*; C: adab – epistle/hunting.

(524) R/5s 253a/11 *Risāla fī al-ṣayd wa-al-ṭard li-man ittaṣala qawmahu wa-uṭṭurida – An Epistle on Trapping and Hunting for He Who Joined His Kin and Was Driven Away*; this title, most likely an anthology/commentary on the popular topic of hunting, is not identifiable. The cataloguer was clearly unsure about this title's authorship as he has it without the definite article and added a description probably drawn from the text itself (or copied from the heading?). VQ: 1; Ṣ; C: adab – epistle/hunting.

(525) R/5s 253a/11–12 *Risālat al-Jāḥiẓ ilā Muḥammad b. ᶜAbd al-Malik al-Zayyāt fī al-ᶜatb wa-al-iᶜtidhār – Al-Jāḥiẓ's Letter to Muḥammad b. ᶜAbd al-Malik al-Zayyāt Concerning Reproval and Excuse*; A: al-Jāḥiẓ (d. 255/868–9); while al-Jāḥiẓ's epistles to the ᶜAbbasid vizier al-Zayyāt (d. 233/847) are well known this title is not identifiable. J. Montgomery, *Jest and Earnest*, has suggested that this title may be identical to the treatise *Fī al-ghaḍab wa-al-riḍā* (Pellat, 'D'inventaire', no. 66). VQ: 1; Ṣ; C: adab – epistle.

(526) R/5s 253a/12-13 *Risālat al-Jāḥiẓ fī al-ḥāsid wa-al-maḥsūd – Al-Jāḥiẓ's Epistle on the Envier and the Envied*; A: al-Jāḥiẓ (d. 255/868–9); S: ed. M. al-Sūd, *Rasāʾil al-Jāḥiẓ*, Beirut: DKI, 2000, 5–19; NC: 4; C: adab – epistle. (cf. no. 1287e)

(527) R/5s 253a/13-14 *Risālat al-Jāḥiẓ fī madḥ al-kutub wa-al-ḥathth ^{c}alā jam^{c}ihā – Al-Jāḥiẓ's Epistle in Praise of Books and Urging to Collect Them*; A: al-Jāḥiẓ (d. 255/868–9); S: Pellat, 'D'inventaire', nos. 124–5; C: adab – epistle. (cf. nos. 499, 1287g)

(528) R/5s 253a/14 *al-Risāla al-mūḍiḥa fī dhikr sariqāt al-Mutanabbī wa-sāqiṭ shi^{c}rihi – The Epistle on Disclosing al-Mutanabbī's Plagiarism and the Deficiency of His Poetry*; A: Muḥammad b. al-Ḥasan al-Ḥātimī (d. 388/998); S: ed. M.Y. Najm, Beirut: DṢ, 1965; VQ: 1; Ṣ; C: poetry – commentary. (cf. nos. 507, 1249j, 1278a)

(529) R/5s 253a/15 *al-Risāla al-Ḥātimīya al-ṣaghīra – Al-Ḥātimī's Short Epistle*; on al-Mutanabbī; A: Muḥammad b. al-Ḥasan al-Ḥātimī (d. 388/998); S: EI^{2}, S.A. Bonebakker, 'al-Ḥātimī'; NC: 2; VQ: 1–45; Ṣ; C: poetry – commentary. (cf. nos. 1249a, 1278a)

(530) R/5s 253a/15–16 *Risāla fīmā yajūzu ^{c}alayhi al-i^{c}āda wa-mā lā yajūzu – An Epistle on when Repetition Is Permissible and when It Should Be Avoided*; no such title is identifiable. It was seemingly also unknown to the cataloguer, who uses the term 'epistle' without the definite article. He ascribes it to al-Ṭabarī who was concerned with the question of repetition throughout his works, stressing particularly in his *tafsīr* that *i^{c}āda* should be avoided in order to keep texts to an appropriate length (Rosenthal, *General Introduction*, 55). A: Muḥammad b. Jarīr al-Ṭabarī (d. 310/923); C: rhetoric.

(531a) R/5s 253a/16–253b/1 *Risālatān li-l-Jāḥiẓ aḥaduhumā fī taqrīẓ ^{c}Abd Allāh b. Ṭāhir – Two Epistles by al-Jāḥiẓ, One in Praise of ^{c}Abd Allāh b. Ṭāhir*; A: al-Jāḥiẓ (d. 255/868–9); this is most likely a – not known – panegyric (Pellat, 'D'inventaire', no. 2 has only a *Risāla ilā ^{c}Abd Allāh b. Yaḥyā*) for the ^{c}Abbasid governor Ibn Ṭāhir (d. 230/844). C: panegyric?

(531b) 253b/1 *wa-al-ukhrā ilā Aḥmad b. ^{c}Abd al-Wahhāb fī al-masā$^{\circ}$il – And the Other [Treatise] Written to Aḥmad b. ^{c}Abd al-Wahhāb on [Theological] Questions*; A: al-Jāḥiẓ (d. 255/868–9); This is the author's *K. al-tarbī^{c} wa-al-tadwīr*, an attack on Rāfiḍism and a defence of Mu^{c}tazilism. S: Montgomery, 'Hellenizing Philosophy'; VQ: 1; Ṣ; C: theology.

(532) R/5s 253b/1-2 *Risāla fī ḥifẓ al-asnān wa-al-litha – Treatise on Preserving Teeth and Gums*; A: Ḥunayn b. Isḥāq (d. 260/873); S: ed. M.F. al-Dhākirī, Aleppo: DQa al-ᶜarabī, 1996; VQ: 1; Ṣ; C: medicine.

(533) R/5s 253b/2 *Risālat al-Maᶜarrī – Al-Maᶜarrī's Epistle*; most likely the *Risālat al-Ighrīḍīya*, which is elsewhere described as '*Risālat Abī al-ᶜAlāᵓ*' (cf. no. 53b); Scr('*bi-khaṭṭ*'): al-Ḥasan al-Qaylawī (d. 633/1236; TI, 631–40, p. 145), a renowned scribe of Damascus and librarian of al-Malik al-Ashraf who copied another manuscript in this library (cf. nos 257, 698, 1253) and was also involved in the transmission of other copies (cf. no. 807); A: Abū al-ᶜAlāᵓ al-Maᶜarrī (d. 449/1058); S: al-Maᶜarrī, *Rasāᵓil*, I, 183–250; VQ: 1; Ṣ; C: adab. (cf. nos. 53b, 1223a, 1306a)

(534) R/5s 253b/2-3 *al-Risāla al-Khwārazmīya – The Khwarazmian Epistle*; this title is unknown but, similar to no. 516, it may be a work authored after the battle at Erzincan in 627/1230 when al-Malik al-Ashraf, in coalition with the Rum Saljuq Sultan ᶜAlāᵓ al-Dīn Kay Qubādh, defeated the Khwarazmshah Jalāl al-Dīn Mingburnu. The name of the author given here, 'al-Tāj al-Ṣarkhadī', does not allow a definite identification. A: Tāj al-Dīn Maḥmūd al-Ṣarkhadī (d. 674/1275, TI, 671–80, pp. 168–70) is possible, especially as he lived in Damascus and was a scholar with strong literary ambitions. VQ: 1; Ṣ; C: history – Ayyūbid? – al-Malik al-Ashraf? (cf. no. 516?)

(535) R/5s 253b/3 *Risālat al-amīr Niẓām al-Dīn ilā al-Qādir bi-Allāh – The Officer Niẓām al-Dīn's Epistle to al-Qādir bi-Allāh*; referring to the Caliph al-Qādir bi-Allāh (d. 422/1031); probably A: Niẓām al-Dīn Maḥmūd b. Sebüktigin of Ghazna (d. 421/1030); VQ: 1; Ṣ; C: history/adab – epistle.

(536) Z/1 253b/4 *Zād al-masīr – Provisioning the Traveller [in the Field of Exegesis]*; A: Ibn al-Jawzī (d. 597/1200); S: *Zād al-masīr fī ᶜilm al-tafsīr*, ed. Beirut: DKI, 2002; MS: Süleymaniye, Sultan Ahmed I 31*; VQ: 5; Ṣ; C: Koran – exegesis (*tafsīr*). (cf. no. 915)

(537) Z/2 253b/4-5 *Zayn al-muqaṣṣiṣ fī al-qiṣaṣ – The Narrator's Ornament on Narrations*; A: Ibn al-Jawzī (d. 597/1200); S: Alwajī, *Muᵓallafāt*, 141: *Zayn al-qiṣaṣ*; VQ: 1; Ṣ; C: sermons.

(538) Z/2 253b/5 *Zubdat al-ḥaqāᵓiq – Quintessence of Realities*; A: ᶜAyn al-Quḍāt ᶜAbd Allāh (or Muḥammad) b. Abī Bakr al-Hamadhānī al-Mayānajī[79] (d. 525/1131); S: ed. ᶜA. ᶜUsayrān, in: *Muṣannafāt-i ᶜAyn*

al-Quḍāt-i Hamadānī, Tehran: Dānishgāh, 1962; VQ: 1; Ṣ; C: theology – mystical. (cf. no. 1184a)

(539) Z/3 253b/5 *Ziyārāt – [Guide to] Pilgrimage Sites*; A: ʿAlī b. Abī Bakr al-Harawī (d. 611/1215); S: *al-Ishārāt ilā maʿrifat al-ziyārāt*, ed. & Fr. tr. J. Sourdel-Thomine, Damascus 1952–7; VQ: 1; Ṣ; C: rituals – ziyārāt.

(540) Z/4 253b/6 *Zāhir – The Flourishing [Book]*; A: Ibn al-Anbārī (d. 328/940); S: *al-Zāhir fī maʿānī kalimāt al-nās*, ed. Ḥ.Ṣ. al-Ḍāmin, Baghdad: DR, 1979; MS: Süleymaniye, Esad Efendi 3216*; VQ: 1; Ṣ; C: lexicography.

(541) Z/8 253b/6 *Zahr al-ādāb – The Flowers of Adab [and Fruits of Hearts]*; A: Ibrāhīm b. ʿAlī al-Ḥuṣrī al-Qayrawānī (d. 413/1022); S: *Zahr al-ādāb wa-thamar al-albāb*, ed. ʿA.M. al-Bajāwī, Cairo: DIKA, 1953; MS: Süleymaniye, Ayasofya 4028**; NC: 2; VQ: 8, 44; Ṣ; C: adab – anthology. (cf. nos. 1272, 1500)

(542) Z/8 253b/7 *al-Zahra – [Book of] the Flower*; A: Muḥammad b. Dāwūd al-Iṣfahānī (d. 297/909); S: ed. I. al-Sāmarrāʾī, al-Zarqāʾ: al-Manār, 1985; VQ: 3; Ṣ; C: adab/poetry – love literature – anthology. (cf. nos. 1532, 1552, 1560)

(543) Z/8 253b/7 *al-Zahr wa-al-ṭuraf wa-al-nūr wa-al-tuḥaf – Flower of Curiosities and Light of Rarities*; probably A: Ibrāhīm b. ʿAlī al-Ḥuṣrī al-Qayrawānī (d. 413/1022) who authored *Nūr al-ṭarf wa-nūr al-ẓarf* ('K. al-nurayn', cf. no. 1362); S: ed. L. ʿA. Abū Ṣāliḥ, Beirut: MR, 1996; VQ: 1–40; Ṣ; C: adab – anthology.

(544) Z/9 253b/7 *al-Zīj al-zāhir – The Brilliant Astronomical Handbook*; A: attr. Muḥammad b. Muḥammad al-Būzjānī (d. c.388/998); S: Ḥājjī Khalīfa, *Kashf*, II, 968 mentions this title together with al-Būzjānī's *al-Zīj al-shāmil*, which is also known as *al-Zīj al-wāḍiḥ* (EI^3, U. Rebstock, 'Abū l-Wafāʾ al-Būzjānī'); VQ: 1–39; Ṣ; C: astronomy.

(545) Z/15 253b/8 *Zīnat al-dahr – Adornment of Time*; A: Saʿd b. ʿAlī b. al-Qāsim al-Ḥaẓīrī Dallāl al-Kutub (d. 568/1172); S: MU, III, 1350; NC: 2; VQ: 1; Ṣ; C: poetry – anthology – Saljūq.

(546) Z/15 253b/8 *Zajr al-nābiḥ – Chiding the Barking Dog*; A: Abū al-ʿAlāʾ al-Maʿarrī (d. 449/1058); S: ed. A. al-Ṭarābulusī, Damascus: MLA, 1965; defending his own poetry; VQ: 1; Ṣ; C: poetry – Ḥamdānid/Mirdāsid.

(547) S/1 253b/9 *Sīrat al-Nabī ᶜalayhi al-salām – The Life of the Prophet (may peace be upon him)*; possibly A: Ibn Isḥāq (d. 150/767)/Ibn Hishām (d. 218/833 or 213/828); S: ed. M.Ḥ. Allāh, *Sīrat Ibn Isḥāq al-musammā bi-Kitāb al-mubtadaᵓ wa-al-mabᶜath wa-al-maghāzī*, Rabat 1976; NC: 3; FI: '*mujalladān*'/'*two bound volumes*' *[first copy]*; VQ: 6; C: biography of the Prophet (*sīra*). (cf. no. 575)

(548) S/1 253b/9 *Siyar al-salaf al-ṣāliḥ*[80] – *Biographies of the Pious Predecessors*; this is most likely the *Siyar al-salaf al-ṣāliḥīn* by A: Ismāᶜīl b. Muḥammad al-Iṣfahānī (d. 535/1140–1); S: ed. K. b. Ḥilmī b. Farḥāt b. Aḥmad, Riyad: Dār al-rāya, 1999; VQ: 1; Ṣ; C: biography – early Islam/ḥadīth.

(549) S/1 253b/10 *Sīrat ᶜUmar b. ᶜAbd al-ᶜAzīz – The Life of ᶜUmar b. ᶜAbd al-ᶜAzīz*; the work by Muḥammad b. Masᶜūd al-ᶜAyyāshī (d. early 4th/10th c.; IN, I/1, 687) is possible. However, in light of the many works by A: Ibn al-Jawzī (d. 597/1200) in the Ashrafiya library and the large number of manuscripts preserved of this work (e.g. Süleymaniye, Ayasofya 3239, Ayasofya 3240/1, Ayasofya 3240/2, Reisülküttab 633/2) his authorship is more likely. S: ed. M. al-Khaṭīb, Cairo: Maṭbaᶜat al-Muᵓayyad, 1913; VQ: 1; Ṣ; C: biography – Umayyad.

(550) S/4 253b/10 *Sībawayh – Sībawayh['s Book]*; A: ᶜAmr b. ᶜUthmān Sībawayh (d. 180/796); S: ed. ᶜA.M. Hārūn, Cairo: DQa, 1968–77; FI: '*tāmm*'/'*complete [manuscript]*'; VQ: 1; Ṣ; C: grammar. (cf. no. 1408)

(551) S/4 253b/10 *Sirr al-adab – The Secret of Adab*; the *Sirr al-adab wa-sabk al-dhahab* by Aḥmad Ibn Burd al-Aṣghar (d. 445/1054; EI^{2}, H. Monés, 'Ibn Burd') is unlikely in this category as it is an anthology of his own oeuvre. Fitting category 4 this is most likely *Fiqh al-lugha wa-sirr al-ᶜarabīya* also known as *Sirr al-adab fī majārī kalām al-ᶜArab*. A: al-Thaᶜālibī (d. 429/1038); S: Orfali, 'Works', no. 7; VQ: 1; Ṣ; C: lexicography. (cf. nos. 958a, 1406)

(552) S/5 253b/11 *Sīrat Ṣalāḥ al-Dīn – The Life of Ṣalāḥ al-Dīn*; two main possibilities: 1) Bahāᵓ al-Dīn Yūsuf b. Rāfiᶜ Ibn Shaddād (d. 632/1235) (*al-Nawādir al-sulṭānīya*) or 2) al-Asᶜad b. Muhadhdhab Ibn Mammātī (d. 606/1209) (*Muntakhab*, no. 522); VQ: 2; Ṣ; C: biography – Ayyūbid.

(553) S/5 253b/11 *Sanā al-Barq al-Shāmī – The Clarity of The Syrian Bolt*; summary of *al-Barq al-Shāmī* by ᶜImād al-Dīn al-Kātib al-Iṣfahānī

(d. 597/1201); A: al-Fatḥ b. ᶜAlī al-Bundārī (d. after 623/1226); S: eds R. Şeşen and E. İhsanoğlu, Istanbul 2004; VQ: 2; C: history – Ayyūbid.

(554) S/6 253b/11 *al-Siyāsa* – *Politics*; A: pseudo-Aristotelian work; S: *Sirr al-asrār: al-siyāsa wa-al-farāsa fī tadbīr al-riʾāsa*, ed. S.S. al-Aᶜwar, Beirut: Dār al-ᶜulūm al-ᶜarabīya, 1995; C: political thought – non-Muslim.

(555) S/6 253b/12 *Sīrat al-Iskandar* – *The Life of Alexander the Great*; anonymous; S: Doufikar-Aerts, *Alexander Magnus Arabicus*, 195–277; VQ: 1; Ṣ; C: biography – popular.

(556) S/6 253b/12 *Siqṭ al-zand* – *Spark of the Blazing Stick*; Scr('*bi-khaṭṭ*'): probably Yaḥyā b. ᶜAlī al-Khaṭīb al-Tibrīzī (d. 502/1109) who wrote a commentary on this work (cf. no. 639); A: Abū al-ᶜAlāʾ al-Maᶜarrī (d. 449/1058); S: ed. al-S. ᶜIbāda, Cairo: MMA, 2003; C: poetry – Ḥamdānid/Mirdāsid. (cf. no. 566)

(557a) S/6 253b/12-13 *al-Sabᶜ al-ṭiwāl wa-tatimmat al-ᶜashar* – *The Seven Long Poems and the Completion to Ten*; the *muᶜallaqāt* collection of pre-Islamic Arabic poems; Scr('*ākhirayhā bi-khaṭṭihi ayḍan*'/'*the two last [qaṣīdas] are also in his hand*'): referring to the previous entry's scribe, Yaḥyā b. ᶜAlī al-Khaṭīb al-Tibrīzī (d. 502/1109); S: for the seven *muᶜallaqāt*-poems see al-Qurashī, *Jamharat*, 124–428; for those included in collections of ten see, for instance, Ḥusayn al-Zawzanī (d. 486/1093), *Sharḥ al-Muᶜallaqāt al-ᶜashar*, Damascus: Raslān, 2007; VQ: 1; Ṣ; C: poetry – anthology – pre-Islamic.

(557b) 253b/13 second manuscript as above except Scr('*bi-khaṭṭ*'): Mawhūb b. Aḥmad Ibn al-Jawālīqī (d. 539/1144) (EI^{2}, H. Fleisch, 'al-Djawālīḳī'). C: poetry – anthology – pre-Islamic.

(558) S/7 253b/13–14 *Sulwān al-muṭāᶜ* – *The Ruler's Consolation [During the Hostility of Subjects]*; A: Muḥammad b. Muḥammad al-Ṣiqillī Ibn Ẓafar (d. 565/1169–70); S: *Sulwān al-muṭāᶜ fī ᶜudwān al-atbāᶜ*, ed. A.ᶜA. al-Buḥayrī, Cairo 1999; MS: Süleymaniye, Fatih 3930**; NC: 2; FI: '*nuskha thāniya fī al-thāmina*'/'*a second copy is in [category] eight*';[81] this work advises rulers on proper conduct and rule. It was probably placed in category 7 on account of the prominent role of material such as animal fables and princely characters from ancient Persian history. C: political thought – mirror for princes/adab.

(559) S/8 253b/14 *Sirāj al-mulūk – The Light for Kings*; A: Muḥammad b. al-Walīd al-Ṭurṭūshī (d. 520/1126?); S: ed. J. al-Bayātī, London 1990; MS: Süleymaniye, Ayasofya 1850**; NC: 3; VQ: 2; C: political thought – mirror for princes. (cf. no. 1571)

(560) S/8 253b/14–15 *al-Sulṭān – The Ruler*; part of the author's *ᶜUyūn al-akhbār*; A: ᶜAbd Allāh b. Muslim al-Dīnawarī Ibn Qutayba (d. 276/889); S: eds M.M. Qamīḥa and Y.ᶜA. Ṭawīl, *ᶜUyūn al-akhbār*, Beirut: DKI, 1985; MS: Süleymaniye, Fazıl Ahmed Paşa 1344** ('*Kitāb ᶜUyūn al-akhbār wa-huwa kitāb al-sulṭān*'); VQ: 1; Ṣ; C: political thought.

(561) S/8 253b/15 *al-Siyāsa – [Communal] Governance*; A: Muḥammad b. Muḥammad al-Fārābī (d. 339/950); S: *al-Siyāsa al-madanīya*, ed. M.F. al-Jabr, Damascus: DY, 2006; VQ: 1; Ṣ; C: political thought.

(562) S/8 253b/15 *Siyāsat al-mamālik wa-al-duwal – Ruling Provinces and Realms*; no such title is identifiable. VQ: 1; Ṣ; C: political thought.

(563) S/8 253b/16 *al-Sīrat al-Hubayrīya – The Life of Ibn Hubayra*; on the ᶜAbbasid vizier Yaḥyā b. Muḥammad Ibn Hubayra (d. 560/1165); A: ᶜUbayd Allāh b. ᶜAlī Ibn al-Māristānī (d. 599/1203); S: Abū Shāma, *al-Mudhayyal*, I, 129; VQ: 1; Ṣ; C: biography – ᶜAbbāsid.

(564) S/8 253b/16 *Safar al-mulūk – The Travel of Kings*; probably the *K. Zād safar al-mulūk: fī al-safar wa-madḥihi wa-dhammihi wa-maḥāsin al-akhlāq fīhi*; A: al-Thaᶜālibī (d. 429/1038); S: eds R. Baᶜlbākī and B. Orfali, Beirut: DOI, 2011; C: political thought – mirror for princes/adab.

(565) S/8 253b/16 *Sīrat Aḥmad b. Ṭūlūn – The Life of Aḥmad b. Ṭūlūn*; the Egyptian governor and ruler, d. 270/884; two possibilities: 1) ᶜAbd Allāh b. Muḥammad al-Balawī (fl. 4th/10th c.) (ed. M. Kurd ᶜAlī, Damascus: al-Maktaba al-ᶜarabīya, 1939) or 2) Aḥmad b. Yūsuf Ibn al-Dāya (d. 340/951?) (not extant, incorporated into *al-Mughrib fī ḥula al-Maghrib* by ᶜAlī b. Mūsā al-Maghribī (d. 685/1286) (ed. Sh. Dayf, Cairo: DM, 1953–5); NC: 3; VQ: 1; Ṣ; C: biography – Ṭūlūnid. (cf. no. 1466)

(566) S/11 253b/17 *Siqṭ al-zand – Spark of the Blazing Stick*; A: Abū al-ᶜAlāᵓ al-Maᶜarrī (d. 449/1058); S: ed. al-S. ᶜIbāda, Cairo: MMA, 2003; MS: Süleymaniye, Ayasofya 3767/3 (fols. 58a–146b)**; NC: 8; VQ: 1–39; Ṣ; C: poetry – Ḥamdānid/Mirdāsid. (cf. no. 556)

(567) S/13 253b/17-254a/1 *al-Sab^c al-mu^callaqāt – The Seven Suspended Ones*; Scr(*'bi-khaṭṭ'*): ^cAlī b. Ismā^cīl Ibn Sīda (d. 458/1066) (IKH, III, 330); S: al-Qurashī, *Jamharat*, 124–428; VQ: 1; Ṣ; C: poetry – anthology – pre-Islamic. (cf. nos. 569, 852, 1230m, 1686)

(568) S/13 254a/1 *al-Sab^c al-mu^callaqāt sharḥ Ibn al-Anbārī – The Seven Suspended Ones, Ibn al-Anbārī's Commentary*; A: Ibn al-Anbārī (d. 328/940); S: ed. ^cA.M. Hārūn, Cairo: DM, 1963; C: poetry – commentary – anthology – pre-Islamic.

(569) S/13 254a/1-2 *al-Sab^c al-mu^callaqāt – The Seven Suspended Ones*; S: al-Qurashī, *Jamharat*, 124–428; FI: *'munakkata'/'with vowel marks'*; VQ: 1; Ṣ; C: poetry – anthology – pre-Islamic. (cf. nos. 567, 852, 1230m, 1686)

(570) S/13 254a/2 *Saqīṭ al-durar – Falling Pearls [and Plucked Flowers]*; lost work on poetry of al-Mu^ctamid Ibn al-^cAbbād (d. 487/1095) (ruler of Seville); A: Muḥammad b. ^cĪsā Ibn al-Labbāna (d. 507/1113); S: al-Ziriklī, *al-A^clām*, VII, 214: *Saqīṭ al-durar wa-laqīṭ al-zahr*; VQ: 1; Ṣ; C: poetry – Andalusian.

(571) S/15 254a/2 *Siḥr al-balāgha – The Enchantment of Rhetoric*; A: al-Tha^cālibī (d. 429/1038); S: ed. ^cA. al-Ḥūfī, Beirut: DKI, 1984; MS: Süleymaniye, Fazıl Ahmed Paşa 1283***; VQ: 1; Ṣ; C: rhetoric.

(572) S/15 254a/3 *Subuḥāt al-Jawhar – Al-Jawhar's Additional Prayers*; no such title is identifiable. It may refer to prayers drawn from a book entitled *al-Jawhar* or to the Fatimid general Jawhar al-Ṣiqillī (d. 381/992). VQ: 1–44; Ṣ; C: prayer book?

(573) S/3s 254a/3 *Sariqāt al-Naḥwī min al-shu^carā^ʾ – Plagiarisms from the Poets, by al-Naḥwī*; no such title is identifiable. It may refer to the work *Sariqāt al-Mutanabbī* that survives in a unique manuscript (ed. M. al-Ṭāhir ibn ^cĀshūr, Tunis: DTu, 1970), copied in 615/1218. In this manuscript the author identifies himself as 'Ibn Bassām al-Naḥwī' and another hand added that he is one and the same as ^cAlī b. Bassām al-Shantarīnī (d. 543/1147), the author of the *Dhakhīra* (cf. no. 456). However, owing to the title's syntax here in the catalogue it is also possible that 'al-Naḥwī', whoever he is, was himself the plagiarist, and that the author is not mentioned here. VQ: 51–47; Ṣ; C: poetry – commentary.

(574) S/5s 254a/4 *Sīrat al-Nabī ṣallā Allāh ᶜalayhi wa-sallam wa-dhikr al-ᶜashara raḍiya Allāh ᶜanhum – The Life of the Prophet (may God's blessing and peace be upon him) and Mentioning of the Ten [Companions Who Were Promised Paradise] (may God be pleased with them)*; probably A: ᶜAbd al-Ghanī b. ᶜAbd al-Wāḥid al-Maqdisī (d. 600/1203) who authored *Sīrat al-nabī wa-aṣḥābihi al-ᶜashara*; S: ed. H. al-Ḍinnāwī, Beirut: Dār al-jinān, 1986; VQ: 1; Ṣ; C: biography of the Prophet (*sīra*).[82]

(575a) S/5s 254a/4–5 *Sūd al-nasab al-zakī al-thamīn – The Illustrious and Precious Genealogy*; this is most likely another copy of the biography of the Prophet by Ibn Hishām. The title's wording can be explained by the incept that is found in some manuscripts: '*Sūd al-nasab al-zakī min Muḥammad [invocation] ilā Ādam [invocation]*' (e.g. *al-Sīra al-nabawīya*, Konya Mawlānā Museum 1166, see Ismāᶜīl, 'al-Makhṭūṭāt al-ᶜarabīya', 393). A: Ibn Isḥāq (d. 150/767) and Ibn Hishām (d. 218/833 or 213/828); S: ed. M.Ḥ. Allāh, *Sīrat Ibn Isḥāq al-musammā bi-Kitāb al-mubtadaᵓ wa-al-mabᶜath wa-al-maghāzī*, Rabat 1976; C: biography of the Prophet (*sīra*). (cf. no. 547)

(575b) 254a/5 *wa-Qiṣṣat ᶜĀᵓisha maᶜa Muᶜāwiya – The Tale of ᶜĀᵓisha and Muᶜāwiya*; no such title is identifiable. Most likely this is a short extract on the meeting between ᶜĀᵓisha and Muᶜāwiya in Medina after the latter's execution of Ḥujr b. ᶜAdī al-Kindī (for example, in Morony (tr.): *History of al-Ṭabarī*, XVIII, 153–4). Al-Suhaylī's 6th-/12th-c. commentary on the Prophet's biography by Ibn Isḥāq/Ibn Hishām refers to this meeting (*al-Rawḍ al-unuf*, ed. ᶜA. al-Wakīl, VI, 191; cf. no. 465) and may explain why the text was included in this multiple-text manuscript. VQ: 1–47; Ṣ; C: history – early Islamic.

(576) Sh/2 254a/5–6 *al-Shihāb – The Flame*; the name of the author given in the catalogue most likely reads 'F/q-f/q-āᶜī'. However, no title by an author carrying such a name (such as the Damascene courtier (*sharabdār*) and poet Muḥammad b. Ghāzī al-Fuqqāᶜī, d. 629/1232, TI, 621–30, p. 375) is identifiable, which is surprising as the work was so popular that it was held in five copies. As the work is placed in category 2, which has the majority of *ḥadīth* collections, it is thus likely that the intended author is rather A: Muḥammad b. Salāma al-Quḍāᶜī (d. 454/1062) who authored the *ḥadīth* collection

al-Shihāb or *Shihāb al-akhbār*. S: ed. Ḥ. al-Salafī, Beirut: MR, 1985; NC: 5; VQ: 1; Ṣ; C: ḥadīth – collection.

(577) Sh/2 254a/6 *al-Shifā᾿ bi-taᶜrīf ḥuqūq al-Muṣṭafā* – *The Cure by Knowing the Chosen One's Rights*; A: ᶜIyāḍ b. Mūsā al-Yaḥṣubī (d. 544/1149); S: ed. ᶜA.M. Amīn, Beirut: DKI, 2000; VQ: 2; C: Prophet Muḥammad – devotional.

(578) Sh/2 254a/6–7 *Sharaf al-Nabī ṣallā Allāh ᶜalayhi wa-sallam wa-ahl baytihi* – *The Prophet's and His Family's Nobility (may God's blessing and peace be upon him)*; A: ᶜAbd al-Malik b. Muḥammad al-Khargūshī (d. 406/1015 or 407/1016), the author of *Sharaf al-Muṣṭafā*, which is repeatedly cited in subsequent literature as *Sharaf al-Nabī* (e.g. al-Sha᾿mī, *Subul*, VII, 130); S: Abd Al-Rahman, *Sharaf Al-Mustafa*; VQ: 1; Ṣ; C: Prophet Muḥammad – devotional?

(579) Sh/3 254a/7 *Sharḥ* – *Commentary [on the Problematic Traditions]*; A: Aḥmad b. Muḥammad al-Ṭaḥāwī (d. 321/933); S: *Sharḥ mushkil al-āthār*, ed. Sh. al-Arnā᾿ūṭ, Beirut: MR, 1994; MS: Süleymaniye, Ayasofya 1202**; VQ: 2; C: ḥadīth – study of.

(580) Sh/4 254a/7-8 *Sharḥ al-lumaᶜ* – *Commentary on the Lumaᶜ*; referring to the work by Abū al-Fatḥ Ibn Jinnī (d. 392/1002); A: al-Qāsim b. Muḥammad Ibn Mubāshir al-Wāsiṭī (fl. 5th/11th c.); S: ed. R.ᶜU. Muḥammad, Cairo: MK, 2000; NC: 2; VQ: 1; C: grammar. (cf. no. 1308c)

(581) Sh/4 254a/8 *Sharḥ muqaddimat al-Jarmī* – *Commentary on al-Jarmī's Introduction*; referring to the work by Ṣāliḥ b. Isḥāq al-Jarmī (d. 225/839) (cf. no. 957); A: two possibilities: 1) ᶜAlī b. ᶜUbayd Allāh al-Daqīqī (d. 415/1024) (al-Ziriklī, *al-Aᶜlām*, V, 124 '*Sharḥ al-Jarmī*') or 2) ᶜAbd Allāh b. Jaᶜfar Ibn Durustawayh (d. 346/957) (IKH, II, 44: '*tafsīr kitāb al-Jarmī*'); C: grammar.

(582) Sh/4 254a/8 *Sharḥ al-durūs* – *Commentary on the Lessons*; possibly a commentary on the author's own work; A: Saᶜīd b. al-Mubārak Ibn al-Dahhān (d. 569/1174); S: IKH, II, 382: '*al-Durūs fī al-naḥw*'; VQ: 1; Ṣ; C: grammar. (cf. no. 1307e)

(583) Sh/4 254a/9 *Sharḥ abyāt Iṣlāḥ al-manṭiq* – *Commentary on the Verses Cited in Iṣlāḥ al-manṭiq*; referring to the work by Ibn al-Sikkīt (d. 244/858) (cf. no. 25); A: Yūsuf b. al-Ḥasan al-Sīrāfī (d. 385/995); S: ed. Y. M. al-

Sawwās, Damascus: al-Dār al-muttaḥida, 1992; MS: Süleymaniye, Fazıl Ahmed Paşa 1296*; VQ: 1–42; Ṣ; C: lexicography/poetry – commentary.

(584) Sh/4 254a/9 *al-Shāʾ wa-al-maᶜz – The Book of the Sheep and the Goat*; probably the *K. al-shāʾ* by A: ᶜAbd al-Malik b. Qurayb al-Aṣmaᶜī (d. 213/828?); S: ed. Ṣ. al-Tamīmī, Beirut: Dār Usāma, 1987; VQ: 1; Ṣ; C: lexicography.

(585) Sh/6 254a/9–10 *Shiᶜr al-Shanfarā – Al-Shanfarā's Poetry*; A: al-Shanfarā; S: *Dīwān*, in *Dīwān al-ṣaᶜālīk*, Beirut: DJ, 1992; NC: 4; C: poetry – pre-Islamic.

(586) Sh/6 254a/10 *Shiᶜr al-Mawj b. al-Zimmān – Al-Mawj b. al-Zimmān's Poetry*; A: al-Mawj b. al-Zimmān b. Qays b. Maᶜdī Karib al-Taghlibī; S: mentioned in MU, I, 78; NC: 12; C: poetry – early Islamic.

(587) Sh/6 254a/10 *Shiᶜr Salāma b. Jandal – Salāma b. Jandal's Poetry*; A: Salāma b. Jandal; S: ed. F. Qabāwa, Aleppo: al-Maktaba al-ᶜarabīya, 1968; NC: 15; C: poetry – pre-Islamic.

(588) Sh/6 254a/11 *Shiᶜr Ḥātim – Ḥātim's Poetry*; A: Ḥātim al-Ṭāʾī; S: ed. S. Jamāl, Cairo: MK, 1990; NC: 4; C: poetry – pre-Islamic.

(589) Sh/6 254a/11 *Shiᶜr al-Mutalammis – Al-Mutalammis' Poetry*; A: al-Mutalammis; S: ed. M. Altūnjī, Beirut: DṢ, 1998; MS: Süleymaniye, Ayasofya 3931/1 (fols. 1a–25b)**; NC: 7; C: poetry – pre-Islamic. (cf. no. 1213a)

(590) Sh/6 254a/11-12 *Shiᶜr ᶜUrwa b. Ḥizām – ᶜUrwa b. Ḥizām's Poetry*; A: ᶜUrwa b. Ḥizām (d. about 30/650 or some decades later); S: eds I. al-Sāmarrāʾī and A. Maṭlūb, Baghdad 1961; NC: 4; C: poetry – early Islamic.

(591) Sh/6 254a/12 *Shiᶜr ᶜUrwa b. al-Ward – ᶜUrwa b. al-Ward's Poetry*; A: ᶜUrwa b. al-Ward; S: ed. ᶜA. al-Mallūḥī, Damascus: WTh, 1966; C: poetry – pre-Islamic.

(592) Sh/6 254a/12 *Maqṣūrat Abī Ṣafwān – Abū Ṣafwān's Maqṣūra Poem*; A: Abū Ṣafwān al-Asadī; S: cited in Ismāᶜīl al-Qālī, *al-Amālī*, Beirut 1980, II, 237–40; authorship disputed; see GAS, II, 460; NC: 4; C: grammar. (cf. no. 973)

(593) Sh/6 254a/12 *Shiᶜr Abī Dahbal – Abū Dahbal's Poetry*; A: Wahb b. Zamᶜa Abū Dahbal al-Jumaḥī (d. after 96/715); S: ed. ᶜA. ᶜAbd al-Muḥsin, al-Najaf: Maṭbaᶜat al-thaqāfa, 1972; NC: 2; C: poetry – early Islamic.

(594) Sh/6 254a/13 *Shi^{c}r Muṣarrif b. al-A^{c}lam – Muṣarrif b. al-A^{c}lam's Poetry*; A: Muṣarrif b. al-A^{c}lam al-^{c}Āmirī; S: al-Ziriklī, *A^{c}lām*, VIII, 128; NC: 2; C: poetry – pre-Islamic.

(595a) Sh/6 254a/13 *Shi^{c}r Ṭahmān – Ṭahmān's Poetry*; A: Ṭahmān b. ^{c}Amr al-Kilābī (fl. late 1st/early 8th c.); S: ed. M.J. al-Mu^{c}aybid, Baghdad: MI, 1968; NC: 5; C: poetry – Umayyad.

(595b) 254a/13 Sixth copy of same work; Scr('*bi-khaṭṭ*'): Ibn al-Bawwāb (d. 413/1022); C: poetry – Umayyad.

(596) Sh/6 254a/14 *Shi^{c}r al-Ḥuṭayʾa – Al-Ḥuṭayʾa's Poetry*; A: Jarwal b. Aws al-Ḥuṭayʾa (d. after 41/661?); S: ed. N.A. Ṭāhā, Cairo: MBḤ, 1958; NC: 5; C: poetry – pre-Islamic/early Islamic. (cf. nos. 686, 1451)

(597) Sh/6 254a/14 *Shi^{c}r Qays al-Majnūn – Qays al-Majnūn's Poetry*; part of the Majnūn Laylā romance; S: *Dīwān Majnūn Laylā*, ed. A. Farrāj, Cairo: MMi, 1958; C: poetry – Umayyad. (cf. no. 1449)

(598) Sh/6 254a/14 *Shi^{c}r al-Khansāʾ – Al-Khansāʾ's Poetry*; A: Tumāḍir bt. ^{c}Amr al-Khansāʾ (d. 24/644?); S: ed. K. al-Bustānī, Beirut: DṢ, 1963; C: poetry – pre-Islamic/early Islamic. (cf. no. 679)

(599) Sh/6 254a/14-15 *Shi^{c}r ^{c}Umar b. Abī Rabī^{c}a – ^{c}Umar b. Abī Rabī^{c}a's Poetry*; A: ^{c}Umar (b. ^{c}Abd Allāh) b. Abī Rabī^{c}a (d. 93/712 or 103/721); S: ed. P. Schwarz, Leipzig 1901–9; NC: 5; C: poetry – Umayyad. (cf. no. 1215b)

(600) Sh/6 254a/15 *Shi^{c}r al-A^{c}shā Bāhila – Al-A^{c}shā Bāhila's Poetry*; A: ^{c}Āmir b. al-Ḥārith A^{c}shā Bāhila (d. early 7th c.?); S: ed. R. Geyer, *Gedichte von ʾAbû Baṣîr Maimûn ibn Qais al-ʾA^{c}šâ*, London 1928, 266–9; NC: 2; C: poetry – pre-Islamic.

(601) Sh/6 254a/15 *Shi^{c}r ^{c}Ulayya – ^{c}Ulayya's Poetry*; A: ^{c}Ulayya bt. al-Mahdī (d. 210/825); S: ed. R. Sim^{c}ān, *al-Shā^{c}ira ^{c}Ulayya bint al-Mahdī wa-dīwān shi^{c}rihā*, *al-Karmil* 5 (1984) 21–35, 6 (1985) 73–127; NC: 2; C: poetry – ^{c}Abbāsid.

(602) Sh/6 254a/15 *Shi^{c}r Suḥaym – Suḥaym's Poetry*; as the cataloguer further down (cf. no. 1332) employs 'Suḥaym' to unequivocally refer to A: Suḥaym ^{c}Abd Banī al-Ḥasḥās (d. 37/657–8) this is most likely the poet meant here (and not Suḥaym b. Wathīl, d. *c.*40/661; GAS, II, 202–3); S: *Dīwān*, ed. ^{c}A.

al-Maymanī, Cairo: DQ, 1950; NC: 2; C: poetry – pre-Islamic/early Islamic. (cf. nos. 972, 1332a)

(603) Sh/6 254a/16 *Shi^{c}r ^{c}Abd Allāh b. Rawāḥa – ^{c}Abd Allāh b. Rawāḥa's Poetry*; A: ^{c}Abd Allāh b. Rawāḥa (d. 8/629); S: EI^{3}, S. Mirza, '^{c}Abdallāh b. Rawāḥa'; C: poetry – pre-Islamic/early Islamic.

(604) Sh/6 254a/16 *Shi^{c}r Abī al-Hindī – Abū al-Hindī's Poetry*; A: ^{c}Abd Allāh (?) Abū al-Hindī (fl. 130/747?); S: ed. ^{c}A. al-Jubūrī, Najaf: al-Nu^{c}mān, 1969; C: poetry – Umayyad/^{c}Abbāsid.

(605) Sh/6 254a/16 *Shi^{c}r ^{c}Amr b. Kulthūm – ^{c}Amr b. Kulthūm's Poetry*; A: ^{c}Amr b. Kulthūm[83]; S: ed. F. Krenkow, Beirut: MKa, 1922; C: poetry – pre-Islamic.

(606) Sh/6 254a/16–17 *Shi^{c}r Tawba – Tawba's Poetry*; A: Tawba b. al-Ḥumayyir (d. 55/674?); S: ed. Kh.I. al-^{c}Aṭīya, Baghdad: MI, 1968; MS: Süleymaniye, Fatih 4189**; NC: 2; C: poetry – early Islamic.

(607) Sh/6 254a/17 *Shi^{c}r Khalīfa – Khalīfa's Poetry*; A: Khalīfa b. ^{c}Āmir Dhū al-Khiraq; S: GAS, II, 195; this may be his lost *K. Banī Ṭuhayya* mentioned by the 4th-/10th-c. author al-Āmidī, *al-Mu$^{\circ}$talif*, 139. The interlinear note right on top of this entry seems to be an addition to the name in the form of 'B/T/Th/N/Y-l-b/t/th/n/y-^{c}/gh b.'. Yet no poet with any of the possible variants is identifiable and the cataloguer probably misread this obscure poet's name. The fact that not a single diacritical mark is used for this insertion, although marks are reasonably well used in this section of the catalogue, shows the cataloguer's incertitude. VQ: 1; C: poetry – pre-Islamic.

(608) Sh/6 254a/17 *Shi^{c}r ^{c}Alqama b. ^{c}Abada – ^{c}Alqama b. ^{c}Abada's Poetry*; A: ^{c}Alqama b. ^{c}Abada al-Faḥl; S: eds L. al-Saqqāl and D. al-Khaṭīb, Aleppo: DKiA, 1969; C: poetry – pre-Islamic. (cf. no. 1450)

(609) Sh/6 254a/17 *Shi^{c}r ^{c}Antara – ^{c}Antara's Poetry*; probably A: ^{c}Antara b. Shaddād; S: ed. W. Ahlwardt, London 1870; C: poetry – pre-Islamic.

(610) Sh/6 254a/17–254b/1 *Shi^{c}r Qa^{c}nab – Qa^{c}nab's Poetry*; A: Qa^{c}nab b. Ḍamra b. Umm Ṣāḥib al-Ghaṭafānī (fl. 86/705); S: Muḥammad Ibn Ḥabīb, *Man nusiba ilā ummihi min al-shu^{c}arā$^{\circ}$*, *Nawādir al-makhṭūṭāt* 3, ed. ^{c}A. Hārūn, Cairo 1951; NC: 3, C: poetry – Umayyad.

(611) Sh/6 254b/1 *Shiʿr al-Baʿīth – Al-Baʿīth's Poetry*; A: Khidāsh b. Bishr al-Mujāshiʿī al-Baʿīth (fl. Umayyad period); S: GAS, II, 363–4; C: poetry – Umayyad.

(612) Sh/6 254b/1 *Shiʿr Ṭufayl – Ṭufayl's Poetry*; A: Ṭufayl b. ʿAwf/Kaʿb al-Ghanawī; S: ed. M.ʿA. Aḥmad, Beirut: DKJ, 1968; C: poetry – pre-Islamic.

(613) Sh/6 254b/1 *Shiʿr ʿĀmir b. al-Ṭufayl – ʿĀmir b. al-Ṭufayl's Poetry*; A: ʿĀmir b. al-Ṭufayl; S: ed. Ch. Lyall, Leiden 1913; C: poetry – pre-Islamic/early Islamic.

(614) Sh/6 254b/2 *Shiʿr Imruʾ al-Qays – Imruʾ al-Qays' Poetry*; probably A: Imruʾ al-Qays b. Ḥujr al-Kindī; S: ed. M.A. Ibrāhīm, Cairo: DM, 1958; NC: 3; C: poetry – pre-Islamic.

(615) Sh/6 254b/2 *Shiʿr al-Ṣimma al-Qushayrī*[84] *– Al-Ṣimma al-Qushayrī's Poetry*; A: al-Ṣimma b. ʿAbd Allāh al-Qushayrī (d. *c.*90/708); S: GAS, II, 342–3; Ṣ; C: poetry – Umayyad. (cf. no. 114)

(616) Sh/6 254b/2 *Shiʿr Abī Ḥayya al-Numayrī – Abū Ḥayya al-Numayrī's Poetry*; A: al-Haytham b. al-Rabīʿ Abū Ḥayya al-Numayrī (d. between 158/775 and 180/796); S: Y. al-Jubūrī, *Shiʿr Abī Ḥayya al-Numayrī*, Damascus: WTh, 1975; C: poetry – Umayyad. (cf. no 1315c)

(617) Sh/6 254b/3 *Shiʿr ʿAlī b. Abī Ṭālib karrama Allāh wajhahu – ʿAlī b. Abī Ṭālib's Poetry (may God honour his countenance)*; A: ʿAlī b. Abī Ṭālib, the fourth Caliph and first Shiʿite *imām* (d. 40/661); possibly extracted from or similar to S: Muḥammad b. al-Ḥusayn al-Kaydarī (or al-Kaydharī) (fl. 576/1180), *Dīwān Imām ʿAlī/Anwār al-ʿuqūl min ashʿār waṣī al-rasūl*, ed. K. S. al-Jubūrī, Beirut: Dār maḥajjat al-bayḍāʾ, 1999; VQ: 1; Ṣ; C: poetry – early Islamic.

(618) Sh/6 254b/3 *Shiʿr al-Ḥasan wa-al-Ḥusayn raḍiya Allāh ʿanhumā – Al-Ḥasan's and al-Ḥusayn's Poetry (may God be pleased with them)*; A: al-Ḥasan b. ʿAlī b. Abī Ṭālib, the second Shiʿite *imām* (d. 49/669–70?)/al-Ḥusayn b. ʿAlī b. Abī Ṭālib, the third Shiʿite *imām* (d. 61/680); S: M.Sh. Ḥassānī/Ḥ. al-Zarqānī, *Dīwān al-imām al-Ḥusayn*, Beirut: al-Hilāl, 2006; C: poetry – early Islamic.

(619) Sh/6 254b/4 *Shiʿr Kaʿb b. Saʿd – Kaʿb b. Saʿd's Poetry*; A: Kaʿb b. Saʿd; S: GAS, II, 226; Ṣ; C: poetry – pre-Islamic/early Islamic?

(620) Sh/6 254b/4 *Shi^{c}r al-Ashhab b. Rumayla – Al-Ashhab b. Rumayla's Poetry*; A: al-Ashhab b. Rumayla al-Nahshalī (fl. mid-1st/7th c.); S: Kilpatrick, *Making*, 327; VQ: 1; Ṣ; C: poetry – Umayyad.

(621) Sh/6 254b/4 *Shi^{c}r Muḥammad b. ^{c}Umar al-^{c}Anbarī – Muḥammad b. ^{c}Umar al-^{c}Anbarī's Poetry*; A: Muḥammad b. ^{c}Umar al-^{c}Anbarī (d. 412/1021); S: al-Ziriklī, *A^{c}lām*, VII, 202; VQ: 1; Ṣ; C: poetry.

(622) Sh/6 254b/5 *Shi^{c}r A^{c}shā Qays – A^{c}shā Qays' Poetry*; A: Maymūn b. Qays al-A^{c}shā (d. after 625); S: EI^{3}, B. Jockers, 'al-A^{c}shā'; Ṣ; C: poetry – early Islamic.

(623) Sh/6 254b/5 *Shi^{c}r al-Samawʾal – Al-Samawʾal's Poetry*; A: al-Samawʾal b. ^{c}Ādiyā (fl. 6th c. CE); S: ed. L. Cheikho, *Diwan d'as-Samaouʾal d'après la récension de Niftawaihi*, Beirut 1909 and M.Ḥ. Āl Yāsīn, Baghdad 1955; Ṣ; C: poetry – pre-Islamic.

(624) Sh/6 254b/5 *Shi^{c}r Jamīl b. Ma^{c}mar – Jamīl b. Ma^{c}mar's Poetry*; A: Jamīl b. Ma^{c}mar al-^{c}Udhrī (d. 82/701); S: *Dīwān*, ed. Ḥ. Naṣṣār, Cairo: Dār Miṣr, 1985; Jagonak, *Bild der Liebe*; C: poetry – early Islamic/love literature.

(625) Sh/6 254b/5 *Shi^{c}r Ziyād b. Munqidh – Ziyād b. Munqidh's Poetry*; A: Ziyād/al-Marrār b. Munqidh b. ^{c}Amr (fl. 96/715); S: GAS, II, 383; C: poetry – Umayyad.

(626) Sh/6 254b/6 *Shi^{c}r al-Ḥakam b. Ma^{c}mar – Al-Ḥakam b. Ma^{c}mar's Poetry*; A: al-Ḥakam b. Ma^{c}mar (fl. 2nd/8th c.); S: GAS, II, 443; C: poetry – early ^{c}Abbāsid.

(627) Sh/6 254b/6 *Shi^{c}r ^{c}Ubayd Allāh*[85] *b. Qays al-Ruqayyāt – ^{c}Ubayd Allāh b. Qays al-Ruqayyāt's Poetry*; A: ^{c}Ubayd Allāh b. Qays al-Ruqayyāt (d. 72/691); S: ed. ^{c}U.F. al-Ṭabbā^{c}, Beirut: DQa, 1995; C: poetry – Umayyad. (cf. no. 1705)

(628) Sh/6 254b/6 *Shi^{c}r Ka^{c}b b. al-Ashraf – Ka^{c}b b. al-Ashraf's Poetry*; A: Ka^{c}b b. al-Ashraf (d. 3/624?); S: GAS, II, 296; C: poetry – pre-Islamic/early Islamic.

(629) Sh/6 254b/6–7 *Shi^{c}r al-Ḥārith b. Ḥilliza – Al-Ḥārith b. Ḥilliza's Poetry*; A: al-Ḥārith b. Ḥilliza al-Yashkurī: S: ed. H. al-Ṭa^{cc}ān, Baghdad: MI, 1969; C: poetry – pre-Islamic.

(630) Sh/6 254b/7 *Shi^{c}r Abī Ḥizām al-^{c}Uqaylī – Abū Ḥizām al-^{c}Uqaylī's Poetry*; A: Abū Ḥizām Ghālib b. al-Ḥārith al-^{c}Uklī[86] (fl. 158/775); S: GAS, II, 628; C: poetry – ^{c}Abbāsid.

(631) Sh/6 254b/7 *Shi^{c}r Rāshid b. Shihāb – Rāshid b. Shihāb's Poetry*; A: Rāshid b. Shihāb; S: GAS, II, 160–1; C: poetry – pre-Islamic.

(632) Sh/6 254b/7–8 *Shi^{c}r al-Aqra^{c} b. Mu^{c}ādh – Al-Aqra^{c} b. Mu^{c}ādh's Poetry*; A: al-Ashja^{c} al-Aqra^{c} b. Mu^{c}ādh al-Qushayrī; S: ed. H. Nāji, in: *al-Mawrid*, 7/3 (1978) 187–200; GAS, II, 451; C: poetry – early ^{c}Abbāsid.

(633) Sh/6 254b/8 *Shi^{c}r Ja^{c}far b. ^{c}Ulba – Ja^{c}far b. ^{c}Ulba's Poetry*; A: Ja^{c}far b. ^{c}Ulba (d. 145/762?); S: GAS, II, 451; C: poetry – Umayyad/^{c}Abbāsid.

(634) Sh/6 254b/8 *Shi^{c}r Ibrāhīm al-Ṣūlī – Ibrāhīm al-Ṣūlī's Poetry*; A: Ibrāhīm b. al-^{c}Abbās al-Ṣūlī (d. 243/857); S: GAS, II, 578–80; C: poetry – ^{c}Abbāsid. (cf. no. 646)

(635) Sh/6 254b/8–9 *Shi^{c}r Ibrāhīm al-Ṣābi$^{\circ}$ – Ibrāhīm al-Ṣābi$^{\circ}$'s Poetry*; A: Ibrāhīm b. Hilāl al-Ṣābi$^{\circ}$ (d. 384/994); S: *Shi^{c}r Abī Isḥāq al-Ṣābi$^{\circ}$*, ed. M. Gharīb, Alexandria: Markaz al-Babāṭīn, 2010; C: poetry – Būyid. (cf. nos. 1042, 1305b)

(636) Sh/6 254b/9 *Shi^{c}r ^{c}Amr b. Aḥmar – ^{c}Amr b. Aḥmar's Poetry*; the MS clearly has '*^{c}Umar b. Aḥmad*', but no famous poet is known by this name. It is highly unlikely that it referred to ^{c}Umar b. Aḥmad Ibn al-^{c}Adīm (d. 660/1262). Although he was well known to the audience of the catalogue and was contemporaneous to it, he is not famous as a poet. The context of early poetry in this section implies rather that the cataloguer left out the final '*waw*' of '^{c}Amr' as he does elsewhere (cf. nos. 605, 684). A: ^{c}Amr b. Aḥmar Abū al-Khaṭṭāb al-Bāhilī; S: GAS, II, 195–6; C: poetry – early Islamic.

(637) Sh/6 254b/9 *Shi^{c}r Ḥassān b. Thābit – Ḥassān b. Thābit's Poetry*; A: Ḥassān b. Thābit b. Mundhir (d. 40/659?); S: ed. Ḥ. Ḥasanayn, Cairo: HMAK, 1974; C: poetry – pre-Islamic/early Islamic.

(638) Sh/6 254b/9–10 *Shi^{c}r Yazīd b. Mufarrigh – Yazīd b. Mufarrigh's Poetry*; A: Yazīd b. Ziyād Ibn Mufarrigh (d. 69/689); S: D. Sallūm, *Shi^{c}r Ibn Mufarrigh al-Ḥimyarī*, Baghdad: Maktabat al-Andalus, 1968; C: poetry – early Islamic.

(639) Sh/6 254b/10 *Sharḥ Siqṭ al-zand* – *The Commentary on Siqṭ al-zand*; referring to *Spark of the Blazing Stick* by al-Maᶜarrī (d. 449/1058); Scr(‘*bi-khaṭṭ*’) & A: Yaḥyā b. ᶜAlī al-Khaṭīb al-Tibrīzī (d. 502/1109); S: ed. M. al-Saqqā *et al.*, in: *Shurūḥ Siqṭ al-zand*, Cairo: DQ, 1945–9; FI: ‘*wa-qīla innahu bi-khaṭṭihi*’/‘*and it is said that it is in his hand*’; C: poetry – commentary.

(640) Sh/8 254b/10 *Shajarat al-ᶜaql* – *Tree of Reason*; the *ḥadīth*-related work by al-Walīd b. Aḥmad al-Zawzanī (d. 376/986) (quoted in later works such as al-Suyūṭī, *al-Lumaᶜ fī asbāb wurūd al-ḥadīth*, Beirut 1996, 83) is unlikely on account of the thematic category. This is arguably the work by the secretary, *adīb* and poet A: Sahl b. Hārūn b. Rāhawayh (d. 215/830); S: IN, I/2, 373; VQ: 1; Ṣ; C: adab?

(641) Sh/8 254b/11 *Sharḥ risālat Adab al-kātib* – *Commentary on the Treatise Adab al-kātib [The Secretary's Manual]*; this is possibly a work on the treatise by Ibn Qutayba (d. 276/889) that attracted eleven commentaries (Lecomte, *Ibn Qutayba*, 104–5). As he plays a prominent role in the library's stock, this may be the work by Mawhūb b. Aḥmad Ibn al-Jawālīqī (d. 539/1144). MS: Süleymaniye, Nuruosmaniye 3954*; VQ: 1; Ṣ; C: administrative handbook – manual for secretaries – commentary.

(642) Sh/8 254b/11 *Shāfī al-ghalīl fī maᶜrifat al-taʾwīl* – *Curing He Who Is Thirsty for Mastering Interpretation*; no such title is identifiable. The term ‘*taʾwīl*’ may indicate, especially in earlier periods, Koranic interpretation or divination. Yet it would be rather surprising to have such a title in the thematic category 8.

(643) Sh/11 254b/12 *Shiᶜr al-Bustī al-mujānis al-lafẓ bi-ikhtilāf al-maᶜnā* – *Al-Bustī's Poetry, Which Is Identical in Pronunciation but Different in Meaning*; A: ᶜAlī b. Muḥammad al-Bustī (d. 354/965); S: *Dīwān Abī al-Fatḥ al-Bustī*, ed. Sh. al-ᶜĀshūr, Damascus: DY, 2006; NC: 2; C: poetry – Ghaznawid.

(644) Sh/12 254b/12 *Shiᶜr al-Malik al-Afḍal* – *Al-Malik al-Afḍal's Poetry*; arguably the Ayyubid prince A: ᶜAlī b. Yūsuf Ṣalāḥ al-Dīn (d. 622/1225) whose poetry is cited by contemporaries such as Ibn Khallikān; S: IKH, III, 419–21; C: poetry – Ayyūbid.

(645) Sh/12 254b/13 *Sharḥ Dīwān Abī Tammām* – *The Commentary on Abū Tammām's Dīwān*; popular title with numerous possibilities (cf. GAS, II, 555–7); VQ: 2; Ṣ; C: poetry – commentary.

(646) Sh/12 254b/13 *Shi*ᶜ*r Ibrāhīm b. al-*ᶜ*Abbās al-Ṣūlī – Ibrāhīm b. al-*ᶜ*Abbās al-Ṣūlī's Poetry*; A: Ibrāhīm b. al-ᶜAbbās al-Ṣūlī (d. 243/857); S: GAS, II, 578–80; C: poetry – ᶜAbbāsid. (cf. no. 634)

(647) Sh/12 254b/13 *Shi*ᶜ*r al-Ṭirimmāḥ – Al-Ṭirimmāḥ's Poetry*; probably A: al-Ṭirimmāḥ b. Ḥakīm al-Ṭāʾī (d. 126/743?); S: ed. ᶜI. Ḥasan, Damascus: WTh, 1994; C: poetry – Umayyad.

(648) Sh/12 254b/13–14 *Shi*ᶜ*r al-Ballanūbī – Al-Ballanūbī's Poetry*; A: ᶜAlī b. ᶜAbd al-Raḥmān al-Ballanūbī al-Ṣiqillī (fl. early 6th/12th c.); S: ed. Ḥ. Nājī, Baghdad: Dār al-risāla, 1976; C: poetry – Fatimid.

(649) Sh/12 254b/14 *Shi*ᶜ*r Abī al-Jawāʾiz – Abū al-Jawāʾiz's Poetry*; A: Abū al-Jawāʾiz al-Ḥasan b. ᶜAlī al-Wāsiṭī (d. 460/1067–8); S: IKH, II, 111–13; C: poetry – Būyid.

(650) Sh/12 254b/14 *Shi*ᶜ*r Khālid b. Yazīd – Khālid b. Yazīd's Poetry*; A: Khālid b. Yazīd al-Kātib al-Tamīmī (d. 269/883?); S: ed. K. Ṣādir, Damascus: WTh, 2006; VQ: 1; Ṣ; C: poetry – ᶜAbbāsid.

(651) Sh/12 254b/14 *Shi*ᶜ*r al-*ᶜ*Ābid b. al-Ẓarīf al-Fāriqī – Al-*ᶜ*Ābid b. al-Ẓarīf al-Fāriqī's Poetry*; A: al-ᶜĀbid Abū al-Riḍā b. Manṣūr b. al-Ẓarīf al-Fāriqī (d. 430/1038–9); S: Ibn al-Najjār, *Dhayl*, XVII, 51 (name); Ibn al-Athīr, *al-Kāmil*, IX, 466 (poetry); C: poetry. (cf. no. 1289b)

(652) Sh/12 254b/15 *Shi*ᶜ*r al-adīb Ibn al-Labbāna – Ibn al-Labbāna's Poetry*; A: Muḥammad b. ᶜĪsā Ibn al-Labbāna (d. 507/1113); S: contemporaneous authors quote verses by this poet (IKH, V, 31; VI, 20 and 193); C: poetry – Andalusian.

(653) Sh/12 254b/15 *Shi*ᶜ*r* ᶜ*Aḍud al-Dawla Abī Shujā*ᶜ *–* ᶜ*Aḍud al-Dawla Abū Shujā*ᶜ*'s Poetry*; A: Buyid ruler ᶜAḍud al-Dawla Abū Shujāᶜ (d. 372/983); S: IKH, IV, 50–5; C: poetry – Būyid.

(654) Sh/12 254b/15 *Shi*ᶜ*r Rukn al-Dawla – Rukn al-Dawla's Poetry*; possibly the Buyid ruler A: al-Ḥasan Rukn al-Dawla (d. 366/976); C: poetry – Būyid.

(655) Sh/12 254b/16 *Shi*ᶜ*r Ẓāfir al-Ḥaddād – Ẓāfir al-Ḥaddād's Poetry*; A: Ẓāfir b. al-Qāsim al-Barqī al-Ḥaddād (d. 528–9/1134); S: *Dīwān*, ed. Ḥ. Naṣṣār, Cairo: MMi, 1969; C: poetry – Fatimid. (cf. no. 1182a)

(656) Sh/12 254b/16 *Shi*ᶜ*r al-wazīr Abī al-Qāsim – The Vizier Abū al-Qāsim's Poetry*; A: Abū al-Qāsim al-Ḥusayn al-Wazīr al-Maghribī (d. 418/1027); S:

I. ᶜAbbās, *al-Wazīr al-Maghribī, dirāsa fī sīratihī wa-adabihī maᶜa mā tabqā min āthārihī*, Amman: Dār al-Shurūq, 1988; C: poetry – Fatimid/ᶜAbbāsid/ᶜUqaylid/Marwānid.

(657) Sh/12 254b/16 *Shiᶜr al-wazīr Abī Shujāᶜ Muḥammad – The Vizier Abū Shujāᶜ Muḥammad's Poetry*; A: Abū Shujāᶜ Muḥammad b. al-Ḥusayn al-Rūdhrāwarī (d. 488/1095); S: contemporaneous authors quote his poetry (IKH, V, 136–7); C: poetry – ᶜAbbāsid.

(658) Sh/12 254b/17 *Shiᶜr al-Malik al-ᶜAzīz b. Jalāl al-Dawla – Al-Malik al-ᶜAzīz b. Jalāl al-Dawla's Poetry*; A: Buyid prince al-Malik al-ᶜAzīz b. Jalāl al-Dawla b. Buwayh (d. 441/1049); S: Ibn al-Athīr, *Kāmil*, IX, 561 '*shiᶜr ḥasan*'; C: poetry – Būyid. (cf. nos. 668, 1631)

(659) Sh/12 254b/17 *Shiᶜr Abī al-Faraj al-Waʾwāʾ – Abū al-Faraj al-Waʾwāʾ's Poetry*; A: Abū al-Faraj Muḥammad al-Waʾwāʾ al-Ghassānī (d. between 370/980–1 and 390/1000); S: ed. S. al-Dahhān, Damascus: MIA, 1950; C: poetry – Ḥamdānid.

(660) Sh/13 254b/18 *Shiᶜr al-Shahriyārī – Al-Shahriyārī's Poetry*; two main possibilities: 1) ᶜImādī al-Shahriyārī (d. 573/1177–8?; EI^2, M.Sh. Israeli, 'ᶜImādī') or 2) Shahryārī (d. after 552/1157; de Blois, *Persian Literature*, 535); L: Persian; VQ: 1; Ṣ; C: poetry – Ghaznawid/Saljūq.

(661) Sh/13 254b/18 *Shiᶜr al-Ḍaḥḥāk al-Alūsī – Al-Ḍaḥḥāk al-Alūsī's Poetry*; A: al-Ḍaḥḥāk b. Salmān Abū al-Azhar al-Alūsī (d. 563/1167–8); S: MU, IV, 1451–2; C: poetry.

(662) Sh/13 254b/18 *Shiᶜr al-wazīr Abī Muḥammad al-Muhallabī – The Vizier Abū Muḥammad al-Muhallabī's Poetry*; A: Abū Muḥammad al-Ḥasan b. Muḥammad al-Muhallabī al-Wazīr (d. 352/963); S: IKH, II, 124–7; C: poetry – Būyid.

(663) Sh/13 254b/19 *Shiᶜr Tāj al-Mulūk – Tāj al-Mulūk's Poetry*; A: Burid ruler Būrī b. Ayyūb Tāj al-Mulūk (d. 526/1132); S: ed. M.ᶜA. Sālim, Cairo: Hajar, 1988; C: poetry – Būrid.

(664) Sh/13 254b/19 *Shiᶜr al-Malik al-Muᶜaẓẓam – Al-Malik al-Muᶜaẓẓam's Poetry*; arguably A: ᶜĪsā b. al-Malik al-ᶜĀdil Sayf al-Dīn al-Malik al-Muᶜaẓẓam (d. 624/1227), al-Malik al-Ashraf's predecessor in Damascus who composed poetry, according to Ibn Khallikān; S: IKH, III, 494–6; C: poetry – Ayyūbid.

(665) Sh/13 254b/19 *Shi^{c}r Ibn Zaydūn al-^{c}Umānī* [87] – *Ibn Zaydūn al-^{c}Umānī's Poetry*; A: Aḥmad b. ^{c}Abd Allāh b. Aḥmad Ibn Zaydūn al-Wazīr (d. 463/1070); S: ed. K. al-Bustānī, Beirut: DṢ, 1960; C: poetry – Andalusian (^{c}Abbādid).

(666) Sh/13 255a/1 *Shi^{c}r A^{c}shā Taghlib – A^{c}shā Taghlib's Poetry*; A: Rabī^{c}a b. Yaḥyā A^{c}shā Taghlib (d. 92/710); S: EI^2 'al-A^{c}shā'; C: poetry – Umayyad, court.

(667) Sh/13 255a/1 *Shi^{c}r Sālim wa-^{c}Abd al-Raḥmān b.* [88] *Dāra – Sālim's and ^{c}Abd al-Raḥmān b. Dāra's Poetry*; A: Sālim Ibn Dāra (d. *c.*30/650) and ^{c}Abd al-Raḥmān b. Dāra (d. after 41/661); S: GAS, II, 238–9; C: poetry – early Islamic.

(668) Sh/13 255a/1–2 *Shi^{c}r al-Malik al-^{c}Azīz b. Buwayh – Al-Malik al-^{c}Azīz b. Buwayh's Poetry*; A: Buyid prince al-Malik al-^{c}Azīz b. Jalāl al-Dawla b. Buwayh (d. 441/1049); S: Ibn al-Athīr, *Kāmil*, IX, 561 '*shi^{c}r ḥasan*'; C: poetry – Būyid. (cf. nos. 658, 1631)

(669) Sh/15 255a/2 *Sharḥ al-Ḥamāsa – Commentary on the Ḥamāsa*; referring to Abū Tammām's work (cf. no. 335); A: Aḥmad b. Muḥammad al-Marzūqī (d. 421/1030); S: eds A. Amīn/^{c}A. Hārūn, Cairo: LTTN, 1951; MS: Süleymaniye, Fatih 3942 & 3943**; C: poetry – commentary – anthology. (cf. nos. 670, 671, 1526, 1557)

(670) Sh/15 255a/2 *Sharḥ al-Ḥamāsa – Commentary on the Ḥamāsa*; referring to Abū Tammām's work (cf. no. 335); A: Yaḥyā b. ^{c}Alī al-Khaṭīb al-Tibrīzī (d. 502/1109); S: ed. M.^{c}A. ^{c}Azzām, Cairo: DM, 1964–5; MS: Süleymaniye, Fatih 3946**; NC: 4; C: poetry – commentary – anthology. (cf. nos. 669, 671, 1526, 1557)

(671) Sh/15 255a/3 *Sharḥ al-Ḥamāsa – Commentary on the Ḥamāsa*; referring to Abū Tammām's work (cf. no. 335); A: Ḥusayn b. ^{c}Alī al-Namarī (d. 385/995–6); S: ed. ^{c}A.^{c}A. ^{c}Usaylān, *Ma^{c}ānī abyāt al-Ḥamāsa*, Cairo: MK, 1983; C: poetry – commentary – anthology. (cf. nos. 669, 670, 1526, 1557)

(672) Sh/15 255a/3 *Sharḥ al-Mufaḍḍalīyāt – Commentary on the Mufaḍḍalīyāt*; original work ascribed to al-Mufaḍḍal al-Ḍabbī (d. 164/780 or 170/786); popular title with several possibilities, among them Ibn al-Anbārī (d. 328/940) and Aḥmad al-Marzūqī (d. 421/1030) with a preference for A: Yaḥyā b. ^{c}Alī

al-Khaṭīb al-Tibrīzī (d. 502/1109) on account of his other commentaries in this section (cf. nos. 639, 670, 677) and MS: Süleymaniye, Fatih 3963*; S: GAS, II, 54; *Sharḥ ikhtiyārāt al-Mufaḍḍal*, ed. F. Qabāwa, Damascus: MLA, 1971; NC: 3; C: poetry – commentary – anthology – pre-Islamic.

(673) Sh/15 255a/3–4 *Sharḥ Siqṭ al-zand – The Commentary on Siqṭ al-zand*; referring to *Spark of the Blazing Stick* by al-Maᶜarrī (d. 449/1058); popular title with several possibilities, among them Yaḥyā al-Tibrīzī (d. 502/1109), Ibn al-Sīd al-Baṭalyawsī (521/1127) and Ṣadr al-Afāḍil al-Qāsim al-Khwārazmī (d. 617/1220); S: GAL, I, 255 and S, I, 452–3 (for the different commentaries preserved); ed. M. al-Saqqā *et al.*, *Shurūḥ Siqṭ al-zand*, Cairo: DQ, 1945–9; However, the surviving manuscript makes Yaḥyā al-Tibrīzī's authorship most likely. MS: Süleymaniye, Fatih 3961**; NC: 4; C: poetry – commentary. (cf. no. 639)

(674) Sh/15 255a/4 *Sharḥ al-muhimmāt min al-maqāmāt – Commentary on the Important Passages from the Maqāmāt [by al-Ḥarīrī]*; A: ᶜAbd Allāh b. al-Ḥusayn al-ᶜUkbarī (d. 566/1219); S: al-ᶜUkbarī authored a commentary on the *maqāmāt*, referred to as '*Sharḥ al-maqāmāt al-Ḥarīrīya*' (IKH, III, 100) or '*al-Muhimmāt fī sharḥ al-maqāmāt*' (e.g. King Faysal Centre for Research and Islamic Studies, Riyad, MS 2222-1-f); MS: Süleymaniye, Reisülküttab 852* (by al-ᶜUkbarī, but title page missing, copied in 607/1211 by ᶜAbd al-Raḥmān b. Isḥāq b. Mawhūb b. Aḥmad al-Jawālīqī); C: adab – commentary.

(675) Sh/15 255a/4 *Sharḥ al-Mutanabbī – The Commentary on al-Mutanabbī*; A: ᶜAlī b. Aḥmad al-Wāḥidī (d. 468/1076); S: ed. F. Dieterici, Berlin 1861; MS: Süleymaniye, Fatih 3959**; NC: 2; C: poetry – commentary.

(676) Sh/15 255a/4-5 *Sharḥ al-Duraydīya [fī al-maqṣūr wa-al-mamdūd] – Commentary on Ibn Durayd's Qaṣīda [on the Short and Long Alif]*; Ibn Durayd's *qaṣīda* is well represented in this library and attracted a high number of commentaries over the centuries. However, none of the known commentators (see overview in al-Lakhmī, *al-Fawāʾid al-Maḥṣūra*, 42–9) fits the *nisba* given here, 'al-Farrāʾ'. This could be one of the anonymous commentaries (see GAS, IX, 86), which would be here ascribed to a scholar with this *nisba* or – more likely – the cataloguer made a mistake here and confused a commentary on Ibn Durayd's work with *al-Maqṣūr wa-al-mamdūd* by A: Yaḥyā b. Ziyād

al-Farrāʾ (d. 200/822); S: IN, I/1, 200; C: grammar. (cf. nos. 384a, 384b, 1203b, 1230j, 1238g, 1268b, 1307b, 1313a, 1326b)

(677) Sh/15 255a/5 *Sharḥ al-qaṣāʾid al-ᶜashar – Commentary on the Ten Qaṣīdas*; A: Yaḥyā b. ᶜAlī al-Khaṭīb al-Tibrīzī (d. 502/1109); S: ed. F. al-Shaᶜār, Beirut: Muʾassasat al-maᶜārif, 2006; MS: Süleymaniye, Ayasofya 4095/1 (fols. 1a–110b)**; C: poetry – commentary – anthology – pre-Islamic. (cf. no. 876)

(678) Sh/15 255a/5 *Sharḥ muqaddimat shiᶜr Ibn Aflaḥ – Commentary on Ibn Aflaḥ's Introduction to Poetry*; no such title is identifiable. This work refers to ᶜAlī Ibn Aflaḥ (d. 535/1141) (ed. G.J. van Gelder, *Two Arabic Treatises on Stylistics*, Leiden 1987; cf. no. 1207b). C: poetry – commentary.

(679) Sh/15 255a/5–6 *Shiᶜr al-Khansāʾ wa-al-mujānis ᶜalā al-ḥurūf – Al-Khansāʾ's Poetry and Paronomasia Organised According to the Alphabet*; A: Tumāḍir bt. ᶜAmr al-Khansāʾ (d. 24/644?); S: ed. K. al-Bustānī, Beirut: DṢ, 1963; C: poetry – commentary – pre-Islamic/early Islamic. (cf. no. 598)

(680) Sh/1s 255a/6 *Shiᶜr Umayya Ibn Abī al-Ṣalt – Umayya Ibn Abī al-Ṣalt's Poetry*; A: Umayya Ibn Abī al-Ṣalt; S: EI[2], J.E. Montgomery, 'Umayya b. Abi 'l-Ṣalt'; alternatively, this entry could refer to Abū al-Ṣalt Umayya b. ᶜAbd al-ᶜAzīz b. Abī al-Ṣalt al-Andalusī (d. 529/1134), but the focus on pre-Islamic and early Islamic poetry in the preceding entry and the following entries makes this unlikely. C: poetry – pre-Islamic.

(681) Sh/1s 255a/6-7 *Shiᶜr Aws b. Ḥajar – Aws b. Ḥajar's Poetry*; A: Aws b. Ḥajar al-Tamīmī; S: ed. M.Y. Najm, Beirut: DṢ, 1960; C: poetry – pre-Islamic.

(682) Sh/1s 255a/7 *Shiᶜr Ṭarafa b. al-ᶜAbd – Ṭarafa b. al-ᶜAbd's Poetry*; A: Ṭarafa ᶜAmr b. al-ᶜAbd b. Sufyān; S: ed. D. al-Khaṭīb, Damascus: MLA, 1975; C: poetry – pre-Islamic. (cf. no. 1185a)

(683) Sh/1s 255a/7 *Shiᶜr Kuthayyir ᶜAzza – Kuthayyir ᶜAzza's Poetry*; A: Kuthayyir ᶜAzza = Kuthayyir b. ᶜAbd al-Raḥmān al-Mulaḥī (d. 105/723); S: ed. I. ᶜAbbās, Beirut: DTh, 1971; C: poetry – Umayyad. (cf. no. 1586)

(684) Sh/1s 255a/7 *Shiᶜr ᶜAmr b. Maᶜdīkarib – ᶜAmr b. Maᶜdīkarib's Poetry*; A: ᶜAmr b. Maᶜdīkarib al-Zubaydī (d. 21/642?);[89] S: H. al-Ṭaᶜᶜān, Baghdad: WTh, 1970; C: poetry – pre-Islamic/early Islamic.

(685) Sh/1s 255a/7-8 *Shi*ᶜ*r al-*ᶜ*Abdī – Al-*ᶜ*Abdī's Poetry*; several possible poets, chief among them, and most likely on account of the other pre-Islamic titles in this section, the pre-Islamic poets al-Muthaqqib al-ᶜAbdī and Ṭarafa b. al-ᶜAbd, who is also called al-ᶜAbdī (e.g. Aḥmad b. Muḥammad al-Marzūqī, *Sharḥ Dīwān al-Ḥamāsa*, eds A. Amin and ᶜA. Hārūn, Cairo: LTTN, 1951, II, 529), (cf. no. 682); C: poetry – pre-Islamic.

(686) Sh/3s 255a/8 *Shi*ᶜ*r al-Nābighā wa-al-Ḥuṭay*ʾ*a – Al-Nābighā's and al-Ḥuṭay*ʾ*a's Poetry*; probably A: al-Nābigha al-Jaᶜdī (d. 79/698–9?) rather than the pre-Islamic al-Nābigha al-Dhubyānī, as the second poet is also early Islamic; Jarwal b. Aws al-Ḥuṭayʾa (d. after 41/661?); S: al-Nābigha: ed. M. Nallino, Rome: Bardi, 1953; al-Ḥuṭayʾa: ed. N.A. Ṭāhā, Cairo: MBḤ, 1958; C: poetry – pre-Islamic/early Islamic. (al-Ḥuṭayʾa: cf. nos. 596, 1451)

(687) Sh/3s 255a/8-9 *Shakwā al-gharīb* ᶜ*an al-awṭān ilā* ᶜ*ulamā*ʾ *al-buldān – The Complaint of Exiles to the Scholars of the Lands*; A: ᶜAyn al-Quḍāt ᶜAbd Allāh (or Muḥammad) b. Abī Bakr al-Hamadhānī al-Mayānajī (d. 525/1131); S: Engl. tr. A.J. Arberry, *A Sufi Martyr. The Apologia of* ᶜ*Ain al-Quḍāṭ al-Hamadhānī*, London 1969; VQ: 45; C: sufism.

(688) Sh/3s 255a/9 *Shi*ᶜ*r al-Rammāḥ Ibn Mayyāda – Al-Rammāḥ Ibn Mayyāda's Poetry*; A: al-Rammāḥ b. Abrad/Yazīd Ibn Mayyāda al-Murrī (d. 136/754?); S: *Shi*ᶜ*r Ibn Mayyāda*, ed. Ḥ.J. Ḥaddād, Damascus: MLA, 1982; C: poetry – Bedouin. (cf. no. 1305a)

(689) Sh/5s 255a/9 *Shi*ᶜ*r al-Zibriqān b. Badr – Al-Zibriqān b. Badr's Poetry*; A: Ḥusayn al-Zibriqān b. Badr (d. after 41/661); S: ed. S.M. ᶜAbd al-Jābir, Beirut: MR, 1984; VQ: 1; Ṣ; C: poetry – early Islamic.

(690) Sh/5s 255a/10 *al-Shabāb – Youth*; probably poetry anthology by A: Muḥammad b. Yaḥyā al-Ṣūlī (d. 335/947) on the theme of youth (and age); S: IN, I/2, 465 '*al-Shubbān*'; C: poetry – anthology – ᶜAbbāsid.

(691) Sh/5s 255a/10 *Shi*ᶜ*r – Poetry*; anonymous work with generic title; FI: '*fī waraq ḥarīr maktūb bi-al-Kūfī* / *'on silk paper written in Kūfī script*'; C: poetry – anthology.

(692) Sh/5s 255a/10 *Shi*ᶜ*r Muslim b. al-Walīd Ṣarī*ᶜ *al-Ghawānī – Muslim b. al-Walīd Ṣarī*ᶜ *al-Ghawānī's Poetry*; A: Muslim b. al-Walīd Ṣarīᶜ al-Ghawānī

al-Anṣārī (d. 208/823); S: *Sharḥ dīwān Ṣarīᶜ al-Ghawānī*, ed. S. Dahhān, Cairo: DM, 1958; C: poetry – ᶜAbbāsid. (cf. no. 1641)

(693) Sh/6s 255a/11 *al-Shawārid – Linguistic Anomalies*; title with popular key word and thus several possibilities; placed in category no. 6 this is most probably a philological work such as the *K. al-Shawārid* (IN, I/1, 151) by Abū ᶜUbayda Maᶜmar b. al-Muthannā al-Taymī (d. between 207/822 and 213/828), *al-Shawārid fī al-rasāʾil* (IN, I/2, 432) by a certain Ibn ᶜAbdūs or *al-Shawārid fī al-lugha* (ed. ᶜA.ᶜA. al-Dūrī, Baghdad 1983) by al-Ḥasan b. Muḥammad al-Ṣaghānī (d. 650/1252). FI: '*ᶜatīq raththʼ/ʻold and worn-out [manuscript]*' (cf. no. 462 on '*atīq*'); C: lexicography?

(694) Sh/7s 255a/11 *Shiᶜr Taʾabbaṭa Sharran – Taʾabbaṭa Sharran's Poetry*; A: Taʾabbaṭa Sharran; S: ed. ᶜAlī Dh. Shākir, Beirut: DGI, 1984; C: poetry – pre-Islamic.

(695) Ṣ/1 255a/12 *Ṣaḥīḥ Muslim – Muslim's Sound [Collection]*; A: Muslim b. al-Ḥajjāj al-Nīsābūrī (d. 261/875); S: M.F. ᶜAbd al-Bāqī, Cairo: DIKA, 1955–6; NC: 8?[90]; C: ḥadīth – collection.

(696) Ṣ/1 255a/12 *Ṣaḥīḥ al-Bukhārī – Al-Bukhārī's Sound [Collection]*; A: Muḥammad b. Ismāᶜīl al-Bukhārī (d. 256/870); S: eds M. Khaṭīb and M.F. ᶜAbd al-Bāqī, Cairo: al-Salafīya, 1979; NC: 5; VQ: 14; Ṣ; C: ḥadīth – collection.

(697) Ṣ/1 255a/12 *Ṣiḥāḥ Razīn b. Muᶜāwiya – Razīn b. Muᶜāwiya's Sound Traditions*; A: Razīn b. Muᶜāwiya al-ᶜAbdarī (d. 524/1129 or 535/1140); S: EI^2, M. Fierro, 'Razīn b. Muᶜāwiya'; VQ: 3; Ṣ; C: ḥadīth – collection. (cf. no. 1435)

(698) Ṣ/4 255a/13 *Ṣiḥāḥ al-Jawharī – Al-Jawharī's Sound [Dictionary]*; Scr: al-Ḥasan al-Qaylawī (d. 633/1236; TI, 631–40, p. 145), a renowned scribe of Damascus and librarian of al-Malik al-Ashraf who copied this work for '*al-khizāna al-sulṭānīya al-malakīya al-Ashrafīya*' in 609/1212 (cf. Süleymaniye, Süleymaniye 1008, fol. 1a), whose copies of this work were famous (*Wāfī*, XII, 218), who appears elsewhere as scribe in this library (cf. no. 257, 533, 1253) and who was also involved in the transmission of other copies (cf. no. 807); A: Ismāᶜīl (b. Naṣr?) b. Ḥammād al-Jawharī (d. 398/1007–8); S: ed. A.ᶜA. ᶜAṭṭār, Cairo: DKiA, 1956; MS:

Süleymaniye, Süleymaniye 1007 & 1008***; NC: 2; C: lexicography. (cf. no. 1413)

(699) Ṣ/5 255a/13 *Ṣafwat al-ta'rīkh Ṣiffīn – The Quintessence of History, [The Passage on?] Ṣiffīn*; this summary of al-Ṭabarī was authored by A: ᶜAlī b. ᶜAbd al-ᶜAzīz al-Jurjānī (d. 392/1001–2?). S: Ibn Qāḍī Shuhbah, *Ṭabaqāt al-shāfiᶜīya*, I, 161; VQ: 1; Ṣ; C: history – early Islamic.

(700) Ṣ/8 255a/14 *al-Ṣadīq wa-al-ṣadāqa – The Friend and Friendship*; A: Abū Ḥayyān al-Tawḥīdī (d. 414/1023); S: ed. I. al-Kīlānī, Damascus: DF, 1964; NC: 2; C: adab.

(701) Ṣ/9 255a/14 *al-Ṣādiḥ wa-al-bāghim – The Singer and the Wailer*; A: Muḥammad b. Muḥammad al-ᶜAbbāsī Ibn al-Habbārīya (d. 509/1115–16?); S: ed. Ḥ. ᶜĀṣī, in: *Kashf al-asrār ᶜan ḥikam al-ṭuyūr wa-al-azhār*, Beirut: DMa, 1995; NC: 2; FI: '*muṣawwar*[an]'/'*illustrated*'; C: poetry/adab – anthology. (cf. nos. 705, 1288a)

(702) Ṣ/9 255a/15 *Ṣurradurr – Ṣurradurr*; A: Abū Manṣūr ᶜAlī b. al-Ḥasan Ibn al-Faḍl Ṣurradurr (d. 465/1074), probably extracts from his diwan; S: facs. ed. Cairo: DKM, 1995; FI: '*mujalladān*'/'*two bound volumes*'; C: poetry. (cf. nos. 414, 415)

(703) Ṣ/9 255a/15 *al-Ṣabāba wa-naᶜt al-kitāba – Arduous Love Concerning the Praise of Penmanship*; no such title is identifiable and the combination of *ṣabāba* and *kitāba* sounds quite unusual.

(704) Ṣ/10 255a/15 *Ṣifāt al-khayl – Characteristics of Horses*; no such title is identifiable. Placed in category 10 this may either be an unknown veterinary treatise or an extract from a lexicographical work such as *al-Khayl* by Abū ᶜUbayda Maᶜmar b. al-Muthannā al-Taymī (d. between 207/822 and 213/828) (ed. M.ᶜA. Aḥmad, Cairo: Maṭbaᶜat al-nahḍa al-ᶜarabīya, 1986), which contains material relevant for veterinary medicine, such as chapters on '*min ᶜuyūb al-khayl*'. C: veterinary medicine/lexicography?

(705) Ṣ/12 255a/16 *al-Ṣādiḥ wa-al-bāghim – The Singer and the Wailer*; A: Muḥammad b. Muḥammad al-ᶜAbbāsī Ibn al-Habbārīya (d. 509/1115–16?); S: ed. Ḥ. ᶜĀṣī, in: *Kashf al-asrār ᶜan ḥikam al-ṭuyūr wa-al-azhār*, Beirut: DMa, 1995; MS: Süleymaniye, Laleli 1873*; NC: 6; C: poetry/adab – anthology. (cf. nos. 701, 1288a)

(706) Ṣ/15 255a/16 *al-Ṣinaᶜatayn – [The Book of] the Two Crafts [Writing and Poetry]*; A: al-Ḥasan b. ᶜAbd Allāh b. Sahl al-ᶜAskarī (fl. 4th/10th c.); S: *Kitāb al-ṣināᶜatayn al-kitāba wa-al-shiᶜr*, eds ᶜA. al-Bijāwī and M.A. Ibrāhīm, Cairo: DIKA, 1952; MS: Süleymaniye, Fatih 3891***; NC: 2; C: rhetoric.

(707) Ṣ/4s 255a/17 *al-Ṣaḥīfa al-gharrā᾿ – The Most Illustrious Book*; A: revelations ascribed to the pre-Islamic Messenger Idrīs/Enoch; S: University of Beirut Library, MS 170, fols. 1–4; C: pre-Islamic revelation.

(708) Ṣ/4s 255a/17 *al-Ṣalāt ᶜalā al-Muṣṭafā ṣallā Allāh ᶜalayhi wa-sallam – The Prayer on The Chosen One (may God's blessing and peace be upon him)*; C: prayer book.

(709) Ṭ/2 255a/17–255b/1 *al-Ṭarīq al-sālim – [The Scholar's Reminder Concerning] the Right Path*; A: ᶜAbd al-Sayyid b. Muḥammad Ibn al-Ṣabbāgh (d. 477/1084); S: IKH, III, 217: '*Tadhkirat al-ᶜālim wa-al-ṭarīq al-sālim*'; MS: Süleymaniye, Ayasofya 2004***; VQ: 5; C: adab of scholars.

(710) Ṭ/2 255b/1 *al-Ṭarīq al-maslūk fī waᶜẓ al-mulūk – The Path to Be Followed when Admonishing Kings*; possibly A: Muḥammad b. Futūḥ al-Ḥumaydī (d. 488/1095) who authored *al-Dhahab al-masbūk fī waᶜẓ al-mulūk* (cf. no. 1269a); S: eds A. al-Ẓāhirī and ᶜA. ᶜUways, Riyad: DAK, 1982; However, Süleymaniye, Fatih 3502/1 (fols. 1a–37b) has an *al-Ṭarīq al-maslūk fī siyāsat al-mulūk* copied in Damascus in 764/1363, which may be a minor local work that had already existed in the previous century. C: political thought – adab of scholar.

(711) Ṭ/4 255b/1–2 *al-Ṭīb – The Perfume*; A: al-Mufaḍḍal b. Salama[91] (fl. 3rd/9th c.); S: GAL S, I, 181; IN, I/1, 224: '*Muṭayyab*'; placed in category 4 and taking into account the author's background in philological fields of knowledge this is most likely a work on grammar or lexicography. C: grammar/lexicography?

(712) Ṭ/5 255b/2 *Ṭarīq al-ṭalīq – Path of the Freed*; A: al-Asᶜad b. Muhadhdhab Ibn Mammātī (d. 606/1209); S: Ibn Faḍl Allāh al-ᶜUmarī, *Masālik al-abṣār fī mamālik al-amṣār*, eds K. al-Jubūrī and M. al-Najm, Beirut: DKI, 2010, XVIII, 68: '*kitābuhu al-musammā Ṭarīq al-ṭalīq*'; this work by Ibn Mammātī is lost and al-ᶜUmarī only quotes two lines of poetry, which do not give any hint of this book's possible content. As this work is placed in category 5 and

as Ibn Mammātī authored a versified biography of Saladin (cf. no. 552?) this is arguably another historical work. VQ: 1; Ṣ; C: history?

(713) Ṭ/8 255b/2 *Ṭayf al-khayāl – The Vision of the Beloved*; possibly A: ᶜAlī b. al-Ḥusayn al-Sharīf al-Murtaḍā (d. 436/1044); S: ed. H. al-Ṣayrafī, Cairo: DIKA, 1962; C: poetry – commentary.

(714) Ṭ/8 255b/2 *Ṭarāʾif al-akhbār – Choicest Reports*; possibly A: ᶜAlī b. al-Ḥusayn al-Masᶜūdī (d. 345/956) who authored *K. mazāhir al-akhbār wa-ṭarāʾif al-āthār fī akhbār Āl al-Nabī*; S: EI², Ch. Pellat, 'al-Masᶜūdī'; C: history – ᶜAlīd?

(715) Ṭ/15 255b/3 *Ṭabaqāt al-shuᶜarāʾ – The Generations of Poets*; Scr('*bi-khaṭṭ*'): Muḥammad b. Khazraj al-Dimashqī (d. 654/1256) who, according to *Wāfī*, III, 37, also made a splendid copy ('*nuskha ᶜaẓīma*') of the *Istīᶜāb* by Ibn ᶜAbd al-Barr (cf. no. 1392), which was in al-Ṣafadī's time still endowed in the Ashrafiya library; A: ᶜAbd Allāh Ibn al-Muᶜtazz (d. 296/908); S: ed. ᶜA.A. Farrāj, Cairo: DM, 1956; C: biographical dictionary – poets.

(716) Ṭ/15 255b/3 *al-Ẓarāʾif wa-al-laṭāʾif – Rarities and Subtleties*; if the title given in the catalogue, *al-Ṭarāʾif wa-al-laṭāʾif*, is correct this is either an anonymous collection of sayings or a key word title. If the latter is the case this probably refers to *Laṭāʾif al-Dhakhīra wa-ṭarāʾif al-Jazīra* by al-Asᶜad b. Muhadhdhab Ibn Mammātī (d. 606/1209), a summary of Ibn Bassām's (d. 543/1147) anthology of Andalusian writers and poets (ed. N. Mijallī, Cairo: HMAK, 2001; cf. no. 456). However, it is more likely that the cataloguer made a mistake here and that the letter *ẓāʾ* already starts at this point. The title is thus most probably *al-Ẓarāʾif wa-al-laṭāʾif* by A: al-Thaᶜālibī (d. 429/1038). S: This work was mainly transmitted in Abū Naṣr al-Maqdisī's recension *al-Laṭāʾif wa-al-ẓarāʾif*, ed. ᶜU. al-Asᶜad, *Laṭāʾif al-luṭf*, Beirut: Dār al-Masīra, 1980; C: adab – anthology. (cf. nos. 908, 958b, 1242a, 1707)

(717) Ẓ/? 255b/4 *al-Ẓaʾāt – The Letter ẓāʾ*; probably A: ᶜAlī b. Yūsuf Ibn al-Qifṭī (d. 646/1248) who authored a *K. al-ḍād wa-al-ẓāʾ*; S: MU, V, 2028; owing to the absence of the thematic numbering system in the *ẓāʾ*-section, the thematic classification of titles proves difficult for such 'borderline' cases. Works with this title could belong to the field of Koran recitation, focusing on possible misunderstandings in the Koran, or to the field of lexicography, discussing possible confusions between the letters *ḍāʾ* and *ẓāʾ*. On account

of the thematic profile of al-Qifṭī's works the latter is the more probable category in this case. VQ: 41; C: lexicography.

(718) Ẓ/? 255b/4 *al-Ẓāhirāt – Phaenomena*; A: Euclid/Uqlīdis; S: ed. ᶜA.M.H. Sulaymān, *Ẓāhirāt al-falak li-Uqlīdis bi-taḥrīr Naṣīr al-Dīn al-Ṭūsī*, Beirut: DNA, 1996; C: astronomy – spherical.

(719) Ẓ/? 255b/4–5 *al-Ẓarf wa-al-mutaẓarrifin – Refinement and People Displaying Refinement*; this title is ascribed to al-Māwardī but no such author, including the famous al-Māwardī (d. 450/1058), is identifiable as having authored such a work. There is also no passage from a work by this author that could have been extracted here. Most likely this is an erroneous ascription of one of the books on 'refined people', such as *K. al-Muwashshā/al-Ẓarf wa-al-ẓurafāʾ* by Ibn al-Washshāʾ (d. 325/936–7) (ed. R. Brünnow, Leiden 1886). C: adab.

(720) ᶜ/1 255b/5-6 *al-ᶜArāʾis fī al-majālis – The Brides of Sessions [on the Stories of the Prophets]*; A: al-Thaᶜlabī (d. 427/1035); S: *al-ᶜArāʾis fī al-majālis fī qiṣaṣ al-anbiyāʾ*, Engl. tr. Brinner, '*Lives of the Prophets*'; NC: 2[92]; C: qiṣaṣ al-anbiyāʾ. (cf. nos. 773, 1687)

(721) ᶜ/2 255b/6 *ᶜUlūm al-ḥadīth – Sciences of* ḥadīth; A: ᶜUthmān b. ᶜAbd al-Raḥmān Ibn al-Ṣalāḥ (d. 643/1245); S: ed. ᶜĀ. ᶜAbd al-Raḥmān, *Muqaddimat Ibn al-Ṣalāḥ*, Cairo: HMAK, 1974–6; MS: Süleymaniye, Ayasofya 448**; C: ḥadīth – study of.

(722) ᶜ/2 255b/6 *Min ᶜAwālī al-Furāwī – [Parts] of al-Furāwī's Elevated isnāds*; A: Muḥammad b. al-Faḍl al-Furāwī (d. 530/1136); S: IKH, IV, 290–1 (title not mentioned); C: ḥadīth – collection. (cf. no. 1394)

(723) ᶜ/2 255b/6–7 *ᶜAwārif al-maᶜārif – Benefits of Discernment*; A: Shihāb al-Dīn ᶜUmar al-Suhrawardī (d. 632/1234); S: Germ. tr. R. Gramlich, *Die Gaben der Erkenntnisse des ᶜUmar as-Suhrawardī*, Wiesbaden 1978; C: sufism – manual.

(724) ᶜ/3 255b/7 *al-ᶜUmda – The Pillar*; A: ᶜAbd al-Raḥmān b. Muḥammad al-Fūrānī (d. 461/1069); S: Ibn Qāḍī Shuhbah, *Ṭabaqāt al-shāfiᶜīya*, I, 148–9: '*al-ᶜAmd*'; C: fiqh – shāfiᶜī?

(725) ᶜ/3 255b/7–8 *al-ᶜAqīda al-mawsūma bi-al-adilla al-ᶜaqlīya – The Creed Characterised by Rational Arguments*; this unknown theological work

was most likely authored by the jurisprudent and theologian A: al-Qāsim b. Muḥammad al-Qaffāl al-Shāshī (d. 336/947) (al-Subkī, *Ṭabaqāt*, III, 472–7). It is not clear why the cataloguer emphasises the 'rational arguments'. C: theology.[93]

(726) ᶜ/4 255b/8 *ᶜAyn al-ᶜayn – Essence of the [K.] al-ᶜAyn*; no such title is identifiable. As this entry is in thematic category 4 this is most likely a lexicographical work and thus a summary of/commentary on the dictionary *al-ᶜAyn* ascribed to al-Khalīl b. Aḥmad al-Farāhīdī (d. 175/791?). Such summaries were, for instance, authored by the 4th-/10th-c. scholar Muḥammad al-Zubaydī (*Mukhtaṣar al-ᶜAyn*, ed. N. al-Shādhilī, Beirut: AK, 1996). The title here is ascribed to a certain al-Shīrāzī. The most famous scholar by this name in 7th-/13th-c. Damascus, Ibrāhīm b. ᶜAlī al-Fīrūzābādī al-Shīrāzī (d. 476/1083), was not active in lexicography. This may thus be a lost work ascribed to another scholar with this name, such as the grammarian and poet Hibat Allāh b. al-Ḥusayn al-Shīzārī (d. 377/987–8) (MU, VI, 2768/9). C: lexicography.

(727) ᶜ/6 255b/8 *ᶜUrāḍat al-adīb – The* adīb's *Present*; A: Muḥammad b. Muḥammad al-ᶜAbbāsī Ibn al-Habbārīya (d. 509/1115–16?) (IKH, IV, 453–7); No such title by this author is identifiable and this is most likely a little-known anthology of his poetry. C: poetry – anthology – Saljūq. (cf. no. 749)

(728) ᶜ/6 255b/9 *ᶜArūḍ Ibn ᶜAbbād – Ibn ᶜAbbād's Metrics*; A: Ismāᶜīl Ibn ᶜAbbād (d. 385/995); S: ed. M.Ḥ. Āl Yāsīn, *al-Iqnāᶜ fī al-ᶜarūḍ wa-takhrīj al-qawāfī*, Baghdad: MMa, 1960; C: poetry – metrics.

(729) ᶜ/6 255b/9 *ᶜUnwān al-maʾāthir al-mujāhidīya – Indicating Deeds of al-Mujāhid*; no such title is identifiable, but this may be a panegyric work written for the Ayyubid ruler of Homs al-Malik al-Mujāhid Shīrkūh b. Nāṣir al-Dīn (r. 589–637/1193–1240). C: panegyric – Ayyūbid? – al-Malik al-Mujāhid?

(730) ᶜ/7 255b/9 *al-ᶜIqd – The [Unique] Necklace*; A: Aḥmad b. Muḥammad Ibn ᶜAbd Rabbih (d. 328/940); S: *al-ᶜIqd al-farīd*, eds A. Amīn, A. al-Zayn and I. al-Ibyārī, Cairo: LTTN, 1940–65; VQ: 5; Ṣ; C: adab – anthology. (cf. nos. 1549?, 1555, 1590)

(731) ᶜ/7 255b/10 *ᶜAjāʾib al-ashᶜār wa-gharāʾib al-akhbār – Marvellous Poems and Unique Reports*; A: Amīn al-Dīn Muslim b. Maḥmūd b. Niᶜma

al-Shayzārī (fl. 622/1225); S: MM, III, 852; ed. Ismāʿīl al-ʿAqlāwī, PhD thesis al-Jāmiʿa al-islāmīya al-ʿālamīya/International Islamic University (Islamabad) 2008 (http://prr.hec.gov.pk/Thesis/2443.pdf); VQ: 44–2; Ṣ; C: poetry/adab – anthology.

(732) ʿ/7 255b/10 *ʿUqalāʾ al-majānīn – Wise Fools*; possibly A: al-Ḥasan b. Muḥammad al-Nīsābūrī (d. 406/1015); S: ed. ʿU. al-Asʿad, Beirut 1987; other possible authors include Muḥammad (b. Aḥmad?) b. Mazyad Ibn Abī al-Azhar (d. 325/937), *Akhbār ʿuqalāʾ al-majānīn* (IN, I/2, 456). C: adab.

(733) ʿ/8 255b/11 *ʿUyūn al-akhbār – Choicest Reports*; A: ʿAbd Allāh b. Muslim al-Dīnawarī Ibn Qutayba (d. 276/889); S: ed. M.M. Qamīḥa/Y. ʿA. Ṭawīl, Beirut: DKI, 1985; NC: 2; C: adab – anthology. (cf. no. 1544)

(734) ʿ/8 255b/11 *al-ʿUmda – The Pillar [on the Merits of Poetry and Its Etiquette]*; A: Ḥasan b. Rashīq al-Qayrawānī (d. 456/1063–4 or 463/1070–1); S: *al-ʿUmda fī maḥāsin al-shiʿr wa-ādābihi*, ed. M.M. ʿAbd al-Ḥamīd, Beirut: DJ, 1981; C: adab/poetry – literary criticism.

(735) ʿ/8 255b/11 *ʿIbārāt al-ishārāt – Interpreting Allusions*; no such title is identifiable and the *Talkhīṣ al-ʿibārāt bi-laṭīf al-ishārāt fī al-qirāʾāt al-sabʿ* by al-Ḥasan b. Khalaf Ibn Ballīma (d. 514/1120) (ed. J. Sharaf, Ṭanṭā: Dār al-ṣaḥāba li-l-turāth, *c.*2000) is unlikely as a work on Koran recitation does not fit thematic category 8. This may be an unknown compilation of adab material, which would fit this category and the preceding titles. C: adab?

(736) ʿ/8 255b/12 *ʿAhd Ardashīr – The Testament of Ardashīr*; A: ʿAbd Allāh Ibn al-Muqaffaʿ (d. 139/756?); S: IN, II/1, 391; C: political thought – non-Muslim – mirror for princes. (cf. no. 1176)

(737) ʿ/9 255b/12 *ʿIlāl taʿbīr al-ruʾyā – Causes of Dream Interpretation*; Scr('*bi-khaṭṭ*'): possibly the Saljuq author and secretary Asʿad b. Masʿūd al-ʿUtbī (d. 474/1081–2) (MU, II, 633–5); possibly A: al-Kindī (d. *c.*252/866), author of *ʿIlal al-nawm wa-al-ruʾyā*; S: Fahd, *Divination*, 345; VQ: 1; Ṣ; C: oneiromancy.

(738) ʿ/9 255b/12–13 *ʿIlm al-raml – Geomancy*; no author fitting 'Ibn M-d/dh-b/t/th/n/y-l-j/ḥ/kh' can be identified, probably on account of the relative marginality of geomancy in our standard sources. A comparable obscure case contemporaneous to al-Malik al-Ashraf's rule in Damascus is the geomantic

work *ᶜUmdat al-ṭālib wa-tuḥfat al-rāghib* by a certain Abū Ḥāmid al-Ashrafī, which was authored in 630/1232–3 (Baghdādī, *Īḍāḥ al-Maknūn*, II, 122). C: geomancy.

(739) ᶜ/9 255b/13 *al-ᶜAmal bi-al-aṣṭurlāb[sic]* – *Using the Astrolabe*; popular title with numerous possibilities (cf. IN, index); C: astronomy.

(740) ᶜ/12 255b/13 *al-ᶜIrāqīyāt* – *The Iraqi Poems*; one of the two sections of the *Dīwān* by A: Fakhr al-ᶜArab Abū al-Muẓaffar Muḥammad b. Aḥmad al-Abīwardī (d. 507/1113); S: ed. ᶜU. al-Asᶜad, Damascus: MLA, 1974–5; C: poetry – anthology.

(741) ᶜ/13 255b/14 *ᶜUyūn al-ashᶜār* – *Choicest Poems*; A: al-Ḥusayn b. Muḥammad al-Rāghib al-Iṣfahānī (d. early 5th/11th c.?); S: al-Iṣfahānī, *Muḥāḍarāt al-udabāᵓ*, I, 13 where the author mentions that he wrote a work entitled *ᶜUyūn al-ashᶜār*; VQ: 1; Ṣ; C: poetry – anthology – Būyid? (cf. nos. 742, 1259b)

(742) ᶜ/13 255b/14 *ᶜUyūn al-ashᶜār* – *Choicest Poems*; A: al-Ḥusayn b. Muḥammad al-Rāghib al-Iṣfahānī (d. early 5th/11th c.?); S: al-Iṣfahānī, *Muḥāḍarāt al-udabāᵓ*, I, 13 where the author mentions that he wrote a work entitled *ᶜUyūn al-ashᶜār*; FI: the cataloguer adds the letter *ẓ* after the title. Most likely this abbreviation stands here for *aẓunnuhu* ('I think it to be') or *fīhi naẓar* ('it requires consideration') (Gacek, *Vademecum*, 80) as he was not certain whether this title is the same work as the preceding or a different one (such as *ᶜUyūn al-akhbār wa-al-ashᶜār* by Abū ᶜAṣīda Aḥmad b. ᶜUbayd (d. 273/886) (GAS, II, 82); VQ: 1; Ṣ; C: poetry – anthology – Būyid? (cf. nos. 741, 1259b)

(743) ᶜ/15 255b/14 *ᶜUhdat al-sulṭān* – *The Sultan's Decree*; no such title is identifiable. It is unlikely that this refers to a specific Sultan's decree (such as a decree by al-Malik al-Ashraf), so this may be a book-in-the-making in the mirror for princes genre. C: political thought – mirror for princes?

(744) ᶜ/15 255b/15 *al-ᶜAjāᵓib wa-al-ṭuraf wa-al-hadāyā wa-al-tuḥaf* – *Marvels, Curiosities, Presents and Rarities*; A: Abū al-Ḥasan/Ḥusayn Aḥmad b. ᶜAlī b. Ibrāhīm Ibn al-Zubayr (d. 563/1167); S: *Kitāb al-dhakhāᵓir wa-al-tuḥaf*, ed. M. Ḥamīd Allāh, Kuwait: MḤK, 1959; this work is quoted in Mamluk-period literature with the title given here in the catalogue, cf., for example, al-Maqrīzī, *Ittiᶜāẓ*, II, 331. C: adab – anthology – Fatimid.

(745) ᶜ/15 255b/15 *al-ᶜArūḍ – Metrics*; no such title of an author by the name given in the catalogue is known. As this is a treatise on metres, this may be the poet Marwān b. Abī al-Junūb b. Marwān[94] (d. 247/861) (IKH, V, 193). C: poetry – metrics.

(746) ᶜ/15 255b/15-16 *al-ᶜArūḍ – Metrics*; this is arguably a work ascribed to A: ᶜAbd al-Raḥmān b. ᶜĪsā al-Hamadhānī (d. 320/932), who is referred to elsewhere in this catalogue also as 'ᶜAbd al-Raḥmān' (cf. nos. 27 and 1311a). Although al-Hamadhānī is not known to have authored a work on metrics, it is possible that such a work was ascribed to this poet and philologist. C: poetry – metrics.

(747) ᶜ/15 255b/16 *ᶜAhd Adriyānūs*[95] *al-Malik ilā ibnihi – The Testament of King Hadrian to His Son*; A: pseudo-Plato, probably an extract from the *K. al-ᶜuhūd al-yūnānīya* by Aḥmad b. Yūsuf Ibn al-Dāya (d. *c.*331/942–3); S: Badawī, *al-Uṣūl al-yūnānīya*; C: political thought – non-Muslim – mirror for princes.[96] (cf. no. 1180b)

(748) ᶜ/15 255b/16 *ᶜAhdat al-shāᶜir – The Poet's Secret Depository*;[97] this title is unidentifiable and it is most probably an anonymous anthology. C: poetry – anthology.

(749) ᶜ/15 255b/16–17 *ᶜUrāḍat al-adīb – The* adīb's *Present*; Scr('*bi-khaṭṭ*'): two main possibilities 1) Aḥmad Ibn al-Khāzin (d. 518/1124) (IKH, I, 149–51 and 2) al-Ḥusayn b. ᶜAlī Ibn al-Khāzin (d. 502/1109) (MU, III, 1105), who were both renowned calligraphers or scribes; most likely A: Muḥammad b. Muḥammad al-ᶜAbbāsī Ibn al-Habbārīya (d. 509/1115–16?) who is named as the author of a work by this title in no. 727; no such title by this author is identifiable and this is most likely a book-in-the-making anthology of his poetry. C: poetry – Saljūq. (cf. no. 727)

(750) ᶜ/3s 255b/17 *ᶜAhd al-Maᵓmūn – The Testament of al-Maᵓmūn*; The Testament by A: ᶜAbbasid Caliph al-Maᵓmūn (r. 198–218/813–33) to his brother and successor al-Muᶜtaṣim; This is included in various sources, including S: Bosworth (tr.): *The History of al-Ṭabarī*, XXXII, 225–8; C: political thought – ᶜAbbāsid. (cf. no. 1209c)

(751) ᶜ/4s 255b/17 *al-ᶜAmal fī Rajab – Conduct during the Month of Rajab*; A: Aḥmad Ibn ᶜAyyāsh al-Jawharī (d. 401/1010–11); S: Kohlberg, *Ibn Ṭāwūs*, 107; this work has been lost, but excerpts are quoted in later texts. These

excerpts consist of prayers ascribed to Twelver Shi^{c}ite imams and a prophetic tradition. It is debatable to what extent this was indeed an independent text or combined with similar pieces on conduct in Ramaḍān and Sha^{c}bān. Rajab was one of the most 'devotional' months of the year (similar to nos. 809 and 934). The issue of some rituals' permissiveness led to conflicts in 7th-/13th-c. Damascus (Pouzet, *Damas*, 138 and 344) and the treatise could be linked to these conflicts. Another reflection on these practices and the debates surrounding them is arguably no. 1313e on *Ṣalāt al-raghā$^{\circ}$ib*. C: rituals.

(752) ^{c}/4s 255b/18 *^{c}Ūdhat al-Nabī ṣallā Allāh ^{c}alayhi wa-sallam – The Prophet's Invocation (may God's blessing and peace be upon him)*; C: prayer book.

(753) ^{c}/5s 255b/18 *^{c}Arā$^{\circ}$is al-albāb wa-gharā$^{\circ}$is al-ādāb – The Brides of Hearts and the Seeds of Adab*; no such title is identifiable and this is most likely a book-in-the-making. Judging from title and the thematic category this is most likely an anthology of prose and verse. C: adab/poetry – anthology.

(754) ^{c}/5s 256a/1–2 *al-^{c}Arabīyāt al-muntakhabāt allatī tadkhulu fī al-^{c}ibārāt wa-al-kutub – Chosen Arabic Terms that Enter Phrases and Books*; FI: '*wa-hiya alfāẓ gharība mashrūḥa bi-al-^{c}ajamī*/'*and these are difficult expressions explained in Persian*'; L: Persian/Arabic; VQ: 1; Ṣ; C: lexicography.

(755a) ^{c}/6s 256a/2 *^{c}Uddat al-kuttāb – Secretaries' Tools*; A: Muḥammad b. ^{c}Alī Ibn Muqla (d. 328/940); S: ed. H. Nājī, *Ibn Muqla: khaṭṭāṭ^{an} wa-adīb^{an} wa-insān^{an}. Ma^{c}a taḥqīq risālatihī fī al-khaṭṭ wa-al-qalam*, Baghdad 1991; C: administrative handbook.

(755b) 256a/2 *Dhakhīrat al-ādāb fī al-tarassul – The Treasure of Adab on Composing Letters*; no such title is identifiable. It may be the same as no. 460 (^{c}Alī b. ^{c}Abd al-^{c}Azīz Ibn Ḥājib al-Nu^{c}mān (d. 423/1031), *Dhakhīrat al-kuttāb*); C: administrative handbook.

(756) ^{c}/7s 256a/2–3 *^{c}Ishrūna mas$^{\circ}$ala su$^{\circ}$ila ^{c}anhā al-Shāfi^{c}ī raḍiya Allāh ^{c}anhu – Twenty Problematic Issues on Which al-Shāfi^{c}ī (may God be pleased with him) Was Asked*; referring to Muḥammad b. Idrīs al-Shāfi^{c}ī (d. 204/820); C: fiqh – shāfi^{c}ī.

(757) ^{c}/9s 256a/3 *Dustūr al-lugha – The Counsellor on Speech*; A: Ḥusayn b. Ibrāhīm al-Naṭanzī (d. 497/1103); S: GAL, I, 288: '*Dustūr al-lugha min al-asmā$^{\circ}$ wa-al-af^{c}āl wa-al-^{c}adawāt*'; L: Persian; VQ: 1; Ṣ; C: lexicography.[98]

(758) ᶜ/9s 256a/3-4 *al-Kāfī fī al-ᶜarūḍ – The Sufficient [Book] on Metrics*; A: Yaḥyā b. ᶜAlī al-Khaṭīb al-Tibrīzī (d. 502/1109); S: ed. al-Ḥ.Ḥ. ᶜAbdallāh, Cairo: JDA, 1966; this is a work on metrics and thus so language-specific that a translation into Persian seems very unlikely. However, this title is clearly not in its alphabetical place and there must have been some connection with the Persian-language section. Interestingly, further down another work on metrics, that by Ibn Jinnī (cf. no. 953b), is bound together with a lexicographical work on Arabised words from Persian. L: Persian?; C: poetry – metrics. (cf. nos. 890, 1216a)

(759) ᶜ/9s 256a/4 *Uṣūl al-Ḥarb – The Principles of (Ibn) Ḥarb*; A: Jaᶜfar b. Ḥarb (d. 236/850); S: IN, I/2, 591; Mandelung, *Muᶜtazilitische Häresiographie*; L: Persian; C: theology – doxography.

(760) ᶜ/9s 256a/4 *Shiᶜr al-Ḥakam al-Rūmī wa-ghayrihi – The Poetry of al-Ḥakam al-Rūmī and Others*; the standard bibliographical works for Persian poetry do not list a poet known as al-Ḥakam al-Rūmī. L: Persian; C: poetry – anthology.

(761) ᶜ/9s 256a/4–5 *Dīwān al-Rashīd Waṭwāṭ – Al-Rashīd Waṭwāṭ's Diwan*; A: Rashīd al-Dīn Muḥammad b. Muḥammad Waṭwāṭ al-ᶜUmarī (d. 578/1182–3?); S: ed. S. Nafīsī, Shāhābād: Kitābkhāna-i Bārānī, 1960; L: Persian; C: poetry – Khwārazmshāh. (cf. no. 770)

(762) ᶜ/9s 256a/5 *al-Irshād fī al-fiqh – Guidance on Jurisprudence*; three main possibilities: 1) Muḥammad b. Aḥmad al-Hāshimī (d. 428/1037) (TI, 421–40, p. 240:'*Irshād*'); C: fiqh – ḥanbalī; 2) ᶜAlī b. ᶜUqayl al-Baghdādī (d. 513/1119) (Baghdādī, *Hadīyat*, I, 695); C: fiqh – ḥanbalī; 3) Muḥammad b. Muḥammad al-Shaykh al-Mufīd (d. 413/1032) (Engl. tr. Howard, *Book of Guidance*); L: Persian?; C: fiqh – imāmī. (cf. no. 20)

(763) ᶜ/9s 256a/5 *Maqāmāt – Maqāmāt*; possibly the Persian *maqāmāt* by A: ᶜUmar b. Maḥmūd Ḥamīdī (d. 559/1164); S: Behmardi, 'Arabic and Persian Intertextuality'; NC: 2; L: Persian; C: adab.

(764) ᶜ/9s 256a/5-6 *Wasīlat al-ṭālib – The Student's Guide*; A: ᶜAyn al-Quḍāt ᶜAbd Allāh (or Muḥammad) b. Abī Bakr al-Hamadhānī al-Mayānajī[99] (d. 525/1131); no such title is identifiable, either by ᶜAyn al-Quḍāt or another scholar. This is most likely a work similar to al-Ghazālī's *Bidāyat al-hidāya* (cf. nos. 199, 1170b) and belongs to the Persian works ascribed to

ᶜAyn al-Quḍāt (EI³, H. Landolt, 'ᶜAyn al-Quḍāt al-Hamadhānī'). NC: 2; L: Persian; C: ethics? – Islamic.

(765) ᶜ/9s 256a/6 *Dīwān Jamāl al-Dīn al-Naqqāsh – Jamāl al-Dīn al-Naqqāsh's Diwan*; A: Jamāl al-Dīn Muḥammad al-Naqqāsh (fl. late 6th/12th c.); S: de Blois, *Persian Literature*, 345–7 (who is doubtful whether the poet Jamāl al-Dīn Muḥammad and the miniaturist Jamāl-i Naqqāsh are one and the same person, but this diwan seems to confirm this); L: Persian; C: poetry – Saljūq. (cf. no. 797)

(766) ᶜ/9s 256a/6 *Dīwān al-Baylaqānī – Al-Baylaqānī's Diwan*; A: Mujīr al-Dīn Baylaqānī (d. *c.*594/1197–8); S: ed. M. Ābādī, Tabriz: Muᵓassasa-i Tārīkh, 1979; L: Persian; C: poetry.

(767) ᶜ/9s 256a/6 *Dīwān Bundār – Bundār's Diwan*; A: Bundār (Pindār?) al-Rāzī (d. early 5th/11th c.); S: de Blois, *Persian Literature*, 103; L: Persian; C: poetry – Būyid.

(768) ᶜ/9s 256a/7 *Nuzhat al-ᶜushshāq – The Pleasure of Lovers [and the Passionate One's Opportunity]*; A: ᶜAyn al-Quḍāt ᶜAbd Allāh (or Muḥammad) b. Abī Bakr al-Hamadhānī al-Mayānajī (d. 525/1131); S: EI³, H. Landolt, 'ᶜAyn al-Quḍāt al-Hamadhānī'; *Nuzhat al-ᶜushshāq wa-nuhzat al-mushtāq* is a collection of Arabic verses and it is unclear whether the cataloguer misplaced this title or whether this is indeed a Persian translation. L: Persian?; C: adab – love literature/theory.

(769) ᶜ/9s 256a/7 *al-[sic]Dīwān al-Asadī – Al-Asadī's Diwan*; A: ᶜAlī b. Aḥmad al-Asadī al-Ṭūsī (d. 465/1072–3?); S: de Blois, *Persian Literature*, 83–90 (does not mention a diwan); L: Persian; C: poetry.

(770) ᶜ/9s 256a/7 *al-[sic]Dīwān al-ᶜUmarī – Al-ᶜUmarī's Diwan*; A: Rashīd al-Dīn Muḥammad b. Muḥammad Waṭwāṭ al-ᶜUmarī (d. 578/1182–3?); S: ed. S. Nafīsī, Shāhābād: Kitābkhāna-i Bārānī, 1960; L: Persian; C: poetry – Khwārazmshāh. (cf. no. 761 where the same poet is named '*al-Rashīd Waṭwāṭ*'?)

(771) ᶜ/9s 256a/7 *Kalīla wa-Dimna – Kalīla and Dimna*; A: ᶜAbd Allāh Ibn al-Muqaffaᶜ's (d. 139/756?) work, possibly in the Persian translation by Niẓām al-Dīn Naṣr Allāh b. Muḥammad b. ᶜAbd al-Ḥamīd (fl. 6th/12th c.); S: *Tarjama-i Kalīla wa-Dimna*, ed. M. Mīnuwī, Tehran: Dānishgāh, 1362

[1983]; MS: Süleymaniye, Carullah 1727*; L: Persian; C: political thought – non-Muslim – mirror for princes.

(772) ^{c}/9s 256a/7–8 *Dīwān Abī al-Mafākhir – Abū Mafākhir's Diwan*; A: Abū Mafākhir al-Rāzī (fl. 6th/12th c.); S: al-Ṭihrānī, *al-Dharī^{c}a*, IX/1, 50; L: Persian; C: poetry.

(773) ^{c}/9s 256a/8 *Qiṣaṣ al-anbiyāʾ – Stories of the Prophets*; this is arguably the work by A: al-Tha^{c}ālibī (d. 429/1038), of which a Persian 7th-/13th-c. manuscript is in MS: Süleymaniye, Fatih 4449**. S: *Qiṣaṣ al-anbiyāʾ/dāstānhā-yī payghāmbarān*, ed. Ḥ. Yaghmāʾī, Tehran: Intishārāt-i Bungāh-i Tarjuma va Nashr-i Kitāb, 1961; L: Persian; C: qiṣaṣ al-anbiyāʾ. (cf. nos. 720, 1687)

(774) ^{c}/9s 256a/8 *Daf^{c} maḍārr al-aghdhiya – Avoiding Harms of Nutriments*; possibly A: al-Rāzī (Rhazes) (d. 313/925 or 323/935); S: IN, II/1, 311; L: Persian; C: medicine. (cf. no. 1031c)

(775) ^{c}/9s 256a/8 *Tarājim al-a^{c}ājim – Biographies of the Persians*; probably A: Shāhfūr b. Ṭāhir Isfarāʾinī (fl. 5th/11th c.); S: *Tāj al-tarājim fī tafsīr al-Qurʾān li-l-a^{c}ājim*, eds N.M.Haravī and ^{c}A.A. Khurāsānī, Tehran: Shirkat-i Intishārāt-i ^{c}Ilmī va Farhangī, 1996. Potentially this entry could also refer to the biographical dictionary *Kāfī al-tarājim bi-lisān al-a^{c}ājim* by Muḥammad b. Abī al-Qāsim al-Baqqāl(ī) (d. 562/1167) (TI, 561–70, p. 139). However, the MS: Süleymaniye, Fatih 302/2 (fols. 282a–531b)*** makes Isfarāʾinī's title more likely. L: Persian; C: Koran – exegesis (*tafsīr*).

(776) ^{c}/9s 256a/8-9 *Majmū^{c} Shi^{c}r warathat ^{c}Allūn – Collection of Poetry by the Heirs of ^{c}Allūn*; no such Persian poetry is identifiable, but there is a reference to a Kurdish elder called Ibn ^{c}Allūn in the 5th/11th c. in northern Mesopotamia who offered patronage to local poets (al-Qāḍī ^{c}Iyāḍ (d. 544/1149), *al-Ghunya*, 115). L: Persian; C: poetry.[100]

(777) ^{c}/9s 256a/9 *Majmū^{c} Shi^{c}r – Collection of Poetry*; anonymous work with generic title; FI: '*mujadwal*'/'*in columns*'; L: Persian; C: poetry – anthology.

(778) ^{c}/9s 256a/9 *Nafthat al-maṣdūr – The Consumptive's Sigh*; this could be the memoirs of Anūshirwān b. Khālid (fl. 6th/12th c.) on his life as a public official (EI^{3}, C.L. Klausner, 'Anūshirwān b. Khālid'), but more likely is the authorship of A: Muḥammad b. Aḥmad al-Khurandizī al-Nasawī (d. 647/1249–50) who authored this autobiographical report in Persian

during his service for the Ayyubid ruler of Mayyāfāriqīn, al-Malik al-Muẓaffar Ghāzī. S: ed. A.Ḥ. Yazdagirdī, Teheran: Intishārāti Idāra-i Kull-i Nigarish wa Wizarāt-i Āmūzish wa Parwarish, 1343/1964; L: Persian; C: autobiography.

(779) ^{c}/9s 256a/9 *Majmū^{c} shi^{c}r – Collection of Poetry*; anonymous work with generic title; L: Persian; C: poetry – anthology.

(780) ^{c}/9s 256a/9-10 *Majmū^{c} ākhar – Another Collection*; anonymous work with generic title; L: Persian; C: poetry – anthology.

(781) ^{c}/9s 256a/10 *Tarassul ^{c}ajamī – Persian Correspondence*; anonymous work with generic title; L: Persian; C: adab – epistle?

(782) ^{c}/9s 256a/10 *Majmū^{c} shi^{c}r – Collection of Poetry*; anonymous work with generic title; FI: '*^{c}atīq*'/'*old [manuscript]*' (cf. no. 462 on '*atīq*'); L: Persian; C: poetry – anthology.

(783) ^{c}/9s 256a/10 *Majmū^{c} shi^{c}r – Collection of Poetry*; anonymous work with generic title; FI: '*^{c}atīq*'/'*old [manuscript]*' (cf. no. 462 on '*atīq*'); L: Persian; C: poetry – anthology.

(784) Gh/1 256a/11 *Gharīb al-ḥadīth – Uncommon Words in ḥadīth*; A: Ibn al-Jawzī (d. 597/1200); S: ^{c}A.A. Qal^{c}ajī, Beirut: DKI, 1985; C: ḥadīth – collection/lexicography.

(785) Gh/1 256a/11 *Gharīb al-ḥadīth – Uncommon Words in ḥadīth*; A: ^{c}Abd Allāh b. Muslim al-Dīnawarī Ibn Qutayba (d. 276/889); S: ^{c}A. al-Jubūrī, Baghdad: Wizārat al-awqāf, 1977; C: ḥadīth – collection/lexicography. (cf. no. 1443)

(786) Gh/1 256a/12 *Gharīb al-ḥadīth – Uncommon Words in ḥadīth*; A: Abū[101] ^{c}Ubayd al-Qāsim b. Sallām al-Harawī (d. 224/838); S: ed. Ḥ.M.M. Sharaf, Cairo: MLA, 1984–94; MS: Süleymaniye, Fatih 4008**; C: ḥadīth – collection/lexicography. (cf. no. 1442)

(787) Gh/1 256a/12 *Gharīb al-Qur$^{\circ}$ān – Uncommon Words in the Koran*; A: Muḥammad b. ^{c}Uzayr/^{c}Azīz al-Sijistānī (d. *c.*330/942); S: ed. M.al-Ṣ. Qamḥāwī, *Tafsīr gharīb al-Qur$^{\circ}$ān*, Cairo: Maktabat al-Jindī, 1970; MS: Süleymaniye, Ayasofya 426**; C: Koran/lexicography. (identical with no. 789)

(788) Gh/1 256a/12-13 *Gharībā al-Qur$^{\circ}$ān wa-al-ḥadīth – Uncommon Words in Koran and ḥadīth*; A: Abū ^{c}Ubayd Aḥmad b. Muḥammad al-Harawī

(d. 401/1010–11); S: ed. A.F. al-Mazīdī, Beirut: MAṢ, 1999; MS: Süleymaniye, Fazıl Ahmed Paşa 377***; NC: 4; C: Koran/ḥadīth – collection/lexicography.

(789) Gh/2 256a/13 *Gharīb al-Qurʾān – Uncommon Words in the Koran*; A: Muḥammad b. ᶜUzayr/ᶜAzīz al-Sijistānī (d. *c.*330/942); S: ed. M.al-Ṣ. Qamḥāwī, *Tafsīr gharīb al-Qurʾān*, Cairo: Maktabat al-Jindī, 1970; NC: 3; C: Koran/lexicography. (identical with no. 787)

(790) Gh/2 256a/13–14 *Ghurar al-fawāʾid – The Finest of Wise Sayings*; A: ᶜAlī b. al-Ḥusayn al-Sharīf al-Murtaḍā (d. 436/1044); S: *Ghurar al-fawāʾid wa-durar al-qalāʾid*, ed. M.A. Ibrāhīm, Cairo: DIKA, 1954; MS: Süleymaniye, Ragıp Paşa 711*; NC: 2; C: Koran – exegesis (*tafsīr*)/ḥadīth – Exegesis/adab. (cf. no. 824)

(791) Gh/7 256a/14 *al-Ghurra – The Bright Star*; no such title nor the named author ᶜAbd Allāh al-Tāʾib is identifiable. The name of ᶜAbd Allāh Ibn Abī al-Tāʾib does not fully match, he is rather late (b. *c.*642–3/1244–6) and no titles are mentioned for him (al-Ṣafadī, *Aᶜyān*, II, 895). This may be a minor author of local prominence who authored what could be – judging from the thematic category – an adab anthology. C: adab?

(792) Gh/7 256a/14–15 *Ghurūs al-barāᶜāt – Shoots of Eloquence*; no such title is identifiable and this may be an unknown adab anthology. C: adab?

(793) Gh/8 256a/15 *al-Ghārāt – The Book of Raids*; popular title with several possibilities (see IN, index), including the well-known work by Ibrāhīm b. Muḥammad al-Thaqafī (d. 283/896) on the conflict between ᶜAlī and Muᶜāwiya (ed. ᶜA. al-Khaṭīb, Beirut: DAḍ, 1987); FI: '*mujallad*'/'*one bound volume*'; C: history – early Islam. (cf. no. 1318a)

(794) Gh/12 256a/15 *Ghazal – Love Poetry*; A: Muḥammad b. ᶜAlī Ibn al-Muᶜallim (d. 592/1196); S: IKH, V, 5–9; C: poetry – ghazal. (cf. nos. 422, 1624)

(795) Gh/13 256a/16 *Ghazal Ibn Hāniʾ – Ibn Hāniʾ's Love Poetry*; A: Abū al-Qāsim Muḥammad Ibn Hāniʾ al-Andalusī (d. 362/973); the name could also refer to al-Ḥasan b. Hāniʾ Abū Nuwās, but the cataloguer does not use this name element in his other references to this poet. FI: '*huwa Durr al-maᶜānī fī ghurar Ibn Hāniʾ*'/'*this is the Pearl of Meanings Concerning the*

Finest of Ibn Hāniʾ'; no such title is identifiable and the cataloguer preferred to enter the work under the generic title '*Ghazal Ibn Hāniʾ*', rather than the title he provided in the FI, as he seemingly thought readers would be more likely to find it in this way. This is thus most likely a minor commentary on Ibn Hāniʾ's poetry (see his *Dīwān*, ᶜU.F. al-Ṭabbāᶜ, Beirut: DAr, 1998); C: poetry – ghazal.

(796) Gh/13 256a/16 *Ghazal – Love Poetry*; A: Muslim b. al-Khiḍr b. Qasīm al-Ḥamawī (d. 541/1146); S: *Dīwān Ibn Qasīm al-Ḥamawī*, ed. S.M. ᶜAbd al-Jābir, Amman: Dār al-bashīr, 1995; C: poetry – ghazal.

(797) Gh/13 256a/16-17 *Ghazal Dīwān al-Naqqāsh – Love Poetry from al-Naqqāsh's Diwan*; A: Jamāl al-Dīn Muḥammad al-Naqqāsh (fl. late 6th/12th c.); S: de Blois, *Persian Literature*, 345–7; L: Persian?; C: poetry – ghazal. (cf. no. 765)

(798) Gh/13 256a/17 *Ghazal – Love Poetry*; A: Mihyār b. Marzawayh al-Daylamī (d. 428/1037); S: ed. A. Nasīm, Beirut: MA, 1999; C: poetry – ghazal. (cf. nos. 396, 1613)

(799a) Gh/13 256a/17 *Ghazal – Love Poetry*; A: al-Walīd al-Buḥturī (d. 284/897); S: ed. Ḥ. al-Ṣayrafī, Cairo: DM, 1963–5; C: poetry – ghazal.

(799b) 256a/17 *Ghazal – Love Poetry*; A: Muḥammad b. al-Ḥusayn al-Sharīf al-Raḍī (d. 406/1016); S: I. ᶜAbbās, Beirut: DṢ, 1994; C: poetry – ghazal.

(800) Gh/13 256a/17 *Ghazal – Love Poetry*; probably A: Asᶜad b. Aḥmad al-Sinjārī (d. 622/1225); S: IKH, I, 214–17 who mentions that he only found this poet's diwan in the Ashrafiya library; C: poetry – ghazal. (cf. no. 1054)

(801) Gh/13 256b/1 *Ghazal – Love Poetry*; A: ᶜAlī b. Rustam Ibn al-Sāᶜātī (d. *c.*604/1207); S: ed. A. al-Maqdisī, Beirut: American Press, 1938–9; MS: Süleymaniye, Ayasofya 3872***; C: poetry – ghazal. (cf. nos. 399, 1229c)

(802) Gh/13 256b/1 *Ghazal – Love Poetry*; A: Muḥammad b. al-Ḥusayn al-Sharīf al-Raḍī (d. 406/1016); S: I. ᶜAbbās, Beirut: DṢ, 1994; NC: 6; C: poetry – ghazal.

(803) Gh/15 256b/1 *al-Ghilmān al-mughannīn – Singing Youths*; A: Abū al-Faraj al-Iṣfahānī (d. 356/967); S: Kilpatrick, *Making*, 23; C: adab – love literature/theory. (cf. no. 1188d)

(804) Gh/6s 256b/2 *Ghurar al-balāgha – Blazes of Eloquence*; A: Hilāl b. al-Muḥassin al-Ṣābiʾ (d. 448/1056); S: ed. M. al-Dībājī, Beirut: DṢ, 2000; C: rhetoric. (cf. nos. 501b, 1323a)

(805) F/2 256b/2 *Faḍāʾil al-aᶜmāl – Merits of Devotional Works*; A: Ḍiyāʾ al-Dīn Muḥammad b. ᶜAbd al-Wāḥid al-Maqdisī (d. 643/1245); S: ed. ᶜĀ.A. Ḥaydar, Beirut: MKTh, 1985; C: ḥadīth – merits.

(806) F/2 256b/3 *Faḍāʾil Dimashq – Merits of Damascus*; arguably A: ᶜAlī b. Muḥammad al-Rabaᶜī (d. 444/1052), whose *K. Faḍāʾil al-Shām wa-Dimashq* was well known and, for instance, used by Ibn ᶜAsākir (d. 571/1176) in the introduction to his *Taʾrīkh madīnat Dimashq*; S: ed. Ṣ. al-Munajjid, Damascus: MIA, 1950; C: ḥadīth – merits.

(807) F/2 256b/3 *Faḍāʾil al-ṣaḥāba wa-ahl al-bayt – Virtues of the Prophet's Companions and His Family*; this is a popular title, but among the numerous possible authors of *Faḍāʾil al-ṣaḥāba* works this is arguably A: Aḥmad b. Ḥanbal (d. 241/855). A copy of this work is held in the Süleymaniye library and one of its transmission notes mentions al-Ḥasan al-Qaylawī (d. 633/1236) (TI, 631–40, p. 145), a renowned scribe of Damascus and librarian of al-Malik al-Ashraf who appears elsewhere as scribe in the Ashrafiya library (cf. nos. 257, 533, 698, 1253). MS: Süleymaniye, Yeni Cami 878***. C: ḥadīth – merits.

(808) F/2 256b/3 *Faḍāʾil al-Quds – Merits of Jerusalem*; popular title with numerous possibilities (cf. ᶜAsalī, *Makhṭūṭāt*); C: ḥadīth – merits.

(809) F/2 256b/3-4 *Fuṣūl ḥisān fī faḍl Shaᶜbān – Pleasing Chapters on the Merits on the Month of Shaᶜbān*; possibly A: Amīn al-Dīn ᶜAbd al-Muḥsin b. Ḥamūd al-Ḥalabī (d. 643/1245) (TI, 641–50, pp. 181–2), poet and administrator whose biographers focus on his pious poetry, but this title is not identifiable; on this issue's topicality in 7th-/13th-c. Damascus cf. no. 751. C: ḥadīth – merits?

(810) F/3 256b/4 *Farāʾiḍ – Shares of Inheritance*; A: al-Jamāl ᶜAlī b. Muḥammad b. Aḥmad al-Miṣrī (d. 338/950); S: IN, I/2, 663 (neither here nor in other biographical dictionaries is this scholar's *laqab* mentioned, so 'al-Jamāl' cannot be confirmed, e.g. *Wāfī*, XXI, 405; *Siyar*, XV, 381); C: fiqh.

(811) F/4 256b/5 *Fiqh al-lugha – The Understanding of Lexicography*; A: al-Thaᶜālibī (d. 429/1038); S: *Fiqh al-lugha wa-sirr al-ᶜarabīya*, ed. M. al-Saqqā, I. al-Ibyārī and ᶜA. Shalabī, Cairo: MTK, 1938; MS: Süleymaniye, Laleli 3582*; NC: 12; C: lexicography.

(812) F/4 256b/5 *Farāᵓid al-kharāᵓid – The Unique Pearls*; summary of al-Maydānī's (d. 518/1124) *Majmaᶜ al-amthāl*; A: Yūsuf b. Ṭāhir al-Khuwayyī/Khūwī (d. 549/1154?); S: *Farāᵓid al-kharāᵓid fī al-amthāl*, ed. ᶜA.al-Ḥ. Ḥusayn, al-Dammām 1994; MS: Süleymaniye, Ayasofya 4865/1 (fols. 1a–83b)**; C: adab – proverbs.

(813) F/4 256b/5-6 *al-Farq bayna al-ẓāᵓ wa-al-ḍād – The Difference between the Letters ẓāᵓ and ḍād*; A: Muḥammad b. ᶜAbd Allāh Ibn Mālik al-Jayyānī (d. 672/1274); S: al-Ziriklī, *al-Aᶜlām*, VII, 111; C: lexicography. (cf. no. 1230f)

(814) F/5 256b/6 *Futūḥ – The Conquests*; A: Aḥmad Ibn Aᶜtham al-Kūfī (fl. 3rd/9th c.); S: ed. M. Khān, Hyderabad: DMU, 1968; VQ: 3; Ṣ; C: history – early Islam. (cf. no. 1458)

(815) F/5 256b/6 *Futūḥ – The Conquests*; A: Sayf b. ᶜUmar (fl. 2nd/8th c.); S: EI[2], F.M. Donner, 'Sayf b. ᶜUmar'; VQ: 2; C: history – early Islam.

(816) F/5 256b/6 *al-Fatḥ al-qussī – Eloquent Rhetoric [on the Conquest of Jerusalem]*; A: Muḥammad b. Muḥammad ᶜImād al-Dīn al-Kātib al-Iṣfahānī (d. 597/1201); S: *al-Fatḥ al-qussī fī al-fatḥ al-qudsī*, ed. M.M. Ṣubḥ, Cairo: DQ, 1965; MS: Süleymaniye, Ayasofya 3346**; VQ: 1; Ṣ; C: history – Ayyūbid. (cf. no. 1548)

(817) F/5 256b/7 *Futūḥ al-nawāḥī wa-al-buldān – The Conquests of the Regions and Lands*; A: Aḥmad b. Yaḥyā al-Balādhurī (d. *c.*279/892); S: ed. Ṣ. al-Munajjid, *K. futūḥ al-buldān*, Cairo: MNM, 1956–7; C: history – early Islam.

(818) F/5 256b/7 *Futūḥ al-Shām – The Conquests of Greater Syria*; A: Abū Mikhnaf Lūṭ b. Yaḥyā al-Azdī (d. 157/774); S: EI[3], Kh. Athamina, 'Abū Mikhnaf'; C: history – early Islam.

(819) F/5 256b/7–8 *Faḍāᵓil Miṣr wa-dhikr mā khaṣṣahā Allāh taᶜālā bihi – The Merits of Egypt and Mentioning by What God (may He be exalted) Singled It Out*; two main possibilities: 1) *Faḍāᵓil Miṣr* by ᶜUmar b. Muḥammad

al-Kindī (d. after 350/961) (eds I.A. al-ᶜAdawī and ᶜA.M. ᶜUmar, Cairo: Wahba, 1971) or 2) *Faḍāᵓil Miṣr wa-akhbāruhā wa-khawāṣṣuhā* by al-Ḥasan b. Ibrāhīm Ibn Zūlāq (d. 386/996) (ed. ᶜA.M. ᶜUmar, Cairo: MK, 2000); C: history/merits.

(820) F/5 256b/8 *Fihrist kutub al-umam – Catalogue of the Books of [All] Peoples*; A: Muḥammad b. Isḥāq al-Warrāq Ibn al-Nadīm (d. 385/995); S: IN, I/1, 3: '*Fihrist kutub jamīᶜ al-umam*'; MS: Süleymaniye, Fazıl Ahmed Paşa 1135**; C: bibliography.

(821) F/6 256b/8-9 *Faṣl fī faḍl al-faqr ᶜalā al-ghinā – Chapter on the Merit of Poverty over Riches*; Scr('*bi-khaṭṭ*'): Shihāb al-Dīn ᶜUmar al-Suhrawardī (d. 632/1234) (IKH, III, 446–8); possibly A: al-Jamāl ᶜAlī b. Muḥammad b. Aḥmad al-Miṣrī (d. 338/950); S: IN, I/2, 663; C: sufism.

(822) F/6 256b/9 *al-Fatḥ ᶜalā Abī al-Fatḥ – The Unlocking of Abū al-Fatḥ*; A: Muḥammad b. Aḥmad Fūrraja (d. after 437/1045); S: ed. ᶜA. al-Dujaylī, Baghdad 1974; criticising Abū al-Fatḥ Ibn Jinnī's (d. 392/1002) commentary on Aḥmad al-Mutanabbī's (d. 354/955) diwan (cf. nos. 1108, 1518, 1580, 1584); C: poetry – commentary.

(823) F/7 256b/9 *al-Faraj baᶜda al-shidda – Relief after Hardship*; popular title with several possibilities, but most likely this is the famous book by A: al-Muḥassin b. ᶜAlī al-Tanūkhī (d. 384/994) (S: ed. ᶜA. al-Shāljī, Beirut: DṢ, 1978; C: adab – anthology). (cf. nos. 1498, 1510)

(824) F/7 256b/10 *al-Fawāᵓid min ghurar al-farāᵓid – Wise Sayings from the Finest Pearls*; no such title is identifiable. This is probably a summary of *Ghurar al-fawāᵓid* by ᶜAlī b. al-Ḥusayn al-Sharīf al-Murtaḍā (d. 436/1044) (cf. no. 790), which is also referred to in the period's sources as '*ghurar al-farāᵓid*'. Placed in category 7 the *fawāᵓid* probably focus on the adab element in this work. C: adab?

(825) F/7 256b/10 *Funūn al-fawāᵓid – Various Sorts of Wise Sayings*; FI: '*wa-huwa majmūᶜ ashᶜār wa-ghayruhu*' / '*and this is a collection of poetry and Other [Writings]*'; probably an anonymous and little-known book-in-the-making as the cataloguer felt the need to describe it; C: poetry – anthology. (cf. no. 838)

(826) F/8 256b/10-11 *Faḍl Zibdīn – The Merit of Zibdīn*; arguably A: ᶜAlī Ibn ᶜAsākir (d. 571/1176) who has a *ḥadīth* treatise concerned with this

village in the Damascene Ghūṭa (*Aḥādīth Zibdīn*); S: Ibn ʿAsākir, *Taʾrīkh madīnat Dimashq*, ed. Ṣ. al-Munajjid, Damascus: MIA, 1951, ed. intro. 29; C: ḥadīth – merits.

(827) F/8 256b/11 *al-Futūwa wa-al-murūwa – Qualities of the Young and the Mature Man*; no such title is identifiable. C: adab?

(828) F/8 256b/11 *al-Farāʾid wa-al-qalāʾid – Pearls and Necklaces*; A: Muḥammad al-Ṣaghānī al-Ahwāzī (fl. 5th/11th c.); S: ed. I.Dh. al-Thāmirī, Beirut: DIḤ, 2006; NC: 4; C: adab – proper conduct – proverbs. (cf. nos. 1180a, 1198a)

(829) F/10 256b/11–12 *al-Filāḥa – [Nabatean] Agriculture*; A: Aḥmad b. ʿAlī Ibn Waḥshīya (d. 218/930-1); S: on the disputed origin and content of *al-Filāḥa al-nabaṭīya* see Hämeen-Anttila, *Last Pagans of Iraq*; C: agriculture.

(830) F/10 256b/12 *al-Furūsīya – Equitation*; A: Abū ʿAbd Allāh Muḥammad b. Yaʿqūb Ibn Akhī Ḥizām al-Khuttalī (fl. late 3rd/9th c.); this is either the author's book on hippiatrics *al-Furūsīya wa-al-bayṭara* (ed. & Germ. tr. Heide, *Hippiatrie*) or his lost work on equitation (Heide, *Hippiatrie*, 4). VQ: 4; C: veterinary medicine/equitation.

(831) F/10 256b/12 *al-Firdaws fī al-Ṭibb – Paradise [of Wisdom] Concerning Medicine*; A: ʿAlī b. Sahl Rabban al-Ṭabarī (fl. first half 3rd/9th c.); S: M.Z. al-Ṣiddīqī, *Firdaws al-ḥikma fī al-ṭibb*, Berlin 1928; MS: Süleymaniye, Ayasofya 4857/3 (fols. 5b–57b)*; C: medicine.

(832) F/10 256b/12–13 *Fann min al-funūn fī maʿrifat ṣufr al-ʿuyūn – A Tract on Understanding the Eyes' Yellowing*; unidentified; C: medicine.

(833) F/10 256b/13 *al-Furūsīya – Equitation*; generic/popular title with numerous possibilities (cf. Al-Sarraf, 'Mamluk Furūsīyah Literature'); FI: '*muṣawwar*' / '*illustrated*'; C: equitation.

(834) F/10 256b/13 *al-Furūsīya ākhar – Another [Work on] Equitation*; generic/popular title with numerous possibilities (cf. Al-Sarraf, 'Mamluk Furūsīyah Literature'); C: equitation.

(835) F/10 256b/13 *al-Furūsīya ākhar – Another [Work on] Equitation*; generic/popular title with numerous possibilities (cf. Al-Sarraf, 'Mamluk Furūsīyah Literature'); C: equitation.

(836) F/13 256b/13–14 *Faraḥ al-qulūb fī madāʾiḥ Banī Ayyūb – The Hearts' Pleasure Concerning the Panegyrics for the Banū Ayyūb*; no such title is identifiable and this is most likely a book-in-the-making anthology. C: poetry – panegyrics – Ayyūbid.

(837) F/15 256b/14 *Fulk al-maᶜānī – The Ship of Meanings*; A: Muḥammad b. Muḥammad al-ᶜAbbāsī Ibn al-Habbārīya (d. 509/1115–16?); S: MU, I, 339 and IKH, VI, 156; NC: 2; C: adab – anthology.

(838) F/15 256b/14 *Funūn al-fawāʾid – Various Sorts of Wise Sayings*; probably anonymous book-in-the-making; C: poetry – anthology. (cf. no. 825)

(839) F/15 256b/15 *al-Fāḍil fī al-adab al-kāmil – The Excellent [Book] on Perfect Education*; A: Muḥammad b. Aḥmad Ibn al-Washshāʾ (d. 325/937); S: ed. Y.W. al-Jabbūrī, *K. al-fāḍil fī ṣifat al-adab al-kāmil*, Beirut: DGI, 1991; C: rhetoric.

(840) F/3s 256b/15 *Faḍāʾil al-jihād wa-shahr Ramaḍān – Merits of Jihad and the Month of Ramadan*; A: ᶜAlī Ibn ᶜAsākir (d. 571/1176); S: MU, IV, 1701: '*K. faḍl al-jihād*'; Ibn ᶜAsākir, *Taʾrīkh madīnat Dimashq*, ed. Ṣ. al-Munajjid, Damascus: MIA, 1951, ed. intro. 40: '*Faḍl Ramaḍān*'; C: ḥadīth – merits. (cf. no. 842)

(841) F/3s 256b/16 *Faḍāʾil al-jihād – Merits of Jihad*; arguably A: Bahāʾ al-Dīn Yūsuf b. Rāfiᶜ Ibn Shaddād (d. 632/1235); S: ed. S. Zakkār, *Arbaᶜat kutub fī al-jihād min ᶜaṣr al-ḥurūb al-Ṣalībīya*, Damascus: al-Takwīn, 2007, 183–273; Ibn Shaddād's work was the first *jihād* treatise dedicated to an Ayyubid ruler. Its presence in this library is especially likely because all of the other great works of the preceding decades, such as those by Ibn ᶜAsākir (cf. nos. 840, 842), were held. As Ibn Shaddād's treatise is not mentioned anywhere else in the catalogue this entry thus arguably refers to it. C: ḥadīth – merits.

(842) F/5s 256b/16 *Faḍāʾil al-jihād – Merits of Jihad*; A: ᶜAlī Ibn ᶜAsākir (d. 571/1176); S: MU, IV, 1701: '*K. faḍl al-jihād*'; C: ḥadīth – merits. (cf. no. 840)

(843) F/5s 256b/16 *Fiqar wa-ḥikam wa-nawādir – Prose, Pieces of Wisdom and Anecdotes*; anonymous work with generic title; C: adab – anthology.

(844) F/6s 256b/17 *Fuṣūṣ al-fuṣūl wa-ᶜuqūd al-ᶜuqūl – Bezels of Discernment and Necklaces of Insight*; A: Hibat Allāh b. Jaᶜfar Ibn Sanāʾ al-Mulk

(d. 608/1211); S: EI², Ch. Pellat, 'Ibn Sanāʾ al-Mulk'; C: adab/poetry – anthology – Ayyūbid.

(845) F/6s 256b/17 *Fuṣūl al-bulaghāʾ* – *The Eloquents' Aphorisms*; no such title is identifiable and this is most likely a book-in-the-making. This is probably an anonymous collection similar to Süleymaniye, Esad Efendi 3542 (fols. 153b–154b), *Fuṣūl al-ḥikam wa-al-balāgha*. C: adab – anthology.

(846) F/6s 256b/17 *Fuṣūl mustaḥabba fī al-mukātabāt* – *Esteemed Chapters on Correspondence*; no such title is identifiable and this is probably an anonymous collection. C: adab – epistle.

(847) F/6s 256b/18 *Faḍīlat al-mujāhidīn ᶜalā al-qāᶜidīn* – *The Excellence of Those Engaging in Jihad over Those Remaining Idle*; no such title is identifiable. This is probably a treatise with prose texts and poetry referring to the Koranic verse *al-Nisāʾ*, 95; C: jihād.

(848) Q/1 256b/18 *Qirāʾat Yaᶜqūb wa-ghayrihi* – *The Recitation of Yaᶜqūb and Others*; arguably A: Yaᶜqūb b. Isḥāq al-Ḥaḍramī (d. 205/820–1), one of the accepted reciters in the system of ten recitations; S: F. Leemhuis, 'Readings of the Qurʾān', in McAuliffe, *Encyclopaedia*; C: Koran – recitation.

(849) Q/2 257a/1 *Qiṣaṣ al-anbiyāʾ* – *Stories of the Prophets*; arguably A: Muḥammad b. ᶜAbd Allāh al-Iskāfī (d. 240/854), although IN, I/2, 592/3 does not mention this title; C: qiṣaṣ al-anbiyāʾ.

(850) Q/2 257a/1 *Qūt al-qulūb* – *Nourishment of the Hearts*; A: Muḥammad b. ᶜAlī al-Makkī (386/998); S: ed. ᶜA. Madkūr/ᶜĀ. al-Najjār, Cairo: HMAK, 2005-7; Germ. tr. Gramlich, *Nahrung der Herzen*; MS: Süleymaniye, Fatih 2765**; C: sufism. (cf. no. 1446)

(851) Q/3 257a/1-2 *Qaḍāyā ᶜAlī b. Abī Ṭālib karrama Allāh wajhahu* – *Legal Decisions by ᶜAlī b. Abī Ṭālib (may God honour his countenance)*; referring to ᶜAlī b. Abī Ṭālib, the fourth Caliph and first Shiᶜite *imām* (d. 40/661); popular title with numerous possibilities (cf. e.g. al-Ṭihrānī, *al-Dharīᶜa*, XVII, 151–3); C: fiqh – imāmī.

(852) Q/6 257a/2 *al-Qaṣāʾid al-sabᶜ* – *The Seven Qaṣīdas*; most likely the seven 'suspended' (*muᶜallaqāt*)-poems; S: al-Qurashī, *Jamharat*, 124–428; C: poetry – anthology – pre-Islamic. (cf. nos. 567, 569, 1230m, 1686)

(853) Q/6 257a/2-3 *Qaṣīd Zuhayr bi-sharḥihā – The Qaṣīdas of Zuhayr and Their Commentary*; Scr('*khaṭṭ*'): Mawhūb b. Aḥmad Ibn al-Jawālīqī (d. 539/1144) (EI^2, H. Fleisch, 'al-Djawālīḳī'); A: Zuhayr b. Abī Sulmā Rabīᶜa al-Muzanī (d. 609 CE?); commentary: probably either al-Aᶜlam al-Shantamarī (d. 476/1083) or Thaᶜlab (d. 291/904); S: EI^2, L. Bettini, 'Zuhayr'; C: poetry – commentary – pre-Islamic.

(854) Q/6 257a/3 *Qiṭᶜat shiᶜr – Fragment of Poetry*; anonymous work with generic title; Scr('*khaṭṭ*'): Yaḥyā b. ᶜAlī al-Khaṭīb al-Tibrīzī (d. 502/1109) who is called 'al-Khaṭīb' at other places in the catalogue and appears also as scribe (cf. no. 639); C: poetry.

(855) Q/7 257a/3 *Qalāʾid al-ᶜiqyān – The Golden Necklaces*; an anthology of rhymed prose and verse referring to members of the political elite, judges and scholars. A: al-Fatḥ b. Muḥammad Ibn Khāqān al-Ishbīlī (d. 529/1134?); S: ed. M. al-Ṭāhir ibn ᶜĀshūr, Tunis: DTu, 1990; MS: Süleymaniye, Ayasofya 3359***; NC: 3; C: adab/poetry – anthology.

(856) Q/8 257a/4 *al-Qāʾif – The Minute Observer*; commentary on *Kalīla and Dimna*; A: Abū al-ᶜAlāʾ al-Maᶜarrī (d. 449/1058); S: MU, I, 333; C: political thought – non-Muslim – mirror for princes – commentary.

(857) Q/8 257a/4 *Qurāḍat al-dhahab – The Clipped Gold Piece [on Criticising the Arabs' Poems]*; A: Ḥasan b. Rashīq al-Qayrawānī (d. 456/1063–4 or 463/1070–1); S: *Qurāḍat al-dhahab fī naqd ashᶜār al-ᶜArab*, ed. Ch. Bouyahia, Tunis 1972; C: poetry – commentary – anthology.

(858) Q/9 257a/4–5 *Qurᶜat al-sharāb – Choice of Syrup*; no such title is identifiable. Taking into account the thematic category this is most likely a pharmacological work on the preparation of medical beverages. NC: 2; FI: '*muṣawwar*'/'*illustrated*'; C: pharmacology.

(859) Q/9 257a/5 *al-Qādirī fī al-taᶜbīr – The Qādirī on Oneiromancy*; dedicated to the Caliph al-Qādir bi-Allāh (r. 381–422/991–1031); A: Naṣr b. Yaᶜqūb al-Dīnawarī (fl. 397/1006); S: F. Saᶜd, Beirut: AK, 1997; NC: 2; C: oneiromancy.

(860) Q/9 257a/5 *Qiyās al-māʾ bi-al-khamr – Comparing Water with Wine*; no such title is identifiable. As thematic category 9 occasionally has pharmacological and medical works (just above cf. no. 858) this may be a treatise on

mixing wine and water for medical purposes, as, for instance, discussed in Ibn Ḥamdūn, *Tadhkira*, VIII, 349. C: medicine?

(861) Q/10 257a/5–6 *Qānūn Ibn Sīnā – Ibn Sīnā's Canon*; A: Ibn Sīnā (d. 428/1037); S: ed. M.A. al-Ḍannāwī, Beirut: DKI, 1999; MS: Süleymaniye, Fatih 3595***; NC: 2; C: medicine. (cf. no. 1477)

(862) Q/10 257a/6 *Quṣtā b. Lūqā fī al-?*[102] – *Quṣtā b. Lūqā on?*; A: Quṣtā b. Lūqā al-Baᶜlabakkī (d. *c.*300/912–13); MS: Süleymaniye, Fatih 3439/1 (fols. 2a–65b)***; the cataloguer was clearly unsure about this entry: He misspelled the name of 'Quṣtā' as 'Quṣtār' and he did not finish the last word. Most likely he could not make sense of this work on Euclidian geometry entitled *Uqlīdis fī al-uṣūl al-handasīya* in the Fatih manuscript. The multiple-text manuscript Fatih 3439 contains other titles that are similar to Ashrafīya entries (cf. nos. 89, 94, 331). C: mathematics – geometry.

(863) Q/13 257a/6 *al-Qaṣāᵓid al-Ashrafīyāt – The Qaṣīdas for al-Ashraf*; this is most likely panegyric poetry for al-Malik al-Ashraf, the mausoleum's patron. The most probable poet is al-Ashraf's secretary A: ᶜAlī b. Muḥammad Kamāl al-Dīn Ibn al-Nabīh (d. 619/1222) renowned for his *Ashrafīyāt* and the poet who has the largest corpus of panegyrics for al-Ashraf. S: al-Asᶜad, *Dīwān Ibn al-Nabīh*, 123–363; C: poetry – panegyric – Ayyūbid – al-Malik al-Ashraf. (cf. nos. 190, 288, 315, 868, 1049, 1055, 1229d)

(864) Q/13 257a/7 *Qaṣīdat al-shaykh Saᶜd Allāh – Al-Shaykh Saᶜd Allāh's Qaṣīda*; A: al-Shaykh Saᶜd Allāh b. Abī al-Fatḥ al-Manbijī (d. 651/1254) whom Ibn al-ᶜAdīm calls 'al-Shaykh Saᶜd Allāh' and who composed poetry for the mausoleum's patron al-Malik al-Ashraf; S: Ibn al-ᶜAdīm, *Bughyat*, IX, 4239/40; C: poetry – Ayyūbid – edifying. (cf. no. 458)

(865) Q/15 257a/7 *Qānūn al-wizāra – Ordinance of the Vizier's Office*; A: al-Māwardī (d. 450/1058); S: ed. F.ᶜA. Aḥmad/M.S. Dāwūd, *Qawānīn al-wizāra*, Alexandria: Muᵓassasat shabāb al-jāmiᶜa, 1991; C: political thought – adab of vizier.

(866a) Q/15 257a/7 *al-Qawāfī – Rhymes*; probably A: al-Khalīl b. Aḥmad al-Farāhīdī (d. 175/791?) although his biographers do not mention such a title (e.g. IN, I/1, 113–16; MU, III, 1271); C: poetry – rhyme.

(866b) 257a/8 *al-Qawāfī – Rhymes*; A: Sa^{c}īd b. Mas^{c}ada al-Akhfash al-Awsaṭ (d. 215/830); S: ed. ^{c}I. Ḥasan, Damascus: Mudīrīyat iḥyāʾ al-turāth al-qadīm, 1970; C: poetry – rhyme. (cf. no. 872)

(866c) 257a/8 *al-Qawāfī – Rhymes*; A: Ṣāliḥ b. Isḥāq al-Jarmī (d. 225/839); S: IN, I/1, 162; C: poetry – rhyme.

(867) Q/1s 257a/8 *Qaṣīd Ka^{c}b b. Zuhayr mashrūḥa – Ka^{c}b b. Zuhayr's Qaṣīdas with Explanation*; the *Bānat Su^{c}ād* or *Burda* poem recited to the Prophet and subject to numerous commentaries over the centuries; A: Ka^{c}b b. Zuhayr; S: Diem, *Überlieferung*; C: poetry – commentary – early Islamic. (cf. nos. 1215c, 1230d)

(868) Q/3s 257a/8–9 *al-Qaṣāʾid al-Ḥalabīya fī al-faḍāʾil al-Ashrafīya – The Aleppian Qaṣīdas on the Ashrafian Merits*; Al-Malik al-Ashraf never ruled Aleppo, but he established informal control over the city in the 610s/1210s. In order to consolidate this control he spent several months in the city in 615/1218–19. During this period his main panegyrist Ibn al-Nabīh sent him a poem from northern Mesopotamia and the title here may refer to this piece. Probably A: ^{c}Alī b. Muḥammad Kamāl al-Dīn Ibn al-Nabīh (d. 619/1222); S: al-As^{c}ad, *Dīwān Ibn al-Nabīh*, 329–36; C: poetry – panegyric – Ayyūbid – al-Malik al-Ashraf. (cf. nos. 190, 288, 315, 863, 1049, 1055, 1229d)

(869a) Q/3s 257a/9 *Qaṣīdat al-A^{c}shā – Al-A^{c}shā's Qaṣīda*; most likely A: Maymūn b. Qays al-A^{c}shā (d. after 625); S: EI^{3}, B. Jockers, 'al-A^{c}shā'; C: poetry – early Islamic.

(869b) 257a/9 *Tuḥfat al-ẓurafāʾ – The Refined Persons' Precious Rarity*; arguably the *Bulghat al-ẓurafāʾ fī taʾrīkh al-khulafāʾ*; A: ^{c}Alī b. Muḥammad b. Abī al-Surūr al-Rawḥī (d. after 648/1250); S: ed. ^{c}I. Hilāl, Cairo: Wizārat al-awqāf, 2004; FI: '*dhukirat fī al-tāʾ*'/'*[also] mentioned in [the section on the letter] tāʾ [cf. no. 280]*'; C: history – Islamic.

(870) Q/5s 257a/10 *al-Qaṣāʾid al-mashhūrāt*[103] *– The Famous Qaṣīdas*; this is probably a book-in-the-making with a generic title and with what one anthologist perceived to be famous *qaṣīdas*. C: poetry – anthology.

(871) Q/5s 257a/10 *Qaṣāʾid – Qaṣīdas*; anonymous work with generic title; Scr('*bi-khaṭṭ*'): probably ^{c}Abd al-Salām al-Baṣrī (fl. 5th/11th c.) (IKH, VII, 73; cf. nos. 186 and 313); C: poetry – anthology.

(872) Q/5s 257a/10 *al-Qawāfī – Rhymes*;[104] A: Saᶜīd b. Masᶜada al-Akhfash al-Awsaṭ (d. 215/830); S: ed. ᶜI. Ḥasan, Damascus: Mudīrīyat iḥyā᾽ al-turāth al-qadīm, 1970; C: poetry – rhyme. (cf. no. 866b)

(873) Q/5s 257a/11 *Qaṣīd fī madḥ Ṣalāḥ al-Dīn – Qaṣīdas in Praise of Ṣalāḥ al-Dīn*; A: al-Ḥasan b. ᶜAlī al-Juwaynī (d. 586/1190?), Zangid and Ayyubid secretary whose panegyrics for Saladin are quoted by the ruler's biographers (e.g. Abū Shāma, *al-rawḍatayn*, III, 30) and who has several titles in the Ashrafiya library (cf. nos. 142, 347, 348, 874); S: MU, II, 940/1; C: poetry – panegyric – Ayyūbid – Ṣalāḥ al-Dīn.

(874) Q/5s 257a/11 *Qaṣid fī madḥ al-Malik al-ᶜĀdil Sayf al-Dīn – Qaṣīdas in Praise of al-Malik al-ᶜĀdil Sayf al-Dīn*; referring to al-Malik al-Ashraf's father al-Malik al-ᶜĀdil (d. 615/1218); A: al-Ḥasan b. ᶜAlī al-Juwaynī (d. 586/1190?), Zangid and Ayyubid secretary who has several titles in the Ashrafiya library (cf. nos. 142, 347, 348, 873); S: MU, II, 940–1; C: poetry – panegyric – Ayyūbid – al-Malik al-ᶜĀdil.

(875) Q/5s 257a/12 *Qaṣīd Ashrafiya – Ashrafiyan Qaṣīdas*; these *qaṣīdas* are probably by A: Muḥammad b. Aḥmad b. ᶜAlī Ibn (al-)Amsīnā (fl. 606/1209). The fate of this secretary after he lost his position in the Caliphal administration in Baghdad in 606/1209 at the age of 57 (lunar) years (*Wāfī*, II, 109) is unknown. He may have moved to al-Malik al-Ashraf's court in northern Mesopotamia, where the latter had built up a major principality. The cataloguer clearly does not know these panegyrics, because he does not use – similar to the epistles by the same author in no. 484 – the definite article. C: poetry – panegyric – Ayyūbid? – al-Malik al-Ashraf? (cf. no. 484)

(876) Q/7s 257a/12 *al-Qaṣā᾽id al-thalāth tatimmat al-ᶜashar sharḥ al-Khaṭīb – The Three Qaṣīdas Completing the Ten, al-Khaṭīb's Commentary*; referring to the poems by Ziyād al-Nābigha al-Dhubyānī, ᶜAbīd b. al-Abraṣ and Maymūn b. Qays al-Aᶜshā; A: Yaḥyā b. ᶜAlī al-Khaṭīb al-Tibrīzī (d. 502/1109); S: *Sharḥ al-qaṣā᾽id al-ᶜashar*, ed. F. al-Shaᶜār, Beirut: Mu᾽assasat al-maᶜārif, 2006; C: poetry – commentary – anthology – pre-Islamic/early Islamic.

(877) K/1 257a/13 *al-Kashf wa-al-bayān fī tafsīr al-Qur᾽ān – Exposition and Elucidation on Interpreting the Koran*; A: al-Thaᶜlabī (d. 427/1035); S: ed. S. Kasrawī, Beirut: DKI, 2004; MS: Süleymaniye, Şehid Ali Paşa 156*; C: Koran – exegesis (*tafsīr*).

(878) K/3 257a/14 *al-Kashf ᶜan masāwī – The Revelation of [the] Faults [of al-Mutanabbī's Poetry]*; A: Ismāᶜīl Ibn ᶜAbbād (d. 385/995); S: *al-Kashf ᶜan masāwī shiᶜr al-Mutanabbī*, ed. M.Ḥ. Āl-Yāsīn, Baghdad: MN, 1965; C: poetry – commentary. (cf. nos. 1020, 1248b)

(879) K/3 257a/14 *al-Kifāya fī al-fiqh – The Sufficient Book on fiqh*; popular title with several possibilities, most likely (as it was written some decades before the library was set up and as it is the only *fiqh* work with this title cited by Ibn Khallikān) A: Muḥammad b. Ibrāhīm al-Jājarmī (d. 613/1216); S: IKH, IV, 256; C: fiqh – shāfiᶜī.

(880) K/4 257a/14 *Kifāyat al-mutaḥaffiẓ – The Sufficient [Book] for He Who Memorizes*; A: Ibrāhīm b. Ismāᶜīl al-Ajdābī (d. *c.*650/1251); S: *Kifāyat al-mutaḥaffiẓ wa-nihāyat al-mutalaffiẓ fī al-lugha al-ᶜarabīya*, ed. ᶜA. Al-Hilālī, Baghdad: DSh, 1986; MS: Süleymaniye, Fazıl Ahmed Paşa 1325/2 (fols. 81a–107b)**; C: lexicography.

(881) K/6 257a/15 *Kunnāsh al-khiff – Compendium of Comfort*; A: Isḥāq b. Ḥunayn al-ᶜIbāḍī (d. *c.*289/910–11); S: IAU, II, 159; C: medicine.

(882) K/6 257a/15 *al-Kalāᵓ wa-al-shajar – [Names of] Herbs and Trees*; A: Abū Zayd Saᶜīd b. Aws al-Anṣārī (d. 215/830); S: A. Abū Suwaylim and M. al-Shawābika, *K. al-shajar wa-al-kalāᵓ*, Amman: Dār al-Abjadīya, 1995; GAS, VIII, 78; C: lexicography.

(883) K/9 257a/15 *Kunnāsh ṭibbī nujūmī – Compendium of Astrological Medicine*; anonymous work with generic title, on astrological medicine cf. Ullmann, *Medizin*, 254–6; a work with this title, although written within a multiple-text manuscript, can be found in Süleymaniye, Ayasofya 3724/18, fols. 203b–215b. C: medicine – astrological.

(884) K/9 257a/16 *al-Kunnāsh al-mughīth – The Supporting Compendium*; no such title is identifiable and this is most likely a book-in-the-making. Based on the preceding title, the terminology ('*kunnāsh*') and the category this is most likely a treatise on astrological medicine (cf. Ullmann, *Medizin*, 254–6). C: medicine – astrological.

(885) K/10 257a/16 *Kashf al-alibbāᵓ ᶜan aḥwāl al-aṭibbāᵓ – Elucidating Intelligent Persons as to the Circumstances of Physicians*; no such title is identifiable and it is probably a biographical dictionary of physicians similar to

Muḥammad b. Ibrāhīm Ibn al-Akfānī's (d. 749/1348) *Rawḍat al-alibbāʾ fī ishārat al-aṭibbāʾ* (cf. Witkam, *Egyptische arts*, 51); C: biographical dictionary – physicians?

(886) K/10 257a/16–17 *Kunnāsh al-Sāhir – Al-Sāhir's Medical Compendium*; A: Yūsuf al-Sāhir (fl. late 3rd/early 10th c.); S: IN, II/1, 305; C: medicine.

(887) K/10 257a/17 *al-Kalbaza – Hounds*; A: Hippocrates[105]; S: *Kalbaza* refers to dogs or hounds. ᶜAlī al-Ghuzūlī, *Maṭāliᶜ al-budūr fī manāzil al-surūr*, Cairo: Idārat al-waṭan, 1299 h. [1881], II, 211 (quoting Jamāl al-Dīn Waṭwāṭ's *Mabāhij al-fikar*) uses this term, for instance, when he discusses the origin of Salūqī dogs: '*kamā ḥakāhu ahl al-kalām fī al-kalbaza*'. The standard primary (e.g. IAU, I, 202–21) and secondary sources (e.g. Ullmann, *Medizin*, 25–35) do not mention such a text ascribed to Hippocrates. C: veterinary medicine.

(888) K/15 257a/17 *al-Kāmil – The Perfect Book [on Adab]*; A: Muḥammad b. Yazīd al-Mubarrad (d. 286/900); S: *al-Kāmil fī al-adab*, ed. M.A. al-Dālī, Beirut: MR, 1986; MS: Süleymaniye, Fatih 4022***; NC: 3; C: adab – anthology. (cf. nos. 1539, 1545?)

(889) K/15 257b/1 *al-Kināya wa-al-taᶜrīḍ – Metonymy and Allusion*; A: al-Thaᶜālibī (d. 429/1038); S: ed. ᶜĀ.Ḥ. Farīd, Cairo: Dār Qabāʾ, 1998; MS: Süleymaniye, Fazıl Ahmed Paşa 1353/2 (fols. 35a–54b)**; C: rhetoric.

(890) K/15 257b/1 *al-Kāfī fī al-ᶜarūḍ – The Sufficient [Book] on Metrics*; A: Yaḥyā b. ᶜAlī al-Khaṭīb al-Tibrīzī (d. 502/1109); S: ed. al-Ḥ.Ḥ. ᶜAbdallāh, Cairo: JDA, 1966; NC: 2; C: poetry – metrics. (cf. nos. 758, 1216a)

(891) K/15 257b/1 *Kanz al-kuttāb – The Secretaries' Treasure*; popular title with three possibilities: 1) Maḥmūd Kushājim (d. c.350/961) (repeatedly cited in al-Qalqashandī, *Ṣubḥ al-aᶜshā*); C: administrative handbook?; 2) al-Thaᶜālibī (d. 429/1038) or perhaps al-Mīkālī (d. 436/1044), published under the title *al-Muntaḥal*, Alexandria 1901; C: adab of secretary; 3) Ibrāhīm b. ᶜAlī al-Fihrī (d. 651/1253–4) (ed. Ḥ. Qāra, Abu Dhabi: al-Majmaᶜ al-thaqāfī, 2004); C: adab/poetry – anthology.

(892) K/5s 257b/2 *K. Rūfus fī dalāʾil al-ṣiḥḥa allatī tuḥtāju ilayhā ᶜinda shirāʾ al-mamālīk – Rūfus' Book on the Proofs of Health You Need to Consider*

when Purchasing Slaves; A: Rufus of Ephesus (fl. *c.*100 BCE); S: Ullmann, *Medizin*, 74 (*Maqāla fī shirāʾ al-mamālīk*); C: medicine.

(893) K/5s 257b/2-3 *K. katabahu al-Muʿizz li-Dīn Allāh taʿālā ilā fatāhu al-kātib Jawhar – Letter Composed by al-Muʿizz li-Dīn Allāh (may He be exalted) for His Freedman and Secretary Jawhar*; Letter by the A: Fatimid Caliph al-Muʿizz (r. 341–65/953–75) to his general Jawhar al-Ṣiqillī (d. 381/992) several of which can be found in S: al-Jūdharī, *Vie de l'Ustadh Jaudhar*, Fr. tr. M. Canard; C: history – Fatimid.

(894) K/5s 257b/3 *K. ʿan al-Mustarshid – Letter from al-Mustarshid*; referring to the ʿAbbasid Caliph al-Mustarshid (r. 512–29/1118–35); C: history – ʿAbbāsid.

(895) L/2 257b/4 *Lawāmiʿ anwār al-qulūb – Flashes of the Hearts' Lights [on the Collection of the Beloved's Mysteries]*; A: ʿAzīzī b. ʿAbd al-Malik al-Jīlī/Jīlānī (d. 494/1100); S: Prozorov, *Sufi Tradition* (*Lawāmiʿ anwār al-qulūb fī jamʿ asrār al-maḥbūb*); C: sufism.

(896) L/2 257b/4 *[al-]Lumaʿ fī ʿulūm al-ṣūfiya – Shafts of Light on Sufism's Fields of Knowledge*; A: ʿAbd Allāh b. ʿAlī al-Sarrāj[106] (d. 378/988); S: Germ. tr. R. Gramlich, *Schlaglichter über das Sufitum*, Wiesbaden 1990; C: sufism.

(897) L/4 257b/5 *Lumaʿ – Shafts of Light*; A: Abū al-Fatḥ Ibn Jinnī (d. 392/1002); S: ed. F. Fāris, Amman: Dār al-Amal, 2001; MS: Süleymaniye, Ayasofya 4578**; C: grammar. (cf. no. 901)

(898) L/5 257b/5 *al-Lubāb fī tahdhīb al-ansāb – Kernels on Refining Genealogies*; A: ʿAlī Ibn al-Athīr (d. 630/1233); S: ed. Baghdad: MMu, [1972]; C: onomastics.

(899) L/6 257b/6 *Luzūm mā lā yalzam – Self-Imposed Constraints*; A: Abū al-ʿAlāʾ al-Maʿarrī (d. 449/1058); S: ed. I. al-Ibyārī, Cairo: WTa, 1959; C: poetry – Ḥamdānid/Mirdāsid. (cf. nos. 905, 1505, 1525)

(900) L/6 257b/6 *al-Libaʾ wa-al-laban – Bee Stings and Milk*; Scr('*khaṭṭ*'): Mawhūb b. Aḥmad Ibn al-Jawālīqī (d. 539/1144) (EI[2], H. Fleisch, 'al-Djawālīḳī'); several possible authors (e.g. IN, I/1, 155, 159 and 168), including the surviving work by Abū Zayd Saʿīd b. Aws al-Anṣārī (d. 215/830) (eds A. Haffner and L. Shaykhū, *Dix anciens traités de philologie arabe*, Beirut: MKa, 1914); C: lexicography.

(901) L/6 257b/6-7 *Lumaᶜ – Shafts of Light*; Scr('*khaṭṭ*'): possibly ᶜAlī b. Zayd al-Qāsānī (fl. 411/1020) renowned for his calligraphy and student of Ibn Jinnī (MU, IV, 1759); A: Abū al-Fatḥ Ibn Jinnī (d. 392/1002); S: ed. F. Fāris, Amman: Dār al-Amal, 2001; C: grammar. (cf. no. 897)

(902) L/7 257b/7 *Lubb al-ādāb – Kernel of Adab*; A: Ibrāhīm b. Muḥammad Ibn Abī ᶜAwn (fl. 3rd/9th c.); S: EI^2, M.A. Muᶜīd Khan, 'Ibn Abī ᶜAwn': '*Lubb al-ādāb fī radd jawāb dhawī al-albāb*'; this *adīb* is renowned for titles such as *al-Ajwiba al-muskita*/*The Book of Quick-Witted Replies* (ed. M.A. Yūsuf, Cairo: ᶜAyn li-l-dirāsāt wa-al-buḥūth, 1996). C: adab – anthology.

(903) L/8 257b/7 *al-Laᵓāliᵓ al-muḍīya fī manāqib al-Kamālīya – The Blazing Pearls: On the Virtues of al-Kamāl*; no such title is identifiable and this is either a panegyric on a certain Kamāl al-Dīn or, more likely, a commentary on a work with the key word '*Kamāl*'. A likely candidate for this would be a near-contemporaneous work that had a short-term impact (and thus generated such titles) without gaining a long-lasting reputation, thus explaining the absence of any subsequent references to this commentary, such as the biographical dictionary *al-Kamāl fī maᶜrifat al-rijāl* by Muḥibb Allāh b. Maḥāsin Ibn al-Najjār (d. 578/1183) (MU, VI, 2645), which has only survived in fragments. Placed in the thematic category 8 this is most likely an adab work. C: adab?

(904) L/9 257b/8 *Lubāb al-lubāb – Kernels of Kernels*; several books with this popular title are known. Due to the work's classification in category 9 the two main possibilities are 1) ᶜAlī b. Muḥammad al-Qaysī (d. 601/1204) (*Lubāb al-lubāb fī bayān masāᵓil al-ḥisāb – Kernels of Kernels: On Elucidating the Problems of Arithmetic*, see al-Marrākushī, *al-Dhayl wa-al-takmila*, V, 376); C: mathematics; or 2) Muḥammad b. ᶜUthmān al-Zanātī (fl. before 629/1232) (*Lubāb al-lubāb fī ᶜilm al-khuṭūṭ wa-ashkāl al-turāb – Kernels of Kernels: On Geomancy*; see Baghdādī, *Īḍāḥ al-maknūn*, II, 399); C: geomancy.

(905) L/13 257b/8 *Luzūm mā lā yalzam – Self-Imposed Constraints*; A: Abū al-ᶜAlāᵓ al-Maᶜarrī (d. 449/1058); S: ed. I. al-Ibyārī, Cairo: WTa, 1959; C: poetry – Ḥamdānid/Mirdāsid. (cf. nos. 899, 1505, 1525)

(906) L/15 257b/8 *Lumaḥ al-mulaḥ – Flashes of Pleasant Poetry/Anecdotes*; A: Saᶜd b. ᶜAlī b. al-Qāsim al-Ḥaẓīrī Dallāl al-Kutub (d. 568/1172); S: ed. Y. ᶜAbd al-ᶜAẓīm, Cairo: Dār al-Kutub wa-al-Wathāᵓiq al-

Qawmīya, 2007; MS: Süleymaniye, Ayasofya 4246*; NC: 3; C: poetry – anthology – Saljūq.

(907) L/15 257b/9 *Lumaḥ al-mulaḥ – Flashes of Pleasant Poetry/Anecdotes*; A: ᶜAlī b. (al-)Munjib Ibn al-Ṣayrafī (d. 542/1147); S: MU, V, 1972; C: adab or poetry – Fatimid.

(908) L/15 257b/9 *al-Laṭāʾif – Subtleties*; probably one of the works by A: al-Thaᶜālibī (d. 429/1038): 1) *al-Ẓarāʾif wa-al-laṭāʾif*, which was mainly transmitted in Abū Naṣr al-Maqdisī's recension *al-Laṭāʾif wa-al-ẓarāʾif*, ed. ᶜU. al-Asᶜad, *Laṭāʾif al-luṭf*, Beirut: Dār al-Masīra, 1980 (cf. no. 716?); 2) *al-Luṭf wa-al-laṭāʾif*, ed. M.ᶜA. al-Jādir, Kuwait: DA, 1984 (cf. no. 1312b); C: adab – anthology. (cf. nos. 958b, 1242a, 1707)

(909) L/15 257b/9 *Laṭāʾif al-maᶜārif – Curious and Entertaining Information*; A: al-Thaᶜālibī (d. 429/1038); S: eds I. al-Ibyārī and H. al-Ṣayrafī, Cairo: DIKA, 1960, Engl. tr. C.E. Bosworth, *The Book of Curious and Entertaining Information*, Edinburgh 1968; C: adab – anthology.

(910) L/3s 257b/10 *Lumaᶜ min akhbār al-Barāmika – Shafts of Light on the Reports of the Barmakid Family*; probably a summary of one of the two main *Akhbār al-Barāmika*: 1) Muḥammad b. ᶜImrān al-Marzubānī (d. 384/994) (MU, VI, 2583); 2) ᶜUmar al-Kirmānī (dates unknown, cited in later works; cf. ᶜAbbās, *Kutub mafqūda*); C: history – ᶜAbbāsid. (cf. nos. 911, 1646)

(911) L/5s 257b/10 *Lumaᶜ min akhbār al-Barāmika – Shafts of Light on the Reports of the Barmakid Family*; probably another summary of one of the two main *Akhbār al-Barāmika*, but different from no. 910: 1) Muḥammad b. ᶜImrān al-Marzubānī (d. 384/994) (MU, VI, 2583); 2) ᶜUmar al-Kirmānī (dates unknown, cited in later works; cf. ᶜAbbās, *Kutub mafqūda*); C: history – ᶜAbbāsid. (cf. nos. 910, 1646)

(912) L/5s 257b/10-11 *al-Laṭāʾif al-ḥalīya min al-mawāqif al-ᶜalīya – The Pleasant Subtleties Concerning the Elevated Sites*; the most famous author with the *nisba* given in the catalogue is Ṣāliḥ b. Isḥāq al-Jarmī[107] (d. 225/839). Yet, no such title is identifiable for him or another 'al-Jarmī'.

(913) L/9s 257b/11 *Ladhdhat al-qulūb wa-nuzhat li-nafs al-makrūb – The Hearts' Delight and the Afflicted Soul's Pleasure*; no such title is identifiable and thematic category 9s is too broad to speculate on this work's content.

(914) M/1 257b/12 *Musnad – Musnad*; A: ʿAbd Allāh b. ʿAbd al-Raḥmān al-Dārimī (d. 255/869); S: ed. M.A. Dahmān, Beirut: DKI, 1990?; C: *ḥadīth* – collection.

(915) M/1 257b/12 *Mukhtaṣar zād al-masīr fī al-tafsīr – Summary of Provisioning the Traveller in the Field of Exegesis*; this summary refers to Ibn al-Jawzī's (d. 597/1200) work. No such title is identifiable, but Süleymaniye, Fatih 5300/13 (fols. 189b–190b) contains extracts (*manāfiʿ*) from the author's *Zād al-masīr*. As this Fatih multiple-text manuscript originates from the Ashrafiya library (or was at least composed with reference to works originally held in the Ashrafiya library; cf. nos. 261, 1115, 1132, 1135a, 1256b) these extracts were probably part of the *Summary* referred to here. C: Koran – exegesis (*tafsīr*). (cf. no. 536)

(916) M/1 257b/12 *Maʿālim al-tanzīl – Signposts of Revelation*; A: al-Ḥusayn b. Masʿūd (Ibn) al-Farrāʾ al-Baghawī (d. 516/1122?); S: ed. Beirut: DKI, 1993; C: Koran – exegesis (*tafsīr*).

(917) M/2 257b/13 *Maṣābīḥ – Lanterns [of the Sunna]*; A: al-Ḥusayn b. Masʿūd (Ibn) al-Farrāʾ al-Baghawī (d. 516/1122?); S: *Maṣābīḥ al-sunna*, ed. Y. Marʿashlī, Beirut: Dār al-maʿrifa, 1987; C: *ḥadīth* – collection.

(918) M/2 257b/13 *al-Mutaḥābbīn fī Allāh – Mutual Lovers in God*; A: ʿAbd Allāh b. Aḥmad Ibn Qudāma al-Maqdisī al-Muwaffaq (d. 620/1223); S: ed. Kh. al-Sharīf, Damascus: Dār al-ṭabbāʿ, 1991; C: ḥadīth – collection.

(919) M/2 257b/13 *Musnad al-Shāfiʿī*[108] *– Al-Shāfiʿī's Musnad*; A: Muḥammad b. Idrīs al-Shāfiʿī (d. 204/820); S: ed. A. Abū Khashrīf, Damascus: Dth al-ʿarabīya, 2002; C: ḥadīth – collection. (cf. no. 1262b)

(920) M/2 257b/13 *Muwaṭṭaʾ riwāyat Yaḥyā b. Yaḥyā – The Muwaṭṭaʾ in the Recension of Yaḥyā b. Yaḥyā*; A: Mālik b. Anas (d. 179/796); transmitted by Yaḥyā b. Yaḥyā al-Maṣmūdī (d. 234/848–9); S: ed. B.ʿA. Maʿrūf, Beirut: DGI, 1996; C: ḥadīth – collection/fiqh – māliki.

(921) M/2 257b/14 *Muwaṭṭaʾ riwāyat Maʿn – The Muwaṭṭaʾ in the Recension of Maʿn*; A: Mālik b. Anas (d. 179/796); transmitted by Maʿn b. ʿĪsā al-Qazzāz (d.198/814); S: TI, 191–200, pp. 406–7; C: ḥadīth – collection/fiqh – māliki.

(922) M/2 257b/14 *Muwaṭṭaʾ riwāyat Abī Muṣʿab – The Muwaṭṭaʾ in the Recension of Abū Muṣʿab*; A: Mālik b. Anas (d. 179/796); transmitted by Abū Muṣʿab al-Zuhrī (d. 242/856); S: ed. B.ʿA. Maʿrūf/M.M. Khalīl, Beirut: MR, 1993; C: ḥadīth – collection/fiqh – māliki.

(923) M/2 257b/14 *Man ʿāsha baʿda al-mawt – Those Who Lived after Death*; A: ʿAbd Allāh b. Muḥammad Ibn Abī al-Dunyā (d. 281/894); S: ed. ʿA.A. Jāballāh, Beirut: DKI, 1987; C: eschatology/afterlife.

(924) M/2 257b/14-15 *al-Musʿida fī al-qirāʾāt – The Assistant on Koranic Recitation*; A: ʿAlī b. ʿAbd al-Raḥmān Ibn al-Jarrāḥ (d. 497/1103–4); S: *Wāfī*, XXI, 224–5: '*al-Qaṣīda al-Musʿida*'; C: Koran – recitation.

(925) M/2 257b/15 *Mashyakhat Ibn al-Jawzī – The Book of Ibn al-Jawzī's Teachers*; A: Ibn al-Jawzī (d. 597/1200); S: ed. M. Mahfūẓ, Beirut: DGI, 1980; C: biographical dictionary – mashyakha.

(926) M/2 257b/15 *al-Mudhish – The Astounding*; A: Ibn al-Jawzī (d. 597/1200); S: ed. M. Qabbānī, Beirut: DKI, 1985; MS: Süleymaniye, Fatih 4081**; C: sermons.

(927) M/2 257b/15 *al-Mubtadaʾ – The Beginning*; A: Muḥammad b. ʿAbd Allāh al-Kisāʾī, on this 'author' see EI², T. Nagel, 'al-Kisāʾī'; S: ed. I. Eisenberg, *Qiṣaṣ al-anbiyāʾ*, Leiden 1922; some manuscripts have the title '*Badʾ al-dunyā wa-qiṣaṣ al-anbiyāʾ*' (GAL S, I, 592); C: history – biblical.

(928) M/2 257b/16 *Manāqib al-abrār – Virtues of the Righteous*; A: al-Ḥusayn b. Naṣr Ibn Khamīs al-Mawṣilī al-Shāfiʿī (d. 552/1157); S: *Manāqib al-abrār min maḥāsin al-akhyār*, ed. S. ʿAbd al-Fattāḥ, Beirut: DKI, 2006; C: sufism – biographies.

(929) M/2 257b/16 *Muthīr al-gharām al-sākin ilā ashraf al-amākin – Arousing Calm Desire for the Noblest of All Places*; A: Ibn al-Jawzī (d. 597/1200); S: ed. M.M.Ḥ. al-Dhahabī, Beirut: Dār al-ḥadīth, 1995; MS: Süleymaniye, Fatih 4469*; C: rituals – ḥajj.

(930) M/2 257b/16 *Manāfiʿ al-Qurʾān ʿan Jaʿfar al-Ṣādiq – The Benefits of the Koran on the Authority of Jaʿfar al-Ṣādiq*; A: Jaʿfar al-Ṣādiq, the sixth Shiʿite *imām* (d. 148/765); S: GAS, I, 530 '*Manāfiʿ suwar al-Qurʾān*'; C: Koran – divination.

(931) M/2 257b/17 *Maqtal al-Ḥusayn b. ᶜAlī raḍiya Allāh ᶜanhumā – The Killing of al-Ḥusayn b. ᶜAlī (may God be pleased with them)*; referring to al-Ḥusayn b. ᶜAlī b. Abī Ṭālib, the third Shiᶜite *imām* (d. 61/680); popular title with numerous possibilities (e.g. IN, I/2, 292, 294, 309, 333); C: biography – martyrology.

(932) M/2 257b/17 *al-Malāḥim – Battles*; A: Aḥmad b. Jaᶜfar Ibn al-Munādī; S: *Wāfī*, VI, 290 (title not mentioned); C: eschatology/afterlife.

(933) M/2 258a/1 *Marāfiq al-Muwāfiq*[109] – *Benefits of the Successful*; A: Ibn al-Jawzī (d. 597/1200); S: ed. ᶜA.I. Azharī, *Marāfiq al-muwāfiq fī al-waᶜẓ*, Beirut: DKI, 2002; MS: Süleymaniye, Reisülküttab 927/1 (fols. 1a–83b)** with the same inverted title as given here in the Ashrafiya catalogue; C: sermons.

(934) M/2 258a/1 *Mawāᶜiẓ fī faḍāʾil Rajab wa-Shaᶜbān – Sermons on Merits of the Months of Rajab and Ramadan*; identical to or based on *faḍāʾil* treatises such as the '*Faḍāʾil al-ashhur al-thalātha, Rajab, Shaᶜbān, Ramaḍān*' by Muḥammad Ibn Bābūya al-Qummī (d. 381/991) (ed. Beirut 1997) or the *Faḍāʾil Rajab* by ᶜAbd al-Ghanī b. ᶜAbd al-Wāḥid al-Maqdisī (d. 600/1203; TI, 591–600, p. 442). On this issue's topicality in 7th-/13th-c. Damascus cf. no. 751. C: sermons.

(935) M/2 258a/2 *Manāqib Abī Ḥanīfa – Virtues of Abū Ḥanīfa*; popular title with numerous possibilities (cf. GAS, I, 411–12), but in light of the more than twenty works by A: Ibn al-Jawzī (d. 597/1200) in this library, of which some are the preceding entries, it is likely that this is his work; S: *The Virtues of the Imam Aḥmad ibn Ḥanbal*, ed. & Engl. tr. M. Cooperson, New York 2013; C: biography – praise of scholar.

(936) M/2 258a/2 *Manāqib ᶜAlī b. Abī Ṭālib karrama Allāh wajhahu – Virtues of ᶜAlī b. Abī Ṭālib* (*may God honour his countenance*); referring to ᶜAlī b. Abī Ṭālib, the fourth Caliph and first Shiᶜite *imām* (d. 40/661); popular title with numerous possibilities (cf. EI², Ch. Pellat, 'Manāḳib'); C: biography – hagiography.

(937) M/3 258a/3 *al-Maḥṣūl – The Outcome*; A: Muḥammad b. ᶜUmar Fakhr al-Dīn al-Rāzī Ibn al-Khaṭīb (d. 606/1210); S: *al-Maḥṣūl fī ᶜilm uṣūl al-fiqh*, ed. Ṭ.J. al-ᶜAlwānī, Beirut: MR, 1992; NC: 2; C: fiqh – uṣūl al-fiqh.

(938) M/3 258a/3 *Manāsik al-ḥajj – Pilgrimage Rituals*; A: Yaḥyā b. al-Qāsim al-Asadī (d. 150/767); S: MU, III, 1015; C: rituals – ḥajj.

(939) M/3 258a/3–4 *al-Mustaṣfā – The Sifted*; A: al-Ghazālī (d. 505/1111); S: *al-Mustaṣfā min ᶜilm al-uṣūl*, ed. Cairo: Būlāq, 1904–6; NC: 3; MS: Süleymaniye, Fatih 1465**; C: fiqh – uṣūl al-fiqh. (cf. no. 1395)

(940) M/3 258a/4 *Maqāṣid al-falāsifa – The Philosophers' Intentions*; A: al-Ghazālī (d. 505/1111); S: ed. S. Dunyā, Cairo: DM, 1961, C: philosophy – doxography.

(941) M/3 258a/4 *Muᶜāyāt fī al-ṭalāq – Problematic Issues Concerning Divorce*; no such title is identifiable and the fact that the cataloguer (or the manuscript's title page) has the key word *muᶜāyāt* without the definite article implies that this is a generic title for an anonymous collection/note book of material on this legal issue. On the term *muᶜāyāt* see Wizārat al-awqāf wa-al-shuᵓūn al-islāmīya, *al-Mawsūᶜa al-fiqhīya*, Kuwait: Dār al-ṣafwa, 1998, XXXVIII, 188–91. C: fiqh.

(942) M/3 258a/4-5 *Majmūᶜ masāᵓil fiqhīya – Collection of Legal Problems*; anonymous work with generic title; C: fiqh.

(943) M/3 258a/5 *al-Maqālāt al-ṣaghīra – Brief Tracts*; A: ᶜAbd Allāh b. Muḥammad al-Nāshiᵓ al-Akbar (d. 293/906); probably a shorter version of the author's *K. al-Awsaṭ fī al-maqālāt* (ed. J.v. Ess, *Frühe muᶜtazilitische Häresiographie*, Beirut and Wiesbaden 1971); C: philosophy – doxography?

(944) M/3 258a/5-6 *al-Muḥīṭ fī al-fiqh ᶜalā madhhab Abī Ḥanīfa raḍiya Allāh ᶜanhu – The Comprehensive [Treatise] on Jurisprudence according to the School of Abū Ḥanīfa (may God be pleased with him)*; two main possibilities: 1) Maḥmūd Ibn Māza al-Bukhārī (d. 616/1219–20, *al-Muḥīṭ al-Burhānī*, ed. N. Aḥmad, Karachi: Idārat al-ᶜUlūm/Johannesburg: al-Majlis al-ᶜIlmī, 2004) or 2) Muḥammad b. Muḥammad al-Sarakhsī (d. 544/1149, *al-Muḥīṭ al-Raḍāwī*); C: fiqh – ḥanafī.

(945) M/3 258a/6 *Majmūᶜ – Collection*; as the manuscript is untitled (or has a very generic title) the possible authors with the name 'Muḥammad b. Yaḥyā' are numerous. However, the cataloguer must have assumed that this is a sufficient identifier for the readers. The manuscript is placed in category 3, and is thus most probably a *fiqh*-work, so this Muḥammad b. Yaḥyā must

have had a strong profile as jurisprudent excluding, for instance, candidates such as the 3rd-/9th-c. *ḥadīth* scholar Muḥammad b. Yaḥyā al-Dhuhlī or the *adīb* Muḥammad b. Yaḥyā al-Ṣūlī (d. 335/947). The most probable author is the jurisprudent A: Muḥammad b. Yaḥyā al-Nīsābūrī (d. 548/1153) who was prominent enough in mid-7th-/13th-c. Syria to receive an entry in Ibn Khallikān's biographical dictionary (IKH, IV, 223). C: fiqh – shāfiᶜī?

(946) M/3 258a/6 *Mukhtaṣar – The Summary [of Jurisprudence]*; A: Aḥmad b. Muḥammad al-Ṭaḥāwī (d. 321/933); S: *al-Mukhtaṣar fī al-fiqh*, ed. A. al-Afghānī, Cairo 1951; C: fiqh – ḥanafī.

(947) M/3 258a/6-7 *Manāsik al-ḥajj – Pilgrimage Rituals*; the naming of the author is slightly unusual as it does not seem to be his shuhra, the name by which a person is famous, but simply the given name and the father's name. This implies that the author was not a prominent scholar, but known to the cataloguer and (he probably assumed) the users of the catalogue. The most likely candidate for this is Aḥmad b. ᶜĪsā (d. 643/1245–6), a not very prominent member of the Damascene Qudāma family, which played a crucial role in the city's learned culture during the 7th/13th c. (Pouzet, *Damas*, 80–3). According to al-Ṣafadī (*Wāfī*, VII, 273), he wrote 'drafts that he was not able to finalise' ('*sawwada musawwadāt lam yatamakkan min tabyīḍihā*') and this entry may be one of these unfinished drafts. C: rituals – ḥajj.

(948) M/3 258a/7 *Mukhtaṣar mā yataᶜallaqu bi-al-Sulṭān min al-aḥkām – Summary of What Relates to the Sultan Regarding Ordinances*; no such title is identifiable and this is most likely a summary of a mirror for princes. The obvious candidate for the original work is al-Māwardī's (d. 450/1058) *al-Aḥkām al-sulṭānīya* (Engl. tr. Wahba, *Ordinances of Government*). This summary may either relate to the entire work or to specific chapters such as *aḥkām al-iqṭāᶜ*, *aḥkām al-jarāʾim* and *aḥkām al-ḥisba*. C: political thought – mirror for princes?

(949) M/3 258a/7-8 *Milḥa fī muᶜtaqad ahl al-ḥaqq – Oath on the Belief of Righteous People*; A: ᶜAbd al-ᶜAzīz b. ᶜAbd al-Salām al-Sulamī (d. 660/1262); S: Arberry, *Handlist*, IV, 32 (no. 3849, fols. 62–74); this is a work on the question of anthropomorphism directed against the '*ḥashwīya*'. In Damascus of the 7th/13th c. this term was used against Hanbalite anthropomorphism (Pouzet, *Vie et Structures*, 155). C: theology (*kalām*).

(950) M/3 258a/8 *al-Mūjaz fī al-manṭiq – Summary of Logic*; two main possibilities: 1) Afḍal al-Dīn Muḥammad b. Nāmāwar al-Khūnajī (d. 646/1248) (EI[3], Kh. El-Rouayheb, 'al-Khūnajī, Afḍal al-Dīn') or 2) Ibn Sīnā (d. 428/1037) (a work by this title was ascribed to Ibn Sīnā, although Gutas, *Avicenna and the Aristotelian Tradition*, 439 argues that scribes invented the title); C: logic.

(951) M/4 258a/8 *al-Mujmal – Summary [on Lexicography]*; A: Aḥmad Ibn Fāris (d. 395/1004); S: *al-Mujmal fī al-lugha*, ed. H.Ḥ. Ḥammūdī, Kuwait: al-Munaẓẓama al-ᶜarabīya, 1985; NC: 7; C: lexicography. (cf. no. 1423)

(952) M/4 258a/9 *al-Muqtaṣid fī sharḥ al-Īḍāḥ – Concise Explanation of Elucidating [Grammar]*; a commentary on Abū ᶜAlī al-Ḥasan al-Fārisī's (d. 377/987) *al-Īḍāḥ fī al-naḥw*; A: ᶜAbd al-Qāhir b. ᶜAbd al-Raḥmān al-Jurjānī (d. 471/1078); S: ed. K.B. al-Marjan, Baghdad: Wth, 1982; MS: Süleymaniye, Fazıl Ahmed Paşa 1473**; C: grammar.

(953a) M/4 258a/9 *al-Muᶜarrab – [The Book] of Arabised Words*; A: Mawhūb b. Aḥmad Ibn al-Jawālīqī (d. 539/1144); S: *al-Muᶜarrab min al-kalām al-aᶜjamī*, ed. A.M. Shākir, Cairo: DKM, 1995; MS: Süleymaniye, Laleli 3629*; NC: 3; C: lexicography.

(953b) 258a/10 *ᶜArūḍ – Metrics*; A: Abū al-Fatḥ Ibn Jinnī (d. 392/1002); S: F. ᶜĪsā, Cairo: Dār al-maᶜrifa al-jāmiᶜīya, 2003; FI: '*wa-maᶜa aḥadihā ᶜArūḍ Ibn Jinnī*/'*in one of them [the three copies of Ibn al-Jawālīqī's al-Muᶜarrab] is Ibn Jinnī's [Book of] Metrics*'; C: poetry – metrics.

(954) M/4 258a/10 *al-Muḥsiba – The Sufficient [Introduction to Grammar]*; A: Ṭāhir b. Aḥmad Ibn Bābashādh (d. 469/1077); S: *al-Muqaddima al-Muḥsiba fī al-naḥw*, ed. Ḥ.S. al-Nuᶜaymī, *Majallat kullīyat al-islāmīya* (Baghdad) 3 (1970), 338–84; NC: 2; C: grammar.

(955) M/4 258a/10 *al-Mūjaz fī al-naḥw – Summary of Grammar*; among authors of such a title, such as Muḥammad b. al-Sarī Ibn al-Sarrāj (d. 316/929) (MU, VI, 2536), Muḥammad b. Aḥmad Ibn al-Khayyāṭ (d. 320/932) (MU, V, 2309) and Muḥammad b. ᶜAbd Allāh al-Kirmānī (d. 329/940–1) (MU, VI, 2548), none bears the *nisba* al-Harawī. Among those grammarians bearing the *nisba* al-Harawī, in turn, such as Shamir b. Ḥamdawayh (d. 255/868–9) (MU, III, 1420–1), Junāda b. Muḥammad al-Harawī (d. 399/1008–9) (MU, II, 800–1), Muḥammad b. ᶜAlī al-Harawī (d. 433/1041) (MU, VI, 2579),

the latter's father ᶜAlī b. Muḥammad al-Harawī (d.?; MU, V, 1923) and Ādam b. Aḥmad al-Harawī (d. 536/1142) (MU, I, 35–7) none is known to have authored such a title. C: grammar.

(956) M/4 258a/11 *al-Mudkhal ilā kitāb Sībawayh – Introduction to Sībawayh's Book*; referring to Sībawayh's (d. *c.*180/796) founding text of grammatical science; three main possibilities: 1) Muḥammad b. Yazīd al-Mubarrad (d. 286/900) (GAS, IX, 80); 2) al-Ḥasan b. ᶜAbd Allāh al-Sīrāfī (d. 368/979) (GAS, IX, 100); 3) Isḥāq b. Aḥmad al-Ṣaffār (d. 405/1014) (GAS, IX, 195/6) with a slight preference for al-Sīrāfī's work (the only one to have 7th-/13th-c. manuscripts in the Süleymaniye: Hamidiye 1313 (609/1212), Şehid Ali Paşa 2466 (640/1242) and 2467 (645/1247)); C: grammar.

(957) M/4 258a/11 *Muqaddimat al-Jarmī wa-ghayruhā – Al-Jarmī's Introduction and Other [Writings]*; A: Ṣāliḥ b. Isḥāq al-Jarmī (d. 225/839); S: probably referring to the author's introductory work on grammar, which is also called *Mukhtaṣar naḥw li-l-mutaᶜallimīn* (IN, I/1, 162) and *Mukhtaṣar fī al-naḥw* (IKH, II, 485–7); C: grammar. (cf. no. 1317a?)

(958a) M/4 258a/11 *Majmūᶜ fīhi min Sirr al-adab – Multiple-Text Manuscript with Extracts from The Secret of Adab*; most likely *Fiqh al-lugha wa-sirr al-ᶜarabīya* also known as *Sirr al-adab fī majārī kalām al-ᶜArab*; A: al-Thaᶜālibī (d. 429/1038); S: Orfali, 'Works', no. 7; C: lexicography. (cf. nos. 551, 1406)

(958b) 258a/12 *wa-al-Laṭāʾif – and Subtleties*; on account of the other two works in this multiple-text manuscript this is probably one of the works by A: al-Thaᶜālibī (d. 429/1038): 1) *al-Ẓarāʾif wa-al-laṭāʾif*, which was mainly transmitted in Abū Naṣr al-Maqdisī's recension *al-Laṭāʾif wa-al-ẓarāʾif*, ed. ᶜU. al-Asᶜad, *Laṭāʾif al-luṭf*, Beirut: Dār al-Masīra, 1980 (cf. no. 716?); 2) *al-Luṭf wa-al-laṭāʾif*, ed. M.ᶜA. al-Jādir, Kuwait: DA, 1984 (cf. no. 1312b); C: adab – anthology. (cf. nos. 908, 1242a, 1707)

(958c) 258a/12 *wa-al-Mubhij – and The Book, Which Makes One Rejoice*; A: al-Thaᶜālibī (d. 429/1038); S: ed. I. Ṣāliḥ, Damascus: DB, 1999; C: adab – anthology. (cf. nos. 1005, 1192)

(959) M/4 258a/12 *al-Muqniᶜ fī al-naḥw – The Sufficient [Book] on Grammar*; possibly a title with a popular key word and thus three possibilities: 1) Ibrāhīm b. Muḥammad Nifṭawayh (d. 323/935) (IN, I/1, 251); 2) Muḥammad b. Aḥmad Ibn al-Khayyāṭ (d. 320/932) (IN, I/1, 149); 3)

Aḥmad b. Muḥammad al-Naḥḥās (d. 338/950) (*al-Muqni*ᶜ *fī ikhtilāf al-Baṣrīyīn wa-al-Kufīyīn fī al-naḥw*; GAS, IX, 208); C: grammar.

(960) M/4 258a/12 *Muqaddimat Ibn al-Jawālīqī – The Introduction of Ibn al-Jawālīqī*; A: Mawhūb b. Aḥmad Ibn al-Jawālīqī (d. 539/1144); his biographers do not mention this title (e.g. IKH, V, 342–4; MU, VI, 2735–7). Placed in category 4 this is most likely a philological work and the term *muqaddima* signals an introductory text. These were especially popular in the field of grammar (see the works by Ṭāhir Ibn Bābashādh, d. 469/1077 and Muḥammad Ibn Ājurrūm, d. 723/1323), in which the author was also active. C: grammar?

(961) M/4 258a/12–13 *al-Mukhtār min alfāẓ al-abrār – The Selection from the Sayings of the Pious*; no such title is identifiable. The term '*abrār*' seems to hint at a biographical/hagiographical work such as Majd al-Dīn Abū al-Saᶜādāt al-Mubārak Ibn al-Athīr's (d. 606/1210) *al-Mukhtār fī manāqib al-akhyār* (IKH, VII, 326) on pious men and women of the early Islamic period, which in some manuscripts carries the title *al-Mukhtār fī manāqib al-abrār* (GAL S, I, 609). However, placed in philological category 4 the main term seems rather to be '*alfāẓ*' and this is most likely a lexicographical commentary on edifying aphorisms. C: lexicography?

(962a) M/4 258a/13 *al-Maṭar wa-al-nabāt – The Rain and Plants*; this is most likely a multiple-text manuscripts of three works. The first two works on '*maṭar*' and '*nabāt*' are lexicographical treatises of which numerous examples exist. However, as the two treatises are bound together it may be that they were both authored by A: Abū Zayd Saᶜīd b. Aws al-Anṣārī (d. 215/830) the main scholar who has two such titles in his oeuvre. S: MU, III, 1359–63; C: lexicography.

(962b) 258a/13 *wa-Malāhī al-*ᶜ*arab – Instruments of the Arabs*; no work with the title '*Malāhī al-*ᶜ*arab*' is known and al-Anṣārī did not write in this field at all. This is plausibly the work by the grammarian A: al-Mufaḍḍal b. Salama (fl. 3rd/9th c.) whose treatise '*al-Malāhī*' stressed the Arab tradition of instruments. S: ed. Gh. ᶜA. Khashaba, Cairo: HMAK, 1984; C: music.

(963) M/4 258a/13 *Mukhtaṣar fī al-qawāfī – Summary on Rhymes*; A: Muḥammad b. (Abī) al-Ḥasan/Ḥusayn Ibn al-Ardakhl al-Mawṣilī (d. 628/1231); S: IKH, V, 336; the reading of the name is far from being

straightforward, but the fact that this poet was among the courtiers and panegyrists of al-Malik al-Ashraf, the mausoleum's patron, (IKH, V, 336) makes this reading likely. His biographies only mention a diwan, not such a treatise on metrics, but the entry makes clear that this was not a well-known work. In contrast to other entries the cataloguer has the term *mukhtaṣar* without the definite article, making this a generic title and clearly implying that this was merely 'a' summary that he did not expect the users of the catalogue to know. C: poetry – rhyme.

(964) M/4 258a/14 *Mā yalḥanu fīhi al-ᶜāmma – What the Commoners Pronounce Incorrectly*; A: Mawhūb b. Aḥmad Ibn al-Jawālīqī (d. 539/1144); S: ed. Ḥ.Ṣ. al-Ḍāmin, *Takmilat iṣlāḥ mā taghlaṭu fīhī al-ᶜāmma*, Beirut: DB, 2007; C: lexicography.

(965) M/4 258a/14 *al-Murtajal fī sharḥ al-Jumal – Improvised [Book] on Explaining the Book of Summaries*; commentary on ᶜAbd al-Qāhir b. ᶜAbd al-Raḥmān al-Jurjānī's (d. 471/1078), grammar (cf. no. 293); A: ᶜAbd Allāh b. Aḥmad Ibn al-Khashshāb (d. 567/1172); S: ed. ᶜA. Ḥaydar, Damascus 1972; MS: Süleymaniye, Fazıl Ahmed Paşa 1485**; C: grammar.

(966) M/4 258a/14-15 *Mufḥim al-anām fī naẓm Faṣīḥ al-kalām – What Silences Dumb Mankind: Versifying Pure Speech*; no such title is identifiable, but this is clearly one of the versifications of *Faṣīḥ al-kalām* by Aḥmad b. Yaḥyā Thaᶜlab (d. 291/904) (on versifications see GAS, VIII, 144/5). C: lexicography.

(967) M/4 258a/15 *Mulḥat al-iᶜrāb – Pleasantry of Inflection*; A: al-Qāsim b. ᶜAlī al-Ḥarīrī al-Baṣrī (d. 516/1122); S: ed. B.Y. Habbūd, Sidon: MAṢ, 1997; C: grammar – didactic verse. (cf. no. 1522)

(968) M/5 258a/15 *Maghāzī – [The Book of] Raids*; A: Muḥammad b. ᶜUmar al-Wāqidī (d. 207/822); S: ed. J.M. Jones, London 1966; C: history – early Islam. (cf. no. 1276b)

(969) M/5 258a/15–16 *Mukhtaṣar taᵓrīkh al-Balādhurī – Summary of al-Balādhurī's History*; referring to the 3rd-/9th-c. *Futūḥ al-Buldān* by Aḥmad b. Yaḥyā al-Balādhurī; A: Yaḥyā b. ᶜĪsā Ibn Jazla (d. 493/1100); the sources on Ibn Jazla do not mention such a work. However, they are aware of another historical work by this physician, *Mukhtār mukhtaṣar Taᵓrīkh Baghdād*, (EI^2, J. Vernet, 'Ibn Djazla') so that the title of this work is probably a mistake.

The Süleymaniye, Reisülküttab copy, written by the Damascene physician al-Dakhwār (d. 628/1230) and arguably identical with the Ashrafiya manuscript mentioned here, is entitled *K. al-Mukhtār min mukhtaṣar Taʾrīkh al-Baghdādī*. MS: Süleymaniye, Reisülküttab 692**ʻ; C: history – regional.

(970) M/5 258a/16 *al-Mustaẓhirī fī al-taʾrīkh – The Mustaẓhirī on History*; A: al-Ghazālī (d. 505/1111); S: ed. ᶜA. Badawī, Paris 2006; FI: '*dhukira fī al-alif*' / '*mentioned in [the section on the letter] alif*' (cf. no. 44); C: political thought.

(971) M/5 258a/16–258b/1 *Murūj al-dhahab – The Meadows of Gold*; A: ᶜAlī b. al-Ḥusayn al-Masᶜūdī (d. 345/956); S: Engl. tr. P. Lunde, London 1989; ed. M.M. ᶜAbd al-Ḥamīd, Beirut: MAṢ, 1988; MS: Süleymaniye, Fatih 4481*; NC: 3; C: history – universal. (cf. no. 1428)

(972a) M/6 258b/1 *Majmūᶜ wa-shiᶜr Suḥaym – Multiple-Text Manuscript [with] Suḥaym's Poetry*; Scr('*bi-khaṭṭ*'): possibly Mūsā b. al-Maʾmūn al-Baṭāʾiḥī Sharaf al-Khilāfa Jamāl al-Dīn (d. 588/1192); as the cataloguer further down (cf. no. 1332a) employs 'Suḥaym' to unequivocally refer to A: Suḥaym ᶜAbd Banī al-Ḥasḥās (d. 37/657–8) this is most likely the poet meant here (and not Suḥaym b. Wathīl (d. *c.*40/661) (GAS, II, 202–3)). S: *Dīwān*, ed. ᶜA. al-Maymanī, Cairo: DQ, 1950; C: poetry – pre-Islamic/early Islamic. (cf. nos. 602, 1332a)

(972b) 258b/1 *wa-al-Ḥādira – and al-Ḥādira['s Poetry]*; Scr('*bi-khaṭṭ*'): possibly Mūsā b. al-Maʾmūn al-Baṭāʾiḥī Sharaf al-Khilāfa Jamāl al-Dīn (d. 588/1192); A: Quṭba al-Ḥādira; S: GAS, II, 213/4; C: poetry – pre-Islamic. (cf. no. 1226c)

(972c) 258b/1-2 *wa-marāthī fī al-Nabī ṣallā Allāh ᶜalayhi wa-sallam – and Elegies on the Prophet (may God's blessing and peace be upon him)*; Scr('*bi-khaṭṭ*'): possibly Mūsā b. al-Maʾmūn al-Baṭāʾiḥī Sharaf al-Khilāfa Jamāl al-Dīn (d. 588/1192); C: poetry – anthology – elegies – Prophet Muḥammad.

(973) M/6 258b/2 *Maqṣūrat Abī Ṣafwān – Abū Ṣafwān's Maqṣūra Poem*; A: Abū Ṣafwān al-Asadī; S: cited in Ismāᶜīl al-Qālī, *al-Amālī*, Beirut: Dār al-Āfāq, 1980, II, 237–40; authorship disputed, see GAS, II, 460; NC: 4; C: grammar. (cf. no. 592)

(974) M/6 258b/2–3 *Majmūᶜ fīhi ashᶜār jamāᶜa min al-ᶜarab awwaluhu shiᶜr ᶜAbd Allāh b. ᶜUtba b. Masᶜūd – Multiple-Text Manuscript with Poems*

of a Number of Arabs, the First One Being by ᶜAbd Allāh b. ᶜUtba b. Masᶜūd; generic title; A: mostly anonymous and ᶜAbd Allāh b. ᶜUtba b. Masᶜūd (fl. 1st/7th c.) (IKH, II, 372); the term '*al-ᶜarab*' in connection with poetry, used at several points in this catalogue, most likely refers to pre-Islamic and early Islamic poets, such as in al-Qurashī, *Jamharat*. FI: '*bi-khaṭṭ*'/'*in calligraphy*'; C: poetry – anthology – pre-Islamic/early Islamic.

(975) M/6 258b/3 *Majmūᶜ – Multiple-Text Manuscript*; Scr('*bi-khaṭṭ*'): ᶜAbd Allāh b. Muḥammad Ibn Abī al-Jūᶜ al-Warrāq (d. 395/1004–5) (IKH, IV, 379); on account of the thematic category and the fact that this scribe appears elsewhere in the context of poetry (cf. nos. 1270b, 1606) this is most likely an anonymous anthology with a generic title. C: poetry – anthology.

(976) M/6 258b/4 *Mulḥat Ibn ᶜAbbād fī al-farq bayna al-ẓāʾ wa-al-ḍād – The Pleasantry of Ibn al-ᶜAbbād on the Difference Between the letters ẓāʾ and ḍād*; this author's lexicographical work is well known, but the first term of the title given here is unusual. This is either a slightly amended title or a derivative work, for instance, didactic verse. A: Ismāᶜīl Ibn ᶜAbbād (d. 385/995); S: ed. M.Ḥ. Āl-Yāsīn, *al-Farq bayna al-ḍād wa-al-ẓāʾ*, Baghdad: MMa, 1958; MS: Süleymaniye, Fatih 5413/1 (fols. 1a–13a)**; C: lexicography. (cf. no. 32?)

(977) M/6 258b/4 *al-Muᶜjiza al-ᶜarabīya fī manāqib al-dawla al-Ashrafīya – The Arabic Miracle on the Virtues of al-Ashraf's Reign*; no such title is identifiable and this is most likely a book-in-the-making in verse and/or prose dedicated to the mausoleum's patron al-Malik al-Ashraf. C: panegyric – Ayyūbid – al-Malik al-Ashraf.

(978) M/6 258b/5–6 *Majmūᶜ fīhi akhbār wa-asānīd wa-qaṣāʾid min Istaghfir wa-istaghfirī wa-ghayr dhālika – Multiple-Text Manuscript with Reports, Chains of Transmissions and Qaṣīdas from The Book of Forgiveness and Similar [Texts]*; Scr('*bi-khaṭṭ*'): Mawhūb b. Aḥmad Ibn al-Jawālīqī (d. 539/1144) (EI^2, H. Fleisch, 'al-Djawālīḳī'); A: Abū al-ᶜAlāʾ al-Maᶜarrī (d. 449/1058); S: al-Qifṭī, *Inbāh*, I, 65; the author's *Istaghfir wa-istaghfirī* is a collection of poetry on 'homiletics, asceticism and forgiveness' ('*al-ᶜiẓa wa-al-zuhd wa-al-istighfār*') not to be confused with his *Epistle of Forgiveness*/*Risālat al-ghufrān* (G.J. van Gelder and G. Schoeler, New York 2013). C: poetry – zuhdīya.

(979) M/6 258b/6 *Majmūᶜ fawāʾid – Multiple-Text Manuscript of Wise Sayings*; anonymous with generic title; Scr('*dhukira anna aktharahu*

bi-khaṭṭ' l' it is mentioned that most of it is in the hand of'): Muḥammad b. ᶜAlī Ibn Muqla (d. 328/940); FI: '*tisᶜ qawāᵓim' l' nine leaves/folios*'.[110]

(980) M/6 258b/6–7 *al-Maṭar – [Describing] Rain [and Clouds]*; A: Ibn Durayd (d. 321/933); S: *K. waṣf al-maṭar wa-al-saḥāb*, ed. ᶜI. al-Tanūkhī, Damascus: MIA, 1963; C: lexicography/adab.

(981) M/6 258b/7 *Majmūᶜ shiᶜr fīhi ᶜUmāra b. ᶜAqīl wa-ghayr dhālika – Multiple-Text Manuscript of Poetry Including ᶜUmāra b. ᶜAqīl and Other*; generic title; A: mostly anonymous and ᶜUmāra b. ᶜAqīl (fl. early 3rd/9th c.); S: *Dīwān*, ed. Sh. al-ᶜĀshūr, Damascus: DY, 2006; C: poetry – anthology.

(982) M/6 258b/7-8 *al-Maqṣūr wa-al-mamdūd – On the Short and Long Alif*; A: Abū ᶜAlī al-Ḥasan al-Fārisī (d. 377/987); S: ᶜA.Ḥ. al-Ḥārithī, *Maqāyīs al-maqṣūr wa-al-mamdūd*, al-Ṭāᵓif: Dār al-Ṭarafayn, 2001; C: grammar.

(983) M/6 258b/8 *al-Masᵓala allatī jarat bayna Sībawayh wa-al-Kisāᵓī – The Discussion that Took Place between Sībawayh and al-Kisāᵓī*; this title refers to the famous *al-Masᵓala al-zunbūrīya* between ᶜAmr b. ᶜUthmān Sībawayh (d. 180/796) and al-Ḥasan ᶜAlī b. Ḥamza al-Kisāᵓī (d. 189/805?) (on this discussion see al-Qifṭī, *Inbāh*, II, 358–9). No such title is identifiable and this is most likely a (an anonymous?) treatise with selected material on this discussion. C: grammar.

(984) M/7 258b/9 *Muḥāḍarāt – Conversations [of the adībs]*; A: al-Ḥusayn b. Muḥammad al-Rāghib al-Iṣfahānī (d. early 5th/11th c.?); S: *Muḥāḍarāt al-udabāᵓ*, ᶜU. al-Ṭabbāᶜ, Beirut: DAr, 1999; MS: Süleymaniye, Fazıl Ahmed Paşa 1377**; NC: 3; C: adab – anthology.

(985) M/7 258b/9 *Majmūᶜ Ibn Shams al-Khilāfa – Multiple-Text Manuscript of Ibn Shams al-Khilāfa['s Writings]*; A: Jaᶜfar b. Shams al-Khilāfa al-Afḍalī (d. 622/1225); S: TI, 621–30, pp. 103–4; NC: 2; C: poetry – Fatimid/Ayyūbid/adab.

(986) M/7 258b/9 *al-Muᶜammarīn – [The Book of] Those Who Lived to an Advanced Age*; no such title by an author Abū/Ibn ᶜUbayda is identifiable. Most likely the cataloguer erroneously assumed that the book by Abū Ḥātim al-Sijistānī (255/869) (ed. I. Goldziher, *K. al-Muᶜammarīn, Abhandlungen zur arabischen Philologie*, ii, Leiden 1889) was authored by al-Sijistānī's teacher Abū ᶜUbayda Maᶜmar b. al-Muthannā al-Taymī (d. between 207/822 and

213/828), who is prominently quoted in al-Sijistānī's book. C: biographies. (cf. no. 1513)

(987) M/7 258b/10 *Mulaḥ al-mumālaḥa – Pleasant Poetry/Anecdotes of Table Companionship*; A: ʿAbd Allāh b. Muḥammad Ibn Nāqiyā (d. 485/1092); S: IKH, III, 98: '*majmūʿ*'; NC: 4; C: adab/poetry – anthology.

(988) M/7 258b/10 *Mulaḥ al-funūn – The Marvels of the Arts*; this is arguably the paraenetic work by A: Ibn al-Jawzī (d. 597/1200) who plays a prominent role in this library. The title is generally given simply as '*Mulāḥ*' (Alwajī, *Muʾallafāt*, 220), but appears also as '*Mulaḥ fī al-mawʿiẓa*' (Ḥājjī Khalīfa, *Kashf*, II, 1817). However, the manuscript S: Süleymaniye, Laleli, 1502 has '*Mulaḥ al-funūn*'. C: sermons.

(989) M/7 258b/10 *Maṣāriʿ al-ʿushshāq – Calamities of Lovers*; A: Jaʿfar b. Aḥmad al-Sarrāj (d. 500/1106); S: ed. Beirut: DṢ, 1958; anthology of prose texts and poems about love and lovers; C: adab/love literature. (cf. no. 1689)

(990) M/7 258b/10 *Muntakhab al-adhkiyāʾ – Choices from The Wise*; probably an anonymous selection from Ibn al-Jawzī's *al-Adhkiyāʾ*; C: adab – anthology. (cf. no. 59)

(991) M/7 258b/11 *al-Mudhahhab – The Golden [Book Concerning the Reports on Poets and Their Classes]*; A: Muḥammad Ibn Ḥabīb[111] (d. 245/860); S: IN, I/2, 328: '*al-Mudhahhab fī akhbār al-shuʿarāʾ wa-ṭabaqātihim*'; C: adab/ poetry.

(992) M/7 258b/11 *al-Mustajād min faʿlāt al-ajwād – The Admirable Deeds of Munificent Men*; A: al-Muḥassin b. ʿAlī al-Tanūkhī (d. 384/994) (authorship disputed); S: ed. L. Pauly, Stuttgart 1939; NC: 2; C: adab.

(993) M/7 258b/11–12 *al-Muḥdath fī al-Aghānī – The Innovated Concerning the Songs*; A: ʿAbd Allāh b. Muḥammad Ibn Nāqiyā (d. 485/1092); this work is generally referred to as '*Aghānī al-muḥdathīn*' (e.g. MU, IV, 1561), but some authors such as Ibn Faḍl Allāh al-ʿUmarī, *Masālik al-abṣār fī mamālik al-amṣār*, B.M. Bārūd *et al.*, Abu Dhabi: al-Majmaʿ al-thaqāfī, 2003–4 call it '*al-Muḥdath fī al-Aghānī*' (e.g. X, 409). C: adab – anthology.

(994) M/7 258b/12 *al-Mudabbaj – The Ornate [Book]*; A: Muḥammad b. ʿImrān al-Marzubānī (d. 384/994); S: IN, I/2, 413: '*K. al-Mudabbaj fī al-walāʾim wa-al-daʿawāt wa-al-sharāb*'; C: adab – wine.

(995) M/7 258b/12 *al-Muntahā fī al-kamāl – The [Book of] Utmost Perfection*; A: Muḥammad b. Sahl Ibn al-Marzubān al-Karkhī (d. *c.*345/956); S: ed. S.M. al-Hadrusi, Berlin 1988; R. Bostan, Berlin 1988; C: adab – anthology. (cf. nos. 12, 1107, 1260f)

(996) M/7 258b/12 *al-Muqtabas – [Book of] Extracts*; A: Ibn Durayd (d. 321/933); S: IKH, IV, 324; NC: 2; C: adab?

(997) M/8[112] 258b/13 *Maqātil al-Fursān – Slain Heroes*; popular title with numerous possibilities (see e.g. indices IN and MU), including Abū ᶜUbayda Maᶜmar b. al-Muthannā al-Taymī (d. between 207/822 and 213/828); Muḥammad Ibn Ḥabīb (d. 245/860); Aḥmad Ibn Abī Ṭāhir Ṭayfūr (d. 280/893); Ismāᶜīl b. al-Qāsim al-Qālī (d. 356/967); Yaḥyā b. ᶜAlī al-Khaṭīb al-Tibrīzī (d. 502/1109); C: adab. (cf. no. 1547)

(998) M/8 258b/13 *Maqālat Jawāhir al-sulūk – The Tract Entitled Gems of Deportment*; no such title, or passage '*Jawāhir al-sulūk*' within a larger work, is identifiable. The category and the title indicate an adab book-in-the-making. C: adab – anthology?

(999) M/8 258b/13 *Maᶜārif – [The Book of] Noteworthy Information*; A: ᶜAbd Allāh b. Muslim al-Dīnawarī Ibn Qutayba (d. 276/889); S: *K. al-maᶜārif*, ed. Th. ᶜUkāsha, Cairo: WTh, 1960; MS: Süleymaniye, Fatih 4441**; C: history – early Islamic. (cf. no. 1464)

(1000) M/8 258b/13–14 *al-Muᵓnis, ashᶜār – The Companion, Poems*; several works with the popular key word '*Muᵓnis*' exist, but the cataloguer explicitly specified that this is a work of poetry. This excludes those works dealing with other fields such as music. Most probably this is the anthology of ᶜAbbasid-period poems entitled '*Muᵓnis al-waḥda*' by A: Ḍiyāᵓ al-Dīn Abū al-Fatḥ Naṣr Allāh Ibn al-Athīr (d. 637/1239); S: GAL S, I, 521; MS: Süleymaniye, Fazıl Ahmed Paşa 1400*; C: poetry – anthology.

(1001) M/8 258b/14 *al-Majmūᶜ al-ᶜudhrī – The ᶜUdhrite Collection*; no such title is identifiable. This (anonymous?) anthology refers to the popular theme of *al-ḥubb al-ᶜUdhrī* in classical Arabic poetry and prose (EI^2, R. Jacobi, 'ᶜUdhri'). C: adab/love literature.

(1002) M/8 258b/14 *Maḥāsin al-muḥāḍarāt – Virtues of Conversations*; no such title is identifiable and this is probably a commentary/summary on the

Muḥāḍarāt al-udabā' by al-Ḥusayn b. Muḥammad al-Rāghib al-Iṣfahānī (d. early 5th/11th c.?). C: adab – anthology. (cf. no. 984)

(1003) M/8 258b/14 *al-Mukāfa'a ᶜalā al-ḥusn wa-al-qabīḥ – Reward and Punishment for the Good and the Bad*; A: Aḥmad b. Yūsuf Ibn al-Dāya (d. 340/951?); S: ed. ᶜA.M. ᶜUmar, *K. al-Mukāfa'a wa-ḥusn al-ᶜuqbā*, Cairo: MK, 2001; C: ethics.

(1004) M/8 258b/15 *al-Maḥẓūẓ fī al-rizq wa-al-manḥūs fīhi – The Fortunate Wealthy and the Unfortunate*; no such title is identifiable, but placed in category 8 this is most likely an adab anthology on this theme. C: adab?

(1005) M/8 258b/15 *al-Mubhij – The Book, Which Makes One Rejoice*; A: al-Thaᶜālibī (d. 429/1038); S: ed. I. Ṣāliḥ, Damascus: DB, 1999; C: adab – anthology. (cf. nos. 958c, 1192b)

(1006) M/8 258b/15–16 *Majmūᶜ awwaluhu akhlāq Rasūl Allāh ṣallā Allāh ᶜalayhi wa-sallam – Multiple-Text Manuscript with the Prophet's Morals in the Beginning (may God's blessing and peace be upon him)*; A: ᶜAbd Allāh b. Muḥammad Abū al-Shaykh (d. 369/979); S: ed. ᶜI.S. al-Ṣabābiṭī, *Akhlāq al-Nabī wa-ādābuhu*, Cairo: DML, 1991; C: ethics.

(1007) M/8 258b/16 *al-Mamādiḥ wa-al-madhāmm – Praise and Dispraise*; A: Ḥasan b. Rashīq al-Qayrawānī (d. 456/1063–4 or 463/1070–1); S: IKH, II, 88. Placed in category 8 this is most likely an adab work by this *adīb* and poet. C: adab?

(1008) M/8 258b/16 *al-Mūjaz – The Summary*; A: Muḥammad b. Yazīd al-Mubarrad (d. 286/900); no such work by the grammarian and philologist is identifiable (cf. the list of his works in al-Mubarrad, *al-Mudhakkar*, 45–61). Placed in category 8 this is most likely a work of adab. C: adab?

(1009) M/8 258b/16–17 *Muḍāhāt Kalīla wa-Dimna – The Emulation of Kalīla and Dimna*; A: Muḥammad b. Ḥusayn al-Yamanī (fl. 4th/10th c.); S: ed. M.Y. Najm, *K. Muḍāhāt amthāl kitāb Kalīla wa-Dimna bimā ashbahahā min ashᶜār al-ᶜarab*, Beirut: DTh, 1961; C: political thought – non-Muslim – mirror for princes. (cf. no. 1021)

(1010) M/8 258b/17 *Maᶜālī man ismuhu ᶜAlī – Merits of Those Named Ali*; no such title is identifiable, but placed in category 8 this is most likely an adab work on this theme. C: adab – merits.

(1011) M/8 258b/17 *al-Muwāzana wa-al-tarjīḥ fī al-Mutanabbī – Comparing and Preferring al-Mutanabbī*; no such title is identifiable, but it roughly describes the content of *al-Wasāṭa bayna al-Mutanabbī wa-khuṣūmihi* by ᶜAlī b. ᶜAbd al-ᶜAzīz al-Jurjānī (d. 392/1001–2?), eds M.A. Ibrāhīm and ᶜA.M. al-Bajāwī, Cairo: MAṢ, 1934 (cf. no. 1542); C: poetry – commentary.

(1012) M/8 258b/17 *al-Muwashshā – The Brocaded*; A: Muḥammad b. Aḥmad (Ibn) al-Washshāᵓ (d. 325/937); S: ed. R.E. Brünnow, Leiden 1886; C: adab – anthology. (cf. no. 1102)

(1013) M/8 259a/1 *al-Maṣūn fī sirr al-hawā al-maknūn – The Well-Guarded [Book] Concerning the Secret of Hidden Passion*; A: Ibrāhīm b. ᶜAlī al-Ḥuṣrī al-Qayrawānī (d. 413/1022); S: ed. al-N.ᶜA. Shaᶜlān, Cairo: Dār al-ᶜArab li-l-Bustānī, 1989; C: adab/love literature. (cf. nos. 1104, 1502)

(1014) M/8 259a/1 *Man ghāba ᶜanhū al-muṭrib – [The Book of] Those Who Have None (Other) to Delight Them*; A: al-Thaᶜālibī (d. 429/1038); S: al-N. ᶜA. Shaᶜlān, Cairo: MK, 1984; MS: Süleymaniye, Laleli 1946*; C: adab – anthology. (cf. no. 1274b)

(1015) M/8 259a/1 *Miṣbāḥ al-mujtahid – The Mujtahid's Lantern*; A: Muḥammad b. al-Ḥusayn al-Naqqāsh al-Tanūkhī (fl. 599/1203); S: Baghdādī, *Īḍāḥ al-Maknūn*, II, 493. This work and its author are only known from this source. Based on the thematic category this may be an adab work. C: adab?

(1016) M/8 259a/2 *al-Muntahā fī al-mushtahā – The Utmost Desire*; the title recalls Ibn al-Jawzī's (d. 597/1200) homiletic *Muntahā al-mushtahā* (TI, 591–600, p. 290). However, this work would not fit thematic category 8 very well and this is more likely an unknown anthology similar to *al-Mushtahā bi-naẓm ashᶜār wa-nawādir wa-ḥikāyāt wa-āthār* authored by a minor member of the grand Damascene al-Sulamī family (MS Yale, Landberg MSS 637). C: poetry/adab – anthology.

(1017) M/8 259a/2 *Muqaṭṭaᶜāt al-Nīl – Short Poems of the Nile*; A: ᶜAlī b. Rustam Ibn al-Sāᶜātī (d. *c.*604/1207); S: IKH, III, 396; C: poetry – Ayyūbid.

(1018) M/8 259a/2 *Mirᵓāt al-murūwāt – The Mirror of Honour and Virtues*; A: al-Thaᶜālibī (d. 429/1038); S: ed. M.Kh.R. Yūsuf, Beirut: DIḤ, 2004; NC: 2; C: adab – collection of material under rubric of honour/virtues.

(1019) M/8 259a/3 *Man nusiba min al-shu^carā^ɔ ilā amīr – Those among the Poets Who Derive Their Nisba from a Commander*; no such title is identifiable, but this seems to be a biographical treatise similar to Muḥammad Ibn Ḥabīb's (d. 245/860) *Man nusiba ilā ummihi min al-shu^carā^ɔ* (*Those among the Poets Who Derive Their Nisba from Their Mother*, ed. ᶜA. Hārūn, *Nawādir al-makhṭūṭāt*, Cairo: LTTN, 1951, I, 83–96). C: biographical dictionary – poets.

(1020) M/8 259a/3 *Masāwī shiᶜr al-Mutanabbī – The Faults of al-Mutanabbī's Poetry*; A: Ismāᶜīl Ibn ᶜAbbād (d. 385/995); S: ed. M.Ḥ. Āl-Yāsīn, *al-Kashf ᶜan masāwī shiᶜr al-Mutanabbī*, Baghdad: MN, 1965; C: poetry – commentary. (cf. nos. 878, 1248b)

(1021) M/9 259a/3–4 *Muḍāhāt Kalīla wa-Dimna – The Emulation of Kalīla and Dimna*; A: Muḥammad b. Ḥusayn al-Yamanī (fl. 4th/10th c.); S: ed. M.Y. Najm, *K. Muḍāhāt amthāl kitāb Kalīla wa-Dimna bimā ashbahahā min ashᶜār al-ᶜarab*, Beirut: DTh, 1961; FI: '*muṣawwara*' / '*illustrated*'; C: political thought – non-Muslim – mirror for princes. (cf. no. 1009)

(1022) M/9 259a/4 *al-Majisṭī – Almagest*; A: Ibn Sīnā (d. 428/1037); this is probably a summary of the *Almagest*, which Gutas, *Avicenna and the Aristotelian Tradition*, 465–6 argues to be identical with the author's *al-Arṣād al-kullīya* (*Comprehensive Observations)*. C: astronomy.

(1023) M/9 259a/4 *al-Mawālīd wa-ghayruhu – Horoscopes and Other [Writings]*; popular title with numerous possibilities (cf. IN, index); C: astronomy/genethlialogy.

(1024) M/9 259a/4 *Mawāqīt al-aṭibbā^ɔ – The Physicians' Horology*; 'Mawāqīt' in its astronomical sense refers to determining the prayer times and the tables resulting from these efforts (King, *Synchrony with the Heavens*) and this is most likely a work on astrological medicine (cf. Ullmann, *Medizin*, 254–6). C: astronomy – horology/medicine.

(1025) M/9 259a/5 *Mukhtaṣar fī siyāsat al-ḥurūb – Summary of Conducting Wars*; A: al-Shaᶜrānī al-Harthamī (fl. 3rd/9th c.); S: eds ᶜA. ᶜAwn and M.M. Ziyāda, Cairo: al-Muɔassasa al-Miṣrīya al-ᶜāmma, 1964; C: warfare.

(1026) M/9 259a/5 *Mudāwāt*[113] *jarā^ɔiḥ al-jawāriḥ – Treating Injuries of Beasts of Prey*; no such title is identifiable. Most likely this is an extract from one of the works on falconry (cf. nos. 214–19, 307, 1041), in which as much as half of the text can be devoted to the illnesses and treatment of birds of prey (see Ullmann, *Medizin*, 218). C: veterinary medicine.

(1027) M/9 259a/5–6 *Mabdaʾ jawāmiᶜ Kitāb Jālīnūs wa-ghayruhu – The Beginning of the Summaries of Galen's Book and Other [Writings]*; it is not clear to which 'book' by A: Galen the title is referring (for Arabic texts ascribed to Galen see Ullmann, *Medizin*, 35–67). Arguably this could be MS: Süleymaniye, Fatih 3538 & 3539**, which are vols. 1 and 2 of a work entitled *Kitāb jawāmiᶜ al-iskandarīyīn li-kutub Jālīnūs fī al-ṭibb naqala Ḥunayn b. Isḥāq*. This manuscript was written in 571/1175 and circulated in the early 7th/13th c. among Damascene physicians, such as Maḥmūd b. ᶜUmar al-Mutaṭayyib al-Ḥānawī (d. 635/1238) (TI, 631–40, pp. 264–5; cf. Fatih 3539, fol. 1a). C: medicine.

(1028) M/9 259a/6 *Manṣūbāt al-shaṭranj – Chess Problems*; A: Muḥammad b. ᶜUbayd Allāh al-Lajlāj (fl. 4th/10th c.); S: IN, II/1, 480–1; C: chess.

(1029) M/10 259a/6 *al-Miʾa – [The Book of] One Hundred [Medical Questions]*; A: ᶜĪsā b. Yaḥyā al-Masīḥī al-Jurjānī (d. 401/1010); S: ed. F. Sanagustin, Damascus: IFD, 2000; NC: 2; C: medicine.

(1030) M/10 259a/7 *Minhāj al-bayān – The Method of Demonstrating [What Man Uses]*; A: Yaḥyā b. ᶜĪsā Ibn Jazla (d. 493/1100); S: *Minhāj al-bayān fīmā yastaᶜmiluhu al-insān*, eds M.M. Badawī and F. al-Ḥafyān, Cairo: JDA, 2010; MS: Süleymaniye, Ayasofya 3755***; NC: 8; C: pharmacology. (cf. no. 1480)

(1031a) M/10 259a/7 *Majmūᶜ fīhi al-Aghdhiya – Multiple-Text Manuscript with the Book of Dietetics*; popular title with numerous possible authors such as (cf. Ullmann, *Medizin*, 199–203), Rufus of Ephesus (fl. *c.*100 BCE), Ḥunayn b. Isḥāq (d. 260/873), and ᶜAbd al-Malik Ibn Zuhr (d. 557/1162) (cf. no. 108); C: medicine – dietetics.

(1031b) 259a/7 *wa-Tadbīr al-aṣiḥḥāʾ – Regimen of the Healthy*; A: Hippocrates; no such title by Hippocrates is known (cf. Ullmann, *Medizin*, 25–35) and this is possibly Galen's *Tadbīr al-aṣiḥḥāʾ* (Ullmann, *Medizin*, 46) wrongly ascribed. C: medicine – dietetics.

(1031c) 259a/8 *wa-Dafᶜ maḍārr al-aghdhiya* – *Avoiding Harms of Nutriments*; A: al-Rāzī (Rhazes) (d. 313/925 or 323/935); S: IN, II/1, 311; C: medicine. (cf. no. 774)

(1032) M/10 259a/8 *al-Mughnī* – *The Sufficient [Book]*; most likely this is an otherwise unknown medical treatise by the Fatimid court physician A: Isḥāq b. Ibrāhīm (fl. early 4th/10th c.), the successor to Manṣūr b. Sahlān (cf. no. 264). S: IAU, III, 354–5; C: medicine.

(1033) M/10 259a/8 *al-Mustaṭraf fī al-ṭibb* – *The Utmost on Medicine*; no such (key word?) title is identifiable. C: medicine.

(1034) M/10 259a/8-9 *Maṣāliḥ al-abdān wa-al-anfus* – *Sustenance for Body and Soul*; A: Aḥmad b. Sahl al-Balkhī (d. 322/934); S: ed. M. Miṣrī, Cairo: MMA, 2005; C: medicine.

(1035) M/10 259a/9 *al-Manṣūrī* – *The Manṣūri [Book of Medicine]*; A: al-Rāzī (Rhazes) (d. 313/925 or 323/935); S: *K. al-ṭibb al-Manṣūrī*, P. de Koning, *Trois traités d'anatomie arabes*, Leiden 1903; MS: Süleymaniye, Ayasofya 3751*; NC: 2; C: medicine. (cf. no. 1484)

(1036) M/10 259a/9 *Manāfiᶜ al-fawākih* – *The Benefits of Fruits*; no such title is identifiable, but this is probably similar to ᶜAlī b. Rabban al-Ṭabarī's (d. *c.*240/855) *Manāfiᶜ al-aṭᶜima wa-al-ashriba wa-al-ᶜaqāqīr* (IN, II/1, 297). This treatise drew from discussions on the benefits of fruits that IAU reports, for example, a discussion that purportedly took place at the pre-Islamic Persian court (IAU, I, 387–92). C: medicine – dietetics.

(1037) M/10 259a/9 *al-Mughnī* – *The Sufficient [Book Concerning the Treatment of Illnesses and the Knowledge of Afflictions and Affections]*; A: Saᶜīd b. Hibat Allāh b. al-Ḥusayn (d. 495/1101); S: Ullmann, *Medizin*, 160: '*al-Mughnī fī tadbīr al-amrāḍ wa-maᶜrifat al-ᶜilal wa-al-aᶜrāḍ*'; NC: 3; C: medicine.

(1038) M/10 259a/10 *Maᶜrifat al-jawāhir*[114] – *Knowledge of Precious Stones*; possibly A: al-Bīrūnī (d. after 442/1050); S: ed. H. Said, *K. al-Jamāhir fī maᶜrifat al-jawāhir*, Karachi 2001; C: mineralogy. (cf. nos. 306, 269)

(1039) M/10 259a/10 *al-Mulūkī*[115] – *Royal [Medicine]*; A: al-Rāzī (Rhazes) (d. 313/925 or 323/935); S: IN, II/1, 310: '*al-Ṭibb al-mulūkī*'; C: medicine.

(1040) M/10 259a/10–11 *Majmū*ᶜ *fī jawāmi*ᶜ *Jālīnūs fī al-faṣd – Multiple-Text Manuscript with the Summary of Galen's [Book] on Phlebotomy*; A: Thābit b. Qurra al-Ḥarrānī (d. 288/901); S: IAU, II, 201: '*Jawāmi*ᶜ *K. al-faṣd*'; FI: '*wa-fīhi shay*ᵓ *bi-khaṭṭ al-Masīḥī*'/'*and in it [Thābit's book] is something in the hand of al-Masīḥī* [ᶜ*Īsā b. Yaḥyā* <u>*al-Masīḥī*</u> *al-Jurjānī (d. 401/1010)]*; C: medicine.

(1041) M/10 259a/11 *Mukhtaṣar al-jamhara fī* ᶜ*ulūm al-bayzara – Summary of the Compilation Concerning the Disciplines of Falconry*; this summary probably refers to A: ᶜĪsā al-Azdī's (4th/10th c.?) work on falconry, *al-Jamhara* (EI², F. Viré, 'Bayzara'). This manuscript, copied in 672/1273, but without title page, is held in MS: Süleymaniye, Ayasofya 3813***. C: falconry.

(1042) M/11 259a/12 *Mukhtār min shi*ᶜ*r al-Ṣābi*ᵓ *– Selection of al-Ṣābi*ᵓ*'s Poetry*; most likely referring to A: Ibrāhīm b. Hilāl <u>al-Ṣābiᵓ</u> (d. 384/994), whose poetry is included in several places in this catalogue (cf. nos. 635, 1305); S: *Shi*ᶜ*r Abī Isḥāq al-Ṣābi*ᵓ, ed. M. Gharīb, Alexandria: Markaz al-Babāṭīn, 2010; C: poetry – Būyid. (cf. no. 1492)

(1043) M/11 259a/12 *Mukhtār min shi*ᶜ*r Ibn Munīr – Selection of Ibn Munīr's Poetry*; A: Aḥmad <u>b. Munīr</u> al-Ṭarābulusī al-Raffāᵓ (d. 548/1153); S: *Dīwān Ibn Munīr*, ed. ᶜU.ᶜA. Tadmurī, Beirut: DJ, 1986; C: poetry – Zangid. (cf. nos. 1491, 1622, 1657)

(1044) M/12 259a/13 *Mukhtār shi*ᶜ*r Ibn Qalāqis – Selection of Ibn Qalāqis' Poetry*; A: Naṣr (Allāh) b. ᶜAbd Allāh <u>Ibn Qalāqis</u> (d. 567/1172); S: *Dīwān*, ed. S. al-Furayḥ, Kuwait 1988; C: poetry – Fatimid.

(1045) M/12 259a/13 *al-Mustajād min shi*ᶜ*r al-*ᶜ*Imād – The Most Excellent of al-*ᶜ*Imād's Poetry*; no such title is identifiable and arguably this refers to A: Muḥammad b. Muḥammad ᶜ<u>Imād</u> al-Dīn al-Kātib al-Iṣfahānī (d. 597/1201), certainly the most renowned 'al-ᶜImād' in this period. C: poetry – Ayyūbid. (cf. nos. 1489, 1659)

(1046) M/12 259a/13 *Mukhtār min shi*ᶜ*r al-Bustī – Selection of al-Bustī's Poetry*; A: ᶜAlī b. Muḥammad <u>al-Bustī</u> (d. 354/965); S: *Dīwān Abī al-Fatḥ al-Bustī*, ed. Sh. al-ᶜĀshūr, Damascus: DY, 2006; C: poetry – Ghaznawid.

(1047) M/12 259a/13–14 *Mukhtār min shi*ᶜ*r Ibn al-Rīwandī – Selection of Ibn al-Rīwandī's Poetry*; A: Aḥmad b. Yaḥyā <u>Ibn al-Rīwandī</u> (*c.*298/912);

some lines of verse have been attributed to him, e.g. in al-ᶜAbbāsī, *Maᶜāhid*, I, 53 and 57. Yet this attribution is disputed and they seem to be by al-Qiṣāfī (d. 247/861) (see Ibn al-Muᶜtazz, *Ṭabaqāt*, 446). On Ibn al-Rīwandī (Rāwandī/Rawandī) see Stroumsa, *Freethinkers of Medieval Islam*. C: poetry.

(1048) M/13 259a/14 *al-Manāʾiḥ*[116] *al-Saᶜīdīya* – *The Saidian Offerings*; no such title is identifiable, but this may be panegyrics for the Hamdanid ruler of Aleppo, Saᶜīd al-Dawla (d. 392/1002). This would fit the regional profile of the library, which had a solid corpus of Hamdanid poetry (for example, nos. 1051, 1110, 1181b). C: poetry – panegyric – Ḥamdānid?

(1049) M/13 259a/14 *al-Madāʾiḥ al-Ashrafīya* – *The Ashrafian Panegyrics*; probably al-Malik al-Ashraf's secretary A: ᶜAlī b. Muḥammad Kamāl al-Dīn Ibn al-Nabīh (d. 619/1222) renowned for his *Ashrafīyāt* and the poet who has the largest corpus of panegyrics for al-Ashraf; S: al-Asᶜad, *Dīwān Ibn al-Nabīh*, 123–363; C: poetry – panegyric – Ayyūbid – al-Malik al-Ashraf. (cf. nos. 190, 288, 315, 863, 868, 1055, 1229d)

(1050) M/13 259a/15 *Mukhtār min shiᶜr al-Farazdaq* – *Selection of al-Farazdaq's Poetry*; A: Tammām b. Ghālib al-Farazdaq (d. *c.*114/732); S: *Sharḥ dīwān al-Farazdaq*, ed. ᶜA.I. al-Ṣāwī, Cairo: MTK, 1936; C: poetry – Umayyad. (cf. nos. 1073, 1290c)

(1051) M/13 259a/15 *Mukhtār min shiᶜr al-Mutanabbī* – *Selection of al-Mutanabbī's Poetry*; A: Aḥmad al-Mutanabbī (d. 354/955); S: *Dīwān*, ed. ᶜA. ᶜAzzām, Cairo: LTTN, 1944; C: poetry – Ḥamdānid.

(1052) M/13 259a/15 *Mukhtār al-Ḥulī wa-al-ḥulal* – *Selection from al-Ḥulī wa-al-ḥulal*; no such title is identifiable. 2 main possibilities: 1) selection and commentary on this *qaṣīda* by Hibat Allāh b. Jaᶜfar Ibn Sanāʾ al-Mulk (d. 608/1211) (*Dīwān*, ed. I. Naṣr, Cairo: DKA, 1967–9), 2) selection from the work by Aḥmad Ibn Abī Ṭāhir Ṭayfūr (d. 280/893) (IN, I/2, 452); C: poetry.

(1053) M/13 259a/15–16 *Manāʾiḥ*[117] *al-qarāʾiḥ* – *Bestowal of Talents*; the *kalām* summary by the theologian Sayf al-Dīn ᶜAlī al-Āmidī (d. 631/1233) (IKH, III, 293) can be discarded owing to the thematic category. It is thus most probably the work of poetry by A: ᶜAlī b. (al-)Munjib Ibn al-Ṣayrafī (d. 542/1147); S: MU, V, 1971–2; C: poetry – Fatimid.

(1054) M/13 259a/16 *Madāʾiḥ fī al-Malik al-ᶜĀdil – Panegyrics on al-Malik al-ᶜĀdil*; referring to al-Malik al-Ashraf's father al-Malik al-ᶜĀdil Sayf al-Dīn (d. 615/1218); A: Asᶜad b. Aḥmad al-Sinjārī (d. 622/1225); S: IKH, I, 214–17 who mentions that he found this poet's diwan only in the Ashrafīya library; C: poetry – panegyric – Ayyūbid – al-Malik al-ᶜĀdil. (cf. no. 800)

(1055) M/13 259a/16 *Mulaḥ al-madāʾiḥ*[118] *al-ᶜĀdilīya – Pleasant Poetry/ Anecdotes of the ᶜĀdilian Panegyrics*; referring to al-Malik al-Ashraf's father al-Malik al-ᶜĀdil Sayf al-Dīn (d. 615/1218); arguably al-Malik al-Ashraf's secretary A: ᶜAlī b. Muḥammad Kamāl al-Dīn Ibn al-Nabīh (d. 619/1222) who composed a series of ᶜĀdilīyāt-poems; S: al-Asᶜad, *Dīwān Ibn al-Nabīh*, 110–21; C: poetry – panegyric – Ayyūbid – al-Malik al-ᶜĀdil. (cf. nos. 190, 288, 315, 863, 868, 1049, 1229d)

(1056) M/13 259a/16-17 *Mukhtār shiᶜr Ibn Munqidh – Selection of Ibn Munqidh's Poetry*; A: Usāma b. Munqidh (d. 584/1188); S: *Dīwān Usāma Ibn Munqidh*, ed. A.A. Badawī/Ḥ. ᶜAbd al-Majīd, Cairo: al-Maṭbaᶜa al-amīrīya, 1953; the other possibility would be the early Islamic poet Ziyād/ al-Marrār b. Munqidh b. ᶜAmr (fl. 96/715). However, he is named 'Ziyād b. Munqidh' (cf. no. 625) elsewhere in the catalogue and the context of the surrounding titles makes poetry by Usāma much more likely. C: poetry – Zangid/Ayyūbid. (cf. no. 1621)

(1057) M/13 259a/17 *Mukhtār shiᶜr al-Ablah – Selection of al-Ablah's Poetry*; A: Muḥammad al-Ablah (d. *c.*579/1183); S: IKH, IV, 463–5; C: poetry – Saljūq.

(1058) M/13 259a/17 *Mukhtār Dīwān al-Sarrāj – Selection from al-Sarrāj's Diwan*; A: Jaᶜfar b. Aḥmad al-Sarrāj (d. 500/1106); S: MU, II, 777–81 who mentions his poetry; C: poetry – zuhdīya?

(1059) M/13 259a/17–18 *al-Mufaḍḍalīyāt – Mufaḍḍal al-Dīn's Compilation*; A: attr. al-Mufaḍḍal al-Ḍabbī (d. 164/780 or 170/786); S: eds A.M. Shākir and ᶜA.M. Hārūn, Cairo: DM, 1942; FI: '*mujarrada ᶜan gharībihā*'/'*without the uncommon words*'; C: poetry – anthology – pre-Islamic. (cf. nos. 1285c, 1635)

(1060) M/13 259a/18 *al-Mubtazz min Dīwān Ibn al-Muᶜtazz – The Haul from Ibn al-Muᶜtazz's Diwan*; such a title is not identifiable, but it is clearly a selection from ᶜAbd Allāh Ibn al-Muᶜtazz's (d. 296/908) diwan (ed.

B. Lewin, Istanbul 1945–50); C: poetry – ᶜAbbāsid. (cf. nos. 395, 1075, 1596, 1617, 1638)

(1061) M/13 259a/18 *Mukhtār shiᶜr al-Khālidīyayn – Selection from the Two Khālidīs' Poetry*; referring to the two court poets Abū ᶜUthmān Saᶜd/Saᶜīd (d. 350/961) and Abū Bakr Muḥammad (d. 380/990); C: poetry – ᶜAbbāsid. (cf. no. 1283)

(1062) M/13 259a/18–259b/1 *Muntakhab min Dīwān Ibn Abī al-Ṣaqr – Choices from Ibn Abī al-Ṣaqr's Diwan*; A: Muḥammad b. ᶜAlī Ibn Abī al-Ṣaqr (d. 498/1105); S: IKH, IV, 450–1 who states that he saw this diwan in the Ashrafiya library; C: poetry.

(1063) M/13 259b/1 *Mukhtār min shiᶜr Abī Tammām – Selection from Abū Tammām's Poetry*; A: Ḥabīb b. Aws Abū Tammām (d. 231/845 or 232/846); S: *Dīwān Abī Tammām bi-sharḥ al-Khaṭīb al-Tibrīzī*, ed. M. ᶜAzzām, Cairo: DM, 1957–65; C: poetry – ᶜAbbāsid. (cf. nos. 409, 1626)

(1064) M/13 259b/1 *al-Muntakhal min shiᶜr al-qabāʾil – The Sifted of Tribal Poetry*; A: al-Ḥasan b. Bishr al-Āmidī (d. 370/980 or 371/981); S: GAS, II, 44: '*Muntakhal al-qabāʾil*'; C: poetry – anthology – pre-Islamic. (cf. no. 1704)

(1065) M/13 259b/2 *al-Muntakhal – The Sifted*; A: Abū al-Faḍl ᶜUbayd Allāh b. Aḥmad al-Mīkālī[119] (d. 436/1044); S: ed. Y.W. al-Jubūrī, Beirut: DGI, 2000; also ascribed to al-Thaᶜālibī (d. 429/1038); C: poetry – anthology – Sāmānid/Ghaznawid. (cf. nos. 1066, 1208a)

(1066) M/13 259b/2 *al-Muntakhal – The Sifted*; A: Abū al-Faḍl ᶜUbayd Allāh b. Aḥmad al-Mīkālī (d. 436/1044); S: ed. Y.W. al-Jubūrī, Beirut: DGI, 2000; FI: '*mudhahhab*'/'*gilded*'; also ascribed to al-Thaᶜālibī (d. 429/1038); C: poetry – anthology – Sāmānid/Ghaznawid. (cf. nos. 1065, 1208a)

(1067) M/13 259b/2 *Maṭlab al-maᶜānī wa-muṭrib al-Aghānī – The Place to Seek Meanings and the Delightful of the Songs*; A: Abū al-Faḍl ᶜUbayd Allāh b. Aḥmad al-Mīkālī[120] (d. 436/1044); this is probably a summary or commentary on the *Book of Songs* by Abū al-Faraj al-Iṣfahānī (d. 356/967). No such title by the poet and litterateur al-Mīkālī is known, but it would fit his profile as he authored a summary or commentary on another great work of poetry, the *Book of Bravery* by Ḥabīb b. Aws Abū Tammām (d. 231/845 or

232/846) (GAS, II, 643). C: poetry – commentary – Sāmānid/Ghaznawid/adab.

(1068) M/13 259b/3 *Mukhtār maṭlab al-maᶜānī* – *The Selection from The Place to Seek Meanings*; no such title is identifiable, but this is most likely a (an anonymous) summary of the preceding work. C: poetry/adab – anthology.

(1069) M/13 259b/3 *al-Mukhtazal min al-madīḥ wa-al-ghazal* – *Extract of Elegies and Love Poetry*; the only identifiable work entitled *al-Mukhtazal* is the summary that Aḥmad b. ᶜAbd al-Jalīl al-Tudmīrī (d. 555/1160) made of his own commentary on al-Zajjājī's (d. 337/948 or 339–40/949–50?) grammatical treatise (Ibn al-Abbār (d. 658/1260), *Takmila*, I, 60). This neither fits the category nor the description given here. This is thus most probably a poetry anthology of the book-in-the-making type. C: poetry – anthology.

(1070) M/13 259b/3–4 *Mukhtār shiᶜr al-Shihāb Fityān* – *Selection from al-Shihāb Fityān's Poetry*; A: Fityān b. ᶜAlī al-Shihāb al-Shāghūrī (d. 615/1228); S: IKH, IV, 24–6 who states that he saw a small version of this poet's diwan with his dūbaytī verses in Damascus; C: poetry – dūbaytī.

(1071) M/13 259b/4 *Majmūᶜ ashᶜār min ᶜiddat dawāwīn* – *Multiple-Text Manuscript of Poetry from Several Diwans*; anonymous work with generic title; C: poetry – anthology.

(1072) M/13 259b/4 *Mukhtār Dīwān Jarīr* – *Selection from Jarīr's Diwan*; A: Jarīr b. ᶜAṭīya (d. *c.*110/728–9); S: *Dīwān*, ed. N. Ṭaha, Cairo: DM, 1969–71; C: poetry – Umayyad. (cf. nos. 404, 1229e, 1290b, 1610, 1630, 1653)

(1073) M/13 259b/5 *Mukhtār Dīwān al-Farazdaq* – *Selection from al-Farazdaq's Diwan*; A: Tammām b. Ghālib al-Farazdaq (d. *c.*114/732); S: *Sharḥ dīwān al-Farazdaq*, ed. ᶜA.I. al-Ṣāwī, Cairo: MTK, 1936; C: poetry – Umayyad. (cf. nos. 1050, 1290c)

(1074) M/13 259b/5 *Mukhtār al-Naqāʾiḍ* – *Selection from the Polemical Poems*; this summary is most likely referring to the poems exchanged between Jarīr b. ᶜAṭīya (d. *c.*110/728–9) and Tammām b. Ghālib al-Farazdaq (d. *c.*114/732) (*Naqāʾiḍ Jarīr wa-al-Farazdaq*, ed. A.A. Bevan, Leiden 1905) because the preceding two entries refer to these two poets and because the *Polemical Poems* are explicitly ascribed to these two poets in no. 1349. Another less likely possibility would be the poems exchanged between Jarīr and Ghiyāth b. Ghawth al-Akhṭal (d. 92/710) (*Naqāʾiḍ Jarīr wa-al-Akhṭal*, ed. A. Ṣāliḥānī, Beirut: Dār al-Mashriq, 1922). C: poetry – Umayyad. (cf. nos. 1285b, 1290a, 1349, 1356, 1359, 1607)

(1075) M/13 259b/5 *Mukhtār shi^{c}r Ibn al-Mu^{c}tazz – Selection from Ibn al-Mu^{c}tazz's Poetry*; A: ^{c}Abd Allāh Ibn al-Mu^{c}tazz (d. 296/908); S: ed. B. Lewin, Istanbul 1945–50; C: poetry – ^{c}Abbāsid. (cf. nos. 395, 1060, 1596, 1617, 1638)

(1076) M/13 259b/6 *Mukhtār shi^{c}r al-amīr ^{c}Īsā b. Mawdūd – Selection from the Commander ^{c}Īsā b. Mawdūd's Poetry*; A: al-Amīr Abū al-Manṣūr Fakhr al-Dīn ^{c}Īsā b. Mawdūd, ruler of Tikrīt (d. 584/1188); S: IKH, III, 498–500; C: poetry – Saljūq.

(1077) M/13 259b/6 *Mukhtār shi^{c}r al-^{c}Abbās b. al-Aḥnaf – Selection from al-^{c}Abbās b. al-Aḥnaf's Poetry*; A: al-^{c}Abbās b. al-Aḥnaf (d. 193/808); S: EI^{3}, S. Enderwitz, 'al-^{c}Abbās b. al-Aḥnaf'; C: poetry – ^{c}Abbāsid.

(1078) M/13 259b/7 *Mukhtār shi^{c}r Ibn al-Qayṣarānī – Selection from Ibn al-Qayṣarānī's Poetry*; A: Muḥammad b. Naṣr Ibn al-Qayṣarānī (d. 548/1154); S: Muḥammad, *Shi^{c}r Ibn al-Qayṣarānī*; C: poetry – Zangid.

(1079) M/13 259b/7 *Mukhtār shi^{c}r al-Buḥturī wa-al-Raḍī – Selection from al-Buḥturī's and al-Raḍī's Poetry*; no such title is identifiable and this is a probably an anonymous selection referring to al-Walīd al-Buḥturī (d. 284/897) (*Dīwān al-Buḥturī*, ed. Ḥ. al-Ṣayrafī, Cairo: DM, 1963–5) and Muḥammad b. al-Ḥusayn al-Sharīf al-Raḍī (d. 406/1016) (*Dīwān al-Sharīf al-Raḍī*, ed. I. ^{c}Abbās, Beirut: DṢ, 1994). C: poetry – ^{c}Abbāsid/Būyid. (for al-Raḍī cf. nos. 394, 1081, 1181c, 1576, 1666)

(1080) M/13 259b/7-8 *Mukhtār shi^{c}r ^{c}Abd al-Muḥsin al-Ṣūrī – Selection from ^{c}Abd al-Muḥsin al-Ṣūrī's Poetry*; A: ^{c}Abd al-Muḥsin Ibn Ghalbūn al-Ṣūrī (d. 419/1028); S: *Dīwān al-Ṣūrī*, ed. Sh.H. Shukr, Baghdad: DḤ, 1980; C: poetry.

(1081) M/13 259b/8 *Mukhtār shi^{c}r al-Sharīf al-Raḍī – Selection from al-Sharīf al-Raḍī's Poetry*; A: Muḥammad b. al-Ḥusayn al-Sharīf al-Raḍī (d. 406/1016); S: *Dīwān al-Sharīf al-Raḍī*, ed. I. ^{c}Abbās, Beirut: DṢ, 1994; C: poetry – Būyid. (cf. nos. 394, 1079, 1181c, 1576, 1666)

(1082) M/13 259b/8–9 *Mukhtār min shi^{c}r Ibn al-Rūmī – Selection from Ibn al-Rūmī's Poetry*; referring to ^{c}Alī b. al-^{c}Abbās Ibn al-Rūmī (d. 283/896?); A:

(anthologists): al-Khālidīyān, the two court poets Abū ᶜUthmān Saᶜd/Saᶜīd (d. 350/961) and Abū Bakr Muḥammad (d. 380/990); S: IN, I/2, 545–6: '*Ikhtiyār shiᶜr Ibn al-Rūmī*'; C: poetry – ᶜAbbāsid. (cf. nos. 393, 1514)

(1083) M/13 259b/9 *Mukhtār shiᶜr al-Andalusīyīn – Selection from the Andalusians' Poetry*; most likely the anthology by A: Abū al-Ṣalt Umayya b. ᶜAbd al-ᶜAzīz b. Abī al-Ṣalt al-Andalusī (d. 529/1134) that was known under various titles such as S: MU, II, 741: '*al-Ḥadīqa fī mukhtār min ashᶜār al-muḥdathīn*'; Pons Boigues, *Ensayo bio-bibliográfico*, 200: '*Ḥadīqa fī shuᶜarāᵓ al-Andalus*'; C: poetry – anthology – Andalusian.

(1084) M/13 259b/9–10 *Mukhtār shiᶜr al-Andalusīyīn – Selection from the Andalusians' Poetry*; possibly the *adīb* and poet A: ᶜAlī b. Muḥammad b. Arslān Ibn al-Muntajab (d. 536/1141); S: MU, V, 1959–60; C: poetry – anthology – Andalusian.

(1085) M/13 259b/10 *Mukhtār mā yatamaththalu bihi al-ruᵓasāᵓ min al-abyāt al-sāᵓira – Selection of What the Great Recite from Well-Known Verses*; no such title is identifiable and this may be a different title for one of the *al-Abyāt al-sāᵓira* anthologies by authors such as ᶜAbd Allāh b. Khulayd Abū al-ᶜAmaythal (d. 240/854) (IN, I/1, 135) and al-Sukkarī (d. 275/888) (IN, I/1, 240); C: poetry – anthology.

(1086) M/13 259b/10–11 *al-Mujarrad min ghazal al-Sharīf – The Love Poetry of al-Sharīf without the Uncommon Words*; no such title is identifiable, but this seems to be an anthology referring to A: Muḥammad b. al-Ḥusayn al-Sharīf al-Raḍī (d. 406/1016); C: poetry – ghazal.

(1087) M/13 259b/11 *Maᶜānī al-shiᶜr – Themes in Poetry*; A: ᶜAbd al-Raḥmān b. ᶜAbd Allāh Ibn Akhī al-Aṣmaᶜī (fl. 3rd/9th c.); S: IN, I/1, 158; C: poetry – commentary.

(1088) M/13 259b/11 *Maᶜānī al-shiᶜr – Themes in Poetry*; A: Ibn al-Sikkīt (d. 244/858); S: IN, I/1, 220; C: poetry – commentary.

(1089) M/13 259b/12 *Mukhtār shiᶜr al-Buḥturī – Selection from al-Buḥturī's Poetry*; A: al-Walīd al-Buḥturī (d. 284/897); S: *Dīwān al-Buḥturī*, ed. Ḥ. al-Ṣayrafī, Cairo: DM, 1963–5; C: poetry – ᶜAbbāsid. (cf. no. 1601)

(1090) M/13 259b/12 *Maᶜānī al-Amhāndānī – Themes [in Poetry by] al-Amhāndānī*; on account of the category and the preceding entries this is very likely a *ma^cānī al-shi^cr* work. The author is not identifiable and this is most likely a miswritten form of A: Sa^cīd b. Hārūn al-Khaṭīb al-Ushnāndānī (d. 288/901?); S: IN, I/1, 174; whose *ma^cānī* work has an entry further down. C: poetry – commentary. (cf. no. 1101)

(1091) M/13 259b/12–13 *Majmū^c fīhi madā^ɔiḥ ahl al-bayt – Multiple-Text Manuscript with Eulogies on the Prophet's Family*; anonymous work with generic title; C: poetry – anthology – praise of religious figures – ahl al-bayt.

(1092) M/13 259b/13 *Majmū^c fīhi anwā^c al-tashbīh – Multiple-Text Manuscript with Different Kinds of Similes*; anonymous work with generic title; C: poetry.

(1093) M/13 259b/13 *Majmū^c b. Khushnām – Multiple-Text Manuscript of Ibn Khushnām*; this work with a generic title was probably written and 'authored' by A: Muḥammad b. Ibrāhīm b. Khushnām al-Ḥalabī al-Kātib, an otherwise unknown individual who copied the manuscript no. 1162b. Placed in category 13 this is probably a poetry anthology. C: poetry?

(1094) M/13 259b/13–14 *Manādiḥ al-mamādiḥ – Plains of Praiseworthy Deeds*; A: ^cAbd al-Mun^cim b. ^cUmar al-Jilyānī Ḥakīm al-Zamān (d. 602/1206); S: TI, 601–10, pp. 120–1; Khalidi Library MS 1631 *adab ^carabī* 238; C: poetry – panegyric – Ayyūbid – Ṣalāḥ al-Dīn.

(1095) M/15 259b/14 *Maqāmāt – Sessions*; A: al-Qāsim b. ^cAlī al-Ḥarīrī al-Baṣrī (d. 516/1122); S: ed. ^cĪ. Ṣābā, Beirut: DṢ, 2008; NC: 15; C: adab.

(1096) M/15 259b/14–15 *al-Maqāmāt*[121] *– [Sixty] Sessions*; Scr('*bi-khaṭṭihi*') & A: Yaḥyā b. Yaḥyā Ibn Mārī al-Masīḥī (d. 589/1193); S: MU, VI, 2835: '*al-Maqāmāt al-sittūn*'; C: adab.

(1097) M/15 259b/15 *al-Maqāmāt al-luzūmīya – The Luzūmīya Sessions*; title referring to the *Luzūm mā lā yalzam* by Abū al-^cAlā^ɔ al-Ma^carrī (d. 449/1058); A: Muḥammad b. Yūsuf Ibn al-Ashtarkūwī (d. 538/1143); S: Engl. tr. J.T. Monroe, Leiden 2001; C: adab.

(1098a) M/15 259b/15 *Maqāmāt al-Ḥusayn b. Ibrāhīm – Al-Ḥusayn b. Ibrāhīm's Sessions*; possibly A: Abū al-Ḥasan/Ḥusayn Aḥmad b. ^cAlī b. Ibrāhīm Ibn al-Zubayr (d. 563/1167), author of a *maqāmāt* work and mentioned elsewhere in the catalogue (cf. no. 744)?; S: MU, I, 399/400; C: adab.

(1098b) 259b/15 *wa-Dīwān al-Ablah – Al-Ablah's Diwan*; A: Muḥammad al-Ablah (d. *c.*579/1183); S: IKH, IV, 463–5; C: poetry – Saljūq. (cf. no. 1634)

(1099) M/15 259b/16 *al-Muḥibb wa-al-maḥbūb wa-al-mashmūm wa-al-mashrūb – The Lover and the Beloved, the Perfume and the Drink*; A: al-Sarī b. Aḥmad al-Raffāʾ (d. 362/972–3); S: ed. M. Ghalāwinjī, Damascus: MLA, 1986–7; NC: 3; C: poetry – anthology – Ḥamdānid/Būyid. (cf. no. 1570)

(1100) M/15 259b/16 *Maᶜānī al-shiᶜr – Themes in Poetry*; arguably A: Aḥmad b. Ḥātim al-Bāhilī (d. 231/855); S: IN, I/1, 158–9: '*Abyāt al-maᶜānī*'; C: poetry – commentary.

(1101) M/15 259b/17 *Maᶜānī al-shiᶜr – Themes in Poetry*; A: Saᶜīd b. Hārūn al-Khaṭīb al-Ushnāndānī (d. 288/901?); S: IN, I/1, 174; C: poetry – commentary. (cf. no. 1090?)

(1102) M/15 259b/17 *al-Muwashshā – The Brocaded*; A: Muḥammad b. Aḥmad (Ibn) al-Washshāʾ (d. 325/937); S: ed. R.E. Brünnow, Leiden 1886; C: adab – anthology. (cf. no. 1012)

(1103) M/15 259b/17–18 *al-Mūḍiḥ fī sharḥ al-Mutanabbī – The Elucidating [Book] Concerning the Explanation of al-Mutanabbī['s Poetry]*; A: Yaḥyā b. ᶜAlī al-Khaṭīb al-Tibrīzī (d. 502/1109); S: ed. Kh.R. Nuᶜmān, Baghdad: DSh, 2000–2; C: poetry – commentary. (cf. no. 1579)

(1104) M/15 259b/18 *al-Maṣūn fī sirr al-hawā al-maknūn – The Well-Guarded [Book] Concerning the Secret of Hidden Passion*; A: Ibrāhīm b. ᶜAlī al-Ḥuṣrī al-Qayrawānī (d. 413/1022); S: ed. al-N.ᶜA. Shaᶜlān, Cairo: Dār al-ᶜArab li-l-Bustānī, 1989; C: adab/love literature. (cf. nos. 1013, 1502)

(1105) M/15 259b/18 *Majmūᶜ yashtamilu ᶜalā kull fann – Collection on All Fields of Knowledge*; no such title is identifiable and this is most likely a generic title. On account of the category this is probably an anonymous collection with poetry and/or adab similar to the manuscript Süleymaniye, Ayasofya 4842 entitled '*Majmūᶜ laṭīf min kull fann ẓarīf*'. C: poetry/adab?

(1106) M/15 259b/18–260a/1 *al-Munīr fī akhbār Abī Tammām – The Illuminating Book on the Reports on Abū Tammām*; no such title is identifiable, but this is most likely a commentary on one of the numerous *Akhbār Abī Tammām* works (cf. no. 83) with a key word title. C: poetry – commentary.

(1107) M/15 260a/1 *al-Muntahā fī al-kamāl – The Utmost Perfection*; A: Muḥammad b. Sahl Ibn al-Marzubān al-Karkhī (d. *c.*345/956); S: ed. S.M. al-Hadrusi, Berlin 1988; R. Bostan, Berlin 1988; C: adab – anthology. (cf. nos. 12, 995, 1254f)

(1108) M/15 260a/1 *Mukhtaṣar al-Fasr – The Summary of the Disclosure*; summary of the book by Abū al-Fatḥ Ibn Jinnī (d. 392/1002) (ed. R. Rajab, Damascus: DY, 2004). A: ᶜĪsā b. ᶜAbd al-ᶜAzīz al-Juzūlī (d. *c.*610/1213); S: IKH, III, 488; FI: '*wa-huwa sharḥ al-Mutanabbī*'/'*and this is the explanation of al-Mutanabbī['s poetry]*; C: poetry – commentary. (cf. nos. 1518, 1580, 1584 for Ibn Jinnī's *Sharḥ*)

(1109) M/15 260a/1-2 *al-Muqābasāt – Borrowings*; A: Abū Ḥayyān al-Tawḥīdī (d. 414/1023); S: ed. M.T. Ḥusayn, Baghdad: MI, 1970; C: adab.

(1110) M/15 260a/2 *al-Maṣāyid wa-al-maṭārid – Traps and Spears*; A: Maḥmūd Kushājim (d. *c.*350/961); S: ed. M.A. Ṭalas, Baghdad: Dār al-yaqdha, 1954; MS: Süleymaniye, Fatih 4090**; C: poetry – anthology – Ḥamdānid.

(1111) M/15 260a/2 *Mukhtaṣar fī al-siyāsa wa-ādāb al-riʾāsa – A Summary on Good Governance and the Conduct in Rule*; no such title is identifiable. This is possibly a work in the vein of Ibn Rushd/Averroes' translation of Plato's text, *al-Ḍarūrī fī al-siyāsa: mukhtaṣar K. al-Siyāsa*, retransl. from Hebrew into Arabic A. Shaḥlān, Beirut: MDWA, 1998; C: political thought – mirror for princes. (cf. no. 1269d)

(1112) M/15 260a/3 *Manthūr al-manẓūm li-l-Bahāʾī – Prosifying Poetry for Bahāʾ al-Dawla*; referring to the Buyid ruler Bahāʾ al-Dawla (d. 403/1012); A: Muḥammad b. ᶜAlī al-Nayramānī (d. 413/1022); S: facs. ed. Frankfurt 1984; prosification of Abū Tammām's *al-Ḥamāsa*; C: adab/poetry – Būyid. (cf. no. 1192a)

(1113) M/15 260a/3 *al-Muntakhab min al-uns wa-al-furs – The Choices from The [Fruits of] Ease [Concerning the Similes of] the Persians*; no title with *al-uns wa-al-furs* (or alternative vocalisations) is known. The cataloguer (or the compiler of this work) thus most likely used two key words in order to identify the original work. This original work is probably *Thimār al-uns fī tashbīhāt al-furs* by Naṣr b. Yaᶜqūb al-Dīnawarī (fl. 397/1006) (*Wāfī*, XXVII, 91). C: poetry.

(1114) M/15 260a/3–4 *al-Manṭiq wa-al-hijāʾ wa-al-ḥilā wa-al-shiyāt – Speech & Spelling and Characteristics & Qualities*; this is either an anthology with a generic title drawing together material on these themes or with key words referring to other works, which are quoted and summarised. If these are indeed references to other titles one would have expected these to have been authored by one and the same scholar. However, I have not been able to find such an overlap in the bibliography of a single scholar. C: adab?

(1115) M/15 260a/4 *al-Muʾallaf li-l-Malik al-Ashraf fī ḥall al-tarājim – [The Book] Composed for al-Malik Ashraf Concerning Translated Word Puzzles*; this work was specifically written for the mausoleum's patron by A: ᶜAlī b. ᶜAdlān al-Mawṣilī (d. 666/1267); S: Ibn Shākir, *Fawāt*, III, 44: '*Muṣannaf fī ḥall al-mutarjam li-l-Malik al-Ashraf*'. Al-Mawṣilī was a translator and famous for his skills in composing and solving enigmas (*al-alghāz*) and word puzzles with translated words. The term *mutarjam* probably goes back to *al-Muᶜammā al-mutarjam*, a word puzzle in which a Persian word is employed and then translated into Arabic as we find, for instance, in the poetry of the Indo-Persian poet Amīr Khusraw (d. 725/1325) (Ahmed, *Writings*, 87). MS: Süleymaniye, Fatih 5300/4 (fols. 89a–118b)***; The multiple-text manuscript Fatih 5300 holds additional titles, which were identical with or similar to Ashrafiya titles (cf. nos. 261, 915, 1132, 1135a, 1256b). L: Persian/Arabic; C: adab.

(1116) M/15 260a/4 *Muᶜāqarat al-sharāb – Incessant Wine-Drinking*; A: Ibrāhīm b. al-Qāsim (Ibn) al-Raqīq (d. after 418/1027–8); S: EI², J.E. Bencheikh, 'Kh̲amriyya': '*Kitāb muᶜāqarat al-sharab*'; C: adab – wine.

(1117) M/15 260a/4-5 *Mufākharat al-kirām al-ajwād – Boasting of Noble and Generous Persons*; no such title is identifiable, but it most likely belongs to the rich literature on the merits of generosity and the blameworthiness of avarice. This topic was dealt with in numerous treatises, such as *al-Jūd wa-al-karam* by Muḥammad b. Ḥusayn al-Burjulānī (d. 238/852), and was also discussed in the large adab anthologies, such as Ibn ᶜAbd Rabbih's *ᶜIqd al-Farīd* (on these writings see Zakeri, *Wisdom*, 285–91). C: adab – anthology.

(1118) M/15 260a/5 *al-Maqāma al-Dimashqīya – The Damascene Session*; A: ᶜAbd al-Raḥmān b. Najm Nāṣiḥ al-Dīn (d. 634/1236); S: TI, 631–40, p. 197: '*wa-lahu maqāmāt*'; C: adab/sermon.

(1119) M/15 260a/5 *Muntakhab al-amthāl – Choice of Proverbs*; this is probably an anonymous collection based on one or several of the *amthāl*-works by authors such as al-Maydānī (d. 518/1124) (cf. no. 33), Ḥamza al-Iṣfahānī (d. after 350/961) (cf. no. 37) and Abū ᶜUbayd al-Qāsim b. Sallām al-Harawī (d. 224/838) (cf. no. 38). C: adab – proverbs.

(1120) M/15 260a/5–6 *Muntakhab al-amthāl – Choice of Proverbs*; this is probably an anonymous collection based on one or several of the *amthāl*-works by authors such as al-Maydānī (d. 518/1124) (cf. no. 33), Ḥamza al-Iṣfahānī (d. after 350/961) (cf. no. 37) and Abū ᶜUbayd al-Qāsim b. Sallām al-Harawī (d. 224/838) (cf. no. 38). FI: '*qaṭᶜ muᶜtazil*'/'*unusual format*'[122]; C: adab – proverbs.

(1121) M/15 260a/6 *al-Mudārāt*[123] *– Interacting [with Other People]*; A: ᶜAbd Allāh b. Muḥammad Ibn Abī al-Dunyā (d. 281/894); S: *Mudārāt al-nās*, ed. M.Kh. Yūsuf, Beirut: DIḤ, 1998; MS: Süleymaniye, Laleli 3664 (fols. 110a–121b)*** ('*K. Mudārāt al-nās*'); C: ethics – Islamic.

(1122) M1s 260a/6–7 *al-Madāʾiḥ al-durrīya fī al-manāqib al-Ashrafīya – The Blazing Praises Concerning the Virtues of al-Malik al-Ashraf*; no such title is identifiable and this is probably a book-in-the-making in verse and/or prose dedicated to the mausoleum's patron al-Malik al-Ashraf. C: panegyric – Ayyūbid – al-Malik al-Ashraf.

(1123) M1s 260a/7 *Mukhtār min al-Mutanabbī – Selection from al-Mutanabbī['s poetry]*; Scr('*wa-ᶜalayhi khaṭṭuhu*') & A: Aḥmad al-Mutanabbī (d. 354/955); S: *Dīwān*, ed. ᶜA. ᶜAzzām, Cairo: LTTN, 1944; C: poetry – Ḥamdānid.

(1124) M/3s 260a/7 *Masāʾil suʾila ᶜanhā al-Mutanabbī min shiᶜrihi – Issues on Which al-Mutanabbī Was Asked Concerning His Poetry*; no such title is identifiable, but it is probably an extract from the numerous commentaries on al-Mutanabbī's poetry (cf. nos. 1196c, 1248b, 1410, 1580, 1597, 1598). Such questions were also cited in other works such as biographical dictionaries (e.g. IKH, III, 248 citing Ibn Jinnī's commentary, cf. nos. 1108, 1518, 1580, 1584); C: poetry – commentary.

(1125) M/3s 260a/8 *Mukhtār min ṭabaqāt al-shuᶜarāʾ – Selection from the Poets' Generations*; no such selection is identifiable. The title arguably refers to the *Ṭabaqāt* by either 1) Muḥammad Ibn Sallām al-Jumaḥī (d. 231/845 or 232/846) (eds J. Hell and Ṭ.A. Ibrāhīm, Beirut: DKI, 1982) or 2) ᶜAbd Allāh Ibn al-Muᶜtazz (d. 296/908) (ed. ᶜA.A. Farrāj, Cairo: DM, 1956); C: biographical dictionary – poets. (cf. no. 1232d)

(1126) M/3s 260a/8 *Munāẓarat al-shams wa-al-sharāb – The Contest Between Sun and Wine*; no such title is identifiable, but it belongs to the literary genre of living beings or objects competing for precedence, which could include pairs such as heart and eye as well as rooster and dove. In poetry, wine is repeatedly described as a sun (see e.g. Abū Nuwās, *Dīwān*, ed. Ewald Wagner, Wiesbaden 1988, III, 195): '*muqtaṣiran | li-ṣabūḥi mūfiyatin ᶜalā l-shamsī*' ('restricting (my desire) to a morning drink of (a wine) superior to the sun') and Ibn al-Muᶜtazz, *Dīwān*, ed. M.B. Sharīf, Cairo: DM, 1977, II, 269: '*wa-ka-anna . . . fī aqdāḥinā qiṭaᶜan mina l-shamsī*').[124] C: poetry.

(1127) M/3s 260a/8–9 *Majmūᶜ fīhi kutub lughawīya – Multiple-Text Manuscript with Lexicographical Books*; anonymous work with generic title; Scr('*wa-ᶜalayhi khaṭṭ*'): Mawhūb b. Aḥmad Ibn al-Jawālīqī (d. 539/1144) (EI², H. Fleisch, 'al-Djawālīḳī'); C: lexicography.

(1128) M3/s 260a/9 *Mukhtār Ḥilyat al-muḥāḍara – Selection from the Ornament of Disputation*; no such summary is identifiable, but it clearly refers to the work by Muḥammad b. al-Ḥasan al-Ḥātimī (d. 388/998); C: rhetoric. (cf. no. 1645)

(1129) M/3s 260a/9 *Mā wujida min ādāb Aflāṭūn*[125] *– What Is Found of Plato's Writings on Good Conduct*; no such title is identifiable, but this is probably a selection from Plato's writings as quoted by Arab authors, such as IAU, I, 264–70. C: adab – pre-Islamic. (cf. no. 1652)

(1130) M/3s 260a/9–10 *Madāᵓiḥ fī al-Ashraf – Panegyrics on al-Ashraf*; possibly A: ᶜAbd Allāh b. ᶜAbd al-Ḥamīd Ibn Māḍī (d. 655/1257); S: TI, 651–60, p. 200; C: poetry – panegyric – Ayyūbid – al-Malik al-Ashraf.

(1131) M/3s 260a/10 *Mudhahhabat Dhī al-Rumma – Dhū al-Rumma's Excellent Poem*; A: Ghaylān b. ᶜUqba Dhū al-Rumma (d. 117/735); Dhū al-Rumma does not belong to the seven poets said to have authored one of the pre-Islamic/early Islamic *mudhahhabāt* (gilded poems). According to authors such as al-Qurashī in the 4th/10th c. (*Jamharat*, 614–65) these included: Ḥassān b. Thābit b. Mundhir, ᶜAbd Allāh b. Rawāḥa, ᶜAbd Allāh/ᶜAmr b. (al-)ᶜAjlān, Qays

b. al-Khaṭīm b. ᶜAdī al-Ẓafarī, Uḥayḥa b. al-Julāḥ al-Awsī, Abū Qays b. al-Aslat and ᶜAmr b. Imriᵓ al-Qays. The cataloguer may have confused the various groupings of pre-Islamic/early Islamic poetry and classified this poem as a *mudhahhaba* rather than one of the seven *mulḥamāt* poems where al-Qurashī had it (*Jamharat*, 931–82). More likely is that the cataloguer used the term *mudhahhaba* here in the sense of 'excellent poem'. This entry thus refers to Dhū al-Rumma's best-known and longest poem, the *bāᵓīya* (*Poem Rhyming on the Letter b*), S: *Dīwān*, ed. ᶜA. Abū Ṣāliḥ, Damascus: MLA, 1972–3, I, 6–136, which contemporaries also simply described as '*Qaṣīdat Dhī al-Rumma*' (al-Birzālī, *al-Muqtafā*, IV, 89). C: poetry – Umayyad – Bedouin. (cf. nos. 411, 1133a, 1174a, 1230a, 1640)

(1132) M/3s 260a/10 *Min kalām al-Muᶜammā fī adab al-nafs – [Excerpts] from al-Muᶜammā on Good Conduct*; this is either a work by an unidentifiable author, 'al-M-ᶜ/gh/f/q-m-y' or a title in the form of key word + *fī* + content description. In the latter case the construction *kalām al-muᶜammā* (and not *al-kalām al-muᶜammā*) would imply that *al-muᶜammā* refers to a known title. The best known title with this key word is *al-Madkhal fī maᶜrifat al-muᶜammā min al-shiᶜr* by Ibn Ṭabāṭabā (d. 323/934), although it is far from clear how a work on cryptic poetry would be related to the issue of good conduct. Most likely this work is identical with MS: Süleymaniye, Fatih 5300/5 (fols. 119b–133a)**, which has no title page, but is a summary of Ibn Ṭabāṭabā's work. The multiple-text manuscript Fatih 5300 holds additional titles, which were identical with or similar to Ashrafīya titles (cf. nos. 261, 915, 1115, 1135a, 1256b). C: adab.

(1133a) M/3s 260a/10–11 *Mudhahhabat Dhī al-Rumma – Dhū al-Rumma's Excellent Poem*; cf. no. 1131 for comments; A: Ghaylān b. ᶜUqba Dhū al-Rumma (d. 117/735); S: *Dīwān*, ed. ᶜA. Abū Ṣāliḥ, Damascus: MLA, 1972–3, I, 6–136; C: poetry – Umayyad – Bedouin. (cf. nos. 411, 1131, 1174a, 1230a, 1640)

(1133b) 260a/11 *wa-Mīmīya wa-lāmīya – Two Poems Rhyming on the Letters mīm and lām*; probably by same poet A: Ghaylān b. ᶜUqba Dhū al-Rumma (d. 117/735); S: *Dīwān*, ed. ᶜA. Abū Ṣāliḥ, Damascus: MLA, 1972–3, 2202–3; C: poetry – Umayyad – Bedouin. (cf. no. 1133b)

(1134) M/4s 260a/11–12 *Miᵓat jawhara min kalām ᶜAlī b. Abī Ṭālib karrama Allāh wajhahu – One Hundred Gems from ᶜAlī b. Abī Ṭālib's Sayings (may God honour his countenance)*; attr. to A: al-Jāḥiẓ (d. 255/868–9); S: *One Hundred Proverbs* (*Mi$^{\circ}$at kalima min kalām amīr al-Mu$^{\circ}$minīn ^{c}Alī b. Abī Ṭālib)*, in: Engl. tr. & ed. Qutbuddin, *Treasury of Virtues*, 220–33; NC: 2; C: ^{c}Alī – sayings attributed to. (cf. nos. 289, 312, 1658)

(1135a) M/4s 260a/12 *Mukhtaṣar al-sīra al-nabawīya – Summary of the Prophet's Biography*; A: Aḥmad Ibn Fāris (d. 395/1004); S: *Sīrat al-nabī: al-mukhtaṣara*, ed. M.K. ^{c}Izz al-Dīn, Beirut: AK, 1989; MS: Süleymaniye, Fatih 5300/7 (fols. 142b–150a)***. The multiple-text manuscript Fatih 5300 holds additional titles, which were identical with or similar to Ashrafīya titles (cf. nos. 261, 915, 1115, 1132, 1256b). C: biography of the Prophet (*sīra*). (cf. no. 1162a)

(1135b) 260a/12 *wa-Ad^{c}iya sharīfa marwīya – Noble Prayers Transmitted by Riwāya*; generic title; C: prayer book.

(1136) M/4s 260a/12–13 *Munājāt Zayn al-^{c}Ābidīn – Zayn al-^{c}Ābidīn's Whispered Prayers*; A: ^{c}Alī b. al-Ḥusayn b. ^{c}Alī b. Abī Ṭālib Zayn al-^{c}Ābidīn, the fourth Shi^{c}ite *imām* (d. 94/712?); S: Engl. tr. Chittick, *Psalms of Islam*, 232–59; C: prayer book. (cf. nos. 154, 1424)

(1137) M/4s 260a/13 *Mā yud^{c}ā bihi fī a^{c}qāb al-ṣalawāt – What Is Prayed for after the Ritual Prayers*; generic title; C: prayer book.

(1138) M/4s 260a/13 *Mā yud^{c}ā bihi ba^{c}da ṣalāt al-fajr – What Is Prayed for after the Ritual Dawn Prayer*; generic title; C: prayer book.

(1139) M/4s 260a/14 *Mā yud^{c}ā bihi ba^{c}da ṣalāt al-ṣubḥ – What Is Prayed for after the Ritual Morning Prayer*; generic title; C: prayer book.

(1140) M/4s 260a/14 *Mā yuqālu fī al-fajr kull yawm – What Is Said Every Day at Dawn*; generic title; C: prayer book.

(1141) M/4s 260a/14–15 *Mā yud^{c}ā bihi ba^{c}da ṣalāt al-fajr kull yawm – What Is Prayed for Every Day after the Ritual Morning Prayer*; generic title; C: prayer book.

(1142a) M/5s 260a/15 *Majmū^{c} fīhi al-nawādir – Multiple-Text Manuscript with Anecdotes*; anonymous work with generic title; '*Nawādir*' could refer to a wide variety of material. However, placed in historical category 5 and taking into account the contemporaneous usage of this term (most prominently Ibn Shaddād (d. 632/1235), *al-Nawādir al-sulṭānīya*) this is possibly a text of historical nature. C: history?

(1142b) 260a/15 *wa-Iḍmār al-khayl – Training Horses*; on account of the other grammatical works in this multiple-text manuscript this is most likely an extract from the lexicographical/equestrian work by the grammarian A: ᶜAbd Allāh b. Muḥammad al-Tawwazī (d. 233/847–8?). S: IN, I/1, 165 '*al-khayl wa-sabquhā wa-asnānuhā wa-shiyātuhā wa-ᶜuyūnuhā wa-iḍmāruhā wa-man nusiba ilā farasihi*'; C: lexicography.

(1142c) 260a/15–16 *wa-Mā lā tadkhuluhu al-hāʾ min al-muʾannath – Feminine Forms Without the Letter hāʾ [al-taʾnīth]*; most likely an extract from one of the numerous grammatical works on masculine and feminine, *al-Madhkūr wa-al-muʾannath* (cf. IN for references) with a slight preference for A: ᶜAbd al-Malik b. Qurayb al-Aṣmaᶜī (d. 213/828); S: IN, I/1, 157 who could also have been the author of other titles in this multiple-text manuscript; C: grammar.

(1142d) 260a/16 *wa-al-Durrāt – Pearls*; popular key word, similar to terms such as *nawādir* and *fawāʾid*, indicating a choice of noteworthy short texts; C: poetry/adab – anthology?

(1142e) 260a/16 *wa-al-Awqāt – The [Book of] Time*; popular title with numerous possibilities with a slight preference for A: ᶜAbd al-Malik b. Qurayb al-Aṣmaᶜī (d. 213/828); S: IN, I/1, 157 who could also have been the author of other titles in this multiple-text manuscript; C: astronomy.

(1142f) 260a/16 *wa-al-Aṣwāt – Phonetics*; popular title with numerous possibilities with a slight preference for A: ᶜAbd al-Malik b. Qurayb al-Aṣmaᶜī (d. 213/828); S: IN, I/1, 157 who could also have been the author of other titles in this multiple-text manuscript; C: grammar.

(1142g) 260a/16 *wa-al-Hamz – The Letter Hamza*; popular title with several possibilities with a slight preference for A: ᶜAbd al-Malik b. Qurayb al-Aṣmaᶜī (d. 213/828); S: IN, I/1, 157 who could also have been the author of other titles in this multiple-text manuscript; C: grammar.

(1142h) 260a/16–17 *wa-Ṣifat al-nakhl wa-ghayruhu – The Characteristics of the Palm Tree and Other [Writings]*; two main possibilities: 1) Muḥammad b. Ziyād Ibn al-Aᶜrābī (d. *c.*231/846) (MU, VI, 2533) or 2) al-Qāsim b. Maᶜn (IN, I/1208); C: adab/lexicography.

(1143) M/5s 260a/17 *Masāʾil suʾila ^{c}anhā Aflāṭūn – Problems on Which Plato was Asked*; anonymous; C: philosophy.

(1144) M/5s 260a/17 *Majmū^{c} ash^{c}ār wa-akhbār – Multiple-Text Manuscript with Poems and Reports*; anonymous work with generic title; FI: '*mujallad*' / '*one bound volume*'; C: poetry – anthology.

(1145) M/5s 260b/1 *Majmū^{c} Ibn al-Khāzin – Multiple-Text Manuscript of Ibn al-Khāzin*; two main possibilities: 1) Aḥmad Ibn al-Khāzin (d. 518/1124) (IKH, I, 149–51) or 2) al-Ḥusayn b. ^{c}Alī Ibn al-Khāzin (d. 502/1109) (MU, III, 1105); owing to these authors' literary profiles this is most likely poetry. C: poetry?

(1146) M/5s 260b/1 *al-Maqāma al-ṣāḥibīya al-shukrīya – The Session by the Ṣāḥib Abū Shukr*; A: ^{c}Abd Allāh b. ^{c}Alī al-Ṣāḥib Ṣafī al-Dīn Ibn Shukr (d. 622/1125) (TI, 621–30, pp. 109–12); S: ed. O. Rescher, *Beiträge zur Maqamen-Litteratur*, Istanbul 1913, IV, 153–99; C: adab.

(1147) M/5s 260b/1-2 *Madāʾiḥ al-Yārūkī*[126] *li-l-Malik al-Ashraf – Panegyrics by al-Yārūkī for al-Malik al-Ashraf*; A: ^{c}Alī b. ^{c}Umar al-Yārūqī (d. 656/1258); S: *Dīwān*, ed. M.^{c}A. al-Ḥabbāzī, Jerusalem 2002. Although al-Yārūqī's diwan has no poems dedicated to al-Ashraf this poet was a renowned panegyrist of numerous Ayyubid rulers in Syria and Egypt, especially for al-Malik al-Nāṣir Yūsuf (d. 658/1260) in Damascus and al-Malik al-Ṣāliḥ Ayyūb (d. 647/1249). Possibly the poet excluded from his diwan poems for al-Ashraf, which he would have written at a younger age. C: poetry – panegyric – Ayyūbid – al-Malik al-Ashraf.

(1148a) M/5s 260b/2 *Majmū^{c} fīhi ash^{c}ār mustaṭrafa – Multiple-Text Manuscript with Exquisite Poems*; anonymous work with generic title; C: poetry – anthology.

(1148b) 260b/2–3 *wa-Qaṣīd Yaḥyā b. Abī al-Khaṣīb – Yaḥyā b. Abī al-Khaṣīb's Qaṣīdas*; Scr('*bi-khaṭṭ*'): al-Ṣūlī (most likely Muḥammad b. Yaḥyā al-Ṣūlī, d. 335/947); A: Yaḥyā b. Abī al-Khaṣīb (fl. 279/892); S: al-Marzubānī, *Mu^{c}jam al-shu^{c}arāʾ*, ed. F. Krenkow, Beirut: DKI, 1982, I, 502; C: poetry – ^{c}Abbāsid.

(1148c) 260b/3 *wa-Shi^{c}r Mālik b. al-Rayb al-Māzinī – Mālik b. al-Rayb al-Māzinī's Poetry*; Scr('*bi-khaṭṭ*'): al-Ḥasan b. Hāniʾ Abū Nuwās (d. between mid-198 and early 200/813–15); generally Abū Nuwās is identified in this catalogue with his *kunya*, the patronymic, and this entry referring to his *ism*, the given name, and that of his father is an outlier. However, there is no other person by this name who is an obvious candidate. A: Mālik b. al-Rayb al-Māzinī (d. 60/680); S: GAS, II, 401; C: poetry – early Islam.

(1149) M/5s 260b/3–4 *Majmūᶜ fī al-futūwa – Multiple-Text Manuscript on The Qualities of Young Men*; anonymous collection of texts, which had not yet received (and perhaps never received) a non-generic title; this entry could be similar to the manuscript *Majmūᶜ fī al-futūwa* (Süleymaniye, Ayasofya 2049) with Sufi texts studied by Taeschner (1932). C: Sufism?

(1150) M/5s 260b/4 *al-Muᶜashsharāt al-nabawīya*[127] – *Ten-line Stanzas on the Prophet*; this form of poetry is mentioned with a number of adjectives, such as *zuhdīya* and *ghazalīya*, but none that would fit the adjective given here. The most likely version is that these are poems in praise of the Prophet. C: Prophet Muḥammad – devotional.

(1151) M/5s 260b/4 *Mukhtār fī al-madāʾiḥ al-Manṣūrīya al-Quṭbīya – Selection from the Panegyrics for al-Manṣūr Quṭb*; these are most likely panegyric poems composed for the Zangid ruler of the northern Mesopotamian principality of Sinjār, al-Malik al-Manṣūr Quṭb al-Dīn Muḥammad (r. 594/1197–616/1219). The Sinjār court displayed a high level of literary activity during this period (EI², C.P. Haase, 'Sindjār') and as the mausoleum's patron al-Malik al-Ashraf took over this principality in 617/1220 it is likely that some of the court's literary production came with his royal library to Damascus. C: poetry – panegyric – Zangid.

(1152) M/5s 260b/5 *al-Mulaḥ al-ᶜaṣrīya min ashᶜār ahl al-Andalus – Pleasant Poetry/Anecdotes from the Andalusians' Poems*; A: Abū al-Ṣalt Umayya b. ᶜAbd al-ᶜAzīz b. Abī al-Ṣalt al-Andalusī (d. 529/1134); S: EI³, M. Comes, 'Abū l-Ṣalt Umayya b. ᶜAbd al-ᶜAzīz'; C: poetry – anthology – Andalusian.

(1153) M/5s 260b/5–6 *Majmūᶜ ashᶜār – Collection of Poems*; book-in-the-making with generic title; Scr('*bi-khaṭṭ*') & A: 'compiler' ('*bi-jamᶜihi*'): al-Ḥasan b. ᶜAlī al-Juwaynī (d. 586/1190?); S: MU, II, 940–1; C: poetry – anthology.

(1154) M/5s 260b/6 *Mukhtār min ashᶜār fuṣaḥāʾ al-aᶜrāb – Selection of Poems of the Eloquent Among the Arabs*; Scr('*bi-khaṭṭ*') & A: al-Ḥasan b. ᶜAlī al-Juwaynī (d. 586/1190?); S: MU, II, 940–1 (title not mentioned); for '*al-a*ᶜ*rāb*' cf. no. 974; C: poetry – anthology – pre-Islamic/early Islamic.

(1155) M/5s 260b/6–7 *Maḥāsin al-ādāb wa-al-amthāl* – *The Beauties of Adab and Proverbs*; no such title is identifiable and this is probably one of the well-known *Maḥāsin al-ādāb* books by authors such as ᶜAbd Allāh b. ᶜAbd al-Raḥmān al-Dīnawarī (d. *c.*390/1000) (al-Ziriklī, *al-A*ᶜ*lām*, IV, 230) or Yaᶜqūb b. Sulaymān al-Isfarāyīnī (d. 488/1090) (*Wāfī*, XXVIII, 498) with additional proverbs. C: adab/proverbs.

(1156) M/6s 260b/7 *Mukhtār min tarassul al-Ḥarīrī wa-al-Babbaghā*ᵓ – *Selection from al-Ḥarīrī's and al-Babbaghā*ᵓ*'s Letters*; A: al-Qāsim b. ᶜAlī al-Ḥarīrī al-Baṣrī (d. 516/1122) and ᶜAbd al-Wāḥid al-Babbaghāᵓ (d. 398/1007); S: al-Ḥarīrī: contemporaneous authors mention a collection of his epistles: MU, V, 2207: '*Kitāb rasā*ᵓ*ilihi al-mudawwana*'; al-Babbaghāᵓ: Nājī, *al-Babbaghā*ᵓ, 91–132; C: adab – epistle. (cf. nos. 481, 489, 1683)

(1157) M/6s 260b/7-8 *Mulaḥ al-mukātaba* – *Anecdotes of Correspondence*; A: ᶜAbd Allāh b. Muḥammad Ibn Nāqiyā (d. 485/1092); S: MU, VII, 3475 (*Mulaḥ al-mukātib*); C: adab – epistle. (cf. no. 1303c)

(1158) M/6s 260b/8 *Mukhtār min rasā*ᵓ*il Ibn* ᶜ*Abd Mānī* (?) – *Selections from Ibn* ᶜ*Abd Mānī's Epistles*; no author by this name is known. The poet Ibn ᶜAbd Hāniᵓ b. Ḥubaysh, a cousin of Tammām b. Ghālib al-Farazdaq (d. *c.*114/732), and mentioned in al-Āmidī (d. 370/980 or 371/981), *al-Mu*ᵓ*talif*, I, 173 is too early for *rasā*ᵓ*il*-literature. IN, I/2, 551 mentions *Rasā*ᵓ*il Ibn* ᶜ*Abdakān* by the Egyptian head of the diwan Abū Jaᶜfar Muḥammad b. ᶜAbd Kān (d. 278/868).[128] To change a *kāf* to a *mīm* would be rather unusual for the cataloguer, but is not impossible. C: adab – epistle.

(1159) M/7s 260b/8–9 *Masā*ᵓ*il al-malik al-wārid min al-Yaman* ᶜ*alā* ᶜ*Alī b. Abī Ṭālib karrama Allāh wajhahu* – *Questions by the King coming from Yemen to* ᶜ*Alī b. Abī Ṭālib (may God honour his countenance)*; referring to ᶜAlī b. Abī Ṭālib, the fourth Caliph and first Shiᶜite *imām* (d. 40/661); no such title is identifiable and this is most likely a treatise in which aspects of Muslim ritual/dogma are explained to a non-Muslim challenger, similar to the *Ihlīlaja* by al-Ṣādiq (cf. no. 1320a). C: rituals/theology?[129]

(1160a) M/7s 260b/9–10 *Majmū*ᶜ *awwaluhu fiqh* ᶜ*alā madhhab Abī Ḥanīfa wa-ba*ᶜ*ḍ multaqāt al-farā*ᵓ*iḍ*[130] – *Multiple-Text Manuscripts with Jurisprudence according to the Madhhab of Abū Ḥanīfa in the Beginning and with Extracts on Inheritance Shares*; anonymous work with generic title; C: fiqh – ḥanafi.

(1160b) 260b/10 *wa-Qiṭ*ᶜ*a min ta*ᶜ*bīr al-ru*ᵓ*yā* – *Fragment of a Work on Dream Interpretation*; anonymous work with generic title; C: oneiromancy.

(1161a) M/7s 260b/11 *Majmū*ᶜ *fīhi* ᶜ*ishrūna mas*ᵓ*ala su*ᵓ*ila* ᶜ*anhā al-Shāfi*ᶜ*ī* – *Multiple-Text Manuscript with Twenty Questions on Which al-Shāfi*ᶜ*ī Was Asked*; referring to Muḥammad b. Idrīs al-Shāfiᶜī (d. 204/820); C: fiqh – shāfiᶜī.

(1161b) 260b/11–12 *wa-Waṣīyat* ᶜ*Alī b. Abī Ṭālib li-waladihi al-Ḥusayn raḍiya Allāh* ᶜ*anhumā* – ᶜ*Alī b. Abī Ṭālib's Last Advice to His Son al-Ḥusayn (may God be pleased with them)*; treatise on the last advice by A: ᶜAlī b. Abī Ṭālib, the fourth Caliph and first Shiᶜite *imām* (d. 40/661), to Ḥusayn as reported in sources such as S: Hawting (tr.): *The History of al-Ṭabarī*, XVII, 219–22; C: political thought – imāmate theory. (cf. nos. 1384, 1663)

(1162a) M/7s 260b/12–13 *Majmū*ᶜ *fīhi Mukhtaṣar sīrat Rasūl Allāh ṣallā Allāh* ᶜ*alayhi wa-sallam* – *Multiple-Text Manuscript with the Summary of the Prophet's Biography (may God's blessing and peace be upon him)*; A: Aḥmad Ibn Fāris (d. 395/1004); S: *Sīrat al-nabī: al-mukhtaṣara*, ed. M.K. ᶜIzz al-Dīn, Beirut: AK, 1989; C: biography of the Prophet (*sīra*). (cf. no. 1135a)

(1162b) 260b/13 *wa-al-Arba*ᶜ*ūna al-buldānīya* – *The Forty ḥadīth of Various Cities*; two possibilities: 1) Aḥmad b. Muḥammad al-Silafī al-Shāfiᶜī (d. 576/1180) (ed. Abū ᶜA.M. al-Saᶜdanī, Riyad: Aḍwāᵓ al-salaf, 1997) or 2) ᶜAlī Ibn ᶜAsākir (d. 571/1176) ('*K. al-Arba*ᶜ*īn al-buldānīya:* ᶜ*an arba*ᶜ*īn min arba*ᶜ*īn li-arba*ᶜ*īn fī arba*ᶜ*īn*', ed. M.M. al-Ḥāfiẓ, Beirut/Damascus: Dār al-fikr al-muᶜāṣir/DF, 1992) who were both well-known to Damascene authors of the following generations (e.g. al-Birzālī, *al-Muqtafā*, I, 47, 62, 70, 353, II, 339, 390 and TI, 571–80, p. 129; 641–50, p. 99; 671–80, p. 174; 691–700, p. 160); in light of the MS: Süleymaniye, Şehid Ali Paşa 360/1 (fols. 2a–33b)*** it is highly likely that this entry refers to Ibn ᶜAsākir's work. This manuscript was written in 585/1189 by Muḥammad b. Ibrāhīm b. Khushnām al-Ḥalabī al-Kātib, who probably also appears as the author/scribe of no. 1093. C: ḥadīth – collection (40).

(1163a) M/7s 260b/13 *Majmū^c fīhi qirā^ɔat Abī ^cAmr b. al-^cAlā^ɔ – Multiple-Text Manuscript with the Koran Reading According to Abū ^cAmr b. al-^cAlā^ɔ*; A: Abū ^cAmr b. al-^cAlā^ɔ b. al-^cUryan al-Māzinī (d. *c.*154–6/770–2); S: EI³, A. Afsaruddin, 'Abū ^cAmr b. al-^cAlā^ɔ'; C: Koran – recitation.

(1163b) 260b/13–14 *wa-Risāla fī uṣūl al-mukhtaṣar – Treatise on Uṣūl, Summary*; anonymous; C: uṣūl al-dīn?

(1163c) 260b/14 *wa-al-Nāsikh wa-al-mansūkh – The Abrogative and the Abrogated*; A: Ibn al-Jawzī (d. 597/1200); S: Ḥ.S.al-Dārānī, Damascus: Dār al-thaqāfa al-^carabīya, 1990; C: Koran.

(1163d) 260b/14–15 *wa-Sharḥ masā^ɔil ḥamīl al-talkhīṣ fī al-mawārīth – Commentary on the Problems from the Summary's Companion on Inheritance*; no such commentary is identifiable, but it is referring to the work by ^cAbd Allāh b. Ibrāhīm al-Khabrī (d. 476/1083–4), *K. al-Talkhīṣ fī ^cilm al-farā^ɔiḍ*, ed. N. al-Farīdī, Medina: Maktabat al-^culūm wa-al-ḥikam, 1995; C: fiqh.

(1163e) 260b/15 *wa-al-^cUqūd fī al-ḥisāb – [The Book of] Computation on Arithmetic*; this is a title in the form of key word + *fī* + content description, which is not identifiable, but that is clearly situated in the field of arithmetic as *ḥisāb al-^cuqūd* refers to dactylonomy. One possibility is the work *^cUqūd al-abniya* by the mathematician Muḥammad b. al-Ḥasan al-Karājī (d. after 410/1019) (GAS, V, 324); C: mathematics.

(1164a) M/7s 260b/15 *Majmū^c fīhi mukhtaṣarāt Mu^cashsharāt al-Ḥuṣrī – Multiple-Text Manuscript with Summaries of al-Ḥuṣrī's Ten-Line Stanzas*; summaries not identified, most likely anonymous; main work: A: ^cAlī b. ^cAbd al-Ghanī al-Ḥuṣrī (d. 488/1095); S: al-Marzūqī and al-Ḥājj Yaḥyā, *al-Qayrawāni*, 212–40; C: poetry – Andalusian. (cf. no. 1241c)

(1164b) 260b/15–16 *wa-Munājāt – Whispered Prayers*; A: Ibn al-Jawzī (d. 597/1200); S: Alwajī, *Mu^ɔallafāt*, 221; C: prayer book.

(1164c) 260b/16 *wa-Adab al-aṣdiqā^ɔ fī al-mukātabāt wa-al-liqā^ɔ – Etiquette of Friends in Correspondence and Meeting*; possibly A: Muḥammad b. Futūḥ al-Ḥumaydī (d. 488/1095) author of *Adab al-aṣdiqā^ɔ*; S: Ibn ^cAsākir, *Ta^ɔrīkh madīnat Dimashq*, ed. al-^cAmrawī, Beirut: DF, 1995, LV, 80; C: adab.

(1165a) M/7s 260b/16–17 *Majmū^c fīhi Mukhtār lawāmi^c anwār al-qulūb – Multiple-Text Manuscript with The Flashes of the Hearts' Lights*; A: ^cAzīzī b.

ᶜAbd al-Malik al-Jīlī/Jīlānī (d. 494/1100); S: Prozorov, 'Sufi Tradition'; C: sufism.

(1165b) 260b/17 *wa-Rawnaq al-majālis fī al-ḥikāyāt* – *The Glamorous Book of Sessions on Narrations*; possibly A: ᶜUmar al-Samarqandī (fl. second half 5th/11th c.); S: Ess, *Ungenützte Texte*, 30–41; this work was originally authored in Persian with the title *Rawnaq al-qulūb*, but its Arabic version has the title *Rawnaq al-majālis*. C: sufism – biographies.

(1166a) M/7s 260b/17–261a/1 *Majmūᶜ al-Ghazālī al-Masāʾil al-Baghdādīya* – *Multiple-Text al-Ghazālī Manuscript: The Baghdad Questions*; A: al-Ghazālī (d. 505/1111); S: Badawī, *Muʾallafāt al-Ghazālī*, no. 297.

(1166b) 261a/1 *wa-Masāʾil al-ukhrawīya* – *Questions about the Afterlife*; also known as *al-Ajwiba al-ghazālīya fī masāʾil al-ukhrawīya* (GAL S, I, 747) or *al-Maḍnūn al-ṣaghīr*. A: al-Ghazālī (d. 505/1111); S: *Majmūᶜat rasāʾil al-Imām al-Ghazālī*, ed. A. Shams al-Dīn, Beirut: DKI, 1986–8; C: theology.

(1166c) 261a/1 *wa-al-Masāʾil al-arbaᶜūna* – *Forty Questions*; A: al-Ghazālī (d. 505/1111); S: *Kitāb al-arbaᶜīna fī uṣūl al-dīn*, ed. M.M. Jābir, Cairo: Maktabat al-Jundī, *[1964]*; C: theology.[131]

(1166d) 261a/1 *wa-al-Maḍnūn* – [The Book] *to Be Held [from Those for Whom It Is not Written]*; A: al-Ghazālī (d. 505/1111); S: *al-Maḍnūn bihi ᶜalā ghayr ahlihi*, ed. M. Afifi al-Akiti: *The Maḍnūn of al-Ghazālī: A Critical Edition of the Unpublished Major Maḍnūn with Discussion of His Restricted, Philosophical Corpus*, DPhil Oxford 2008; MS: Süleymaniye, Ayasofya 1816/4 (fols. 41a–52a)***; C: theology.

(1166e) 261a/1 *wa-al-Miṣbāḥ* – *The Lantern*; A: al-Ghazālī (d. 505/1111); alternative title for the author's *Mishkāt al-anwār* (*The Niche for Lights*); S: ed. A. ᶜAfīfī, Cairo: DQ, 1963; MS: Süleymaniye, Ayasofya 1816/1 (fols. 1a–3b)***; C: theology. (cf. no. 1701e)

(1166f) 261a/2 *wa-Khawātīm al-bāṭinīya*[132] – *The Bāṭinīya's Seals*; placed in this *majmūᶜ* this is most likely another work by A: al-Ghazālī (d. 505/1111). This is clearly a polemical work against the Ismāᶜīlis, but no such title is known. Perhaps the cataloguer got the title wrong and this is *Qawāṣim al-bāṭinīya* (*The Bāṭinīya's Weak Positions*, ed. A. Ateş, Ilâhiyat Fakültesi Dergisi (Ankara) 3/1–2 (1954), 23–54). C: theology.[133]

(1166g) 261a/2 *wa-Ibṭāl al-dawr al-lafẓī – Abolishing Circular Reasoning in Speech*; no such title is identifiable and this is probably a brief extract from one of al-Ghazālī's legal works or a commentary thereon. In 7th-/13th-c. Damascus, 'a productive period of Ghazālī reception' among the city's Shafiᶜi School (Griffel, *Philosophical Theology*, 76) al-Nawawī (d. 676/1277) took up the issue of circular reasoning in his *Rawḍat al-ṭālibīn wa-ᶜumdat al-muftīn*, a commentary on Ghazālī's *al-Wajīz* (see, for example, *Rawḍat*, ed. Z. al-Shāwīsh, Beirut: al-Maktab al-islāmī, 1991, XII, 125). C: fiqh – shāfiᶜī.[134]

(1167a) M/7s 261a/2 *Majmūᶜ al-Ghazālī Minhāj al-ᶜārifīn – Multiple-Text al-Ghazālī Manuscript: The Way of the Knowledgeable*; A: al-Ghazālī (d. 505/1111); S: *Majmūᶜat rasāʾil al-Imām al-Ghazālī*, ed. A. Shams al-Dīn, Beirut: DKI, 1986–8; C: sufism.

(1167b) 261a/3 *wa-Miᶜrāj al-sālikīn – Ascension of the Wayfarers*; the MS has '*al-ᶜārifīn*', instead of '*al-sālikīn*', but the cataloguer was clearly not sure about this entry. As this is a multiple-text manuscript with works by al-Ghazālī his *Miᶜrāj al-sālikīn* seems to be a straightforward option. A: al-Ghazālī (d. 505/1111); S: *Majmūᶜat rasāʾil al-Imām al-Ghazālī*, ed. A. Shams al-Dīn, Beirut: DKI, 1986—8; MS: Süleymaniye, Ayasofya 1816/3 (fols. 13a–40b)***; FI: The cataloguer adds the letter ẓ for *aẓunnuhu* ('I think it to be') or *fīhi naẓar* ('it requires consideration') (cf. no. 742 for this abbreviation). C: sufism.

(1168) M/7s 261a/3 *Majmūᶜ fīhi tafṣīl al-nashʾatayn wa-taḥṣīl al-saᶜādatayn*[135] *– Multiple-Text Manuscript with Separating the Two Creations and Attaining the Two Felicities*; A: al-Ḥusayn b. Muḥammad al-Rāghib al-Iṣfahānī (d. early 5th/11th c.?); S: ed. ᶜA. al-Najjār, Beirut: DGI, 1988; C: ethics. (cf. no. 1264c)

(1169a) M/7s 261a/3-4 *Majmūᶜ mukhtaṣar uṣūl al-fiqh wa-jadal – Multiple-Text Manuscript with Summary on Legal Theory and Disputation*; anonymous work with generic title; C: fiqh – uṣūl al-fiqh.

(1169b) 261a/4 *wa-Taʾsīs al-naẓāʾir [al-fiqhīya] – The Foundation of [Legal] Similarities*; A: Abū al-Layth Naṣr b. Muḥammad al-Samarqandī (d. between 373/983–4 and 393/1002–3); S: *Taḥqīq makhṭūṭ Taʾsīs al-naẓāʾir*, ᶜAlī M.M. Ramaḍān, MA Azhar University, Kullīyat al-sharīᶜa, 1981; C: fiqh – uṣūl al-fiqh.

(1170a) M/7s 261a/4 *Majmū^{c} fīhi al-Targhīb wa-al-tarhīb – Multiple-Text Manuscript with Encouragement and Warning*; popular title with several possibilities including 1) Ḥumayd b. Zanjawayh (d. 247/861) (*Siyar*, XII, 20), 2) Aḥmad b. al-Ḥusayn al-Bayhaqī (d. 458/1066) (*Siyar*, XVIII, 166), 3) Ismā^{c}īl b. Muḥammad al-Iṣfahānī (d. 535/1140–1) (*Wāfī*, IX, 208–11), 4) ^{c}Abd al-^{c}Aẓīm b. ^{c}Abd al-Qawī al-Mundhirī (d. 656/1285) (ed. M.M. ^{c}Amāra, Cairo: MBḤ, 1968); C: ḥadīth.

(1170b) 261a/5 *wa-Bidāyat al-hidāya – The Beginning of Guidance*; A: al-Ghazālī (d. 505/1111); S: ed. ^{c}A.M. al-Darwīsh, Beirut: DṢ, 1998; C: ethics – Islamic. (cf. no. 199)

(1170c) 261a/5 *wa-Ad^{c}iyat al-ayyām al-sab^{c}a – Prayers of Invocation for the Seven Days*; several possibilities, but this could be (cf. no. 151) A: Fatimid Caliph al-Mu^{c}izz (r. 341–65/953–75); S: ed. I.K. Poonawala, Beirut: DGI, 2006; C: prayer book. (cf. nos. 151, 1198b, 1661)

(1171a) M/7s 261a/5 *Majmū^{c} fīhi al-Nāsikh wa-al-mansūkh – Multiple-Text Manuscript with The Abrogative and the Abrogated*; A: Hibat Allāh b. Naṣr Ibn Salāma (d. 410/1019); to write just 'Hibat' in lieu of 'Hibat Allāh' is unusual, but the cataloguer does so in this title's other entry as well (cf. no. 1339). S: ed. Z. al-Shāwīsh, Beirut: al-Maktab al-islāmī, 1986; MS: Süleymaniye, Ayasofya 65/2 (fols. 107a–126b)**; C: Koran. (cf. no. 1339)

(1171b) 261a/5–6 *wa-Qirāʾāt marmūza*[136] – *Koranic Readings Provided with Reading Marks*; possibly A: Muḥammad b. ^{c}Abd Allāh Ibn Mālik al-Jayyānī (d. 672/1274) of Damascus who composed a '*Qaṣīda dālīya marmūza fī qadr al-Shāṭibīya*' on the various Koranic readings; S: *Wāfī*, III, 359–64; C: Koran – recitation.

(1171c) 261a/6 *wa-Arājīz fī ^{c}adad āy al-Qurʾān – Poems in Rajaz Metre on the Number of Verses in the Koran*; anonymous; C: Koran. (cf. no. 1238b)

(1172a) M/7s 261a/6 *Majmū^{c} fīhi al-^{c}Unwān – Multiple-Text Manuscript with The Book of Indication [on the Seven Readings]*; A: Ismā^{c}īl b. Khalaf Saraqusṭī (d. 455/1063); S: *al-^{c}Unwān fī al-qirāʾāt al-sab^{c}*, eds Z. Zāhid and Kh. al-^{c}Aṭīya, Beirut: AK, 1985; the *Kitāb al-^{c}Unwān* by Agapius b. Maḥbūb, ed. & Engl. tr. A. Vasiliev, Patrologia Orientalis VIII/3, Turnhout 1971 is much less likely because of (1) the focus on Koran recitation in this section of the catalogue and (2) the fact that the recitation work with this title was transmitted in contemporaneous Damascus (e.g. al-Birzālī, *al-Muqtafā*, IV, 88). C: Koran – recitation.

(1172b) 261a/6 *wa-Mutashābih al-Qurʾān* – *The Ambiguous Passages of the Koran*; popular title with numerous possibilities (cf. IN, index); C: Koran.

(1173a) M/7s 261a/7 *Majmūᶜ fīhi Talkhīṣ al-rawḍ* – *Multiple-Text Manuscript with the Garden's Summary*; no book with the title *Talkhīṣ al-rawḍ* is identifiable. The original work with the key word *Rawḍ* is, judging from the references in contemporaneous sources (e.g. IKH, III, 143) and the context of the previous titles, most likely the *Rawḍ al-unuf* by ᶜAbd al-Raḥmān al-Suhaylī (d. 581/1185) (cf. no. 465); C: biography of the Prophet (*sīra*).

(1173b) 261a/7 *wa-Mafātīḥ al-ᶜulūm* – *Keys to the Sciences*; A: Muḥammad b. Aḥmad al-Khwārazmī (fl. 4th/10th c.); S: ed. G.v. Vloten, Leiden 1895; C: lexicography.

(1174a) M/7s 261a/7 *Mudhahhabat Dhī al-Rumma* – *Dhū al-Rumma's Excellent Poem*; cf. no. 1131 for commentary; A: Ghaylān b. ᶜUqba Dhū al-Rumma (d. 117/735); S: *Dīwān*, ed. ᶜA. Abū Ṣāliḥ, Damascus: MLA, 1972–3, I, 6–136; C: poetry – Umayyad – Bedouin. (cf. nos. 411, 1131, 1133a, 1230a, 1640)

(1174b) 261a/7 *wa-Sharḥuhā* – *The Commentary [on the Mudhahhaba]*; several commentaries of Dhū al-Rumma's *bāʾīya qaṣīda* were composed (GAL, II, 397), which is probably meant by the term *mudhahhaba* (cf. no. 1131); C: poetry – commentary.

(1175a) M/7s 261a/7-8 *Majmūᶜ fīhi Dīwān ᶜAlī b. al-Jahm* – *Multiple-Text Manuscript with ᶜAlī b. al-Jahm's Diwan*; A: ᶜAlī b. al-Jahm b. Badr al-Sāmī (d. 249/863); S: ed. Kh. Mardam Bik, Damascus: MIA, 1949; C: poetry.

(1175b) 261a/8 *wa-al-Musawwamāt wa-al-muntakhabāt wa-al-jamarāt wa-al-fursān* – *Poetry on Marked and Chosen Horses as well as Poetry on Parties of Horsemen and Cavaliers*; in combination with the preceding entry, this title seems to refer to the content of poems in this *majmūᶜ*. The terms can be read in various ways (e.g. *muntajabāt* instead of *muntakhabāt*), but it is clear that this *majmūᶜ* was organised around the theme of horses (on *musawwamāt* see Seidensticker, *Das Verbum "'sawwama'* and for an example of the term's usage in poetry *Wāfī*, XIII, 351). C: poetry – anthology.[137]

(1176a) M/7s 261a/8–9 *Majmūᶜ fīhi ᶜAhd Ardashīr – Multiple-Text Manuscript with The Testament of Ardashīr*; ascribed to the Persian monarch A: Ardashīr (*c.*226–40) and purportedly given to his successor/son Shāpūr; S: ed. I. ᶜAbbās, Beirut: DṢ, 1967; C: political thought – non-Muslim – mirror for princes. (cf. no. 736)

(1176b) 261a/9 *wa-Ḥadīth Khusraw Abarwīz wa-ibnuhu Shīrūya – The Speech by Khusraw Abarwīz and His Son Shīrūya*; this is a treatise with a rebuttal and advice ascribed to the Persian monarch Khusraw II Parvīz/Abharvēz (r. 590–628) after his imprisonment by his son and successor. The monarch's speech/message (or parts thereof) is included in various early Arabic sources, one of the most detailed being al-Ṭabarī (d. 310/923) (Bosworth (tr.): *The History of al-Ṭabarī*, V, 386–95). Shorter pieces can be found, for example, in the work by Abū Ḥanīfa Aḥmad b. Dāwūd al-Dīnawarī (fl. 3rd/9th c.; *al-Akhbār al-ṭiwāl*, ed. ᶜA. ᶜĀmir, Cairo: DIKA, 1960, 108–10) and Ibn ᶜAbd Rabbih (d. 328/940) (*al-ᶜIqd al-farīd*, eds A. Amīn, A. al-Zayn and I. al-Ibyārī, Cairo: LTTN, 1940–65, I, 30–2). Ibn Qutayba (d. 276/889) already mentioned that he had come across such Persian material in one of the *kutub al-ᶜajam* (Marlow, *Hierarchy and Egalitarianism*, 85). Later authors such as Ibn Ḥamdūn (d. 562/1166?) (*al-Tadhkira*, I, 301) and al-Qalqashandī (d. 821/1418) (*Ṣubḥ al-aᶜshā*, I, 282) start to refer to a 'book (*kitāb*)' that Abharvēz wrote for his son Shīrūya and the present title is probably such a 'book' that had come into circulation. C: political thought – non-Muslim – mirror for princes.

(1176c) 261a/9–10 *wa-Inqiḍāʾ dawlat al-ᶜajam wa-ibtidāʾ amr khayr al-anbiyāʾ li-khayr al-umam – The End of the Persians' Dynasty and the Beginning of the Affairs of the Best Prophet for the Best Community*; no such title is identifiable and this is probably a treatise that is again drawing on material that had previously been included within larger historical works. C: history – early Islamic.

(1177) M/7s 261a/10–11 *Majmūᶜ yataḍammanu ashyāʾ ḥasana taᶜlīq al-Ḥasan b. Yūsuf al-Āmirī – Multiple-Text Manuscript with Good Things Commented upon by al-Ḥasan b. Yūsuf al-Āmirī*; the named author cannot be identified and the 'title' of this *majmūᶜ* is of little help. Perhaps the author misspelled the name of Abū al-Ḥasan Muḥammad b. Yūsuf al-ᶜĀmirī

(d. 381/992) who appears elsewhere in this catalogue (cf. no. 1184b), but this would be a blatant mistake. The de facto absence of thematic categories in this section with multiple-text manuscripts makes it also impossible to rely on this information to identify the entry.

(1178a) M/7s 261a/11 *Majmū*ᶜ *fīhi al-Minḥa bi-sharḥihā – Multiple-Text Manuscript with the Minḥa and Its Explanation*; this may be the *K. fī miḥnat ḥisāb al-nujūm* by Thābit b. Qurra (d. 288/991) (GAS, II, 163–70), who also authored commentaries on the following title. However, the cataloguer clearly writes '*minḥa*'. C: astronomy?

(1178b) 261a/11 *wa-*ᶜ*Ilal al-zīj al-Ma*ᵓ*mūnī – Explanation of the Ma*ᵓ*mūnī Astronomical Handbook*; no such title is identifiable, but this is most likely a commentary on either *al-Zīj al-ma*ᵓ*mūnī al-mumtaḥan* by Yaḥyā b. Abī Manṣūr (facs. ed. Frankfurt 1986), the astrologer at the court of al-Maᵓmūn (d. 218/833) or Ḥabash b. ᶜAbd Allāh (IN, II/1, 237). FI: '*ghayr tāmm*'/'*incomplete*'; C: astronomy.

(1179a) M/7s 261a/11 *Majmū*ᶜ *fīhi Fanā*ᵓ *al-fanā*ᵓ *– Multiple-Text Manuscript with The Passing-Away of Passing-Away*; no such title is identifiable and this is most likely a (an anonymous) treatise that draws on material on the mystic annihilation of the self. C: sufism.

(1179b) 261a/12 *wa-Zajal* ᶜ*Abd al-Qādir –* ᶜ*Abd al-Qādir's Zajal Poetry*; in light of the previous entry this is most likely Sufi-inspired *zajal*-poetry as it was pioneered by ᶜAlī b. ᶜAbd Allāh al-Shushtarī (d. 668/1269) in al-Andalus and Egypt. There is no famous *zajal*-poet called ᶜAbd al-Qādir nor is there a famous scholar by this name who would have been renowned for Sufi tendencies and for composing *zajal* poetry. In consequence, this is thus most likely poetry by a minor scholar from Egypt/Syria with Sufi inclinations such as ᶜAbd al-Qādir b. ᶜAbd al-Wahhāb (d. 665/1267 in Cairo); TI, 661–70, p. 198). C: poetry – zajal – sufism.

(1179c) 261a/12 *wa-Law*ᶜ*at al-mushtāq – The Enamoured's Affliction*; no such title is identifiable and this arguably refers – in light of the previous entries – to a Sufi poem starting with these words. C: poetry? – sufism?

(1180a) M/7s 261a/12 *Majmū*ᶜ *al-Farā*ᵓ*id wa-al-qalā*ᵓ*id – Multiple-Text Manuscript with The Pearls and Necklaces*; A: Muḥammad al-Ṣaghānī al-

Ahwāzī (fl. 5th/11th c.); S: ed. I.Dh. al-Thāmirī, Beirut: DIḤ, 2006; C: adab – proper conduct – proverbs. (cf. nos. 828, 1198a)

(1180b) 261a/12–13 *wa-Risāla fī al-^{c}uhūd al-yūnānīya – A Treatise on the Greek Testaments*; most likely the *K. al-^{c}uhūd al-yūnānīya* by A: pseudo-Plato, authored by Aḥmad b. Yūsuf Ibn al-Dāya (d. *c.*331/942–3); S: Badawī, *al-Uṣūl al-yūnānīya*; C: political thought – non-Muslim – mirror for princes. (cf. no. 747)

(1181a) M/7s 261a/13 *Majmū^{c} Dīwān al-Rustamī – Multiple-Text Manuscript with al-Rustamī's Diwan*; A: Muḥammad b. Muḥammad al-Rustamī (fl. 4th /10th c.); S: GAS, II, 645; C: poetry – Būyid.

(1181b) 261a/13 *wa-Mukhtār shi^{c}r Abī Firās – Selection from Abū Firās' Poetry*; A: Abū Firās al-Ḥārith b. Sa^{c}īd al-Ḥamdānī (d. 357/968); S: *Dīwān Abī Firās*, ed. ^{c}A. ^{c}Abd al-Sātir, Beirut: DKI, 1983; C: poetry – Ḥamdānid.

(1181c) 261a/13-14 *wa-Mukhtār shi^{c}r al-Sharīf – Selection from al-Sharīf's Poetry*; A: Muḥammad b. al-Ḥusayn al-Sharīf al-Raḍī (d. 406/1016); S: *Dīwān al-Sharīf al-Raḍī*, ed. I. ^{c}Abbās, Beirut: DṢ, 1994; C: poetry – Būyid. (cf. no. 394, 1079, 1081, 1576, 1666)

(1181d) 261a/14 *wa-al-Samāḥa wa-al-shajā^{c}a – Generosity and Boldness*; No such title is cited for A: ^{c}Alī b. Aḥmad al-Wāḥidī (d. 468/1076). This is most likely an extract from al-Wāḥidī's commentary on al-Mutanabbī's *Dīwān* (ed. F. Dieterici, Berlin 1861). C: poetry – commentary.

(1182a) M/7s 261a/14 *Majmū^{c} fīhi shi^{c}r Ẓāfir – Multiple-Text Manuscript with Ẓāfir's Poetry*; A: Abū Manṣūr, Naṣr and al-Qāsim b. al-Qāsim Ẓāfir al-Ḥaddād (d. 528–9/1134); S: *Dīwān*, ed. Ḥ. Naṣṣār, Cairo: MMi, 1969; C: poetry – Fatimid. (cf. no. 655)

(1182b) 261a/14–15 *wa-min Shi^{c}r Muḥammad b. Muḥammad al-Ṣiqillī – [Parts] of Muḥammad b. Muḥammad al-Ṣiqillī's Poetry*; A: Muḥammad b. Muḥammad al-Ṣiqillī Ibn Ẓafar (d. 565/1169–70); S: IKH, IV, 395–7, who quotes some verses by this *adīb* and poet who settled in Syria; C: poetry.

(1182c) 261a/15 *wa-min Kalām al-Wahrānī – [Parts] of the Writings of al-Wahrānī*; A: Muḥammad b. Muḥriz al-Wahrānī (d. 575/1179) who composed *maqāmāt, rasā$^{\circ}$il* and *manāmāt*; S: IKH, IV, 385/6; C: adab? (cf. no. 1685)

(1183) M/7s 261a/15 *Majmū^{c} al-Najm al-Qaṣrī – Multiple-Text Manuscript by al-Najm al-Qaṣrī*; possibly the theologian, jurisprudent and grammarian A: al-Fatḥ b. Mūsā Najm al-Dīn al-Qaṣrī (d. 663/1265) who was born in the Maghrib and subsequently lived in Syria and Egypt; S: TI, 661–70, pp. 153–4.

(1184a) M/7s 261a/15–16 *Majmū^{c} fīhi Zubdat al-ḥaqā$^{\circ}$iq – Multiple-Text Manuscript with The Quintessence of Realities*; A: ^{c}Ayn al-Quḍāt ^{c}Abd Allāh (or Muḥammad) b. Abī Bakr al-Hamadhānī al-Mayānajī (d. 525/1131); S: ed. ^{c}A. ^{c}Usayrān, in: *Muṣannafāt-i ^{c}Ayn al-Quḍāt-i Hamadānī*, Tehran: Dānishgāh, 1962; C: theology – mystical. (cf. no. 538)

(1184b) 261a/16 *wa-Nahj al-taqdīr – The Way of Predestination*; no such title is identifiable, but in conjunction with the following title in this *majmū^{c}* this is arguably a text ascribed to A: Abū al-Ḥasan Muḥammad b. Yūsuf al-^{c}Āmirī (d. 381/992). This older contemporary of Ibn Sīnā authored *al-Taqrīr li-awjuh al-taqdīr* (*The Determination of the Various Aspects of Predestination*) (see Rowson, *Muslim Philosopher*, 10–11). C: theology.

(1184c) 261a/16 *wa-I^{c}tirāḍāt Ibn Sīnā wa-ajwibatuhā – Ibn Sīnā's Objections and Replies*; This may be the *Ajwiba li-su$^{\circ}$ālāt sa$^{\circ}$alahu ^{c}anhā Abū al-Ḥasan al-^{c}Āmirī* (IAU, III, 17) although in this case al-^{c}Āmirī is the questioner. Gutas, *Avicenna and the Aristotelian Tradition*, 431–2, however, argues on the basis of Süleymaniye, Ragıp Paşa 1461 that the questioner could rather be Ibn Sīnā, similar to what the present title implies. C: theology. (cf. 1320b)

(1185a) M/7s 261a/16–261b/1 *Majmū^{c} fīhi shi^{c}r Ṭarafa – Multiple-Text Manuscript with Ṭarafa's Poetry*; A: Ṭarafa ^{c}Amr b. al-^{c}Abd b. Sufyān; S: ed. D. al-Khaṭīb, Damascus: MLA, 1975; C: poetry – pre-Islamic. (cf. no. 682)

(1185b) 261b/1 *wa-Dīwān Labīd – The Diwan of Labīd*; the *mu^{c}allaqāt* poet A: Labīd b. Rabī^{c}a (d. 40/660–1?); S: al-Ṭūsī, *Sharḥ dīwān Labīd b. Rabī^{c}a*, ed. I. ^{c}Abbās, Kuwait: MḤK, 1962; C: poetry – early Islamic.

(1185c) 261b/1 *wa-Ibn Ḥilliza – [The Diwan of] Ibn Ḥilliza*; the *mu^{c}allaqāt* poet A: al-Ḥārith b. Ḥilliza al-Yashkurī; S: ed. H. al-Ṭa^{cc}ān, Baghdad: MI, 1969; C: poetry – pre-Islamic.

(1186a) M/7s 261b/1 *Majmūᶜ fihi ashᶜār mukhtalifa – Multiple-Text Manuscript with Various Poems*; anonymous work with generic title; C: poetry – anthology.

(1186b) 261b/1–2 *wa-Asmāʾ al-ᶜūd alladhī yutabakhkharu bihi wa-ghayr dhālika – Words for Fragrant Wood that Is Used as Incense and Other [Writings]*; no such 'title' is identifiable and this is probably rather the description of a text without title. C: lexicography.

(1187a) M/7s 261b/2 *Majmūᶜ Narjis al-qulūb – The Hearts' Narcissus*; anthology of prophetic *ḥadīth* and other transmissions from the early Islamic period on various topics; A: Ibn al-Jawzī (d. 597/1200); S: Alwajī, *Muʾallafāt*, 538; C: sermon?

(1187b) 261b/2 *wa-Sharḥ Ḥaqāʾiq al-tawba – Commentary on Achieving [the State of] Repentance*; no such title is identifiable. This is most likely a minor commentary on the issue of repentance, which is, for example, discussed in *K. manāzil al-sāʾirīn* by ᶜAbd Allāh al-Anṣārī al-Harawī (d. 481/1089) (Beirut: DKI, 13–15). Ibn Qayyim al-Jawzīya (d. 751/1350), for instance, commented on this passage in his *Madārij al-sālikīn bayna manāzil īyāka naᶜbudu wa-īyāka nastaᶜīnu* (ed. M. al-Baghdādī, Beirut: DKiA, 1996, I, 202–5 '*Ḥaqāʾiq al-tawba wa-ᶜalāmat qabūlihā*' and I, 213–17 '*Min ḥaqāʾiq al-tawba ṭalab aᶜdhār al-khalīqa*'). C: theology.

(1187c) 261b/3 *wa-al-Lubāb fī sharḥ al-shihāb – The Kernels of the Commentary on al-Shihāb*; no such title is identifiable. This is most likely one of the commentaries on *K. al-shihāb* of Muḥammad al-Quḍāᶜī (d. 454/1062). Similar titles include *al-Albāb fī sharḥ al-Shihāb* by Yūsuf b. ᶜAbd Allāh al-Andalusī (d. 575/1180) (TI, 571–80, pp. 191–2) and *Rūḥ al-lubāb fī sharḥ al-shihāb* by al-Ḥusayn b. ᶜAlī al-Rāzī (d. 552/1157) (MM, I, 627); C: ḥadīth.

(1188a) M/7s 261b/3 *Majmūᶜ udabāʾ al-ghurabāʾ – Multiple-Text Manuscript with The Book of Strangers*; possibly A: Abū al-Faraj al-Iṣfahānī (d. 356/967) (authorship disputed); S: *K. Adab al-ghurabāʾ*, ed. Ṣ. al-Munajjid, Beirut: DKJ, 1972; Engl. tr. by Moreh and Crone, *Medieval Arabic Graffiti*. C: adab – anthology. (cf. no. 64)

(1188b) 261b/3 *wa-al-Khammārīn wa-al-khammārāt – The Book of Innkeepers and Tavern Maids*; A: Abū al-Faraj al-Iṣfahānī (d. 356/967); S: GAS, II, 64; C: poetry – wine. (cf. no. 1283b)

(1188c) 261b/4 *wa-Akhbār al-ṭilsamāt – Reports of the Talismans*; no such title is identifiable. This treatise could draw on material such as that mentioned by, for instance, al-Masᶜūdī (d. 345/956) when he states in a passage on the wonder of the world 'according to what we mentioned in (or regarding) *akhbār al-ṭilsamāt*' (*Murūj al-dhahab wa-maᶜādin al-jawhar*, ed. K.Ḥ. Marᶜī, Beirut: MAṢ, 2007, II, 202); C: history?

(1188d) 261b/4 *al-Mughannīn – Singers*; since there are other works by the same author in this multiple-text manuscript, this is arguably *al-Ghilmān al-mughannīn – Singing Youths* or at least an extract from it; A: Abū al-Faraj al-Iṣfahānī (d. 356/967); S: Kilpatrick, *Making*, 23; C: adab – love literature/theory. (cf. no. 803)

(1188e) 261b/4 *al-Diyārāt – [The Book of] Monasteries*; ascribed to A: Abū al-Faraj al-Iṣfahānī (d. 356/967); S: ed. J. al-ᶜAṭīya, London 1991; C: adab – anthology. (cf. no. 386)

(1189a) M/7s 261b/4 *Majmūᶜ Faḍāʾil al-aᶜmāl – Multiple-Text Manuscript with The Merits of Devotional Works*; no such title by an author with the *nisba* al-Hakkārī is identifiable. However, the *nisba* is relatively rare and *Faḍāʾil al-aᶜmāl* works are generally situated within the field of *ḥadīth*. The most likely author of this work is thus the minor *ḥadīth* scholar A: Shaykh al-Islām ᶜAlī b. Muḥammad al-Hakkārī (d. 486/1093) (IKH, III, 345). It is said that he authored several books, although only one title, *ᶜAqīdat al- Shāfiᶜī*, is known (*Siyar*, X, 79). C: ḥadīth – merits.

(1189b) 261b/5 *wa-Waᶜẓ ᶜajamī – Persian Sermon*; anonymous work with generic title; L: Persian; C: sermons.

(1190) M/7s 261b/5 *Majmūᶜ Jadal al-Sharīf – Multiple-Text Manuscript on Disputation by al-Sharīf*; probably a collection of writings on the art of disputation by either 1) ᶜAlī b. al-Ḥusayn al-Sharīf al-Murtaḍā (d. 436/1044) or 2) Muḥammad b. al-Ḥusayn al-Sharīf al-Raḍī (d. 406/1016).

(1191a) M/7s 261b/5 *Majmūᶜ Durar al-sunna – Multiple-Text Manuscript with Pearls of the Sunna*; A: Aḥmad b. Muḥammad b. Maḥmūd/Nūḥ al-Ghaznawī (d. 593/1196–7); S: Ibn al-Mustawfī, *Taʾrīkh Irbil*, I, 121; C: ḥadīth.

(1191b) 261b/5 *wa-Manāfiʿ al-Qurʾān – The Benefits of the Koran*; possibly A: Muḥammad b. Aḥmad b. Saʿīd al-Tamīmī (d. 390/1000); S: al-Ziriklī, *al-Aʿlām*, VI, 202; C: Koran.

(1191c) 261b/6 *wa-al-Munabbihāt – The Reminders*; among the works with this term in the title, the most likely possibility is *Munabbihāt al-Qurʾān* by A: ʿAbd al-Raḥmān b. ʿAbd Allāh al-Suhaylī (d. 581/1185) due to the thematic overlap with the preceding work and as it is the only work with this key word mentioned in pre-modern literature, e.g. in al-Sakhāwī, *al-Ghāya*, 333. C: Koran.

(1192a) M/7s 261b/6 *Majmūʿ al-Manthūr al-Bahāʾī – Multiple-Text Manuscript with Prosifying [Poetry] for Bahāʾ al-Dawla*; for the Buyid ruler Bahāʾ al-Dawla (d. 403/1012); A: Muḥammad b. ʿAlī al-Nayramānī (d. 413/1022); S: facs. ed. Frankfurt 1984; prosification of Abū Tammām's *al-Ḥamāsa*; C: adab/poetry – Būyid. (cf. no. 1112)

(1192b) 261b/6 *wa-al-Mubhij – [The Book,] Which Makes One Rejoice*; A: al-Thaʿālibī (d. 429/1038); S: ed. I. Ṣāliḥ, Damascus: DB, 1999; C: adab – anthology. (cf. nos. 958c, 1005)

(1193) M/7s 261b/6 *Waqʿat al-Adham – The Battle of Adham*; A: Muḥammad b. al-Ḥasan al-Ḥātimī (d. 388/998); S: MU, VI, 2506; no description of this *adīb*'s and poet's 'epistle' (*risāla*) seems to exist, but taking into account the thematic category this is most likely an adab anthology. This could be the third text of the preceding multiple-text manuscript, but the '*wa-*' is missing. C: adab? (cf. no. 1380)

(1194a) M/7s 261b/6–7 *Majmūʿ fihi Rajaz Ḥumayd al-Arqaṭ – Multiple-Text Manuscript with Ḥumayd al-Arqaṭ's Rajaz*; A: Ḥumayd al-Arqaṭ (fl. 1st-2nd/7th-8th c.); S: ed. Hämeen-Anttila, *Five Rağaz Collections*, 194–215; C: poetry – Umayyad.

(1194b) 261b/7 *wa-Dukayn*[138] *– [Rajaz by] Dukayn*; no poet by the name *dh-k-r* is known. As this multiple-text manuscript consists of Umayyad-period *rajaz* poets this is most likely the misspelled name of Dukayn al-Rājiz, the name for either A: Dukayn b. Rajāʾ (d. 105/723) (GAS, II, 372) or Dukayn b. Saʿīd (d. 109/727) (GAS, II, 372/3); S: ed. Hämeen-Anttila, *Minor Rağaz Collections*, 198–209; C: poetry – Umayyad.

(1194c) 261b/7 *wa-al-Faqᶜasī – [Rajaz by] al-Faqᶜasī*; A: ᶜAbd Allāh al-Faqᶜasī (fl. Umayyad period?); S: ed. Hämeen-Anttila, *Minor Rağaz Collections*, 216–44; C: poetry – Umayyad.

(1194d) 261b/7 *wa-Suʾr al-Dhiʾb – [Rajaz by] Suʾr al-Dhiʾb*; A: Suʾr al-Dhiʾb; S: Ibn Manẓūr, *Lisān al-ᶜarab*, Beirut: DṢ, 1994, entry 'ḥ-j-f' quotes *rajaz* poetry by this obscure poet; C: poetry.

(1195) M/7s 261b/7-8 *Majmūᶜ Akhbār al-khulafāʾ – Reports on the Caliphs*; several possibilities including Muḥammad b. Yazīd Ibn Māja (d. 273/887) (*Taʾrīkh al-khulafāʾ*, ed. M.M. al-Ḥāfiẓ, Damascus: MLA, 1979), Aḥmad Ibn Abī Ṭāhir Ṭayfūr (d. 280/893) (*Taʾrīkh Baghdād*, ed. ᶜI.M. al-Ḥājj ᶜAlī, Beirut: DKI, 2009, called *Taʾrīkh Baghdād fī akhbār al-khulafāʾ*), ᶜAlī b. Muḥammad al-Madāʾinī (d. 215/830?) (MU, IV, 1856); Scr('*wa-ᶜalayhi khaṭṭ Jamāl al-Dīn*'): possibly Sharaf al-Khilāfa Jamāl al-Dīn Mūsā b. al-Maʾmūn al-Baṭāʾiḥī (d. 588/1192) who is mentioned as a scribe elsewhere in this *fihrist*, cf. no. 972a and probably 1244a. The cataloguer most likely was also not sure about this work's author as he added: FI: '*taʾrīkh qadīm*'/'*an ancient chronicle*'; C: history.

(1196a) M/7s 261b/8 *Majmūᶜ al-Ṭīb wa-al-taṭayyub – Multiple-Text Manuscript with Perfume and Using It*; no such title is identifiable. This may be a collection of *ḥadīths*, reports, anecdotes and poetry similar to the section *Dhikr mā jāʾa fī al-ṭīb wa-al-taṭayyub* in al-Ibshīhī's (d. after 850/1446) *al-Mustaṭraf fī kull fann mustaẓraf*, Beirut: AK, 1999, 278/9.[139] C: adab – anthology.

(1196b) 261b/8 *wa-Mukhtaṣar al-ishtiqāq – Summary of the Etymology*; several possibilities including the *Ishtiqāq* by ᶜAbd al-Malik b. Qurayb al-Aṣmaᶜī (d. 213/828?) (ed. S. al-Nuᶜaymī, Baghdad: Asᶜad, 1968) and by Ibn Durayd (d. 321/933) (ed. ᶜA.M. Hārūn, Cairo: MK, 1958). Since this multiple-text manuscript contains other works on the *Ḥamāsa* this may be a summary of the work by Abū al-Fatḥ Ibn Jinnī (d. 392/1002), *al-Manhaj fī ishtiqāq asmāʾ shuᶜarāʾ al-Ḥamāsa* (IKH, III, 247). C: poetry – commentary. (cf. no. 73)

(1196c) 261b/9 *wa-al-Risāla al-murtajala fī tafsīr lafẓ al-Ḥamāsa – The Improvised Epistle on Interpreting the Ḥamāsa's Wording*; no such title is identifiable among the many commentaries of Abū Tammām's (d. 231/845 or 232/846) *Book of Bravery* (cf. GAS, II, 555–7). C: poetry – commentary.

(1196d) 261b/9 *wa-Īḍāḥ mushkil shi^c^r al-Mutanabbī – Elucidating the Difficult Passages in al-Mutanabbī's Poetry*; two main possibilities: 1) ^c^Alī b. Ismā^c^īl Ibn Sīda (d. 458/1066) (*Sharḥ al-mushkil min shi^c^r al-Mutanabbī*, ed. M. al-Saqqā, Cairo: DKM, 1996) or 2) Yaḥyā b. ^c^Alī al-Khaṭīb al-Tibrīzī (d. 502/1109) (*al-Mūḍiḥ fī sharḥ shi^c^r al-Mutanabbī*, ed. Kh.R. Nu^c^mān, Baghdad: DSh, 2000); C: poetry – commentary.

(1196e) 261b/9–10 *wa-Sirr al-ṣinā^c^a fī al-t-r-?-l* (?) – *The Secret of the Craft Concerning?*; A: Abū al-Fatḥ Ibn Jinnī (d. 392/1002); S: *Sirr ṣinā^c^at al-i^c^rāb*, ed. M.Ḥ. Ismā^c^īl, Beirut: DKI, 2000; Ibn Jinnī's book was far more famous than the *Sirr al-ṣinā^c^a* by Muḥammad b. al-Ḥasan al-Ḥātimī (d. 388/998), which makes Ibn Jinnī's authorship more likely. The last term could be read as *tarassul*, but that would not fit this work on phonetics and grammar. C: grammar.

(1197) M/7s 261b/10 *Majmū^c^ Jadal wa-qiyās – Multiple-Text Manuscript of Disputation and Reasoning by Analogy*; this is clearly not a stable book title, but a generic title with the cataloguer describing the content of this multiple-text manuscript. The terms *jadal* and *qiyās* could in isolation refer to different fields of knowledge, but in combination they most likely refer to the study and practice of law. However, there is no obvious candidate for the author A: al-Ḥawārī. C: fiqh?

(1198a) M/7s 261b/10 *Majmū^c^ al-Farā^ɔ^id wa-al-qalā^ɔ^id – Multiple-Text Manuscript with The Pearls and Necklaces*; A: Muḥammad al-Ṣaghānī al-Ahwāzī (fl. 5th/11th c.); S: ed. I.Dh. al-Thāmirī, Beirut: DIḤ, 2006; C: adab – proper conduct – proverbs. (cf. nos. 828, 1180a)

(1198b) 261b/11 *wa-Ad^c^iyat al-ayyām al-sab^c^a – Prayers of Invocation for the Seven Days*; several possibilities, but this could be (cf. no. 151) A: Fatimid Caliph al-Mu^c^izz (r. 341–65/953–75); S: ed. I.K. Poonawala, Beirut: DGI, 2006; C: prayer book. (cf. nos. 151, 1170c, 1661)

(1199a) M/7s 261b/11 *Manāqib al-Shāfi^c^ī – Virtues of al-Shāfi^c^ī*; popular title with numerous possibilities (including Aḥmad b. al-Ḥusayn al-Bayhaqī (d. 458/1066) (ed. A. Ṣaqr, Cairo: DT, 1970–1), Muḥammad b. ^c^Umar Fakhr al-Dīn al-Rāzī Ibn al-Khaṭīb (d. 606/1210) (ed. A.Ḥ. Saqqā, Cairo: MKA, 1986) and Aḥmad b. ^c^Alī al-Khaṭīb al-Baghdādī (d. 463/1071) with a slight preference for Ismā^c^īl b. Aḥmad al-Qarrāb (d. 414/1023) whose

Manāqib al-Shāfiʿī was held in the following century in the library of the mausoleum's sister institution in Damascus, the Dār al-ḥadīth al-Ashrafiya (al-Subkī, *Ṭabaqāt*, IV, 266); C: biography – praise of scholar. (cf. no. 1277b)

(1199b) 261b/11 *wa-Juzʾ – A ḥadīth Volume*; A: Hishām b. ʿUrwa (d. 146/763); S: GAS, I, 88–9; C: ḥadīth – collection.

(1199c) 261b/11–12 *wa-[al-]Manāmāt – Dream Stories*; A: ʿAbd Allāh b. Muḥammad Ibn Abī al-Dunyā (d. 281/894); S: ed. ʿA.A. ʿAṭā, Beirut: MKTh, 1993; C: oneiromancy.

(1200a) M/7s 261b/12 *Majmūʿ ʿajamī – Multiple-Text Manuscript (with) Persian (Writings)*; anonymous work with generic title; L: Persian.

(1200b) 261b/12 *wa-Dūbaytī – Dūbaytī* (*Poems)*; anonymous work with generic title; L: Persian?; C: poetry – anthology – dūbaytī.

(1200c) 261b/12 *wa-Nudbat Zayn al-ʿĀbidīn – Zayn al-ʿĀbidīn's Lamentation Prayer of Supplication*; this prayer is generally ascribed to the sixth Shiʿite *imām* Jaʿfar al-Ṣādiq (d. 148/765), but here it is ascribed to A: ʿAlī b. al-Ḥusayn b. ʿAlī b. Abī Ṭālib Zayn al-ʿĀbidīn, the fourth Shiʿite *imām* (d. 94/712?); S: Majlisī, *Zād al-maʿād*, 303–9 and Kohlberg, *Ibn Ṭāwūs*, 222; L: Persian?; C: prayer book.[140] (cf. no. 1269c)

(1200d) 261b/12 *wa-Maqtal al-Ḥallāj – The Killing of al-Ḥallāj*; A: Muḥammad b. Ismāʿīl Ibn Zanjī (d. 334/945–6); S: *Dhikr Maqtal al-Ḥallaj*, ed. M. al-Hindī, Cairo: Dār Qibāʾ, 1998; L: Persian?; C: biography – hagiography.

(1201) M/7s 261b/12–13 *Majmūʿ shiʿr marāthī – Multiple-Text Manuscript with Elegies*; anonymous work with generic title; C: poetry – anthology – elegies.

(1202a) M/7s 261b/13 *Majmūʿ mukhtār shiʿr al-Baḥrānī – Multiple-Text Manuscript with Selections of al-Baḥrānī's Poetry*; A: Muḥammad b. Yūsuf al-Baḥrānī (d. 585/1190); S: IKH, V, 9–12; C: poetry – Begtiginid/Ayyūbid.

(1202b) 261b/13 *wa-Abī al-Shīṣ al-Khuzāʿī – and Abū al-Shīṣ al-Khuzāʿī's [Poetry]*; A: Abū al-Shīṣ Muḥammad al-Khuzāʿī (d. *c*.200/915); S: *Ashʿār Abī al-Shīṣ al-Khuzāʿī wa-akhbāruhu*, ed. ʿA. al-Jubūrī, al-Najaf: Maṭbaʿat al-Ādāb, 1386 *[1967]*; C: poetry – ʿAbbāsid.

(1203a) M/7s 261b/13 *Majmūʿ Mulqā al-sabīl – Multiple-Text Manuscript with Thrown on the Road*; A: Abū al-ʿAlāʾ al-Maʿarrī (d. 449/1058); S: ed.

al-S. ᶜIbāda, Cairo: Dār al-baṣāʾir, 2007; C: adab/poetry – Ḥamdānid/Mirdāsid.

(1203b) 261b/14 *wa-al-Maqṣūr [wa-al-mamdūd]* – *The Short [and Long Alif]*; A: Ibn Durayd (d. 321/933); S: *Dīwān*, ed. B. al-ᶜAlawī, Cairo: LTTN, 1946, 29–37; C: grammar. (cf. nos. 384a, 384b, 676 *[sharḥ]*, 1230j, 1238g, 1268b, 1307b, 1313a, 1326b)

(1203c) 261b/14 *wa-Mā yalḥanu fīhi al-ᶜāmma wa-ghayr dhālika* – *What the Commoners Pronounce Incorrectly and Other [Writings]*; A: ᶜAlī b. Ḥamza al-Kisāʾī (d. 189/805?); S: ed. R. ᶜAbd al-Tawwāb, Cairo: MK, 1982; C: lexicography.

(1204) M/7s 261b/14–15 *Mukhtār min shiᶜr Abī al-Murhaf*[141] *al-Numayrī* – *Selection from Abū al-Murhaf al-Numayrī's Poetry*; A: Naṣr b. al-Ḥasan Abū al-Murhaf al-Numayrī (d. 588/1192); S: IKH, V, 383–4; this poet of Baghdad was renowned for praising the Caliphs, viziers and grandees. C: poetry – Saljūq – panegyric?

(1205a) M/8s 261b/15 *Majmūᶜ Risālat waṣf al-shiyam wa-al-akhlāq* – *Multiple-Text Manuscript with the Epistle on the Description of Dispositions and Characters*; no such work is identifiable and the reading of *shiyam* is tentative. Al-Masᶜūdī in his *Murūj al-dhahab* reports, however, that the ᶜAbbasid Caliph al-Qāhir (r. 320–2/932–4) summoned Muḥammad al-ᶜAbdī, an expert on the 'characters and dispositions' of the ᶜAbbasid Caliphs, who duly reported on their biographies (cited in Cooperson, *Classical Arabic Biography*, 21). With the second text in this *majmūᶜ* also being concerned with biographical information, the present title may refer to such biographical information. C: biography/history.

(1205b) 261b/15–16 *wa-Risālat hafawāt al-alibbāʾ wa-ᶜatharāt al-aṭibbāʾ* – *Epistle on the Intelligent Persons' Faults and the Physicians' Gaffes*; no such title is identifiable and the best known work containing the key word *hafawāt*, *K. al-Hafawāt al-nādira* by Muḥammad b. Hilāl Ghars al-Niᶜma (d. 480/1088) (ed. Ṣ. al-Ashtar, Damascus: MLA, 1967), does not fit the title given here; C: medicine?

(1206) M/8s 261b/16–17 *Majmūᶜ akhbār wa-ḥikāyāt wa-ṭuraf ashᶜār* – *Multiple-Text Manuscript with Reports, Narrations and Curiosities of Poems*; anonymous work with generic title; FI: '*awwaluhu akhbār al-Maʾmūn wa-risālatān*' I' *in its beginning are reports on al-Maʾmūn and two epistles*'; referring to ᶜAbbasid Caliph al-Maʾmūn (r. 198–218/813–33); C: adab/poetry/history.

(1207a) M/8s 261b/17 *Majmūᶜ fihi min Rasāʾil al-Khwārazmī – Multiple-Text Manuscript with al-Khwārazmī's Epistles*; A: Muḥammad b. al-ᶜAbbās al-Khwārazmī (d. 383/993); S: ed. N.W. al-Khāzin, Beirut: DMḤ, 1970; C: adab – epistle.

(1207b) 261b/17–262a/1 *wa-Risālat Ibn Aflaḥ fī ᶜilm al-shiᶜr – Ibn Aflaḥ's Epistle on Poetry*; arguably the *Muqaddima* by the same author (cf. no. 678), A: ᶜAlī Ibn Aflaḥ (d. 535/1141); S: ed. G.J. van Gelder, *Two Arabic Treatises on Stylistics*, Leiden 1987; C: poetry – commentary.

(1207c) 262a/1 *wa-qiṭᶜa min shiᶜrihi – Fragment of His [Ibn Aflaḥ's] poetry*; A: ᶜAlī Ibn Aflaḥ (d. 535/1141); S: cf. no. 1207b; C: poetry – Saljūq.

(1207d) 262a/1 *wa-min Shiᶜr al-Arrajānī wa-ghayr dhālika – [Parts] of Al-Arrajānī's Poetry and Other [Writings]*; A: Aḥmad b. Muḥammad al-Arrajānī (d. 544/1149); S: ed. M.Q. Muṣṭafā, Baghdad: WTh, 1979–81; C: poetry – Saljūq.

(1208a) M/8s 262a/1–2 *Majmūᶜ fihi Muntakhal al-Mīkālī – Multiple-Text Manuscript with The Sifted*; A: Abū al-Faḍl ᶜUbayd Allāh b. Aḥmad al-Mīkālī (d. 436/1044); S: ed. Y.W. al-Jubūrī, Beirut: DGI, 2000; also ascribed to al-Thaᶜālibī, d. 429/1038; C: poetry – anthology – Sāmānid/Ghaznawid. (cf. nos. 1065, 1066)

(1208b) 262a/2 *wa-Khayl al-ᶜarab – The Horses of the Arabs*; probably *Asmāʾ khayl al-ᶜarab* by A: Muḥammad b. Ziyād Ibn al-Aᶜrābī (d. *c*.231/846); S: ed. M.ᶜA. Sulṭānī, Beirut: MR, 1981; GAS, VIII, 127–8; C: lexicography. (cf. no. 31)

(1208c) 262a/2 *wa-mukhtār Maḥāsin Nathr al-durr – Selections from The Beauties of Scattering the Pearls*; no such title is identifiable. This entry probably refers to *Nathr al-durr* by A: Manṣūr b. al-Ḥusayn al-Ābī (d. 421/1030); S: ed. M.ᶜA. Qurana *et al.*, Cairo: HMAK, 1980–90; C: adab – anthology. (cf. no. 1350 for *Nathr al-durar*, 1564)

(1208d) 262a/2 *wa-al-Rāʾiq wa-al-shāʾiq – The Pure and the Yearning*; possibly referring to *al-Khaṭṭ al-rāʾiq wa-al-faḍl al-fāʾiq wa-al-lafẓ al-shāʾiq* by

A: al-Ḥasan b. ᶜAlī al-Juwaynī (d. 586/1190?) who is well represented in this catalogue (cf. nos. 142, 347, 348, 873, 874, 1153, 1154); S: *Siyar*, XXI, 233; C: adab.

(1208e) 262a/2–3 *wa-Muntakhab Jāwīdhān* – *Choices from The Eternal Wisdom*; this anthology of pre-Islamic gnomes (*ḥikma*) was supposedly translated from Sasanian texts and has come down in A: Aḥmad b. Muḥammad Miskawayh's (d. 421/1030?) version. S: Zakeri, *Wisdom*, 73–82; *al-Ḥikma al-khālida: Jāwīdān khirad*, ed. ᶜA. Badawī, Cairo: MNM, 1952; C: political thought – non-Muslim – mirror for princes. (cf. no. 1263a)

(1208f) 262a/3 *wa-Ādāb Ibn al-Muᶜtazz wa-ghayr dhālika* – *Sayings Illustrating the Moral Qualities and Behaviour of an Educated Man and Other [Writings]*; A: ᶜAbd Allāh Ibn al-Muᶜtazz (d. 296/908), S: ed. S. Radīf, Baghdad: MḤ, 1972; C: adab. (cf. no. 51?)

(1209a) M/8s 262a/3–4 *Majmūᶜ* – *Multiple-Text Manuscript*; anonymous work with generic title; FI: '*mutarjam bi-nuzhat al-farīd fīhi bayt fī al-tafsīr wa-raqāᵓiq*'/'*with the heading*[142] '*Nuzhat al-farīd*' *and in it is a verse on interpretation and pious sayings*'; the cataloguer was uncertain whether *Nuzhat al-farīd* was a title or not so he added further description. No such title is identifiable and it is unclear what this text's content is.

(1209b) 262a/4 *wa-akhbār wa-ḥikāyāt wa-samar Nadīm al-farīd* – *Reports, Narrations and the Tale from Nadīm al-farīd*; mostly anonymous material with a generic title (or extracts from Miskawayh's work?) except for Miskawayh's *Nadīm al-farīd* (Ḥājjī Khalīfa, *Kashf*, II, 1937), another title for his *Uns al-farīd* (cf. no. 1538); A: Aḥmad b. Muḥammad Miskawayh (d. 421/1030?); C: adab – anthology.

(1209c) 262a/4–5 *wa-Wilāyat ᶜahd al-Maᵓmūn wa-fawāᵓid* – *The Testament of al-Maᵓmūn and Wise Sayings*; the testament by A: ᶜAbbasid Caliph al-Maᵓmūn (r. 198–218/813–33) to his brother and successor al-Muᶜtaṣim, included in various sources such as S: Bosworth (tr.): *The History of al-Ṭabarī*, XXXII, 225–8; C: political thought – ᶜAbbāsid. (cf. no. 750)

(1210) M/8s 262a/5–6 *Majmūᶜ mutarjam bi-Akhbār al-khulafāᵓ* – *Multiple-Text Manuscript with Heading* '*Reports on the Caliphs*'; FI: '*awwaluhu dhikr al-ṣabūḥ wa-ākhiruhu min al-nuᶜūt*'/'*in its beginning mention is made of the morning drink and in its end [are selections from] descriptions (in poetry)*'; there are several possibilities for the *Akhbār al-khulafā*ᵓ including Muḥammad b. Yazīd Ibn Māja (d. 273/887) (ed. M.M. al-Ḥāfiẓ, Beirut: MR, 1986), Aḥmad Ibn Abī Ṭāhir Ṭayfūr (d. 280/893) (*Taᵓrīkh Baghdād*, ed. ᶜI.M. al-Ḥājj ᶜAlī, Beirut: DKI, 2009, called *Taᵓrīkh Baghdād fī akhbār al-khulafā*ᵓ), ᶜAlī b. Muḥammad al-Madāᵓinī (d. 215/830?) (MU, IV, 1856). However, this is most likely an extract from the *K. al-Awrāq* by A: Muḥammad b. Yaḥyā al-Ṣūlī (d. 335/947) (cf. nos. 43, 1551), which contains the *Urjūza fī dhamm al-ṣabūḥ* by Ibn al-Muᶜtazz (d. 296/908). S: ed. J. Heyworth-Dunne, London and Cairo 1934, III, 251–8.[143] Since this collection of accounts about the ᶜAbbasid Caliphs contains an abundant number of poems *nuᶜūt* may also refer to extracts from the same work. C: history/poetry.

(1211a) M/8s 262a/6 *Majmūᶜ ṭibbī fīhi al-Ruhbān – Multiple-Text Medical Manuscript with The Monks*; referring to the *Tadbīr al-amrāḍ*, a treatise on homely remedies, particularly for the benefit of monks; A: al-Mukhtār b. al-Ḥasan Ibn Buṭlān (d. 458/1066); S: ed. S.Y. Jadon, *The Arab Physician Ibn Buṭlān's (d. 1066) Medical Manual for the Use of Monks and Country People*, PhD thesis, University of California (Los Angeles) 1968; C: pharmacology.

(1211b) 262a/6 *wa-Jālīnūs fī ᶜalāmāt al-ṭabāᵓiᶜ – Galen on the Signs of Natures*; A: Galen; no such title of Galen is known and this may refer to one of his medical titles, such as *Kitāb al-ᶜalāmāt* (GAS, III, 130) or *K. ilā Ighlawqun fī ism al-ṭabīᶜa wa-fī shifāᵓ al-amrāḍ* (Ullmann, *Medizin*, 45); C: medicine.

(1211c) 262a/6–7 *wa-al-Dalālāt ᶜalā maᶜrifat al-awjāᶜ – Guidance Concerning the Knowledge of Types of Pain*; no such title is identifiable. Ḥunayn b. Isḥāq (d. 260/873) authored *K. maᶜrifat awjāᶜ al-maᶜida* (Ullmann, *Medizin*, 118), but the cataloguer would have most likely mentioned the focus on stomach pain if this was the title meant here. This is thus either an unknown independent treatise on types of pain or an extract from a more general medical work such as the book by Yūḥannā b. Māsawayh (d. 243/857) dedicated to the ᶜAbbasid Caliph al-Maᵓmūn, which included sections on human anatomy, the body parts, organs, bones and also '*maᶜrifat asbāb al-awjāᶜ*' (IAU, II, 126). C: medicine.

(1211d) 262a/7 *wa-ᶜAlāmāt al-mawt – Signs of [Immanent] Death*; attr. to A: Hippocrates; S: Ullmann, *Medizin*, 33–4; C: medicine.

(1211e) 262a/7 *wa-al-Adwiya al-mushila – Laxative Drugs*; popular title with several possibilities (cf. Ullmann, *Medizin*) including Isḥāq b. Ḥunayn al-^{c}Ibāḍī (d. *c.*289/910–11) (IAU, II, 159) and Ḥubaysh b. al-Ḥasan al-Dimashqī al-A^{c}sam (fl. 3rd/9th c.). As the multiple-text manuscript contains other works by Galen it is most likely that the entry refers to the treatise ascribed to him. A: Galen; S: IAU, I, 355; C: medicine.

(1212a) M/8s 262a/7–8 *Majmū^{c} fihi min taʾrīkh Ibn Abī al-Azhar – Multiple-Text Manuscript including [parts] of Ibn Abī al-Azhar's Chronicle*; A: Muḥammad (b. Aḥmad?) b. Mazyad Ibn Abī al-Azhar (d. 325/937); S: ^{c}Abbās, *Kutub mafqūda*, 21–7; C: history.

(1212b) 262a/8 *wa-min Mukhtār al-adawāt – [Parts] of The Selection of [The Book of] Instruments/Particles*; no such *mukhtār* is identifiable, but the original title probably refers to a grammatical work, such as Muḥammad b. ^{c}Alī al-Naḥwī (d. 550/1155–6) (*al-Adawāt fi al-naḥw*, MU, VI, 2571) and Muḥammad b. Aḥmad al-Azharī (d. 370/980) (*K. al-adawāt*, MU, V, 2322). C: grammar?

(1213a) M/8s 262a/8 *Majmū^{c} fihi Dīwān al-Mutalammis – Multiple-Text Manuscript with al-Mutalammis' Diwan*; A: al-Mutalammis; S: ed. M. Altūnjī, Beirut: DṢ, 1998; C: poetry – pre-Islamic. (cf. no. 589)

(1213b) 262a/8-9 *wa-inshādāt wa-ghayr dhālika – Recitations and Other [Writings]*; anonymous work with generic title.

(1214) M/8s 262a/9 *Majmū^{c} fihi funūn tashtamilu ^{c}alā al-^{c}aql wa-al-dhāt wa-nawādir al-ḥukamāʾ wa-ad^{c}iya wa-istighfār – Multiple-Text Manuscript with Different Fields of Knowledge Including on the Intellect and the Essence, Anecdotes of the Wise Teachers, Prayers of Invocation and [Asking] Forgiveness*; anonymous work with generic title; C: philosophy/prayer book. (*nawādir al-ḥukamāʾ*: cf. no. 1292c)

(1215a) M/8s 262a/10 *Majmū^{c} fihi Dīwān al-Afwah – Multiple-Text Manuscript with al-Afwah's Diwan*; A: Ṣalāʾa b. ^{c}Amr al-Afwah al-Awdī; S: ed. M. Altūnjī, Beirut: DṢ, 1998; C: poetry – pre-Islamic.

(1215b) 262a/10 *wa-min Shi^{c}r Ibn Abī Rabī^{c}a – [Parts] of Ibn Abī Rabī^{c}a's Poetry*; A: ^{c}Umar (b. ^{c}Abd Allāh) b. Abī Rabī^{c}a (d. 93/712 or 103/721); S: *Der Diwan des ^{c}Umar Ibn Abi Rebi^{c}a*, ed. P. Schwarz, Leipzig 1901–9; C: poetry – Umayyad. (cf. no. 599)

(1215c) 262a/10 *wa-Qaṣīd Ka*[c]*b* – *Ka*[c]*b's Qaṣīdas*; probably A: Ka[c]b b. Zuhayr; S: Diem, *Überlieferung*; C: poetry – early Islamic. (cf. nos. 867, 1230d)

(1215d) 262a/10 *wa-Lāmīya al-Shanfarā* – *The Poem Rhyming on lām*; A: al-Shanfarā; S: *Dīwān*, in *Dīwān al-ṣa*[c]*ālīk*, Beirut: DJ, 1992; C: poetry – pre-Islamic.

(1215e) 262a/11 *wa-Shi*[c]*r Qays al-Ẓafarī* – *Qays al-Ẓafarī's Poetry*; A: Qays b. al-Khaṭīm b. [c]Adī al-Ẓafarī; S: *Dīwān*, eds I. al-Sāmarrā[ɔ]ī and A. Maṭlūb, Baghdad: M[c]A, 1962; C: poetry – pre-Islamic. (cf. no. 1305d)

(1216a) M/8s 262a/11 *Majmū*[c] *fīhi Mīzān al-*[c]*arūḍ* – *Multiple-Text Manuscript with The Balance of Metrics*; no such title is identifiable, although it recalls *al-Qisṭāṣ al-mustaqīm fī* [c]*ilm al-*[c]*arūḍ* by Maḥmūd b. [c]Umar al-Zamakhsharī (d. 538/1144) (ed. Baghdad: Maktabat al-Andalus, 1969). However, the catalogue explicitly mentions that it was authored by 'al-Khaṭīb' and this is thus most likely an altered title of the work *al-Kāfī fī al-*[c]*arūḍ* mentioned above. A: Yaḥyā b. [c]Alī al-Khaṭīb al-Tibrīzī (d. 502/1109); S: ed. al-Ḥ.Ḥ. [c]Abdallāh, Cairo: JDA, 1966; C: poetry – metrics. (cf. nos. 758, 890)

(1216b) 262a/11 *wa-al-Jumal fī al-naḥw* – *The Comprehensive Grammar*; A: al-Khalīl b. Aḥmad al-Farāhīdī (d. 175/791?); S: ed. F. Qabāwa, Beirut: MR, 1985; MS: Süleymaniye, Ayasofya 4456/3 (fols. 6a–81a)*; C: grammar.

(1216c) 262a/12 *wa-Mukhtaṣar mā yajūzu ṣarfuhu li-l-shā*[c]*ir* – *Summary of What the Poet Has Licence to Inflect*; neither the summary nor the original title is identifiable for this (most likely anonymous) treatise on morphology. C: grammar/poetry.

(1217a) M/8s 262a/12–13 *Majmū*[c] *yashtamilu* [c]*alā maqālatay Ghulām Zuḥal fī māhīyat al-shu*[c]*ā*[c]*āt wa-*[c]*ilaluhā* – *Multiple-Text Manuscript Containing Two Tracts by Ghulām Zuḥal [the First] on the Nature of the Rays and Their Causes*; A: [c]Ubayd Allāh b. al-Ḥasan Ghulām Zuḥal ('Saturn's Servant') (d. 376/986–7); S: GAS, VII, 168 (*K. al-shu*[c]*ā*[c]*āt*); C: astronomy.

(1217b) 262a/13 *wa-Subul al-tasyīrāt* – *[And the Second Tract on] Ways of Prognosticating Future Events*; A: [c]Ubayd Allāh b. al-Ḥasan Ghulām Zuḥal ('Saturn's Servant') (d. 376/986–7); S: GAS, VII, 168 (*K. al-tasyīrāt*); C: astronomy.

(1218a) M/8s 262a/13 *Majmūᶜ awwaluhu fī mawlid al-Nabī ṣallā Allāh ᶜalayhi wa-sallam – Multiple-Text Manuscript with the Prophet's Birth in the beginning (may God's blessing and peace be upon him)*; anonymous work with generic title; C: poetry – mawlid.

(1218b) 262a/13–14 *wa-Waṣīyatuhu li-ᶜAlī b. Abī Ṭālib karrama Allāh wajhahu – Conferring the Trusteeship to ᶜAlī b. Abī Ṭālib (may God honour his countenance)*; anonymous treatise building on material found in sources such as *Ithbāt al-waṣīya li-l-Imām ᶜAlī b. Abī Ṭālib* (attr. Abū al-Ḥasan ᶜAlī b. al-Ḥusayn al-Masᶜūdī, d. 345/956, ed. Najaf, *c.*1955); C: political thought – imāmate theory. (cf. no. 19)

(1218c) 262a/14 *wa-Thulāthīyāt al-Bukhārī – Al-Bukhārī's 'Thulāthīya' ḥadīths*; there are several collections of those *ḥadīths* in which only three intermediaries separate al-Bukhārī from the Prophet. For a list of such works see al-Kattānī, *Rubāᶜīyāt*, 138–9. C: ḥadīth – collection.

(1218d) 262a/14 *wa-Adᶜiya wa-ghayruhā – Prayers and Other [Writings]*; anonymous work with generic title; C: prayer book.

(1219a) M/8s 262a/14–15 *Majmūᶜ ᶜuwadh wa-ḥurūz – Multiple-Text Manuscript with Talismans and Prayer Amulets*; anonymous work with generic title; C: prayer amulets.

(1219b) 262a/15 *wa-Qalᶜ al-āthār – Removing Stains [from Clothes]*; A: al-Kindī (d. *c.*252/866); S: *Wāfī*, XXVIII, 479–88, here 485: '*Qalᶜ al-āthār min al-thiyāb*'; C: chemistry.

(1219c) 262a/15 *wa-min al-Khawāṣṣ – [Parts] of the Book on Sympathetic Qualities*; A: al-Rāzī (Rhazes) (d. 313/925 or 323/935); S: Ullmann, *Natur- und Geheimwissenschaften*, 407 (*khawāṣṣ al-ashyā'*); C: medicine – sympathetic qualities.

(1220) M/8s 262a/15–16 *Majmūᶜ ashᶜār wa-akhbār wa-ḥikam wa-nawādir wa-ḥikāyāt wa-ghayr dhālika – Multiple-Text Manuscript with Poems, Reports, Pieces of Wisdom, Anecdotes, Narrations and Other [Writings]*; anonymous work with generic title; FI: '*kamā dhukira fī tarjama*'/'*as mentioned in heading*'; C: adab/poetry – anthology.

(1221a) M/8s 262a/16 *Majmūᶜ fīhi al-khayl wa-faḍluhā – Multiple-Text Manuscript with The Horses and Their Merits*; most likely extract from one of the numerous books on horses (*K. al-khayl*), some of which are mentioned in this catalogue (cf. nos. 361, 374, 704); C: lexicography.

(1221b) 262a/17 *wa-al-Ṭīb wa-ajnāsuhu – Perfume and Its Varieties*; most likely extract from a book on scents such as *K. al-ṭīb* by Ibrāhīm b. al-Mahdī (d. 224/839); C: lexicography.

(1221c) 262a/17 *wa-al-Ḥubb min al-jamāhīr – The Kernel of the Essence*; arguably an extract from the *K. al-jamāhīr* on grammar by A: Muḥammad b. al-Mustanīr Quṭrub (d. 206/821); S: al-Tanūkhī, *al-ʿUlamāʾ al-naḥwīyīn*, I, 83; C: grammar.

(1222a) M/8s 262a/17 *Majmūʿ ʿArūḍ al-Zanjānī – Multiple-Text Manuscript with al-Zanjānī's Metrics*; A: ʿAbd al-Wahhāb b. Ibrāhīm al-Khazrajī al-Zanjānī (fl. 660/1261); S: *Miʿyār al-nuẓẓār fī ʿulūm al-ashʿār*, ed. M.ʿA.R. al-Khafājī, Cairo: DM, 1991;[144] FI: *'jayyid'/'magnificent [collection?]'*; C: poetry – metrics.

(1222b) 262a/17–18 *wa-Qawāfī Ibn Jinnī – Ibn Jinnī's [Book on] Rhymes*; A: Abū al-Fatḥ Ibn Jinnī (d. 392/1002); S: *Mukhtaṣar al-qawāfī*, ed. Ḥ.Sh. Farhūd, Cairo: DT, 1975; C: poetry – rhyme. (cf. no. 1313b?)

(1222c) 262a/18 *wa-al-Sīra*[145] – *The [Prophet's] Biography*; A: Aḥmad Ibn Fāris (d. 395/1004); S: MU, I, 410; C: biography of the Prophet (*sīra*).

(1222d) 262a/18 *wa-Fawāʾid – Wise Sayings*; anonymous work with generic title.

(1222e) 262a/18 *wa-Fuḥūl al-ʿarab – The Great Arabs*; A: Hishām b. Muḥammad Ibn al-Kalbī (d. 204/819 or 206/821); S: MU, VI, 2780: '*Asmāʾ fuḥūl al-ʿarab*'; C: adab – anthology.

(1222f) 262a/18 *wa-Ādāb al-wuzarāʾ wa-al-kuttāb – Rules for Viziers and Secretaries*; possibly A: Muḥammad b. ʿAbdūs al-Jahshiyārī (d. 331/942); S: *K. al-wuzarāʾ wa-al-kuttāb*, ed. M. al-Saqā, Cairo: MBḤ, 1938 – although this is rather a chronicle and changing the title to '*ādāb*' would be surprising; C: political thought – adab of vizier. (cf. nos. 69, 1263b for *ādāb al-wuzarāʾ*-works)

(1223a) M/8s 262b/1 *Majmūʿ fīhi al-Ighrīḍīya – Multiple-Text Manuscript with the Ighrīḍīya Epistle*; A: Abū al-ʿAlāʾ al-Maʿarrī (d. 449/1058); S: al-Maʿarrī, *Rasāʾil*, I, 183–250; C: adab. (cf. nos. 53b, 533, 1306a)

(1223b) 262b/1 *wa-Fawāʾid* – *Wise Sayings*; anonymous work with generic title.

(1223c) 262b/1 *wa-al-Wuḥūsh* – *The Wild Animals*; A: ᶜAbd al-Malik b. Qurayb al-Aṣmaᶜī (d. 213/828?); S: ed. Ay.M.ᶜA. Maydān, Jidda 1990; C: lexicography. (cf. no. 1297b)

(1223d) 262b/1 *wa-Shiᶜr* – *Poetry*; A: Zuhayr b. Abī Sulmā Rabīᶜa al-Muzanī (d. 609 CE?); S: *Dīwān*, ed. K. al-Bustānī, Beirut 1960; C: poetry – pre-Islamic. (cf. no. 417)

(1223e) 262b/2 *wa-al-Mudhahhaba* – *The Mudhahhaba Poem*; this is either one of the seven *mudhahhaba* poems as listed by al-Qurashī, *Jamharat*, 614–65 or the term *mudhahhaba* is meant here in the sense of an 'excellent poem' as above (cf. no. 1131). As the cataloguer determined the term *mudhahhaba* here (in contrast to no. 1230l) he seems to be referring to a specific poem, perhaps one by the poet mentioned in the previous entry, Zuhayr b. Abī Sulmā Rabīᶜa al-Muzanī. C: poetry.

(1224a) M/8s 262b/2 *Majmūᶜ awwaluhu shiᶜr li-baᶜḍ shuᶜarāʾ Ṣalāḥ al-Dīn* – *Multiple-Text Manuscript with Poetry by One of Ṣalāḥ al-Dīn's Poets in the Beginning*; anonymous work with generic title; C: poetry – panegyric – Ayyūbid – Ṣalāḥ al-Dīn.

(1224b) 262b/2 *wa-Maᶜrifat ᶜuyūb al-shiᶜr* – *Knowledge of the Shortcomings of Poetry*; no such title is identifiable. This is possibly an extract from one of the works on literary criticism (see Ouyang, *Literary Criticism*). Owing to chronological proximity the *ᶜUyūb al-shiᶜr* by Muḥammad b. ᶜAlī al-ᶜIrāqī (d. *c.*560/1165) (TI, 551–60, pp. 361–3) is a possible contender. C: poetry – commentary.

(1224c) 262b/2 *wa-al-Qawāfī* – *Rhymes*; popular title with several possibilities including Abū al-Fatḥ Ibn Jinnī (d. 392/1002) (*Mukhtaṣar al-qawāfī*, ed. Ḥ.Sh. Farhūd, Cairo: DT, 1975); Saᶜīd b. Masᶜada al-Akhfash al-Awsaṭ (d. 215/830) (ed. ᶜI. Ḥasan, Damascus 1970); Ṣāliḥ b. Isḥāq al-Jarmī al-Naḥwī (d. 225/839–40) (S: IN, I/1, 162); C: poetry – rhyme. (cf. no. 1226b)

(1224d) 262b/3 *wa-Sharḥ al-masāʾil al-thalāth* – *Commentary on the Three Questions*; 'Three Questions/Problems' developed in a wide variety of fields such as *tafsīr* (e.g. the question of '*al-rūḥ wa-al-kahf wa-dhī al-qarnayn*' in

Ibn ^{c}Aṭīya, *al-Muḥarrar*, III, 494) and *fiqh*. However, no such commentary is identifiable.

(1224e) 262b/3 *wa-Sharḥ al-masāʾil al-sab^{c}* – *Commentary on the Seven Questions*; 'Seven Questions/Problems' developed in a wide variety of fields such as philosophy (e.g. Muḥammad b. ^{c}Abd al-Karīm al-Shahrastānī (d. 548/1153), *Muṣāra^{c}at al-falāsifa*, ed. M.F. al-Jabar, Damascus: Dār Mu^{c}add, 1997). Again, no such commentary is identifiable.

(1224f) 262b/3 *wa-Makhārij al-ḥurūf wa-ghayr dhālika* – *Points of Articulation and Other [Writings]*; popular title with numerous possibilities including Ibn Sīnā (d. 428/1037; alternative title: *Asbāb ḥudūth al-ḥurūf*, Engl. tr. by Khalīl I. Semaan, Lahore 1963) and ^{c}Uthmān b. ^{c}Alī al-Ṣiqillī (*Wāfī*, XX, 87–8); C: phonetics.

(1225a) M/8s 262b/3–4 *Majmū^{c} fīhi al-khaṭṭ wa-al-qalam* – *Multiple-Text Manuscript with the Script and the Pen*; popular title with numerous possibilities including al-Mufaḍḍal b. Salama (fl. 3rd/9th c.) (MU, VI, 2709) and *Risālat al-khaṭṭ wa-al-qalam* attr. to ^{c}Abd Allāh b. Muslim al-Dīnawarī Ibn Qutayba (d. 276/889) (ed. H.Ṣ. al-Dāmin, Beirut: MR, 1989, cf. no. 379); C: calligraphy.

(1225b) 262b/4 *wa-Tahānī wa-ta^{c}āzī wa-waṣāyā* – *Felicitations, Condolences and Advice*; anonymous work with generic title; C: adab – anthology.

(1226a) M/8s 262b/4–5 *Majmū^{c} awwaluhu rasāʾil wa-^{c}Arūḍ al-Khalīl wa-al-durūs fīhā* – *Multiple-Text Manuscript with Epistles in the Beginning and the Metrics as well as Teaching Material on It*; *rasāʾil*: not identifiable; *^{c}Arūḍ*: A: al-Khalīl b. Aḥmad al-Farāhīdī (d. 175/791?); S: IN, I/1, 116; C: poetry – metrics.

(1226b) 262b/5 *wa-al-Qawāfī* – *Rhymes*; several possibilities cf. no. 1224c; C: poetry – rhyme.

(1226c) 262b/5 *wa-Shi^{c}r al-Ḥādira* – *Al-Ḥādira's Poetry*; A: Quṭba al-Ḥādira; S: GAS, II, 213/4; C: poetry – pre-Islamic. (cf. no. 972b)

(1226d) 262b/5 *wa-min-Shi^{c}r li-Ibn Abī Zunbūr* – *[Parts] of Ibn Abī Zunbūr's Poetry*; A: Aḥmad b. ^{c}Alī Ibn Abī Zunbūr (d. *c*.613/1216–17) who wrote panegyrics for Saladin; S: *Wāfī*, VII, 200; C: poetry – Ayyūbid.

(1226e) 262b/5–6 *wa-Urjūzatuhu fī ṣifāt al-khayl* – *His Poem on the Characteristics of Horses*; A: Aḥmad b. ^{c}Alī Ibn Abī Zunbūr (d. *c*.613/1216 17);

his biographies such as *Wāfī*, VII, 200 do not mention any titles and only state that he composed panegyrics and that he was an *adīb*. C: lexicography.

(1226f) 262b/6 *wa-Ad^{c}iya – Prayers*; generic title; C: prayer book.

(1227a) M/8s 262b/6 *Majmū^{c} fīhi mukhtār Nishwār al-muḥāḍara – Multiple-Text Manuscript with the Selection from the Assembly's Elegant Talks*; referring to A: al-Muḥassin b. ^{c}Alī al-Tanūkhī (d. 384/994); S: *Nishwār al-muḥāḍara wa-akhbār al-mudhākara*, ed. ^{c}A. al-Shāljī, Beirut: DṢ, 1971–3, C: adab – anthology. (cf. nos. 1507, 1523)

(1227b) 262b/6–7 *wa-al-Azhār al-dhakīya fī al-mabāḥith al-qiyāsīya – Fragrant Flowers on Studying Reasoning by Analogy*; no such title is identifiable, yet it is similar to the legal treatise *al-Nihāya al-Bahāʾiya fī al-mabāḥith al-qiyāsīya* by Muḥammad b. ^{c}Umar Fakhr al-Dīn al-Rāzī Ibn al-Khaṭīb (d. 606/1210) (al-Zarkān, *Fakhr al-Dīn al-Rāzī*, no. 60); C: fiqh – uṣūl al-fiqh.

(1228) M/8s 262b/7 *al-Maṣūn li-l-Rayḥānī*[146] *yashtamilu ^{c}alā ^{c}iddat kutub min tawālīfihi – Al-Rayḥānī's The Hidden Containing Several Books of His Writings*; A: ^{c}Alī b. ^{c}Ubayda al-Rayḥānī (d. 219/834), S: Zakeri, *Wisdom*, 230–4; C: adab – gnomic literature.

(1229a) M/8s 262b/7–8 *Majmū^{c} akhbār wa-ash^{c}ār wa-min shi^{c}r al-Ghazzī – Multiple-Text Manuscript with Reports, Poems and [parts] of al-Ghazzī's Poetry*; mostly generic title and A: Ibrāhīm *[b. Yaḥyā?]* b. ^{c}Uthmān al-Ghazzī (d. 524/1129); S: *Dīwān* ed. ^{c}A. Ḥusayn, Dubai: Markaz Jum^{c}a al-Mājid, 2008; C: poetry – panegyric?

(1229b) 262b/8 *wa-Dīwān Imriʾ al-Qays al-Kindī – Imruʾ al-Qays al-Kindī's Diwan*; probably A: Imruʾ al-Qays b. Ḥujr al-Kindī; S: ed. M.A. Ibrāhīm, Cairo 1958; MS: Süleymaniye, Laleli 1820*; C: poetry – pre-Islamic.

(1229c) 262b/8 *wa-min-Shi^{c}r Ibn al-Sā^{c}ātī – [Parts] of Ibn al-Sā^{c}ātī's Poetry*; A: ^{c}Alī b. Rustam Ibn al-Sā^{c}ātī (d. *c.*604/1207); S: *Dīwān*, ed. A. al-Maqdisī, Beirut: American Press, 1938/9; C: poetry – Zangid/Ayyūbid. (cf. nos. 399, 801)

(1229d) 262b/9 *wa-Ibn al-Nabīh – Ibn al-Nabīh's [Poetry]*; A: ^{c}Alī b. Muḥammad Kamāl al-Dīn Ibn al-Nabīh (d. 619/1222); S: al-As^{c}ad, *Dīwān Ibn al-Nabīh*; C: poetry – panegyric? – Ayyūbid? – al-Malik al-Ashraf? (cf. nos. 190, 288, 315, 863, 868, 1049, 1055)

(1229e) 262b/9 *wa-Jarīr – Jarīr's [Poetry]*; A: Jarīr b. ᶜAṭīya (d. *c.*110/728–9); S: ed. N. Ṭaha, Cairo: DM, 1986; C: poetry – Umayyad. (cf. nos. 404, 1072, 1290b, 1610, 1630, 1653)

(1230a) M/8s 262b/9 *Majmūᶜ fīhi Mudhahhabat Dhī al-Rumma – Multiple-Text Manuscript with Dhū al-Rumma's Excellent Poem*; cf. no. 1131 for commentary; A: Ghaylān b. ᶜUqba Dhū al-Rumma (d. 117/735); S: *Dīwān*, ed. ᶜA. Abū Ṣāliḥ, Damascus: MLA, 1972–3, I, 6–136; C: poetry – Umayyad – Bedouin. (cf. nos. 411, 1131, 1133a, 1174a, 1640)

(1230b) 262b/9 *wa-Qaṣīd Diᶜbil – Diᶜbil's Qaṣīdas*; A: Muḥammad b. ᶜAlī b. Razīn al-Khuzāᶜī Diᶜbil (d. *c.*246/860); S: *Dīwān Diᶜbil*, ed. ᶜA.ᶜI. al-Dujaylī, Beirut: DKL, 1972; C: poetry – ᶜAbbāsid.

(1230c) 262b/9 *wa-al-Shanfarā – Al-Shanfarā's [Qaṣīdas]*; A: al-Shanfarā; S: *Dīwān*, in *Dīwān al-ṣaᶜālīk*, Beirut: DJ, 1992; C: poetry – pre-Islamic.

(1230d) 262b/10 *wa-Kaᶜb – Kaᶜb's [Qaṣīdas]*; probably A: Kaᶜb b. Zuhayr; S: Diem, *Überlieferung*; C: poetry – early Islamic. (cf. nos. 867, 1215c)

(1230e) 262b/10 *wa-Thāʾīyat Ibn Durayd – Ibn Durayd's Poem on the Rhyme Letter thāʾ [Amāṭat lithām^an]*; A: Ibn Durayd (d. 321/933); S: *Dīwān*, ed. B. al-ᶜAlawī, Cairo: LTTN, 1946, 42–64; The first term is undotted and could also indicate another rhyme letter, but his *Qaṣīda* starting with *Amāṭat lithām^an* is one of his longer poems.[147] C: poetry – ᶜAbbāsid. (cf. no. 1332b)

(1230f) 262b/10 *wa-Qaṣīd fī al-ẓāʾāt wa-Urjūza fī al-farq bayna al-ḍād wa-al-ẓāʾ – Qaṣīdas on Words with the Letter ẓāʾ and a Didactic Poem on The Difference between the Letters ẓāʾ and ḍād*; *urjūza*: arguably by A: Muḥammad b. ᶜAbd Allāh Ibn Mālik al-Jayyānī (d. 672/1274); S: ed. Ṭ. Muḥsin, Damascus: DY, 2009; C: lexicography. (cf. no. 813)

(1230g) 262b/11 *wa-min Shiᶜr Ibn al-Ḥarīrī – [Parts] of Ibn al-Ḥarīrī's Poetry*; A: al-Qāsim b. ᶜAlī al-Ḥarīrī al-Baṣrī (d. 516/1122) who was often called 'Ibn' al-Ḥarīrī; S: EI², D.S. Margoliouth ad Ch. Pellat, 'al-Ḥarīrī'; his diwan has been lost; C: poetry

(1230h) 262b/11 *wa-Qaṣīd Diᶜbil Afīqī – Diᶜbil's Qaṣīda [Starting with] 'Wake up, woman!'*; A: Muḥammad b. ᶜAlī b. Razīn al-Khuzāᶜī Diᶜbil (d. *c.*246/860); S: *Dīwān Diᶜbil*, ed. ᶜA.ᶜI. al-Dujaylī, Beirut: DKL, 1972, 291–5; the poet's famous *qaṣīda* refuting the long poem by al-Kumayt b. Zayd with the same metre and rhyme.[148] C: poetry.

(1230i) 262b/11 *wa-Qaṣīd Abī al-Baydā᾽ – Qaṣīdas [Compiled] by Abū al-Baydā᾽*; A: Abū al-Baydā᾽ Asᶜad b. ᶜIṣma al-Riyāḥī (fl. 2nd/8th c.); S: IN, I, 521 and MU, II/2, 630; FI: *'allatī lā yuᶜrafu qā᾽iluhā' l' of which it is not known who composed them'*; C: poetry.

(1230j) 262b/12 *wa-Maqṣūr [wa-mamdūd] – The Short [and Long Alif]*; A: Ibn Durayd (d. 321/933); S: *Dīwān*, ed. B. al-ᶜAlawī, Cairo: LTTN, 1946, 29–37; C: grammar. (cf. nos. 384a, 384b, 676 *[sharḥ]*, 1203b, 1238g, 1268b, 1307b, 1313a, 1326b)

(1230k) 262b/12 *wa-Qaṣīdatuhu fīhi wa-lahu muntakhab – His [Ibn Durayd's] Qaṣīda on It [the Maqṣūra] and a Selection [from His Works?]*; A: Ibn Durayd (d. 321/933); S: *Dīwān*, ed. B. al-ᶜAlawī, Cairo: LTTN, 1946; C: grammar. (cf. nos. 1250e, 1268a, 1270a)

(1230l) 262b/12 *wa-Mudhahhaba – A Mudhahhaba Poem*; this is either one of the seven *mudhahhaba* poems as listed by al-Qurashī, *Jamharat*, 614–15 (more likely on account of following entry), or the term *mudhahhaba* is meant here in the sense of an 'excellent poem' as above (cf. no. 1131). C: poetry.

(1230m) 262b/12 *wa-al-Sabᶜ [al-muᶜallaqāt] – The Seven [Suspended Qaṣīdas]*; S: al-Qurashī, *Jamharat*, 124–428; C: poetry – anthology – pre-Islamic. (cf. nos. 567, 569, 852, 1686)

(1230n) 262b/12 *wa-Hal bi-al-ṭulūl – [The Poem Starting with] hal bi-al-ṭulūl*; also known as *al-Qaṣīda al-yatīma*, ascribed to various poets such as Dawqala al-Manbijī and Abū al-Shīṣ Muḥammad (b. ᶜAbd Allāh) b. Razīn al-Khuzāᶜī (d. *c.*200/915), see *al-Qaṣīda al-yatīma*, ed. Ṣ. al-Munajjid, Beirut: DKJ, 1974; C: poetry. (cf. no. 1241d)

(1230o) 262b/13 *wa-Yā dāra mayyata – [The Muᶜallaqa Poem Starting with] Yā dāra Mayyata*; A: Ziyād al-Nābigha al-Dhubyānī; S: EI², A. Arazi, 'al-Nābigha al-Dhubyānī'; C: poetry – pre-Islamic.

(1230p) 262b/13 *wa-Qaṣīd Suwayd – Suwayd's Qaṣīdas*; A: several possibilities including Suwayd b. Kurāᶜ (early Islamic) (GAS, II, 223) and Suwayd b. al-Khadhdhāk (pre-Islamic) (GAS, II, 188); C: poetry.

(1231) M8/s 262b/13–14 *Majmūᶜ Shiᶜr Abī al-Shās wa-ashᶜār wa-akhbār wa-ghayr dhālika – Multiple-Text Manuscript with Poetry by Abū al-Shās, Poems, Reports and Other [Writings]*; generic title and A: Abū Shās (Shaᵓs) Munīr; S: al-Shābushtī, *al-Diyārāt*, 181–3; the reading of this obscure poet is tentative as the MS seems to have 'al-Shāᵓis'. C: poetry.

(1232a) M/8s 262b/14 *Majmūᶜ Awzān al-ashᶜār – Multiple-Text Manuscript with the Poems' Metres*; most likely A: Muḥammad b. ᶜAbd al-Malik Ibn al-Sarrāj (d. *c.*549/1154); S: *al-Miᶜyār fī awzān al-ashᶜār*, ed. M.R. Dāya, Beirut: Dār al-anwār, 1968; C: poetry – metrics.

(1232b) 262b/14 *wa-Qawāfī – Rhymes*; A: Muḥammad b. Yazīd al-Mubarrad (d. 286/900); S: ed. R. ᶜAbd al-Tawwāb, Cairo: Maṭbaᶜat Jāmiᶜat ᶜAyn Shams, 1972; C: poetry – rhyme.

(1232c) 262b/14 *wa-Kunā al-shuᶜarāᵓ – The Poets' kunyas*; A: Aḥmad b. Yaḥyā Thaᶜlab (d. 291/904); No such work by Thaᶜlab is known, probably this is the well-known work by Muḥammad Ibn Ḥabīb (d. 245/860) (*Asmāᵓ al-mughtālīn. . .*, ed. S.K. Ḥasan, Beirut: DKI, 2001); C: biographical dictionary – poets.

(1232d) 262b/15 *wa-Ṭabaqātuhum – Their [the Poets'] Generations*; A: Muḥammad Ibn Sallām al-Jumaḥī (d. 231/845 or 232/846), S: eds J. Hell and Ṭ.A. Ibrāhīm, Beirut: DKI, 1982; C: biographical dictionary – poets. (cf. no. 1125)

(1232e) 262b/15 *wa-Risālat al-Babbaghāᵓ fī al-dawāt – Al-Babbaghāᵓ's Epistle on Inkwells*; A: ᶜAbd al-Wāḥid al-Babbaghāᵓ (d. 398/1007); S: extracts cited in al-Qalqashandī, *Ṣubḥ al-aᶜshā*, IX, 124; C: adab – epistle.

(1233a) M8/s 262b/15 *Majmūᶜ al-Akhlāq – Multiple-Text Manuscript with The Morals*; A: al-Ḥasan b. al-Ḥasan/Ḥusayn Ibn al-Haytham al-Baṣrī (d. 430/1039), authorship disputed; S: *Maqālat fī al-akhlāq*, ed. ᶜA. Badawī, *Dirāsāt wa-nuṣūṣ fī al-falsafa wa-al-ᶜulūm ᶜinda al-ᶜArab*, Beirut: MAr, 1981, 107–45; C: ethics.

(1233b) 262b/16 *wa-Zajr al-nafs – Chiding the Soul*; A: Plato (authorship also ascribed to Hermes Trismegistus, Socrates, and Aristotle); S: ed. ascribed to Hermes Trismegistus, Beirut: MKa, 1903; C: ethics.

(1233c) 262b/16 *wa-Siyāsat al-badan wa-faḍl al-sharāb – Provisioning the Body and the Merit of Wine*; A: Ibn Sīnā (d. 428/1037); S: Gutas, *Avicenna and the Aristotelian Tradition*, 519; C: medicine.

(1234a) M/8s 262b/16–17 *Majmū^{c} awzān al-af^{c}āl wa-al-asmāʾ – Multiple-Text Manuscript with the Pattern of Verbs and Nouns*; not identified, the *K. amthilat al-gharīb ^{c}alā awzān al-al-af^{c}āl* by ^{c}Alī b. al-Ḥasan al-Hunāʾī (fl. 307/919–20) is quite close; C: morphology.

(1234b) 262b/17 *wa-Risālat Ibn al-Habbārīya ilā al-Khaṭīb – Ibn al-Habbārīya's Epistle to al-Khaṭīb*; A: Muḥammad b. Muḥammad al-^{c}Abbāsī Ibn al-Habbārīya (d. 509/1115–16?) to Yaḥyā b. ^{c}Alī al-Khaṭīb al-Tibrīzī (d. 502/1109); S: for instance, cited in Ibn Ḥamdūn, *al-Tadhkira*, VI, 425; FI: '*nāqiṣa*'/'*incomplete*'; C: adab – epistle.

(1234c) 262b/17–18 *wa-Maqāla fī al-nafs wa-fawāʾid – Tract on the Soul and Wise Sayings*; anonymous.

(1235a) M/8s 262b/18 *Majmū^{c} fīhi al-iqtibās min kalām rabb al-nās – Multiple-Text Manuscript with Citations from the Lord of Mankind's Words*; anonymous, probably poetry referring to the Koran, as, for instance, quoted by al-Bākharzī (d. 467/1075), *Dumyat al-qaṣr*, II, 795; C: poetry?

(1235b) 262b/18–19 *wa-min Amālī Ibn Durayd wa-ghayr dhālika – [Parts] of Ibn Durayd's Dictations and Other [Writings]*; A: Ibn Durayd (d. 321/933); S: *Ta^{c}līq min Amālī Ibn Durayd*, ed. al-S.M. al-Sanūsī, Kuwait: al-Majlis al-Waṭanī, 1984; C: adab.

(1236) M/8s 262b/19–263a/1 *Majmū^{c} – Multiple-Text Manuscript*; FI: '*dhukira fī tarjama juzʾ fīhi faḍāʾil suwar al-Qurʾān wa-fī al-uṣūl wa-faḍl al-wuḍūʾ wa-al-hadya ilā al-mawtā wa-al-ṣalāt*'/'*in heading is mentioned: a volume on the merits of the Koran's chapters, on the principles, on the merits of the minor ablution, on alms in the name of the dead and on the ritual prayer*'; anonymous work with generic title; C: Koran/rituals.

(1237a) M/8s 263a/1–2 *Majmū^{c} mukhtār min Risālat Ibn ^{c}Abbād fī amthāl* [149] *shi^{c}r al-Mutanabbī – Multiple-Text Manuscript with Selections from Ibn ^{c}Abbād's Epistle on Proverbial Passages in al-Mutanabbī's Poetry*; A: Ismā^{c}īl Ibn ^{c}Abbād (d. 385/995); S: ed. J.^{c}A ^{c}Uwayḍa, s.l., 2009; C: poetry – commentary.

(1237b) 263a/2–3 *wa-Akhbār wa-inshādāt min al-Bayān – Reports and Recitations from the Bayān*; probably referring to A: al-Jāḥiẓ (d. 255/868–9), *al-Bayān wa-al-tabyīn*; S: ed. ᶜA.M. Hārūn, Cairo: MK, 1948–50; C: adab. (cf. nos. 205, 1249i, 1516, 1528)

(1237c) 263a/3 *wa-Risālat Arisṭāṭālīs fī tadbīr al-akhlāq ilā al-Iskandar – Aristotle's Letter on Ethics to Alexander the Great*; S: Maróth, *Aristotle and Alexander the Great*; C: political thought – non-Muslim – mirror for princes/ adab – epistle/history. (cf. no. 509)

(1238a) M/8s 263a/4 *Majmūᶜ baᶜḍ Mukhtār fiqh – Multiple-Text Manuscript with a Selection of fiqh*; anonymous work with generic title; C: fiqh.

(1238b) 263a/4 *wa-Qaṣīd fī ᶜadad āy al-Qurᵓān – Qaṣīdas on the Number of Verses in the Koran*; anonymous work with generic title; C: Koran. (cf. no. 1171c)

(1238c) 263a/4 *wa-Mawāᶜiẓ – Sermons*; anonymous work with generic title; C: sermons.

(1238d) 263a/4 *wa-al-Muthallath – Words with Triple Vocalization*; arguably A: Muḥammad b. ᶜAbd Allāh Ibn Mālik al-Jayyānī (d. 672/1274) who composed this *rajaz* versification for al-Malik al-Ashraf's predecessor in Damascus al-Malik al-Nāṣir Dāwūd (d. 656/1258); S: *al-Iᶜlām bi-muthallath al-kalām*, ed. Cairo: Maṭbaᶜat al-Jamālīya, 1329/*c.*1908; C: grammar. (cf. no. 1328c)

(1238e) 263a/5 *wa-Naḥw – Grammar*; anonymous work with generic title; C: grammar.

(1238f) 263a/5 *wa-Ashᶜār wa-khaṭṭ – Poems and Calligraphy*; anonymous work with generic title; C: poetry/adab.

(1238g) 263a/5 *wa-al-Maqṣūr wa-al-mamdūd – The Short and Long Alif*; A: Ibn Durayd (d. 321/933); S: *Dīwān*, ed. B. al-ᶜAlawī, Cairo: LTTN, 1946, 29–37; C: grammar. (cf. nos. 384a, 384b, 676 *[sharḥ]*, 1203b, 1230j, 1268b, 1307b, 1313a, 1326b)

(1239) M/8s 263a/5-6 *Majmūᶜ Muwashshaḥāt wa-ashᶜār mukhtāra – Multiple-Text Manuscript with Poetry in the Muwashshaḥ Rhyme Scheme and Selected Poems*; anonymous work with generic title; C: poetry – anthology.

(1240a) M/8s 263a/6 *Majmūᶜ Risālat al-Baṭīkha – Multiple-Text Manuscript with the Baṭīkha Epistle*; no such title is identifiable and the vocalisation of the term *Baṭīj/ḥ/kha* is unclear. It may refer to a place name connected to this epistle. This may be al-Baṭīḥa on the lower course of the Euphrates and Tigris in southern Iraq, but no such epistle is known. More likely is thus that it refers to the castle/palace near Raʾs al-ʿAyn where al-Malik al-Ashraf's panegyrist and secretary Ibn al-Nabīh (d. 619/1222) composed one of his poems. In the manuscripts the name appears as *Baṭīkhān/B-t-n-ja/B-t-n-jān* (al-Asʿad, *Dīwān Ibn al-Nabīh*, 296). C: adab – epistle?

(1240b) 263a/6 *wa-Dīwān Ẓahīr-i Fāryābī – Ẓahīr-i Fāryābī's Diwan*; A: Ṭāhir b. Muḥammad Ẓāhir al-Dīn al-Fāryābī (d. 598/1201); S: ed. Ḥ. Yazdgirdī, Tehran: Qaṭra, 1381h.š. *[2002/03]*; L: Persian; C: poetry.

(1240c) 263a/6-7 *wa-Ashʿār bi-al-ʿajamī – Persian Poetry*; anonymous work with generic title; L: Persian; C: poetry – anthology.

(1241a) M8/s 263a/7 *Majmūʿ Urjūza fī al-farāʾiḍ*[150] – *Multiple-Text Manuscript with an urjūza on the Ritual Obligations/Shares of Inheritance*; anonymous; C: fiqh.

(1241b) 263a/7 *wa-Qaṣīd Abī Muzāḥim – Abū Muzāḥim's Qaṣīdas*; A: Mūsā b. ʿUbayd Allāh Abū Muzāḥim (d. 325/937); S: GAS, I, 14–15; Abū Muzāḥim was a poet, grammarian and scholar of Koran recitation. On account of the previous title it can be posited that this entry includes his *qaṣīda* on recitation, *Qaṣīda fī al-tajwīd.* C: poetry – Koran recitation?

(1241c) 263a/7 *wa-Muʿashsharāt al-Ḥuṣrī – Al-Ḥuṣrī's Ten-Line Stanzas*; A: ʿAlī b. ʿAbd al-Ghanī al-Ḥuṣrī (d. 488/1095); S: al-Marzūqī and al-Ḥājj Yaḥyā, *al-Qayrawānī*, 212–40; MS: Süleymaniye, Fazıl Ahmed Paşa 1611/3 (fols. 58a–70b)*; C: poetry – Andalusian. (cf. no. 1164a)

(1241d) 263a/8 *wa-Hal bi-al-ṭulūl – The Poem Starting with 'hal bi-al-ṭulūl'*; also known as *al-Qaṣīda al-yatīma*, ascribed to various poets and thus several possibilities such as Dawqala al-Manbijī and Abū al-Shīṣ Muḥammad (b. ʿAbd Allāh) b. Razīn al-Khuzāʿī (d. *c.*200/915), see *al-Qaṣīda al-yatīma*, ed. Ṣ. al-Munajjid, Beirut: DKJ, 1974; C: poetry. (cf. no. 1230n)

(1241e) 263a/8 *wa-Qaṣīd naḥw – Qaṣīdas on Grammar*; anonymous work with generic title; C: grammar.

(1241f) 263a/8 *wa-Muwāfaqāt al-ṣaḥīḥ – Points of Agreement*; A: Ḍiyāʾ al-Dīn Muḥammad b. ʿAbd al-Wāḥid al-Maqdisī (d. 643/1245); *Siyar*, XXIII,

128 mentions a work of grammar called '*muwāfaqāt*', but the term *ṣaḥīḥ* makes a work in the field of *ḥadīth* more likely. '*Muwāfaqāt*' are traditions with a specific form of elevated *isnāds* and al-Maqdisi wrote such a work on Ibn Ḥanbal, edited as S: *Min ᶜawālī ḥadīth al-Ḥāfiẓ Ḍiyāᵓ al-Dīn al-Maqdisī: takhrījuhu min al-muwāfaqāt fī mashāyikh al-Imām Aḥmad ibn Ḥanbal*, ed. M.M. al-Ḥāfiẓ, Beirut: DB, 2001. The present entry must be a similar work on either of the two *ṣaḥīḥ*-collections (cf. nos. 695 and 696). C: ḥadīth – collection.

(1241g) 263a/8–9 *wa-Sharḥ gharīb al-Muwaṭṭaᵓ* – *Explanation of the Difficult Passages/Words in the Muwaṭṭaᵓ*; referring to the *Muwaṭṭaᵓ* by Mālik b. Anas (d. 179/796) cf. nos. 920, 921, 922); A: ᶜAbd al-Malik b. Ḥabīb al-Sulamī al-Qurṭubī (d. 238/853); S: ed. M. ᶜUthmān, Beirut: DKI, 2011; C: ḥadīth – collection/lexicography.

(1242a) M8/s 263a/9 *Majmūᶜ al-Laṭāᵓif* – *Multiple-Text Manuscript with The Subtleties*; probably one of the works by A: al-Thaᶜālibī (d. 429/1038): 1) *al-Ẓarāᵓif wa-al-laṭāᵓif*, which was mainly transmitted in Abū Naṣr al-Maqdisī's recension *al-Laṭāᵓif wa-al-ẓarāᵓif*, ed. ᶜU. al-Asᶜad, *Laṭāᵓif al-luṭf*, Beirut: Dār al-Masīra, 1980 (cf. no. 716?); 2) *al-Luṭf wa-al-laṭāᵓif*, ed. M.ᶜA. al-Jādir, Kuwait: DA, 1984 (cf. no. 1312b); C: adab – anthology. (cf. nos. 908, 958b, 1707)

(1242b) 263a/9 *wa-min Shiᶜr Abī al-Ghanāᵓim al-Rabaᶜī* – *[Parts] of Abū al-Ghanāᵓim al-Rabaᶜī's Poetry*; the *ghazal* poet A: Abū al-Ghanāᵓim Sālim b. al-Muḥsin al-Rabaᶜī (d. c.519/1125); S: Ibn al-ᶜAdīm, *Bughyat*, IX, 4160; C: poetry – Fatimid – ghazal.

(1242c) 263a/9 *wa-min Shiᶜr Fakhr al-ᶜArab* – *[Parts] of Fakhr al-ᶜArab's Poetry*; A: Fakhr al-ᶜArab Abū al-Muẓaffar Muḥammad b. Aḥmad al-Abīwardī (d. 507/1113); for the use of 'Fakhr al-ᶜArab' for al-Abīwardī see, for example, *Siyar*, XIX, 285; S: *Dīwān*, ed. ᶜU. al-Asᶜad: MLA, Damascus, 1974–5; C: poetry.

(1243a) M8/s 263a/10 *Majmūᶜ Mā istawā min Khalq al-insān* – *Multiple-Text Manuscript with What Is Correct in Human Anatomy*; no such title is identifiable. It refers to Abū al-Ḥusayn Aḥmad Ibn Fāris's (d. 395/1004) well-known work (MU, I, 412: '*khalq al-insān*'); C: lexicography.

(1243b) 263a/10 *wa-Mukhtaṣar Khalq al-insān – Summary of The Human Anatomy*; no such title is identifiable. It refers most likely to Aḥmad Ibn Fāris's (d. 395/1004) well-known work (MU, I, 412: '*khalq al-insān*'); C: lexicography.

(1243c) 263a/10 *wa-Khalq al-faras – Anatomy of the Horse*; popular title with several possibilities such as Muḥammad b. al-Mustanīr Quṭrub (d. 206/821) (IN, I/1, 148, cf. no. 367) and ᶜAbd al-Malik b. Qurayb al-Aṣmaᶜī (d. 213/828?) (IKH, III, 176, cf. no. 1297); C: lexicography.

(1243d) 263a/11 *wa-Asmāʾ al-Birr – Names [of the Poets?] in the Birr*; the reading of '*birr*' is tentative, but it seems that this is a work comparable to the *Names of the Poets in the Ḥamāsa* (cf. no. 73). In this case the *Asmāʾ al-birr* is a summary of the *Dīwān al-birr* by ᶜAlī b. ᶜĪsā Ibn al-Jarrāḥ (d. 334/946) (MU, IV, 1824). C: poetry.

(1243e) 263a/11 *wa-[al-]Maqṣūr [wa-al-mamdūd] – The Short [and Long] Alif*; A: Muḥammad b. al-Mustanīr Quṭrub (d. 206/821); this title is not among the works ascribed to Quṭrub (cf. GAS, IX, 64–5). C: grammar.

(1243f) 263a/11 *wa-[al-]Maqṣūr [wa-al-mamdūd] – The Short [and Long] Alif*; A: Ibrāhīm b. Muḥammad Nifṭawayh (d. 323/935); S: ed. H. Shādhilī Farhūd, Cairo: DT, 1980; C: grammar.

(1243g) 263a/11–12 *wa-Risālat al-maᶜād al-dīnīya fī al-yawm wa-al-sāᶜa wa-al-daqīqa – Treatise on the Place of Resurrection in the Hereafter Concerning Judgement Day and the Hour of Resurrection*; no such title is identifiable. C: eschatology/afterlife.

(1243h) 263a/12 *wa-al-Risāla al-muwashshā fī taḍᶜīf buyūt al-shāh – The Embroidered Epistle on Doubling the King's Squares*; No such title is identifiable. This refers to the tale of the Indian sage who bankrupted a king by demanding that the king put a single grain of rice/wheat on the first square of a chessboard and double it on every consequent one (cf. Osti, L. (2005), 'The Grain on the Chessboard: Travels and Meanings', in F. Bauden/A. Chraïbi/A. Ghersetti (eds), *Le répertoire narratif arabe médiéval: transmission et ouverture, Geneva 2008, 231–51).* Fascinatingly, the first fully-fledged report of this tale in Arabic literature is in the biographical dictionary by Ibn Khallikān who was contemporaneous with the library and who frequented it (IKH, IV, 357–9). C: adab – epistle.

(1244a) M8/s 263a/12–13 *Majmūʿ fīhi handasa – Multiple-Text Manuscript with Geometry*; anonymous work with generic title; FI: '*kamā dhakara Jamāl al-Dīn*' / '*as Jamāl al-Dīn mentioned*'; this comment probably refers to a scribe's note at the beginning of this multiple-text manuscript. The cataloguer mentions a 'Jamāl al-Dīn' as scribe (cf. no. 1195: possibly Sharaf al-Khilāfa Jamāl al-Dīn Mūsā b. al-Maʾmūn al-Baṭāʾiḥī (d. 588/1192) and elsewhere). For a similar use of *dh-k-r* for introducing the content of a multiple-text manuscript cf. no. 1249. C: mathematics – geometry.

(1244b) 263a/13 *wa-al-Juzʾ al-fard – The Ultimate Part*; no such title is identifiable, but this treatise on the atomistic conception of the world could draw on the respective discussions in philosophical and theological (*kalām*) works (EI^3, A. Dhanani, 'Atomism'). C: theology?

(1244c) 263a/13 *wa-al-Akhlāq – Ethics*; A: Ibn Sīnā (d. 428/1037); S: ʿIlm al-akhlāq, in: *Majmūʿat al-rasāʾil*, Cairo 1328 *[1910]*; C: ethics.

(1244d) 263a/13 *wa-min Kalāmihi wa-kalām ghayrihi – [Parts] of His [Ibn Sīnā's] Writings and Those by Others*; A: Ibn Sīnā (d. 428/1037).

(1245a) M/8s 263a/14 *Majmūʿ li-l-Rāzī Abdāl al-adwiya – Multiple-Text Manuscript of al-Rāzī [with] Substitutes for Drugs*; A: al-Rāzī (Rhazes) (d. 313/925 or 323/935); S: Engl. tr. M. Levey, in: *Substitute Drugs in Early Arabic Medicine*, Stuttgart 1971, 7-62; C: pharmacology. (cf. no. 110)

(1245b) 263a/14 *wa-Manāfiʿ al-ṭīn wa-maḍārruhu – The Benefits of Soil and Its Harm*; A: al-Rāzī (Rhazes) (d. 313/925 or 323/935); S: IN, II/1, 309: '*K. fī anna al-ṭīn al-muntaqal bihi fīhi manāfiʿ*'; C: medicine.

(1245c) 263a/14 *wa-Ḥaṣā al-kulā wa-al-mathāna – Stones in the Kidney and Bladder*; A: al-Rāzī (Rhazes) (d. 313/925 or 323/935); S: ed. & Fr. tr. P. de Koning, *Traité sur le calcul dans les reins et dans la vessie*, Leiden 1896; FI: '*nāqiṣa*' / '*incomplete*'; C: medicine.

(1245d) 263a/15 *wa-al-Adwiya al-mawjūda bi-kull makān – Drugs Available Everywhere*; A: al-Rāzī (Rhazes) (d. 313/925 or 323/935); S: IN, II/1, 310; C: pharmacology.

(1245e) 263a/15 *wa-Fī al-sharāb – On Wine*; A: al-Rāzī (Rhazes) (d. 313/925 or 323/935); S: IAU, III, 44; C: pharmacology.

(1245f) 263a/15 *wa-al-Faṣd – On Phlebotomy*; A: al-Rāzī (Rhazes) (d. 313/925 or 323/935); S: IAU, III, 46; C: medicine.

(1246) M/8s 263a/15-16 *Majmū^{c} Ikhtiyārāt shi^{c}r al-^{c}arab – Multiple-Text Manuscript with Selections from the Poetry of the Arabs*; generic title; Scr('*bi- khaṭṭ*'): Tawfīq b. Muḥammad (IKH, IV, 458); for '*shi^{c}r al-^{c}arab*' cf. no. 974; C: poetry – anthology – pre-Islamic/early Islamic.

(1247) M/8s 263a/16 *Majmū^{c} al-Yamīnī wa-ghayr dhālika – Multiple-Text Manuscript with the Yamīnī [History] and Other [Writings]*; A: Muḥammad b. ^{c}Abd al-Jabbār al-^{c}Utbī (d. 427/1036 or 431/1040); S: *al-Yamīnī fī sharḥ akhbār al-sulṭān Yamīn al-Dawla wa-Amīn al-Milla Maḥmūd al-Ghaznawī*, ed. I.Dh. al-Thāmirī, Beirut: Dār al-ṭalī^{c}a, 2004; C: history – Ghaznawid. (cf. no. 1387)

(1248a) M/8s 263a/16–17 *Majmū^{c} al-Adab al-jāmi^{c} wa-rasāʾil wa-ash^{c}ār – Multiple-Text Manuscript with The Adab Compendium, Epistles and Poems*; A: ^{c}Abd Allāh Ibn al-Muqaffa^{c} (d. 139/756?); most likely referring to his *al-Adab al-kabīr*, also known as *al-Durra al-yatīma*; S: *al-Durra al-yatīma*, ed. A.R. al-Badrāwī, Beirut: DN, 1974; C: political thought – mirror for princes. (cf. nos. 1284a, 1312a, 1330a, 1391)

(1248b) 263a/17 *wa-Risālat Ibn ^{c}Abbād fī shi^{c}r al-Mutanabbī wa-tarassul – Ibn ^{c}Abbād's Epistle on al-Mutanabbī's Poetry and Letters*; A: Ismā^{c}īl Ibn ^{c}Abbād (d. 385/995); S: ed. M.Ḥ. Āl-Yāsīn, *al-Kashf ^{c}an masāwī shi^{c}r al-Mutanabbī*, Baghdad: MN, 1965; C: poetry – commentary. (cf. nos. 878, 1020)

(1249a) M/8s 263b/1-2 *Majmū^{c} – Multiple-Text Manuscript*; anonymous work with generic title; FI: '*dhakara annahu yashtamilu ^{c}alā mukhtār al-^{c}ilm wa-al-bayān wa-al-sharūd wa-min Kitāb al-nisāʾ*'/'*which mentions that it contains selections of knowledge, eloquence and current verses as well as [selections] from The Book on Women*'; the reading of the term '*sharūd*' is tentative, but the content of this multiple-text manuscript makes a term linked to poetry most likely. *K. al-nisāʾ*: several works with the title *K. al-nisāʾ* exist such as those by ^{c}Abd Allāh b. Muslim al-Dīnawarī Ibn Qutayba (d. 276/889) and Muḥammad b. Sahl Ibn al-Marzubān al-Karkhī (d. *c.*345/956). C: adab – anthology.

(1249b) 263b/2 *wa-min Shi^{c}r al-Babbaghāʾ – [Parts] of al-Babbaghāʾ's Poetry*; A: ^{c}Abd al-Wāḥid al-Babbaghāʾ (d. 398/1007); S: Nājī, *al-Babbaghāʾ*, 23–91; C: poetry.

(1249c) 263b/2 *wa-Risālat al-Isfarāyīnī – Al-Isfarāyīnī's Epistle*; A: Ibrāhīm

b. Muḥammad al-Isfarāyīnī (d. 418/1027); in view of the following entry by al-Ghazālī this is most likely a theological epistle. C: theology?

(1249d) 263b/2 *wa-al-Ghazālī – [And writings by] al-Ghazālī*; A: al-Ghazālī (d. 505/1111); normally the cataloguer does not use isolated names of authors for his entries. The brevity here may be explained by the length of this multiple-text manuscript, which contains twelve different texts and the cataloguer already had in 1249a an unusually brief description. In view of the preceding entry by al-Isfarāyīnī this is most likely a theological epistle. C: theology?

(1249e) 263b/2-3 *wa-Mukhtār min al-Baṣāʾir – Selections from [The Treasures of] Insightful Perception*; A: Abū Ḥayyān al-Tawḥīdī (d. 414/1023); S: *al-Baṣāʾir wa-al-dhakhāʾir*, ed. W. al-Qāḍī, Beirut: DṢ, 1984–8; C: adab – anthology. (cf. nos. 204, 303)

(1249f) 263b/3 *wa-min Shiᶜr Dīk al-Jinn – [Parts] of Dīk al-Jinn's Poetry*; A: ᶜAbd al-Salām b. Raghbān Dīk al-Jinn (d. 235–6/849–51); S: ed. A. Qawwāl, *Dīwān*, Beirut: DKiA, 1992; C: poetry – ᶜAbbāsid. (cf. nos. 406, 1605)

(1249g) 263b/3 *wa-min ᶜUyūn al-ḥikam – [Parts] of The Choicest Pieces of Wisdom*; A: Aḥmad Ibn Fāris (d. 395/1004). Such a title authored by an Ibn Fāris is not identifiable. However, the cataloguer repeatedly uses this name in the catalogue to refer to the famous Ibn Fāris (cf. nos. 951, 1135a, 1162a, 1222c, 1243a, 1423). It is thus likely that this is a little-known collection of 'wise sayings' ascribed to this author, which did not acquire the status of an independent book (similar to no. 298). C: adab.

(1249h) 263b/4 *wa-min Shiᶜr al-Ibrī – [Parts] of al-Ibrī's Poetry*; A: ᶜAlī b. Muḥammad Ibn al-Ibrī (549/1154); S: al-Iṣfahānī, *Kharīdat al-qaṣr* (al-ᶜIrāq), 144–6 who cites some of his poetry; C: poetry – Saljūq.

(1249i) 263b/4 *wa-min al-Bayān wa-al-tabyīn – [Parts] of The Book of Clarity and Clarification*; A: al-Jāḥiẓ (d. 255/868–9); S: ed. ᶜA.M. Hārūn, Cairo: MK, 1948–50; C: adab – anthology. (cf. nos. 205, 1237b?, 1516, 1528)

(1249j) 263b/4 *wa-al-Ḥātimīya – Al-Ḥātimī's Epistle*; this is most likely al-Ḥātimī's epistle *al-Risāla al-Mūḍiḥa* against al-Mutanabbī. In contrast to no. 529 the epistle is not described here as '*al-ṣaghīra*'. A: Muḥammad b.

al-Ḥasan al-Ḥātimī (d. 388/998); S: ed. M.Y. Najm, Beirut: DṢ, 1965; C: poetry – commentary. (cf. nos. 507, 528, 1278a)

(1249k) 263b/4–5 *wa-min Shi*ᶜ*r al-Khwārazmī wa-ghayr dhālika – [Parts] of al-Khwārazmī's Poetry and Other [Writings]*; A: Muḥammad b. al-ᶜAbbās al-Khwārazmī (d. 383/993); S: *Dīwān Abī Bakr al-Khwārazmī*, ed. Ḥ. Sidqī, Tehran: Maktab nashr al-turāth al-makhṭūṭ, 1997; C: poetry.

(1249l) 263b/5 *wa-al-Anīs fī ghurar al-tajnīs – The Close Friend on the Blazes of Paronomasia*; A: attr. al-Thaᶜālibī (d. 429/1038); S: ed. H. Nājī, in *Majallat al-Majma*ᶜ *al-*ᶜ*Ilmī al-*ᶜ*Irāqī* 33 (1982), 369–80; C: rhetoric. (cf. no. 133)

(1250a) M/8s 263b/5 *Majmū*ᶜ *Akhbār Kalfā*ᵓ *al-jinn – Multiple-Text Manuscript with Reports on Kalfā*ᵓ *the [Lady of the] Jinn*; no such title is identifiable. Most likely this refers to the story included in texts such as *al-Jalīs al-ṣāliḥ* on a mysterious Kalfāᵓ, a dark or freckled old woman (al-Jarīrī (d. 390/1000), *al-Jalīs al-ṣāliḥ*, III, 393–5). Although the term '*jinn*' is not mentioned in this story, the rather otherworldly description of her, as well as her transformation, while singing, into a beautiful girl, all make an association with *jinn* very likely. C: poetry/adab.

(1250b) 263b/6 *wa-Qaṣīd al-dalāla – The Dalāla Qaṣīdas*; A: Muḥammad b. Sāmī al-Shaᶜbānī (fl. 4th/10th c.); S: IN, I/2, 538: '*qaṣīdat al-dalāla*'; C: poetry.

(1250c) 263b/6 *wa-Ba*ᶜ*ḍ khamrīyāt Abī Nuwās – One of Abū Nuwās' Wine Poems*; A: al-Ḥasan b. Hāniᵓ Abū Nuwās (d. between mid-198 and early 200/813–5); S: al-ᶜAshmāwī, *Khamrīyāt Abī Nuwās*; C: poetry – wine – ᶜAbbāsid. (cf. no. 1258b)

(1250d) 263b/6 *wa-Adab al-nadīm – Convivial Etiquette*; A: Maḥmūd Kushājim (d. c.350/961); S: ed. N.ᶜA. Shaᶜlān, Cairo: MK, 1999; C: adab.

(1250e) 263b/7 *wa-Maqṣūrat Durayd wa-ash*ᶜ*ār – The Short [and Long Alif] and [Other] Poems*; A: Ibn Durayd (d. 321/933); S: *Dīwān*, ed. B. al-ᶜAlawī, Cairo: LTTN, 1946, 29–37; C: grammar/poetry. (cf. nos. 1230k, 1268a, 1270a)

(1251a) M/8s 263b/7-8 *Majmū*ᶜ *min al-Lahw wa-al-malāhī – Multiple-Text Manuscript with [Parts] of [the Book of] Playing and Musical Instruments*; two main possibilities for the authorship of this work: 1)

Ibn Khurradādhbih (d. *c*.300/911) (ed. I.ʿA. Khalīfa, *Mukhtār min kitāb al-Lahw wa-al-malāhī*, Beirut: Dār al-mashriq, 1969) or 2) Aḥmad b. al-Ṭayyib al-Sarakhsī (d. 286/899) (IN, II/1, 197); FI: '*fihi annahu ʿulliqa min majmūʿ ustuʿīra min Amīn al-Dawla kātib al-sirr*'/'*in it is stated that it was extracted from a multiple-text manuscript lent from Amīn al-Dawla, the kātib al-sirr*'. As it is rather unlikely that this refers to the Ayyubid *adīb* and administrator Amīn al-Dawla Ibn Ghazāl (d. 648/1250) (MM, I, 406 and IAU, IV, 306–17) this probably refers either to the ʿAbbasid administrator Amīn al-Dawla al-ʿAlāʾ b. al-Ḥasan Ibn al-Mūṣalāyā (d. 497/1104) (IKH, III, 480) or (with a slight preference due to the library's Fatimid links) the Fatimid scholar and administrator Amīn al-Dawla al-Ḥasan b. ʿAmmār al-Kalbī (d. 390/1000) (al-Ziriklī, *al-Aʿlām*, II, 225). S: music.

(1251b) 263b/8–9 *wa-min Shiʿr Ibn al-Muʿadhdhal – [Parts] of Ibn al-Muʿadhdhal's Poetry*; A: ʿAbd al-Ṣamad b. al-Muʿadhdhal al-ʿAbdī (d. 240/854–5); S: *Dīwān*, ed. Z. Zāhid, Beirut: DṢ, 1998; C: poetry.

(1252) M/8s 263b/9 *Majmūʿ rasāʾil al-Badīʿ wa-rasāʾil ʿajamīya wa-fawāʾid wa-ashʿār – Multiple-Text Manuscript with al-Badīʿs Epistles, Persian Epistles, Wise Sayings and Poems*; generic title and A: Aḥmad Badīʿ al-Zamān al-Hamadhānī (d. 398/1008); S: ed. Constantinople: Maṭbaʿat al-Jawāʾib, 1298 *[1880]*; L: Persian; C: adab.

(1253) M/8s 263b/10 *Majmūʿ Ikhtiyārāt ashʿār wa-nawādir wa-ghayr dhālika – Multiple-Text Manuscript with Selections of Poems, Anecdotes and Other [Writings]*; anonymous work with generic title; this could be MS: Süleymaniye, Ayasofya 4242***, which has no title, but where the compiler states in the introduction that he chose (*ikhtiyār*) poetry. The compiler of this manuscript is al-Ḥasan al-Qaylawī (d. 633/1236) (TI, 631–40, p. 145), a renowned scribe of Damascus and librarian of al-Malik al-Ashraf who appears elsewhere as scribe in this library (cf. nos. 257, 533, 698) and who was also involved in the transmission of other copies (cf. no. 807). C: poetry/adab – anthology.

(1254a) M/8s 263b/10–11 *Majmūʿ – Multiple-Text Manuscript*; FI: '*aktharuhu ashʿār ʿajamīya*'/'*most of it are Persian poems*'; anonymous work with generic title; L: Persian; C: poetry – anthology.

(1254b) 263b/11 *wa-Risālat As^{c}ad ilā Waṭwāṭ – As^{c}ad's Epistle to Waṭwāṭ*; Rashīd al-Dīn Muḥammad b. Muḥammad Waṭwāṭ al-^{c}Umarī (d. 578/1182–3?); possibly A: Qāḍī As^{c}ad b. Ya^{c}qūb in whose favour Rashīd al-Dīn wrote a letter (*Majmū^{c}at rasāʾil Rashīd al-Dīn al-Waṭwāṭ*, Cairo: MMa, 1897, I, 69–71); C: adab – epistle.

(1255a) M/8s 263b/11 *Majmū^{c} wa^{c}ẓ – Multiple-Text Manuscript of Sermons*; anonymous work with generic title; C: sermons.

(1255b) 263b/11 *wa-Ādāb – Adab*; anonymous work with generic title; C: adab.

(1255c) 263b/11 *wa-Ad^{c}iya – Prayers*; generic title; C: prayer book.

(1256a) M/8s 263b/11–12 *Majmū^{c} al-mulaḥ – Multiple-Text Manuscript with Pleasant Poetry/Anecdotes*; anonymous; C: poetry/adab – anthology.

(1256b) 263b/12 *wa-Ikhtiyār Masāʾil Ḥunayn – Selections from the Questions of Ḥunayn*; A: Ḥunayn b. Isḥāq (d. 260/873); S: *Masāʾil fī al-ṭibb li-l-muta^{c}allimīn*, eds M. Abū Rayyān and M. ^{c}Arab/J. Mūsā, Cairo: DJM, 1978; MS: Süleymaniye, Fatih 5300/10 (fols. 164a–178a)** *Mukhtaṣar masāʾil Ḥunayn b. Isḥāq al-ṭabīb*; the multiple-text manuscript Fatih 5300 holds additional titles, which were identical with or similar to Ashrafīya titles (cf. nos. 261, 915, 1115, 1132, 1135a). C: pharmacology. (cf. no. 277)

(1257) M/8s 263b/12–13 *Majmū^{c} al-I^{c}jāz wa-al-ījāz wa-ash^{c}ār wa-ghayr dhālika – Multiple-Text Manuscript with Inimitability and Conciseness, Poems and Other [Writings]*; '*al-I^{c}jāz wa-al-ījāz*': A: al-Tha^{c}ālibī (d. 429/1038); S: ed. M.I. Salīm, Cairo: MQ, 1999; C: adab – anthology/proverbs. (cf. no. 50)

(1258a) M/8s 263b/13 *Majmū^{c} Amthāl al-muwalladīn min al-Maydānī – Multiple-Text Manuscript with Proverbs of the Moderns [Taken] from al-Maydānī['s Proverbs]*; no such title is identifiable. This work is derived from al-Maydānī's (d. 518/1124) *al-Amthāl* (ed. M.M. ^{c}Abd al-Ḥamīd, Beirut: DF, 1972); C: adab – proverbs.

(1258b) 263b/14 *wa-Khamrīyāt Abī Nuwās – Abū Nuwās' Wine Poems*; A: al-Ḥasan b. Hāniʾ Abū Nuwās (d. between mid-198 and early 200/813–15); S: al-^{c}Ashmāwī, *Khamrīyāt Abī Nuwās*; C: poetry – wine – ^{c}Abbāsid. (cf. no. 1250c)

(1258c) 263b/14 *wa-Akhbār wa-nawādir wa-ash^{c}ār wa-nukat wa-ghayruhā –*

Reports, Anecdotes, Poems, Charming Remarks and Other [Writings]; anonymous work with generic title; C: adab/poetry – anthology.

(1259a) M/8s 263b/15 *Majmūᶜ min Shiᶜr al-Bāriᶜ al-Dabbās – Multiple-Text Manuscript with [Parts] of al-Bāriᶜ al-Dabbās' Poetry*; A: al-Ḥusayn b. Muḥammad al-Bāriᶜ al-Dabbās (d. 524/1130); S: IKH, II, 181–4; C: poetry.

(1259b) 263b/15-264a/1 *wa-ᶜUyūn al-ashᶜār wa-nawāẓir al-ashjār – The Choicest Poetry and the Gazes of Trees*; A: al-Ḥusayn b. Muḥammad al-Rāghib al-Iṣfahānī (d. early 5th/11th c.?); S: al-Iṣfahānī, *Muḥāḍarāt al-udabāᵓ*, I, 13 where the author mentions that he authored a work entitledᶜ *Uyūn al-ashᶜār*; the second part of the title is not mentioned by al-Iṣfahānī and this could refer to another work. However, a work by this title is not known and the rhyme scheme as well as the use of the terms *ᶜuyūn* and *nawāẓir* indicate that the two phrases belong to one single title. C: poetry – anthology – Būyid? (cf. nos. 741, 742)

(1260a) M/9s 264a/1 *Majmūᶜ Minhāj al-ᶜābidīn – Multiple-Text Manuscript with the Worshippers' Path*; ascribed to A: al-Ghazālī (d. 505/1111); S: *Minhāj al-ᶜābidīn ilā jannat rabb al-ᶜālamīn*, M.M. Ḥalāwī, Beirut: DB, 2001; C: sufism.

(1260b) 264a/2 *wa-Naḥw – Grammar*; A: ᶜAlī Ibn Faḍḍāl Mujāshiᶜī (d. 479/1086); S: MU, IV, 1834–8; C: grammar.

(1260c) 264a/2 *wa-Tarassul – Epistles*; anonymous work with generic title; C: adab – epistle.

(1260d) 264a/2 *wa-al-Munqidh – Deliverance [from Error]*; A: al-Ghazālī (d. 505/1111); S: *al-Munqidh min al-ḍalāl*, Engl. tr. W.M. Watt, *The Faith and Practice of Al-Ghazali*, London 1953; MS: Süleymaniye, Ayasofya 1816/6 (63a–79a)***; C: autobiography – spiritual.

(1260e) 264a/2 *wa-Abyāt al-futūwa – Verses of Futūwa Poetry*; verses by an author such as Abū al-ᶜAlāᵓ al-Maᶜarrī (d. 449/1058) who was said to have composed poetry on this topic (*Siyar*, XVIII, 33); C: poetry – anthology.

(1260f) 264/2-3 *wa-min al-Muntahā fī al-kamāl – [Parts] of The Utmost Perfection*; A: Muḥammad b. Sahl Ibn al-Marzubān al-Karkhī (d. *c.*345/956); S: ed. S.M. al-Hadrusi, Berlin 1988; R. Bostan, Berlin 1988; C: adab – anthology. (cf. nos. 12, 995, 1107)

(1260g) 264a/3 *wa-min Ḥilyat al-muḥāḍara – [Parts] of The Ornament of*

Disputation; A: Muḥammad b. al-Ḥasan al-Ḥātimī (d. 388/998); S: ed. H. Nājī, Beirut: DMḤ, 1978; C: rhetoric. (cf. no. 1644)

(1260h) 264a/3 *wa-min Natāʾij al-ḥikma – [Parts] of The Results of Wisdom*; no such title is identifiable. Several works written during the 6th/12th and 7th/13th centuries start with *Natāʾij*, e.g. *Natāʾij al-afkār* by ᶜAlī b. Yaḥyā al-Mukharrimī (d. 646/1248) (TI, 641–50, pp. 323–4) but a conclusive identification is not possible.

(1261a) M/9s 264a/3–4 *Majmūᶜ al-ādāb wa-al-mawāᶜiẓ – Multiple-Text Manuscript with Adab and Sermons*; A: al-Khalīl b. Aḥmad al-Sijzī (d. 378/988–9); S: MU, III, 1271–4 (title mentioned II, 515); C: sermons.

(1261b) 264a/4 *wa-Arbaᶜūn – Forty [ḥadīth]*; A: Muḥammad b. ᶜAbd Allāh al-Ḥākim al-Nīsābūrī (d. 405/1014); S: cited in Ṣadr al-Dīn al-Bakrī, *Kitāb al-arbaᶜīn ḥadīthan*, ed. M. Maḥfūẓ, Beirut: DGI, 88-91; C: ḥadīth – collection (40).[151]

(1262a) M/9s 264a/4–5 *Majmūᶜ Risālat al-Shāfiᶜī wa-asmāʾ man ḥaddatha ᶜanhu – Multiple-Text Manuscript with al-Shāfiᶜī's Treatise and Names of Those Who Transmitted from Him*; A: Muḥammad b. Idrīs al-Shāfiᶜī (d. 204/820); S: A.M. Shākir, Cairo: MBḤ, 1940; Eng. tr. M. Khadduri, Cambridge 1987; C: fiqh – uṣūl al-fiqh.

(1262b) 264a/5 *wa-al-Sunan – The Customs*; on account of the first text in this multiple-text manuscript, this title is most likely referring to an extract from al-Shāfiᶜī's *Musnad*; A: Muḥammad b. Idrīs al-Shāfiᶜī (d. 204/820); S: ed. A. Abū Khashrīf, Damascus: Dth al-ᶜarabīya, 2002; C: ḥadīth – collection. (cf. no. 919)

(1263a) M/9s 264a/5-6 *Majmūᶜ Jāwīdhān Khirad – Multiple-Text Manuscript with The Eternal Wisdom*; this anthology of pre-Islamic gnomes (*ḥikma*) was supposedly translated from Sasanian texts and has come down in A: Aḥmad b. Muḥammad Miskawayh's (d. 421/1030?) version. S: Zakeri, *Wisdom*, 73–82; ed. ᶜA. Badawī, Cairo: MNM, 1952; C: political thought – non-Muslim – mirror for princes. (cf. no. 1208e)

(1263b) 264a/6 *wa-Ādāb al-wuzarāʾ wa-ghayr dhālika – Rules for Viziers and Other [Writings]*; possibly A: Aḥmad b. Jaᶜfar b. Shādhān (fl. 3rd/9th c.?); S: Kohlberg, *Ibn Ṭāwūs*, 99–100; C: political thought – adab of vizier. (cf. no. 69)

(1264a) M/9s 264a/6–7 *Majmū^c Mīzān al-^camal – Multiple-Text Manuscript with The Scales of Deeds*; A: al-Ghazālī (d. 505/1111); S: S. Dunyā, Cairo: DM, 1964; MS: Süleymaniye, Fatih 2877**; C: ethics.

(1264b) 264a/7 *wa-Adab al-dīn wa-al-dunyā – On Conduct in Religious and Worldly Matters*; A: al-Māwardī (d. 450/1058); S: ed. M. al-Saqqā, *Adab al-dunyā wa-al-dīn*, Beirut 1955; Germ. tr. by O. Rescher, Stuttgart 1932; C: ethics. (cf. no. 9)

(1264c) 264a/7 *wa-Tafṣīl al-nash^atayn – Separating the Two Creations [and Attaining the Two Felicities]*; A: al-Ḥusayn b. Muḥammad al-Rāghib al-Iṣfahānī (d. early 5th/11th c.?); S: *Tafṣīl al-nash^atayn wa-taḥṣīl al-sa^cādatayn*, ed. ^cA. al-Najjār, Beirut: DGI, 1988; MS: Süleymaniye, Ayasofya 2897/2 (fols. 100a–121b)***; C: ethics. (cf. no. 1168)

(1264d) 264a/7 *wa-al-Dharī^ca – Means [to the Virtues of Islamic Law]*; A: al-Ḥusayn b. Muḥammad al-Rāghib al-Iṣfahānī (d. early 5th/11th c.?); S: *al-Dharī^ca ilā makārim al-sharī^ca*, ed. A. al-^cAjamī, Cairo: Dār al-wafā^, 1985; MS: Süleymaniye, Ayasofya 2897/1 (fols. 1a–99a)***; C: ethics.

(1265a) M/9s 264a/7–8 *Majmū^c mukhtār shi^cr min al-^cArūs – Multiple-Text Manuscript with Poetry from the Book al-^cArūs*; selection of poetry probably by A: Ḥamd/Aḥmad b. Muḥammad al-Khaṭṭābī al-Bustī (d. 388/998); S: MU, II, 486: '*K. al-^carūs*'; C: poetry.

(1265b) 264a/8 *wa-Bahjat al-qalb wa-ghayr dhālika – The Heart's Splendour and Other [Writings]*; the reading of the title is tentative and no such title is identifiable, including the likely variant *Muhjat*. This is possibly, similar to the first title in this multiple-text manuscript, another anthology of poetry. C: poetry?

(1266a) M/9s 264a/8–9 *Majmū^c Tashīl al-naẓar – Multiple-Text Manuscript with Aiding Examination*; A: al-Māwardī (d. 450/1058); S: *Tashīl al-naẓar wa-ta^cjīl al-ẓafar*, M.H. Sarḥān, Beirut: DNA, 1981; C: political thought.

(1266b) 264a/9 *wa-Tawqī^cāt al-khulafā^ al-Umawīyīn wa-al-^cAbbāsīyīn – The Decrees of the Umayyad and ^cAbbāsid Caliphs*; no independent book with such decrees is known, but they were included in a wide variety of works, such as *K. khāṣṣ al-khāṣṣ* by al-Thaᶜālibī (d. 429/1038; ed. Ḥ. al-Amīn, Beirut: DMḤ, *[1966]*, 84–94). On such decrees see al-Dukhayyil, 'al-Tawqīᶜāt al-adabīya'. C: adab/history.

(1267a) M/9s 264a/9–10 *Majmūᶜ Rawḍat al-ādāb – Multiple-Text Manuscript with The Garden of Adab*; A: Muḥammad b. ᶜAlī b. Muḥammad (d. *c.*570/1174); S: *Wāfī*, IV, 163: '*Rawḍat al-ādāb fī al-lugha*'; C: lexicography.

(1267b) 264a/10 *wa-al-Wudd – [Book on] Fondness*; title with popular key word and thus several possibilities including the mystical work by Muḥammad Ibn Khafīf al-Shīrāzī (d. 371/982), *K. al-wudd wa-al-ulfa* (Bell and Al-Shafie, *Mystical Love*, XLIX) with a slight preference, due to the other work in this multiple-text manuscript, for the *Rāʾid al-wudd* by the *adīb* ᶜAlī b. ᶜUbayda al-Rayḥānī (d. *c.*219/834; Zakeri, *Wisdom*, 245–6); FI: '*thamāniya maḥdhūfa*' / '*eight [leaves?] curtailed*'; C: adab?

(1268a) M/9s 264a/10 *Majmūᶜ Maqṣūrat Ibn Durayd – Multiple-Text Manuscript with The Short [and Long Alif]*; A: <u>Ibn Durayd</u> (d. 321/933); S: *Dīwān*, ed. B. al-ᶜAlawī, Cairo: LTTN, 1946, 29–37; C: grammar. (cf. nos. 1230k, 1250e, 1270a)

(1268b) 264a/10–11 *wa-al-Maqṣūr wa-al-mamdūd lahu – The Short and Long Alif by Him*; A: <u>Ibn Durayd</u> (d. 321/933); S: *Dīwān*, ed. B. al-ᶜAlawī, Cairo: LTTN, 1946, 29–37; FI: '*wa-ᶜan al-Aṣmaᶜī*' / '*[and material] transmitted from al-Aṣmaᶜī*'; referring to ᶜAbd al-Malik b. Qurayb al-Aṣmaᶜī (d. 213/828?) (IN, I/157); such a line of transmission is, for instance, mentioned by the contemporaneous Yāqūt al-Ḥamawī (*Muᶜjam al-buldān*, I, 11): 'Abū Saᶜīd al-Aṣmaᶜī whose work I chanced upon in the narration by Ibn Durayd'; C: grammar. (cf. nos. 384a, 384b, 676 *[sharḥ]*, 1203b, 1230j, 1238g, 1307b, 1313a, 1326b)

(1269a) M/9s 264a/11 *Majmūᶜ al-Dhahab al-masbūk – Multiple-Text Manuscript with The Molten Gold [on the Admonition of Kings]*; A: Muḥammad b. Futūḥ al-Ḥumaydī (d. 488/1095); S: *al-Dhahab al-masbūk fī waᶜẓ al-mulūk*, eds A. al-Ẓāhirī and ᶜA. ᶜUways, Riyad: DAK, 1982; C: political thought – adab of scholar. (cf. no. 710?)

(1269b) 264a/11 *Islām Jabala – The Conversion of Jabala*; no such title is identifiable. This entry refers to the conversion of Jabala b. al-Ayham, the last Ghassānid ruler (d. *c.*24/645) and is probably either an extract from chronicles such as al-Ṭabarī (Blankinship (tr.): *The History of al-Ṭabarī*, XI, 58–9) or a poem from another work such as Abū al-Faraj's *K. al-aghānī* (eds I. ^{c}Abbās, I. al-Sa^{cc}āfīn and B. ^{c}Abbās, Beirut: DṢ, 2004, XV, 109–12). C: biography – early Islam.

(1269c) 264a/12 *wa-al-Nudba – Lamentation [Prayer of Supplication]*; A: generally ascribed to the sixth Shi^{c}ite *imām* Ja^{c}far al-Ṣādiq (d. 148/765); S: Majlisī, *Zād al-ma^{c}ād*, 303–9: '*Du^{c}ā al-Nudba*' and Kohlberg, *Ibn Ṭāwūs*, 222; C: prayer book. (cf. no. 1200c)

(1269d) 264a/12 *wa-Mukhtaṣar fī al-siyāsa wa-ghayr dhālika – A Summary of Good Governance and Other [Writings]*; no such title is identifiable. This is possibly a work in the vein of Ibn Rushd/Averroes' translation of Plato's work, *al-Ḍarūrī fī al-siyāsa: mukhtaṣar Kitāb al-Siyāsa*, retransl. from Hebrew into Arabic A. Shaḥlān, Beirut: MDWA, 1998; C: political thought. (cf. no. 1111)

(1270a) M/9s 264a/12 *Majmū^{c} al-Duraydīya [fī al-maqṣūr wa-al-mamdūd] – Multiple-Text Manuscript with Ibn Durayd's Qaṣīda [on the Short and Long Alif]*; A: Ibn Durayd (d. 321/933); S: *Dīwān*, ed. B. al-^{c}Alawī, Cairo: LTTN, 1946, 29–37; C: grammar. (cf. nos. 1230k, 1250e, 1268a)

(1270b) 264a/12 *wa-Qaṣīd marthiya – Elegies*; generic title; Scr('*bi-khaṭṭ*'): ^{c}Abd Allāh b. Muḥammad Ibn Abī al-Jū^{c} al-Warrāq (d. 395/1004–5) (IKH, IV, 379) (cf. nos. 975, 1606); C: poetry – anthology – elegies.

(1271a) M/9s 264a/13 *Majmū^{c} al-Sarj wa-al-lijām – Multiple-Text Manuscript with Saddle and Reins*; popular title with numerous possibilities (cf. no. 359), but as the following work in this multiple-text manuscript is by the same author, this is probably A: Ibn Durayd (d. 321/933); S: ed. M.M. Muḥammad, *Ṣifat al-sarj wa-al-lijām*, Cairo: MMA, 1992; This is even more likely given the fact that MS: Süleymaniye, Şehid Ali Paşa 2719/7 (fols. 125a–125a)*** contains a fragment of this text, followed by the same text as here in the Ashrafīya. This manuscript was written by Yāqūt al-Mawṣilī (d. 622/1225) whose manuscripts were being traded in Damascus at the time of the establishment of the Ashrafīya library (IKH, VI, 122–6). C: lexicography.

(1271b) 264a/13 *wa-Ṣifat al-saḥāb – Characteristics of Clouds*; A: Ibn Durayd (d. 321/933); S: ed. ^{c}I. al-Tanūkhī, *K. waṣf al-maṭar wa-al-saḥāb*, Damascus:

MIA, 1963; IN, I/1, 180: '*Ṣifat al-saḥāb wa-al-ghayth*'; MS: Süleymaniye, Şehid Ali Paşa 2719/8 (fols. 126a–142b)***; C: lexicography/adab.

(1271c) 264a/13–14 *Talqīb al-qawāfī – Naming Rhymes*; A: Muḥammad b. Aḥmad Ibn Kaysān (d. 320/932?); S: ed. in M.I. al-Bannā, *Dirāsāt wa-nuṣūṣ lughawīya*, Mecca: al-Maktaba al-Makkīya, 2006; C: poetry – rhyme.

(1272) M/9s 264a/14 *Majmūᶜ Mukhtār min Zahr – Multiple-Text Manuscript with Selections from [the] Flower*; it is unusual that the cataloguer has a book title without article, but based on Ibn Khallikān's repeated use of the term in his *Wafayāt* (I, 54, 55; III, 322, 378) it is most likely that the reference here is to *Zahr al-ādāb [wa-thamar al-albāb]* (*The Flowers of ādāb [and Fruits of Hearts]*) by A: Ibrāhīm b. ᶜAlī al-Ḥuṣrī al-Qayrawānī (d. 413/1022); S: ed. ᶜA.M. al-Bajāwī, Cairo: DIKA, 1953; C: adab – anthology. (cf. nos. 541, 1500)

(1273a) M/9s 264a/14–15 *Majmūᶜ al-Riyāḍ wa-ikhtiyārāt ukhar – Multiple-Text Manuscript with The Garden and Other Selections*; *al-Riyāḍ*: popular title with several possibilities including *al-Riyāḍ* by Makkī b. Abī Ṭālib al-Qaysī al-Andalusī (d. 437/1045) and the *Zahr al-Riyāḍ* by Saᶜīd b. al-Mubārak Ibn Dahhān (d. 569/1169).

(1273b) 264a/15 *wa-Ashᶜār bi-al-ᶜajamī – Poems in Persian*; anonymous work with generic title; L: Persian; C: poetry – anthology.

(1274a) M/9s 264a/15 *Majmūᶜ Iᶜtilāl al-qulūb – Multiple-Text Manuscript with Lovelornness [Concerning the Reports on Lovers]*; A: Muḥammad b. Jaᶜfar al-Kharāʾiṭī (d. 327/939); S: *Iᶜtilāl al-qulūb fī akhbār al-ᶜushshāq*, ed. Gh. al-Shaykh, Beirut: DKI, 2001; C: ḥadīth – collection/love literature. (cf. no. 13)

(1274b) 264a/15 *Man ghāba ᶜanhū al-muṭrib – [The Book of] Those Who Have None (Other) to Delight Them*; A: al-Thaᶜālibī (d. 429/1038); S: al-N.ᶜA. Shaᶜlān, Cairo: MK, 1984; C: adab – anthology. (cf. no. 1014)

(1275a) M/9s 264a/16 *Majmūᶜ Qaṣāʾid al-shawārid – Multiple-Text Manuscript with Qaṣīdas from the Shawārid*; '*Shawārid*' can refer to different titles such as *K. al-shawārid* by Abū ᶜUbayda Muᶜammar b. al-Muthannā (d. *c.*210/825) (MU, VI, 2708) and *al-Shawārid* by al-Ḥasan b. Muḥammad al-Ṣāghānī (d. 650/1252) (*Siyar*, XXIII, 293); C: poetry – anthology.

(1275b) 264a/16 *wa-Naẓm al-sulūk* – *The Mystic's Progress*; A: ᶜUmar b. ᶜAlī Ibn al-Fāriḍ (d. 632/1235); S: Engl. tr. A.J. Arberry, *The Poem of the Way*, London 1952; C: sufism.

(1276a) M/9s 264a/16 *Majmūᶜ al-Mubtadaᵓ* – *Multiple-Text Manuscript with The Beginning*; the term '*al-Mubtadaᵓ*' is generally used in grammatical or historical works (such as the history by Wahb b. Munabbih (d. 110/728?) (GAS, I, 306). On account of the second title in this multiple-text manuscript a historical work seems to be more likely, but no such work by a scholar bearing the *nisba* al-Ṭūsī/al-Ṭuwaytī is known. This may be an erroneous ascription of the historical work by Abān b. ᶜUthmān b. Yaḥyā, which Yāqūt al-Ḥamawī, for instance, only knows via a reference by Muḥammad b. al-Ḥasan al-Ṭūsī (d. 459/1066 or 460/1067) (MU, I, 39); C: history/qiṣaṣ al-anbiyāᵓ?

(1276b) 264b/1 *wa-min Maghāzī al-Wāqidī* – *[Parts] of [The Book of] Raids*; A: Muḥammad b. ᶜUmar al-Wāqidī (d. 207/822); S: ed. J.M. Jones, London 1966; C: history – early Islam. (cf. no. 968)

(1277a) M/9s 264b/1 *Majmūᶜ ᶜIṣmat al-anbiyāᵓ ᶜalayhim al-salām* – *Multiple-Text Manuscript with The Prophets' Infallibility (may peace be upon them)*; A: Muḥammad b. ᶜUmar Fakhr al-Dīn al-Rāzī Ibn al-Khaṭīb (d. 606/1210); S: ed. M. Ḥijāzī, Cairo: Maktabat al-thaqāfa al-dīnīya, 1986; C: theology.

(1277b) 264b/1–2 *wa-Manāqib al-Shāfiᶜī* – *Virtues of al-Shāfiᶜī*; popular title with numerous possibilities (including Aḥmad b. al-Ḥusayn al-Bayhaqī (d. 458/1066) (ed. A. Ṣaqr, Cairo: DT, 1970–1), Muḥammad b. ᶜUmar Fakhr al-Dīn al-Rāzī Ibn al-Khaṭīb (d. 606/1210) (ed. A.Ḥ. Saqqā, Cairo: MKA, 1986) and Aḥmad b. ᶜAlī al-Khaṭīb al-Baghdādī (d. 463/1071) with a slight preference for Ismāᶜīl b. Aḥmad al-Qarrāb (d. 414/1023), whose *Manāqib al-Shāfiᶜī* was held in the following century in the library of the mausoleum's sister institution in Damascus, the Dār al-ḥadīth al-Ashrafīya (al-Subkī, *Ṭabaqāt*, IV, 266); C: biography – praise of scholar. (cf. no. 1199a)

(1278a) M/9s 264b/2 *Majmūᶜ al-Ḥātimīya* – *Multiple-Text Manuscript with al-Ḥātimī's Epistle*; this is most likely al-Ḥātimī's epistle *al-Risāla al-Mūḍiḥa* against al-Mutanabbī (cf. no. 1249j). In contrast to no. 529 the epistle is here not described as '*al-ṣaghīra*'. A: Muḥammad b. al-Ḥasan al-Ḥātimī (d. 388/998); S: ed. M.Y. Najm, Beirut: DṢ, 1965; C: poetry – commentary. (cf. nos. 507, 528, 1249j)

(1278b) 264b/2 *wa-al-Khilāf bayna ṣāḥibay Abī ^{c}Umar – The Dispute between Abū ^{c}Umar's Two Companions*; no such title is identifiable and it is not evident who is meant here by Abū ^{c}Umar. Within the context of the 7th-/13th-c. Damascus this may refer to the member of the prominent Maqdisī family Muḥammad b. Aḥmad b. Qudāma, known as Abū ^{c}Umar (d. 607/1210), a scholar and holy man of the city (Meri, *Cult of Saints*, 85–90). Abū ^{c}Umar became a subject of hagiographical writings (such as Muḥammad al-Maqdisī, *Manāqib al-Shaykh Abū ^{c}Umar al-Maqdisī*, ed. A ^{c}A. al-Kandarī/H. al-Murrī, Beirut: DIḤ, 1997) and this may be another treatise on an episode of his life. C: biography?

(1279) M/9s 264b/2–3 *Majmū^{c} Ḥāmil al-^{c}arūḍ – Multiple-Text Manuscript with The Carrier of Metrics*; A: Sa^{c}īd b. Hārūn al-Khaṭīb al-Ushnāndānī (d. 288/901?); S: title of work and 'al-Khaṭīb' not mentioned in entries such as in IN, I, 174 and MU, III, 1377, but the *nisba* clearly identifies him as author; C: poetry – metrics.

(1280a) M/9s 264b/3 *Majmū^{c} Mukhtār min tarassul al-Fāḍil – Multiple-Text Manuscript with Selections of al-Fāḍil's Epistles*; A: ^{c}Abd al-Raḥīm b. ^{c}Alī al-Qāḍī al-Fāḍil al-Baysānī (d. 596/1200); S: *Rasā^{c}il al-Qāḍī al-Fāḍil*, ed. ^{c}A.N. ^{c}Īsā, Beirut: DKI, 2005; MS: Süleymaniye, Beşir Ağa(Eyüp) 127***; C: adab – epistle. (cf. no. 1682)

(1280b) 264b/4 *wa-Dūbaytī al-^{c}Imād – Al-^{c}Imād's Dūbaytī Poems*; A: Muḥammad b. Muḥammad ^{c}Imād al-Dīn al-Kātib al-Iṣfahānī (d. 597/1201); S: EI^{2}, W. Stoetzer, 'Rubā^{c}ī'; C: poetry – dūbaytī – Ayyūbid.

(1280c) 264b/4 *wa-min al-Ḥamāsa – [Parts] of the [Book of] Bravery*; A: Ḥabīb b. Aws Abū Tammām (d. 231/845 or 232/846); S: ed. M. Khafājī, Cairo: ^{c}Alī Ṣabīḥ, 1955; C: poetry – anthology – ^{c}Abbāsid. (cf. nos. 335, 1526, 1554, 1557, 1561)

(1281) M/9s 264b/4 *Majmū^{c} min Shi^{c}r Ibn Wakī^{c} wa-ghayr dhālika – Multiple-Text Manuscript with [Parts] of the Poetry of Ibn Wakī^{c} and Other [Writings]*; A: al-Ḥasan b. ^{c}Alī Ibn Wakī^{c} al-Tinnīsī (d. 393/1003); S: ed. H. Nājī, Baghdad: DSh, 1998; C: poetry.

(1282) M/9s 264b/5 *Majmū^{c} fī al-qirā$^{\circ}$āt – Multiple-Text Manuscript on the Readings of the Koran*; anonymous work with generic title; FI: '*safīna*'/'*Safīna-shaped*';[152] C: Koran – recitation.

(1283a) M/9s 264b/5 *Majmū^{c} fīhi al-Adyira – Multiple-Text Manuscript with The [Book of] Monasteries*; A: al-Khālidīyān, the two court poets Abū ^{c}Uthmān Sa^{c}d/Sa^{c}īd (d. 350/961) and Abū Bakr Muḥammad (d. 380/990); the cataloguer uses here an unusual plural form, as the standard title for this work in contemporaneous sources was '*Diyārāt*' (e.g. IKH, III, 319). C: poetry – ^{c}Abbāsid. (cf. no. 1061)

(1283b) 264b/5-6 *wa-al-Khammārīn wa-al-khammārāt – The Book of Innkeepers and Tavern Maids*; A: Abū al-Faraj al-Iṣfahānī (d. 356/967); S: GAS, II, 64; C: poetry – wine. (cf. no. 1188b)

(1284a) M/9s 264b/6 *Majmū^{c} [al-]Durra – Multiple-Text Manuscript with The [Unique] Pearl [on the Conduct of Kingship]*; also known as *al-Adab al-kabīr*; A: ^{c}Abd Allāh Ibn al-Muqaffa^{c} (d. 139/756?); S: *al-Durra al-yatīma*, ed. A.R. al-Badrāwī, Beirut: DN, 1974; C: political thought – mirror for princes. (cf. nos. 1248a, 1312a, 1330a, 1391)

(1284b) 264b/6 *wa-nathr wa-naẓm bi-al-^{c}ajamī – Prose and Verse in Persian*; anonymous work with generic title; L: Persian; C: poetry/adab.

(1285a) M/9s 264b/7 *Majmū^{c} min ash^{c}ār al-^{c}arab – Multiple-Text Manuscript with Poems by the Arabs*; anonymous work with generic title; for '*ash^{c}ār al-^{c}arab*' cf. no. 974; C: poetry – anthology – pre-Islamic/early Islamic.

(1285b) 264b/7 *wa-Mukhtār min al-naqā$^{\circ}$iḍ – Selection from the Polemical Poems*; this selection most likely refers to the poems exchanged between Jarīr b. ^{c}Aṭīya (d. *c.*110/728–9) and Tammām b. Ghālib al-Farazdaq (d. *c.*114/732) (*Naqā$^{\circ}$iḍ Jarīr wa-al-Farazdaq*, ed. A.A. Bevan, Leiden 1905); see comments in no. 1074; C: poetry – Umayyad. (cf. nos. 1074, 1290a, 1349, 1356, 1359, 1607)

(1285c) 264b/7 *wa-min al-Mufaḍḍalīyāt – [Parts] of Mufaḍḍal al-Dīn's Compilation*; A: al-Mufaḍḍal al-Ḍabbī (d. 164/780 or 170/786); S: ed. A.M. Shākir and ^{c}A.M. Hārūn, Cairo: DM, 1942; C: poetry – anthology – pre-Islamic. (cf. nos. 1059, 1635)

(1286a) M/9s 264b/8 *Majmūᶜ Akhlāq al-mulūk – Multiple-Text Manuscript with The Morals of the Kings*; as the following work is said to be by al-Jāḥiẓ this is most probably also the work attributed to him, but authored by A: Muḥammad b. al-Ḥārith al-Thaᶜlabī (fl. 3rd/9th c.); S: Fr. tr. (attr. to al-Jāḥiẓ) Pellat, *Livre de la couronne*; C: political thought – mirror for princes. (cf. no. 67)

(1286b) 264b/8 *wa-Mufākharat al-shitāᵓ wa-al-ṣayf – The Boasting Match between Winter and Summer*; A: attr. al-Jāḥiẓ (d. 255/868–9); S: Pellat, 'D'inventaire', no. 204; C: adab.[153] (cf. no. 1697)

(1287a) M/9s 264b/8–9 *Majmūᶜ li-l-Jāḥiẓ shiᶜruhu – Multiple-Text Manuscript by al-Jāḥiẓ with His Poetry*; A: al-Jāḥiẓ (d. 255/868–9); Al-Jāḥiẓ, known rather for his prose writings, did not leave an anthology to which this entry may refer. C: poetry – ᶜAbbāsid.

(1287b) 264b/9 *wa-al-Maḍāḥik – [The Book of] Jokes*; A: al-Jāḥiẓ (d. 255/868–9); S: Pellat, 'D'inventaire', no. 131, C: adab. (cf. no. 1314b)

(1287c) 264b/9 *wa-al-Mulaḥ – [The Book of] Anecdotes*; A: al-Jāḥiẓ (d. 255/868–9); probably his *K. al-Mulaḥ wa-al-ṭuraf*; S: Pellat, 'D'inventaire', no. 150, C: adab.

(1287d) 264b/9 *wa-Dhamm al-hawā – Censure of Passion*; A: al-Jāḥiẓ (d. 255/868–9); S: Pellat, 'D'inventaire', no. 84; C: adab – love literature/theory.[154]

(1287e) 264b/9 *wa-al-Ḥāsid wa-al-maḥsūd – The Envier and the Envied*; A: al-Jāḥiẓ (d. 255/868–9); S: ed. M. al-Sūd, *Rasāᵓil al-Jāḥiẓ*, Beirut: DKI, 2000, 5–19; C: adab. (cf. no. 526)

(1287f) 264b/9 *wa-Istihdāᵓ – Request [for a Gift]*; A: al-Jāḥiẓ (d. 255/868–9); no such title is identifiable and the term cannot be possibly connected to the following title. As it is without the definite article, this entry is most likely an extract from one of al-Jāḥiẓ's works similar to requests for gifts in adab works such as in Ibn Zubayr's *Book of Gifts and Rarities* (cf. no. 744), Engl. tr. Gh.al-Ḥ. al-Qaddūmī, Cambridge (MA) 1996, 80–2 (Caliph al-Mutawakkil requesting a gift from the ruler of India). C: adab.

(1287g) 264b/10 *wa-al-Ḥathth ᶜalā ittikhādh al-kutub – Urging to Choose Books*; A: al-Jāḥiẓ (d. 255/868–9); S: Pellat, 'D'inventaire', no. 125; C: adab. (cf. no. 527)

(1288a) M/9s 264b/10 *Majmūʿ al-Ṣādiḥ wa-al-bāghim – Multiple-Text Manuscript with the Singer and the Wailer*; A: Muḥammad b. Muḥammad al-ʿAbbāsī Ibn al-Habbārīya (d. 509/1115–16?); S: ed. Ḥ. ʿĀṣī, in: *Kashf al-asrār ʿan ḥikam al-ṭuyūr wa-al-azhār*, Beirut: DMa, 1995; C: poetry/adab – anthology. (cf. nos. 701, 705)

(1288b) 264b/10 *wa-min Shiʿr Ibn al-Khāzin – [Parts] of Ibn al-Khāzin's Poetry*; two main possibilities: 1) Aḥmad Ibn al-Khāzin (d. 518/1124) (IKH, I, 149–51) or 2) al-Ḥusayn b. ʿAlī Ibn al-Khāzin (d. 502/1109) (MU, III, 1105); C: poetry. (cf. nos. 749, 1145)

(1289a) M/9s 264b/11 *Majmūʿ Shiʿr Abī al-Ḥakam – Multiple-Text Manuscript with Abū al-Ḥakam's Poetry*; A: Abū al-Ḥakam ʿUbayd Allāh b. al-Muẓaffar al-Andalusī (d. 549/1155) who composed a diwan and died in Damascus; S: Gelder, 'Joking Doctor'; a second possibility would be the Umayyad poet al-Ḥazīn b. Sulaymān al-Dīlī (d. *c.*90/709) (al-Ziriklī, *Aʿlām*, II, 187 and GAS, II, 426). However, as the other poet in this multiple-text manuscript lived in the 5th/11th and 6th/12th centuries this is not very likely. C: poetry – Zangid/Munqidhite.

(1289b) 264b/11 *wa-Shiʿr Ibn al-Ẓarīf al-Fāriqī – Ibn al-Ẓarīf al-Fāriqī's Poetry*; A: al-ʿĀbid Abū al-Riḍā b. Manṣūr b. al-Ẓarīf al-Fāriqī (d. 430/1038–9); S: Ibn al-Najjār, *Dhayl*, XVII, 51 (name); Ibn al-Athīr, *Kāmil*, IX, 466 (poetry); C: poetry. (cf. no. 651)

(1290a) M/9s 264b/11–12 *Majmūʿ mukhtār al-Naqāʾiḍ – Multiple-Text Manuscript with Selection from the Polemical Poems*; most likely the poems exchanged between Jarīr b. ʿAṭīya (d. *c.*110/728–9) and Tammām b. Ghālib al-Farazdaq (d. *c.*114/732) (*Naqāʾiḍ Jarīr wa-al-Farazdaq*, ed. A.A. Bevan, Leiden 1905); see comments in no. 1074; C: poetry – Umayyad. (cf. nos. 1074, 1285b, 1349, 1356, 1359, 1607)

(1290b) 264b/12 *wa-Shiʿr Jarīr – Jarīr's Poetry*; A: Jarīr b. ʿAṭīya (d. *c.*110/728–9); S: ed. N. Ṭaha, Cairo: DM, 1986; C: poetry – Umayyad. (cf. nos. 404, 1072, 1229e, 1610, 1630, 1653)

(1290c) 264b/12 *wa-al-Farazdaq – Farazdaq's [Poetry]*; A: Tammām b. Ghālib al-Farazdaq (d. *c.*114/732); S: *Sharḥ dīwān al-Farazdaq*, ed. ʿA.I. al-Ṣāwī, Cairo: MTK, 1936; C: poetry – Umayyad. (cf. nos. 1073, 1050)

(1291) M/9s 264b/12 *Majmū^{c} fīhi ash^{c}ār al-Anṣār – Multiple-Text Manuscript with Poems by the Prophet's Companions*; anonymous work with generic title; C: poetry – anthology – early Islamic.

(1292a) M/9s 264b/12–13 *Majmū^{c} al-Tamthīl wa-al-muḥāḍara – Multiple-Text Manuscript with The Book of Exemplification and Discussion*; A: al-Tha^{c}ālibī (d. 429/1038); S: ed. ^{c}A. al-Ḥulw, Cairo: D^{c}AK, 1961; C: adab – anthology. (cf. nos. 253, 1463)

(1292b) 264b/13 *wa-al-Asjā^{c} – Rhymed Prose*; no such title is identifiable and the author is given as 'al-^{c}Ijlī'. The most famous work with this term in the title is *Anwā^{c} al-asjā^{c}* by Ibn Abī al-Zalāzil (d. 354/965), but the catalogue has the full title elsewhere (cf. no. 1643) and no element of this author's name corresponds even remotely with al-^{c}Ijlī. This may thus be the *Anwā^{c} al-riqā^{c} fī al-asjā^{c}* by ^{c}Alī b. al-Ḥasan Shumaym al-Ḥillī (d. 601/1204) (MU, IV, 1691) who lived in northern Mesopotamia and Syria and who dedicated works to Saladin. This would assume that العجلي has to be read as الحلي. C: adab.

(1292c) 264b/13 *wa-Risāla fī nawādir al-ḥukamāʾ wa-min kalāmihim – Epistle on Anecdotes of the Wise Teachers and [Parts] of Their Words*; C: philosophy? (*nawādir al-ḥukamāʾ*: cf. no. 1214)

(1293) M/9s 264b/13–14 *Majmū^{c} ikhtiyār jamā^{c}a min shu^{c}arāʾ al-^{c}arab wa-ash^{c}ārihim – Multiple-Text Manuscript with Selections from a Group of Poets of the Arabs and Their Poems*; anonymous work with generic title; for '*shu^{c}arāʾ al-^{c}arab*' cf. no. 974; FI: '*radīʾ*'/'*of inferior quality*' (cf. no. 165); C: poetry – anthology – pre-Islamic/early Islamic.

(1294a) M/9s 264b/14–15 *Majmū^{c} Mukātabāt bayna al-Sharīf wa-al-Ṣābiʾ – Multiple-Text Manuscript with The Correspondence Between al-Raḍī and al-Ṣābiʾ*; A: Muḥammad b. al-Ḥusayn al-Sharīf al-Raḍī (d. 406/1016) and Ibrāhīm b. Hilāl al-Ṣabiʾ (d. 384/994); S: *Rasāʾil al-Ṣābiʾ wa-al-Sharīf al-Raḍī*, ed. M. Najm, Kuwait: MḤK, 1961; C: adab – epistle. (cf. no. 485b)

(1294b) 264b/15 *wa-Dīwān Ibn Qasīm – The Diwan of Ibn Qasīm*; A: Muslim b. al-Khiḍr b. Qasīm al-Ḥamawī (d. 541/1146); S: *Dīwān Ibn Qasīm al-Ḥamawī: min shu^{c}arāʾ Nūr al-Dīn Zankī*, ed. S.M. ^{c}Abd al-Jābir, Amman: Dār al-bashīr, 1995; C: poetry – panegyric – Zangids.

(1295) M/9s 264b/15 *Majmū^{c} thamāniyat ^{c}ashar qaṣīda li-l-^{c}arab – Multiple-Text Manuscript with Eighteen Qaṣīdas by the Arabs*; anonymous work with generic title; for '*qaṣīda li-l-^{c}arab*' cf. no. 974; C: poetry – anthology – pre-Islamic/early Islamic.

(1296) M/9s 264b/15–16 *Majmū^{c} mukhtār min shi^{c}r thalathat ^{c}ashar shā^{c}ir^{an} min al-^{c}arab – Multiple-Text Manuscript with Poetry of Thirteen Poets of the Arabs*; Scr('*bi-khaṭṭ*') & A: 'anthologist' ('*ikhtiyār*'): Mihyār b. Marzawayh al-Daylamī (d. 428/1037); for '*shā^{c}ir^{an} min al-^{c}arab*' cf. no. 974; while Mihyār's *Dīwān* is well-known (ed. A. Nasīm, Cairo: DKM, 1925–31) no such 'title' is known. From the cataloguer's use of a generic title this does not seem to be an anthology with a stable title. This could be identical with parts of the multiple-text manuscript MS: Süleymaniye, Esad Efendī 3542**, which contains more than 30 textual units. Among them are selections from thirteen poets: 3542/10 Ibn al-Mu^{c}tazz; 3542/12 ^{c}Alī al-Tihāmī; 3542/13 Ibn Nubāta; 3542/14 Ibn al-Rūmī; 3542/15 Abū Firās al-Taghlibī; 3542/16 Mihyār; 3542/17 Abū Tammām; 3542/20 Shanfarā; 3542/21 Muslim b. al-Walīd; 3542/22 Ibn Abī Rabī^{c}a; 3542/23 Abū Nuwās; 3542/24 Ibn al-Hāni$^{\circ}$; 3542/25 al-Mutanabbī; C: poetry – anthology – pre-Islamic/early Islamic.

(1297a) M/9s 264b/16-17 *Majmū^{c} Khalq al-faras – Multiple-Text Manuscript with Anatomy of the Horse*; A: ^{c}Abd al-Malik b. Qurayb al-Aṣma^{c}ī (d. 213/828?); S: IKH, III, 176; C: lexicography.

(1297b) 264b/17 *wa-al-Waḥsh – The Wild Animal*; referring to *al-Wuḥūsh*: A: ^{c}Abd al-Malik b. Qurayb al-Aṣma^{c}ī (d. 213/828?); S: ed. Ay.M.^{c}A. Maydān, Jidda 1990; C: lexicography. (cf. no. 1223c)

(1297c) 264b/17 *wa-Alfāẓ Ibn al-^{c}Arābī – The Words*; A: Muḥammad b. Ziyād Ibn al-A^{c}rābī (d. c.231/846); S: MU, VI, 2533: '*K. al-alfāẓ*'; FI: '*bi-ziyādāt Ibn Khālawayh*' / *with additions by Ibn Khālawayh [d. 370/980–1]*'; C: lexicography.

(1297d) 264b/17 *wa-Ḥadīth Qays – Qays' Words*; no such title is identifiable. Arguably it is a short treatise with the speech ascribed to Qays b. Dharīḥ (d. 68/687?) concerning his marriage to Lubnā, which is repeatedly transmitted via Ibn al-A^{c}rābī, the author of the preceding title (e.g. al-Qālī, *al-Amālī*, Cairo: DKM, 1926, II, 75). C: adab.

(1298a) M/9s 264b/18 *Majmū^{c} Mukhtār al-Mutanabbī – Multiple-Text Manuscript with Selections from al-Mutanabbī*; A: Aḥmad al-Mutanabbī (d. 354/955); S: *Dīwān*, ed. ^{c}A. ^{c}Azzām, Cairo: LTTN, 1944; C: poetry – Ḥamdānid.

(1298b) 264b/18 *wa-al-Buḥturī – [And Selections from] al-Buḥturī*; A: al-Walīd al-Buḥturī (d. 284/897); S: *Dīwān*, ed. Ḥ. al-Ṣayrafī, Cairo: DM, 1963–5; C: poetry – ^{c}Abbāsid.

(1298c) 264b/18 *wa-Abī Tammām – [And Selections from] Abū Tammām*; A: Ḥabīb b. Aws Abū Tammām (d. 231/845 or 232/846); S: *Dīwān Abī Tammām bi-sharḥ al-Khaṭīb al-Tibrīzī*, ed. M. ^{c}Azzām, Cairo: DM, 1957–65; C: poetry – ^{c}Abbāsid.

(1298d) 264b/18 *wa-al-Multaqaṭ min al-amthāl wa-al-mulḥa – The Collection of Proverbs and the Anecdote*; anonymous; C: adab – anthology.

(1299a) M/9s 264b/19 *Majmū^{c} Qaṣīdat Ibn Ḥilliza al-sab^{c}a – Multiple-Text Manuscript with Ibn Ḥilliza's Mu^{c}allaqāt Qaṣīda*; A: al-Ḥārith b. Ḥilliza al-Yashkurī; S: *Dīwān*, ed. H. al-Ṭa^{cc}ān, Baghdad: MI, 1969; C: poetry – pre-Islamic.

(1299b) 264b/19 *wa-Qaṣīdat Ibn Khamīs – Ibn Khamīs' Qaṣīda*; one would expect here another pre-Islamic poet in accordance with the manuscript's two other entries, but no such poet with the name form Ḥ/J/Kh-a/i/u-m-ī/ay-s/sh is identifiable. A certain al-Ḥusayn b. Naṣr Ibn Khamīs al-Mawṣilī Shāfi^{c}ī (d. 552/1157) is named by Ibn Khallikān as a transmitter of poetry (IKH, II, 139). However, this scholar was first and foremost a jurisprudent and it is difficult to see how he would fit into this multiple-text manuscript. C: poetry.

(1299c) 264b/19 *wa-Qaṣīdat ^{c}Antar[a] – ^{c}Antar[a]'s Qaṣīda*; A: ^{c}Antara b. Shaddād; S: ed. W. Ahlwardt, London 1870; C: poetry – pre-Islamic.

(1300a) M/9s 264b/19–265a/1 *Majmū^{c} Bard al-akbād – Multiple-Text Manuscript with The Alleviation of Hearts [Concerning Numbers]*; A: al-Tha^{c}ālibī (d. 429/1038); S: *Bard al-akbād fī al-a^{c}dād*, ed. I. Thāmirī, Beirut: DIḤ, 2006; C: adab – anthology. (cf. no. 222)

(1300b) 265a/1 *wa-Adab al-nafs – Training the Soul*; A: Muḥammad b. ^{c}Alī al-Tirmidhī al-Ḥakīm[155] (fl. 3rd/9th c.); S: ed. A.^{c}A. al-Sāyiḥ, Cairo: DML, 1993; C: sufism.

(1300c) 265a/1 *wa-Mukhtār al-Jazūrī – Selections from al-Jazūrī*; most likely the poet A: ᶜAbd al-ᶜAzīz b. Khalūf al-Jazūrī/Jarūrī (fl. late 4th/10th–early 5th/11th c.); S: *Wāfī*, XVIII, 377–9; C: poetry.

(1301) M/9s 265a/1–2 *Majmūᶜ fīhi shiᶜr jamāᶜa min al-ᶜarab – Multiple-Text Manuscript with Poems of a Group from among the Arabs*; FI: '*wa-aẓunnuhu min al-Hudhalīyīn*'/'*and I believe that they are from the Hudhalī Tribe*'; S: *Dīwān al-Hudhalīyīn*, ed. M. Abū al-Wafāᵓ/A. Zayn, Cairo: DKM, 1945–50; C: poetry – anthology – pre-Islamic/early Islamic. (cf. nos. 113, 1488, 1575)

(1302a) M/9s 265a/2 *Majmūᶜ [al-]Faṣīḥ – Multiple-Text Manuscript with The Pure Speech*; A: Aḥmad b. Yaḥyā Thaᶜlab (d. 291/904); S: GAS, VIII, 141–2; C: lexicography. (cf. nos. 1307a, 1317b)

(1302b) 265a/2 *wa-[al-]ᶜArūḍ – Metrics*; A: ᶜAlī b. ᶜĪsā al-Rabaᶜī (d. 420/1029); S: ed. M.A. Badrān, Berlin 2000; C: poetry – metrics.

(1303a) M/9s 265a/2–3 *Majmūᶜ al-Risāla al-Ḥukmīya – Multiple-Text Manuscript with the Jurisdictional Epistle*; A: al-Ḥasan b. ᶜAbd Allāh b. Sahl al-ᶜAskarī (fl. 4th/10th c.); S: *K. mā iḥtakama bihi al-khulafāᵓ ilā al-quḍāh*, ed. & Fr. tr. M. Tillier, *Le Livre des Caliphes qui s'en remirent au jugement d'un cadi*, Cairo 2011. The title given here is not known for this treatise. However, no other work by al-ᶜAskarī fits the title even remotely and the fact that it is a very short work probably explains why it is called '*risāla*'. C: political thought – mirror for princes.

(1303b) 265a/3 *wa-al-Nājim – The [Book] of the Morning Star*; there are two books with this title by al-Marwazī (d. 274/887) and ᶜAlī b. ᶜUbayda al-Rayḥānī (d. 219/834). None of these fits the name mentioned in the catalogue (al-Nabhānī?), but this may be a misspelled version of the latter's name, whose work is in another multiple-text manuscript (cf. no. 1324a). C: adab?

(1303c) 265a/3 *wa-Mulaḥ al-mukātabāt – Anecdotes of Correspondence*; A: ᶜAbd Allāh b. Muḥammad Ibn Nāqiyā (d. 485/1092); S: MU, VII, 3475: '*Mulaḥ al-mukātib*'; C: adab – epistle. (cf. no. 1157)

(1303d) 265a/3 *wa-Adᶜiyat al-ayyām – Prayers of Invocation for the Days*; generic title; C: prayer book.

(1304a) M/9s 265a/4 *Majmūᶜ Ikhtilāf manẓar al-nayyirayn – Multiple-Text Manuscript with The Parallax of Sun and Moon*; no such title is identifiable, but it is similar to works such as the anonymous *Risāla fī ḥarakāt al-nayyirayn* (GAS, VI, 286) and Ibn al-Haytham's (d. 430/1039) *Qawl/Masʾala fī ikhtilāf manẓar al-qamar* (GAS, VI, 258). C: astronomy.[156]

(1304b) 265a/4 *wa-Risālat al-Fārābī fī al-juzʾ wa-mā [lā] yatajazzaʾ – Al-Fārābī's Treatise on the Atom*; A: Muḥammad b. Muḥammad al-Fārābī (d. 339/950); S: IAU, IV, 27. This is al-Fārābī's work entitled '*al-Kalām fī al-juzʾ wa-mā lā yatajazzaʾ*' (the indivisible part). The rather sketchy hand of the cataloguer indicates that he was not entirely sure about the entries in this multiple-text manuscript. In the present entry the crucial '*lā*' is missing, although it is also missing in the main manuscript used for the IAU edition cited here. C: natural philosophy.[157]

(1304c) 265a/5 *wa-Tabyīn* (?) *al-sabab bayna awtād al-*(?); this is a very tentative reading. As the preceding title is by al-Fārābī, this may refer to a treatise on prosody by him. In his *K. al-Mūsīqā al-kabīr* (eds Gh. Kashaba and M. Ḥifnī, Cairo: DKA, 1965, pp. 1076–9), for instance, al-Fārābī discusses *sabab* and *watid* (for these terms see EI², W.P. Heinrichs, 'Sabab – In prosody' and EI², W. Stoetzer 'Watid') and this entry may be drawing on such passages. C: poetry – rhyme.

(1305a) M/9s 265a/5 *Majmūᶜ Shiᶜr Ibn Mayyāda – Multiple-Text Manuscript with Ibn Mayyāda's Poetry*; A: al-Rammāḥ b. Abrad/Yazīd Ibn Mayyāda al-Murrī (d. 136/754?); S: *Shiᶜr Ibn Mayyāda*, ed. Ḥ.J. Ḥaddād, Damascus: MLA, 1982; C: poetry – Bedouin. (cf. no. 688)

(1305b) 265a/5 *wa-al-Ṣābiʾ – Al-Ṣābiʾ's [Poetry]*; most likely A: Ibrāhīm b. Hilāl al-Ṣābiʾ (d. 384/994); S: *Shiᶜr Abī Isḥāq al-Ṣābiʾ*, ed. M. Gharīb, Alexandria: Markaz al-Babāṭīn, 2010; C: poetry – Būyid. (cf. nos. 635, 1042)

(1305c) 265a/5–6 *wa-al-Ḥakam b. ᶜAbd Allāh – Al-Ḥakam b. ᶜAbd Allāh's [Poetry]*; A: al-Ḥakam b. ᶜAbd Allāh al-Ẓulaymī; S: Ibn al-Athīr, *Lubāb*, II, 299: '*al-shāᶜir*'; C: poetry.

(1305d) 265a/6 *wa-Qays b. al-Khaṭīm – Qays b. al-Khaṭīm's [Poetry]*; A: Qays b. al-Khaṭīm b. ᶜAdī al-Ẓafarī; S: *Dīwān*, eds I. al-Sāmarrāʾī and A. Maṭlūb, Baghdad: MᶜA, 1962; C: poetry – pre-Islamic. (cf. no. 1215e)

(1305e) 265a/6 *wa-Jirān al-ᶜAwd – Jirān al-ᶜAwd's [Poetry]*; A: Jirān al-ᶜAwd al-Numayrī (fl. 1st/7th c.); S: *Dīwān Jirān al-ᶜAwd al-Numayrī: riwāyat Abī Saᶜīd al-Sukkarī*, Cairo: DKM, 1931; C: poetry – Umayyad. (1331b)

(1306a) M/9s 265a/6 *Majmūᶜ Risālat al-Ighrīḍīya – Multiple-Text Manuscript with the Ighrīḍīya Epistle*; A: Abū al-ᶜAlāᵓ al-Maᶜarrī (d. 449/1058); S: al-Maᶜarrī, *Rasāᵓil*, I, 183–250; C: adab. (cf. nos. 53b, 533, 1223a)

(1306b) 265a/7 *wa-al-Malāᵓika – The Angels*; A: Abū al-ᶜAlāᵓ al-Maᶜarrī (d. 449/1058); S: ed. M.S. al-Jundī, Beirut: DṢ, 1992; C: morphology.

(1307a) M/9s 265a/7 *Majmūᶜ [al-]Faṣīḥ – Multiple-Text Manuscript with The Pure Speech*; A: Aḥmad b. Yaḥyā Thaᶜlab (d. 291/904); S: GAS, VIII, 141–2; C: lexicography. (cf. nos. 1302a, 1317b)

(1307b) 265a/7 *wa-al-Maqṣūr wa-al-mamdūd – The Short and Long Alif*; A: Ibn Durayd (d. 321/933); S: *Dīwān*, ed. B. al-ᶜAlawī, Cairo: LTTN, 1946, 29–37; C: grammar. (cf. nos. 384a, 384b, 676 [sharḥ], 1203b, 1230j, 1238g, 1268b, 1313a, 1326b)

(1307c) 265a/8 *wa-al-Malāḥin – Ambiguities of Speech*; A: Ibn Durayd (d. 321/933); S: ed. ᶜA. Nabhān, Beirut: Maktabat Lubnān, 1996; C: lexicography.

(1307d) 265a/8 *wa-mā yuktabu bi-al-alif wa-al-yāᵓ – What Is Written with the Letter alif and What Is Written with the Letter yāᵓ*; A: Abū al-Fatḥ Ibn Jinnī (d. 392/1002); S: ed. ᶜA. al-Khazrajī, Jidda: Dār al-wafāᵓ, 1987; C: morphology/orthography.

(1307e) 265a/8 *wa-durūs fī al-naḥw – Lessons in Grammar*; as the cataloguer has the '*durūs*' without the definite article this is probably anonymous teaching material with a generic and not a stable title such as *al-Durūs fī al-naḥw* by Saᶜīd b. al-Mubārak Ibn al-Dahhān (d. 569/1174); S: IKH, II, 382. C: grammar. (cf. no. 582)

(1308a) M/9s 265a/8–9 *Majmūᶜ Naḥw – Multiple-Text Manuscript on Grammar*; A: Aḥmad b. al-Ḥusayn Ibn Shuqayr (d. *c.*315/927); either the author's *al-Jumal fī al-naḥw* or his *al-Mukhtaṣar fī al-naḥw*. S: GAS, IX, 162–3; C: grammar.

(1308b) 265a/9 *wa-Qaṣīd fī ẓāᵓāt al-Qurᵓān mashrūḥa – Qaṣīdas on the Letter ẓāᵓ in the Koran with a Commentary*; anonymous work with generic title; C: Koran – recitation.

(1308c) 265a/9 *wa-Sharḥ al-lumaᶜ – Commentary on the Lumaᶜ*; referring to the work by Abū al-Fatḥ Ibn Jinnī (d. 392/1002); A: al-Qāsim b. Muḥammad

Ibn Mubāshir al-Wāsiṭī (fl. 5th/11th c.); S: ed. R.ᶜU. Muḥammad, Cairo: MK, 2000; C: grammar. (cf. no. 580)

(1309a) M/9s 265a/10 *Majmūᶜ al-Maqṣūr wa-al-mamdūd – Multiple-Text Manuscript with The Short and Long Alif*; A: Abū ᶜUbayd al-Qāsim b. Sallām al-Harawī (d. 224/838); S: GAS, IX, 70/1; C: grammar.

(1309b) 265a/10 *Faᶜala wa-afᶜala – [The Book on] the Verbal Patterns 'faᶜala' and 'afᶜala'*; A: Yaḥyā b. Ziyād al-Farrāᵓ (d. 200/822); S: GAS, IX, 133; C: morphology.

(1310a) M/9s 265a/10–11 *Majmūᶜ taᶜziya – Multiple-Text Manuscript with an Elegy*; A: Abū al-ᶜAlāᵓ al-Maᶜarrī (d. 449/1058); on account of the following text in this multiple-text manuscript this is most likely his elegy for Abū al-Qāsim al-Ḥusayn al-Wazīr al-Maghribī. C: poetry – anthology – Ḥamdānid/Mirdāsid.

(1310b) 265a/11 *wa-Risālat al-wazīr ilayhi wa-ilā akhīhi [illegible words] – The Vizier's Letter to Him [al-Maᶜarrī] and to His Brother [. . .]*; A: Abū al-Qāsim al-Ḥusayn al-Wazīr al-Maghribī (d. 418/1027); S: al-Maᶜarrī, *Rasāᵓil*, I, 251–5; C: adab – epistle.

(1310c) 265a/11–12 *Mukhtaṣar iṣlāḥ al-manṭiq wa-ghayr dhālika – Summary of Iṣlāḥ al-manṭiq and Other [Writings]*; on account of the preceding texts in this multiple-text manuscript this is most likely al-Maghribī's recension of *Iṣlāḥ al-manṭiq* by Ibn Sikkīt (cf. no. 25, 1414), which he sent prior to its 'publication' to Abū al-ᶜAlāᵓ al-Maᶜarrī (d. 449/1058) and who praised it in his *al-Risālat al-Ighrīḍīya/Risālat al-ighrīḍ* (cf. nos. 53b, 533, 1223, 1306). A: Abū al-Qāsim al-Ḥusayn al-Wazīr al-Maghribī (d. 418/1027); S: *al-Munakhkhal: mukhtaṣar Iṣlāḥ al-manṭiq*, ed. J. Ṭulba, Beirut: DKI, 1994. C: lexicography.

(1311a) M/9s 265a/12 *Majmūᶜ Alfāẓ ᶜAbd al-Raḥmān – Multiple-Text Manuscript with The Words*; A: ᶜAbd al-Raḥmān b. ᶜĪsā al-Hamadhānī (d. 320/932); S: IN, I/2, 425: '*al-Alfāẓ*', ed. *K. al-Alfāẓ al-kitābīya*, Beirut: DKI, 1991; C: lexicography. (cf. no. 27)

(1311b) 265a/12 *wa-ᶜIlal al-ᶜarūḍ – Metric Deviations*; A: Ibrāhīm b. al-Sarī al-Zajjāj (d. 311/923); no such title for al-Zajjāj is identifiable and this is most likely an extract from his *K. al-ᶜarūḍ*, which was well known to contemporaneous authors (MU, I, 63 and IKH, I, 49). C: poetry – metrics.

(1311c) 265a/12–13 *wa-Anwāʾ Abī ᶜUbayd – Setting and Rising of Asterisms*; A: Abū ᶜUbayd al-Qāsim b. Sallām al-Harawī (d. 224/838); this is very likely what the author meant by 'Abū ᶜUbayd' as the cataloguer refers to him with this *kunya* elsewhere in the catalogue (cf. nos. 38, 786, 1309a, 1417, 1442). This is most likely an extract from this author's encyclopaedic work *al-Gharīb al-muṣannaf* in which he deals also with astronomical and meteorological themes (GAS, VII, 345). C: astronomy/meteorology.

(1312a) M/9s 265a/13 *Majmūᶜ al-Durra al-yatīma – Multiple-Text Manuscript with The Unique Pearl [on the Conduct of Kingship]*; no known work by the 4th-/10th-c. Christian author Severus Ibn al-Muqaffaᶜ matches the title given in the manuscript. The title can thus be best read as a corrupted version of *al-Durra al-Yatīma* (also known as *al-Adab al-kabīr*) by A: ᶜAbd Allāh Ibn al-Muqaffaᶜ (d. 139/756?); S: ed. A.R. al-Badrāwī, Beirut: DN, 1974; C: political thought – mirror for princes. (cf. nos. 1248a?, 1284a, 1330a, 1391)

(1312b) 265a/13 *al-Luṭf wa-al-laṭāʾif – Subtleties*; A: al-Thaᶜālibī (d. 429/1038); S: ed. M.ᶜA. al-Jādir, Kuwait: DA, 1984; C: adab – anthology. (cf. nos. 908, 958b, 1242a, 1707)

(1313a) M/9s 265a/13–14 *Majmūᶜ Qaṣīd Ibn Durayd fī al-maqṣūr wa-al-mamdūd – Multiple-Text Manuscript with Ibn Durayd's Qaṣīdas on The Short and Long Alif*; A: Ibn Durayd (d. 321/933); S: *Dīwān*, ed. B. al-ᶜAlawī, Cairo: LTTN, 1946, 29–37; C: grammar. (cf. nos. 384a, 384b, 676 [sharḥ], 1203b, 1230j, 1238g, 1268b, 1307b, 1326b)

(1313b) 265a/14 *wa-Mukhtaṣar Qawāfī – Summary of [a Book of] Rhymes*; the lack of the definite article is slightly odd for a well-known work, but this is possibly A: Abū al-Fatḥ Ibn Jinnī (d. 392/1002); S: *Mukhtaṣar al-qawāfī*, ed. Ḥ.Sh. Farhūd, Cairo: DT, 1975; C: poetry – rhyme. (cf. no. 1222b?)

(1313c) 265a/14–15 *wa-Mā qaruba isnāduhu – Where the isnād Is Short*; A: ᶜUmar b. Aḥmad Ibn Shāhīn (d. 385/995); S: GAS, I, 209–10 (title not mentioned); C: ḥadīth.

(1313d) 265a/15 *wa-Manāfiᶜ Ḥamza – The Benefits by Ḥamza*; A: Ḥamza al-Iṣfahānī (d. after 350/961); 'Al-Iṣfahānī' is most likely what the author meant by 'Ḥamza' as the cataloguer refers to him with this *ism* elsewhere in the catalogue (cf. nos. 37, 42, 390, 1486). No such title by this author (or by any other Ḥamza) is identifiable. The term *manāfi*^{c} was regularly used for titles on medicine/dietetics (cf. nos. 1036, 1245b, 1481) and Koran (cf. nos. 930 and 1191b). However, considering the literary profile of al-Iṣfahānī this is most likely an extract from one of his works on poetry such as *Maḍāḥik al-ash*^{c}*ār* (MU, III, 1221) on the benefits of poetry, similar to passages that we find in works such as *al-*^{c}*Umda fī maḥāsin al-shi*^{c}*r wa-ādābihi* by Ḥasan b. Rashīq al-Qayrawānī (d. 456/1063–4 or 463/1070–1; ed. M.M. ^{c}Abd al-Ḥamīd, Beirut: DJ, 1981, I, 69–75). C: poetry – literary criticism?

(1313e) 265a/15 *wa-Ṣalāt al-raghā*$^{\circ}$*ib* – *The Prayer of Supplications*; no such title is identifiable. This is most likely a book-in-the-making on the mid-Sha^{c}bān prayer and thus linked to similar titles such as nos. 751, 809, 934. The *Ṣalāt al-raghā*$^{\circ}$*ib*, accompanied by carnivalesque celebrations that led to intensive debates, had its heyday in Mamluk Damascus (Talmon-Heller and Ukeles, 'Lure of a Controversial Prayer'). Among the writings on this ritual was *Risāla fī jawāz ṣalāt al-raghā*$^{\circ}$*ib* by ^{c}Uthmān b. ^{c}Abd al-Raḥmān Ibn al-Ṣalāḥ (d. 643/1245) and *Risāla fī dhamm ṣalāt al-raghā*$^{\circ}$*ib* by ^{c}Abd al-^{c}Azīz b. ^{c}Abd al-Salām al-Sulamī (d. 660/1262) (published together Beirut: DF, 2001). C: rituals.

(1313f) 265a/15 *wa-*^{c}*Arūḍ* – *Metrics*; anonymous work with generic title; C: poetry – metrics.

(1313g) 265a/15 *wa-Futyā faqīh al-*^{c}*arab* – *Riddles for the Learned Among the Arabs*; A: Aḥmad Ibn Fāris (d. 395/1004); S: ed. Ḥ.^{c}A. Maḥfūẓ, Damascus: MIA, 1377 *[1958]*; C: philology.

(1313h) 265a/16 *wa-Mukhtār al-Futyā* – *Selections from the Futyā*; extracts from preceding work, not identified; C: philology.

(1313i) 265a/16 *wa-Akhbār fī al-numūw* – *Reports on Growth*; no such title is identifiable and this entry may be linked to the following one, which would give *Akhbār fī al-Numūw [wa-]khalq al-insān*.

(1313j) 265a/16 *[wa-]Khalq al-insān* – *Human Anatomy*; A: Ibrāhīm b. al-Sarī al-Zajjāj (d. 311/923); S: ed. I. al-Sāmarrā$^{\circ}$ī, Baghdad: MII, 1963; C: lexicography. (cf. no. 362)

(1313k) 265a/16 *wa-Aḥādīth Abī Manẓūr* – *Abū Manẓūr's Ḥadīths*; A: Abū Manẓūr al-Shāmī, minor *ḥadīth* transmitter; S: Ibn Ḥajar al-^{c}Asqalānī, *Lisān al-mīzān*, IX, 484; C: ḥadīth – collection.

(1313l) 265a/17 *wa-Nukat – Points [on the Koran's Inimitability]*; A: ᶜAlī b. ᶜĪsā al-Rummānī (d. 384/994); S: *Nukat [fī iᶜjāz al-Qurʾān], in: Thalāth rasāʾil fī iᶜjāz al-Qurʾān*, eds M. Khalafallāh and M.Z. Salām, Cairo: DM, 1955, 75–133; C: Koran.

(1313m) 265a/17 *wa-min ḥaythu Abī Muḥammad al-Juwaynī – As Regards Abū Muḥammad al-Juwaynī*; this entry's reading and thus meaning is unclear, but it definitely refers to the Shafiᶜi jurisprudent A: Abū Muḥammad ᶜAbd Allāh b. Yūsuf al-Juwaynī (d. 438/1047) (IKH, III, 47); C: fiqh?

(1313n) 265a/17 *wa-Khamsa min amālī al-Silafī – Five of al-Silafī's Dictations*; A: Aḥmad b. Muḥammad al-Silafī al-Shāfiᶜī (d. 576/1180); S: IKH, I, 105–7; C: ḥadīth – collection.

(1314a) M/9s 265a/17–18 *Majmūᶜ Madḥ al-sakhāʾ wa-al-sakhī wa-dhamm al-bukhl wa-al-bakhīl – Multiple-Text Manuscript with Praise of Generosity & The Generous and Condemnation of Avarice & The Avaricious*; as al-Jāḥiẓ is mentioned at the end of this multiple-text manuscript this is probably his *K. al-bukhalāʾ*. A: al-Jāḥiẓ (d. 255/868–9); S: Engl. tr. R.B. Serjeant, *The Book of Misers*, Reading 1997; C: adab.

(1314b) 265a/18–19 *wa-al-Yāqūt fī al-maḍāḥik wa-al-nawādir – The Gem on Jokes and Anecdotes*; A: al-Jāḥiẓ (d. 255/868–9); although a *K. al-maḍāḥik* is known (cf. no. 1287b) this is clearly an independent title with the key word *al-Yāqūt*. No such title by al-Jāḥiẓ is known. C: adab.

(1315a) M/9s 265a/19 *Majmūᶜ Shiᶜr Ibn ᶜUllayq – Multiple-Text Manuscript with Ibn ᶜUllayq's Poetry*; A: Ḥibbān/Ḥayyān b. ᶜUllayq b. Rabīᶜa; S: al-Āmidī (d. 370/980 or 371/981), *al-Muʾtalif*, I, 122; C: poetry – pre-Islamic.

(1315b) 265a/19 *wa-Ibn Dharīḥ – And Ibn Dharīḥ['s Poetry]*; A: Qays b. Dharīḥ (d. c.68/687); S: GAS, II, 411–12; C: poetry – early Islamic.

(1315c) 265a/19 *wa-Abī Ḥayya – And Abū Ḥayya['s Poetry]*; tentative reading and problematic because all other texts in this multiple-text manuscript are pre-Islamic or early Islamic; A: al-Haytham b. al-Rabīᶜ Abū Ḥayya al-Numayrī (d. between 158/775 and 180/796); S: Y. al-Jubūrī, *Shiᶜr Abī Ḥayya al-Numayrī*, Damascus: WTh, 1975; C: poetry – Umayyad. (cf. no. 616)

(1315d) 265a/19 *wa-Muhalhil – And Muhalhil['s Poetry]*; A: Imruᵓ al-Qays/ᶜAdī b. Rabīᶜa al-Taghlibī Muhalhil; S: GAS, II, 148–9; C: poetry – pre-Islamic.

(1315e) 265a/20 *wa-ᶜAbd Allāh b. ᶜAjlān wa-waladihi – And [Poetry] by ᶜAbd Allāh b. ᶜAjlān and His Son*; A: ᶜAbd Allāh/ᶜAmr b. (al-)ᶜAjlān; S: GAS, II, 147–8; C: poetry – pre-Islamic/early Islamic.

(1315f) 265a/20 *wa-al-Find – And al-Find['s Poetry]*; A: Shahl b. Shaybān al-Zimmānī al-Find; S: GAS, II, 156; C: poetry – pre-Islamic.

(1316a) M/9s 265a/20–265b/1 *Majmūᶜ al-Qawl al-Mūjaz fī akhbār dawlat al-Muwaḥḥidīn bi-al-Maghrib – Multiple-Text Manuscript with The Concise Discourse Concerning the Almohads' History in the Maghreb*; no such title is identifiable. This history of the 6th-/12th-c. Almohad dynasty may have been a local Damascene work that originated within the city's considerable Maghrebi community (see Chapter 2), perhaps to introduce the following work. For other Maghrebi historical works cf. nos. 84, 295, 1531. C: history – Almohad.

(1316b) 265b/1 *wa-ᶜAqīdat al-Mahdī – The Mahdī's Creed*; A: Ibn Tūmart (Mahdī of the Almohads) (d. 524/1130); S: *Le Livre de Mohammed Ibn Toumert*, Algiers: Imprimerie Orientale, 1903, 229–33; C: theology.

(1317a) M/9s 265b/1 *Majmūᶜ Muqaddimat naḥw – Multiple-Text Manuscript with an Introduction to Grammar*; anonymous work with generic title; this could be identical with the manuscript MS: Süleymaniye, Fatih 5413/3 (fols. 40a–69b)* entitled *ᶜIlal al-taṣrīf taᵓlīf baᶜḍ al-udabāᵓ*, which is bound together with the following text. C: grammar.

(1317b) 265b/2 *wa-al-Faṣīḥ – Pure Speech*; most likely the work by A: Aḥmad b. Yaḥyā Thaᶜlab (d. 291/904); S: GAS, VIII, 141–2; MS: Süleymaniye, Fatih 5413/2 (fols. 14a–39a)**; C: lexicography. (cf. nos. 1302a, 1307a)

(1317c) 265b/2 *wa-al-Jarmīya – The al-Jarmīyan Work*; uncertain reading, but this refers most likely to the grammarian A: Ṣāliḥ b. Isḥāq al-Jarmī (d. 225/839); S: IKH, II, 485–7; C: grammar? (cf. no. 957)

(1318a) M/9s 265b/2 *Majmūᶜ al-Ghārāt – Multiple-Text Manuscript [with The Book of Raids]*; popular title with several possibilities (cf. IN, index), including the well-known work by Ibrāhīm b. Muḥammad al-Thaqafī

(d. 283/896) on the conflict between ᶜAlī and Muᶜāwiya; S: ᶜA. al-Khaṭīb, Beirut: DAḍ, 1987; C: history – early Islam. (cf. no. 793)

(1318b) 265b/2–3 *wa-Iftirāq al-ᶜarab min Maᶜadd wa-ayna nazalat* – *The Dispersion of the Arabs of the Maᶜadd Tribes and Where They Settled*; possibly A: al-Ḥaytham b. ᶜAdī al-Ṭāʾī (d. *c.*207/822); S: IKH, VI, 106: '*Iftirāq al-ᶜarab wa-nuzūl manāzilihā*'; C: history – pre-Islamic.

(1318c) 265b/3 *wa-al-Muḥabbar* – *[The] Elaborately Ornamented [Book]*; A: Muḥammad Ibn Ḥabīb (d. 245/860); S: ed. I. Lichtenstadter, Hyderabad: DMU, 1942; C: history – pre-Islamic.

(1318d) 265b/3 *wa-Masāʾil fī baᶜḍ tanbīh al-Muᶜtazila* – *Questions on a Warning of the Muᶜtazila*; the reading of '*tanbīh*' is tentative and the construction is awkward as one would have expected '*ᶜalā al-Muᶜtazila*'. I take this to be an anonymous treatise that is an extract from an anti-Muᶜtazilite work, such as *al-Tanbīh wa-al-radd ᶜalā ahl al-ahwāʾ wa-al-bidaᶜ* (*The Book of Warning and Refuting the People of Desire and Innovation*) by Muḥammad b. Aḥmad al-Malaṭī (d. 377/987) (ed. S. Dedering, Istanbul and Leipzig 1939). C: theology – doxography – Muᶜtazila.

(1318e) 265b/3 *wa-min Nasab wuld al-ᶜAbbās* – *[Parts]* of the ᶜAbbāsids' *Genealogy*; probably the genealogical *K. wuld al-ᶜAbbās* by A: Hishām b. Muḥammad Ibn al-Kalbī (d. 204/819 or 206/821); S: IN, I/2, 306; C: biography – ᶜAbbāsid.

(1319a) M/9s 265b/3–4 *Majmūᶜ Maqtal ᶜUmar b. al-Khaṭṭāb raḍiya Allāh ᶜanhu* – *Multiple-Text Manuscript with ᶜUmar b. al-Khaṭṭāb's (may God be pleased with him) Assassination*; no such title is identifiable and contemporaneous authors do not mention such an independent title on the second Caliph ᶜUmar b. al-Khaṭṭāb (d. 23/644). This is probably extracted from a chronicle such as Smith (tr.): *The History of al-Ṭabarī*, XIV, 89–93. C: biography – early Islam.

(1319b) 265b/4 *wa-Ḥikāyāt ᶜan al-Shāfiᶜī raḍiya Allāh ᶜanhu* – *Reports on al-Shāfiᶜī (may God be pleased with him)*; anonymous work with generic title, referring to Muḥammad b. Idrīs al-Shāfiᶜī (d. 204/820).

(1320a) M/9s 265b/4-5 *Majmūᶜ Ihlīlajat*[158] *al-Ṣādiq* – *Multiple-Text Manuscript with al-Ṣādiq's Ihlīlaja*; ascribed to A: Jaᶜfar al-Ṣādiq, the sixth Shiᶜite *imām* (d. 148/765); S: Kohlberg, *Ibn Ṭāwūs*, 187; C: theology.

(1320b) 265b/5 *wa-Ithnā ᶜashar masᵓala suᵓila ᶜanhā al-ᶜĀmirī wa-ghayr dhālika – Twelve Questions on Which al-ᶜĀmirī Was Asked and Other [Writings]*; such a title is not identifiable, but this is most likely a treatise with questions that had been put to the philosopher and theologian Abū al-Ḥasan Muḥammad b. Yūsuf al-ᶜĀmirī (d. 381/992) (Rowson, *Muslim Philosopher*). Contemporaneous authors repeatedly quote al-ᶜĀmirī's disputations and the questions put to him (e.g. MU, II, 909). C: philosophy/theology? (cf. no. 1184c)

(1321) M/9s 265b/5–6 *Majmūᶜ Shiᶜr Laylā wa-Tawba – Multiple-Text Manuscript with Poetry on Laylā and Tawba*; referring to Tawba b. al- Ḥumayyir (d. *c.*55/674) and Laylā al-Akhyalīya; A: attr. Laylā al-Akhyalīya; S: *Dīwān Laylā Akhyalīya*, ed. Kh.I. al-ᶜAṭīya, Baghdad: Dār al-Jumhūrīya, 1967; C: adab – love literature/theory.

(1322a) M/9s 265b/6 *Majmūᶜ? al-Akhlāq – Multiple-Text Manuscript with Ethics*?; the reading of the second term is unclear. If read as 'li-l-Layth' this could refer to al-Layth b. al-Muẓaffar (d. 187/803), the Barmarkid secretary and philologist, and the work would be most presumably one of advice for cultivating personal virtue. C:?

(1322b) 265b/6 *wa-Alfāẓ al-ḥukamāᵓ – Words of the Learned*; either *al-Mubīn fī sharḥ maᶜānī alfāẓ al-ḥukamāᵓ wa-al-mutakallimīn* by Sayf al-Dīn ᶜAlī al-Āmidī (d. 631/1233) (ed. Ḥasan Maḥmūd al-Shāfiᶜī, Cairo 1983) or an anonymous treatise similar to other such items in this library (cf. nos. 143, 1214, 1292c); C: philosophy/theology?

(1322c) 265b/6–7 *wa-Masāᵓil suᵓila ᶜanhā Ibn al-ᶜAbbās – Issues on Which Ibn al-ᶜAbbās Was Asked*; prominent scholars referred to as Ibn al-ᶜAbbās include the early scholar of Koran exegesis ᶜAbd Allāh b. ᶜAbbās al-Qurashī al-Hāshimī (d. *c.*68/687–8; EI³, Cl. Gilliot, 'ᶜAbdallāh b. ᶜAbbās') and the physician ᶜAlī b. al-ᶜAbbās al-Majūsī (fl. 4th/10th c.; 'Haly Abbas', EI³, F. Micheau, 'ᶜAlī b. al-ᶜAbbās al-Majūsī'). However, even assuming that there was some homogeneity in the material bound in one manuscript it is not possible to make an informed guess on this title as the contents of the other two entries are not sufficiently clear.

(1323a) M/9s 265b/7 *Majmūᶜ Ghurar al-balāgha – Multiple-Text Manuscript with Blazes of Eloquence*; A: Hilāl b. al-Muḥassin al-Ṣābiᵓ (d. 448/1056); S: ed. M. al-Dībājī, Beirut: DṢ, 2000; C: rhetoric. (cf. nos. 501b, 804)

(1323b) 265b/7 *wa-Mā waqaᶜa ᶜalayhi al-ikhtiyār min al-ashᶜār wa-al-akhbār – What Was Selected from Poetry and Reports*; anonymous work with generic title; C: poetry/adab – anthology.

(1324a) M/9s 265b/8 *Majmūᶜ al-Rayḥānī al-Nājim – Multiple-Text Manuscript of al-Rayḥānī with The Morning Star*; A: ᶜAlī b. ᶜUbayda <u>al-Rayḥānī</u> (d. 219/834); S: Zakeri, *Wisdom*, 244–5; IN, I/2, 371–2; C: adab? (cf. no. 1303b?)

(1324b) 265b/8 *wa-al-Ṭāriq – The Evening Star*; A: ᶜAlī b. ᶜUbayda al-Rayḥānī (d. 219/834); S: Zakeri, *Wisdom*, 244; IN, I/2, 371–2; C: adab?

(1324c) 265b/8 *wa-al-Zimām – The Bridle*; A: ᶜAlī b. ᶜUbayda al-Rayḥānī (d. 219/834); S: Zakeri, *Wisdom*, 215–18 (suggests that this could also refer to the administrative office *Dīwān al-zimām*); IN, I/2, 371–2; C: lexicography?

(1324d) 265b/8 *wa-ᶜ-r-s*? *al-Q-ṭ-r*; a title by al-Rayḥānī fitting any of the possible readings is not known. Perhaps this is an anthology with extracts from his works that never developed into a widely known text ('book-in-the-making'). Alternatively, this may be a work on *ᶜUrs al-Qaṭr* (as a short form of *ᶜUrs Qaṭr al-Nadā*), the famous wedding of the daughter of Khumārawayh (d. 282/896), the second Ṭūlūnid ruler of Egypt, to the future ᶜAbbasid Caliph al-Muᶜtaḍid (d. 289/902) in 272/892. As al-Rayḥānī had died two generations earlier he is obviously not the author, but this work may have subsequently been ascribed to him. A: ᶜAlī b. ᶜUbayda al-Rayḥānī (d. 219/834).

(1325a) M/9s 265b/8-9 *Majmūᶜ Murabbaᶜat Ibn Durayd – Multiple-Text Manuscript with Ibn Durayd Four-Line Poems*; A: <u>Ibn Durayd</u> (d. 321/933); S: *Dīwān*, ed. B. al-ᶜAlawī, Cairo: LTTN, 1946, 115–23; C: poetry – ᶜAbbāsid.

(1325b) 265b/9 *wa-Ṣifat al-Muᶜaqqir wa-mā yaṣīru ilayhi – Descriptive Poetry by al-Muᶜaqqir and What Is Coming Upon Him*; the reading of the name is very tentative, but as the preceding entry was poetry this may be the pre-Islamic poet (al-)Muᶜaqqir b. Aws al-Bāriqī. In this case '*ṣifat*' would refer to 'descriptions' as we find it, for instance, as one of the chapters in Abū Tammām's anthology of poetry, the *Ḥamāsa*. The second part of the title is entirely unclear and it may be a quote from an unknown poem. C: poetry? – pre-Islamic?

(1325c) 265b/9 *wa-Risālat Ibn al-Ṣūrī – Ibn al-Ṣūrī's Epistle*; although a medical work is somewhat odd in the context of this multiple-text manuscript, contemporaneous authors only use this name for the Damascene physician who served at the city's Ayyubid court A: Rashīd al-Dīn Ibn al-Ṣūrī (d. 639/1242). Ibn al-Ṣūrī authored a splendid illustrated book on pharmacology, but the '*risāla*' referred to here was probably a more modest piece of writing, such as the medical advice and information mentioned by Ibn Abī Uṣaybiᶜa (IAU, IV, 270: '*fawāʾid wa-waṣāyā ṭibbīya*'). C: medicine.

(1325d) 265b/9–10 *wa-Khumāsīya zuhdīya – Khumāsīya ḥadīths on Renunciation*; *Khumāsīya* collections of *ḥadīths* in which only five intermediaries separate the transmitter and the Prophet belong to the typical post-canonical genres of *ḥadīth* scholarship (cf. Davidson, *Carrying on the Tradition*). This was seemingly an anonymous collection that the cataloguer left without definite article. C: ḥadīth – collection.

(1325e) 265b/10 *wa-Dhikr al-mawt – Remembrance of Death*; works with this title (e.g. Ibn Abī al-Dunyā (d. 281/894) ed. A.M. Āl-Salmān, ᶜAjmān: Maktabat al-Furqān, 2002) or the chapter from al-Ghazālī's *Iḥyāʾ* (*The Remembrance of Death and the Afterlife*, Engl. tr. T.J. Winter, Cambridge 1989) are well known. The author given here (al-K-r-l-j) is not identifiable. C: eschatology/afterlife.

(1325f) 265b/10 *wa-Ḥikāyat al-ᶜAbbās [illegible word] – The Story of al-ᶜAbbās [. . .]*; not identified; narrative sources refer to a *Ḥikāyat al-ᶜAbbās b. ᶜAbd al-Muṭallab* (e.g. Ibn Ḥajar al-ᶜAsqalānī, *Lisān al-mīzān*, VIII, 273). This title could thus be linked to *Akhbār al-ᶜAbbās [b. ᶜAbd al-Muṭallab]* by Hishām b. Muḥammad Ibn al-Kalbī (d. 204/819 or 206/821) (cf. no. 85). C: history – ᶜAbbāsid.

(1325g) 265b/10 *wa-Islām ᶜUmar raḍiya Allāh ᶜanhu – The Conversion of ᶜUmar (may God be pleased with him)*; unidentified work on the conversion of the second Caliph ᶜUmar b. al-Khaṭṭāb (d. 23/644); C: biography – early Islam.

(1326a) M/9s 265b/11 *Majmūᶜ mukhtaṣar al-Jarmī min al-Muntahā fī al-balāgha li-Ibn al-Ashall – Multiple-Text Manuscript with the Summary of al-Jarmī from Ibn al-Ashall's The Utmost on Rhetoric*; the second part of this entry refers probably to the '*K. ṣifat al-balāgha*' (MU, VI, 2542), which was part of the *Muntahā fī al-kamāl* by Muḥammad b. Sahl Ibn al-Marzubān al-Karkhī (d. *c.*345/956) (cf. nos. 12, 995, 1107, 1260f) whom al-Yāqūt al-Ḥamawī also names as 'al-Ashall' (MU, VI, 2542). The 'al-Jarmī' mentioned here is most likely Ḥubaysh b. ᶜAbd al-Raḥmān/Munqidh, a transmitter of poetry (MU, II, 804). C: adab.

(1326b) 265b/11–12 *wa-Qaṣīd Ibn Durayd fī al-Mamdūd – Ibn Durayd's Qaṣīdas on the [Short and] Long Alif*; A: Ibn Durayd (d. 321/933); S: *Dīwān*, ed. B. al-ᶜAlawī, Cairo: LTTN, 1946, 29–37; C: grammar. (cf. nos. 384a, 384b, 676 [sharḥ], 1203b, 1230j, 1238g, 1268b, 1307b, 1313a)

(1327a) M/9s 265b/12 *Majmūᶜ al-Muntakhab al-mulūkī – Multiple-Text Manuscript with the Royal Choices*; this title cannot be identified, but there are at least three books entitled *al-Mulūkī* to which this secondary work could refer: 1) the genealogical *al-Mulūkī fī al-ansāb* by Hishām b. Muḥammad Ibn al-Kalbī (d. 204/819 or 206/821) (MU, VI, 2781); 2) *[al-Ṭibb] al-Mulūkī* by al-Rāzī (Rhazes) (d. 313/925 or 323/935) on medicine (cf. no. 1039); 3) *al-Taṣrīf al-mulūkī* or *Jumal al-taṣrīf* by Abū al-Fatḥ Ibn Jinnī (d. 392/1002) on morphology (cf. no. 299). There is no thematic overlap between either of these works and the following text in this multiple-text manuscript. However, on account of the preceding entry on grammar the present selection most likely refers to Ibn Jinnī's work, which generated a high number of commentaries (GAS, IX, 178–9). C: grammar?

(1327b) 265b/12–13 *wa-Fiqh al-kalām ᶜalā taqāsīm khiṣāl al-kirām – Understanding the Words on the Classes of the Pious' Merits*; no such title is identifiable and this is most likely a book-in-the-making.

(1328a) M/9s 265b/13 *Majmūᶜ Maqṣūr al-Farrāᵓ wa-mamdūduhu – Multiple-Text Manuscript with al-Farrāᵓ's Short and Long Alif*; A: Yaḥyā b. Ziyād al-Farrāᵓ (d. 200/822); S: ed. ᶜA. al-M. al-Rājkūtī, Cairo: DM, 1967; C: grammar.

(1328b) 265b/13 *wa-Fāᵓit al-Faṣīḥ – Supplement to the Faṣīḥ*; A: Muḥammad b. ᶜUthmān al-Shaybānī (d. *c.*320/932); S: GAS, VIII, 156. The reading of 'al-Fāᵓit' is very tentative, but of all the works on *Faṣīḥ al-kalām* by Aḥmad b. Yaḥyā Thaᶜlab (d. 291/904), this is the most likely version. C: lexicography.

(1328c) 265b/13 *wa-al-Muthallath – Words with Triple Vocalization*; arguably A: Muḥammad b. ^{c}Abd Allāh Ibn Mālik al-Jayyānī (d. 672/1274); S: *al-I^{c}lām bi-muthallath al-kalām*, ed. Cairo: Maṭba^{c}at al-Jamālīya, 1329; C: grammar. (cf. no. 1238d)

(1329a) M/9s 265b/13–14 *Majmū^{c} Tawjīh al-qawlayn – Multiple-Text Manuscript with Directing the Two Opinions*; possibly A: al-Ghazālī (d. 505/1111) who authored the S: *K. Ḥaqīqat al-qawlayn fī tawjīh takhrīj al-Imām al-Shāfi^{c}ī li-ba^{c}ḍ al-masā$^{\circ}$il ^{c}alā qawlayn*, ed. A. Āl Zahwī, Beirut: Mu$^{\circ}$assasat al-Rayyān, 2007; C: fiqh? – Shāfi^{c}ī.

(1329b) 265b/14 *wa-Ikhtilāf al-maqālāt – The Difference in the Teachings*; A: Muḥammad b. Shaddād al-Misma^{c}ī Zurqān (d. 278/891) who authored the lost *K. al-maqālāt*; S: D. Thomas (2008), 'Heresiographical Works', in I.R.Netton (ed.), *Encyclopedia of Islamic Civilization and Religion*, Abingdon, 226–9; C: theology – doxography.

(1330a) M/9s 265b/14 *Majmū^{c} Ādāb Ibn al-Muqaffa^{c} al-kabīr – Multiple-Text Manuscript with The Great Adab Compendium*; *also known as al-Durra al-yatīma*; A: ^{c}Abd Allāh Ibn al-Muqaffa^{c} (d. 139/756?); S: *al-Durra al-yatīma*, ed. A.R. al-Badrāwī, Beirut: DN, 1974; C: political thought – mirror for princes. (cf. nos. 1248?, 1284, 1312, 1391)

(1330b) 265b/15 *wa-Risālat Ibn Abī al-Ṣalt wa-ghayr dhālika – Ibn Abī al-Ṣalt's Epistle and Other [Writings]*; A: Abū al-Ṣalt Umayya b. ^{c}Abd al-^{c}Azīz b. Abī al-Ṣalt al-Andalusī (d. 529/1134); one of the author's epistles of which the most famous are *al-Risāla al-miṣrīya* (history), *al-Risāla fī al-mūsīqā* (music) and *Risāla fī al-^{c}amal bi-l-asṭurlāb* (astronomy); S: EI^{3}, M. Comes, 'Abū l-Ṣalt Umayya b. ^{c}Abd al-^{c}Azīz'.

(1331a) M/9s 265b/15 *Majmū^{c} Miskīn al-Dārimī – Multiple-Text Manuscript with Miskīn al-Dārimī['s Poetry]*; A: Miskīn al-Dārimī, Rabī^{c}a b. ^{c}Āmir (fl. 1st/7th c.); S: ^{c}A. al-Jubūrī/I. al-^{c}Atijja, Baghdad: Dār al-Baṣrī, 1389 *[1970]*; C: poetry – early Islamic.

(1331b) 265b/15-16 *wa-Jirān al-^{c}Awd – Jirān al-^{c}Awd['s Poetry]*; A: Jirān al-^{c}Awd al-Numayrī (fl. 1st/7th c.); S: GAS, II, 217; *Dīwān Jirān al-^{c}Awd al-Numayrī: riwāyat Abī Sa^{c}īd al-Sukkarī*, Cairo: DKM, 1931; C: poetry – Umayyad. (cf. no. 1305)

(1332a) M/9s 265b/16 *Majmūᶜ fīhi Qaṣīdatā Suḥaym ᶜUmayrata waddiᶜ – Multiple-Text Manuscript with Two Qaṣidas [the First One Being] 'Say farewell to ᶜUmayra'*; A: Suḥaym ᶜAbd Banī al-Ḥasḥās (d. 37/657–8); S: *Dīwān*, ed. ᶜA. al-Maymanī, Cairo: DQ, 1950, 16–33. As in other places, the cataloguer quotes the poem's first verse here to identify the poem. C: poetry – pre-Islamic/early Islamic. (cf. nos. 602, 972a)

(1332b) 265b/16 *wa-Ibn Durayd Amāṭat lithām*^{an} *– [and the second Qaṣida] by Ibn Durayd [starting with] 'She Removed (her) Veil'*; A: Ibn Durayd (d. 321/933); S: *Dīwān*, ed. B. al-ᶜAlawī, Cairo: LTTN, 1946, 42–64; C: poetry – ᶜAbbāsid. (cf. no. 1230e)

(1333) N/1 265b/17 *Nihāyat al-bayān fī tafsīr al-qurʾān – The Utmost Elucidation on Koran Exegesis*; A: al-Muᶜāfā b. Ismāᶜīl al-Mawṣilī (d. 630/1233); S: Ibn al-Mustawfī, *Taʾrīkh Irbil*, II, 61; MS: Süleymaniye, Fatih 398*; C: Koran – exegesis (*tafsīr*).

(1334) N/2 265b/18 *Nawādir al-uṣūl – Rare Principles*; A: Muḥammad b. ᶜAlī al-Tirmidhī al-Ḥakīm (fl. 3rd/9th c.); S: ed. T.M. Takla, Beirut: Dār al-nawādir, 2010; C: sufism/ḥadīth.

(1335) N/2 265b/18 *al-Naṣīḥa fī al-adᶜiya al-ṣaḥīḥa – Advice on the Sound Prayers of Invocation*; A: ᶜAbd al-Ghanī b. ᶜAbd al-Wāḥid al-Maqdisī (d. 600/1203); S: ed. M. al-Arnāʾūṭ, Beirut: MR, 1982; C: prayer book/ḥadīth.

(1336) N/2 265b/19–20 *Nahj al-balāgha min kalām amīr al-muʾminīn ᶜAlī b. Abī Ṭālib karrama Allāh wajhahu – The Path of Eloquence from the Words of the Commander of the Believers ᶜAlī b. Abī Ṭālib (may God honour his countenance)*; A: Muḥammad b. al-Ḥusayn al-Sharīf al-Raḍī (d. 406/1016); S: ed. Ḥ. al-Aᶜlamī, Beirut: MA, 1993; NC: 6; C: ᶜAlī – sayings attributed to. (cf. no. 1393)

(1337) N/2 265b/20 *Naṣīḥat al-mulūk – Advice of Rulers*; A: al-Ghazālī (d. 505/1111); S: *Book of Counsel for Kings*, Engl. tr. F. Bagley, eds J. Humāʾī and H.D. Isaacs, Oxford 1964; NC: 2; Even though this text is not in the library's Persian section it is surely a Persian text. Arabic versions generally bear the title *Tibr al-masbūk fī naṣīḥat al-mulūk* (e.g. MS Süleymaniye, Fatih 3478, dated 790/1388), while Persian versions (e.g. MS Süleymaniye, Fatih

5406/1, dated 709/1309) have the title given here. L: Persian; C: political thought – mirror for princes.

(1338) N/2 265b/20 *al-Nuṣḥ fī al-Dīn – Counsel on Faith*; unidentified work, probably similar to Süleymaniye, Şehid Ali Paşa 1502 '*al-Nuṣḥ fī al-Dīn wa-maʾārib al-qāṣidīn fī mawāʿiẓ al-mulūk wa-al-salāṭīn* (Counsel on Faith and on the Necessities for Those Aiming to Admonish Kings)' by a certain A: Muḥammad b. Abī Bakr al-Mawṣilī Ibn al-Muḥiqq (d. before 745/1344–5); The scribe of Şehid Ali Paşa 1502 states that this work is a summary of the author's *Minhāj al-sulūk fī mawāʿiẓ al-mulūk*. C: political thought – adab of scholar.

(1339) N/2 265b/20–266a/1 *al-Nāsikh wa-al-mansūkh – The Abrogative and the Abrogated*; A: Hibat Allāh b. Naṣr Ibn Salāma (d. 410/1019); to write just 'Hibat' in lieu of 'Hibat Allāh' is unusual, but the cataloguer does so in this title's other entry as well (cf. no. 1171a). S: ed. Z. al-Shāwīsh, Beirut: al-Maktab al-islāmī, 1984; C: Koran. (cf. no. 1171a)

(1340) N/2 266a/1 *al-Nashīd al-ʿUqaylī* (?) – *The ʿUqaylid* (?) *Chant*; tentative reading and unidentified; C: music?

(1341) N/2 266a/1-2 *Naẓm al-sulūk fī waʿẓ al-mulūk – The Poem on the Way to Admonish Kings*; A: ʿAbd al-Raḥīm b. Muḥammad Ibn Nubāta (fl. 4th/10th c.); S: Ibn Shākir, *Fawāt*, IV, 27; C: political thought – adab of scholar.

(1342) N/2 266a/2 *al-Nūr fī faḍl al-ayyām wa-al-shuhūr – The Light on the Merit of Days and Months*; A: Ibn al-Jawzī (d. 597/1200); S: Alwajī, *Muʾallafāt*, 558; FI: '*mujallad*'/'*one bound volume*'; C: sermons?

(1343) N/3 266a/3 *Nihāyat al-maṭlab – The Ultimate Place of Seeking*; A: ʿAbd al-Malik b. ʿAbd Allāh al-Juwaynī (d. 478/1085); S: *Nihāyat al-maṭlab fī dirāyat al-madhhab*, ed. M. ʿUthmān, Beirut: DKI, 2010; MS: Süleymaniye, Ayasofya 1500*; C: fiqh – shāfiʿī.

(1344) N/4 266a/3 *Naḥw – A Grammar*; anonymous work with generic title; FI: '*bi-khaṭṭ daqīq*'/'*in small calligraphy*'; C: grammar.

(1345) N/4 266a/3–4 *al-Nabāt – Plants*; A: Abū Ḥanīfa Aḥmad b. Dāwūd al-Dīnawarī (fl. 3rd/9th c.); S: ed. B. Lewin, *The Book of Plants*, Wiesbaden 1974; C: lexicography.

(1346) N/4 266a/4 *Naḥw – A Grammar*; A: al-Layth b. al-Muẓaffar/Ibn Rāfiʿ (d. *c.*190/805); S: GAS, VIII, 159. Although no title by this secretary is known, he was renowned for his knowledge in lexicography and poetry. FI: '*taṣnīf*' / '*author-(or compiler)ship*'. This is the only instance in the catalogue where this term is employed for authorship, which indicates that the cataloguer was not certain whether Ibn Rāfiᶜ was indeed the author. C: grammar.

(1347) N/4 266a/4 *Naḥw ᶜan al-Farrāᵓ – A Grammar [transmitted on authority] of al-Farrāᵓ*; A: Yaḥyā b. Ziyād al-Farrāᵓ (d. 200/822); S: GAS, IX, 131–4; C: grammar.

(1348) N/5 266a/5 *Nasab Quraysh – The Quraysh's Genealogy*; A: al-Zubayr Ibn Bakkār (d. 256/870); S: ed. M.M. Shākir, *Jamharat Nasab Quraysh wa-akhbārihā*, Cairo: Dār al-ᶜurūba, 1381 *[1961]*; MS: Süleymaniye, Fazıl Ahmed Paşa 1141**; C: history – ᶜAbbāsid.

(1349) N/6 266a/5 *al-Naqāᵓiḍ bayna Jarīr wa-al-Farazdaq – The Polemical Poems between Jarīr and Farazdaq*; A: Jarīr b. ᶜAṭīya (d. *c.*110/728–9) and Tammām b. Ghālib al-Farazdaq (d. *c.*114/732); S: *Naqāᵓiḍ Jarīr wa-al-Farazdaq*, ed. A.A. Bevan, Leiden 1905; C: poetry – Umayyad. (cf. nos. 1074, 1285b, 1290a, 1356, 1359, 1607)

(1350) N/7 266a/6 *Nathr al-durr – Scattering the Pearl*; A: Manṣūr b. al-Ḥusayn al-Ābī (d. 421/1030); S: *Nathr al-durr*, ed. M.ᶜA. Qurana *et al.*, Cairo: HMAK, 1980–90; MS: Süleymaniye, Reisülküttab 930*; NC: 5; C: adab – anthology. (cf. nos. 1208c?, 1564)

(1351) N/8 266a/6 *Naqṭ al-ᶜarūs – The Bride's Beauty Spots [Concerning the History of the Caliphs]*; A: ᶜAlī b. Aḥmad Ibn Ḥazm (d. 456/1064); S: *Naqṭ al-ᶜarūs fī tawārīkh al-khulafāᵓ*, ed. I. ᶜAbbās, *Rasāᵓil Ibn Ḥazm al-Andalusī*, vol. II, Beirut: MAr, 1980–3; C: adab/history – Andalusian.

(1352) N/8 266a/7 *al-Nukat wa-al-ishārāt – Remarks and Directives*; most likely *al-Nukat wa-al-ishārāt ᶜalā alsun al-Ḥayawānāt*; A: Saᶜīd b. al-Mubārak Ibn al-Dahhān (d. 569/1174); S: MU, III, 1371; a second possibility is *al-Nukat wa-al-ishārāt fī al-masāᵓil al-mufradāt* by Muḥammad b. Muḥammad Abū Yaᶜlā al-Ṣaghīr (d. 560/1165) (al-Ziriklī, *Aᶜlām*, VII, 251), but this is rather unlikely as grammar works are generally not classified in category 8, but rather in the categories 4 (and occasionally 6). C: adab.

(1353) N/9 266a/7 *Nuskhat kitāb Jibrīl b. Bukhtīshū*[c] – *A Copy of Jibrīl b. Bukhtīshū*[c]*'s Book*; A: Jibrīl b. Bukhtīshū[c] (d. 212/827); S: GAS, III, 226–7 (exclusively medical works); C: medicine.

(1354) N/10 266a/8 *al-Nihāya fī al-kuḥl – The Utmost on Ophthalmology*; this is a title with key word + *fī* + content description; A: [c]Abd Allāh b. Qāsim al-Ḥarīrī (d. *c*.654/1256); S: *Nihāyat al-afkār wa-nuzhat al-abṣār*, ed. Ḥ. al-Bakrī/M.Sh. al-[c]Ānī, Baghdad: WTh, 1979–80; NC: 2; the Baghdad manuscript on which the edition is based is an autograph composed in 624/1227 for 'Shāh Arman' (ed., pp. 18–19). As seen above (cf. no. 315), this title can refer to the mausoleum's patron al-Malik al-Ashraf. C: medicine – ophthalmology.

(1355) N/10 266a/8 *Nawādir ṭibbīya – Medical Aphorisms*; an *al-Nawādir al-ṭibbīya* was authored by the physician Yūḥannā Ibn Māsawayh (d. 243/857) (eds & Fr. trs D. Jacquart and G. Troupeau, Paris 1980). However, as this title is without the definite article the cataloguer was either not sure about the authorship or, more likely, this is an anonymous collection of aphorisms. C: medicine.

(1356) N/12 266a/9 *al-Naqā*[ɔ]*iḍ – The Polemical Poems*; most likely the poems exchanged between Jarīr b. [c]Aṭīya (d. *c*.110/728–9) and Tammām b. Ghālib al-Farazdaq (d. *c*.114/732) (*Naqā*[ɔ]*iḍ Jarīr wa-al-Farazdaq*, ed. A.A. Bevan, Leiden 1905); see comments in no. 1074; C: poetry – Umayyad. (cf. nos. 1074, 1285b, 1290a, 1349, 1359, 1607)

(1357) N/12 266a/9 *Nukhbat al-Bāri*[c] – *The Pick of The Excellent Book*; no such title is identifiable. It refers to the anthology *al-Bāri*[c] by Hārūn Ibn al-Munajjim (d. 288/901 or to 289/902). C: poetry – anthology. (cf. no. 220)

(1358) N/13 266a/9–10 *Nuzhat al-riyāḍ wa-shifā*[ɔ] *al-qulūb al-mirāḍ – The Gardens' Delight on Curing Sick Hearts*; no such title is identifiable, but this is probably the *Zahrat al-riyāḍ wa-nuzhat al-qulūb al-mirāḍ* (given as *Nuzhat al-riyāḍ wa-nuzhat al-qulūb al-mirāḍ* in Ḥājjī Khalīfa, *Kashf*, II, 1942), a work on sermons in sixty-seven *majālis*, by: A: Sulaymān b. Dāwūd al-Saqsīnī (fl. 550/1155); S: Süleymaniye, Ayasofya 4329, fol. 1a, l. 13; C: sermons.

(1359) N/13 266a/10 *al-Naqā*[ɔ]*iḍ – The Polemical Poems*; most likely the poems exchanged between Jarīr b. [c]Aṭīya (d. *c*.110/728–9) and Tammām b. Ghālib al-Farazdaq (d. *c*.114/732) (*Naqā*[ɔ]*iḍ Jarīr wa-al-Farazdaq*, ed.

A.A. Bevan, Leiden 1905); see comments in no. 1074; NC: 3; C: poetry – Umayyad. (cf. nos. 1074, 1285b, 1290a, 1349, 1356, 1607)

(1360) N/15 266a/10–11 *Nuzhat al-abṣār fī naᶜt al-fawākih wa-al-azhār – The Eyes' Delight Concerning the Description of Fruits and Flowers*; A: Sharaf al-Dīn Muḥammad b. Naṣr Allāh Ibn al-Athīr (d. 622/1225) who also authored a *majmūᶜ* for al-Malik al-Ashraf (IKH, V, 397); S: al-Ziriklī, *al-Aᶜlām*, VII, 347; C: adab.

(1361) N/15 266a/11 *al-Nawādir al-mustaṭrafa – Exquisite Anecdotes*; no such (probably generic) title is identifiable. It is probably an anonymous adab collection with a generic title. C: adab.

(1362) N/15 266a/11–12 *al-Nūrayn – The Two Lights*; short title for *Nūr al-ṭarf wa-nawr al-ẓarf* by A: Ibrāhīm b. ᶜAlī al-Ḥuṣrī[159] al-Qayrawānī (d. 413/1022); S: ed. L.ᶜA. Abū Ṣāliḥ, Beirut: MR, 1996; NC: 2; C: adab – anthology. (cf. no. 543)

(1363) N/15 266a/12 *Nuzhat al-ᶜuyūn wa-rāḥat al-maḥzūn – The Eyes' Delight and Consolation of the Afflicted*; no such title is identifiable. The genealogical work *Nuzhat al-ᶜuyūn* by ᶜAbd Allāh b. al-Ḥasan al-Nassāba (*Wāfī*, XVII, 129) is rather unlikely as neither title nor thematic category match.

(1364) N/15 266a/12–13 *Nuzhat al-nāẓir wa-rāḥat al-khāṭir – Beholder's Delight and Repose of the Mind*; this is most likely *Nuzhat al-nāẓir wa-tanbīh al-khāṭir* by A: al-Ḥusayn b. Muḥammad al-Ḥulwānī (fl. 5th/11th c.); S: ed. n.n., Mashhad: Maṭbaᶜat Saᶜīd, 1404 *[1983/4]*). This is a collection of *hadīths* or wisdom sentences attributed to the Prophet and all the Shiᶜite *imāms*. Arguably, it is placed in adab category 15 because al-Ḥulwānī suggests that he collected the material from the works of Ibn al-Muqaffaᶜ, ᶜAlī b. ᶜUbayda al-Rayḥānī, Sahl b. Hārūn b. Rāhawayh and other adab authors to give it back to its rightful owners. C: adab/*imāms* – sayings attributed to.[160]

(1365) N/15 266a/13 *Nafthat al-ᶜaqīd – The 'Spellbinding' [Work]*; no such title, including the alternative *al-faqīd*, is identifiable. The translation here follows a suggestion by G.J. van Gelder with reference to Koran 113:4 ('*al-naffāthāti fī al-ᶜuqad*' / '*witches when they blow on knots*'). Placed in category 15 this is most likely not a work on magic, but rather a spellbinding work of adab. C: adab?

(1366) N/4s 266a/13 *Naskhat al-raf^catayn – Abrogation of Raising the Hands during Prayer*; no such title is identifiable and this reading raises a number of problems. '*Naskha*' for the act of abrogation is rare and the standard use of this first term would be rather '*nuskha*' (copy). However, the title is in the alphabetical section of the letter *nūn* and one would thus expect this first term to be part of the title and not a mere statement that there was one copy of this work. The disputed question of raising the hands during prayer was mostly discussed under the heading '*raf^c al-yadayn*', but some contemporaneous scholars also refer to the issue as '*raf^cayn/raf^catayn*' (e.g. al-Nawawī, *al-muhadhdhab*, III, 397). This treatise must have discussed the abrogation of some of the relevant traditions (for a discussion of the main traditions see Fierro, 'La polémique'). The reading of the author's name as al-Kishmardī, especially because of the final '-īh/-īya', is very tentative. In this case this could be the *ḥadīth* scholar Muḥammad b. ^cAlī al-Kishmardī (d. 541/1146–7) (TI, 541–50, p. 81). C: rituals – prayer.

(1367) N/5s 266a/14 *Nasab al-Nabī ṣallā Allāh ^calayhi wa-sallam wa-mawliduhu wa-al-khulafā^ɔ ba^cdahu – The Prophet's Genealogy (may God's blessing and peace be upon him), His Birth and the Caliphs after Him*; anonymous work with generic title; FI: '*muṣawwar*'/'*illustrated*'; '*makshūṭ al-ṣuwar*'/'*the illustrations are out of place*';[161] one such undated, but probably later, illustrated work is Süleymaniye, Ayasofya 3128/3, fols. 20a–26b '*Kitāb nasab al-Nabī*'. C: biography of the Prophet (*sīra*)/history – early Islam.

(1368) N/7s 266a/15 *al-Naṣṣ wa-al-qiyās fī faḍl Banī ^cAbbās – Textual and Other Evidence on the ^cAbbāsids' Merits*; no such text is identifiable. The legal terms *naṣṣ* (authoritative text) and *qiyās* (reasoning by analogy) are slightly unusual, but the rhymed title clearly indicates that they belong to the title and are thus meant in a figurative sense. C: adab/panegyric?

(1369) H/3s 266a/16 *al-Hadīya al-Ashrafīya fī al-hadāyā al-khafīya – The Ashrafian Offering on Concealed Gifts*; no such title is identifiable and the reading of the last term is tentative. This is probably a book-in-the-making with verse and/or prose dedicated to the mausoleum's patron al-Malik al-Ashraf. C: panegyric – Ayyūbid – al-Malik al-Ashraf.

(1370) H/4s 266a/16–17 *al-Hayākil al-sab^ca ^canhu – The Magic Formulae and Prayers Transmitted from Him [the Prophet Muḥammad] to be Said on*

Each of the Seven Days; for an undated *al-Hayākil al-sabᶜa* see Süleymaniye, Aşir Efendi 426/25, fols. 235a–237a, which is ascribed to the Prophet Muḥammad. The *ᶜanhu* in this title most likely also refers to him (cf. no. 177 for a similar blunt reference '*huwa*'). C: prayer book.

(1371) H/8s 266a/17 *al-Hidāya fī al-rimāya – The Guidance to Archery*; the catalogue has '*Bidāya*', but this is most likely a mistake as it does not fit the alphabetical order. No such title is identifiable, but this may be a text similar to the 7th-/13th-c. treatise *al-Nihāya fī ᶜilm al-rimāya* (GAL S, I, 905). C: warfare?

(1372) W/1 266a/18 *Wajīz al-Wāḥidī – Al-Wāḥidī's Concise Book*; A: ᶜAlī b. Aḥmad al-Wāḥidī (d. 468/1076); S: *al-Wajīz fī maᶜānī al-Qurᵓān al-ᶜAzīz*, ed. S.ᶜA. Dāwūdī, Damascus: DQa, 1995; MS: Süleymaniye, Fazıl Ahmed Paşa 152**; FI: '*mujallad*'/'*one bound volume*'; C: Koran – exegesis (*tafsīr*). (cf. no. 1433)

(1373) W/1 266a/18 *Wasīṭ al-Wāḥidī – Al-Wāḥidī's Intermediate Book*; A: ᶜAlī b. Aḥmad al-Wāḥidī (d. 468/1076); S: *al-Wasīṭ fī tafsīr al-Qurᵓān al-majīd*, ed. ᶜĀ.A. ᶜAbd al-Mawjūd, Beirut: DKI, 1994; MS: Süleymaniye, Carullah 248*; NC: 2; C: Koran – exegesis (*tafsīr*).

(1374) W/1 266a/18-266b/1 *al-Wāḍiḥ fī al-tafsīr – The Clarification on Koran Exegesis*; A: ᶜAbd Allāh b. al-Mubārak al-Dīnawarī (fl. c.300/912–3); S: Motzki, *Dating* and *Tafsīr Ibn Wahb [sic] al-musammā al-wāḍiḥ fī tafsīr al-Qurᵓān al-karīm*, Beirut: DKI, 2003, MS: Süleymaniye, Ayasofya 221 & 221**; C: Koran – exegesis (*tafsīr*).

(1375) W/1 266b/1 *al-Waqf wa-al-ibtidāᵓ – Pauses and Beginnings*; A: Ibn al-Anbārī (d. 328/940); This is probably identical to the author's well-known *al-Īḍāḥ fī al-Waqf wa-al-ibtidāᵓ*. S: ed. M.ᶜA. Ramaḍān, Damascus: MLA, 1971; C: Koran – recitation. (cf. no. 3)

(1376) W/3 266b/2 *Wasīṭ – The Intermediate Book*; A: al-Ghazālī (d. 505/1111); S: *al-Wasīṭ fī al-madhhab*, ed. A.M. Ibrāhīm, Cairo: Dār al-salām, 1997; MS: Süleymaniye, Fatih 2214**; NC: 3; C: fiqh – shāfiᶜī. (cf. no. 1397)

(1377) W/4 266b/2-3 *al-Wujūh wa-al-naẓāᵓir – Polysemes and Synonyms*; FI: '*wa-huwa Mā ittafaqa lafẓuhū wa-ikhtalafa maᶜnāhū*'/'*and this is what is similar in pronunciation and different in meaning*'; placed in the philological category 4 the lexicographical/exegetical *K. Mā ittafaqa lafẓuhu wa-ikhtalafa maᶜnāhu min al-Qurʾān al-majīd* (ed. M.R. al-Dāya, Damascus: DB, 1992) by Muḥammad b. Yazīd al-Mubarrad (d. 286/900) is possible. Yet this would have been rather placed in category 1 where we have, for instance, the works on uncommon words in the Koran (cf. nos. 787 and 788). This is thus probably the lexicographical work by A: Hibat Allāh b. ᶜAlī Ibn al-Shajarī (d. 542/1148); S: *Mā ittafaqa lafẓuhū wa-ikhtalafa maᶜnāhū*, ed. ᶜA. Rizq, Stuttgart 1992; C: lexicography. (cf. no. 1416)

(1378) W/5 266b/3 *Wulāt Khurāsān – Khurāsān's Governors*; A: al-Ḥusayn b. Aḥmad al-Sallāmī (fl. 4th/10th c.); S: EI², C.E. Bosworth, 'al-Sallāmī'; C: history – regional.

(1379) W/5 266b/3–4 *Wasāʾiṭ al-ᶜuqūd al-muqtanāh – The Innermost Stones of The Acquired Necklaces*; unidentified; C:?

(1380) W/8 266b/4 *Waqᶜat al-Adham – The Battle of Adham*; A: Muḥammad b. al-Ḥasan al-Ḥātimī (d. 388/998); S: MU, VI, 2506; NC: 4; no description of this *adīb* and poet's 'epistle' (*risāla*) seems to exist, but taking into account the thematic category this is most likely an adab anthology. C: adab? (cf. no. 1193)

(1381) W/13 266b/5 *al-Withāq wa-al-istirāq – The Firm Bond and Thievery*; no such title is identifiable and the reading is tentative. '*Istirāq*' may refer to poetic borrowing/'plagiarism', but the normal term for this is *sarīqa* and *withāq* does not fit this topic. However, as the title is placed in category 13 this may be a work of poetry. C: poetry?

(1382) W/3s 266b/5–6 *Waṣīyat ᶜAlī b. Abī Ṭālib karrama Allāh wajhahu li-waladihi al-Ḥasan raḍiya Allāh ᶜanhu – ᶜAlī b. Abī Ṭālib's* (*may God honour his countenance*) *Last Advice to His Son Ḥasan* (*may God be pleased with him*); probably a treatise on the advice by A: ᶜAlī b. Abī Ṭālib, the fourth Caliph and first Shiᶜite *imām* (d. 40/661) to his son Ḥasan, which was, for instance, included in the S: *Treasury of Virtues* (*Dustūr maᶜālim al-ḥikam*) by Muḥammad al-Quḍāᶜī (d. 454/1062) (Engl. tr. & ed. Qutbuddin, *Treasury of Virtues*, 89–93, 101); NC: 3; C: political thought – imāmate theory. (cf. no. 14c)

(1383a) W/3s 266b/6 *Waṣīyat al-Manṣūr li-l-Mahdī – Al-Manṣūr's Last Advice for al-Mahdī*; A: ᶜAbbasid Caliph al-Manṣūr (r.136–58/754–5) advising his son and successor al-Mahdī; this advice is included in various sources including S: Kennedy (tr.): *The History of al-Ṭabarī*, XXIX, 149–55; C: political thought – ᶜAbbāsid.

(1383b) 266b/7 *wa-Risālat al-Ghazālī – Al-Ghazālī's Epistle*; A: al-Ghazālī (d. 505/1111); there is no further indication that '*risāla*' is meant here. As it was bound with the preceding advice treatise it is possible that this is linked to al-Ghazālī's *Book of Counsel for Kings* (cf. no. 1337). The interlinear note FI: '*fīhi naẓar*'/'*it requires consideration*' (cf. no. 742 for this term) shows that the cataloguer was unsure about the exact nature of this text. C: political thought – mirror for princes?

(1384) W/4s 266b/7 *Waṣīyat ᶜAlī b. Abī Ṭālib li-waladihi al-Ḥusayn raḍiya Allāh ᶜanhumā – ᶜAlī b. Abī Ṭālib's Last Advice to His Son Ḥusayn* (*may God be pleased with them*); treatise on the last advice by A: ᶜAlī b. Abī Ṭālib, the fourth Caliph and first Shiᶜite *imām* (d. 40/661), to Ḥusayn as reported in sources such as S: Hawting (tr.): *The History of al-Ṭabarī*, XVII, 219–22; C: political thought – imāmate theory. (cf. no. 1161b, 1663)

(1385) W/4s 266b/8 *Wāḥid wa-alf ism min asmāʾ Allāh subḥānahu wa-taᶜālā – A Thousand and One Names of God* (*may He be praised and exalted*); C: prayer book?

(1386) W/5s 266b/8–9 *Wasīlat al-Rājī – The Supplicant's Guide*; A: ᶜAlī b. (al-)Munjib Ibn al-Ṣayrafī (d. 542/1147); no such title is identifiable for this secretary and poet. Judging from the author's background, the list of his works (MU, V, 1971–2) and the thematic category 5s this is most likely an anthology of verse or prose. C: poetry – Fatimid/adab?

(1387) Y/5 266b/9 *al-Yamīnī – The Yamīnī [History]*; A: Muḥammad b. ᶜAbd al-Jabbār al-ᶜUtbī (d. 427/1036 or 431/1040); S: *al-Yamīnī fī sharḥ akhbār al-sulṭān Yamīn al-Dawla wa-Amīn al-Milla Maḥmūd al-Ghaznawī*, ed. I.Dh. al-Thāmirī, Beirut: Dār al-ṭalīᶜa, 2004; MS: Süleymaniye, Ayasofya 2949**; NC: 4; C: history – Ghaznawid. (cf. no. 1247)

(1388) Y/5 266b/9 *Yatīmat al-dahr – The Unique/Orphaned Book of the Ages*; A: al-Thaᶜālibī (d. 429/1038); S: *Yatīmat al-dahr fī maḥāsin ahl al-ᶜaṣr*, ed.

M. ^{c}Abd al-Ḥamīd, Beirut: DKI, 1979; NC: 4; C: poetry/adab – anthology. (cf. nos. 1499, 1501, 1506, 1509, 1520, 1524, 1558)

(1389) Y/8 266b/10 *al-Yawāqīt fī al-mawāqīt – Precious Stones of the Meeting Places*; A: al-Tha^{c}ālibī (d. 429/1038); S: ed. N.M. Jād, Cairo: DKM, 2006; MS: Süleymaniye, Fatih 5432*; C: adab/poetry – anthology.

(1390) Y/9 266b/10–11 *Alyānūs fī ta^{c}biyat al-ḥurūb – Aelianus on Preparation for Warfare*; translation of the Greek military treatise by A: Aelianus Tacticus (fl. 2nd c. CE); S: Germ. tr. F. Wüstenfeld, *Das Heerwesen der Muhammedaner und die Arabische Uebersetzung der Taktik des Aelianus*, Göttingen 1880; C: warfare.

(1391) Y/15 266b/11–12 *al-Yatīma fī siyāsat al-mulk – The Unique [Pearl] on the Conduct of Kingship*; A: ^{c}Abd Allāh Ibn al-Muqaffa^{c} (d. 139/756?); S: *al-Durra al-yatīma*, ed. A.R. al-Badrāwī, Beirut: DN, 1974; C: political thought – mirror for princes. (cf. nos. 1248a? 1284a, 1312a, 1330a)

(1392) Makh/1 266b/12 *Min al-Istī^{c}āb – [Parts] of The Complete [Book for Knowing the Prophet's Companions]*; A: Yūsuf b. ^{c}Abd Allāh Ibn ^{c}Abd al-Barr (d. 463/1071); S: *al-Istī^{c}āb fī ma^{c}rifat al-aṣḥāb*, ed. ^{c}A.M. al-Bijāwī, Cairo: MN; probably copied by Muḥammad b. Khazraj al-Dimashqī (d. 654/1256,) (cf. no. 715) as a splendid copy ('*nuskha ^{c}aẓīma*') of this work was still endowed in this library in the 8th/14th c. (*Wāfī*, III, 37); C: biographical dictionary – early Islam.

(1393) Makh/2 266b/13 *Nahj al-Balāgha – The Path of Eloquence*; A: Muḥammad b. al-Ḥusayn al-Sharīf al-Raḍī (d. 406/1016); S: ed. Ḥ. al-A^{c}lamī, Beirut: MA, 1993; FI: '*nāqiṣa*'/'*incomplete manuscript*' and '*nuqilat ilā al-rābi^{c}a ^{c}ashara*'/'*moved to category 14*' (cf. nos. 1428, 1429); C: ^{c}Alī – sayings attributed to. (cf. no. 1336)

(1394) Makh/2 266b/13 *Min ^{c}Awālī al-Furāwī – [Parts] of al-Furāwī's Elevated isnāds*; A: Muḥammad b. al-Faḍl al-Furāwī (d. 530/1136); S: IKH, IV, 290–1 (title not mentioned); FI: '*dhukira fī al-^{c}ayn*'/'*mentioned under the letter ^{c}ayn*' (cf. no. 722); C: ḥadīth – collection.

(1395) Makh/3 266b/14 *al-Mustaṣfā – The Sifted*; A: al-Ghazālī (d. 505/1111); S: *al-Mustaṣfā min ^{c}ilm al-uṣūl*, ed. Cairo: Būlāq, 1904–6; FI: '*makhrūm al-awwal*'/'*incomplete in the beginning*'; C: fiqh – uṣūl al-fiqh. (cf. no. 939)

(1396) Makh/3 266b/14 *Min Baḥr*[162] *al-madhhab – [Parts] of The Sea of the [Shāfiᶜī] School*; A: ᶜAbd al-Wāḥid b. Ismāᶜīl al-Rūyānī (d. 502/1108); S: IKH, III, 198–9; Q: '1st, 2nd and 3rd'; C: fiqh – shāfiᶜī.

(1397) Makh/3 266b/14–15 *Min al-Wasīṭ – [Parts] of The Intermediate Book*; on account of category and the preceding titles most likely A: al-Ghazālī (d. 505/1111); S: *al-Wasīṭ fī al-madhhab*, ed. A.M. Ibrāhīm, Cairo: Dār al-salām, 1997; Q: '1st, 3rd and 1st, 2nd and 2nd, this is half of the total (*wa-huwa niṣf al-jumla*)'; C: fiqh – shāfiᶜī. (cf. no. 1376)

(1398) Makh/3 266b/15–16 *Min al-Asrār – [Parts] of The Secrets*; A: Abū Zayd ᶜAbd Allāh b. ᶜUmar al-Dabūsī (d. 430/1039); S: IKH, III, 48: '*al-Asrār fī al-uṣūl wa-al-furūᶜ*'; MS: Süleymaniye, Murad Molla 751*; C: fiqh – uṣūl al-fiqh – ḥanafī.

(1399) Makh/3 266b/16 *Min al-Mudhahhab – [Parts] of The Golden Book*; on account of category mostly likely a *fiqh* work, which would be – taking into account how contemporaneous sources such as Ibn Khallikān in his *Wafayāt* use this term – *al-Muhadhdhab fī fiqh al-Imām al-Shāfiᶜī* by A: Ibrāhīm b. ᶜAlī al-Fīrūzābādī al-Shīrāzī (d. 476/1083); S: ed. Z. ᶜUmayrāt, Beirut: DKI, 1995; Q: '2nd, 3rd and 3rd also'; C: fiqh – shāfiᶜī.

(1400) Makh/3 266b/16-17 *Min Taᶜlīq al-Qāḍī Ḥusayn – [Parts] of al-Qāḍī Ḥusayn's Commentary*; A: al-Qāḍī al-Ḥusayn b. Muḥammad (d. 462/1069–70); S: IKH, II, 134–5; Q: '1st, 2nd'; C: fiqh – shāfiᶜī.

(1401) Makh/3 266b/17 *Min al-Shāmil – [Parts] of The Comprehensive [Book]*; most likely *al-Shāmil fī uṣūl al-dīn* by A: ᶜAbd al-Malik b. ᶜAbd Allāh al-Juwaynī (d. 478/1085) on account of the following title; S: ed. ᶜA.S. al-Nashshār, Alexandria: Munshaᵓat al-Maᶜārif, 1969; MS: Süleymaniye, Fazıl Ahmed Paşa 826*; Q: '1st, 2nd, 3rd'; C: theology (kalām).

(1402) Makh/3 266b/17 *Min Tabṣirat al-muwaḥḥidīn – [Parts] of The Elucidation of Those Professing the Oneness of God*; no such title is identifiable, but it recalls the Shiᶜite *Rawḍat al-wāᶜiẓīn* by Muḥammad b. Aḥmad al-Fattāl al-Nīsābūrī (fl. 6th/12th c.) that is also known as *Ḥilyat al-muwaḥḥidīn* or *Tabṣirat al-muttaᶜiẓīn* (ed. Ḥ. al-Aᶜlamī, Beirut: MA, 1986). Q: '1st'; C: theology.

(1403) Makh/3 266b/18 *Mukhtaṣar fī al-fiqh – A Summary on fiqh*; anonymous work with generic title; FI: '*makhrūm*'/'*incomplete*'; C: fiqh.

(1404) Makh/4 266b/18 *Jamharat al-amthāl – Compilation of Proverbs*; A: al-Ḥasan b. ᶜAbd Allāh b. Sahl al-ᶜAskarī (fl. 4th/10th c.); S: ed. A. Zaghlūl, Beirut: DKI, 1988; FI: '*nāqiṣ min ākhirihi*'/'*incomplete in the end*'; C: adab – proverbs. (cf. no. 292)

(1405) Makh/4 266b/18–19 *al-Naḥl – The [Book of] Bees*; popular title with several possibilities including al-Zubayr Ibn Bakkār (d. 256/870) (Ibn al-Sāᶜī, *Durr*, 371) and Muḥammad b. Isḥāq al-Ahwāzī (fl. 3rd/9th c.); (GAS, VIII, 199); alternatively this could be *K. al-nakhl* by Abū Ḥātim al-Sijistānī (255/869); (ed. I. al-Sāmarrāʾī, Riyad: Dār al-liwāʾ/Beirut: MR, 1985). FI: '*makhrūm al-awwal*'/'*incomplete in the beginning*'; C: lexicography.

(1406) Makh/4 266b/19 *Min Sirr al-adab – [Parts] of The Secret of Adab*; most likely *Fiqh al-lugha wa-sirr al-ᶜarabīya* also known as *Sirr al-adab fī majārī kalām al-ᶜArab*; A: al-Thaᶜālibī (d. 429/1038); S: Orfali, *Works*, no. 7; Q: '1st'; C: lexicography. (cf. nos. 551, 958a)

(1407) Makh/4 266b/19 *Alfāẓ – Words*; A: Ibn al-Sikkīt (d. 244/858); S: IN, I/1, 220; FI: '*wa-fīhā naqṣ yasīr*'/'*minor lacunae*'; C: lexicography. (cf. no. 36)

(1408) Makh/4 267a/1 *Min Sībawayh – [Parts] of [The Book by] Sībawayh*; A: ᶜAmr b. ᶜUthmān Sībawayh (d. 180/796); S: ed. ᶜA.M. Hārūn, Cairo: DQa, 1968–77; C: grammar. (cf. no. 550)

(1409) Makh/4 267a/1 *Min al-Jamhara – [Parts] of The Gathering Together*; A: Ibn Durayd (d. 321/933); S: *Jamharat al-lugha*, ed. I. Shams al-Dīn, Beirut: DKI, 2005; C: lexicography.

(1410) Makh/4 267a/1 *Min al-Lāmiᶜ – [Parts] of The Radiant*; commentary on al-Mutanabbī's poetry; A: Abū al-ᶜAlāʾ al-Maᶜarrī (d. 449/1058); S: *al-Lāmiᶜ al-ᶜazīzī sharḥ dīwān al-Mutanabbī*, ed. M. Mawlawī, Riyad: MMF, 2008; Q: '2nd, 3rd'; C: poetry – commentary.

(1411) Makh/4 267a/1 *Min Tadhkirat Abī ᶜAlī – [Parts] of Abū ᶜAlī's Treatise*; A: Abū ᶜAlī al-Ḥasan al-Fārisī (d. 377/987); S: contemporaneous authors are aware of this work (e.g. IKH, II, 80); Q: '3rd'; C: grammar/poetry – commentary (on difficult verses).

(1412) Makh/4 267a/2 *Min Uṣūl Ibn al-Sarrāj – [Parts] of Ibn al-Sarrāj's Principles*; A: Muḥammad b. al-Sarī Ibn al-Sarrāj (d. 316/929); S: *al-Uṣūl fī al-naḥw*, ed. ᶜA. al-Fatlī, Beirut: MR, 1985; Q: '2nd, 4th, *[in]* different *[hands]* (*mukhtalifa*)'; C: grammar.

(1413) Makh/4 267a/2 *Min al-Ṣiḥāḥ – [Parts] of The Sound [Dictionary]*; theoretically this could be any work by this title. However, the cataloguer clearly assumes that this term sufficiently identifies the work and it is thus likely that he is referring to a work he had mentioned before. As the thematic category 4 focuses on grammar, poetry and lexicography a *ḥadīth* work such as *al-Ṣiḥāḥ* by Razīn b. Muᶜāwiya al-ᶜAbdarī (d. 524/1129 or 535/1140) (cf. no. 697) is rather unlikely (especially as this title is explicitly ascribed to the author farther down (cf. no. 1435) and it is arguably *al-Ṣiḥāḥ* by A: Ismāᶜīl (b. Naṣr?) b. Ḥammād al-Jawharī (d. 398/1007–8) (cf. no. 698); S: ed. A.ᶜA. ᶜAṭṭār, Cairo: DKiA, 1956; Q: '8th, last *[*quire/*al-akhīr]*'; C: lexicography.

(1414) Makh/4 267a/2–3 *Min Iṣlāḥ al-manṭiq – [Parts] of Correcting Speech*; A: Ibn al-Sikkīt (d. 244/858); S: ed. ᶜA.M. Hārūn, Cairo: DM, 1949; Q: '1st'; C: lexicography. (cf. no. 25)

(1415) Makh/4 267a/3 *Min Sharḥ al-īḍāḥ – [Parts] of The Explanation of the Elucidation*; this popular title could refer to a variety of works, but the context of this section makes one of the commentaries on the grammar *al-Īḍāḥ fī al-naḥw* by Abū ᶜAlī al-Ḥasan al-Fārisī (d. 377/987) very likely (cf. no. 30a). The most likely author is A: ᶜAbd Allāh b. al-Ḥusayn al-ᶜUkbarī (d. 566/1219). A manuscript of this work, copied in 674/1275, is in Istanbul, Süleymaniye, Fatih 4908. Q: '8th'; C: grammar.

(1416) Makh/4 267a/3–4 *Mā ittafaqa lafẓuhū wa-ikhtalafa maᶜnāhū – What is Similar in Pronunciation and Different in Meaning*; most likely A: Hibat Allāh b. ᶜAlī Ibn al-Shajarī (d. 542/1148); S: ed. ᶜA. Rizq, Stuttgart 1992; Q: '1st'; C: lexicography. (cf. no. 1377)

(1417) Makh/4 267a/4 *al-Nuᶜūt – The Good Qualities*; A: Abū[163] ᶜUbayd al-Qāsim b. Sallām al-Harawī (d. 224/838); this is most likely the author referred to by the cataloguer as 'Abū ᶜUbayd', as the cataloguer refers to him with this *kunya* elsewhere in the catalogue (cf. nos. 38, 786, 1309a, 1311c, 1442). No such title is identifiable for this author (or for any other Ibn/Abū ᶜUbayd). *Nuᶜūt* was used in literary criticism in contradistinction to the *ᶜuyūb*, the bad qualities of a given poem or prose writing. Most likely this is an extract from one of his works on poetry such as his *K. al-shuᶜarāʾ* (IN, I/1, 216). Q: '2nd'; C: poetry – criticism?

(1418) Makh/4 267a/4 *al-Awsaṭ – The Middle-Sized Book*; A: Saᶜīd b. Masᶜada al-Akhfash al-Awsaṭ (d. 215/830); S: IN, I/1, 147: '*al-Awsaṭ fī al-naḥw*'; Q: '2nd'; C: grammar.

(1419) Makh/4 267a/4 *Min al-Fākhir – [Parts] of The Magnificent Book*; there are numerous possibilities for this title with a popular key word, but the thematic category makes a philological title most likely. The lexicographical work *al-ᶜUbāb al-zākhir wa-al-lubāb al-fākhir* by al-Ḥasan b. Muḥammad al-Ṣaghānī (d. 650/1252) is not very likely as '*al-Fākhir*' is not the most characteristic term of the title. It is more likely that it refers to the well-known *al-Fākhir*, the anthology of proverbs by A: al-Mufaḍḍal b. Salama (fl. 3rd/9th c.); S: ed. ᶜA. al-Ṭaḥāwī/ᶜA. al-Najjār, Cairo: IBḤ/DIKA, 1960. This is, for example, the only work that Ibn Khallikān cites with this title (IKH, IV, 205). Q: '2nd, 2nd'; C: adab – proverbs.

(1420) Makh/4 267a/4–5 *Min al-Thiyāb – [Parts] of [the Book of] Cloth*; A: Muḥammad b. Masᶜūd al-ᶜAyyāshī (d. early 4th/10th c.); S: IN, I/2, 686; Q: '3rd'; C: lexicography?

(1421) Makh/4 267a/5 *Min Mujarrad Kurāᶜ – [Parts] of The Purified*; A: ᶜAlī b. al-Ḥasan Kurāᶜ al-Naml (d. 310/922); S: *al-Mujarrad fī gharīb kalām al-ᶜarab wa-lughātihā*, ed. M. al-ᶜUmarī, Cairo: DM, 1992; Q: '1st'; C: lexicography.

(1422) Makh/4 267a/5–6 *Min Nawādir al-Qālī – [Parts] of al-Qālī's Rare Occurrences*; A: Ismāᶜīl b. al-Qāsim al-Qālī (d. 356/967); S: *K. dhayl al-Amālī wa-al-nawādir*, Cairo: Dār al-kutub, 1926; Q: '1st, 2nd, 3rd, 4th, 5th and [parts] of another manuscript (*min nuskha ukhrā*)'; C: philology.

(1423) Makh/4 267a/6 *Min Mujmal Ibn Fāris – [Parts] of The Summary [on Lexicography]*; A: Aḥmad Ibn Fāris (d. 395/1004); S: *al-Mujmal fī al-lugha*, ed. H.Ḥ. Ḥammūdī, Kuwait: al-Munaẓẓama al-ᶜarabīya, 1985; Q: '1st, 1st' '2nd, 3rd from another manuscript (*min nuskha ukhrā*)'; C: lexicography. (cf. no. 951)

(1424) Makh/5 267a/7 *Min al-Fākhir fī al-ḥawādith fī ayyām al-imām al-Nāṣir – [Parts] of The Magnificent Book on the Events in the Days of al-Nāṣir*;

referring to the ᶜAbbasid Caliph al-Nāṣir li-Dīn Allāh (d. 622/1225); A: Ibn al-Jawzī (d. 597/1200); S: Alwajī, *Muʾallafāt*, 161: '*al-Fākhir fī ayyām al-imām al-Nāṣir*'; C: history – ᶜAbbāsid.

(1425) Makh/5 267a/7 *Min Taʾrīkh Ibn al-Ṣābiʾ – [Parts] of Ibn al-Ṣābiʾ's Chronicle*; A: Hilāl b. al-Muḥassin al-Ṣābiʾ (d. 448/1056); S: IKH, V, 127; FI: '*dhukira fī al-tāʾ*' /'*mentioned under the letter tāʾ*' (cf. no. 243); C: history – Būyid.

(1426) Makh/5 267a/8 *Mukhtaṣar taʾrīkh – Summary of a Chronicle*; anonymous work with generic title; FI: '*ghayr tāmm al-ākhir*' /'*not complete in the end*'; C: history.

(1427) Makh/5 267a/8 *Taʾrīkh – A Chronicle*; anonymous work ('*ghayr maᶜrūf al-muṣannif*' /'*author not known*') with generic title; FI: '*makhrūm al-awwal*' /'*incomplete in beginning*'; C: history.

(1428) Makh/5 267a/8–9 *Min Murūj al-dhahab – [Parts] of The Meadows of Gold*; A: ᶜAlī b. al-Ḥusayn al-Masᶜūdī (d. 345/956); S: Engl. tr. P. Lunde, London 1989; ed. M.M. ᶜAbd al-Ḥamīd, Beirut: MAṢ, 1988; FI: '*nuqilat ilā al-rābiᶜa ᶜashara*' /'*moved to category 14*' (cf. nos. 1393, 1429);[164] C: history – universal. (cf. no. 971)

(1429) Makh/5 267a/9 *Min Futūḥ Miṣr – [Parts] of The Conquest of Egypt*; A: ᶜAbd al-Raḥmān b. ᶜAbd Allāh Ibn ᶜAbd al-Ḥakam (d. 257/871); S: ed. C.C. Torrey, New Haven 1922; FI: '*nuqilat ilayhā ayḍān*' /'*moved to it [category 14] as well*' (cf. nos. 1393, 1428); C: history – early Islamic.

(1430) Makh/6 267a/10 *Min [al-]Tafsīr – [Parts] of The Commentary*; also known as *al-Tafsīr al-kabīr* or *Mafātīḥ al-ghayb*; A: Muḥammad b. ᶜUmar Fakhr al-Dīn al-Rāzī Ibn al-Khaṭīb (d. 606/1210); S: ed. M. Muḥyī al-Dīn, Cairo: al-Bāhīya, 1933; This entry is most likely identical with MS: Süleymaniye, Fatih 313 & 314**, which is an unfinished copy from 604/1207 with gaps where the subheadings should be in the latter part of the manuscript. C: Koran – exegesis (*tafsīr*).[165]

(1431) Makh/6 267a/10 *Min Maᶜādin al-ibrīz – [Parts] of The Mines of Gold*; A: Yūsuf Sibṭ Ibn al-Jawzī (d. 654/1256); S: *Wāfī*, XXIX, 277; Q: '1st'; C: Koran – exegesis (*tafsīr*).

(1432) Makh/6 267a/11 *al-Tibyān fī iᶜrāb al-Qurʾān – The Exposition of the Koran's Inflexion*; A: ᶜAbd Allāh b. al-Ḥusayn al-ᶜUkbarī (d. 566/1219);

S: ed. ᶜA.M. al-Bajāwī, Cairo: IBḤ, 1976; Q: '2nd'; C: Koran – inflexion (*iᶜrāb*).

(1433) Makh/6 267a/11 *Wajīz al-Wāḥidī – Al-Wāḥidī's Concise Book*; A: ᶜAlī b. Aḥmad al-Wāḥidī (d. 468/1076); S: *al-Wajīz fī maᶜānī al-Qurᵓān al-ᶜAzīz*, ed. S.ᶜA. Dāwūdī, Damascus: DQa, 1995; Q: '2nd'; C: Koran – exegesis (*tafsīr*). (cf. no. 1372)

(1434) Makh/6 267a/11 *al-Kashshāf – The Revealer*; on account of the preceding works on the Koran, this is arguably A: Maḥmūd b. ᶜUmar al-Zamakhsharī (d. 538/1144); S: A.J. Lane, *A Traditional Muᶜtazilite Qurᵓān Commentary*, Leiden 2006; Q: '6th'; C: Koran – exegesis (*tafsīr*).

(1435) Makh/6 267a/12 *Min al-Ṣiḥāḥ – [Parts] of The Sound Traditions*; A: Razīn b. Muᶜāwiya al-ᶜAbdarī (d. 524/1129 or 535/1140); S: EI², M. Fierro, 'Razīn b. Muᶜāwiya'; Q: '1st, 3rd, 4th'; C: ḥadīth – collection. (cf. no. 697)

(1436) Makh/6 267a/12 *Min Sharḥ al-sunna – [Parts] of Explaining the Sunna*; popular title with several possibilities including al-Qāḍī al-Ḥusayn b. Muḥammad (d. 462/1069–70); (IKH, II, 134/5), al-Ḥasan b. ᶜAlī al-Barbahārī (d. 329/941); (*Wāfī*, XII, 147) and al-Ḥusayn b. Masᶜūd (Ibn) al-Farrāᵓ al-Baghawī (d. 516/1122?) (IKH, II, 136) with a preference for the latter because of the high number of summaries written of this work in the following decades and because 7th-/13th-c. manuscripts of works entitled '*Sharḥ al-sunna*' in the Süleymaniye collection are almost exclusively those by al-Baghawī (e.g. Süleymaniye, Fatih 809). Q: '1st'; C: ḥadīth – study of.

(1437) Makh/6 267a/12–13 *Min Akhbār Makka – [Parts] of the Reports on Mecca*; popular title with several possibilities, including Muḥammad b. Isḥāq al-Fākihī (fl. 3rd/9th c.) (ed. ᶜA. Ibn Duhaysh, Beirut: Dār Khiḍr, 1998), Muḥammad b. ᶜAbd Allāh al-Azraqī (d. 222/837) (ed. F. Wüstenfeld, Leipzig 1858) and Muḥammad b. ᶜUmar al-Wāqidī (d. 207/822) (IN, I/2, 308); Q: '1st'; C: history – regional.

(1438) Makh/6 267a/13 *Min Jamᶜ al-Ḥumaydī – [Parts] of Bringing Together and Comparing [the Two Ṣaḥīḥs]*; A: Muḥammad b. Futūḥ al-Ḥumaydī (d. 488/1095); S: *al-Jamᶜ bayna al-ṣaḥīḥayn*, ed. ᶜA.Ḥ. al-Bawwāb, Beirut: DIḤ, 1998; Q: '2nd, 4th, *[in]* different [hands] (*mukhtalif*)'; C: ḥadīth – study of.

(1439) Makh/6 267a/13 *Min [al-]Jam^{c} – [Parts] of Bringing Together and Comparing [the Two Ṣaḥīḥs]*; A: Muḥammad b. ^{c}Abd Allāh al-Jawzaqī (d. 388/998); S: GAS, I, 211: '*al-Jam^{c} bayna al-ṣaḥīḥayn*'; C: ḥadīth – study of.

(1440) Makh/6 267a/13 *Min al-Tirmidhī – [Parts] of al-Tirmidhī['s ḥadīth Collection]*; A: Muḥammad b. ^{c}Īsā al-Tirmidhī (d. 279/892); on account of the context of this section this is S: *al-Jāmi^{c} al-ṣaḥīḥ*, ed. A.M. Shākir; Cairo: MBḤ, 1937–65; Q: '5th'; C: ḥadīth – collection.

(1441) Makh/6 267a/14 *Min Ad^{c}iyat al-Ṭabarānī – [Parts] of al-Ṭabarānī's [Book of] Prayers*; A: Sulaymān b. Ayyūb al-Ṭabarānī (d. 360/971); S: GAL, I, 196 ('*Kitāb al-du^{c}ā$^{\circ}$*'); Q: '2nd'; C: prayer book.

(1442) Makh/6 267a/14 *Min [al-]Gharīb – [Parts] of Uncommon Words [in ḥadīth]*; on account of the preceding *ḥadīth* works this is most probably the *Gharīb al-ḥadīth* rather than his *al-Gharīb al-muṣannaf* or *Gharīb al-Qur$^{\circ}$ān*. A: Abū ^{c}Ubayd al-Qāsim b. Sallām al-Harawī (d. 224/838); S: *Gharīb al-ḥadīth*, Ḥ.M.M. Sharaf, Cairo: MLA, 1984–94; Q: '1st' '2nd from another manuscript (*min nuskha ukhrā*)'; C: ḥadīth – collection/lexicography. (cf. no. 786)

(1443) Makh/6 267a/14–15 *Min [al-]Gharīb – [Parts] of Uncommon Words [in ḥadīth]*; on account of the preceding *ḥadīth* works this is most probably *Gharīb al-ḥadīth* rather than his *Tafsīr gharīb al-Qur$^{\circ}$ān*, A: ^{c}Abd Allāh b. Muslim al-Dīnawarī Ibn Qutayba (d. 276/889); S: *Gharīb al-ḥadīth*, ed. ^{c}A. al-Jubūrī, Baghdad: Wizārat al-awqāf, 1977; Q: '2nd'; C: ḥadīth – collection/lexicography. (cf. no. 785)

(1444) Makh/6 267a/15 *Min al-Firdaws – [Parts] of The Paradise [of Wisdom]*; owing to the preceding *ḥadīth* works this is most probably a *ḥadīth* collection rather than works from other fields such as medicine (cf. no. 831), A: Shīrawayh b. Shahradār (d. 509/1115); S: *K. Firdaws al-akhbār*, ed. F.A. al-Zimirlī, Beirut: DKiA, 1987; MS: Süleymaniye, Laleli 648* (vol. 3); Q: '3rd' '2nd from another manuscript (*min nuskha ukhrā*)'; C: ḥadīth – collection.

(1445) Makh/6 267a/15–16 *Min Ṣifat al-ṣafwa – [Parts] of The Chosen Ones' Characteristics*; A: Ibn al-Jawzī (d. 597/1200); S: ed. M. Fākhūrī, Beirut: Dār al-ma^{c}rifa, 1985; Q: '1st', '2nd, 3rd, 8th, 10th in different hands (*mukhtalifat al-khaṭṭ*)'; C: sufism.

(1446) Makh/6 267a/16–17 *Min Qūt al-qulūb – [Parts] of The Nourishment of the Hearts*; A: Muḥammad b. ʿAlī al-Makkī (386/998); S: ed. ʿA. Madkūr/ʿĀ. al-Najjār, Cairo: HMAK, 2005–7; Germ. tr. Gramlich, *Nahrung der Herzen*; Q: '1st' '1st from another manuscript (*min nuskha ukhrā*)'; C: sufism. (cf. no. 850)

(1447) Makh/6 267a/17 *Min Sūq al-ʿarūs – [Parts] of The Bride's Place*; this entry could refer to the works by either ʿAbd al-Karīm b. ʿAbd al-Ṣamad al-Qaṭṭān (d. 478/1085) (MM, II, 207) on *qirāˀāt* or Ḥusayn b. Muḥammad al-Dāmaghānī (d. 478/1085) (MM, I, 633) on preaching. However, in light of his strong presence in this library (cf. no. 1445) this is arguably the work by A: Ibn al-Jawzī (d. 597/1200). S: Alwajī, *Muˀallafāt*, 143; Q: '1st' '2nd from another manuscript (*min nuskha ukhrā*)'; C: sermons.

(1448) Makh/6 267a/17–18 *Min al-Iḥyāˀ – [Parts] of The Revival [of the Religious Sciences]*; A: al-Ghazālī (d. 505/1111); S: ed. Cairo: Lajnat Nashr al-thaqāfa al-islāmīya, 1937–9; Q: 'of one exemplar six [quires] (*min aṣl*[166] *sitta*)' 'and three quires in different hands: 6th, 7th, 8th (*wa-minhu thalātha mukhtalifat al-khaṭṭ wa-huwa al-sādis wa-al-sābiʿ wa-al-thāmin*)'; C: sufism. (cf. no. 11)

(1449) Makh/6 267a/18–19 *Shiʿr Qays al-Majnūn – Poetry of Qays al-Majnūn*; part of the Majnūn Laylā romance; anonymous; S: *Dīwān Majnūn Laylā*, ed. A. Farrāj, Cairo: MMi, 1958; FI: '*makhrūm al-awwal*'/'*incomplete in the beginning*'; C: poetry – Umayyad. (cf. no. 597)

(1450) Makh/6 267a/19 *Shiʿr ʿAlqama b. ʿAbada – ʿAlqama b. ʿAbada's Poetry*; A: ʿAlqama b. ʿAbada al-Faḥl; S: eds L. al-Saqqāl and D. al-Khaṭīb, Aleppo: DKiA, 1969; C: poetry – pre-Islamic. (cf. no. 608)

(1451) Makh/6 267a/19 *Shiʿr al-Ḥuṭayˀa – Al-Ḥuṭayˀa's Poetry*; if this is indeed al-Ḥuṭayˀa the name is rather carelessly written. A: Jarwal b. Aws al-Ḥuṭayˀa (d. after 41/661?); S: ed. N.A. Ṭāhā, Cairo: MBḤ, 1958; the addition 'al-Ṭarrāz' is unclear, as no such *nisba* is known for this poet. Reading it as 'al-Ṭirāz', it may be a key word to identify a specific poem. FI: '*makhrūm al-awwal*'/'*incomplete in the beginning*'; C: poetry – pre-Islamic/early Islamic? (cf. nos. 596, 686)

(1452) Makh/6 267a/19–20 *Min Shiʿr ʿAdī b. al-Riqāʿ – [Parts] of ʿAdī b. al-Riqāʿ's Poetry*; A: ʿAdī b. Zayd b. al-Riqāʿ (d. shortly after 100/718); S:

Dīwān, ed. N.Ḥ. al-Qaysī/Ḥ.Ṣ. al-Ḍāmin, Baghdad: MII, 1987; Q: '4th quire (*al-juzʾ al-rābi*^{c})'; C: poetry – Umayyad.

(1453) Makh/6 267a/20 *Min Gharīb al-Qurʾān – [Parts] of The Uncommon Words in the Koran*; popular title with numerous possibilities, including the work by al-Sijistānī (d. c.330/942) (cf. no. 787), see also the index in IN; Q: 'a quire (*juzʾ*)'; C: Koran/lexicography.

(1454) Makh/6 267a/20 *Min al-Qurʾān al-*^{c}*azīz – [Parts] of The Venerated Koran*; C: Koran – text.

(1455) Makh/6 267a/20-267b/1 *Min Khuṭab Ibn Nubāta – [Parts] of The Sermons of Ibn Nubāta*; Scr('*khaṭṭ*'): Yaḥyā b. ^{c}Alī al-Khaṭīb al-Tibrīzī (d. 502/1109); A: ^{c}Abd al-Raḥīm b. Muḥammad Ibn Nubāta (fl. 4th/10th c.); S: ed. *Dīwān khuṭab*, Cairo: ^{c}Abbās Shaqrūn, 1982; C: sermons (*khuṭab*). (cf. nos. 350, 355)

(1456) Makh/7 267b/1 *Min Tajārib al-umam – [Parts] of The Experiences of Communities*; A: Aḥmad b. Muḥammad Miskawayh (d. 421/1030?); S: ed. H.F. Amedroz, Cairo: al-Tamaddun, 1914; Engl. tr. D.S. Margoliouth, *The Eclipse of the Abbasid Caliphate*, Oxford 1920–1; C: history – universal.

(1457) Makh/7 267b/1 *Min al-*^{c}*Umda – [Parts] of The Pillar*; numerous possibilities for this title with a popular key word from different fields of knowledge such as *al-*^{c}*Umda fī maḥāsin al-shi*^{c}*r wa-ādābihi* by al-Qayrawānī (d. 456/1063–4 or 463/1070–1) (cf. no. 734), *al-*^{c}*Umda* by al-Fūrānī (d. 461/1069) (cf. no. 724) and ^{c}*Umdat al-masālik fī siyāsat al-mamālik* by al-Manjanīqī (d. 626/1229) (cf. no. 562?); Q: '1st'[167] '1st, 1st of *[another]* exemplar (*min aṣl 1 1*)' 'and of it *[al-*^{c}*Umda]* of [another] exemplar 6th and of it 7th (*wa-minhu min aṣl 6 wa-minhu 7*)'; Ṣ.

(1458) Makh/7 267b/2 *Min Futūḥ Ibn A*^{c}*tham – [Parts] of Ibn A*^{c}*tham's Conquests*; A: Aḥmad Ibn A^{c}tham al-Kūfī (fl. 3rd/9th c.); S: ed. M. Khān, Hyderabad: DMU, 1968; Q: '7th, 7th'; Ṣ; C: history – early Islam. (cf. no. 814)

(1459) Makh/7 267b/2–3 *Min al-Mukhtār min Rabī*^{c} *al-abrār – [Parts] of The Selections from The Righteous' Spring*; alternative title for *Zahr al-rabī*^{c} *min rabī*^{c} *al-abrār* by Muḥammad b. Abī Bakr al-Rāzī (fl. 666/1268) (MM, III, 168), which is a summary of Maḥmūd b. ^{c}Umar al-Zamakhsharī's

(d. 538/1144) work *Rabī^{c} al-abrār wa-fuṣūṣ al-akhbār*; manuscripts bearing this title include, for instance, Süleymaniye, Laleli 1921. Q: '1st [quire]' 'another [quire] of *Rabī^{c} al-abrār*, on it [is written] "*A Selection from Rabī^{c} al-abrār*" (*ākhar min Rabī^{c} al-abrār ^{c}alayhi mukhtār Rabī^{c} al-abrār*)'; Ṣ; C: adab – anthology.

(1460) Makh/7 267b/3 *Min Madḥ al-Marzubānī – [Parts] of al-Marzubānī's Praise*; possibly *Akhbār al-awlād wa-al-zawjāt wa-al-ahl wa-mā jā$^{\circ}$a fīhim min madḥ wa-dhamm* by A: Muḥammad b. ^{c}Imrān al-Marzubānī (d. 384/994); S: IN, I/2, 413; Q: '1st'[168]; C: adab.

(1461) Makh/7 267b/3–4 *Min Tadhkirat Ibn Ḥamdūn – [Parts] of Ibn Ḥamdūn's Handbook*; A: Muḥammad b. al-Ḥasan Ibn Ḥamdūn (d. 562/1166–7); S: eds I. ^{c}Abbās and B. ^{c}Abbās, Beirut: DṢ, 1996; C: adab – anthology. (cf. no. 1556)

(1462) Makh/7 267b/4 *Min Tuḥfat al-albāb – [Parts] of The Gift of the Hearts*; FI: '*wa-huwa al-Mu^{c}rib ^{c}an akhbār al-mashriq wa-al-maghrib*'/'*and this is the eloquent book on the reports of east and west*'; A: Muḥammad b. ^{c}Abd al-Raḥmān/al-Raḥīm al-Māzinī (d. 565/1169–70) who authored *Tuḥfat al-albāb wa-nukhbat al-a^{c}jāb* (ed. A. Ramos, Madrid 1990) and *al-Mu^{c}rib an ba^{c}ḍ ^{c}ajā$^{\circ}$ib al-Maghrib* (ed. I. Bejarano, Madrid 1991). Either the cataloguer confused these two works or this copy combines them. Such travel writings contain a broad range of material, including natural history, cosmography and *^{c}ajā$^{\circ}$ib* (wonders/marvels). C: geography/adab.

(1463) Makh/8 267b/5 *Min al-Tamthīl – [Parts] of The Book of Exemplification*; A: al-Tha^{c}ālibī (d. 429/1038); S: *al-Tamthīl wa-al-muḥāḍara*, ed. ^{c}A. al-Ḥulw, Cairo: D^{c}AK, 1961; FI: '*nuskha thālitha min al-Tamthīl dhukirat fī al-tā$^{\circ}$*'/'3rd *[incomplete]* copy of the *Tamthīl* that was mentioned in the [alphabetical section on the letter] *tā$^{\circ}$*';[169] C: adab – anthology. (cf. nos. 253, 1292a)

(1464) Makh/8 267b/5 *Min Ma^{c}ārif Ibn Qutayba – [Parts] of Ibn Qutayba's [Book of] Noteworthy Information*; A: ^{c}Abd Allāh b. Muslim al-Dīnawarī Ibn Qutayba (d. 276/889); S: ed. Th. ^{c}Ukāsha, Cairo: WTh, 1960; FI: '*makhrūm*'/'*incomplete*'; C: history – early Islamic. (cf. no. 999)

(1465) Makh/8 267b/5-6 *Min Baṣā$^{\circ}$ir al-Tawḥīdī – [Parts] of al-Tawḥīdī's Treasures of Insightful Perception*; A: Abū Ḥayyān al-Tawḥīdī (d. 414/1023);

S: *al-Baṣāʾir wa-al-dhakhāʾir*; ed. W. al-Qāḍī, Beirut: DṢ, 1984–8; C: adab – anthology. (cf. nos. 204, 303, 1249e)

(1466) Makh/8 267b/6 *Sīrat Ibn Ṭūlūn* – *The Life of Ibn Ṭūlūn*; either by 1) ᶜAbd Allāh b. Muḥammad al-Balawī (fl. 4th/10th c.) (ed. M. Kurd ᶜAlī, Damascus 1939) or 2) Aḥmad b. Yūsuf Ibn al-Dāya (d. 340/951?) (not extant, incorporated into *al-Mughrib fī ḥula al-Maghrib* by ᶜAlī b. Mūsā al-Maghribī (685/1286), ed. Sh. Dayf, Cairo: DM, 1953–5); NC: 3; FI: '*fī baᶜḍihā naqṣ*' / '*with some lacunae*'; C: biography – Ṭūlūnid. (cf. no. 565)

(1467) Makh/9 267b/6 *Min Ṣuwar al-aqālīm* – *[Parts] of The Climes' Illustrations*; attr. to A: Aḥmad b. Sahl al-Balkhī (d. 322/934); S: EI[3], H.H. Biesterfeldt, 'al-Balkhī, Abū Zayd'; C: geography.

(1468) Makh/9 267b/7 *Min al-Wāfidīn wa-al-wāfidāt* – *[Parts] of the Male and Female Envoys*; A: al-ᶜAbbās b. Bakkār al-Ḍabbī (d. 222/837); S: *Akhbār al-wāfidīn min al-rijāl min ahl al-Baṣra wa-al-Kūfa ᶜalā Muᶜāwiya Ibn Abī Sufyān*, ed. S. al-Shihābī, Beirut: MR, 1984, 19–38; *Akhbār al-wāfidāt min al-nisāʾ ᶜalā Muᶜāwiya*, ed. S. al-Shihābī, Beirut: MR, 1983; C: history/adab.

(1469) Makh/9 267b/7 *Min al-Masālik wa-al-mamālik* – *[Parts] of Routes and Kingdoms*; popular title with several possibilities, including Ibn Khurradādhbih (d. *c.*300/911) (IN, I/2, 458) and Aḥmad b. al-Ṭayyib al-Sarakhsī (d. 286/899) (IN, I/2, 459); C: geography?

(1470) Makh/9 267b/7 *Min Manāsik al-ḥajj* – *[Parts] of the Pilgrimage Rituals*; FI: '*muṣawwar*' / '*illustrated*'; as this is an illustrated manuscript it is unlikely that it is the draft by Aḥmad b. ᶜĪsā Ibn Qudāma (d. 643/1245–6) held in the library's section of complete manuscripts (cf. no. 947). There are numerous other possibilities, including Ibrāhīm b. Isḥāq al-Ḥarbī (d. 285/898) (MU, I, 50), Makkī b. Abī Ṭālib al-Qaysī al-Andalusī (d. 437/1045) (MU, VI, 2714), al-Ḥusayn b. Naṣr Ibn Khamīs al-Mawṣilī Shāfiᶜī (d. 552/1157) (IKH, II, 139), ᶜUthmān b. ᶜAbd al-Raḥmān Ibn al-Ṣalāḥ (d. 643/1245) (IKH, III, 244) and al-Asadī (d. 150/767) (cf. no. 938); C: rituals – ḥajj.

(1471) Makh/9 267b/7–8 *Min al-Shifāʾ* – *[Parts] of The Book of Healing*; A: Ibn Sīnā (d. 428/1037); S: eds S.Z. Qanawātī, M.R. Madwar, I. Aḥmad *et al.*, Cairo: al-Amīrīya, HMAK *et al.*, 1952–83; MS: Süleymaniye, Fatih 3211**; C: philosophy.

(1472) Makh/9 267b/8 *Taᶜbīr al-ruʾyā – Dream Interpretation*; popular title with numerous possibilities including the manuals by Khargūshī (d. 406/1015 or 407/1016) (cf. no. 206), ᶜAbd al-Wāḥid (fl. 4th/10th c.) (cf. no. 260) and Muḥammad Ibn Sīrīn (d. 110/728) (cf. no. 261); FI: '*makhrūm al-awwal*'/'*incomplete in the beginning*'; C: oneiromancy.

(1473) Makh/9 267b/8 *Min al-Āthār al-ᶜulwīya – [Parts] of The Meteorological Phenomena*; referring to the Meteorology of Aristotle and of Theophrastus; S: EI², B. Lewin, 'al-Āthār al-ᶜUlwiyya'; Q: '1st'; C: astronomy/meteorology (influence of the spheres).

(1474) Makh/9 267b/8 *Min al-Furūsīya – [Parts] of Equitation*; generic/popular title with numerous possibilities (cf. Al-Sarraf, 'Mamluk Furūsīyah Literature') including the work by Abū ᶜAbd Allāh Muḥammad b. Yaᶜqūb Ibn Akhī Ḥizām al-Khuttalī (fl. late 3rd/9th c.) (cf. no. 830), but in most instances the catalogue lists these works without an author (cf. nos. 833, 834, 835); Q: '1st'; C: equitation.

(1475) Makh/9 267b/9 *K. Arṭāmīdūrūs fī taᶜbīr – Artemidorus on Dreams*; A: Artemidorus of Ephesus (fl. 2nd c. CE); S: ed. T. Fahd, *Artémidore d'Éphèse. Le livre des songes. Traduit du grec en arabe par Ḥunayn b. Isḥāq*, Damascus: IFD, 1964; Q: 'second tract'/'*al-maqāla al-thāniya*'; C: oneiromancy.

(1476) Makh/9 267b/9–10 *Min Tafsīr Jālīnūs li-Fuṣūl Buqrāṭ – [Parts] of Galen's Commentary on Hippocrates' Aphorisms*; A: Galen; S: Ullmann, *Medizin*, 50; Q: '1st'; C: medicine.

(1477) Makh/9 267b/10–11 *Min Qānūn Ibn Sīnā – [Parts] of Ibn Sīnā's Canon*; A: Ibn Sīnā (d. 428/1037); S: M.A. al-Ḍannāwī, Beirut: DKI, 1999; FI: '*16 mujallad*ᵃⁿ *mutadākhila mukhtalifat al-khaṭṭ wa-al-qaṭ*ᶜ'/'*sixteen bound volumes, overlapping, in different hands and different formats*'; C: medicine. (cf. no. 861)

(1478) Makh/9 267b/11 *Min al-Fākhir fī al-Ṭibb – [Parts] of The Magnificent Book on Medicine*; A: al-Rāzī (Rhazes) (d. 313/925 or 323/935); S: IAU, III, 38/9; Q: '1st, 2nd'; C: medicine.

(1479) Makh/9 267b/11 *Min al-adwiya al-mufrada – [Parts] of The Simple Drugs*; see comments in no. 105; probably A: Rashīd al-Dīn Ibn al-Ṣūrī (d. 639/1242); S: *Wāfī*, XIV, 125; Q: '3rd'; C: pharmacology. (cf. no. 105, 193)

(1480) Makh/9 267b/11-12 *Min Minhāj – [Parts] of The Method [of Demonstrating What Man Uses]*; A: Yaḥyā b. ^{c}Īsā Ibn Jazla (d. 493/1100); S: *Minhāj al-bayān fīmā yasta^{c}miluhu al-insān*, eds M.M. Badawī and F. al-Ḥafyān, Cairo: JDA, 2010; Q: '1st'; C: pharmacology. (cf. no. 1030)

(1481) Makh/9 267b/12 *Min Manāfi^{c} al-a^{c}ḍāʾ – [Parts] of [the Treatise on] the Organs' Functions*; A: Galen; S: Savage-Smith, *Shelflist*, 63–4; Q: '2nd, 3rd', '1st, 2nd'; C: medicine.

(1482) Makh/9 267b/12–13 *Min al-Mukhtār fī al-ṭibb – [Parts] of the Choice Book on Medicine*; A: ^{c}Alī b. Aḥmad Ibn Hubal (d. 610/1213); S: ed. Hyderabad: DMU, 1943–4; FI: '*mukhtalifat al-khaṭṭ wa-al-qaṭ^{c}*'/'*in different hands and different formats*'; C: medicine.

(1483) Makh/9 267b/13 *Min al-Malikī fī al-ṭibb – [Parts] of the Royal Book on Medicine*; A: ^{c}Alī b. al-^{c}Abbās al-Majūsī (fl. 4th/10th c.) ('Haly Abbas'); S: EI^{3}, F. Micheau, "^{c}Alī b. al-^{c}Abbās al-Majūsī'; FI: '*mukhtalifat al-khaṭṭ wa-al-qaṭ^{c}*'/'*in different hands and different formats*'; C: medicine.

(1484) Makh/9 267b/13–14 *Min al-Manṣūrī fī al-ṭibb – [Parts] of The Manṣūri Book of Medicine*; A: al-Rāzī (Rhazes) (d. 313/925 or 323/935); S: P. de Koning, *Trois traités d'anatomie arabes*, Leiden 1903; Q: '1st'; FI: '*makhrūm fī ākhirihi*'/'*incomplete in the end*'; C: medicine. (cf. no. 1035)

(1485) Makh/10 267b/14 *al-Bayṭara – The Book on Veterinary Medicine*; A: Aḥmad b. al-Ḥasan b. al-Aḥnaf (d.?); S: Grube, *Hippiatrica Arabica Illustrata*; C: veterinary medicine.

(1486) Makh/11 267b/15 *Min Dīwān Abī Nuwās Riwāyat Ḥamza – [Parts] of Abū Nuwās' Diwan in the Transmission of Ḥamza [al-Iṣfahānī]*; A: al-Ḥasan b. Hāniʾ Abū Nuwās (d. between mid-198 and early 200/813–5); S: eds E. Wagner and G. Schoeler, Wiesbaden and Beirut 1958–2006; MS: Süleymaniye, Fatih 3775**; C: poetry – ^{c}Abbāsid. (cf. no. 390)

(1487) Makh/11 267b/15 *Min Dīwān Ḥayṣa*[170] *Bayṣa – [Parts] of Ḥayṣa Bayṣa's Diwan*; Scr('*bi-khaṭṭ*') & A: Sa^{c}d b. Muḥammad Ḥayṣa Bayṣa (d. 574/1179); S: eds M. Jāsim and Sh. Shukr, Baghdad: Wizārat al-i^{c}lām, 1974–5; C: poetry – Saljūq. (cf. nos. 407, 1618)

(1488) Makh/12 267b/15–16 *Min Ash^{c}ār al-Hudhalīyīn*[171] *– [Parts] of the Poems of Those Belonging to the Hudhalī Tribe*; Scr('*wa-minhā ayḍan* *[bi-khaṭṭihi]*' probably in the sense of referring back to the previous entry's scribe who seemingly copied part of this entry as well): Sa^c^d b. Muḥammad Ḥayṣa Bayṣa (d. 574/1179); S: *Dīwān al-Hudhalīyīn*, eds M. Abū al-Wafā' and A. Zayn, Cairo: DKM, 1945–50; C: poetry – anthology – pre-Islamic/ early Islamic. (cf. nos. 113, 1301, 1575)

(1489) Makh/12 267b/16 *Min Shi^c^r al-^c^Imād al-Kātib – [Parts] of al-^c^Imād al-Kātib's Poetry*; A: Muḥammad b. Muḥammad ^c^Imād al-Dīn al-Kātib al-Iṣfahānī (d. 597/1201); S: *Dīwān*, ed. N. Rashīd, Mosul: Jāmi^c^at al-mawṣil, 1983; C: poetry – Ayyūbid. (cf. nos. 1045, 1659)

(1490) Makh/12 267b/16 *Min Azjāl Ibn Quzmān – [Parts] of Ibn Quzmān's Zajal Poems*; A: Muḥammad Ibn Quzmān (d. 555/1160); S: *Todo Ben Quzmān*, ed. E.G. Gómez, Madrid 1972; C: poetry – zajal. (cf. nos. 1589, 1594)

(1491) Makh/13 267b/17 *Min Dīwān Ibn Munīr – [Parts] of Ibn Munīr's Diwan*; A: Aḥmad b. Munīr al-Ṭarābulusī al-Raffā' (d. 548/1153); S: ed. ^c^U.^c^A. Tadmurī, Beirut: DJ, 1986; C: poetry – Zangid. (cf. nos. 1043, 1622, 1657)

(1492) Makh/13 267b/17 *Min Shi^c^r al-Ṣābi' – [Parts] of al-Ṣābi''s Poetry*; most likely A: Ibrāhīm b. Hilāl al-Ṣābi' (d. 384/994), whose poetry is included in several places in this catalogue (cf. nos. 635, 1305); S: *Shi^c^r Abī Isḥāq al-Ṣābi'*, ed. M. Gharīb, Alexandria: Markaz al-Babāṭīn, 2010; Q: '1st'; C: poetry – Būyid. (cf. no. 1042)

(1493) Makh/13 267b/17 *Dīwān ^c^Arqala – [Parts] of ^c^Arqala's Diwan*; A: Ḥassān b. Numayr ^c^Arqala al-Kalbī (d. *c.*567/1171–2) (cf. no. 82?); S: ed. A. al-Jindī, Damascus: MLA, 1970; FI: '*makhrūm*'/'*incomplete*'; C: poetry – Zangid/Ayyūbid.

(1494) Makh/13 267b/17–18 *Min Shi^c^r Ṣāliḥ b. ^c^Abd al-Quddūs – [Parts] of Ṣāliḥ b. ^c^Abd al-Quddūs' Poetry*; A: Ṣāliḥ b. ^c^Abd al-Quddūs al-Baṣrī (d. 167/783); S: ^c^A. Khaṭīb, *Ṣāliḥ b. ^c^Abd al-Quddūs al-Baṣrī*, Baghdad: Dār Manshūrāt al-Baṣrī, 1967; C: poetry – Umayyad/^c^Abbāsid.

(1495) Makh/13 267b/18 *Min Dīwān Bashshār – [Parts] of Bashshār's Diwan*; A: Bashshār b. Burd (d. 167/783); S: GAS, II, 455–7; the reading of 'Bashshār' is not certain, but the context of the preceding entry makes it likely: both authors lived during the same period and were executed by the ᶜAbbasid Caliph al-Mahdī for unbelief in the same year. C: poetry – Umayyad/ᶜAbbāsid.

(1496) Makh/13 267b/18 *Min Shiᶜr Ibn Ḥajjāj – [Parts] of Ibn Ḥajjāj's Poetry*; A: al-Ḥusayn b. Aḥmad Ibn al-Ḥajjāj (d. 391/1001); S: Ibn Nubāta, *Talṭīf al-mizāj min shiᶜr Ibn al-Ḥajjāj*, ed. N.ᶜA. Muṣṭafā, Sūsa: Dār al-Maᶜārif, 2001; contemporary authors such as Ḥāzim al-Qarṭājannī (d. 684/1285) name him also as 'Ibn Ḥajjāj' without article (cited in v. Gelder, *Bad and the Ugly*, 110); C: poetry – Būyid. (cf. nos. 1599, 1649, 1672, 1688)

(1497) Makh/13 267b/18 *Muwashshaḥāt Ibn Sanāᵓ al-Mulk – Ibn Sanāᵓ al-Mulk's Poems in the Muwashshaḥ Rhyme Scheme*; A: Hibat Allāh b. Jaᶜfar Ibn Sanāᵓ al-Mulk (d. 608/1211); S: *Dār al-ṭirāz: poétique du muwashshaḥ*, ed. J. Rikābī, Damascus 1949; C: poetry – Ayyūbid.

(1498) Makh/14 268a/1 *Min al-Faraj baᶜda al-shidda – [Parts] of Relief after Hardship*; popular title with several possibilities, but most likely is the famous book by A: al-Muḥassin b. ᶜAlī al-Tanūkhī (d. 384/994); S: ed. ᶜA. al-Shāljī, Beirut: DṢ, 1978; Q: '1st'; C: adab – anthology. (cf. nos. 823, 1510)

(1499) Makh/14 268a/1 *Min Yatīmat al-dahr – [Parts] of The Unique/Orphaned Book of the Ages*; A: al-Thaᶜālibī (d. 429/1038); S: *Yatīmat al-dahr fī maḥāsin ahl al-ᶜaṣr*, ed. M. ᶜAbd al-Ḥamīd, Beirut: DKI, 1979; Q: '1st'; C: poetry/adab – anthology. (cf. nos. 1388, 1501, 1506, 1509, 1520, 1524, 1558)

(1500) Makh/14 268a/1 *Min Zahr al-ādāb – [Parts] of The Flowers of Adab [and Fruits of Hearts]*; A: Ibrāhīm b. ᶜAlī al-Ḥuṣrī al-Qayrawānī (d. 413/1022); S: *Zahr al-ādāb wa-thamar al-albāb*, ed. ᶜA.M. al-Bajāwī, Cairo: DIKA, 1953; Q: '3rd'; C: adab – anthology. (cf. nos. 541, 1272)

(1501) Makh/14 268a/2 *Min Yatīmat al-dahr – [Parts] of The Unique/Orphaned Book of the Ages*; A: al-Thaᶜālibī (d. 429/1038); S: *Yatīmat al-dahr fī maḥāsin ahl al-ᶜaṣr*, ed. M. ᶜAbd al-Ḥamīd, Beirut: DKI, 1979; Q: '3rd'; C: poetry/adab – anthology. (cf. nos. 1388, 1499, 1506, 1509, 1520, 1524, 1558)

(1502) Makh/14 268a/2 *Min al-Durr al-maknūn – [Parts] of The Hidden Pearls*; the book is referred to elsewhere in the catalogue as '*al-Maṣūn fī sirr al-hawā al-maknūn*' (cf. nos. 1013, 1104), but Yāqūt al-Ḥamawī cites it also as '*al-Maṣūn wa-durr al-maknūn*' (MU, I, 160). A: Ibrāhīm b. ᶜAlī al-Ḥuṣrī al-Qayrawānī (d. 413/1022); S: ed. al-N.ᶜA. Shaᶜlān, Cairo: Dār al-ᶜArab li-l-Bustānī, 1989; Q: '2nd'; C: adab/love literature.

(1503) Makh/14 268a/2 *Min Zahr al-riyāḍ – [Parts] of The Gardens' Flower*; A: Muḥammad b. ᶜImrān al-Marzubānī (d. 384/994); S: MU, VI, 2583: '*al-Riyāḍ fī akhbār al-mutayyamīn*'; FI: '*ghayr mutawāliya*' / '*[the quires/leaves are] non-consecutive*'; C: adab – love literature/theory.

(1504) Makh/14 268a/3 *Min al-Aghānī – [Parts] of [the Book] of Songs*; A: Abū al-Faraj al-Iṣfahānī (d. 356/967); S: eds I. ᶜAbbās, I. al-Saᶜᶜāfīn and B. ᶜAbbās, Beirut: DṢ, 2004; Q: '8th, 30th'; C: poetry/adab.

(1505) Makh/14 268a/3 *Min Luzūm mā lā yalzam – [Parts] of Self-Imposed Constraints*; A: Abū al-ᶜAlāᵓ al-Maᶜarrī (d. 449/1058); S: ed. I. al-Ibyārī, Cairo: WTa, 1959; Q: '1st, 3rd'; C: poetry – Ḥamdānid/Mirdāsid. (cf. nos. 899, 905, 1525)

(1506) Makh/14 268a/3 *Min Yatīmat al-dahr – [Parts] of The Unique/Orphaned Book of the Ages*; A: al-Thaᶜālibī (d. 429/1038); S: *Yatīmat al-dahr fī maḥāsin ahl al-ᶜaṣr*, ed. M. ᶜAbd al-Ḥamīd, Beirut: DKI, 1979; Q: '2nd, 3rd'; C: poetry/adab – anthology. (cf. nos. 1388, 1499, 1501, 1509, 1520, 1524, 1558)

(1507) Makh/14 268a/4 *Min Nishwār al-muḥāḍara – Multiple-Text Manuscript with the Assembly's Elegant Talks*; A: al-Muḥassin b. ᶜAlī al-Tanūkhī (d. 384/994); S: *Nishwār al-muḥāḍara wa-akhbār al-mudhākara*, ed. ᶜA. al-Shāljī, Beirut: DṢ, 1971–3, Q: '1st'; C: adab – anthology. (cf. nos. 1227a, 1523)

(1508) Makh/14 268a/4 *Min al-Ṣāhil wa-al-shāḥij – [Parts] of The Neigher and the Brayer*; A: Abū al-ᶜAlāᵓ al-Maᶜarrī (d. 449/1058); S: *Risālat al-Ṣāhil wa-al-shāḥij*, ed. ᶜĀ.ᶜA. Bint al-Shāṭiᵓ, Cairo: DM, 1975; Q: '1st'; C: political thought – mirror for princes.

(1509) Makh/14 268a/4 *Min Yatīmat al-dahr – [Parts] of The Unique/Orphaned Book of the Ages*; A: al-Thaᶜālibī (d. 429/1038); S: *Yatīmat al-dahr fī maḥāsin ahl al-ᶜaṣr*, ed. M. ᶜAbd al-Ḥamīd, Beirut: DKI, 1979; FI: '*bi-ghayr jild*' / '*without binding*'; C: poetry/adab – anthology. (cf. nos. 1388, 1499, 1501, 1506, 1520, 1524, 1558)

(1510) Makh/14 268a/5 *Min al-Faraj ba^{c}da al-shidda – [Parts] of Relief after Hardship*; popular title with several possibilities, but most likely is the famous book by A: al-Muḥassin b. ^{c}Alī al-Tanūkhī (d. 384/994); S: ed. ^{c}A. al-Shāljī, Beirut: DṢ, 1978; Q: '1st'; C: adab – anthology. (cf. nos. 823, 1498)

(1511) Makh/14 268a/5 *Min Naṣīḥat al-ṭullāb – [Parts] of Advice for the Seeker*; A: al-Ḥārith b. Asad al-Muḥāsibī (d. 243/857); S: GAS, I, 642: '*al-Naṣīḥa li-l-ṭālibīn wa-al-farq bayna al-taḥqīq wa-al-mudda^{c}īn*'; Q: '1st'; C: sufism?

(1512) Makh/14 268a/5–6 *Min Bustān al-adab – [Parts] of The Garden of Adab*; FI: '*raththh*[172] *mukhtār talīhi ajzā' fī mujallad*' / '*worn-out [manuscript], selection followed by parts in a volume*'; no such title is identifiable, but as this volume consists of a select abridgment of the work and volumes (of the original text?) it must have been a fairly well-known text. Consequently, this may be *al-Bustān wa-qā^{c}idat al-ḥikma wa-shams al-ādāb* by the physician Yuḥannā/Yaḥyā Ibn Māsawayh (d. 243/857) (GAS, III, 234). C: medicine?

(1513) Makh/14 268a/6 *al-Mu^{c}ammarīn – [The Book of] Those Who Lived to an Advanced Age*; no such title by an author Abū/Ibn ^{c}Ubayda is identifiable. Most likely the cataloguer erroneously assumed that the book by Abū Ḥātim al-Sijistānī (255/869) (ed. I. Goldziher, *K. al-Mu^{c}ammarīn, Abhandlungen zur arabischen Philologie*, ii, Leiden 1889) was authored by al-Sijistānī's teacher Abū ^{c}Ubayda Ma^{c}mar b. al-Muthannā al-Taymī (d. between 207/822 and 213/828), who is prominently quoted in al-Sijistānī's book. C: biographies. (cf. no. 986)

(1514) Makh/14 268a/6–7 *Min Shi^{c}r Ibn al-Rūmī – [Parts] of Ibn al-Rūmī's Poetry*; A: ^{c}Alī b. al-^{c}Abbās Ibn al-Rūmī (d. 283/896?); S: *Dīwān*, ed. H. Naṣṣār, Cairo: HMAK, 1973–81; Q: '1st, 1st, 1st, 1st, 3rd, 5th'; C: poetry – ^{c}Abbāsid. (cf. nos. 393, 1082)

(1515) Makh/14 268a/7 *Min Anwā^{c} al-Ṣūlī – [Parts] of al-Ṣūlī's Species*; A: Muḥammad b. Yaḥyā al-Ṣūlī (d. 335/947); S: EI^{2}, S. Leder, 'al-Ṣūlī'; Q: '1st'; C: poetry – commentary?

(1516) Makh/14 268a/7 *Min al-Bayān – [Parts] of the Book of Clarity [and Clarification]*; A: al-Jāḥiẓ (d. 255/868–9); S: *al-Bayān wa-al-tabyīn*, ed. ^{c}A.M. Hārūn, Cairo: MK, 1948–50; Q: '1st'; C: adab – anthology. (cf. nos. 205, 1237b?, 1249i, 1516, 1528)

(1517) Makh/14 268a/7 *Min al-Rawḍa – [Parts] of The Garden*; popular title with several possibilities (see IN, I/2, 457; I/2, 461; II/2, 454), but on the basis of contemporaneous references (e.g. MU, II, 793, 805; VI, 2472, 2684) the most likely work is A: Muḥammad b. Yazīd al-Mubarrad (d. 286/900); Q: '1st'; C: poetry – anthology.

(1518) Makh/14 268a/7–8 *Min al-Fasr wa-al-ma^{c}ānī – [Parts] of The Disclosure [: The Explanation of al-Mutanabbī's Diwan] and [its] Meanings*; A: Abū al-Fatḥ Ibn Jinnī (d. 392/1002); S: *al-Fasr: sharḥ Ibn Jinnī al-kabīr ^{c}alā Dīwān al-Mutanabbī*, ed. R. Rajab, Damascus: DY, 2004; Q: '2nd', '3rd'; Ibn Jinnī's book is generally only entitled 'al-Fasr', but the cataloguer presumably added the '*ma^{c}ānī*' for further clarification. Another – less likely – possibility would be that this is a second independent title. C: poetry – commentary. (cf. nos. 822, 1108, 1580, 1584)

(1519) Makh/14 268a/8 *Min al-Wuzarā$^{\circ}$ – [Parts] of [the Book] of Viziers*; A: Muḥammad b. Yaḥyā al-Ṣūlī (d. 335/947); S: Sourdel, 'Fragments d'al-Ṣūlī'; Q: '1st, 2nd, 3rd'; C: history – ^{c}Abbāsid.

(1520) Makh/14 268a/8 *Min al-Yatīma – [Parts] of The Unique/Orphaned Book [of the Ages]*; A: al-Tha^{c}ālibī (d. 429/1038); S: *Yatīmat al-dahr fī maḥāsin ahl al-^{c}aṣr*, ed. M. ^{c}Abd al-Ḥamīd, Beirut: DKI, 1979; Q: '3rd'; C: poetry/adab – anthology. (cf. nos. 1388, 1499, 1501, 1506, 1509, 1524, 1558)

(1521) Makh/14 268a/8–9 *Min al-Imtā^{c} wa-al-mu$^{\circ}$ānasa – [Parts] of [The Book of] Delightful and Intimate Conversations*; A: Abū[173] Ḥayyān al-Tawḥīdī (d. 414/1023); S: eds A. Amīn and A. al-Zayn, Cairo: LTTN, 1953; Q: '1st'; C: adab/philosophy. (cf. nos. 58, 81a)

(1522) Makh/14 268a/9 *al-Mulḥa bi-sharḥihā – The Pleasantry [of Inflection] Together with its Commentary*; A: al-Qāsim b. ^{c}Alī al-Ḥarīrī al-Baṣrī (d. 516/1122); S: ed. B.Y. Habbūd, Sidon: MAṢ, 1997; there are additional works with this title that may have been intended here. However, biographical dictionaries employ '*al-Mulḥa wa-sharḥuhā*' as a reference to al-Ḥarīrī (e.g. *Siyar*, XIX, 462) and this is confirmed by the corpus of surviving manuscripts of commentaries on '*al-Mulḥa*' (e.g. Süleymaniye, Laleli 3451/1, 3452/2, 3453, 3454/2 and 3524/2). C: grammar – didactic verse. (cf. no. 967)

(1523) Makh/14 268a/9 *Min Nishwār al-muḥāḍara – Multiple-Text Manuscript with The Assembly's Elegant Talks*; A: al-Muḥassin b. ᶜAlī al-Tanūkhī (d. 384/994); S: *Nishwār al-muḥāḍara wa-akhbār al-mudhākara*, ed. ᶜA. al-Shāljī, Beirut: DṢ, 1971–3; C: adab – anthology. (cf. nos. 1227a, 1507)

(1524) Makh/14 268a/9–10 *Min Yatīmat al-dahr – [Parts] of The Unique/ Orphaned Book of the Ages*; A: al-Thaᶜālibī (d. 429/1038); S: *Yatīmat al-dahr fī maḥāsin ahl al-ᶜaṣr*, ed. M. ᶜAbd al-Ḥamīd, Beirut: DKI, 1979; Q: '1st'; C: poetry/adab – anthology. (cf. nos. 1388, 1499, 1501, 1506, 1509, 1520, 1558)

(1525) Makh/14 268a/10 *Luzūm mā lā yalzam – Self-imposed Constraints*; A: Abū al-ᶜAlāᵓ al-Maᶜarrī (d. 449/1058); S: ed. I. al-Ibyārī, Cairo: WTa, 1959; C: poetry – Ḥamdānid/Mirdāsid. (cf. nos. 899, 905, 1505)

(1526) Makh/14 268a/10 *Min al-Ḥamāsa bi-sharḥihā – [Parts] of the [Book of] Bravery with its Commentary*; 'Ḥamāsa': A: Ḥabīb b. Aws Abū Tammām (d. 231/845 or 232/846); S: ed. M. Khafājī, Cairo: ᶜAlī Ṣabīḥ, 1955; 'Commentary': popular title with several possibilities, cf. GAS, II, 555–7; Q: '2nd'; C: poetry – anthology – commentary – ᶜAbbāsid. (cf. no. 1557; cf. nos. 335, 1280c, 1554, 1561 for the *Ḥamāsa* and nos. 669, 670, 671 for commentaries)

(1527) Makh/14 268a/10 *Min Bahjat al-majālis – [Parts] of The Gatherings' Splendour*; A: Ibn ᶜAbd al-Barr (d. 463/1070); S: eds M. al-Khūlī and ᶜA. al-Qiṭṭ, Cairo: al-Dār al-Miṣrīya, 1969–72; Q: '2nd'; FI: '*bi-ghayr jild*' / '*without binding*'; C: ḥadīth/adab. (cf. no. 196)

(1528) Makh/14 268a/10–11 *Min al-Bayān – [Parts] of The Book of Clarity [and Clarification]*; A: al-Jāḥiẓ (d. 255/868–9); S: *al-Bayān wa-al-tabyīn*, ed. ᶜA.M. Hārūn, Cairo: MK, 1948-50; C: adab – anthology. (cf. nos. 205, 1237b?, 1249i, 1516)

(1529) Makh/14 268a/11 *Min al-Furūsīya – [Parts] of [The Book on] Equitation*; A: Abū ᶜAbd Allāh Muḥammad b. Yaᶜqūb Ibn Akhī Ḥizām al-Khuttalī (fl. late 3rd/9th c.); this is either the author's book on hippiatrics *al-Furūsīya wa-al-bayṭara* (ed. & Germ. tr. Heide, *Hippiatrie*) or his lost work on equitation (Heide, *Hippiatrie*, 4). Q: '1st'; C: veterinary medicine/ equitation. (cf. no. 830)

(1530) Makh/14 268a/11 *Min al-Bayṭara – [Parts] of The Book on Veterinary Medicine*; popular title with numerous possibilities, but as the preceding title is ascribed to him, this is arguably A: Abū ᶜAbd Allāh Muḥammad b. Yaᶜqūb Ibn Akhī Ḥizām al-Khuttalī (fl. late 3rd/9th c.); S: ed. & Germ. tr. Heide, *Hippiatrie*; Q: '2nd'; C: veterinary medicine. (cf. no. 211)

(1531) Makh/14 268a/11–12 *Min Akhbār al-ruʾasāʾ wa-al-Jalīya – [Parts] of the Reports on Leading Men and Brilliant [Lights]*; this is most likely *al-Anwār al-jalīya fi akhbār al-dawla al-murābiṭīya*, which is also referred to as *K. akhbār al-ruʾasāʾ bi-al-Andalus*. A: Yaḥyā b. Muḥammad Ibn al-Ṣayrafī (d. 570/1174); S: Ṭāhā, *al-Taʾrīkh al-andalusī*, 239; Q: '3rd'; C: history – Andalusian. (cf. no. 84)

(1532) Makh/14 268a/12 *Min al-Zahra – [Parts] of [The Book of] the Flower*; most likely the work held elsewhere in the library by A: Muḥammad b. Dāwūd al-Iṣfahānī (d. 297/909); S: ed. I. al-Sāmarrāʾī, al-Zarqāʾ: al-Manār, 1985; Q: '2nd, 3rd'; C: adab/poetry – love literature – anthology. (cf. nos. 542, 1552, 1560)

(1533) Makh/14 268a/12 *Zaharāt al-alfāẓ – Flowers of Expressions*; no such title is identifiable. The key word '*zaharāt*' was rarely used in titles and the '*Zaharāt al-basātīn*' by the contemporaneous al-Qāsim b. Muḥammad al-Anṣārī (d. 642/1244) (al-Marrākushī, *al-Dhayl wa-al-takmila*, V/2, 566) would seem like a possibility. Yet this is a biographical dictionary of his teachers whereas the title here indicates rather an anthology of poetry or adab. C: adab/poetry?

(1534) Makh/14 268a/12 *Min Riyāḍ al-afkār – [Parts] of The Gardens of Consideration*; no such title is identifiable and this is most likely an anthology of prose and/or poetry. Q: '2nd, 3rd'; C: adab/poetry?

(1535) Makh/14 268a/12–13 *Min al-Ḥayawān – [Parts] of The Animals*; A: al-Jāḥiẓ (d. 255/868–9); S: ed. ᶜA. Hārūn, Cairo: MBḤ, 1938–45; C: adab. (cf. no. 339 where this manuscript was already mentioned; also cf. no. 1604)

(1536) Makh/14 268a/13 *Min Kitāb Ṭuᶜma – [Parts] of Ṭuᶜma's Book*; perhaps the *ḥadīth* transmitter Ṭuᶜma b. ᶜAmr al-ᶜĀmirī al-Kūfī (d. 168/784–5) (*Wāfī*, XVI, 443), yet a '*K. Ṭuᶜma*' is not known and the adab context of this section makes a *ḥadīth* work rather unlikely; Q: '2nd'.

(1537) Makh/14 268a/13 *Aḥsan mā sami*ᶜ*tu* – *The Best That I have Heard*; A: al-Thaᶜālibī (d. 429/1038); S: eds A. Tammām and S. ᶜĀṣim, Beirut: MKTh, 1989; C: poetry – anthology – Ghaznawid/Khwārazmshāh/adab.

(1538) Makh/14 268a/13 *Uns al-farīd* – *The Companion for the Lonely*; A: Aḥmad b. Muḥammad Miskawayh (d. 421/1030?); S: MU, II, 495; C: adab – anthology. (cf. no. 1209)[174]

(1539) Makh/14 268a/13–14 *Min al-Kāmil* – *[Parts] of The Perfect [Book on Adab]*; A: Muḥammad b. Yazīd al-Mubarrad (d. 286/900); S: *al-Kāmil fī al-adab*, ed. M.A. al-Dālī, Beirut: MR, 1986; Q: '1st, 2nd'; C: adab – anthology. (cf. nos. 888, 1545?)

(1540) Makh/14 268a/14 *Min al-Jalīs al-ṣāliḥ* – *The Good Companion [and the Intimate Adviser]*; this could be *al-Jalīs al-ṣāliḥ al-kāfī wa-al-anīs al-naṣīḥ al-shāfī* by Muᶜāfā b. Zakarīyāᵓ al-Jarīrī (d. 390/1000). However, the cataloguer referred to this book earlier as *al-Jalīs al-ṣāliḥ al-kāfī* (cf. no. 300). It is thus more likely the book by A: Yūsuf Sibṭ Ibn al-Jawzī (d. 654/1256); S: *al-Jalīs al-ṣāliḥ wa-al-anīs al-nāṣiḥ*, ed. F. Fawwāz, London 1989; Q: '3rd'; C: political thought – mirror for princes. (cf. no. 301)

(1541) Makh/14 268a/14 *Min Mukhtār al-Anwār* – *[Parts] of The Selection from the Book of Lights*; such a selection could refer to several works, including al-Ghazālī (d. 505/1111) (*Mishkāt al-anwār*, ed. A. ᶜAfīfī, Cairo: DQ, 1963) on sufism, Muḥammad b. Aḥmad Ibn al-Washshāᵓ (d. 325/937) (*al-Zāhir fī al-anwār*, MU, V, 2304) probably in the field of adab and the poetry anthology by ᶜAlī b. Muḥammad al-Shimshāṭī (fl. 4th/10th c.) (*al-Anwār wa-maḥāsin al-ash*ᶜ*ār*, ed. al-S.M. Yūsuf, Kuwait: Wizārat al-iᶜlām, 1977–8). Q: '3rd'. (cf. no. 1565)

(1542) Makh/14 268a/14–15 *Min al-Wasāᵓiṭ bayna al-Mutanabbī wa-khaṣmihi* – *[Parts] of the Mediations Between al-Mutanabbī and His Rival*; most likely *al-Wasāṭa bayna al-Mutanabbī wa-Khuṣūmihi* by A: ᶜAlī b. ᶜAbd al-ᶜAzīz al-Jurjānī (d. 392/1001–2?); S: eds M.A. Ibrāhīm and ᶜA.M. al-Bajāwī, Cairo: MAṢ, 1934; C: poetry – commentary. (cf. no. 1011?)

(1543) Makh/14 268a/15 *Min al-Ishārāt al-ilāhīya* – *[Parts] of the Divine Intimations*; A: Abū Ḥayyān al-Tawḥīdī (d. 414/1023); S: ed. W. al-Qāḍī, Beirut: DTh, 1973; Q: '1st, 2nd'; C: sufism.

(1544) Makh/14 268a/15 *Min ᶜUyūn al-akhbār – [Parts] of The Choicest Reports*; A: ᶜAbd Allāh b. Muslim al-Dīnawarī Ibn Qutayba (d. 276/889); S: eds M.M. Qamīḥa and Y.ᶜA. Ṭawīl, *ᶜUyūn al-akhbār*, Beirut: DKI, 1985; Q: '1st'; C: adab – anthology. (cf. no. 733)

(1545) Makh/14 268a/16 *Min al-Kāmil – [Parts] of The Perfect [Book]*; numerous possibilities for this title with a popular key word, but as the cataloguer had explicitly ascribed a '*Kāmil*' to al-Mubarrad six entries previously and as this section with incomplete manuscripts repeatedly lists the same titles separately but near to one another (cf. the *Yatīmat al-dahr* entries in this section nos. 1499, 1501, 1506, 1509, 1520, 1524, 1558) the most likely version is: A: Muḥammad b. Yazīd al-Mubarrad (d. 286/900); S: *al-Kāmil fī al-adab*, ed. M.A. al-Dālī, Beirut: MR, 1986; Q: '2nd'; C: adab – anthology. (cf. nos. 888, 1539)

(1546) Makh/14 268a/16 *Min Akhbār al-wuzarāᵓ – [Parts] of the Viziers' Reports*; several possibilities, including the history of viziers by Muḥammad b. Yaḥyā al-Ṣūlī (d. 335/947) (cf. no. 1519), Muḥammad b. ᶜAbdūs al-Jahshiyārī (d. 331/942) (*K. al-wuzarāᵓ wa-al-kuttāb*, ed. M. al-Saqā, Cairo: MBḤ, 1938, cited in IKH, IV, 29 as '*akhbār al-wuzarāᵓ*', cf. no. 1222f), Abū Ḥamza b. ᶜAlī ᶜUmāra al-Yamanī (d. 569/1174) (*K. fīhi al-nukat al-ᶜaṣrīya fī akhbār al-wuzarāᵓ al-miṣrīya*, ed. H. Derenbourg, Paris 1897) and Muḥammad b. Aḥmad al-Qādisī (d. 621/1224) (IKH, I, 329); Q: '2nd, 3rd, 4th'; C: history.

(1547) Makh/14 268a/16 *Min Maqātil al-fursān – [Parts] of Slain Heroes*; popular title with numerous possibilities (cf. indices IN and MU) including Abū ᶜUbayda Maᶜmar b. al-Muthannā al-Taymī (d. between 207/822 and 213/828); Muḥammad Ibn Ḥabīb (d. 245/860); Aḥmad Ibn Abī Ṭāhir Ṭayfūr (d. 280/893); Ismāᶜīl b. al-Qāsim al-Qālī (d. 356/967); Yaḥyā b. ᶜAlī al-Khaṭīb al-Tibrīzī (d. 502/1109); Q: '2nd'; C: adab. (cf. no. 997)

(1548) Makh/14 268a/16–17 *Min al-Fatḥ al-qudsī – [Parts] of [The Eloquent Rhetoric on] the Conquest of Jerusalem*; A: Muḥammad b. Muḥammad ᶜImād al-Dīn al-Kātib al-Iṣfahānī (d. 597/1201); S: *al-Fatḥ al-qussī fī al-fatḥ al-qudsī*, ed. M.M. Ṣubḥ, Cairo: DQ, 1965; Q: '2nd'; C: history – Ayyūbid. (cf. no. 816)

(1549) Makh/14 268a/17 *Min Ikhtiyār al-ᶜIqd – [Parts] of Choice of The [Unique] Necklace*; referring to Ibn ᶜAbd Rabbih (d. 328/940), *al-ᶜIqd al-farīd*; This is possibly the summary by A: Muḥammad b. Mukarram Ibn Manẓūr (630/1233–711/1311–2); S: Werkmeister, *Quellenuntersuchungen*, 38, although he would be quite late. C: adab – anthology.[175] (cf. nos. 730, 1555, 1590)

(1550) Makh/14 268a/17 *Min al-Muntaẓam fī taʾrīkh al-umam – [Parts] of The Well-Ordered History of Communities*; A: Ibn al-Jawzī (d. 597/1200); S: eds M. ᶜAṭā and M. ᶜAṭā, Beirut: DKI, 1992; Q: '2nd'; C: history – universal.

(1551) Makh/14 268a/17–18 *Min Awrāq al-Ṣūlī – [Parts] of The Book of Leaves*; A: Muḥammad b. Yaḥyā al-Ṣūlī (d. 335/947); S: part. ed. J. Heyworth-Dunne, London and Cairo 1934; IN, I/2, 464; Q: '1st'; C: adab/history. (cf. no. 43)

(1552) Makh/14 268a/18 *Min al-Zahra – [Parts] of [The Book of] the Flower*; most likely the work held elsewhere in the library by A: Muḥammad b. Dāwūd al-Iṣfahānī (d. 297/909); S: ed. I. al-Sāmarrāʾī, al-Zarqāʾ: al-Manār, 1985; Q: '1st'; C: adab/poetry – love literature – anthology. (cf. nos. 542, 1532, 1560)

(1553) Makh/14 268a/18 *Min al-Muwaffaqīyāt – [Parts] of the Blessed Tidings*; A: al-Zubayr Ibn Bakkār (d. 256/870); S: *al-Akhbār al-muwaffaqīyāt*, ed. S.M. al-ᶜĀnī, Baghdād: MᶜA, 1972; Q: '1st, 2nd, 4th'; C: history – ᶜAbbāsid/adab.

(1554) Makh/14 268a/18 *Min al-Ḥamāsa – [Parts] of the [Book of] Bravery*; A: Ḥabīb b. Aws Abū Tammām (d. 231/845 or 232/846); S: ed. M. Khafājī, Cairo: ᶜAlī Ṣabīḥ, 1955; Q: '2nd'; C: poetry – anthology – ᶜAbbāsid. (cf. nos. 335, 1280c, 1526, 1557, 1561)

(1555) Makh/14 268a/18 *Min al-ᶜIqd – [Parts] of The [Unique] Necklace*; A: Aḥmad b. Muḥammad Ibn ᶜAbd Rabbih (d. 328/940); S: *al-ᶜIqd al-farīd*, eds A. Amīn, A. al-Zayn ad I. al-Ibyārī, Cairo: LTTN, 1940–65; Q: '1st'; C: adab – anthology. (cf. nos. 730, 1549?, 1590)

(1556) Makh/14 268b/1 *Min al-Tadhkira al-Ḥamdūnīya – [Parts] of the Ḥamdūnian Handbook*; A: Muḥammad b. al-Ḥasan Ibn Ḥamdūn (d. 562/1166–7); S: eds I. ᶜAbbās and B. ᶜAbbās, Beirut: DṢ, 1996; C: adab – anthology. (cf. no. 1461)

(1557) Makh/14 268b/1 *Min al-Ḥamāsa bi-sharḥihā – [Parts] of the [Book of] Bravery with Its Commentary*; 'Ḥamāsa': A: Ḥabīb b. Aws Abū Tammām (d. 231/845 or 232/846); S: ed. M. Khafājī, Cairo: ᶜAlī Ṣabīḥ, 1955; 'Commentary': several possibilities, cf. GAS, II, 555–7; Q: '2nd'; C: poetry – anthology – commentary – ᶜAbbāsid. (cf. no. 1526; cf. nos. 335, 1280c, 1554, 1561 for the *Ḥamāsa* and nos. 669, 670, 671 for commentaries)

(1558) Makh/14 268b/1–2 *Min Yatīmat al-dahr – [Parts] of The Unique/ Orphaned Book of the Ages*; A: al-Thaᶜālibī (d. 429/1038); S: *Yatīmat al-dahr fī maḥāsin ahl al-ᶜaṣr*, ed. M. ᶜAbd al-Ḥamīd, Beirut: DKI, 1979; Q: '1st, 2nd, 3rd, 6th, 7th'; C: poetry/adab – anthology. (cf. nos. 1388, 1499, 1501, 1506, 1509, 1520, 1524)

(1559) Makh/14 268b/2 *Min Ansāb al-Munīra – [Parts] of the Genealogies of the Luminous [Book]*; insecure reading, probably extract of genealogies from a book entitled *al-Munīra*, such as *al-Shams al-munīra* by al-Ḥasan b. Muḥammad al-Ṣaghānī (d. 650/1252) (TI, 641–50, pp. 443–6); Q: '1st'.

(1560) Makh/14 268b/2 *Min al-Zahra – [Parts] of [The Book of] the Flower*; most likely the work held elsewhere in the library by A: Muḥammad b. Dāwūd al-Iṣfahānī (d. 297/909); S: ed. I. al-Sāmarrāᵓī, al-Zarqāᵓ: al-Manār, 1985; Q: '1st, 2nd'; C: adab/poetry – love literature – anthology. (cf. nos. 542, 1532, 1552)

(1561) Makh/14 268b/2–3 *Min al-Ḥamāsa – [Parts] of the [Book of] Bravery*; A: Ḥabīb b. Aws Abū Tammām (d. 231/845 or 232/846); S: ed. M. Khafājī, Cairo: ᶜAlī Ṣabīḥ, 1955; Q: '3rd, 4th, 5th, 6th'; C: poetry – anthology – ᶜAbbāsid. (cf. nos. 335, 1280c, 1526, 1554, 1557)

(1562) Makh/14 268b/3 *Min al-Taᵓrīkh – [Parts] of The History*; A: Muḥammad b. Yazīd al-Mubarrad (d. 286/900); this is most likely the author's genealogical work S: *Nasab ᶜAdnān wa-Qaḥṭān*, ed. ᶜA. al-Maymanī, Cairo: LTTN, 1936; Q: '1st'; C: history – pre-Islamic.

(1563) Makh/14 268b/3 *Min al-Kharāj – [Parts] of the [Book on] Taxation*; popular title with numerous possibilities, including Qudāma b. Jaᶜfar (d. 328/939–40 or 337/948?) (cf. no. 370) and Aḥmad Ibn Sahl (d. 270/883) (cf. no. 373); FI: '*mujallad*'/'*one bound volume*'; C: administrative handbook.

(1564) Makh/14 268b/3–4 *Min Nathr al-durr – [Parts] of Scattering the Pearls*; A: Manṣūr b. al-Ḥusayn al-Ābī (d. 421/1030); S: ed. M.ᶜA. Qurana *et al.*, Cairo: HMAK, 1980–90; Q: '2nd, 3rd'; C: adab – anthology. (cf. nos. 1208c?, 1350)

(1565) Makh/14 268b/4 *Min Mukhtār al-Anwār – [Parts] of The Selection from the Book of Lights*; no such title is identifiable and this selection could refer to several works (cf. no. 1541). Q: '1st, 3rd, 4th'. (cf. no. 1541)

(1566) Makh/14 268b/4 *Min Nuzhat al-qulūb – [Parts] of the Hearts' Delight*; the exegetical work by al-Sijistānī (d. *c.*330/942) that is known under this title (Kohlberg, *Ibn Ṭāwūs*, 345–6) or as *Gharīb al-Qurᵓān* (cf. nos. 787 and 789) is rather unlikely in this section. Arguably this is the adab work by A: Qudāma b. Jaᶜfar (d. 328/939–40 or 337/948?); S: MU, V, 2235; Q: '2nd'; C: adab.

(1567) Makh/14 268b/5 *Min Ḥilyat al-ādāb – [Parts] of The Ornament of Adab*; as no such title is identifiable, this is likely to be *Ḥilyat al-udabāᵓ* by A: Muḥammad b. Aḥmad al-Ḥakīmī (d. 336/948); S: MU, V, 2305; Q: '1st, 3rd'; C: adab/poetry – anthology.

(1568) Makh/14 268b/5 *Min al-Riyāsh al-muṣṭaniᶜī – [Parts] of The Splendid Attire*; commentary on the anthology *al-Ḥamāsa al-Riyāshīya* by Abū Riyāsh al-Qaysī (d. 339/950–1); EI³, G.J. van Gelder, 'Abū Riyāsh'); A: Abū al-ᶜAlāᵓ al-Maᶜarrī (d. 449/1058); S: MU, I, 182; Q: '1st'; C: poetry – commentary.

(1569) Makh/14 268b/5–6 *Min Nathr al-naẓm wa-ḥall al-ᶜaqd – [Parts] of Prosifying Poetry*; A: al-Thaᶜālibī (d. 429/1038); S: ed. A. Tammām, Beirut: MKTh, 1990; Q: '2nd'; C: adab/poetry – Ghaznawid/Khwārazmshāh. (cf. no. 342)

(1570) Makh/14 268b/6 *Min al-Muḥibb wa-al-maḥbūb – [Parts] of The Lover & the Beloved [and the Perfume & the Drink]*; A: al-Sarī b. Aḥmad al-Raffāᵓ (d. 362/972–3); S: *al-Muḥibb wa-al-maḥbūb wa-al-mashmūm wa-al-mashrūb*, ed. M. Ghalāwinjī, Damascus: MLA, 1986–7; Q: '1st'; C: poetry – anthology – Ḥamdānid/Būyid. (cf. no. 1099)

(1571) Makh/14 268b/6 *Min Sirāj al-mulūk – [Parts] of The Light for Kings*; A: Muḥammad b. al-Walīd al-Ṭurṭūshī (d. 520/1126?); S: ed. J. al-Bayātī, London 1990; Q: '1st, 1st'; C: political thought – mirror for princes. (cf. no. 559)

(1572) Makh/14 268b/6–7 *Min Tanjīf Taʾrīkh Baghdād – [Parts] of the Extract* (?) *from the History of Baghdad*; the reading of the second term is very tentative. No summary or continuation of the *History of Baghdad* by Aḥmad b. ᶜAlī al-Khaṭīb al-Baghdādī (d. 463/1071) with this (or a similar title) is known. Q: '1st'; C: history – regional.

(1573) Makh/14 268b/7 *Min al-Aḥkām al-sulṭānīya – [Parts] of The Ordinances of Government*; A: Muḥammad b. al-Ḥusayn Ibn al-Farrāʾ (d. 458/1066); S: ed. Ḥ. al-Fiqī, Cairo: MBḤ, 1938; Q: '3rd'; C: political thought.

(1574) Makh/14 268b/7–8 *Min al-Ḥulal al-mawshīya wa-al-ikhtiyārāt al-ṣāliḥīya – [Parts] of Embroidered Cloaks and Good Choices*; the title's first part seems to be the Andalusian chronicle of this name (authorship disputed, see EI[2], A. Huici-Miranda, 'al-Ḥulal al-Mawshiyya', ed. I.S. ᶜAllūsh, Rabat 1936), but for chronological reasons this is impossible as the chronicle goes up to the late 8th/14th c. There is no independent work identifiable for '*al-ikhtiyārāt al-ṣāliḥīya*'. Q: '1st, 2nd'.

(1575) Makh/14 268b/8 *Min Ashᶜār al-Hudhalīyīn – [Parts] of the Poems of Those Belonging to the Hudhalī Tribe*; S: *Dīwān al-Hudhalīyīn*, ed. M. Abū al-Wafāʾ and A. Zayn, Cairo: DKM, 1945–50; FI: '*mujallad*'/'*one bound volume*'; C: poetry – anthology – pre-Islamic/early Islamic. (cf. nos. 113, 1301, 1488)

(1576) Makh/14 268b/8–9 *Min Shiᶜr al-Sharīf al-Raḍī – [Parts] of al-Sharīf al-Raḍī's Poetry*; A: Muḥammad b. al-Ḥusayn al-Sharīf al-Raḍī (d. 406/1016); S: *Dīwān al-Sharīf al-Raḍī*, ed. I. ᶜAbbās, Beirut: DṢ, 1994; FI: '*arbaᶜ mujalladāt*'/'*4 bound volumes*'; Q: '[and in addition] 3rd, 1st, 2nd, 3rd, 3rd, 4th, 5th, 2nd, 2nd [quires]'; C: poetry – Būyid. (cf. nos. 394, 1079, 1081, 1181c, 1666)

(1577) Makh/14 268b/9 *Min Shiᶜr al-Samarqandī – [Parts] of al-Samarqandī's Poetry*; there is no obvious poet with this *nisba*. It may refer to the religious scholar ᶜUmar b. Muḥammad al-Nasafī al-Samarqandī (d. 537/1142) who composed 'decent poetry in the way of the jurisprudents and scholars' (*shiᶜr ḥasan ᶜalā ṭarīqat al-fuqahāʾ wa-al-ḥukamāʾ*, TI, 521–40, p. 448) and whose poetry is quoted by Yāqūt al-Ḥamawī (MU, V, 2099). Q: '1st, 3rd'; C: poetry.

(1578) Makh/14 268b/9–10 *Min Shiᶜr Miqdād al-Maṭāmīrī – [Parts] of Miqdād al-Maṭāmīrī's Poetry*; A: Miqdād b. al-Mukhtār al-Maṭāmīrī (d. 538/1143–4); S: TI, 521–40, p. 490; Q: '1st'; C: poetry.

(1579) Makh/14 268b/10 *Min Sharḥ al-Mutanabbī – [Parts] of the Explanation of al-Mutanabbī['s Poetry]*; A: Yaḥyā b. ᶜAlī al-Khaṭīb al-Tibrīzī (d. 502/1109); S: *al-Mūḍiḥ fī sharḥ al-Mutanabbī*, ed. Kh.R. Nuᶜmān, Baghdad: DSh, 2000–2; Q: '1st, 2nd'; C: poetry – commentary. (cf. no. 1103)

(1580) Makh/14 268b/10 *Min Sharḥihi – [Parts] of the Explanation of [al-Mutanabbī's Poetry]*; A: Abū al-Fatḥ Ibn Jinnī (d. 392/1002); S: *al-Fasr: sharḥ Ibn Jinnī al-kabīr ᶜalā Dīwān al-Mutanabbī*, ed. R. Rajab, Damascus: DY, 2004; Q: '1st'; C: poetry – commentary. (cf. no. 822, 1108, 1518, 1584)

(1581) Makh/14 268b/10-11 *Min Sharḥihi – [Parts] of the Explanation of [al-Mutanabbī's Poetry]*; A: Abū al-ᶜAlāᵓ al-Maᶜarrī (d. 449/1058); most likely al-Maᶜarrī's *Muᶜjiz Aḥmad* edited as S: *Sharḥ Dīwān al-Mutanabbī*, ed. ᶜA. Diyāb, Cairo: DM, 1992; alternatively this entry may refer to al-Maᶜarrī's '*K. al-lāmiᶜ al-ᶜazīzī fī sharḥ shiᶜr al-Mutanabbī*' (cf. no. 1410). FI: '*mujallad*'/'*one bound volume*'; C: poetry – commentary.

(1582) Makh/14 268b/11 *al-Mutanabbī – Al-Mutanabbī['s Diwan]*; A: Aḥmad al-Mutanabbī (d. 354/955); S: *Dīwān*, ed. ᶜA. ᶜAzzām, Cairo: LTTN, 1944; FI: '*nāqiṣ mujallad*'/'*incomplete, one bound volume*'; C: poetry – Ḥamdānid. (cf. nos. 397, 1583, 1591, 1606)

(1583) Makh/14 268b/11 *Min al-Mutanabbī – [Parts] of al-Mutanabbī['s Diwan]*; A: Aḥmad al-Mutanabbī (d. 354/955); S: *Dīwān*, ed. ᶜA. ᶜAzzām, Cairo: LTTN, 1944; Q: '1st, 2nd'; C: poetry – Ḥamdānid. (cf. nos. 397, 1582, 1591, 1606)

(1584) Makh/14 268b/11–12 *Min Sharḥ al-Mutanabbī – [Parts] of al-Mutanabbī's Explanation*; A: Abū al-Fatḥ Ibn Jinnī (d. 392/1002); S: *al-Fasr: sharḥ Ibn Jinnī al-kabīr ᶜalā Dīwān al-Mutanabbī*, ed. R. Rajab, Damascus: DY, 2004; Q: '4th'; C: poetry – commentary. (cf. nos. 822, 1108, 1518, 1580)

(1585) Makh/14 268b/12 *Min al-Jawāhir al-sanīya – [Parts] of The Resplendent Gems*; this is arguably the lost collection of panegyric poetry for the Rum Saljuq Sultan ᶜAlāᵓ al-Dīn Kay Qubādh (d. 634/1237), *al-Jawāhir al-sanīya fī al-madāᵓiḥ al-ᶜAlāᵓīya*, written by ᶜAlī b. Anjab Ibn al-Sāᶜī (d. 674/1276) (Ibn al-Sāᶜī, *al-Durr*, 369). However, as Ibn al-Sāᶜī lived in Baghdad it is debatable whether this work would have made it into a Damascene library within such a short time period. Another possibility arises from the fact that

Ibn al-Sāᶜī got the material for this work from his colleague Dāwūd b. ᶜAbd al-Wahhāb al-Taghlibī (d. 665/1267), who went in his younger years on a mission to the Rum Sultanate. It is thus possible that the oral line of transmission of this panegyric poetry was also put to writing elsewhere, for example in northern Mesopotamia. Q: '1st'; C: poetry – panegyrics – Rūm Saljūq.

(1586) Makh/14 268b/12 *Min Shiᶜr Kuthayyir ᶜAzza – [Parts] of Kuthayyir ᶜAzza's Poetry*; A: Kuthayyir ᶜAzza = Kuthayyir b. ᶜAbd al-Raḥmān al-Mulaḥī (d. 105/723); S: ed. I. ᶜAbbās, Beirut: DTh, 1971; Q: '2nd'; C: poetry – Umayyad. (cf. no. 683)

(1587) Makh/14 268b/12 *Sayfiyāt al-Mutanabbī – The Panegyrics for Sayf al-Dawla by al-Mutanabbī*; composed for the Hamdanid ruler of Aleppo; A: Aḥmad al-Mutanabbī (d. 354/955); S: Hamori, *Panegyrics*; FI: '*bi-khaṭṭ riwāyatuhu*' / '*in calligraphy; [with] its line of transmission*'; C: poetry – panegyric – Ḥamdānid.

(1588) Makh/14 268b/13 *Min Maᶜānī al-shiᶜr – [Parts] of Themes in Poetry*; A: Aḥmad b. Yaḥyā Thaᶜlab (d. 291/904); S: IN, I/1, 226; Q: '2nd'; C: poetry – commentary.

(1589) Makh/14 268b/13 *Min Azjāl Ibn Quzmān – [Parts] of Ibn Quzmān's Zajal Poems*; A: Muḥammad Ibn Quzmān (d. 555/1160); S: *Todo Ben Quzmān*, ed. E.G. Gómez, Madrid 1972; C: poetry – zajal. (cf. nos. 1490, 1594)

(1590) Makh/14 268b/13 *Min al-ᶜIqd – [Parts] of The [Unique] Necklace*; A: Aḥmad b. Muḥammad Ibn ᶜAbd Rabbih (d. 328/940); S: *al-ᶜIqd al-farīd*, ed. A. Amīn, A. al-Zayn and I. al-Ibyārī, Cairo: LTTN, 1940–65; Q: '3rd'; C: adab – anthology. (cf. nos. 730, 1549?, 1555)

(1591) Makh/14 268b/13–14 *Min Shiᶜr al-Mutanabbī – [Parts] of al-Mutanabbī's Poetry*; A: Aḥmad al-Mutanabbī (d. 354/955); S: ed. ᶜA. ᶜAzzām, Cairo: LTTN, 1944; FI: '*mujallad*' / '*one bound volume*', '*wa-ᶜalayhi khaṭṭuhu*' / '*and on it [the manuscript] is his [al-Mutanabbī's] writing*'; C: poetry – Ḥamdānid. (cf. nos. 397, 1582, 1583, 1606)

(1592) Makh/14 268b/14 *Min Dīwān al-Akhṭal – [Parts] of al-Akhṭal's Diwan*; A: Ghiyāth b. Ghawth al-Akhṭal (d. 92/710); S: *Shiᶜr al-Akhṭal*, ed. F. Qabāwa, Aleppo: Dār al-aṣmaᶜī, 1970/1; Q: '2nd'; C: poetry – Umayyad. (cf. no. 1608)

(1593) Makh/14 268b/14 *al-Maḍāʾiḥ al-Ayyūbīya* – *The Ayyūbid Praises*; no such title is identifiable and this is most likely a book-in-the-making. FI: '*mujallad*'/'*one bound volume*'; C: poetry – panegyrics – Ayyūbid.

(1594) Makh/14 268b/14 *Min Azjāl Ibn Quzmān* – *[Parts] of Ibn Quzmān's Zajal Poems*; A: Muḥammad Ibn Quzmān (d. 555/1160); S: *Todo Ben Quzmān*, ed. E.G. Gómez, Madrid 1972; Q: '2nd'; C: poetry – zajal. (cf. nos. 1490, 1589)

(1595) Makh/14 268b/15 *Min Azjāl Ibn Baqī* – *[Parts] of Ibn Baqī's Zajal Poems*; A: Yaḥyā b. Aḥmad Ibn Baqī (d. *c.*545/1150–1); S: *Dīwān*, ed. I.Kh. al-Dannān, Beirut: DKI, 2012; Q: '4th'; C: poetry – zajal.[176]

(1596) Makh/14 268b/15 *Min Shiʿr Ibn al-Muʿtazz* – *[Parts] of Ibn al-Muʿtazz's Poetry*; A: ʿAbd Allāh Ibn al-Muʿtazz (d. 296/908); S: *Dīwān*, ed. B. Lewin, Istanbul 1945–50; Q: '3rd'; C: poetry – ʿAbbāsid. (cf. nos. 395, 1060, 1075, 1617, 1638)

(1597) Makh/14 268b/15 *Min Shiʿr al-Mutanabbī bi-sharḥihi* – *[Parts] of al-Mutanabbī's Poetry with Explanation*; one of the previously mentioned explanations that the cataloguer could not identify, for example those by Ibn Jinnī (cf. nos. 1108, 1518, 1580, 1584), Abū al-ʿAlāʾ al-Maʿarrī (cf. no. 1581), al-Khaṭīb al-Tibrīzī (cf. no. 1579) and Ibn Sīda (cf. no. 1196d?) or an anonymous work; Q: '8th'; C: poetry – commentary – Ḥamdānid.

(1598) Makh/14 268b/15–16 *Min Shiʿrihi bi-sharḥihi* – *[Parts] of His [al-Mutanabbī's] Poetry with Explanation*; same as preceding entry; Q: '5th'; C: poetry – commentary – Ḥamdānid.

(1599) Makh/14 268b/16 *Min Shiʿr Ibn Ḥajjāj* – *[Parts] of Ibn Ḥajjāj's Poetry*; A: al-Ḥusayn b. Aḥmad Ibn al-Ḥajjāj (d. 391/1001); S: Ibn Nubāta, *Talṭīf al-mizāj min shiʿr Ibn al-Ḥajjāj*, ed. N.ʿA. Muṣṭafā, Sūsa: Dār al-Maʿārif, 2001; FI: '*mujallad*'/'*one bound volume*'; C: poetry – Būyid. (cf. nos. 1496, 1649, 1672, 1688)

(1600) Makh/14 268b/16 *Min Maghānī al-maʿānī* – *[Parts] of the Themes' Abodes*; A: Yaʿqūb b. Ṣābir al-Manjanīqī (d. 626/1229); S: IKH, VII, 37; Q: '1st'; C: poetry – anthology.

(1601) Makh/14 268b/16–17 *Min Dīwān al-Buḥturī* – *[Parts] of al-Buḥturī's Diwan*; A: al-Walīd al-Buḥturī (d. 284/897); S: ed. Ḥ. al-Ṣayrafī, Cairo: DM, 1963–5; Q: '1st, 3rd, 6th'; C: poetry – ʿAbbāsid. (cf. nos. 389, 1089)

(1602) Makh/14 268b/17 *Min al-Mufīd al-Khāṣṣ fī ᶜilm al-khawāṣṣ – [Parts] of the Instructive and Special [Book] on Sympathetic Qualities*; A: al-Rāzī (Rhazes) (d. 313/925 or 323/935); S: GAS, III, 285; Q: '1st'; C: medicine – sympathetic qualities.

(1603) Makh/15 268b/17 *Min al-Jawāhir – [Parts] of Gems [of Speech]*; A: Isḥāq b. Ibrāhīm al-Mawṣilī (d. 235/849); S: IN, I/2, 437: '*Jawāhir al-kalām*'; Zakeri, *Wisdom*, 16; Q: '1st'; C: adab – gnomic literature. (cf. no. 309)

(1604) Makh/15 268b/18 *al-Ḥayawān – [Parts] of The Animals*; A: al-Jāḥiẓ (d. 255/868–9); S: ed. ᶜA. Hārūn, Cairo: MBḤ, 1938–45; FI: '*bi-naqṣa*'/'*incomplete*'; C: adab. (cf. nos. 339, 1535)

(1605) Makh/1s 268b/18 *Min Shiᶜr Dīk al-Jinn – [Selections] from Dīk al-Jinn's Poetry*; A: ᶜAbd al-Salām b. Raghbān Dīk al-Jinn (d. 235–6/849–51); S: ed. A. Qawwāl, *Dīwān*, Beirut: DKiA, 1992; C: poetry – ᶜAbbāsid. (cf. nos. 406, 1249f)

(1606) Makh/1s 268b/18 *Min al-Mutanabbī – [Parts] of al-Mutanabbī['s Poetry]*; Scr('*bi-khaṭṭ*'): most likely ᶜAbd Allāh b. Muḥammad Ibn Abī al-Jūᶜ al-Warrāq (d. 395/1004–5) (IKH, IV, 379, cf. nos. 975, 1270b); A: Aḥmad al-Mutanabbī (d. 354/955); S: ed. ᶜA. ᶜAzzām, Cairo: LTTN, 1944; C: poetry – Ḥamdānid. (cf. nos. 397, 1582, 1583, 1591)

(1607) Makh/2s 268b/19 *Min al-Naqāʾiḍ – [Parts] of The Polemical Poems*; Scr('*bi-khaṭṭ*'): Yūsuf b. Muḥammad al-Muwaffaq Ibn al-Khallāl (d. 566/1171) (IKH, VII, 219–25); most likely the poems exchanged between Jarīr b. ᶜAṭīya (d. *c.*110/728–9) and Tammām b. Ghālib al-Farazdaq (d. *c.*114/732) (*Naqāʾiḍ Jarīr wa-al-Farazdaq*, ed. A.A. Bevan, Leiden 1905); see comments in no. 1074; Q: '2nd, 2nd to 6th in hand of Ibn al-Khallāl, 1st'; C: poetry – Umayyad. (cf. nos. 1285b, 1290a, 1349, 1356, 1359)

(1608) Makh/2s 268b/19–20 *Min Dīwān al-Akhṭal*[177] *– [Parts] of al-Akhṭal's Diwan*; A: Ghiyāth b. Ghawth al-Akhṭal (d. 92/710); S: *Shiᶜr al-Akhṭal*, ed. F. Qabāwa, Aleppo: Dār al-aṣmaᶜī, 1970–1; Q: '1st'; C: poetry – Umayyad. (cf. no. 1592)

(1609) Makh/2s 268b/20 *Min Shiᶜr al-Arrajānī – [Parts] of al-Arrajānī's Poetry*; A: Aḥmad b. Muḥammad al-Arrajānī (d. 544/1149–50); S: ed. Q. Māyū, Beirut: DJ, 1998; Q: '1st'; C: poetry – Saljūq – panegyrics.

(1610) Makh/2s 268b/20 *Min Shi^c^r Jarīr – [Parts] of Jarīr's Poetry*; A: Jarīr b. ^c^Aṭīya (d. *c.*110/728–9); S: ed. N. Ṭaha, Cairo: DM, 1986; Q: 'a quire (*juz*^ɔ^)'; C: poetry – Umayyad. (cf. nos. 404, 1072, 1229e, 1290b, 1630, 1653)

(1611) Makh/2s 268b/20 *Min Dīwān Ibn Ruzzīk – [Parts] of Ibn Ruzzīk's Diwan*; A: Ṭalā^ɔ^i^c^ b. Ruzzīk al-Malik al-Ṣāliḥ (d. 556/1161); S: ed. A.A. Badawī, al-Fajjāla: MNM, 1958; Q: '1st'; C: poetry – Fatimid.

(1612) Makh/2s 268b/21 *Min Dīwān Ibn Abī Ḥuṣayna – [Parts] of Ibn Abī Ḥuṣayna's Diwan*; A: al-Ḥasan b. ^c^Abd Allāh Ibn Abī Ḥuṣayna (d. 457/1065); S: ed. M.A. Ṭalas, Damascus: MIA, 1956–7; Q: '1st, 2nd, 2nd'; C: poetry – Mirdasid.

(1613) Makh/2s 268b/21 *Min Shi^c^r Mihyār – [Parts] of Mihyār's Poetry*; A: Mihyār b. Marzawayh al-Daylamī (d. 428/1037); S: *Dīwān*, ed. A. Nasīm, Beirut: MA, 1999; Q: '1st, 2nd'; C: poetry – Būyid. (cf. nos. 396, 798)

(1614) Makh/2s 268b/21–269a/1 *Min Dīwān Abī Fātik – [Parts] of Abī Fātik's Diwan*; the MS reads 'Ibn Fātik' but none of the scholars with this name, for instance Ayman b. Khuraym b. Fātik (fl. 1st/7th c.) and al-Mubashshir b. Fātik (fl. 5th/11th c.), were renowned as poets or left a diwan. Most likely this is 'Abī Fātik' and thus refers to the Yemenite Najāḥid ruler and poet A: Jayyāsh b. Najāḥ Abū Fātik (d. *c.*500/1107); S: *Wāfī*, XI, 228; al-Ziriklī, *al-A^c^lām*, II, 147; Q: '1st, 1st, 4th'; C: poetry.

(1615) Makh/2s 269a/1 *Min Shi^c^r Ibn al-Zubayr – [Parts] of Ibn al-Zubayr's Poetry*; A: Abū al-Ḥasan/Ḥusayn Aḥmad b. ^c^Alī b. Ibrāhīm Ibn al-Zubayr (d. 563/1167); S: IKH, I, 160–1: '*lahu dīwān shi^c^r*'; Q: '2nd, 3rd'; Aḥmad had a brother, al-Ḥasan b. ^c^Alī Ibn al-Zubayr (d. 561/1166) (IKH, I, 161), who was also a poet and to whom this entry could refer. However, ^c^Alī was the more renowned of the two. Finally, the entry could also refer to the pre-Islamic poet ^c^Abd Allāh b. al-Zabīr al-Asadī (GAS, II, 329–30), but this is unlikely as the other poets in this section are from a later period. C: poetry – Fatimid.

(1616) Makh/2s 269a/1 *Min Shi^c^r Ibn Nubāta – [Parts] of Ibn Nubāta's Poetry*; A: ^c^Abd al-^c^Azīz b. ^c^Umar Ibn Nubāta (d. 405/1015); S: *Dīwān*, ed. ^c^A. al-Ṭā^ɔ^ī, Baghdad: DḤ, 1977; Q: '2nd, 2nd'; C: poetry – Ḥamdānid. (cf. no. 420)

(1617) Makh/2s 269a/1–2 *Min Shi^{c}r Ibn al-Mu^{c}tazz – [Parts] of Ibn al-Mu^{c}tazz's Poetry*; A: ^{c}Abd Allāh Ibn al-Mu^{c}tazz (d. 296/908); S: *Dīwān*, ed. B. Lewin, Istanbul 1945–50; Q: '1st'; C: poetry – ^{c}Abbāsid. (cf. nos. 395, 1060, 1075, 1596, 1638)

(1618) Makh/2s 269a/2 *Min Shi^{c}r Ḥayṣa*[178] *Bayṣa – [Parts] of Ḥayṣa Bayṣa's Poetry*; A: Sa^{c}d b. Muḥammad Ḥayṣa Bayṣa (d. 574/1179); S: eds M. Jāsim and Sh. Shukr, Baghdad: Wizārat al-i^{c}lām, 1974–5; Q: '1st, 1st, 1st, 2nd'; C: poetry – Saljūq. (cf. nos. 407, 1487)

(1619) Makh/2s 269a/2 *Min Shi^{c}r al-Muṭarriz – [Parts] of al-Muṭarriz's Poetry*; most likely A: ^{c}Abd al-Wāḥid b. Muḥammad al-Muṭarriz, the father of Ghulām Tha^{c}lab (d. 345/957); S: IKH, IV, 333; Q: '2nd'; C: poetry.

(1620) Makh/2s 269a/2–3 *Min Shi^{c}r Abī Naṣr al-Fāriqī – [Parts] of Abū Naṣr al-Fāriqī's Poetry*; A: Abū Naṣr al-Ḥasan b. Asad al-Fāriqī (d. 487/1094); S: MU, II, 841–7; Q: '2nd'; C: poetry – Saljūq.

(1621) Makh/2s 269a/3 *Min Shi^{c}r Ibn Munqidh – [Parts] of Ibn Munqidh's Poetry*; A: Usāma b. Munqidh (d. 584/1188); S: *Dīwān Usāma Ibn Munqidh*, ed. A.A. Badawī/Ḥ. ^{c}Abd al-Majīd, Cairo: al-Maṭba^{c}a al-amīrīya, 1953; the other possibility would be the early Islamic poet Ziyād/al-Marrār b. Munqidh b. ^{c}Amr (fl. 96/715). However, he is named elsewhere in this catalogue 'Ziyād b. Munqidh' (cf. no. 625) and the chronological context of the surrounding titles makes poetry by Usāma in this section much more likely. Q: '1st'; C: poetry – Zangid/Ayyūbid. (cf. no. 1056)

(1622) Makh/2s 269a/3 *Min Dīwān Ibn Munīr – [Parts] of Ibn Munīr's Diwan*; A: Aḥmad b. Munīr al-Ṭarābulusī al-Raffāʾ (d. 548/1153); S: ed. ^{c}U.^{c}A. Tadmurī, Beirut: DJ, 1986; Q: '3,[179] 2nd, 1st, a [further] quire (*juzʾ*); C: poetry – Zangid. (cf. nos. 1043, 1491, 1657)

(1623) Makh/2s 269a/3–4 *Min Dīwān Abī Nuwās – [Parts] of Abū Nuwās' Diwan*; A: al-Ḥasan b. Hāniʾ Abū Nuwās (d. between mid-198 and early 200/813–15); as this entry includes various, partly parallel parts, the cataloguer refrains here from mentioning the respective transmitter (cf. nos. 390, 1486 (Ḥamza), 391 (al-Ṣūlī) and 392 (Tūzūn) for the various possibilities); Q: '1st,1st,1st,1st, 2nd, 2nd, 3rd'; C: poetry – ^{c}Abbāsid.

(1624) Makh/2s 269a/4 *Min Dīwān Ibn al-Mu^callim – [Parts] of Ibn al-Mu^callim's Diwan*; A: Muḥammad b. ^cAlī Ibn al-Mu^callim (d. 592/1196); S: IKH, V, 5–9; MS Bodleian Marsh. 516; Q: '1st, 1st, 2nd'; C: poetry. (cf. nos. 422, 794)

(1625) Makh/2s 269a/4–5 *Min Shi^cr al-Sarī al-Raffā^ɔ – [Parts] of al-Sarī al-Raffā^ɔ's Poetry*; A: al-Sarī b. Aḥmad al-Raffā^ɔ (d. 362/972–3); S: *Dīwān*, ed. Ḥ. al-Ḥasanī, Baghdad: DR, 1981; Q: '1st'; C: poetry – Ḥamdānid/Būyid. (cf. no. 421)

(1626) Makh/2s 269a/5 *Min Dīwān Abī Tammām – [Parts] of Abū Tammām's Diwan*; A: Ḥabīb b. Aws Abū Tammām (d. 231/845 or 232/846); S: *Dīwān Abī Tammām bi-sharḥ al-Khaṭīb al-Tibrīzī*, ed. M. ^cAzzām, Cairo: DM, 1957–65; Q: '1st, 1st, 2nd, another quire (*juz^ɔ ākhar*)'; C: poetry – ^cAbbāsid. (cf. nos. 409, 1063)

(1627) Makh/2s 269a/5 *Min Shi^cr Ibn al-Ta^cāwīdhī – [Parts] of Ibn al-Ta^cāwīdhī's Poetry*; A: Muḥammad b. ^cUbayd Allāh Ibn al-Ta^cāwīdhī (Sibṭ Ibn al-Ta^cāwīdhī) (d. 584/1188); S: ed. D.S. Margoliouth, Cairo: al-Muqtaṭaf, 1903; Q: '1st, 2nd'; C: poetry – Ayyūbid.

(1628) Makh/2s 269a/5–6 *Min Shi^cr Ibn Sanā^ɔ al-Mulk – [Parts] of Ibn Sanā^ɔ al-Mulk's Poetry*; A: Hibat Allāh b. Ja^cfar Ibn Sanā^ɔ al-Mulk (d. 608/1211); S: ed. I. Naṣr, Cairo: DKA, 1967–9; Q: '2nd'; C: poetry – Ayyūbid. (cf. no. 400)

(1629) Makh/2s 269a/6 *Min Shi^cr Ibn Ḥayyūs – [Parts] of Ibn Ḥayyūs' Poetry*; A: Muḥammad b. Sulṭān Ibn Ḥayyūs (d. 473/1081); S: ed. Kh. Mardam, Damascus: MIA, 1951; Q: '2nd'; C: poetry – Mirdāsid. (cf. no. 405)

(1630) Makh/2s 269a/6 *Min Shi^cr Jarīr – [Parts] of Jarīr's Poetry*; A: Jarīr b. ^cAṭīya (d. *c.*110/728–9); S: ed. N. Ṭaha, Cairo: DM, 1986; Q: '2nd'; C: poetry – Umayyad. (cf. nos. 404, 1072, 1229e, 1290b, 1610, 1653)

(1631) Makh/2s 269a/6–7 *Min Shi^cr al-Malik al-^cAzīz – [Parts] of al-Malik al-^cAzīz's Poetry*; A: Buyid prince al-Malik al-^cAzīz b. Jalāl al-Dawla b. Buwayh (d. 441/1049) who according to Ibn al-Athīr, *al-Kāmil*, IX, 561 composed '*shi^cr ḥasan*'; FI: '*makhrūm al-awwal wa-al-ākhir*' / '*incomplete in the beginning and in the end*'; C: poetry – Būyid. (cf. nos. 658, 668)

(1632) Makh/2s 269a/7 *Min Shi*ᶜ*r al-Faḍl b. al-*ᶜ*Abbās – [Parts] of al-Faḍl b. al-*ᶜ*Abbās' Poetry*; A: al-Faḍl b. al-ᶜAbbās b. ᶜUtba Ibn Abī Lahab (fl. late 1st/early 8th c.); S: *Wāfī*, XXIV, 50–2; GAS, II, 420; FI: '*makhrūm al-awwal*' / '*incomplete in the beginning*'; C: poetry – Umayyad.

(1633) Makh/2s 269a/7 *Min Shi*ᶜ*r* ᶜ*Umar* (?) *al-[illegible] b. Qaṣr* (?); unidentified; FI: '*makhrūm al-awwal*' / '*incomplete in the beginning*'; C: poetry.

(1634) Makh/2s 269a/7–8 *Min Dīwān al-Ablah – [Parts] of al-Ablah's Diwan*; A: Muḥammad al-Ablah (d. *c.*579/1183); S: IKH, IV, 463–5; Q: '2nd'; C: poetry – Saljūq. (cf. no. 1098b)

(1635) Makh/3s 269a/8 *Min al-Mufaḍḍalīyāt – [Parts] of Mufaḍḍal al-Dīn's Compilation*; A: al-Mufaḍḍal al-Ḍabbī (d. 164/780 or 170/786); S: eds A.M. Shākir and ᶜA.M. Hārūn, Cairo: DM, 1942; Q: '3rd, 1st'; C: poetry – anthology – pre-Islamic. (cf. nos. 1059, 1285c)

(1636) Makh/3s 269a/8 *Min Nasab Banī al-*ᶜ*Abbās – [Parts] of the* ᶜ*Abbāsids' Genealogy*; A: Hārūn b. Muḥammad b. Isḥāq al-Hāshimī (d. 167/783–4); S: this lost work is repeatedly cited in later works such as Ibn al-ᶜAdīm, *Bughyat* (e.g. I, 451, 531; VII, 3449), for the author see Rosenthal (tr.): *The History of al-Ṭabarī*, XXVIII, 5, n31; Q: '1st'; C: history – ᶜAbbāsid.

(1637) Makh/3s 269a/8–9 *Min Mulaḥ al-arājīz – [Parts] of the Interesting Poems in Rajaz Metre*; A: al-Ḥasan b. Bishr al-Āmidī (d. 370/980 or 371/981); this is most likely the author meant by 'al-Āmidī', as the cataloguer refers to him with this *nisba* elsewhere in the catalogue (cf. nos. 1064, 1704), although the sources do not mention such a *nisba* (cf. GAS, II, 614). Q: '1st'; C: poetry – rajaz.

(1638) Makh/3s 269a/9 *Min Dīwān Ibn al-Mu*ᶜ*tazz – [Parts] of Ibn al-Mu*ᶜ*tazz's Diwan*; A: ᶜAbd Allāh Ibn al-Muᶜtazz (d. 296/908); S: ed. B. Lewin, Istanbul 1945–50; Q: '1st, a *[further]* quire (*juz*ʾ)'; C: poetry – ᶜAbbāsid. (cf. nos. 395, 1060, 1075, 1596, 1617)

(1639) Makh/3s 269a/9 *Min Ikhtiyār al-ash*ᶜ*ār – [Parts] of the Selection of Poems*; anonymous work with generic title; Q: '2nd'; C: poetry – anthology.

(1640) Makh/3s 269a/9–10 *Min Shi*ᶜ*r Dhī al-Rumma – [Parts] of Dhū al-Rumma's Poetry*; A: Ghaylān b. ᶜUqba Dhū al-Rumma (d. 117/735); S:

Dīwān, ed. ᶜA. Abū Ṣāliḥ, Damascus: MLA, 1972–3; Q: 'a fragment (*qiṭᶜa*)'; C: poetry – Umayyad – Bedouin. (cf. nos. 411, 1131, 1133a, 1174a, 1230a)

(1641) Makh/3s 269a/10 *Min Shiᶜr Muslim Ibn al-Walīd wa-akhbāruhu – [Parts] of Muslim b. al-Walīd's Poetry and His Reports*; A: Muslim b. al-Walīd Ṣarīᶜ al-Ghawānī al-Anṣārī (d. 208/823); S: *Sharḥ dīwān Ṣarīᶜ al-Ghawānī*, ed. S. Dahhān, Cairo: DM, 1958; Q: '1st, 3rd'; C: poetry – commentary – ᶜAbbāsid. (cf. no. 692)

(1642) Makh/3s 269a/10–11 *Min Akhbār al-mutamaththilīn bi-al-shiᶜr – Reports on Those Who Recite Poetry as Proverbs*; A: ᶜAlī b. Muḥammad al-Madāᵓinī (d. 215/830?); S: MU, IV, 1857: '*K. al-mutamaththilīn, K. man tamaththala bi-shiᶜr fī maraḍihi*'; Q: '1st'; C: poetry/adab – anthology – ᶜAbbāsid.

(1643) Makh/3s 269a/11 *Min Anwāᶜ al-asjāᶜ – [Parts] of the Different Kinds of Rhymed Prose*; A: al-Ḥusayn b. ᶜAbd al-Raḥīm Ibn Abī al-Zalāzil (d. 354/965); S: MU, III, 1129; Q: '1st'; C: adab – sajᶜ.

(1644) Makh/3s 269a/11 *Min Ḥilyat al-muḥāḍara – [Parts] of The Ornament of Disputation*; A: Muḥammad b. al-Ḥasan al-Ḥātimī (d. 388/998); S: ed. H. Nājī, Beirut: DMḤ, 1978; Q: '1st'; C: rhetoric. (cf. no. 1260g)

(1645) Makh/3s 269a/11 *Min mukhtārihā [Ḥilyat al-muḥāḍara] – [Parts] of the Selection from It [the Ornament of Disputation]*; no such title is identifiable. This summary refers to the work by Muḥammad b. al-Ḥasan al-Ḥātimī (d. 388/998); Q: '1st'; C: rhetoric. (cf. no. 1128)

(1646) Makh/3s 269a/11–12 *Min Akhbār al-Barāmika – [Parts] of The Reports of the Barmakid Family*; two main possibilities: 1) Muḥammad b. ᶜImrān al-Marzubānī (d. 384/994) (MU, VI, 2583) or 2) ᶜUmar al-Kirmānī (dates unknown) (cited in later works, e.g. ᶜAbbās, *Kutub mafqūda*); MS: Süleymaniye, Fatih 4828/2 (fols. 24a–103b)***, no author given; Q: '3 quires (*karārīs*)'; C: history – ᶜAbbāsid. (cf. nos. 910, 911)

(1647) Makh/3s 269a/12 *Min Ashᶜār al-Andalusīyīn – [Parts] of The Andalusians' Poems*; probably an anonymous collection or a work that the cataloguer could not identify such as Ṣafwān b. Idrīs al-Tujībī al-Mursī's (d. 598/1201) anthology and biographical dictionary (ed. *Zād al-musāfir wa-ghurrat muḥayyā al-adab al-sāfir: ashᶜār al-andalusīyīn min ᶜaṣr al-dawla al-muwaḥḥidīya*, ed. ᶜA. Maḥdād, Beirut: DRA, 1970); Q: '1st'; C: poetry – anthology – Andalusian. (cf. no. 1674)

(1648) Makh/3s 269a/12 *Min kalām al-ḥukamāʾ fī adab al-nafs – [Parts] of the Sayings of the Wise on Good Conduct*; probably anonymous collection drawn from adab works on this issue such as Aḥmad b. al-Ṭayyib al-Sarakhsī's (d. 286/899) work mentioned by Ibn Nadīm (IN, I/2, 550 '*K. al-Sarakhsī ilā al-Muᶜtaḍid fī adab al-nafs*') and Aḥmad Muḥammad b. Khālid al-Kūfī's work mentioned by Yāqūt al-Ḥamawī (MU, I, 431); C: adab – anthology.

(1649) Makh/3s 269a/12–13 *Min Shiᶜr Ibn Ḥajjāj – [Parts] of Ibn Ḥajjāj's Poetry*; A: al-Ḥusayn b. Aḥmad Ibn al-Ḥajjāj (d. 391/1001); S: Ibn Nubāta, *Talṭīf al-mizāj min shiᶜr Ibn al-Ḥajjāj*, ed. N.ᶜA. Muṣṭafā, Sūsa: Dār al-Maᶜārif, 2001; FI: '*makhrūm al-awwal wa-al-ākhir*'/'*incomplete in the beginning and end*'; C: poetry – Būyid. (cf. nos. 1496, 1599, 1672, 1688)

(1650a) Makh/3s *Min Naẓm al-jawāhir – [Parts] of The String of Gems*; A: Asᶜad b. al-Batrīq (d. 357/968); S: Baghdādī, *Īḍāḥ al-maknūn*, II, 658; C: history.

(1650b) 269a/13 *Akhbār al-luṣūṣ wa-min shiᶜr – [and] Reports on the Thieves and Parts of [Their] Poetry*; probably referring to *Ashᶜār al-luṣūṣ by* al-Sukkarī (d. 275/888); FI: '*makhrūm al-awwal wa-al-ākhir*'/'*incomplete in the beginning and end*'; C: poetry – commentary. (cf. nos. 79, 131)[180]

(1651) Makh/3s 269a/13 *Min Shiᶜr al-Ḥāfiẓ al-Silafī – [Parts] of al-Ḥāfiẓ al-Silafī's Poetry*; A: Aḥmad b. Muḥammad al-Silafī al-Shāfiᶜī (d. 576/1180); S: MU, I, 105–7; C: poetry – Fatimid (sunni).

(1652) Makh/3s 269a/14 *Min Ādāb Aflāṭūn* [181] – *[Parts] of Plato's Writings on Good Conduct*; not identified; probably selection from Plato's writings as quoted by Arab authors such as IAU (I, 264–70); in the undated, but most likely Ottoman-period multiple-text manuscript Süleymaniye, Ayasofya 2456, treatise no. 11 is entitled *Ādāb Aflāṭūn.* C: adab – pre-Islamic. (cf. no. 1129)

(1653) Makh/3s 269a/14 *Min Shiᶜr Jarīr – [Parts] of Jarīr's Poetry*; the reading of the name is tentative, but supported by the poet's prominence in this library. Scr('*ka-annahu khaṭṭ*'/'*[it seems] as if it is in the hand of*'): Amīn al-Dīn ᶜAbd al-Muḥsin b. Ḥamūd al-Ḥalabī (d. 643/1245) (TI, 641–50, pp. 181–2); A: Jarīr b. ᶜAṭīya (d. *c.*110/728–9); S: ed. N. Ṭaha, Cairo: DM, 1986; NC: 2; C: poetry – Umayyad. (cf. nos. 404, 1072, 1229e, 1290b, 1610, 1630)

(1654) Makh/3s 269a/14 *Min al-Madāᵓiḥ al-Baghawīya – [Parts] of al-Baghawī's Eulogies*; the reading of 'Baghawīya' is tentative, but the *madāᵓiḥ* may refer to religious eulogies. In this case the entry could refer to al-Ḥusayn b. Masᶜūd (Ibn) al-Farrāᵓ al-Baghawī (d. 516/1122?) whose main works were held elsewhere in this library (cf. nos. 916 and 917). Q: '1st'; C: poetry.

(1655) Makh/3s 269a/14–15 *Shiᶜr Khams qaṣāᵓid – Poetry: Five Qaṣīdas*; anonymous work with generic title; C: poetry – anthology.

(1656) Makh/3s 269a/15 *Min al-Nafy – [Parts] of the Book of Negation*; A: Muḥammad b. Aḥmad Ibn Kaysān (d. 320/932?); no such title is mentioned in Ibn Kaysān's bibliographies (such as IN, I/1, 248) so this is probably an extract from one of his grammatical works. C: grammar.

(1657) Makh/3s 269a/15 *Min Shiᶜr Ibn Munīr – [Parts] of Ibn Munīr's Poetry*; Scr('*khaṭṭ*'): probably ᶜAlī b. al-Ḥasan b. Ṣadaqa (d. 554/1159) (praised, for instance, by MU, IV, 1689 for his calligraphy; cf. no. 156); A: Aḥmad b. Munīr al-Ṭarābulusī al-Raffāᵓ (d. 548/1153); S: *Dīwān*, ed. ᶜU.ᶜA. Tadmurī, Beirut: DJ, 1986; C: poetry – Zangid. (cf. nos. 1043, 1491, 1622)

(1658) Makh/3s 269a/15–16 *Min Kalām ᶜAlī b. Abī Ṭālib karrama Allāh wajhahu – [Parts] of ᶜAlī b. Abī Ṭālib's Sayings (may God honour his countenance)*; attr. to A: al-Jāḥiẓ (d. 255/868–9); S: *One Hundred Proverbs* (*Miᵓat kalima min kalām amīr al-Muᵓminīn ᶜAlī b. Abī Ṭālib)*, in: Engl. tr. & ed. Qutbuddin, *Treasury of Virtues*, 220-33; C: ᶜAlī – sayings attributed to. (cf. nos. 289, 312, 1134)

(1659) Makh/3s 269a/16 *Min Shiᶜr al-ᶜImād al-Iṣfahānī – [Parts] of al-ᶜImād al-Iṣfahānī's Poetry*; A: Muḥammad b. Muḥammad ᶜImād al-Dīn al-Kātib al-Iṣfahānī (d. 597/1201); S: *Dīwān*, ed. N. Rashīd, Mosul: Jāmiᶜat al-mawṣil, 1983; C: poetry – Ayyūbid. (cf. nos. 1045, 1489)

(1660) Makh/3s 269a/16 *Juzᵓ Shiᶜr Munyat al-nafs wa-Ṭīb al-uns – A Volume of Poetry [Including the Poems] Munyat al-nafs and Ṭīb al-uns*; the two clauses *Munyat al-nafs* and *Ṭīb al-uns* do not exist as book titles so here the cataloguer is presumably describing a manuscript with neither a title nor an identifiable author in more detail by quoting poetry. *Munyat al-nafs*, for instance, occurs in an often-cited line by ᶜAlī b. al-ᶜAbbās Ibn al-Rūmī (d. 283/896?) (cited, for example, in ᶜAbd al-Raḥmān b. Isḥāq al-Zajjājī, d. 337/948 or 339–40/949–50?, *al-Amālī*, ed. ᶜA. Hārūn, Beirut: DJ, 1987, 170); FI: '*mujallad ṣaghīr*' / '*one small bound volume*'; C: poetry.

(1661) Makh/3s 269a/17 *Adᶜiyat al-ayyām al-sabᶜa – Prayers of Invocation for the Seven Days*; several possibilities, but this could be (cf. no. 151) A: Fatimid Caliph al-Muᶜizz (r. 341–65/953–75); S: ed. I.K. Poonawala, Beirut: DGI, 2006; FI: '*nuskha rābiᶜa makhrūm al-ākhir*' / '*fourth copy, incomplete in the end*', 'fourth copy' as three other copies of the work have been mentioned previously; C: prayer book. (cf. nos. 151, 1170c, 1198b)

(1662) Makh/5s 269a/17–18 *Min Duᶜāᵓ – [Parts] of a Prayer of Invocation*; Scr('*bi-khaṭṭ*', '*bi-ghayr shakk*' / '*without doubt*'): Ibn al-Bawwāb (d. 413/1022); FI: '*khams qawāᵓim*' / '*five folios*'[182], '*bi-qalam al-muḥaqqaq*' / '*in muḥaqqaq script*', '*fī mujallad*' / '*one bound volume*'; C: prayer book.

(1663) Makh/5s 269a/18–269b/1 *Min Waṣīyat amīr al-muᵓminīn ᶜAlī b. Abī Ṭālib li-waladihi al-Ḥusayn raḍiya Allāh ᶜanhumā – [Parts] of the Last Advice by the Commander of the Believers ᶜAlī b. Abī Ṭālib to His Son Ḥusayn (may God be pleased with them)*; treatise on the last advice by A: ᶜAlī b. Abī Ṭālib, the fourth Caliph and first Shiᶜite *imām* (d. 40/661), to Ḥusayn as reported in sources such as S: Hawting (tr.): *The History of al-Ṭabarī*, XVII, 219– 22; Q: '5th'; C: political thought – imāmate theory. (cf. nos. 1161b, 1384)

(1664) Makh/5s 269b/1 *Min Kalām ᶜAlī b. ᶜUbayda al-Rayḥānī – [Parts] of ᶜAlī b. ᶜUbayda al-Rayḥānī's Sayings*; most likely this is a work of proverbs ascribed to al-Rayḥānī, which may be similar to the *Jawāhir al-kilam* (unique MS Cairo, Dār al-kutub, adab-71, dated to 637/1239); A: ᶜAlī b. ᶜUbayda al-Rayḥānī (d. 219/834); S: Zakeri, *Wisdom*, 305–15; C: adab – proverbs.

(1665) Makh/5s 269b/1 *Mā yukhṭiᵓ fīhi al-ᶜāmma – Commoners' Errors*; A: ᶜAbd al-Malik b. Qurayb al-Aṣmaᶜī (d. 213/828?); such a title by al-Aṣmaᶜī is not included in the standard lists of his works (IN, I/1, 157; IKH, III, 176); FI: '*makhrūm al-ākhir*' / '*incomplete in the end*'; C: grammar/lexicography.

(1666) Makh/5s 269b/1–2 *Min Shiᶜr al-Sharīf al-Raḍī – [Parts] of al-Sharīf al-Raḍī's Poetry*; Scr('*bi-khaṭṭ*'): al-Raḍī's son Abū *[Aḥmad]* ᶜAdnān (EI²,

Moktar Djebli, 'al-Sharīf al-Raḍī'); A: Muḥammad b. al-Ḥusayn al-Sharīf al-Raḍī (d. 406/1016); S: *Dīwān al-Sharīf al-Raḍī*, ed. I. ^{c}Abbās, Beirut: DṢ, 1994; C: poetry – Būyid. (cf. nos. 394, 1079, 1081, 1181c, 1576)

(1667) Makh/5s 269b/2 *Min Amālī al-Qāḍī Abī Ja^{c}far* [183] *Ibn al-Buhlūl – [Parts] of Ibn al-Buhlūl's Dictations*; A: Abū Ja^{c}far Aḥmad b. Isḥāq Ibn (al-) Buhlūl (d. 318/930); S: MU, I, 188–98; C: ḥadīth – collection.

(1668) Makh/5s 269b/2–3 *Mukhtaṣar al-Naṣā$^{\circ}$iḥ al-sāmiya – The Summary of Lofty Advice*; neither the summary nor the original work is identifiable, but it may refer to the *Naṣ$^{\circ}$iḥ* by al-Ḥārith b. Asad al-Muḥāsibī (d. 243/857) (GAS, I, 640). FI: '*makhrūm al-ākhir*'/'*incomplete in the end*'.

(1669) Makh/5s 269b/3 *Min Shi^{c}r Muḥammad b. Ṣādiq – [Parts] of Muḥammad b. Ṣādiq's Poetry*; probably the son (by Ḥamīda) of Ja^{c}far al-Ṣādiq, the sixth Shi^{c}ite *imām* (d. 148/765) who was accepted by some as legitimate successor; C: poetry – imāmate.

(1670) Makh/5s 269b/3 *Min Ḥadīth Majnūn Laylā*[184] – *[Parts] of the Majnūn Laylā Narration*; anonymous; S: *Dīwān Majnūn Laylā*, ed. A. Farrāj, Cairo: MMi, 1958; FI: '*makhrūm al-ākhir*'/'*incomplete in the end*'; C: adab.

(1671) Makh/5s 269b/3–4 *Min Mā lā yasa^{c}u al-kātib jahlahu – [Parts] of What the Secretary Cannot Afford to Ignore*; such a title is not identifiable, but this is most likely an administrative handbook with advice for the secretary. In the early 9th/15th c. al-Qalqashandī (d. 821/1418) used the phrase '*lā yasa^{c}u al-kātib jahlahā*' in the preamble to his famous administrative manual (*Ṣubḥ al-a^{c}shā*, I, 35) when discussing earlier works, such as *al-Ta^{c}rīf bi-al-muṣṭalaḥ al-sharīf* by al-^{c}Umarī (d. 749/1349) and *Tathqīf al-ta^{c}rīf* by Ibn Nāẓir al-Jaysh (d. 786/1384). This fragment in the Ashrafīya was most likely a minor local manual, which was superseded by the great administrative manuals of the following two centuries. Q: '1st'; C: administrative handbook.

(1672) Makh/5s 269b/4 *Min Shi^{c}r Ibn Ḥajjāj – [Parts] of Ibn Ḥajjāj's Poetry*; A: al-Ḥusayn b. Aḥmad Ibn al-Ḥajjāj (d. 391/1001); S: Ibn Nubāta, *Talṭīf al-mizāj min shi^{c}r Ibn al-Ḥajjāj*, ed. N.^{c}A. Muṣṭafā, Sūsa: Dār al-Ma^{c}ārif, 2001; Q: '5th, 6th in one quire (*fī juz$^{\circ}$ wāḥid*)'; C: poetry – Būyid. (cf. nos. 1496, 1599, 1649, 1688)

(1673) Makh/5s 269b/4 *Min Jinān al-Janān – [Parts] of the Soul's Paradise [and the Mind's Garden]*; A: Abū al-Ḥasan/Ḥusayn Aḥmad b. ᶜAlī b. Ibrāhīm Ibn al-Zubayr (d. 563/1167); S: MU, I, 400: '*Jinān al-Janān wa-rawḍat al-adhhān*'; this is probably a work of poetry because this section of the catalogue has a distinct focus on poetry. The ascription of this title to Abū al-Futūḥ al-Rāzī (fl. 525/1131), author of the Shiᶜite Koran commentary *[Rawḍ al-] Jinān [wa-Rawḥ] al-Janān* is thus rather unlikely (K. Bauer, 'Exegete', 307). Q: '1st'; C: poetry – anthology. (cf. nos. 1675, 1676)

(1674) Makh/5s 269b/5 *Min Ashᶜār ahl al-Andalus – [Parts] of The Andalusians' Poems*; probably an anonymous collection or a work that the cataloguer could not identify such as Ṣafwān b. Idrīs al-Tujībī al-Mursī's (d. 598/1201) anthology and biographical dictionary (ed. *Zād al-musāfir wa-ghurrat muḥayyā al-adab al-sāfir: ashᶜār al-andalusīyīn min ᶜaṣr al-dawla al-muwaḥḥidīya*, ed. ᶜA. Maḥdād, Beirut: DRA, 1970); Q: '1st'; C: poetry – anthology – Andalusian. (cf. no. 1647)

(1675) Makh/5s 269b/5 *Min al-Jinān fīhi ashᶜār al-Qayrawānīyīn – [Parts] of the [Soul's] Paradise*; A: Abū al-Ḥasan/Ḥusayn Aḥmad b. ᶜAlī b. Ibrāhīm Ibn al-Zubayr (d. 563/1167); S: MU, I, 400 and IKH who quotes this work as '*al-jinān*' (I, 55, 196, 245) and quotes from it poets with the *nisba* 'al-Qayrawānī' (e.g. I, 55: Ibrāhīm b. ᶜAlī al-Ḥuṣrī al-Qayrawānī, d. 413/1022); C: poetry – anthology. (cf. nos. 1673, 1676)

(1676) Makh/5s 269b/5–6 *Min Ashᶜār al-Ṭāriʾīn ᶜalā Miṣr – [Parts] of the Poems of Those Who Migrated to Egypt*; either an anonymous collection of poetry or, more likely, another extract from above *Jinān al-Janān wa-rawḍat al-adhhān* by A: Abū al-Ḥasan/Ḥusayn Aḥmad b. ᶜAlī b. Ibrāhīm Ibn al-Zubayr (d. 563/1167); S: MU, I, 400 who states that the book '*yashtamilu ᶜalā shiᶜr shuᶜarāʾ miṣr wa-man ṭaraʾa ᶜalayhim*'; C: poetry – anthology. (cf. nos. 1673, 1675)

(1677) Makh/5s 269b/6 *Min Ashᶜār al-shāmīyīn – [Parts] of The Syrians' Poems*; this is most likely an anonymous anthology, which is in structure similar to ᶜImād al-Dīn al-Iṣfahānī, *Kharīdat al-qaṣr wa-jarīdat al-ᶜaṣr: qism shuᶜarāʾ al-Shām*, ed. Sh. Fayṣal, Damascus 1955–64. C: poetry – anthology.

(1678) Makh/5s 269b/6 *Min al-Dhayl al-Sāhī – [Parts] of the Sāhī Continuation*; such a book title is not identifiable. Perhaps this is a *dhayl* to a work with *al-Sāhī* in its title (although the article for *Dhayl* would be erroneous in this case), such as *Nuzhat al-mufakkir al-sāhī* by Aḥmad b. al-Ṭayyib al-Sarakhsī (d. 286/899) (IAU, II, 194) and *Tanbīh al-sāhī bi-al-ᶜilm al-ilāhī* by Muḥammad b. Aḥmad al-Iskāfī Ibn al-Junayd (d. 381/991) (IN, I/2, 688).

(1679) Makh/6s 269b/6–7 *Min Rasāᵓil al-Ṣābiᵓ – [Parts] of al-Ṣābiᵓ's Epistles*; A: Ibrāhīm b. Hilāl al-Ṣābiᵓ (d. 384/994); S: Hachmeier, 'Letters'; Q: '1st, 2nd, 4th, 3rd, 3rd, 1st ('on birds'/'*fī ṭayr*')', 10th'; C: adab – epistle.

(1680) Makh/6s 269b/7 *Min Tarassul – [Parts] of Correspondence*; anonymous work with generic title; Q: '1st, the second part (?) (*al-qism al-thānī*)'; C: adab – epistle.

(1681) Makh/6s 269b/7 *Min al-ᶜItāb – [Parts] of [Epistles of] Friendly Reproach*; FI: '*aẓunnuhu li-Ibn al-Athīr*'/'*I believe it is by Ibn al-Athīr*'; A: Ḍiyāᵓ al-Dīn Abū al-Fatḥ Naṣr Allāh Ibn al-Athīr (d. 637/1239); this litterateur authored a diwan with his epistles (*Dīwān rasāᵓil Ibn al-Athīr*, ed. H. Nājī, Mosul: Jāmiᶜat al-mawṣil, 1982). These epistles contain several exchanges with friends after the exchange of letters had stopped for a while and in which the sender either reproaches the addressee or justifies himself (for example, *Dīwān*, nos. 18, 24, 25 and 54). It is also likely that Ḍiyāᵓ al-Dīn is the author meant here because his son Sharaf al-Dīn Muḥammad (585–622/1189–225) authored a *majmūᶜ* for al-Malik al-Ashraf with, among others, prose and his father's epistles (IKH, V, 397). C: adab – epistle.

(1682) Makh/6s 269b/8 *Min Rasāᵓil al-Qāḍī al-Fāḍil – [Parts] of al-Qāḍī al-Fāḍil's Epistles*; A: ᶜAbd al-Raḥīm b. ᶜAlī al-Qāḍī al-Fāḍil al-Baysānī (d. 596/1200); S: *Rasāᵓil al-Qāḍī al-Fāḍil*, ed. ᶜA.N. ᶜĪsā, Beirut: DKI, 2005; MS: Süleymaniye, Şehid Ali Paşa 2808/5 (fols. 88a–131a)**; FI: '*mujalladān muqābalān*'/'*2 collated bound volumes*'; Q: 'a quire, a quire, a quire, a quire, a quire (*juzᵓ*)'; C: adab – epistle. (cf. no. 1280a)

(1683) Makh/6s 269b/8–9 *Mukātabāt Ibn al-Ḥarīrī – Ibn al-Ḥarīrī's Correspondence*; probably A: al-Qāsim b. ᶜAlī al-Ḥarīrī al-Baṣrī (d. 516/1122) who was also called 'Ibn' al-Ḥarīrī; this refers probably to his *rasāᵓil*, which are mentioned elsewhere in this catalogue (cf. nos. 481, 489, 1156). FI: '*nāqiṣ min ākhirihī*'/'*incomplete in the end*'; C: adab – epistle?

(1684) Makh/6s 269b/9 *Min Rasā*ᵓ*il Abī* ᶜ*Abd Allāh Ibn al-Marzubān – [Parts] of Abū* ᶜ*Abd Allāh Ibn al-Marzubān's Epistles*; the generic term '*rasā*ᵓ*il*' in combination with 'Ibn al-Marzubān' leaves many potential authors. However, the cataloguer specifies the *kunya* as 'Abū ᶜAbd Allāh' so that A: Abū ᶜAbd Allāh Aḥmad b. Khalaf Ibn al-Marzubān (d. 310/922) is possible. His brother is named elsewhere (cf. nos. 137, 256) and may explain the use of the *kunya* here. His works must have circulated in contemporaneous Damascus as the only surviving manuscript was copied in the city in 634/1236 (Chester Beatty MS 3493, cf. A. J. Arberry, 'Two Rare Manuscripts', *Journal of Arabic Literature* 1 (1970), 109–16); FI: '*ka-annahu awwal ba*ᶜ*ḍ mukātabat Ibn al-Shilḥī*'/'*[it seems] as if it is the beginning of some correspondence by Ibn al-Shilḥī [Muḥammad b. Muḥammad b. Sahl al-Shilḥī, d. 423/1032]*'; C: adab – epistle?[185] (cf. no. 483)

(1685) Makh/6s 269b/9–10 *Min Tarassul al-Wahrānī – [Parts] of al-Wahrānī's Correspondence*; A: Muḥammad b. Muḥriz al-Wahrānī (d. 575/1179) who composed *maqāmāt, rasā*ᵓ*il* and *manāmāt*; S: IKH, IV, 385/6; C: adab – epistle. (cf. no. 1182c)

(1686) Makh/7s 269b/10 *al-Qaṣā*ᵓ*id al-sab*ᶜ *– The Seven Qaṣīdas*; most likely the seven 'suspended' (*mu*ᶜ*allaqāt*)-poems; S: al-Qurashī, *Jamharat*, 124–428; FI: '*makhrūm al-ākhir*'/'*incomplete in the end*'; C: poetry – anthology – pre-Islamic. (cf. nos. 567, 569, 852, 1230m)

(1687) Makh/7s 269b/10 *Min al-*ᶜ*Arā*ᵓ*is fī al-majālis – [Parts] of The Brides of Sessions [on the Stories of the Prophets]*; A: al-Thaᶜlabī (d. 427/1035); S: *al-*ᶜ*Arā*ᵓ*is fī al-majālis fī qiṣaṣ al-anbiyā*ᵓ, Engl. tr. Brinner, '*Lives of the Prophets*'; Q: '2nd'; C: qiṣaṣ al-anbiyāᵓ. (cf. nos. 720, 773)

(1688) Makh/7s 269b/10–11 *Min Shi*ᶜ*r Ibn Ḥajjāj – [Parts] of Ibn Ḥajjāj's Poetry*; A: al-Ḥusayn b. Aḥmad Ibn al-Ḥajjāj (d. 391/1001); S: Ibn Nubāta, *Talṭīf al-mizāj min shi*ᶜ*r Ibn al-Ḥajjāj*, ed. N.ᶜA. Muṣṭafā, Sūsa: Dār al-Maᶜārif, 2001; FI: '*bi-ghayr jild*'/'*without binding*'; C: poetry – Būyid. (cf. nos. 1496, 1599, 1649, 1672)

(1689) Makh/7s 269b/11 *Maṣāri*ᶜ *al-*ᶜ*ushshāq – Calamities of Lovers*; A: Jaᶜfar b. Aḥmad al-Sarrāj (d. 500/1106); S: ed. Beirut: DṢ, 1958; Q: '1st'; C: adab/love literature. (cf. no. 989)

(1690) Makh/7s 269b/11 *Min Rāḥat al-albāb – [Parts] of The Hearts' Repose*; FI: '*wa-huwa min majmū*ᶜ *shi*ᶜ*r li-Maḥmūd al-Na*ᶜᶜ*āl*' /'*and this is from a multiple-text manuscript of poetry by Maḥmūd al-Na*ᶜᶜ*āl*'; the title *Rāḥat al-albāb* is not identifiable, which is not surprising as the FI indicates that this is probably only a single poem. The main candidate for the author is the minor scholar Maḥmūd b. ᶜUthmān al-Naᶜᶜāl (d. 609/1212) (TI, 601–10, pp. 348–9) who lived in Baghdad but travelled also to Damascus. C: poetry.

(1691) Makh/7s 269b/12 *Majmū*ᶜ *Ash*ᶜ*ār – Multiple-Text Manuscript with Poems*; anonymous work with generic title; FI: '*makhrūm al-awwal wa-al-ākhir*' /'*incomplete in the beginning and end*'; C: poetry – anthology.

(1692) Makh/7s 269b/12 *Min Shi*ᶜ*r Ibn al-Bayyāḍī – [Parts] of Ibn al-Bayyāḍī's Poetry*; A: Masᶜūd b. ᶜAbd al-ᶜAzīz <u>al-Bayyāḍī</u> (d. 468/1076); S: IKH, V, 197–9; FI: '*raqq*' /'*parchment*'; C: poetry.

(1693) Makh/7s 269b/12–13 *Majmū*ᶜ *Ash*ᶜ*ār wa-ḥikāyāt – Multiple-Text Manuscript with Poems and Narrations*; anonymous work with generic title; FI: '*maktūb* ᶜ*alayhi Uns al-Muḥibbīn*' /'*Lovers' Companion is written on it*'; C: poetry – anthology.

(1694) Makh/7s 269b/13–14 *Majmū*ᶜ *– Multiple-Text Manuscript*; FI: '*mubawwab bi-abwāb shibh abwāb al-sijill*' /'*organised by topics in chapters similar to the register's chapters*'; '*wa-ghayruhu li-ba*ᶜ*ḍ al-muta*ᵓ*akhkharīn*' /'*and another [work] by a recent author*'; '*wa-huwa ghayr tāmm*' /'*it is not complete*' '*kātibuhu al-awwal mu*ᵓ*allifuhu ba*ᶜ*da sanat* ᶜ*ishrīn wa-sitt mi*ᵓ*a*' /'*the scribe of the first part is the author [who wrote it] after the year 620[/1223–4]*'.

(1695) Makh/7s 269b/14 *Min al-Tadhkira ghayr al-Ḥamdūnīya wa-fīhi funūn – [Parts] of the Handbook, but not the Ḥamdūnian, with Different Fields of Knowledge*; anonymous work with generic title, probably similar to the early Mamluk encyclopaedia of the Damascene administrator and *adīb* ᶜAlī b. al-Muẓaffar al-Wadāᶜī (d. 716/1316), with which the Ashrafīya catalogue is bound today (see Chapter 5); C: adab?

(1696) Makh/7s 269b/15 *Min al-Shi*ᶜ*r – [Parts] of Poetry*; anonymous work with generic title; Scr('*bi-khaṭṭ*'): ᶜAlī b. ᶜAbd al-ᶜAzīz <u>Ibn Ḥājib al-Nu</u>ᶜ<u>mān</u> (d. 423/1031) (MU, IV, 1806–7), Muḥammad <u>Ibn Asad</u> al-Kātib (d. 410/1019) (IKH, III, 342–3), <u>al-Ṭabarī</u> (? possibly Ibrāhīm b. Aḥmad, fl.

4th/10th c. who was a renowned scribe and broadly contemporaneous with the two other scribes) (MU, I, 39/40); C: poetry – anthology.

(1697) Makh/7s 269b/15-16 *Mufākharat al-shitāʾ wa-al-ṣayf – The Boasting Match between Winter and Summer*; attr. to A: al-Jāḥiẓ (d. 255/868–9); S: Pellat, 'd'inventaire', no. 204; Q: 'a quire (*juzʾ*)'; FI: '*nāqiṣa*' / '*incomplete*'; C: adab. (cf. no. 1286b)

(1698) Makh/7s 269b/16 *Min Kitāb – [Parts] of a Book*; perhaps A: al-Thaᶜlabī (d. 427/1035); '*majhūl al-muṣannif wa-ka-annahu min taʾlīf al-Thaᶜlabī*' / '*author unknown and [it seems] as if it was authored by al-Thaᶜlabī*'; FI: '*mujallad*' / '*one bound volume*'; '*mubawwab*' / '*organised in chapters*'; '*bi-raqq*' / '*in parchment*'.

(1699) Makh/7s 269b/16–17 *Min Naẓāʾir al-Khālidīyayn – [Parts] of [The Book of] Similarities by the two Khālidīs*; A: the two court poets Abū ᶜUthmān Saᶜd/Saᶜīd (d. 350/961) and Abū Bakr Muḥammad (d. 380/990); S: *K. al-Ashbāh wa-al-naẓāʾir*, ed. M. Yūsuf, Cairo: LTTN, 1958; Q: '1st, 2nd, a [further] quire (*juzʾ*), another (*ākhar*) [quire]'; C: poetry – anthology – ᶜAbbāsid.

(1700a) Makh/7s 269b/17 *Majmūᶜ fīhi al-shuhūr al-Qibṭīya – Multiple-Text Manuscript with The Coptic Months*; anonymous; probably similar to the *Fāʾida fī maᶜrifat al-shuhūr al-qibṭīya* (Leiden Or. 2805 (6), see J.J. Witkam, *Inventory of the Oriental Manuscripts of the Library of the University of Leiden*, online publication, III, 205); C: dates.

(1700b) 269b/17 *wa-Akhbār Miṣr – The Reports on Egypt*; A: Sharaf al-Khilāfa Jamāl al-Dīn Mūsā b. al-Maʾmūn al-Baṭāʾiḥī (d. 588/1192); S: ed. F. Sayyid, *Nuṣūṣ min akhbār Miṣr li-Ibn al-Maʾmūn*, Cairo: IFAO, 1983; FI: '*makhrūm al-ākhir*' / '*incomplete in the end*'; C: history – Fatimid. (cf. no. 248)

(1701a) Makh/7s 269b/17–18 *Majmūᶜ al-Qisṭās – Multiple-Text Manuscript with the Just Balance*; A: al-Ghazālī (d. 505/1111); S: Badawī, *Muʾallafāt al-Ghazālī*, no. 42: '*al-Qisṭās al-mustaqīm*'; MS: Süleymaniye, Ayasofya 1816–18 (93b–111b)***; FI: '*makhrūm al-awwal wa-al-ākhir*' / '*incomplete in the beginning and end*'; C: logic/theology.

(1701b) 269b/18 *wa-min al-Farāʾiḍ – [Parts] of The [Book on] Ritual Obligations/Shares of Inheritance*; owing to preceding title most probably A:

al- Ghazālī (d. 505/1111); S: Badawī, *Mu$^{\circ}$allafāt al-Ghazālī*, no. 388; C: rituals/fiqh.

(1701c)[186] 269b/18 *Lawāmi^{c} al-adab – Flashes of Adab*; FI: '*bi-al-^{c}ajamī wa-al-^{c}arabī*'/'*in Persian and Arabic*', '*nāqiṣ min awwalihi*'/'*incomplete in the beginning*'; anonymous; Q: 'a quire (*juz$^{\circ}$*)'; L: Persian/Arabic; adab – anthology.

(1701d) 269b/19 *Min al-A^{c}māl – [Parts] of [the Book] of Deeds*; anonymous: '*min ta$^{\circ}$līf al-thiqa*'/'*by a trustworthy author*'; C: ethics – Islamic.

(1701e) 269b/19 *Min al-Miṣbāḥ – [Parts] of The Lantern*; A: al-Ghazālī (d. 505/1111); alternative title for the author's *Mishkāt al-anwār* (*The Niche for Lights*); S: ed. A. ^{c}Afīfī, Cairo: DQ, 1963; Q: '2nd'; C: theology. (cf. no. 1166e)

(1702a) Makh/7s 269b/19 *Majmū^{c} Mukhtaṣar al-tadlīs fī al-ri$^{\circ}$āsa – Multiple-Text Manuscript with the Summary of the Deceiver Concerning Leadership*; no such title is identifiable, arguably a summary of the *K. al-tadlīs* by Muḥammad b. Aḥmad al-Iskāfī Ibn al-Junayd (d. 381/991) (Baghdādī, *Īḍāḥ al-maknūn*, II, 281).

(1702b) 269b/19–20 *wa-Kitāb fīhi al-Bustān min ash^{c}ār al-fursān – A Book with the Garden on the Heroes' Poems*; FI: '*makhrūm min ākhirihi*'/'*incomplete in the end*'; probably anonymous; C: poetry – anthology.

(1703a) Makh/7s 269b/20 *Majmū^{c} Maqālat al-^{c}Ilal – Multiple-Text Manuscript with the Tract on Illnesses/Defects*; excerpt from one of the many works entitled *^{c}Ilal* that cover a wide range of fields including metrics (al-Zajjāj (d. 311/923), *^{c}Ilal al-^{c}arūḍ*, cf. no. 1311b) and medicine (al-Rāzī (Rhazes) (d. 313/925 or 323/935), *Taqāsīm al-^{c}ilal*, cf. no. 276).

(1703b) 269b/20–270a/1 *wa-Maqāla fī al-ḥisāb – A Tract on Arithmetic*; anonymous work with generic title; FI: '*makhrūm al-awwal wa-al-thālith*'/'*incomplete in the beginning and in the third [quire?]*'. C: mathematics?

(1704) Makh/7s 270a/1 *Min al-Mukhtār min ash^{c}ār al-qabā$^{\circ}$il – [Parts] of the Selection from the Tribes' Poems*; A: al-Ḥasan b. Bishr al-Āmidī (d. 370/980 or 371/981); this is an extract from the author's anthology of pre-Islamic tribal poetry, which was mentioned earlier in this catalogue ('*al-Muntakhal min shi^{c}r al-qabā$^{\circ}$il*'); C: poetry – anthology – pre-Islamic. (cf. no. 1064)

(1705) Makh/7s 270a/1 *Shi^{c}r [Ibn] Qays al-Ruqayyāt – [Ibn] Qays al-Ruqayyāt's Poetry*; A: ^{c}Ubayd Allāh b. Qays al-Ruqayyāt (d. 72/691); S: ed. ^{c}U.F. al-Ṭabbā^{c}, Beirut: DQa, 1995; FI: '*makhrūm al-awwal*' / '*incomplete in the beginning*'; C: poetry – Umayyad. (cf. no. 627)

(1706a) Makh/7s 270a/2 *Majmū^{c} al-R/Z [illegible word] – Multiple-Text Manuscript by [illegible word]*; the illegible author's name appears in the following entry as the author of an *al-Maqṣūr wa-al-mamdūd* work, but no known author would fit the form given here. Al-Jūmānī, *Fihrist*, reads 'al-Hadīya' without identifying the work and I cannot see the basis for this reading. FI: '*nāqiṣa min awwalihā*' / '*incomplete from the beginning*'.

(1706b) 270a/2 *wa-al-Maqṣūr wa-al-mamdūd – The Short and Long Alif*; A: '*lahu*', the illegible author's name that appears in the preceding entry; C: grammar.

(1707) Makh/7s 270a/2 *Majmū^{c} al-laṭāʾif – Multiple-Text Manuscript with The Subtleties*; probably one of the works by A: al-Tha^{c}ālibī (d. 429/1038): 1) *al-Ẓarāʾif wa-al-laṭāʾif* that was mainly transmitted in Abū Naṣr al-Maqdisī's recension *al-Laṭāʾif wa-al-ẓarāʾif*, ed. ^{c}U. al-As^{c}ad, *Laṭāʾif al-luṭf*, Beirut 1980 (cf. no. 716?); 2) *al-Luṭf wa-al-laṭāʾif*, ed. M.^{c}A. al-Jādir, Kuwait: DA, 1984 (cf. no. 1312b); C: adab – anthology. (cf. nos. 908, 958b, 1242a)

Notes

1. Fihrist al-Ashrafiya, Engl. tr. no. 9.
2. Fihrist al-Ashrafiya, Engl. tr. nos. 1144, 138, 781.
3. For example, Fihrist al-Ashrafiya, Engl. tr. nos. 160–5.
4. Fihrist al-Ashrafiya, Engl. tr. no. 1144 (*Majmū^{c} ash^{c}ār wa-akhbār*): '*in one bound volume*'; no. 1662 (*Du^{c}āʾ*): '*in five folios*', '*in muḥaqqaq script*', '*in one bound volume*'; no. 979 (*Majmū^{c} fawāʾid*): '*in nine leaves/folios*'.
5. Fihrist al-Ashrafiya, Engl. tr. no. 691 (*Shi^{c}r*): '*on silk paper written in Kūfī script*'; no. 317 (*Jawāb kitāb wa-ta^{c}ziya*): '*in thuluth script*', '*parchment*'; no. 427 (*Du^{c}āʾ sharīf*): '*bound in black parchment with silver*'.
6. Fihrist al-Ashrafiya, Engl. tr. no. 782 (*Majmū^{c} shi^{c}r*): '*old [manuscript]*'; no. 783 (*Majmū^{c} shi^{c}r*): '*old [manuscript]*'.
7. Fihrist al-Ashrafiya, Engl. tr. no. 777 (*Majmū^{c} Shi^{c}r*): '*in columns*'; no. 1694 (*Majmū^{c}*): '*organised by topics in chapters similar to the register's chapters*'; no. 217 (*al-Bayzara*): '*in 62 chapters*'.

8. Fihrist al-Ashrafīya, Engl. tr. no. 1282 (*Majmūᶜ fī al-qirāᵓāt*): '*safina-shaped*'; no. 169 (*Adᶜiya maᵓthūra*): '*in large format*'; no. 322 (*Ḥirz*): '*to be worn as a necklace*'.
9. Fihrist al-Ashrafīya, Engl. tr. no. 160 (*Adᶜiya*): '*in proportioned script*'; no. 164 (*Adᶜiya*):'*in Kufi Script*'; no. 1344 (*Naḥw*): '*in small calligraphy*'.
10. Fihrist al-Ashrafīya, Engl. tr. no. 1293 (*Majmūᶜ ikhtiyār jamāᶜa min shuᶜarāᵓ al-ᶜarab wa-ashᶜārihim*): '*of inferior quality*'; no. 165 (*Adᶜiya*): '*of inferior quality*'; no. 314 (*Juzᵓ*): '*loose folios*'.
11. Fihrist al-Ashrafīya, Engl. tr. no. 1209a (*Majmūᶜ*): '*with the heading* '"*Nuzhat al-farīd*"' *and in it is a verse on Interpretation and pious sayings*'; no. 1249a (*Majmūᶜ*): '*which mentions that it contains selections of knowledge, eloquence and current verses as well as [selections] from The Book on Women*'; no. 1236 (*Majmūᶜ*): '*in heading are mentioned: a volume on the merits of the Koran's chapters, on the principles and on the merits of the minor ablution, of alms in the name of the dead and of the ritual prayer*'.
12. Fihrist al-Ashrafīya, Engl. tr. nos. 904 and 808.
13. Fihrist al-Ashrafīya, Engl. tr. no. 1413.
14. Fihrist al-Ashrafīya, Engl. tr. nos. 697 and 1435.
15. Fihrist al-Ashrafīya, Engl. tr. no. 1154. Another example is no. 1153, which is only given as *Majmūᶜ ashᶜār*, but the catalogue explicitly states that al-Juwaynī is not only the scribe of the work, but also its compiler ('*bi-jamᶜihi*').
16. On book titles see Gacek, *Vademecum*, 37; Ambros, 'Beobachtungen'; Hirschler, *Medieval Arabic Historiography*, 66–72; al-Jūmānī, 'al-Fahāris al-makhṭūṭa', 23–5; al-Jūmānī, 'al-Fihrist', 77–78.
17. For these short titles see Serikoff, *Marginal- und Schnitttitel.*
18. Fihrist al-Ashrafīya, Engl. tr. no. 1391.
19. Fihrist al-Ashrafīya, Engl. tr. no. 1284a.
20. Fihrist al-Ashrafīya, Engl. tr. no. 264.
21. Fihrist al-Ashrafīya, Engl. tr. nos. 326 and 461.
22. As far as is evident al-Jūmānī, 'Fihris'and 'al-Fahāris' relied in his identification of Ashrafīya entries primarily on later works.
23. On books that he consulted in the Ashrafīya library see IKH, I, 214 (Fihrist al-Ashrafīya, Engl. tr. no. 800); IKH, IV, 450 (no. 1062); and possibly IKH, IV, 24–6 (no. 1070).
24. TI, 641–50, p. 325.
25. *Wāfī*, III, 37 (Fihrist al-Ashrafīya, Engl. tr. no. 1392).
26. *Al-Muntakhab*, ed. Sbath, IX.

27. On the Salem foundation cf. Río Sánchez, *Catalogue*. I thank the author for providing further background on the collection as well as establishing contact with the curator.
28. Sbath, *al-Fihris*.
29. Blog Roger Pearse, posting 28/4/2009, http://www.roger-pearse.com/weblog/2008/09/09/1000-arabic-manuscripts-destroyed-in-ww2/ (last accessed 16/3/2015).
30. Blog Roger Pearse, posting 11/4/2010, http://www.roger-pearse.com/weblog/2008/09/09/1000-arabic-manuscripts-destroyed-in-ww2/ (last accessed 16/3/2015).
31. On Ibn al-Nabīh (d. 619/1222) see Rikabi, *Poésie profane*, 87–104; Ibn Wāṣil, *Mufarrij*, III, 157–8; IKH, V, 336. More than 50% of all poems are dedicated to al-Ashraf in his diwan (al-As^{c}ad, *Dīwān Ibn al-Nabīh*). Fihrist al-Ashrafīya, Engl. tr. nos. 315, 863, 868, 1049 and 1055.
32. Ibn ^{c}Unayn (d. 630/1233): Bāshā, *al-Adab fī bilād al-Shām*, 297–322; IKH, V, 336; Sibṭ Ibn al-Jawzī, *Mir$^{\circ}$āt*, XV, 48; Ibn Wāṣil, *Mufarrij*, IV, 101–2 and V, 43; Ibn ^{c}Unayn, *Dīwān*, 9–12, 12–14, 14–15, 103; al-Talla^{c}farī (d. 675/1277): Bāshā, *al-Adab fī bilād al-Shām*, 356–77; Ibn al-Ardakhl (d. 628/1231): IKH, V, 336; Fihrist al-Ashrafīya, Engl. tr. no. 963; As^{c}ad al-Sinjārī (d. 622/1225): IKH, V, 336; Fihrist al-Ashrafīya, Engl. tr. nos. 800, 1054; al-Ḥillī (d. 627/1230): IKH, V, 336; Ibn Wāṣil, *Mufarrij*, III, 185–6; IKH, IV, 7–9; al-Kutubī, *Fawāt*, II, 7–15; Ibn Raqīqa (d. 635/1237–8): IAU, IV, 295.
33. *Qaṣīdas*: Fihrist al-Ashrafīya, Engl. tr. no. 875; *epistles*: no. 484.
34. For instance, Isḥāq b. Ṭarkhān Ibn Māḍī (d. 639/1242) (TI, 631–40, pp. 392–3); ^{c}Abd al-Ḥamīd b. Muḥammad Ibn Māḍī (d. 639/1242) (TI, 631–40, pp. 401–2); ^{c}Abd al-Raḥīm b. ^{c}Abd al-Ḥamīd (d. 677/1278) (TI, 671–80, p. 275); Taqī al-Dīn ^{c}Abd al-Sātir b. ^{c}Abd al-Ḥamīd Ibn Māḍī (d. 679/1280) (TI, 671–80, pp. 323–4).
35. Pouzet, *Damas*, 91.
36. Fihrist al-Ashrafīya, Engl. tr. no. 1147; al-Yārūqī (d. 656/1258), *Dīwān*.
37. I thank Suleiman Mourad (Smith College) for advice on this entry.
38. MS has '*al-Ījād*'.
39. I thank Swantje Bartschat (Marburg) for advice on this entry.
40. I thank Suleiman Mourad (Smith College) for advice on this entry.
41. MS has '*Ibn*'.
42. I thank Frank Griffel (Yale) for advice on this entry.

43. The MS has '*al-Aᶜmāl*', but a work with this title by this author is not identifiable. The reading '*Ikmāl*' is likely because the only other onomastic work in this library is also in category 5 (cf. no. 898).
44. On this comment see Chapter 2.
45. The cataloguer forgot to note thematic category 7 in the line. He immediately realised this mistake and inserted the category under line 10 before he wrote the following line. The wider spacing between lines 10 and 11 clearly shows that he did not squeeze the category between these lines at a later point. The category thus clearly refers to the preceding line and the positioning under this title leaves no doubt that the cataloguer intended the category to start with this title.
46. MS has '*ūdabāʾ*'.
47. MS has '140', but this number would be a complete outlier (the next highest number is 51) and it is thus safe to assume that the cataloguer meant '1–40'.
48. I thank Natalia Bachour (Zürich) for suggesting this reading.
49. MS has '*al-Hudhaylīyīn*'.
50. MS has '*al-rijāl*'. Yet this is neither grammatically possible nor does it fit the alphabetical order of the catalogue. This miswriting is probably related to the fact that the cataloguer had made his main mistake – and corrected it – in the preceding passage (lines 5–10) when erroneously jumping several letters.
51. The term '*muqaddam*' in the margins does not belong to the title, but draws attention to the erroneous transposition of entries starting with the letter *dāl* in the preceding lines.
52. MS has '*dār*'.
53. Before this entry the cataloguer inserts '*al-sādisa wa-hiya ūlā al-thānīya*'/'sixth *[thematic category]*, which is the beginning of the second' (same as in 251b/2–3, 252b/1 and 267a/9–10). This has to be read in light of the similar insertion in 251a/11–12: '*al-sādisa wa-hiya al-ūlā min al-ṣaff al-thānī*'/'sixth *[thematic category]*, which is the beginning of the second shelf'.
54. I thank Sonja Brentjes (Berlin) for advice on this entry.
55. I thank Hidemi Takahashi (Tokyo), Erica Hunter (SOAS) and Jack B. Tannous (Princeton) for advice on the entries 207–9.
56. I thank Anna Akasoy (New York) for directing me to the pertinent secondary literature.
57. MS has '*Ibn Burhān*'.
58. MS has 'ترب' (?).
59. I thank David King (Frankfurt) for advice on this entry.

60. I thank Thomas Bauer (Münster) for advice on this entry.
61. I thank Ulrich Rebstock (Freiburg) and Moustafa Mawaldi (Aleppo) for advice on entries 329 and 330.
62. The catalogue has this title under 'Ḥ', but *Ḥalāʾiq* is impossible.
63. Before this entry the cataloguer inserted '*al-adab fī al-rābiʿa ashara*' because he had overseen this thematic category and had already embarked on listing the titles of category 15. It also has to be underlined that these are the only category 14 titles in the entire catalogue that are not in the section of incomplete manuscripts.
64. The cataloguer has this and the following three lexicographical works in category 3. However, it is most likely that he simply forgot to insert the heading for category 4 here as these titles would be very odd in category 3, which has no other lexicographical or philological titles whatsoever.
65. Before this entry the cataloguer inserts '*al-sādisa wa-hiya al-ūlā min al-ṣaff al-thānī*'/'sixth *[thematic category]*, which is the beginning of the second shelf' (same as in 267a/9–10 and similar to 249a/14, 251b/2–3 and 252b/1).
66. For *darj* in sense of scroll see Gacek, *Vademecum*, 225.
67. The manuscript has '*al-khāj*' (?).
68. The following 'ṣ' is mostly likely an abbreviation for *ṣaḥīfa/ṣafīḥa* (for these terms see Gacek, *Tradition*, 45), although this would make the manuscript surprisingly brief.
69. Before this entry the cataloguer erroneously wrote category 4 '*rābiʿat al-ṣighār*', realised his mistake and wrote the correct category 3 '*thālitha*' without crossing out the wrong entry, which he just repeated in the following line when the category 4 entries did indeed start.
70. MS has '*Ibn*'.
71. This entry is followed by the word 'درر', which is not an independent entry and nor does there seem to be a connection with the following number for the next thematic category. It seems to be out of place, but the cataloguer inserted it on purpose because it also appears on folio 248a, l. 5 where he had already registered this title by mistake.
72. Before this entry the cataloguer inserts '*al-sādisa wa-hiya ūlā al-thānīya*'/'sixth *[thematic category]*, which is the beginning of the second' (same as in 249a/14 and 252b/1). This has to be read in light of the similar insertions in 251a/11–12 and 267a/9–10: '*al-sādisa wa-hiya al-ūlā min al-ṣaff al-thānī*'/'sixth *[thematic category]*, which is the beginning of the second shelf'.
73. The heading for thematic category 11 is followed by the numeral 42.

74. The number here, unusually, is without definite article.
75. Before this entry the cataloguer inserts '*al-sādisa wa-hiya ūlā al-thānīya*'/'sixth *[thematic category]*, which is the beginning of the second' (same as in 249a/14 and 251b/2–3). This has to be read in light of the similar insertions in 251a/11–12 and 267a/9–10: '*al-sādisa wa-hiya al-ūlā min al-ṣaff al-thānī*'/'sixth *[thematic category]*, which is the beginning of the second shelf'.
76. At this point the cataloguer returns, very unusually, to the normal-sized entries up to folio 253a, l. 2 (cf. no. 511). See comments in Chapter 2 on this.
77. I thank Istvan Kristo-Nagy (Exeter) for advice on this entry.
78. I thank Andrew Peacock (St Andrews) for his advice on this title.
79. MS has '*al-Mayānī*' in reference to his hometown Mayāna (cf. no. 764).
80. MS has '*Sīrat*'.
81. In contrast to the other 'a second/another manuscript is in'-constructions (cf. nos. 73, 371, 385, 415) here it does not refer to the number of volumes/folia. Rather it refers to the thematic category, which is indicated by the fact that the number is spelled out and determined just as the thematic categories themselves in the catalogue.
82. I thank Caterina Bori (Bologna) for advice on this entry.
83. The cataloguer repeatedly left out the final '*waw*' for ᶜAmr (e.g. cf. nos. 636, 684).
84. The cataloguer was clearly unsure about this *nisba*.
85. MS has '*ᶜAbd Allāh*'.
86. Assuming that the cataloguer mistook '*al-ᶜUklī*' as '*al-ᶜUqaylī*'.
87. No such *nisba* is mentioned in Ibn Zaydūn's biographical entries. '*Al-ᶜUmānī*' is listed in Ibn al-Athīr's dictionary of *nisbas* (Ibn al-Athīr, *al-Lubāb*, II, 356–7) and seems the most probable reading.
88. MS has '*Abī*'.
89. The cataloguer repeatedly left out the final '*waw*' for ᶜAmr (e.g. cf. nos. 605, 636).
90. Only the word 'eight' is added after the title without the usual 'copies/*nusakh*'.
91. As in other instances in this catalogue the *ᶜan* here merely signifies authorship and not 'transmitted by'. I am not sure why the cataloguer decided to use this construction in some instances rather than the *li-* that he has in most cases to express authorship for a determined title.
92. One copy is in thematic category 1 and the other copy is in thematic category 2.
93. I thank Ayman Shihadeh (SOAS) for advice on this entry.
94. MS has 'مرون ابن'.

95. MS has '*Ardiyānūs*'.
96. I thank Louise Marlow (Wellesley) for advice on this entry.
97. For *ᶜahdat*, see Lane, *Lexicon*.
98. Before this entry the cataloguer inserted '*al-kutub bi-al-ᶜajamīya fī al-tāsiᶜa*'/'Books in Persian in *[thematic category]* nine'.
99. MS has '*al-Mayānī*' in reference to his hometown Mayāna (cf. no. 538).
100. Alternatively, this term could be read as ᶜUlwān ('title page', Gacek, *Tradition*, 56). I thank Frédéric Bauden (Liège) for advice on this entry.
101. MS has '*Ibn*'.
102. Incomplete word. None of the titles by this prolific author of medical works match what seems to be a word starting with *fā*ᵓ/*qāf*/ᶜ*ayn*/*ghayn*.
103. MS has 'المهورات'.
104. Authorship indicated with '*ᶜan*'.
105. Using the rather rare form '*Buqrāṭīs*' instead of Buqrāṭ.
106. MS has '*Ibn Sarrāj*'.
107. The name can be read as '*al-J/Ḥ/Khūmī*', but the only known scholar with this *nisba* is the Andalusian Koran recitator and scholar Aḥmad b. Khalaf al-Ḥūmī (d.?; Ibn al-Jazarī, *Ghāyat al-nihāya*, I, 52), who is not renowned for producing any work that would fit this title and/or this category.
108. MS has 'الشعافي', which seems to be a scribal error, although it is difficult to imagine that such a clear error escaped the cataloguer's attention, especially as the remainder of the catalogue shows that he is willing to correct his mistakes. However, there is no scholar known by this *nisba*.
109. MS has '*Muwāfiq al-marāfiq*'.
110. On the term '*qawāᵓim*' see Gacek, *Tradition*, 120.
111. MS has 'لاحبيب'.
112. Manuscript has '2', but this is clearly a slip of the pen.
113. MS has '*mudawāt*'.
114. MS has '*jawhar*'.
115. The cataloguer continued with a '*fī al-*' and a further stroke, probably in order to add the typical '*fī*' + content description element to the title's key word.
116. MS lacks the initial letter *mīm*.
117. MS has '*madāᵓiḥ*'.
118. MS has '*madḥ*'.
119. MS has '*al-Mīkāᵓilī*'.
120. MS has '*al-Mīkāᵓilī*'.
121. MS has '*muqāt*'.

122. For 'Muᶜtazil' see R. Dozy, *Supplément aux dictionnaires arabes*, Leiden 1881. Al-Jūmānī, 'Fihris', 81 reads المعتدلي and sees it as an unknown paper format.
123. MS has '*dāra*', but this is the closest title by Ibn Abī Dunyā that would also fit under the letter *mīm*.
124. I thank G.J. van Gelder (Oxford) for suggesting this reading and providing these references.
125. MS has '*Aflāṭun*'.
126. MS has '*al-Yārjūkī*'.
127. MS has '*yawmīya*'. This mistake is so basic that it seems very odd. However, it may be that the cataloguer was not familiar with this genre and that this led to glaring mistakes. In another entry on *muᶜashsharāt* on the same folio 260b, l. 15 he gets the term wrong and has to cross the erroneous version out (cf. no. 1165).
128. I thank G.J. van Gelder (Oxford) for the reference to Ibn ᶜAbd Khān.
129. I thank Teresa Bernheimer (SOAS) for advice on this entry.
130. MS has 'ملقيات'.
131. I thank Frank Griffel (Yale) for advice on this entry.
132. MS has *al-Bāṭina.*
133. I thank Frank Griffel (Yale) for advice on this entry.
134. I thank Ayman Shihadeh (SOAS) for advice on this entry.
135. MS has, as in the preceding entry, '*al-ᶜārifīn*', but no title *Taḥṣīl al-ᶜārifīn* is identifiable and as the other three words clearly match this title (that is also mentioned elsewhere in the catalogue) this is the most likely version.
136. On the term '*marmūz*' see Gacek, *Tradition*, 60.
137. I thank Tilman Seidensticker (Jena) and G.J. van Gelder (Oxford) for advice on this entry.
138. The MS has ذكر.
139. I thank G.J. van Gelder (Oxford) for this reference.
140. I thank Omid Ghaemmaghami (Binghamton) and Derek Mancini-Lander (SOAS) for advice on this entry.
141. MS lacks article.
142. For '*tarjama*' see Gacek, *Vademecum*, 57.
143. I thank G.J. van Gelder (Oxford) for this reference.
144. I thank G.J. van Gelder (Oxford) for this reference.
145. This reading is very uncertain, but the other main option 'المرة' (for *al-marʾa*) is no more satisfying as no such title is known.
146. In MS '*Rayḥān*'.

147. I thank G.J. van Gelder (Oxford) for this reference.
148. I thank G.J. van Gelder (Oxford) for this reference.
149. The MS has here a different term, but this is the only known epistle by Ibn ᶜAbbād that fits this title.
150. MS has '*qarāʾiḍ*', but a reference to the poetic term is highly unlikely.
151. I thank Swantje Bartschat (Münster) for advice on this entry.
152. See Chapter 2 on this term.
153. I thank James Montgomery (Cambridge) for advice on this entry.
154. I thank James Montgomery (Cambridge) for advice on this entry.
155. MS '*al-Ḥākimī*'.
156. I thank David King (Frankfurt) for suggesting this reading.
157. I thank G.J. van Gelder (Oxford) for advice on this entry.
158. MS has '*Hilīlaja*'.
159. MS has 'الحطري'.
160. I thank Mohsen Zakeri (Göttingen) for advice on this entry.
161. Cf. Biberstein-Kazimirski, *Dictionnaire, k-sh-ṭ*: 'au passif, être déplacé, ôté de sa place'.
162. MS has '*al-Baḥr*'.
163. MS has 'Ibn'.
164. On this comment and the same comment in the following entry see Chapter 2.
165. Before this entry the cataloguer inserted, but then crossed out: '*al-sādisa wa-hiya al-ūlā min al-ṣaff al-thānī*'/'sixth *[thematic category]*, which is the beginning of the second shelf' (same as in 251a/11–12 and similar to 249a/14, 251b/2–3 and 252b/1).
166. For '*aṣl*' in the sense of exemplar see Gacek, *Tradition*, 78.
167. Here and in the following two entries the cataloguer changes his system of how to record volumes of incomplete manuscripts. Whereas he generally spells out the volumes ('fourth', 'eighth', etc.), in this section he uses numerals (4, 8, etc.). This is linked to the 'Ṣ'-sign, which he suddenly uses here again and that he arguably used to earmark entries for later revisions (see Chapter 2). The cataloguer uses a numeral once again in no. 1622, although without an 'Ṣ' sign.
168. At this point the cataloguer reverts to his original system of spelling out the volume numbers.
169. In that entry the cataloguer had already mentioned three copies, so he counted this manuscript twice.
170. In MS with article.
171. MS has '*al-Hudhaylīyīn*'.

172. Tentative reading as in MS with article.
173. MS has 'Ibn'.
174. This entry is preceded by '*wa-yamurruhu*' (?), which may be read as 'and *[the text of Uns al-farīd]* goes along with it *[the text of Aḥsan mā sami*ᶜ*tu]*', and the two texts would thus be intertwined.
175. I thank Isabel Toral-Niehoff (Berlin) for advice on this entry.
176. I thank Gregor Schoeler (Basel) for advice on this entry.
177. MS has '*Ibn al-Akhṭal*'.
178. In MS with article.
179. The cataloguer, very unusually, uses a numeral here and refers to '3' (volumes?). For the previous use of numerals for recording volumes of incomplete manuscripts cf. nos. 1457–9.
180. This entry has an unusual format (asyndetic enumeration of the two titles) as this is a collective manuscript.
181. MS has '*Aflāṭun*'.
182. On the term '*qawā*ʾ*im*' see Gacek, *Tradition*, 120.
183. MS has 'جعر'.
184. The preceding حامل (?) is unclear.
185. I thank Mohsen Zakeri (Göttingen) for advice on this entry.
186. It is not entirely clear whether the cataloguer starts a new entry at this point or not. However, as this section is on incomplete collective manuscripts it is most likely that each new entry starts with the term '*majmū*ᶜ'.

5

The Ashrafīya Catalogue: Edition

The Ashrafiya catalogue has been preserved in a unique manuscript in the Fatih collection in Istanbul, presently housed in the Süleymaniye Library (Fatih 5433, folia 246b–270a). Fatih 5433 is a multiple-text manuscript with texts that, judging from the binding, were most likely bound together in the Ottoman period. The shared characteristic of these texts is that they are all linked with Damascus and that they were all composed in the late Ayyubid/early Mamluk period. The manuscript thus starts on folia 1b to 53b with an anonymous summary of the chronicle *The Mirror of Times* (*Mirʾāt al-zamān*) by the Damascene scholar Sibṭ Ibn al-Jawzī (d. 654/1256), who was closely attached to the city's Ayyubid rulers, among them al-Malik al-Ashraf.[1] Epistles, anecdotes, poems and historical material appear on the following folia up to the Ashrafiya catalogue. These are most likely from the early Mamluk encyclopaedia of the Damascene administrator and *adīb* ᶜAlī b. al-Muẓaffar al-Wadāᶜī (d. 716/1316).[2] The summary and the encyclopaedia are repeatedly interlaced with other texts, such as the 'spiritual testament' (*waṣīya*) by the Sufi al-Suhrawardī (d. 632/1234) on folia 104a–105a. After the Ashrafiya catalogue we find on folia 271b to 282b again material from a minor untitled manual by the low-ranking early Mamluk administrator Sulaymān b. Mūsā Abū al-ᶜAlāʾ (d. 713/1314).[3]

The Ashrafiya catalogue has no colophon but was, as discussed in Chapter 1, most likely written in Damascus in the 670s/1270s by the librarian Aḥmad al-Anṣārī. The manuscript consists of twenty-five folia of differently coloured wove paper. It is in a very good state of preservation with no lacunae and only occasional stains. The catalogue is written in *naskh* with partially pointed letters and occasional use of vocalisation. The script is of decreasing quality as the catalogue progresses from a very clear hand in the beginning to a rather sloppy script towards the end. Even though the hand changes, the entire catalogue was written by one scribe.[4] The text is monochrome in black ink. For rubrications, wider word spacing and larger letter sizes are employed. The manuscript is bound in an Ottoman full leather binding on pasteboard without fore-edge flaps. The front and back cover are identically decorated with a framed square.

The catalogue's page format measures 195 x 135mm with page trimmings on the left. The trimmings were probably undertaken to fit the catalogue with the size of the other titles when it was bound into the Fatih 5433 multiple-text manuscript. It is a *safīna*-shaped manuscript with the lines running horizontal to the spine. The written area varies considerably between the pages. For the height *c.*170mm is the average with a variation from *c.*161mm (folio 261a; Plate 36) to *c.*178mm (folio 267a; Plate 48). For the width the average is *c.*120mm with a variation from *c.*110mm (folio 268b; Plate 51) to *c.*125mm (folia 259b, 266a; Plates 33, 46). The forty-seven full pages have from fifteen to twenty-one lines (see *Figure 2.1*).[5] The line spacing is accordingly irregular and there are no marks of pricking and ruling. The Arabic foliation is in pencil on the top left and European numerals are on the middle to lower left. Catchwords are, as seen in Chapter 2, inconsistently used and appear on roughly a third of the folia. The catalogue consists of three quires: two quaternions (folia 246–53 and 254–61) and a quinion (folia 262–71). With the catalogue ending at the top of folio 270a (Plate 54) this left almost four pages blank that were used at a later point. The remainder of folio 270a was filled with scribal verses and probatio pennae. Folia 270b and 271a have extracts from an anonymous mirror for princes and on folio 271b the above-mentioned early Mamluk administrative manual begins.

One guiding principle in editing the catalogue was to represent its organisation according to alphabet, size and themes, which the cataloguer indicated in display script. These structural terms are thus set in bold in the edition below. For ease of legibility commas were used in order to separate the individual entries. An entry could consist of (1) the title, (2) the number of additional manuscripts of a previously cited title or (3) the title and the total number of manuscripts. The division between (1) and (2) seems somewhat artificial, but here we follow the cataloguer's system. In the early parts of the catalogue, al-Anṣārī clearly saw the title and the number of manuscripts as distinct entries and neatly separated them until he gradually changed to system (3).[6]

For the sake of legibility, the orthography has been standardised to bring it into a form familiar to modern readers. The text is reproduced with fully pointed letters, although they are inconsistently used in the manuscript. By contrast, the *fatḥa*, *kasra*, *ḍamma* and *shadda* signs that the writer occasionally inserted are not reproduced. The *hamza* is generally weakened in the manuscript, typical for Middle Arabic, but it is reproduced in the edition, that is, رياسة is reproduced as رئاسة / *riʾāsa*. Nouns are given in accordance with post-classical conventions, for instance, ابرهيم as إبراهيم / Ibrāhīm, اسحق as إسحاق / Isḥāq, افلاطن as أفلاطون / Aflāṭūn, رحمن as رحمان / *raḥmān*, ثلث as ثلاث / *thalāth*. The *hamza* is inconsistently used in '*ibn*' and this has not been changed in the edition. Especially towards the end, al-Anṣārī hardly differentiates between '*abī*' and '*ibn*' and the editor's choice has only been highlighted if relevant for the identification of the title.[7] Substantial errors are corrected and indicated with square brackets in the English text, but simple slips of the pen are corrected without comment. One single page exists in two versions, as al-Anṣārī mixed up the order of folia at one point and wrote by mistake a section on the title page's recto (folio 246a; Plate 6). After he realised his mistake he rewrote the same section in its correct place (folio 253a; Plate 20) (see Chapter 2 on this) and any differences between the two versions are indicated in the footnotes with '246a'.

Symbols used in editing the Arabic text

,	new entry
/	line break (with line number in superscript)
. . .	text illegible or obscure
( )	doubtful or tentative reading
{ }	text to be deleted (e.g. unintentionally repeated words)
[ ]	editor's insertion of letters or words and folio numbers
[[ ]]	text erased in the manuscript
| |	interlinear addition
|| ||	marginal addition

[246ب] بسم الله الرحمان الرحيم وبه نستعين /2 فهرست كتب خزانة الأشرفية التي في تربة الملك الأشرف رحمة الله عليه شمالي /3 الكلاسة بجامع الأموي ||**الألف الأولى**|| اختصار صحيح مسلم للملك الكامل، الأربعون الجهادية /4 للمرادي، إيضاح الوقف والابتداء لابن الأنباري 2، الإنجاد في الجهاد اص، أخبار /5 روح العارفين اص، أربعون حديث جهادية لعبد الرحيم بن منصور اص، الآيات الواردة /6 في فضل الجهاد اص، الأسباب الجهادية لسبط أبي سعيد، أدب الدين والدنيا للماوردي اص، /7 الاختيار في الحكايات، إحياء علوم الدين، الأعزية والتهاني، اعتلال /8 القلوب، إعراب سورة الإخلاص يتضمن أمثالاً عن علي بن أبي طالب ووصية /9 لولده رضي الله عنهما، أصول الدين لابن خلاد، الإشارة لسليم، آداب الاجتهاد، /10 الإتمام لفضائل الأنام، إثبات إمامة علي بن أبي طالب رضي الله عنه، الإرشاد /11 في الفقه، الاعتبار والنظر، إشارة النظار، الإفصاح والبيان في معرفة الله /12 تعالى من القرآن، الإرشاد إلى ما ليس للسلاطين تفويضه إلى القضاة، **الرابعة** /13 إصلاح المنطق، أدب الكاتب، ألفاظ عبد الرحمان، ألفاظ محمد بن الحسن، /14 الأضداد لابن السكيت، الإيضاح والتكملة، أسماء خيل العرب لابن الأعرابي، /15 الألفاظ (لمغى ولقد الأسماء) في الفرق بين الضاد والظاء، الأمثال للميداني، الأنواء /16 لأبي حنيفة، الإنصاف لابن الأنباري، الألفاظ لابن السكيت، الأمثال [247أ] الأمثال لحمزة، الأمثال لأبي عبيد، الأمثال للمفضل، أمثال الأصمعي، /2 الأنموذج في النحو، أمثال حمزة، **الخامسة** الأوراق للصولي، /3 الاستظهار أمر القضاة وهو المستظهري، الأخبار الطوال لأبي حنيفة /4 الدينوري، (الإكمال) لابن ماكولا، أمثال أمر |الملك| المعظم في ترجمة أخبار العجم 5، /5 نسخة ثانية منه 5، **السادسة وهي الأولى من النسبة** أشعار فهم وعدوان ا، /6 أشعار بني {ا} بدر بن جوية ا، نسخة ثانية منه اص، الإعجاز[[39]] والإيجاز 39، /7 نسخة ثانية 45، نسخة ثالثة، نسخة رابعة 15، الآداب الذهبية لابن المعتز اص،/8 اسم المفعول {الثاني} [الثلاثي] لابن جني ويعرف بالمعتصب اص، أسماء الأسد ورسالة أبي العلاء /9 وهي الإغريضية اص، إجمال عوامل الإعراب لابن بري اص، الأنواء لابن دريد اص، /10 |**السابعة**| الأبيات السائرة مائة بخط ابن مقلة اص،الأعيان والأماثل اص 43، /11 الإمتاع والمؤانسة 3ص 43، الأذكياء لابن الجوزي اص 43، نسخة ثانية /12 منه ا 44، الأمثال والحكم للماوردي ا 38، نسخة ثانية ا 44، /13 نسخة ثالثة ا 44، أخبار وحكايات وأمثال وأشعار اص، أخبار/14 ابن حجاج اص، نسخة ثانية منه مصورة في 9، أجناس الأعداد والأخبار اص،/15 أدباء الغرباء (140)، اختيارات ابن العميد من كتب الجاحظ ا 45، **الثامنة** /16 آداب الملوك اص 41، أخلاق الملوك ا 39، اختيار الوزراء |3| 4، [247ب] آداب الوزراء ا، الأوصاف المختلفة الأصناف 3ص 41، أخلاق /2 الوزيرين التوحيدي 2ص 40، نسخة ثانية منه اص، الأنواء لأحمد الرازي اص 41، /3 أسماء شعراء الحماسة ا، نسخة ثانية اص في 15، أشجان الإخوان ا 40، أخبار /4 الحسين بن الضحاك اص 39، الإشارة إلى سلوك نهج الإمارة 46، الإشارة /5 إلى محاسن التجارة، أخبار العدائين وأشعارهم اص 40، نسخة ثانية /6 منه اص 42، أشعار اللصوص وأخبارهم اص، الأوائل لابن شبة اص 41، /7 الإمتاع والموازنة اص، الارتسام وفوائد الاغتنام اص 36، نسخة ثانية (لعرقلة) اص 41، /8 أخبار أبي التمام اص، أخبار الرؤساء، أخبار العباس اص، (الانتخاب) في حفظ /9 الأصحاب اص، اختيارات من سماعات محمد بن سهل الشلحي اص،

التاسعة /10 الأحجار لأرسطاطاليس اص، نسخة ثانية منه اص، أبواب مجموعة في علم النجوم اص، /11 أصول صناعة الأحكام في النجوم اص، أسباب الندأ[ة] والظل اص، أقوال جماعة /12 من الحكماء اص، آداب الفلاسفة اص، الآلات النجومية، **العاشرة** اقتناء /13 الخيل وعلاجها 3ص، الابتهاج في أصناف العلاج اص، أدب الطبيب اص، /14 الأشربة لابن مسكويه اص، الإرشاد في حفظ صحة بن (حماد) اص، أدب الفلاحين اص، /15 الإيضاح في الرماية اص، الأطعمة المختارة اص، أقراباذين (مرهم)، اختصار /16 جالينوس لكتابه حيلة البرء اص، الأدوية المفردة اص، أقراباذين منزوع من [248أ] من عدة أقراباذينات اص، أقراباذين سابور اص، الأغذية لابن زهر اص، /2 إظهار حكمة الرحمان في خلق الإنسان وغيره اص،أبدال الأدوية المفردة /3 والمركبة اص، الإكليل للرازي اص، أقراباذين يوحنا اص، **الثانية عشرة** /4 أشعار الهذليين 5ص، نسخة ثانية منه ااص، الأغاني لابن القشيري اص، /5 [[**الدال الثانية** دستور معالم الحكم اص، الدعاء للمحاملي اص، درر، /6 **السادسة وهي أولى الثانية**، الدريدية منكتة اص، نسخة أخرى وتعاليق وفوائد /7 بخط ابن العصار اص، **الثامنة** دمية القصر اص 39، نسخة أخرى ثانية في 15، /8 الديارات للإصفهاني اص، (الدلجيين) اص 38، نسخة ثانية منه اص 40، **التاسعة** /9 الدلائل لابن البهلول اص، **الحادية عشرة** 42 ديوان البحتري اص، نسخة /10 ثانية 2 ص]] أزجال المدغليس اص، موجز الأزجال في 13ص، **الثالثة عشرة** || مقدمِ || /11 أشعار دوبيتي اص في 12، أشعار دوبيتي اص في 2، أشعار الستة اص، الأغراض /12 في ذكر الأعراض اص، أشعار الستة اص، أشعار وأخبار جمع الثعالبي وبخطه، /13 **الخامسة عشرة** أخبار مجنون ليلى وأشعاره اص،الإعجاز في الأحاجي /14 والألغاز اص، أزهار الأنهار 3ص، الآداب لابن شمس الخلافة اص 38، نسخة /15 ثانية منه اص، أخبار الحماسة لأبي رياش اص 46، آداب الملوك والعلماء للنحاس اص، /16 أخبار أبي نواس اص 42، أخبار العدائين وسعاة العرب اص، أخبار/17 اللصوص، أحسن ما قيل في البلاغة اص، أجناس في التجنيس والمنهج للثعالبي اص، [248ب] أدب المظالم اص 45، أفراد المعاني اص، آلات الرئاسة اص، أخبار /2 عبد الله بن جعفر اص، أخبار وأشعار ونوادر اص، أنيس الأمير وجليس /3 الوزير اص 42، أجزاء حديث اص، **أولى الصغار** أشعار بني نهد بن /4 موعد اص، **ثالثة** أشعار وأخبار ونوادر بخط الجويني اص، اختيارات /5 من كلام الحكماء بخط منوجهر اص، أشعار في أهل البيت وأخبار مستحسنة اص، /6 أشعار وفقر منتخبة اص 47، أخبار البحتري اص 47، أسباب ... /7 الطاهرة اص 46، أشعار وأخبار وفقر اص، الألفاظ المقتضبات والكلمات /8 المهديات اص، **رابعة الصغار** أسماء الله الحسنى اص، أدعية الأيام /9 السبعة، أدعية شريفة ا، أدعية عن النبي صلى الله عليه وسلم خط ابن /10 ريش اص، أدعية ومناجاة علي بن الحسين اص، أدعية مأثورة اص، أدعية خط /11 ابن صدقة اص، أدعية النصر والاحتراس اص، أدعية شريفة مجربة لقضاء /12 الحوائج اص، أدعية شريفة مجربة عن السلف الصالح اص، أدعية بخط منسوب اص، /13 أدعية نثر ونظم اص، أدعية بخط كوفي اص، أدعية بخط كوفي اص، أدعية بخط /14 كوفي اص، أدعية مكتوبة بأحمر وأصفر وأسود رديء اص، أدعية مباركة اص، /15 أدعية مباركة بخط منسوب اص، أدعية مباركة عن النبي صلى الله عليه وسلم بخط /16 ابن ريش اص، أدعية مأثورة كبيرة القطع اص، الإصابة في دعوات المستجابة اص، /17 أدعية مباركة مأثورة مروية عن السلف اص، أدعية عن النبي عليه السلام، /18 أدعية منقولة من خط ابن البواب اص، أدعية بخط

المراكشي، أدعية [249ا] أدعية أوله ما جاء في فضل الدعوات، أدعية الوسائل إلى المسائل اص، /2 أدعية هو دعاه يوم الأحزاب اص، أدعية مختارة بخط (منجر) اص، أدعية /3 شريفة ورثت عن أهل البيت، أدعية عن السلف 5، أدعية مستجابة /4 عن النبي عليه السلام اص، أدعية عن الإمام الشافعي رحمه الله اص، أسماء ألف اسم /5 واسم اص، أدعية بخط المراكشي، أدعية مروية عن النبي عليه السلم اص، /6 **خامسة الصغار** أخبار وإنشادات بخط عبد السلام البصري ا 5، /7 أشعار في الجوار اص، قصة دلة المحتالة اص، أشعار وعظية لأبي العتاهية اص، /8 الألفاظ التعزية والمدائح الأشرفية اص، أغاني (جزء) اص، **السادسة** /9 ألفاظ فائقة وكلمات رائقة في الرسائل اص، **السابعة** الأدوية /10 المفردة، **الباء الأولى** بستان المبتدئ في القرآت اص، البعث لابن /11 الأشعث والمائة الشريحية اص، **الثانية** بهجة المجالس لابن عبد البر 2ص، بهجة /12 الأسرار مجهول المصنف اص، بهجة الأسرار لابن جهضم خط بن الشواء 5، بداية /13 الهداية اص، نسخة أخرى اص، بستان العارفين اص، **الثالثة** البحر الحاوي /14 لجوهر الفتاوي، **الخامسة** البرق الشامي 6ص، **السادسة وهي أولى الثانية** /15 البسالة اختيار ثعلب اص 45، **الثامنة** البصائر والذخائر للتوحيدي، /16 **التاسعة** البيان والتبيين اص 4، البشارة والنذارة اص، البستان /17 ... 3ص، (بشورع دنا) في الآثار العلوية اص، **العاشرة** [249ب] ياربوقا في السموم 6ص، البيطرة الكبير 3ص، البيطرة لعبد الله بن يعقوب 2ص، /2 البيطرة تصنيف آخر اص، البيطرة تصنيف آخر اص، البيزرة مصور اص، البيزرة /3 لابن (حيد) اص، البيزرة لمحمد بن عبد الله بن عمر اص، البيزرة اثنان وستون /4 باباً اص، البزاة لخمارويه بن أحمد اص، البزاة بخط كوفي رث اص، **الثالثة عشرة** /5 البارع لابن المنجم 2ص، **الخامسة عشرة** بهجة الأسرار اص، برد الأكباد /6 في الأعداد اص، نسخة ثانية منه اص، بستان الناظر ونزهة الخاطر اص 40، نسخة ثانية /7 منه ا 5، بدائع البدائه اص، بدائع ما نجم من متخلفي كتاب العجم اص 44، **التاء الأولى** /8 تذكرة الغريب في تفسير القرآن لابن الجوزي اص، التبيان في تفسير القرآن لابن مريم 5ص، /9 تفسير القرآن لأبي الليث 4ص، تفسير آي الجهاد لابن عساكر 2ص، **الثانية** /10 تفسير سورة يوسف للشهرستاني اص، تنوير الغبش في فضل السود والحبش لابن الجوزي /11 وبخطه اص 2، التوابين للموفق اص، **الثالثة** تقريب الأحكام على فقهاء الإسلام 2ص، /12 تتمة الإبانة 10ص، نسخة ثانية 9، تلخيص الأقسام لمذاهب الأنام اص، تقويم النظر لابن برهان اص، /13 تعليق الشريف 2ص، تفريع ابن الجلاب اص، تهذيب إصلاح جيوش الجهاد اص، **الرابعة** /14 تصريف عبد القاهر اص، تهذيب إصلاح المنطق اص، التقفية لليمان بن اليمان 2ص، /15 **الخامسة** من تأريخ ابن الصابئ 29ص، تأريخ بن جرير 26، التأريخ الأتابكي اص، /16 تأريخ ثابت بن سنان بن قرة 6ص، التأريخ البدري لابن منقذ 5ص، تأريخ جمال الدين /17 ابن المأمون 2ص، التبيين في نسب القرشيين، التأريخ التاجي للصابئ 4ص، /18 **السابعة** تتمة اليتيمة اص، ست نسخ، التصحيف والتحريف 2ص، التمثيل والمحاضرة 2ص، /19 ثلاث نسخ، التحف والظرف اص، **الثامنة** تعظيم الملوك اص، تفضيل /20 الكلاب على كثير ممن لبس الثياب اص 44، التنبيه والتوقيف على (فضائل) الخريف، [250ا] **التاسعة** تقويم سنة خمس وعشرين وستمائة اص، تحفة الملوك في التعبير اص، تعبير /2 الرؤيا لعبد الواحد اص، تعبير الرؤيا عن ابن سيرين اص، تحويل المواليد وغيره اص، /3 تركيب العود والعمل به اص، **العاشرة** التبصرة في النبض والتفسرة اص، التدارك لأنواع /4 خطاء التدبير اص،

التذكرة الأشرفية ١ص، تقويم الصحة، أحد عشر نسخة، تقويم الأبدان، /5 أربع نسخ، التبصرة في معرفة الجواهر ١ص، الترياق الكبير، خمس نسخ، ترياق (بن) شعثاء ١ص، /6 التأتي لشفاء الأمراض ١ص، تدبير الصحة لحنين ١ص، نسخة ثانية ١ص، تذكرة الكحالين ١ص، التحبير /7 لعلي بن عبد الله ١ص، تقاسيم العلل وعلاجها ١ص، تقاسيم مسائل حنين ١ص، تفسير /8 أسنان الدواب ١ص، **الخامسة عشرة** توقيعات كسرى أنوشروان ١ص، **ثالثة** /9 **الصغار** تحفة الظرفاء في تأريخ الخلفاء ومعه قصيدة الأعشى ونذكره في القاف، /10 **رابعة** تحفة العباد في بيان الأوراد ١ص، ترجمة الناقوس عن علي بن أبي طالب /11 رضي الله عنه ١ص، تحفة الأديب وحلية الأريب ١ص من 4، **خامسة** التوحيد /12 عن الأئمة ١ص، **سادسة** التشبيبات والطلب ١ص، (ترسل) الخصكفي ١ص، **سابعة** /13 تدبير المسافرين وتنبيه (المختلسين) لصحتي الأبدان والأديان ١ص، **الثاء الثالثة عشرة** /14 الثناء المشرف بصفات الملك الأشرف 3ص، **الجيم الثانية** جواهر الكلام عن /15 علي بن أبي طالب كرم الله وجهه ١ص، جواهر القرآن للغزالي ١ص، **الثالثة** جامع شرائط /16 الأحكام ١ص، **الرابعة** جمهرة الأمثال للعسكري ١ص، جمل عبد القاهر ١ص، /17 جمل الزجاجي ١ص، **الخامسة** الجمع والبيان في أخبار القيروان 2ص، **السادسة** /18 جزء حديث بخط بن الجواليقي ١ص، جزء آخر بخطه أيضاً ١ص، الجمان لابن فارس وبخطه ١ص، [250ب] جمل التصريف لابن جني ١ص، **السابعة** الجليس الصالح الكافي 4ص، /2 الجليس الصالح لابن الج(و)زي ١ص 43، الجوهر البديع في ملتقط المجاميع ١ص، /3 **الثامنة** الجواهر المنتخبة من البصائر والذخائر 2ص 41، الجوابات لابن /4 (باعوراء)، **التاسعة** الجامع لتفسير صورة الإنسان ١ص، **العاشرة** الجماهر /5 في الجواهر ١ص، ثلاث نسخ، الجوارح والضواري، ثلاث نسخ، **الثانية عشرة** الجواهر /6 المؤلفة في المدائح المستطرفة ١ص 43، **الخامسة عشرة** الجواهر لإسحاق الموصلي ١ص 44، /7 الجامع الكبير في المنظوم والمنثور ١ص، **ثالثة الصغار** جلاء الهموم والأحزان ١ص 39، /8 **رابعة** جواهر الكلام عن علي بن أبي طالب رضي الله عنه، **خامسة** جزء حديث بخط /9 عبد السلام البصري ١ص، جزء أوراق ذكر أنها بخط مؤلف القوت ١ص، الجوهر /10 المثمن في مدح شاه أرمن ١ص، جامع الأنس ومبهج النفس ١ص 42، **ثامنة** /11 جواب كتاب (ثلثية) وتعزية لا أعرف مؤلفه برق ١ص، **الحاء الثالثة** الحاوي /12 للماوردي 4 ١ص، **الخامسة** الحجة المشرفية للدولة الأشرفية ١ص، **السادسة** /13 (الحشرات) ورسالة بن أبي طاهر في سرقات البحتري ١ص، حرز مروي عن جعفر الصادق ص، /14 حرز آخر في هيكل حمائلي، **السابعة** حكمة الآداب ١ص، **الثامنة** الحروب /15 بواسط وغيرها 42، الحنين حكايات وأخبار ١ص، حاوي الفنون ١ص، **التاسعة** /16 حديث جميل وبثينة ١ص، الحيل لبني موسى ١ص، الحساب الهندي ١ص، الحساب المعروف /17 بالزعفران ١ص، **العاشرة** حساب ١ص، الحاوي في الطب 4ص، ثلاث نسخ، (ال[خ]لائق) /18 الأشرفية ١ص، الحيل في الحرب ١ص، **الثانية عشرة** الحماسة لأبي تمام، عشر نسخ، الحماسة [251ا] الوحشية ١ص، الحديقة لأبي الصلت، **الثالثة عشرة** حديقة الحدق ١ص 42، /2 نسخة ثانية، **الخامسة عشرة** الحيوان للجاحظ ١ص ناقص ذكر في المخاريم، الحيل في الأدب ١ص، /3 **الأدب من الرابعة عشرة** حل الشعر والميدان في الغزل بالغلمان ١ص، حل العقد للثعالبي ١ص، /4 حديث ملك من ملوك الهند ١ص، **أولى الصغار** حل التتمة لابن شمس الخلافة ١ص، /5 **ثالثة** حكايات ونوادر ١ص، **خامسة** حكم ومواعظ من كلام جعفر الصادق، حكم وأشعار /6 ونوادر وأخبار بخط الجويني ١ص، حكم وأخبار وأشعار

للجويني وبخطه اص، **الخاء الثانية** /7 الخواتم لابن الجوزي وبخطه اص 44، الخطب النباتية اص، الخطب للكيزاني وغيره اص 40، /8 خطب بن شيث 40، خطب جهادية للهروي اص، خطب مجموعة اص، خطب الجلال بن نباتة اص، /9 خاصيات الخواص العشرة، **الثالثة** الخصال والعقود اص، الخلاصة على مذهب أبي حنيفة /10 رضي الله عنه 2ص، الخيل والسرج واللجام اص، خلق الإنسان للأصمعي اص، الخيل للأصمعي ولأبي زيد اص، /11 خلق الإنسان للزجاج اص، **الخامسة** الخريدة للعماد الكاتب الإصفهاني 12ص، **السادسة** /12 **وهي الأولى من الصف الثاني** ختمة كريمة بخط بن البواب اص، ختمة كريمة في درج كثيرة الإذهاب، /13 خدمة الملوك السرخسي اص، خلق الفرس عن قطرب اص 46، الخط للمبرد بخط (توزون) اص 45، /14 **الثامنة** (الخراج) لابن الأصباغي اص، ثلاث نسخ، الخراج لقدامة 2ص، خصائص الطرب اص، نسخة /15 أخرى في 3ص ص، **الثالثة عشرة** (الخراجية الطليقية) اص، **الخامسة عشرة** الخراج لابن سهل اص، /16 الخيل لأبي عبيدة اص، الخطب الدرية في المناقب الأشرفية اص، **رابعة الصغار ثالثة** /17 الخمس عشرية في المدائح الكاملية للحلاوي اص، **رابعة** خبر بيت النعم ودعا عند /18 الصباح اص 45، **خامسة** خبر أبي عارم وذئب لنمر اص، الخط والقلم لابن /19 قتيبة اص، خلق الإنسان لابن منصور الكاتب وشيء من شعر المتنبي وغير ذلك، [251ب] **السابعة** الخطبة الموجزة الزاهرة في بعض مناقب الأشرفية الزاهرة اص، /2 **الدال الثانية** دستور معالم الحكم اص، الدعاء للمحاملي اص، درر **السادسة** /3 **وهي أولى الثانية**، الدريدية منكتة اص، نسخة أخرى وتعاليق وفوائد بخط بن العصار اص، /4 **الثامنة** دمية القصر اص 39، نسخة أخرى في 15، الديارات للإصفهاني اص، /5 (الدلجيين) اص 38، نسخة ثانية منه اص 40، **التاسعة** الدلائل لابن البهلول اص، **الحادية** /6 **عشرة** 42 ديوان البحتري اص، تسع نسخ، ديوان أبي نواس رواية حمزة أربع نسخ، /7 رواية الصولي اثنا عشر نسخة، رواية توزون اص، ديوان بن الرومي أربع نسخ، ديوان /8 الشريف الرضي ثلاث نسخ، ديوان عبد الله بن المعتز ثلاث نسخ، ديوان مهيار /9 تسع نسخ، ديوان المتنبي ثماني نسخ وفي الثامنة عليها خطه، ديوان أبي القاسم بن هانئ /10 عشر نسخ، ديوان بن الساعاتي أربع نسخ، ديوان بن سناء الملك خمس نسخ، ديوان /11 ابن القيصراني خمس نسخ، ديوان إبراهيم بن هلال الصابئ نسختين، ديوان كشاجم ست /12 نسخ، **ثانية عشرة** ديوان جرير نسختان، ديوان بن حيوس عشر نسخ، ديوان /13 ديك الجن نسختان، ديوان الحيص بيص خمس نسخ، ديوان بن شبل نسختان، /14 ديوان أبي تمام حبيب نسختان، ديوان أبي الشيص ثلاث نسخ، ديوان ذي /15 الرمة نسختان، ديوان علي بن القاسم الحظيري ثلاث نسخ، ديوان (أبي) الفضل أربع نسخ، /16 ديوان أبي منصور بن الفضل ستة نسخ، ديوان صردر نسخة في 13ص، ديوان الخفاجي /17 خمس نسخ، ديوان زهير بن أبي سلمى خمس نسخ، ديوان أبي الفضل بن الحارث /18 نسختان، ديوان العصفري نسختان، ديوان بن نباتة نسختان، ديوان /19 السري الرفاء ثلاث نسخ، ديوان بن المعلم ثلاث نسخ، ديوان بن الزبير نسختان، [252ا] دعاء الصحيفة، دعاء الصحيفة نسخة أخرى وفيها مناجاة علي بن الحسين رضي الله عنهما، /2 دعاء مستجاب خط ابن شيث، دعاء رواه زيد بن ثابت عن النبي صلى الله عليه وسلم، دعاء /3 شريف في رق أسود يليقه فضة اص، الدعاء بأسماء الله العظام، دعاء مروي عن /4 رسول الله صلى الله عليه وسلم، دعاء عن جعفر الصادق رضي الله عنه، دعاء الجرس وعوذة /5 الباقر، دعاء بخط منسوب،

دعاء جعفر الصادق، الدعاء من أسماء الله العظام، /6 دعاء النبي صلى الله عليه وسلم عند كل شدة شديدة، دعاء الحاجات عن السلف، دعاء الاعتذار /7 من الظلم، دعاء ليلة الجمعة عن زين العابدين رضي الله عنه، دعاء عن أئمة السلف، /8 دعاء شريف مروي عن السلف، دعاء شريف، دعاء النصر والجهاد، دعاء الختم، نسخة ثانية، /9 دعاء الفرج، دعاء الصلوات الخمس، دعاء الصباح، دعاء الصباح، دعاء الصباح، /10 الدعاء بعد صلوة الصبح، دعاء مذهب الأول والأخير، دعاء يوم الخميس، الدعاء في /11 {في} الصباح، الدعاء بعد الصباح، دعاء مكتوب عليه أنه خط بن البواب، **الذال** /12 **الثالثة** الذخيرة للبندنيجي 6ص، الذخيرة لابن بسام 8ص، نسخة ثانية، ذيل /13 الوزير أبي شجاع، **السادسة** ذكر روحاني من كلام سعد الله المنبجي، الذهب /14 والفضة بخط بن الجواليقي، **السابعة** ذخيرة الكتاب، **الثالثة عشرة** ذات /15 الفنون وسلوة المحزون، **الخامسة عشرة** الذخائر عتيق، ذيل بدائع البدائه، **ثالثة** /16 **الصغار** ذم الجزع وحمد الصبر، **الراء الأولى** الروض الأنف 2ص، نسخة أخرى 2ص، /17 **الثانية** روضة المحققين اص، رسالة القشيري اص، رسالة في التصوف مجهول /18 المصنف اص، الرد على المتعصب العنيد المانع من ذم يزيد اص، **الثالثة** رموز [252ب] الكنوز اص، **السادسة وهي أولى الثانية** رجز أبي المنجم اص، روائع الآثار وبدائع /2 الأخبار اص 45، **السابعة** ريحانة المهج المختار من كتاب الفرج 2ص 44، **الثامنة** روضة /3 العاشق اص، ريحان الأفاضل اص 44، روضة المناظر ا، **العاشرة** الرمي عن القوس اص، /4 **الخامسة عشرة** رسل الملوك اص، رقاع الوزير أنوشروان اص، **سادسة الصغار** رسائل /5 أبي حيان التوحيدي اص، رسائل الحريري وأجوبة بن جيا (والصباحات القوام) اص، /6 نسخة أخرى اص، رسائل بن حمدون 2ص، رسائل بن المرزبان اص، رسائل أشرفية على /7 حروف المعجم لابن امسينا اص، رياضة الكمال في صنعة الرسائل ونسخ المكاتبات /8 بين الرضي والصابئ، رسائل ولي الدولة بن خيران اص، رسائل بن المعتز اص، /9 رسائل الحيص بيص اص، رسائل بن الحريري اص، نسخة ثانية، رسائل العزيز بن شجاع اص، /10 رسائل لابن شيث اص، رسائل لابن ناقيا اص، رسائل قابوس بن وشمكير اص، /11 رسا[[ئل]] |لة| جعفر بن ورقاء اص 4، رسا[[ئل]] |لة| أبي بكر وعمر إلى علي اص في 2، رسالة /12 عبد الحميد إلى جماعة الكتاب 16، رسالة أحمد بن الواثق بخط الولي 16ص، رسالة /13 عبد الحميد في وصية الكتاب وغير ذلك خط بن الجواليقي، رسالة الجاحظ في /14 مدح الكتب اص 45، رسالة بخط القصاري اص، **السابعة** رسالة في /15 الخط وثلاث رسائل من غرر البلاغة، **الثامنة** رسالة بن الزبير لابن منقذ، /16 رسالة لابن المنجب الح...، رسالة بن المقفع في آداب الوزراء اص، **التاسعة** /17 رسالة حي بن يقظان لابن سينا اص، رسالة في امتحان الأطباء اص، **الخامسة عشرة** /18 رسالة جبهة الأدب اص، رسالة السعيدية لابن الدهان اص، رسالة أرسطا [253ا] طاليس إلى إسكندر اص 45، رسالة الموسومة بكوكب المتأمل ا 45، /2 **ثالثة الصغار**[8] **خامسة الصغار** الرسالة المأمونية /3 الملقبة بالذهبية، رسالة الأبيوردي إلى صدقة بن دبيس شكره على صنيعه /4 عقيب فراغه من جوهر الأنساب اص، رسالة أبي بكر بن طرخان (المكتتبة) نسخها /5 في رمضان اص،[9] رسالة أحمد بن [[الواثق]] أبي طاهر في الكشف عن شهاب الشعر اص، /6 رسالة سقراطيس في سياسة الملك اص، رسالة (السبيلة) في النصرة على الخوارزمية، /7 رسالة سينية وشينية[10] لعبد المنعم الحنفي، رسالة في البله والعقل اص 42، /8 رسالة الجاحظ في العاشق

المتلاشي والعاشق الناشي اص 47، رسالة /9 أحمد بن الواثق إلى أبي العباس المبرد اص، الرسالة الطردية للصابئ اص، رسالة /10 الجاحظ إلى مويس بن عمران، رسالتا الصابئ في الصيد والبندق، /11 رسالة في الصيد والطرد لمن اتصل قومه واطرد اص، رسالة الجاحظ /12 إلى محمد بن عبد الملك الزيات في العتب والاعتذار اص، رسالة الجاحظ /13 في الحاسد والمحسود أربع نسخ، رسالة الجاحظ في مدح الكتب والحث على /14 جمعها، الرسالة الموضحة في ذكر سرقات المتنبي وساقط شعره للحاتمي اص، /15 الرسالة الحاتمية الصغيرة اص 45 نسختين[11]، رسالة فيما يجوز عليه الا[[عتذار]]عادة /16 وما لا يجوز للطبري، رسالتان للجاحظ أحدهما في تقريظ عبد الله [253ب] ابن طاهر والأخرى إلى أحمد بن عبد الوهاب في المسائل اص، رسالة في حفظ /2 الأسنان واللثة اص، رسالة المعري بخط القيلوي اص، الرسالة الخوارزمية /3 للتاج الصرخدي اص، رسالة الأمير نظام الدين إلى القادر بالله اص، **الزاى** /4 **الأولى** زاد المسير لابن الجوزي 5ص، **الثانية** زين المقصص /5 في القصص لابن الجوزي اص، زبدة الحقائق للمياني اص، زيارات الهروي اص، /6 **الرابعة** زاهر بن الأنباري اص، **الثامنة** زهر الآداب 8ص، نسخة ثانية 44 /7 الزهرة للإصبهاني 3ص، الزهر والطرف والنور والتحف اص 40، **التاسعة** الزيج الزاهر اص 39، /8 **الخامسة عشرة** زينة الدهر اص، نسخة ثانية، زجر النابح للمعري اص، **السين الأولى** /9 سيرة النبي عليه السلام مجلدان، نسخة ثانية 6، نسخة ثالثة، سيرة السلف الصالح اص، /10 سيرة عمر بن عبد العزيز اص، **الرابعة** سيبويه تام اص، سر الأدب اص، **الخامسة** /11 سيرة صلاح الدين 2ص، سنا البرق الشامي 2، **السادسة** السياسة لأرسطو، /12 سيرة الإسكندر اص، سقط الزند بخط الخطيب، السبع الطوال وتتمة /13 العشر آخريها بخطه أيضاً اص، ونسخة أخرى بخط الجواليقي، **السابعة** سلوان /14 المطاع، نسخة ثانية في الثامنة، **الثامنة** سراج الملوك 2، ثلاث نسخ، السلطان /15 لابن قتيبة اص، السياسة للفارابي اص، سياسة الممالك والدول اص، /16 السيرة الهبيرية اص، سفر الملوك، سيرة أحمد بن طولون اص، ثلاث نسخ، **الحادية عشرة** /17 سقط الزند لأبي العلاء اص 39، ثماني نسخ، **الثالثة عشرة** السبع المعلقات بخط [254ا] بن سيدة اص، السبع المعلقات شرح بن الأنباري، السبع المعلقات /2 منكتة اص، سقيط الدرر لابن اللبانة اص، **الخامسة عشرة** سحر البلاغة اص، /3 سبحات الجوهر اص 44، **ثالثة الصغار** سرقات النحوي من الشعراء 51 47، /4 **خامسة** سيرة النبي صلى الله عليه وسلم وذكر العشرة رضي الله عنهم اص، سود /5 النسب (الزكي) الثمين وقصة عائشة مع معاوية اص 47، **الشين الثانية** الشهاب /6 للفقاعي اص، خمس نسخ، الشفاء بتعريف حقوق المصطفى لعياض 2، شرف النبي /7 صلى الله عليه وسلم وأهل بيته اص، **الثالثة** شرح الطحاوي 2، **الرابعة** شرح اللمع /8 لابن مباشر ا، نسخة ثانية، شرح مقدمة الجرمي، شرح الدروس لابن الدهان اص، /9 شرح أبيات إصلاح المنطق اص 42، الشاء والمعز اص، **السادسة** شعر الشنفرى، /10 أربع نسخ، شعر الموج بن الزمان اثني عشر نسخة، شعر سلامة بن جندل خمسة عشرة نسخة، /11 شعر حاتم أربع نسخ، شعر المتلمس سبع نسخ، شعر عروة بن حزام أربع نسخ، شعر /12 عروة بن الورد، مقصورة أبي صفوان أربع نسخ، شعر أبي دهبل نسختان، /13 شعر مصرف بن الأعلم نسختان، شعر طهمان خمس نسخ ونسخة سادسة بخط ابن البواب، /14 شعر الحطيئة خمس نسخ، شعر قيس المجنون، شعر الخنساء، شعر عمر بن أبي ربيعة /15 خمس نسخ، شعر أعشى باهلة نسختان،

شعر علية نسختان، شعر سحيم نسختان، /16 شعر عبد الله بن رواحة، شعر أبي الهندي، شعر عمر بن كلثوم، شعر /17 توبة نسختان، شعر |(بليغ بن)| خليفة ا، شعر علقمة بن عبدة، شعر عنترة، شعر قعنب [254ب] ثلاث نسخ، شعر البعيث، شعر طفيل، شعر عامر بن الطفيل، /2 شعر امرئ القيس ثلاث نسخ، شعر الصمة القشيري[ص]، شعر أبي حية النميري، /3 شعر علي بن أبي طالب كرم الله وجهه ا[ص]، شعر الحسن والحسين رضي الله عنهما، /4 شعر كعب بن سعد [ص]، شعر الأشهب بن رميلة ا[ص]، شعر محمد بن عمر العنبري ا[ص]، /5 شعر أعشى قيس [ص]، شعر السموأل[ص]، شعر جميل بن معمر، شعر زياد بن منقذ، /6 شعر الحكم بن (معمر)، شعر عبيد الله بن قيس الرقيات، شعر كعب بن الأشرف، شعر /7 الحارث بن الحلزة، شعر أبي حزام العقيلي، شعر راشد بن شهاب، شعر /8 الأقرع بن معاذ، شعر جعفر بن علبة، شعر إبراهيم الصولي، شعر /9 إبراهيم الصابئ، شعر عمرؤ بن أحمر، شعر حسان بن ثابت، شعر يزيد بن /10 مفرغ، شرح سقط الزند للخطيب وقيل إنه بخطه، **الثامنة** شجرة العقل ا[ص]، /11 شرح رسالة أدب الكاتب ا[ص]، شافي الغليل في معرفة التأويل، **الحادية عشرة** /12 شعر البستي المجانس اللفظ باختلاف المعنى نسختان، **الثانية عشرة** شعر الملك الأفضل، /13 شرح ديوان أبي تمام 2[ص]، شعر إبراهيم بن العباس الصولي، شعر الطرماح، شعر /14 البلنوبي، شعر أبي الجوائز، شعر خالد بن يزيد ا[ص]، شعر العابد بن الظريف الفارقي، /15 شعر الأديب ابن اللبانة، شعر عضد الدولة أبي شجاع، شعر ركن الدولة، /16 شعر ظافر الحداد، شعر الوزير أبي القاسم، شعر الوزير أبي الشجاع محمد، /17 شعر الملك العزيز بن جلال الدولة، شعر أبي الفرج الوأواء، **ثالثة عشرة** /18 شعر الشهرياري ا[ص]، شعر الضحاك الألوسي، شعر الوزير أبي محمد المهلبي، /19 شعر تاج الملوك، شعر الملك المعظم، شعر بن زيدون (العماني)، [255ا] شعر أعشى تغلب، شعر سالم وعبد الرحمان أبي دارة، شعر الملك العزيز /2 بن بويه، **الخامسة عشرة** شرح الحماسة للمرزوقي، شرح الحماسة للتبريزي أربع نسخ، /3 شرح الحماسة للنمري، شرح المفضليات ثلاث نسخ، شرح سقط الزند أربع /4 نسخ، شرح المهمات من المقامات، شرح المتنبي للواحدي نسختان، شرح الدريدية /5 للفراء، شرح القصائد العشر للخطيب، شرح مقدمة شعر بن أفلح، شعر الخنساء /6 والمجانس على الحروف، **أولى الصغار** شعرأمية بن أبي الصلت، شعر أوس بن /7 حجر، شعر طرفة بن العبد، شعر كثير عزة، شعر عمر بن معدي كرب، وشعر /8 العبدي، **ثالثة** شعر النابغة والحطيئة، شكوى الغريب عن الأوطان إلى /9 علماء البلدان 45، شعر الرماح بن ميادة، **خامسة** شعر الزبرقان بن بدر ا[ص]، /10 الشباب للصولي، شعر في ورق حرير مكتوب بالكوفي، شعر مسلم بن الوليد صريع الغواني، /11 **سادسة** الشوارد عتيق رث، **السابعة** شعر تأبطة شراً، **الصاد الأولى** /12 صحيح مسلم ثمانية، صحيح البخاري 14[ص]، خمس نسخ، صحاح رزين بن مع[ا]وية 3[ص]، /13 **الرابعة** صحاح الجوهري نسختان، **الخامسة** صفوة التأريخ صفين ا[ص]، /14 **الثامنة** الصديق والصداقة نسختان، **التاسعة** الصادح والباغم مصوراً نسختان، /15 صر در مجلدان، الصبابة ونعت الكتابة، **العاشرة** صفات الخيل، **الثانية عشرة** /16 الصادح والباغم ست نسخ، **الخامسة عشرة** الصناعتين للعسكري نسختان، **رابعة الصغار** /17 الصحيفة الغراء، الصلاة على المصطفى صلى الله عليه وسلم، **الطاء الثانية** الطريق [255ب] السالم لابن الصباغ 5، الطريق المسلوك في وعظ الملوك، **الرابعة** الطيب /2 عن المفضل، **الخامسة** طريق

الطليق اص، **الثامنة** طيف الخيال، طرائف الأخبار /3 **الخامسة عشرة** طبقات الشعراء بخط بن خزرج، الطرائف واللطائف، **الظاء** /4 الظاءات لعلي بن يوسف 41، الظاهرات لأقليدس، الظرف والمتظرفين /5 للماوردي، **العين الأولى** العرائس في المجالس للثعلبي، **الثانية** العرائس، نسخة /6 ثانية، علوم الحديث لابن الصلاح، من عوالي الفراوي، عوارف المعارف /7 للسهروردي، **الثالثة** العمدة للفوراني، العقيدة الموسومة بالأدلة العقلية /8 للشاشي، **الرابعة** عين العين للشيرازي، **السادسة** عراضة الأديب لابن الهبارية، /9 عروض بن عباد، عنوان المآثر المجاهدية، **السابعة** العقد لابن عبد ربه 5ص، /10 عجائب الأشعار وغرائب الأخبار 44 2ص، عقلاء المجانين، **الثامنة** /11 عيون الأخبار لابن قتيبة نسختان، العمدة لابن رشيق، عبارات الإشارات /12 عهد أردشير لابن المقفع، **التاسعة** علل تعبير الرؤيا بخط العتبي اص، علم الرمل /13 (لابن مدبلج)، العمل بالأصطرلاب، **الثانية عشرة** العراقيات لأبي المظفر /14 **الثالثة عشرة** عيون الأشعار اص، عيون الأشعار ظ اص، **الخامسة عشرة** عهدة السلطان، /15 العجائب والطرف والهدايا والتحف، العروض لابن (مرون)، العروض لعبد /16 الرحمان، عهد أدريانوس الملك إلى ابنه، عهدة الشاعر، عراضة الأديب /17 بخط بن الخازن، **ثالثة الصغار** عهد المأنون، **رابعة** العمل في رجب /18 عوذة النبي صلى الله عليه وسلم، **خامسة** عرائس الألباب وغرائس الآداب، ||العربيات|| [256ا] العربيات المنتخبات التي تدخل في العبارات والكتب وهي ألفاظ غريبة مشروحة /2 بالعجمي اص، **سادسة** عدة الكتاب وذخيرة الآداب في الترسل، **سابعة** عشرون مسئلة سئل /3 عنها الشافعي رضي الله عنه، **الكتب بالعجمية في التاسعة** دستور اللغة اص، الكافي /4 في العروض، أصول الحرب، شعر الحكم الرومي وغيره، ديوان الرشيد /5 وطواط، الإرشاد في الفقه، مقامات نسختان، وسيلة الطالب للمياني /6 نسختان، ديوان جمال الدين النقاش، ديوان البيلقاني، ديوان بندار، /7 نزهة العشاق، الديوان الأسدي، الديوان العمري، كليلة ودمنة، ديوان /8 أبي المفاخر، قصص الأنبياء، دفع مضار الأغذية، تراجم الأعاجم، مجموع /9 شعر (ورثة) علو[[ا]]ن، مجموع شعر مجدول، نفثة المصدور، مجموع شعر، مجموع /10 آخر، ترسل عجمي، مجموع شعر عتيق، مجموع شعر عتيق، **الغين** /11 **الأولى** غريب الحديث لابن الجوزي، غريب الحديث لابن قتيبة، /12 غريب الحديث لأبي عبيد، غريب القرآن لابن عزير، غريبا القرآن والحديث /13 للهروي أربع نسخ، **الثانية** غريب القرآن لابن عزير ثلاث نسخ، غرر الفوائد /14 للشريف المرتضى، نسخة ثانية، **السابعة** الغرة لعبد الله التائب، غروس /15 البراعات، **الثامنة** الغارات مجلد، **الثانية عشرة** غزل ابن المعلم، **الثالثة** [**عشرة**] /16 غزل بن هانئ هو در المعاني في غرر بن هانئ، غزل بن قسيم الحموي، غزل /17 ديوان النقاش، غزل مهيار، غزل البحتري والرضي، غزل السنجاري، [256ب] غزل بن الساعاتي، غزل الشريف ست نسخ، **الخامسة عشرة** الغلمان المغنين، /2 **سادسة الصغار** غرر البلاغة للصابئ، **الفاء الثانية** فضائل الأعمال للضياء، /3 فضائل دمشق، فضائل الصحابة وأهل البيت، فضائل القدس، فصول /4 حسان في فضل شعبان للأمين الحلبي، **الثالثة** فرائض للجمال المصري، **الرابعة** /5 فقه اللغة للثعالبي اثني عشرة نسخة، فرائد الخرائد، الفرق بين الظاء والضاد /6 لمحمد بن عبد الله، **الخامسة** فتوح ابن أعثم 3ص، فتوح سيف بن عمر 2، الفتح القسي اص، /7 فتوح النواحي والبلدان للبلاذري، فتوح الشام للأزدي، فضائل مصر وذكر /8 ما خصها

الله تعالى به، فهرست كتب الأمم، **السادسة** فصل في فضل الفقر على الغني /9 بخط شهاب الدين السهروردي، الفتح على أبي الفتح، **السابعة** الفرج بعد الشدة، /10 الفوائد من غرر الفرائد، فنون الفوائد وهو مجموع أشعار وغيره، **الثامنة** فضل /11 زبدين، الفتوة والمروة، الفرائد والقلائد أربع نسخ، **العاشرة** الفلاحة لابن /12 وحشية، الفروسية لمحمد بن يعقوب 4، الفردوس في الطب، فن من الفنون في معرفة /13 صفر العيون، الفروسية مصور، الفروسية آخر، الفروسية آخر، **الثالثة عشرة** فرح /14 القلوب في مدائح بني أيوب، **الخامسة عشرة** فلك المعاني لابن الهبارية |نسختان|، فنون الفوائد، /15 الفاضل في الأدب الكامل، **ثالثة الصغار** فضائل الجهاد وشهر رمضان لابن عساكر، /16 فضائل الجهاد، **خامسة** فضائل الجهاد لابن عساكر، فقر وحكم ونوادر، **السادسة** /17 فصوص الفصول وعقود العقول، فصول البلغاء، فصول مستحبة في المكاتبات، /18 فضيلة المجاهدين على القاعدين، **القاف الأولى** قراءة يعقوب وغيره [257أ] وغيره، **الثانية** قصص الأنبياء للإسكافي، قوت القلوب، **الثالثة** قضايا /2 علي بن أبي طالب كرم الله وجهه، **السادسة** القصائد السبع، قصيد زهير بشرحها /3 خط بن الجواليقي، قطعة شعر خط الخطيب، **السابعة** قلائد العقيان ثلاث نسخ، /4 **الثامنة** القائف لأبي العلاء، قراضة الذهب، **التاسعة** قرعة الشراب مصور /5 نسختان، القادري في التعبير نسختان، قياس الماء بالخمر، **العاشرة** قانون /6 ابن سينا نسختان، قسطا بن لوقا في ال...، **الثالثة عشرة** القصائد الأشرفيات، /7 قصيدة الشيخ سعد الله، **الخامسة عشرة** قانون الوزارة للماوردي، القوافي للخليل /8 والأخفش والجرمي، **أولى الصغار** قصيد كعب بن زهير مشروحة، **ثالثة** القصائد /9 الحلبية في الفضائل الأشرفية، قصيدة الأعشى وتحفة الظرفاء ذكرت في التاء، **خامسة** /10 القصائد (المشهورات)، قصائد بخط عبد السلام البصري، القوافي عن الأخفش، /11 قصيد في مدح صلاح الدين للجويني، قصيد للجويني في مدح الملك العادل سيف الدين [[الدولة]]، /12 قصيد أشرفية لابن أمسينا، **السابعة** القصائد الثلاث تتمة العشر شرح الخطيب، /13 **الكاف الأولى** الكشف والبيان في تفسير القرآن للثعلبي، **الثالثة** /14 الكشف عن مساوي، الكفاية في الفقه، **الرابعة** كفاية المتحفظ، **السادسة** /15 كناش الخف، الكلاء والشجر لأبي زيد، **التاسعة** كناش طبي نجومي، /16 الكناش المغيث، **[ال]عاشرة** كشف الألباء عن أحوال الأطباء، كناش /17 الساهر، الكلبزة لبقراطيس، **الخامسة عشرة** الكامل للمبرد ثلاث نسخ، [257ب] الكناية والتعريض، الكافي في العروض نسختان، كنز الكتاب، **خامسة الصغار** /2 كتاب روفس في دلائل الصحة التي تحتاج إليها عند شراء المماليك، كتاب /3 كتبه المعز لدين الله تعالى إلى فتاه الكاتب جوهر، كتاب عن المسترشد /4 **اللام الثانية** لوامع أنوار القلوب، لمع بن السراج في علوم الصوفية، /5 **الرابعة** لمع أبي الفتح بن جني، **الخامسة** اللباب في تهذيب الأنساب، /6 **السادسة** لزوم ما لا يلزم، اللبأ واللبن خط بن الجواليقي، لمع بن جني /7 خط القاساني، **السابعة** لب الآداب، **الثامنة** اللآلئ المضية في مناقب الكمالية، /8 **التاسعة** لباب اللباب، **الثالثة عشرة** لزوم ما لا يلزم، **خامسة عشرة** لمح الملح للحظيري ثلاث نسخ، /9 لمح الملح لابن الصيرفي، اللطائف للثعالبي، لطائف المعارف، **ثالثة الصغار** /10 لمع من أخبار البرامكة، **خامسة** لمع من أخبار البرامكة، اللطائف الحلية من /11 المواقف العلية (للجرمي)، **تاسعة** لذة القلوب ونزهة لنفس المكروب، **الميم الأولى** /12 مسند الدارمي، مختصر زاد المسير في التفسير، معالم التنزيل للبغوي، **الثانية** /13 مصابيح البغوي،

المتحابين في الله، مسند الشافعي، موطأ رواية يحيى بن يحيى، /14 موطأ رواية معن، موطأ رواية أبي مصعب، من عاش بعد الموت، المسعدة في /15 القراءات، مشيخة بن الجوزي، المدهش لابن الجوزي، المبتدأ للكسائي، /16 مناقب الأبرار لابن خميس، مثير الغرام الساكن إلى أشرف الأماكن، منافع القرآن /17 عن جعفر الصادق، مقتل الحسين بن علي رضي الله عنهما، الملاحم لابن المنادي، [258أ] مرافق الموافق لابن الجوزي، مواعظ في فضائل رجب وشعبان، /2 مناقب أبي حنيفة، مناقب علي بن أبي طالب كرم الله وجهه، **الثالثة** /3 المحصول لابن الخطيب نسختان، مناسك الحج للأسدي، المستصفى للغزالي /4 ثلاث نسخ، مقاصد الفلاسفة، معاياة في الطلاق، مجموع مسائل /5 فقهية، المقالات الصغيرة للناشئ، المحيط في الفقه على مذهب أبي /6 حنيفة رضي الله عنه، مجموع لمحمد بن يحيى، مختصر الطحاوي، مناسك الحج /7 لأحمد بن عيسى، مختصر ما يتعلق بالسلطان من الأحكام، ملحة في معتقد /8 أهل الحق، الموجز في المنطق، **الرابعة** المجمل لابن فارس سبع نسخ، /9 المقتصد في شرح الإيضاح، المعرب لابن الجواليقي نسختان ثلاث نسخ ومع /10 أحدها عروض بن جني، المحسبة لابن باب شاذ نسختان، الموجز في النحو للهروي، /11 المدخل إلى كتاب سيبويه، مقدمة الجرمي وغيرها، مجموع فيه من سر الأدب /12 واللطائف والمبهج، المقنع في النحو، مقدمة ابن الجواليقي، المختار من ألفاظ /13 الأبرار، المطر والنبات وملاهي العرب، مختصر في القوافي لابن الأردخل، /14 ما يلحن فيه العامة لابن الجواليقي، المرتجل في شرح الجمل، مفحم الأنام في /15 نظم فصيح الكلام، ملحة الإعراب، **الخامسة** مغازي الواقدي، مختصر تأريخ /16 البلاذري لابن جزلة، المستظهري في التأريخ ذكر في الألف، مروج الذهب [258ب] ثلاث نسخ، **السادسة** مجموع بخط بن المأمون وشعر سحيم والحادرة ومراثي /2 في النبي صلى الله عليه وسلم، مقصورة أبي صفوان أربع نسخ، مجموع بخط فيه /3 أشعار جماعة من العرب أوله شعر عبد الله بن عتبة بن مسعود، مجموع بخط بن أبي الجوع، /4 ملحة بن عباد في الفرق بين الظاء والضاد، المعجزة العربية في مناقب الدولة الأشرفية، /5 مجموع بخط بن الجواليقي فيه أخبار وأسانيد وقصائد من استغفر واستغفري /6 وغير ذلك، مجموع فوائد تسع قوائم ذكر أن أكثره بخط بن مقلة، المطر /7 لابن دريد، مجموع شعر فيه عمارة بن عقيل وغير ذلك، المقصور والممدود /8 لأبي علي الفارسي، المسئلة التي جرت بين سيبويه والكسائي، **السابعة** /9 محاضرات الراغب ثلاث نسخ، مجموع بن شمس الخلافة نسختان، المعمرين لأبي عبيدة، /10 ملح الممالحة لابن ناقيا أربع نسخ، ملح الفنون، مصارع العشاق، منتخب الأذكياء، /11 المذهب لا[بن] حبيب، المستجاد من [[فعلاة]] فعلات الأجود نسختان، المحدث /12 في الأغاني، المدبج للمرزباني، المنتهى في الكمال، المقتبس لابن دريد نسختان، /13 {الثانية} **[الثامنة]** مقاتل الفرسان، مقالة جواهر السلوك، معارف بن قتيبة، المؤنس /14 أشعار، المجموع (العذري)، محاسن المحاضرات، المكافأة على الحسن والقبيح، /15 المحظوظ في الرزق والمنحوس فيه، المبهج للثعالبي، مجموع أوله أخلاق رسول الله /16 صلى الله عليه وسلم لأبي الشيخ، الممادح والمذام، الموجز للمبرد، مضاهاة /17 كليلة ودمنة، معالي من اسمه علي، الموازنة والترجيح في المتنبي، الموشا للوشاء، [259أ] المصون في سر الهوى المكنون، من غاب عنه المطرب، مصباح المجتهد، /2 المنتهى في المشتهى، مقطعات النيل،[[مراعات]] |مرآة| المروات نسختان،

/3 من نسب من الشعراء إلى أمير، مساوي شعر المتنبي، **التاسعة** مضاهاة /4 كليلة ودمنة مصورة، المجسطي لابن سينا، المواليد وغيره، مواقيت الأطباء، /5 مختصر في سياسة الحروب، مدواة جرائح الجوارح، مبدأ [[كتاب]] جوامع /6 كتاب جالينوس وغيره، منصوبات الشطرنج، **العاشرة** المائة للمسيحي نسختان، /7 منهاج البيان لإبي جزلة ثماني نسخ، مجموع فيه الأغذية وتدبير الأصحاء لبقراط /8 ودفع مضار الأغذية، المغني لإسحاق بن إبراهيم، المستطرف في الطب، مصالح /9 الأبدان والأنفس، المنصوري نسختان، منافع الفواكه، المغني لسعيد بن /10 هبة الله بن الحسين ثلاث نسخ، معرفة الجوهر، الملوكي {في ال ا}، مجموع في /11 جوامع جالينوس في الفصد وفيه شيء بخط المسيحي، مختصر الجمهرة في علوم البيزرة، /12 **الحادية عشرة** مختار من شعر الصابئ، مختار من شعر بن منير، **الثانية عشرة** /13 مختار شعر بن قلاقس، المستجاد من شعر العماد، مختار من شعر البستي، مختار /14 من شعر بن الريوندي، **الثالثة عشرة** المنائح السعيدية، المدائح الأشرفية، /15 مختار من شعر الفرزدق، مختار من شعر المتنبي، مختار الحلي والحلل، مدائح /16 القرائح، مدائح في الملك العادل للسنجاري، ملح المدح العادلية، مختار /17 شعر بن منقذ، مختار شعر الأبله، مختار ديوان السراج، المفضليات مجردة /18 عن غريبها، المبتز من ديوان بن المعتز، مختار شعر الخالديين، منتخب من ديوان [259ب] ابن أبي الصقر، مختار من شعر أبي تمام، المنتخل من شعر القبائل للآمدي، /2 المنتخل للميكائلي، المنتخل مذهب، مطلب المعاني ومطرب الأغاني للميكائلي، /3 مختار مطلب المعاني، المختزل من المديح والغزل، مختار شعر الشهاب، /4 فتيان، مجموع أشعار من عدة دواوين، مختار {ديوان} ديوان جرير، /5 مختار ديوان الفرزدق، مختار النقائض، مختار شعر بن المعتز، /6 مختار شعر الأمير عيسى بن مودود، مختار شعر العباس بن الأحنف، /7 مختار شعر بن القيصراني، مختار شعر البحتري والرضي، مختار شعر عبد /8 المحسن الصوري، مختار شعر الشريف الرضي، مختار من شعر بن الرومي /9 للخالديين، مختار شعر الأندلسيين لابن أبي الصلت، مختار شعر الأندلسيين /10 لابن المنتجب، مختار ما يتمثل به الرؤساء من الأبيات السائرة، المجرد من غزل /11 الشريف، معاني الشعر للأصمعي، معاني الشعر [[للأصمعي]] لابن السكيت، /12 مختار شعر البحتري، معاني (الأمهانداني)، مجموع فيه مدائح أهل /13 البيت، مجموع فيه أنواع التشبيه، مجموع بن خشنام، منادح الممادح /14 لحكيم الزمان، **الخامسة عشرة** مقامات الحريري خمسة عشرة نسخة، مقا[ما]ت للمسيحي /15 بخطه، المقامات اللزومية، مقامات الحسين بن إبراهيم وديوان الأبله، /16 المحب والمحبوب والمشموم والمشروب ثلاث نسخ، معاني الشعر للباهلي، /17 معاني الشعر للأشنانداني، الموشا للوشاء، الموضح في شرح المتنبي للخطيب /18 التبريزي، المصون في سر الهوى المكنون، مجموع يشتمل على كل فن، المنير في [260أ] أخبار أبي تمام، المنتهى في الكمال، مختصر الفسر وهو شرح المتنبي، المقابسات /2 للتوحيدي، المصايد والمطارد، مختصر في السياسة وآداب الرئاسة، /3 منثور المنظوم للبهائي، المنتخب من الأنس والفرس، المنطق والهجاء والحلا /4 والشيات، المؤلف للملك الأشرف في حل التراجم، معاقرة الشراب، مفاخرة /5 الكرام الأجواد، المقامة الدمشقية للناصح، منتخب الأمثال، منتخب الأمثال /6 قطع معتزل، المداراة لابن أبي دنيا، **أولى الصغار** المدائح الدرية في المناقب /7 الأشرفية، مختار من المتنبي وعليه

خطه، **ثالثة الصغار** مسائل سئل عنها المتنبي من شعره، /[8] مختار من طبقات الشعراء، مناظرة الشمس والشراب، مجموع فيه كتب لغوية وعليه /[9] خط بن الجواليقي، مختار حلية المحاضرة، ما وجد من آداب أفلاطون، مدائح في /[10] الأشرف لابن ماضي، مذهبة ذي الرمة، من كلام المعمى في أدب النفس، مذهبة /[11] ذي الرمة وميمية ولامية، **رابعة** مائة جوهرة من كلام علي بن أبي طالب كرم الله وجهه، /[12] نسخة ثانية، مختصر [[الس]] السيرة النبوية لابن فارس وأدعية شريفة مروية، مناجآت /[13] زين العابدين، ما يدعا به في أعقاب الصلوات، ما يدعا به بعد صلوة الفجر، /[14] ما يدعا به بعد صلوة الصبح، ما يقال في الفجر كل يوم، ما [[ص]] يدعا به بعد صلوة /[15] الفجر كل يوم، **خامسة** مجموع فيه النوادر وإضمار الخيل وما لا تدخله الهاء /[16] من المؤنث والدرات والأوقات والأصوات والهمز وصفة النخل /[17] وغيره، مسائل سئل عنها أفلاطون، مجموع أشعار وأخبار مجلد، [260ب] مجموع بن الخازن، المقامة الصاحبية الشكرية، مدائح (اليارجوكي) /[2] للملك الأشرف، مجموع فيه أشعار مستطرفة وقصيد يحيى بن أبي الخصيب /[3] بخط الصولي وشعر مالك بن الريب بن المازني بخط الحسن بن هانئ، مجموع /[4] في الفتوة، المعشرات (النبوية)، مختار في المدائح المنصورية القطبية، /[5] الملح العصرية من أشعار أهل الأندلس، مجموع أشعار بخط الجويني /[6] وجمعه، مختار من أشعار فصحاء الأعراب للجويني وبخطه، محاسن /[7] الآداب والأمثال، **سادسة** مختار من ترسل الحريري والببغاء، ملح /[8] المكاتبة لابن ناقيا، مختار من رسائل بن عبد (ماني)، **سابعة** مسائل /[9] الملك الوارد من اليمن على علي بن أبي طالب كرم الله وجهه، مجموع أوله فقه /[10] على مذهب أبي حنيفة وبعض (ملقيات) الفرائض وقطعة من تعبير الرؤيا، /[11] مجموع فيه عشرون مسئلة سئل عنها الشافعي ووصية علي بن أبي طالب لولده /[12] الحسين رضي الله عنهما، مجموع فيه مختصر سيرة رسول الله صلى الله عليه وسلم لابن /[13] فارس والأربعون البلدانية، مجموع فيه قراءة أبي عمرو بن العلاء ورسالة /[14] في أصول المختصر والناسخ والمنسوخ لابن الجوزي وشرح مسائل حميل التلخيص في /[15] المواريث والعقود في الحساب، مجموع فيه مختصرات معشرات الحصري ومناجاة /[16] ابن الجوزي وأدب الأصدقاء في المكاتبات واللقاء، مجموع فيه مختار لوامع /[17] أنوار القلوب ورونق المجالس في الحكايات، مجموع الغزالي المسائل [261أ] البغدادية ومسائل الأخروية والمسائل الأربعون والمضنون والمصباح /[2] وخواتيم (الباطنية) وإبطال الدور اللفظي، مجموع للغزالي منهاج العارفين /[3] ومعراج {العارفين} [السالكين] |ظا|، مجموع فيه تفصيل النشأتين وتحصيل {العارفين} [السعادتين]، مجموع /[4] مختصر أصول الفقه وجدل وتأسيس النظائر، مجموع فيه الترغيب والترهيب /[5] وبداية الهداية وأدعية الأيام السبعة، مجموع فيه الناسخ والمنسوخ لهبة وقرآت /[6] مرموزة وأراجيز في عدد آي القرآن، مجموع فيه العنوان ومتشابه القرآن، /[7] مجموع فيه تلخيص الروض ومفاتيح العلوم، مذهبة ذي الرمة وشرحها، مجموع /[8] فيه ديوان علي بن الجهم والمسومات والمنتخبات والجمرات والفرسان، مجموع /[9] فيه عهد أردشير وحديث خسروى ابرويز وابنه شيروية وانقضاء دولة العجم /[10] وابتداء أمر خير الأنبياء لخير الأمم، مجموع يتضمن أشياء حسنة تعليق الحسن بن يوسف /[11] (الآمري)، مجموع فيه المنحة بشرحها وعلل الزيج المأموني غير تام، مجموع فيه فناء الفناء /[12] وزجل عبد القادر ولوعة المشتاق، مجموع الفرائد والقلائد ورسالة في /[13] {في} العهود

{و} اليونانية، مجموع ديوان الرستمي ومختار شعر أبي فراس ومختار /14 شعر الشريف والسماحة والشجاعة للواحدي، مجموع فيه شعر ظافر ومن شعر /15 محمد بن محمد الصقلي ومن كلام الوهراني، مجموع النجم القصري، مجموع فيه زبدة /16 الحقائق ونهج التقدير واعتراضات ابن سينا وأجوبتها، مجموع فيه شعر [261ب] طرفة وديوان لبيد وابن حلزة، مجموع فيه أشعار مختلفة وأسماء العود /2 الذي يتبخر به وغير ذلك، مجموع نرجس القلوب وشرح حقائق التوبة /3 واللباب في شرح الشهاب، مجموع أدباء الغرباء والخمارين والخمارات /4 وأخبار الطلسمات المغنين والديارات، مجموع فضائل الأعمال للهكاري /5 ووعظ عجمي، مجموع جدل الشريف، مجموع درر السنة ومنافع القرآن /6 والمنبهات، مجموع المنثور البهائي والمبهج وقعة الأدهم، مجموع فيه /7 رجز حميد الأرقط (ودكين) والفقعسي وسؤر الدئب، مجموع أخبار الخلفاء /8 عليه خط جمال الدين تأريخ قديم، مجموع الطيب والتطيب ومختصر الاشتقاق /9 والرسالة المرتجلة في تفسير لفظ الحماسة وإيضاح مشكل شعر المتنبي وسر الصناعة /10 في (الترسل)، مجموع جدل وقياس للحواري، مجموع الفرائد والقلائد [[ورسالة]] /11 [[في العهود]] وأدعية الأيام السبعة، مناقب الشافعي وجزء ابن عروة ومنامات ابن /12 أبي الدنيا، مجموع عجمي ودوبيتي وندبة زين العابدين ومقتل الحلاج، مجموع شعر /13 مراثي، مجموع مختار شعر البحراني وأبي الشيص الخزاعي، مجموع ملقى (السبيل) /14 والمقصور لابن دريد وما يلحن فيه العامة للكسائي وغير ذلك، مختار من شعر أبي /15 مرهف النميري، **الثامنة** مجموع رسالة وصف (الشيم) والأخلاق ورسالة هفوات /16 الألباء وعثرات الأطباء، مجموع أخبار وحكايات وطرف أشعار أوله أخبار /17 المأمون ورسالتان، مجموع فيه من رسائل الخوارزمي ورسالة بن أفلح في علم [262أ] الشعر وقطعة من شعره ومن شعر الأرجاني وغير ذلك، مجموع فيه منتخل /2 الميكالي وخيل العرب ومختار محاسن نثر الدر والرائق والشائق ومنتخب /3 جاويذان وآداب ابن المعتز وغير ذلك، مجموع مترجم بنزهة الفريد /4 فيه بيت في التفسير ورقائق وأخبار وحكايات وسمر نديم الفريد وولاية عهد /5 المأمون وفوائد، مجموع مترجم بأخبار الخلفاء أوله ذكر الصبوح وآخره من /6 النعوت، مجموع طبي فيه الرهبان والجالينوس في علامات الطبائع والدلالات /7 على معرفة الأوجاع وعلامات الموت والأدوية المسهلة، مجموع |فيه من| تأريخ بن أبي /8 الأزهر ومن مختار الأدوات، مجموع فيه ديوان المتلمس وإنشادات وغير /9 ذلك، مجموع فيه فنون تشتمل على العقل والذات ونوادر الحكماء وأدعية واستغفار، /10 مجموع فيه ديوان الأفوه ومن شعر بن أبي ربيعة وقصيد كعب ولامية الشنفرى /11 وشعر قيس الظفري، مجموع فيه ميزان العروض للخطيب والجمل في النحو للخليل /12 ومختصر ما يجوز صرفه للشاعر، مجموع يشتمل على مقالتي غلام زحل في ماهية الشعاعات /13 وعللها وسبل التسيرات، مجموع أوله في مولد النبي صلى الله عليه وسلم ووصيته /14 لعلي بن أبي طالب كرم الله وجهه وثلاثيات البخاري وأدعية وغيرها، مجموع عوذ /15 وحروز وقلع الآثار ومن الخواص للرازي، مجموع أشعار وأخبار وحكم /16 ونوادر وحكايات وغير ذلك كما ذكر في ترجمة، مجموع فيه الخيل وفضلها /17 والطيب وأجناسه والحب من [[البوا]] الجماهير، مجموع جيد عروض الزنجاني وقوافي /18 بن جني و(السيرة) لابن فارس وفوائد وفحول العرب وآداب الوزراء والكتاب، [262ب] مجموع فيه الإغريضية

وفوائد والوحوش للأصمعي وشعر لابن أبي سلمى /2 والمذهبة، مجموع |أوله| شعر لبعض شعراء صلاح الدين ومعرفة عيوب الشعر والقوافي /3 وشرح المسائل الثلاث وشرح المسائل السبع ومخارج الحروف وغير ذلك، مجموع /4 فيه الخط والقلم وتهاني وتعازي ووصايا، مجموع أوله رسائل وعروض الخليل /5 والدروس فيها والقوافي وشعر الحادرة ومن شعر لابن أبي زنبور وأرجوزته /6 في صفات الخيل وأدعية، مجموع فيه مختار نشوار المحاضرة والأزهار الذكية في /7 المباحث القياسية، المصون للريحان[ي] يشتمل على عدة كتب من تواليفه، مجموع أخبار /8 وأشعار ومن شعر الغري وديوان امرئ القيس الكندي ومن شعر ابن الساعاتي /9 وابن النبيه وجرير، مجموع فيه مذهبة ذي الرمة وقصيد دعبل والشنفرى /10 وكعب وثائية بن دريد وقصيد في الظاآت وأرجوزة في الفرق بين الضاد والظاء /11 ومن شعر بن الحريري وقصيد دعبل أفيقي وقصيد أبي البيداء التي لا يعرف قائلها /12 ومقصور لابن دريد وقصيدته فيه وله منتخب ومذهبة والسبع وهل بالطلول /13 ويادارمية وقصيد سويد، مجموع شعر أبي (الشاس) وأشعار وأخبار /14 وغير ذلك، مجموع أوزان الأشعار وقوافي المبرد وكنى الشعراء لثعلب /15 وطبقاتهم للجمحي ورسالة الببغاء في الدواة، مجموع الأخلاق لابن الهيثم /16 وزجر النفس لأفلاطون وسياسة البدن وفضل الشراب، مجموع أوزان /17 الأفعال والأسماء ورسالة بن الهبارية إلى الخطيب ناقصة ومقالة في النفس /18 وفوائد، مجموع فيه الاقتباس من كلام رب الناس ومن أمالي بن دريد وغير /19 ذلك، مجموع ذكر في ترجمة جزء فيه فضائل سور القرآن وفي الأصول [263أ] الأصول وفضل الوضوء والهدية إلى الموتى والصلوة، مجموع مختار /2 من رسالة ابن عباد في [أمثال] ... شعر المتنبي وأخبار وإنشادات /3 من البيان ورسالة أرسطاطاليس في تدبير الأخلاق الى الإسكندر، /4 مجموع بعض مختار فقه وقصيد في عدد آي القرآن ومواعظ والمثلث /5 ونحو وأشعار وخط والمقصور والممدود لابن دريد، مجموع موشحات /6 وأشعار مختارة، مجموع رسالة البطيحة وديوان ظاهر الفاريابي وأشعار /7 بالعجمي، مجموع أرجوزة في الفرائض وقصيد أبي مزاحم ومعشرات الحصري /8 وهل بالطلول وقصيد نحو وموافقات الصحيح للمقدسي وشرح غريب /9 الموطأ، مجموع اللطائف ومن شعر أبي الغنائم الربعي ومن شعر فخر العرب، /10 مجموع ما استو[ى] من خلق الإنسان لابن فارس ومختصر خلق الإنسان وخلق الفرس /11 وأسماء (البر) ومقصور قطرب ولنفطويه ورسالة المعاد الدينية في اليوم /12 والساعة والدقيقة والرسالة الموشأة في تضعيف بيوت الشاه، مجموع فيه /13 هندسة كما ذكر جمال الدين والجزء الفرد والأخلاق لابن سينا ومن كلامه وكلام غيره، /14 مجموع للرازي أبدال الأدوية ومنافع الطين ومضاره وحصى الكلى واالمثانة ناقصة /15 والأدوية الموجودة بكل مكان وفي الشراب والفصد، مجموع بخط توفيق بن محمد /16 اختيارات شعر العرب، مجموع اليميني وغير ذلك، مجموع الأدب الجامع /17 لابن المقفع ورسائل وأشعار ورسالة بن عباد في شعر المتنبي وترسل، [263ب] مجموع ذكر أنه يشتمل على مختار العلم والبيان و(الشرود) ومن /2 كتاب النساء ومن شعر الببغاء ورسالة الاسفرايني والغزالي ومختار /3 من البصائر وشعر ديك الجن ومن عيون الحكم لابن فارس /4 ومن شعر الابري ومن البيان و(التبيين) والحاتمية ومن شعر الخوارزمي /5 وغير ذلك والأنيس في غرر التجنيس، **مجموع** أخبار كلفاء الجن /6 وقصيد الدلالة وبعض خمريات أبي نواس وأدب النديم

لكشاجم /7 ومقصورة [ابن] دريد وأشعار، مجموع فيه أنه علق من مجموع استعير /8 من أمين الدولة كاتب السر ومن اللهو والملاهي ومن شعر ابن /9 المعذل، مجموع رسائل البديع ورسائل عجمية وفوا[[د]]ئد وأشعار، /10 مجموع اختيارات أشعار ونوادر وغير ذلك، مجموع أكثره أشعار /11 عجمية ورسالة أسعد إلى وطواط، مجموع وعظ وآداب وأدعية، مجموع /12 الملح واختيار مسائل حنين، **مجموع** الإعجاز والإيجاز /13 وأشعار وغير ذلك، **مجموع** أمثال المولدين من الميداني /14 وخمريات أبي نواس وأخبار ونوادر وأشعار ونكت وغيرها، /15 **مجموع** من شعر البارع الدباس وعيون الأشعار [264ا] الأشعار ونواظر الأشجار، **التاسعة مجموع** منهاج العابدين /2 ونحو لابن فضال وترسل والمنقذ وأبيات الفتوة ومن المنتهى في /3 الكمال ومن حلية المحاضرة ومن نتائج الحكمة، **مجموع** الآداب /4 والمواعظ للخليل السجزي وأربعون للحاكم، **مجموع** رسالة /5 الشافعي وأسماء من حدث عنه والسنن، **مجموع** [[حاوند...]] /6 جاويذان خرد وآداب الوزراء وغير ذلك، **مجموع** ميزان /7 العمل وأدب الدين والدنيا وتفصيل النشأتين والذريعة، **مجموع** /8 مختار شعر من العروس وبهجة القلب وغير ذلك، **مجموع** تسهيل /9 النظر وتوقيعات الخلفاء الأمويين والعباسيين، **مجموع** روضة /10 الآداب والود ثمانية محذوفة، **مجموع** مقصورة بن دريد والمقصور /11 والممدود له وعن الأصمعي، **مجموع** الذهب المسبوك وإسلام جبلة /12 والندبة ومختصر |في| السياسة وغير ذلك، مجموع الدريدية وقصيد مرثية بخط /13 ابن أبي الجوع، **مجموع** السرج واللجام وصفة السحاب وتلقيب /14 القوافي، **مجموع** مختار من زهر، **مجموع** الرياض واختيارات /15 أخر وأشعار بالعجمي، **مجموع** اعتلال القلوب ومن غاب عنه المطرب، /16 مجموع قصائد الشوارد ونظم السلوك، **مجموع** المبتدأ (للطوسي) [264ب] ومن {معاني} [مغازي] الواقدي، **مجموع** عصمة الأنبياء عليهم السلام ومناقب /2 الشافعي، **مجموع** الحاتمية والخلاف بين صاحبي أبي عمر، **مجموع** /3 حامل العروض للخطيب الأشنانداني، **مجموع** مختار من ترسل الفاضل /4 ودوبيتي العماد ومن الحماسة، **مجموع** من شعر بن وكيع وغير ذلك، /5 **مجموع** سفينة في القرآت، **مجموع** فيه الأديرة للخالديين /6 والخمارين والخمارات للاصفهاني، **مجموع** درة بن المقفع ونثر ونظم بالعجمي، /7 **مجموع** من أشعار العرب ومختار من النقائض ومن المفضليات، /8 **مجموع** أخلاق الملوك ومفاخرة الشتاء والصيف، **مجموع** /9 للجاحظ شعره والمضاحك والملح وذم الهوى والحاسد والمحسود واستهداء /10 والحث على اتخاذ الكتب، **مجموع** الصادح والباغم ومن شعر بن الخازن، /11 **مجموع** شعر أبي الحكم وشعر بن الظريف الفارقي، **مجموع** مختار /12 النقائض وشعر جرير وفرزدق، **مجموع** فيه أشعار الأنصار، مجموع /13 التمثيل والمحاضرة والأسجاع (للعجلي) ورسالة في نوادر الحكماء ومن كلامهم، **مجموع** /14 اختيار جماعة من شعراء العرب وأشعارهم رديء، **مجموع** مكاتبات بين الشريف /15 والصابئ وديوان بن قسيم، **مجموع** ثمانية عشر قصيدة للعرب، **مجموع** /16 مختار من شعر ثلاثة عشر شاعراً من العرب اختيار مهيار بخطه، **مجموع** خلق /17 الفرس للأصمعي والوحش له وألفاظ بن الأعرابي بزيادات ابن خالويه وحديث قيس، /18 **مجموع** مختار المتنبي والبحتري وأبي تمام والملتقط من الأمثال والملحة، /19 **مجموع** قصيدة بن الحلزة السبعة وقصيدة بن (خميس) وقصيدة عنتر، **مجموع** برد [265ا] برد الأكباد وأدب النفس للحاكمي ومختار الجزوري، **مجموع** |فيه| شعر

جماعة من العرب /2 وأظنه من الهذليين، **مجموع** فصيح ثعلب وعروض بن عيسى الربعي، **مجموع** /3 الرسالة الحكمية للعسكري والناجم (للنبهاني) وملح المكاتبات لابن ناقيا وأدعية الأيام، /4 **مجموع** اختلاف منظر النيرين ورسالة الفارابي في الجزء وما [لا] يتجزأ /5 و(تبيين) السبب بين أوتاد (العتيبي)، **مجموع** شعر بن ميادة والصابئ والحكم /6 بن عبد الله وقيس بن الخطيم وجيران العود، **مجموع** رسالة الإغريضية /7 والملائكة لأبي العلاء، **مجموع** فصيح ثعلب ولابن دريد المقصور والممدود /8 والملاحن وما يكتب بالألف والياء لابن جني ودروس في النحو، **مجموع** /9 نحو لابن شقير وقصيد في ظاآت القرآن مشروحة وشرح اللمع لابن مباشر، /10 مجموع المقصور والممدود لأبي عبيد وفعل وأفعل للفراء، **مجموع** /11 تعزية لأبي العلاء ورسالة الوزير إليه وإلى أخيه ...الي، مختصر إصلاح المنطق /12 وغير ذلك، **مجموع** ألفاظ عبد الرحمان وعلل العروض للزجاج وأنواء أبي /13 عبيد، **مجموع** (الدرة اليتيمة) لابن المقفع واللطف واللطائف، **مجموع** /14 قصيد بن دريد في المقصور والممدود ومختصر قوافي وما قرب إسناده /15 لابن شاهين ومنافع حمزة وصلاة الرغائب وعروض وفتيا فقيه العرب /16 ومختار الفتيا وأخبار في النمو وخلق الإنسان للزجاج وأحاديث أبي منظور /17 ونكت الرماني و(من حيث) أبي محمد الجويني وخمسة من أمالي السلفي، **مجموع** /18 مدح السخاء والسخي وذم البخل والبخيل والياقوت في المضاحك والنوادر /19 للجاحظ، **مجموع** شعر بن عليق وبن ذريح و(أبي حية) ومهلهل /20 وعبد الله بن عجلان وولده والفند، **مجموع** القول الموجز في أخبار [265ب] دولة الموحدين بالمغرب وعقيدة المهدي، **مجموع** مقدمة نحو /2 والفصيح و(الجرمية)، **مجموع** الغارات وافتراق العرب من معد وأين /3 نزلت والمحبر ومسائل في بعض (تنبيه) المعتزلة ومن نسب ولد العباس، **مجموع** /4 مقتل عمر بن الخطاب رضي الله عنه وحكايات عن الشافعي رضي الله عنه، **مجموع** /5 [ا]هليلجة الصادق واثنا عشر مسئلة سئل عنها العامري وغير ذلك، **مجموع** /6 شعر ليلى وتوبة، **مجموع** (الليث) الأخلاق وألفاظ الحكماء ومسائل سئل /7 عنها ابن العباس، **مجموع** غرر البلاغة وما وقع عليه الاختيار من الأشعار والأخبار، /8 **مجموع** الريحاني الناجم والطارق والزمام و(عرس القطر)، **مجموع** /9 مربعة بن دريد وصفة (المعقر) وما يصير إليه ورسالة ابن الصوري وخماسية /10 زهدية وذكر الموت (للكرلج) وحكاية العباس عا... وإسلام عمر رضي الله عنه، /11 **مجموع** مختصر الجرمي من المنتهى في البلاغة لابن الأشل وقصيد بن دريد /12 في المدمود، **مجموع** المنتخب الملوكي وفقه [[الك...]] الكلام على تقاسيم خصال /13 الكرام، **مجموع** [مقصور] الفراء وممدوده و(فائت) الفصيح والمثلث، **مجموع** /14 توجيه القولين واختلاف المقالات للمسمعي، **مجموع** آداب بن المقفع الكبير /15 ورسالة ابن أبي الصلت وغير ذلك، **مجموع** مسكين الدارمي وجران /16 العود، **مجموع** فيه قصيدتا سحيم وابن دريد عميرة ودع واماطت لثاما، /17 **النون الأولى** نهاية البيان في تفسير القرآن، **الثانية** /18 نوادر الأصول للحكيم الترمذي، النصيحة في الأدعية الصحيحة، /19 نهج البلاغة من كلام أمير المؤمنين علي بن أبي طالب كرم الله وجهه ست /20 نسخ، نصيحة الملوك للغزالي نسختان، النصح في الدين، الناسخ [266ا] والمنسوخ لهبة، (النشيد) العقلي، نظم السلوك في وعظ /2 الملوك لابن نباتة، النور في فضل الأيام والشهور مجلد، /3 **الثالثة** نهاية المطلب، **الرابعة** نحو بخط دقيق، النبات /4 لأبي حنيفة الدينوري، نحو تصنيف ابن رافع، نحو

عن الفراء، **الخامسة** /5 نسب قريش لابن بكار، **السادسة** النقائض بين جرير والفرزدق، /6 **السابعة** نثر الدر للآبي خمس نسخ، **الثامنة** نقط العروس /7 النكت والإشارات، **التاسعة** نسخة كتاب جبريل بن بختيشوع، /8 **العاشرة** النهاية في الكحل نسختان، نوادر طبية، **الثانية عشرة** /9 النقائض، نخبة البارع لابن المنجم، **الثالثة عشرة** نزهة الرياض /10 وشفاء القلوب المراض، النقائض ثلاث نسخ، **الخامسة عشرة** نزهة الأبصار /11 في نعت الفواكه والأزهار، النوادر المستطرفة، النورين للحصري /12 نسختان، نزهة العيون وراحة المحزون، نزهة الناظر وراحة /13 الخاطر، نفثة العقيد، **رابعة الصغار** نسخة (الرفعتين) (للكشمردي)، /14 **خامسة** نسب النبي صلى الله عليه وسلم ومولده والخلفاء بعده مصور مكشوط /15 الصور، **السابعة** النص والقياس في فضل بني العباس، **الهاء** /16 **الثالثة من الصغار**الهدية الأشرفية في الهدايا (الخفية)، **رابعة** الهياكل /17 السبعة عنه، **ثامنة الصغار** ال{ب}[ه]داية في الرماية، **الواو الأولى** /18 وجيز الواحدي مجلد، وسيط الواحدي نسختان، الواضح في التفسير [266ب] لابن المبارك، الوقف والابتداء لابن الأنباري، **الثالثة** /2 وسيط الغزالي ثلاث نسخ، **الرابعة** الوجوه والنظائر وهو ما /3 اتفق لفظه واختلف معناه، **الخامسة** ولاة خراسان، وسائط العقود /4 [[المقق]] المقتناة، **الثامنة** وقعة الأدهم للحاتمي أربع نسخ، /5 **الثالثة عشرة** (الوثاق والاستراق)، **ثالثة الصغار** وصية علي بن أبي طالب /6 كرم الله وجهه لولده الحسن رضي الله عنه [[نسختان]] |ثلاث نسخ|، وصية [[المهدي]] المنصور للمهدي، /7 ورسالة الغزالي |فيه نظر|، **رابعة** وصية علي بن أبي طالب لولده الحسين رضي الله عنهما، /8 واحد وألف اسم من أسماء الله سبحانه وتعالى، **خامسة** وسيلة الراجي لابن /9 منجب، **الياء الخامسة** اليميني للعتبي أربع نسخ، يتيمة الدهر أربع نسخ، /10 **الثامنة** اليواقيت في المواقيت، **التاسعة** اليانوس /11 في تعبية الحروب، **الخامسة عشرة** اليتيمة في سياسة الملك لابن /12 المقفع، **المخاريم الأولى** من الاستيعاب لابن عبد البر، **الثانية** /13 نهج البلاغة ناقصة نقلت الى الرابعة عشرة، من عوالي الفراوي ذكر في العين، /14 **الثالثة** المستصفى مخروم الأول، من البحر المذهب أول وثاني وثالث، من الوسيط /15 ومنه أول وثالث ومنه أول وثاني ومنه الثاني وهو نصف الجملة، من الأسرار لأبي /16 زيد الدبوسي، من المهذب ثاني وثالث ومنه ثالث أيضاً، من تعليق القاضي /17 حسين أول وثاني، من الشامل أول وثاني وثالث، من (تبصرة) الموحدين أول، /18 مختصر في الفقه مخروم، **الرابعة** جمهرة الأمثال ناقص من آخرة، (النحل) /19 مخروم الأول، من سر الأدب أول، ألفاظ بن السكيت وفيها نقص يسير، من [267أ] من سيبويه، من الجمهرة لابن دريد، من اللامع ثاني وثالث، من تذكرة أبي علي ثالث، /2 من أصول بن السراج ثاني ورابع مختلفة، من الصحاح ثامن والأخير، من إصلاح /3 المنطق أول، من شرح الإيضاح ثامن، أول ما اتفق لفظه واختلف معناه، /4 ثاني النعوت لابن عبيد، ثاني الأوسط للأخفش، من الفاخر ثاني وثاني، من /5 الثياب ثالثه، من مجرد كراع أوله، من نوادر القالي أول وثاني وثالث ورابع وخامس /6 من نسخة أخرى، من مجمل بن فارس أول وأول ومن نسخة أخرى ثاني وثالث، **الخامسة** /7 من الفاخر في الحوادث في أيام الإمام الناصر، من تأريخ بن الصابئ ذكر في التاء، /8 مختصر تأريخ غير تام الآخر، تأريخ مخروم الأول غير معروف المصنف، من مروج /9 الذهب نقلت إلى الرابعة عشرة، من فتوح [[الشام]] مصر نقلت إليها أيضاً، **السادسة** /10 [[وهي الأولى من الصف الثاني]] من تفسير

فخر الدين الرازي، من معادن الأبريز أوله، /[11] ثاني التبيان في إعراب القرآن، ثاني وجيز الواحدي، سادس الكشاف، /[12] من الصحاح رزين أول وثالث ورابع، من شرح السنة أول، من أخبار مكة /[13] أول، من جمع الحميدي ثاني ورابع مختلف، من جمع الجوزقي، من الترمذي خامسه، /[14] من أدعية الطبراني ثانيه، من غريب أبي عبيد أوله ومن نسخة أخرى ثانيه، من غريب بن /[15] قتيبة ثانيه، من الفردوس ثالثه ومنه من نسخة أخرى ثانيه، من صفة الصفوة أول /[16] وثاني وثالث وثامن وعاشر مختلفة الخط، من قوت القلوب أوله ومن نسخة أخرى /[17] أول، من سوق العروس أول ومن نسخة أخرى ثاني، من الإحياء من أصل ستة /[18] ومنه ثلاثة مختلفة الخط وهي السادس والسابع والثامن، شعر قيس المجنون مخروم /[19] الأول، شعر علقمة بن عبدة، شعر (الحطيئة) الطراز مخروم الأول، من شعر عدي بن /[20] الرقاع الجزء الرابع، من غريب القرآن جزء، من القرآن العزيز، من خطب بن نباتة خط [267ب] التبريزي، **السابعة** من تجارب الأمم، من العمدة ا من أصل ا اص ومنه من /[2] أصل 6ص ومنه 7، من فتوح ابن أعثم 7 و7ص، من المختار من ربيع الأبرار اص/[3] آخر من ربيع الأبرار عليه مختار ربيع الأبرار، من مدح المرزباني أوله، من تذكرة /[4] بن حمدون، من تحفة الألباب وهو [[العرب]] المعرب عن أخبار المشرق والمغرب، /[5] نسخة ثالثة من التمثيل ذكرت في التاء، **الثامنة** من معارف بن قتيبة مخروم، من /[6] بصائر التوحيدي، سيرة بن طولون في بعضها نقص، **التاسعة** من صور الأقاليم، /[7] من الوافدين والوافدات، من [[الما]] المسالك والممالك، من مناسك الحج مصور، من الشفاء /[8] لابن سينا، تعبير الرؤيا مخروم الأول، من الآثار العلوية أوله، من الفروسية أوله، /[9] المقالة [[الثالثة]] الثانية من كتاب أرطاميدوروس في التعبير، من تفسير جالينوس /[10] لفصول بقراط ومنه أول، من قانون بن سينا ستة عشر مجلداً متداخلة مختلفة /[11] الخط والقطع، من الفاخر في الطب أول وثاني، من الأدوية المفردة ثالثه، من منهاج /[12] بن جزلة أوله، من منافع الأعضاء لجالينوس ثاني وثالث ومنه أول وثاني، من المختار /[13] في الطب مختلفة الخط والقطع، من الملكي في الطب مختلفة الخط والقطع، من المنصوري /[14] في الطب أول مخروم في آخره، **العاشرة** البيطرة لأحمد بن الحسن بن الأحنف، **الحادية عشرة** /[15] من ديوان أبي نواس رواية حمزة، من ديوان الحيص بيص وبخطه، **الثانية عشرة** من أشعار /[16] الهذليين ومنها أيضاً، من شعر العماد الكاتب، من أزجال بن قزمان، **الثالثة عشرة** /[17] من ديوان بن منير، من شعر الصابئ أول، ديوان عرقلة مخروم، من شعر صالح بن عبد /[18] القدوس، من ديوان بشار، من شعر بن حجاج، موشحات بن سناء الملك، **الرابعة** [268ا] **عشرة** من الفرج بعد الشدة أوله، من يتيمة الدهر أوله، من زهر الآداب ثالثه، /[2] من يتيمة الدهر ثالثه، من الدر المكنون ثانيه، من زهر الرياض للمرزباني غير متوالية، /[3] من الأغاني ثامن وثلاثون، من لزوم ما لا يلزم أوله وثالثه، من يتيمة الدهر ثاني وثالث، /[4] من نشوار المحاضرة أوله، من الصاهل والشاحج أوله، من يتيمة الدهر بغير جلد، /[5] من الفرج بعد الشدة أوله، من نصيحة الطلاب أوله، من بستان الأدب (الرث) مختار /[6] تليه أجزاء في مجلد، المعمرين لابن عبيدة، من شعر بن الرومي أوله أول وأول وأول /[7] وثالث وخامس، من أنواع الصولي أول، من البيان للجاحظ أوله، من الروضة أوله، من (الفسر) /[8] والمعاني ثانيه وثالثه، من الوزراء للصولي أول وثاني وثالث، من اليتيمة ثالث، من الإمتاع /[9] والمؤانسة لأبي حيان أوله، الملحة بشرحها، من

نشوار المحاضرة، من يتيمة الدهر /10 أوله، لزوم ما لا يلزم، من الحماسة بشرحها ثانيه، من بهجة المجالس بغير جلد ثانيه، من البيان /11 للجاحظ، من الفروسية للخ[[ل]]تلي أوله، من البيطرة ثانيه، من أخبار الرؤساء والجلية /12 ثالثه، من الزهرة ثانيه وثالثه، زهرات الألفاظ، من رياض الأفكار ثانيه وثالثه، من /13 الحيوان للجاحظ، من كتاب (طعمة) ثانيه، أحسن ما سمعت، (ويمره) أنس الفريد، من الكامل /14 للمبرد أوله وثانيه، من الجليس الصالح ثالثه، من مختار الأنوار ثالثه، من الوسائط بين /15 المتنبي وخصمه، من الإشارات الال[ا]هية أوله ومنه ثانيه، من عيون الأخبار أوله، /16 من الكامل ثانيه، من أخبار الوزراء ثانيه وثالثه ورابعه، من مقاتل الفرسان ثانيه، من /17 الفتح القدسي ثانيه، من اختيار العقد، من المنتظم في تأريخ الأمم ثانيه، من أوراق الصولي /18 أوله، من الزهرة أوله، من الموفقيات أول وثاني ورابع، من الحماسة ثانيه، من العقد أوله [268ب] من التذكرة الحمدونية، من الحماسة بشرحها ثانيه، من يتيمة الدهر أول وثاني وثالث /2 وسادس وسابع، من (أنساب) (المنيرة) أوله، من الزهرة أول وثاني، من الحماسة ثالث /3 ورابع وخامس وسادس، من التأريخ للمبرد أول، من الخراج مجلد، من [[ال]] نثر الدر /4 الثاني والثالث، من مختار الأنوار أول وثالث ورابع، من نزهة القلوب ثانيه، /5 من حلية الآداب أول وثالث، من الرياش المصطنعي أوله، من نثر النظم وحل العقد /6 ثانيه، من المحب والمحبوب أوله، من سراج الملوك أول وأول، من (تنجيف) تأريخ بغداد /7 أوله، من الأحكام السلطانية لابن الفراء ثالثه، من الحلل الموشية والاختيارات الصالحية أول /8 وثاني، من أشعار الهذليين مجلد، من شعر الشريف الرضي أربع مجلدات وثالث وأول وثاني /9 وثالث وثالث ورابع وخامس وثاني وثاني، من شعر السمرقندي أوله وثالث، من شعر مقداد /10 المطاميري أول، من شرح المتنبي للخطيب أول وثاني، من شرحه لابن جني أوله، من شرحه لأبي /11 العلاء المعري مجلد، المتنبي ناقص مجلد، من المتنبي أوله ومنه ثانيه، من شرح المتنبي لابن /12 جني رابعه، من الجواهر السنية أوله، من شعر كثير عزة ثانيه، سيفيات المتنبي بخط روايته، /13 من معاني الشعر لثعلب ثانيه، من أزجال بن قزمان، من العقد ثالثه، من شعر المتنبي وعليه خطه /14 مجلد، من ديوان الأخطل ثانيه، المدائح الأيوبية مجلد، من أزجال بن قزمان ثانيه، /15 من أزجال بن بقي رابعه، من شعر بن المعتز ثالثه، من شعر المتنبي بشرحه ثامنه، من شعره بشرحه /16 خامسه، من شعر بن حجاج مجلد، من مغاني المعاني أوله، من ديوان {بن} البحتري أول وثالث /17 وسادس، من المفيد الخاص في علم الخواص أوله، **الخامسة عشرة** من الجواهر لإسحاق أوله، /18 الحيوان للجاحظ بنقصة، **أولى الصغار** من شعر ديك الجن، من المتنبي بخط بن [أبي] الجوع، /19 **الثانية** من النقائض ثانيه ومنها من الثاني إلى السادس بخط بن الخلال وأول منها، من /20 ديوان [بن] الأخطل أوله، من شعرالأرجاني أوله، من شعر جرير جزء، من ديوان بن رزيك أوله، /21 من ديوان بن أبي حصينة أول وثاني وثاني، من شعر مهيار أول وثاني، من ديوان (أبي) فاتك [269ا] أول وأول ورابع، من شعر بن الزبير ثاني وثالث، من شعر بن نباتة ثاني وثاني، من شعر بن المعتز /2 أول، من شعر الحيص بيص أول وأول وأول وثاني، من شعر المطرز ثاني، من شعر أبي نصر الفارقي /3 ثاني، من شعر بن منقذ أول، من ديوان بن منير 3 ومنه ثاني وأول جزء منه، من ديوان أبي نواس /4 أول وأول وأول وأول وثاني وثاني وثالث، من ديوان بن المعلم أول وأول وثاني، من شعر السري /5

الرفاء أول، من ديوان أبي تمام أول وأول وثاني وجزء آخر، من شعر بن التعاويذي أول وثاني، من شعر /6 بن سناء الملك ثانيه، من شعر بن حيوس ثانيه، من شعر جرير ثانيه، من شعر الملك العزيز مخروم الأول /7 والآخر، من شعر الفضل بن العباس مخروم الأول، من شعر (عمر ال... بن قصر) مخروم الأول، من ديوان /8 الأبله ثاني، **الثالثة** من المفضليات ثالثه ومنه أول، من نسب بني العباس [[أوله]] أوله، من /9 ملح الأراجيز للآمدي أول، من ديوان بن المعتز أول جزء، من اختيار الأشعار ثاني، من شعر /10 ذي الرمة قطعة، من شعر مسلم بن الوليد وأخباره أول [[ومن ال]] وثالث، من أخبار المتمثلين /11 بالشعر أول، من أنواع الأسجاع أول، من حلية المحاضرة أول، من مختارها أول، من أخبار البرامكة /12 ثلاث كراريس، من أشعار الأندلسيين أوله، من كلام الحكماء في أدب النفس، من شعر بن حجاج مخروم الأول /13 والآخر، من نظم الجواهر أخبار اللصوص ومن شعر مخروم الأول والآخر، من شعر الحافظ السلفي، /14 من آداب أفلاطون، من شعر (جرير) كأنه خط الأمين الحلبي، من المدائح (البغوية) أول، شعر خمس /15 قصائد، من النفي لابن كيسان، من شعر بن منير خط ابن صدقة، من كلام علي بن أبي طالب كرم الله وجهه /16 للجاحظ، من شعر العماد الإصفهاني، جزء شعر مجلد صغير منية النفس وطيب الأنس، /17 أدعية الأيام السبعة نسخة رابعة مخروم [[الأول]] الآخر، **خامسة** من دعاء خمس قوائم بخط بن البواب /18 بغير شك بقلم المحقق في مجلد، من وصية أمير المؤمنين علي بن أبي طالب لولده (الحسين) رضي الله عنهما [269ب] خامسه، من كلام علي بن عبيدة الريحاني، ما يخطئ فيه العامة للأصمعي مخروم [[الأول]] الآخر، من شعر /2 الشريف الرضي بخط ولده أبي عدنان، من أمالي القاضي أبي جعفر بن البهلول، مختصر النصائح /3 (السامية) مخروم الآخر، من شعر محمد بن صادق، من (حامل) حديث مجنون ليلى مخروم الآخر، من ما لا /4 يسع الكاتب جهله أوله، من شعر بن حجاج خامس وسادس في جزء واحد، من جنان الجنان أول، /5 من أشعار أهل الأندلس أول، من الجنان فيه أشعار (القيروانيين)، من أشعار الطارئين على /6 مصر، من أشعار الشاميين، من الذيل الساهي، **سادسة** من رسائل الصابئ أول وثاني ورابع، /7 وثالث وثالث والأول في الطير والعاشرة، من ترسل أوله القسم الثاني، من العتاب أظنه لابن الأثير، /8 من رسائل القاضي الفاضل مجلدان مقابلان وجزء وجزء وجزء وجزء، مكاتبات بن الحريري /9 ناقص من آخره، من رسائل أبي عبد الله بن المرزبان كأنه أول بعض مكاتبات بن الشلحي، من ترسل /10 الوهراني، **سابعة** القصائد السبع مخروم الآخر، من العرائس في المجالس ثانيه، من شعر بن حجاج /11 بغير جلد، مصارع العشاق أوله، من (راحة) الألباب وهو من مجموع شعر لمحمود (النعال)، /12 مجموع أشعار مخروم الأول والآخر، من شعر بن البياضي رق، مجموع أشعار وحكايات /13 مكبوب عليه أنس المحبين، مجموع مبوب بأبواب شبه أبواب السجل وغيره لبعض المتأخرين /14 وهو غير تام كاتبه الأول مؤلفه بعد سنة عشرين وستمائة، من التذكرة غير الحمدونية وفيه فنون، /15 من الشعر بالخط بن حاحب النعمان وابن أسد والطبري، مفاخرة الشتاء والصيف للجاحظ /16 ناقصة جزء، من كتاب مجهول المصنف مبوب وكأنه من تأليف الثعلبي وهو مجلد برق، من نظائر /17 الخالديين أول وثاني وجزء وآخر، مجموع فيه الشهور القبطية وأخبار مصر مخروم الآخر، مجموع /18 القسطاس ومن الفرائض مخروم الأول والآخر، لوامع الأدب بالعجمي والعربي

ناقص من أوله /19 جزء ومن الأعمال من تأليف الثقة والثاني من المصباح، مجموع مختصر التدليس في الرئاسة وكتاب فيه /20 البستان من أشعار الفرسان مخروم من آخره، مجموع مقالة العلل ومقالة في الحساب مخروم [270ا] الأول والثالث، من المختار من أشعار القبائل للآمدي، مختصر قيس الرقيات مخروم الأول، /2 مجموع ال... ناقصة من أوله والمقصور والممدود له، مجموع اللطائف

Notes

1. This summary is described (fol. 2a, margin) as '*Kitāb multaqaṭ min Kitāb Mirʾāt al-zamān*'. The passages included in this summary correspond to pp. 110–214 (with substantial lacunae) in the *Mirʾāt*-edition by K.S. al-Jubūrī, Dār al-kutub al-ᶜilmīya 2013.
2. On this scholar see IT, 701–46, p. 140 and *Wāfī*, XXII, 199–213. Fol. 115a explicitly mentions the title: '*manqūl min al-juzʾ al-sābiᶜ min al-tadhkira al-Kindīya*'.
3. This work is described as '*mimmā ᶜamilaha al-shaykh Ṣafī al-Dīn Abū al-ᶜAlāʾ fī waḍᶜ ṣināᶜat al-kitāba*' (fol. 271b). Al-Ṣafadī describes this work as '*Muqaddima fī ṣināᶜat al-ḥisāb wa-al-dīwān*' (al-Ṣafadī, *Aᶜyān*, II, 457–8).
4. See, for instance, the two strikingly dissimilar ways of writing the word '*fī*' when the scribe inadvertently repeats it on fol. 260a, ll. 12 and 13 and the word '*min*' as written on fol. 263b, l. 4 and l. 15.
5. Excluded from this count are fol. 246a, which was written by mistake and the final fol. 270a, which has only two lines.
6. However, in the analysis of the catalogue in Chapters 1–3, as well as in Chapter 4, (2) has not been counted as an independent entry.
7. For example, Fihrist al-Ashrafīya, Engl. tr. nos. 38, 380a, 667, 786, 1521.
8. Followed by blank (same in fol. 246a).
9. 246a omits 'المكتتبة نسخها في رمضان'.
10. 253a: 'سينية', 246a: شينية.
11. 246a omits 'نسختين'.

Bibliography

Abbreviations

AI	Annales Islamologiques
AK	^{c}Ālam al-kutub
BEO	Bulletin d'Études Orientales
CBMLC	Corpus of British Medieval Library Catalogues
DA	Dār al-^{c}arabīya
DAḍ	Dār al-aḍwāᵓ
DAJ	Dār al-āfāq al-jadīda
DAK	Dār ^{c}ālam al-kutub
D^{c}AK	al-Dār al-^{c}arabīya li-l-kitāb
DAr	Dār al-arqam
DB	Dār al-bashāᵓir
DF	Dār al-fikr
DGI	Dār al-gharb al-islāmī
DḤ	Dār al-ḥurrīya
DIḤ	Dār Ibn Ḥazm
DIKA	Dār iḥyāᵓ al-kutub al-^{c}arabīya
DJ	Dār al-jīl
DJM	Dār al-jāmi^{c}āt al-Miṣrīya
DKA	Dār al-kātib al-^{c}arabī
DKḤ	Dār al-kutub al-ḥadītha
DKI	Dār al-kutub al-^{c}ilmīya
DKiA	Dār al-kitāb al-^{c}arabī
DKJ	Dār al-kitāb al-jadīd

DKL	Dār al-kitāb al-Lubnānī
DKM	Dār al-kutub al-Miṣrīya
DM	Dār al-maᶜārif
DMa	Dār al-mawāsim
DMḤ	Dār maktabat al-ḥayāt
DML	al-Dār al-Miṣrīya al-Lubnānīya
DMU	Dāᵓirat al-maᶜārif al-ᶜuthmānīya
DN	Dār al-najāḥ
DNA	Dār al-nahḍa al-ᶜarabīya
DOI	Deutsches Orient-Institut
DQ	al-Dār al-qawmīya
DQa	Dār al-qalam
DR	Dār al-rashīd
DRA	Dār al-rāᵓid al-ᶜarabī
DṢ	Dār ṣādir
DSh	Dār al-shuᵓūn al-thaqāfīya al-ᶜāmma
DT	Dār al-turāth
DTh	Dār al-thaqāfa
DTu	al-Dār al-Tūnisīya
DY	Dār al-yanābīᶜ
EI^2	Bearman *et al.*, *Encyclopaedia*
EI^3	Krämer *et al.*, *Encyclopaedia*
GAL	Brockelmann, *Geschichte*
GAS	Sezgin, *Geschichte*
HMAK	al-Hayᵓa al-miṣrīya al-ᶜāmma li-l-kitāb
IAU	Ibn Abī ᶜUṣaybiᶜa, *ᶜUyūn al-anbāᵓ*
IBḤ	ᶜĪsā al-Bābī al-Ḥalabī
IFAO	Institut Français d'Archéologie Orientale
IFD	Institut Français de Damas
IKH	Ibn Khallikān, *Wafayāt*
IN	Ibn al-Nadīm, *Fihrist*
JDA	Jāmiᶜat al-duwal al-ᶜarabīya
LTTN	Lajnat al-taᵓlīf wa-al-tarjama wa-al-nashr
MA	Muᵓassasat al-aᶜlamī
MᶜA	Maṭbaᶜat al-ᶜĀnī
MAr	al-Muᵓassasa al-ᶜarabīya
MAR	al-Majlis al-aᶜlā li-riᶜāyat al-funūn wa-al-ādāb wa-al-ᶜulūm al-ijtimāᶜīya

MAṢ	al-Maktaba al-ᶜaṣrīya
MBḤ	Muṣṭafā al-Bābī al-Ḥalabī
MDWA	Markaz dirāsāt al-waḥda al-ᶜarabīya
MḤ	Maṭbaᶜat al-ḥawādith
MḤK	Maṭbaᶜat ḥukūmat al-Kuwayt
MI	Maṭbaᶜat al-irshād
MIA	al-Majmaᶜ al-ᶜilmī al-ᶜarabī
MII	al-Majmaᶜ al-ᶜilmī al-ᶜIrāqī
MK	Maktabat al-Khānjī
MKa	al-Maṭbaᶜa al-kāthūlīkīya
MKA	Maktabat al-kullīyāt al-azharīya
MKTh	Muᵓassasat al-kutub al-thaqāfīya
MLA	Majmaᶜ al-lugha al-ᶜarabīya
MM	al-Kaḥḥāla, *Muᶜjam*
MMa	Maṭbaᶜat al-maᶜārif
MMA	Maᶜhad al-makhṭūṭāt al-ᶜarabīya
MMF	Markaz al-Malik Fayṣal
MMi	Maktabat Miṣr
MMu	Maktabat al-Muthannā
MN	Maktabat al-nahḍa
MNM	Maktabat al-nahḍa al-Miṣrīya
MQ	Maktabat al-Qurᵓān
MR	Muᵓassasat al-risāla
MTK	al-Maktaba al-tijārīya al-kubrā
MU	Yāqūt al-Ḥamawī, *Muᶜjam al-udabāᵓ*
Siyar	al-Dhahabī, *Siyar*
TI	al-Dhahabī, *Taᵓrīkh al-islām*
Wāfī	al-Ṣafadī, *al-Wāfī*
WTa	Wizārat al-tarbīya
WTh	Wizārat al-thaqāfa

Primary Sources

Al-ᶜAbbāsī, ᶜAbd al-Raḥīm, *Maᶜāhid al-tanṣīṣ*, Cairo: Būlāq, 1316h.

Abū Shāma, *K. al-rawḍatayn fī akhbār al-dawlatayn al-Nūrīya wa-al-Ṣalāḥīya*, ed. I. al-Zaybaq, Beirut: MR, 1997.

Abū Shāma, *al-Mudhayyal ᶜalā al-Rawḍatayn*, ed. I. al-Zaybaq, Beirut: DB al-islāmīya, 2010.

Al-Āmidī, *al-Muʾtalif wa-al-mukhtalif*, ed. F. Krenkow, Beirut: DJ, 1991.

Al-Badrī, *Nuzhat al-anām fī maḥāsin al-Shām*, Beirut: DRA, 1980.

Al-Bākharzī, *Dumyat al-qaṣr wa-ʿuṣrat ahl al-ʿaṣr*, ed. M. Altūnjī, Beirut: DJ, 1993.

Al-Baṭalyawsī, *Sharḥ al-ashʿār al-sitta al-jāhilīya*, ed. N.S. ʿAwwād, Beirut and Berlin: Klaus Schwarz, 2008.

Al-Birzālī, al-Qāsim, *al-Muqtafā ʿalā Kitāb al-rawḍatayn*, ed. ʿU.ʿA. Tadmurī, Beirut: MAṢ, 2006.

Blankinship, Kh.Y. (tr.), *The History of al-Ṭabarī; vol. 11 The Challenge to the Empires*, Albany, 1993.

Bosworth, C.E. (tr.), *The History of al-Ṭabarī; vol. 5 The Sāsānids, the Byzantines, the Lakhmids, and Yemen*, Albany, 1985.

Bosworth, C.E. (tr.), *The History of al-Ṭabarī; vol.* 32 *The Reunification of the ʿAbbāsid Caliphate*, Albany, 1987.

Brinner, W.M., *ʿArāʾis al-majālis fī qiṣaṣ al-anbiyāʾ or 'Lives of the Prophets'*, Leiden, 2002.

Al-Buṣrawī, *Taʾrīkh al-Buṣrawī: ṣafaḥāt majhūla min taʾrīkh Dimashq fī ʿaṣr al-Mamālīk*, ed. A.Ḥ. al-ʿUlabī, Damascus: Dār al-Maʾmūn li-l-turāth, 1988.

Al-Dhahabī, *Siyar al-aʿlām al-nubalāʾ*, eds Sh. al-Arnāʾūṭ and B. ʿAwād, Beirut: MR, 1981–8.

Al-Dhahabī, *al-ʿIbar fī khabar man ghabar*, ed. A. Zaghlūl al-Abyānī, Beirut: DKI, 1985.

Al-Dhahabī, *Taʾrīkh al-islām wa-wafayāt al-mashāhīr wa-al-aʿlām*, ed. ʿU.ʿA. Tadmurī, Beirut: DKiA, 1987–2000.

Al-Dhahabī, *Muʿjam al-shuyūkh al-kabīr*, ed. M. al-Ḥabīb al-Hīla, al-Ṭāʾif: Maktabat al-Ṣiddīq, 1988.

Al-Dhahabī, *Maʿrifat al-qurrāʾ al-kibār ʿalā al-ṭabaqāt wa-al-aʿṣār*, ed. M. Ismāʿīl, Beirut: DKI, 1997.

Al-Farābī, *Iḥṣā al-ʿulūm*, ed. A. ʿUthmān, Cairo: DF al-ʿarabī, 1949.

Al-Fārisī, Kamāl al-Dīn, *K. tanqīḥ al-manāẓir li-dhawī al-abṣār wa-al-baṣāʾir*, ed. M. Ḥijāzī, Cairo: HMAK, 1984.

Fihrist kutub khizānat al-Ashrafiya, MS Istanbul, Süleymaniye Library, Fatih 5433, fols. 246v–270r.

Al-Ghazzī, *al-Kawākib al-sāʾira*, ed. Kh. al-Manṣūr, Beirut: DKI, 1997.

Ḥājjī Khalīfa (Kātib Çelebi), *Kashf al-ẓunūn*, eds Ş. Yaltkaya and K.R. Bilge, Istanbul, 1941–3.

Al-Ḥākim al-Naysābūrī, *al-Mustadrak ʿalā al-Ṣaḥiḥāyn*, ed. M.ʿA. ʿAṭā, Beirut: DKI, 1990.

Hawting, G.R. (tr.), *The History of al-Ṭabarī; vol. 17 The First Civil War*, Albany, 1996.

Ibn al-Abbār, *al-Takmila li-kitāb al-ṣila*, ed. ʿA. al-Harrās, Beirut: DF, 1995.

Ibn ʿAbd al-Hādī, *Fihrist al-kutub*, MS Damascus, al-Assad National Library, 3190 (written before 896/1491).

Ibn Abī al-Dam, *K. adab al-qaḍāʾ*, ed. M.ʿA. Aḥmad ʿAtā, Beirut: DKI, 1987.

Ibn Abī ʿUṣaybiʿa, *ʿUyūn al-anbāʾ fī ṭabaqāt al-aṭibbāʾ*, ed. ʿĀ. al-Najjār, Cairo: HMAK, 1986.

Ibn al-ʿAdīm, *Bughyat al-ṭalab fī taʾrīkh Ḥalab*, ed. S. Zakkār, Beirut: DF, 1988.

Ibn ʿAsākir, *Taʾrīkh madīnat Dimashq*, eds Ṣ. al-Munajjid and S. al-Shihābī *et al.*, Damascus: MIA/MLA/MR, 1951–.

Ibn al-Athīr, *al-Kāmil fī al-taʾ*rīkh, ed. C.J. Tornberg, repr. Beirut: DF, 1965–7.

Ibn al-Athīr, *al-Lubāb fī tahdhīb al-ansāb*, Baghdad: MMu, 1972.

Ibn ʿAṭīya, ʿAbd al-Ḥaqq, *al-Muḥarrar al-wajīz fī tafsīr al-Kitāb al-ʿazīz*, ed. ʿA.ʿA. Muḥammad, Beirut: DKI, 1993.

Ibn al-Fuwaṭī (pseudo), *al-Ḥawādith al-jāmiʿa wa-al-tajārib al-nāfiʿa fī al-miʾa al-sābiʿa*, ed. M. Jawād, Baghdad: al-Maktaba al-ʿarabīya, 1932.

Ibn al-Fuwaṭī, *Talkhīṣ majmaʿ al-ādāb fī muʿjam al-alqāb*, ed. M. Jawād, Damascus: WTh, 1962.

Ibn Ḥajar al-ʿAsqalānī, *al-Durar al-kāmina fī aʿyān al-miʾa al-thāmina*, ed. M. Jād al-Ḥaqq, Cairo: DKḤ, 1966–7.

Ibn Ḥajar al-ʿAsqalānī, *Lisān al-mīzān*, ed. ʿA. Abū Ghudda, Beirut: DB, 2002.

Ibn Ḥamdūn, *al-Tadhkira al-ḥamdūnīya*, eds I. ʿAbbās and B. ʿAbbās, Beirut: DṢ, 1996.

Ibn al-ʿImād, *Shadharāt al-dhahab fī akhbār man dhahab*, eds ʿA. al-Arnāʾūṭ and M. al-Arnāʾūṭ, Damascus and Beirut: Dār Ibn Kathīr, 1986–95.

Ibn Iyās, *Badāʾiʿ al-zuhūr fī waqaʾiʿ al-duhūr*, ed. M. Muṣṭafā, Cairo and Wiesbaden: Steiner, 1972–5 (vols I & II), 1960–32 (vols III–V).

Ibn Jamāʿa, *Tadhkirat al-sāmiʿ wa-al-mutakallim fī ādāb al-ʿālim wa-al-mutaʿallim*, Hayderabad: DMU, 1934.

Ibn al-Jazarī, *Ghāyat al-nihāya fī ṭabaqāt al-qurrāʾ*, eds G. Bergsträsser and O. Pretzl, Cairo: Saʿāda, 1933–7.

Ibn Kathīr, *al-Bidāya wa-al-nihāya*, ed. ʿA. Shīrī, Beirut: Dār iḥyāʾ al-turāth al-ʿarabī, 1987.

Ibn Khallikān, *Wafayāt al-aʿyān wa-abnāʾ al-zamān*, ed. I. ʿAbbās, Beirut: DTh, 1968–72 (reprint Beirut: DṢ).

Ibn Munqidh, *K. al-ʿAṣā*, ed. Ḥ. ʿAbbās, Alexandria: HMAK, 1978.

Ibn al-Mustawfī, *Taʾrīkh Irbil*, ed. S. al-Saqār, Baghdad: DR, 1980.

Ibn al-Muᶜtazz, *Ṭabaqāt al-shuᶜarāʾ*, ed. ᶜA.A. Farrāj, Cairo: DM, 1956.

Ibn al-Nadīm, *Kitāb al-Fihrist*, ed. A.F. Sayyid, London 2009.

Ibn al-Najjār, *Dhayl Taʾrīkh Baghdād*, in *Taʾrīkh Baghdād wa-dhuyūluhu*, ed. M.ᶜA. ᶜAṭā, Beirut, 1997.

Ibn Qāḍī Shuhbah, *Ṭabaqāt al-shāfiᶜīya*, ed. ᶜA. Khān, Beirut: AK, 1987.

Ibn al-Qifṭī, *Taʾrīkh al-ḥukamāʾ*, ed. J. Lippert, Leipzig 1903.

Ibn Rajab, *Dhayl Ṭabaqāt al-Ḥanābila*, ed. ᶜA. al-ᶜUthaymīn, Riyad: Maktabat al-ᶜAbīkān, 2005.

Ibn al-Sāᶜī, *al-Durr al-thamīn fī asmāʾ al-muṣannifīn*, eds A.Sh. Binbīn and M.S. Ḥanashī, Tunis: DGI, 2009.

Ibn Shaddād, *al-Nawādir al-sulṭānīya wa-al-maḥāsin al-yūsufīya*, ed. J. al-Shayyāl, Cairo: Dār al-Miṣrīya, 1964.

Ibn Shākir, *Fawāt al-wafayāt*, ed. I. ᶜAbbās, Beirut: DṢ, 1973/4.

Ibn Sīda, *al-Muḥkam wa-al-muḥīṭ al-aᶜẓam*, ed. ᶜA. Hindawī, Beirut: DKI, 2000.

Ibn Taymīya, *Minhāj al-sunna al-nabawīya*, ed. M.R. Sālim, Riyad: Jāmiᶜat al-Imām Muḥammad Ibn Saᶜūd al-islāmīya, 1406h *[1985/6]*.

Ibn Taymīya, *al-Risāla al-ṣafadīya*, ed. M.R. Sālim, Cairo: Maktabat Ibn Taymīya, 1406h *[1985/6]*.

Ibn al-Ṭuwayr, *Nuzhat al-muqlatayn fī akhbār al-dawlatayn*, ed. A.F. Sayyid, Beirut: Steiner, 1992.

Ibn ᶜUnayn, *Dīwān*, ed. Kh. l. Mardam, Damascus: MIA, 1365 *[1946]*.

Ibn Wāṣil, *Mufarrij al-kurūb fī akhbār banī Ayyūb*, eds J. al-Shayyāl, Ḥ. al-Rabīᶜand S. ᶜĀshūr, vols 1–5, Cairo, 1953–77, vol. 6: ed. M. Rahim, *Die Chronik des ibn Wasil. Kritische Edition des letzten Teils (646/1248–659/1261) mit Kommentar. Untergang der Ayyubiden und Beginn der Mamlukenherrschaft*, Wiesbaden, 2010.

Al-Iṣfahānī, ᶜImād al-Dīn, *Kharīdat al-qaṣr wa-jarīdat al-ᶜaṣr*, ed. M.B. al-Atharī, Baghdad: MII, 1955 (al-ᶜIrāq).

Al-Iṣfahānī (d. early 5th/11th century?), al-Ḥusayn al-Rāghib, *Muḥāḍarāt al-udabāʾ*, ed. ᶜU. al-Ṭabbāᶜ, Beirut: DAr, 1999.

Al-Iṣfahānī, Abū al-Faraj, *Mukhtār al-aghānī*, ed. I. Ibyārī, Cairo: al-Muʾassasa al-Miṣrīya al-ᶜāmma, 1965/6.

Al-Jarīrī, *al-Jalīs al-ṣāliḥ al-kāfī*, eds M. al-Khūlī and I. ᶜAbbās, Beirut: AK, 1981–7.

Al-Jūdharī, *Vie de l'Ustadh Jaudhar (contenant sermons, lettres et rescrits des premiers califes fâtimides) écrite par Mansûr le secrétaire à l'époque du calife al-'Azîz billâh (365–386/875–996)*, Fr. tr. M. Canard, Algiers, 1958.

Kairouan catalogue-cum-inventory [untitled], MS Raqqāda, Centre d'Études de la Civilisation et des Arts Islamiques, box 289.

Kennedy, H. (tr.), *The History of al-Ṭabarī; vol. 29 Al-Manṣūr and al-Mahdī*, Albany, 1990.

Al-Kutubī, *Fawāt al-wafayāt wa-al-dhayl ʿalayhā*, ed. I. ʿAbbās, Beirut: DṢ, 1973–4.

Al-Lakhmī, *al-Fawāʾid al-Maḥṣūra fī sharḥ al-Maqṣūra*, ed. A.ʿA. ʿAṭṭār, Beirut: Dār maktabat al-ḥayāt, 1980.

Al-Maʿarrī, *Rasāʾil Abī al-ʿAlāʾ al-Maʿarrī*, ed. I. ʿAbbās, Beirut: Dār al-shurūq, 1982.

Al-Maʿarrī, *The Epistle of Forgiveness [Risālat al-ghufrān]*, eds and trs G.J. van Gelder and G. Schoeler, New York, 2013.

Majlisī, M., *Zād al-maʿād*, Beirut: MA, 2003.

Al-Maqrīzī, *Ittiʿāẓ al-ḥunafāʾ bi-akhbār al-aʾimma al-Fāṭimīyīn al-khulafāʾ*, eds J. al-Shayyāl and M.Ḥ.M. Aḥmad, Cairo: Lajnat iḥyāʾ al-turāth al-islāmī, 1967–73.

Al-Maqrīzī, *al-Mawāʿiẓ wa-al-iʿtibār fī dhikr al-khiṭaṭ wa-al-athār*, ed. A.F. Sayyid, London 2002.

Al-Mardāwī, *Maʿrifat al-rājiḥ min al-khilāf*, ed. M.Ḥ. al-Fiqī, Cairo, 1955–8.

Al-Marrākushī, Muḥammad b. Maymūn, 'K. al-azhār fī ʿamal al-aḥbār', ed. I. Shabbūḥ, *Zeitschrift für Geschichte der arabisch-islamischen Wissenschaften* 14 (2001), 41–133.

Al-Marrākushī, Muḥammad b. Muḥammad, *al-Dhayl wa-al-takmila li-kitābay al- Mawṣūl wa-al-Ṣila*, eds M. Ibn Sharīfa and I. ʿAbbās, Beirut: DTh, 1965.

Morony, M.G. (tr.), *The History of al-Ṭabarī; vol. 18 Between Civil Wars: The Caliphate of Muʿāwiyah*, Albany, 1987.

Al-Mubarrad, *al-Mudhakkar wa-al-muʾannath*, ed. R. ʿAbd al-Tawwāb, Cairo: DKM, 1980.

Al-Muntakhab mimmā fī khazāʾin al-kutub bi-Ḥalab, ed. P. Sbath, Choix de livres qui se trouvaient dans les bibliothèques d'Alep (au XIIIe siècle), Cairo: IFAO, 1946.

Al-Muqaddasī, *Aḥsan al-taqāsīm fī maʿrifat al-aqālīm*, ed. M.J. de Goeje, Leiden, 1877 (reprint Beirut: DṢ, 1991).

Al-Najāshī, *K. al-rijāl*, ed. M.J. al-Nāʾinī, Beirut: Dār al-aḍwāʾ, 1988.

Al-Nawawī, *al-Majmūʿ sharḥ al-muhadhdhab*, Beirut: DF, 2000.

Al-Nuʿaymī, *al-Dāris fī taʾrīkh al-madāris*, ed. J. al-Ḥasanī, Damascus: MIA, 1948–51.

Al-Qāḍī ʿIyāḍ, *al-Ghunya: fihrist shuyūkh al-qāḍī ʿIyāḍ*, ed. M.Z. Jarrār, Beirut: DGI, 1982.

Al-Qāḍī ʿIyāḍ, *Tartīb al-madārik wa-taqrīb al-masālik*, ed. S.A. Aʿrāb, Rabat: Wizārat al-awqāf, 1981.

Al-Qalʿī, *Tahdhīb al-riʾāsa wa-tartīb al-siyāsa*, ed. I.M. ʿAjū, al-Zarqāʾ: al-Manār, 1985.

Al-Qalqashandī, *Ṣubḥ al-aʿshā fī ṣināʿat al-inshāʾ*, ed. M.Ḥ. Shams al-Dīn, Beirut: DKI, 1987.

Al-Qifṭī, *Inbāh al-ruwāt ʿalā anbāh al-nuḥāt*, Cairo: DKM, 1950–73.

Al-Qurashī, *Jamharat ashʿār al-ʿarab*, ed. ʿA.M. al-Bajāwī, Cairo: Dār nahḍat Miṣr, 1967.

Al-Rāfiʿī, *al-Tadwīn fī akhbār Qazwīn*, Beirut: DKI, 1987.

Rosenthal, F. (Engl. tr. and introd.), *The History of al-Ṭabarī; vol. 1 General Introduction and from the Creation to the Flood*, Albany, 1989.

Rosenthal, F. (tr.), *The History of al-Ṭabarī; vol. 38 The Return of the Caliphate to Baghdad*, Albany, 1985.

Al-Ṣafadī, *al-Wāfī bi-al-wafayāt*, ed. H. Ritter *et al.*, Istanbul, 1931–97.

Al-Ṣafadī, *Aʿyān al-ʿaṣr wa-aʿwān al-naṣr*, ed. ʿA. Abū Zayd, Beirut: DF al-muʿāṣir, 1998.

Al-Sakhāwī, *al-Ghāya fī sharḥ al-hidāya fī ʿilm al-riwāya*, ed. ʿA. Ibrāhīm, Cairo: Maktabat awlād al-shaykh, 2001.

Al-Sakhāwī, *al-Jawāhir wa-al-durar fī tarjmat Shaykh al-islām Ibn Ḥajar*, ed. al-Nashshār, in al-Nashshār, *Taʾrīkh al-maktabāt*.

Al-Shābushtī, *al-Diyārāt*, ed. G. ʿAwwād, Baghdad: MMu, 1966.

Al-Shaʾmī, *Subul al-hudā wa-al-rashād*, ed. ʿA. al-Mawjūd, Beirut: DKI, 1993.

Al-Shantamarī, *Ashʿār al-shuʿarāʾ al-sitta al-jāhilīyīn: ikhtiyārāt min al-shiʿr al-jāhilī*, Beirut: DAJ, 1979.

Al-Shayzarī, *Nihāyat al-rutba fī ṭalab al-ḥisba*, ed. al-S. al-ʿArīnī, Cairo: LTTN, 1947.

Sibṭ Ibn al-Jawzī, *Mirʾāt al-zamān fī taʾrīkh al-aʿyān*, ed. K.S. al-Jubūrī, Abu Dhabi: Hayʾat Abū Ẓabī li-l-thaqāfa wa-al-turāth, 2007.

Smith, G.R. (tr.), *The History of al-Ṭabarī; vol. 14 The Conquest of Iran*, Albany, 1993.

Al-Subkī, *Fatāwā*, 2 vols, Beirut: Dār al-maʿrifa, n.d.

Al-Subkī, *Ṭabaqāt al-Shāfiʿīya al-kubrā*, eds M. al-Ṭanāḥī and ʿA. al-Ḥulw, Cairo: IBḤ, 1964–76.

Al-Suyūṭī, *Bughyat al-wuʿāt fī ṭabaqāt al-lughawīyyīn wa-al-nuḥāt*, ed. M.A. Ibrahīm, Beirut: DF, 1979.

Al-Suyūṭī, *Abwāb al-saʿāda fī asbāb al-shahāda*, ed. N.ʿA. Khalaf [S.l.]: al-Maktaba al-qayyima, 1981.

Al-Tanūkhī, *Taʾrīkh al-ʿulamāʾ al-naḥwīyīn*, ed. ʿA.M. al-Ḥulw, Riyad: Idārat al-thaqāfīya wa-al-nashr bi-al-jāmiʿa, 1981.

Williams, J.A. (tr.), *The History of al-Ṭabarī; vol. 27 The ᶜAbbāsid Revolution*, Albany, 1985.

Yāqūt al-Ḥamawī, *Muᶜjam al-udabāʾ: Irshād al-arīb ilā maᶜrifat al-adīb*, ed. I. ᶜAbbās, Beirut: DGI, 1993.

Yāqūt al-Ḥamawī, *Muᶜjam al-buldān*, Beirut: DṢ,[2]1995.

Al-Yārūqī, *Dīwān*, ed. M.ᶜA. al-Ḥabbāzī, Jerusalem, 2002.

Al-Yūnīnī, *Dhayl Mirʾāt al-zamān*, ed. K.S. al-Jubūrī, Abu Dhabi: Hayʾat Abū Ẓabī li-l-thaqāfa wa-al-turāth, 2007 (volume numbering consecutive with above-cited edition of Sibṭ Ibn al-Jawzī, *Mirʾāt al-zamān*).

Secondary Literature

ᶜAbbās, I. (1988a), *Shadharāt min kutub mafqūda fī al-taʾrīkh*, Beirut.

ᶜAbbās, I. (1988b), *ᶜAbd al-Ḥamīd b. Yaḥyā al-Kātib wa-mā tabqā min rasāʾilihi wa-rasāʾil Sālim Abī al-ᶜAlāʾ*, Amman.

ᶜAbd al-Ḥalīm, F. (2003), *al-ᶜImāra al-islāmīya fī ᶜaṣr al-mamālīk al-jarākisa, ᶜaṣr al-Sulṭān al-Muʾayyad Shaykh*, Cairo.

ᶜAbd al-Mahdī, ᶜA. (1980), *al-Ḥaraka al-fikrīya fī ẓill al-masjid al-aqṣā fī al-ᶜaṣrayn al-ayyūbī wa-al-mamlūkī*, ᶜAmmān.

Abd Al-Rahman, D.S. (1986 *[1424h]*), *A Critical Edition of Kitab Sharaf Al-Mustafa, PhD*, University of Exeter and Mecca.

Adang, C., S. Schmidtke and D. Sklare (eds) (2007), *A Common Rationality: Muᶜtazilism in Islam and Judaism*, Würzburg.

Ahmed, H. (2007), *The Writings of Amir Khusrau*, Forest Park, IL.

Ahmed, Sh. (2000), 'Mapping the World of a Scholar in Sixth/Twelfth Century Bukhara: Regional Tradition in Medieval Islamic Scholarship as Reflected in a Bibliography', *Journal of the American Oriental Society* 120/1, 24–43.

Alhamzah, Kh.A. (2009), *Late Mamluk Patronage: Qansuh al-Ghuri's Waqfs and his Foundation in Cairo*, Boca Raton.

Ali, S. (2010), *Arabic Literary Salons in the Islamic Middle Ages: Poetry, Public Performance, and the Presentation of the Past*, Notre Dame.

Allony, N. (2006), *The Jewish Library in the Middle Ages: Book Lists from the Cairo Genizah*, eds M. Frenkel and H. Ben-Shammai with the participation of M. Sokolow, Jerusalem: Ben-Zvi Institute *[Hebrew]*.

Alwajī, ᶜA. (1992), *Muʾallafāt Ibn al-Jawzī*, Kuwait.

Ambros, A. (1990), 'Beobachtungen zu Aufbau und Funktion des gereimten klassisch-arabischen Buchtitels', *Wiener Zeitschrift für die Kunde des Morgenlandes* 80, 13–57.

Ansari, H. and S. Schmidtke (2010), 'The Zaydī Reception of Ibn Khallād's Kitāb al-Uṣūl. The Ta[c]līq of Abū Ṭāhir b. [c]Alī al-Ṣaffār', *Journal Asiatique* 298/2, 275–302.

Ansari, H. and S. Schmidtke (2014), 'Al-Shaykh al-Ṭūsī: His Writings on Theology and Their Reception', in F. Daftary and G. Miskinzoda (eds), *The Study of Shi[c]i Islam: History, Theology and Law*, London, pp. 475–97.

Antoon, S. (2014), *The Poetics of the Obscene in Premodern Arabic Poetry: Ibn al-Ḥajjāj and* Sukhf, New York.

Arberry, A.J. (1952), *A Second Supplementary Hand-List of the Muhammadan Manuscripts in the University & Colleges of Cambridge*, Cambridge.

Arberry, A.J. (1955–66), *A Handlist of the Arabic Manuscripts*, Dublin.

Al-As[c]ad, [c]U.M. (1969), *Dīwān Ibn al-Nabīh*, Beirut.

[c]Asalī, K.J. (1981), *Makhṭūṭāt faḍā[ʾ]il Bayt al-Maqdis: dirāsa wa-bībliyūghrāfiyā*, Amman: MLA al-Urdunnīya.

Al-[c]Ashmāwī, A.M.Z. (1998), *Khamrīyāt Abī Nuwās*, Alexandria.

Azar, H. (2008), *The Sage of Seville*, Cairo.

Badawī, [c]A. (1954), *al-Uṣūl al-yūnānīya li-l-naẓarīyāt al-siyāsīya fī al-islām = Fontes graecae doctrinarum politicarum islamicarum*, Cairo.

Badawī, [c]A. (1961), *Mu[ʾ]allafāt al-Ghazālī*, Cairo.

Baghdādī, I. (1945–7), *Īḍāḥ al-maknūn fī al-dhayl [c]alā Kashf al-ẓunūn*, Istanbul: Milli Eğitim Basımevi.

Baghdādī, I. (1951), *Hadīyat al-[c]ārifīn: asmā[ʾ] al-mu[ʾ]allifīn wa-āthār al-muṣannifīn*, Istanbul (repr. Beirut, n.d.).

Bakar, O. (1998), *Classification of Knowledge in Islam. A Study in Islamic Philosophies of Science*, Cambridge.

Bandt, C. and A. Rattmann (2011), 'Die Damaskusreise Bruno Violets 1900/1901 zur Erforschung der Qubbet el-Chazne', *Codices Manuscripti* 76/77, 1–20.

Bāshā, [c]U.M. (1972), *al-Adab fī bilād al-Shām: [c]aṣr al-zankīyīn wa-al-ayyūbīyīn wa-al-mamālīk*, Damascus.

Bauer, K. (2011), 'The Muslim Exegete and His Audience, 5th/11th–6th/12th Centuries', in A. Ahmed, M. Bonner and B. Sadeghi (eds), *The Islamic Scholarly Tradition: Studies in History, Law and Thought in Honor of Professor Michael Allan Cook*, Leiden, pp. 293–315.

Bauer, Th. (2003), 'Literarische Anthologien der Mamlūkenzeit', in St. Conermann and A. Pistor-Hatam (eds), *Die Mamlūken. Studien zu ihrer Geschichte und Kultur. Zum Gedenken an Ulrich Haarmann (1942–1999)*, Hamburg, pp. 71–122.

Bauer, Th. (2011), *Die Kultur der Ambiguität: Eine andere Geschichte des Islams*, Berlin.

Bauer, Th. (2013), 'Mamluk Literature as a Means of Communication', in St. Conermann (ed.), *Ubi sumus? Quo vademus?: Mamluk Studies-State of the Art*, Göttingen, pp. 23–56.

Bearman, P. *et al.* (1960–2004), *Encyclopaedia of Islam, Second Edition*, Leiden: Brill.

Behmardi, V. (2011), 'Arabic and Persian Intertextuality in the Seljuq Period: Ḥamīdī's maqāmāt as a Case Study', in Ch. Lange and M. Songul (eds), *The Seljuqs. Politics, Society and Culture*, Edinburgh, pp. 240–55.

Bell, D.N. (1992), *The Libraries of the Cistercians, Gilbertines and Premonstratensians*, CBMLC III, London.

Bell, J.N. and H.M. Al-Shafie (2005), *A Treatise on Mystical Love*, Edinburgh.

Berkey, J.P. (1992), *The Transmission of Knowledge in Medieval Cairo*, Princeton.

Biberstein-Kazimirski, A. (1860), *Dictionnaire Arabe-Français*, Paris.

Binbaş, I.E. (2011), 'Structure and Function of the "Genealogical Tree" in Islamic Historiography', in I.E. Binbaş and N. Kılıc-Schubel (eds), *Horizons of the World: Festschrift for Isenbike Togan*, Istanbul, pp. 465–544.

Blois, F. de (2004), *Persian Literature, a Bio-Bibliographical Survey*, Volume V, London.

Bora, F. (2015), 'Did Ṣalāḥ al-Dīn Destroy the Fatimids' Books? An Historiographical Enquiry', *Journal of the Royal Asiatic Society* 25, 21–39.

Bosworth, C.E. (2003), 'Arabic, Persian and Turkish Historiography in the Eastern Iranian World', in *History of Civilizations of Central Asia*, vol. IV/2, Delhi, pp. 142–52.

Brentjes, S. (2010), 'Ayyubid Princes and their Scholarly Clients from the Ancient Sciences', in Fuess/Hartung, *Court Cultures*, pp. 326–56.

Brentjes, S. (2011), 'The Prison of Categories – "Decline" and Its Company', in D. Reisman and F. Opwis (eds), *Islamic Philosophy, Science, Culture, and Religion, Studies in Honor of Dimitri Gutas*, Leiden, pp. 131–56.

Brett, M. (1970), *Fitnat Al Qayrawān: A Study of Traditional Arabic Historiography*, PhD, University of London.

Briquel-Chatonnet, F. (1997), *Manuscrits syriaques de la Bibliothèque nationale de France (nos 356–435 entrés depuis 1911), de la Bibliothèque Méjanes d'Aix-en-Provence, de la Bibliothèque municipale de Lyon et de la Bibliothèque nationale et universitaire de Strasbourg: catalogue*, Paris.

Brockelmann, C. (1898–1949), *Geschichte der arabischen Litteratur*, Leiden.

Cahen, Cl. (1947–8), 'Un traité d'armurerie composé pour Saladin', *BEO* 12, 1–47 and 150–63.

Chamberlain, M. (1994), *Knowledge and Social Practice in Medieval Damascus, 1190–1350*, Cambridge.

Chamberlain, M. (2005), 'Military Patronage States and the Political Economy of the Frontier, 1000–1250', in Y.M. Choueiri (ed.), *A Companion to the History of the Middle East*, Malden (MA), pp. 135–53.

Chittick, W.C. (1988), *The Psalms of Islam: al-Ṣaḥīfa al-kāmila al-sajjādiyya*, London.

Clarke, P.D. (2002), *The University and College Libraries of Cambridge*, CBMLC X, London.

Contadini, A. (2009), 'Ayyubid Illustrated Manuscripts and their North Jaziran and ʿAbbasid Neighbours' in R. Hillenbrand and S. Auld (eds), *Ayyubid Jerusalem. The Holy City in Context 1187–1250*, London, pp. 179–94.

Cooperson, M. (2008), *Classical Arabic Biography: The Heirs of the Prophets in the Age of al-Maʾmūn*, Cambridge.

Daiber, H. (1992), 'The Meteorology of Theophrastus in Syriac and Arabic Translation', in W. Fortenbaugh and D. Gutas (eds), *Theophrastus: His Psychological, Doxographical, and Scientific Writings*, New Brunswick, NJ, 166–293.

Daïm, A. (1958), *L' oniromancie arabe d'après Ibn Sîrîn*, Damascus.

Davidson, G. (2014), *Carrying on the Tradition: An Intellectual and Social History of Post-Canonical Hadith Transmission*, PhD, University of Chicago.

Dickinson, E. (2002), 'Ibn al-Ṣalāḥ al-Shahrazūrī and the Isnād', *Journal of the American Oriental Society* 122/3, 481–505.

Diem, W. (2010), *Studien zur Überlieferung*, Wiesbaden.

D'Ottone, A. (2013a), 'Manuscripts as Mirrors of a Multilingual and Multicultural Society: The Case of the Damascus Find', in B. Crostini and S. La Porta (eds), *Negotiating Co-Existence: Communities, Cultures and Convivencia in Byzantine Society*, Trier, 63–88.

D'Ottone, A. (2013b), 'La bibliothèque d'un savant Yéménite du XIIIe siècle d'après une note manuscrite autographe', in Ch. Müller and M. Roiland-Rouabah (eds), *Les non-dits du nom. Onomastique et documents en terres d'Islam. Mélanges offerts à Jacqueline Sublet*, Damascus, 67–84.

Doufikar-Aerts, F. (2010), *Alexander Magnus Arabicus: A Survey of the Alexander Tradition through Seven Centuries*, Leuven.

Drory, R. (1996), 'The Abbasid Construction of the Jahiliyya: Cultural Authority in the Making', *Studia Islamica* 83, 33–49.

Al-Dukhayyil, Ḥ.N. (1429/2008), 'Fī al-tawqīʿāt al-adabīya fī al-ʿaṣr al-islāmī wa-al-umawī wa-al-ʿabbāsī', *Majallat jāmīʿat Umm al-Qurā li-l-ʿulūm al-sharīʿa wa-al-lugha al-ʿarabīya wa-ādābuhā* 13/22, 1083–129.

Eastmond, A. (forthcoming), *Tamta's World: One Woman's Encounters from the Mediterranean to Mongolia in the Thirteenth Century*.

Eche, Y. (1967), *Les bibliothèques arabes publiques et semipubliques en Mésopotamie, en Syrie et en Égypte au Moyen Âge*, Damascus.

Eco, U. (2008), *The Name of the Rose*, London.

El-Aswad, A. (1977), *Der Diwan des Ibn al-Haǧǧāǧ: Der Reimbuchstabe nūn*, PhD Giessen.

Elayyan, R.M. (1990), 'The History of the Arabic-Islamic Libraries: 7th to 14th Centuries', *International Library Review* 22, 119–35.

Erünsal, İ.E. (1987), 'Catalogues and Cataloguing in the Ottoman Libraries', *Libri* 37, 333–49.

Erünsal, İ.E. (1989), 'The Establishment and Maintenance of Collections in the Ottoman Libraries: 1400–1839', *Libri* 39, 1–17.

Erünsal, İ.E. (2007), 'Ottoman Foundation Libraries: Their History and Organization', *Osmanlı Araştırmaları/Journal of Ottoman Studies* 30, 31–86.

Erünsal, İ.E. (2008), *Ottoman Libraries: A Survey of the History, Development and Organization of Ottoman Foundation Libraries*, Cambridge, MA.

Erünsal, İ.E. (2014), 'Fethedilen Arap Ülkelerindeki Vakıf Kütüphaneleri Osmanlılar Tarafından Yağmalandı mı?', *Osmanlı Araştırmaları/Journal of Ottoman Studies* 43, 19–66.

Ess, J.v. (1980), *Ungenützte Texte zur Karrāmīya: eine Materialsammlung*, Heidelberg.

Fahd, T. (1987), *La divination arabe: études religieuses, sociologiques et folkloriques sur le milieu natif de l'Islam*, Paris.

Fierro, M.I. (1987), 'La polémique à propos de *rafʿ al-yadayn fī l-ṣalāt* dans al-Andalus', *Studia Islamica* 65, 69–90.

Fiey, J.M. (1966), 'Îchô'dnah métropolite de Basra, et son oeuvre', *L'Orient Syrien* 11, 431–50.

Friis-Jensen, K. and J.M.W. Willoughby (2001), *Peterborough Abbey*, CBMLC VIII, London.

Fuess, A. and J.-P. Hartung (eds) (2010), *Court Cultures in the Muslim World: Seventh to Nineteenth Centuries*, London.

Gacek, A. (1983), 'Some Remarks on the Cataloguing of Arabic Manuscripts', *British Society for Middle Eastern Bulletin* 10, 173–9.

Gacek, A. (2001), *The Arabic Manuscript Tradition: A Glossary of Technical Terms and Bibliography*, Leiden.

Gacek, A. (2009), *Arabic Manuscripts. A Vademecum for Readers*, Leiden.

Gameson, R. (2006), 'The Medieval Library (to c. 1450)', in E. Leedham-Green and T. Webber (eds), *The Cambridge History of Libraries in Britain and Ireland, vol. 1: To 1640*, Cambridge, pp. 13–50.

Gelder, G.J.v. (1988), *The Bad and the Ugly: Attitudes towards Invective Poetry (hijāʾ) in Classical Arabic Literature*, Leiden.

Gelder, G.J.v. (1995), 'The Joking Doctor: Abū l Ḥakam ʿUbayd Allāh Ibn al Muẓaffar (d. 549/1155)', in C. Vázquez de Benito and M.Á.M. Rodríguez (eds), *Actas XVI Congreso UEAI [Salamanca, Aug–Sept. 1992]*, Salamanca, pp. 217–28.

Gelder, G.J.v. (2012), *Sound and Sense in Classical Arabic Poetry*, Wiesbaden.

Ghanem, I. (1969), *Zur Bibliotheksgeschichte von Damaskus 549/1154–922/1516*, PhD, University of Bonn.

Görke, A. and K. Hirschler (eds) (2011), *Manuscript Notes as Documentary Sources*, Würzburg.

Gramlich, R. (1992), *Die Nahrung der Herzen*, Stuttgart.

Green, A. (1988), 'The History of Libraries in the Arab World. A Diffusionist Model', *Libraries & Culture* 23/4, 454–73.

Griffel, F. (2009), *Al-Ghazali's Philosophical Theology*, Oxford and New York.

Grube, E.J. (1967), 'The Hippiatrica Arabica Illustrata: Three 13th-Century Manuscripts and Related Material', in A.U. Pope and P. Ackermann (eds), *A Survey of Persian Art*, Oxford, pp. 3138–55.

Gründler, B. (forthcoming), *The Arab Book Revolution*, Cambridge, MA.

Günther, S. (2005), 'Advice for Teachers: The 9th Century Muslim Scholars Ibn Saḥnūn and al-Jāḥiẓ on Pedagogy and Didactics', in S. Günther (ed.), *Ideas, Images, and Methods of Portrayal: Insights into Classical Arabic Literature and Islam*, Leiden, pp. 89–128.

Gutas, D. (^{2}2014), *Avicenna and the Aristotelian Tradition*, Leiden.

Haarmann, U. (1984), 'The Library of a Fourteenth-Century Jerusalem Scholar', *Der Islam* 61, 327–33.

Hachmeier, K. (2010/11), 'The Letters of Abū Isḥāq Ibrāhīm al-Ṣābiʾ – A Large Buyid Collection Established from Manuscripts and Other Sources', *Mélanges de l'Université Saint-Joseph* LXIII, 107–221.

Halm, H. (1997), *The Fatimids and their Traditions of Learning*, London.

Hämeen-Anttila, J. (1995), *Five Rağaz Collections: al-Aghlab al-ʿIğlī, Bashīr ibn an-Nikth, Ǧandal ibn al-Muthannā, Ḥumayd al-Arqaṭ, Ghaylān ibn Ḥurayth*, Helsinki.

Hämeen-Anttila, J. (1996), *Minor Raǧaz Collections: Khiṭām al-Muǧāshiᶜī, the two Dukyans, al-Qulākh ibn Ḥazn, Abū Muḥammad al-Faqᶜasī, Manẓūr ibn Marthad, Himyān ibn Quḥāfa*, Helsinki.

Hämeen-Anttila, J. (2006), *The Last Pagans of Iraq: Ibn Waḥshiyya and His Nabatean Agriculture*, Leiden.

Hamori, A. (1992), *The Composition of Mutanabbī's Panegyrics to Sayf al-Dawla*, Leiden.

Hartmann, A. (1986), 'Les ambivalences d'un sermonnaire ḥanbalite: Ibn al-Ǧawzī (m. en 597/1201), sa carrière et son ouvrage autographe, le Kitāb al-Ḫawātīm', *AI* 22, 51–115.

Heide, M. (2008), *Das Buch der Hippiatrie*, Wiesbaden.

Heidemann, St. (2009), 'Economic Growth and Currency in Ayyubid Palestine', in R. Hillenbrand and S. Auld (eds), *Ayyubid Jerusalem: The Holy City in Context 1187–1250*, London, pp. 276–300.

Hillenbrand, C. (2012), 'The Shīᶜīs of Aleppo in the Zengid Period: Some Unexploited Textual and Epigraphic Evidence', in H. Biesterfeldt and V. Klemm (eds), *Differenz und Dynamik im Islam. Festschrift für Heinz Halm zum 70. Geburtstag*, Würzburg, pp. 163–79.

Hirschler, K. (2006), *Medieval Arabic Historiography: Authors as Actors*, London.

Hirschler, K. (2012a), *The Written Word in the Medieval Arabic Lands: A Social and Cultural History of Reading Practices*, Edinburgh.

Hirschler, K. (2012b), '"Catching the Eel" – Documentary Evidence for Concepts of the Arabic Book in the Middle Period', *Journal of Arabic and Islamic Studies* 12, 224–34.

Hirschler, K. (2016), 'From Archive to Archival Practices. Rethinking the Preservation of Mamlūk Administrative Documents', *Journal of the American Oriental Society* 135/1.

Hodgson, M.G.S. (1974–7), *The Venture of Islam: Conscience and History in a World Civilization*, Chicago.

Howard, I.K.A. (1981), *The Book of Guidance*, London.

Humphreys, K.W. (1990), *The Friars' Libraries*, CBMLC I, London.

Humphreys, St. (1977), *From Saladin to the Mongols: The Ayyubids of Damascus, 1193–1260*, Albany.

Ibn Badrān, ᶜA. (1985), *Munādamat al-aṭlāl wa-musāmarat al-khayāl*, ed. Z. al-Shāwīsh, Beirut.

Ibn Dohaish, A. (1989), 'Growth and Development of Islamic Libraries', *Der Islam* 66, 289–302.

Ibrāhīm, ᶜA. (1962), 'Maktaba fī wathīqa, dirāsa li-l-maktaba wa-nashr li-l-wathīqa', in ᶜA. Ibrāhīm, *Dirāsāt fī al-kutub wa-al-maktabāt al-islāmīya*, Cairo.

Ismāᶜīl, ᶜA.S. (1979), 'al-Makhṭūṭāt al-ᶜarabīya fī maktabat Mawlānā fī Qunyā', *al-Mawrid* 8, 393–420.

Jagonak, M. (2008), *Das Bild der Liebe im Werk des Dichters Ǧamīl ibn Maᶜmar*, Wiesbaden.

Al-Jūmānī, S.Ḍ. (2008), 'Fihrist kutub khizānat al-turba al-ashrafīya', *Turāthīyāt* 12, 71–89.

Al-Jūmānī, S.Ḍ. (2009), 'al-Fahāris al-makhṭūṭa li-l-maktabāt al-islāmīya', *Turāthīyāt* 14, 9–75.

Al-Kaḥḥāla, ᶜU.R. (1993), *Muᶜjam al-muᵓallifīn*, Beirut.

Al-Kattānī, Y. (1984), *Rubāᶜīyāt al-imām al-Bukhārī*, Rabat: Maktabat al-maᶜārif.

Kaya, Ö. (2007), *Selahaddin sonrası Dönemde Anadolu'da Eyyûbiler*, Istanbul.

Kaya, Ö. (2012), 'Eyyubi Meliklerinden el-Eşref Musa'nın Artuklu Melikleri ile Ilişkileri', in Ö. Kaya (ed.), *Eyyubiler: Yönetim, Diplomasi, Kültürel Hayat*, Istanbul, pp. 263–88.

Khulayyif, Y. (1959), *al-Shuᶜarāᵓ al-ṣaᶜālīk fī al-ᶜaṣr al-jāhilī*, Cairo.

Kilpatrick, H. (2010), *Making the Great Book of Songs*, London.

King, D.A. (2004), *In Synchrony with the Heavens, vol 1: The Call of the Muezzin*, Leiden.

King, D.A. and J. Samsó (2001), 'Astronomical Handbook and Tables from the Islamic World (750–1900): An Interim Report', *Suhayl* (Barcelona) 2, 9–105.

Kister, M. (1986), 'Mecca and the Tribes of Arabia: Some Notes on Their Relations', in M. Sharon (ed.), *Studies in Islamic History and Civilization in Honour of Professor David Ayalon*, Jerusalem and Leiden, pp. 33–57.

Kohlberg, E. (1992), *A Medieval Muslim Scholar at Work: Ibn Ṭāwūs and His Library*, Leiden.

Korn, L. (2004), *Ayyubidische Architektur in Ägypten und Syrien: Bautätigkeit im Kontext von Politik und Gesellschaft 564–658/1169–1260*, Heidelberg.

Korn, L. (2010), 'Art and Architecture of the Artuqid Courts', in Fuess and Hartung, *Court Cultures*, 385–407.

Krämer, G. *et al.* (2007–), *Encyclopaedia of Islam, Third Edition*, Leiden.

Kügelgen, A.v. (2005), 'Bücher und Bibliotheken in der islamischen Welt des "Mittelalters"', in M. Stolz and A. Mettauer (eds), *Buchkultur im Mittelalter: Schrift, Bild, Kommunikation*, Berlin and New York, pp. 147–76.

Lamoreaux, J. (2002), *Early Islamic Tradition of Dream Interpretation*, Albany.

Lane, E. (1863), *Arabic-English Lexicon*, London.

Lecomte, G. (1965), *Ibn Qutayba (mort en 276/889): l'homme, son oeuvre, ses idées*, Damascus.

Liebrenz, B. (2012), 'Die Rifā'īya. Neue Forschungen zur Geschichte einer Familienbibliothek aus dem osmanischen Damaskus', in Th. Fuchs, Ch. Mackert and R. Scholl (eds), *Das Buch in Antike, Mittelalter und Neuzeit. Sonderbestände der Universitätsbibliothek Leipzig*, Wiesbaden, pp. 265–79.

Leiser, G. and N. Al-Khaledy (2004), *Questions and Answers for Physicians: A Medieval Arabic Study Manual by ᶜAbd al-ᶜAzīz al-Sulamī*, Leiden.

Lindstedt, I. (2011), 'Anti-Religious Views in the Works of Ibn al-Rāwandī and Abū l-ᶜAlāᵓ al-Maᶜarrī', *Studia Orientalia* 111, 131–57.

Lovatt, R. (2002), 'Introduction', in Clarke, *Libraries of Cambridge*.

McAuliffe, J.D. *et al.* (2001–6), *Encyclopaedia of the Qurᵓān*, Leiden.

Makdisi, G. (1981), *The Rise of Colleges: Institutions of Learning in Islam and the West*, Edinburgh.

Mandelung, W. (1980), 'Frühe muᶜtazilitische Häresiographie: das K. al-uṣūl des Ǧaᶜfar b. Ḥarb?', *Der Islam* 57, 220–36.

Marlow, L. (1997), *Hierarchy and Egalitarianism in Islamic Thought*, Cambridge.

Marlow, L. (2013), 'Among Kings and Sages: Greek and Indian Wisdom in an Arabic Mirror for Princes', *Arabica* 60, 1–57.

Maróth, M. (2006), *The Correspondence Between Aristotle and Alexander the Great: An Anonymous Greek Novel in Letters in Arabic Translation*, Piliscsaba.

Al-Marzūqī, M. and J. b. al-Ḥājj Yaḥyā (1963), *Abū al-Ḥasan al-Ḥuṣrī al-Qayrawāni*, Tunis.

Mayer, H.E. (1992), 'Abū ᶜAlīs Spuren am Berliner Tiergarten', *Archiv für Diplomatik* 38, 114–33.

Meisami, J.S. (1991), *The Sea of Precious Virtues: A Medieval Islamic Mirror for Princes*, Salt Lake City.

Melvin-Koushki, M.S. (2012), *The Quest for a Universal Science: The Occult Philosophy of Ṣāᵓin al-Dīn Turka Iṣfahānī (1369–1432) and Intellectual Millenarianism in Early Timurid Iran*, PhD Yale.

Meri, J.W. (2002), *The Cult of Saints Among Muslims and Jews in Medieval Syria*, Oxford.

Meri, J.W. (ed.) (2006), *Medieval Islamic Civilization: An Encyclopedia*, New York.

Michot, Y.J. (2003), 'A Mamlūk Theologian's Commentary on Avicenna's Risāla Aḍḥawiyya: Being a Translation of a Part of the Darᵓ al-taᶜāruḍ of Ibn

Taymiyya, with Introduction, Annotation, and Appendices Part I', *Journal of Islamic Studies* 14/2, 149–203.

Moaz, A. (1987–8), 'Note sur la mausolée de Saladin à Damas', *BEO* 39–40, 183–9.

Möller, D. (1965), *Studien zur mittelalterlichen arabischen Falknereiliteratur*, Berlin.

Montgomery, J. (2007), 'Al-Ǧāḥiẓ and Hellenizing Philosophy', in C. D'Ancona (ed.), *The Libraries of the Neoplatonists*, Leiden, pp. 443–56.

Montgomery, J. (2009), 'al-Jāḥiẓ on Jest and Earnest', in G. Tamer (ed.), *Humor in der arabischen Kultur*, Berlin, pp. 209–39.

Moreh, Sh. and P. Crone (2000), *Medieval Arabic Graffiti on the Theme of Nostalgia*, Princeton.

Morimoto, K. (2012), 'How to Behave toward Sayyids and Sharifs: A Trans-sectarian Tradition of Dream Accounts', in K. Morimoto (ed.), *Sayyids and Sharifs in Muslim Societies*, London, pp. 15–36.

Morimoto, K. (2014), 'The Prophet's Family as the Perennial Source of Saintly Scholars: Al-Samhūdī on ᶜIlm and Nasab', in C. Mayeur-Jaouen and A. Papas (eds), *Family Portraits with Saints: Hagiography, Sanctity, and Family in the Muslim World*, Berlin, pp. 106–24.

Mostafa, S. (1968), *Kloster und Mausoleum des Farağ ibn Barqūq in Kairo*, Glückstadt.

Motzki, H. (2006), 'Dating the So-Called Tafsīr Ibn ᶜAbbās: Some Additional Remarks', *Jerusalem Studies in Arabic and Islam* 31, 147–63.

Mouton, J.-M. (1993), 'De quelques reliques conservées à Damas au Moyen Age, stratégie politique et religiosité populaire sous les Bourides', *AI* 27, 245–62.

Mouton, J.-M. (1994), *Damas et sa principauté sous les Saljoukides et les Bourides (468–549/1076–1154): vie politique et religieuse*, Cairo.

Muḥammad, ᶜĀ.J. Ṣāliḥ (1991), *Shiᶜr Ibn al-Qayṣarānī*, al-Zarqāᵓ: al-Wakāla al-ᶜArabīya.

Mulder, St. (2014), *The Shrines of the ᶜAlids in Medieval Syria: Sunnis, Shiᶜis and the Architecture of Coexistence*, Edinburgh.

Müller, K. (1999), 'al-Ḥanīn ilā l-awṭān in Early Adab Literature', in A. Neuwirth (ed.), *Myths, Historical Archetypes and Symbolic Figures in Arabic Literature*, Beirut, pp. 33–58.

Al-Munajjid, Ṣ. (1976), *Qawāᶜid fahrasat al-makhṭūṭāt al-ᶜarabīya*, Beirut.

Nājī, H. (1998), *al-Babbaghāᵓ, ḥayātuhū – dīwānuhū – rasāᵓiluhū – qiṣaṣuhū*, Beirut.

Al-Nashshār, al-S. (1993), *Taᵓrīkh al-maktabāt fī Miṣr al-ᶜaṣr al-mamlūkī*, Cairo.

Nef, A. (2008), 'L'histoire des "mozarabes" de Sicile. Bilan provisoire et nouveaux matériaux', in C. Aillet, M. Penelas and Ph. Roisse (eds), *¿Existe una identidad* *mozárabe? Historia, lengua y cultura de los cristianos de al-Andalus (siglos IX–XII)*, Madrid, pp. 255–86.

O'Kane, B. (2003), *Early Persian Painting: Kalila and Dimna Manuscripts of the late 14th Century*, Cairo.

Orfali, B. (2009), 'The Works of Abū Manṣūr al-Thaᶜālibi', *Journal of Arabic Literature* 40, 273–318.

Ouyang, W.-Ch. (1997), *Literary Criticism in Medieval Arabic-Islamic Culture*, Edinburgh.

Pellat, Ch. (1954), *Le Livre de la couronne/Kitāb al-Tāj fī akhlāq al-mulūk*, Paris.

Pellat, Ch. (1984), 'Nouvel essai d'inventaire de l'oeuvre Ǧāḥiẓienne', *Arabica* 31, 117–64.

Pellat, Ch. (1986), *Cinq calendriers égyptiens*, Cairo.

Petroski, H. (1999), *The Book on the Bookshelf*, New York.

Pfeiffer, J. (2014a), 'Confessional Ambiguity vs. Confessional Polarization: Politics and the Negotiation of Religious Boundaries in the Ilkhanate', in Pfeiffer (ed.), *Tabriz*, pp. 129–68.

Pfeiffer, J. (ed.) (2014b), *Politics, Patronage and the Transmission of Knowledge in 13th–15th Century Tabriz*, Leiden.

Pons Boigues, F. (1898), *Ensayo bio-bibliográfico sobre los historiadores y geógrafos arábigo-españoles*, Madrid.

Pourhadi, I.V. (2003), 'Muslim Libraries During the Middle Ages in the Works of Orientalists', in M.H. Faghfoory (ed.), *Beacon of Knowledge: Essays in Honor of Seyyed Hossein Nasr*, Louisville, KY: Fons Vitae, pp. 439–67.

Pouzet, L. (1975), 'Maghrébiens à Damas au VIIe/XIIIe siècle', *BEO* 28, 167–99.

Pouzet, L. ([2]1991), *Damas au VIIe/XIIe siècle. Vie et structures religieuses dans une métropole islamique*, Beirut: Dar el-machreq.

Prozorov, S. (2010), 'Prophet Muhammad in the Sufi Tradition', in *East and West: Common Spiritual Values, Scientific–Cultural Links*, Istanbul, pp. 559–76.

Qutbuddin, T. (2013), *A Treasury of Virtues: Sayings, Sermons, and Teachings of Ali, with the One Hundred Proverbs, attributed to al-Jahiz*, New York.

Renard, J. (ed.) (1998), *Windows on the House of Islam: Muslim Sources on Spirituality and Religious Life*, Berkeley.

Rikabi, J. (1949), *La poésie profane sous les Ayyûbides et ses principaux représentants*, Paris.

Río Sánchez, F. del (2008), *Catalogue des manuscrits de la Fondation Georges et Mathilde Salem (Alep, Syrie)*, Wiesbaden.

Ron-Gilboa, G. (forthcoming), 'Pre-Islamic Brigands in Mamlūk Historiography:

Taqī al-Dīn Al-Maqrīzī's Account of "the Brigands among the Arabs"', *Annales Islamologiques* 49.

Rouse, R.H. and M.A. Rouse (1991), *Registrum Anglie de libris doctorum et auctorum veterum*, CBMLC II, London.

Rouse, R.H. and M.A. Rouse (2004), *Henry of Kirkestede. Catalogus de libris autenticis et apocrifis*, CBMLC XI, London.

Rowson, E.K. (1988), *A Muslim Philosopher on the Soul and its Fate*, New Haven.

Sack, D. (1989), *Damaskus. Entwicklung und Struktur einer orientalisch-islamischen Stadt*, Mainz.

Al-Sarraf, Sh. (2004), 'Mamluk Furūsīyah Literature and Its Antecedents', *Mamlūk Studies Review* VIII/1, 141–200.

Savage-Smith, E. (1996), *A Shelflist of Islamic Medical Manuscripts at the National Library of Medicine*, Bethesda, MD.

Sayyid, A.F. (1996), *Dār al-kutub al-miṣrīya: taʾrīkhuhā wa-taṭawwuruhā*, Cairo.

Sayyid, A.F. (1997), *al-Kitāb al-ʿarabī al-makhṭūṭ wa-ʿilm al-makhṭūṭāt*, Cairo.

Sbath, P. (1938–40), *al-Fihris. Catalogue de manuscrits arabes*, Cairo.

Schmidtke, S. (2014), 'Jewish Reception of Twelver Shīʿī *kalām*: A Copy of al-Sharīf al-Murtaḍā's *Kitāb al-Dhakhīra* in the Abraham Firkovitch Collection, St. Petersburg', *Intellectual History of the Islamicate World* 2, 50–74.

Schwarb, G. (2006), 'Sahl b. al-Faḍl al-Tustarī's Kitāb al-Īmāʾ', *Ginzei Qedem: Genizah Research Annual* 2, 61*–105*.

Schwarb, G. (2011), 'Muʿtazilism in the Age of Averroes', in P. Adamson (ed.), *In the Age of Averroes: Arabic Philosophy in the 6th/12th Century*, London, pp. 251–82.

Seidensticker, T. (1986), *Das Verbum 'sawwama'. Ein Beitrag zum Problem der Homonymenscheidung im Arabischen*, München.

Serikoff, N. (2011), 'Beobachtungen über die Marginal- und Schnitttitel in christlich-arabischen und islamischen Büchersammlungen', in Görke and Hirschler, *Manuscript Notes*, pp. 163–71.

Şeşen, R. (1970), 'Cāḥīz'in Eserleri Hakkında Bāzı Yeni Malzemeler', *Tarih Enstitüsü Dergisi* 1, 231–72.

Şeşen, R. (1997), *Mukhtārāt min al-makhṭūṭāt al-ʿarabīya al-nādira fī maktabāt Turkiyā*, Istanbul.

Şeşen, R. (2007), *Salahaddin'den Baybars'a: Eyyubiler – Memluklar (1193–1260)*, Istanbul.

Sezgin, F. (1967–84), *Geschichte des arabischen Schrifttums*, Leiden.

Shabbūḥ, I. (1956), 'Sijill qadīm li-maktabat jāmiʿ al-Qayrawān', *Majallat maʿhad al-makhṭūṭāt al-ʿarabīya* 2, 339–72.

Sharpe, R. (1998), 'Reconstructing the Medieval Library of Bury St Edmunds: The Lost Catalogue of Henry of Kirkstead', in A. Gransden (ed.), *Bury St Edmunds: Medieval Art, Architecture, Archaeology and Economy*, Leeds, pp. 204–18.

Sharpe, R. (2003), *Titulus: Identifying Medieval Latin Texts. An Evidence-Based Approach*, Turnhout.

Sharpe, R. (2006), 'The Medieval Librarian', in E. Leedham-Green and T. Webber (eds), *The Cambridge History of Libraries in Britain and Ireland, vol. 1: To 1640*, Cambridge, pp. 218–41.

Sharpe, R. (2008), 'Library Catalogues and Indexes', in N.J. Morgan and R.M. Thomson (eds), *The Cambridge History of the Book in Britain, vol. 2: 1100–1400*, Cambridge, pp. 197–218.

Sharpe, R., J.P. Carley, R.M. Thomson and A.G. Watson (1996), *English Benedictine Libraries*, CBMLC IV, London.

Shatzmiller, M. (2015), *An Early Knowledge Economy: The Adoption of Paper, Human Capital and Economic Change in the Medieval Islamic Middle East, 700–1300 AD*, Centre for Global Economic History Working Paper Series no. 64, Utrecht.

Al-Shihābī, Q. (1995), *Mushayyadāt Dimashq dhawāt al-aḍriḥa wa-ʿanāṣiruhā al-jamālīya (= Mausolean Monuments of Damascus & Its Ornaments)*, Damascus: WTh.

Sibai, M.M. (1987), *Mosque Libraries: An Historical Study*, London and New York.

Soden, D.H. v. (1903), 'Bericht über die in der Kubbet in Damaskus gefundenen Handschriftenfragmente', *Sitzungsberichte der Königlich Preussischen Akademie der Wissenschaften. Philosophisch-historische Classe*, Halbband II, 825–30.

Sourdel, D. (1957), 'Fragments d'al-Ṣūlī I'Histoire des vizirs ʿabbāsides', *BEO* 15, 99–108.

Sourdel, D. and J. Sourdel-Thomine (1974), 'Un texte d'invocations en faveur de deux princes ayyūbides', in D.K. Kouymjian (ed.), *Near Eastern Numismatics, Iconography, Epigraphy, and History: Studies in Honor of George C. Miles*, Beirut, pp. 347–52.

Sourdel, D. and J. Sourdel-Thomine (2006), *Certificats de pèlerinage d'époque Ayyoubide*, Paris.

Sourdel-Thomine, J. (1961–2), 'Les conseils du šayḫ al-Harawī à un prince ayyūbide', *BEO* XVII, 205–66.

Stanley, T. (2004), 'The Books of Umur Bey', *Muqarnas* XXI, 323–32.

Stewart, D. (2007), 'The Structure of the *Fihrist*: Ibn al-Nadim as Historian of

Islamic Legal and Theological Schools', *International Journal of Middle East Studies* 39/3, 369–87.

Stoneman, W.P. (1999), *Dover Priory*, CBMLC V, London.

Stroumsa, S. (1999), *Freethinkers of Medieval Islam: Ibn Al-Rāwandī, Abū Bakr Al-Rāzī and Their Impact on Islamic Thought*, Leiden.

Su^{c}ūd, T. (1992), *Aḥmad ibn Fāris – ḥayātuhu wa-ārā$^{\circ}$uhu fī al-lugha wa-al-naḥw*, al-Ribāṭ: MMa al-jadīda.

Tabbaa, Y. (1997), *Constructions of Power and Piety in Medieval Aleppo*, University Park, PA.

Taeschner, F. (1932), 'Futuwwa-Studien. Die Futuwwabünde in der Türkei und ihre Literatur. Die Achibünde und ihr Verhältnis zum Nāṣirkreis', *Islamica* 5, 285–333.

Ṭāhā, ^{c}A.Dh. (2004), *Dirāsāt fī al-ta$^{\circ}$rīkh al-andalusī*, Beirut: Dār al-madār al-islāmī.

Talmon-Heller, D. (2007), *Islamic Piety in Medieval Syria: Mosques, Cemeteries and Sermons under the Zangids and Ayyūbids (1146–1260)*, Leiden.

Talmon-Heller, D. and R. Ukeles (2012), 'The Lure of a Controversial Prayer. *Ṣalāt al-raghā$^{\circ}$ib* (the Prayer of Great Rewards) in Sixth/Twelfth-Eighth/Fifteenth Century Arabic Texts and from a Socio-Legal Perspective', *Der Islam* 89/2, 141–66.

Tardy, J. (1993), 'Traduction d'al-Adab al-Kabīr d'Ibn al-Muqaffa^{c}', *AI* XXVII, 181–223.

Al-Ṭihrānī, Āghā Buzurg (1983–8), *al-Dharī^{c}a ilā taṣānīf al-Shī^{c}a*, Beirut.

Tillier, M. (2011), *Le Livre des Caliphes qui s'en remirent au jugement d'un cadi*, Cairo.

Touati, H. (2003), *L'Armoire à sagesse. Bibliothèques et collections en Islam*, Paris.

Ullmann, M. (1970), *Die Medizin im Islam*, Leiden and Cologne.

Ullmann, M. (1972), *Die Natur- und Geheimwissenschaften im Islam*, Leiden.

Vajda, G. (1982), 'Trois manuscrits de la bibliothèque du savant damascain Yūsuf ibn ^{c}Abd al-Hādī', *Journal Asiatique* 270, 229–56.

Varisco, D.M. (1993), 'A Rasulid Agricultural Almanac for 808/1425–6', *New Arabian Studies* 1, 108–223 (repr. D.M. Varisco, *Medieval Folk Astronomy and Agriculture in Arabia and the Yemen*, Aldershot 1997, XV).

Voguet, E. (2003), 'L'inventaire des manuscrits de la Bibliothèque de la grande mosquée de Kairouan (693/1293–4)', *Arabica* 50, 532–44.

Wahba, W.H. (1996), *The Ordinances of Government*, Reading.

Walker, P. (2013), 'An Ismā^{c}īli Answer to the Problem of Worshiping the Unknowable, Neoplatonic God', *Ishraq: Islamic Philosophy Yearbook* (Russian Academy of Sciences, Institute of Philosophy), Moscow, 186–98 (revised version of the article originally published in *American Journal of Arabic Studies* 2 (1974), 7–21 and reprinted in *Ilm* (London, Ismailia Association) 2 (1976), 12–22).

Webb, P. (2014), 'Al-Jāhiliyya: Uncertain Times of Uncertain Meanings', *Der Islam* 91/1, 69–94.

Webber, T. and A.G. Watson (1998), *The Libraries of the Augustinian Canons*, CBMLC VI, London.

Werkmeister, W. (1983), *Quellenuntersuchungen zum Kitāb al-ᶜIqd al-farīd des Andalusiers Ibn ᶜAbdrabbih (246/860–328/940)*, Berlin.

Wing, P. (2014), 'Rich in Goods and Abounding in Wealth', in Pfeiffer (ed.), *Tabriz*, pp. 301–20.

Winter, M. (2006), 'Historiography in Arabic during the Ottoman Period', in R. Allen and D.S. Richards (eds), *Arabic Literature in the Post-Classical Period*, Cambridge, pp. 171–88.

Witkam, J.J. (1989), *De Egyptische arts Ibn al-Akfani (gest. 749/1348) en zijn indeling van de wetenschappen*, Leiden.

Woods, J.E. (1976), *The Aqquyunlu: Clan, Confederation, Empire*, Minneapolis.

Wulzinger, K. and C. Watzinger (1924), *Damaskus. Die islamische Stadt*, Berlin.

Yılmaz, H. (2012), 'Dımaşk Eyyubi Meliki el-Melikü'l-Muazzam'ın İlmî Hayatı', in Ö. Kaya (ed.), *Eyyubiler: Yönetim, Diplomasi, Kültürel Hayat*, Istanbul, pp. 329–47.

Zakeri, M. (2002), 'Some Early Persian Apophthegma', *Jerusalem Studies in Arabic and Islam* 27, 283–304.

Zakeri, M. (2006), *Persian Wisdom in Arabic Garb*, Leiden.

Al-Zarkān, M.Ṣ. (1963), *Fakhr al-Dīn al-Rāzī wa-ārāᵓuhu al-kalāmīya wa-al-falsafiya*, Cairo.

Al-Ziriklī, Kh. (1970), *al-Aᶜlām. Qāmūs tarājim li-ashhar al-rijāl wa-al-nisāᵓ min al-ᶜArab wa-al-mustaᶜribīn wa-al-mustashriqīn*, 3rd edition, Beirut.

Index of Subjects

References are to page numbers and references to images in *italics*. In all indexes the article 'al-', diacritics and 'b.' are disregarded in the alphabetical order.

Index of Titles

This index references the titles in the Ashrafiya catalogue as listed in Chapter 4. The numbers refer to the respective entry number. Numbers in brackets refer to page numbers in Chapters 1 to 3. Titles in the form of *'Shi*ᶜ*r/Dīwān/Qaṣīd/Akhbār/Azjāl/Ghazal* + name', *'Mukhtār shi*ᶜ*r* + name' and *'Risāla/rasā*ᵓ*il* + name' are not indexed as they can be easily identified via the author index. Generic titles such as *'majmū*ᶜ *shi*ᶜ*r'*, *'Qiṭ*ᶜ*at shi*ᶜ*r'* and *'Du*ᶜ*ā*ᵓ*'* are also not indexed as they can be more easily identified via the index of external categories.

Index of Authors

This index primarily lists authors and the numbers refer to the respective entry number as listed in Chapter 4. Numbers in brackets refer to page numbers in Chapters 1 to 3. Numbers in italics refer to persons who are named in Chapter 4 for reasons other than authoring the work in question, for instance because they authored the summarised work, were the dedicatee or acted as scribe.

Index of External Categories

This index lists the external categories ('C:') in the Ashrafiya catalogue.